Personal Injury Sch

Calculating Damages

3rd edition

Personal Injury Schedules

Calculating Damages

3rd edition

General Editor
William Latimer-Sayer
LLB (Hons), MA
Barrister, Cloisters, London

Advisory Editor and Author
Mr Justice Langstaff

Authors
Andrew Buchan
LLB (Hons)
Barrister, Cloisters, London

Rodney Nelson-Jones
MA (Oxon)
Partner, Field Fisher Waterhouse

William Audland
BA (Oxon)
Barrister, 12 KBW, London

Julian Chamberlayne
LLB (Hons)
Partner, Stewarts Law LLP, London

Bloomsbury Professional

Bloomsbury Professional Ltd, Maxwelton House, 41–43 Boltro Road, Haywards Heath, West Sussex, RH16 1BJ

A CIP Catalogue record for this book is available from the British Library.

ISBN 978 1 84766 373 3

Typeset by Phoenix Photosetting, Chatham, Kent
Printed in Great Britain by Hobbs the Printers, Totton, Hampshire

Foreword to the Third Edition

I am delighted to have the opportunity of welcoming the third edition of *Personal Injury Schedules*. The editors have again achieved the difficult task of producing an authoritative text that can be relied upon as containing a comprehensive and up to date analysis of the relevant principles and case law, but in the form of an eminently practical handbook. I have no doubt that the third edition will take the place of its predecessors as a permanent fixture on the desks of those who are concerned with the assessment of damages and the preparation and presentation of personal injury claims.

Sir Robert Owen
June 2010

Foreword to the Second Edition

On 1 April 2005 the statutory provisions enabling the Court to award damages for future loss in the form of periodical payments came into effect. It is a fundamental change to the law, and one on which clear and authoritative guidance is essential. Such guidance is provided in the second edition in a chapter that contains a masterly analysis of the effect of the statutory provisions and the problems that they will present for practitioners and judges alike.

The text has also been expanded to incorporate chapters on a number of important subjects, damages for the dying, professional negligence claims, claims for 'lost years', and schedules in the Employment Tribunal. Furthermore, it now includes a new and substantial opening chapter setting out the general principles applicable to the assessment of damages in personal injury and clinical negligence claims, in an admirably succinct but comprehensive form.

The first edition showed all the promise of youth; the second has more than fulfilled that promise. Its authors are again to be congratulated.

Sir Robert Owen
June 2005

The Authors

General Editor – William Latimer-Sayer

William is a barrister at Cloisters Chambers. He has been involved in a number of the highest awards in recent years including *Sarwar v (1) Ali (2) MIB* (gross award of £9.5 m); *A v Powys Health Board* (damages award equivalent to £10.7 m), and *XXX v A Strategic Health Authority* (gross award equivalent to £9.4 m). He is recommended as a leading junior in *Chambers & Partners*, *Legal 500* and *Legal Experts*. In 2008 William was named *Chambers and Partners'* Personal Injury Junior of the Year. Sheer talent and an impressive worth ethic were said to mark William out as 'one of the best juniors of his generation'. He was nominated for the same award again in 2009. In 2010 he was elected to sit on the Executive Committee of the Personal Injury Bar Association.

Advisory Editor – Mr Justice Langstaff

Mr Justice Langstaff is a former Chairman of the Personal Injury Bar Association. In 2002 he was invited to chair the Master of the Rolls' Working Party into Structured Settlements. Prior to being appointed to the High Court bench in October 2005 he was a leading personal injury and clinical negligence silk representing both claimants and defendants. He appeared in numerous high profile cases including *Jolley v Sutton BC* [2000] 1 WLR 1082; *Fairchild & others v Glenhaven Funeral Services Ltd & others* [2002] UKHL 22; *Barker v Somerset CC* [2004] UKHL 13; *Majrowski v Guys & St Thomas's NHS Trust* [2005] EWCA Civ 251; and *JD v East Berkshire Community Health* NHS Trust [2005] UKHL 23. He was also instructed as lead counsel to the Bristol Injury (children's heart surgery). Since his appointment he has given judgment in several significant quantum cases including *Warrilow v Norfolk and Norwich Hospitals NHS Trust* [2006] EWHC 801 (QB) and *Van Wees v (1) Karkour v (2) Walsh* [2007] EWHC 165 (QB).

Andrew Buchan

Andrew Buchan is a barrister at Cloisters. He has considerable experience in personal injury and clinical negligence cases. He has been instructed in a number of leading cases involving the interface between employment and personal injury including *Sheriff v Klyne Tugs (Lowestoft) Ltd* [1999] ICR 1170; *Waters v Commissioner of Police for the Metropolis* [2000] UKHL 50; *Barber v Somerset County Council* [2004] UKHL 13; and *Eastwood and another v Magnox Electricity plc* [2004] UKHL 35. In addition to being a co-author of the Schedules Book Andrew is also the Editor and co-author of '*Personal Injury Practice, the guide to litigation in the County Court and High Court*' (5th edition published by Tottel Publishing, 2008).

Rodney Nelson-Jones

Rodney Nelson-Jones has specialised in personal injury claims on behalf of victims for 30 years. The Association of Personal Injury Lawyers awarded him the APIL Award for Outstanding Achievement in 2002. He was a member of the Solicitors Steering Committee arising out of the M1 air crash and is a member of FOCIS (The Forum of Complex Injury Solicitors), incorporating the Richard Grand Society for leading personal injury solicitors. He is highly rated by the legal directories and is listed by *Chambers & Partners* as one of only two star rated individuals in the country in the field of personal injury being described as 'absolutely first-rate in the field of industrial disease'. Rodney is the author of numerous legal texts on matters such as personal injury damages statistics, limitation and multiplier tables.

William Audland

William is a barrister at 12 KBW who has a strong specialist personal injury and clinical negligence practice. He is recognised as a leading junior in the *Legal 500* (for personal injury) and in *Chambers and Partners* in the fields of both Personal Injury (Band 1) and Travel Law (Band 2), where he is described as 'wonderfully clever and inspiring' with a 'strong analytical approach and a straightforward friendly manner'.

Julian Chamberlayne

Julian Chamberlayne is the Knowledge Management Partner and Head of the Travel Law Team at Catastrophic Injury Specialists, Stewarts Law. For the last five years, he has recovered in excess of £70 million for Personal Injury clients, including acting for the Claimants in *Sarwar v Ali and the MIB* [2007] EWHC 1255 (QB) and right up to the House of Lords in *Harding v Wealands* [2007] 2 AC 1. Julian is rated in Band 1 for personal injury by *Chambers and Partners*, is a past Times 'Lawyer of the Week' and is Treasurer of the Forum of Complex Injury Solicitors (FOCIS).

Acknowledgements

The authors would like to acknowledge and thank the following people who assisted with the writing of all editions of this work.

On the Third Edition, we would like to thank Dan Herman from Stewarts who assisted with research in relation to security of funding and Simon Philpott from Smith & Williamson who assisted with the pension loss calculations.

We would like to thank Keith Carter of Keith Carter & Associates for his help and expert guidance regarding the use of employment consultants covered in Chapter C.

Permission was given by Simon Levene to use the *Heil v Rankin* conversion table at the end of Chapter D.

We are grateful to William Norris QC who provided assistance and useful material for the drafting of Chapters F and H, including an advance copy of an article he wrote regarding the case of *Brown v King's Lynn and Wisbech NHS Hospitals Trust*.

We would like to thank Rowland Hogg for his expert guidance in relation to discount rates and the selection of multipliers, particularly in Fatal Accident Act claims.

We are indebted to the Honourable Mr Justice Jackson (as he then was) for checking and commenting upon the draft of Chapter N.

We are grateful to Douglas Hall and Simon Philpott of Smith Williamson for their assistance with the pension loss section of Chapter H and their considerable patience in checking and rechecking the pension loss calculations which appear in Chapter Q.

Our thanks are due to the following people who provided assistance and anonymous schedules and counter-schedules in preparation of the example schedules which appear in Chapter Q: Richard Vallance and Edwina Rawson of Charles Russell; Michael Tuner and Kathryn Lee; Alison Millar of Leigh Day & Co; Stuart Dench of Stewarts; and Simon Taylor, Patricia Hitchcock, Joel Donovan, Simon Dyer and Casper Glyn of Cloisters.

We would also like to thank the following people who provided assistance and sample accident questionnaires which assisted in the preparation of the examples which appear in Chapter Q: John Davis of Irwin Mitchell; Maria Crowley of How & Co; and Chris Kennett of Hawkridge & Co.

Contents

Table of Statutes

References are to paragraph numbers. Chapters are indicated in **bold**

Table of Statutory Instruments

References are to paragraph numbers. Chapters are indicated in **bold**

Table of Cases

References are to paragraph numbers. Chapters are indicated in **bold**

C

M

Q

R

S

T

A General Principles

I Introduction

[A1] One of the most important questions a client will ask, whether claimant or defendant, is 'how much is the claim worth?' In this chapter we provide an overview of the guiding principles involved in the assessment of damages for personal injury and clinical negligence claims. The reader is referred to subsequent chapters for a more detailed analysis regarding the entitlement to claim particular heads of loss and the methods by which specific items of injury, loss and damage are calculated.

2 The Constituent Elements

[A2] There are a number of different ways to break down a claim for personal injury into its constituent elements. The two main traditional methods of categorisation are set out below:

Method I	Method 2
General Damages	Non-pecuniary Loss
Special Damages	Pecuniary Loss
Interest	Interest

[A3] Following the introduction of the CPR in 1999, there has been a greater emphasis than ever on providing a detailed breakdown of the claim that is advanced. There has also been a slight change in terminology[1]. In considering each potential head of loss, we have adopted the following system of classification of the main elements of every personal injury claim and have dedicated a separate section to each:

- non-pecuniary loss (general damages)[2];
- interest on non-pecuniary loss (general damages)[3];
- past expenses and losses (pecuniary loss);
- interest on past losses and expenses (pecuniary loss); and
- future expenses and losses (pecuniary loss).

---

[1]   For example, the phrase 'schedule of special damages' has now disappeared and para 4.2 of the PD to CPR, Pt 16 requires a claimant in any personal injury action to attach to his particulars of claim 'a schedule of details of any past and future expenses and losses which he claims'.

[2]   The term 'general damages' is used here in the loose sense described below, covering all heads of loss which are incapable of precise quantification, eg pain, suffering and loss of amenity, loss of congenial employment, loss of leisure time etc.

[3]   Interest on general damages is considered separately to interest on past losses and expenses because different principles apply to the assessment of each.

3 Terminology

(i) General and Special Damages

General damages

[A4] Although the term 'general damages' has a variety of different meanings, in a personal injury context it is commonly used to describe all heads of damage which by their very nature cannot be assessed as precise sums but have to be assessed[1]. Examples include awards for:

- pain, suffering and loss of amenity;
- handicap on the open labour market/loss of earnings capacity[2];
- loss of congenial employment;
- loss of use (eg of a vehicle); and
- loss of enjoyment (eg of a holiday).

---

[1]   However, perhaps with the exception of awards for handicap on the labour market, this does not necessarily mean that a reasonably accurate assessment cannot be made. See further Chapter D regarding the assessment of the main different heads of general damage.

[2]   The award for handicap on the labour market is notoriously difficult to assess and has been described judicially as 'nothing more than a guess': *Eaton v Concrete (Northern) Ltd* [1979] CA Transcript 30, per Megaw LJ. See further Chapter H.

[A5] Technically, the term 'general damages' also applies to all claims for future expenses and losses (both pecuniary and non-pecuniary). Of course, all awards made for such expenses and losses must necessarily be approximate, given the difficulty of predicting what will happen in the future and the uncertainties surrounding the length of time for which any such expenses and losses will continue. However, the usage of the term is inconsistent amongst practitioners. For example, the term is occasionally used as shorthand to refer only to the award in respect of pain, suffering and loss of amenity[1]. Alternatively, it is used for all 'personal' aspects of the claim, ie pain, suffering and loss of amenity, handicap on the labour market and loss of congenial employment. In the circumstances, particular care should be taken, especially when negotiating with an opponent, to ensure that all parties share the same meaning when using the expression 'general damages'[2].

---

[1]   See eg *Williams v Devon County Council* [2003] EWCA Civ 365, in which Latham LJ frequently used the term 'general damages' to connote the award for 'pain, suffering and loss of amenity'. This should be contrasted with Lord Woolf's judgment in *Heil v Rankin* [2001] PIQR Q16, CA, in which the Master of the Rolls was careful to use the expressions '[general] damages for pain, suffering and loss of amenity' or 'non-pecuniary loss' rather than simply 'general damages' on its own.

[2]   Failure to take such care can lead to the professional negligence trap where an offer of £X is put forward by a defendant to settle the claimant's claim for 'general damages', meaning all heads of non-pecuniary loss, and this is accepted by the claimant on the mistaken understanding that the offer only related to the award for 'pain, suffering and loss of amenity'.

Special damages

[A6] In contrast, the term 'special damages' is used to connote all items of loss or damage which have an exact monetary value, eg the costs that have been incurred repairing a damaged vehicle or undergoing medical treatment. Technically, the term does not apply to losses and expenses which are yet to be incurred at the time of trial because, by reason of uncertainty, these are impossible to assess with point accuracy. However, again, the term is used inconsistently amongst practitioners and may sometimes be used (wrongly) as a synonym for 'pecuniary loss'.

(ii)   Pecuniary and Non-pecuniary Loss

[A7]   An alternative and more precise method of categorising heads of loss is the distinction drawn between pecuniary and non-pecuniary loss.

Pecuniary loss

[A8]   Pecuniary loss may be defined as all financial loss which is attributable to the defendant's wrongdoing. The claimant is obliged to itemise such loss in a detailed schedule of loss attached to his or her particulars of claim[1]. Pecuniary loss is further subdivided into two parts[2]:
- pre-trial losses and expenses together (known as 'past expenses and losses'); and
- post-trial losses and expenses (known as 'future expenses and losses').

---

[1]   Paragraph 4.2 of the PD to CPR, Pt 16.
[2]   See below at para [A13] for the reasons why past and future expenses and losses need to be considered separately.

Non-pecuniary loss

[A9]   Generally speaking, the term 'non-pecuniary loss' or 'non-economic loss' in a personal injury context[1] relates to the award for pain, suffering, and loss of amenity[2]. Although it is usual for one global award to be made for pain, suffering and loss of amenity, the concepts of 'pain and suffering' and 'loss of amenity' are separate and distinct[3]. Generally speaking, the award for 'pain and suffering' reflects the subjective feelings resulting from the injuries such as physical pain, mental distress, anxiety and embarrassment, whereas the award for 'loss of amenity' reflects the objective consequences of the injuries upon the claimant's activities such as restriction of mobility and movement, loss of senses, inability to communicate, impairment of intellectual function, loss of sexual function and the inability to pursue former hobbies or leisure interests. In some cases, it is possible to claim for only 'pain and suffering' or 'loss of amenity' but not both. Perhaps the most obvious example is the unconscious claimant. Whilst such a person is unable to experience any pain or suffering, nonetheless the total loss of amenity justifies an award at the top end of the scale[4].

---

[1]   In other contexts, it is possible to claim for loss of reputation, interference with enjoyment of property and mental distress.
[2]   Historically, it also used to be possible to claim an award for loss of expectation of life; however, this was removed by s 1 of the Administration of Justice Act 1982 for all claims whose cause of action accrued on or after 1 January 1983. By virtue of s 1(1)(b) of the 1982 Act, if the claimant's expectation of life has been reduced by the injuries, the court when assessing the appropriate award for pain and suffering must take into account any suffering which has been or is likely to be caused to the claimant by reason of his or her awareness that his or her life expectancy has been reduced.

3   See further Chapter D. In *Heil v Rankin* [2001] QB 272, Lord Woolf stated at 298 [39]: 'In determining what is the correct level of damages for PSLA, it is not usual for the Court to attribute differing sums for different aspects of the injury. The Court's approach involves trying to find the global sum which most accurately in monetary terms reflects or can be regarded as reflecting a fair, reasonable and just figure for the injuries which have been inflicted and the consequences which they will have in PSLA. A sophisticated analytical approach distinguishing between pain and suffering and loss of amenity is not usually required.'

4   *Lim Poh Choo v Camden and Islington Area Health Authority* [1980] AC 174.

[A10]   Arguably, the term 'non-pecuniary loss' may also be applied to other claims, such as the loss of enjoyment of a specific event (eg a holiday) or the loss of use of a chattel (eg a car). However, since these heads of loss often have a readily identifiable financial value (eg the cost of the holiday or the cost of hiring a replacement car), they are more often than not thought of and claimed as items of pecuniary loss[1].

1   Although cf *Ichard v Frangoulis* [1977] 2 All ER 461 in which Peter Pain J held that a larger sum of general damages in respect of pain, suffering and loss of amenity would be awarded for the loss of enjoyment of a tourist's holiday. See also *Bygrave v Thomas Cook Tour Operations Ltd* [2003] EWCA Civ 1631, in which Ward LJ suggested that it would have been appropriate for the trial judge to have made an award of general damages of £2,500 to reflect the claimant's increased expenditure on taxis as a result of her injuries.

[A11]   There is no requirement to list the items of non-pecuniary loss claimed in the schedule of loss, but the claimant's date of birth and brief details of the personal injury must be included in the particulars of claim[1]. If the claimant is relying upon the evidence of a medical practitioner, the claimant must attach to or serve with his or her particulars of claim 'a report from a medical practitioner about the personal injuries which he or she alleges in the claim'[2]. General guidance in relation to the expected contents and format of medical reports is contained within CPR, Pt 35, but there is no specific guidance in relation to what exactly should be covered in the initial report served with the proceedings. It is suggested that, in order to avoid an application for strike out under r 3.4 or a request for further information under Pt 18, it would be prudent for any medical evidence served with the particulars of claim at least to identify the broad nature of the injuries sustained and relate them to the matters complained of[3]. It is also good practice to set out any claims for handicap on the open labour market, loss of congenial employment, loss of use etc, either in the particulars of claim or perhaps more appropriately in the schedule of loss[4].

1   Paragraph 4.1 of the PD to CPR, Pt 16.
2   Paragraph 4.3 of the PD to CPR, Pt 16. Note that the rule does not state that the claimant must serve or attach to the particulars of claim the report from the medical practitioner on which he or she relies, rather the claimant is only obliged to serve 'a report from a medical practitioner about the personal injuries which he alleges in his claim'. The inference is that the report served does not necessarily have to be from the same medical practitioner whom the claimant wishes to rely upon at trial. Usually the claimant will want to rely upon the report served with the particulars of claim. However, there are exceptions to this. For example, where a client approaches a solicitor close to the expiry of the limitation period, it might be necessary to obtain a short form report from a GP which in due course will be superseded by the evidence of a specialist such as an orthopaedic surgeon. Also, in clinical negligence cases the claimant will often only want to serve a brief condition and prognosis report with the particulars of claim and wait for mutual exchange of expert evidence before serving reports on breach of duty and causation.
3   Under the old rules, RSC Ord 18, r 12 required the plaintiff to serve a medical report substantiating all the personal injuries alleged in the statement of claim which the plaintiff proposed to adduce

in evidence as part of his or her case at trial. This was interpreted as requiring the plaintiff to serve a medical report which verified the plaintiff's complaints and attributed them to the matters complained of: *Nur v John Wyeth & Bros Ltd* [1996] 7 Med LR 300; *Lort v Thames Water Utilities Ltd* (29 January 1993), CA; *B v John Wyeth & Bros Ltd* [1992] 1 WLR 172; *L & W v John Wyeth & Bros Ltd* (6 May 1992), Ian Kennedy J. Whilst the wording of the new rule does not go as far as the old, the court may be persuaded to exercise its case management powers against the claimant if the medical evidence served with the particulars of claim does not at least outline the broad nature of the injuries that were sustained and, without necessarily giving away the claimant's whole case in respect of causation, attribute them to the defendant's alleged wrongdoing.

[4]   See further, *Thorn v Powergen* [1997] PIQR Q71 and *Chan Wai Tong v Li Ping Sum* [1985] AC 446 in which it was decided under the old rules that it was not necessary specifically to plead a claim for handicap on the open labour market if such a claim was disclosed on the face of the medical evidence. Some doubt may now be cast on these decisions by reason of the new 'cards on the table approach' and the obligation upon the claimant by virtue of CPR, para 4.2 of the PD to Pt 16 to attach to his or her particulars of claim 'a schedule of details of any past and future expenses and losses claimed'. However, it is worth noting that CPR, r 16.2(5) states that the court may grant any remedy to which the claimant is entitled, even if that remedy is not specified in the claim form.

Overlap between pecuniary and non-pecuniary loss

[A12]   On occasions, there will be examples where pecuniary and non-pecuniary loss may appear to overlap[1]. However, whether there was any overlap between pecuniary loss and non-pecuniary loss was doubted by Lord Scarman in the leading case of *Lim Poh Choo v Camden and Islington Area Health Authority*[2]. In *Arafa v Potter*[3] the claimant, who had been a restaurant manager working in excess of 70 hours per week with only two weeks' holiday a year, was prevented from continuing in his pre-accident job by reason of his injuries. He retrained and became a teacher. Although he received approximately the same level of remuneration, he was only contracted to work 40 hours per week and had the benefit of school holidays amounting to 12 weeks a year. The Court of Appeal refused to take into account the intangible benefit to the claimant of working shorter hours and enjoying longer holidays against his claim for loss of earnings[4]. It is submitted that this correctly states the position in English law that a perceived benefit can only be set off against a claim of the same type[5]. Therefore, non-pecuniary advantage should not be used to restrict pecuniary loss[6].

[1]   See eg *Harris v Harris* [1973] 1 Lloyd's Rep 445, CA, in which there was a claim for the lost chance of marriage prospects and starting a family, together with a full claim for loss of earnings. See also *Musmar v Kalala* [1999] CLY 1565 in which Recorder Digney held that the claim for loss of amenity in respect of the claimant's inability to drive, due to a phobic reaction, overlapped with a damages claim for loss of use. And, in *Brown v Merton Health Authority (Teaching)* [1982] 1 All ER 650, CA, a claim for a greenhouse and raised flower beds was rejected on the basis that these costs were properly met out of the award for pain, suffering and loss of amenity.

[2]   [1980] AC 174 at 192, where Lord Scarman stated: 'Upon the point of principle whether damages for non-pecuniary loss can properly be reduced to avoid an overlap with damages for pecuniary loss I express no final opinion. I confess, however, that I doubt the possibility of overlap: and I note the Pearson Commission (Cmnd 7054-I, para 759) considers it wrong in principle to reduce the one by reason of the size of the other.'

[3]   [1994] PIQR Q73.

[4]   See also the speech of Lord McCluskey in the Court of Session's decision in *McFarlane v Tayside Heath Board* 1998 SLT 307, where he said at 316: 'But not all the benefits that might accrue to the victim of a legal wrong are brought into account. We were offered the example of a coal miner who, while working in a deep pit, is rendered unfit to work by an accident, caused by his employer's fault, and resulting in the loss of an arm. He leaves the coal industry and becomes a park attendant

at a lower wage. Instead of the dust, darkness and dangers of the pit, his environment becomes one of fresh air bird song and sweet smelling flowers. No-one would dream of suggesting that a price has to be put on such non-patrimonial benefits accruing to him as an incident of his working in a park rather than a pit, and that that price should be deducted either from his calculated wage loss or even from the money awarded by way of solatium given to mark the pain, suffering and deprivation flowing from the loss of the limb. It would be possible to multiply such examples.'

5   The general rule is that only like can be set off against like. See eg *Parry v Cleaver* [1970] AC 1, in which the House of Lords held that a pension received on account of injury is not to be taken into account against a claim for loss of earnings. In the Court of Appeal in the same case, Winn LJ had stated that 'Damages for pain, loss of mobility or enjoyment of life are different in kind from damages for monetary loss; the two are not to be set off': [1968] 1 QB 195 at 211. Further, in *Rialas v Mitchell* (1984) Times, 17 July, the Court of Appeal rejected the argument that there was any overlap between a claim for loss of amenity and the cost of buying technical aids. See also the speech of Lord Hope in *Longden v British Coal Corpn* [1997] 3 WLR 1336 at 1347F–1348 and Dixon CJ in the High Court of Australia in *Espagne's case* (1961) 105 CLR 569. This principle is mirrored in the statutory framework for the deduction of benefits (see further, Chapter J, Recovery of State and Collateral Benefits). A recent example is provided by *Samuels v Benning* [2002] EWCA Civ 858, in which the trial judge had held that a claim for DIY costs in the future was to be equated with the loss of a rewarding hobby and was adequately compensated from within the award for pain, suffering and loss of amenity. The Court of Appeal held that there had not been adequate compensation for this loss (particularly as the claim for past loss had been made out) and awarded an additional £5,000 (applying a multiplier of 10 to the claimed multiplicand of £500 per annum).

6   Cf the House of Lords' decision in *McFarlane v Tayside Health* [2000] 2 AC 59, where it was held that it was not just, fair and reasonable to hold a doctor responsible for the costs of bringing up a child born as a result of an unwanted pregnancy. The birth of a healthy child was considered to be a blessing. Since it was impossible to value the pleasure derived from the child's existence which would counteract the financial burden placed on the parents, the cost of upbringing was not a recoverable head of damages.

(iii)   Past and Future Expenses and Losses

[A13]   There are three main reasons for differentiating between past and future expenses and losses. First, past losses are more easily assessable and tend to have fewer uncertainties than future losses which, unless periodical payments are awarded, should usually, though not always, be calculated using the conventional multiplier/ multiplicand method[1]. Secondly, it is necessary to split past and future losses so that interest may be added accurately to those expenses and losses which have already been incurred[2]. Lastly, periodical payments may only be awarded in respect of future loss[3].

1   *Taylor v O'Connor* [1971] AC 115; *Lim Poh Choo v Camden and Islington Area Health Authority* [1980] AC 174; *Hodgson v Trapp* [1989] AC 807; *Wells v Wells* [1999] AC 345. See further *Coates v Curry* (1997) Times, 22 August and *Cornell v Green* [1998] CLY 1485, in which the Court of Appeal held that it was wrong to make one broad brush assessment of the claims for past and future loss of earnings instead of using the conventional multiplier/multiplicand method of assessment. Such an assessment is only justified where the uncertainties are so great that a reasoned calculation would be artificial: see eg *Blamire v South Cumbria Health Authority* [1993] PIQR Q1; *Goldborough v Thompson* [1996] PIQR Q86; *Michael v Ashdown* (2 December 1998, unreported), CA; *Hannon v Pearce* (24 January 2001, unreported), QBD; *Willemse v Hesp* [2003] EWCA Civ 994; *Bullock v Atlas Ward Structures Ltd* [2008] EWCA Civ 194. As to the multiplier/multiplicand see further at para **[A18]** and Chapter H.

2   See further *Jefford v Gee* [1970] 2 QB 130. Of course, no interest is payable on items of future loss because, by definition, this loss has not yet been incurred and the claimant has therefore not been kept out of his or her money.

3   See further Chapter O.

Past expenses and losses[1]

[A14] The claimant will be able to recover any reasonably foreseeable[2] expenses or losses he or she proves to have been reasonably incurred as a result of the defendant's wrongdoing[3]. Whether an expense is reasonably and necessarily incurred will depend upon the facts of the particular case and the evidence available to support the claim[4]. The reasonable course of action is not necessarily the cheapest[5]. However, since damages are purely 'compensatory', the claimant's recoverable loss is limited to the loss which he or she has actually suffered, as opposed to any notional or hypothetical loss[6]. Further, the claimant is only entitled to claim his or her net loss[7]. So, for example, deductions must be made from a claim for loss of earnings to reflect tax[8], National Insurance[9] and any expenses that would have been incurred earning the money[10]. Discounts must also be made to take account of the risk that the loss might have occurred in any event or to reflect uncertainties[11]. Lost opportunities arising between the date of injury and date of trial may also be claimed, such as the chance of obtaining a promotion or a pay rise[12]. As long as the lost chance was 'real' or 'substantial', such claims do not need to be proved on the balance of probabilities and can be put forward as a percentage increase on top of the basic claim[13]. Claims may also be advanced for multiple lost chances, eg where a number of different career options were open to the claimant at the time of injury[14].

[1] For a much more detailed explanation of the principles governing the assessment of individual heads of past expenses and losses, see further Chapter F, Past Expenses and Losses.

[2] Only the type of loss needs to be reasonably foreseeable; neither the extent of the loss nor the precise mechanism of the loss needs to be foreseeable: *Hughes v Lord Advocate* [1963] AC 837; *Overseas Tankship (UK Ltd) v Miller Steamship Co Pty (The Wagon Mound No 2)* [1967] 1 AC 617; *Jolley v Sutton LBC* [2000] 1 WLR 1082.

[3] *Roberts v Roberts* (1960) Times, 11 March; *Cassel v Riverside Hospital Health Authority* [1992] PIQR Q1; *Hunt v Severs* [1993] QB 815; *Parry v North West Surrey Health Authority* (29 November 1999, unreported), QBD; *Thrul v Ray* [2000] PIQR Q71, CA. Note that the expenses/loss must actually have been incurred in order to be recoverable. For example, the claimant who owns a sports car which is damaged in an accident, and hires a more modest vehicle whilst his car is being repaired, can only recover the hire charges spent on hiring the more modest vehicle and not the notional hire charges of a replacement sports car: *Clark v Tull* [2002] EWCA Civ 510, upheld in *Lagden v O'Connor* [2003] UKHL 64.

[4] Contrast *Biesheuval v Birrell* [1999] PIQR Q40, in which a claim for Viagra was disallowed, with *Re McCarthy (CICA: Quantum: 2000)* [2001] CLY 1555 in which a similar claim succeeded. Contrast also *Cassel v Riverside Hospital Health Authority* [1992] PIQR Q1, in which a claim for a swimming pool was denied, with *Haines v Airedale NHS Trust* (2 May 2000, unreported), QBD, in which the evidence supported the claim for a hydrotherapy pool.

[5] *Rialas v Mitchell* (1984) Times, 17 July. See also *Cunningham v Kensington, Chelsea and Westminster* [1998] CLY 1480 in which the care home selected for the claimant was held to be reasonable despite the availability of a significantly cheaper alternative, which was found to be less advantageous. These principles have recently been applied in numerous first instance cases such as *Massey v Tameside & Glossop Acute Services NHS Trust* [2007] EWHC 317 (QB); *Wakeling v (1) McDonagh and (2) MIB* [2007] EWHC 1201 (QB); *A v Powys Health Board* [2007] EWHC 2996 (QB); *Smith v East and North Hertfordshire Hospitals NHS Trust* [2008] EWHC 2234 (QB) and *XXX v A Strategic Health Authority* [2008] EWHC 2727 (QB); *Smith v LC Window Fashions Ltd* [2009] EWHC 1532 (QB).

[6] *Hunt v Severs* [1994] 2 AC 350, per Lord Bridge at 357H; *Lagden v O'Connor* [2003] UKHL 64.

[7] As stated by Lord Bridge in *Hodgson v Trapp* [1989] AC 807 at 819E: 'the basic rule is that it is the net consequential loss and expense which the court must measure'.

[8] *British Transport Commission v Gourley* [1956] AC 185.

[9] *Cooper v Firth Brown* [1963] 1 WLR 418.

10   *Lim Poh Choo v Camden and Islington Area Health Authority* [1980] AC 174.
11   See below at paras **[A97]** and **[A100]** regarding the sorts of deductions and discounts commonly
      made.
12   See eg *Anderson v Davis* [1993] PIQR Q87.
13   *Domsalla v Barr* [1969] 1 WLR 630; *Davies v Taylor* [1974] AC 207; *Anderson v Davis* [1993]
      PIQR Q87; *Allied Maples v Simmons & Simmons* [1995] WLR 1602; and *Doyle v Wallace* [1998]
      PIQR Q146. 'Substantial' here does not mean more than likely. It means just enough to avoid being
      dismissed as 'insubstantial'.
14   *Langford v Hebran* [2001] EWCA Civ 361, cf *Herring v Ministry of Defence* [2003] EWCA Civ
      528.

Future expenses and losses[1]

[A15]   In theory, the same principle for the recovery of past expenses and losses
applies to the assessment of future expenses and losses, ie the claimant is entitled
to recover full compensation[2] for all net[3] expenses and losses which are reasonably
foreseeable and necessary as a result of the defendant's negligence. In general,
therefore, the same heads of past loss may be claimed as future loss, assuming that
the loss is ongoing or there is a chance that the loss will recur at some point in the
future[4]. In practice, however, the quantification of future expenses and losses is more
complex, particularly when awarding damages on a lump sum basis, because account
must be taken of:

- Greater uncertainties: having considered what has happened in the past
  (particularly as between the date of the defendant's negligence and the date of
  the trial), the court will do its best, with the benefit of lay and expert evidence,
  to predict what is likely to happen in the future. However, there will always
  remain a number of imponderables, including when a future loss is likely to be
  incurred, the likely period of time that the loss will continue to be incurred, and
  what would have happened in the absence of the negligence in any event (which
  will often depend upon the intentions of the claimant). In order to take account
  of these uncertainties, a variety of discounts are applied to reflect the chances
  that the loss might not occur, will not occur until later than expected, the period
  of loss might not be as long as expected, or the loss would have occurred in any
  event[5]. The further the contingency is away from the date of assessment, the
  greater the discount will be[6]. A discount must be given to reflect the chance that
  the claimant will not survive to 'normal' life expectancy; however, there is no
  room for an additional discount to reflect the fact that the claimant might not live
  to his or her life expectancy where that expectancy is agreed as a figure[7].
- Accelerated receipt: if a claimant is awarded full compensation now for a loss
  which will not occur for some time, the claimant could invest that money and earn
  interest on it. This will result in over-compensation once the loss materialises.
  Therefore, the court assumes that the claimant will invest his or her award of
  damages and earn interest on it at a particular rate (which is net of tax), known as
  the 'discount rate'[8]. The discount rate is presently fixed by the Lord Chancellor
  at 2.5% under his powers conferred by s 1 of the Damages Act 1996[9]. In other
  words, the court will assume that in respect of any loss occurring in the future
  the claimant will be able to invest his or her money now to achieve an annual
  net rate of return of 2.5% after inflation has been accounted for. A factor by
  which to multiply the loss in order to take account of the accelerated receipt,

called the 'multiplier', is taken from the Ogden Tables[10]. These Tables (now in their 6th edition) are produced on a regular basis by the Government Actuary's Department[11].

[1]   For a much more detailed explanation of the principles governing the assessment of individual heads of future expenses and losses, see further Chapter H, Future Expenses and Losses.

[2]   *Wells v Wells* [1999] AC 345.

[3]   As with past expenses and losses, the claimant may only claim the net loss and must give credit for all relevant deductions, eg in respect of a claim for future loss of earnings the claimant must give credit from the gross amount for tax (*British Transport Commission v Gourley* [1956] AC 185) and National Insurance (*Cooper v Firth Brown* [1963] 1 WLR 418) as well as any significant expenses associated with the work, eg travel expenses, equipment or tools (*Lim Poh Choo v Camden and Islington Area Health Authority* [1980] AC 174).

[4]   There are, however, a few heads of loss which may only be claimed for the future, eg handicap on the open labour market.

[5]   See further at para **[A100]** as regards the discounts that are commonly made to reflect contingencies.

[6]   *Mallett v McMonagle* [1970] AC 166.

[7]   *Wells v Wells* [1999] AC 345. As Lord Lloyd stated at 378: '… there is no room for any discount in the case of a whole life multiplier with an agreed expectation of life. In the case of loss of earnings the contingencies can work only in one direction – in favour of the defendant. But in the case of life expectancy, the contingency can work in either direction. The [claimant] may exceed his normal expectation of life, or he may fall short of it.'

[8]   It is considered desirable to fix a single rate to be applied to the vast majority of cases, in order to facilitate settlements and to save the expense of expert evidence at trial: *Wells v Wells* [1999] AC 345.

[9]   Damages (Personal Injury) Order 2001, SI 2001/2301. It should be noted that the court can adopt a different rate of return under s 2 of the Damages Act 1996 if 'it is more appropriate in the case in question'. However, this has been interpreted by the Court of Appeal in *Warriner v Warriner* [2002] EWCA Civ 81 as applying only where (a) a case has special features material to the rate of return, and (b) such features were not taken into account by the Lord Chancellor in his reasons for setting the discount rate. In practice, therefore, as noted by Dyson LJ, s 1(2) will only successfully be invoked in comparatively few cases. An example of this might be where the claimant will be subjected to unusually high tax payments: see further *Hodgson v Trapp* [1989] AC 807; *Wells v Wells* [1999] AC 345; and *Biesheuval v Birrell* [1999] PIQR Q40; cf *Van Oudenhaven v Griffin Inns Ltd* [2000] 1 WLR 1413.

[10]   Following *Wells v Wells* [1999] AC 345, in any case where there is an agreed or decided life expectancy, the Ogden Tables are to be used as a starting point rather than a check, and the court must be slow to depart from the actuarial tables purely on impressionist grounds. Section 10 of the Civil Evidence Act 1995 was designed to allow the Tables to be proved in evidence by the production of a copy published by The Stationery Office. Although this section has not been brought into force as of yet, the courts routinely adopt the Ogden Tables without requiring formal evidence from someone at the Government Actuary's Office. It should be noted that employment tribunals are also permitted to use the Ogden Tables for cases of unfair dismissal once it is established that there is a prima facie career-long loss: *Dunnachie v Kingston Upon Hull City Council* (No 2) [2004] ICR 227. They will probably use them for other forms of employment claim without restriction.

[11]   The Ogden Tables can be found fully set out in *Personal Injury Damages Statistics* by Rodney Nelson-Jones, and in 'Facts & Figures' produced by the Professional Negligence Bar Association. Life expectancy in the UK continues to improve. They can also be downloaded from the Government Actuary's Office website at: www.gad.gov.uk.

(I)   One-off items of future loss

[A16]   Where there is a particular item of expense or loss which might occur at some point in the future, it is fairly straightforward to calculate the lump sum loss by obtaining the current day value of the item and discounting for accelerated receipt and the chance that such loss might not be incurred. Take, eg, the case of a claimant who has a 50% chance of needing a knee replacement operation ten years from the date of trial and where the current cost of the operation (including all surgical, anaesthetic, hospital and nursing fees) is £10,000. The loss is calculated as follows:

$$£10,000 \times 0.7812^1 \times 0.5^2 = £3,906.$$

[1]   The discount factor to be applied for accelerated receipt of ten years (table 27 of the Ogden Tables at a discount rate of 2.5%). Note that, with appropriate evidence, it might be possible to prove that the real cost of medical treatment and surgery has been increasing annually in excess of inflation which justifies a discount for accelerated receipt at less than the discount set by the Lord Chancellor under the Damages Act 1996: cf *Cooke v United Bristol Health Care* [2003] EWCA Civ 1370. However, an argument that can be made in response is that advances in medicine may mean that, when the claimant in fact comes to undergo the necessary treatment, there may be new methods of treatment available which are less invasive, have more chance of success, and require less recovery time than the current form of treatment.

[2]   The chance that the surgery will be required.

[A17]   It should be noted that only losses which have more than a speculative chance of being incurred will be recoverable. In *Howarth v Whittaker*[1] the claimant suffered extensive injuries including a moderately severe brain injury. Given the claimant's very poor work history (he had not worked for at least 13 years prior to the accident) and drinking problem, his claim for future loss of earnings was rejected, since the prospect of him obtaining remunerative employment was too low and speculative to justify any award under this head. In *Parkhouse v North Devon Healthcare NHS Trust*[2], notwithstanding an agreement in the joint statement between the parties' respective IT experts that the claimant should be awarded £100,000 in order to cover technical aids which were not currently available but might become available in the future, the claim was rejected on the basis that it was almost 'pure speculation'. Likewise a claim for dependency on the basis of the deceased's pension was rejected in *D and D v Donald*[3] because it was a matter of 'sheer speculation' whether and to what extent the claimant might have become dependent on the deceased's pension, bearing in mind his infidelity at the time of the accident.

[1]   [2003] Lloyd's Rep Med 235.
[2]   [2002] Lloyd's Rep Med 100.
[3]   [2001] PIQR Q44.

(2)   ONGOING ITEMS OF EXPENSE OR LOSS

[A18]   Traditionally, in respect of future loss, the court has attempted to award a lump sum which is of sufficient size to meet the claimant's annual needs arising from the defendant's negligence until those needs come to an end (usually on the claimant's death), but no more[1]. Ongoing losses and expenses, or those which are likely to persist over a period of time that are not awarded by way of periodical payments, are usually calculated using a multiplier/multiplicand method[2]. The annual loss is known as the 'multiplicand'. Once the multiplicand has been calculated[3], it is multiplied by a factor known as 'the multiplier' in order to arrive at the appropriate lump sum to meet the claimant's needs[4]. Current day figures are used since future inflation is ignored[5]. For the above reasons, the multiplier is not the number of years which make up the period of the loss but a reduced figure in order to take account of uncertainties and accelerated receipt. The starting point multiplier is taken from the

Ogden Tables but, save in respect of the whole life multiplier[6], is further discounted in order to take account of contingencies other than mortality[7]. The multiplier for future loss is calculated from the date of trial in respect of a living claimant[8], or from the date of death in a case brought under the Fatal Accidents Act 1976[9]. Where there are varying periods of loss and different costs applying to each, the multiplier may be split to cover the different periods[10]. In cases involving a proved admitted chance that, at some definite point in the future, the claimant will develop some serious disease or suffer some serious deterioration in his or her physical or mental condition, an award of provisional damages may be made entitling the claimant to come back to court to seek further damages[11].

[1]   *Taylor v O'Connor* [1971] AC 115; *Cookson v Knowles* [1979] AC 556; *Lim Poh Choo v Camden and Islington Area Health Authority* [1980] AC 174; *Hodgson v Trapp* [1989] AC 807; *Wells v Wells* [1999] AC 345. In *Hodgson v Trapp* [1989] AC 807 at 826D, Lord Oliver of Aylmerton elegantly expressed the law as follows: 'Essentially what the court has to do is to calculate as best it can the sum of money which will on the one hand be adequate, by its capital and income, to provide annually for the injured person a sum equal to his estimated annual loss over the whole of the period during which that loss is likely to continue, but which, on the other hand, will not, at the end of that period, leave him in a better financial position than he would have been apart from the accident'.

[2]   Where there are too many imponderables to make an accurate assessment of a particular head of loss using the usual multiplier/multiplicand method, the court may instead decide to make a broad brush assessment and award a single global lump sum. This is most common in relation to awards for future loss of earnings/handicap on the labour market: see eg *Blamire v South Cumbria Health Authority* [1993] PIQR Q1; *Goldborough v Thompson* [1996] PIQR Q86; *Tait v Pearson* [1996] PIQR Q92; and *Hannon v Pearce* (24 January 2001, unreported), QBD. However, lump sums may also be awarded for other heads of loss, eg DIY/decorating (see eg *Worral v Powergen plc* [1999] PIQR Q103) and care (see eg *Pollitt v Oxfordshire Health Authority* (16 July 1998, unreported), QBD).

[3]   In *Wells v Wells* [1999] 1 AC 345, Lord Lloyd emphasised the importance of focusing upon the individual multiplicands for each head of loss. He said at 377E: 'In my view the Court of Appeal was right to scrutinise the individual items which went to make up the multiplicand. Since the effect of reducing the rate of discount will be to increase the multiplier in every case, it is all the more important to keep firm control of the multiplicand. [Claimants] are entitled to a reasonable standard of care to meet their requirements, but that is all'.

[4]   Note that, since the multiplier is based on a mixture of educated guesswork and assumptions (involving predictions as to the likely course of the claimant's condition and prognosis, the claimant's life expectancy, the discount rate, the cost of future care, the claimant's residual earning capacity etc), the resultant lump sum figure will almost certainly be an inaccurate prediction of the actual future loss. This is an inherent weakness of the lump sum system of compensation. As Lord Scarman observed in *Lim Poh Choo v Camden and Islington Area Health Authority* [1980] AC 174 at 183, 'there is really only one certainty: the future will prove the award to be either too high or too low'. However, given the actuarial approach adopted by the courts following *Wells v Wells* [1999] AC 345, it is perhaps less of a guess now than it used to be.

[5]   *Mallet v McMonagle* [1970] AC 166; *Taylor v O'Connor* [1971] AC 115; *Mitchell v Mulholland (No 2)* [1972] 1 QB 65; *Young v Percival* [1975] 1 WLR 17; *Cookson v Knowles* [1979] AC 556; *Lim Poh Choo v Camden and Islington Area Health Authority* [1980] AC 174; *Auty v NCB* [1985] 1 WLR 784; *Wells v Wells* [1999] AC 345.

[6]   Where there is agreed medical evidence as to the claimant's life expectancy, or by analogy where the court makes a finding in relation to the claimant's life expectancy, there is no further justification for any discount in respect of the 'contingencies of life': *Wells v Wells* [1999] AC 345.

[7]   *Wells v Wells* [1999] AC 345. In respect of the level of contingencies to be applied, the appropriate discount must be made following a consideration of the claimant's individual circumstances: *Pearce v Lindfield* [2003] EWCA Civ 647. But, in order to justify a substantially higher discount by reason of additional future contingencies to those envisaged in the Introduction to the Ogden Tables, there must be tangible reasons relating to the personality or likely future circumstances of the claimant, going beyond the purely speculative: *Herring v Ministry of Defence* [2003] EWCA Civ 528.

8   *Pritchard v J H Cobden Ltd* [1987] 1 All ER 300.

9   *Cookson v Knowles* [1979] AC 556. Under the current system, the multiplier in a Fatal Accidents Act case is calculated from the date of death, with the actual period from death to trial deducted from the whole multiplier to produce the future loss multiplier, although, in cases where there has been a long delay between date of death and trial, the multiplier may be increased to allow for the fact that time has removed many of the uncertainties for which a multiplier assessed at the date of death would have allowed: *Corbett v Barking Havering and Brentwood Health Authority* [1991] 2 QB 408. However, the present law has been heavily criticised by the Law Commission, the Ogden Working Party and leading commentators such as *Kemp & Kemp* and *McGregor on Damages*. See further Chapter L.

10   *Hunt v Severs* [1993] QB 815. However, it is important to ensure that the multipliers are correctly split and apportioned because (a) there is much more chance that a claimant will survive early years rather than later years, and (b) the discount for accelerated receipt must inevitably be greater for years which are further away in the future than those which are nearer. If this factor is not taken into account, the defendant may face a much larger claim because the multiplicand for the later years is generally more expensive, whether the claim is for loss of earnings or for care. See further Chapter K, Counter-schedules of Division I, for a worked example.

11   See further at paras **[A135]–[A139]** and Senior Courts Act 1981, s 32A (or County Courts Act 1984, s 51).

[A19]   Alternatively, since 1 April 2005 the court has had the power to award periodical payments in respect of future loss[1]. Such payments are usually paid annually or quarterly although can be made as frequently as required in order to meet the claimant's needs. The payments can be increased or decreased at particular times to take account of fluctuations in the claimant's level of needs, and may be indexed to a suitable measure so that they keep pace with inflation. The aim is to match more closely the claimant's needs so that the money does not run out, and periodical payments have significant advantages, particularly where the claimant's needs are significant and/or life expectancy is short or heavily contested. The guidance issued by the Department of Constitutional Affairs when implementing periodical payments stated that the policy behind the Government introducing the new system was that the existing system of compensation for future losses was unsatisfactory, and that periodical payments were usually a 'much better and fairer' way of compensating those facing long term future loss and care needs[2]. In cases begun on or after 1 April 2005, variable periodical payment orders may be made allowing the court to adjust the level of the payments in the event that the claimant suffers from a serious deterioration or enjoys some significant improvement in his or her physical or mental condition[3].

1   Courts Act 2003, ss 100 and 101, amending s 2 of the Damages Act 1996. See further Chapter O.

2   See further paragraph 6 of the DCA Guidance of Periodical Payments published on 1 April 2005 which can be downloaded at www.dca.gov.uk/pubs/pps-guidance-final.pdf. See also the Regulatory Impact Assessment: 'Courts Bill: Power to Order Periodical Payments for Future Loss' issued by the Lord Chancellor's Department in November 2002 which stated, at paragraph 2, that the 'Government considers that it is generally preferable for claimants to receive periodical payments, rather than a lump sum, where significant damages are awarded for future care costs and loss of earnings'.

3   See further Chapter O.

(3)   CONTINGENCY AWARDS

[A20]   In certain cases, an additional lump sum may be recoverable on top of the pleaded claim in respect of a particular head of loss or generally, on the basis that there is a chance in the future that the costs for the item in question will increase. Such an award is often referred to as a 'contingency award'. Examples where such awards have been made include:

- *Goldfinch v Scannell*[1] – Staughton LJ said that the correct approach to the assessment of the claimant's future care was 'to make an award based upon at least that degree of care which [the claimant] will certainly need, on a generous scale, and then to add some amount to reflect the contingencies that may occur'[2]. The main contingency that needed to be catered for was the inability of the claimant's mother to continue providing gratuitous care.
- *Bristow v Judd*[3] – The Court of Appeal awarded a lump sum of £15,000 in order to provide for the contingency that the claimant's girlfriend would not be able to continue providing housekeeping services.
- *Stuart v Martin*[4] – an award of £100,000 was made for 'contingencies'. The claimant was hit by a drunken driver and suffered a very severe head injury. There was a high chance that the claimant would suffer from further episodes of psychiatric illness and that her marriage would break down. If her marriage broke down, she would be very vulnerable and would require a greater level of guidance and support[5].
- *Blair v Michelin Tyre*[6] – an additional 15% of the total claim for care was awarded in order to reflect the risk that the claimant would go on to suffer terminal cancer and require greater care and assistance.
- *Finnis v Caulfield*[7] – HHJ Grenfell awarded an additional lump sum of £50,000 to reflect the chance that the claimant's marriage might break up, in which case the future care rates would be higher.
- *Whyte v Barber*[8] – an additional award was made on the basis that, although the agreed life expectancy evidence was that the claimant would live to the age of 18, there was a 22.5% risk that the claimant would go on to live to the age of 25. The court approved the claim for 22.5% of the increased costs of care between the ages of 19 and 25.
- *Kidd v Plymouth Health Authority*[9] – an increased multiplicand was used in respect of the claimant's future care needs to reflect the chance that her current care regime might break down, requiring increased accommodation and care costs at a secure unit or a rehabilitation unit.

---

[1]   [1993] PIQR Q143, CA.

[2]   At **[Q155]**.

[3]   [1993] PIQR Q 117. Beldam LJ said at Q127: '... in my judgment the [claimant] is also entitled to a sum to provide for the contingency that he would have to replace Mrs. Vivien's ordinary housekeeping services if he was left on his own. A starting point for the evaluation of this contingency is the number of hours needed to replace those services by someone already engaged to provide the additional care given by Mrs Vivien. On the basis of the evidence given at the trial her housekeeping services could hardly be replaced at less than an additional £40–£50 per week based on an extra one hour per day and taking into account the enhanced rate for weekends. The [claimant] would qualify for no extra benefit and to guard him against the risk that in future he is left on his own, I consider he is entitled to an additional sum of £15,000'.

[4]   [2001] All ER (D) 401 (Oct).

[5]   An alternative approach to making a contingency award might be to increase the multiplier or ask the court to make an educated guess as to when the claimant's wife would probably stop being able to provide care for her husband and apply a split multiplier. In *Potts v Buckley* (21 December 1992, unreported), QBD, Tuckey J accepted the argument that the claimant's wife was unlikely to be able

to care for her husband after he reached the age of 65 and that he should receive an allowance for 24-hour care costed on a commercial basis.

6   (25 January 2002, unreported), HHJ Marr-Johnson sitting as a judge of the Queen's Bench Division.

7   [2002] All ER (D) 353.

8   (February 2003, unreported), QBD, Smith J. See further 'Claims for Catastrophic Injury' by William Norris QC and John Pickering in [2004] JPIL, Issue 1/04.

9   [2001] Lloyd's Law Rep Med 165 at 172.

[A21]   It should be noted, however, that separate contingency awards will not necessarily be made where there are numerous different imponderables. Where there are a number of factors which could influence the cost of a future claim, it might be more appropriate to increase the claim or not apply the usual discount. In *Willbye v Gibbons*[1] the trial judge had made a number of increased awards to reflect the chances that the claimant might incur additional care costs as a result of having children, her partner leaving her or wanting to go on holiday alone. The Court of Appeal set aside the three separate contingency awards that had been made and substituted the original figure for care without any discount (the pleaded claim for future care had been discounted by 25% in order to reflect the 'gratuitous element' of the care provided). In effect the Court of Appeal awarded a single uplift of 25% on the claim for future care to reflect all the contingencies envisaged by the claimant's representatives that might give rise to increased care costs in the future. The position was put by Scott Baker LJ as follows[2]:

'On the question of future care, this is a compendious term that covers the various aspects of assistance that the appellant may need in the years ahead. Her future is full of uncertainties and the nature and extent of the assistance she will require depends on many factors, not least whether she continues to have a partner, whether and at what age she has children and if she does, how many. To split up the award into separate elements, as the judge did, is in my view to clothe the future with a greater degree of certainty than the circumstances warrant. There are likely to be periods in her life when, for one reason or another, she will need additional support but it is impossible to predict with any precision when these periods will occur or for how long they will last. An award under this head is very much a matter of feel with the judge keying in the various uncertainties about the appellant's future life and using her experience as to the appropriate range for a global award. In my judgment, the additional help that the appellant will need if she has children and/or has to live alone are matters that ought to be taken into account, but in the award for care and assistance as a whole rather than as discrete heads of damage.'

1   [2003] EWCA Civ 372.
2   At [20].

(iv)   Interest

[A22]   There is a general presumption that interest will be awarded on all awards for personal injury worth in excess of £200[1]. However, interest on general damages is calculated differently to interest on past expenses and losses[2]. No interest is payable on future expenses and losses because, by their definition, they have not yet been incurred and the object of the award of interest – ie to compensate the claimant from being kept out of his or her money – is not relevant[3].

1   Senior Courts Act 1981, s 35A and County Courts Act 1984, s 69, as interpreted by the Court of Appeal in *Davies v Inman* [1999] PIQR Q 20. However, this presumption may be displaced in exceptional circumstances, eg the where the claimant has issued prematurely in breach of the Personal Injury Pre-action Protocol or where the claimant has been guilty of gross delay in pursuing the claim.

2   See further Chapters E, Interest on General Damages, and G, Interest on Past Expenses and Losses. Note there are also special rules which apply to the calculation of interest in Fatal Accidents Act claims, and the reader is referred to Chapter L.

3   *Jefford v Gee* [1970] 2 QB 130, per Lord Denning MR at 147: 'Where the loss or damage to the [claimant] is future pecuniary loss, eg loss of future earnings, there should in principle be no interest. The judges always give the present value at the date of trial, ie, the sum which, invested at interest, would be sufficient to compensate the [claimant] for his future loss, having regard to all contingencies. There should be no interest awarded on this: because the [claimant] will not have been kept out of any money. On the contrary, he will have received it in advance'.

4   The Aim of Compensation

(i)   Different Causes of Action

[A23]   The ultimate aim of any personal injury claim is to compensate the injured party for the damage that he or she has suffered. There are subtle theoretical differences in the court's approach to the assessment of damages depending upon the nature of the particular cause of action which is being pursued. The vast majority of personal injury claims are brought in tort. In tort the general rule is that the court strives, so far as possible in monetary terms, to put the claimant back into the position he or she would have been in had the tort not occurred[1]. This principle is known as 'restitutio in integrum'. The same principle applies to a claim based upon breach of statutory duty, ie the court attempts to put the claimant back into the position her or she would have been, had the breach of statutory duty not occurred[2]. As regards contractual claims, the object of compensation is to put the claimant into the position as if the contract had been properly performed[3]. This allows a claimant to claim, for example, the loss of bargain that was expected from performance of the contract.

1   *Livingstone v Rawyards Coal Co* (1880) 5 App Cas 25; *Admiralty Commissioners v SS Valeria* [1922] 2 AC 242; *Liesbosch Dredger (Owners) v SS Edison* [1933] AC 449; *Lim Poh Choo v Camden and Islington Area Health Authority* [1980] AC 174.

2   An actionable breach of statutory duty will give rise to a statutory tort, and the measure of damages is calculated in the same way as if the claim was brought as a tortious action under the common law. See eg *Hurley v Mustoe (No 2)* [1983] ICR 422 in relation to the measure of damages following a breach of the Sex Discrimination Act 1975. See also *Ministry of Defence v Cannock* [1994] IRLR 509, EAT (another case brought under the Sex Discrimination Act 1975) where Morrison J stated at 517 that, where compensation was awarded, 'as best as money can do it, the [applicant] must be put into the position she would have been in but for the unlawful conduct of [her employer]'.

3   *Robinson v Harman* (1848) 1 Ex 850; *Nykredit Mortgage Bank plc v Edward Erdman Group Ltd (No 2)* [1997] 1 WLR 1627; *Senate Electrical Wholesalers Ltd v Alcatel Submarine Networks* [1999] 2 Lloyd's Rep 423.

[A24]   In practice, the nature of the cause of action pursued will have little, if any, impact upon the assessment of damages. This is because, whether the loss arose from a breach of tortious duty, a breach of contract or a breach of statutory duty, the goal will still be the same, ie to assess the appropriate award of damages resulting from the claimant's injury. This necessarily involves a comparison between the claimant's pre- and post-injury position.

[A25]   It should be noted, however, that in particular circumstances the cause of action upon which the claim is based might conceivably have an impact upon the scope of the defendant's liability. In particular, differences in the rules of remoteness may allow a party with a contractual claim to recover a kind of loss that would be precluded from a party in the same position with a tortious claim[1].

1   A detailed analysis of the rules of remoteness is beyond the scope of this work, and the reader is referred to the relevant section in other works such as *Clerk & Lindsell on Torts, Chitty on Contracts* and *McGregor on Damages.*

(ii)   Pecuniary Loss

[A26]   In terms of pecuniary loss, so far as possible, the fundamental principle is that the claimant is entitled to full compensation, ie 100% of the value of his or her proven net expenses and losses[1]. This is known as the 100% principle and applies equally to the assessment of lump sum damages as it does to assessment of periodical payments[2].

1   *Livingstone v Rawyards Coal Co* (1880) 5 App Cas 25; *Lim Poh Choo v Camden and Islington Area Health Authority* [1980] AC 174; *Hodgson v Trapp* [1989] AC 807; *Pickett v Pickett* [1980] AC 136; *Wells v Wells* [1999] AC 345. In *Wells v Wells* [1999] AC 345, Lord Steyn said at 382–383: 'The premise of the debate was that as a matter of law a victim of a tort is entitled to be compensated as nearly as possible in full for all pecuniary losses. For present purposes this mainly means compensation for loss of earnings and medical care, both past and future. Subject to the obvious qualification that perfection in the assessment of future compensation is unattainable, the 100 per cent. principle is well established and based on high authority: *Livingstone v Rawyards Coal Co* (1880) 5 App Cas 25, 39; *Lim Poh Choo v Camden and Islington Area Health Authority* [1980] AC 174, 187E, per Lord Scarman'. Note that, as explained in *Parry v North West Surrey Health Authority* (29 November 1999, unreported), QBD, where earlier views have been expressed, particularly by Lord Denning, that the calculation of damages must be 'fair, just and reasonable' (suggesting that the 100% principle might be moderated by overriding considerations of unspecific 'fairness'), these sentiments generally apply to non-pecuniary loss as opposed to pecuniary loss. The need for 'fairness' in assessing damages, as expressed by Brett J in *Rowley v London and North Western Rly* (1873) LR 8 Ex 221 and Lord Denning in *Fletcher v Autocar and Transporters Ltd* [1968] 2 QB 322 at 335, has little or no application to the assessment of pecuniary loss. Thus, the House of Lords in *Wells v Wells* [1999] 1 AC 345 adopted the principle of 'full compensation' for pecuniary loss without any mention of fairness to the parties. In other words, the claimant is entitled to claim 100% of his or her losses attributable to the defendant's wrongdoing without any need for the award to be 'fair' to the defendant. See further *Heil v Rankin* [2001] QB 272; *McGregor on Damages*; and *Clerk & Lindsell on Torts.*

2   *Flora v Wakom (Heathrow) Ltd* [2006] EWCA Civ 1103, [2007] 1 WLR 482; *Thompstone v Tameside and Glossop NHS Trust* [2008] EWCA Civ 5, [2008] 1 WLR 2207.

[A27]   The classic statement of the full compensation principle was expressed by Lord Blackburn in *Livingstone v Rawyards Coal Co*[1]:

'[W]here any injury is to be compensated by damages, in settling the sum of money to be given for reparation of damages you should as nearly as possible get at that sum of money which will put the party who has been injured, or who has suffered, in the same position as he would have been in if he had not sustained the wrong for which he is now getting his compensation or reparation.'

1   (1880) 5 App Cas 25 at 39.

[A28] There is no limit on the award that the court can make in relation to pecuniary loss and no reason to discount the award because it seems too high or unfair[1]. It was put in this way by Lord Lloyd in *Wells v Wells*[2]:

> 'The purpose of the award is to put the [claimant] in the same position, financially, as if he had not been injured. The sum should be calculated as accurately as possible, making just allowance, where this is appropriate, for contingencies. But once the calculation is done, there is no justification for imposing an artificial cap on the multiplier. There is no room for a judicial scaling down. Current awards in the most serious cases may seem high. The present appeals may be taken as examples. But there is no more reason to reduce the awards, if properly calculated, because they seem high than there is to increase the awards because the injuries are very severe.'

[1] As Lord Scarman stated in *Lim Poh Choo v Camden and Islington Area Health Authority* [1980] AC 174 at 187: 'There is no room here for considering the consequences of a high award upon the wrongdoer or those who finance him'.

[2] [1999] AC 345 at 364.

(iii) Non-pecuniary loss

[A29] The principle of 'full compensation' also applies to non-pecuniary loss[1]. However, the assessment of compensation for pain, suffering and loss of amenity poses its own special problems, because there is no immediately apparent way of valuing the appropriate damages to be awarded for particular injuries, eg how do you value the loss of a limb?[2] In the circumstances, the award for pain, suffering and loss of amenity is necessarily an arbitrary figure designed to be 'fair, just and reasonable' monetary compensation for the injuries sustained[3]. The Court of Appeal is charged with the responsibility of setting the applicable guidelines and keeping them up to date[4]. The tariffs are conventional sums which take into account both social and economic factors[5].

[1] *Heil v Rankin* [2001] QB 272, per Lord Woolf at 293 [23].

[2] See further *H West & Son Ltd v Shephard* [1964] AC 326, in particular per Lord Pearce at 365.

[3] *Rowley v London and North Western Ry Co* (1873) LR 8 Exch 221 at 231; *Pickett v British Railways Board Ltd* [1980] AC 136 at 168; *Lim Poh Choo v Camden Area Health Authority* [1980] AC 174 at 187; and *Heil v Rankin* [2001] QB 272.

[4] *Wright v BRB* [1983] 2 AC 773; *Heil v Rankin* [2001] QB 272.

[5] *Heil v Rankin* [2001] QB 272.

5 Jurisdiction[1]

[A30] Where an injury occurs abroad, the question of jurisdiction arises in three main ways:

(i)   whether or not the claimant has jurisdiction to start an action in this country;

(ii) whether the law of this country or another country governs liability (and causation); and

(iii) whether the law of this country or another country governs quantum and the assessment of damages.

It is this third issue which concerns us in this section. By virtue of s 11 of the Private International Law (Miscellaneous Provisions) Act 1995, the general rule is that the applicable law is the law of the country in which the events constituting the tort occur, and s 12 of the 1995 Act the court may decide to apply the law regarding the assessment of damages of a different country if it is 'substantially more appropriate for the applicable law for determining the issues arising in the case, or any of those issues, to be the law of the other country'. However, under s 14(3)(b), any rules of evidence, pleading, practice or procedure are to be determined by the law of the forum. In *Harding v Wealands*[2] the House of Lords unanimously held that, under s 14(3)(b) of the 1995 Act, questions regarding the quantification or assessment of damages were procedural rather than substantive. Therefore, in relation to proceedings issued in this country involving a foreign accident, damages would be assessed in accordance with English law[3]. Whether or not a particular head of damage is permitted is considered a substantive matter to be determined by the law of the country where the events constituting the tort occurred (unless English law is considered 'substantially more appropriate' under s 12). However, if a particular head of loss is recognised by the foreign jurisdiction, the assessment of the loss is quantified according to English principles. This meant that Mr Harding, who had suffered a serious accident in New South Wales, Australia, had his damages assessed by reference to English law, which led to a settlement which was 30% higher than if his damages had been assessed in accordance with Australian law. Although provisions of the Motor Accidents Compensation Act 1999 restricted the recovery of damages for road traffic accidents in Australia, these provisions were considered to be procedural rather than substantive law, and therefore of no application to the assessment of damages in England.

[1]	See further *Dicey & Morris on the Conflict of Laws* and 'Foreign Compensation Systems and Personal Injury Claims' by Michael McParland [2007] JPIL, Issue 3/07 (September) pp 273–286.
[2]	[2006] UKHL 32.
[3]	This interpretation was clearly supported by Ministerial statements at the time that the 1995 Act was implemented, stating that there was no need to worry about American-sized awards since quantum would continue to be regulated by our own domestic law of damages.

[A31]   Whilst the clarification of the law in *Harding v Wealands*[1] was very much welcomed, the position in relation to accidents occurring on or after 19 August 2007 has now been changed by virtue of Regulation (EC) 864/2007 on the Law Applicable to Non-Contractual Obligations ('Rome II Regulation') which came into force on 11 January 2009[2]. Under Art 15(c) the foreign applicable law will now govern '[t]he existence, the nature and the assessment of damage or the remedy claimed'. Although there may be arguments regarding precisely what is covered by the assessment of damages, English courts will now be obliged to assess damages in accordance with where the injury took place[3]. This is likely to result in a reduction of damages in many cases. However, there are three exceptions. First, the foreign law will not apply if the claimant and the defendant both had their habitual residence in the same country when the damage occurred[4]. Secondly, if in all the circumstances another country's law is 'manifestly more closely connected to the tort', then the law of that country will apply[5]. Thirdly, Recital 33 suggests that, in relation to road traffic accidents when quantifying damages for personal injury, the court seised of the matter should take into account all the relevant circumstances of the specific victim, including in particular the actual losses and costs of after-care and medical attention. It remains to be seen how this Regulation and exceptions will be applied in practice. Although the Regulation applies to all member states apart from Denmark, on its face the provisions apply to accidents which occur outside Europe. So, whilst some claimants who suffer injuries in countries such as Spain and Germany may see a reduction in damages, other claimants who are injured in countries such as the USA may see an increase. But, in the case of road traffic accidents, Recital 33 may have the effect of awarding damages commensurate with the extent of the loss that will actually be incurred.

1	[2006] UKHL 32. See also *Maher and Maher v Groupama Grand Est* [2009] EWCA Civ 1191.
2	See further 'Tort Injuries Abroad and the Rome II Regulation: A Brief Wake-Up Call for Existing Claims' by Michael McParland in [2008] JPIL Issue 3/08, pp 221–223; 'An Introductory Guide to Rome II for Personal Injury Practitioners' by Charles Dougherty and Marie Louise Kinsler, available from www.2tg.co.uk; and 'All Change for Rome II' by Alan Saggerson, available from www.no1chancerylane.com.
3	See further Art 4(1) which states: 'Unless otherwise provided for in this Regulation, the law applicable to a non-contractual obligation arising out of a tort/delict shall be the law of the country in which the damage occurs irrespective of the country in which the event giving rise to the damage occurred and irrespective of the country or countries in which the indirect consequences of that event occurred'.
4	Art 4(2).
5	Art 4(3).

6 The Time of Assessment

(i) Generally

[A32]   The normal rule is that damages fall to be assessed once and for all at the date of trial[1]. There is a strong public interest in the finality of litigation and preventing relitigation of matters, even though the assessment of damages may have been uncertain at the date of trial[2]. The court has to make its best assessment of the claimant's past and future losses and expenses at that time[3]. This means that, whilst account may be taken of any change in the claimant's condition between the date of injury and the date of trial, the quantification of many heads of claim may still be uncertain. Where the claimant is still undergoing treatment, the court will often be amenable to delaying the assessment of damages until a final prognosis is available. However, given the emphasis in today's modern litigation upon dealing with cases justly, which includes an obligation to ensure that cases are pursued expeditiously whilst allotting a proportionate amount of court time to each case[4], there may come a time when the court will not be inclined to prolong assessment any further, and the court will have to do its best to assess quantum on the basis of the available evidence. Having said that, there are a number of presumptions which come into play in order to assist with the assessment, and various discounts can be made in order to take account of uncertainties and future contingencies[5].

1	*Mulholland v Mitchell* [1971] AC 666, per Lord Pearson at 681: 'The normal rule in accident cases is that the sum of damages falls to be assessed once at for all at the time of the hearing. When the assessment is made, the court has to make the best assessment it can as to events which may happen in the future. If further evidence as to new events were too easily admitted, there would be no finality in such litigation'. See also *Pritchard v J H Cobden Ltd* [1987] 1 All ER 300. However, where appropriate, the court has the power under CPR, Pt 3 to adjourn or stay the assessment of one or more heads of loss. See further 'Adjournment and/or Stay' at para [A133].

2   This is encompassed in the maxim 'interest reipublicae ut sit finis litium'. See further *Brown v Dean* [1910] AC 373 at 374; *Murphy v Stone-Wallwork (Charlton) Limited* [1969] 1 WLR 1023; *Mulholland v Mitchell* [1971] AC 666 at 681.

3   Although it should be noted that, where the trial is long or there have been one or more adjournments, the assessment is carried out at the end of the trial when all the evidence has been heard. See eg *Ford v GKR* [2000] 1 WLR 1397, CA, in which the defendant carried out video surveillance of the claimant during an adjournment after the claimant had already been cross-examined. Judge LJ stated: 'Sometimes claimants do lie, embellish or fantasise, but if that is to be the defendants' case fairness demands that the claimant should have a reasonable opportunity to deal with these allegations. Sometimes sensible grounds for maintaining surveillance on a claimant may arise after the trial has begun. If they do, the defendants cannot be criticised for taking advantage of the opportunity given by an adjournment to do so'.

4   See further the overriding objective, CPR, r 1.1.

5   See further at paras [A100], [A101].

[A33]   When assessing damages at the date of trial, the court is able to take account of all known facts, including any change of circumstances since the injury. Developments may be considered right up to the end of the final hearing, so that even evidence obtained during an adjournment of the trial may be admitted with the court's permission[1]. Changes of circumstance that may have a bearing on the likely award of damages include the following:

- Any increase or decrease in salary to which the claimant would have been entitled.
- Whether or not the claimant would have developed a supervening illness or disease in any event[2].
- Any increase or decrease in the cost of items purchased as a result of the injuries.
- Any increase or decrease in the cost of care or accommodation[3].
- Any promotion or job prospect that would have become available.
- Any changes in the industrial or economic climate.
- The fact that the claimant may have voluntarily taken a particular course[4].
- Any increase in the applicable tariff in respect of general damages for pain, suffering and loss of amenity[5].
- Any changes in law, practice or procedure[6].
- Changes to the amount of recoupable benefits received[7].

1   See eg *Ford v GKR Construction Ltd* [2000] 1 WLR 1397, CA, in which the trial judge permitted the defendant to rely upon video surveillance evidence of the claimant obtained during an adjournment of the trial.

2   For example, in *Jobling v Associated Dairies Ltd* [1982] AC 794 the claimant developed a serious spinal disease between the date of the accident and the date of trial which would have prevented the claimant from working in any event. The House of Lords held that this supervening illness had to be taken into account when assessing damages.

3   See eg *Mulholland v Mitchell* [1971] AC 666; and *Lim Poh Choo v Camden and Islington Area Health Authority* [1980] AC 174.

4   For example, in *Carter v British Steam Navigation Co Ltd and France (William) Fenwick & Co Ltd* [1974] 1 Lloyd's Rep 419.

5   Such as a change in the discount rate set by the Lord Chancellor under s 1 of the Damages Act 1996.

6   See eg *Van Oudenhaven v Griffin Inns Ltd* [2000] 1 WLR 1413, in which the claimant was awarded an additional 8.5% in respect of general damages for pain, suffering and loss of amenity following the Court of Appeal's decision in *Heil v Rankin* [2001] QB 272.

7   Sometimes, delay in relation to the final hearing can cause prejudice to a defendant because they become liable to pay more under the Social Security (Recovery of Benefits) Act 1997. This prejudice may sometimes result in cases being struck out, although the court now has a lot of flexibility under the CPR, especially where a fair trial is still possible. See further Chapter J, Recovery of State and Collateral Benefits.

(ii) Special Cases

[A34] It should be noted that, whilst the time for assessment of damages will be at the date of trial, there are a number of heads of loss which the court will assess by reference to an earlier period. The main categories of these special cases are listed below.

Damaged or destroyed chattels

[A35] Where the claimant's clothing or possessions have been damaged in an accident, the appropriate measure of damages is the diminution in their value which is usually measured by the cost of repair[1]. Where clothing or possessions have been destroyed or damaged beyond economical repair, the claimant is entitled to recover the market value of the item as at the date of the accident (less any salvage value of the destroyed item)[2]. Exceptionally, where an item is unique or has a high salvage value, it may be appropriate to adjourn the trial so that the item can be put on the market and/or sold in order to obtain evidence to assist with the assessment of the diminution in value[3].

[1]   *Darbishire v Warran* [1963] 1 WLR 1067.
[2]   *The Clyde* (1856) Swab 23. See further chapter 32 of *McGregor on Damages*.
[3]   *Constantine v Totalfinaelf UK Ltd* [2003] EWHC 428 (QB).

Reasonableness of decision-making

[A36] Whilst the time for assessment of past expenses and losses is at the date of trial, when considering the reasonableness of the claimant's decisions and actions the court will generally only take into account what could or should have been known at the time the expenses or losses were incurred. For example, when considering the reasonableness of past medical treatment, the court will not take into account the fact that the treatment has ultimately failed or made the claimant's condition worse[1]. Hindsight is revealing, but the issue for the court is whether or not it was reasonable for the claimant to have undergone the particular treatment at the time, bearing in mind what he or she was told about the treatment and what was then known about the risks and benefits of the same.

[1]   See eg *Rubens v Walker* [1946] SC 215. See also *Morris v Richards* [2003] EWCA Civ 232, where the claimant was unable to continue in her pre-accident employment by reason of her injuries and took up a new job. In hindsight, the claimant appreciated that she did not have the relevant skills or experience necessary for the new job. She decided to resign before she was pushed. The Court of Appeal held that she had acted reasonably, observing that many people when embarking upon a new career make a false start, and the chances of making a false start are, if anything, magnified when being forced to choose a second career because of an accident.

Fatal accidents

[A37] Another example of an exception to the general rule regarding the time for assessment of damages is the calculation of multipliers in claims brought under the Fatal Accidents Act 1976. Unlike a living claimant, the multiplier in a fatal accident claim is traditionally fixed as at the date of death and not from the date of trial[1]. The reason for this is that the court takes into account potential uncertainties in the deceased's life, had he lived, which could have affected his expenses/losses between death and trial. The multiplier is calculated from death (when there are the least number of uncertainties), and then the period from death to trial is deducted from the overall multiplier to give the multiplier to be adopted for future loss[2]. However, the traditional approach to the assessment of the value of dependencies under the Fatal Accidents Act 1976 has been criticised by a number of leading commentators[3]. In its paper No 263 entitled 'Claims for Wrongful Death' (November 1999), the Law Commission recommended that the law in this area should be reformed. However, to date there have been a number of failed attempts[4] to persuade the court to bring the assessment of multipliers in fatal accident claims in line with personal injury cases, and it appears that all lower courts will consider themselves bound by the approach taken by the House of Lords in *Cookson v Knowles*[5].

[1]   *Cookson v Knowles* [1979] AC 556, HL.
[2]   For example, in *Cookson v Knowles* [1979] AC 556, HL, a final future loss multiplier of 8.5 was used. This was calculated from an initial multiplier of 11 from death: the trial was 2½ years after death.
[3]   See eg *Kemp & Kemp*; *McGregor on Damages* and David Kemp and Rowland Hogg 'How to Determine Multipliers in Assessing Damages under the Fatal Accidents Acts, Using the Revised "Ogden Tables" ' [2000] JPIL, Issue 2–3/00, pp 142–155 and also [1999] JPIL, Issue 1/99, p 42.
[4]   *A Train & Sons Ltd v Fletcher* [2008] 4 All ER 699; *ATH v MS* [2002] EWCA Civ 792; *White v ESAB Group UK* [2002] PIQR Q76; and *Wilkins v William Press Ltd* (30 November 2000, unreported), QBD, Wilkinson QC.
[5]   [1979] AC 556, HL.

Professional negligence[1]

[A38]   In proceedings for professional negligence against solicitors or counsel arising out of failure to pursue a case to trial, two dates are relevant for assessment. First, the date at which, but for the negligence, the case probably would have been heard ('the notional trial date') and, secondly, the date of hearing of the professional negligence action. The quantification of damage in such cases takes place in three stages:

- assessment of the chances that the original action would have succeeded at trial;
- assessment of the value of the claim as it would have been at the notional trial date; and
- interest on the judgment sum from the notional trial date to the date of the professional negligence hearing, together with any other losses (eg legal fees).

[1]   See further Chapter N.

[A39]   The assessment is a matter of judgement for the court hearing the professional negligence claim. Consideration must be given to the evidence which would have been available to the trial judge at the notional date of trial. However, the court may not necessarily ignore subsequent events and, in appropriate circumstances, the court may admit evidence which might be relevant to an existing head of damage. In particular, it is unlikely that the court will assume that the notional trial judge would have made mistaken findings of fact and/or exercised his or her discretion wrongly.

Thus the notional trial judge is likely to be held to have determined matters which could only have been predicted with uncertainty at the notional trial date, but which have since become certain one way or the other in accordance with what is now known to be the case. For example, in *Charles v Hugh James Jones & Jenkins*[1] the court took account of medical evidence that had been obtained after the notional trial date but which clarified what had previously been an uncertain prognosis in relation to a condition that was already manifest. Swinton Thomas LJ stated[2]:

> '... it would be absurd, and in my judgment wrong, if, for example, at the notional trial date the medical evidence indicated that there was a strong probability that the claimant would in future suffer some adverse medical consequence as a result of the injuries sustained in the accident, but it was shown as at the date of the actual hearing that there was no such risk, that the claimant should recover damages in respect of it. Similarly, if there was evidence as at the notional trial date that the probability was that the claimant would never work again, but at the actual trial date he or she had obtained remunerative employment, it would be wrong not to take that fact into account. Equally, if the evidence was less certain as to the claimant's prospects of obtaining employment at the notional trial date, but it was quite certain as at the actual trial date that she would be unable to go back to work again, that is a fact which can properly be considered by the judge. In my judgment, it would be absurd and wrong in principle to disregard such evidence.'

---

[1]   [2000] 1 WLR 1278. See also *Dudarec v Andrew and others* [2006] EWCA Civ 256, [2006] 1 WLR 3002.

[2]   At 1290–1291.

[A40]   As regards the position in relation to completely new conditions or events arising after the notional trial date, the Court of Appeal left open the question of whether such developments should be taken into account by the trial judge in *Charles v Hugh James Jones & Jenkins*[1] and the subsequent case of *Dudarec v Andrew and others*[2]. However, the point did arise for consideration in *Whitehead v Searle and another*[3], where it was held that the *Bwllfa*[4] principle applied, ie that 'where facts are available they are to be preferred to prophecies'[5] and 'the court should never speculate where it knows'[6]. Thus a professional negligence action failed which was based on a wrongful birth claim being brought on for trial before the original claimant committed suicide where damages would have been assessed on the false basis that there was continuing future loss claim beyond the date of her death. Laws LJ (with whom Rix and Rimmer LLJ agreed) held that the defendants were not liable for failing to secure an uncovenanted benefit based upon the premise that the original claimant was still living (and had a normal life expectancy) when events occurring after the putative trial contradicted that assumption. However, Laws LJ specifically confined his judgment to supervening events occurring after the notional trial date which, if taken into account, would diminish rather than swell the damages[7].

---

[1]   [2000] 1 WLR 1278; see per Swinton Thomas LJ at 1290 and Sir Richard Scott at 1295.

[2]   [2006] EWCA Civ 256, [2006] 1 WLR 3002. See also *Snowden v Thurstan Hoskins & Partners (a firm) and Jewill Hill & Bennett (a firm)* (14 November 2002, unreported).

[3]   [2008] EWCA Civ 285, [2009] 1 WLR 549.

[4]   *Bwllfa and Merthyr Dare Steam Collieries (1891) Ltd v Pontypridd Waterworks Co* [1903] AC 426.

[5]   *In re Bradberry* [1943] Ch 35, 45, per Uthwatt J.

[6]   *Curwen v James* [1963] 1 WLR 748, 753, per Harman LJ.

[7]   [2009] 1 WLR 549 at 563, para [29].

Appeals

[A41] In exceptional circumstances the court will admit fresh evidence in order to reassess the appropriate award of damages calculated as at the date of trial[1]. The most obvious example is the fraudulent claimant who is not caught until after trial. For example, in *Liverpool City Council v Hill*[2] the claimant falsely claimed he had tripped on a defective pavement and damaged his knee. He was awarded £11,000. Shortly thereafter, the council became suspicious when the claimant's name appeared as a goal scorer for his Sunday football team in the local paper. Covert surveillance was carried out and the claimant was ordered to repay the money with £1,100 interest. However, where fraud is alleged, there is an alternative remedy in the form of fresh proceedings to set aside the fraudulently obtained judgment[3]. Where the fraud is 'not clearly established' or is 'hotly contested', it may be preferable for the aggrieved party to bring fresh fraud proceedings, particularly where the matter is complex and detailed findings of fact need to be made[4]. In *Kuwait Airways Corpn v Iraqi Airways Co and another (No 2)*[5], when refusing to entertain an application to review its previous decision in a complex case, Lord Slynn of Hadley said:[6]

'... there is well established authority that where a final decision has been made by a court a challenge to the decision on the basis that it has been obtained by fraud must be made by a fresh action alleging and proving the fraud.'

[1]   In *Curwen v James* [1963] 1 WLR 748 at 753, Harman LJ stated, 'the court should never speculate where it knows'..
[2]   (1996) Times, 26 September, HHJ Hamilton. See also *Prentice v Hereward Housing Association and Cambridgeshire District Council* [2001] EWCA Civ 437.
[3]   *Flower v Lloyd* (1877) 6 Ch D 297; *Jonesco v Beard* [1930] AC 298; *Pell v (1) Express Newspapers and (2) Watts* [2005] EWCA Civ 46; and *Jaffray and others v Society of Lloyd's* [2008] 1 WLR 75.
[4]   *Wood v Gahlings* (unreported, 4 November 1996, CA); *Kuwait Airways Corpn v Iraqi Airways Co and another (No 2)* [2001] 1 WLR 429; *Sohal v Sohal* [2002] EWCA Civ 1297; *Pell v (1) Express Newspapers and (2) Watts* [2005] EWCA Civ 46; and *Jaffray and others v Society of Lloyd's* [2008] 1 WLR 75.
[5]   [2001] 1 WLR 429.
[6]   Para 24 at page 433.

[A42] In other cases not necessarily involving fraud, the court retains a general discretion to allow further evidence to be adduced on appeal[1]. The court may also be willing to admit fresh evidence after the conclusion of a trial where there is a danger that it has been misled into making findings on an incorrect factual basis. For example, in *Mulholland v Mitchell*[2] the House of Lords upheld the Court of Appeal's decision to allow fresh evidence regarding the increased costs of nursing care following the claimant's unexpected deterioration after trial and his emergency admission to hospital. Further, in *Vernon v Bosley (No 2)*[3] the claimant failed to disclose the existence of medical reports obtained in relation to proceedings under the Children Act 1989 by the same experts he was relying upon in a personal injury action for nervous shock. The reports in the family proceedings concerning the question of whether or not the claimant was fit enough to look after his children painted a much rosier picture regarding the claimant's condition and prognosis than the reports in the civil action, where the main issues centred upon the claimant's ability to return to gainful employment and the level of care he required. The Court of Appeal held that the reports obtained during the family proceedings were clearly relevant to the issues to be decided in the civil claim and were not protected by litigation privilege. Permission was therefore granted to hear further evidence relevant to the claimant's mental condition and prognosis for the future, which would or might have affected the judge's assessment of the quantum of damages at the time it was made.

---

1   See generally *Ladd v Marshall* [1954] 1 WLR 1489; *Curwen v James* [1963] 1 WLR 748; *Mulholland v Mitchell* [1971] AC 666; *Hertfordshire v Bubb and Bubb* [2000] 1 WLR 2318; *Hamilton v Mohamed Al Fayed* [2001] EMLR 394; *Cooper v Reed and Atlas Radio Cars* [2001] EWCA Civ 224; *Gillingham, Gillingham and Gillingham v Gillingham* [2001] EWCA Civ 906; *Jones v South Tyneside Health Authority* [2001] EWCA Civ 1701; and *Saluja v Gill (t/a Gill Estate Agents Property Services) and Netlink Property Services Ltd* [2002] EWHC 1435 (Ch).

2   [1971] AC 666.

5   [1997] 2 WLR 683.

[A43]   Generally speaking, it will be more difficult to appeal on the basis of fresh evidence in quantum cases because of the need for finality in litigation and the fact that the judge has to do his or her best to predict the future on the basis of the available evidence[1]. A particular consideration is that applications to overturn a previous decision, especially long after the time for appeal has run out, have to be confined to 'very special and exceptional cases', bearing in mind 'the general evil of allowing judgment to be disturbed and thereby prolonging and extending litigation'[2]. However, one example of where the court did exercise its discretion is provided by *McCann v Sheppard*[3], in which the trial judge had awarded the claimant loss of earnings using a multiplier of 15 but the claimant died of a drugs overdose only four months after trial. The defendant was granted permission to adduce fresh evidence regarding the claimant's death and, accordingly, the award for loss of earnings was recalculated up to the date of the claimant's death. It was held that it would be an 'affront to common sense' if the court closed its eyes to the fact of the death[4]. Since the damages were intended for the injured man himself and not for the benefit of his dependants, the damages would be reduced to reflect his actual lifespan. It was doubted whether his dependants could bring an action under the Fatal Accidents Act 1976 for the shortfall in his damages[5].

---

1   Only in very special and exceptional circumstances will fresh evidence as to the assessment of damages be admitted on appeal: *Curwen v James* [1963] 1 WLR 1963; *McCann v Sheppard* [1973] 1 WLR 540; *Jenkins v Richard Thomas & Baldwins* [1966] 1 WLR 476; *Murphy v Stone-Wallwork (Charlton) Limited* [1969] 1 WLR 1023; *Mulholland v Mitchell* [1971] 1 AC at 681. See further *Phipson on Evidence*, at paragraph 13-12 of the main work.

2   *Murphy v Stone-Wallwork (Charlton) Limited* [1969] 1 WLR 1023 per Lord Upjohn at 1031D–F and Lord Pearce at 1028C–D.

3   [1973] 1 WLR 540.

4   Per Lord Denning at 546.

5   This is because of the wording of s 1 of the Fatal Accidents Act 1976, which assumes that only one action can be brought either by the deceased or alternatively by the dependants where the deceased would have been entitled to bring such an action. See further *Jameson v Central Electricity Generating Board (No 1)* [2000] 1 AC 455, in which the House of Lords held that a claim could not be brought by dependants under the Fatal Accidents Act 1976 against a tortfeasor where the deceased had already accepted settlement against a concurrent tortfeasor.

7   Entitlement to Claim

[A44]   Generally speaking, a claimant is only entitled to claim legally recognised losses which he or she has suffered personally and that are not too remote.

(i)   Entitlement in Law

[A45]   There are a number of heads of loss for which damages are not recoverable. For example, the costs of raising and caring for a healthy baby are prohibited by reasons of public policy[1], and compensation is not recoverable for gratuitous services provided by the tortfeasor[2]. Whilst the list of unrecoverable heads is not exhaustive, see Chapter K for further examples of heads of loss which are not recognised in law.

[1]   *McFarlane v Tayside Health Board* [2000] 2 AC 59.
[2]   *Hunt v Severs* [1994] 2 AC 350.

(ii)   The Claimant's Loss

[A46]   In the ordinary course of events, a claimant may not recover damages for the loss suffered by a third party, since the defendant does not owe the third party any duty of care to avoid causing the loss[1]. However, there are a number of recognised exceptions to this general principle:

- Where a parent or guardian has incurred expenses or losses on behalf of an injured minor.
- Where the person who would have been the claimant has died and an action is pursued under the Law Reform (Miscellaneous Provisions) Act 1934 for the benefit of the deceased's estate or under the Fatal Accidents Act 1976 for the benefit of the deceased's dependants.
- Where others have provided gratuitous services on behalf of the claimant (such as care, domestic assistance or gardening), reasonable recompense for these services is recoverable by the claimant but held on trust for the care providers[2].
- Where friends or family members have incurred travel expenses visiting the claimant in hospital which has aided the claimant's recovery[3].
- Where the claimant was (lawfully) in possession of a third party's chattels which were damaged or destroyed by the defendant's negligence[4].
- Where members of the claimant's family have benefited from accommodation bought to re-house the claimant[5].
- Where the claimant's parents have incurred costs moving home as a result of the claimant's disability[6].
- Where the claimant is no longer able to provide gratuitous care to another by reason of his or her injuries[7].
- Subrogated claims for damages, eg recovery for an employer's outlay in continuing to pay the claimant's wages[8], an insurer's outlay for the repair or replacement of the claimant's vehicle or possessions, and a private healthcare insurer's outlay for providing private medical treatment.
- Subrogated claims for interest on expenses/losses incurred by third parties[9].

1   *Best v Samuel Fox & Co* [1952] AC 176; *Buckley v Farrow* [1997] PIQR Q78; *Swain v LAS NHS Trust* [1999] All ER (D) 260. See also *Lee v Sheard* [1956] 1 QB 192 and *Kent v BRB* [1995] PIQR Q42 regarding the calculation of loss of earnings in respect of a partnership: the claimant's loss is limited to the claimant's share in the profits and not the whole of the partnership loss. Although cf *Ward v Newalls Insulation* [1998] 1 WLR 1722, where an equal share of profits between partners was not held to be appropriate when two of the partners were 'sleeping partners' who were included in the partnership as a tool to reduce tax.

2   *Hunt v Severs* [1994] 2 AC 350. See further *ATH v MS* [2002] EWCA Civ 792.

3   See further *Schneider v Eisovitch* [1960] 2 QB 430 and *Havenhand v Jeffrey* (24 February 1997, unreported), CA.

4   *The Winkfield* [1902] P 42; *Morrison Steamship Co Ltd v SS Greystoke Castle* [1947] AC 265; *Hepburn v A Tomlinson (Hauliers) Ltd* [1966] AC 451; and *The Albazero* [1977] AC 774. A bailee in possession of a chattel may sue for any injury inflicted upon that chattel, and may recover in full the cost of replacement or repair, irrespective of whether the chattel has been destroyed or merely damaged and irrespective of whether he or she has suffered any personal loss as a result of the defendant's misconduct. See further *Palmer on Bailment* (2nd edn).

5   *M (a child) v Leeds Health Authority* [2002] PIQR Q46.

6   *Parkhouse v North Devon Healthcare NHS Trust* [2002] Lloyd's Rep Med 100. Note that it was held in this case that it was speculative that the claimant's parents would have moved in any event but for the claimant's injuries.

7   *Lowe v Guise* [2002] EWCA Civ 197.

8   *Davies v Inman* [1999] PIQR Q26.

9   Any interest received is held on trust for the third party who incurred the loss/expense under the principle in *Hunt v Severs* [1994] 2 AC 350. See eg *Davies v Inman* [1999] PIQR Q26 regarding an employer who continued to pay the claimant's loss of earnings for the 13 weeks he was off as a result of an accident, on the undertaking that the claimant would repay his employer from any subsequent award of damages.

(iii)   The Rule Against Double Recovery

[A47]   A claimant must give credit against his or her loss for money or benefits in kind which he or she would not have received but for his or her injuries[1]. There are two recognised exceptions to this: insurance; and the benevolence of third parties[2]. Thus a claimant who has obtained free medical treatment on the NHS has not suffered any loss and may not recover the notional costs of the treatment[3]. Likewise, a claimant who receives state benefits not covered by the statutory recoupment scheme must give credit for the same[4], and a claimant who obtains free car hire from a third party because the third party failed to ensure that the hire agreement complied with the Consumer Credit Act 1974 cannot claim the notional cost of the hire charges from the defendant[5]. Additionally, individual heads of loss may overlap, resulting in double recovery. For example, a claim cannot be made both for the notional value of gratuitous services provided by a relative and also the relative's loss of earnings sustained in order to have time for the injured claimant[6]. On occasions, it may appear that pecuniary and non-pecuniary heads of damage can overlap, resulting in double recovery[7]. However, whether or not different types of damage can actually overlap in this way is doubtful[8].

1   *Hodgson v Trapp* [1989] 1 AC 807.

2   *Parry v Cleaver* [1970] AC 1 at 14.

3   *Harris v Bright's Asphalt Contractors Ltd* [1953] 1 QB 617; see further *Hunt v Severs* [1994] 2 AC 350, per Lord Bridge at 360–361.

4   *Hodgson v Trapp* [1989] 1 AC 807.

5   *Dimond v Lovell* [2002] 1 AC 384.

6   *Fish v Wilcox* [1994] 5 Med LR 230.
7   See eg *Harris v Harris* [1973] 1 Lloyd's Rep 445, CA; *Brown v Merton Health Authority (Teaching)* [1982] 1 All ER 650, CA; and *Musmar v Kalala* [1999] CLY 1565.
8   See further Lord Scarman's speech in *Lim Poh Choo v Camden and Islington Area Health Authority* [1980] AC 174. See further at para **[A12]**.

(iv)   Actionable Injury

[A48]   Some causes of action, such as trespass to the person and breach of contract, are actionable even without proof of damage. If no actual damage is proved, the claimant is entitled to nominal damages. However, claims in negligence require actionable damage and the principle 'de minimis non curat lex' prohibits claims being brought for trivial injury. In order to succeed in a negligence claim the claimant must prove he is worse off as a result of the defendant's negligence. But how much worse off must one be to establish a claim in negligence? This point was considered by the House of Lords in *Rothwell v Chemical & Insulating Co Ltd*[1] concerning whether or not pleural plaques were an actionable injury. Lord Hoffmann cited with approval the words of Harman LJ, Pearson LJ, Lord Reid and Lord Evershed in *Cartledge v E Jopling & Sons Ltd* [1963] AC 758, who spoke of the damage being 'not insignificant', 'beyond what can be regarded as negligible' and 'real damage as distinct from purely minimal damage'[2]. It was held that Holland J's finding that the pleural plaques were not in themselves damage which could sustain a cause of action was unassailable. Further, the so-called aggregation theory was rejected, and it was held that taking pleural plaques together with anxiety (falling short of a recognisable psychiatric condition) at the prospect of developing future injury was insufficient to make what would not otherwise be considered an actionable injury become actionable. The Government subsequently carried out a consultation regarding those who suffer from pleural plaques, and on 25 February 2010, Justice Secretary Jack Straw announced that the Government did not intend to change the law to permit such sufferers to bring a claim[3]. However, payments made under the Pneumoconiosis etc (Workers' Compensation) Act 1979 and the Child Maintenance and Other Payments Act 2008 would be increased.

1   [2008] 1 AC 281.
2   [2008] 1 AC 281 at 289–290.
3   The announcement can be found at www.justice.gov.uk/news/announcement250210a.htm.

(v)   Remoteness

[A49]   A defendant is not liable for damage which is not reasonably foreseeable[1]. However, only slight damage of the type of loss in question must be foreseeable, not the exact nature and extent of the loss, nor the precise mechanism of the loss[2]. Where it is reasonably foreseeable that a defendant's conduct would expose the claimant to risk of personal injury, the claimant will be able to recover for any personal injury, whether physical or psychiatric, resulting from the defendant's wrongdoing, even if psychiatric injury was not foreseeable[3]. Where the claimant commits suicide as a result of the defendant's breach of duty, the claimant need not prove that the suicide was foreseeable, and all that needs to be foreseen is the risk of some personal injury (whether physical or psychiatric)[4]. Foreseeability is judged objectively and, for example, in an accident at work, foreseeability is judged as at the date of the accident and with reference to the very accident which occurred, but with reference not to the actual victim but to a hypothetical employee so as to give effect to the principle that the tortfeasor must take his victim as he finds him[5]. Some damage has been considered too remote and therefore not recoverable, such as side-effects in consequence of a drug prescribed for injuries[6], an exacerbation of injuries caused by the claimant's neurotic mother[7], a dependency claim based upon the presumption that the deceased infant would have cared for his parents when older[8], and a dependency claim based upon the deceased's pension which was a matter of sheer speculation[9].

[1] *McKew v Holland & Hannen & Cubitts* [1970] SC (HL) 20, 25 per Lord Reid; *Bourhill v Young* [1943] AC 92, 101 per Lord Russell of Killowen; *Allan v Barclay* 2 M 873, 874 per Lord Kinloch; *Simmons v British Steel plc* [2004] ICR 585 per Lord Rodger at 609C–D, subsequently cited with approval by Lord Bingham in *Corr v IBC Vehicles* [2008] UKHL 13.

[2] *Smith v Leech Brain & Co Ltd* [1962] 2 QB 405; *Hughes v Lord Advocate* [1963] AC 837; *Overseas Tankship (UK) Ltd v Miller Steamship Co Pty (The Wagon Mound (No 2)* [1967] 1 AC 617; *Ogwo v Taylor* [1988] 1 AC 431; *Corr v IBC Vehicles Ltd* [2008] UKHL 13. For examples of the application of these principles in clinical negligence cases, see *Wisniewski v Central Manchester Health Authority* [1998] PIQR 324; *Hepworth v Kerr* [1995] Med LR 139; and *Loraine v Wirral University Teaching Hospital NHS Foundation Trust* [2008] EWHC 1565 (QB).

[3] *Page v Smith* [1996] AC 155; *Simmons v British Steel plc* [2004] ICR 585.

[4] *Corr v IBC Vehicles Ltd* [2008] UKHL 13.

[5] *Corr v IBC Vehicles Ltd* [2008] 1 AC 902A per Lord Bingham of Cornhill. Different principles apply in psychiatric injury cases, such as stress or bullying at work, where the court considers whether the injury to the particular claimant was foreseeable, knowing what the employer knew or ought to have known about the claimant and any pre-existing vulnerability: see *Hatton v Sutherland* [2002] EWCA Civ 76.

[6] *Alston v Marine and Trade Insurance Co* 1964 (4) SA.

[7] *Mclaren v Bradstreet* (1969) 113 Sol Jo 471, CA.

[8] *Barnett v Cohen* [1921] All ER Rep 528.

[9] *D and D v Donald* [2001] PIQR Q44.

8 Proof

(i) The Burden of Proof

[A50] The general rule of evidence is that 'he who asserts must prove'[1]. Therefore, where a claimant asserts that he or she has suffered a particular head of loss as a result of the defendant's wrongdoing, the claimant bears the burden of proving that he or she has in fact suffered the alleged loss and the extent of the same[2]. Of course, to be recoverable the claimant must show that the loss suffered was a foreseeable type of damage[3] which is recognised by the law[4] and attributable to the defendant's wrongdoing[5]. It is unclear, however, who bears the burden of proving that an item of loss is too remote, and there are conflicting authorities on this point. Where there is no evidence of a loss, a claimant will not be able to claim for that loss. Where there is evidence of a loss, but the extent of the loss is unclear, the court's assessment of that loss will depend crucially upon the evidence actually brought before it. It may be that the evidence is insufficient to show any damage, thus permitting an award other than for nominal damages[6]. Occasionally, although there is no specific evidence regarding the item of loss in question, it will be possible to infer or presume such loss from the rest of the available evidence[7]. In other cases, although the extent of the loss may not be capable of assessment with precision, the court will do its best to assess the appropriate award of damages[8]. A classic example of this is an award for future disadvantage on the open labour market[9]. Where it is alleged that the claimant failed to mitigate his or her loss, the defendant bears the burden of proving that the claimant has acted unreasonably[10]. Likewise, the defendant bears the burden of proving an allegation of malingering[11] or conscious exaggeration[12]. Since the allegation of malingering is tantamount to an allegation of fraud[13], the allegation must be pleaded[14] and, in practice, a high degree of evidence is required[15].

1   *Robins v National Trust Co* [1927] AC 515; *Huyton-with-Roby UDC v Hunter* [1955] 1 WLR 603.

2   *The Clarence* (1850) 2 W Rob (Adm) 283; *Bonham-Carter v Hyde Park Hotel* (1948) 64 TLR 178; *Ashcroft v Curtain* [1971] 1 WLR 1731; *Tate & Lyle Food and Distribution v GLC* [1982] 1 WLR 149; *Harrison v Leake* (1989) Times, 12 October, CA; *Hughes (Gordon Clifford) v Addis (John)* (23 March 2000, unreported), CA; *Smith v McCrae* [2003] EWCA Civ 505. However, this duty should not be taken to extremes. For example, in *Eden v West & Co* [2002] EWCA Civ 991, the Court of Appeal overturned the trial judge's refusal to award anything for loss of earnings, due to lack of evidence. There was unchallenged evidence that the claimant was working before the accident, and the agreed medical evidence supported the fact that the claimant was unfit to work for a period of six months by reason of the accident. In the event, a global award of £5,000 was substituted against a claim for past loss of earnings in the schedule of loss amounting to £11,500, and a further £1,000 was awarded in respect of loss of future earnings.

3   *The Wagon Mound* [1961] AC 388.

4   There are a number of claims for which the law does not permit recovery. The most obvious of these is a claim for loss of earnings based upon illegality – see eg *Burns v Edman* [1970] 2 QB 541. See further Chapter K, Counter-schedules.

5   *The Solholt v Sameiet Solholt* [1983] 1 Lloyd's Rep 605; *Wilsher v Essex Area Health Authority* [1988] 2 WLR 557; *Pickford v ICI plc* [1998] 1 WLR 1189; *Tahir v Haringey Health Authority* [1998] Lloyd's Rep Med 104; *Hooper v Young* [1998] Lloyd's Rep Med 61; *Holtby v Brigham & Cowan (Hull) Ltd* [2000] 3 All ER 421; although sometimes it may be inferred that the defendant's negligence has caused the claimant's damage: see eg *J (a child) v North Lincolnshire County Council* [2000] PIQR P84; *McGhee v National Coal Board* [1973] 1 WLR 1; *Fairchild v Glenhaven Funeral Services* [2002] UKHL 22. A detailed analysis of the law of causation is beyond the scope of this section. See further *Clerk & Lindsell on Torts; Charlesworth & Percy on Negligence; McGregor on Damages*; Michael A Jones *Medical Negligence*; and *Kennedy & Grubb Principles of Medical Law*. In addition, see paras **[A75]–[A77]** and Chapter K, Counter-schedules.

6   *Mappouras v Waldrons Solicitors* [2002] EWCA Civ 842; cf *Experience Hendrix LLC v PPX Enterprises Inc* [2003] EWCA Civ 323 where it was held, in the exceptional circumstances of the case, that the claimant was entitled to damages for breaches of a compromise agreement even though the claimant could not prove any loss flowing from the breaches.

7   See further chapter 45 of *McGregor on Damages* (18th edn) and *Bygrave v Thomas Cook Tour Operations Ltd* [2003] EWCA Civ 1631, where the Court of Appeal accepted that it was reasonable for the judge to infer that the claimant would suffer increased expenditure on taxis as a result of her injuries.

8   *Chaplin v Hicks* [1911] 2 KB 786 at 792; *The Mediana* [1900] AC 113 at 116–117; *Otter v Church* [1953] Ch 280; and *Moeliker v A Reyrolle & Co Ltd* [1977] 1 WLR 132 at 141; *Thompson v Smith Shiprepairers (North Shields)* [1984] QB 405. In *Chaplin v Hicks* [1911] 2 KB 786, Vaughan Williams LJ stated, 'The fact that damages cannot be assessed with certainty does not relieve the wrongdoer of the necessity of paying damages'. See also *Eden v West & Co* [2002] EWCA Civ 991 and *Felicia Andrina George (Administratrix of the Estate of Hughes Williams, Deceased) v Eagle Air Services Limited* [2009] UKPC 34, in which the Privy Council awarded $3,000 for funeral expenses against a claim of $5,000 notwithstanding the lack of any specific evidence proving the level of costs incurred.

9   *Moeliker v A Reyrolle & Co Ltd* [1977] 1 WLR 132.

10   *Geest v Lansiquot* [2002] UKPC 48. See further *Froggatt v LEP International* [2002] EWCA Civ 600 and *Morris v Richards* [2003] EWCA Civ 232. Although it should be noted that para 9.2(8) of

the PD to CPR, Pt 16 says that the claimant must specifically set out in the particulars of claim 'any facts relating to mitigation of loss or damage'.

11   *Stojalowski v Imperial Smelting Corpn* (NSC) (1976) 121 SJ 118, CA; *Cooper v P&O Stena Line Ltd* [1999] 1 Lloyd's Rep 734. There is a general presumption of innocence in civil cases which applies in cases where there is an allegation of fault, fraud or other wrongdoing: *Constantine Line v Imperial Smelting* [1942] AC 154, per Lord Wright at 192; *Emanuel v Emanuel* [1946] P 115.

12   Conscious exaggeration must be distinguished from unconscious exaggeration or litigation neurosis. See further *James v Woodall Duckham Construction Co* [1969] 1 WLR 903, CA, and *Digby v Essex County Council* [1994] PIQR 54. For examples of recent cases where the claimant has been found to be consciously exaggerating his injuries, see *McNally v RG Manufacturing Ltd* [2001] Lloyd's Rep IR 379; and *Smith v Rod Jenkins* [2003] EWHC 1356 (QB).

13   *Stojalowski v Imperial Smelting Corpn (NSC)* (1976) 121 SJ 118, CA.

14   In *Jonesco v Beard* [1930] AC 298, in which Lord Buckmaster said at 300: 'It has long been the settled practice of the Court that the proper method of impeaching a completed judgment on the ground of fraud is by action in which, as in any other action based on fraud, the particulars of the fraud must be exactly given and the allegation established by the strict proof such a charge requires'. See also *Cooper v P&O Stena Line Ltd* [1999] 1 Lloyd's Rep 734; *Scruton v Bone* (20 November 2001, unreported) in which Sir Andrew Morritt held that allegations of dishonesty must be pleaded clearly and with particularity, and are not to be left to inferencealone; *Pickering v JA McConville* [2003] EWCA Civ 554; *Lawrenson v Lawrenson and Equity Red Star* LTL 15/8/05; and *Noble v Owens* [2010] EWCA Civ 284, in which Elias LJ said at para [37]: '... where allegations of fraud are made they should be particularised and established to the appropriate standard of proof. This is a hallowed principle of law which has been repeated by the courts on many occasions'.

15   *Hornal v Neuberger Products Ltd* [1957] 1 QB 247; *Re Dellow's Wills Trusts* [1964] 1 WLR 451; and *Blyth v Blyth* [1966] 1 All ER 524, HL. In *Re H (minors)* [1996] AC 536 Lord Nicholls stated at 563: '... the more serious the allegation the less likely it is that the event occurred and hence, the stronger should be the evidence before the court concludes that the allegation is established on the balance of probabilities'.

(ii)   The Standard of Proof

[A51]   In civil cases, each party must prove the essential elements of its case on the balance of probabilities[1].

1   *Miller v Minister of Pensions* [1947] 2 All ER 372; *Bater v Bater* [1951] P 35, CA; *Bonnington Castings v Wardlow* [1956] AC 613; *Hornal v Neuberger Products Ltd* [1957] 1 QB 247; *Re H (minors)* [1996] AC 563; *Re Doherty* [2008] UKHL 33; *Re B (Children) (FC)* [2008] UKHL 35. There are some exceptions to this rule which require separate examination, and are unusual.

(iii)   The Need for Evidence

[A52]   If there is insufficient evidence to assess the value of a particular head of loss, the court may not make any award under that head[1]. However, as long as loss is not too small[2] or speculative[3] to be measured/claimed, the fact that the assessment of a particular head of loss might be difficult, eg because there are a number of imponderables, should not be a bar to recovery[4]. Whilst there might not be specific evidence regarding a particular head of loss, the court may be able to draw inferences from other evidence[5]. The court has to do its best in order to assess the appropriate level of compensation on the available evidence[6]. In respect of future expenses and losses, the claimant must also prove that he or she is likely to take advantage of or make use of the item claimed. For example, where the costs of future private medical treatment are claimed, the claimant will not be able to recover them unless it can be shown that he or she will probably undergo, or there is a significant chance that he or she will undergo, the medical treatment on a private basis as opposed to having the treatment on the NHS[7]. Likewise the claimant is unable to recover the costs of aids and equipment unless he or she would actually make use of them if they were purchased. In this regard, witness evidence is crucial. In *Blair v Michelin Tyre*[8], HHJ Marr-Johnson sitting as a judge of the High Court rejected a claim for a second wheelchair because the claimant did not seem keen on it and it 'might seldom, if ever, be used'. Further, in *Dorrington v Lawrence*[9], Hooper J disallowed a claim for a computer and £600-worth of software because the claimant already had a computer which he did not use and it was unclear whether he had the capacity to make use of the software that was recommended.

[1]   *Ashcroft v Curtin* [1971] 1 WLR 1731; *Hughes (Gordon Clifford) v Addis (John)* (23 March 2000, unreported), CA; *Harrison v Leake* (1989) Times, 12 October, CA.

[2]   In respect of torts requiring actionable damage, a claimant will not be able to recover for a trivial injury (such as pleural plaques) due to the principle 'de minimis non curat lex': *Rothwell v Chemical & Insulating Co Ltd and anor* [2008] 1 AC 281. Whether or not an injury is sufficiently serious to found a claim for compensation is a question of degree. The injury must be 'beyond what can be regarded as negligible': per Lord Reid in *Cartledge v E Jopling & Sons Ltd* [1963] AC 758 at 771–2. See also *Harwood v Cross Paperware* [1975] CLY 107u, CA.

[3]   Claims which are no more than speculative will not be recoverable. See eg *Howarth v Whittaker* [2003] Lloyd's Rep Med 235 (a claim for loss of earnings); *Parkhouse v North Devon Healthcare NHS Trust* [2002] Lloyd's Rep Med 100 (a claim for future IT); *D and D v Donald* [2001] PIQR Q44 (a claim for dependency based upon deceased's pension); and *Firth v Geo Ackroyd Jnr Ltd* [2000] Lloyd's Law Rep Med 312 (a claim for indemnity or a lump sum to reflect the chance that there would be a change of law in the future requiring the claimant to pay for his accommodation or care charges).

[4]   *Chaplin v Hicks* [1911] 2 KB 786 at 792; *The Mediana* [1900] AC 113 at 116–117; *Otter v Church* [1953] Ch 280; *Moeliker v A Reyrolle & Co Ltd* [1977] 1 WLR 132 at 141; and *Thompson v Smith Shiprepairers (North Shields)* [1984] QB 405. In *Chaplin v Hicks* [1911] 2 KB 786, Vaughan Williams LJ stated, 'The fact that damages cannot be assessed with certainty does not relieve the wrongdoer of the necessity of paying damages'. See also *Eden v West & Co* [2002] EWCA Civ 991.

[5]   See eg *Bygrave v Thomas Cook Tour Operations Ltd* [2003] EWCA Civ 1631, where the Court of Appeal held that it was reasonable for the trial judge to draw an inference from the evidence that the claimant would spend more on taxis in the future because of her injuries, and upheld the award of £100 per annum under this head of loss (although it was suggested that a more appropriate way of reflecting this loss might have been an award of general damages of say £2,500).

[6]   See eg *Moeliker v A Reyrolle & Co Ltd* [1977] 1 WLR 132 and, more recently, *Eden v West & Co* [2002] EWCA Civ 991, in which the Court of Appeal was critical of the trial judge's dismissive approach to the claim for loss of earnings because of the paucity of supporting documentary evidence.

[7]   *Woodrup v Nicol* [1993] PIQR Q104, CA.

[8]   (25 January 2002, unreported), QBD.

[9]   [2001] All ER (D) 145 (Nov).

(iv) Types of Evidence

[A53]   The following main categories of evidence are likely to be relied upon in support of, or in response to, a claim for personal injury or clinical negligence[1]:

- Factual witness evidence.
- Expert evidence (including any specialist literature relied upon and joint statements of meetings between experts).
- Medical records[2].

- Payslips/earnings details/business accounts/pension scheme details[3].
- Employment records including occupational health file, absence/sickness records, personnel file etc.
- Records from Government departments such as the DWP, HMRC etc.
- Reports from public servants, eg the police, fire service etc.
- Invoices/estimates/receipts.
- Statistics, research and studies[4].
- Actuarial tables.
- Photographic and video evidence.
- Hearsay evidence including letters, notes etc[5].

[1]   See further Chapter C, Compiling the Evidence.
[2]   This would include GP records, hospital records, radiology (including X-rays, MRI scans and CT scans), test results, correspondence, together with records of any private treatment undergone, eg physiotherapy, osteopathy, acupuncture and chiropractic treatment.
[3]   Note that, where the claimant is self-employed and business accounts have been prepared, it will not normally be legitimate to go beyond these accounts in order to calculate the claimant's loss of earnings: *Phillips v Holliday* [2001] EWCA Civ 1074.
[4]   In *Stefanovic v Carter* [2001] EWCA Civ 452 the Court of Appeal approved the use of the National Average Earnings Statistics as a guide for calculating the claimant's loss. See also *Smith v Rod Jenkins* [2003] EWHC 1356 (QB) where, in the absence of evidence regarding the claimant's likely increase in salary but for the accident, Gibbs J used the National Average Earnings Index to indicate the year-by-year increase on a broad percentage basis.
[5]   The admissibility of hearsay evidence is governed by CPR, Pt 33 and the Civil Evidence Act 1995.

(v)   Amount of Evidence

[A54]   Obviously, little or no evidence is required to prove an item of loss which has been agreed or admitted[1]. Where an item is disputed, the parties need to exercise judgement and discretion as to how much evidence is adduced. Whilst there is no limit to the amount of evidence that may be required in order to prove or to challenge a particular head of claim, generally speaking, the amount of evidence which is presented should be proportionate to the complexity of the issues, the importance of the claim to the parties, and the value of the particular item in dispute[2].

[1]   Where the defendant agrees an item in the counter-schedule, it will be difficult for the defendant to later withdraw from the admission: *Parkhouse v North Devon Healthcare NHS Trust* [2002] Lloyd's Rep Med 100, Gage J.
[2]   This accords with the aims of the CPR as set out in the overriding objective, Pt 1. It should be noted that under CPR, r 32.1 the court retains a far-reaching power to control the evidence in a case, which includes the power to exclude evidence that would otherwise be admissible.

(vi)   Disclosure

Pre-action disclosure

[A55]   Until proceedings are issued, the disclosure of evidence in personal injury claims is largely governed by the Personal Injury Pre-action Protocol and, in clinical negligence cases, by the Pre-action Protocol for the Resolution of Clinical Disputes.

(1)   THE PERSONAL INJURY PRE-ACTION PROTOCOL (PIPAP)

[A56]   One of the stated aims of the PIPAP is to promote 'better and earlier exchange of information'[1]. The intention is that, by front-loading the investigation of claims, the parties will be in a better position to be able to settle without resorting to litigation[2]. Although the PIPAP is primarily designed to cover cases with a value of or less than the fast track limit, a 'cards on the table approach' should be followed for multi-track matters, and representatives are still expected to follow the spirit if not the letter of the protocol[3]. The claimant is required to send a Letter of Claim in standard form outlining the background to the claim, the reasons why fault is being alleged and indicating the documents that should be disclosed[4]. The claimant is obliged to send to the defendant as soon as practicable a Schedule of Special Damages with supporting documents, particularly where the defendant has admitted liability[5]. Where a defendant denies liability, he or she should enclose, with his or her letter of reply, copies of documents in his or her possession which are material to the issues between the parties, and which would be likely to be ordered to be disclosed by the court, either on application for pre-action disclosure, or on disclosure during proceedings[6]. The defendant should also disclose any documents relevant to issues of contributory negligence[7].

[1]   PIPAP, para 1.2.
[2]   PIPAP, para 1.2.
[3]   PIPAP, paras 2.3 and 2.4.
[4]   PIPAP, paras 2.7 and 3.11.
[5]   PIPAP, para 3.14.
[6]   PIPAP, para 3.10.
[7]   PIPAP, para 3.12.

(2)   PRE-ACTION PROTOCOL FOR THE RESOLUTION OF CLINICAL DISPUTES (RCDPAP)

[A57]   Again, one of the expressed objectives of the RCDPAP is to ensure that sufficient information is disclosed by both parties to enable each to understand the other's perspective and case, and to encourage early resolution[1]. The patient or adviser is under an obligation to provide sufficient information to alert the healthcare provider where an adverse outcome has been serious or had serious consequences[2]. Medical records are to be requested as specifically as possible[3] using the Law Society and Department of Health standard forms (at Annex B to the RCDPAP)[4] and copies provided within 40 days[5]. In the rare event that the healthcare provider has difficulties complying with the request, the problem should be explained quickly and details given of what is being done to resolve it[6]. Should the records still not be provided, the patient may apply for an order for pre-action disclosure, and the court may impose costs sanctions for unreasonable delay[7]. The Letter of Claim should: contain a clear summary of the facts, and the main allegations of negligence; describe the patient's injuries (including present condition and prognosis); outline the heads of damage to be claimed and the scale of the same (unless impracticable)[8]; provide a chronology (in more complex cases)[9]; refer to any relevant documents[10]; and provide sufficient information to enable the healthcare provider to commence investigations and to put an initial valuation on the claim[11]. Any offers to settle which are made at an early stage should generally be accompanied by a medical report and a schedule of loss, together with supporting documentation[12]. The response to the Letter of Claim should provide reasons, if the claim is denied, and copies of any additional documents relied upon, eg internal protocols[13]. Any offers to settle should be responded to, preferably with reasons, any counter-offer and copies of any other evidence in relation to the value of the claim within the healthcare provider's possession[14].

[1]   RCDPAP, para 2.2.
[2]   RCDPAP, para 3.5.
[3]   RCDPAP, para 3.7.
[4]   RCDPAP, para 3.8.
[5]   RCDPAP, para 3.9.
[6]   RCDPAP, para 3.10.
[7]   RCDPAP, para 3.12.
[8]   RCDPAP, para 3.16.
[9]   RCDPAP, para 3.17.
[10]   RCDPAP, para 3.18.
[11]   RCDPAP, para 3.19.
[12]   RCDPAP, para 3.22.
[13]   RCDPAP, para 3.25.
[14]   RCDPAP, para 3.26.

(3)   Failure to comply with the protocols

[A58] The court will not be concerned with a minor breach of the pre-action protocols, eg failure by a short period to provide relevant information[1]. However, a significant breach, eg failing to provide any disclosure at all or issuing proceedings prematurely, is likely to lead to costs penalties[2]. In *Ford v GKR Construction Ltd*[3], Lord Woolf said[4]:

> 'The principle to which Lord Justice Judge referred as to the parties conducting their litigation making full and proper disclosure is even more important now that the CPR have come into force. Under the CPR it is possible for the parties to make offers to settle before litigation commences. As to the disclosure required in relation to that procedure, protocols in specific areas of litigation make express provision. Even where there is no express provision contained in a relevant protocol which applies to the particular litigation, the approach reflected in the protocols should be adopted by parties generally in the conduct of their litigation.
>
> If the process of making Part 36 offers before the commencement of litigation is to work in the way which the CPR intends, the parties must be provided with the information which they require in order to assess whether to make an offer or whether to accept that offer. Where offers are not accepted, the CPR make provision as to what are to be the cost consequences (CPR, r 36.20 and 36.21). Both those rules deal with the usual consequences of not accepting an offer which, when judged in the light of the litigation, should have been accepted.'

[1]   PIPAP, para 1.5 and RCDPAP, para 1.14.
[2]   See RCDPAP, para 3.12 which specifically refers to the court's power to impose sanctions for unreasonable delay in providing records. See also PIPAP, para 2.11 in respect of reasons for early issue, and *Paul Thomas Construction Ltd v Damian Hyland and Jackie Power* [2001] CILL 1748, where indemnity costs were ordered in the Technology and Construction Court for clear breach of the relevant pre-action protocol. See also *Straker v Tudor Rose* [2007] EWCA Civ 368, where the Court of Appeal reduced the claimant's costs by 40% for failing to comply with the PIPAP.
[3]   [2000] 1 WLR 1397.
[4]   At 1403.

[A59]   In the event that it is suspected that a party has failed to comply with its obligation of disclosure under the relevant protocol, an application for pre-action disclosure can be sought against any party who is 'likely to be a party to subsequent proceedings'[1].

---

[1]   The power to make such an application is conferred by Senior Courts Act 1981, s 33, as supplemented by CPR, r 31.16. See further *Herbert Black v Sumitomo Corpn* [2002] EWCA Civ 1819; and *Bermuda International Securities Ltd v KPMG* [2001] EWCA Civ 269. It should be noted that the starting point under CPR, r 48.1(2) is that the general rule regarding applications for pre-action disclosure is that the court will order the person against whom the order is sought the costs of the application; however, the position may be different where there has been a clear breach of the relevant pre-action protocol. However, see RCDPAP, para 3.12 which specifically refers to the court's power to impose sanctions for unreasonable delay in providing records.

Disclosure during the currency of proceedings

[A60]   Once proceedings have been issued, the CPR takes over. Part 31 governs the obligations of parties to disclose documents. Unless the court directs otherwise or the parties agree, the ordinary course is for each party to provide standard disclosure by way of a list including a disclosure statement[1]. Standard disclosure requires a party to disclose documents upon which they rely, which adversely affect their own or another party's case, or which support another party's case[2]. The duty is a continuing duty until the proceedings have concluded[3]. Therefore, if relevant documents become available which have not been previously disclosed and are not protected by privilege, the party in possession must be advised to disclose any such documents forthwith to the other parties[4]. Where there is a danger that the court could be misled, it is the duty of a party's representative to advise his or her client that disclosure should be made[5]. A party may resist disclosure if he or she is no longer in control of a document, has a right or duty to withhold inspection, or it would be disproportionate to permit inspection[6]. Where a party considers that the disclosing party has provided inadequate disclosure, he or she may make an application for specific disclosure identifying the documents that are sought[7]. A party who has a right to inspect a document may request a copy of the document, which must be supplied within seven days after the date on which the request was received, assuming that an undertaking is given to pay the disclosing party's reasonable copying charges[8]. Where a document which is privileged is inadvertently inspected, the inspecting party may only use that document with the permission of the court[9].

---

[1]   See further CPR, rr 31.5, 31.6 and 31.10. 'Disclosure' is defined under r 31.2 as 'stating that the document exists or has existed'.

[2]   CPR, r 31.6.

[3]   CPR, r 31.11. Rule 31.11(2) reads: 'If documents to which that duty extends come to a party's notice at any time during the proceedings, he must immediately notify every other party'.

[4]   *Vernon v Bosley (No 2)* [1997] 3 WLR 683.

[5]   *Vernon v Bosley (No 2)* [1997] 3 WLR 683.

[6]   CPR, r 31.3.

[7]   CPR, r 31.12. Also see paras 5.1–5.5 of the PD to Pt 31.

[8]   CPR, r 31.15.

[9]   CPR, r 31.20.

Non-party disclosure

[A61] Sometimes, documents in the possession of non-parties such as the police, social services, employers or the DWP will also prove useful, if not necessary, for the proper investigation of a claim. Increasingly, information from bodies such as NICE and CHI will be relevant. If necessary, an application can be made to the court in order to enforce disclosure of such documents[1]. Of particular interest to personal injury and clinical negligence practitioners is the disclosure of documents prepared for inquests. Ever since the Divisional Court case of *R v HM Coroner at Hammersmith, ex p Peach*[2], it has been considered that interested parties had no right to advance disclosure of statements under r 37 of the Coroners' Rules 1984[3]. However, considerable inroads have recently been made regarding this issue, most notably by the decision of Mr Justice Sullivan in *R v HM Coroner District of Avon, ex p Bentley*.[4] In this case the applicant successfully judicially reviewed the decision of a coroner who refused to give prior disclosure of documents and statements that were relied upon at the inquest without providing any reasons for that decision. Mr Justice Sullivan stated[5]:

> 'The request for advance disclosure was, on the face of it, a perfectly reasonable one. Certainly no reason has been advanced by the Coroner as to why it should have been refused. The fact that the Rules do not require advance disclosure is not a sufficient answer. There is an overriding obligation to conduct the inquest in a fair manner. The requirements of natural justice, or fairness, are not immutable. What was considered a fair procedure 20 years ago may well be regarded as unfair by today's standards. By way of example, the view that fairness very often requires the giving of reasons for a decision has been steadily gaining ground over recent years.'

1   Applications for pre-action disclosure are governed by Senior Courts Act 1981, s 33, as supplemented by CPR, r 31.17. See further *Three Rivers District Council v Bank of England* [2002] EWCA Civ 1182 and *Clark v Ardington Electrical Services & Helphire UK Ltd* [2001] EWCA Civ 585.
2   [1980] QB 211. Note, however, that the verdict of the inquest itself is not admissible evidence in support (or in dispute of) a claim: *Bird v Keep* [1918] 2 KB 692.
3   See eg *R v HM Coroner for Lincoln, ex p Hay* [2000] Lloyd's Rep Med 264.
4   [2001] EWHC Admin 170. Although see also *R v HM Coroner South East & Cumbria* [2009] EWHC 1653 (Admin), in which the application for advance disclosure was refused where there was a pending criminal investigation.
5   [2001] EWHC Admin 170 at [63].

Medical records

[A62] In order for a thorough medical report to be prepared, it will be necessary for the reporting expert to consider a copy of the claimant's medical records detailing any relevant history. In any event, the combined effect of CPR, rr 31.3, 31.6 and 31.8 is that the defendant has a right to inspect the claimant's medical records[1]. Where damages for future loss arising out of injury are claimed, it is likely that disclosure of the claimant's entire medical records will be held to be relevant and necessary[2]. However, in the ordinary course of events it will be for the claimant (and/or his or her advisers) to obtain a copy of the medical records and for the defendant to request inspection of the same, rather than the defendant being granted authority to obtain the records directly from the relevant bodies[3]. In exceptional cases, it may be necessary to apply to the court for an order that the defendant be given authority to obtain copies of the claimant's medical records directly, in default of which the claim be stayed[4]. Care should be taken to ensure that the terms of any such order are clearly and carefully defined in order to protect the claimant's rights, whether under the European Convention on Human Rights or otherwise[5]. To this end, the order should detail the exact records which are to be disclosed, to whom they are to be disclosed, and for what purpose. Although the court does have the power to order pre-action disclosure of the claimant's medical records under CPR, r. 31.16 prior to proceedings being issued, such disclosure is unlikely to be considered desirable in order to dispose fairly of the anticipated proceedings or to assist the dispute to be resolved without proceedings pursuant to r 31.16(3)(d), and it may well be an uphill struggle to persuade a court to order disclosure against the claimant's wishes[6].

[1]   *Bennett v Compass Group UK* [2002] EWCA Civ 642, per Clarke LJ at [20].
[2]   *Dunn v British Coal Corpn* [1993] PIQR 275; *Hipwood v Gloucester Health Authority* [1995] PIQR P447. It should be noted, however, that Art 8 of the European Convention on Human Rights may come into play in relation to disclosure of medical records. In *MS v Sweden* (1997) 3 BHRC 248 the ECtHR held that the applicant's medical records and medical history were part of her private life. However, under Art 8(2), disclosure in that particular case was justified because it was held to be in accordance with law, was founded on a legitimate aim, and was necessary in a democratic society. The material suggested that the applicant was obtaining benefit unlawfully.
[3]   *Bennett v Compass Group UK* [2002] EWCA Civ 642, per Clarke LJ at [14]. At [72], Chadwick LJ stated: 'The normal – and by far the most satisfactory course – is for the medical records to be produced by the claimant's advisers for inspection and consideration by the defendant's experts. It should not be necessary for the defendant's advisers to approach the GP or the hospital directly. But I cannot say that there are not circumstances in which it may be necessary – in order to break through what appears to be a wall of unresponsive silence ...'.
[4]   The court does have the jurisdiction to make such an order: *Bennett v Compass Group UK* [2002] EWCA Civ 642; *Dunn v British Coal Corpn* [1993] PIQR 275.
[5]   *Bennett v Compass Group UK* [2002] EWCA Civ 642, per Clarke LJ at [41].
[6]   See further *OCS Group Ltd v Wells* [2008] EWHC 919 (QB) in which Nelson J, applying the principles in *Bennett v Compass Group UK* [2002] EWCA Civ 642 that claimants bringing a personal injury claim should be prepared to reveal their medical records but only at the appropriate time to the appropriate people, upheld an appeal from a judge refusing to order pre-action disclosure of medical records.

[A63]   Where a defendant wishes to challenge the claimant's pleaded case based upon inconsistent entries in the claimant's medical records, notice should be given to the claimant, either formally in the defence or counter-schedule, or informally in correspondence[1]. The claimant should then consider whether or not he or she objects to the records and what steps (if any) are required to challenge the authenticity of the records. If the defendant relies upon the inconsistent statement at trial, it must be put to the claimant under s 4 of the Criminal Procedure Act 1865. If the claimant admits to having made the statement, then the statement can be admitted in evidence. Where the claimant does not admit to making the statement, the circumstances surrounding the making of the statement need to be put to the claimant and before asking again whether or not the statement is admitted. Thereafter, the statement may be admitted under s 6(5) of the Civil Evidence Act 1995, and becomes evidence for any relevant purpose[2]. Whilst such statements are technically hearsay, hearsay is admissible in civil proceedings by virtue of the Civil Evidence Act 1995, and the failure to give advance notice of intention to rely upon such a previous inconsistent statement does not render the statement inadmissible, but may affect the weight that is put on it and may lead to the imposition of costs sanctions[3].

¹   *Denton Hall Legal Services v Fifield* [2006] EWCA Civ 169.
²   To the extent that Buxton LJ's obiter dicta suggests otherwise in *Denton Hall Legal Services v Fifield* [2006] EWCA Civ 169, it is respectfully submitted that this is wrong: see further 'Inconsistent Statements in Medical Records – False Alarm or Timely Reminder?' by David Sanderson in [2006] JPIL Issue 2/06, pp 207–213.
³   See s 2(4) of the Civil Evidence Act 1995.

Legal professional privilege

[A64]   A party may object to disclosing relevant documents if they are privileged, the most common form of which is legal professional privilege. Documents will only attract such privilege where the sole or dominant purpose of the document when it first came into being was for legal advice in actual or contemplated litigation¹. It should be noted that, despite claims to the contrary, the following documents often do not attract this protection:

*   Documents arising out of previous or outstanding claims for the same or similar injuries, especially if the documents have been disclosed².
*   Medical reports and documents arising out of Children Act proceedings³.
*   Adverse outcome/incident reports⁴.
*   Complaints files⁵.
*   Internal protocols and statistical data.
*   Documents arising out of disciplinary proceedings⁶.
*   Independent reviews⁷.

¹   *Waugh v British Railways Board* [1980] AC 521.
²   *Murrell v Healy* [2001] EWCA Civ 486.
³   *Vernon v Bosley (No 2)* [1999] QB 18; *Re L (a minor) (Police Investigation: Privilege)* [1997] AC 16.
⁴   *Lask v Gloucester Health Authority* (1991) 2 Med LR 379.
⁵   *Hatcher v Plymouth Hospital NHS Trust* (7 August 1999, unreported); *Hewlett-Parker v St Georges Healthcare NHS Trust* (20 February 1998, unreported), Owen J.
⁶   Although it should be noted that records of in camera discussions held by the GMC's professional conduct committee will be protected from disclosure by reason of public interest immunity: *Dr Roylance v GMC* (1999) Times, 27 January.
⁷   *Mercer v St Helens & Knowsley Hospitals NHS Trust* [1995] CLY 4125.

Late disclosure

[A65]   It should be noted that late disclosure of evidence in support of the claim might lead to the adjournment of the trial and an order for wasted costs¹. Likewise, late applications to amend a schedule of loss are likely to be met with resistance. Applications for late amendments, particularly ones which may necessitate an adjournment of the final hearing, are especially likely to receive a frosty reception in cases which have been allocated to the small claims or fast track. For example, in *Taylor v Brock*², shortly before the disposal hearing, the claimant in a fast track case applied to re-allocate the claim to the multi-track, to adjourn the disposal hearing and to obtain updated medical evidence. The trial judge refused the claimant's application for an adjournment. Quantum was assessed and the claimant failed to beat the payment into court. The claimant then appealed to the Court of Appeal on the basis that the prejudice suffered by the claimant in not granting the appeal far outweighed the prejudice that would be caused to the defendant by permitting the adjournment. Tuckey LJ (with whom Mance LJ agreed) refused the appeal, stating:

'The procedure demands, as one would expect, that defendants to such claims should be given ample notice of what claims they face. The procedure is designed (by exchange of witness statements, experts reports and the like in the run up to the hearing) to inform defendants of the nature and extent of the claims they face. The original claims were based on medical reports obtained in 1995 and 1997. Nothing had been done to update the medical reports although the solicitors must or should have known that the claimant was saying that she had not recovered from the accidents.

This was a case which had been allocated to the fast-track. The fast-track means what it says. The adherence to a fixed timetable is all important. The Practice Direction makes it clear that in such cases "litigants and lawyers must be in no doubt that the court will regard the postponement of a trial as an order of last resort". No evidence was filed to support the application for an adjournment. If, as the claimant said, she was still suffering from symptoms and her work was in jeopardy, then a statement could and should have been taken from her setting this out supported, as necessary, by statements from employers or former employers. The psychiatrist's report which we have seen was not put before the court and no attempt had been made to amend the pleadings to make this part of the claim. So when the judge came to decide the matter, he had nothing upon which to form a view as to whether these further claims could be substantiated. In these circumstances it was inevitable that the judge would refuse to adjourn and would proceed with the case on the basis that it had always been put.

I can see nothing wrong with the judge's decision not to adjourn, certainly nothing which would justify this court in interfering with this decision. Decisions about adjournment are pre-eminently for the trial judge in the exercise of his discretion and not for this court.

I have to add that I feel extremely sorry for the claimant. We are not in a position to judge whether the further claims which have been intimated on her behalf are good ones or not. But if they are they could and should have been advanced in these proceedings long before they were. As they were not, then, on the face of it (and I do not attempt to prejudge the matter) the reason why they were not was the fault of the claimant's solicitors. However, that is no answer to this appeal. I am afraid she must suffer the failings of her own advisers. No doubt she will be advised to seek separate advice as to her position in the light of our decision.'

---

1   *Brown v BM Group plc* (12 July 1996, unreported). For an example when an extremely late application to amend a schedule of loss was permitted, albeit under the old rules, see *Haines v T H Sutcliffe (Meat Wholesalers) Ltd* (17 November 1998, unreported), CA, where the claimant was granted permission to amend his pleaded claim for loss of future earnings from £20,000 to £170,000, even though the trial was to take place the following day.

2   [2001] CP Rep 11. See also *Maguire v Molin* [2002] EWCA Civ 1083.

[A66]   Further, in *Baron v Lovell*[1], Brooke LJ said as follows[2]:

'Pre-trial disclosure obliges the parties to disclose to each other the substance of the evidence on which they intend to rely at the trial. If a claimant's symptoms are continuing, this must be made clear in the witness statements served on his side. It is not legitimate to serve out of date statements and then hope to be allowed to update them in a radical way just before the trial. The reason for this is that each party is afforded by the rules the opportunity to make a well informed valuation of the claim, and to make a well informed Part 36 offer, or payment into court in the case of a defendant, well before the trial takes place. This regime simply will not work effectively if the former laxities in serving late statements (or updated statements with no warning that a significant change is likely) are allowed to persist ...

[The defendant's solicitor] reveals that she intended to disclose Mr Wetherill's report for the first time on 26 April 1999, more than two months after she received it. She complains that the claimant's solicitors had not pursued the question of Mr Wetherill's report after 3 March or sought a debarring order. In my judgment they were not obliged to do so. She overlooked the fact that she now required the permission of the court if her client was to be allowed to rely on it, so that it was in his interests that such permission should be sought promptly. It was therefore not in her client's interests to delay disclosing it one day longer than was necessary. It was also not, in the judge's language, in the spirit of Woolf to delay disclosing it deliberately, as she intended, until the day a Part 36 payment was made. Under CPR, r 36.11 the claimant only has an absolute right to accept a Part 36 payment in the 21 days after payment is made. The defendant's solicitor therefore intended to create a situation in which the claimant's advisers had to consider whether to accept the payment during those 21 days without giving them any prior opportunity, in consultation with their client and Mr Marchon, to consider Mr Wetherill's report before the payment was made. They might have wished to make a Part 36 offer as soon as they had absorbed its effect.'

1   [2000] PIQR P20.
2   [2000] PIQR P20 at P28 and P29.

[A67] However, there may be an exception to this principle in respect of video evidence, where the defendant has obtained video surveillance evidence but wants the claimant to serve his or her witness statement and/or schedule of loss prior to disclosing video evidence[1].

1   See further *Uttley v Uttley* [2002] PIQR P123; and *Booth v Britannia Hotels Ltd* [2002] EWCA Civ 579.

Failure to disclose

[A68] A party may not rely upon any document which he or she fails to disclose, or in respect of which he or she fails to permit inspection, unless the court gives permission[1].

1   CPR, r 31.21.

9 Presumptions and Judicial Notice

[A69] The assessment of quantum is aided by the operation of a number of legal and factual presumptions, and occasionally by the operation of judicial notice. In run-of-the-mill cases, these presumptions save the expense of calling evidence to prove certain, usually uncontentious, elements of the claim. Most presumptions are rebuttable, which means that a state of affairs will be presumed only if reasons are not provided or evidence is not called to challenge the applicability of the presumption in the individual case. There are two main types of general presumption: legal and factual. In certain cases, the facts may also lend themselves to the application of additional presumptions (or inferences)[1].

¹   For example, where injury would not normally occur in the absence of negligence, a rebuttable evidential presumption of negligence may apply (traditionally described as 'res ipsa loquitur' or 'the matter speaks for itself'): *Scott v London and St Katherine Dock Co* (1865) 3 H&C 596. However, an inference of negligence may not be drawn in a complex matter which requires the assistance of expert evidence to resolve, such as a neurological defect following a spinal injection: *Ratcliffe v Plymouth and Torbay Health Authority* [1998] PIQR P170.

(i)   Legal Presumptions

[A70]   The law makes a number of presumptions by way of primary and secondary legislation, application of court rules and the common law. The presumption will operate to shift the persuasive or evidential burden of proof onto the party seeking to disprove the presumption. Examples of legal presumptions which may apply in personal injury and clinical negligence cases include the following:

- A party has the capacity to manage his or her own affairs[1].
- A party is competent to make treatment decisions and consent to treatment on his or her own behalf[2].
- An admission of liability will be binding[3].
- The real rate of return on investments, ie the rate received after inflation has been allowed for (known as the discount rate), is 2.5%[4].
- The standard rates of tax will stay the same in the future[5].
- A party is innocent of fault until proven guilty[6].
- Profits will be shared equally within a partnership[7].
- Interest is payable on awards of damages for personal injury[8].
- A bailee in possession of a chattel has title as against a wrongdoer[9].
- A person who was convicted of a criminal offence committed that offence[10].
- A marriage which is celebrated by a ceremony is presumed to be valid[11].
- A child born during wedlock is legitimate[12].
- For the purposes of the rule against perpetuities, men under the age of 14, and women under the age of 12 or over the age of 55, are presumed to be infertile[13].
- A person who has not been heard of for seven years by those who, if he or she had been alive, would be likely to have heard of him or her is presumed to be dead[14].
- The authenticity of a disclosed document is deemed to be admitted unless a notice is served requesting that the document is proved at trial[15].

Generally speaking, a legal presumption may be rebuttable if sufficient evidence is provided to challenge the application of the presumption on the facts of a particular case. However, it should be noted that there are a few irrebuttable legal presumptions. An example is provided by s 50 of the Children and Young Persons Act 1933, as amended, which conclusively presumes that no child under ten is capable of committing a criminal offence.

¹   *Masterman-Lister v Brutton & Co* [2003] 1 WLR 1511.
²   *Re MB* [1997] 8 Med LR 217.
³   PIPAP, para 3.9 and RCDPAP, para 3.25. See further *Gale v Superdrug Stores plc* [1996] 1 WLR 1089; *Sollitt v DJ Broadly Ltd* [2000] CPLR 259; *Hackman v Hounslow London Borough Council* [2000] CLY 354; *Flinn v Wills* [2001] CLY 412; *Thomas v Davies* [2000] CLY 353.
⁴   Damages (Personal Injury) Order 2001, SI 2001/2301; although it should be noted that the court does have a discretion to adopt a different rate of return under s 2 of the Damages Act 1996 if 'it is

more appropriate in the case in question'. In *Warriner v Warriner* [2002] EWCA Civ 81 the Court of Appeal held that this exception only applied where (a) a case has special features material to the rate of return, and (b) such features were not taken into account by the Lord Chancellor in his reasons for setting the discount rate. In practice, therefore, as noted by Dyson LJ, s 1(2) will only successfully be invoked in comparatively few cases. An example of this might be where the claimant will be subjected to unusually high tax payments: see further *Hodgson v Trapp* [1989] AC 807; *Wells v Wells* [1999] AC 345; and *Biesheuval v Birrell* [1999] PIQR Q40, cf *Van Oudenhaven v Griffin Inns Ltd* [2000] 1 WLR 1413.

5   *Hodgson v Trapp* [1989] AC 807; *Wells v Wells* [1999] AC 345.

6   The presumption of innocence equally applies in civil cases as it does to criminal cases: *Constantine Line v Imperial Smelting* [1942] AC 154, per Lord Wright at 192; *Emanuel v Emanuel* [1946] P 115.

7   Partnership Act 1890, s 24. See further *Lee v Sheard* [1956] 1 QB 192; and *Kent v British Railways Board* [1995] PIQR Q42. See also *Ward v Newalls Insulation* [1998] 1 WLR 1722 where the presumption was rebutted.

8   Insofar as an award is in respect of pain, suffering and loss of amenity, interest is awarded in order to compensate the claimant from being kept out of his or her money: *Pickett v British Rail Engineering Ltd* [1980] AC 136; *Wright v British Railways Board* [1983] 2 AC 773. But it is calculated at a low rate since it is appreciated that inflation will enhance such an award: see further Chapter E, Interest on General Damages. As regards pecuniary loss, Senior Courts Act 1981, s 35A(2) and County Courts Act 1984, s 69(2) create a presumption that interest will be paid on all awards in excess of £200. See further *Davies v Inman* [1999] PIQR Q26. However, the court retains a discretion to displace this presumption where there are special reasons, eg where the claimant has issued prematurely in breach of the PIPAP or where the claimant has been guilty of gross delay in pursuing the claim.

9   *The Winkfield* [1902] P 42.

10 Civil Evidence Act 1968, s 11.

11 *Piers v Piers* (1849) 2 HL Cas 331.

12 Family Law Reform Act 1969, s 26. The presumption may be displaced by a party adducing evidence to show that it is more probable than not that the child is illegitimate.

13 See further Perpetuities and Accumulations Act 1964, s 2.

14 *Prudential Assurance Co v Edmonds* (1877) 2 App Cas 487; *Chipchase v Chipchase* [1939] P 391; *Chard v Chard* [1956] P 259; *Bullock v Bullock* [1960] 1 WLR 975.

15 CPR, r 32.19.

(ii)   Factual Presumptions

[A71]   A number of inferences are commonly drawn from the facts in personal injury and clinical negligence cases, examples of which include:

- The claimant will have a normal life expectancy (in accordance with the actuarial tables prepared by the Government Actuary's Department)[1].

- The claimant is in the position of a prudent investor, who will avoid risk so far as possible and will invest in Government Index Linked Stock rather than gilts or equities[2].

- When calculating the level of dependency in a claim brought under the Fatal Accidents Act 1976 where the deceased's earnings were pooled with those of the dependent partner, it is conventionally assumed that 33.3% of the deceased's earnings were spent on him or herself, 33.3% on the dependent partner and 33.33% on the joint expenses; where there are dependent children, the appropriate proportions become 25% on the deceased, 25% on the dependent partner, 25% on the children and 25% on joint expenses[3].

- When calculating a claim for 'lost years', the available surplus which it is assumed will accrue to the claimant's estate is 50% of the claimant's earnings[4].

- A claimant who has suffered serious injuries will have suffered some pain and suffering or loss of amenity.
- A party intends the natural or foreseeable consequences of his or her actions[5].
- A person will continue to earn at the same level of salary as before[6].
- The claimant's care needs will continue at the same level[7].
- Ongoing expenses or losses will continue at the same rate (unless evidence suggests they will increase, cease or diminish).
- People become less capable of physical tasks as they become older[8].
- The law will remain as it is[9].

[1] *Rowley v London and North Western Railway* (1873) LR 8 Ex 221. Following *Wells v Wells* [1999] AC 345, in any case where there is an agreed or decided life expectancy, the Ogden Tables are to be used as a starting point rather than a check, and the court must be slow to depart from the actuarial tables purely on impressionist grounds. It has since been held that Tables 19–38 (based upon projected mortality figures) should be preferred over Tables 1–20 (based upon actual mortality figures): *Worrall v Powergen plc* [1999] PIQR Q103; *Biesheuval v Birrell* [1999] PIQR Q40; *Jenkins v Groscott and Hoyte* [2000] PIQR Q17; *Barry v Ablerex* [2000] PIQR Q263; and *Ved v Caress* (9 April 2001, unreported), QBD, HHJ Chapman.

[2] *Wells v Wells* [1999] AC 345.

[3] *Harris v Empress Motors* [1984] 1 WLR 212; and *Coward v Comex Houlder Driving Ltd* (1984) Independent, 25 July, CA. Any rule to this effect is disavowed (see per O'Connor LJ in *Harris*) but the figures are almost invariably used as a starting point.

[4] *Gammell v Wilson* [1982] AC 27; *Harris v Empress Motors* [1984] 1 WLR 212; *White v LTE* [1982] QB 489; *Phipps v Brooks Dry Cleaning* [1996] PIQR Q100.

[5] See eg *Kaslefsky v Kaslefsky* [1950] 2 All ER 398. In a different context, see also *R v Hyam* [1975] AC 55; and *R v Maloney* [1985] AC 905.

[6] Such a presumption is dependent upon the individual facts of a case and will only apply where there is no evidence regarding a chance of promotion or career advancement or, alternatively, redundancy or the expiry of fixed-term employment. See eg *Roach v Yates* [1938] 1 KB 256 at 269. It should be noted that a greater discount for 'contingencies other than mortality' would usually be applied to the multiplier for loss of future earnings where the claimant was involved in a physically demanding job or one which was particularly hazardous or dangerous.

[7] This is dependent upon the medical evidence, in particular as regards prognosis. Such a presumption is often easily displaced where there is evidence that the claimant's condition is likely to deteriorate as he or she gets older (and/or the claimant will need more assistance because of his or her increased weight/size), in which case the care costs are likely to increase accordingly: see eg *Whyte v Barber* (February 2003, unreported), QBD, Smith J. However, it should be noted that the multiplicand in future care claims can sometimes be reduced because the claimant's increasing care needs may ultimately result in the claimant being institutionalised at public expense: see eg *Mitchell v Mulholland (No 2)* [1972] 1 QB 65, CA.

[8] See eg *Smith v McCrae* [2003] EWCA Civ 505, in which the Court of Appeal reduced the multiplier in respect of the claim for future DIY in order to take account of the fact that the claimant might have not been doing heavy DIY jobs as time went on in any event.

[9] See eg *Firth v Geo Ackroyd Jnr Ltd* [2000] Lloyd's Law Rep Med 312, in which HHJ Robert Taylor sitting as a deputy High Court judge refused to make an award for damages to take account of the risk that the law might change in the future to allow the local authority to seek repayment of charges for the provision of care. However, it should be noted that the award was rejected because there was no evidence or material before the judge to establish that there was a real or substantial risk of the law changing in the future. On different facts, it may be possible successfully to claim for such an award.

(iii)   Presumptions Which Are Not Made

[A72]

- No presumption is made as to how the claimant will use or spend his or her money in the future[1].
- Just because the claimant is receiving gratuitous care from his or her friends or relatives does not mean this will continue indefinitely[2].
- Just because a claimant is receiving free care from a local authority does not mean this will necessarily continue (especially once a substantial award of damages including a claim for care has been made by the court)[3].

[1]   *Wells v Wells* [1999] AC 345. However, it is assumed that the claimant is in the position of a prudent investor, and will therefore invest in Government Index Linked Stock rather than in gilts and equities.

[2]   *Biesheuval v Birrell* [1999] PIQR Q40. Consideration should be given to the age, health and personal circumstances of the care provider and intentions of the claimant/care provider. See eg *Potts v Buckley* (21 December 1992, unreported), QBD, in which Tuckey J accepted that the claimant's wife was unlikely to be able to care for her husband after he reached the age of 65.

[3]   In *Howarth v Whittaker* [2003] Lloyd's Rep Med 235, Elias J rejected the argument that it could be assumed that the local authority would continue providing the claimant with seven hours of care per week free of charge.

(iv)   Judicial Notice

[A73]   In certain instances, the court may take judicial notice of various facts or matters which are general knowledge or evident from inquiries carried out by the judge, such as:

- A fortnight is too short a period for human gestation[1].
- The streets of London are full of traffic, and a boy riding a bicycle in them runs the risk of injury[2].
- Medical inflation is higher than ordinary inflation[3].
- The increased cost of food and outgoing for carers[4].

[1]   *R v Luffe* (1807) 8 East 193.

[2]   *Dennis v A J White & Co* [1916] 2 KB 1 at 6.

[3]   See eg *Houghton v Drayton* (16 December 1992, unreported), HHJ Crawford QC sitting as a judge of the High Court, although cf *Cooke v United Bristol Health Care* [2003] EWCA Civ 1370.

[4]   *Iqbal v Whipps Cross University Hospital NHS Trust* [2007] LS Law Medical 97 at para [37].

10   The Assessment

(i)   Pecuniary Loss

[A74]   The assessment of quantum in any given case must depend upon the facts of that particular case. However, there are a number of general factors which may or may not impact upon the assessment of quantum, some of the most common of which are listed below.

Relevant factors

(1)   CAUSATION

[A75]   Causation of a given loss is a necessary ingredient of liability to compensate for that loss. For a claimant to be entitled to an award of damages, it must be shown that he or she suffered a type of damage which was reasonably foreseeable and attributable to the defendant's wrongdoing. In this regard, it is sufficient that the wrongdoing probably caused or contributed to the claimant's injury[1]. Thus if the evidence demonstrates that, 'but for' the contribution of the tortious cause, the injury would probably not have occurred, the claimant will succeed in establishing liability. But in a case where medical science cannot establish the probability that, 'but for' an act of negligence, the injury would not have happened but can establish that the negligent cause made a material (ie more than negligible) contribution to the injury, the 'but for' test is modified, and the claimant will succeed[2]. Once some loss can be attributed to the defendant's wrongdoing, the degree and nature of the defendant's breach of duty and the extent of the defendant's contribution to the claimant's injury, loss and damage may impact upon the quantification of damages. In essence, the extent of the loss that the defendant is held responsible for is a value judgement which depends heavily upon the facts of the individual case[3]. For example:

- The claimant may not claim for any injury, loss or damage which is due to events which pre-existed the defendant's negligence[4].
- Where the causal link between the defendant's negligence and the claimant's injury, loss or damage has been broken by a supervening event[5], the claimant's unreasonable behaviour[6] or voluntary decision[7], the claimant will not be able to claim damages beyond that point.
- Where the claimant's conduct following his or her injuries is not so unreasonable as to break the chain of causation but does attract some culpability, the claimant's damages may nonetheless be reduced because of contributory negligence[8].
- No claim can be made for injury, loss or damage complained of which would have happened in any event, unless it occurs earlier than it otherwise would have done[9].
- No claim can be made for the lost chance of a better medical outcome[10].
- Where there are multiple potential causes of an injury, a claimant can demonstrate causation by proving that the tortious exposure has at least doubled the risk arising from the non-tortious cause(s)[11].
- Where separate and distinct damage is caused by multiple defendants, each defendant is liable for the injury, loss or damage arising out of his or her wrongdoing (and the degree of blameworthiness of each defendant is not relevant)[12].
- Where there are multiple divisible torts and the damage is cumulative, each defendant is only liable for the extent that his or her tortious conduct contributed to the injury, loss or damage complained of[13]; however, the position in relation to the apportionment of psychiatric injury is controversial[14].
- Where there are multiple defendants but the damage is indivisible, the defendants will each be jointly and severally liable for the totality of the claimant's damage (as between the defendants, liability will be apportioned depending upon each

defendant's degree of blameworthiness and the causative potency of their tortious conduct, but this does not affect the claimant)[15].

- A defendant who is responsible for causing injuries in a first accident may be liable for subsequent injuries sustained in a second accident arising out of the claimant's disabilities resulting from the first accident[16].

1 *McGhee v National Coal Board* [1973] 1 WLR 1; *Bonnington Castings v Wardlow* [1956] AC 613.

2 *Bonnington Castings v Wardlow* [1956] AC 613; *Nicholson v Atlas* [1957] 1 WLR 613, HL; *Bailey v MOD* [2008] EWCA Civ 883, per Waller LJ at para [46].

3 See *Kuwait Airways Corpn v Iraqi Airways Co (No 4 and 5)* [2002] UKHL 19 per Lord Nicholls at paras [69] and [70].

4 *Jobling v Associated Dairies Ltd* [1982] AC 794; *Kenth v Heimdale Hotel Investments Ltd* [2001] EWCA Civ 1283; and *Morgan v Millett* [2001] EWCA Civ 1641. The event must be something 'ultroneous': per Lord Wright in *The Oropesa* [1943] P 32 at 39.

5 For example, see *West v Versil Ltd* (1996) Times, 31 August, CA; *Weait v Jayanbee Joinery* [1963] 1 QB 239.

6 See eg *McKew v Holland & Hannen & Cubitts* [1969] 3 All ER 1621; and *Sabri-Tabrizi v Lothian Health Board* (1998) 43 BMLR 190.

7 This argument often overlaps with an argument that the claimant has failed to mitigate his or her loss. See further *Carter v British India Steam Navigation Co Ltd* [1974] 1 Lloyd's Rep 419; *Jeffries v Mills Scaffold Co* (1963) Guardian, 27 April, CA; and *Morris v Richards* [2003] EWCA Civ 232.

8 *Spencer v Wincanton Holdings Ltd* [2009] EWCA Civ 1404.

9 *Barnett v Chelsea and Kensington Hospital Management Committee* [1969] 1 QB 428; *Jobling v Associated Dairies Ltd* [1982] AC 794; *Hotson v East Berkshire Health Authority* [1987] AC 750; *Kenth v Heimdale Hotel Investments Ltd* [2001] EWCA Civ 1283; *Morgan v Millett* [2001] EWCA Civ 1641.

10 *Gregg v Scott* [2005] 2 AC 176.

11 *Novartis Grimsby Ltd v Cookson* [2007] EWCA Civ 1271; *Sienkiewicz v Greif (UK) Ltd* [2009] EWCA Civ 1159.

12 *Rhaman v Arearose Ltd University College London NHS Trust* [2001] QB 351.

13 *Allen v British Rail Engineering* [2001] EWCA Civ 242, [2001] ICR 942; *Holtby v Brigham & Cowan (Hull) Ltd* [2000] 3 All ER 421, CA.

14 Contrast *Hatton v Sutherland* [2002] EWCA Civ 76 and *Hartman & others v SE Mental Health and Community Care NHS Trust* [2005] EWCA Civ 06 with *Dickins v O2 Plc* [2008] EWCA Civ 1144, [2009] IRLR 58.

15 *Dingle v Associated Newspapers Ltd* [1962] 3 WLR 229; *Nicholson v Atlas Steel Foundry Co* [1957] 1 All ER 776; *Rhaman v Arearose Ltd University College London NHS Trust* [2001] QB 35; *Barker v Corus UK Ltd* [2006] 2 AC 575 (although subsequently reversed by s 3 of the Compensation Act 2006); *Dickins v O2 Plc* [2008] EWCA Civ 1144; [2009] IRLR 58, cf *Hatton v Sutherland* [2002] EWCA Civ 76. In *Rhaman v Arearose Ltd University College London NHS Trust* [2001] QB 351, Laws LJ stated at [18]: 'The reason for the rule that each concurrent tortfeasor is liable to compensate for the whole of the damage is not hard to find. In any such case, the claimant cannot prove that either tortfeasor singly caused the damage, or caused any particular part or portion of the damage. Accordingly his claim would fall to be dismissed, for want of proof of causation. But that would be the plainest injustice; hence the rule'.

16 *Wieland v Cyril Lord Carpets* [1969] 3 All ER 1006, followed in *Pyne v Wilkenfeld* (1981) 26 SASR 441. Cf *McKew v Holland & Hannen & Cubitts* [1969] 3 All ER 1621, HL, in which the House of Lords held that the second accident was caused by the claimant's unreasonable behaviour.

[A76]   It should be noted that it is not always necessary to show the exact aetiology of the claimant's continuing symptoms to be able to recover for damages in respect of their consequences. For example, where a claimant continues to suffer chronic pain following an accident but medical evidence cannot provide the precise pathological reason for the same, assuming the claimant is found to be genuine, it may be that there is a psychological component to the claimant's injuries which is secondary to the physical effects. The Court of Appeal so found in *McMylor v Firth Rixson plc*[1], in which the claimant continued to complain of pain and swelling in his left leg following an accident at work. Notwithstanding the absence of any direct psychiatric or psychological evidence, Parker J (with whom Kennedy LJ agreed) held that the trial judge was entitled to accept the medical evidence which had been called from a Consultant in Accident & Emergency Medicine and a Consultant Orthopaedic Surgeon to the effect that there was a consistent history of complaint since the accident, the pain was genuine and may have been related to a degree of psychological overlay.

[1]   [2002] EWCA Civ 1863. See also *Mullins v Gray* [2004] EWCA Civ 1483.

[A77]   Special principles of causation apply in some industrial disease cases[1]. In *Fairchild v Glenhaven Funeral Services Ltd*[2] the House of Lords held that, subject to certain conditions, there was an exception in mesothelioma cases to the general rule of legal causation (that the claimant must show that the tort had probably caused the disease) and it was sufficient for the claimant to show that the tortious exposure had made a material contribution to the risk of developing the disease. Although the *Fairchild* exception was held to be applicable in the vibration white finger case of *Transco v Griggs*[3], generally the courts have been reluctant to extend the exception to other scenarios and it has been held not to be applicable to a single incident[4], to acceleration cases[5] or to cases involving the lost chance of a better medical outcome[6]. Where the *Fairchild* exception does apply, the House of Lords subsequently held in *Barker v Corus (UK) Ltd*[7] that it is enough for the claimant to show that the defendant's negligence made a material contribution to the risk of injury, even though the injury might in fact have been caused by some non-negligent factor, including a natural phenomenon or by the claimant's own negligence. The decision in *Barker*, that liability should be apportioned between different defendants in accordance with the degree of contribution to the overall risk of injury, has subsequently been overruled by s 3 of the Compensation Act 2006.

[1]   The law in this area is complex, and the reader is referred to more detailed texts regarding liability causation for a full analysis of the relevant principles involved. A useful article is 'Causation: the search for principle' by Smith LJ in [2009] JPIL Issue 2/09 pp 101–113.

[2]   [2003] 1 AC 32.

[3]   [2003] EWCA Civ 564.

[4]   *Clough v First Choice Holidays and Flights Ltd* [2006] EWCA Civ 15.

[5]   *Environment Agency v Ellis* [2008] EWCA Civ 117.

[6]   *Gregg v Scott* [2005] 2 AC 176.

[7]   [2006] 2 AC 572. The Court of Appeal subsequently held in *Sienkiewicz v Greif (UK) Ltd* [2009] EWCA Civ 1159 that s 3 of the Damages Act 2006 applies to cases involving tortious as well as environmental exposure.

(2)   CONTRIBUTORY NEGLIGENCE

[A78]   A claimant's award of damages will be reduced by the extent to which he or she is to blame for the damage they have suffered. If contributory negligence is to be alleged, it must be pleaded[1], and documents in support of the allegation of contributory negligence must be disclosed in accordance with the PIPAP[2]. Unless there is agreement between the parties, the court will have to consider: (i) whether or not the claimant was partly responsible for his or her injuries; and (ii) if so, the extent of this responsibility. This will depend upon the degree of causative potency and blameworthiness of each party's actions or inactions[3]. The better view is that, since contributory negligence is a partial defence which depends upon primary liability being established, there cannot be a finding that the claimant was 100% contributory negligent[4]. Were the court to find that the claimant was 100% responsible for an accident, this is in effect a finding that the claimant's damage did not result from any wrongdoing on the part of the defendant but was wholly the fault of the claimant[5]. Once the appropriate degree of contributory negligence has been ascertained, this should be deducted from the total award of damages to which the claimant is found to be entitled before apportionment is carried out as between joint tortfeasors[6]. Contributory negligence is not limited in time to conduct surrounding the original injuries, and the claimant may be found partly to blame for aggravating injuries caused by the defendant's negligence such that his or her damages are reduced to reflect the proportion of the aggravation that he or she is to blame for[7].

[1]   *Fookes v Slaytor* [1978] 1 WLR 1293, CA.
[2]   PIPAP, para 3.12.
[3]   *Davies v Swan Motor Co* [1949] 2 KB 291; *Stapley v Gypsum Mines Ltd* [1953] AC 663; *Baker v Willoughby* [1970] AC 497; *Froom v Butcher* [1976] QB 286; *Madden v Quirke* [1989] 1 WLR 702; *Fitzgerald v Lane* [1989] AC 328; *Jones v Wilkins* [2001] RTR 283; *Cleminson v John Addley Ltd* (11 May 1999, unreported), CA; *Eagle v Chambers* [2003] EWCA Civ 1107.
[4]   *Boyle v Kodack* [1969] 1 WLR 661; *Pitts v Hunt* [1991] 1 QB 24; *Anderson v Newham College of Further Education* [2002] EWCA Civ 505; cf *Jayes v IMI (Kynoch) Ltd* [1985] ICR 155 and *Marshall v Lincolnshire Roadcar Co Ltd* (7 December 2000, unreported), CA. The position may, however, be different where a breach of statutory duty is proved. See eg *Jayes v IMI (Kynoch) Ltd* [1985] ICR 155, cf *Anderson v Newham College of Further Education* [2002] EWCA Civ 505.
[5]   See further *Pitts v Hunt* [1991] 1 QB 24 per Beldam LJ at 48. As Sedley LJ stated in *Anderson v Newham College of Further Education* [2002] EWCA Civ 505 at [18]:'The relevant principles are straightforward. Whether the claim is in negligence or for breach of statutory duty, if the evidence, once it has been appraised as the law requires, shows the entire fault to lie with the claimant there is no liability on the defendant. If not, then the court will consider to what extent, if any, the claimant's share in the responsibility for the damage makes it just and equitable to reduce his damages. The phrase "100 per cent contributory negligence", while expressive, is unhelpful, because it invites the court to treat a statutory qualification of the measure of damages as if it were a secondary or surrogate approach to liability, which it is not. If there is liability, contributory negligence can reduce its monetary quantification, but it cannot legally or logically nullify it'.
[6]   *Fitzgerald v Lane* [1989] AC 328. See also *Sharpe v Michael Addison* [2003] EWCA Civ 1189 in relation to the approach as regards contributory negligence in a professional negligence claim arising out of a personal injury case.
[7]   *Spencer v Wincanton Holdings Ltd* [2009] EWCA Civ 1404.

[A79]   It should be noted that there is an argument to suggest that, where a claimant's contributory negligence is significant, this may operate to further reduce the appropriate award of damages. The argument is based on the principle in *Woodrup v Nicol*[1] that a claimant is not entitled to recover the cost of future private medical expenses where, on the balance of probabilities, he or she is unlikely to incur such private fees. Take, for example, a claimant who is seriously injured and needs special accommodation. The purchase of a suitable property might cost £350,000. On a full liability basis the claimant's claim including loss of earnings, care, accommodation etc is worth £2,000,000. But if the claimant were found to be 90% to blame for the accident, he would only receive £200,000. Could the claimant still claim for 10% of the special accommodation even though, because of his contributory negligence, he would not be able to afford to buy the property claimed? The Court of Appeal has recently confirmed in *Sowden v Lodge*[2] that the answer to this question is Yes. In *Sowden* the trial judge, Smith J, rejected the claimant's claim for private accommodation. On the facts, it was held that the claimant's best interests were actually met by continuing to stay in the residential accommodation funded by the local authority. Although it was not necessary to decide the point in order to reach his decision, Smith J also accepted the defendant's argument that, as a matter of principle, since the claimant was 50% contributory negligent and would be unlikely to afford a private care arrangement, she was not entitled to recover the same. The Court of Appeal disagreed with the trial judge on this point. Although technically obiter, the Court of Appeal accepted the claimant's submission that, when assessing damages, the court calculates the claimant's entitlement to damages on a 100% basis and shuts its eyes to contributory negligence at that stage. The wording of s 1(2) of the Law Reform (Contributory Negligence) Act 1945, which envisages that the 'damages recoverable' are assessed before any deduction is made for contributory negligence, supports this approach. Pill LJ concluded that 'the finding of contributory negligence has no bearing upon the manner of the assessment of damages in this case'[3]. In our view, this decision correctly states the law and may be supported by the following additional arguments not canvassed in *Sowden*:

- It is contrary to the accepted practice of valuing an award of compensatory damages. The value of a claim is worked out on a full liability basis first and then, if necessary, a deduction is made for contributory negligence[4]. Assuming the items claimed are reasonable and would be incurred by the claimant assuming he or she had the funds, there is no room to further reduce the award by reason of the practical consequences of the finding of contributory negligence[5]. In other words, contributory negligence should not affect the value of a claim; only the final payment that is made to the claimant. An analogy here can be drawn with apportionment cases. Where a defendant is responsible for causing 50% of the claimant's symptoms, and 50% of the claimant's symptoms stem from a pre-existing condition, there is no reason to further reduce the award on the basis that the claimant is unlikely to be able to afford certain items of expense/loss. The appropriate level of compensation is first calculated on a full liability basis, and the claimant is entitled to claim 50% of the reasonable expenses and losses flowing from the injuries.
- It is a fundamental principle that how the claimant spends his or her award of damages is irrelevant[6]. The defendant must take his or her victim as he or she finds them, and the claimant's means should not influence the applicable principles when assessing quantum[7]. For example, when considering the issue of mitigation, the claimant's impecuniosity is not taken into account[8]. It is therefore not legitimate to start an inquiry into what purchases a claimant will or will not make using their reduced award of damages[9]. If it were legitimate to do so, by parity of argument, it should be equally possible to say that account should be taken of the defendant's resources, and a rich defendant should pay more than a poor defendant[10].
- There are public policy reasons against further reducing an award of damages to a claimant, who already has a reduced award, to take account of his or her blame for the accident. If their blameworthiness has already been taken account in the calculation of the award, why should it operate again to lower the applicable

level of compensation? This means that claimants who badly need every penny of an award (since, by definition, it will not represent the full extent of their expenses and losses) will have even less money to meet their needs.

¹   *Woodrup v Nicol* [1993] PIQR Q104, CA.

²   [2004] EWCA Civ 1370.

³   At [84].

⁴   *Kelly v Stockport Corporation* [1949] 1 All ER 893; *Fitzgerald v Lane* [1989] AC 328; *Cassel v Riverside* [1992] PIQR Q1; *Fitzgerald v Ford* [1996] PIQR Q72.

⁵   See eg *Willbye v Gibbons* [2003] EWCA Civ 372, in which the Court of Appeal accepted that it was reasonable to claim for the cost of fees for a receiver notwithstanding that, because of a finding that the claimant was 75% contributory negligent, there was a relatively small fund of damages which would be diminished by spending on professional services.

⁶   *Lim Poh Choo v Camden and Islington Area Health Authority* [1980] AC 174, per Lord Scarman at 191; *Wells v Wells* [1999] AC 345; *Heil v Rankin* [2001] QB 272. See also *Fitzgerald v Ford* [1996] PIQR Q72 at Q83, where the Court of Appeal refused an application from the defendant to see if the claimant, who had recovered damages on the basis of 75% liability, was spending damages in the way anticipated by the claimant's expert.

⁷   In *Heil v Rankin* [2001] QB 272 at 296 [33], Lord Woolf agreed with the defendant's submission that 'in making an award of damages the court is not concerned with whether the claimant is a pauper or a millionaire'. Whilst it is accepted that this case was involved with setting guideline figures for pecuniary loss, it was specifically stated (at [23]) that the principle of full compensation applies to both pecuniary and non-pecuniary damage alike.

⁸   *Clippens Oil Co v Edinburgh and District Water Trustees* [1907] AC 291; *Liesbosch Dredger v SS Edison* [1933] AC 449; *Robbins of Putney v Meek* [1971] RTR 345; *Martindale v Duncan* [1973] 1 WLR 574, CA; *Alcoa Minerals of Jamaica plc v Broderick* [2000] 3 WLR 23, PC.

⁹   On this basis, the decision in *Woodrup v Nicol* [1993] PIQR Q104 may be distinguished because it relates to the claimant's intentions (irrespective of means) as opposed to the claimant's resources.

¹⁰   As a matter of principle, however, the means of a defendant are not relevant to the calculation of damages: *Lim Poh Choo v Camden and Islington Area Health Authority* [1980] AC 174; *Wells v Wells* [1999] AC 345; *Heil v Rankin* [2001] QB 272.

(3) MITIGATION OF LOSS

[A80] The claimant is under a duty to take reasonable steps in order mitigate his or her loss[1]. Failure to take such steps will result in the claimant being limited to the damages which would have applied had those steps been taken. The burden is upon the defendant to prove that the claimant has failed to mitigate his or her loss[2]. The defence must be pleaded[3] and, generally speaking, specific evidence should be called by the defendant to make out the allegation[4]. Further, the claimant is also under an obligation to plead any facts relating to mitigation of loss or damage on which he or she wishes to rely at trial[5]. The question of whether or not the claimant has failed to mitigate his or her loss is a question of fact not law[6]. The claimant's reasonable expenses may be recovered in minimising his or her losses, eg medication and treatment expenses[7]. Should the mitigation prove unsuccessful or worsen the claimant's condition, assuming the steps taken were reasonable and the chain of causation has not been broken, the defendant will remain liable for the extent of the claimant's injuries including any deterioration[8]. Likewise, if the treatment takes longer than expected or the expense incurred in pursuit of mitigation is greater than first anticipated, assuming the claimant has acted reasonably and the chain of causation is not broken, any additional loss will be recoverable[9]. However, if the steps taken to mitigate loss are successful, the defendant is entitled to the benefit of the same[10].

1   Although see *The Solholt v Sameiet Solholt* [1983] 1 Lloyd's Rep 605, in which Lord Donaldson MR stated: 'A [claimant] is under no duty to mitigate his loss, despite the habitual use by lawyers of the phrase "duty to mitigate". He is completely free to act as he judges to be in his best interests. On the other hand, a defendant is not liable for all loss suffered by the claimant in consequence of his so acting. A defendant is only liable for such part of the [claimant's] loss as is properly to be regarded as caused by the defendant's breach of duty'.

2   *Roper v Johnson* (1873) LR 8 CP 167, as affirmed in *Garnac Grain Co v Faure & Fairclough* [1968]; *Geest plc v Lansiquot* [2002] UKPC 48, which expressly disapproved of its earlier decision in *Selvanayagam v University of West Indies* [1983] 1 WLR 585; *Eaton v Johnstone* [2008] UKPC 1.

3   In *Geest plc v Lansiquot* [2002] UKPC 48, Lord Bingham stated at [16]: 'It should be clearly understood that if a defendant intends to contend that a [claimant] has failed to mitigate his or her damage, notice of such contention should be clearly given to the [claimant] long enough before the hearing to enable the [claimant] to prepare to meet it. If there are no pleadings, notice should be given by letter'.

4   In *Froggatt v LEP International* [2002] EWCA Civ 600, the Court of Appeal referred to the conspicuous lack of evidence called on behalf of the defendant in order to establish a mitigation of loss argument. No prior notice of the point had been given to the claimant and was raised for the first time in cross-examination. It was held that the claimant's failure to leave the defendant's employment (from which he was not receiving any income but did continue to receive a contribution to his pension) in order to look for alternative work was not unreasonable in the circumstances of the case.

5   CPR, PD 16, para 9.2(8).

6   *Payzu v Saunders* [1919] 2 KB 581, CA; and *The Solholt v Sameiet Solholt* [1983] 1 Lloyd's Rep 605.

7   Although it should be noted that the expenses claimed must be reasonable. Where a treatment is claimed whose long-term efficacy or side-effects are unknown, or the claimant undergoes alternative therapies with no proven medical benefit, recovery may be refused. See eg *Biesheuval v Birrell* [1999] PIQR Q40, in which Eady J disallowed a claim for Viagra; cf *Re McCarthy* [2001] 6 Ch 172.

8   *Rubens v Walker* [1946] SC 215; *Hoffberger v Ascot* (1976) 120 Sol Jo 130, CA; although this claim was in contract, the same principles apply in tort.

9   *Mattocks v Mann* [1973] RTR 13; *Candlewood Navigation Corpn Ltd v Mitsui OSK Lines Ltd* [1986] 1 AC 1; *Lagden v O'Connor* [2003] UKHL 64. In *Mattocks v Mann* [1993] RTR 13 the repair of the claimant's car should have taken 6 weeks but was actually not completed for 12 weeks. Beldam LJ stated at 18: 'For a supervening cause or a failure to mitigate to relieve a defendant of a period of hire there must, in my judgment, be a finding of some conduct on her [Mrs Mattocks] part or on the part of someone for whom she is in law responsible, or indeed of a third party, which can truly be said to be an independent cause of loss of her car for that period'. See also *Bygrave v Thomas Cook Tour Operations Ltd* [2003] EWCA Civ 1631, in which the claimant took a full-time job in mitigation of her loss, which then rendered her too tired to carry out her domestic chores. The Court of Appeal upheld the judge's award for domestic assistance.

10   *British Westinghouse Electric and Manufacturing Co Ltd v Underground Electric Railways Co of London Ltd* [1912] AC 673; *Bellingham v Dhillon* [1973] QB 304; *Birch v Aslam* [2001] CLY 1532; *Dimond v Lovell* [2002] 1 AC 384, cf *Woodrow v Whitbread plc* (10 December 2001, unreported), QBD, Rougier J, where the claimant retrained as a result of an accident and was thereby likely to receive more than he otherwise would in his pre-accident job.

[A81] It should be remembered that the claimant needs only to act 'not unreasonably', having regard to all the circumstances[1]. The test for judging the claimant's actions is not high[2]. The test is objective, ie what a reasonable man would have done in the claimant's position[3]. Account is only taken of matters known to the claimant at the time, and subsequent knowledge with the benefit of hindsight is ignored[4]. The claimant's impecuniosity is not to be held against him or her[5]. Further, a mistaken judgment may be considered a natural consequence for which the defendant is responsible[6].

1   *Richardson v Redpath Brown & Co Ltd* [1944] AC 62. See further Chapter K, Failure to Undergo Medical Treatment in respect of the relevant factors when considering whether the claimant has failed to mitigate his or her loss by refusing recommended medical treatment.

2   See para **[A84]** below as regards the test to be applied.

3   *Morgan v T Wallis* [1974] 1 Lloyd's Rep 165.

4   *See eg Rubens v Walker* [1946] SC 215. See also *Morris v Richards* [2003] EWCA Civ 232.

5   A claimant who is under a duty to mitigate is not obliged to do that which he or she cannot afford to do: *Clippens Oil Co v Edinburgh and District Water Trustees* [1907] AC 291; *Liesbosch Dredger v SS Edison* [1933] AC 449; *Robbins of Putney v Meek* [1971] RTR 345; *Martindale v Duncan* [1973] 1 WLR 574, CA; *Dodd Properties Ltd v Canterbury City Council* [1980] 1 WLR 433 at 435; *Alcoa Minerals of Jamaica plc v Broderick* [2000] 3 WLR 23, PC; *Lagden v O'Connor* [2003] UKHL 64. In *Lagden v O'Connor* [2003] UKHL 64, Lord Hope said at [34]: '... It is for the defendant who seeks a deduction from expenditure in mitigation on the ground of betterment to make out his case for doing so. It is not enough that an element of betterment can be identified. It has to be shown that the claimant had a choice, and that he would have been able to mitigate his loss at less cost. The wrongdoer is not entitled to demand of the injured party that he incur a loss, bear a burden or make unreasonable sacrifices in the mitigation of his damages. He is entitled to demand that, where there are choices to be made, the least expensive route which will achieve mitigation must be selected. So if the evidence shows that the claimant had a choice, and that the route to mitigation which he chose was more costly than an alternative that was open to him, then a case will have been made out for a deduction. But if it shows that the claimant had no other choice available to him, the betterment must be seen as incidental to the step which he was entitled to take in the mitigation of his loss and there will be no ground for it to be deducted'.

6   Per Lord Haldane in *The Metagama* [1927] 29 Ll L Rep 253; *Morris v Richards* [2003] EWCA Civ 232.

[A82] As regards loss of earnings and residual earning capacity, the court will take into account the claimant's pre-existing ambitions and interests. For example, a claimant is unlikely to be required to undertake a better-paid sedentary job if he had always wanted to work on a farm, assuming that this ambition was reasonable and could still be realised with assistance[7]. Likewise, the court will be slow to find a claimant has acted unreasonably by failing to move to another country in order to realise a higher earning capacity, especially if that would involve uprooting the claimant's whole family[8].

1   See eg *Woodrup v Nicol* [1992] PIQR Q104 per Russell LJ at Q111.

2   *Limbu v MOD* LTL 17/7/08.

[A83] As regards medical treatment, before the claimant can be held unreasonable in refusing to undergo any proposed treatment, it must be shown that there is a proven benefit on the balance of probabilities[1]. The claimant is not necessarily expected to submit to invasive medical treatment or surgery which carries with it significant risks or has an uncertain outcome[2]. Likewise, the claimant cannot be expected to undergo medical treatment where there is conflicting evidence about the likely benefit of the same[3]. The court will also take into account the circumstances and subjective qualities of the claimant. For example, the court will not say that a claimant who does not believe in abortions acted unreasonably by refusing to terminate an unwanted pregnancy[4]. But the court will take into account past actions of the claimant and advice he or she has received, so that where, for example, the claim arises in relation to an alleged negligently performed abortion and sterilisation procedure, if the claimant was aware of the risk of falling pregnant after the procedure, she may be held to have acted unreasonably by exposing herself to that risk, thereby breaking the chain of causation[5]. It is important to note that each case is fact sensitive, and consideration must be given to the particular factors influencing the claimant to refuse particular treatment[6]. Factors likely to be important include[7]: (i) the prospects of success; (ii) the risk of complications (and their severity); (iii) the claimant's anxieties about the treatment (including any past adverse experiences of similar treatment); (iv) advice received from treating doctors about the treatment; (v) advice received from the claimant's GP; (vi) advice received from medico-legal experts; and (vii) whether or not the experts instructed in the case consider that it is reasonable for the claimant to refuse to undergo the treatment in all the circumstances. These factors should be considered cumulatively[8]. Additional potentially relevant factors include the degree of understanding and education of the claimant, and whether the claimant has to pay (and can afford the treatment) or if it can be obtained free of charge on the NHS[9].

[1]   *Morgan v T Wallis* [1974] 1 Lloyd's Rep 165.
[2]   See eg *Geest v Lansiquot* [2002] UKPC 48, in which the Privy Council held that the claimant had not failed to mitigate her loss by failing to undergo surgery to her spine for a disc prolapse which had no guarantee of success and might have actually made her condition worse. Although, in *Noble v Owens* [2008] EWHC 359 (QB), Field J found the claimant had failed to mitigate his loss by refusing to undergo urodynamic studies under general anaesthetic and treatment for his urinary incontinence. Furthermore, it is easier for a defendant to prove a failure to mitigate where the proposed treatment is non-invasive and carries with it little risk: see eg *Birch v Aslam* [2001] CLY 1532.
[3]   *McAuley v London Transport Executive* [1957] 2 Lloyd's Rep 500 at 505.
[4]   *Emeh v Kensington and Chelsea and Westminster Area Health Authority* [1984] 3 All ER 1044. Although see *Richardson v LRC Products Ltd* [2000] PIQR P164 in which Kennedy J held, in a claim under the Consumer Protection Act 1987 involving a burst condom, that the claimant had acted unreasonably by failing to take advice in relation to the morning-after pill.
[5]   *Sabri-Tabrizi v Lothian Health Board* 1998 SLT 607; (1998) 43 BMLR 190. See also *Richardson v LRC Products Ltd* [2000] PIQR P164.
[6]   In *Edmonds v Lloyds Group Plc* [2004] EWCA Civ 1526, Gage LJ said at [15]: 'Both counsel, in their skeleton arguments and, to some extent, in argument before us today, have referred to decisions in other cases dealing with alleged failures to mitigate damages. Some of them are personal injury cases. For my part, I gain little assistance from these authorities. In personal injury cases the issue of whether or not a claimant has acted reasonably will, in my judgment, almost invariably be very fact specific. I glean little by way of assistance from those authorities other than that they demonstrate some factors which have caused the court to rule one or other side of the line'.
[7]   See eg the factors considered in *Edmonds v Lloyds Group Plc* [2004] EWCA Civ 1526.
[8]   *Edmonds v Lloyds Group Plc* [2004] EWCA Civ 1526, per Gage LJ at [25].
[9]   See *Bouchouk v MOD* [2009] EWHC 2614 (QB), per Cooke J at para [17].

[A84]   As regards the appropriate test to be applied, Sachs LJ said in *Melia v Key Terrain Ltd*[1]:

'As between a claimant and a tortfeasor the onus is on the latter to show that the former has unreasonably neglected to mitigate the damages. The standard of reasonable conduct required must take into account that a claimant in such circumstances is not to be unduly pressed at the instance of the tortfeasor. To adopt the words of Lord Macmillan in the well-known Waterlow case, the claimant's conduct ought not to be weighed in nice scales at the instance of the party which has occasioned the difficulty.'

[1]   (1969) No 155B. These remarks were recently cited with approval by the Court of Appeal in *Morris v Richards* [2003] EWCA Civ 232.

[A85]   For a good example of this test in action, it is worthwhile considering the facts of *Morris v Richards*[1]. The claimant was involved in a road traffic accident and was forced to give up her job as a radiographer. In an attempt to mitigate her loss, she took up a job as a marketing manager with Toshiba. Her new job paid much better than her old job but she struggled to perform her duties. It was the claimant's case that she did not possess the relevant skills or experience for her new job (which was accepted by the trial judge). She got wind that her new employers were about to dismiss her and decided to 'jump before she was pushed'. The Court of Appeal held that the issue in the case was correctly decided to be a question of mitigation rather than remoteness (as argued by the defendant). Since the trial judge had made a positive finding that the claimant did not have the required qualities for the Toshiba job, it was held not to have been unreasonable for her to resign. In the words of Keene LJ[2]:

> 'The liability of a tortfeasor is not to be reduced because the injured party, having lost employment because of the injury, takes a different job in an attempt to mitigate his or her damage but loses that job because it is beyond his or her capabilities.'

[1]   [2003] EWCA Civ 232. See also *McKeown v Ford Motor Co Ltd* [2006] EWCA Civ 336, in which the defendant unsuccessfully attempted to argue at first instance and on appeal that the claimant gave up work with the defendant and accepted early retirement too soon.

[2]   [2003] EWCA Civ 232 at [6].

[A86] Where a claimant obtains a better-paid job as a result of the defendant's wrongdoing, should he or she have to give credit for this? Although on the facts this situation arose in *Morris v Richards*[1], it was not in issue before the Court of Appeal because the claimant did not seek any loss of earnings until she resigned from her job at Toshiba. But what if a claimant is able to continue in a new job which remunerates him or her more than their pre-injury job or has the potential to do so in the future? Such a position arose in *Woodrow v Whitbread plc*[2]. The claimant sustained a wedge compression fracture of a vertebra and was unable to pursue his pre-accident employment as a bricklayer. In order to mitigate his loss, the claimant started training as a production manager. The claimant's future earnings from his new career were likely to outstrip the level of earnings from his pre-accident career. The judge held that, where a claimant through his own hard work would be better off financially in the medium to long term as a result of a change of career which had been enforced as a result of personal injury, that was not something upon which a tortfeasor could rely to offset against any future loss of earnings. The loss of earnings claim was therefore allowed, up to the point where the claimant's new earnings were likely to catch up with his pre-accident level of earnings, but no credit was given from that point onwards for the likely increase in his earnings over and above what he would have earned but for the accident.

[1]   [2003] EWCA Civ 232.

[2]   (10 December 2001, unreported), QBD, Rougier J. This case was subsequently mentioned with apparent approval by Sedley LJ in *Orthet Ltd v Vince-Cain* [2004] EWCA Civ 1613.

[A87] However, this decision could arguably be said to run contrary to a long line of authority which holds that, generally speaking, the defendant is entitled to the benefit of any successful steps taken by the claimant in order to mitigate his or her loss[1]. Logically, if the claimant is to be put back into the position he or she would have been in but for the injury, any additional earnings resulting from a change in career should be taken into account against any claim for past or future earnings based upon the old career. As against this, it might be said that the claimant always had the ability to achieve the additional earnings, and the fact that he or she realised such earning potential after the defendant's wrongdoing is not a case of the claimant's injuries 'adding value' to his or her position. Further, it might not fit logically with the principles of calculation and mitigation of loss (since it seeks to transmute the mitigation of the wronged party's loss into a source of benefit to the wrongdoer) and does not appeal to a sense of justice[2]. In any event, 'like' should only be set off against 'like' and, therefore, if actual or potential increased earnings in a new job secured as a result of the accident operate to extinguish a claim for past or future loss of earnings in a pre-injury job, any residual amount should not be set off against other heads of loss[3]. Take, for example, a claimant who retrains to become a computer programmer following a serious accident and earns £50,000 up to the date of trial in his new job. If the accident had not occurred, he probably would have continued in his old job earning a total of £30,000 up to the date of trial. Arguably, the claimant's claim for past loss of earnings would be wholly extinguished by the benefits of his mitigation, but the remaining £20,000 should not be used to reduce any outstanding claims that the claimant may have, such as pain, suffering and loss of amenity, medical expenses etc.

[1]   *British Westinghouse Electric and Manufacturing Co Ltd v Underground Electric Railways Co of London Ltd* [1912] AC 673; *Bellingham v Dhillon* [1973] QB 304; *Dimond v Lovell* [2002] 1 AC 384. See further *McGregor on Damages* (18th edn) at chapter 7.
[2]   *Orthet Ltd v Vince-Cain* [2004] EWCA Civ 1613, per Sedley LJ at [7].
[3]   For examples of this principle, see *Parry v Cleaver* [1970] AC 1; and *Longden v British Coal Corpn* [1997] 3 WLR 1336.

(4)   PRE-EXISTING ILLNESS/CONDITIONS

[A88]   Where the claimant was already suffering from a pre-existing illness/ condition at the time of the accident, a number of interrelated principles come into play. These are as follows:

* The eggshell skull principle – it is no defence to say that the injuries sustained by the proposed claimant are out of proportion to the defendant's wrongdoing. The defendant must take his or her victim as he or she finds them[1]. Therefore, where personal injury was a foreseeable outcome of the defendant's conduct, he or she will be responsible for the entirety of the damage caused notwithstanding the unusually severe reaction suffered by the claimant who was particularly vulnerable to suffering injury by reason of his or her pre-existing condition. For example, in *Smith v Leech Brain*[2] the claimant's husband was struck by a piece of molten metal and suffered a small burn on his lip. Thereafter, because of a predisposition to cancerous cells, he developed cancer and died. The defendant was held liable for his death: some injury was to be foreseen, even if the extent of it was not.
* The eggshell personality principle – there is no difference in principle between pre-existing psychiatric vulnerability factors and pre-existing physical vulnerability factors. Therefore, where a claimant suffers from pre-existing psychological problems, the defendant will be responsible for the entirety of the damage caused notwithstanding that the extent of the same could not have been foreseen. This principle is known as the eggshell personality principle[3].

- Supervening illnesses principle – the defendant will not be liable for the consequences of any supervening illnesses which would have occurred in the absence of the defendant's wrongdoing in any event[4]. This is an extension of the principle that the defendant is not responsible for damage which would have occurred irrespective of his or her wrongdoing[5]. Therefore, the defendant is not responsible for any symptoms or deterioration in the claimant's health that would have occurred naturally.
- The aggravation/exacerbation principle – where a claimant already suffered some symptoms arising from a pre-existing illness or condition prior to the accident, the defendant is only liable for the additional injury he or she has caused[6].
- The acceleration principle – where a claimant suffered from a pre-existing condition the symptoms of which have been brought forward or accelerated by reason of the defendant's negligence, the claimant is restricted to claiming damages for injuries, expenses and losses for the duration of the 'acceleration period'[7]. Of course, the expenses and losses arising after the relevant acceleration period would have occurred in any event and will therefore not be recoverable.
- Discount for pre-existing risk of injury principle – where a claimant had a pre-existing condition at the time of the accident which made it possible that he or she would suffer from similar injuries to those complained of in any event, it is possible that the claim for future loss will be discounted to reflect the chance that the injuries, expenses and losses complained of may have occurred notwithstanding the defendant's negligence[8].

[1] *Bourhill v Young* [1943] AC 92, per Lord Wright at 109–110: 'If the wrong is established the wrongdoer must take the victim as he finds him'. See also *Smith v Leech Brain* [1962] 2 QB 405.
[2] [1962] 2 QB 405.
[3] *Malcolm v Broadhurst* [1970] 3 All ER 508. See also *Mullins v Gray* [2004] EWCA Civ 1483.
[4] *Jobling v Associated Dairies Ltd* [1982] AC 794; *Kenth v Heimdale Hotel Investments Ltd* [2001] EWCA Civ 1283; *Morgan v Millett* [2001] EWCA Civ 1641; and *Gray v Thames Trains Ltd v another* [2009] 3 WLR 167.
[5] See further *Barnett v Chelsea and Kensington Hospital Management Committee* [1969] 1 QB 428; and *Hotson v East Berkshire Health Authority* [1987] AC 750.
[6] *Page v Smith (No 2)* [1996] 1 WLR 855; *Vernon v Bosley* [1997] PIQR P255.
[7] *Kenth v Heimdale Hotel Investments Ltd* [2001] EWCA Civ 1283.
[8] *Page v Smith* [1996] AC 155; *Heil v Rankin* [2001] PIQR Q3.

[A89] Where the claimant was already suffering from a pre-existing illness/ condition at the time of the accident, it is important to consider what the claimant's condition and prognosis would have been irrespective of the defendant's wrongdoing. To this end, it will often be important to obtain detailed factual evidence about the claimant's symptoms and level of activity at the time of the accident. Expert evidence should consider which of the claimed injuries, losses and expenses would have occurred in any event and, if applicable, the relevant acceleration period involved. It should be noted that different acceleration periods might apply to different heads of loss. For example, the claimant might have stopped working due to his pre-existing condition within two years of the accident but might not have needed a chair lift for another ten years after the accident. The individual item of loss must be scrutinised. Most ongoing expenses and losses will be recoverable, eg the acceleration by two years of a shoulder injury requiring monthly physiotherapy means that the claimant will incur an additional 24 sessions of physiotherapy, whereas one-off items of expense and loss will not be recoverable since they would have occurred anyway, eg an accident which accelerates the claimant's back condition bringing forward his need for a spinal fusion operation. However, there are exceptions. Take, for example, the claimant who was working in a good job prior to the accident with private health insurance cover. As a result of the accident, he suffered a back injury accelerating a pre-existing spinal condition by five years and necessitating a spinal fusion operation. But for the accident, his condition may have deteriorated gradually and his company may have paid for the operation. As a result of the accident, the claimant was unable to perform his duties and his contract of employment was terminated before he was able to have the surgery. He therefore paid privately for the surgery. In this case, it is conceivable that the claimant can recover the cost of the private surgery, discounted for the risk that he might have lost his job or entitlement to his pre-accident private health insurance cover.

[A90]   Generally speaking, pre-existing conditions/illnesses will reduce the value of the claimant's claim, in order to take account of the damage which cannot be directly attributed to the defendant's wrongdoing[1]. However, there are some instances where the application of the eggshell skull principle means that the claimant will be entitled to an increased award. For example, a claimant who only had one eye before an accident stands to lose his or her whole eyesight if their remaining eye is damaged, which will result in much more serious consequences than if the claimant had two good eyes to start with[2].

---

[1]   See eg *Haggar v De Placido* [1972] 1 WLR 716, in which the claimant who was rendered incomplete quadriplegic following an accident received less damages than he otherwise would have done in order to take account of his pre-existing extensive disability.

[2]   *Paris v Stepney Borough Council* [1951] AC 367. For further examples of cases in which damages were increased by reason of pre-existing injuries, see *Mustard v Morris* Current Law 1983/62u and *Savory v Burningham* [1996] CLY 2362.

(5)   Multiple torts, multiple accidents and subsequent injuries

[A91]   Where there are a number of potential defendants, the assessment of damages against each defendant will depend upon whether or not the damage caused is divisible or indivisible. Damages are indivisible where the damage, once it eventuates, is such that individual contributions to it cannot separately be identified; put another way, the injury cannot be shown to be any worse or less because of any particular contribution factor. A classic example of this is cancer, to which there might be a number of contributory causes but, once the disease arises, it is no greater or less because of the prior presence of any one of those factors. A further example is provided by a glass of water which is nearly full so that, when another liquid is added, the contents of the glass overflow. The overflow is caused indivisibly by the presence of the water and the presence of the other liquid because they cannot be separated, and the overflow only happens due to the combination of the two liquids. This is to be contrasted with a condition where not only the fact of, but also the extent of, the separate contributions to it can be identified, and the condition may be exacerbated or accelerated by any one of those separately identifiable contributions. A classic example of such a divisible injury is asbestosis, where the severity and prognosis of the disease depends on the extent of the exposure to asbestos. Assuming there is sufficient evidence regarding the extent of the claimant's exposure to asbestos, liability may be apportioned between different tortfeasors in accordance with the contribution they each individually made to the claimant's injury[1].

---

[1] *Holtby v Brigham & Cowan (Hull) Ltd* [2000] 3 All ER 421, CA.

[A92] The damage is likely to be divisible where one accident takes place some time after another[1], or a second distinct tort is committed which results in the claimant sustaining additional injuries[2]. In such cases, the subsequent tortfeasor is only responsible for the further injuries and/or the resulting aggravation/exacerbation of pre-existing injuries caused by his or her wrongdoing[3]. It will be necessary for the court to disentangle the individual responsibility of each defendant for causing the claimant's various injuries and loss. Such an assessment must be attempted even though it is difficult and complex, if necessary apportioning heads of loss such as general damages for pain, suffering and loss of amenity and loss of earnings[4]. Further, where one claim is brought and settled, the documents relating to that claim will be disclosable in relation to any outstanding claim for additional loss arising out of the same or similar injuries[5].

---

[1] *Murrell v Healy* [2001] EWCA Civ 486.
[2] *Rhaman v Arearose Ltd University College London NHS Trust* [2001] QB 351.
[3] *Page v Smith (No 2)* [1996] 1 WLR 855; *Murrell v Healy* [2001] EWCA Civ 486.
[4] *Rhaman v Arearose Ltd University College London NHS Trust* [2001] QB 351.
[5] *Murrell v Healy* [2001] EWCA Civ 486.

[A93] The damage will be indivisible where there are joint tortfeasors each contributing to the same damage, eg the manufacturer and supplier of a dangerous product[1]. Alternatively, the court may judge that the damage is indivisible where each defendant made a material contribution to the claimant's damage but it is impossible to tell, given the current level of medical and scientific knowledge, what element or proportion of the claimant's damage is attributable to which defendant. In this situation, each defendant will be held jointly and severally liable for the resulting damage[2]. In other cases where each defendant's wrongdoing acts cumulatively to cause the claimant's damage, it may be possible to apportion responsibility between each defendant in accordance with the individual contribution they have made to the development of the injury, eg in a vibration white finger case where there is a direct link between the extent of vibration exposure and the severity of the condition[3].

---

[1] See further the Consumer Protection Act 1987. For examples of actions against multiple joint tortfeasors, see *A v The National Blood Authority* [2001] Lloyd's Rep Med 187; *Fairchild v Glenhaven Funeral Services* [2002] UKHL 22; *Gwilliam v West Hertfordshire Hospital NHS Trust* [2002] EWCA Civ 1041; *Pearce v Lindfield* [2003] EWCA Civ 647.
[2] *Bonnington Castings v Wardlaw* [1956] AC 613; *McGhee v NCB* [1973] 1 WLR 1.
[3] *Allen v British Rail Engineering* [2001] EWCA Civ 242, [2001] ICR 942.

[A94] Whether or not the claimant's injuries in a particular case will be classed as divisible or indivisible will usually be determined by the available medical evidence. For example, where two accidents occur very close together, so that it is impossible to tell which accident was responsible for causing what damage, the two individual tortfeasors are likely to be held equally responsible for the totality of the claimant's damage[1]. Further, even though a number of accidents may have been spread out over a period of months, if the medical evidence is to the effect that the accidents were together jointly responsible for causing the claimant's condition, the tortfeasors are likely to be found equally liable for the claimant's loss[2].

1   See eg *Fitzgerald v Lane* [1989] AC 328. If it is possible to tell, although the evidence has not been gathered, the claim may yet fail for want of sufficient proof – see further *Fairchild v Glenhaven Funeral Services* [2002] UKHL 22 for an exposition of the relevant principles.
2   *Pearce v Lindfield* [2003] EWCA Civ 647.

[A95]   Occasionally, having suffered one injury, the claimant subsequently becomes the victim of further injuries or accidents which are related to the initial injury. Whether or not the original tortfeasor will be responsible for any subsequent damage which occurs will largely depend upon the integrity of the chain of causation between the separate events. A common example of this arises where a claimant is negligently treated by doctors following an initial injury. It has been held by the Court of Appeal that the chain of causation in this situation is not broken unless the medical treatment provided is 'so grossly negligent as to be a completely inappropriate response to the injury inflicted'[1]. Thus the defendant responsible for the initial injury and the treating doctors become joint tortfeasors for the same damage. As far as the claimant is concerned, this means that the proceedings only need to be issued as against the original tortfeasor without needing to embark upon often more risky litigation for clinical negligence. If so advised, the original tortfeasor may then bring a claim for a contribution or an indemnity against the negligent doctors[2].

1   *Webb v Barclays Bank plc* [2001] EWCA Civ 1141 at [55].
2   If such a claim is made out against the claimant's doctors, the court will apportion liability between the respective tortfeasors in accordance with the principles under the Civil Liability (Contribution) Act 1978, ie the court will have regard to the blameworthiness of each party and the causative potency of their actions. See further *Webb v Barclays Bank plc* [2001] EWCA Civ 1141.

[A96]   Another example of this arises where a claimant sustains an injury which makes him or her vulnerable to suffering from further injuries. It does not take too much imagination to appreciate that an injury which makes it difficult for the claimant to see where he or she is going might result in the claimant suffering a further injury[1]. In order to succeed, however, it will be necessary to show that the chain of causation between the original injury and the subsequent injury has not been broken[2]. Where the claimant has acted unreasonably, resulting in an aggravation of his or her injuries, but not so unreasonably as to break the chain of causation, the court may reduce the claimant's award of damages by reason of contributory negligence[3].

1   See eg *Wieland v Cyril Lord Carpets* [1969] 3 All ER 1006, followed in *Pyne v Wikenfield* (1981) 26 SASR 441.
2   Contrast *Webb v Barclays Bank plc* [2001] EWCA Civ 1141 with cases where the chain of causation was held to have been broken by the claimant's unreasonable behaviour, such as *McKew v Holland & Hannen & Cubitts* [1969] 3 All ER 1621, HL, and *Sabri-Tabrizi v Lothian Health Board* (1998) 43 BMLR 190.
3   See eg *Spencer v Wincanton Holdings Ltd* [2009] EWCA Civ 1404.

(6)   DEDUCTIONS, CREDIT AND BENEFITS[1]

[A97]   The award made under any particular head will be the net loss to the claimant, taking into account any deductions, credit or benefits that would have applied in any event[2]. Deductions tend to be made on a 'like for like' basis, so that the deduction is applied to the relevant head of loss. For example, in relation to claims for loss of earnings, common deductions include the following:

- Tax[3].
- National Insurance[4].
- Pension contributions[5].
- Receipts from an employer's permanent health insurance policy[6].
- Tax rebates received as a result of the injuries[7] and any tax which would have been saved as a result of the injuries[8].
- Ex gratia payments made by the tortfeasor[9].
- Sick pay[10].
- Redundancy payments where a redundancy might never have otherwise occurred, ie where in the absence of the injuries the claimant would have continued to retirement in his or her pre-injury job[11].
- Any significant expenses that would have been incurred earning the money[12].
- Any state benefits outside the statutory scheme of recoupment which would not have otherwise been received by the claimant but for his or her injuries[13].

[1]   See further generally Chapter J, Recovery of State and Collateral Benefits.
[2]   As stated by Lord Bridge in the leading case of *Hodgson v Trapp* [1989] AC 807 at 819E: '*the basic rule is that it is the net consequential loss and expense which the court must measure. If, in consequence of the injuries sustained, the claimant has enjoyed receipts to which he would not otherwise have been entitled, prima facie, those receipts are to be set against the aggregate of the claimant's losses and expenses in arriving at the measure of his damages*' [emphasis added].
[3]   *British Transport Commission v Gourley* [1956] AC 185.
[4]   *Cooper v Firth Brown* [1963] 1 WLR 418.
[5]   *Dews v National Coal Board* [1988] AC 1.
[6]   *Hussain v New Taplow Paper Mills Ltd* [1987] 1 All ER 417; *Page v Sheerness Steel*, upheld on appeal to the Court of Appeal and House of Lords; *Wells v Wells* [1999] 1 AC 345.
[7]   *Hartley v Sandholme Iron Co* [1975] QB 600.
[8]   *Brayson v Wilmot-Breedon* [1976] CLY 682. This may have particular relevance to the Government's new tax credits scheme.
[9]   *Gaca v Pirellis General Plc & others* [2004] EWCA Civ 373.
[10] *Hussain v New Taplow Paper Mills Ltd* [1988] AC 514.
[11] *Colledge v Bass Mitchells & Butlers Ltd* [1988] 1 All ER 536. See further Chapter J, Recovery of State and Collateral Benefits at paras **[J95]–[J99]**.
[12] See eg *Sparks v Royal Hospitals NHS Trust* (21 December 1998, unreported), QBD; and *Eagle v Chambers (No 2)* [2004] EWCA Civ 1033, where deductions were made to reflect the claimant's travel expenses. However, it is unusual for travel expenses to be taken into account unless they are significant: *Dews v National Coal Board* [1988] AC 1, per Lord Griffiths.
[13] For example, housing benefit (*Clenshaw v Tanner* [2002] EWHC 184 (QB)) and council tax (*Smith v Rod Jenkins* [2003] EWHC 1356 (QB)).

[A98]   In the same way, discounts often need to be made from other heads of loss in order to reflect the net loss to the claimant. For example, where a claimant has entered into a credit hire agreement to replace a vehicle which was damaged or written off by the accident, his gross loss might seem to be the costs payable under that agreement (which, because it extends credit, are not payable until the expiry of a deferred period). However, the agreement will often provide for more than a mere substitute vehicle by adding benefits such as free delivery, legal representation etc. In such a case, the court will assume that the value of these extra benefits is the difference between the ordinary spot hire rate and the credit hire rate[1]. In the ordinary course of events, damages are not recoverable for 'the worry and nuisance caused by the inconvenience of dealing with the accident'[2], and the claimant must give credit to the defendant for the benefits of successful mitigation. Therefore, prima facie, the ordinary spot rate hire charge for the vehicle in question will be the correct measure of the claimant's net loss, and the claimant will be restricted to recovering the same[3].

1   *Dimond v Lovell* [2002] 1 AC 384 at 400–403. This is an operation of the principle that the defendant is entitled to the benefit of any successful steps taken by the claimant in order to mitigate his or her loss: *British Westinghouse Electric and Manufacturing Co Ltd v Underground Electric Railways Co of London Ltd* [1912] AC 673; *Bellingham v Dhillon* [1973] QB 304.
2   *Dimond v Lovell* [2001] 1 QB 216, per Sir Richard Scott V-C at 239. See also *Taylor v Browne* [1995] CLY 1842.
3   *Dimond v Lovell* [2002] 1 AC 384, per Lord Hoffmann at 403. Note that the position may be different where the claimant is impecunious and has no choice but to hire a car using a credit hire scheme since the defendant must take his or her victim as he or she finds him: *Lagden v O'Connor* [2003] UKHL 64.

[A99]   Once the claimant's loss has been calculated, the actual sum payable by the defendant will take into account any deduction for contributory negligence[1], any apportionment between tortfeasors[2] and any recoupable state benefits under the Social Security (Recovery of Benefits) Act 1997. The defendant will be entitled to withhold from any payment to the claimant the amount of any recoupable benefits as shown on the CRU Certificate[3].

1   See further paras **[A78]** and **[A79]**.
2   See further paras **[A75]** and **[A77]**.
3   See further Chapter J, Recovery of State and Collateral Benefits.

(7)   Discounts and uplifts to take account of contingencies

[A100]   Discounts may be applied to take account of a plethora of risks and contingencies which, if they materialised, would operate to reduce the value of the claim. The discount should be individual to the particular claimant and/or circumstances of the claim[1] and be based upon evidence[2]. A non-exhaustive list of common discounts includes:

*   Discounts to claims for loss of earnings for 'contingencies other than mortality' or the 'vicissitudes of life'. The reduction takes into account the risks of redundancy, ill-health, accident/injury, periods of unemployment, early retirement etc[3]. However, it should be noted that, following *Wells v Wells*[4], it may be difficult to substantiate the traditionally high discounts under this head. Now that a more evidence-based approach is taken using actuarial tables as a guide, there must be tangible reasons relating to the claimant's personality, or the likely future circumstances of the claimant going beyond the purely speculative, in order to justify a substantially higher discount for contingencies over and above the discounts set out in Tables A–C of the Introduction to the Ogden Tables[5].
*   Discounts from claims for loss of earnings to reflect the time the claimant would have had out of work in any event[6]; the fact that he or she might have earned less as he or she grew older in any event[7]; that the claimant might return to some form of work in the future[8]; or that his or her residual earning capacity is likely to increase in the future[9].

- Discounts for the 'gratuitous element' of a care claim, ie the fact that the gratuitous carer does not have to pay tax and National Insurance; does not incur travel expenses; and the care may not be as skilled as could be obtained professionally[10].

- Discounts to a care claim to reflect the chance that the claimant's condition might deteriorate, in which case he or she is likely to be cared for by an institution funded by the state[11].

- Discounts to claims for DIY to reflect the assistance the claimant might have needed with heavier work in any event[12].

- Discounts for the 'domestic element' from claims for loss of earnings/care, lost years and lost dependency in order to reflect the living expenses which have been saved[13].

- Credit must be given for expenses saved whilst the claimant was in hospital or residential care[14].

- Discounts from claims for future losses and expenses to reflect the chance that the loss or expenses might have occurred in any event[15].

- Discounts to reflect the fact that the claimant's condition and prognosis might improve in the future following successful treatment[16].

- Discounts from credit hire claims to reflect the additional services provided to the claimant by the credit hire company which are not recoverable from the defendant[17].

---

[1]   See eg *Herring v Ministry of Defence* [2003] EWCA Civ 528; and *Pearce v Lindfield* [2003] EWCA Civ 647 in which Kay LJ stated at [21]: '[Counsel for the defendant] argues that … the judge should have concluded that there was at least an identifiable chance that the claimant would have retired before the age of 60 even if she had not had the three accidents. He submits the judge should therefore have gone on to make an allowance, albeit a relatively small one, for that chance in determining the appropriate multiplier in calculating her loss of earnings. The fallacy in that argument is that the judge was not assessing when any teacher might retire but was instead directing his mind as to when the claimant was likely to retire. He had to consider her as an individual and not merely as one of a class of people. He heard evidence from her that she wanted to go on working until the age of 60. I find it impossible to see how, without even hearing such evidence, this court could conclude that that was not a finding of fact open to the judge'.

[2]   Following *Wells v Wells* [1999] 1 AC 345, the days are gone where impressionist, ie judicial, discounts can be made simply because an award seems too high. As Lord Lloyd put it at 364: 'The purpose of the award [of damages] is to put the [claimant] in the same position, financially, as if he had not been injured. The sum should be calculated as accurately as possible, making just allowance, where this is appropriate, for contingencies. But once the calculation is done, there is no justification for imposing an artificial cap on the multiplier. There is no room for a judicial scaling down. Current award in the most serious cases may seem high. The present appeals may be taken as examples. But there is no more reason to reduce the awards, if properly calculated, because they seem high than there is to increase the awards because the injuries are very severe'.

[3]   See further Chapter K, Counter-schedules (reduction to loss of earnings multiplier) and para **[H91]**–**[H97]**.

[4]   [1999] 1 AC 345.

[5]   *Herring v Ministry of Defence* [2003] EWCA Civ 528, per Potter LJ at [31].

[6]   See eg *Clenshaw v Tanner* [2002] EWHC 184 (QB), in which Silber J discounted the claim for past loss of earnings by 30% in order to take account of the time the claimant would have been out of work in any event. See also *Brown v Berry* (14 October 1997, unreported), QBD, in which Mr Robert Seabrook QC sitting as a deputy judge of the High Court discounted the claim for past loss of earnings by 50% in order to take account of the claimant's lack of qualifications and driving licence and history of low seasonal employment.

[7]   *Newman v Folkes and Dunlop Tyres Ltd* [2002] PIQR Q13.

8   *Froggatt v Chesterfield & North Derbyshire Royal Hospitals NHS Trust* [2002] All ER (D) 218 (Dec).
9   *Longden v Mercury Communications* [2002] PIQR Q1 at 11.
10   See further at paras **[F109]–[F115]**.
11   See Eg *Mitchell v Mulholland (No 2)* [1972] 1 QB 65; and *Sklair v Haycock* [2009] EWHC 3328 (QB).
12   This is often reflected in a reduction of the multiplier to a certain age. See eg *Smith v McCrae* [2003] EWCA Civ 505.
13   *Mitchell v Mulholland (No 2)* [1972] 1 QB 65.
14   Administration of Justice Act 1982, s 5 provides: 'In an action under the law of England and Wales or the law of Northern Ireland for damages for personal injuries (including any such action arising out of a contract) any saving to the injured person which is attributable to his maintenance wholly or partly at public expense in a hospital, nursing home or other institution shall be set off against any income lost by him as a result of his injuries'.
15   See eg *Heil v Rankin & MIB* [2001] PIQR Q16, CA, in which the Court of Appeal upheld a discount to reflect the chance that the claimant might have suffered post-traumatic stress disorder in any event.
16   *Thomas v Bath District Health Authority* [1995] PIQR Q19, CA.
17   *Dimond v Lovell* [2002] 1 AC 384.

[A101]   Equally, in appropriate cases, uplifts may be applied to take account of chances which may occur or contingencies which, if they materialise, would tend to increase the appropriate level of damages. For example, where a claimant had a real or substantial chance of promotion but for his or her injuries, this can be taken into account in either the multiplicand or multiplier when calculating the claim for loss of earnings[1]. Also, in claims brought under the Fatal Accidents Act 1976, awards for dependency can be made to reflect the lost prospect of dependency which was not in existence at the time of death but may have occurred in the future[2]. Further, in appropriate cases, a 'contingency award' can be sought in order to cover additional eventualities giving rise to further expense or loss[3].

1   *Mitchell v Mulholland (No 2)* [1972] 1 QB 65 at 83; *Anderson v Davis* [1993] PIQR Q87; *Doyle v Wallace* [1998] PIQR Q146; *Langford v Hebran* [2001] EWCA Civ 361.
2   *Taff v Vale Rly Co v Jenkins* [1913] AC 1; *Barnett v Cohen* [1921] All ER Rep 528; *Kandalla v British European Airways Corpn* [1980] 1 All ER 341. To be recoverable, the prospect must be more than speculative: *D and D v Donald* [2001] PIQR Q44.
3   See further at para **[A15]**.

(8)   LIFE EXPECTANCY

[A102]   The longer a claimant's life expectancy, the greater the multiplier for future expenses and losses. The presumption is that the claimant will have a normal life expectancy[1]. Following *Wells v Wells*[2], the starting point for the assessment of life expectancy will be the Government's actuarial tables prepared for this purpose, known as the Ogden Tables. The calculation of life expectancy is predominantly a medical issue relating to an individual claimant, but the doctors may be informed by statistical information[3]. Where a claimant's life expectancy is agreed between the parties or is determined by the court, a fixed-term multiplier should be used (which can be gleaned from Table 28 of the Ogden Tables)[4]. In the event that a claimant's life expectancy has been reduced by the defendant's wrongdoing, it is no longer possible to claim a separate award of general damages for this loss[5]. Instead, the claimant's award in respect of general damages for pain, suffering and loss of amenity can be increased to take account of any awareness and anxiety resulting from the knowledge that his or her life expectancy has been reduced. Where there is a significant reduction of life expectancy, a claim for the 'lost years' may be brought in respect of the lost earnings and pension resulting from living a shorter life[6].

1   *Rowley v London and North Western Railway* (1873) LR 8 Ex 221.
2   [1999] 1 AC 345.
3   *B v RVI & Associated Hospital NHS Trust* [2002] EWCA Civ 348.
4   In *Wells v Wells* [1999] 1 AC 345 at 378, Lord Lloyd said: 'But there is no room for any discount in the case of a whole life multiplier with an agreed expectation of life. In the case of loss of earnings the contingencies can work in only one direction – in favour of the defendant. But in the case of life expectancy, the contingency can work in either direction. The [claimant] may exceed his normal expectation of life, or he may fall short of it'. See further *B v RVI & Associated Hospital NHS Trust* [2002] EWCA Civ 348; see also *Brown v King's Lynn & Wisbech NHS Hospitals Trust* (20 December 2000, unreported), QBD.
5   Administration of Justice Act 1982, s 1 which applies to all claims where the cause of action accrued on or after 1 January 1983.
6   See further Chapter I, The Claim for Lost Years.

(9) AGE, SEX, RACE AND RELIGION

[A103]   Generally speaking, everybody is treated equally and a claimant's age, sex and race have little bearing on the appropriate award of damages for non-pecuniary loss[1]. But age, sex and race and religion may have an impact on pecuniary losses. For example:

- A person's age is likely to influence their life expectancy and hence the applicable multiplier for future expenses and losses.
- Traditionally, a higher discount for 'contingencies other than mortality' has been applied to the loss of earnings claim of women of child-bearing age, to take account of the fact that they might take time out to raise and bring up a family[2].
- In certain cultures or religions, it may be customary to incur certain expenses and losses and/or avoid others[3].

1   See further Chapter D.
2   See eg *Harris v Harris* [1973] 1 Lloyd's Rep 445, CA, where the Court of Appeal reduced the trial judge's multiplier for loss of future earnings from 15 to 10 to take account of the fact that, but for the accident, the claimant may have married and taken time off from her career. According to the CBI report *Workforce 2000*, it is estimated that women lose on average seven years of career development having a family. However, as research carried out by the Equal Opportunities Commission and Policy Studies Institute highlights, more and more women are now returning to work after childbirth. It should be noted that the suggested discounts for contingencies other than mortality in the guidance notes to the Ogden Tables (6th edition) already taken into account time off to bring up a family (which is why the discounts for women of child-bearing age are larger than the discounts for men of equivalent age): *A v Powys Health Board* [2007] EWHC 2996 (QB).
3   For example, *Quainoo v Brent & Harrow Area Health Authority* (1982) 132 NLJ 1100, involving a claim brought under the Fatal Accidents Act 1976 arising out of the death of a member of the Ghanaian Royal Family, and *Emeh v Kensington, Chelsea and Westminster Area Health Authority* [1984] 3 All ER 1044, in which it was held that it was not reasonable to expect a claimant to abort an unwanted pregnancy against her beliefs. In *Ahsan v University Hospitals Leicester NHS Trust* [2006] EWHC 2624 (QB), HHJ Hegarty QC sitting as a judge of the High Court held that the religious beliefs of the claimant, who was in a persistent vegetative state, and his family were relevant to the assessment of meeting the claimant's reasonable needs. See also *Rahman (a child) v West Pennine Health Authority* (18 December 2002, unreported), in which it was accepted in principle that the claimant was entitled to claim the increased cost of fulfilling his religious obligation to undertake the

Hadj pilgrimage but that, on the facts, no award was made because there was insufficient evidence to persuade the judge that the pilgrimage would have been undertaken in the absence of the claimant's injuries.

[A104]   In terms of loss of earnings, women are often still paid less than their male counterparts for performing the same job. However, if the court were to take account of any prejudice because of age, sex, sexual orientation, race or religion when assessing the claimant's loss, this may be seen as condoning such discrimination. Therefore, when considering a claim for the loss of future earnings on behalf of a female claimant, arguably the court should take the average loss of earnings figure for men and women, or the higher earnings of men, instead of limiting the claimant to the lower rates applicable to women[1].

[1]   See further *Van Wees v (1) Karkour and (2) Walsh* [2007] EWHC 165 (QB) at para 139; and *Clark v Powell*, Lawtel, 13/7/2004, Document No AM0900740 and [2007] EWHC 165 (QB).

(10) ILLEGALITY

[A105]   For policy reasons, the court will not allow a claimant to benefit from his or her illegal or immoral acts[1]. Therefore, a claim cannot be brought for loss of earnings arising out of unlawful conduct such as theft[2] or for a loss of dependency based upon 'moonlighting', ie working illegally whilst in receipt of statutory benefits[3]. Likewise, a claim for loss of earnings will fail where it is based on a deliberate concealment amounting to the criminal offence of obtaining pecuniary advantage by deception[4]. Additionally, no claim can be brought for damages arising out of criminal behaviour caused by a personality change following an accident[5]. The difficulty, however, often arises where the illegality complained of is collateral to the claim[6], eg where a claimant was working in a legitimate business before the accident but did not pay tax or National Insurance. In such cases, unless there is any other evidence of illegality which taints the claim, an award for loss of earnings will usually succeed for the net loss of earnings after deduction of the tax and National Insurance that should have been paid[7]. However, the claimant is likely to face the risk of being reported to the relevant authorities in respect of previous non-payment of monies together with a claim for back payments and/or prosecution in the criminal courts. Where a claimant has dishonestly exaggerated a genuine claim, it is well established that the claimant will not be deprived of damages to which he is entitled because he has fraudulently attempted to obtain more than his entitlement – the invariable rule is that the judge limits the damages which are appropriate to his findings[8]. Likewise, this principle applies where the claimant's (attempted) fraud consists of lying to support the claim of another person[9].

[1]   This is known as the principle 'ex turpi causa non oritur actio'.

[2]   See eg *Burns v Edman* [1970] 2 QB 541.

[3]   *Hunter v Butler* [1996] RTR 396.

[4]   See eg *Hewison v Meridian Shipping* [2002] EWCA Civ 1821, in which the Court of Appeal upheld the trial judge's decision to reject a claim for loss of earnings as a matter of public policy where a merchant seaman had deliberately concealed his condition of epilepsy from his employer.

[5]   *Worrall v British Railways Board* [1999] CLY 1413, CA; *Clunis v Camden and Islington Health Authority* [1998] QB 968; *Gray v Thames Trains Ltd v another* [2009] 3 WLR 167.

[6]   In order to succeed, the test for illegality that is usually applied is to ask whether or not the claimant has to rely upon the illegality in order to establish his or her case: *Tinsley v Milligan* [1994] 1

AC 340; *Revill v Newberry* [1996] QB 567; *Clunis v Camden and Islington Area Health Authority* [1998] QB 978; *Gray v Thames Trains Ltd v another* [2009] 3 WLR 167.

7   *Le Bagge v Buses* [1958] NZLR 630; *Duller v South East Lincs Engineers* [1981] CLY 585; and *Newman v Folkes & Dunlop Tyres Ltd* [2002] PIQR Q2 (whilst this case was appealed to the Court of Appeal, a decision – which Ward LJ later observed ([2002] EWCA Civ 591 at [14]) was quite correct – was taken not to appeal the trial judge's finding on this point).

8   *Shah v Ul-Haq* [2009] EWCA Civ 542, per Smith LJ at paras [17], [20]. See also *Churchill v Kelly* [2006] EWHC 18 (QB).

9   *Shah v Ul-Haq* [2009] EWCA Civ 542, per Smith LJ at para [20]: 'I can see no logical justification for suggesting that the claimant who lies about another person's claim should be treated more severely than the claimant who lies about his own claim. Both behave disgracefully; both commit the criminal offences of attempting to pervert the course of justice and attempting to obtain property by deception or attempting to obtain a pecuniary advantage by deception. Yet the policy of the law has not been to shut them out from justice altogether – save where the claim relates to an insurance contract'.

(11) HUMAN RIGHTS AND EUROPEAN LAW

[A106]   Primary and subordinate legislation must be read so as to give effect to the European Convention on Human Rights[1]. Likewise, domestic law must be interpreted in accordance with European law and, if there are any inconsistencies between the two, effect must be given to the European position[2].

1   Human Rights Act 1998, s 3(1). For example, see *Cachia v Francis Ola Faluyi* [2001] EWCA Civ 998.

2   European Communities Act 1972. See further *Costa v ENEL* [1964] ECR 585; *Internationale Handelsgesellschaft* [1970] ECR 1125; *Simmenthal* [1978] ECR 629; *R v Secretary of State for Transport, ex p Factortame Ltd* [1990] 2 AC 85; *R v Secretary of State for Employment, ex p Equal Opportunities Commission* [1995] 1 AC 1.

Irrelevant factors

(1) THE DEFENDANT'S MEANS

[A107]   When deciding what the appropriate award of damages should be in a particular case, the court must not be influenced by the means of the defendant[1]. As Lord Woolf stated in *Heil v Rankin*[2]:

'The award for the same injury should be the same irrespective of the defendant's means. This is clear from the authorities.'

1   *Lim Poh Choo v Camden and Islington Area Health Authority* [1980] AC 174; *Wells v Wells* [1999] AC 345; *Heil v Rankin* [2001] QB 272.

2   *Heil v Rankin* [2001] QB 272 at 296, para [33].

(2) THE CLAIMANT'S MEANS

[A108]   The principles of recoverability should be the same, whatever the claimant's means or standing[1]. One of the most common examples of this is when considering whether the claimant has mitigated his or her loss, since it is well established that the claimant's impecuniosity should not affect the amount of compensation received[2]. But, whilst the principles of assessment might remain the same, in practice the means of the claimant may make a difference to the amount of damages received. Indeed, there are a number of heads of loss where the appropriate award of damages may well depend upon the resources and lifestyle of the claimant at the time of the defendant's negligence, eg damaged clothing and property[3], loss of earnings, holidays etc. An obvious example of this is that the wealthy claimant, who has prior to trial been able to fund his or her own private medical treatment, will be able to recover the reasonable cost of the same, whereas the less well-to-do claimant, who had all of his treatment free of charge on the NHS, will receive nothing[4]. Thus, whilst the principles of assessment may not change, obviously what amounts to 'reasonable' recovery in one case may not be appropriate in another.

[1]   In *Heil v Rankin* [2001] QB 272 at 296, para [33], Lord Woolf agreed with the defendant's submission that 'in making an award of damages the court is not concerned with whether the claimant is a pauper or a millionaire'.

[2]   In particular, see the following cases regarding mitigation of loss: *Clippens Oil Co v Edinburgh and District Water Trustees* [1907] AC 291; *Liesbosch Dredger v SS Edison* [1933] AC 449; *Robbins of Putney v Meek* [1971] RTR 345; *Martindale v Duncan* [1973] 1 WLR 574, CA; *Alcoa Minerals of Jamaica plc v Broderick* [2000] 3 WLR 23, PC; and *Lagden v O'Connor* [2003] UKHL 64.

[3]   For example, it would be unreasonable for the claimant to recover the costs of hiring a Rolls Royce to replace his elderly Nissan Sunny damaged as a result of an accident.

[4]   Law Reform (Personal Injuries) Act 1948, s 2(4) provides that, in determining the reasonableness of any expenses, the possibility of avoiding them or part of them by taking advantage of facilities under the NHS shall be disregarded. See further at paras **[F47]** to **[F52]**.

(3)   Amount claimed does not represent full extent of the claim

[A109]   It is not relevant to the assessment of quantum that the amount claimed (as reflected by the statement of value on the claim form) does not reflect the true value of the claim, eg where there is a memorandum of understanding between respective insurers[1].

[1]   *Khiaban v Beard* [2002] EWCA Civ 358.

(4)   The size or consequences of the damages award

[A110]   As stated above, the principle in English law, so far as possible, is full compensation[1]. Thus, the magnitude of the award when totalled up, or the consequences upon the defendant of paying the award, is not relevant. Thus in *Wells v Wells*[2], Lord Lloyd of Berwick, quoting Lord Scarman in *Lim Poh Choo v Camden and Islington Area Health Authority*[3], said[4]:

'There is no room here for considering the consequences of a high award upon the wrongdoer or those who finance him. And, if there were room for any such consideration, upon what principle, or by what criterion, is the judge to determine the extent to which he is to diminish upon this ground the compensation payable?'

[1]   *Livingstone v Rawyards Coal Co* (1880) 5 App Cas 25; *Lim Poh Choo v Camden and Islington Health Authority* [1980] AC 174; *Hodgson v Trapp* [1989] AC 807; *Pickett v Pickett* [1980] AC 136; *Wells v Wells* [1999] AC 345.

[2]   [1999] 1 AC 345.

[3]   [1980] AC 174.

[4]   [1999] 1 AC 345 at 373.

(5) Medical treatment which could have been obtained on the NHS

[A111]   Section 2(4) of the Law Reform (Personal Injuries) Act 1948 provides that:

'In an action for damages for personal injuries ... there shall be disregarded, in determining the reasonableness of any expenses the possibility of avoiding those expenses or part of them by taking advantage of facilities available under the National Health Service.'

[A112]   However, it should be noted that the case law has placed a number of limits on the interpretation of this provision[1], and a claimant will not be able to recover the costs of private medical treatment unless he or she can show on the balance of probabilities that private facilities will be used or that, where there is a risk of future treatment being needed, they would be used[2].

---

[1]   See further Chapter F, Services Provided by the NHS.
[2]   *Woodrup v Nicol* [1993] PIQR Q104.

(6) The loss is difficult to calculate

[A113]   Unless a particular head of loss is too small, speculative or fanciful to calculate, difficulty of calculation is no bar to recovery[1].

---

[1]   See further at para **[A52]**.

(7) Future inflation

[A114]   Save in exceptional circumstances, future inflation is ignored[1]. It should be noted, however, that there is an argument that future inflation should be taken into account for certain heads of loss which have historically risen significantly above the rate of the Retail Prices Index, eg the Hospital and Community Health Service Inflation rose 3.9% per annum from 1997 to 2002, compared with the rise in RPI over the same period of 2.3%[2]. This argument was rejected by the Court of Appeal in a group of test cases[3]. It remains to be seen whether the House of Lords would be willing to adopt different rates of inflation in respect of different heads of loss[4]. Whilst adopting such an approach may enable the court to make a more accurate calculation of the claimant's loss according to the fundamental principle of 100% compensation, it could lead to uncertainty and increased costs and court time to decide the applicable rates in each case. However, periodical payment orders may be made by reference to whatever is the appropriate index[5]. If the claimant requires substantial annual sums to meet his or her long-term care needs, this may be a compelling reason for preferring periodical payments to a lump sum award due to the potential for significant under-compensation if the care costs increase at a rate faster than the RPI[6].

---

[1]   *Mallet v McMonagle* [1970] AC 166; *Taylor v O'Connor* [1971] AC 115; *Mitchell v Mulholland (No 2)* [1972] 1 QB 65; *Young v Percival* [1975] 1 WLR 17; *Cookson v Knowles* [1979] AC 556; *Lim Poh Choo v Camden and Islington Area Health Authority* [1980] AC 174; *Auty v NCB* [1985] 1 WLR 784; *Wells v Wells* [1999] 1 WLR 345.
[2]   See eg *Moran v Miller Construction Ltd* (6 June 2003, unreported), approval of settlement by Master Rose.
[3]   *Cooke v United Bristol Health Care* [2003] EWCA Civ 1370.

4   See the arguments for and against such an approach in Appendices A and B to the Ogden Tables (5th edition) published in *Facts & Figures 2005*, pp 63–69.
5   Damages Act 1996, s 2(9) (as amended by the Courts Act 2003).
6   *Thompstone v Tameside and Glossop NHS Trust* [2008] EWCA Civ 5, [2008] 1 WLR 2207.

(8)   How the claimant will spend his or her award

[A115]   Once an award of damages has been made, the claimant may do with it as he or she pleases. Generally speaking, therefore, the intentions of the claimant regarding whether he or she will decide to invest or spend the money are irrelevant[1]. As Lord Clyde stated in *Wells v Wells*[2]:

> 'One clear principle is that what the successful [claimant] will in the event actually do with the award is irrelevant … it is for the [claimant] to decide how the award is to be applied. Whether he is proposing to invest it or spend it, does not affect the calculation of the award. No distinction is recognised here between misers and spendthrifts. While it may be evident that there are certain ways in which he could prudently invest the award and other ways in which he is entitled in compensation takes no account of the course which he may in the event choose to adopt.'

1   *Lim Poh Choo v Camden and Islington Area Health Authority* [1980] AC 174, per Lord Scarman at 191; *Wells v Wells* [1999] AC 345; *Heil v Rankin* [2001] QB 272.
2   [1999] AC 345 at 394H.

[A116]   It should be noted, however, that there are a few exceptions to this general rule, where the claimant's intentions may have an impact on the appropriate award of damages. For example, the claimant's intentions are likely to be relevant in the following situations:

- Where a claim for private healthcare treatment is brought but, on the balance of probabilities, the claimant would have treatment on the NHS[1].
- Where the claimant voluntarily decides to live off the award of damages and not realise any residual earning capacity[2].
- Where the claimant plans to move somewhere where items such as the cost of care may be more expensive or cheaper, eg moving from Staffordshire to Surrey[3], or moving from central London to India.

1   *Woodrup v Nicol* [1993] PIQR Q104, CA.
2   In such a case, the claimant is likely to be held to have failed to mitigate his or her loss, and the appropriate award of damages is reduced to the applicable level assuming the claimant had satisfied his or her earning potential. See further at paras **[A77]–[A83]**.
3   *XXX v A Strategic Health Authority* [2008] EWHC 2727 (QB).

[A117]   Furthermore, post-*Eeles v Cobham Hire Services Ltd*[1], where the court has ordered a significant interim payment to be used for a specific purpose, the court may be keen to accept an undertaking from the claimant's solicitor that the money will be held in the firm's client account, and reasonable steps will be taken before making a payment out to ensure that it is only made in respect of loss identified in the schedule of loss[2].

1   [2009] EWCA Civ 204.
2   *FP v Taunton & Somerset NHS Trust* [2009] EWHC 1965 (QB).

(9) AGE, SEX, RACE AND RELIGION

[A118] As noted above, save for the odd exception, these factors are largely irrelevant to the assessment of damages for pecuniary loss[1].

1   See further at para **[A99]** for examples of ways in which the claimant's age, sex and race may affect the quantification of pecuniary loss.

(10) CHARITABLE DONATIONS, INSURANCE PAYMENTS, PENSION PAYMENTS, REDUNDANCY PAYMENTS AND BENEFITS[1]

[A119] The general principle is that credit should be given for any benefits received by the claimant as a result of his or her injuries which would not otherwise have been received. For example, common deductions include those made for sick pay[2], payments under an employer's permanent health insurance[3], ex gratia payments made by tortfeasors[4], and redundancy payments resulting from the defendant's negligence[5]. A statutory scheme exists to govern the recoupment of certain statutory benefits[6]. Further, if the claimant receives a benefit as a result of his or her injuries which is not covered by the statutory scheme, the claimant must give credit for past and future payments of the benefit in order to avoid the rule against double recovery[7]. Recognised exceptions to this principle include charitable donations[8], insurance payments[9], pension payments (both disablement pensions[10] as well as retirement pensions[11]) and redundancy payments which are not related to the injuries[12]. It should be noted, however, that the claimant does not have to give credit for an award from the Criminal Injuries Compensation Authority/Board, and any such award is not taken into account when quantifying the claim[13].

1   See further generally Chapter J, Recovery of State and Collateral Benefits.
2   *Parry v Cleaver* [1970] AC 1; *Hussain v New Taplow Paper Mills Ltd* [1987] 1 All ER 417.
3   *Page v Sheerness Steel* [1997] PIQR Q17, upheld on appeal to the Court of Appeal and House of Lords; *Wells v Wells* [1999] 1 AC 345.
4   *Gaca v Pirellis General plc* [2004] EWCA Civ 373.
5   *Colledge v Bass Mitchells & Butlers Ltd* [1988] 1 All ER 536.
6   Social Security (Recovery of Benefits) Act 1997. See further Chapter J, Recovery of State and Collateral Benefits.
7   *Hodgson v Trapp* [1989] 1 AC 807. See further *Smith v Rod Jenkins* [2003] EWHC 1356 (QB) (council tax benefit); and *Clenshaw v Tanner* [2002] EWHC 184 (QB) (housing benefit).
8   *Redpath v Belfast and County Down Rly* [1947] NI 167; *Parry v Cleaver* [1970] AC 1; *Cunningham v Harrison* [1973] QB 942.
9   *Bradburn v Great Western Rly Co* (1874) LR 10 Exch 1; *McCamley v Cammell Laird Ltd* [1990] 1 WLR 963. Although it should be noted that the insurance exception only applies where the claimant has either paid for or contributed to the insurance him or herself: *Gaca v Pirellis General Plc* [2004] EWCA Civ 373. See further Chapter J.
10   *Parry v Cleaver* [1970] AC 1; *Smoker v London Fire and Civil Defence Authority* [1991] 2 AC 502.
11   *Hopkins v Norcros plc* [1994] ICR 11; *Hewson v Downs* [1970] 1 QB 73. See further *Longdon v British Coal Corpn* [1998] AC 653.
12   *Wilson v NCB* 1981 SC(HL) 9; *Mills v Hassalls* [1983] ICR 330.
13   *Oldham v Sharples* [1997] PIQR Q82; *A v Hoare* [2008] EWHC 1573; *AT & others v Dulghieru* [2009] EWHC 225 (QB).

Quality of life

[A120] When assessing damages in accordance with the 100% principle, one factor the relevance of which is somewhat controversial is the claimant's 'quality of life'. Many judges will refer to the potential for a particular loss or expense to improve or restore the claimant's 'quality of life'[1], 'enjoyment of life'[2] or 'level of independence'[3] as a way of justifying the recovery of that particular head of loss. This may just be seen as shorthand for the exercise which the court is performing, ie attempting so far as money can to put the claimant back in the position he or she would have been but for the injury, when the claimant had a much greater ability to enjoy life. However, other judges adopt a more technical and less sympathetic view regarding the relevance of this concept. For example, in *Thrul v Ray*[4], Burton J (as he then was) stated:[5]

> 'It is therefore important in assessing the [claimant's] claim for compensation to bear in mind that it is not the purpose of this court to make allowance for anything which would, as it was put on various occasions by, I think, all the witnesses called by the [claimant], improve her "quality of life". It is not the test that the defendant should be required to pay by way of damages to the [claimant] consequent upon the unfortunate injuries resulting from the accident any sum which will simply make the [claimant] happier or more comfortable ... the provision must be one which is reasonably necessary to compensate for what she has lost, but also no more than is reasonably likely to be expended on her behalf in providing her with the substitute for what she has lost.'

The aim of the court is to restore the claimant to the position he would have been in, but for his injuries – no better, no worse. That may well include a view as to his state of mind (if not unreasonably, part of the consequence of the accident has been to make the claimant miserable). Therefore, there would seem to be no reason in principle why something which improves the claimant's quality of life and makes him or her happier should not be claimed. An expense is unlikely to be unreasonable if it seeks to achieve this aim, even if some of the assessment is inevitably looking to the subjective effects of the differing lifestyles of the claimant. Whether or not it is reasonable will depend upon the facts of the case, the item being claimed and proportionality. However, it is submitted that the court ought to take a holistic view of what the 100% principle of pre-accident state implies.

---

[1]   In *Rahman v West Pennine HA* (18/18/02, QBD); LTL 13/5/03, McCombe J said at para [15]: 'I accept Mr Wingate-Saul's oral submission that the purpose of the award is to restore, so far as possible, this Claimant's quality of life'. In *Page v Sheerness Steel Co Ltd* [1996] PIQR 26 at 40, the cost of care to provide an enabler was described as 'someone who will take the [claimant] out of the house, stimulate his interest in sporting and other activities and generally seek to motivate him and improve the quality of his life'. See also the judgment of Cooke J in *Eagle v Chambers* [2003] EWHC 3135 (QB) regarding improvement in the claimant's quality of life as a reason for justifying a period of intensive rehabilitation in a residential neurological unit which was subsequently upheld on appeal: *Eagle v Chambers (No 2)* [2004] EWCA Civ 1033, in particular per Waller LJ at para [33].

[2]   In *Rialis v Mitchell* (1984) Times, 17 July, Stephenson LJ said at p 25 of the transcript: '... the court must not put the standard of reasonableness too high when considering what is being done to improve a plaintiff's condition *or increase his enjoyment of life*' [emphasis added].

[3]   See eg *Burton v Kingsbury* [2007] EWHC 2091 (QB), in which Flaux J stated when considering the claim for information technology: 'If such technology is available to give the Claimant a level

of independence so that he does not have to summon a carer or his wife to switch on a light or a piece of equipment or to draw a curtain or blind, it seems to me that he should be entitled to it and to recover its cost from the Defendant'.

4   [2000] PIQR Q44.

5   At **[Q47]**.

(ii)   Non-pecuniary Loss

[A121]   The correct approach to the assessment of general damages for pain, suffering and loss of amenity is perhaps most clearly expressed by Lord Diplock in *Wright v British Railways Board*[1]:

> '[Where] judges carry out their duty of assessing damages for non-economic loss in the money of the day at the date of the trial ... this is a rule of practice that judges are required to follow, not a guideline from which they have a discretion to depart if there are special circumstances that justify their doing so ... My Lords, given the inescapably artificial and conventional nature of the assessment of damages for non-economic loss in personal injury actions ... it is an important function of the Court of Appeal to lay down guidelines ... as to the quantum of damages appropriate to compensate for various types of commonly occurring injuries ... The purpose of such guidelines is that they should be simple and easy to apply though broad enough to permit allowances to be made for special features of individual cases which make the deprivation caused to the particular plaintiff by the non-economic loss greater or less than in the general run of cases involving injuries of the same kind. Guidelines laid down by an appellate court are addressed directly to judges who try personal injury actions; but confidence that trial judges will apply them means that all those who are engaged in settling out of court the many thousands of claims that never reach the stage of litigation at all or, if they do, do not proceed as far as trial will know very broadly speaking what the claim is likely to be worth if 100 per cent liability is established. The Court of Appeal, with its considerable case-load of appeals in personal injury actions and the relatively recent experience of many of its members in trying such cases themselves, is, generally speaking, the tribunal best qualified to set the guidelines for judges currently trying such actions, particularly as respects non-economic loss; and this House should hesitate before deciding to depart from them, particularly if the departure will make the guideline less general in its applicability or less simple to apply. A guideline as to quantum of conventional damages ... is not a rule of law nor is it a rule of practice. It sets no binding precedent; it can be varied as circumstances change or experience shows that it does not assist in the achievement of even-handed justice or makes trials more lengthy or expensive or settlements more difficult to reach ... As regards assessment of damages for non-economic loss in personal injury cases, the Court of Appeal creates the guidelines as to the appropriate conventional figure by increasing or reducing awards of damages made by judges in individual cases for various common kinds of injuries. Thus so-called "brackets" are established, broad enough to make allowance for circumstances which make the deprivation suffered by an individual plaintiff in consequence of the particular kind of injury greater or less than in the general run of cases, yet clear enough to reduce the unpredictability of what is likely to be the most important factor in arriving at settlement of claims. "Brackets" may call for alteration not only to take account of inflation, for which they ought automatically to be raised, but also it may be to take account of advances in medical science which may make particular kinds of injuries less disabling or advances in medical knowledge which may disclose hitherto unsuspected long term effects of some kinds of injuries or industrial diseases.'

1   *Wright v British Railways Board* [1983] 2 AC 773 at 782, 784–785, followed in *Heil v Rankin* [2001] QB 272, per Lord Woolf at [43].

[A122]   A single lump sum award will usually be made in respect of general damages for pain, suffering and loss of amenity[1]. Conventional sums[2] are awarded representing 'fair, just and reasonable' compensation for the injuries suffered[3]. A judicial tariff system is set by the Court of Appeal[4], which takes into account social and economic factors[5]. The appropriate sum to be awarded in a given case will depend upon the appropriate bracket of the Judicial Studies Board Guidelines[6] and the level of awards made in previously decided cases with similar facts[7] (updated to current day values using the RPI in order to take account of inflation[8]). Whilst there is no lower limit for the award as long as an identifiable injury has been sustained[9], the upper limit is currently about £260,000[10]. Where there is no appropriate Judicial Studies Board Guideline or comparable reported cases, the court must do its best to assess the appropriate level of award using other sources[11]. The applicable award is made irrespective of the claimant's means[12] and, generally speaking, age, sex and ethnicity do not play a significant role[13]. A subjective assessment is made of the appropriate award in the individual case, having regarding to the following factors amongst others:

- the claimant's age;
- the circumstances giving rise to the injuries;
- the claimant's pre-existing level of health;
- the nature, number and severity of the injuries;
- the extent to which the claimant is or was in pain;
- the effect of the injuries upon the claimant's cognitive abilities, memory and executive function, mobility, senses, appearance, sexual and bodily function etc;
- the claimant's degree of insight and awareness into the nature and severity of the injuries;
- the treatment undergone and length of time in hospital or recuperating;
- the extent of any residual disability;
- the length of time for which the claimant will suffer any disability;
- the impact of the injuries on the claimant's daily activities such as work, domestic activities, leisure interests, sports and hobbies;
- the effect of the injuries upon the claimant's relationships and social life;
- the likely prognosis;
- the need for treatment in the future;
- any increased vulnerability to further injury; and
- any awareness of reduced life expectancy.

1   Although it should be noted that 'pain and suffering' is distinct from 'loss of amenity', and it is possible to have one without the other, eg where the claimant is rendered permanently unconscious: *Lim Poh Choo v Camden and Islington Area Health Authority* [1980] AC 174. See further at para **[A9]** and Chapter D, General Damages. 'Pain and suffering' includes the shock of the events giving rise to the injuries: *Behrens v Bertram Mills Circus Ltd* [1957] 2 QB 1; and *Owens v Liverpool Corpn* [1939] 1 KB 394. Further, where a claimant has suffered multiple injuries, judges will occasionally make separate awards in respect of the different types of injuries suffered by a claimant, particularly where psychiatric injuries have been sustained in addition to physical injuries. See further Chapter D, General Damages.
2   As stated by Diplock LJ in *Wright v British Railways Board* [1983] 2 AC 773: 'Such loss is not susceptible of measurement in money. Any figure at which the assessor of damages arrives cannot

be other than artificial and, if the aim is that justice meted out to all litigants should be even-handed instead of depending on idiosyncrasies of the assessor, whether jury or judge, the figure must be "basically" a conventional figure derived from experience and from awards in comparable cases'.

3   *Rowley v London and North Western Ry Co* (1873) LR 8 Exch 221 at 231; *Pickett v British Railways Board Ltd* [1980] AC 136 at 168; *Lim Poh Choo v Camden and Islington Area Health Authority* [1980] AC 174 at 187; and *Heil v Rankin* [2001] QB 272.

4   In *Wright v BRB* [1983] 2 AC 773, Lord Diplock stated: 'The Court of Appeal, with its considerable case-load of appeals in personal injury actions and the relatively recent experience of many of its members in trying such cases themselves is, generally speaking, the tribunal best qualified to set the guide-lines for judges trying such actions'. See also *Heil v Rankin* [2001] QB 272.

5   *Heil v Rankin* [2001] QB 272. Lord Woolf stated at [36] and [38]: 'Awards must be proportionate and take into account the consequences of increases in the awards of damages on defendants as a group and society as a whole. The considerations are ones which the Court cannot ignore. They are the background against which the fair, reasonable and just figure has to be determined ... When the question is the level of damages for non-pecuniary loss the Court is ... concerned with determining what is the fair, reasonable and just equivalent in monetary terms of an injury and the resultant PSLA. The decision has to be taken against the background of the society in which the Court makes the award ... The level of awards does involve questions of social policy. But the questions are ones with which the courts are accustomed to deal as part of their normal role'.

6   *Arafa v Potter* [1994] PIQR Q73; *Reed v Sunderland HA* (1998) Times, 16 October.

7   In *Every v Miles* (1964, unreported), CA, Diplock LJ stated as follows: 'Any such decision involves an attempt to equate the incommensurable. Such an equation is insoluble, and in the logical sense there is no answer which is right. But since justice is not justice unless even-handed, so that one man gets roughly the same treatment from the courts as another in comparable circumstances, and since the law requires that compensation be awarded for physical injuries, and the only kind of compensation which the courts can award is money, the courts are compelled to make a pragmatic solution. They have done so by fixing arbitrary standards of monetary compensation which ... are not susceptible of analysis. These standards have been evolved from such current consensus of damage-awarding tribunals as is manifested by the amounts they have in fact awarded in broadly similar cases'.

8   *Wright v British Railways Board* [1983] 2 AC 773.

9   See *Parry v English Electric Co Ltd* [1971] 1 WLR 664; *Moore v Maidstone and District Motor Services* (1979, unreported), CA; *Price v Quinn* [1979] CA No 98.

10   Following *Heil v Rankin* [2001] QB 272 (updated for inflation) and the Judicial Studies Board Guidelines (7th edn) (uprated for inflation).

11   See further *Armstrong v British Coal Corpn* [1998] CLY 2842, CA; *C v Flintshire County Council* [2001] EWCA Civ 302; and *Meah v McCreamer* [1985] 1 All ER 367.

12   *Lim Poh Choo v Camden and Islington Health Authority* [1980] AC 174; *Wells v Wells* [1999] AC 345; *Heil v Rankin* [2001] QB 272.

13   Although sometimes these factors will be important. For example, scarring is considered more serious on a young female than on an elderly male. See further Chapter D, General Damages.

[A123]   It should be noted that cases in which there are pre-existing injuries or illnesses[1] or multiple injuries[2] are more difficult to assess.

1   See further at para **[A88]** and Chapter D, General Damages.

2   See *Bracken v Lancashire CCEA* (1 April 1987, unreported), QBD; *Stevens v Simon* (1987) Times, 20 November, CA; *Hicks v Barnes* (13 January 1988, unreported), QBD; *Lloyd v Lloyd* (21 March 1990, unreported), CA; *Brown v Woodall* [1995] PIQR Q36; *Dureau v Evans* [1996] PIQR Q18; *Clarke v South Yorkshire Transport Ltd* [1998] PIQR Q104. See further at para **[A87]** and Chapter D, General Damages.

11   **Exaggeration and Malingering**

(i)   Conscious or Unconscious Exaggeration

[A124]   A distinction needs to be drawn between conscious and unconscious exaggeration[1]. On the one hand, conscious exaggeration or malingering involves a deliberate decision by the claimant to feign his or her injuries or to make out that they are worse than they actually are. In the worst-case scenario the 'claimant' may have never suffered any injury at all[2]. On the other hand, unconscious exaggeration may be totally unintended and may relate to a recognised psychiatric disorder such as anxiety/litigation/compensation neurosis, somatic disorder, a chronic pain disorder or depression. The claimant's representatives owe a duty to be on the look-out for exaggerated claims, and may face a wasted costs order for not taking appropriate steps to prevent an unmeritorious claim from proceeding to trial[3]. In practice, in the absence of conclusive objective evidence (such as video surveillance evidence), many cases are difficult to pigeon-hole. Assuming that the claimant's continuing symptoms cannot be explained organically, additional expert evidence (usually from a psychiatrist/neuropsychiatrist or psychologist/neuropsychologist) will be required to determine whether the claimant's symptoms may be genuinely related to the defendant's wrongdoing. In some cases, it may well be that there are elements of both conscious and unconscious exaggeration[4]. In such a case, it will be necessary for the court to make a finding as regards the extent of each and when, but for the conscious exaggeration, the claimant might have made a good recovery/returned to work etc. The claimant's presentation to expert witnesses, demeanour in the witness box[5], and appearance in any video surveillance evidence[6] will be crucial to this decision, as well as what the claimant tells people about his or her injuries and disability, eg the and employers. Generally speaking, to establish the existence of conscious exaggeration – which is tantamount to an allegation of malingering or fraud – the evidence must be strong and cogent[7]. This does not necessarily mean that a different standard of proof applies. However, fraud is usually inherently less likely than other innocent explanations and 'cogent evidence is generally required to satisfy a civil tribunal that a person has been fraudulent'[8] and a court will 'look closely into the facts grounding an allegation of fraud before accepting that it has been established'[9].

[1]   In *Digby v Essex County Council* [1994] PIQR P53 at P54, Sir Thomas Bingham MR said: 'The upshot of that report, therefore, is that the orthopaedic surgeon, subject to the possibility of the neurological explanation, concludes that there is no organic basis for the symptoms of which the plaintiff complains, and concludes that there is likely to be a functional overlay, that is, a genuine complaint by the patient but one for which there is no organic basis. It is, as I take it, clearly understood that functional overlay is something quite distinct from deliberate malingering and deliberate dishonest exaggeration'.

[2]   See eg *Afzal v Chubb Guarding Services Ltd* [2003] EWHC 822 (QB), in which HHJ Bowsher QC found that the claimant did not suffer any psychiatric or psychological injuries but had deliberately falsified his symptoms. He concluded that the claimant with his wife was engaged in malingering and deception, probably for personal gain and financial reward.

[3]   See eg *Ali v Ali and Provident Insurance* (7 March 2003, unreported). Although it should be noted that an allegation of professional negligence on the part of a solicitor should be approached in an untechnical way and, where there is a conflict of medical evidence, it is not for the claimant's lawyers to decide that conflict of evidence before the trial: *Afzal v Chubb Guarding Services Ltd* [2003] EWHC 822 (QB).

[4]   See eg *Smith v Rod Jenkins* [2003] EWHC 1356 (QB). See also *Shah v Wasim Ul-Haq and others* [2009] EWCA Civ 542, in which Smith LJ said at para [20]: 'Of course, not all exaggerated

claims entail dishonesty; sometimes exaggeration can be innocent, resulting from a subconscious preoccupation, even obsession, with the injury. Judges are always careful to take account of such effects when assessing damages'.

[5]   See eg the impressions formed by: Gorman J in *Thompson v Royal Mail Lines Ltd* [1957] 1 Lloyd's Rep 99 at 100; Saville J in *Coben v Charter Medical of England* (8 October 1987, unreported), QBD; and Judge Jowitt QC, sitting as a judge of the High Court in *Whitehead v Reed Corrugated Cases Ltd* (15 July 1987, unreported), QBD.

[6]   See eg *Jenkins v Wakefield Metropolitan District Council* (23 June 1988, unreported), QBD; *Dunk v Bejam Frozen Food Centres Ltd* (20 December 1990, unreported), QBD; *Drummond v Shrewsbury and Atcham Borough Council* (2 May 1996, unreported), CA; *Ford v GKR Construction* [2000] 1 WLR 1397; *Uttley v Uttley* [2002] PIQR P123; *Booth v Britannia Hotels Ltd* [2002] EWCA Civ 579; *Sutton v Tesco Stores* (30 July 2002, unreported), QBD; and *Jones v University of Warwick* [2003] EWCA Civ 151.

[7]   See further *Hornal v Neuberger Products Ltd* [1957] 1 QB 247; *Re Dellow's Wills Trusts* [1964] 1 WLR 451; and *Blyth v Blyth* [1966] 1 ALL ER 524, HL.

[8]   *Secretary of State for the Home Department v Rehman* [2003] 1 AC 153, per Lord Hoffmann at para [55].

[9]   *Re Doherty* [2008] UKHL 33, per Lord Carswell at para [28].

(ii)   Malingering

[A125]   Malingering may be defined as[1]:

'The intentional production of false or grossly exaggerated physical or psychological symptoms, motivated by external incentives such as avoiding military duty, avoiding work, obtaining financial compensation, evading criminal prosecution, or obtaining drugs.'

[1]   *Diagnostic and Statistical Manual of Mental Disorders IV.*

(iii)   The Need for Psychological or Psychiatric Evidence

[A126]   Obviously, where the deception is blatant, such as a claimant who claims during a medical examination to have pain and difficulty walking but is later seen out of the examination room window running down the street, no psychological or psychiatric input may be needed. However, it is often appropriate to have psychological or psychiatric evidence in a case where malingering is suspected. In particular, as explained above, there may be genuine reasons why a claimant unconsciously exaggerates his or her physical injuries, especially where the claimant suffers from psychiatric injuries or anxiety resulting from the ongoing litigation. Various tests have been developed by experts in order to assist with the assessment of whether or not claimed symptoms are genuine. For example, neuropsychologists use various 'validity' tests in order to distinguish between genuinely reduced cognitive performance following a head injury, and symptoms which may be simulated or exaggerated. Likewise, many orthopaedic surgeons use a variety of tests to attempt to catch out would-be malingerers. Perhaps the most famous of these are the tests developed by Wadell which include the 'compression test' (ie pressing down on the claimant's head) and the 'fake rotation test' (which involves rotating the claimant but not straining the claimant's spinal muscles).

(iv)   Alleging Conscious Exaggeration/Malingering

[A127]   In civil as well as criminal cases, there is a presumption of innocence[1] and the burden is upon the alleging party to prove any wrongdoing[2]. Alleging conscious exaggeration/malingering is tantamount to alleging fraud[3]. It is therefore a serious allegation, must be pleaded if relied upon[4], and should only be pleaded where there is some evidence (although not necessarily admissible evidence) which justifies the same[5]. Low-velocity impact claims are an exception, and it is not necessary to specifically plead fraud when it is alleged that, due to the low speed of the collision, the claimant has not proved that he has suffered the injuries he claims[6]. The onus is on the defendant to prove that the claimant is consciously exaggerating or malingering[7] and cogent evidence is required before a finding of conscious exaggeration or malingering can be found[8]. Generally speaking, any evidence relied upon in support of such allegations should be disclosed in good time[9], although it may be possible to justify delaying service of obtained video evidence until the claimant has committed him or herself to their witness statement and/or schedule of loss[10]. Furthermore, if the defendant's case is that the claimant is lying, this should be put to the claimant in cross-examination; otherwise, it may be difficult for the defendant to rely upon such a submission at a later stage if a decision was taken not to challenge the claimant's credibility[11].

[1]   *Constantine Line v Imperial Smelting* [1942] AC 154, per Lord Wright at 192; *Emanuel v Emanuel* [1946] P 115.

[2]   *Stojalowski v Imperial Smelting Corpn (NSC)* (1976) 121 SJ 118, CA; and *Cooper v P&O Stena Line Ltd* [1999] 1 Lloyd's Rep 734.

[3]   *Stojalowski v Imperial Smelting Corpn (NSC)* (1976) 121 SJ 118, CA.

[4]   In *Jonesco v Beard* [1930] AC 298, in which Lord Buckmaster said at 300: 'It has long been the settled practice of the Court that the proper method of impeaching a completed judgment on the ground of fraud is by action in which, as in any other action based on fraud, the particulars of the fraud must be exactly given and the allegation established by the strict proof such a charge requires'. See also *Cooper v P&O Stena Line Ltd Ferries* [1999] 1 Lloyd's Rep 734; *Scruton v Bone* (20 November 2001, unreported), in which Sir Andrew Morritt held that allegations of dishonesty must be pleaded clearly and with particularity, and are not to be left to inference alone; *Pickering v JA McConville* [2003] EWCA Civ 554; and *Lawrenson v Lawrenson and Equity Red Star* LTL 15/8/05.

[5]   *Medcalf v Mardell* [2002] UKHL 27.

[6]   *Kearsley v Klarfeld* [2005] EWCA Civ 1510

[7]   *Stojalowski v Imperial Smelting Corpn (NSC)* (1976) 121 SJ 118, CA; *Cooper v P&O Stena Line Ltd Ferries* [1999] 1 Lloyd's Rep 734.

[8]   *Hornal v Neuberger Products Ltd* [1957] 1 QB 247; *Re Dellow's Wills Trusts* [1964] 1 WLR 451; and *Blyth v Blyth* [1966] 1 All ER 524, HL; *Secretary of State for the Home Department v Rehman* [2003] 1 AC 153, per Lord Hoffmann at para [55]; *Re Doherty* [2008] UKHL 33, per Lord Carswell at para [28].

[9]   *Ford v GKR Construction* [2000] 1 WLR 1397.

[10]   See further *Uttley v Uttley* [2002] PIQR P123; and *Booth v Britannia Hotels Ltd* [2002] EWCA Civ 579.

[11]   *Coles v Greaves* [2005] All ER (D) 127 at para [54].

(v)   Effect of Exaggeration/Malingering on the Assessment of Damages

Unconscious exaggeration

[A128]   Where the exaggeration is due to an unconscious psychological reaction, the claimant will be entitled to recover the full extent of his or her losses[1]. There is a duty, however, to ensure that the claim is resolved as quickly as possible where there are any issues of functional overlay/malingering[2].

[1]   *Digby v Essex County Council* [1994] PIQR Q54. See also, at first instance, *Page v Smith* [1993] PIQR Q55, in which the trial judge expressly found that the claimant's condition of ME was genuine and he was not guilty of malingering or hysteria. In *Ford v GKR Construction* [2000] 1 WLR 1397 the trial judge made the following express finding noted by the Court of Appeal: 'I do not think that the [claimant] was deliberately lying. I think there is a failure on her part to recognise that there are times when she can do much more than she does, and in fact to recognise that on occasions she does do more for herself. I think there is force in the submission that once the [claimant] was regarded as limited in her capabilities, it was easy for her to regard that as the norm, whereas in fact it may reflect the situation when she is at her worst. It is the nature of the illness that it fluctuates'.

[2]   *Blyth Valley Borough Council v Henderson* [1996] PIQR P64. Potter J said: 'But more important, this is a case where, so far as the medical evidence is concerned, it is alleged to be a case of malingering, and (although neither side appears so to contend with vigour) questions of functional overlay are also likely to arise. I consider that question is always present in the judge's mind when he is faced with two conflicting views in a so-called "malingering" case. He may always be disposed to take the view that although he thinks there is an element of malingering, nonetheless, there is also an element of functional overlay which requires compensation. Whether it is one or both, such cases are *par excellence* cases where damages are required to be tried together with liability as soon as possible. The view of the judge overall, in relation to liability, may be very much conditioned by his view of the [claimant] in relation to the issue of damages and, *in any event, as I say, there is a duty on the adviser to bring the case to trial as quickly as possible*' (emphasis added).

Conscious exaggeration/malingering

[A129]   Where the claimant is caught perverting the course of justice, eg by forging documents or bribing witnesses, the claimant may lose the right to continue participating with the proceedings[1]. If the matter proceeds to trial and the judge makes findings of fact regarding dishonesty, it is likely that the court will refer the matter to the Director of Public Prosecutions for consideration as to whether the claimant should be prosecuted[2]. In such a case, the defendant should be able to recover his or her full costs of defending the action, particularly where the claimant has failed to beat a payment into court[3]. For example, in *Hawker v British Steel*[4], Judge Masterman ordered that the claimant pay the entire costs of one of the defendants because the defendant had been brought into the action completely unnecessarily. Further, the claimant was only awarded half of his costs against the other defendant because he had deliberately exaggerated his schedule of loss and had been untruthful about the circumstances of the accident. Where the level of exaggeration is less serious, the judge must attempt to separate out the elements of conscious and unconscious exaggeration, and award the claimant those sums to which he would have been entitled in the absence of conscious exaggeration/malingering[5]. Where the claimant would only have been entitled to a modest award but for the deliberate exaggeration, the claimant may be restricted to claiming fixed costs in accordance with the small claims track[6]. Even where the level of exaggeration is serious, the court does not have the power to strike out the claim under its case management powers, and the invariable rule is that the judge must make findings about the genuine level of injury and award limited damages appropriate to his findings[7]. However, in such circumstances the court retains a wide discretion in relation to costs[8] and the claimant may also be exposed to subsequent proceedings for contempt of court[9]. The claimant is likely to fare much better if he or she faces the music, eg by accepting the contents of video surveillance evidence and reducing his or her claim accordingly[10]. Before the defendant can be regarded as the winner on an issue of exaggeration, that issue must feature as an important feature of the claim with costs consequences[11].

1   *Arrow Nominees v Blackledge* [2000] 2 BCLC 167. See also *Molloy v Shell UK Ltd* [2001] EWCA Civ 1272, in which Laws LJ stated: 'For my part I entertain considerable qualms as to whether, faced with manipulation of the civil justice system on so grand a scale, the court should once it knows the facts entertain the case at all save to make the dishonest claimant pay the defendant's costs.' However, see the qualification of this principle in *Shah v Wasim Ul-Haq and others* [2009] EWCA Civ 542, per Smith LJ.

2   See eg *Cottrell v Redbridge Healthcare NHS Trust* (2001) 61 BMLR 72, HHJ Richard Seymour, QC, and *Churchill v Kelly* [2006] EWHC 18 (QB), in which Gibbs J referred the claimant to the chief crown prosecutor of Staffordshire for consideration as to whether or not he should be prosecuted.

3   *Molloy v Shell UK Ltd* [2001] EWCA Civ 1272. See also *Painting v University of Oxford* [2005] EWCA Civ 161 and *Carver v BAA* [2009] 1 WLR 113, in which the judge's order that the claimant pay the claimant's costs was upheld in circumstances where the claimant had only beaten the defendant's Part 36 offer by £51 and had acted unreasonably in exaggerating her claim and not making any realistic offers to settle.

4   [2000] CLY 417. See also *Cottrell v Redbridge Healthcare NHS Trust* (2001) 61 BMLR 72; and *Hussein v William Hill Group* [2004] EWHC 208 (QB).

5   *Smith v Rod Jenkins* [2003] EWHC 1356 (QB) at [72]. Gibbs J said that he was impressed with leading counsel for the defendant's submission that he should 'strip out' the effects of the claimant's conscious exaggeration, and assess what would have probably happened had there been none. See also *Day v Bracknell District Council* (17 October 1987, unreported), QBD, where Boreham J said: '... For all these reasons I have come to the conclusion which I have already indicated and that leaves the most difficult question of all, namely what is the proper apportionment between what is genuinely functional and what has been feigned or exaggerated? I think the plaintiff must not complain if, in attempting a fair apportionment, judgment is less than accurate, because the picture has been so significantly clouded ...'.

6   *Devine v Franklin* [2002] EWHC 1846 (QB). See also *Booth v Britannia Hotels Ltd* [2002] EWCA Civ 529, in which Jonathan Parker LJ stated: 'In my judgment, a claimant who pursues an exaggerated and inflated claim for damages must expect to bear the consequences when his costs come to be assessed'.

7   In *Shah v Wasim Ul-Haq and others* [2009] EWCA Civ 542, Smith LJ said at para 17: 'I am unaware of any reported case in which a judge has dismissed the whole of a claim because he has found that the claim has been dishonestly exaggerated. The invariable rule is that, in those circumstances, the judge awards the limited damages which are appropriate to his findings. Of course, a claimant's credibility may be so damaged that he fails to prove any part of his loss, but if he proves some loss, he recovers that even though he has fraudulently attempted to recover far more'.

8   In *Shah v Wasim Ul-Haq and others* [2009] EWCA Civ 542, Smith LJ said at para 28: '[the judge] can mark his disapproval of the way in which the court's time and the parties' money has been wasted by an order for costs'. See also *Carver v BAA* [2009] 1 WLR 113 and *Churchill v Kelly* [2006] EWHC 18 (QB), in which Gibbs J made the claimant pay the costs of the trial below and on appeal on an indemnity basis, and *Sulaman v AXA* [2009] EWCA Civ 1331, where the Court of Appeal upheld an order depriving the successful claimant of two-thirds of her costs because she had lied during the course of her evidence.

9   See eg *Kirk v Walton* [2008] EWHC 1780 (QB) and [2009] EWHC 703 (QB). See further 'In full and final settlement: RIP' by Brian Barr, APIL PI Focus, Vol 19, Issue 6, pp 12–15.

10   See eg *Morgan v UPS* [2008] EWCA Civ 1476, distinguishing *Painting v University of Oxford* [2005] EWCA Civ 161.

11   *Hall v Stone* [2007] EWCA Civ 1354; but see also *Widlake v BAA Ltd* [2009] EWCA Civ 1256, where the Court of Appeal overturned the judge's costs order, making a claimant who had lied to medical experts and exaggerated her claim pay the defendant's costs even though she had beaten the defendant's Part 36 offer, and substituted an order that there be 'no order for costs'.

12   The Mechanics of the Award

(i)   Methods of Payment

The current law

[A130]   At present, once judgment has been entered, the court has five main options as regards the manner in which an award is to be made:

- Make a single lump sum award of damages[1].
- Make an award for provisional damages (assuming the same has been claimed)[2].
- Make a non-variable periodical payment order[3].
- Make a variable periodical payment order[4].
- Adjourn and/or stay the assessment of some or all quantum issues until a later date (and in the meantime, if necessary, make one or more interim payments)[5].

These awards may be mixed and matched as appropriate, eg a lump sum for pain, suffering and loss of amenity and past loss; provisional damages in respect of future loss; a periodical payment order for loss of future earnings; and a variable periodical payment order for future care.

[1]   *Mulholland v Mitchell* [1971] AC 666; *Lim Poh Choo v Camden and Islington Area Health Authority* [1980] AC 174; *Hodgson v Trapp* [1989] AC 807; *Wells v Wells* [1999] AC 345.
[2]   By virtue of para 4.4 of the PD to CPR, Pt 16, where a claimant is seeking an award of provisional damages under either Senior Courts Act 1981, s 32A or County Courts Act 1984, s 51, he or she must specify the disease or type of deterioration in respect of which an application may be made at a future date. See further CPR, Pt 41 and PD and at paras **[A128]–[A131]**.
[3]   Courts Act 2003, ss 100 and 101 came into force on 1 April 2005. See further Chapter O.
[4]   Such orders are only available for cases begun after 1 April 2005: see further Chapter O.
[5]   See eg *A v National Blood Authority* [2002] Lloyd's Rep Med 487.

[A131]   The court presently has no express general power in free-standing proceedings to award an indemnity in respect of future expenses or losses in addition to or instead of an award of damages[1]. Indeed, in *Firth* v *Geo Ackroyd Junior Ltd*[2], HHJ Robert Taylor sitting as a deputy judge of the High Court held that, in the absence of any evidence that there was a real or substantial risk of a change in the law, the claimant was not entitled to an indemnity or an additional award of damages to compensate for the possibility that the law might change in the future resulting in the local authority seeking to recoup payment for the services they had provided to him.

[1]   Note that the Report of the Master of the Rolls' Working Party on Structured Settlements, chaired by Brian Langstaff QC, 9 August 2002, recommended that consideration should be given to creating an express power for the court to grant such indemnities.
[2]   [2001] PIQR Q4.

(1)   SINGLE LUMP SUM

[A132]   The general rule in English law is that damages are assessed on a once-and-for-all basis at the date of trial[1]. As regards future expenses and losses, a single lump sum is awarded of sufficient size so that, when the fund is invested, if capital is gradually drawn to make up income to the level of the continuing loss, the fund will last for precisely the period of the loss[2]. This is known as the annuity method, which was expressed in *Hodgson v Trapp*[3] by Lord Oliver of Aylmerton as follows[4]:

'Essentially what the court has to do is to calculate as best it can the sum of money which will on the one hand be adequate, by its capital and income, to provide annually for the injured person a sum equal to his estimated annual loss over the whole of the period during which that loss is likely to continue, but which, on the other hand, will not, at the end of that period, leave him in a better financial position than he would have been apart from the accident.'

1   *Mulholland v Mitchell* [1971] AC 666; *Lim Poh Choo v Camden and Islington Area Health Authority* [1980] AC 174; *Wells v Wells* [1999] AC 345. See further paras [A32]–[A43].
2   *Taylor v O'Connor* [1971] AC 115; *Lim Poh Choo v Camden and Islington Area Health Authority* [1980] AC 174; *Hodgson v Trapp* [1989] AC 807; *Wells v Wells* [1999] AC 345.
3   [1989] AC 807.
4   At 826D.

[A133]   Save where the claimant is under a disability[1] or where the part of the award is to be paid to or held on trust for a third party[2], the award of the lump sum must be unconditional in the sense that the court cannot require the claimant to satisfy a condition before making the award of damages[3]. Once made, the award is tax free[4]. Interest arising from investment, however, is taxable. Unless appropriate steps are taken, eg by setting up a trust or a structured settlement, the claimant may lose his or her entitlement to means tested benefits and/or face recoupment in respect of accommodation provided by a local authority[5].

1   See further CPR, Pt 21.
2   See further *Hunt v Severs* [1993] QB 815; and *ATH v MS* [2002] EWCA Civ 792.
3   *Banbury v Bank of Montreal* [1918] AC 626.
4   Income and Corporation Taxes Act 1988, s 329(1) although see further [2001] Quantum, Issue 5/2001, 8 October in respect of the position as regards inheritance tax in Fatal Accidents Act cases.
5   See further the Report of the Master of the Rolls' Working Party on Structured Settlements, chaired by Brian Langstaff QC, 9 August 2002, together with the addendum dated 9 October 2002.

[A134]   There are a number of advantages and disadvantages of the traditional method of awarding damages as a lump sum/annuity[1]. On the plus side, the claimant will have direct control over his or her damages and be able to spend as much or as little of it as and when desired. The most notable disadvantage is that, no matter how much care is taken to calculate the appropriate lump sum award, the figure may well prove to be too much or too little[2]. In particular, the claimant may die much sooner than expected or outlive the estimate of his or her life expectancy. Furthermore, there is the responsibility to invest the damages so that they last for the claimant's lifetime and this creates risk. By virtue of CPR, r 41.6 the court is obliged to consider and indicate to the parties as soon as practicable whether periodical payments or a lump sum is likely to be the more appropriate form for all or part of an award of damages.

1   See further the Report of the Master of the Rolls' Working Party on Structured Settlements, chaired by Brian Langstaff QC, 9 August 2002, together with the addendum dated 9 October 2002.
2   *Wells v Wells* [1999] AC 345, per Lord Lloyd at 363. As Lord Scarman observed in *Lim Poh Choo v Camden and Islington Area Health Authority* [1980] AC 174 at 183, 'there is really only one certainty: the future will prove the award to be either too high or too low'.

(2)   PROVISIONAL DAMAGES

[A135]   By virtue of CPR, r 41.2 the court may award provisional damages where such a claim has been pleaded[1] and the court is satisfied that the conditions of s 32A of the Senior Courts Act 1981 or s 51 of the County Courts Act 1984 have been met. Section 32A(1) of the Senior Courts Act reads as follows:

> 'This section applies to an action for damages for personal injuries in which there is proved or admitted to be a chance that at some definite or indefinite time in the future the injured person will, as a result of the act or omission which gave rise to the cause of action, develop some serious disease or suffer some serious deterioration in his physical or mental condition.'

¹ Under CPR, r 16.4(d) the claimant must plead a claim for provisional damages in the particulars of claim and set out the grounds upon which such damages are claimed.

[A136] There have been comparatively few reported cases which have interpreted this provision. The leading case is *Curi v Colina*[1]. Roch LJ stated that there were three questions which needed to be asked in order to see whether or not an award for provisional damages was appropriate in any given case, namely:

- Is the chance of the claimant developing some disease or suffering some other deterioration in physical or mental condition measurable rather than fanciful[2]?
- Can the disease or deterioration in physical or mental condition be described as serious[3]?
- If the above two questions are answered in the affirmative, should the court go on to exercise its discretion to award provisional damages?

¹ [1998] EWCA Civ 1326.
² See further the judgment of Scott Baker J in *Wilson v Ministry of Defence* [1991] 1 All ER 638, which was approved by Roch LJ in *Curi v Colina* [1998] EWCA Civ 1326.
³ In this context, the development of osteo-arthritis is not considered to be a serious deterioration of the condition but rather the natural progression of the condition.

[A137] It should be noted that the claimant bears the burden of proving, on the balance of probabilities, that there is a measurable chance of the disease or deterioration materialising. There should be some clear-cut event which triggers entitlement to further compensation[1]. However, the fact that there may be a subsequent issue, as to whether the injury was actually causative of the deterioration in the claimant's condition which materialises, should not necessarily prevent the court from exercising its power to award provisional damages[2].

¹ *Wilson v Ministry of Defence* [1991] 1 All ER 638, per Scott Baker J at 644h. See further Simon Brown's judgment in *Patterson v Ministry of Defence* [1987] CLY 1194.
² *Mann v Merton & Sutton Health Authority* [1989] CLY 1229.

[A138] As regards the exercise of the court's discretion, in *Curi v Colina*[1] Roch LJ endorsed Michael Davies J's approach in *Allott* v *Central Electricity Generating Board*[2] that the court should not be 'very enthusiastic, [to exercise its power] save in the clearest case …'. The power should be confined to those cases where it is possible to describe with sufficient precision the event which has to occur before the claimant becomes entitled to seek further damages, and that the injury or deterioration which may occur in the future is not speculative or unclear. Further, the power should be used in a situation where paying a claimant at the date of trial, in respect of a risk he or she might suffer which in fact he or she may never suffer, would probably be to order a defendant to pay too much, yet if the risk were actually to materialise the amount would be insufficient to cover it. Examples of cases in which provisional damages have been awarded include the risk of the claimant developing epilepsy[3], the risk of developing syringomyelia[4], the risk of developing spinal curvature that progresses to a level where the claimant requires a brace with a neck extension or surgery[5], the risk of requiring a liver transplant[6], the risk of receiving a kidney transplant or having an unsuccessful transplant[7], myocardial infarction or ruptured coronary artery aneurysm[8], and venous ulceration[9].

1   [1998] EWCA Civ 1326.
2   (19 December 1988, unreported).
3   *Wan v Fung* [2003] CLY 3131.
4   *Mitchell v Royal Liverpool & Broadgreen University Hospitals NHS Trust* LTL 11/9/2008, Lawtel Document No AC0118195; *Sarwar v (1) Ali and (2) MIB* [2007] LS Medical 375; *Davies v Bradshaw and others* [2008] EWHC 740 (QB) (first instance judgment reversed on appeal by consent on this point).
5   *Field v Lewisham Hospital NHS Trust* [2009] LTLPI 2/6/2009, Document No AM0201364.
6   *Longmore v Worcestershire Acute Hospitals NHS Trust* LTLPI 5/6/2006, Lawtel Document No AM0200974.
7   *H v Thomson Holidays Ltd* [2007] EWHC 850 (QB).
8   *Henry-Frost v Essex Rivers Healthcare NHS Trust* LTLPI 24/1/2008, Lawtel Document No AM0201204.
9   *Paintin v Stella Musical Production Ltd* LTLPI 15/8/2002, Lawtel Document No AM0200437.

[A139]   In *Garth v (1) Grant and (2) MIB*[1], HHJ Hickinbottom (as he then was) had to deal with a novel application for provisional damages involving the risk of complications arising from future planned surgery. The claimant sustained multiple severe injuries, the most serious of which was an open book fracture of her pelvis. Hip replacement surgery was planned, which carried with it a 1% chance of a fatal anaesthetic complication, a 5–10% chance of sciatic nerve palsy, and a 10–15% chance of an infection around the prosthesis. In short, there was a risk of about 20% that the claimant would be no better off following the operation and may in fact be worse off. An application was made under s 32A of the Senior Courts Act 1981 for provisional damages on the basis that the claimant does not suffer 'sciatic nerve palsy and/or prosthesis infection and/or any other known or unknown risk of adverse outcome as a result of either primary or secondary hip replacement operation such as to cause her to be in a worse condition with less functionality than she presently has'. HHJ Hickinbottom found the claimant's submission uncompelling that she would suffer a serious deterioration in her condition if she were to suffer a palsy or infection. Confusingly, he said: 'It would not be her condition that would deteriorate in these circumstances; it would be her prognosis'. This is not understood, since prognosis is simply a prediction of future condition. If her condition did deteriorate following surgery then, assuming the need for the surgery was related to the accident, there does not appear to be any good reason why this event could not be the subject of a provisional damages award. However, on the facts of this case, HHJ Hickinbottom found that if she were to suffer a sciatic nerve palsy it would not represent a serious deterioration in her condition. This case should be contrasted with *Chewings v (1) Williams and (2) Abertawe Bro Morgannwg University NHS Trust*[2], in which Mrs Justice Slade had to consider an application for provisional damages regarding the risk of amputation arising from fusion surgery. She held that there was a real (not a fanciful) chance that the claimant would need fusion surgery, due to increasingly unbearable pain which carried with it a small risk that the claimant would need an amputation. She had no difficulty making an award of provisional damages which she thought was the 'very situation for which an award of provisional damages is entirely appropriate'. It is submitted that the reasoning of Mrs Justice Slade is to be preferred.

¹   QBD, Lawtel 17/7/2007.
²   [2009] EWHC 2490 (QB).

(3) Variable and non-variable periodical payments

[A140]   On 1 April 2005, ss 100 and 101 of the Courts Act 2003 came into force, amending s 2 of the Damages Act 1996, giving the court a discretionary power to make an award for future pecuniary loss wholly or in part by way of periodical payments. This created a fundamental change in the way that future loss is assessed, and the reader is referred to Chapter O for a detailed explanation and discussion of the applicable rules and principles. Whenever the court is considering a claim for future pecuniary loss, the court must consider whether or not to make an award for periodical payments as opposed to a lump sum, and regard must be had to the factors set out in para 1 of PD 41B, namely:

(1) the scale of the annual payments taking into account any deduction for contributory negligence;
(2) the form of award preferred by the claimant including –
   (a) the reasons for the claimant's preference; and
   (b) the nature of any financial advice received by the claimant when considering the form of award; and
(3) the form of award preferred by the defendant including the reasons for the defendant's preference.

(4) Adjournment and/or stay

[A141]   CPR, Pt 3 provides the court with the power: to order that any part of proceedings be dealt with as separate proceedings; to stay the whole or part of proceedings; and to try individual issues separately. Where some issues of quantum might be capable of resolution at the date of trial and others not, it is possible to adjourn and/or stay certain elements of the claim for future consideration. For example, *A v National Blood Authority*[1] was a case which concerned group litigation arising out of the contraction of hepatitis from blood products. Burton J (as he then was) approved an order allowing the claimants to claim further general and special damages if they underwent treatment in the future on the advice of a hepatologist. He had no doubt that the court had very wide case management powers under the CPR which were underlain by the overriding objective. In the circumstances, he was content to approve an order which contained the following wording:

> 'For the avoidance of doubt, the claimants shall be entitled to apply for further damages in relation to treatment as referred to ... as a result of the exercise by the court of its powers under rule 3.1(2) of the Civil Procedure Rules 1998, in particular (a) the court directs that the issue of the quantum of such damages be tried separately; (b) the court orders that the trial of such issue be adjourned generally; (c) the parties have liberty to apply.'

¹   [2002] Lloyd's Rep Med 487. In respect of the courts' general powers pre-CPR to adjourn certain elements of quantum, see further *Trans Trust SPRL v Danubian Trading Co Ltd* [1952] 2 QB 297; and *Deeny v Gooda Walker (in liquidation)* [1995] 1 WLR 1206.

[A142]   However, it should be noted that, in *A v National Blood Authority*[1], the adjournment was consented to by all parties. In the subsequent case of *Adan v Securicor Custodial Services*[2], the claimant made an application to adjourn the assessment of his awards for future care and accommodation which was opposed by the defendant. The facts were that the claimant had been injured whilst being driven by the defendant to a court to be sentenced for a criminal offence. He suffered a severe head injury and was detained at Rampton Hospital under the Mental Health Act 1983 where he was likely to remain as an in-patient for the foreseeable future. The claimant sought to postpone the assessment of his claims for future care and accommodation in case he made an improvement[3] such that he could be cared for in the community, in which case he would not be able to afford good care without the means to provide it, which he would have wished to have as part of his award. Eady J rejected the application, holding that there was nothing tangible to take the case out of the normal run of cases where it is still deemed appropriate, despite potential injustice, for the court to make a single award of damages to include the best assessment of future loss. Reliance was placed upon the observations of Lord Pearce in *Murphy v Stone-Wallwork*[4], Lord Hodson in *Mulholland v Mitchell*[5], and Phillips J (as he then was) in *Denny v Gooda Walker Ltd*[6], that the court's function was to bring an end to litigation, with the court doing its best to assess damages once and for all on the available evidence at trial, notwithstanding the fact that predictions have to be made about uncertainties in the future. It was the court which suggested an adjournment in *Ahsan v University Hospitals Leicester NHS Trust*[7]. The claimant, who was in a persistent vegetative state, was being cared for in a private residential home funded by the local Primary Care Trust. The claimant's family wished for her to return home and be cared for at home with a private care regime. The judge declared that such a regime was reasonable and that damages should be assessed on this basis. But an interim payment was made and the case adjourned in order to allow a staged return so as to see whether, as a matter of fact, she was likely to return home for the rest of her life. Also, in *Smith v East and North Hertfordshire Hospitals NHS Trust*[8], Mr Justice Penry-Davey (apparently of his own motion, although it is a little unclear from the judgment) granted the claimant liberty to apply for a trial up to the age of 19 in respect of future education costs, in particular legal costs that might be incurred in challenging the claimant's statement of special educational needs.

¹   [2002] Lloyd's Rep Med 487.
²   [2004] EWHC 394 (QB), [2005] PIQR P6.
³   Arguably, an improvement in condition as envisaged in this case could potentially now meet the criteria for a variable periodical payments order. See further Chapter O.
⁴   [1969] 1 WLR 1023 where, at 1027, Lord Pearce said: 'Our courts have adopted the principle that damages are assessed at the trial once and for all. If later the [claimant] suffers greater loss from an accident than was anticipated at the trial, he cannot come back for more. Nor can the defendant come back if the loss is less than was anticipated. Thus, the assessment of damages for the future is necessarily compounded of prophecy and calculation. The court must do the best it can to reach what seems to be the right figure on a reasonable balance of probabilities, avoiding undue optimism and undue pessimism'.

⁵ [1971] AC 666 where, at 674, Lord Hodson said: 'By our law, unlike that of many other countries, the maxim interest reipublicae ut sit finis litium is, in the usual case, strictly followed. Damages are, accordingly, assessed once and for all at the time of the trial notwithstanding that in many cases, and this applies especially to cases of personal injury, uncertain matters have to be taken into account. The court has to make the best estimate it can as to the future life of the injures person, not only as to his prospects of recovery or improvement but also, as in this case, as to the cost of caring for him either in his own home or in an institution suitably equipped to deal with his condition. This is the function of the court'.

⁶ [1995] 1 WLR 1206 where, at 1214, Phillips J said: 'The desirability of bringing an end to litigation will normally make it appropriate for the court to make a single award of damages which includes the best assessment possible of future loss'.

⁷ [2006] EWHC 2624 (QB).

⁸ [2008] EWHC 2234 (QB).

[A143] When the issue of quantum is adjourned or stayed in whole or in part, the court retains a general discretion to award one or more interim payment[1]. A significant interim payment may well be justified where the principal reason for the adjournment is to allow the claimant to die, so that his or her dependants can be substituted as claimants under the Fatal Accidents Act 1976[2]. Where the claim is adjourned pending an assessment of damages hearing, the court also has the power to make interim periodical payments[3].

¹ CPR, Pt 25.

² See further *Murray v Shuter* [1972] 1 Ll Rep 6, CA, and per Langstaff J in *Thompson v Arnold* LTL 14/8/2007, [2008] PIQR P1, [2008] LS Law Medical 78 at para 28.

³ Damages Act 1996, s 2A(5), as amended by Courts Act 2003, s 100.

(ii) Amount of Award

[A144] Although awards for non-pecuniary loss, in particular the award for pain, suffering and loss of amenity, are conventionally linked to tariffs set by the Court of Appeal[1], with the maximum award for pain, suffering and loss of amenity currently being in the region of £260,000, as regards pecuniary loss the claimant is entitled to 'full compensation'[2] for his or her loss, and there is no artificial limit placed on the award the court can make. For practical purposes, however, it is necessary for a claimant to include a statement of value in the particulars of claim so that the claim may be allocated to the appropriate track[3]. It should be noted that, in order to calculate the statement of value, it is not necessary to include the full value of the claim, eg where the parties agree to limit the claim to a value below the small claims track limit but have a memorandum of understanding to follow the court's decision in respect of liability for other losses[4]. But in any event, notwithstanding any limit placed on the claim by the claimant by way of the statement of value, the court has power to award in excess of the stated limit[5].

¹ *Wright v British Railways Board* [1983] 2 AC 773; *Heil v Rankin* [2001] QB 272.

² *Livingstone v Rawyards Coal Co* (1880) 5 App Cas 25; *Admiralty Commissioners v SS Valeria* [1922] 2 AC 242; *Liesbosch Dredger (Owners) v SS Edison* [1933] AC 449; *Lim Poh Choo v Camden and Islington Area Health Authority* [1980] AC 174. See further at paras **[A22]–[A27]**.

³ See further CPR, Pt 26.

⁴ *Khiaban v Beard* [2002] EWCA Civ 358.

⁵ CPR, r 16.3(7).

(iii)   Currency of Award

[A145]   Generally speaking, awards of damages made in England and Wales are made in the currency of the jurisdiction, ie sterling. However, if appropriate, the court has a discretion to award damages in any currency[1]. The object of the award of damages is to award compensation which best expresses the claimant's loss and sometimes this will involve awarding damages in a foreign currency, especially where an expense has been or will be incurred in that currency[2]. It is for the claimant to choose which currency to claim in and to prove that a judgment in that currency would most truly express his or her loss and compensate them for that loss[3].

1	*Milliangos v George Rank (Textiles) Ltd* [1976] AC 443; *The Despina R* [1979] AC 685.
2	*The Despina R* [1979] AC 685; *Hoffman v Sofaer* [1982] 1 WLR 1350. See also *A v Powys Health Board* [2007] EWHC 2996 (QB), in which Lloyd-Jones J awarded part of the damages in sterling and part in Euros.
3	*The Despina R* [1979] AC 685; *Ozalid Group (Export) v African Continental Bank* [1979] 2 Lloyd's Rep 231.

13   Aggravated and Exemplary Damages

[A146]   The fundamental principle governing the assessment of damages for personal injury is that the claimant is entitled to recover his or her full loss (both pecuniary and non-pecuniary)[1]. The object of the award of damages is to compensate the claimant as opposed to punishing the defendant. There are, however, some exceptional instances in which the claimant might be entitled to claim additional damages over and above the compensatory value of the claim in order to punish the defendant. Such damages fall into two main categories: aggravated and exemplary. Generally speaking, the entitlement to claim punitive damages will arise either out of the circumstances in which the injury was sustained or from the conduct and motive of the defendant (especially where the injury was inflicted deliberately)[2]. The principles relating to when such damages are appropriate, and the assessment of the same, are set out in the following paragraphs.

1	*Livingstone v Rawyards Coal Co* (1880) 5 App Cas 25; *Lim Poh Choo v Camden and Islington Area Health Authority* [1980] AC 174; *Hodgson v Trapp* [1989] AC 807; *Pickett v Pickett* [1980] AC 136; *Wells v Wells* [1999] AC 345. See further para **[A23]** et seq.
2	See further the Law Commission's Report No 247 'Aggravated, Exemplary and Restitutionary Damages' (1997).

(i)   Aggravated Damages
Definition

[A147]   Aggravated damages may be defined as follows[1]:

> 'compensation for the injured feeling of the [claimant] where his sense of injury resulting from the [defendant's wrongful conduct] is justifiably heightened by the manner in which or motive for which the defendant did it.'

1	*Broome v Cassell & Co* [1972] AC 1027 at 1124.

Applicability and assessment

[A148] Aggravated damages may only be awarded when they have been claimed by the claimant[1]. They must be pleaded in the particulars of claim, together with the grounds upon which they are sought[2]. Whilst they cannot be awarded for the tort of negligence or breach of contract[3], they may be awarded for many other causes of action, including assault and battery, false imprisonment, malicious prosecution, defamation, intimidation, discrimination, trespass to land, deceit, nuisance, and unlawful interference with business[4]. The justification for awarding aggravated damages arises out of exceptional elements of the circumstances at the time the injury was sustained causing the claimant mental distress[5]. Aggravating features must be established such as the high-handed, humiliating, insulting, offensive, arrogant, spiteful, malicious or oppressive manner in which the injury was inflicted[6]. Aggravating features may include the way in which the defendant defends a claim, conducts litigation or contests liability at trial, relying upon tainted or false evidence and/or forcing the claimant to give evidence and be cross-examined[7]. It may not be an aggravating feature that an employer fails to institute disciplinary proceedings[8] and there is some doubt that an innocent employer can be vicariously liable for the contumelious conduct of an employee in any event[9]. An award of aggravated damages is primarily to compensate the claimant for the injury to his or her pride, dignity and the consequences of any humiliation suffered[10]. Therefore, no award for aggravated damages can be made where the claimant is unaware of the defendant's exceptional conduct[11]. However, there may also be a penal element in order to punish the defendant for his or her conduct[12]. Aggravated damages may be reduced or eliminated altogether by the claimant's own conduct if this conduct caused or contributed to the behaviour complained of[13]. Evidence showing aggravating or mitigating features is admissible up to the time that damages are assessed[14]. As regards quantum, the Court of Appeal took the opportunity in *Thompson v MPC*[15] to lay down some guidelines for the assessment of aggravated damages. Whilst the guidelines were intended to apply to police cases, in which the jury decided the amount of aggravated damages to be awarded following the judge's summing-up, the Court of Appeal's guidelines moderating such awards may be thought to have wider implications. In summary, the Court of Appeal held that:

- Aggravated damages can be awarded where there are aggravating features about the case which would result in the claimant not receiving sufficient compensation for the injury suffered if the award were restricted to a basic (ie compensatory) award.
- The appropriate award for aggravated damages is unlikely to be less than £1,000[16].
- The award for aggravated damages would not normally be expected to be twice as much as the basic (ie compensatory) award.

[1]   *Thompson v MPC* [1998] QB 498, per Lord Woolf at 514. Although CPR, r 16.2(5) gives the court the power to grant any remedy to which the claimant is entitled, even if that remedy is not specified in the claim form, it does not give the same power if the remedy is not claimed in the particulars of claim, although permission is likely to amend the particulars of claim so as to seek such a remedy in an appropriate case.

[2]   CPR, r 16.4(1)(c).

3   *Kralj v McGrath* [1986] 1 All ER 54. Although note that, following the House of Lords' decision in *Kuddus v Chief Constable of Leicestershire* [2001] UKHL 29, it is arguable that the House of Lords would be persuaded to drop the 'cause of action' test previously applied in *Kralj v McGrath* [1986] 1 All ER 54 in order to bring the law in line with that which applies to exemplary damages.

4   See further the Law Commission's Report No 247 'Aggravated, Exemplary and Restitutionary Damages' (1997) at para 1.10 et seq.

5   The Law Commission, in its Report No 247, considered that there were two preconditions for the availability of an award for aggravated damages: (i) exception or contumelious conduct or motive on the part of the defendant committing the wrong, or, in certain circumstances, subsequent to the wrong; and (ii) mental distress sustained by the claimant as a result. These pre-conditions were accepted as correctly stating the law by Dyson J in *Appleton v Garrett* [1996] PIQR P1.

6   *Rookes v Barnard* [1964] AC 1221; *McCarey v Associated Newspapers Ltd (No 2)* [1965] 2 QB 86; *Broome v Cassell & Co* [1972] AC 1027; *Thompson v MPC* [1998] QB 498. It should be noted that, following the Court of Appeal's decision in *Richardson v Howie* [2004] EWCA Civ 1127, in cases involving assault, aggravated damages may only be awarded where the facts are wholly exceptional, because the award for general damages takes into account compensation for injury to feelings including the indignity, mental suffering, humiliation or distress that might be caused by such an attack, but cf *Gerald v MPC* (1998) Times, 26 June, CA, in which Auld LJ suggested that aggravated damages did include 'humiliation or an affront to dignity' but were not confined to those features. See further below at paras **[A150]–[A152]**.

7   See eg *Warwick v Foulkes* (1844) 12 M&W 506; *Warby v Cascaino* (1989) Times, 27 October; *Marks v Chief Constable of Greater Manchester Police* (1992) Times, 28 January; *C v S (damages: sexual abuse)* [1998] CLY 1508; *Fairweather v Ghafoor* [2001] CLY 4164; *Thompson v MPC* [1998] QB 498.

8   See further *Gerald v MPC* (1998) Times, 26 June, CA. On the facts, the defendant would have been out of time to institute such proceedings, so it could not be taken into account as an aggravating factor. However, the question as to whether a defendant's failure to institute disciplinary proceedings against a culpable employee could ever be taken into account as an aggravating feature was left open by the Court of Appeal.

9   See eg *Thompson v MPC* [1998] QB 498, in which Lord Woolf stated at 512: 'Even if the use of civil proceedings to punish a defendant can in some circumstances be justified it is more difficult to justify the award where the defendant and the person responsible for meeting any award is not the wrongdoer, but his "employer"'. Cf *Racz v Home Office* [1994] 2 AC 45.

10 *Thompson v MPC* [1998] QB 498, per Lord Woolf at 512. See further the Law Commission's Report No 247, paras 1.1–1.38.

11 *Alexander v Home Office* [1988] 1 WLR 968 at 976C–D; *Ministry of Defence v Meredith* [1995] IRLR 539 at 542–543.

12 *Thompson v MPC* [1998] QB 498, per Lord Woolf at 512. See further the Law Commission's Consultation Paper No 132 'Aggravated, Exemplary and Restitutionary Damages' (1993) at para 2.17 et seq.

13 *Lane v Holloway* [1968] 1 QB 379; *O'Connor v Hewitson* [1979] Crim LR 46, CA; *Thompson v MPC* [1998] QB 498, per Lord Woolf at 517.

14 *Walters v Alltools* (1944) 61 TLR 39 at 40.

15 [1998] QB 498. Note, however, that it is unclear how, if at all, the award of aggravated damages has been affected in these cases by the Court of Appeal's decision in *Richardson v Howie* [2004] EWCA Civ 1127. See below at paras **[A150]–[A152]**.

16 Worth approximately £1,383, updated for RPI to August 2009.

Examples of cases in which aggravated damages have been awarded

[A149]   Although it is unusual for aggravated damages to be awarded in a personal injury or clinical negligence context, examples have included[1]:

- cases of rape and indecent assault[2];
- assault and battery[3]; and
- carrying out unnecessary dentistry on healthy teeth for reasons of profit[4].

1   Note that, following the Court of Appeal's decision in *Richardson v Howie* [2004] EWCA Civ 1127,
    it is unclear whether awards for aggravated damages would now be made in similar cases. Judges
    may be inclined to make global awards including basic or compensatory damages and an element
    for the aggravating circumstances: see further *Lawson v Glaves-Smith (Executor of the Estate of
    Christopher Dawes, Deceased)* [2006] EWHC 2865 (QB).

2   See eg *Parrington v Marriott* [1998] CLY 1509, in which HHJ Hall awarded the sum of £30,000
    aggravated damages in addition to £25,000 general damages. See also *B (a child) v D* [2001] CLY
    1585, in which the claimant suffered a very serious and violent sexual assault involving vaginal rape
    and anal penetration. She was awarded £40,000 for PSLA and £20,000 for aggravated damages.
    Most recently, Treacy J made awards of between £82,000 and £125,000 in respect of PSLA for
    each claimant, and a further £30–£35,000 each in respect of aggravated damages, in *AT & others v
    Dulghieru* [2009] EWHC 225 (QB).

3   See further *Thompson v MPC* [1998] QB 498.

4   *Appleton v Garrett* [1996] PIQR P1, where Dyson J held that there had been exceptional, or
    contumelious, conduct or motive on the part of the defendant and the claimants were awarded
    aggravated damages in the sum of 15% of general damages for pain, suffering and loss of amenity
    to reflect the heightened sense of injury or grievance they suffered as a result of knowing that the
    dental treatment they underwent at the hands of the defendant was completely unnecessary.

Cases involving 'assault and similar torts'

[A150]   In *Richardson v Howie*[1] the claimant brought a claim for assault arising out
of an attack which occurred on holiday. The defendant struck the claimant about the
head and neck with a bottle. She was left with a number of small scars. The trial judge
awarded the claimant £10,000 damages including general damages for pain, suffering
and loss of amenity and £5,000 for aggravated damages. The defendant appealed
against the order for aggravated damages, arguing that no such award should have
been made in principle, and also against the level of damages awarded. The appeal
was upheld and the claimant's damages were reduced to £4,500. As regards the claim
for aggravated damages, Thomas LJ delivering the judgment of the court (with which
Jacob LJ agreed) said[2]:

'It is and must be accepted that at least in cases of assault and similar torts, it is
appropriate to compensate for injury to feelings including the indignity, mental suffering,
humiliation or distress that might be caused by such an attack, as well as anger or
indignation arising from the circumstances of the attack. It is also now clearly accepted
that aggravated damages are in essence compensatory in cases of assault. Therefore we
consider that a court should not characterise the award of damages for injury to feelings,
including any indignity, mental suffering, distress, humiliation or anger and indignation
that might be caused by such an attack, as aggravated damages; a court should bring
that element of compensatory damages for injured feelings into account as part of the
general damages awarded. It is, we consider, no longer appropriate to characterise the
award for the damages for injury to feelings as aggravated damages, except possibly in
a wholly exceptional case.

   Where there is an assault, the victim will be entitled to be compensated for any
injury to his or her feelings, including the anger and indignation aroused. Those
feelings may well also be affected by the malicious or spiteful nature of the attack or
the motive of the assailant; if so, then the victim must be properly compensated for that,
particularly where the injured feelings have been heightened by the motive or spiteful
nature of the attack. In our view, damages which provide such compensation should
be characterised and awarded therefore as ordinary general damages which they truly
are. The misapprehension as to the nature of the damages to be awarded for injured

feelings which plainly arose in the trial judge's mind and which led him to award a sum that was wholly extravagant as aggravated damages would not have arisen, if the award had been made as one of ordinary compensatory general damages and not as an award of aggravated damages. The facts of this case clearly did not in any way approach the wholly exceptional case where an award of aggravated damages might still be appropriate.

This was indeed a case of a spiteful attack in an outburst of irrational anger with a weapon which Mr Howie must have appreciated would scar Miss Richardson; her feelings were, as is accepted, plainly injured by the circumstances and nature of the attack. She was entitled to be compensated for that as part of the general damages awarded.'

1   [2004] EWCA Civ 1127.
2   At [23] and [24].

[A151]   It is unclear exactly what Thomas LJ had in mind where he refers to 'wholly exceptional cases' of assault justifying awards for aggravated damages. Whilst a number of cases were cited, including *Westward v Hardy*[1], *W v Meah*[2] and *Appleton v Garret*[3], it is uncertain whether the Court of Appeal endorsed any of the awards made for aggravated damages in these cases or were critical of them all. It is also questionable whether the Court of Appeal's reasoning applies equally to police cases, where claims of assault are commonly made, and it might be difficult to argue that any one particular case is exceptional on its facts. Unfortunately, it appears that the court was not directed to the previous Court of Appeal case of *Gerald v MPC*[4] involving an assault, false imprisonment and malicious prosecution by police officers. Although the Court of Appeal reduced the award made by the jury for aggravated damages, an award of £8,000 was still made in order to compensate for the additional harm other than physical or mental injury resulting from the manner of the wrong including 'humiliation or affront to dignity'.

1   [1964] CLY 994.
2   [1986] 1 All ER 935.
3   *Appleton v Garrett* [1996] PIQR P1.
4   (1998) Times, 26 June, CA. Transcript available on Lawtel.

[A152]   Since *Richardson v Howie*[1], not all judges have followed the guidance regarding making separate awards. In *Lawson v Glaves-Smith (Executor of the Estate of Christopher Dawes, Deceased)*[2], Eady J cited *Richardson* and made a global award encompassing the aggravating elements. However, in *AT & others v Dulghieru*[3], Treacy J made separate awards for aggravated damages of between £30,000 and £35,000 each where the claimants had been kidnapped and forced to carry out sexual activities with large numbers of men. Furthermore, in *Martins v Choudhary*[4] it was denied that there was any hard and fast rule regarding making separate awards for injury to feelings[5] or aggravated damages. Thus, at present, there is conflicting authority on this point, and first-instance judges have a lot of freedom to decide whether they wish to make a separate award or not. In practice, the relevant factors are likely to be whether the case involves an assault by the police (or other state body), where awards for aggravated damages are commonplace, and the severity of the assault or surrounding circumstances. Comparing the relatively mild facts of *Richardson*, where the claimant was left with some mild scarring from a bottle attack, to the much more severe case of *AT & others v Dulghieru*, one can readily see why Treacy J may have been inclined to make separate awards for aggravated damages, given the truly horrendous ordeal the claimants were subjected to.

1   [2004] EWCA Civ 1127.
2   [2006] EWHC 2865 (QB)
3   [2009] EWHC 225 (QB).
4   [2007] EWCA Civ 1379.
5   See also *Vento v Chief Constable of West Yorkshire Police (No 2)* [2003] IRLR 102.

(ii) Exemplary Damages

Definition

[A153] Exemplary damages are damages which are intended to punish the defendant, that may be awarded[1]: (i) in respect of unconstitutional, arbitrary or oppressive behaviour[2] carried out by servants of the Government[3]; (ii) for wrongful conduct calculated by the defendant in order to make a profit[4]; and (iii) where expressly allowed by statute[5]. At the time of writing, the Government considers that the law in relation to exemplary damages should be left to the courts to develop, and there are no plans for new statutory provisions[6].

1   These three categories were set out by Lord Devlin in *Rookes v Barnard* [1964] AC 1221.
2   The terms 'oppressive, arbitrary or unconstitutional' are to be read disjunctively: *Huckle v Money* (1793) 2 Wils KB 205, 95 ER 768; *Broome v Cassell & Co* [1972] AC 1027 at 1128H, 1134D–E; *Holden v Chief Constable of Lancashire* [1987] QB 380 at 388C–D, 388H.
3   The term 'servants of the Government' is to be widely construed: *Broome v Cassell & Co* [1972] AC 1027 at 1077H–1078C, 1088A–B, 1130B–C. It includes any tortfeasors exercising 'governmental power', such as the police: *Holden v Chief Constable of Lancashire* [1987] QB 380. However, this term does not include bodies set up by statute to supply amenities, since such bodies are engaged in conducting commercial operations as opposed to governmental functions: *AB v South West Water Services* [1993] QB 507, CA, overruled by *Kuddus v Chief Constable of Leicestershire* [2002] 2 AC 122, but not on this point.
4   By 'profit' the court means any gain that the defendant seeks to make, and this category is not limited to money-making in the strict sense: *Rookes v Barnard* [1964] AC 1221. It is not necessary that the defendant has made any precise or mathematical calculation as to the gain to be made from its conduct, merely that the conduct in question has been motivated by mercenary consideration: *John v MGN Ltd* [1997] QB 586.
5   The only clear example of a statute expressly authorising exemplary damages is Reserve and Auxiliary Forces (Protection of Civil Interests) Act 1951, s 13(2). See further the Law Commission's Consultation Paper No 247 'Aggravated, Exemplary and Restitutionary Damages' (1997), at paras 1.105–1.107. However, the Government has proposed amending this provision to read 'aggravated damages' instead of 'exemplary damages' – see further clause 9(1) of the draft Civil Law Reform Bill published by the Ministry of Justice on 15 December 2009.
6   Ministry of Justice 'The Law on Damages – Response to Consultation', 1 July 2009.

Applicability and assessment

[A154] A claim for exemplary damages must be pleaded in the particulars of claim, together with the grounds upon which they are sought[1]. Exemplary damages may be claimed across the whole range of tort[2] although are precluded from a claim under the Law Reform (Miscellaneous Provisions) Act 1934[3]. The nature of the award is purely punitive, ie to punish the defendant as opposed to compensating the claimant, and is entirely discretionary[4]. Such an award is only available to the court if, but only if, the measure of compensatory damages is inadequate to punish the defendant for his or her outrageous conduct and to deter others from engaging in similar conduct[5]. It is considered perverse, therefore, for exemplary damages to be awarded but not compensatory damages[6]. Awards for exemplary damages must be kept at moderate levels and should not exceed the minimum sum necessary to meet the public purpose underlying such damages, ie retribution and deterrent[7]. Everything which aggravates or mitigates the defendant's conduct is relevant to the assessment of the appropriate award[8], including the means of the defendant[9] and conduct of the claimant[10]. Exemplary damages are not appropriate where the defendant has already been punished for his or her misconduct, eg by a criminal court[11]. Additionally, the claimant must be a victim of the punishable behaviour so as not to gain a windfall in consequence[12]. If there are multiple defendants, the award for exemplary damages is calculated by reference to the defendant who is least blameworthy[13]. It is unclear on the authorities if and how the doctrine of vicarious liability should apply to exemplary damages[14]. Where there are multiple claimants, the court may decide to fix the level of exemplary damages and then divide the award between the claimants[15].

[1]   CPR, r 16.4(1)(c). Although CPR, r. 16.2(5) gives the court the power to grant any remedy to which the claimant is entitled, even if that remedy is not specified in the claim form, it does not give the same power if the remedy is not claimed in the particulars of claim, although permission is likely to amend the particulars of claim so as to seek such a remedy in an appropriate case.

[2]   *Kuddus v Chief Constable of Leicestershire* [2002] 2 AC 122, overruling *AB v South West Water Services* [1993] QB 507, CA.

[3]   Law Reform (Miscellaneous Provisions) Act 1934, s 1(2)(a)(i). See further *Brown v Robinson & others* [2004] UKPC 56.

[4]   *Broome v Cassell & Co* [1972] AC 1027. Note that the entitlement to exemplary damages must be proved on civil standard of proof, ie the balance of probabilities: *John v MGN* [1997] QB 586. However, where criminal conduct is relied upon, cogent evidence is likely to be required – see further para **[A50]**.

[5]   *Rookes v Barnard* [1964] AC 1221; *Broome v Cassell & Co* [1972] AC 1027; *Thompson v MPC* [1998] QB 498. In *Rookes v Barnard* [1964] AC 1221 at 1228, Lord Devlin stated that when juries are considering exemplary damages they should be directed that: '... if, but only if, the sum which they have in mind to award as compensation (which may, of course, be a sum aggravated by the way in which the defendant has behaved to the [claimant]) is inadequate to punish him for his outrageous conduct, to mark their disapproval of such conduct and to deter him from repeating it, then it can award some larger sum'.

[6]   *Cumber v Chief Constable of Hampshire Constabulary* (1995) 92(08) LSG 39, CA.

[7]   *Broome v Cassell & Co* [1972] AC 1027.

[8]   *Rookes v Barnard* [1964] AC 1221 at 1228.

[9]   *Rookes v Barnard* [1964] AC 1221 at 1228.

[10]   But only if the conduct was the cause of the offending behaviour: *Thompson v MPC* [1998] QB 498.

[11]   *Archer v Brown* [1985] QB 401; and *AB v South West Water Services* [1993] QB 507, CA, overruled by *Kuddus v Chief Constable of Leicestershire* [2002] 2 AC 122, but not on this point. Arguably, the fact that disciplinary proceedings have been or will be brought against the individuals responsible for the reprehensible conduct will be relevant to the decision whether to award exemplary damages: see further *Thompson v MPC* [1998] QB 498; and *Gerald v MPC* (1998) Times, 26 June.

[12]   *Rookes v Barnard* [1964] AC 1221.

[13]   *Broome v Cassell & Co* [1972] AC 1027.

[14]   See eg *Racz v Home Office* [1994] 2 AC 45; and *Makanjuola v MPC* (1998) Times, 8 August. In *Kuddus v Chief Constable of Leicestershire* [2002] 2 AC 122, Lord Scott stated that 'the objection to exemplary damages in vicarious liability cases seems to me to be fundamental' and 'vicarious punishment via an award of exemplary damages is contrary to principle and should be rejected'. See further the Law Commission Report No 247 'Aggravated, Exemplary and Restitutionary Damages' (1997) (Consultation Paper No 132) at paras 2.17 et seq.

Riches v Newsgroup Newspapers Ltd [1986] QB 256; *AT & others v Dulghieru* [2009] EWHC 225 (QB).

[A155] Again, the Court of Appeal took the opportunity in *Thompson v MPC*[1] to lay down some guidelines as regards the assessment of exemplary damages. Whilst the guidelines were for police cases, in which the jury was deciding the amount of exemplary damages to be awarded following the summing-up by the judge, the guidance given may well be of relevance to awards of exemplary damages in other contexts. In summary, the Court of Appeal held that:

- an award of exemplary damages is only appropriate where the award for compensatory and/or aggravated damages is insufficient for punishing the defendant.
- the appropriate award for exemplary damages is unlikely to be under £5,000[2].
- in order to attract an award of £25,000[3] in respect of exemplary damages, the conduct must be particularly deserving of condemnation.
- the absolute maximum award for exemplary damages would be £50,000[4], reserved for very serious misconduct of at least the rank of superintendent.
- it would be unlikely that the award of exemplary damages would be more than three times the amount of the basic (ie compensatory) award, except where the basic award was modest.

[1]   [1998] QB 498 (decision made on 19 February 1997 when the RPI was 155).
[2]   Worth approximately £6,916, updated for RPI to August 2009.
[3]   Worth approximately £34,581, updated for RPI to August 2009.
[4]   Worth approximately £69,161, updated for RPI to August 2009.

Examples of cases in which exemplary damages might be awarded

[A156] Exemplary damages are seldom awarded in a personal injury or clinical negligence context, but examples of cases in which such an award damages may be appropriate include those involving:

- abuse of public office;
- assault and battery;
- kidnap and forced sexual activity (for profit)[1];
- giving false evidence in court;
- making publicly embarrassing wrongful arrest;
- intentional discrimination of a racist or sexual nature leading to psychiatric injury;
- persistent and aggressive questioning of the claimant; and
- deliberate misconduct designed to make a profit.

[1]   *AT & others v Dulghieru* [2009] EWHC 225 (QB).

B Schedules of Loss

I The Need for a Schedule of Loss

(i) The Background

[B1] Prior to 1969, damages for personal injury were awarded on a 'global sum' basis[1]. The change of approach in 1969 occurred because Administration of Justice Act 1969, s 22 required that interest had to be awarded on past losses in a personal injury case, meaning that awards had to be itemised. This also reflected a change of approach by the judiciary. In *Kirby v Vauxhall Motors Ltd*[2], Lord Denning stated:

> '... in the ordinary way it is both proper and helpful for a Judge to itemise the damages: and he should be encouraged to do so for two reasons. First, it shows that the Judge has applied his mind to all the proper considerations and has worked out the damages in the way it should be done. Second, it is a great help to this court on an appeal, so that this court can themselves review the items in computing the overall figure.'

Lord Edmund-Davies LJ said: 'It is helpful to this court also to know how he has solved that problem as a means of arriving at the overall figure.'

[1]   In *Watson v Powles* [1968] 1 QB 596, [1967] 3 All ER 721, Lord Denning observed: 'It is not the Judge's duty to divide up the total award into separate items. He may now do so if he thinks it proper and helpful, but it is not his duty to do so'.
[2]   (1969) 113 Sol Jo 736.

[B2] Thus, since the late 1960s, personal injury lawyers have been dividing up their claims into a number of 'heads of damage'. The categories of these heads of damage are not closed and are constantly evolving. For example, damages for loss of congenial employment only developed as a head of damage during the 1980s[1].

[1]   See further Chapter D, General Damages.

[B3] The two principal heads of damage are pecuniary and non-pecuniary loss. The former has to be itemised in a detailed schedule of loss. Pecuniary loss is divided into two parts[1]:

(1) pre-trial expenses and losses ('past expenses and losses'), and
(2) post-trial expenses and losses ('future expenses and losses').

[1]   For the reasons why past expenses and losses and future expenses and losses are separated, see further *Jefford v Gee* [1970] 2 QB 130, [1970] 1 All ER 1202; *Coates v Curry* (1997) Times, 22 August and at para **[A13]**.

[B4] It will be seen from the above that the calculation of damages in personal injury cases has been transformed over the last 30 years from an art to a science. Considered in this way, it is not so surprising that Lord Steyn stated in *Wells v Wells*[1]:

> 'My Lords, until the Lord Chancellor takes action under his statutory powers it is essential that there should be a firm and workable principle. It should be general and simple in order to enable settlement negotiations and litigation to be conducted with the benefit of a reasonable degree of predictability of the likely outcome of a case.'

[1]   [1999] 1 AC 345 at 388. Note that the Lord Chancellor has exercised his power under Damages Act 1996, s 1 and has fixed the discount rate at 2.5%. See further at paras **[H27]–[H37]**.

[B5] Whereas the pre-trial losses would have accrued item by item over time, and future losses will probably do the same, a lump sum has traditionally been awarded as a 'once and for all' payment in respect of all such losses. However, there has recently been a fundamental change in the way that courts approach the assessment of future pecuniary loss. Since 1 April 2005, the court has had the power to order periodical payments: see further Chapter O. There are a number of advantages of the new system, not least the fact that the payments are guaranteed to continue for the life of the claimant and can be indexed to a more appropriate index than the RPI in order to keep pace with inflation. Periodical payments should reduce the risk of over- or under-compensation, and provide a more closely matched system of compensation to the claimant's needs than is available by way of a lump sum award.

(ii)   The Pre-action Protocols

The Personal Injury Pre-action Protocol

[B6] By virtue of para 3.14 of the Personal Injury Pre-action Protocol, the claimant is obliged to send to the defendant as soon as practicable a 'Schedule of Special Damages with supporting documents, particularly where the defendant has admitted liability'. It is unclear why the language used here is different to that of the PD to CPR, Pt 16 but the intention is clearly the same, ie that the claimant serves on the defendant a schedule detailing all past and future expenses and losses claimed as a result of the defendant's alleged wrongdoing.

The Pre-action Protocol for the Resolution of Clinical Disputes

[B7] By virtue of para 3.19 of the Personal Injury Pre-action Protocol, the Letter of Claim should provide sufficient information to enable the healthcare provider to commence investigations and to put an initial valuation on the claim. In addition, under para 3.22 any offers to settle which are made at an early stage should generally be accompanied by a medical report and a schedule of loss, together with supporting documentation.

(iii)   The Civil Procedure Rules 1998 ('CPR')

[B8] In relation to personal injury claims, para 4.2 of the PD to CPR, Pt 16 states:

'The Claimant must attach to his particulars of claim a schedule of details of any past and future expenses and losses which he claims.'

[B9]   This rule is thought to apply equally to clinical negligence cases, although is often honoured more in the breach than the observance where, at the time of issue, there is simply not enough information to provide details of the value of the claim in the absence of a definitive prognosis[1].

[1]   Para 3.2 of the draft Clinical Negligence Practice Direction suggested that it was not necessary for the claimant to serve a schedule of loss with proceedings, but allowed the defendant to apply within 14 days of service of the particulars of claim for such a schedule. However, this Practice Direction has never been implemented.

2   The Purpose of the Schedule of Loss

[B10]   The schedule of loss is a very important document for the following reasons:

*   It might determine the jurisdiction and track of the case, ie whether the claim should be allocated to the small claims track, the fast track or the multi-track, and whether the claim is appropriate for the High Court as opposed to the county court[1].
*   It sets out the detail of the claim. Any schedule, whether simple or complex, will tell the defendants the experience of the claimant's lawyers. A poorly drafted schedule will not impress defendants and provides them with an opportunity to make lower offers from the start than they otherwise would. Equally, a well-drafted schedule will tell experienced defendant lawyers that the claimant's lawyers are on top of the case and will give them a good run for their money.
*   It should provide the trial judge with a template for his or her approach to the assessment of damages and the appropriate sums to award[2].

[1]   As regards the allocation of claims, see CPR, Pt 26. By virtue of para 9 of the High Court and County Courts Jurisdiction Order 1991, SI 1991/724, as amended, a personal injury claim may not be commenced in the High Court unless its value is £50,000 or more (see also para 2.2 of the PD to CPR, Pt 7). Although note that, in order to calculate the statement of value, it is not always necessary to include the full value of the claim, eg where the parties agree to limit the claim to a value below the small claims track limit but have a memorandum of understanding to follow the court's decision in respect of liability for other losses: *Khiaban v Beard* [2002] EWCA Civ 358, [2003] 3 All ER 362. In any event, the court retains the power under CPR, r 16.3(7) to award in excess of the stated limit which appears on the claim form.

[2]   If periodical payments are sought, it is therefore sensible to quantify the annual loss figures.

[B11]   The aim must be to:

*   identify the heads of claim,
*   quantify them, and
*   explain them (if necessary).

The court will be looking to make an award that is 'fair and reasonable' to both sides[1]. Care must be taken to avoid overlap with other heads of claim[2]. Speculative claims of merest conjecture or chance, rather than substantial claims, should be discouraged[3].

[1]   Following the introduction of the Courts Act 2003, the award may be by way of periodical payments as well as a one-off lump sum. See further Chapter O.

Lim Poh Choo v Camden and Islington Area Health Authority [1980] AC 174 at 191. See further at
       para **[A47]** and Chapter K, Counter-schedules.
Davies v Taylor [1974] AC 207 at 212. For examples of speculative claims which failed, see
       Howarth v Whittaker [2003] Lloyd's Rep Med 235, Elias J; and *D and D v Donald* [2001] PIQR
       Q44. See further at para **[A15]**.

3   The Content of the Schedule of Loss

[B12]   There are no specific requirements or guidelines under the CPR regarding
what is to be included in a schedule of loss. However, it is usual for schedules of loss
to include the following:

* The claimant's date of birth.
* The claimant's pre-accident occupation (if any).
* The date of the accident.
* The claimant's life expectancy (if relevant).
* The date of the schedule.
* The (assumed) trial date or window.
* The heads of past loss.
* The heads of future loss.
* An indication as to whether or not future loss is claimed as a lump sum or by way
  of periodical payments (or both)[1].
* Any relevant multipliers.
* Details of interest claimed on general damages.
* Detailed of interest claimed on past expenses and losses.

[1]   CPR, r 41.5 enables the parties to state in their statements of case whether they regard periodical
        payments or a lump sum as likely to be more appropriate for all or part of an award of damages in
        respect of future loss. See further Chapter O.

[B13]   Traditionally, schedules of loss – which used to be known as schedules of
special damage – only dealt with details regarding past and future pecuniary loss.
However, it is now relatively common for schedules to include heads of loss for non-
pecuniary damage, such as general damages for pain, suffering and loss of amenity,
disadvantage on the labour market and loss of congenial employment. In this way,
it is possible to summarise the entire claim in one document. It is now important to
consider whether claims for future pecuniary loss should be advanced as a lump sum
or by way of periodical payment (or both). This may require additional narrative and
two sets of calculations.

[B14]   The schedule, and any subsequent amendments, must be verified by a
statement of truth[1]. Arguably, this means that the schedule may stand as evidence
of itself without needing to be proved by a witness statement (although it is always
sensible to cover the items claimed in the witness evidence). But this also means
that there may be serious consequences for a claimant who deliberately inflates or
exaggerates his or her claim, including proceedings for contempt of court[2].

[1]   Paragraph 1.4(3) of the PD to CPR, Pt 22.
[2]   See further CPR, r 32.14.

[B15]   Should the schedule of loss omit or exclude any information? Technically, by virtue of CPR, r 25.9, where an interim payment has been made by the defendant voluntarily or by court order, this should not be disclosed to the trial judge until the final decision regarding liability and quantum has been made. However, in practice this rule is often ignored by the parties, particularly where interim payments have been made for specific items and the parties wish to make it clear to the court which items are and are not in dispute.

4   The Timing of the Schedule of Loss

[B16]   As mentioned above, the rules say that a schedule of loss must be served with the particulars of claim. This is unless permission has been obtained from the court to dispense with this requirement. However, a balance has to be struck between deciding whether:

(i)   to issue and apply for dispensation;
(ii) to issue and provide a provisional schedule that will be finalised when further information is to hand; or
(iii) not to issue until all the information is available, so that a fully particularised schedule of loss can be drafted.

[B17]   Current practice generally is as follows:

- Approach (i) above should only be used as a last resort (eg when limitation may be a problem) or where a split trial is appropriate (eg due to the costs of compiling the schedule and/or delay). The problem is that it cannot be relied upon that the court will order a split trial or that a schedule need not be served with the particulars of claim.
- Approach (ii) above used to be the norm, but it is becoming less common now due to the need to front-load cases and the courts' eagerness to have as much information as possible to hand in order to allocate the case to the appropriate track. However, it is still often used where there are limitations or evidential problems and there are reasonable prospects that the further information will be available in good time before the final hearing.
- Approach (iii) above used to be less common due to cost and delay, but is increasing in popularity due to the need in the current climate to obtain all the relevant quantum information at an earlier stage. Proceedings are usually only issued now after extensive attempts have been made to settle the case (presumably after it has been fully quantified!). This is certainly the safest option from the claimant's point of view and has the effect of putting him or her in the driving seat. It is also virtually a necessity in fast track cases, where the idea is that the case will proceed to trial within 30 weeks from the date of issue[1].

---

[1]   See para 3.12 of the PD to CPR, Pt 28.

[B18]   Where an application is made to dispense with the need to file and serve a schedule of loss with the particulars of claim, it should be made in accordance with CPR, Pt 23, ie the application should be made to the relevant court, supported by evidence together with a draft of the order sought, as soon as it becomes apparent that an application is necessary or that it is desirable to make it. Unless one of the exceptions in CPR, r 23.7 applies[1] the other side must be served with a copy of the application notice at least three days before the court is to deal with the application.

[1]   Such as cases of exceptional urgency; where the overriding objective is best furthered by so doing; by consent of all the parties; with the permission of the court; where a date for a hearing has already been fixed; or where a court order, rule or practice direction permits.

[B19]   Of course, the overriding objective will be determinative of any application for an extension of time for serving the schedule of loss. Under the old rules, there was some authority to suggest that claims could still succeed even where the claimant had failed to comply with various orders to serve a schedule of loss within a given time period[1]. However, following the Court of Appeal's decision in *Biguzzi v Rank Leisure*[2], such authority is unlikely to be applicable and the court will focus upon what the interests of justice (and the administration of justice) demand in each case.

[1]   *Willis v Royal Doulton (UK) Ltd* [1997] CLY 785, CA; and *Bheeroo v Camden & Islington NHS Trust* (29 June 2000, unreported), CA; cf *Bourlett v Stagecoach East Kent Road Car Co Ltd* [1999] PIQR P43.
[2]   [1999] 4 All ER 934.

5   The Layout and Form of the Schedule of Loss

[B20]   The layout of the schedule should be designed to:

* Provide focus for the claim.
* Be 'user friendly'.
* Have a logical progression.
* Supply a short summary.
* Invite use by the defendant(s).
* Invite use by the judge at trial.
* Be flexible enough to incorporate amendments, additions, deletions and accommodate new information for changed circumstances.

[B21]   The structure depends upon the complexity of the claim. In a more complicated or less obvious claim, the schedule should contain a narrative for the court, explaining the reason for the expenditure/loss and why (with references to the trial bundle, where this is in existence) it is alleged to be recoverable. The parties may also want to set out in the narrative why assessment on a particular basis is or is not appropriate, eg where there is a significant reduction for contributory negligence, this may be a reason for a competent claimant preferring a lump sum as opposed to a periodical payment order, since any periodical payments will not be able to meet the claimant's needs and he or she might be attracted to the flexibility of a lump sum.

[B22]   Traditionally, a distinction has been drawn between 'special damages', as meaning losses incurred up until the date of trial, and 'general damages', meaning those losses to be incurred in the future, together with damages for pain, suffering and loss of amenity (on the basis that losses up until the trial could be assessed on the balance of probability as having occurred, and further losses are inevitably more speculative). However, schedules of special damage have always included details of future losses. There is now, of course, an implied obligation to include details of all future expenses and losses by reason of the schedule's title.

[B23]   Past expenses and losses should be separated from future expenses and losses[1]. This is so that interest can be claimed for past losses. It is not, of course, awarded on future losses since, by definition, they have yet to be incurred.

---

[1]   *Jefford v Gee* [1970] 2 QB 130, [1970] 1 All ER 1202; *Coates v Curry* (1997) Times, 22 August. See further at paras **A[13]** and **[A22]**.

[B24]   Multipliers, now that they are more precisely calculated by reference to tables, should be included. Sometimes it is appropriate to leave the defendants space (or a column) for their figures, and to leave the judge space (or a column) for his or her figures. This is particularly so in any summary which is prepared, because it shows very clearly which heads of loss are agreed and where the largest disputes are.

[B25]   Normally, the schedule will be produced on A4 sheets of paper in portrait format, unless there is insufficient space for columns, in which case landscape format should be used.

6   Basic Principles

(i)   'If you don't ask, you don't get'

[B26]   Any schedule starts off as a blank sheet of paper. What is inserted usually depends upon the skill and expertise of the drafter. The skill is to get the information from the client; and the expertise is knowing whether the claim is reasonable and not fanciful.

(ii)   'If in doubt, include'

[B27]   As a general rule of thumb (and particularly when drafting the first schedule), lawyers should err on the side of caution and insert items rather than leave them out.

[B28]   Too frequently, items are left out, leading to later amendments. This enables defendants to argue, reasonably in some cases, that they have not been given sufficient information to investigate the claim and make appropriate offers to settle[1]. In the era of pre-action protocols, offers to settle and wasted cost orders, the court is less likely to be sympathetic to sloppily drafted schedules which leave out heads of claim without reasonable excuse. This is particularly important where a later amendment results in the need to review the decision regarding the appropriate tracking of the claim.

---

[1]   This may lead to the trial being adjourned and the claimant paying wasted costs: see eg *Brown v BM Group Plc* (12 July 1996, unreported). See also *Taylor v Brock* [2001] CP Rep 11.

(iii)   'Only claim the arguably recoverable'

[B29]   Some losses are simply not recoverable in law. For example, the claimant cannot claim for credit hire charges arising out of an unlawful credit hire agreement[1].

Not only is it a waste of time to claim such losses, but it alerts the court and the defendants to the lack of knowledge or inexperience of the claimant's lawyers (which then causes the reader to scrutinise the rest of the schedule more closely).

[1]   See *Dimond v Lovell* [2002] 1 AC 384, [2000] 2 All ER 897.

[B30] Also included in this category are losses which are more properly viewed as costs, such as the claimant's travelling expenses to visit his or her legal advisers[1].

[1]   *Morris v Johnson Matthey & Co* (1967) 112 Sol Jo 32; *Van Wees v (1) Karkour and (2) Walsh* [2007] EWHC 165 (QB), per Langstaff J at para 163; *Lane v Lake (Deceased)*, QBD, 18/7/2007, Lawtel Document No AC0114378, per John Leighton Williams QC at para 41.

[B31] Care should, however, be taken to include all subrogated claims which the claimant is entitled to recover. A common example of such a claim is the insurer's outlay in a road traffic accident case. If necessary, the contract alleged to give rise to the rights of subrogation should be obtained and studied in detail.

(iv) 'Be realistic'

[B32] It is important that the schedule of loss is realistic. If the schedule does not appear reasonable, it is likely to antagonise the court and, therefore, where appropriate, proper concessions should be made. For example, if there is a possible need for future medical treatment, a claim should not be made on behalf of the claimant for private health care if the claimant has never used private health care in the past and has no intention of using it in the future[1].

[1]   A claimant cannot recover the cost of private medical treatment if, on the balance of probabilities, the claimant would use the NHS rather than avail him or herself of private facilities: *Woodrup v Nicol* [1993] PIQR Q104.

(v) 'Don't overstate your claim'

[B33] Claims should not be exaggerated or made for items of damage which are patently unsustainable. For example, a claim should not be made for the cost of hiring a Rolls Royce for the period when the claimant's Mini is off the road as a result of the defendant's negligence. Deliberately making such claims exposes the claimant to an adverse order for costs[1].

[1]   By virtue of CPR, r 44.3(5)(d), when deciding what order, if any, to make about costs, the court must have regard to whether or not a claimant who has succeeded in his or her claim, in whole or in part, exaggerated his or her claim. A claimant who is found to have been guilty of conscious exaggeration or malingering may end up paying all the costs, particularly where a Part 36 payment is beaten: *Cottrell v Redbridge NHS Trust* [2001] All ER (D) 174 (Apr), QBD, HHJ Richard Seymour QC; *Molloy v Shell UK Ltd* [2001] EWCA Civ 1272, [2001] All ER (D) 79 (Jul); *Booth v Britannia Hotels Ltd* [2002] EWCA Civ 529, [2002] All ER (D) 422 (Mar); see also *Painting v University of Oxford* [2005] EWCA Civ 161. See further at para **[A122]** and in Chapter K at **K[66]**.

[B34] There are also professional obligations not to claim for items of damage for which there is no supporting evidence[1]. It is possible that legal representatives who claim for heads of loss which never had any chance of succeeding will be hit by an order for wasted costs.

See eg *Medcalf v Mardell* [2002] UKHL 27, [2003] 1 AC 120 in relation to the evidence necessary before counsel may justifiably plead an allegation of fraud.

(vi)   'Double-check your figures'

[B35]   It is important to check and double-check the calculations in the schedule. A schedule of loss is unlikely to commend itself to the court if it is littered with errors. Likewise, it is crucial to make sure that the latest figures have been used. Amending schedules at a late stage to correct errors regarding hourly rates, multipliers or figures for past loss is always troublesome and will often lose you the confidence of the tribunal.

(vii)   'Presentation, presentation, presentation'

[B36]   A schedule which is easy on the eye is more likely to find favour with the court. Drafters of schedules should experiment with different styles of layout in order to achieve the most attractive and efficient way of setting out the relevant information. The schedule of loss must be user friendly. It is helpful, therefore, in the larger claims, where the schedule is likely to run well into double figures in page length, for the schedule to be split into various sections including an index, a summary of the claim, a list of important information, and possibly a chronology of important dates.

C Compiling the Evidence

I Introduction

[C1]   The vast majority of personal injury claims are framed in negligence or additionally, if they arise out of employment, as a breach of the contractual duty to take reasonable care for the health and safety of employees[1]. The fundamental principle is that the claimant should be restored to the position, so far as is possible by way of financial compensation, that he or she would have been in but for the defendant's wrongdoing[2]. In practice, this means that the claimant will be able to claim for all losses and expenses which reasonably result from his or her injuries. The challenge for the drafter of the schedule of loss is to identify those expenses and losses and to calculate their value. This, of course, requires evidence.

[1]   *Matthews v Kuwait Bechtel Corpn* [1959] 2 QB 57, [1959] 2 All ER 345; and *Martin v Lancashire County Council* [2000] 3 All ER 544, CA.
[2]   *Livingstone v Rawyards Coal Co* (1880) 5 App Cas 25 at 39. See further Chapter A at paras **[A26]**–**[A28]**.

[C2]   The onus is upon the claimant, where he or she asserts that a head of loss is attributable to the defendant's wrongdoing, to prove[1]:

* the head of loss has actually been or will be incurred; and
* the extent of the loss.

[1]   *The Clarence* (1850) 2 W Rob (Adm) 283; *Bonham-Carter v Hyde Park Hotel* (1948) 64 TLR 178; *Ashcroft v Curtin* [1971] 1 WLR 1731; *Tate & Lyle Food and Distribution v GLC* [1982] 1 WLR 149; *Harrison v Leake* (1989) Times, 12 October, CA; *Hughes (Gordon Clifford) v Addis (John)* (23 March 2000, unreported), CA; *Smith v McCrae* [2003] EWCA Civ 505.

[C3]   If liability is established but the claimant is unable to prove the extent of his or her loss, he or she will only be entitled to recover nominal damages[1]. Where insufficient evidence is provided to assess the value of a particular head of loss, the court may not award anything for the claimed item[2]. But this principle should not be taken to extremes. As long as the loss is not too small[3] or speculative[4] to be measured, the fact that the assessment of a particular head of loss might be difficult, eg because there are a number of imponderables, should not be a bar to recovery[5]. The court is obliged to do its best to calculate the value of the loss on the available evidence[6]. For example, in *Eden v West & Co*[7] the trial judge rejected the claimant's claim for loss of earnings because there was 'such a paucity of evidence to make any findings of fact in relation to the claimant's net income'. The Court of Appeal held that the trial judge was not entitled to be as robust as he was in his approach. There was uncontested evidence that the claimant was working at the time of the accident (indeed, the accident occurred in the course of his employment with the defendant).

The agreed medical evidence supported the fact that the claimant was unfit to work for a period of six months by reason of the accident. In the event, a global award of £5,000 was substituted against the claim for past loss of earnings in the schedule of loss amounting to £11,500, and a further £1,000 was awarded to cover loss of future earnings.

1   *Mappouras v Waldrons Solicitors* [2002] EWCA Civ 842; cf *Experience Hendrix LLC v PPX Enterprises Inc* [2003] EWCA Civ 323 where it was held, in the exceptional circumstances of the case, that the claimant was entitled to damages for breaches of a compromise agreement, even though the claimant could not prove any loss flowing from the breaches.

2   *Ashcroft v Curtin* [1971] 1 WLR 1731; *Harrison v Leake* (1989) Times, 12 October, CA; *Hughes (Gordon Clifford) v Addis (John)* (23 March 2000, unreported), CA. Although, in certain instances it may be reasonable to infer parties' expenses/losses from the evidence: see further chapter 45 of *McGregor on Damages* (18th edn) and *Bygrave v Thomas Cook Tour Operations Ltd* [2004] EWCA Civ 1631, where the Court of Appeal accepted that it was reasonable for the judge to infer that the claimant would spend more on taxis in the future because of her injuries.

3   The claimant may be unable to recover for very slight damage which falls foul of the de minimis principle: see eg *Harwood v Cross Paperware* [1975] CLY 107u, CA. This principle holds that the law does not worry about very small things. In a different context, see further *Hollins v Russell* [2003] EWCA Civ 718.

4   Claims which are no more than speculative will not be recoverable. See eg *Howarth v Whittaker* [2003] Lloyd's Rep Med 235, Elias J (a claim for loss of earnings); *Parkhouse v North Devon Healthcare NHS Trust* [2002] Lloyd's Rep Med 100 (a claim for future IT requirements); *D and D v Donald* [2001] PIQR Q44 (a claim for dependency based upon deceased's pension); *Firth v Geo Ackroyd Jnr Ltd* [2000] Lloyd's Law Rep Med 312 (a claim for indemnity or a lump sum to reflect the chance that there would be a change of law in the future requiring the claimant to pay for his accommodation or care charges).

5   *Chaplin v Hicks* [1911] 2 KB 786 at 792; *The Mediana* [1900] AC 113 at 116–117; *Otter v Church* [1953] Ch 280; *Moeliker v A Reyrolle & Co Ltd* [1977] 1 WLR 132 at 141; and *Thompson v Smith Shiprepairers (North Shields)* [1984] QB 405. In *Chaplin v Hicks* [1911] 2 KB 786, Vaughan Williams LJ stated: 'The fact that damages cannot be assessed with certainty does not relieve the wrongdoer of the necessity of paying damages'. See also *Eden v West & Co* [2002] EWCA Civ 991.

6   See eg *Moeliker v A Reyrolle & Co Ltd* [1977] 1 WLR 132; and, more recently, *Eden v West & Co* [2002] EWCA Civ 991, in which the Court of Appeal was critical of the trial judge's robustly dismissive approach to the claim for loss of earnings, notwithstanding the paucity of documentary evidence in support of the same.

7   [2002] EWCA Civ 991. See also *Bygrave v Thomas Cook Tour Operations Ltd* [2003] EWCA Civ 1631, where the Court of Appeal accepted that it was reasonable for the judge to infer that the claimant would spend more on taxis in the future because of her injuries.

[C4]   Unless sufficient evidence can be obtained in order to make an accurate calculation of the claimant's loss, the court may be forced to make a broad brush or global assessment instead of using the multiplier/multiplicand method[1]. Understandably, this will usually result in the court applying a relatively cautious or conservative valuation, so that the claimant is not over-compensated. The result is that the claimant will often receive a considerably smaller lump sum than if the traditional multiplier/multiplicand technique had been adopted[2].

1   See eg *Smith v McCrae* [2003] EWCA Civ 505, in which Kennedy LJ stated at [6], [8] and [14] 'The first matter still in dispute is the award made in respect of future loss of earnings. The judge had before him in relation to this issue practically no evidence. In order to calculate on the multiplier/multiplicand basis, it was necessary for the judge to have before him reliable evidence as to the claimant's pre-accident earning capacity and as to his post-accident earning capacity. The claimant here simply had not laid before the court the materials which might well, had they been laid before the court, have enabled the judge to adopt the approach he did [ie a calculation

on the multiplier/multiplicand basis]. But the materials were not there. In the absence of those materials it was not appropriate to attempt to use figures which were patently, for the reasons I have endeavoured to explain, unreliable'. And see *Van Wees v (1) Karkour and (2) Walsh* [2007] EWHC 165 (QB), when Langstaff J adopted a broad-brush assessment of the claimant's future loss of earnings because of the difficulties and uncertainties in calculating future loss on a multiplier/multiplicand basis.

[2]   See eg *Rees v Dewhirst plc* [2002] EWCA Civ 871; *Willemse v Hesp* [2003] EWCA Civ 994; *Crouch v King's Healthcare NHS Trust* [2004] EWCA Civ 853.

2   Quantification of Expenses and Losses

[C5]   A good schedule does not just come 'out of thin air'. It has to be carefully investigated beforehand so that all the items claimed can be proved at trial. When a client first attends for interview, the representative should not only be thinking about proof of liability but also about proof of loss. The claim, after all, is about money. Therefore, the claimant's representative has to investigate quantum, and particularly financial expenses/losses, before issuing proceedings.

[C6]   It is now more important than ever to assess the value of the claim at an early stage because this may well affect funding issues. Should a claim be eligible for public funding, it is necessary to conduct an assessment of the costs/benefit ratio. Alternatively, a legal representative considering taking on a case on a conditional fee basis might think twice if the claim is not worth very much[1].

[1]   Money claims with a value of less than £5,000, or personal injury claims with a value of less than £1,000, will be allocated to the small claims track. Following such an allocation, a successful party will not be able to recover their costs unless they can prove unreasonable behaviour on the part of another party to the litigation. See further CPR, Pt 27 and, in particular, r 27.14.

3   The First Interview

[C7]   The claimant's representative has to be tactful at the first interview. The aim is to ascertain approximately what the claim is worth without building up the client's hopes too much. Experience has shown that most clients, naturally, want to know whether they have a claim and also how much that claim is worth. If they are given certain figures at the first interview, they find it difficult to revise those figures downward in the light of future developments in their case. The representative has to be careful not to raise expectations unnecessarily, yet has an obligation to be accurate in any valuation given.

[C8]   An initial statement should be taken detailing the injuries that the claimant has suffered, how the injuries have impinged upon his or her life, and the expenses and losses that have been incurred to date. All areas of the claimant's life should be considered: work, domestic life, social activities and leisure pursuits. Particular attention should be given to the claimant's likely continuing losses.

[C9]   Efforts should also be made to preserve or photograph any evidence which might be the subject of later dispute, eg broken jewellery or damaged goods.

4   Medical Records

(i)   The Need for Medical Records

[C10]   An important initial step in any personal injury claim is to obtain the claimant's medical records. These records will need to be forwarded to any medical expert in order to prepare his or her report[1]. Additionally, the claimant's medical records are needed for a number of purposes, including:

- Identifying any relevant medical history or problems.
- Supporting the claimant's version of events regarding the circumstances in which the injury was suffered[2].
- Indicating the nature and severity of the injuries sustained.
- Detailing the nature and extent of any past or ongoing treatment[3].
- Assessing the reasonableness of the care/treatment received[4].
- Giving an indication of how the injuries have affected the claimant and the extent of any ongoing disability.
- Indicating whether or not the claimant has made any previous claims for personal injury[5].
- Satisfying the burden of proof, eg establishing that the loss of future earnings or earning capacity is related to the accident rather than some other cause[6].

[1]   Where possible, any medical expert instructed to prepare a report should be provided with a complete set of the claimant's medical records prior to their examination. Although it is sometimes necessary for reasons of expediency for the medical expert to see the claimant and prepare a report without sight of the claimant's medical records, and for a supplementary report then to be prepared once the records subsequently become available, this should be avoided. The difficulty in taking the claimant's instructions at face value in relation to their injuries and previous medical history is that the case might get off on the wrong footing, particularly where the claimant inadvertently forgets to mention something which later turns out to be important.
[2]   Often, the medical records will contain a fairly detailed history describing how the claimant's injuries were inflicted, which may or may not confirm what is later said in the legal process. The records may also provide useful information such as whether or not the claimant was wearing a seat belt and who else was with the claimant at the time of the accident.
[3]   The records may also include details about the cost of the treatment, if performed on a private basis.
[4]   Of course, the claimant's medical records will be necessary to investigate and pursue any claim for clinical negligence.
[5]   If a previous claim for personal injury has been made, there will often be correspondence in the claimant's GP records in relation to the same.
[6]   See *Dunn v British Coal* [1993] ICR 591, [1993] IRLR 396, [1993] PIQR P275.

(ii)   Types of Medical Records

[C11]   There are as many types of medical record as the claimant has had treatment. The most common examples include:

- Ambulance and paramedic records.
- GP notes and records.
- Accident & Emergency records.
- Hospital In-patient and Outpatient records.
- Nursing records.
- Psychiatric records.

- Counselling/therapy records.
- Pain clinic notes and records.
- Physiotherapy records.
- Notes and records kept by alternative practitioners such as providers of (cranial) osteopathy, chiropractic treatment and acupuncture.
- Dental records.
- Records held by opticians.
- Records held by pharmacists.
- Records from travel clinics, day care centres and drop-in treatment centres.
- Rehabilitation records.
- Records relating to private treatment provided by doctors, surgeons and nurses.

[C12]   It is important to appreciate that the claimant's medical notes and records may include a number of different documents. Where a claimant has extensive medical records, a medical sorting agency can provide invaluable help to separate the different records, arrange them in chronological order and advise upon any records that are missing. For example, when considering a claimant's GP records, one might expect to see:

- Old handwritten Lloyd George record cards.
- A typed summary of conditions and complaints.
- Typed attendance notes.
- Results of tests, scans and investigations.
- A list of prescriptions and medication given.
- A vaccination card.
- Correspondence (including referral letters to specialists, letters from hospital doctors, private consultants, specialists and communication with the claimant).

It is not uncommon for the claimant's medical records to be incomplete. There may also be a number of relevant documents which are not kept in the claimant's medical records and are not normally disclosed unless specifically requested. For example, in certain cases it may be necessary to see the original X-rays, CT or MRI scans. Further, the claimant may wish to have sight of adverse outcome/incident reports, and any complaints file or reports from independent reviews/investigations. Unless it can be shown that the sole or dominant purpose of the document when it first came into being was for legal advice in actual or contemplated litigation, it will not be protected from disclosure by privilege[1].

[1]   *Waugh v British Railways Board* [1980] AC 521. See further Chapter A at para [A64].

(iii)   Procedure for Obtaining Medical Records

Entitlement

[C13]   Generally speaking, a claimant has a right to seek access to his or her medical records under the Access to Health Records Act 1990 or the Data Protection Act 1998[1]. The claimant further has a right to be sent copies of any records for a maximum fee (currently £50)[2]. The record holder must supply the claimant with copies within 40 days of receiving the request for disclosure or payment, whichever is later.

1   It should be noted that, in exceptional circumstances, the law may prevent such access, eg where it is feared that the records might have an adverse outcome on the claimant's health.
2   Regulation 6(2) of the Data Protection (Subject Access) (Fees and Miscellaneous Provisions) Regulations 2000. However, there are exceptions to this, eg where the records are all automated, the maximum fee is only £10 (see reg 3).

Disclosure to the defendant

[C14]   Historically, a defendant to a claim for personal injury was entitled to seek disclosure of the claimant's entire medical records because they were considered relevant and necessary to decide the issues[1]. It should be noted, however, that the implementation of the Human Rights Act 1998 means that Art 8 of the European Convention on Human Rights must now be taken into account. In *MS v Sweden*[2] the ECtHR held that the applicant's medical records and medical history were part of her private life. However, under Art 8(2) the disclosure was justified because it was held to be in accordance with law, was founded on a legitimate aim, and was necessary in a democratic society. The position may well be different where the other party is not a public authority and therefore cannot rely upon Art 8(2). More recently, in *Bennett v Compass Group UK*[3], the Court of Appeal held that:

- The combined effect of CPR, rr 31.3, 31.6 and 31.8 is that the defendant has a right to inspect the claimant's medical records.
- In the ordinary course of events, it will be for the claimant (and/or his or her advisers) to obtain a copy of the medical records, and for the defendant to request inspection of the same, rather than the defendant being granted authority to obtain the records directly from the relevant bodies[4].
- In exceptional cases, it may be necessary to apply to the court for an order that the defendant be given authority to obtain copies of the claimant's medical records directly, in default of which the claim be stayed, but care should be taken to ensure that the terms of any such order are clearly and carefully defined in order to protect the claimant's rights, whether under the European Convention on Human Rights or otherwise[5].

1   *Dunn v British Coal Corpn* [1993] PIQR 275; *Hipwood v Gloucester Health Authority* [1995] PIQR P447.
2   (1997) 3 BHRC 248.
3   [2002] EWCA Civ 642.
4   At [72], Chadwick LJ stated: 'The normal – and by far the most satisfactory course – is for the medical records to be produced by the claimant's advisers for inspection and consideration by the defendant's experts. It should not be necessary for the defendant's advisers to approach the GP or the hospital directly. But I cannot say that there are not circumstances in which it may be necessary – in order to break through what appears to be a wall of unresponsive silence …'.
5   To this end, the order should detail the exact records which are to be disclosed, to whom they are to be disclosed, and for what purpose.

5   Collating the Proof

(i)   General

[C15]   The claimant's representative should have in mind a number of heads of damage. The two principal heads of damage are likely to be loss of earnings and costs in respect of the need for services (eg care, medical treatment and DIY). However, the client may already have incurred a number of expenses on a daily basis for which there are no receipts.

[C16] Clients should be told that, unless receipts are kept, the expenditure they incur may well not be recoverable from the defendants. Thus, by failing to keep receipts they are doing the defendants a favour! The simplest method for a client to collect and compile a list of receipts is to draw columns on an A4 envelope as follows:

Date	Receipts	Comments (Item of expenditure)	Cost

[C17] The receipts can be conveniently kept in the envelope. If the client does not have a receipt, he or she should be asked to note down the item of expenditure without ticking the receipts column. The fact that the entry appears in the list in this way, provided it is reasonable and logically incurred, is more likely to persuade the court that the expense was incurred. The client should be given an envelope set out in the correct manner to take away with him or her.

[C18] Other documents may also assist in proving loss. Thus, bank statements or credit card statements also show what money was spent on. Again, provided that this can be reasonably argued as having been necessarily incurred as a result of the injuries, the court is likely to be persuaded that it is recoverable.

[C19] In more serious injury cases, the client or his or her family should be urged to keep a diary of relevant aspects of their life. They should be asked to make a note of all the things that happen which would not have happened had they not been injured.

(ii) Questionnaire

[C20] The client should be given a questionnaire of the items of expenditure that are normally incurred in his or her type of case. He or she should be told to err on the side of caution. Thus, if there is any uncertainty regarding whether an item of expenditure is recoverable, it should be included in the list so that the lawyer can decide whether it is recoverable.

[C21] Two examples of such questionnaires are set out in Chapter Q at paras **[Q2]** and **[Q3]**. It is suggested that such a questionnaire should be provided at the end of the first interview, together with a request for sight of all relevant documents. The completed questionnaire and documents may then help identify some of the likely heads of damage at an early stage.

(iii)　Documentary Evidence

The more the better

[C22]　The more documentary evidence there is to support the claims made in respect of past and future losses and expenses, the more likely the claims are to succeed. Often, claims under certain heads of loss fail due to insufficient proof[1]. Where expenses have been incurred but there is no documentary evidence to support the sums claimed, the claimant is at the mercy of the court as to whether or not any damages will be recovered and, if so, the extent of the same[2].

[1]　See eg *Hughes (Gordon Clifford) v Addis (John)* (23 March 2000, unreported), CA, involving a claim for increased fuel costs arising out of the claimant's car phobia. See also *Ashcroft v Curtin* [1971] 1 WLR 1731; *Harrison v Leake* (1989) Times, 12 October, CA; and *Cornes v Southwood* [2008] EWHC 369 (QB).

[2]　For an example where the court was prepared to make an award in respect of a particular item in the absence of specific evidence regarding the extent of the loss, see eg *Felicia Andrina George (Administratrix of the Estate of Hughes Williams, Deceased) v Eagle Air Services Limited* [2009] UKPC 34, in which the Privy Council awarded $3,000 for funeral expenses against a claim of $5,000 notwithstanding the lack of any specific evidence proving the level of costs incurred.

Employment details

[C23]　If the claimant was employed at the time of the accident, it may be that the claimant has kept copies of his or her payslips. If not, salary details should be obtained from the claimant's employer. It is usual to ask for details regarding the claimant's gross and net pay figures for the 13 weeks prior to the accident; but if, for whatever reason, this period was unlikely to be representative of the claimant's lost salary, a longer period should be taken (eg if bonuses were paid annually and the last 13 weeks do not record this). Alternatively, where the claimant's income is seasonal, it might be worth analysing the claimant's salary over the same period in the preceding years before the accident. The following information may also be requested from the claimant's employer:

- Any changes in rates of pay or hours of work since the accident.
- The claimant's P60 and/or P45.
- Any additional overtime payments (if these are not detailed in the salary information).
- Any additional bonus payments (if these are not detailed in the salary information).
- Any additional profit-related pay (if not detailed in the salary information).
- Any additional holiday pay (if not detailed in the salary information).
- Promotional opportunities.
- Pension details.
- The claimant's personnel file.
- The claimant's medical file.
- A copy of the claimant's contract of employment.
- Confirmation regarding whether or not the claimant is obliged to repay any sick pay payments as a result of a third party's negligence.

[C24]　If the claim is brought against the claimant's employer or former employer, it is prudent to request loss of earnings details in the initial letter of claim[1].

The claimant is entitled to disclosure of these details under the Personal Injury Pre-action Protocol as documents material to a claim where the defendant is the claimant's employer.

[C25] If the claimant was self-employed at the time of the accident, the claimant should be asked to produce copies of his or her business records, business accounts and tax returns for the relevant period of incapacity, together with material which will enable a comparison with previous performance. This will usually involve an examination of any annual accounts, copies of tax returns etc, and in most cases may need the claimant to ask his or her tax adviser to compile up-to-date figures as a matter of urgency.

[C26] If the claimant was unemployed immediately prior to the accident, but was studying/training to start a new job or was just about to start a new job at the time of the accident, the claim for loss of earnings will be a claim for a lost chance[1] or, if the injury is longer term, for disability on the labour market. This latter claim will, in such a case, closely resemble a claim for continuing loss of earnings. As much information as possible should be gleaned in order to support the claimant's chance of succeeding in his or her chosen occupation. The claimant's training, qualifications, knowledge and experience should be ascertained in relation to the job. Details should be obtained regarding salary, promotional opportunities and pension entitlement. Where there was a concrete job offer, documentary evidence should be obtained, if possible, such as the contract of employment, in order to see whether or not the claimant would have been subject to a probationary period or whether any unusual terms would have applied. Evidence may also be sought from the claimant's previous employers regarding the claimant's skills, abilities and general employability, and from the prospective employers regarding their opinion of the claimant's suitability for the position.

[1] *Doyle v Wallace* [1998] PIQR Q146.

[C27] One of the most useful sources of evidence in order to prove a loss of earnings claim (particularly concerning rare or unusual jobs, where statistical information is thin) is to obtain evidence from a comparator. Where the claimant loses a job which someone else is now doing or there are comparable positions in other companies, the court will be greatly assisted by evidence from a comparator stating the level of salary he or she receives, including all benefits and perks, as well as any increases or bonuses which have been received prior to the trial. Alternatively, such evidence may be obtained from a human relations employee or an employment consultant[1]. Care must be taken to ensure a comparator is materially in the same position as the claimant.

[1] See eg *George v Stagecoach* [2003] EWHC 2042 QB), in which Mackay J stated at [20]: 'I would have been better served by evidence from a human relations employee of either his present or another company. I would also have been served better by direct evidence of a specific comparator or comparators, particularly so where figures as high as those involved in this case are in play'.

[C28] If the claimant had been unemployed for a considerable period before the accident, consideration should be given as to whether or not a claim for loss of earnings can be sustained at all. However, it is suggested that almost everyone has an earning capacity, and very few, if any, people are unemployed throughout a lifetime.

Accordingly, the effect of lengthy periods of unemployment/job search prior to the accident (or, for that matter, period of time in prison, in rehabilitation or such like) is to reduce any total award, perhaps by reducing the multiplier for any proposed future loss claim under this head.

HM Revenue and Customs

[C29]   If there is any doubt as regards the claimant's employment history or the claimant has difficulty remembering the dates and periods of his or her previous employment, it is possible to request an employment history for the claimant. Since 1 October 2003, HMRC will supply employment histories free of charge for any criminal injury or personal injury claim (including any industrial injury, claim for medical negligence, serious road traffic accident or claim against the tobacco industry).

Receipts, invoices, valuations and estimates

[C30]   The claimant should be asked to bring in or copy his or her receipts/invoices/valuations and estimates every so often, so that they may be put on file and disclosed to the other side. The claimant should be reminded that any receipts/invoices/valuations and/or estimates for services should only include the labour costs involved.

[C31]   Receipts and invoices are commonly obtained for the following losses/expenses:

- Insurance policy excesses.
- Damaged vehicles.
- Damaged items of clothing and possessions.
- Replacement items of clothing and possessions.
- Repair costs for damaged clothing and possessions.
- Past medical treatment including physiotherapy, osteopathy, chiropractic treatment and acupuncture.
- Past medical tests and investigations including X-rays, MRI scans and CT scans.
- Past medication and prescription costs.
- Past aids and equipment.
- Past travel costs.
- Past DIY, decorating and gardening costs.
- Past care costs.
- Past domestic assistance costs.
- Past additional expenditure on such items as special diets, additional heating costs and higher phone bills.

Valuations and estimates are commonly required regarding:

- Pre-accident value of goods and/or current salvage value.
- Future vehicle repairs (and any anticipated storage costs).
- Hire of replacement vehicles and possessions (particularly profit-earning chattels).

- Future repairs to damaged goods.
- Proposed medical tests and investigations.
- Proposed medical treatment and/or surgery.
- Future care costs.
- Future domestic assistance.
- Future DIY, decorating and gardening.
- House/flat valuations.
- Future aids and equipment.
- Proposed home improvements.

Utility bills

[C32] In cases where the claimant is incapacitated by reason of the accident and therefore spends more time at home, it is possible to claim for the increased heating, lighting and telephone bills that are likely to result. In order to support such a claim, it is sensible to obtain copy bills in the months preceding the accident to calculate the increase in bills caused by the accident (ignoring any increase due to general rises in the cost of utility bills which would have occurred in any event).

[C33] Further, many claimants quickly fall into debt if they are unable to work following an accident. They should be asked to keep details in relation to any of the following:

- Overdraft interest.
- Credit card interest.
- Loan interest.
- Interest on arrears of mortgage or rent.
- Interest on debts to creditors or suppliers.
- Court and solicitor fees arising out of third party debt recovery.

Bank and credit card statements

[C34] Bank and credit card statements may provide a useful alternative to receipts and invoices. A bank or credit card statement will usually show the date and place where a particular item was bought and its cost (including any foreign exchange rate). Unfortunately, however, details of the item bought are often not included, and witness evidence will usually be required to plug the gap.

[C35] If the claimant's wages were paid directly into a bank account, the statements relating to that bank account will also be a useful way of proving lost earnings. This is particularly relevant in cases where the claimant was paid 'cash in hand' but held a business account into which most of the monies were paid.

AA, BNA and other associations

[C36] Information to assist with the calculation of particular heads of loss is available from a wide range of associations, bodies, charities and websites. 'Facts & Figures' published annually by the Professional Negligence Bar Association provides a handy compilation of useful tables and materials. Alternatively, the reader may wish to contact some of the sources directly:

- Automobile Association, Technical Services, who are able to provide information on motoring costs (www.theaa.com).
- Association of Personal Injury Lawyers (APIL), 33 Pilcher Gate, Nottingham NG1 1QE, who hold an experts database and are able to offer assistance with particular personal injury claims (www.apil.org.uk).
- Association for Victims of Medical Accidents (AvMA), 44 High Street, Croydon, Surrey CR0 1YB (www.avma.org.uk), who also keep a database of recommended experts and are able to offer assistance with particular clinical negligence claims.
- Personal Injury Bar Association (www.piba.org.uk).
- Average earnings and other statistics: the Office for National Statistics (www.statistics.gov.uk).
- Back Care, 16 Elmtree Road, Teddington, Middlesex TW11 8ST, who are able to provide information regarding back claims.
- British Nursing Association (BNA), Care Assessment Services, the Colonnades, Beaconsfield Close, Hatfield, Herts AL10 8YD, who are able to provide national rates for the provision of nursing care.
- Company information: www.hemscott.net.
- Equality and Human Rights Commission (www.equalityhumanrights.com).
- Financial information is available from: www.ft.com; www.uk-invest.com; and www.bloomberg.com.
- Headway National Head Injuries Association, Church Lane, Heavitree, Exeter who are able to provide information regarding the care and treatment of head injuries (www.headway.org.uk).
- Queen Elizabeth Foundation for Disabled People, Leatherhead, Surrey, who are able to provide information regarding rehabilitation, mobility centres, driver training etc (www.qefd.org).
- Spinal Injuries Association, 76 Saint James Lane, London N10 3DF, who are able to provide information regarding the care and treatment of spinal injuries (www.spinal.co.uk).

CRU

[C37]   A statement of the recoupable benefits paid to the claimant can be obtained from the Compensation Recovery Unit ('CRU') at the Department for Work and Pensions, Durham House, Washington, Tyne & Wear NE38 7SF.

6   Statistical and Actuarial Evidence

[C38]   Following the House of Lords' decision in *Wells v Wells*[1], there is a growing trend for the courts to admit and accept statistical and actuarial data. The same can be extremely useful where there is a paucity of other direct evidence. For example, in *Stefanovic v Carter*[2] the claimant was a trainee accountant who was injured in a car accident. At trial, the claimant relied upon the national average earnings statistics in order to support his claim for loss of earnings, which was accepted by the judge, who adopted the traditional multiplier/multiplicand method of assessment. The defendant appealed on the basis that there was insufficient evidence upon which the trial judge could have awarded damages on a multiplier/multiplicand basis. The Court of Appeal rejected this argument, Hale LJ (as she then was) stating[3]:

'The judge was indeed hampered by having no evidence to support the claimant's suggestion that his earnings would have risen to £35,000 per annum. But what he did have was the Professional Negligence Bar Association's survey of facts and figures, which we have been handed. (It is good to see the Professional Negligence Bar taking the lead of the Family Bar in producing sensible tables of useful documentation to take along to the Kingston upon Hull County Court.) Included in our bundle were the rates for full-time females on adult rates, which were clearly quite inappropriate, being much lower than the rates for adult males. The rates for adult males' average earnings in business and financial professions were some £675 gross per week (if we did not include those who were absent) and £624 per week for chartered and certified accountants. If one goes on and looks at the earnings for builders and building contractors, the comparable figure was £315 per week.

One is therefore driven to the conclusion that the judge was entitled to take the multiplier/multiplicand approach because there was clear evidence of a loss of earnings and a continuing loss of earnings. It was speculative and difficult for him to do, but, on the most objective basis that was available to him, the difference between the sort of earnings which the claimant could have looked forward to as a successful and ambitious accountant and those that he could now look forward to as a back-room boy in a small building firm was considerable. Simple arithmetic indicates that it would be difficult indeed to reach the conclusion that the £10,000 per annum net which he took over a lifetime's earnings was so out of line as to be capable of challenge in this court.'

[1]   [1999] 1 AC 345.
[2]   [2001] EWCA Civ 452.
[3]   At [12]–[14].

[C39]   National average earnings statistics have since been used as a starting point (if not the end point) for the assessment of damages for loss of earnings in a number of further cases, especially when considering the career potential of young claimants who were still at school or college at the time of the accident[1]. The data is now easily available online from the Office for National Statistics (ONS) which produces the Annual Survey of Hours and Earnings (see www.statistics.gov.uk). However, when considering the applicability of this data to the facts of any particular case, it is important to remember that the figures are statistical averages. Therefore, there is no good reason to reduce the figure because it was unrealistic to have expected the claimant to have reached management level (at the higher end of the average) if it was equally unrealistic to have expected the claimant to have settled for a very menial job involving little responsibility (at the lower end of the average)[2]. But there are other ways in which parties may seek to distinguish the claimant from the average. First and foremost, there are the inherent qualities, character and upbringing of the claimant. For example, in *M (a child) v Leeds Health Authority*[3] the claimant suffered a catastrophic injury at the age of two. In the circumstances, Sullivan J held that it was not sensible to postulate any particular career path regarding the claimant's earning potential. He therefore took the average female net earnings figure of £14,500 for non-manual work as a starting point. However, account was taken of the claimant's father, who was found to be 'a cut above average', and the multiplicand was increased to £16,000. Secondly, there is the geographical region in which the claimant lives. The Annual Survey of Hours and Earnings provides data which can be disaggregated into place of work by local authority or borough of residence or by place of work. Thought should also be given to whether or not the statistical data are entirely reliable for predicting future earnings of a claimant. For instance, all females in employment have a contractual right under the Equal Pay Act 1970 to pay which is equal to that of men doing the same job, work rated as equivalent or work of equal value. Although female earnings are historically lower than male average earnings in many jobs, the law requires an equalisation and gives women a right to it. Therefore, if earnings extend beyond the immediate future, arguably the appropriate data is the average earnings data for male and females[4].

---

1   See eg *Dorrington v Lawrence* [2001] All ER (D) 145 (Nov), Hooper J; *Stuart v Martin* [2001] All ER (D) 401 (Oct), Owen J; *M (a child) v Leeds Health Authority* [2002] PIQR Q46, QBD, Sullivan J; *McKeown v Munday* [2002] EWHC 725.

2   *Stuart v Martin* [2001] All ER (D) 401 (Oct), Owen J.

3   [2002] PIQR Q46. For an example of a case where the claimant's poor family employment history and reliance upon benefits reduced the award for loss of earnings, by the judge applying a higher discount for contingencies other than mortality, see *Peters v East Midlands Strategic Health Authority* [2008] EWHC 778 (QB) at [84].

4   See further *Clarke v Powell* 11/6/04, Lawtel Document No AM0900740 and *Van Wees v (1) Karkour and (2) Walsh* [2007] EWHC 165 (QB).

7   Expert Evidence

(i)   The Need for Expert Evidence

[C40]   Of course, at least some medical evidence is required in all personal injury/ clinical negligence cases of any significance[1]. In the larger cases, it is likely that a number of different experts will be required in order to calculate the value of particular heads of loss. Common examples of the types of experts used to assist with the valuation of certain heads of loss include:

*   Medical experts – expert medical opinion will often be required regarding attributability of the injury to the accident alleged; condition and prognosis of the claimant's injuries; the need for any further treatment and/or surgery; the need for care; life expectancy; the level of disability generally; the ability to continue with current occupation; disadvantage (if any) on the open labour market; and risk of developing future problems such as arthritis and epilepsy.
*   Quasi-medical expert – these include physiotherapists, chiropractors, osteopaths, acupuncture therapists and speech/language therapists. They are usually instructed to report upon specific treatment needs and the cost of such treatment. They may also be used to report upon the effectiveness of current treatment and to review the need for further treatment.
*   Care experts – care experts are widely used to calculate a claimant's gratuitous and professional care needs, both past and present. They are usually either qualified nurses or occupational therapists. These experts may also assist with evaluating the cost of DIY, decorating and gardening expenses.
*   Aids and equipment experts (usually occupational therapists) – where a claimant is significantly disabled, evidence might be required regarding items necessary

in order for the claimant to lead a more 'normal' life. The aids and equipment needed vary from case to case and are usually injury specific. For example, in a back injury the following items might be indicated: an orthopaedic pillow and mattress, a back roll support and a perching stool. In more serious cases, details of wheelchairs, hoists, special bathing or showering equipment and other home and mobility aids will be needed.

- Case managers – in catastrophic injury cases, a case manager is often needed to organise and co-ordinate the efforts of the claimant's carers. The case manager is responsible for advising on the care needs of the claimant, ensuring that an appropriate care plan is adopted, and keeping the situation under review. A clinical case manager owes his or her duties to the claimant alone (on unilateral instructions) and is a witness of fact rather than being constrained by any expert duties[2]. The case manager can attend conferences without privilege being waived in the discussions. However, in certain (more serious) cases, there might be justification for claiming the costs of two case managers: one acting case manager, and one reviewing case manager who reports to the court. Adopting this approach permits an independent and objective assessment to be made of the ongoing care regime.

- Information technology experts – in catastrophic injury cases, such experts are sometimes useful to recommend particular equipment or making certain improvements to the claimant's home in order to increase the claimant's quality of life and independence.

- Employment consultants – these experts help to quantify the claim for future loss of earnings or disadvantage on the labour market in difficult cases. Care must be taken, however, not to be seduced into using such an expert where the case is relatively simple – eg someone on a fixed salary scale or in a local authority service – where the courts will expect the lawyers to be able to provide calculations themselves[3].

- Accountants and financial experts – these experts are often used to calculate loss of earnings in complex cases or to assess future pension loss.

- Mobility experts – such experts are used to assist with assessing the particular transport needs of the claimant. Usually, occupational therapists, or nursing care advisers, will in practice be able to cover this aspect of a claim, and the need for it will be obvious from the medical reports.

- Housing/accommodation experts (usually architects or surveyors) – the claimant's home may no longer offer appropriate accommodation following injury. An accommodation expert will be able to assess the particular housing needs of the claimant and, in particular, whether their present accommodation can be modified in order to suit the claimant's needs, or alternatively whether new accommodation must be found.

- Education experts – in cases where the claimant will require special schooling or training, these experts are able to identify the claimant's specific needs and to calculate the value of the claim in accordance with the facilities available in the local area.

- Mechanical or engineering experts – these are often used to provide an estimate of the repair costs for a damaged vehicle.

- Statisticians or life expectancy experts – where the claimant has suffered an injury which may affect his or her life expectancy, it may be that an expert can examine a statistical database and prepare a report upon the claimant's predicted lifespan[4].

[1]   By virtue of para 4.3 of the PD to CPR, Pt 16, if the claimant is relying on the evidence of a medical practitioner, the claimant must attach to or serve with his or her particulars of claim 'a report from a medical practitioner about the personal injuries which he or she alleges in the claim'.

[2]   *Wright v Sullivan* [2005] EWCA Civ 656.

[3]   Experts must only be used where necessary: *Liddle v Middleton* [1996] PIQR P36; *Hawkes v London Borough of Southwark* (20 February 1998, unreported), CA; and *Bandegari v Norwich Union Fire Insurance Society Ltd* (20 May 1999, unreported), CA. See also *Prynn v Cornwall CC* (unreported, 6 November 1995), CA.

[4]   Although it should be noted that life expectancy is predominantly a clinical as opposed to statistical issue: *B v RVI & Associated Hospital NHS Trust* [2002] EWCA Civ 348. See further Chapter H, Future Expenses and Losses.

[C41]   Obviously, it should be checked that any expert who is instructed is competent to comment upon the issues involved. This particularly applies in cases where the claimant is a child or patient. Whilst an expert might be excellent at assessing competent adults, they might have little or no experience dealing with minors or those who lack capacity.

(ii)   General Principles under the CPR

[C42]   Under the CPR, the courts have become increasingly wary regarding the use of experts[1]. This has probably been most obvious in personal injury work, where traditionally numerous 'pet' experts were employed by each side in order to support their case.

[1]   *Prynn v Cornwall CC* (unreported, 6 November 1995), CA; *Liddle v Middleton* [1996] PIQR P36; *Hawkes v London Borough of Southwark* (20 February 1998, unreported), CA; and *Bandegari v Norwich Union Fire Insurance Society Ltd* (20 May 1999, unreported), CA. The same is true in the Employment Tribunal: *De Keyser Ltd v Wilson* [2001] IRLR 324.

[C43]   Expert evidence has now been restricted by the court to that which is 'reasonably required to resolve the proceedings'[1]. No permission is required to instruct an expert[2]. But no party may rely upon the written or oral evidence of any expert without the express permission of the court[3]. This rule does not apply to adducing factual witness evidence from treating experts such as case managers, doctors and therapists[4]. However, in terms of seeking permission to rely upon the expert opinion of an independent expert, unfortunately to date there has been relatively little guidance regarding when such permission should be granted, and therefore judges have been left with a very wide discretion. That said, it is clear that, when considering the question of expert evidence, the court must make a judgment on at least three matters[5]:

- Cogency – how cogent the proposed expert evidence will be.
- Usefulness – how helpful the proposed expert evidence will be in resolving any of the issues in dispute.
- Proportionality – how much it will cost and the relationship of that cost to the sums at stake.

1   See CPR, r 35.1.
2   *Hajigeorgiou v Vasilou* [2005] EWCA Civ 236, CA.
3   See CPR, r 35.4(1).
4   See *Wright v Sullivan* [2005] EWCA Civ 656, CA, in relation to case managers, and *Kirkman v Euro Exide Corp* [2007] EWCA Civ 66, CA, in relation to treating doctors.
5   *Mann v Chetty & Patel* (26 October 2000, unreported), CA.

[C44] The difficulty for the claimant's representative is to decide how best to approach the question of expert evidence in order to minimise the chance that permission to rely upon the chosen evidence will be refused (which may, in turn, prevent recovery of the costs involved). Unfortunately, for the large part, decisions regarding expert evidence will have to be made at an early stage in the proceedings when little detail is known about the claim. It is submitted that the main questions to consider when looking at the instruction of any particular expert in a case are as follows:

- Why is the expert evidence needed?
- What will the expert be able to provide that cannot be gained from alternative sources or other methods of calculation?
- Is the instruction of the expert likely to make a significant difference to the outcome of the case?
- Can the claim be properly quantified without the assistance of such an expert?
- Are the costs of instructing the expert proportionate to the value of the claim?

[C45] It should be noted that, once permission has been granted for expert evidence, there should be parity between the parties. Thus, if the defendant is allowed to call evidence from two consultants whose clinical judgment is being impugned, the claimant should be permitted to call two experts in the same field[1]. Likewise, the court may impose limits on the fees and expenses of expert evidence[2] and prevent the parties from calling evidence which exceeds that limit[3].

1   *E S v A Health Authority* [2003] EWCA Civ 1284, [2004] Lloyd's Law Rep Med 90.
2   CPR, r 35.4(4).
3   *Kranidiotes v Paschalir* [2001] EWCA Civ 357.

(iii)   The Initial Medical Report

[C46] In all but the slightest cases of personal injury, it will be necessary to instruct a medical practitioner to prepare a report in respect of the claimant's injuries[1]. Indeed, by virtue of para 4.3 of the PD to CPR, Pt 16, if the claimant is relying upon the evidence of a medical practitioner, the claimant must attach to or serve with his or her particulars of claim 'a report from a medical practitioner about the personal injuries which he or she alleges in the claim'. There is no specific guidance as to what should be contained in this report. The British Medical Association publishes a list of the points which should normally appear in a medical report. In broad terms, the report should cover the circumstances in which the injuries were sustained, the nature and severity of the injuries, the effect of the injuries upon the claimant, the treatment received, any relevant pre-accident information, and provide a prognosis for the future. Additionally, the report should attribute the injuries to some act on the part of the defendant, which is said in the claim to be in breach of a duty to the claimant[2]. In personal injury cases, in accordance with the CPR, the report served with the particulars of claim is likely to be from a jointly selected, if not jointly instructed, expert[3]. In clinical negligence cases, the expert is likely to be unilaterally instructed by the claimant[4] and may just deal with condition and prognosis, leaving the breach of duty and/or causation reports (which might be prepared by different experts) to be mutually exchanged at a later date[5]. Where limitation is a problem, it may be necessary to serve a short report from the claimant's GP or treating doctor and thereafter seek the court's permission to rely upon another report prepared by a doctor specialising in the relevant field[6]. It should be noted that, where a party has unilaterally instructed an expert to provide a provisional or preliminary report (eg to be discussed at a conference) before a final report is prepared, the earlier report(s) will not be disclosable to the other parties[7].

[1]   Where the claimant only suffered minor cuts and bruising which healed very quickly, it may be disproportionate to obtain a full medical report and it may be possible to prove the claimant's injuries in other ways, eg photographs, the claimant's witness evidence and/or the claimant's medical records (the claimant's discharge summary or Accident & Emergency admission record can often be a useful document in this regard).

[2]   Under the old procedure, RSC Ord 18, r 12, the plaintiff had to serve a medical report substantiating all the personal injuries alleged in the statement of claim and attributing them to the matters complained of: *Nur v John Wyeth & Brother Ltd* [1996] 7 Med LR 300; *Lort v Thames Water Utilities Ltd* (29 January 1993), CA; *B v John Wyeth & Brother Ltd* [1992] 1 WLR 172; *L & W v John Wyeth & Brother Ltd* (6 May 1992), Ian Kennedy J. Whilst the wording of the new rule does not go as far as the old, the court may be persuaded to exercise its case management powers against the claimant if the medical evidence served with the particulars of claim does not at least outline the broad nature of the injuries that were sustained and, without necessarily giving away the claimant's whole case in respect of causation, attribute them to the defendant's alleged wrongdoing.

[3]   See further at para **[C63]**.

[4]   See further *Oxley v Penwarden* [2001] Lloyd's Rep Med 347, CA; and *Simms v Birmingham Health Authority* [2001] Lloyd's Rep Med 382, Curtis J.

[5]   Notwithstanding the new 'cards on the table' approach, were the defendant to have sight of the claimant's medical evidence dealing with breach of duty and causation served with the particulars of claim, the defendant is likely to gain significant tactical advantage from the same. Therefore, the usual direction in clinical negligence cases is that there be mutual exchange of expert evidence regarding breach of duty and causation.

[6]   Note that para 4.3 of the PD to CPR, Pt 16 does not state that the medical report served with the particulars of claim necessarily has to be from the same medical practitioner that the claimant wishes to rely upon at trial.

[7]   *Jackson v Marley Davenport* [2004] EWCA Civ 1225; *Hajigeorgiou v Vasilou* [2005] EWCA Civ 236, CA.

(iv)   Instructions to the Expert

[C47]   A model letter of instruction to a medical expert is annexed to the Personal Injury Pre-Action Protocol. It should be noted that any information (eg a draft witness statement or another expert's report) supplied to an expert for the purposes of obtaining advice should be considered as part of the material instructions, and should therefore be protected from disclosure under CPR, r 35.10(4)[1]. The exception to this is where there are grounds for believing that the expert's statement of instructions was 'inaccurate or incomplete'[2]. The expert should be reminded of his or her duty to the court and the requirements of CPR, Pt 35[3]. Although there is no assumption that a person employed by a party to the litigation could not give expert evidence[4], in the exercise of its discretion, the court may prevent a person giving expert evidence because of their inability to carry out the role of an independent expert, given their close relationship with one of the parties[5].

1   *Lucas v Barking, Havering & Redbridge Hospitals NHS Trust* [2003] EWCA Civ 1102.
2   CPR, r 35.10(4)(b).
3   Failure to comply with the rules may mean that the expert is prevented from giving evidence. See further *Stevens v Gullis* [2000] 1 All ER 527, in which the Court of Appeal upheld a judge's order prohibiting the defendant from relying upon an expert who had repeatedly failed to comply with para 1.2 of the PD to CPR, Pt 35.
4   *Field v Leeds City Council* (2000) Times, 18 January.
5   *Liverpool Roman Catholic Archdiocesan Trust v David Goldberg QC* [2001] 4 All ER 950.

(v) Problems with Particular Experts

[C48] In the experience of the authors, judges now have to be persuaded by cogent arguments to permit the use of certain experts, particularly in cases which have been allocated to the fast track. However, it is to be noted that, if an expert has been instructed prior to proceedings and that expert's report is already to hand, it is often easier to convince a judge about the usefulness of that evidence. Conversely, where the expert in question has not yet been instructed, the court will often look much more closely at the need for and cost of obtaining such evidence, and thus is more likely to conclude that permission is not warranted. Gaining permission to rely upon the following experts has probably created the most difficulty, and we offer some specific guidance regarding their instruction.

Care experts

[C49] It is often suggested by judges that the claimant's representatives should be able to estimate the amount of care required by the claimant and apply the applicable professional rates (subject to a probable discount if the care was provided gratuitously). Such an approach is certainly both justified and proportionate in a straightforward case involving a limited care claim, eg following a simple broken leg. However, the instruction of a care expert would tend to be indicated in the following situations:

* Where there has been a significant amount of past care provided over an extended period involving numerous different applicable hourly rates.
* Where there is an ongoing need for care which requires assessing and costing for the future.
* Where the claimant has suffered an unusual type of injury and his or her care needs are not readily identifiable.

[C50] In a small claim, it might be appropriate for a care expert to provide a brief report in summary form first before deciding whether or not to seek a full report. In a small to medium-size claim, it might be appropriate for the care expert, assuming that the expert is suitably qualified, to provide a joint opinion in relation to care needs as well as the need for aids and equipment. Some care experts will even address the claimant's needs regarding domestic assistance, DIY, decorating and gardening within one and the same report. This approach keeps the costs down, whilst making the judge's job easier by having everything in one document.

[C51] For catastrophic injury claims, the same approach is not generally recommended. In such cases, there is more likely to be dispute regarding the individual heads of loss due to the sums of money involved, and small differences of emphasis between experts may result in very large differences in cash terms. It is, therefore, prudent to have separate experts providing detailed reports concerning their own specialised area.

Employment consultants

[C52] The use of these experts has particularly faced challenge under the CPR. Their evidence is often criticised as speculative and unnecessary[1]. However, it is submitted that, in some cases, their evidence can be an invaluable aid to assessing quantum.

[1]   See further *Larby v Thurgood* [1993] PIQR 128.

[C53] There are no hard and fast rules regarding when an employment consultant should be instructed in a particular case. Such evidence is usually most helpful in the following scenarios:

- Where the claimant is unable to continue in his or her chosen occupation by reason of the injuries, but has an undefined residual earning capacity which might involve re-training or re-qualifying.
- The claimant is a minor and it is necessary to predict what the claimant's earning capacity would have been but for his or her injuries.
- The claimant had an unusual or unique job for which there are no average earnings statistics.
- The claimant had a professional job with a set hierarchy and pay structure, eg an army officer, a civil servant or a teacher, but where there were clear opportunities for moving up the ladder, yet there is limited information to show what level the claimant would have eventually attained and how long it would have taken to get there. It might also be beneficial to find a comparator who started at the same level as the claimant.
- The claimant had a job which provided remuneration far in excess of the national average for that type of work. For example, a chef working in a prestigious London restaurant might have earnings way above the average earnings for cooks/chefs suggested by the Annual Survey of Hours and Earnings. Another example is that of a successful fashion photographer, who is likely to earn far more than the average wedding photographer.
- There is a real risk that the claimant will lose their job in the foreseeable future by reason of their injuries and it is unclear what alternative work they would be able to do in the local area and how long it would take them to find such work.
- Where there is reason to think that the available national statistics are too compressed in the categories they offer to allow for an accurate comparison. An example might be architects and many manual building trades which are classed generally under broad headings which disguise a great variability of earnings.

[C54] When considering whether or not to instruct an employment consultant, the following checklist may provide a useful guide. The more questions to which the answer is 'Yes', the less likely it is that the instruction of an employment consultant is indicated.

- Are you able to predict:
  (i) loss of earnings up to time of trial; and
  (ii) future career earnings (with promotion, advancement and redundancy)?
- Are you able to comment upon the possible effects of:
  (i) the local labour market; and
  (ii) the vicissitudes of the relevant industrial sector?
- Does the claimant's disability now exclude him or her from the labour market?
- Are you able to assess the claimant's:
  (i) job search period;
  (ii) training options; and
  (iii) future earnings?
- Are you sure that other factors such as planned changes in sheltered employment provision etc are not going to affect the claimant's future employability?

[C55] In smaller or more straightforward cases, employment consultants can be asked just to provide or endorse some statistical data in order to help calculate the loss of earnings claim. In these cases, the relevant material might be in the public domain but it would take the layman a disproportionate amount of time to find the sources. The employment consultant thus takes on the role of adviser and does not provide a full report or give evidence to the court. In an advisory capacity, the employment consultant may also offer assistance with a number of other matters, including identification of the central issues in a case, consideration of any Part 36 offers, and seeking to persuade the court why a full employment assessment might be necessary.

Forensic accountants

[C56] Forensic accountants have often been involved in the past to help calculate loss of earnings in difficult cases and to assist with quantifying pension loss.

[C57] As regards loss of earnings, the assistance of a forensic accountant is generally indicated in the following situations:

- Where a self-employed claimant does not have a steady pattern of earnings, and projection of future loss is not straightforward.
- Where the claimant was a partner in a multi-party business and it is necessary to evaluate his lost share of the profits.
- Where the claimant was a director or owner of a company whose profitability is significantly affected by reason of the claimant's injuries.

[C58] As regards pension loss, this is no longer considered the preserve of accountants. Unless the terms of the pension are particularly complicated, courts will usually require the claimant's representatives to assess this loss themselves. See further the Appendices at **[Q20]–[Q25]** regarding what information is needed to calculate this loss.

(vi)   Refusal of the Claimant to Undergo Examination

[C59]   A general stay of proceedings may be granted in the following situations:
- Where the claimant refuses to disclose his or her medical records[1].
- Where the claimant refuses to submit to a medical examination or test[2].
- Where the claimant fails to submit to a functional evaluation test[3].
- Where the claimant refuses to submit for interview with the defendant's employment expert[4].

[1]   *Bennett v Compass Group UK* [2002] EWCA Civ 642.
[2]   *Laycock v Lagoe* [1997] PIQR P518; *Prescott v Bulldog Tools Ltd* [1981] 3 All ER 869; and *Hill v West Lancashire Health Authority* (1996, April) PMILL at p 18.
[3]   *Rimron v Khan* [1999] CLY 48, cf *Tunstall v Street* [1999] CLY 328.
[4]   *Donnelly v KD Scaffolding* [1996] CLY 2114, cf *Larby v Thurgood* [1993] ICR 66; and *Lackey v Wolfe* [1998] CLY 348.

[C60]   In *Laycock v Lagoe*[1] the Court of Appeal applied a two-stage test. First, it should be asked whether or not the interests of justice require the test which the defendant proposes. If the answer to this question is no, the stay will be refused. However, if the test is in the interests of justice, the court must consider the second question, namely whether or not the claimant has put forward a substantial reason (ie one which is not imaginary or illusory) as to why the test should not be undertaken. Account should be taken of the proposed benefit of the test to the litigation process, on the one hand, and the weight of the objection of the declining party, on the other. On the facts of this case, although the proposed MRI scan was held to be in the interests of justice, the claimant's reasons for refusing the test were held to be substantial and therefore the stay was refused. The claimant's concerns included the possibility that the scan might trigger a further psychotic episode, the possibility that there might be an adverse reaction to the chemical dye used, and the possibility of the claimant requiring sedation or an anaesthetic.

[1]   [1997] PIQR P518.

[C61]   It should be noted that the reason why a stay has to be applied for in the above cases is that the court has no power to require the claimant to submit to a medical examination or test[1]. However, the power to grant a stay is not necessarily of general applicability and, for example, the defendant may not be entitled to a stay of proceedings where the claimant refuses to permit the defendant's solicitor to view his or her injuries or scarring[2]. Further, any stay of proceedings must be proportionate to the claimant's refusal. Therefore, if, for example, the claimant refuses an examination by a psychiatrist, this does not automatically entitle the defendant to a stay of the whole proceedings. It may well be that other aspects of the claimant's claim can still proceed, such as the assessment of pain, suffering and loss of amenity for physical injuries and any past expenses/losses not dependent upon the existence of a psychiatric injury[3].

[1]   In *Edmeades v Thames Board Mills Ltd* [1969] 2 QB 67, CA; cf *Cosgrove v Baker* (14 December 1979, unreported), referred to in vol 1 of *Kemp & Kemp* at 15–038.
[2]   *Francom v Williams* [1999] CLY 1416.
[3]   *James v Bailey Gibson* [2002] EWCA Civ 1690.

(vii) The Single Joint Expert

[C62] The assumption under the CPR[1] is that, whenever possible, expert evidence will be given by a single joint expert[2]. However, it is important to distinguish between the following types of 'joint' expert:

- The 'agreed' or 'jointly selected' expert under the Personal Injury Pre-action Protocol (PIPAP).
- The single 'jointly instructed' expert.
- The court-appointed joint expert.

---

[1] Note that this is also the preferred course in the Employment Tribunal: *De Keyser Ltd v Wilson* [200] IRLR 324.
[2] Note that it is possible to displace this presumption, particularly in the field of clinical negligence. See further *Oxley v Penwarden* [2001] Lloyd's Rep Med 347, CA; and *Simms v Birmingham Health Authority* [2001] Lloyd's Rep Med 382, Curtis J. However, these cases relate to liability experts, and there remains a presumption that non-medical quantum experts will be instructed on a single joint basis, even in catastrophic injury cases: *Re P (a child)* (6 November 2001, unreported), CA.

The agreed or jointly selected expert under the PIPAP

[C63] The PIPAP urges the joint selection of experts by the parties[1]. A party is to give notification to the other parties before any expert is instructed, by supplying a list of one or more suitable experts[2]. The other parties are then given 14 days to object to the list of named experts[3]. However, the Court of Appeal has confirmed that an 'agreed' or 'jointly selected' expert under the PIPAP is different from a 'jointly instructed' expert. In *Carlson v Townsend*[4], the claimant's solicitors refused to disclose a report prepared by an expert they had instructed pursuant to the defendant's agreement under the PIPAP. It was held that it was not possible to override the claimant's privilege in the report and, therefore, the claimant could lawfully withhold its disclosure. The difficulty in this case was that the claimant served a report from a second, non-agreed expert and the defendant realised straightaway that the nominated expert's report must have been unsatisfactory. A way round this problem might be for the claimant to list a number of suggested experts. Assuming that objection is not taken to all of these experts, if an unfavourable report is obtained from one of the nominated experts, a further report may be obtained from one of the other agreed experts on the list without the defendant ever finding out[5].

---

[1] Personal Injury Pre-action Protocol, para 2.14.
[2] Personal Injury Pre-action Protocol, para 3.15.
[3] Personal Injury Pre-action Protocol, para 3.17.
[4] [2001] EWCA Civ 511, [2001] 3 All ER 663.
[5] It should be noted that the defendant who seeks to rely upon a further expert is in a different position and will probably have to disclose any previous report before permission will be granted to rely upon another expert: *Beck v Ministry of Defence* [2003] EWCA Civ 1043. See further at para **[C84]**.

The single jointly instructed expert

[C64] The single jointly instructed expert is an expert whom the parties agree to instruct on a joint basis, usually after proceedings have begun. The expert's fee is split between the parties, and each party is entitled to receive a copy of the expert's report.

However, no party is allowed to hold a conference with the joint expert in the absence of the other parties[1].

> [1]   *Mutch v Allen* [2001] EWCA Civ 76; *Re P (a child)* [2002] 1 WLR 210, CA; *Smith v Stephens* (26 January 2001, unreported), QBD.

[C65]   The use of the single joint expert is most prevalent in fast track cases where, given the size of the claim, it would not be proportionate for each party to instruct their own expert[1]. Once a single joint expert has been agreed, the instructions to that expert should also be agreed. If agreement cannot be reached, then each party should send separate instructions[2]. These instructions must at the same time be sent to the other parties[3].

> [1]   However, it should be noted that the court is generally keen to curtail the use of experts in all cases under the CPR, and the use of single joint experts is not necessarily limited to smaller cases: see eg the Court of Appeal's approach in *Townsend v Superdrive Motoring Ltd* [2000] CLY 323, where the judge's decision was that the orthopaedic expert could also deal with the claimant's facial injuries, and either the psychiatrist or psychologist could deal with other reports if necessary.
> [2]   See *Daniels v Walker* [2000] 1 WLR 1382, per Lord Woolf at 1383g.
> [3]   CPR, r 35.8(2).

[C66]   In the normal course of events, a jointly instructed expert would not need to attend trial or be cross-examined, and any issues can be resolved by way of response to questions. If necessary, the court does retain the power to order that the single joint expert should attend court to be cross-examined[1]. However, in such a case it is obviously sensible if the joint expert is told in advance what topics are to be covered and any fresh material is adduced in advance of the hearing[2]. It should be noted that, if the joint expert does not attend court, this does not mean that the court is bound to accept the evidence or conclusions of the joint expert. For example, where the joint expert has made an obvious error regarding the figures in his or her report, the court is entitled to substitute its own figures[3].

> [1]   *Re P (a child)* [2002] 1 WLR 210, per Lord Woolf at 216A–216B; *Austen v Oxford City Council* (17 April 2002, unreported), QBD.
> [2]   See further *Topek v National Westminster Bank plc* [2002] EWCA Civ 42, per Dyson LJ at [29].
> [3]   See *Woolley v Essex CC* [2006] EWCA Civ 753.

The court-appointed single joint expert

[C67]   Under CPR, r 35.7 the court has the power to appoint a single joint expert for both parties. This power is usually exercised in one of two situations. The first situation arises where both parties wish to instruct a particular kind of expert but are unable to agree which expert should be instructed. In this scenario, assuming it is not appropriate or proportionate for each party to instruct their own expert, an application may be made to the court for it to decide which expert should be instructed. Any application should be supported with cogent reasons for the selection of the preferred expert over and above the alternatives. At the hearing of the application, it is useful to have the following information to put before the court: a detailed curriculum vitae of the expert; a breakdown of the amount of claimant/defendant work that the expert takes on; a summary of the expert's forensic experience (in particular the number of times the expert has given evidence in court); details of the expert's fees; details of the expert's availability; and the timeframe in which the expert is able to examine the claimant and prepare his or her report.

[C68] Secondly, the court may direct that the expert evidence on a particular issue be restricted to that of a single expert where the parties each wish to rely upon an expert they have already instructed. An example of this is *Baron v Lovell*[1], where the defendant served a medical report very late in the day. The judge at first instance held that the medical evidence in the case be restricted to that of the claimant's expert. There were a number of factors influencing the judge's decision, including the fact that the evidence of the defendant's expert did not differ largely from the evidence of the claimant's expert, it was not a sizeable claim, and that permitting the defendant to rely upon the further report was likely to delay the final hearing. In the circumstances, the Court of Appeal upheld the judge's decision.

[1]   [2000] PIQR P20.

[C69] Once the court has appointed a single joint expert, each party may give instructions to that expert[1]. The court may also make orders regarding payment of the expert's fees and any inspection, examination or experiments to be carried out[2].

[1]   See CPR, r 35.8(1).
[2]   See CPR, r 35.8(3), (4). By virtue of CPR, r 35.8(5), unless the court otherwise directs, the instructing parties are jointly and severally liable for the payment of the expert's fees.

(viii)   Challenging a Joint Expert

[C70] Occasionally, where the amount at stake is substantial, the court may permit a party to rely upon the evidence of another expert. In the Court of Appeal case of *Daniels v Walker*[1] the infant claimant had been severely injured in a road traffic accident. A care expert had been instructed on a joint basis who recommended an extensive care regime for the claimant. The defendant was not happy with this care report and wanted facilities to instruct a second care expert of his nomination. It was held that the defendant should be allowed to instruct his own care expert, although it would have been preferable to have first asked questions of the joint expert. Lord Woolf said[2]:

'... the fact that a party has agreed to adopt [a joint expert] does not prevent that party being allowed facilities to obtain a report from another expert, or, if appropriate to rely upon the evidence of another expert.
    In a substantial case such as this, the correct approach is to regard the instruction of an expert jointly by the parties as the first step in obtaining expert evidence on a particular issue. It is to be hoped that in the majority of cases it will not only be the first step but the last step. If, having obtained a joint expert's report, a party, for reasons which are not fanciful, wishes to obtain further information before making a decision as to whether or not there is a particular part (or indeed the whole) of the expert's report which he or she may wish to challenge, then they should, subject to the discretion of the court, be permitted to obtain that evidence.
    In the majority of cases, the sensible approach will not be to ask the court straight away to allow the dissatisfied party to call a second expert. In many cases it would be wrong to make a decision until one is in a position to consider the position in the round. You cannot make generalisations, but in a case where there is a modest sum involved

a court may take a more rigorous approach. It may be said in a case where there is a modest amount involved that it would be disproportionate to obtain a second report in any circumstances. At most what should be allowed is merely to put a question to the expert who has already prepared a report.'

¹   [2000] 1 WLR 1382.
²   [2001] 1 WLR 1382 at 1387d.

[C71] It is interesting to note that, in *Daniels v Walker*[1], the defendant sought to challenge the report of the jointly appointed expert because, in the experience of the defendant's insurers, the costs claimed in the report vastly exceeded the care costs involving other infant claimants with similar disabilities. On this basis, the Court of Appeal held it was just to allow the defendant facilities for their own expert. It was not necessary to have shown that the joint expert's report was flawed in some way, eg by being incorrect, inconsistent or biased. Therefore, as long as the claim is substantial, a party's belief (based on reasonable grounds) that the joint expert's report is plainly wrong might be enough to obtain the court's permission to call a second expert[2].

¹   [2000] 1 WLR 1382.
²   Although see *Kay v West Midlands Strategic Health Authority* LTL 1/2/2008, Lawtel Document No AC0115739, in which HHJ MacDuff QC (as he then was) refused permission to the claimant to rely upon a further expert in the field of assistive technology, even though the new expert's costings added £600,000 to the claim.

[C72] The difficulty is defining what is meant by 'substantial' and deciding when an issue is worth enough to attempt to counter the joint expert's evidence. In *Daniels v Walker*[1] it was said that the issue regarding care could involve 'hundreds of thousands of pounds'. It is submitted that, although it might not always need to involve a six-figure sum, the chances of challenging a joint expert's report in a fast track case are remote. It should be emphasised that the defendant in *Daniels v Walker* had good reasons for thinking (from past experience in apparently similar cases) that the jointly instructed expert was out on a limb compared with that which other experts might advise. The case is not authority for the proposition that, without such good reason, a party to a significant claim may simply expect to be allowed an expert of their own.

¹   [2000] 1 WLR 1382.

[C73] It is worth noting that the claimant will often be in a better position to challenge a joint expert's report than the defendant. This is because the claimant may submit him or herself for a further examination or interview, and a second report can be obtained prior to deciding whether or not to challenge the joint expert's view. If this report is positive, the claimant can then apply to the court armed with the second expert's report. Having the second report available should make it much easier to conceive of reasons which are not fanciful as to why the joint expert's report is open to criticism and why the second expert's evidence should be permitted. For the defendant to obtain a second expert report requires the claimant to consent to having another examination or interview[1]. Such consent is unlikely to be forthcoming if he or she is content with the existing joint expert's report. Therefore, unless the defendant has the benefit of a shadow expert, the defendant's representatives will be left to think up reasons to challenge the joint expert's opinion on their own.

¹   See further *Beck v Ministry of Defence* [2003] EWCA Civ 1043 and at para **[C84]**.

[C74] Some useful guidance was provided by Neuberger J (as he then was) in *Cosgrove v Pattison*[1] regarding the factors to be taken into account when considering an application to permit a further expert to be called:

'In my judgment, although it would be wrong to pretend that this is an exhaustive list, the factors to be taken into account when considering an application to permit a further expert to be called are these. First, the nature of the issue or issues; secondly, the number of issues between the parties; thirdly, the reason the new expert is wanted; fourthly, the amount at stake and, if it is not purely money, the nature of the issues at stake and their importance; fifthly, the effect of permitting one party to call further expert evidence on the conduct of the trial; sixthly, the delay, if any, in making the application; seventhly, any delay that the instructing and calling of the new expert will cause; eighthly, any other special features of the case; and finally, and in a sense all embracing, the overall justice to the parties in the context of the litigation.'

[1]   [2001] CPLR 177. In a personal injury context, these principles were applied in *Kay v West Midlands Strategic Health Authority* LTL 1/2/2008, Lawtel Document No AC0115739, in which HHJ MacDuff QC (as he then was) refused permission to rely upon an alternative expert in assistive technology because there were no exceptional circumstances, the claimant had suggested the original expert and had never criticised his report, and the strong impression was that many of the items recommended by the new expert would not be recovered. The *Cosgrove v Pattison* principles have also been applied to the situation where a party seeks to call a second expert after the joint discussion with the opposing party's expert: see further *Stallwood v (1) David and (2) Adamson* [2006] EWHC 2600 (QB).

(ix) Questions to Experts

[C75] Once the expert has reported, the parties have 28 days to put any written questions to the expert about the contents of their report[1]. Technically, any questions should only be for the purposes of 'clarification' of the report[2]. However, it is common for detailed questions to be put which either raise new matters or ask the expert to consider issues which have been omitted from his or her report[3].

[1]   See further CPR, r 35.6.
[2]   CPR, r 35.6(2)(c).
[3]   Support for this practice was provided in *Mutch v Allen* [2001] EWCA Civ 76, in which the Court of Appeal referred to the following notes in the White Book: '[r 35.6(2)(c)] is a useful provision … It enables a party to obtain clarification of a report prepared by an expert by his opponent or to arrange for a point not covered in the report (but within his expertise) to be dealt with'.

[C76] The expert's answers to the questions raised by the parties will be treated as part of the expert's report[1]. Therefore, assuming the expert's report is admissible in evidence, so will be the answers to the questions. The Court of Appeal also sent a clear warning, regarding the unfairness of refusing to permit the answers to questions raised of experts to be adduced in evidence, in *Mutch v Allen*[2]. In this case, the claimant had instructed a medical expert to report upon the claimant's injuries following a car accident. There was an issue in the case as to whether or not the claimant had been wearing his seat belt and whether the extent of his injuries would have been lessened if he had been wearing one. The answers to the questions asked by the defendant of the claimant's expert indicated that the claimant had not been wearing his seat belt and that his injuries would have been considerably less severe had he been wearing it. At a case management hearing the judge refused the defendant permission to rely upon the expert's answers, since it would mean allowing the defendant to rely upon evidence served outside the time limit provided by an earlier court order. The Court of Appeal had no hesitation in permitting the expert's letter answering the defendant's questions into evidence, and also gave permission for the expert to attend court in order to give oral evidence, with each party having permission to cross-examine him.

1   CPR, r 35.6(3).
2   [2001] EWCA Civ 76.

[C77]   It is now clear that, where a joint expert has prepared a report and one party is not satisfied with it, the first step is for that party to submit written questions to that expert[1]. If the answers to those questions still do not allay that party's concerns regarding the expert's evidence, steps may be taken in order to challenge the joint expert by applying for permission to instruct and admit into evidence the report of a further expert. Failure to put questions to the joint expert first, before seeking to challenge that expert's evidence, is unlikely to find favour with the court[2].

1   *Daniels v Walker* [2000] 1 WLR 1382.
2   See eg *Avery v Gough* [2001] 2 CL 38.

(x)   Expert Discussions/Meetings

General

[C78]   The court may direct that each party's respective experts hold a discussion to (a) identify the issues in the proceedings, and (b) where possible to reach agreement on the issues[1]. Such discussions are now commonplace and often much turns on the outcome of the same. The general presumption appears to be that a discussion/ meeting will take place between respective experts in an attempt to narrow the issues between the parties[2], and it will not be a breach of a party's Art 6 right to a fair trial under the European Convention of Human Rights[3]. The content of the discussion and any correspondence between the experts remains privileged and must not be referred to unless all parties agree[4]. Further, any agreement reached between the experts will not bind a party unless the parties expressly agree to be bound by the agreement[5]. Indeed, there are circumstances in which a party may apply for permission to call a second expert where the first expert had modified his opinion following a joint discussion with the other side's opposing expert for reasons that could not properly and fairly support his revised decision[6].

1   CPR, r 35.12(1).
2   Such a direction appears in the model draft directions for multi-track claims, and also the model directions for clinical negligence claims, in the Queen's Bench Division of the Royal Courts of Justice
3   *Hubbard v Lambeth, Southwark & Lewisham Health Authority* [2001] EWCA Civ 1455.
4   CPR, r 35.12(4). See further *Robin Ellis Ltd v Mal Wright Ltd* [1999] 2 WLR 745.
5   CPR, r 35.12(5).
6   *Stallwood v (1) David and (2) Adamson* [2006] EWHC 2600 (QB), applying *Cosgrove v Pattison* [2001] CPLR 177.

Format and agenda for meetings between experts

[C79] Save in the most straightforward cases, it is appropriate for the parties to draw up an agenda for the discussions between experts of like disciplines[1]. Unless the lawyers become involved in this process, often issues are not discussed and a further meeting has to be arranged. Generally speaking, the agenda should contain a list of closed questions which may be answered 'Yes' or 'No'[2]. Where the parties cannot agree the agenda, each party should send its own agenda to the experts[3].

1   See paras 18.5 and 18.6 of the Protocol for the Instruction of Experts to give Evidence in Civil Claims (the Protocol to CPR, Part 35).
2   See further para 5(1) of the Guidelines on Experts' Discussions published by the Clinical Disputes Forum (Clinical Risk, vol 6, p 149), and para 26(d) of the Code of Guidance on Expert Evidence, published by a working party chaired by Sir Louis Blom-Cooper QC.
3   See further the model directions for use in clinical negligence claims in the Queen's Bench Division of the Royal Courts of Justice, London

Presence of lawyers at expert meetings

[C80] It is rare for lawyers to attend expert meetings, and the general presumption is that lawyers do not need to be present[1]. Indeed, it is relatively uncommon for there to be a meeting at all (and the experts will usually discuss matters over the telephone). However, in rare cases the court may be persuaded to allow each party's lawyer (or a representative for each party) to attend the expert meeting[2]. Such permission is only likely to be granted in high-value, complex cases where the lawyers might assist the experts as regards the appropriate law and it would be proportionate for the lawyers to be present. An alternative might be to have the discussion/meeting recorded or an independent person to be agreed between the parties in order to chair the discussion/meeting[3].

1   *Hubbard v Lambeth, Southwark & Lewisham Health Authority* [2001] EWCA Civ 1455. See also para 18.8 of the Protocol for the Instruction of Experts to give Evidence in Civil Claims (the Protocol to CPR, Part 35).
2   See eg *Woodall v BUPA Hospitals Ltd* (30 October 2000, unreported), QBD.
3   *Hubbard v Lambeth, Southwark & Lewisham Health Authority* [2001] EWCA Civ 1455.

Joint statements

[C81] The court will usually direct that, following any expert discussion/meeting, the experts prepare a statement for the court showing (a) the issues upon which they are agreed, and (b) those issues upon which they disagree and a summary of their reasons for disagreeing[1]. Whilst the content of the discussion remains privileged, the outcome of the discussion – ie the joint statement – is not privileged[2]. A party will not be bound by the contents of a joint statement unless they expressly agreed to be so bound; therefore, even if agreement is reached between opposing experts, a party may indicate that it is simply evidence that must be assessed as part of all the evidence[3].

1   CPR, r 35.12(3).
2   *Robin Ellis Ltd v Mal Wright Ltd* [1999] 2 WLR 745; *Aird v Prime Meridan Ltd* [2006] EWCA Civ 1866.
3   CPR, r 35.12(5). See further *Huntley v Simmonds* [2010] EWCA Civ 54.

Unilateral meetings

[C82]   It is not appropriate for one party to meet with a joint expert without the consent of all the other parties[1].

¹   *Re P (a child)* (6 November 2001, unreported), CA; *Smith v Stephens* (16 October 2001, unreported), QBD.

(xi)   Change of Expert's Opinion

[C83]   In *The Ikarian Reefer*[1], Cresswell J said:

'If, after exchange of reports, an expert witness changes his view on a material matter having read the other side's expert's report or for any other reason, such change of view should be communicated (through legal representatives) to the other side without delay and where appropriate with the court.'

¹   [1993] 2 Lloyd's Rep 68. See further *Vernon v Bosley (No 2)* [1999] QB 18 as regards the lawyer's duty not to mislead the court or his opponent.

(xii)   Change of Expert

[C84]   Where a claimant is not happy with an expert report, it is possible for the claimant to submit him or herself to another examination (if necessary) and for a report to be prepared by a different expert. Assuming it has not already been served, the first report will remain privileged from disclosure[1]. If proceedings have been issued and a court order permits expert evidence in a particular discipline but does not name specific experts, there is no problem in a claimant relying upon the new expert's report[2]. However, where a defendant wants to rely upon a new expert, the position is more difficult because the defendant will usually need to be granted facilities by the claimant for a further examination and the claimant is likely to refuse unless a good reason is provided. If necessary, an application can be made to the court to obtain permission to rely upon a further expert, although the court is unlikely to grant such permission unless the defendant provides a good reason why another expert report is required and discloses the report upon which it no longer wishes to rely[3]. The rationale behind this rule is to prevent 'expert shopping', which is strongly discouraged by the court[4]. However, if there are good reasons for wishing to instruct another expert – eg the original expert has retired or died – the court may order that the claim be stayed until the claimant submits him or herself to a further examination. The Court of Appeal was recently persuaded to make such an order on behalf of a defendant (having given an undertaking that it would disclose the report obtained from the first expert) where it claimed that it had completely lost confidence in the first expert it had instructed[5]. On a like–for–like basis, if permission is granted for the parties to rely upon specific named experts, the court may order a claimant to disclose the first expert's report as a condition before granting permission to rely upon a substitute expert[6].

¹   *Carlson v Townsend* [2001] EWCA Civ 511; *Hajigeorgiou v Vasilou* [2005] EWCA Civ 236, CA.
²   *Hajigeorgiou v Vasilou* [2005] EWCA Civ 236, CA.
³   *Lane v Willis* [1972] 1 WLR 326; *Beck v Ministry of Defence* [2003] EWCA Civ 1043, in which Simon Brown LJ stated: 'I do not say that there could never be a case where it would be appropriate

to allow a defendant to instruct a fresh expert without being required at any stage to disclose an earlier expert's report. For my part, however, I find it difficult to imagine any circumstances in which that would be properly permissible …'.

4   *Hajigeorgiou v Vasilou* [2005] EWCA Civ 236, CA.
5   *Beck v Ministry of Defence* [2003] EWCA Civ 1043.
6   *Hajigeorgiou v Vasilou* [2005] EWCA Civ 236, CA.

(xiii)   Shadow Experts

[C85]   A shadow expert is an expert instructed by a party, without express permission from the court, who advises that party in relation to the expert evidence in his or her area. Such an expert will usually be retained to advise upon the claim as it progresses. It is uncertain how common such experts are, but they are likely to be limited to larger cases.

(xiv)   The Role of Expert Evidence at Trial

[C86]   If a case proceeds to trial, it should be noted that, although expert evidence is important, it is only part of the evidence which the judge needs to assess along with all the other evidence[1]. This equally applies to jointly instructed experts, whose evidence the court is not necessarily bound to accept, even where the expert is not called to give evidence, especially where there is an obvious flaw in the expert's reasoning[2]. Clarke LJ (as he then was) put it this way in *Coopers Payen Limited v Southampton Container Terminal Ltd*[3]:

'All depends upon the circumstances of the particular case. For example, the joint expert may be the only witness on a particular topic, as for instance where the facts on which he expresses an opinion are agreed. In such circumstances it is difficult to envisage a case in which it would be appropriate to decide this case on the basis that the expert's opinion was wrong. More often, however, the expert's opinion will only be part of the evidence in the case. For example, the assumptions upon which the expert gave his opinion may prove to be incorrect by the time the judge has heard all the evidence of fact. In that event the opinion of the expert may no longer be relevant, although it is to be hoped that all relevant assumptions of fact will be put to the expert because the court will or may otherwise be left without expert evidence on what may be a significant question in the case. However, at the end of the trial the duty of the court is to apply the burden of proof and to find the facts having regard to all the evidence in the case, which will or may include both evidence of fact and evidence of opinion which may interrelate.'

1   *Coopers Payen Limited v Southampton Container Terminal Ltd* [2003] EWCA Civ 1223; *Tucker v Watt* [2005] EWCA Civ 1429; *Huntley v Simmonds* [2010] EWCA Civ 54.
2   See eg *Woolley v Essex CC* [2006] EWCA Civ 753.
3   [2003] EWCA Civ 1223. See also *Tucker v Watt* [2005] EWCA Civ 1429.

8   The Claimant's Instructions

(i)   Progress Reports

[C87]   It is important that the claimant is encouraged to keep his or her representatives updated regarding his or her condition and continuing losses/expenses. If liability is not contested, it might be possible to obtain an interim payment to cover these costs.

(ii)   Expert Evidence

[C88]   Many experts will require additional information before they can prepare their reports. Often, this information will be gathered directly by way of an interview with the claimant. However, sometimes the claimant's representatives will have to make specific inquiries.

[C89]   The claimant's instructions should be taken regarding the contents of any expert report. If the report is not a joint report, instructions should be taken before the report is disclosed to the other side. That way, errors can be corrected or an expert might be prevailed upon to alter a damaging section of their report[1]. Alternatively, claimants may indicate that they do not wish to rely upon the report at all, in which case, assuming the report remains privileged, it may be discarded[2]. Such errors are not easily rectifiable after a report has been disclosed without drawing the attention of the other party. Further, where a party has disclosed a report but no longer wishes to rely upon its contents, it is open to any other party to use that expert report at the trial[3].

[1]   Following *Carlson v Townsend* [2001] EWCA Civ 511, [2001] 3 All ER 663, it is not improper to adopt this practice with an 'agreed' or 'jointly selected' expert under the PIPAP.
[2]   *Carlson v Townsend* [2001] EWCA Civ 511, [2001] 3 All ER 663.
[3]   CPR, r 35.11 (although it is at least arguable that the court's permission would be required to rely upon such a report by virtue of CPR, r 35.4).

[C90]   In more complex cases, it is often advisable to arrange a face-to-face meeting with the claimant, the expert(s) and counsel in order to take precise instructions regarding major issues. Care should be taken to limit the expert's involvement in any such conference to the matters upon which expert guidance is sought – in particular, because the expert is in the position of giving evidence to the court, as a primary responsibility, and must detail the sources of his or her instructions. The line between that which is privileged and that which is not is arguably unclear, and prudence dictates the exercise of caution: the expert should advise the litigation team, rather than be part of it. However, it should be noted that only final reports need to be disclosed, and preliminary or provisional reports are protected from scrutiny by the other side[1]. Where there is likely to be a dispute regarding loss of earnings or residual earning capacity (or any other significant part of the claim), it is sensible to assess the claimant's credibility as a witness at an early stage. This is particularly important where there is any issue of malingering or exaggeration of symptoms. If the claimant does not make a reliable witness, he or she should be warned at an early stage regarding the prospects of succeeding on the various proposed heads of loss and the dangers associated with exaggerating the claim[2].

[1]   *Jackson v Marley Davenport* [2004] EWCA Civ 1225. But see further *Vernon v Bosley (No 2)* [1999] QB 18 regarding the duty of ongoing disclosure, particularly where the evidence changes and/or it comes to light that experts have given different opinions regarding the claimant's condition and prognosis in another context, such as in child care proceedings.
[2]   For example, see *Molloy v Shell UK Ltd* [2001] EWCA Civ 1272; *Painting v University of Oxford* [2005] EWCA Civ 161; *Devine v Franklin* [2002] EWHC 1846 (QB); and *Booth v Britannia Hotels Ltd* [2002] EWCA Civ 529.

(iii)   Expenses/Losses

[C91]   Importantly, care should be taken to ensure that the claimant and/or the litigation friend understands what heads of loss are being claimed and the reasons why they are required. In particular, it should be checked that the claimant is able to and wants to take advantage of the aids and appliances claimed on his or her behalf. For example, in *Blair v Michelin Tyre*[1] the trial judge rejected the claim for a second wheelchair because the claimant did not seem keen on it and it 'might seldom, if ever, be used'. Further, in *Dorrington v Lawrence*[2], Hooper J disallowed a claim for a computer and £600-worth of software because the claimant already had a computer which he did not use and it was unclear whether the claimant had the capacity to make use of the software that was recommended.

[1]   LTL 19/3/2002, Lawtel Document No AC0102843, HHJ Marr-Johnson sitting as a judge of the QBD.
[2]   [2001] All ER (D) 145 (Nov).

9   The Claimant's Best Interests

[C92]   Occasionally, it will be necessary to establish that a particular item of expense and/or course of action is or is not in the claimant's best interests. This is generally done through factual witness statements or, alternatively, expert evidence. An example of this is the decision regarding whether or not proposed medical treatment is in the best interests of a claimant who lacks capacity[1].

[1]   *Re F* [1990] 2 AC 1; *Airedale NHS Trust v Bland* [1993] AC 789; *Re C (a minor) (HIV test)* [1999] 2 FLR 1004; *Re A (Mental Patient: Sterilisation)* [2000] 1 FLR 549; *Re S (Adult Patient: Sterilisation: Patient's Best Interests)* [2001] Fam 12; *Re A (Children) (Conjoined Twins: Medical Treatment)* [2001] Fam 147.

10   Witness Statements

(i)   Introduction

[C93]   The schedule of loss has to be supported by evidence. Whilst a lot of the supporting evidence may be contained in various expert reports, each head of loss should be specifically commented upon in the witness evidence[1]. Failure to detail the nature and basis upon which each claim is made may result in that particular claim being struck out.

[1]   By virtue of CPR, r 32.2(1), any fact must be proved by the evidence of witnesses by their oral evidence at trial or their written evidence at any other hearing. This is particularly important in respect of disposal hearings which, by virtue of CPR, r 32.6 and para 12.4(1)(b) of the PD to CPR, Pt 26, are to be conducted on the papers alone, unless the presence of the witnesses is requested at the hearing or the court otherwise directs.

(ii)   Evidence in Chief

[C94]   Under the CPR the general rule is that a witness statement will stand as the witness's evidence in chief[1]. It is possible to ask permission to amplify a statement by oral evidence at court[2], but only if there is no good reason not to confine the evidence of the witness to the contents of his witness statement[3]. It is therefore crucial to make sure that the statement covers all relevant matters.

1   CPR, r 32.5(2).
2   CPR, r 32.5(3).
3   CPR, r 32.5(4).

[C95]   Should it not be possible to serve a witness statement, then a party may apply without notice to serve a witness summary instead[1]. A witness summary should summarise either the evidence which would otherwise be included in a witness statement or, alternatively, the matters upon which the serving party intends to question the witness[2]. Unless the court orders otherwise, a witness summary must include the name and address of the intended witness and be served within the same period for service of the witness statement[3].

1   CPR, r 32.9(1).
2   CPR, r 32.9(2).
3   CPR, r 32.9(3), (4).

(iii)   Form of the Statement

[C96]   Unless a witness statement complies with the form specified in the PD to CPR, Pt 32, the court may refuse to admit it as evidence and may refuse to allow the costs arising from its preparation[1]. The required form of a witness statement may be summarised as follows:

- The witness statement must be headed with the heading title of the proceedings[2].
- The following information should be displayed at the top right hand corner: the party on whose behalf the statement is made; the initials and surname of the witness; the number of the statement in relation to that witness; the identifying initials and number of each exhibit referred to; and the date that the statement was made[3].
- The statement must as far as is practical be in the witness's own words; be expressed in the first person; state the full name of the witness; his or her residential or professional address; his or her occupation; and whether or not he or she is a party to the proceedings or an employee of such a party[4].
- An indication must be given as to which statements are made from the witness's own knowledge and belief and which are made from other sources[5].
- All exhibits referred to by the witness should be verified, clearly marked and remain separate from the statement[6].
- The statement should be on durable A4 paper; with a 3.5cm margin; be fully legible; be securely bound; have each page consecutively numbered; be divided into numbered paragraphs; have all numbers expressed in figures; and give in the margin the reference to any document or documents mentioned[7].
- The statement should usually be in chronological order[8].
- The statement must be verified by a statement of truth[9].

1   See para 25.1 of the PD to CPR, Pt 32.
2   See para 17.1 of the PD to CPR, Pt 32.

3   See para 17.2 of the PD to CPR, Pt 32.
4   See para 18.1 of the PD to CPR, Pt 32.
5   See para 18.2 of the PD to CPR, Pt 32.
6   See para 18.3 of the PD to CPR, Pt 32.
7   See para 19.1 of the PD to CPR, Pt 32.
8   See para 19.2 of the PD to CPR, Pt 32.
9   See para 20.1 of the PD to CPR, Pt 32.

(iv)   Content of the Statement

[C97]   A properly drafted witness statement on behalf of the claimant would usually include details regarding the following matters:

- The circumstances surrounding the cause of the claimant's injuries.
- The injuries themselves, both physical and psychological.
- The treatment received, surgery undergone and/or medication taken.
- Any continuing treatment and/or medication for injuries.
- The need (if any) for future treatment and/or surgery.
- Prior work history including qualifications, training, skills and experience (exhibiting a curriculum vitae and any relevant training certificates).
- The effect of the injuries on the claimant's general lifestyle, including mobility, dressing, sleep, personal hygiene and independence.
- The effect of the injuries upon the claimant's capacity to work.
- The effect of the injuries upon the claimant's domestic situation and ability to carry out household chores such as cooking, cleaning and washing.
- The effect of the injuries upon the claimant's ability to carry out DIY, decorating and/or gardening.
- The effect of the injuries upon the claimant's hobbies and leisure activities.
- The effect of the injuries upon the claimant's social life and relationships.
- The need (if any) for care.
- The need (if any) for domestic assistance.
- Any pre-existing injuries or supervening injuries.
- Any claim for disadvantage on the open labour market.
- Any claim for loss of congenial employment.
- All past losses and expenses arising out of the accident.
- All future losses and expenses arising out of the accident.
- A summary of the claim.

[C98]   Although the situations in which it would be beneficial to prepare witness statements on behalf of people other than the claimant in order to support the schedule of loss are limitless, such statements are usually helpful from the following lay witnesses:

- Providers of gratuitous care and/or domestic assistance to the claimant.
- Close friends and relatives who are able to comment upon the effects of the claimant's injuries, especially where the claimant has suffered a personality change. Similar evidence should also be obtained from any apparently reliable objective observer (eg the class teacher; the vicar; the GP; the community police officer) who is able to speak about these matters and paint a fair picture of the before and after injury situations.

- The claimant's ex-partner where, by reason of the injuries, the claimant's relationship has been strained or has come to an end (care must be taken: the pros of advancing this evidence have to be balanced against the cons that any residue of personal hostility engendered by the break-up of the relationship might colour what the ex-partner has to say).
- The claimant's referees (academic and professional) who might be able to provide an idea as to the claimant's career potential but for his or her injuries.
- Work colleagues (especially supervisors/managers) where the claimant's capacity for work and/or future potential (particularly in terms of promotion/ advancement) is in issue. Other workmates may often be useful as comparators if they were in a similar position to the claimant at the time of the injury but have, for instance, since gained promotion/bonuses etc.
- The claimant's accountant or business adviser (who can exhibit relevant documents and accounts).
- The claimant's sporting/leisure contacts with whom the claimant can no longer enjoy a particular activity.
- The claimant's case manager[1].
- The claimant's carers.
- The claimant's treating doctors or therapists[2].

---

[1]   The Court of Appeal has held that the claimant's case manager giving evidence is a witness of fact and is not bound by the usual CPR, Part 35 regime which applies to experts: *Wright v Sullivan* [2005] EWCA Civ 656.

[2]   In *Kirkman v Euro Exide Corp* [2007] EWCA Civ 66, the Court of Appeal held that a witness statement from the claimant's treating surgeon was a statement of fact and did not require permission from the court, because he was not expressing expert opinion regarding what most competent surgeons would have said in the same situation; he was merely speaking for himself.

[C99]   The amount of detail to put in a witness statement depends upon the type and size of claim. Generally speaking, there are two rules: first, the more detail the better; and secondly, the detail must not go beyond that which is relevant. An attempt should be made to ensure that the amount of detail provided on each point is proportionate to the significance of that particular issue. If the statement is relatively long, it is preferable to split the statement into sections with clear subheadings. As far as possible, all the information should be recorded in chronological order. Any useful documents relating to the points covered in the statement should be exhibited for ease of reference. The danger of detail – especially that which is only of tangential relevance – is that, if it is any less than wholly accurate, it may be challenged, and the challenge may affect the apparent credibility of the witness on crucial matters. It is often difficult to assess whether the detail given by a witness will actually 'stand up' at trial, and if there is any doubt, it is better to leave out the additional information in order to avoid the risk of compromising the claim.

[C100]   By virtue of s 1 of the Civil Evidence Act 1995, evidence is no longer inadmissible due to the fact that it is hearsay. However, a party wishing to rely upon hearsay evidence contained in a statement must serve that statement on the other parties[1]. Interestingly, the service of the statement itself qualifies as the hearsay notice under s 2(1)(a) of the Civil Evidence Act 1995[2]. Should the party not be calling any oral evidence in respect of the hearsay evidence, then that party must notify the others that the witness is not being called and give the reasons why[3].

1   CPR, r 33.2(1).
2   CPR, r 33.2(1)(b).
3   CPR, r 33.2(2).

[C101]   Given the possible consequences of signing an incorrect statement of truth, it is vital that a witness, and particularly the claimant, reads through their statement extremely carefully before signing it[1]. Of course, at the end of the day it is the witness and no one else who will have to speak to his or her statement and be cross-examined upon the same, and it is therefore the maker of the statement who is ultimately responsible for checking the accuracy of what is said.

1   In a worst case scenario, a claimant who deliberately signs an incorrect statement of truth may be found guilty of contempt of court: for an example in a personal injury context where committal proceedings were brought, see further *Kirk v Walton* [2008] EWHC 1780 (QB); [2009] EWHC 703 (QB).

(v)   Supplemental Statements

[C102]   As and when new facts emerge which are relevant to the outcome of the claim, supplemental witness evidence should be prepared. For example, if the claimant's employment position has changed since filing the original statement, then an updated statement should be prepared. Supplemental statements should also be used to explain, so far as is possible, unexpected events such as a claimant's 'good day' acrobatics being caught on video surveillance.

[C103]   If an alteration has to be made to a statement, it must be made by the maker of the statement and correctly initialled[1]. A statement which has been altered without being initialled may only be used in evidence with the permission of the court[2].

1   See para 22.1 of the PD to CPR, Pt 32.
2   See para 22.2 of the PD to CPR, Pt 32.

11   Interim Payments

[C104]   The court retains a power to award interim payments under s 32 of the Senior Courts Act 1981 and s 50 of the County Courts Act 1984. The court also has the power to award periodical payments to be made in the interim[1]. A claimant may make an application for an interim payment not exceeding a 'reasonable proportion' of the damages likely to be recovered under CPR, r 25.6. The application must be served at least 14 days before the hearing of the application and be supported by evidence[2]. But what should this evidence consist of? Generally speaking, what the claimant wants the interim payment for is not strictly relevant, since the court is not concerned with what the claimant does with his or her money[3]. However, in practice it is often desirable, if not necessary, to prepare a witness statement in support of any application for a significant interim payment, in order to persuade the court why it should exercise its discretion in the claimant's favour[4]. Tactically, when acting for claimants in higher value claims, it is prudent to apply for an interim payment at an early stage and, thereafter, appoint a case manager to set up a care regime and/or purchase various aids and equipment on behalf of the claimant. Assuming all goes well and the claimant benefits from the care provided and/or items purchased, this makes it much harder for a defendant subsequently to argue that the care or aids/ equipment claimed were unreasonable. Defendants appreciate this difficulty, and attempts are sometimes made to resist the award of an interim payment in case it might prejudice the level playing field.

1   Damages Act 1996, s 2A(5), as amended by Courts Act 2003, s 100.
2   CPR, r 25.6(3).
3   *Stringman (a minor) v McArdle* [1994] 1 WLR 1653. See also *Tinsely v Sarker* [2004] EWCA Civ 1098.
4   See further *Campbell v Mylchreest* [1999] PIQR Q17, CA, per Sir John Balcombe at Q21.

[C105]   In *Campbell v Mylchreest*, Auld LJ put the position as follows[1]:

'It is true that, as a guide to the exercise of that discretion, it indicates that the court should normally order sought interim payments within the amount of the likely recoverable damages without investigation or consideration of the [claimant's] intended use of the money.

However, there may be instances where there may be another matter or other matters relevant to the exercise of the discretion. Mr Mackay has helpfully suggested possible examples in other circumstances: first, that the payment is sought too close to the trial to justify ordering it; second, that the sought payment may be too small for it to be worthwhile as an exercise of the power; and third, where a [claimant] is not getting on with the claim and simply putting off the day of trial by repeated applications for interim payments.

Returning to this case, where the use to which a [claimant] intends to put money received by way of interim payment might prejudice the fair conduct of the trial in some way, it is, in my view, a relevant factor for consideration by the judge, along with the *Stringman (a minor) v McArdle*[2] starting point, when exercising his discretion whether to order a payment. More particularly, where the use to which the [claimant] intends to put the money might pre-empt in some way the outcome of an important issue in the trial, that is a matter relevant to the exercise of the discretion.'

1   [1999] PIQR Q17 at Q24, CA.
2   [1994] 1 WLR 1653.

[C106]   In larger cases where periodical payments may be awarded for some heads of future pecuniary loss, the Court of Appeal has recently given guidance as to the appropriate approach for first-instance judges when considering interim payment applications. In *Cobham Hire Services Ltd v Eeles*[1], Smith LJ giving the lead judgment of the court (with which Dyson and Thomas LLJ agreed) held that the judge must consider which heads of loss may be awarded by way of periodical payment and only award a reasonable proportion of the likely capital sum (made up of general damages, future accommodation and past losses). However, there are exceptions to this where, for example, there is an urgent need to purchase alternative accommodation, and the judge can confidently predict that more heads of loss will be capitalised by the trial judge in order to fund the purchase of the new home[2].

1   [2009] EWCA Civ 204. See further Chapter O at **[O34]–[O43]**.
2   See *Cobham Hire Services Ltd v Eeles* [2009] EWCA Civ 204 at para [38], and *Braithwaite v Homerton University Hospitals NHS Foundation Trust* [2008] EWHC 353 (QB).

12   Other Evidence

(i)   Photographs

[C107]   Pictures of the claimant's injuries can be an excellent way of conveying the pain and discomfort that must have been suffered. Also, a few pictures taken at various intervals are a very convenient way of depicting the different stages of the claimant's convalescence. For example, in a case involving a serious leg fracture the claimant might spend several days in hospital undergoing surgery, followed by some time in a wheelchair, after which the claimant might be able to start gentle weight-bearing with the aid of crutches before being able to walk normally again.

[C108]   Good-quality, close-up colour photographs are especially useful in cases involving scarring or significant bruising. There are some photographers who specialise in this type of work. In smaller cases, however, the claimant should be encouraged to take his or her own photographs, making sure to use plenty of light. However, no case of scarring should be assessed as to the appropriate level of damages without seeing the claimant's injuries personally. Photographs can be misleading (not only over-dramatising scars but also having the opposite effect) and much depends upon the very personal reaction a claimant has to his or her disfigurement.

[C109]   Photographs may also be useful to show an overrun garden (which can no longer be tended to by the claimant), decoration works that had to be done by builders, or the damage caused to vehicles, possessions or objects.

(ii)   Video Evidence

Admissibility

[C110]   Video evidence may be adduced as long as notice is given not later than the latest date for serving witness statements[1]. Where the video evidence is put in by a party to disprove an allegation which appears in a witness statement, notice must be given at least 21 days before the hearing at which the party intends to rely upon the video evidence[2]. Once a party has given notice of intention to rely upon video evidence, he or she must give every other party an opportunity to inspect it and to agree to its admission without further proof[3].

[1]   CPR, r 33.6(4).
[2]   CPR, r 33.6(5)(b).
[3]   CPR, r 33.6(8).

'Day in the life of' videos

[C111]   In catastrophic cases, a 'day in the life of' video can be a very graphic way of showing the claimant's daily life and care regime. However, the response to such videos varies, and care should be taken to ensure that the video is not over the top.

Specific heads of loss

[C112]   Videos may also be invaluable to explain why a certain head of loss is necessary, eg by showing the benefits of having a hydrotherapy pool at home[1] or showing the advantages of one type of stair lift over another. Such evidence may be particularly useful where there is an issue about the claimant's general level of cognitive ability or insight into his or her condition[2]. A defendant might also wish to use video evidence in order to demonstrate the benefits of (cheaper) alternative aids and equipment or accommodation.

[1]   *Coram v Cornwall & Isles of Scilly Health Authority* (16 April 1996), reported in the APIL Newsletter, vol 6, Issue 4, p 15.
[2]   See eg *M (a child) v Leeds Health Authority* [2002] PIQR Q48 at Q50.

Specific procedures or techniques

[C113]   Video evidence may be a useful way of showing how a technical procedure is carried out. In particular, surgical and laboratory procedures are often more easily understood with the benefit of video evidence.

Surveillance videos

(1)   THE NEED FOR SURVEILLANCE EVIDENCE

[C114]   Sometimes, the defendant will suspect that the claimant is less disabled or has made a better recovery than he or she makes out. Insurers will often be prepared to employ private investigators to videotape claimants performing their daily activities in order to see whether or not they demonstrate a greater degree of mobility than revealed in the medical reports and/or witness statements. The cost of obtaining such evidence may be repaid many times over if the claimant is shown to have been exaggerating or malingering.

(2)   THE USES OF SURVEILLANCE EVIDENCE

[C115]   The main uses of surveillance evidence can be summarised as follows:

- To attack a party's credibility and show that he or she cannot be relied upon as a witness of truth[1].
- To demonstrate that the claimant has made a better recovery from his or her physical injuries and is not as disabled as he or she claims[2].
- To show that the claimant has been working.
- To show that the claimant has been able to partake in leisure activities or holidays.
- To support allegations of contributory negligence.

[1]   See eg *Sutton v Tesco Stores plc* (30 July 2002, unreported), QBD.
[2]   See eg *Morgan v Millet* (29 September 2000, unreported).

(3)   DISCLOSURE OF SURVEILLANCE EVIDENCE

[C116]   Generally speaking, the 'cards on the table approach' of the CPR requires that any relevant evidence (including surveillance evidence) should be disclosed as soon as possible, and cost penalties may result from deliberately withholding the disclosure of such evidence for tactical reasons[1]. However, the court retains a discretion to allow a defendant to delay disclosure of video surveillance evidence for a reasonable time, until the claimant has committed him or herself to updated witness evidence and/or an updated schedule of loss has been served[2]. This limits the claimant's ability to explain away what is shown by the surveillance evidence, and increases the chances that there will be discrepancies between what is said in the claimant's witness statement and what is shown on the video evidence. However, the late admission of surveillance evidence amounting to an 'ambush' may be refused[3].

[1]   *Ford v GKR* [2000] 1 WLR 1397.
[2]   *Uttley v Uttley* [2002] PIQR P123, CA; and *Booth v Britannia Hotels Ltd* [2002] EWCA Civ 579.
[3]   *O'Leary v Tunnelcraft Ltd & Others* [2009] EWHC 3438 (QB).

(4)   Refusal of permission to rely upon evidence

[C117]   The court retains a general discretion to control and exclude evidence[1]. There may be circumstances in which it is proper to prohibit the defendant from obtaining video evidence. For example, where the claimant suffers from a psychiatric condition which has already been made worse by being the subject of video surveillance evidence, the court may prohibit the use of further surveillance evidence in order to prevent harm to the claimant and infringement of his or her rights[2]. Alternatively, permission may be refused where the evidence is served too late and would amount to an 'ambush' necessitating the adjournment of the trial[3].

[1]   CPR, r 32.1(2).
[2]   See eg *Progl v Greenstein* (7 November 2002), QBD, Cox J, reported in the APIL Newsletter, vol 12, Issue 6, p 23.
[3]   *O'Leary v Tunnelcraft Ltd & Others* [2009] EWHC 3438 (QB).

(5)   The impact of the Human Rights Act

[C118]   There is a clear tension between Art 8 of the European Convention on Human Rights, on the one hand, which provides that everyone has the right to respect for his private and family life; and Art 6, on the other, which entitles litigants to a fair hearing. Prior to the CPR, it was generally the case that video evidence could be relied upon even if obtained unlawfully, eg by trespass or deception[1]. Under the CPR, the starting point continues to be that, where video evidence has been obtained which substantially undermines the claimant's case, it will usually be in the interests of justice to admit the evidence and allow the defendant to cross-examine the claimant upon it[2]. Although a clear breach of Art 8 may operate to prevent the admissibility of evidence[3], the Court of Appeal's decision in *Jones v University of Warwick*[4] has limited the scope for arguing that unlawfully obtained surveillance evidence should be excluded. In this case, the defendant had instructed an inquiry agent who had obtained covert surveillance evidence of the claimant in her own home by posing as a market researcher. It was common ground that the inquiry agent was guilty of trespass and had obtained entry to the claimant's home by deception. The claimant contended that the evidence should be excluded under the court's discretion provided by CPR, r 32.1(2) and Art 8(1) of the European Convention on Human Rights. The

Court of Appeal upheld HHJ Harris' decision that the evidence should be admitted. Lord Woolf explained the court's reasoning as follows[5]:

> 'The court must try to give effect to what are here the two conflicting public interests. The weight to be attached to each will vary according to the circumstances. The significance of the evidence will differ as will the gravity of the breach of Article 8, according to the facts of the particular case. The decision will depend upon all the circumstances. Here, the court cannot ignore the reality of the situation. This is not a case where the conduct of the defendant's insurers is so outrageous that the defence should be struck out. The case, therefore, has to be tried. It would be artificial and undesirable for the actual evidence, which is relevant and admissible, not to be placed before the judge who has the task of trying the case. We accept Mr Owen's submission that to exclude the use of the evidence would create a wholly undesirable situation. Fresh medical experts would have to be instructed on both sides. Evidence which is relevant would have to be concealed from them, perhaps resulting in a misdiagnosis; and it would not be possible to cross-examine the claimant appropriately. For these reasons we do not consider it would be right to interfere with the Judge's decision not to exclude the evidence.'

[1]   *R v Sang* [1980] AC 402; *R v Khan* [1997] AC 558.

[2]   *Rall v Hume* [2001] EWCA Civ 146, per Potter LJ at [19]: 'In principle, as it seems to me, the starting point on any application of this kind must be that, where video evidence is available which, according to the defendant, undermines the case of the claimant to an extent that would substantially reduce the award of damages to which she is entitled, it will usually be in the overall interests of justice to require that the defendant should be permitted to cross-examine the plaintiff and her medical advisors upon it, so long as this does not amount to trial by ambush'.

[3]   See eg *Rall v Hume* [2001] EWCA Civ 146, [2001] 3 All ER 248, where video evidence showing the claimant was adduced into evidence save for any footage of the claimant within her own home or within her child's nursery. See further *R v Loveridge* (2001) 2 Cr App R 591; and *Hesketh v Courts plc* (14 May 2001), Weymouth CC, referred to in John Foy 'Videos and The Human Rights Act' [2002] JPIL, Issue 2/02.

[4]   [2003] EWCA Civ 151.

[5]   At [28].

(6)   Costs

[C119]   However, it should be noted that there was a sting in the tail for the defendants in *Jones v University of Warwick*[1], as Lord Woolf continued[2]:

> 'While not excluding the evidence it is appropriate to make clear that the conduct of the insurers was improper and not justified ... The fact that the insurers may have been motivated by a desire to achieve what they considered would be a just result does not justify either commission of trespass or the contravention of the claimant's privacy which took place ...
>
> Excluding the evidence is not, moreover, the only weapon in the court's armoury. The court has other steps it can take to discourage conduct of the type of which complaint is made. In particular it can reflect its disapproval in the orders for costs which it makes. In this appeal, we therefore propose, because the conduct of the insurers gave rise to the litigation over the admissibility of the evidence which has followed upon their conduct, to order the defendants to pay the costs of these proceedings to resolve this issue before the district judge, Judge Harris and this court even though we otherwise dismiss the appeal. This is subject to Mr Owen having an opportunity to persuade us to do otherwise. In addition, we would indicate to the trial judge that when he comes to deal with the question of costs he should take into account the defendant's conduct

which is the subject of this appeal when deciding the appropriate order for costs. He may consider the costs of the inquiry agent should not be recovered. If he concludes, as the complainant now contends, that there is an innocent explanation for what is shown as to the claimant's control of her movements then this is a matter which should be reflected in costs, perhaps by ordering the defendants to pay the costs throughout on an indemnity basis. In giving effect to the overriding objective, the court must while doing justice between the parties, also deter improper conduct of a party while conducting litigation. We do not pretend that this is a perfect reconciliation of the conflicting public interests. It is not; but at least the solution does not ignore the insurer's conduct.'

1   [2003] EWCA Civ 151.
2   At [29] and [30].

Video link evidence

[C120] The court has a general discretion to allow witnesses to give evidence through a video link or by other means[1]. The use of this power is becoming increasingly popular when presenting evidence from foreign experts or witnesses and helps to keep costs down.

1   CPR, r 32.3.

13   Advice on Evidence and Part 18 Requests

(i)   The Need for Advice on Evidence

[C121] The advice on evidence is an essential step in any significant personal injury or clinical negligence claim. It is all too easy for a litigator who is in charge of handling a claim on a day-to-day basis to overlook the weaknesses of their client's case and not focus upon the evidence required to support or challenge each head of loss that is claimed. Whilst there is now a much greater degree of specialisation than ever before, and most personal injury practitioners work in teams or whole departments of skilled professionals, it is often extremely valuable to have independent and objective input from external counsel in relation to the evidence needed to prepare a case for trial. Once familiar with a case, it becomes difficult to put oneself in the position of the judge who has only recently picked up the papers (most judges only see the case papers shortly before the trial begins). Those all-important first impressions can be forgotten. Since cases are won or lost on the quality and presentation of the evidence called, it is prudent to obtain the advice of external counsel to advise upon this issue at a relatively early stage in proceedings.

[C122] A recent example of this is provided by *Smith v McRae*[1], in which Newman J gave the following salutary message[2]:

'I wish only to add a few words on the evidence in this case. I share his concern about the way in which the evidence for the claimant was presented. If the method of preparation and presentation adopted in this case reflects a common circumstance in connection with personal injury cases in the district court it has, in my judgment, departed too far from the basic principle that a claimant must prove his case by evidence capable of supporting the conclusions to which the court is invited to come. It may be that the days of a formal advice on evidence are long gone but the need which such advice fulfils remains. Someone on each side in litigation such as this, with sufficient skill to do so, must, at some timely stage before trial, draw up a list of the issues which remain contentious and then consider whether or not there is evidence available to meet those issues. The lack of concern evident from the judgment in this case from the deputy district judge about the sufficiency and quality of the evidence and the apparent alacrity with which he felt able to make assumptions gives cause for concern. No doubt he had in mind the principles often expressed to the effect that judges must often simply do their best or approach an issue on a broad brush basis, but these principles have limitations. There is a need for evidence and there is a need for an analysis of such evidence; then the judge can make findings of fact by drawing inferences and doing the best he can, but on the evidence which is available.'

1   [2003] EWCA Civ 505.
2   At [31].

[C123]   Of course, the English legal system is adversarial. The role of the court is not to investigate, but to adjudicate. A judge will only make decisions upon the issues before the court (as presented by the pleadings) based upon the evidence which is adduced. It is therefore crucial to ensure that the pleadings correctly identify the issues in dispute and that the evidence called addresses those issues. In the new era of 'cards on the table' litigation, it is no longer permissible to ambush an opponent with arguments raised for the first time at trial. Under the CPR, the court has become much more involved with the management of cases and the control of evidence. Permission is required before expert reports may be relied upon[1], admissible evidence may be excluded[2] and there is a need for proportionality[3]. Failure to comply with the relevant rules and practice directions is likely to lead to the imposition of cost penalties.

1   CPR, r 35.4(1).
2   CPR, r 32.1(2).
3   CPR, r 1.1(2)(c).

(ii) What the Advice Should Cover

[C124]   The following is a check-list of the main issues that external counsel should be asked to consider:

(1) What are the issues in the claim?
(2) Do the pleadings (including the schedule and counter-schedule) accurately reflect those issues, and what amendments, if any, should be made to the same?
(3) What evidence is required to prove the client's case in relation to each issue?
(4) Is a conference needed? If so, who should attend?
(5) Witness evidence:
-   How persuasive is the witness evidence that has been prepared to date? Are the statements ready for service? Do the statements cover everything they need to or are any amendments, deletions or additions needed?
-   Who else should be providing witness statements of fact, and what should be covered by the witnesses in their statements?
-   Which witnesses should attend trial, and should the witness evidence be updated before trial?

(6) Expert evidence:
- How persuasive is the expert evidence that has been obtained to date?
- What amendments, if any, need to be made to the reports?
- Are there any issues which need to be clarified or questions which need to be asked of the experts?
- What further expert evidence is needed? If so, identify the relevant expert discipline and make a suitable recommendation as regards choice of expert.
- If there is a conflict of expert evidence – whose evidence is likely to be preferred and why?
- Which experts should permission be sought to call oral evidence from at trial?

(7) Other evidence:
- Is there any need for photographic or video evidence?
- Is there a need for diagrams or sketch plans?
- Should any other information be sought, eg statistical, actuarial or epidemiological evidence?
- Is there any need for instructing an inquiry agent?

(8) Disclosure:
- Are the witness statements/expert reports ready for disclosure?
- Has the disclosure which has been provided by the other parties (under the pre-action protocol or otherwise) been reasonable, or should any further documents be requested?
- Should any information or documents be sought from any third parties?

(9) What further steps could and should need to be taken in respect of:
- The documentary evidence?
- The witness evidence?
- The expert evidence?

(10) Procedural steps:
- Is this a case in which a periodical payments order is to be sought, and if so, what form should it take and what evidence might be required, eg as regards proving security of future payments or establishing the most appropriate index for uprating future payments?
- Are there any grounds for seeking strike out or summary judgment of an issue or whole claim?
- Is there a need for an interim payment?
- Is an award for provisional damages appropriate?
- Is a split trial appropriate?
- Should any issues be tried as preliminary issues?
- Should a Part 20 claim be made? If so, against whom?
- Is there any need to make an application for specific disclosure? If so, what documents should be sought from whom?
- Is there any need for a Part 18 request – if so, what should such a request be asking?
- Should a notice to admit facts be served? If so, what should the same be covering?
- Should witness summonses be served?
- Should a structured settlement or personal injury trust be considered?
- Are any other procedural steps appropriate or necessary?

(11) Tactics:
- What tactics should be employed in this case in order to maximise the chances of a successful outcome?
- Should mediation or a round table meeting be considered?
- Should a Part 36 offer/payment be made? If so, what form should the offer/payment take and at what level should it be pitched?

(12) Trial bundle:
- What documents should go in the trial bundle?
- Are there any documents which should be excluded or omitted from the bundle?
- How should the evidence be presented?

(13) Next steps:
- Set out any additional steps which need to be taken in order to prepare the case for trial and to meet the case that is likely to be presented by the other parties.

(iii)   Part 18 Requests

The need for a Part 18 request

[C125]   There is no reason why Part 18 requests for further information cannot be directed towards quantum issues. For example, a claimant may wish to know from a defendant employer what the current applicable rates of pay are, and whether he or she would have been eligible for any pay rises. A defendant, on the other hand, may wish to inquire as to the claimant's planned retirement age, pension provision or travel expenses.

The timing of the request

[C126]   Generally speaking, a Part 18 request should be delayed until after: (i) disclosure; (ii) exchange of witness evidence; and (iii) exchange of expert evidence. The reason being that the information required may be supplied in accordance with the ordinary case management directions, and the need to respond to a formal Part 18 request will only serve to increase costs. However, sometimes such information is essential in order to put an accurate value on the claim, especially when considering a Part 36 offer or payment, and therefore the request should be made without undue delay.

D Non-Pecuniary Loss (General Damages)

1 Introduction

(i) Definition

[D1] In this chapter we look at non-pecuniary losses or general damages. The term 'general damages' covers a number of heads of loss, and is used as a collective term for damages which are not special damages, ie those heads of loss which, by their very nature, have to be estimated. This chapter will concentrate on non-pecuniary damages awarded for what is sometimes known as 'personal loss': in other words, the loss that denotes all the harm and disadvantage that is inflicted directly and personally on the victim as a result of their injury.

[D2] Past pecuniary expenses and losses are dealt with in Chapter E, and future pecuniary expenses and losses (which are also technically categorised as general damages, due to the inability precisely to calculate the amount to which the claimant is entitled) are dealt with in Chapter F.

(ii) Heads of General Damage

[D3] The main heads of general damage include:

- Pain, suffering and loss of amenity.
- Handicap on the open labour market/*Smith v Manchester* award[1].
- Loss of congenial employment.
- Loss of enjoyment (eg of a holiday).
- Loss of leisure time.
- Loss of marriage prospects and marriage breakdown.
- Loss of use (eg of a vehicle).

[1] Since this head of loss is more properly considered as a form of future loss of earnings or earning capacity, it is dealt with under Chapter H, Future Pecuniary Loss.

(iii) Inclusion in the Schedule of Loss?

[D4] Traditionally, heads of general damages have not been included in schedules of loss. However, in accordance with the modern 'cards on the table' approach, a number of practitioners have now started at least to indicate in the schedule which heads of general damage they will seek at trial. Some practitioners will even go as far as to put forward a figure for each head of general damages claimed. This, of course, cuts both ways because, if the figure is too low, it is likely to be accepted and an opportunity may have been missed to improve upon that figure; if the figure is too high, the other side is able to prepare arguments as to why damages should be assessed at a lower sum. Essentially, the decision as to whether or not heads of general damages should be included in a schedule of loss (with or without suggested figures) is a matter of judgment and style for the individual drafter.

[D5]   Of course, the most common head of general damages is pain, suffering and loss of amenity (PSLA), and it is upon this head that we focus in this section. However, as illustrated above, there are also a number of other heads of general damages that practitioners need to be aware of in order to be able properly to advise their clients. These additional heads of general damages are dealt with separately towards the end of this chapter.

2   Damages for PSLA

(i)   Compensable Damages

[D6]   Save for claims involving trespass and breach of contract, claims in tort are not complete without proof of damage. But how much worse off must the claimant be to found a claim for damages? The House of Lords addressed this question in *Rothwell v Chemical & Insulating Co Ltd*[1], reaffirming that an injury must be more than merely trivial in order to found a claim: de minimis non curat lex. Whether or not an injury is too trivial to justify a remedy is a question of degree[2]. On the facts, it was held that the mere presence of pleural plaques giving rise to an anxiety regarding the risk of developing a future asbestos-related disease did not amount to damage for the purposes of constituting a cause of action in tort. They were symptomless and either not an injury at all, or an injury too trivial to justify compensation[3].

---

[1]   [2008] 1 AC 281.
[2]   Per Lord Hoffmann at 289E. See further *Cartledge v E Jopling & Sons Ltd* [1963] AC 758.
[3]   On 25 February 2010 the Justice Secretary Jack Straw announced that the Government did not intend to legislate to overturn this decision, but that payments made under the Pneumoconiosis etc (Workers' Compensation) Act 1979 and the Child Maintenance and Other Payments Act 2008 would be increased.

(ii)   The Constituent Elements of PSLA

[D7]   Generally speaking, it is usual for 'pain, suffering and loss of amenity' to be considered globally and for one lump sum to be awarded under this head. As Lord Woolf explained in *Heil v Rankin*[1]:

> 'In determining what is the correct level of damages for PSLA, it is not usual for the Court to attribute differing sums for different aspects of the injury. The Court's approach involves trying to find the global sum which most accurately in monetary terms reflects or can be regarded as reflecting a fair, reasonable and just figure for the injuries which have been inflicted and the consequences which they will have in PSLA. A sophisticated analytical approach distinguishing between pain and suffering and loss of amenity is not usually required.'

---

[1]   [2001] QB 272 at [39].

[D8] However, the concepts of 'pain', 'suffering' and 'loss of amenity' are actually separate and distinct. Occasionally, they need to be considered individually, and we therefore set out the meanings of the individual terms in the following paragraphs.

Pain and suffering

[D9] 'Pain and suffering' are usually taken and considered together. However, it is a misconception that they are one and the same. The two elements tend to be placed together since they complement each other with a view to calculation, but they can and do encapsulate different feelings. Pain is, as would be expected, that felt upon the nerves and brain. This may be the direct consequence of the accident (eg the pain suffered by a broken leg), or it can be that resulting indirectly from the accident (eg a painful medical procedure undergone to treat the injuries).

[D10] The duration of the pain inflicted is of considerable importance. In *Mills v Stanway Coaches Ltd*[1], the claimant survived for only four days, but during all or most of that time was unconscious, so the Court of Appeal reduced the amount of damages for pain and suffering to a token sum. However, although the duration is important, so is the intensity of pain. In *Smith v Bolton Copper Ltd*[2], Senior Master Whitaker awarded £55,000[3] in respect of a man who suffered two to three months of the worst symptoms and medical procedures associated with mesothelioma.

[1]   [1940] 2 KB 334, [1940] 2 All ER 586.
[2]   Unreported, 10 July 2007 (QBD).
[3]   Approximately £57,215 as at August 2009 rates.

[D11] 'Suffering' includes shock[1], anxiety, fright, fear of future disability, fear of future complications, embarrassment or humiliation and general 'sickness'. There must be a recognisable physical or psychiatric injury[2] before liability will attach. However, where there has been a physical injury, it is immaterial that psychological symptoms fall short of a recognised psychiatric disorder if those symptoms serve to exacerbate the physical symptoms or, likewise, if there is a pre-existing personality disorder which exacerbates the symptoms suffered[3]. In cases of assault, suffering also includes injury to feelings such as indignity, mental suffering, humiliation, distress or anger that might be caused by an attack (especially where the nature of the assault was malicious or spiteful)[4]. It is clear that not only the past or present suffering should be accounted for, but also prospective suffering must be considered. As Greer LJ stated in *Heaps v Perrite Ltd*[5]:

> 'We have to take into account not only the suffering which he had immediately after the accident but the suffering that he will have throughout his life in future.'

[1]   The award for PSLA includes the shock of the events giving rise to the injuries: *Behrens v Bertram Mills Circus Ltd* [1957] 2 QB 1, [1957] 1 All ER 583; and *Owens v Liverpool Corpn* [1939] 1 KB 394, [1938] 4 All ER 727.
[2]   See further at paras **[D83]–[D96]** below.
[3]   *Mullins v Gray* [2004] EWCA Civ 1483.
[4]   *Richardson v Howie* [2004] EWCA Civ 1127.
[5]   [1937] 2 All ER 60.

[D12]   Also, since the availability of separate awards in respect of reduced life expectancy was removed by s 1 of the Administration of Justice Act 1982 for all claims whose cause of action accrued on or after 1 January 1983, when assessing the appropriate award for PSLA the court must take into account any suffering which is caused or likely to be caused to the claimant by awareness that his or her life expectancy has been reduced[1]. It should be noted, however, that in order to recover under this head the claimant must show, on the balance of probabilities, that his or her life expectancy was reduced by reason of the defendant's negligence. This sometimes leads to difficulties, especially in cases of clinical negligence arising out of delayed diagnosis of cancer[2].

---

[1]   Administration of Justice Act 1982, s 1(1)(b). See eg the judgment of Mr Patrick Bennett QC sitting as a judge of the High Court in *Mulry v William Kenyon & Son Ltd* (17 December 1990, unreported), QBD; and *Judge v Huntingdon Health Authority* [1995] 6 Med LR 223. See also *Davies v Tenby Corpn* [1974] 2 Lloyd's Rep 469 at 78, CA, where Scarman LJ said: '... But I have no doubt that awards for pain and suffering in quadriplegic cases have taken into account the [claimant's] awareness of the shortening of his life: As the judge remarked, the matter was already "fortified with adequate authority" ...'.

[2]   See further *Gregg v Scott* [2005] UKHL 2.

[D13]   Of course, in any given case it may be difficult to disentangle what amounts to pain and what amounts to suffering. The two terms are not necessarily mutually exclusive and often overlap. In the circumstances, as stated earlier, it is therefore convenient to view 'pain and suffering' together in order to get a complete picture of the damages deserved.

Loss of amenity

[D14]   Again, although general damages are usually assessed as a combined total of pain, suffering and loss of amenity, 'loss of amenity' can be identified as a distinct element in the award.

[D15]   Loss of amenity is simply the claimant's reduction in performance of everyday activities or pleasures. It can include a wide range of activities which have been hindered or prevented because of the accident. For example, loss of amenity can be recoverable even where there is no pain or suffering. If a victim of an accident remains unconscious from the relevant date of injury up until the date of death, he or she cannot be said to have felt pain, nor suffered the unpleasantness of his or her condition. However, for the relevant period, the victim will have been unable to perform any activity and has a loss of amenity of almost everything people take for granted. A claimant suffering such an injury is, therefore, entitled to an award at the top end of the scale[1].

---

[1]   *Lim Poh Choo v Camden and Islington Area Health Authority* [1980] AC 174, in which Lord Scarman stated at 191a: '[there is a ...] clear distinction between damages for pain and suffering and damages for loss of amenities. The former depends on the claimant's personal awareness of pain, her capacity for suffering. But the latter are awarded for the fact of deprivation, a substantial loss, whether the claimant is aware of it or not'.

[D16]   Obvious examples of loss of amenity include the inability to run or walk, to play sports, to partake in hobbies/leisure activities such as travelling, board games, cards and video games, playing with children/grandchildren etc. Loss of amenity can also include loss of sexual function[1] and inability to care for others[2]. However, it should be noted that, just because claimants might be deprived of performing an activity they previously enjoyed, this does not automatically mean that it needs to be assessed as part of the claim for PSLA without any additional claim for pecuniary loss arising out of the need to employ others to carry out the same activity[3].

[1] In *Cook v JL Kier & Co Ltd* [1970] 2 All ER 513, [1970] 1 WLR 774, CA, it was recognised that: '... if a husband is rendered impotent, the wife cannot claim damages. But although the wife cannot claim herself, the husband can get damages for the loss to him which is grievous. And he can get damages for the effect on his family life which takes her into account'.

[2] In *Rourke v Barton* (1982) Times, 23 June, McCullough J took into account the inability of the wife, much as she would have wished, to look after her husband terminally ill with cancer, particularly since the husband was looking to her for support. See further *Lowe v Guise* [2002] EWCA Civ 197.

[3] For example, in *Samuels v Benning* [2002] EWCA Civ 858, [2002] All ER (D) 353 (May), the Court of Appeal held that the trial judge had not made adequate provision for the loss of the ability to carry out DIY. The trial judge declined to make an award under this head, believing the same to be sufficiently covered by the award for PSLA. The Court of Appeal disagreed and awarded an additional £5,000 (applying a multiplier of 10 to the claimed multiplicand of £500 per annum) for future loss under this head. See also *Lowe v Guise* [2002] EWCA Civ 197 regarding compensation for the inability to provide services to a third party that would otherwise have been provided by the claimant in the absence of his or her injuries.

[D17] In certain cases, the loss of amenity will provide a considerable increase on the 'normal' award for PSLA arising out of a particular injury. For instance, in *Watson v Gray*[1] the claimant was a professional footballer aged 25 at the time of the accident who suffered a comminuted transverse fracture of the right tibia and fibula. The agreed general damages of £25,000 reflected the enhanced loss of amenity to a professional footballer, together with the loss of congenial employment[2]. In *Harman v J J Smith Ltd*[3], Caulfield J described the claimant as a 'true guitarist' which 'was a big part of his life'. Ballroom dancing at a high level of expertise was found to be the sole recreation of the claimant in *McGourty v Croudace Ltd*[4]. May J found that, by reason of chest injuries, the claimant was barred entirely from pursuing that recreation. He awarded £17,000 on the basis that the bracket was between £8,500 and £18,000–£20,000 – and that the present case was at the top end. In so doing, he took into account the loss of the pleasure of dancing. In *Middleton v South Yorkshire Transport Executive*[5] the Court of Appeal upheld an award of £7,500 for a PE teacher who had previously greatly enjoyed sports and suffered a reduced ability to take part in the sporting activities that she had previously taught and enjoyed. And in *Hunn v McFralane*[6] the trial judge awarded the claimant, who was a keen horse rider and show jumper, £6,500 instead of £3,500 for a whiplash injury because she had suffered 'a serious loss of amenity' in being unable to exercise her horses or compete in competitions for an 18-month period and had been deprived of the ability to pursue a hobby that had been a lifetime interest.

[1] (1998) Times, 26 November.

[2] See further at paras **[D128]**–**[D139]** regarding the assessment of awards for loss of congenial employment. See also *Collett v Smith* [2008] EWHC 1962 (QB), in which £35,000 was agreed for both PSLA and loss of congenial employment.

[3] (9 October 1987, unreported), QBD.

[4] (16 April 1991, unreported), QBD. See also *Kirk v Laine Theatre Arts* [1995] CLY 1712, in which the claimant was awarded £10,000 for the lost ability to pursue a career as a dancer.

⁵   (28 January 1986, unreported), referred to in *Kemp & Kemp* at G4-001.
⁶   [1997] CLY 1901.

[D18]   Where there might be a significant loss of amenity, legal advisers should be alert not to ignore the proofing of witnesses who are able to substantiate such a claim (eg persons who played sport with the claimant). Other methods can be used as well, such as obtaining photographs of sporting trophies won, team events or trips abroad.

The elements combined

[D19]   From time to time, arguments have been put forward challenging awards in respect of general damages for PSLA. One such argument had regard to the relevance of the claimant's knowledge of his injuries. In basic terms, it was argued that if, for example, a victim claimant was unconscious, then there would be no knowledge of the injuries and therefore no pain or suffering and ultimately no conscious inability to perform activities previously enjoyed. Such an argument was put forward in *Lim Poh Choo v Camden and Islington Area Health Authority*[1]. Lord Scarman made it clear that, although ignorance of the victim's condition may negate a claim for pain and suffering, it could not defeat loss of amenity[2]:

> '[there is a …] clear distinction between damages for pain and suffering and damages for loss of amenities. The former depends on the claimant's personal awareness of pain, her capacity for suffering. But the latter are awarded for the fact of deprivation, a substantial loss, whether the claimant is aware of it or not.'

¹   [1980] AC 174, [1979] 2 All ER 910.
²   [1980] AC 174 at 191a.

[D20]   In *Wise v Kaye*[1] the defendant argued that, as the claimant was unaware of her condition, the award was vastly 'out of sync' with an award of equal amount to a paraplegic. Such a person has lost similar amenity yet is aware of the loss and so suffers all the more. However, Upjohn LJ refused such a comparative argument. He held that the claimant had lost even more amenities than a paraplegic. Although it had to be accepted that paraplegics would have greater pain and suffering, they could still think and play some part in life. The ignorant claimant had been robbed of any such prospects or role. It was not for the courts to measure the damages according to loss of happiness, but according to injury and consequent loss of amenity[2]:

> 'In my judgment, ignorance of the injury or of the damage thereby suffered is no ground for reducing damages, save where ignorance prevents the head of damage arising as in the case of pain and suffering.'

¹   [1962] 1 QB 638.
²   At 661.

[D21]   However, this case can also be read as accepting that a person's awareness can heighten a claim. In *Jeffries v McNeill*[1], Drake J increased the award and stated that the claimant had 'acute insight into his condition … his life has been shattered and he knows it'.

¹   (8 December 1987, unreported), QBD. See further category 2(A)(a) – Very Severe Brain Damage of the JSB Guidelines where, amongst other factors, the level of award is expressly said to be affected by the degree of the claimant's insight.

[D22] A further argument was suggested by the defendant in *Wise v Kaye*. It was argued that a relevant factor in general damages is the claimant's need or, indeed, ability to spend the award. Upjohn LJ stated[1]:

'... once the loss is proved and quantified at the proper figure that sum becomes the absolute property for the claimant, that it matters not that the claimant is incapable of personal enjoyment of the money in the very vague and, as I think indefinable sense of spending it on herself.'

[1] [1962] 1 QB 638 at 658. It is a well-known principle that how the claimant spends his or her award of damages is irrelevant: *Lim Poh Choo v Camden and Islington Area Health Authority* [1980] AC 174, per Lord Scarman at 191; *Wells v Wells* [1999] AC 345, [1998] 3 All ER 481; *Heil v Rankin* [2001] QB 272, [2000] 3 All ER 138. It is noteworthy that, in cases where a claimant is a child or patient, the litigation friend, Court of Protection or professional receiver is likely to make spending decisions on behalf of the claimant.

[D23] Such arguments were again raised in *Croke (a minor) v Wiseman*[1]. It was stated that it did not matter that the claimant was unable to use money or appreciate it. An analogy[2] was a millionaire who lost an arm in an accident. The money awarded for the loss of the limb would actually mean nothing to him, but he was still obviously entitled to it in recompense for the loss sustained. In relation to loss of amenity without awareness of the loss, Shaw LJ said:

'In the present case the claimant had no opportunity of enjoying any significant part of his life at all. Not the innocent joys of childhood or the awkward pleasures of growing up, of adolescence or of young manhood or of achievement. His life was made barren when it had hardly begun. I do not see how for the loss of that measure of living, £35,000 can be said to be too much.'

[1] [1981] 3 All ER 852, [1982] 1 WLR 71, a case involving a 21-month-old infant sustaining an injury which meant his brain would never function correctly. Thus, blindness and total paralysis ensued.
[2] [1981] 3 All ER 852, per Shaw LJ at 862.

[D24] However, the sheer dramatics of Shaw LJ's statement induce an argument from the claimant's side. For such a loss of 'innocent joys' etc, would £50,000 be too much, or indeed would £500,000? Who would exchange life for money[1]? Yet a figure must be reached, and it is the difficult job of the judge to do it.

[1] When Mrs Leung, who had been catastrophically injured, was asked by a reporter whether she thought her award of £3.5 million was too much, she replied, 'I'll swap places with you'. This stunned to silence all the reporters present.

(iii) Investigation

[D25] It is wise, when attempting to estimate a value for general damages for PSLA, to question the claimant extensively (if at all possible)[1]. The lay client will often be unaware of how important the various facets of the injury and their resultant effect on his or her life are. Therefore, questioning can expose areas that may be of huge consequence to the award (eg activities performed before the injury now being impossible or limited).

¹ A useful initial indicator of how the claimant's injuries have affected his or her life can be gleaned from the claimant's answers to the personal injury questionnaire, which we recommend should be sent out in all but the most minor cases. See Chapter Q at para **[Q2]** for an example of this questionnaire.

[D26] Full details of the effects of the injury should be taken, including not only the circumstances in which the injury was sustained, the treatment received and injuries themselves, but also the recovery process, present condition and hope for the future[1]. The level of pain should be assessed, whether it is continuous, how severe it is and the extent to which it is disabling. An account should also be made of how the claimant has suffered. The fear or worry regarding the injury, as well as any embarrassment or humiliation caused, can be significant, especially in cases of scarring. Distress regarding awareness of early death and the effects of the injury on the claimant's family should also be noted.

¹ Obviously, if possible, these should also be covered in and supported by the medical evidence.

[D27] Generally speaking, the three most important aspects to consider when investigating a claim for general damages in respect of PSLA are: (1) the nature and severity of the claimant's injuries (including any treatment necessary as a result); (2) the impact of the injuries upon the claimant's lifestyle and daily activities; and (3) prognosis, ie how long the injuries are going to continue affecting the claimant (and whether there is any reduced life expectancy as a result of the injuries).

[D28] Of course, whilst each of these aspects are important to investigate, often it will not be possible fully to assess the nature and severity of a claimant's injuries or the claimant's prognosis without the benefit of expert medical opinion. Therefore, naturally, the main area for the lawyer's concern (as opposed to the concern of the medical expert) is the extent of the claimant's disabilities and impairments: in other words, how the claimant's injuries affect him or her and impinge upon their pre-injury activities and lifestyle, especially as regards:

- Senses – sight, hearing, touch, taste, smell etc.
- Cognitive function – memory, concentration, motor function, personality change etc.
- Mobility – climbing ladders or stairs, kneeling, squatting, running, jumping, sitting, walking, standing and driving.
- Communication – speech, language, reading, writing etc.
- Psychological/psychiatric symptoms – anxiety, depression, tearfulness, nightmares, flashbacks, phobia etc.
- Personal hygiene – grooming, dressing, bathing and showering.
- Domestic – cooking, cleaning, dusting, ironing, shopping, washing clothes, maintenance and DIY.
- Gardening – mowing the lawn, potting plants, weeding, digging and more physical jobs such as laying patios and erecting sheds.
- Painting and decorating.
- Relationships – sexual functions, social interaction with friends and family (in particular, children).
- Social life – ability to visit friends and family.

- Sleep – whether the claimant is able to sleep through the night, nightmares, the need to be turned, the ability to sleep alone etc.
- Work – loss of satisfying job, having to work longer hours.
- Leisure activities – including sport and other hobbies that the claimant particularly enjoyed.

(iv) The Assessment of PSLA

[D29] The calculation of general damages for PSLA is a skilled art that can only be mastered with practice. The whole point of an award is to compensate a victim in monetary terms for an injury that has caused physical or mental injury. But how can a court assess the amount of money a claimant deserves on, say, losing a leg? How does such an assessment work? One helpful pronouncement can be found in *West (H) & Son Ltd v Shephard*[1] in which Lord Pearce stated[2]:

'If a claimant has lost a leg, the court approaches the matter on the basis that he has suffered a serious physical deprivation, no matter what his condition or temperament or state of mind may be. That deprivation may also create future economic loss which is added to the assessment. Past and prospective pain and discomfort increase the assessment. If there is loss of amenity apart from the obvious and normal loss inherent in the deprivation of the limb – if, for instance, the claimant's main interest in life was some sport or hobby from which he will in future be debarred, that too increases the assessment. If there is a particular consequential injury to the nervous system, that also increases the assessment ... These considerations are not dealt with as separate items but are taken into account by the court in fixing an inclusive sum for general damages.'

[1]   [1964] AC 326, [1963] 2 All ER 625.
[2]   [1964] AC 326 at 365.

[D30] In other words, each case must be subjectively assessed by reference to the individual claimant[1]. The fact that an award of damages might be no or inadequate compensation for a claimant's injuries is irrelevant. An award of damages is the only compensation the court can award and, as Scarman LJ (as he then was) said in *Wagner v Mitchell*[2]:

'... There are cases in which it is far too philosophical to say that money is no compensation for pain and suffering. In cases such as the present, a substantial sum given to a person of the [claimant's] age greatly increases the range of his possible diversions, pleasurable activities which can to some extent distract him from his suffering. Let me explain. A substantial sum of money would enable this man, for example, to take himself and his wife on holiday which he would not otherwise be able to afford – if that is what he wishes to do. It would enable him to enrich his daily life at home by buying something which his wife and himself would like to have which they otherwise would not have. Or he may wish to use his money in order to assist his children and grandchildren. All these activities, made possible by a sum of money which otherwise he would not have, are activities which help him to come to terms with, and (in the words of the learned judge) to compensate for, the constant reminder of the intermittent pain which is bound to afflict him every day of his life which remains. In such a case, it is being far too philosophical to say that money is no compensation for pain and suffering. It provides the opportunity of distraction and diversion which are the only resources left to a man afflicted by permanent pain ...'

1   A case which exemplifies the subjective nature of the award of PSLA is *Dimmock v Miles* (12 December 1969, unreported), referred to in *Kemp & Kemp* at paras 3–018 and E2–002. This case concerned a 35-year-old woman who suffered a number of injuries including lacerations to the forehead resulting in permanent scarring. During the course of his judgment, Phillimore J stated: '... the real difficulty is that, again, she was not asked about her own feelings with regard to the scar and that is a much more serious matter in this sort of case. After all, some may treat a scar on the forehead as comparatively trivial, but to another it would be a source of serious worry'.

2   [1975] CA Transcript 444A.

The theory

[D31]   The principles behind the assessment of general damages for pain, suffering and loss of amenity are perhaps most clearly set out by Lord Diplock in *Wright v British Railways Board*[1]:

'[Where] judges carry out their duty of assessing damages for non-economic loss in the money of the day at the date of the trial ... this is a rule of practice that judges are required to follow, not a guideline from which they have a discretion to depart if there are special circumstances that justify their doing so ... My Lords, given the inescapably artificial and conventional nature of the assessment of damages for non-economic loss in personal injury actions ... it is an important function of the Court of Appeal to lay down guidelines ... as to the quantum of damages appropriate to compensate for various types of commonly occurring injuries ... The purpose of such guidelines is that they should be simple and easy to apply though broad enough to permit allowances to be made for special features of individual cases which make the deprivation caused to the particular [claimant] by the non-economic loss greater or less than in the general run of cases involving injuries of the same kind. Guidelines laid down by an appellate court are addressed directly to judges who try personal injury actions; but confidence that trial judges will apply them means that all those who are engaged in settling out of court the many thousands of claims that never reach the stage of litigation at all or, if they do, do not proceed as far as trial will know very broadly speaking what the claim is likely to be worth if 100 per cent liability is established. The Court of Appeal, with its considerable case-load of appeals in personal injury actions and the relatively recent experience of many of its members in trying such cases themselves, is, generally speaking, the tribunal best qualified to set the guidelines for judges currently trying such actions, particularly as respects non-economic loss; and this House should hesitate before deciding to depart from them, particularly if the departure will make the guideline less general in its applicability or less simple to apply. A guideline as to quantum of conventional damages ... is not a rule of law nor is it a rule of practice. It sets no binding precedent; it can be varied as circumstances change or experience shows that it does not assist in the achievement of even-handed justice or makes trials more lengthy or expensive or settlements more difficult to reach ... As regards assessment of damages for non-economic loss in personal injury cases, the Court of Appeal creates the guidelines as to the appropriate conventional figure by increasing or reducing awards of damages made by judges in individual cases for various common kinds of injuries. Thus so-called "brackets" are established, broad enough to make allowance for circumstances which make the deprivation suffered by an individual [claimant] in consequence of the particular kind of injury greater or less than in the general run of cases, yet clear enough to reduce the unpredictability of what is likely to be the most important factor in arriving at settlement of claims. "Brackets" may call for alteration not only to take account of inflation, for which they ought automatically to be raised, but also it may be to take account of advances in medical science which may make particular kinds of injuries less disabling or advances in medical knowledge which may disclose hitherto unsuspected long term effects of some kinds of injuries or industrial diseases.'

1   [1983] 2 AC 773 at 782, 784–785, followed in *Heil v Rankin* [2001] QB 272, per Lord Woolf at [43].

The aim of the award for PSLA

[D32]   As Lord Woolf stated in *Heil v Rankin*[1]:

'[The] principle of "full compensation" applies to pecuniary and non-pecuniary damage alike. But … this statement immediately raises a problem in a situation where what is in issue is what is the appropriate level of "full compensation" for non-pecuniary injury when the compensation has to be expressed in pecuniary terms. There is no simple formula for converting the pain and suffering, the loss of function, the loss of amenity and disability which an injured person has sustained, into monetary terms. Any process of conversion must be essentially artificial. Lord Pearce expressed it well in *West (H) & Sons Ltd v Shephard*[2] when he said: "The court has to perform the difficult and artificial task of converting into monetary damages the physical injury and deprivation and pain and to give judgment for what it considers to be a reasonable sum. It does not look beyond the judgment to the spending of the damages".'

1   [2001] QB 272 at 23.
2   [1964] AC 326 at 364.

[D33]   In the circumstances, the award for PSLA is a conventional[1] sum which although arbitrary is designed to be 'fair, just and reasonable' monetary compensation for the injuries sustained[2].

1   As stated by Diplock LJ in *Wright v British Railway Board* [1983] 2 AC 773: 'Such loss is not susceptible of measurement in money. Any figure at which the assessor of damages arrives cannot be other than artificial and, if the aim is that justice meted out to all litigants should be even-handed instead of depending on idiosyncrasies of the assessor, whether jury or judge, the figure must be "basically" a conventional figure derived from experience and from awards in comparable cases'.
2   *Rowley v London and North Western Ry Co* (1873) LR 8 Exch 221 at 231; *Pickett v British Railway Board Ltd* [1980] AC 136 at 168; *Lim Poh Choo v Camden and Islington Area Health Authority* [1980] AC 174 at 187; and *Heil v Rankin* [2001] QB 272.

Limits on the award

[D34]   It is the job of the Court of Appeal to lay down the applicable guidelines for awards of PSLA and to keep the guidelines up to date[1]. The tariffs set by the Court of Appeal are conventional sums which take into account both social and economic factors[2]. In *Heil v Rankin*, Lord Woolf said[3]:

'Awards must be proportionate and take into account the consequences of increases in the awards of damages on defendants as a group and society as a whole. The considerations are ones which the Court cannot ignore. They are the background against which the fair, reasonable and just figure has to be determined … When the question is the level of damages for non-pecuniary loss the Court is … concerned with determining what is the fair, reasonable and just equivalent in monetary terms of an injury and the resultant PSLA. The decision has to be taken against the background of the society in which the Court makes the award … The level of awards does involve questions of social policy. But the questions are ones with which the courts are accustomed to deal as part of their normal role.'

1   In *Wright v British Railway Board* [1983] 2 AC 773, Lord Diplock LJ stated: 'The Court of Appeal, with its considerable case-load of appeals in personal injury actions and the relatively recent experience of many of its members in trying such cases themselves is, generally speaking, the tribunal best qualified to set the guide-lines for judges trying such actions'. See also *Heil v Rankin* [2001] QB 272 at [43].

2   *Heil v Rankin* [2001] QB 272.

3   [2001] QB 272 at [36] and [38].

[D35]   Whilst there is no lower limit on the available award for PSLA, assuming there is an identifiable injury that the claimant has suffered[1], the current maximum award for PSLA in the most severe of cases is now perhaps constrained by the Judicial Studies Board Guidelines (9th edition) to about £260,000.

1   See *Parry v English Electric Co Ltd* [1971] 2 All ER 1094, [1971] 1 WLR 664; *Moore v Maidstone and District Motor Services* (1979, unreported), CA No 92; *Price v Quinn* [1979] CA No 98. As regards the definition for an identifiable injury, ie one which is recognised by the law to entitle a claimant to recover damages, see further *Rothwell v Chemical & Insulating Co Ltd* [2008] 1 AC 281.

The Judicial Studies Board Guidelines

[D36]   The Guidelines for the Assessment of General Damages in Personal Injury Cases was first published by the Judicial Studies Board in 1992. The slim book, which is now in its 9th edition, is of substantial use and is likely to be used by the court as the starting point for any assessment of damages for PSLA[1]. Guidelines are given for the assessment of injuries ranging from minor whiplash injuries, in which a full recovery is made within one year, to catastrophic brain injuries where the claimant is left with severe and permanent residual symptoms.

[D37]   The 2002 edition stated the Board's intention of the Guidelines in the foreword by Lord Donaldson of Lymington as follows:

'[These Guidelines were] ... not intended to represent, and [do] not represent, a new or different approach to the problem. Nor is it intended to be a "ready reckoner" or in any way to fetter the individual judgment which must be brought to bear upon the unique features of each particular case. What it is intended to do, and what it does quite admirably, is to distil the conventional wisdom contained in the reported cases, to supplement it from the collective experience of the working party and to present the result in a convenient, logical and coherent form.'

1   As Lord Woolf MR said in the introduction to the 3rd (1996) edition: 'Usually it will be the starting off point rather than the last word on the appropriate award in any particular case'. See also *Arafa v Potter* [1995] IRLR 316, [1994] PIQR Q73; and *Reed v Sunderland Health Authority* (1998) Times, 16 October, in which Sir Christopher Staughton made it clear the guidelines simply summarise the law and, as such, consideration should be given to the source of this summary.

[D38]   The Guidelines are therefore a useful way to obtain a ballpark figure[1]. However, in order to get a better picture of the likely award within the range specified by the Guidelines, or to see whether there is any scope for arguing that a particular case falls outside the Guidelines[2], reliance must be placed on comparable reported authorities. In *Wright v British Railways Board*, Lord Diplock stated[3]:

'[PSLA damages are] not susceptible of measurement in money. Any figure at which the assessor of damages arrives cannot be other than artificial and, if the aim is that justice meted out to all litigants should be even handed instead of depending on idiosyncrasies of the assessor, whether jury or judge, the figure must be "basically" a conventional figure derived from experience and from awards in comparable cases.'

1   In *Arafa v Potter* [1995] IRLR 316, [1994] PIQR Q73, Staughton J referred to the guidelines as being a 'slim and handy volume which anyone can slip into their briefcases on their way to the county court'.

2   For examples of cases where the court has held that the injury falls outside the Guidelines, see *Armstrong v British Coal Corpn* [1998] CLY 2842, CA, involving damages for vibration white finger; and *C v Flintshire County Council* [2001] EWCA Civ 302, [2001] 1 FCR 614, involving damages for psychiatric harm resulting from child abuse.

3   [1983] 2 AC 773 at 777C.

[D39] However, it should be noted that, in one example, the courts have not necessarily followed the guidance suggested in the 9th edition of the Guidelines. In relation to the category of mesothelioma, the 9th edition of the JSB Guidelines suggest that, in cases of unusually short periods of pain and suffering lasting three months or so, an award in the region of £25,000 may be appropriate. Save for a few cases in which this guidance has been followed[1], many judges, including Senior Master Whitaker (Master in charge of the specialist mesothelioma and asbestos related diseases list), have declined to follow the guidance[2].

1   *Cameron v Vinters Defence Systems Ltd* [2007] EWHC 2267 (QB), [2008] PIQR P5, and *Gallagher* (HHJ Walton, 17 January 2007).

2   *Smith v Bolton Copper Ltd*, unreported, 10 July 2007 (QBD). See further 'General Damages for Pain and Suffering and Loss of Amenity for Malignant Asbestos Disease' by Allan Gore QC in [2009] JPIL Issue 3/09.

Sources of case law

[D40] As seen above, the Judicial Studies Board Guidelines are useful for obtaining an initial ballpark figure for PSLA damages, which is usually expressed as a range. Where the individual claimant falls within this range is ultimately determined by consideration of previous decided case law involving similar injuries[1]. However, obviously no two cases are identical, and it is for this reason that skill and experience is needed in order accurately to quantify the likely award under this head[2].

1   In *Pakes v Rodge* [1973] CA Transcript 419A, Edmund Davies LJ said: '... We have had cited to us as is customary, the decisions in other cases. It is an exercise not without its value, provided one always bears in mind that it is rare to find that the other cases are adequately reported, and indeed so rare as to be virtually non-existent to the exact parallel with the instant case. Other cases help to form a rough guide, but their roughness must be recognised, and one must always ultimately address oneself to the details of the instant case ...'.

2   In *Maiden v National Coal Board* [1978] CA Transcript 364, Waller LJ, inter alia, said: '... Each case of damages for personal injuries differs from every other one. The brief account of other cases may be helpful as showing a general range; but at the end of the day one has to ask oneself whether or not the figure the learned judge awarded was within the range that one thinks right, or whether, as has been said once, "Really! as much as that" ...'.

[D41] As Rose J, as he then was, put it in *Cassel v Hammersmith and Fulham Health Authority*[1]:

'… In my judgment no useful purpose is served by a point by point comparison between different cases. The question is what is fair compensation in the instant case, having regard to the general level of roughly comparable awards.'

¹   [1992] 1 PIQR Q168 at Q5.

[D42]   Sources of case law include:

- The Law Reports.
- *Butterworths' Personal Injury Litigation Service*.
- *Kemp & Kemp*.
- Current Law.
- *Halsbury's* Personal Injury and Quantum Reports.
- The Journal of Personal Injury Litigation.
- Butterworths' PI Online.
- Lawtel.
- APIL Journal.
- Clinical Risk & the AVMA Journal.
- The Personal and Medical Injuries Law Letter.
- The Medical Law Monitor.

[D43]   Case summaries should be read carefully with the following points in mind:

- Cases will often have been reported for a reason[1].
- Cases which are decided by higher courts (particularly the Court of Appeal) are more authoritative than cases decided by lower courts[2].
- Cases which are assessed by a judge are more authoritative than cases which were agreed between the parties.
- Due to lack of space and the way the summaries are reported, a number of important details may be missing.
- Older cases may not accurately reflect the attitude of the court to the same injuries today, and therefore tend to be less reliable than more recent cases.
- CICB cases may not be directly comparable[3].

¹   This may be because the case is particularly interesting, the award is exceptionally high or low, or because the author of the case summary wishes to see their name in print and collect the cash payment that is sometimes provided for submissions!

²   Note that the Court of Appeal may only interfere with an award made for PSLA where the award is manifestly excessive (or the reverse) or wrong in principle. Therefore, where it does decide to interfere, the award may nonetheless be at the high point of the applicable range, rather than the mid-point from which guidance is best derived. Where it does not, it means no more than the award is neither excessively high (if it is on a defendant's appeal) nor excessively low (as on a claimant's appeal): it does not say it is a figure their Lord Justices would themselves have awarded.

³   Notwithstanding the fact that CICB cases are determined under the same common law principles, there is a general perception that some of the CICB awards are still too low.

Updating figures from comparable cases

(1)   UPDATE FOR INFLATION

[D44]   Once a comparable case has been found, it needs to be updated[1] using the current Retail Price Index (RPI). The way to do this is to multiply the award by the rate of the current RPI and then to divide by the rate of the RPI at the date that the award was made.

Example

In *Mahoney v Williams*[2], District Judge Keogh awarded the claimant £3,000 for general damages in respect of PSLA on 29 February 1996. At that time the RPI was 150.9. The current RPI (at August 2009) is 214.4. Therefore, the calculation is as follows:

Step 1: $3,000 \times 214.4 = 643,200$

Step 2: $643,200 \div 150.9 = 4,262$ (to the nearest pound)

Therefore, the award in *Mahoney v Williams* is worth £4,262 at today's rates.

---

[1] The principle that awards need to be increased to take into account the declining value of money was accepted in *Wright v British Railways Board* [1983] 2 AC 773 and *Walker v John McLean & Sons Ltd* [1979] 2 All ER 965, [1979] 1 WLR 760.

[2] [1996] 1 WLR 760.

(2) UPDATE FOR HEIL V RANKIN

[D45]   Note that any award over £10,000 that was made before 23 March 2000 now also has to be updated for the '*Heil v Rankin*' factor. See further at paras **[D123]**–**[D126]** and the table at **[D150]**.

A jury question?

[D46]   It has been accepted that the best person to assess the award is the trial judge. As Mantell LJ stated in *Clarke v South Yorkshire Transport Ltd*[1]:

> '… in my judgment an appeal court should always be slow to interfere with the trial judge's assessment, even though it may seem that such assessment falls outside the Judicial Studies Board Guidelines or is out of kilter with other roughly comparable cases. After all, the trial judge will have seen the claimant and, sometimes, as in this case, have had the advantage of visiting the claimant's home and seeing film of her getting about both in the home and outside. The trial judge will have been in the best position to make a judgment as to the effect upon the claimant's life of the injuries and the consequent disabilities[2].'

---

[1] [1998] PIQR Q104 at Q107.

[2] However, the Court of Appeal reduced general damages from £55,000 to £47,500.

[D47]   Juries (it might be thought) would award higher sums by way of general damages but a judge's figure is theoretically a 'jury award'. Although the court retains a discretion to order a trial by jury in a case of personal injury[1], in practice it rarely if ever does so. The leading case on the exercise of this discretion is *Ward v James*[2] in which Lord Denning MR, giving the judgment of the court, expressed the view that a jury should be used in a personal injury case only in exceptional cases. Weight was given to the fact that, whilst a judge would be aware of a conventional figure in relation to damages, a jury would not.

¹   Senior Courts Act 1981, s 69(3) (replacing Administration of Justice (Miscellaneous Provisions) Act 1933, s 6).
²   [1966] 1 QB 273, [1965] 1 All ER 563.

[D48]   In *H v Ministry of Defence*¹ it was held that a jury is inappropriate for a personal injury action except in very exceptional circumstances. An example of such is when there was a deliberate abuse of authority akin to a claim for malicious prosecution and false imprisonment (ie those civil trials in which a claimant has a right to have his or her case determined by a jury).

¹   [1991] 2 QB 103, [1991] 2 All ER 834.

Computer valuation?

[D49]   Some insurers have been using computer programs to assess the value of general damages for pain, suffering and loss of amenity. Reference to such programs, including Colossus, was made in Lord Justice Jackson's preliminary costs review published in 2009¹. The complaints about such computer programs to date are that they are not calibrated correctly and/or struggle to take account of special factors such as the presence of multiple injuries or the inability to continue with an enjoyable hobby or leisure activity. The Association of Personal Injury Lawyers' experience is that court awards of damages are always higher than those generated by Colossus². Insurers have suggested that a similar system, monitored by a senior judge, could be used in the future to generate guideline figures for each case. The Personal Injury Bar Association are strongly opposed to such an idea because they fear that such a system could never be accurate. The question is whether a computer system could be calibrated correctly so as to provide an accurate assessment, especially in more difficult cases such as those involving multiple injuries or where there is significant loss of amenity. In his final report³, Lord Justice Jackson suggested setting up a working party consisting of representatives of claimants, defendants and the judiciary to take the matter further.

¹   Available to download at www.judiciary.gov.uk/about_judiciary/cost-review/preliminary-report. htm.
²   See further para 9.8 of Volume 1 of Jackson LJ's preliminary report.
³   Available to download at www.judiciary.gov.uk/about_judiciary/cost-review/reports.htm.

(v)   Problem Cases

[D50]   The use of the Guidelines and comparable past cases can usually assist in reaching a relatively accurate estimation. However, problems can arise in cases of a unique nature, which either do not have a specific category in the Guidelines or any comparable cases. In *Meah v McCreamer*¹, the claimant was a passenger in a car driven by the defendant and was involved in an accident caused by the defendant's negligence. Owing to the accident, Meah suffered serious head injuries and brain damage which resulted in him suffering a marked change in personality. Although, pre-accident, the claimant had been convicted of relatively minor criminal offences, it was accepted that there was no evidence of his being violent towards women. Following his discharge from hospital he carried out, was convicted of and sentenced for three violent sexual attacks. He was sentenced to three life sentences for rape. It was held that the accident caused the personality change and there was nothing he or anyone else could do about it. Woolf J (as he then was) stated[2]:

'Looking at the matter in the best way that I can, bearing in mind the sort of compensation which is provided by the courts in the case of the worst type of injury (I am here thinking of people who suffer from injuries that cause them to be mere vegetables), [and] bearing in mind the sort of compensation that is provided in cases where people are wrongly imprisoned, though I emphasise that with regard to those cases there is usually compensation for loss of employment as well and that factor plays a part in the amount which is given as compensation, I think the appropriate sum to award by way of general damages is a sum of £60,000[3].'

1   [1985] 1 All ER 367.
2   [1985] 1 All ER 367 at 373h.
3   The award was reduced by 25% to take account of the fact that Meah allowed himself to be driven by a drunk driver. However, note that the illegality defence was not argued in this case, and the outcome may therefore have been quite different. See at paras **[D111]**–**[D115]**.

[D51]   Woolf J (as he then was) expressly stated that he was not able to use comparable cases and had to consider other sources. The award of £60,000 would be worth approximately £165,615 at today's (2009) rates, including an uplift for the *'Heil v Rankin'* factor.

[D52]   This need to use any appropriate source was considered in *Dureau v Evans* by Kennedy J, who stated[1]:

'Help is to be obtained from any source where it happens to be available. To a limited extent, in a case where there are multiple injuries, the figures in the Judicial Studies Board Table can help but I accept Mr Murphy's criticism of them that, where one has a multiplicity of injuries, it is necessary to take an overall view. The off-setting process may mean it is not possible to derive a great deal of benefit from that particular source. One then looks to see if anything can be gained from looking at a comparable award, if one is to be found, in another case. Even that may not prove to be a particularly fruitful source of enquiry. It may be necessary, if it be possible, to select what may be the most serious head of injury, to see if a comparable award can be found in relation to that and, if so, build on it to allow for the other heads of injury which have been sustained by the claimant in the instant case.'

1   [1996] PIQR Q18 at Q21.

(vi)   Factors Influencing the Award for PSLA
Pre-existing disability

[D53]   A defendant in an action for personal injury is obviously liable for the PSLA that is caused by the injury sustained. In most cases, this will be simple to work out as the suffering is entirely due to the relevant injury. However, it naturally follows that a tortfeasor cannot be liable for pain etc that would have occurred, without the injury, in any event. The defendant cannot be expected to pay a victim for a disability that was there in the first place and, in effect, has nothing to do with the incident[1]. Therefore, a pre-existing disability may operate to reduce the appropriate award of damages for PSLA. An example of this is where the claimant might have suffered some of the symptoms described in the appropriate category of the JSB Guidelines for the injury in question by reason of an unrelated or pre-existing condition. An example of such a deduction in practice is provided by *Taylor v Weston AHA*[2] in which the claimant, who already suffered from Crohn's disease, developed a spinal subdural and subarachnoid haematoma resulting in permanent spinal cord damage. Pitchers J took the appropriate award for the claimant's injuries from the bottom of the category for quadriplegia in the JSB Guidelines of £165,000, and discounted this by £35,000 reflecting the disability arising from the claimant's pre-existing Crohn's disease, resulting in a net award for PSLA of £130,000.

[1]   See eg *Jobling v Associated Dairies Ltd* [1982] AC 794, [1981] 2 All ER 752, in which the claimant's claim for loss of earnings was disallowed because, following the accident caused by the defendant's negligence, the claimant suffered from a disease which would have prevented him from working in any event.

[2]   [2003] All ER (D) 50 (Dec).

[D54]   In *Cutler v Vauxhall Motors Ltd*[1] the Court of Appeal upheld the decision to reject a claim for loss of earnings following time off work for an operation. Although the accident meant the operation was immediately necessary, the claimant's pre-accident condition was such that an operation was inevitable. This applies in relation to general damages also. As Butler-Sloss LJ stated in *Salih v Enfield Health Authority*[2]:

'... Not only must the tortfeasor take the claimant as he finds him to the disadvantage of the tortfeasor, he may also take him as he is to the advantage of the tortfeasor in an appropriate case ...'

[1]   [1971] 1 QB 418, [1970] 2 All ER 56. See further *Adamson v Kingston-Upon-Hull City Council* (22 June 1990, unreported); *Galbraith v Marley Buildings Ltd* 1984 SLT 155n; and *Robertson v Aberdeen University* 1984 SLT 341n.

[2]   [1991] 3 All ER 400, [1991] 2 Med LR 235.

[D55]   A problem arises, however, in assessing how much of the injury has been caused by the tortfeasor in cases where a condition pre-dated any accident. Consideration must be given not only to an aggravation of the condition but also to whether the injury accelerated the arrival of a latent injury or disease[1]. An example of the courts' technique is *Wallhead v Ruston & Hornsby Ltd*[2] in which it was held that, although the defendant's breach of duty did not cause the claimant's chronic lung illness, the illness had been aggravated by the noxious dust the claimant had inhaled from 1950 to 1964. Therefore, the claimant was entitled to compensation for the disability to the extent that the total aggravation extended beyond the injury that would have occurred without exposure to the noxious dust.

[1]   *Sutton v Population Services Family Planning Programme Ltd* [1981] 2 Lancet 1430, in which the claimant was awarded damages for the acceleration of cancer and menopause by some four years.

[2]   (1973) 14 KIR 285. See also *Allen v British Rail Engineering Ltd* [2001] PIQR Q10; and *Holtby v Brigham & Cowan (Hull) Ltd* [2000] 3 All ER 421, [2000] ICR 1086.

[D56]   Where the claimant suffers from a pre-existing condition which might have given rise to the losses/expenses claimed in any event, the court will sometimes apply a discount to reflect this contingency. For example, in *Heil v Rankin*[1] the claimant was a police officer who suffered from post-traumatic stress disorder as a result of a serious shooting incident in 1987. In 1993 the claimant was the victim of a road traffic accident which exacerbated his psychiatric condition and ultimately led to his permanent discharge from the police force in 1994 on the grounds of ill-health. The trial judge discounted his claim to reflect the chance that the claimant might have suffered another triggering event which would have exacerbated his pre-existing condition in any event. The claimant appealed. The Court of Appeal held that there was no general rule that subsequent hypothetical tortious acts should be ignored when assessing damages for personal injury. Although the discount applied was found to be a little high, it was reasonable to make the deduction in order to take account of what might have happened in any event in the absence of the defendant's negligence.

1   [2001] QB 272, [2000] 3 All ER 138, CA.

[D57]   Whilst, generally speaking, a pre-existing illness/condition will usually operate to reduce the appropriate level of damages to take account of the disability which would have occurred in any event, occasionally such a condition will actually lead to an increase in the appropriate award of damages. For example, in *Mustard v Morris*[1] the claimant who was a diabetic suffered an injury which caused him more trouble than it would have done someone else without his pre-existing illness. The Court of Appeal held that a person who, through natural causes, suffers ill-health and then suffers grave injuries which reduce their capacity to bear their natural ill-health is likely to receive an increased rather than a decreased level of damages. Another example is provided by *Savory v Burningham*[2], which involved a claimant who suffered from congenital spastic quadriplegia. She was injured in a road traffic accident, sustaining a whiplash injury, an injury to her shoulder and post-traumatic stress disorder. The Recorder commented that the very fact of her previously highly restricted state made her injury a serious matter. As a result of the accident, she had all but lost her hard-won independence. It was held that her loss of amenity was much greater than would normally have arisen from such an injury.

1   [1982] 1 CLY 11. See also *Brown v Vosper Thornycroft* [2004] EWHC 400 (QB), in which the claimant had a pre-existing condition of Gilbert's syndrome, which meant that he suffered an adverse reaction to certain painkillers prescribed for the injuries and was entitled to an uplift in his award for PSLA as a result.
2   [1996] CLY 2362.

Acceleration cases

[D58]   In some cases, the defendant's negligence merely accelerates or brings forward the symptoms of a pre-existing condition by a certain period of time. This is particularly common in back injury cases where the claimant has pre-existing degenerative changes. In such a case, where there is clear medical evidence regarding the 'acceleration period', the claimant is likely to be limited to only claiming damages for that period[1]. It should be noted that, where the medical evidence is disputed on the issue of the acceleration period, it is open to the trial judge to examine the claimant's life and work and make his or her own assessment of the likely acceleration period[2].

1   See *Kenth v Heimdale Hotel Investments Ltd* [2001] EWCA Civ 1283, [2001] All ER (D) 27 (Jul), in which the Court of Appeal endorsed the 'acceleration period' approach. In that case, an alternative

method of calculation was put forward by the claimant at the appeal stage. Although the Court of Appeal noted that it would be theoretically possible to advance the claim on a different basis – namely on the basis of lost chance – the court was not willing to interfere with the trial judge's approach because the case had not been presented in this way at trial and the alternative approach had not been canvassed in the medical evidence. See further *Morgan v Millet* [2001] EWCA Civ 1641, [2001] All ER (D) 254 (Oct).

2   *Skerman v H Bollman Manufacturers Ltd* [2002] EWCA Civ 919.

[D59]   Of course, the defendant must take his or her victim as he or she finds them[1]. This is known as the 'eggshell skull' principle. Therefore, even though the claimant was particularly vulnerable to suffering an injury, the defendant will be responsible for all the consequences of that injury if his or her negligence causes it to materialise.

1   *Bourhill v Young* [1943] AC 92, per Lord Wright at 109–110: 'If the wrong is established the wrongdoer must take the victim as he finds him.' See also *Smith v Leech Brain* [1962] 2 QB 405, [1961] 3 All ER 1159.

[D60]   There is a qualification which must be considered where the claimant's vulnerability was such that, in the absence of the defendant's negligence, the condition he or she complains of may have occurred in any event. This was a problem which confronted Popplewell J in *Drayton Thomas v Southend Health Authority*[1], where a door swung open, coming into contact with the claimant and she being found to have sustained a wedge fracture to vertebra L2. The case for the defendants was that the fracture was not caused by the incident, but was most probably caused by the effect of osteoporosis on the back itself over a period of time. The defendant further contended that the claimant had a very vulnerable back, and the incident was of such a sort that it would not cause damage to a normal person and it was not foreseeable that it was likely to exacerbate the pre-existing disability which attached to the claimant. The court held for the claimant on the 'eggshell skull' principle – but then had to go on to consider what the defendant was liable for. The issues were: what damage did the claimant in fact sustain in the accident; and secondly, had the claimant established that there was any causal connection between the extent of her injury and the defendant's act of negligence? In this context, Popplewell J cited *Bailey v Hain Steamship Co Ltd*[2]:

'... It is necessary then to look at the matter of the incident of 22 February coming upon the top, not merely of a state of emotional tension, or obsessional temperament, but one that had already been brought near to the brink by two earlier incidents, for neither of which were these defendants responsible. The injured man was therefore on the brink of a nervous collapse. It is, of course, no answer for them to say that the injury was quite trivial and if the man had not been on the brink of a nervous collapse nothing at all would have happened to him; that by itself is no answer unless they can show that the injury was not the cause in the legal sense. The fact that they injured a man who was prone to this is not, of course, conclusive, but was the injury a cause? In my judgment it was not. The real cause at the time, whatever it may have been in December 1949, was that the man was on the brink of a nervous collapse and anything could have happened – any comparatively trivial matter, whether a slight bump or a fright, or anything that would have frightened an ordinary man, would have precipitated the disease. That is not enough; the case that I believe is always relevant on these matters is the case of the *Leyland Shipping Co Ltd v Norwich Union Fire Insurance Society Ltd* [1918] AC 350 ...

I interpolate to say that that was a case in which a ship had been torpedoed. It was then taken into berth. As a result of a storm it had to be beached. It then holed, and the court took the view that the cause of its loss was the torpedo and not a peril of the sea.

That, of course, was dealing with the cause, but it provides the sort of test which can be applied to causation generally. The court in that case said that the ship was already a doomed ship before the disaster happened; so in this case the man was for all ordinary purposes doomed to suffer this nervous collapse. He had already sustained two nervous shocks, and anything would have set off the third. If, therefore, it be necessary, even on that limited application of the case, to consider whether any damage had been caused, I should have found that it was not.

I do not think it is necessary to make any provision for, or assessment of, the damages in this case. It is very largely a matter of arithmetic, except for one factor, the factor that no doubt would be important, and the factor that I could not in the circumstances accurately assess; that is the relevance to the amount of damage of the matters that I have just been considering. When a man is suffering from a disease which a comparatively trivial accident sets off, there are two ways of dealing with it: the first is the way in which I have just dealt with it, namely, by saying that the precipitating factor is so trivial and played so small a part and would have been so likely to have occurred anyway that it cannot be regarded as a cause at all. But, assuming that it can be regarded as a cause, it would still be very necessary to limit the damages very considerably by considering that this was a man to whom any small accident would cause this to happen. If he had escaped anything on 22 February something may have happened on 23 or 24 February which would have precipitated the same state, and that is the sort of matter which must properly be taken into account in assessing the amount of damage for which a wrongdoer is responsible. As I do not find that this is the case at all clearly, I should not be right in determining what, if it were the case, should be the proper weight to be given to it in the assessment of damages.

On the best case that the [claimant] could have put forward, if she had been struck by a trolley and this fracture had occurred on 9 February, it is accepted by the doctors that she would have been entitled to be off work for a period of a year and should then have sought some sort of employment. She was at the time of the accident in part-time employment. The [claimant] called (against objection by the defendant) a witness, Mrs Wren, who was a Senior Nurse of the District Occupational Health Service of the West Berkshire Health Authority, to speak about the difficulty that somebody in the [claimant's] position would have in getting work. She observed that if you were going to go into industry you would need to have further training; that somebody with a back injury, in any event, would not be an ideal person for that job; that although somebody in a health centre or out-patients department would not be required to do physical handling on a regular basis, there might be occasions when that would be required and, therefore, she would not encourage anybody in the [claimant's] position to take up that sort of job.

The difficulty in the [claimant's] way is that, apart from going back on one occasion to this hospital, she has, as I understand it, made not the slightest effort to obtain any other job. It is true that she has been in nursing all her life and that some form of office job may present some difficulty, although there is no reason why, for instance, hospital records should not be the sort of job which she could take on, provided the job was available. But, in the absence of any evidence about the steps she has taken to obtain work or the absence of suitable jobs I take the view that if indeed she had been entitled to full damages for the period of the year after the accident, that would be a determinable point.

I, therefore, come back to what Devlin LJ said as to the approach of the court in the sort of case where an injury has been caused to the [claimant], which is not the defendants' fault, leaving the [claimant] in a state where, as a result of what the defendants have done, the [claimant] has had the pre-existing disability very substantially accelerated, and Devlin LJ took the view in his case that as a matter of causation he was going to find against the [claimant]. He observed that the alternative view was to give damages on a limited basis on the proper assumption, given the evidence, that given the [claimant's] condition any small accident, trivial or unrelated to negligence, might have reduced the [claimant] to the condition in which she now finds herself.

I prefer the latter approach. I think it would be quite wrong in this case to say that there was no causation. But, having said that, in the light of the evidence given by Mr Spivey, the amount of damages must be strictly limited. It is the aggravation of a pre-existing fracture, unrelated to this incident, which might at any time, as a result of some trivial blow or tripping have created the same situation. I have to make the best judgment I can of how soon after February the [claimant] would have been reduced to the condition in which she now is but for the incident of the trolley. I think that 6 or 9 months is the best that she could have expected, and for that, by way of general damages – the pain and suffering for that period – I award her the sum of £1,500 ...'

---

[1]   (26 March 1990, unreported), QBD. See also *Heil v Rankin* [2001] QB 272, [2000] 3 All ER 138, CA.

[2]   [1956] 1 Lloyd's Rep 641 at 653.

Further intervening injury – novus actus interveniens

[D61]   It is not uncommon for a claimant to be injured by a further tortfeasor or by a non-tortfeasor. He or she may have a car accident, be taken to hospital and be treated negligently by the hospital staff. Alternatively, he or she may have a further accident which aggravates or extinguishes the prior injury.

[D62]   How the law approaches these difficult questions of 'novus actus interveniens' depends upon whether the later act was tortious or not. If the intervening act was a tort, the original tortfeasor is liable for injuries/damages sustained as a result of the original tort, but not for any exacerbation or attenuation caused by the second tort[1]. The second wrongdoer is not liable for any injury that already exists[2]. If the intervening act/omission was not tortious, it may act as a 'novus actus' if it attenuates any of the claimant's suffering or damages[3].

---

[1]   *Baker v Willoughby* [1970] AC 467; the tortfeasor who causes the initial injury is fully liable if the second accident results in the continuance of the same loss (eg in *Baker* the claimant recovered his full loss of earnings despite the second act causing the amputation of his leg).

[2]   *Performance Cars v Abraham* [1962] 1 QB 33, [1961] 3 All ER 413 (not liable for the cost of a respray when the car was already in need of one).

[3]   *Jobling v Associated Dairies Ltd* [1982] AC 794, [1981] 2 All ER 752, HL.

[D63]   A common example of 'novus actus' in operation in personal injury cases is negligent treatment or surgery following an accident. This issue was considered by the Court of Appeal in *Webb v Barclay's Bank plc*[1]. The claimant in that case had tripped over a protruding stone in the forecourt of her employer's premises. She was treated with physiotherapy and bracing of the knee. Thereafter, when her symptoms did not resolve because of complications relating to her pre-existing condition of polio, she was negligently advised to undergo an above-knee amputation of the leg. Henry LJ relied upon the Australian case of *Mahoney v Kruschick (Demolitions) Pty Ltd*[2] and approved the following passage in *Clerk and Lindsell on Torts*[3]:

'... only medical treatment so grossly negligent as to be a completely inappropriate response to the injury inflicted by the defendant should operate to break the chain of causation.'

1   [2001] EWCA Civ 1141. But see also *Robson v Post Office* [1974] 2 All ER 737, [1974] 1 WLR 1176, CA; *Rothwell v Caverswall Stone Co* [1944] 2 All ER 350, CA; and *Hogan v Bentinck Collieries* [1949] 1 All ER 588, HL, in which Lord Normand said at 596: 'I start from the proposition which seems to me to be axiomatic, that if a surgeon, by lack of skill or failure in reasonable care, causes additional injury or aggravates an existing injury and so renders himself liable in damages, the reasonable conclusion must be that his intervention is a new cause, and that the additional injury or the aggravation of the existing injury should be attributed to it and not to the original accident. On the other hand, an operation prudently advised and carefully carried out should not be treated as a new cause, whatever its consequences may be'.

2   (1985) 156 CLR 522.

3   18th edn at para 2–55.

[D64] On the facts, the Court of Appeal held that the doctor's negligence was not grossly negligent and did not eclipse the first defendant's negligence in failing properly to maintain its forecourt. However, the Trust, which was vicariously liable for the actions of the doctor, was held to be much more responsible for the amputation and all that went with it. In the circumstances, liability was apportioned 25% against the bank and 75% against the Trust.

Subsequent injuries

[D65] Occasionally, one injury might make a person more vulnerable to suffering a further injury. For example, a claimant suffering a whiplash injury who is given a neck collar to wear might have difficulty seeing where they are walking and fall down some stairs. These were the facts in *Wieland v Cyril Lord Carpets Ltd*[1] where it was held that the claimant's ability to cope with the vicissitudes of life was diminished, so that another reasonably foreseeable injury resulted. Since the chain of causation had not been broken, the defendant responsible for causing the original injury was held liable for the second injury and its consequences.

1   [1969] 3 All ER 1006, per Eveleigh J, followed in *Pyne v Wikenfeld* (1981) 26 SASR 441.

[D66] As seen above, a common example of this principle occurs in practice when a claimant who is injured in an accident is taken to hospital and suffers further injuries (or an exacerbation of their existing injuries) by reason of clinical negligence. As long as the medical treatment provided is not so grossly negligent as to be a completely inappropriate response to the injury inflicted, the chain of causation will not be broken[1]. The original defendant will therefore remain responsible for the subsequent injuries and consequent damage (although can claim a contribution or an indemnity in respect of the damage caused by reason of the clinical negligence from the health professionals responsible for providing the same).

1   *Webb v Barclays Bank plc* [2001] EWCA Civ 1141, which approved the Australian case of *Mahoney v Kruschick (Demolitions) Pty Ltd* (1985) 156 CLR 522. See also *Robinson v Post Office* [1974] 1 WLR 1176, CA; *Rothwell v Caverswall & Co* [1944] 2 All ER 350, CA; and *Hogan v Bentinck Collieries* [1949] 1 All ER 588.

[D67]   In some instances, the chain of causation between the first and the second injury will be broken, usually by the claimant's own unreasonable behaviour, in which case the defendant responsible for the initial injury will not be held liable for the subsequent injury. For example, in *McKew v Holland & Hannen & Cubitts*[1] the claimant suffered an initial injury to his left leg during the course of his employment. His employers admitted liability for the injury which, it was agreed, made him vulnerable to suffering further injuries because his left leg occasionally gave way. The claimant's left leg gave way as he was coming down some stairs and he decided to jump down some ten steps. The House of Lords held that the claimant's act of attempting to descend steep stairs without a hand rail and without adult assistance or, alternatively, jumping down the stairs was unreasonable. The chain of causation was therefore broken and the defendant was not liable for the subsequent injury (a severe ankle fracture). This case was followed in the Scottish case of *Sabri-Tabrizi v Lothian Health Board*[2]. Here, the claimant underwent a sterilisation procedure which failed, causing her to become pregnant. The claimant decided to terminate that pregnancy but then subsequently re-exposed herself to the risk of pregnancy, without taking adequate precautions against the same, resulting in a second pregnancy. The Outer House held that, following the first termination, the claimant knew that there was a risk of becoming pregnant and it was unreasonable for her to expose herself to this risk again, thus breaking the chain of causation. When will a claimant's conduct be so unreasonable as to break the chain of causation? The courts have generally been reluctant to lay down any prescriptive rules although, in *Emeh v Kensington etc AHA*[3], Waller LJ described Lord Reid's view of the degree of unreasonable conduct required in *McKew* as being 'very high'[4]. However, where the claimant's conduct is not so unreasonable as to break the chain of causation, it may be held to be sufficiently unreasonable so as to justify a finding of contributory negligence. Thus, in *Spencer v Wincanton Holdings Ltd*[5] the Court of Appeal upheld the trial judge's ruling that the claimant's decision to try to get petrol without using crutches or any other walking aid despite his above-knee amputation, which resulted in a fall aggravating his original injuries, justified a finding of contributory negligence of one-third. The defendant was therefore held two-thirds responsible for the further injuries caused by the fall.

[1]   [1969] 3 All ER 1621, HL.
[2]   (1988) 43 BMLR 190.
[3]   [1984] 3 All ER 1044.
[4]   At 1049.
[5]   [2009] EWCA Civ 1404.

Suicide

[D68]   In *Corr v IBC Vehicles Ltd*[1] the House of Lords had to consider the case of a man who committed suicide almost six years following an accident at work. A claim had initially been started on his behalf for personal injury, but then his widow was substituted as the claimant for the purposes of bringing a claim under the Fatal Accidents Act 1976. The defendant employers mounted a number of arguments to resist paying for the financial dependency arising out of the death, which was found to be a foreseeable consequence of Mr Corr's severe depressive illness. In summary, it was held that: (i) the suicide was within the employer's scope of duty; (ii) it was only necessary to prove depression, and not that suicide was a foreseeable consequence of the defendant's breach of duty; (iii) since Mr Corr's capacity to make reasoned and informed judgments about his future was impaired by suffering from a severe depressive illness, the suicide was not a 'novus actus' or an unreasonable act breaking the chain of chain of causation; (iv) Mr Corr had not voluntarily consented to his suicide with 'his eyes open' but the suicide was an act performed because of the psychological condition which the employer's breach of duty had induced; and (v) the claimant's damages should not be reduced by reason of contributory negligence. However, their Lordships specifically left open the possibility in the future that an individual who committed suicide could be held contributory negligent, it being for the defendant to establish any deduction on the basis of evidence and argument[2]. In short, the loss was not too remote and therefore was recoverable.

1   [2008] 1 AC 884.
2   Per Lord Neuberger of Abbotsbury at 919F–G.

Multiple injuries

[D69]   Where a claimant suffers more than one injury, the assessment of the appropriate award for PSLA becomes more complicated. It is necessary for the court to take an overall view as regards the injuries as a whole and their impact upon the victim. As stated by Sir John May in *Brown v Woodall*[1]:

> 'In this type of case, in which there are a number of separate injuries, all adding up to one composite effect upon a claimant, it is necessary for a learned judge, no doubt having considered the various injuries and fixed a particular figure as reasonable for each, to stand back and look at which should be the global aggregate figure and ask if it is reasonable compensation for the totality of the injury to the claimant or to consider whether it would in the aggregate be larger than was reasonable.'

1   [1995] PIQR Q36 at Q39.

[D70]   The danger is that, unless the injuries are considered globally, the claimant will receive too much by way of damages, given the overlap between the respective injuries. The overlap is perhaps most evident in respect of loss of amenity, where different injuries may each be sufficient to prevent the claimant from enjoying a particular hobby or pastime, and to award loss of amenity in relation to each injury would over-compensate the claimant. An example of the overlap between different injuries, and the potential for over-compensation if a global view is not taken in relation to the disability resulting from the claimant's different injuries, is provided by *Fitzgerald v Ford*[1]. In this case, the claimant suffered very severe multiple injuries and was awarded £125,000 by the trial judge. However, this amount was subsequently reduced by the Court of Appeal on the basis that, despite the severity of the claimant's injuries, she was still better off than a tetraplegic. In particular, she had more mobility than the average tetraplegic, could transfer from her chair to the lavatory, could go up and down stairs, and was by and large continent of both urine and faeces. She could also wash her upper body, clean her teeth and feed herself if her food was cut up. The court held that, since the 'conventional' award for a typical middle-of-the-road tetraplegic at that time (July 1993) was £111,000, the appropriate figure for the claimant's injuries was £100,000, and reduced her award for PSLA accordingly.

¹   [1996] PIQR Q72. See also *Sharpe v Woods* (16 July 1993, unreported), in which Potter J assessed
the claimant's injuries on the basis that the claimant was in a worse position than a paraplegic but a
better position than a quadriplegic.

[D71]   But each case must be decided on its facts, since each claimant will be
affected and react in a different way to their injuries. What might be an appropriate
method of assessment for one claimant might be unfair to another. In some cases,
the combination of injuries will have a much more serious impact on the claimant
than simply adding up awards for the separate injuries and applying a discount to
reflect the perceived overlap. The obvious example is a claimant who sustains two
broken legs at the same time. The resulting level of disability may not be adequately
compensated by awarding a (discounted) figure representing double the appropriate
amount in respect of one broken leg¹.

¹   See eg *Welch v Albright & Wilson Ltd* (28 May 1993, unreported), QBD, Birmingham, in which
Kay J was confronted with a nasty above-knee amputation and an injury to the remaining foot:
'Having said that, [the amputation] is not the only element in this case; there is the injury to the
other foot. It is submitted, on behalf of the defendants, that in a sense the two overlap. I think it is
right that in a sense the two do overlap because the period that he spent in hospital, for example,
was a period relevant to both and some of the other matters, loss of mobility. The loss of the leg
makes the loss of mobility in relation to the foot less significant, but, in my judgment, there is a
counterbalancing factor. A man who loses one leg requires as good a second leg as he can possibly
have. This man lost a significant part of his right foot. He has been left with pain in that right foot. In
those circumstances it is clear that this figure must exceed the sort of maximum simply considering
the amputation'.

[D72]   So how does this work in practice? The answer is that the courts have
developed a number of different approaches, depending upon the facts of the case.
The three main methods that are used to assess multiple injuries are set out below.

(1) THE OVERALL IMPRESSION APPROACH

[D73]   This technique involves the court making a one-off broad brush global
assessment regarding the totality of the claimant's injuries. In *Brown v Woodall*, Sir
John May put it as follows¹:

'It is accepted that sometimes there may be a genuine overlap of damages if the sum
awarded for multiple injuries is reached merely by adding together the appropriate award
for each separate injury. For example, an award for a simple leg fracture would include
some damages for the time spent in hospital and in convalescence, as would an award
for a simple arm fracture. If both fractures occurred at the same time and the award for
the multiple injury were calculated by adding together the damages which would be
awarded for each fracture separately, there would be an overlap of the damages awarded
for the time in hospital and convalescence. Accordingly, in such case some discount
should be made from the aggregate of the two sums to allow for the overlap. But there
may also be cases where the effect on the victim of multiple injuries warrants an award
greater than the aggregate of the damages appropriate for each injury taken separately.
For example, the devastating combination of the loss of both legs and the loss of both
arms would warrant a considerably higher award than the aggregate of the award for the
loss of the arms or the legs sustained separately. In every case the court should consider
the total effect of the multiple injuries on the particular claimant.'

¹   [1995] PIQR Q36 at Q39.

[D74] In practice, this can either be done by considering previous awards in other cases of similar multiple injuries or awards in cases involving a similar level of overall disability. In *Hicks v Barnes*[1], Turner J had to compensate for loss of a year's study, a man who was aged 17 at the time of the accident and 20 at trial. He said:

'There is no satisfactorily rational way in which to evaluate a claim such as this. It would be unrealistic to approach the individual injury or groups of injuries and award a sum for each and arrive at a total. What has to be done is for the judge, as best he may, to sit back from it all and try to form an overall impression, both of the impact of the injuries and how as best, but imperfectly as he may, evaluate that in terms of money. It is not just the individual judge's assessment of money because, of course, his award has to be more or less in line with awards in broadly comparable cases, and I lay emphasis on the word "broadly", because no two of these cases are strictly comparable. No two individuals respond equally to the same insult, whether it is of a physical or non-physical kind.'

[1]   (13 January 1988, unreported), QBD.

[D75] The 'overall impression' approach was subsequently endorsed by the Court of Appeal in *Lloyd v Lloyd*[1], in which Farquharson LJ stated:

'There are obvious dangers in making individual awards in the way that has been described. It is then possible to attack each award individually and say that on its own it is excessive, having regard to comparable decisions of the court. For my part, in so far as one is dealing with the case in this way, I am inclined to agree with Mr Bethell's submission that, if there was to be a split, it would have been proper for an award in respect of the orthopaedic injuries, that is to say to the knee and to the arm, to have included the associated scarring with those injuries, and that if one was going to take a separate approach in regard to scarring at all, it should have been restricted to those scars which were the most serious, namely on the forehead and on the abdomen. Those could, no doubt, be separately assessed, thus giving two heads of damage. Finally, I am for my part quite clear that on the findings of the learned judge with regard to the psychological damage it was not right that it should be separately assessed. The depression suffered by the unfortunate respondent as a result of this accident could properly have been reflected as part of the post-traumatic injury she sustained under those first two heads of damage. The danger is, as has been repeatedly pointed out, that if one deals with them separately in this way one tends to come up to an accumulative figure which is in excess of that properly awarded ...'

[1]   (21 March 1990, unreported). See also *Santos v Eaton Square Garage Ltd* [2007] EWCA Civ 225 as regards the aggregation of orthopaedic and psychiatric injuries, where the psychological symptoms relate to pain or the perception of pain caused by the physical injuries.

[D76] This approach was later refined by *Dureau v Evans*[1] by suggesting that, when assessing the appropriate award of PSLA for multiple injuries, the court should start by assessing the claimant's most serious injury and then uplift the resulting figure for that injury in order to take account of the claimant's other injuries. As explained by Kennedy LJ:

'To a limited extent, in a case where there are multiple injuries, the figures in the Judicial Studies Board table can help but I accept Mr Murphy's criticism of them that, where one has a multiplicity of injuries, it is necessary to take an overall view. The off-setting process may mean it is not possible to derive a great deal of benefit from that particular source. One then looks to see if anything can be gained from looking at a comparable award, if one is to be found, in another case. Even that may not prove to be a particularly fruitful source of inquiry. It may be necessary, if it be possible, to select what may be the most serious head of injury to see if a comparable award can be found in relation to that and, if so, build on it to allow for the other heads of injury which have been sustained by the claimant in the instant case.'

1   [1996] PIQR Q18. This approach was approved and followed in *Clarke v South Yorkshire Transport Ltd* [1998] PIQR Q104. See also *Pinnington v Crossleigh Construction* [2003] EWCA Civ 1684.

(2) AGGREGATE OF AWARDS FOR SEPARATE INJURIES WITH DISCOUNT FOR PERCEIVED OVERLAP

[D77] This approach involves the court making an individual assessment of the value of each (significant) injury or group of injuries. The various separate figures are then added together and discounted by a factor to take account of the perceived 'overlap' between them. For example, a calculation might be performed as follows:

Head injury	£20,000
Orthopaedic injuries	£10,000
Dental injuries	£5,000
Pneumothorax	£2,500
Psychiatric injuries	£7,500
Subtotal:	£45,000
Less discount for overlap	(£7,500)
Award for PSLA	£37,500

[D78] Such an assessment was carried out by Wood J in *Bracken v Lancashire County Council Education Authority*[1]:

'... Now, I have been greatly assisted from the Bar in assessing a difficult matter and Mr Donovan broke down the various headings and put a figure against them; the accident, the present disability, the loss of amenities, psoriasis, the surgical scars – and there was a nasty scar of some nine inches down the outside of his hip – and risk of osteoarthritis and he put figures on those, bringing them together and adding them up, and he reached a figure of £17,000. Well, there is a danger of some degree of overlap when one is merely adding together the items in that way, as anyone with experience knows, but nevertheless, I think this young man has suffered a nasty injury and I assess his general damages at £16,000 ...'

1   (1 April 1987, unreported), QBD.

[D79] In *Stevens v Simon*[1] the Court of Appeal confirmed that the approach adopted by Wood J was proper, provided the court does not fall into the trap of awarding damages in the area of the overlap involved in loss of amenity.

1   (1987) Times, 20 November, CA.

[D80] It should be noted that the level of discount to be applied depends upon the degree of overlap between the different injuries. For example, where all of the injuries are of a similar nature, eg orthopaedic, the discount will be higher than where the injuries are more distinct, such as a laceration to the spleen and psychiatric injuries. Whilst discounts of between 10% and 20% are perhaps the norm[1], discounts of 25%

or more are not uncommon². However, the court must make sure that all the injuries are considered in the global award. If the discount applied to take account of the overlap between the injuries is too great, the award will be amenable to appeal. For example, in *Lee v Clark*³ the judge awarded £12,500 in respect of multiple physical injuries involving a serious comminuted fracture of the mid-shaft of the left femur, a fractured rib with traumatic right pneumothorax, anterior dislocation of the right shoulder and loss of sensation in the right forearm. On appeal, the award for PSLA was increased to £15,000. Beldam J said:

'When he sustained his injuries the claimant was only 27 years of age and he did not make a full recovery from his orthopaedic injuries for two-and-a-half years. Although the award of damages must take account of the multiple injuries he sustained, he is not compensated as if he suffered each of the injuries separately. Nevertheless, his award must include compensation for all the injuries. He is left with two permanent consequences which, whilst not in themselves serious, are significant. He has aching in his lower back and in his right hip as a consequence of the shortening of his leg after prolonged standing and walking. Further, he has a loss of sensation on the anterior and medial aspect of the right forearm due to tearing of the nerve in the brachial plexus. These two consequences will be with him for the rest of his life. In my view the judge did under-estimate the severity of the [claimant's] injuries and discount [sic] too greatly these continuing effects. I would increase the award for general damages to GBP15,000 and to that extent would allow the appeal.'

1	See eg *Patterson v Bunclark* [2000] CLY 1501; and *Storey v Phillips* [2001] CLY 1565.
2	See eg *Gubbins v Bailie* [2001] CLY 1564.
3	(April 28 1998, unreported), CA.

(3) AGGREGATE OF AWARDS FOR SEPARATE INJURIES WITHOUT DISCOUNT

[D81]   In some cases, the overlap between different injuries will be slight if it exists at all. In these circumstances, the court may be disinclined to apply any discount at all. For example, in the first-instance decision of *Smith v Rod Jenkins*¹, the claimant suffered a head injury, a fracture to the temporal bone, and fractures of the right jaw and cheek bone. Gibbs J considered the multiplicity of the claimant's injuries and decided not to apply a discount. He reasoned as follows²:

'In assessing the appropriate award under this head, I bear in mind that in most cases in which a claimant suffers from two or more distinct categories of injury, it may not be appropriate simply to aggregate the figures which might be awarded for each injury considered separately. A discount may be appropriate in arriving at a suitable total figure. Here, I think that a discount would be inappropriate. In the case of each of the categories of injury suffered, the effect of the one has in my view made it if anything more difficult for the claimant to cope with the other, even after making allowance for the exaggeration already discussed. I assess damages under this head at £37,000.'

1	[2003] EWHC 1356 (QB).
2	At para 81.

[D82]   Further, in *George v Stagecoach*¹, Mackay J had to consider the appropriate award of general damages for PSLA in relation to a head injury and a degloving injury to the left foot. He also declined to apply a discount to the aggregate award for the separate injuries. He said²:

'Normally I would not simply have added these components. In this case I do, for these reasons. They are three rather discrete pieces of injury. There is really very little way in which they overlap each with the other. Secondly, I do not propose to make a separate award for loss of congenial employment. This case is very much borderline for that; indeed, it probably does not cross the borderline. But that justifies me in making an overall award for pain, suffering and loss of amenity of £59,000.'

1   [2003] EWHC 2042 (QB).
2   At para [52].

[D83]   So, which method will the court use to assess damages for PSLA in any given case? Unfortunately, there are no hard and fast rules. Ultimately, the court retains a discretion to assess damages using the method considered most appropriate to the facts of the individual case. However, the following guidance might provide a few pointers. Where the claimant suffers a number of related injuries, such as a number of orthopaedic injuries and/or scarring resulting from the same, and there is a high degree of overlap between the respective injuries, the first method of assessment, ie the overall impressionistic approach, is likely to be adopted. If the claimant suffers a number of different injuries or types of injury (eg orthopaedic injuries as well as abdominal injuries and psychiatric injuries) and there is some degree of overlap between the respective injuries or types of injury, the second method of assessment is likely to be used, ie an aggregate of the amount for each type of injury, with a discount to account for the overlap. Only where the different injuries sustained are completely separate and distinct, such that there is no overlap between them, is the third method of assessment likely to be appropriate, ie an aggregate of the different awards without discount. In this regard, it should be noted that, notwithstanding what was said by Farquharson LJ in *Lloyd v Lloyd*[1], the case reports are littered with examples showing that the courts are often prepared to assess the appropriate sum for PSLA by making separate awards in respect of physical and psychiatric/psychological injuries[2]. However, the situation may be different where the psychological sequelae are related to the pain or perception of pain initially caused by an orthopaedic injury. For example, in *Santos v Eaton Square Garage Ltd*[3] the Court of Appeal reduced the overall award by £3,000 to £32,000 when aggregating an award of £24,000 for Chronic Pain Syndrome, £3,000 for PTSD and £8,000 for an orthopaedic injury.

1   (21 March 1990, unreported), see quotation at para **[D75]**.
2   See eg *Terry v Sand Farm House Hotel* [2000] CLY 1643; *Jowitt v McNeice* [2001] CLY 1581; *Bajjawi v NE Davies (Engineering) Ltd* [2001] CLY 1679; *Corkish v Harrison* [2002] 3562; and *Kennedy v Queen's Medical Centre University Hospital NHS Trust* [2002] CLY 3524.
3   [2007] EWCA Civ 225. Maurice Kay LJ stated at para [22]: 'Compensation for pain, suffering and loss of amenity has to take into account that where there is a plurality or duality of conditions simple aggregation would produce over-compensation for pain, suffering and loss of amenity. That is particularly so where, as here, the psychological sequelae are related to the pain or perception of pain which was initially caused by the orthopaedic injury'.

Cases of shock

[D84]   If a victim has suffered shock, anxiety and fear without any other injuries, then no liability can attach. To qualify for damages shock must cause some physical, nervous or mental injury or illness[1]. Mere anxiety (falling short of psychiatric injury) regarding the risk of developing a future condition is not sufficient to establish liability[2]. But where physical injury is sustained and thereafter the claimant develops a psychiatric condition or an exacerbation of an existing condition, liability may attach for both the physical and mental illness where it could have reasonably been foreseen that the defendant's conduct would expose the claimant to a risk of injury even if the condition or exacerbation of the mental illness was not foreseeable[3]. Cases involving alleged psychiatric 'injury' must consist of a recognised psychiatric illness to found a claim[4]. Examples include depression, post-traumatic stress disorder, pathological grief disorder, adjustment disorder and car phobia. Once, however, a clinical illness results, perhaps because grief is so extreme as to go beyond the normal into the pathological, there is no warrant for limiting the damage to that element of the suffering which exceeds 'normal' limits[5].

[1] See as examples: *McLoughlin v O'Brian* [1983] 1 AC 410; *Nicholls v Rushton* (1992) Times, 19 June; and *Simpson v ICI Ltd* 1983 SLT 601.

[2] *Rothwell v Chemical & Insulating Co Ltd* [2008] 1 AC 281.

[3] *Page v Smith* [1996] AC 155. See further *Simmons v British Steel plc* [2004] ICR 585, where the House of Lords held that a claimant who had suffered physical injuries in an accident at work (a severe blow to the head) was able to recover for the exacerbation of his psoriasis and the depressive illness resulting from it which was not foreseeable and had been brought on by worry and anger following the accident (which was in part the fault of the defendant).

[4] *Page v Smith* [1996] AC 155. See also *Nicholls v Rushton* (1992) Times, 19 June, CA, in which it was held that there could be no recovery for a nervous reaction which fell short of an identifiable psychological illness. See also *Reilly and Reilly v Merseyside Regional Health Authority* [1995] 6 Med LR 246, where the Court of Appeal disallowed the claim by a husband and wife who were trapped in a lift and suffered from 'apprehension, fear, discomfort and shortness of breath'. It was held that, in the absence of a recognised psychiatric injury, they could not recover for the normal emotion in the face of a most unpleasant experience. See also *Afzal v Chubb Guarding Services Ltd* [2003] EWHC 822, in which HHJ Bowsher QC found that the claimant was malingering rather than suffering from any recognised psychiatric disorder.

[5] *Vernon v Bosley (No 1)* [1997] PIQR P255, in particular per Evans LJ at P313–4.

[D85] However, shock (plus grief and other emotional feelings) is taken into account when assessing general damages if other injuries exist[1].

[1] *Kralj v McGrath* [1986] 1 All ER 54.

Psychiatric Injury

[D86] Where the claimant has suffered an identifiable psychiatric illness[1] by reason of the defendant's wrongdoing, a claim may be made in respect of these injuries and any consequent expenses/losses, assuming that a number of conditions are met. The legal principles surrounding such claims – which used to be known as 'nervous shock' claims – have developed rapidly over the last two decades or so[2]. Indeed, several cases have reached the House of Lords regarding the recoverability for psychiatric injury in recent years (as detailed below), and the law has benefited from significant clarification in this area as a result.

[1] There can be no recovery for a nervous reaction which falls short of a recognised mental injury or illness unless it is accompanied by a physical injury: *Nicholls v Rushton* (1992) Times, 19 June, CA; *Reilly and Reilly v Merseyside Regional Health Authority* [1995] 6 Med LR 246; *Page v Smith* [1996] AC 155.

² See further the Law Commission Report No 249 'Liability for Psychiatric Injury' (1996). In particular, there have been a number of recent cases dealing with psychiatric injury in the context of clinical negligence. See eg *Farrell v Merton Sutton & Wandsworth Health Authority* (2001) 57 BMLR 158; *Farrell v Avon Health Authority* [2001] Lloyd's Rep Med 458; *Walters v North Glamorgan NHS Trust* [2002] EWCA Civ 1792; *Froggatt v Chesterfield* [2002] All ER (D) 218 (Dec); *Atkinson v Seghal* [2003] EWCA Civ 697. It is clear that the normal principles governing recovery for psychiatric injury will apply, notwithstanding the fact that the injury might have occurred in the context of clinical negligence: *Walters v North Glamorgan NHS Trust* [2002] EWCA Civ 1792. Also, since this is still a developing area of law, the court will be reluctant to strike out novel claims before the facts have been tried: *W v Essex County Council* [2000] 2 WLR 601.

[D87] The first case to reach the House of Lords in this area was *McLoughlin v O'Brian*[1]. The claimant's husband and children were injured in a car accident. She was informed of the injuries and the death of a child and she saw the extensive injuries in hospital. The House of Lords upheld her claim in relation to the psychiatric injury suffered as a result of the accident and its aftermath. Lord Bridge, in his judgment, stated:

'The basic difficulty of the subject arises from the fact that the crucial answers to the questions which it raises lie in the difficult field of psychiatric medicine. The common law gives no damages for the emotional distress which any normal person experiences when someone else he loves is killed or injured. Anxiety and depression are normal human emotions. Yet an anxiety neurosis or a reactive depression may be recognisable psychiatric illnesses, with or without psychosomatic symptoms. So the first hurdle which a claimant claiming damages of the kind in question must surmount is to establish that he is suffering, not merely grief, distress or any other normal emotion, but a positive psychiatric illness ... A [claimant] must then establish the necessary chain of causation in fact between his psychiatric illness and the death or injury of one or more third parties negligently caused by the defendant.'

¹ [1983] 1 AC 410.

[D88] A distinction has initially to be made between what have become known as 'primary' and 'secondary' victims of an accident[1]. A 'primary' victim is a claimant who was directly involved in the accident and well within the range of foreseeable injury. On the other hand, a 'secondary' victim has suffered injury by reason of observing or learning of harm done to another person involved in an accident (ie a 'primary' victim)[2]. A 'primary' victim is entitled to recover damages for psychiatric injuries suffered, even where no physical injury has occurred.

¹ See the Law Commission Report No 249 'Liability for Psychiatric Injury' (1996); see also *Page v Smith* [1996] AC 155 and *White v Chief Constable of South Yorkshire Police* [1999] 2 AC 455.
² If the particular claimant falls between the two definitions, then he or she will still be a 'secondary' victim (see below for discussion on rescuers).

[D89] The position concerning 'secondary victims' is governed by the House of Lords' decision in *Alcock v Chief Constable of South Yorkshire Police*[1]. This case arose out of the tragic events that surrounded the Hillsborough disaster. The civilian claimants were not 'victims' in the primary sense, as they saw the events either within the stadium or on television, or had heard about it from others. All the claimants later discovered that their relatives were among the dead. It was accepted that the claimants had suffered psychiatric injury because of this experience. Even though the injury was accepted as attributable to the disaster, the House of Lords prescribed certain qualifications, known as 'control mechanisms', as being necessary for a claim to be successful:

(1) The psychiatric injury must have been caused by direct perception[2] of a 'shocking event'[3] or its immediate aftermath.
(2) The claimant must have either been present at the accident itself or its immediate aftermath[4].
(3) The claimant must have close ties of love and affection with the victim[5]. Such a tie may be presumed in some cases (eg child, parent or spouse), but other relationships may, by evidence, establish such a tie[6].

[1]   [1992] 1 AC 310.
[2]   Colloquially known as the 'Hearness' test.
[3]   There must be shock through the sudden appreciation by sight or sound of an event or its immediate aftermath: *Alcock v Chief Constable of South Yorkshire Police* [1992] 1 AC 310; *White v Chief Constable of South Yorkshire Police* [1999] 2 AC 455; *Walters v North Glamorgan NHS Trust* [2002] EWCA Civ 1792. Although note that it has recently been confirmed that an event may be made up of a number of components: *Walters v North Glamorgan NHS Trust* [2002] EWCA Civ 1792; *Atkinson v Seghal* [2003] EWCA Civ 697.
[4]   Colloquially known as the 'Nearness' test.
[5]   Colloquially known as the 'Dearness' test.
[6]   See eg *McLoughlin v O'Brian* [1983] 1 AC 410.

[D90]   All the claimants in *Alcock*[1] failed in their action for one reason or another. Mr Harrison was present at the ground and his two brothers died. He clearly fulfilled conditions (1) and (2). However, the court was not satisfied that a brother relationship (without further evidence) provided the necessary ties. Mr and Mrs Copac failed as, although the tie was presumed (as it was their son who died), they were not present at the ground and saw the incident only on television[2]. Mr Alcock identified his brother-in-law later that evening at the mortuary. However, he failed as this was not classed as the immediate aftermath of the accident. The other claimants failed for similar reasons.

[1]   *Alcock v Chief Constable of South Yorkshire Police* [1992] 1 AC 310.
[2]   An argument regarding the simultaneous nature of television was rejected, and actual presence is required in any but the most remarkable of cases.

[D91]   Therefore, there are quite extensive control mechanisms placed on 'secondary victim' psychological injury claims. In reality, there are few instances where a person of such close ties will be present and not involved in an accident themselves.

[D92]   The House of Lords had again to consider claims arising out of the Hillsborough disaster in *White v Chief Constable of South Yorkshire Police*[1]. In this case, four police officers had been successful in their appeals to the Court of Appeal, which held that the police officers were owed duties as employees, and were not mere bystanders or spectators and, as such, were owed a duty of care as a rescuer and not a standard secondary victim[2]. The Court of Appeal followed the decision in *Chadwick v British Railways Board*[3]. In *Chadwick* the claimant suffered psychiatric injury following his experiences in assisting the victims of a railway accident. These consisted of a gruelling 12 hours spent crawling in the wreckage helping the victims, either by assisting removal or administering first aid. It was held that Mr Chadwick could recover damages. He was owed a duty of care and it did not matter that the injuries were psychiatric. It was foreseeable that a rescuer would go into the accident site and foreseeable that some injury could occur to that person. The Court of Appeal therefore accepted this as an example of rescuers being in their own class of claimant. Lord Hoffmann[4] chose not to apply such a finding. He held that the rescuer cases are 'quite simple illustrations of the application of general principles of foreseeability and causation to particular facts'. He continued and pointed out that there are no authorities that classify rescuers in any special position regarding liability. The rescuer will still need to be within the range of foreseeable physical injury to qualify as a 'primary victim' and avoid the *Alcock*[5] control mechanisms.

1   [1999] 2 AC 455.

2   A further duty of care was established by way of employment.

3   [1967] 1 WLR 912.

4   In *White v Chief Constable of South Yorkshire Police* [1999] 2 AC 455.

5   [1992] 1 AC 310.

[D93]   The House of Lords held (by a 3:2 majority) that the police officers were not 'primary victims'. Their Lordships rejected extending the liability for psychiatric injury to the officers as 'rescuers' (although Lord Hoffmann accepted, on the authorities, they were free to do so). Lord Hoffmann expressed his view that to do so would be unacceptable not only due to a difficulty of definition but, more importantly, due to the extensive restrictions placed on relatives' and loved ones' claims. The police should be in no better a position than secondary victims when they, too, had not been direct and immediate victims of the tort.

[D94]   Lord Steyn came to a similar conclusion. He stated that:

> 'In order to contain the concept of rescuer in reasonable bounds for the purposes of the recovery of compensation for pure psychiatric harm the claimant must at least satisfy the threshold requirement that he objectively exposed himself to danger or reasonably believed he was doing so.'

[D95]   Therefore, in conclusion, the authorities now offer some guidance as to those who can and cannot claim for psychiatric injury, although whether or not a particular claimant will succeed on a particular set of facts is not always easy to determine[1]. Any extension must be left to Parliament[2]. Following *Page v Smith*[3] a primary victim (that is one within the range of foreseeable physical injury) can claim for purely psychiatric injury. Such claimants could include 'rescuers', but only if they could show on the evidence that they were within the necessary range of danger. Secondary victims who are not actually 'involved' in the shocking event(s) cannot claim for any resultant psychiatric injury unless they qualify under the *Alcock*[4] control mechanisms (namely close ties, proximity and direct perception).

1   A detailed analysis of the applicable legal principles, which predominantly concern questions of liability rather than quantum, is beyond the scope of this work. However, it is noteworthy that, in *Frost v Chief Constable of South Yorkshire Police* [1999] 2 AC 455 at 500, Lord Steyn described the law in this area as 'a patchwork quilt of distinctions which are difficult to justify'. Certainly, the law appears to have been shaped considerably by questions of policy.

2   Per Lord Hoffmann.

3   [1996] 1 AC 155.

4   [1992] 1 AC 310.

[D96] It is not necessary for the secondary victim to distinguish between the extent of the injury caused by the trauma of witnessing the accident and the trauma resulting from the subsequent bereavement[1].

1   *Vernon v Bosley* [1997] 1 All ER 577.

[D97] The Law Commission has recommended that the only control test for a secondary victim should be 'dearness', which should be presumed in the case of certain close relations[1]. However, the Government has rejected the suggestion of implementation of legislation in this area. As at the time of writing, the Government's stated view is that it is preferable for the courts to continue to develop the law rather than attempt to impose a statutory solution[2].

1   See further the Law Commission Report No 249 'Liability for Psychiatric Injury' (1996).
2   Ministry of Justice 'The Law on Damages', response to consultation, 1 July 2009.

Stress and bullying cases

[D98] All employers have a duty to take reasonable care for the safety of their employees: to see that reasonable care is taken to provide them with a safe place of work, safe tools and equipment, and a safe system of working[1]. In the landmark case of *Walker v Northumberland County Council*[2], Colman J held that an employer was liable for the foreseeable psychiatric injury suffered by an employee due to pressure of work (which had already caused the claimant to suffer a previous breakdown). Given the special employer/employee relationship, it was not necessary to apply the tests set out in *White v Chief Constable of South Yorkshire Police*[3]. The decision in *Walker* was subsequently endorsed by the House of Lords in *Barber v Somerset CC*[4].

1   *Wilsons & Clyde Coal Co Ltd v English* [1938] AC 57.
2   [1995] 1 All ER 737.
3   [1999] 2 AC 455.
4   [2004] UKHL 13.

[D99] The law in relation to stress claims was clarified by the Court of Appeal in *Hatton v Sutherland*[1]. Hale LJ (as she then was), giving the judgment for the court, summarised the legal principles applicable to stress claims as follows:

(1) There are no special control mechanisms applying to claims for psychiatric (or physical) illness or injury arising from the stress of doing the work the employee is required to do. The ordinary principles of employer's liability apply.
(2) The threshold question is whether this kind of harm to this particular employee was reasonably foreseeable: this has two components, (a) an injury to health (as distinct from occupational stress) which (b) is attributable to stress at work (as distinct from other factors).
(3) Foreseeability depends upon what the employer knows (or ought reasonably to know) about the individual employee. Because of the nature of mental disorder, it is harder to foresee than physical injury, but may be easier to foresee in a known individual than in the population at large. An employer is usually entitled to assume that the employee can withstand the normal pressures of the job, unless it knows of some particular problem or vulnerability.

(4)   The test is the same whatever the employment: there are no occupations which should be regarded as intrinsically dangerous to mental health.

(5)   Factors likely to be relevant in answering the threshold question include:

(a)   The nature and extent of the work done by the employee. Is the workload much more than is normal for the particular job? Is the work particularly intellectually or emotionally demanding for this employee? Are demands being made of this employee unreasonable when compared with the demands made of others in the same or comparable jobs? Or are there signs that others doing this job are suffering harmful levels of stress? Is there an abnormal level of sickness or absenteeism in the same job or the same department?

(b)   Signs from the employee of impending harm to health. Has he or she a particular problem or vulnerability? Has he or she already suffered from illness attributable to stress at work? Have there recently been frequent or prolonged absences which are uncharacteristic of him or her? Is there reason to think that these are attributable to stress at work, eg because of complaints or warnings from him or her or others?

(6)   The employer is generally entitled to take what it is told by its employee at face value, unless it has good reason to think to the contrary. It does not generally have to make searching inquiries of the employee or seek permission to make further inquiries of his or her medical advisers[2].

(7)   To trigger a duty to take steps, the indications of impending harm to health arising from stress at work must be plain enough for any reasonable employer to realise that it should do something about it.

(8)   The employer is only in breach of duty if it has failed to take the steps which are reasonable in the circumstances, bearing in mind the magnitude of the risk of harm occurring, the gravity of the harm which may occur, the costs and practicability of preventing it and the justifications for running the risk.

(9)   The size and scope of the employer's operation, its resources and the demands it faces are relevant in deciding what is reasonable; these include the interests of other employees and the need to treat them fairly, eg in any redistribution of duties.

(10) An employer can only reasonably be expected to take steps which are likely to do some good – the court is likely to need expert evidence on this.

(11) An employer who offers a confidential advice service, with referral to appropriate counselling or treatment services, is unlikely to be found in breach of duty[3].

(12) If the only reasonable and effective step would have been to dismiss or demote the employee, the employer will not be in breach of duty in allowing a willing employee to continue in the job[4].

(13) In all cases, therefore, it is necessary to identify the steps which the employer both could and should have taken before finding it in breach of its duty of care.

(14) The claimant must show that that breach of duty has caused or materially contributed to the harm suffered. It is not enough to show that occupational stress has caused the harm.

(15) Where the harm suffered has more than one cause, the employer should only pay for that proportion of the harm suffered which is attributable to its wrongdoing, unless the harm is truly indivisible[5]. It is for the defendant to raise the question of apportionment.

(16) The assessment of damages will take account of any pre-existing disorder or vulnerability and of the chance that the claimant would have succumbed to a stress-related disorder in any event.

1   [2002] EWCA Civ 76. See also *Barber v Somerset CC* [2004] UKHL 13 in which the House of Lords emphasised the importance of employers keeping up to date with developments impacting upon the safety of their workers; and *Hartman & others v SE Mental Health and Community Care NHS Trust* [2005] EWCA Civ 06 with regard to foreseeability and apportionment of damages. See further Andrew Buchan, 'Stress at Work – Law and Practice since *Hatton v Sutherland*' [2007] JPIL Issue 1/07 pp 49–69.

2   This principle was in issue before the House of Lords in *Barber v Somerset CC* [2004] UKHL 13. The guiding principle to be adopted is that of the reasonable and prudent employer taking positive thought for the safety of his workmen, ensuring that he has sufficient up-to-date information to do so: the dictum of Swanwick J in *Stokes v Guest, Keen and Nettlefold (Bolts and Nuts) Ltd* [1968] 1 WLR 1776.

3   It has since been recognised by the Court of Appeal that the provision of a confidential counselling service is not a defence which automatically discharges the defendant's duty of care, and all depends upon the particular circumstances: *Daw v Intel Corp (UK) Ltd* [2007] EWCA Civ 70, [2007] 2 All ER 126; *Dickins v O2 Plc* [2008] EWCA Civ 1144, [2009] IRLR 58.

4   But query this as appropriate to all cases.

5   This aspect of the guidelines is controversial and by no means agreed: see eg 'Causation – the search for principle' by Janet Smith LJ in [2009] JPIL 2/09 p 101 at 103. The Court of Appeal has now reaffirmed that liability for psychiatric illness cannot easily be apportioned in many cases – see eg. *Dickins v O2 Plc* [2008] EWCA Civ 1144, [2009] IRLR 58. The usual tortious principles of causation are to apply and, unless there is evidence regarding the aetiology of the injury making it truly divisible, the lower courts are likely to take their cue from the material contribution principle endorsed by the Court of Appeal in *Bailey v Ministry of Defence* [2008] EWCA Civ 883 rather than obiter dicta of Hale LJ (as she then was) regarding apportionment.

Loss of life expectancy and fear of impending death

[D100] General damages cannot be claimed for a claimant's shortened life. However, damages may be awarded where the claimant's knowledge of his or her reduction in life caused by the injury in turn causes particular distress. Administration of Justice Act 1982, s 1(1)(b) states:

'If the injured person's expectation of life has been reduced by the injuries, the court, in assessing damages in respect of pain and suffering caused by the injuries, shall take account of any suffering caused or likely to be caused to him by awareness that his expectation of life has been so reduced.'

[D101] It is suggested that the courts will be prepared to make significant awards under this head of claim, particularly by virtue of the abolition of the traditional claim in respect of any loss of expectation of life, where the (conventional) figure was in the region of £1,500: Administration of Justice Act 1982, s 1(1). Prior to the change in the law, this head of claim had been recognised in *Davies v Tenby Corpn*, where Scarman LJ said[1]:

'... But I have no doubt that awards for pain and suffering in quadriplegic cases have taken into account the [claimant's] awareness of the shortening of his life: As the judge remarked, the matter was already "fortified with adequate authority" ...'

1   [1974] 2 Lloyd's Rep 469 at 478, CA.

[D102]   Knowledge and fear of impending death from a sudden or traumatic event is not relevant to the calculation of general damages for PSLA. Lord Bridge in *Hicks v Chief Constable of South Yorkshire Police* said[1]:

> 'It is perfectly clear law that fear by itself, of whatever degree, is a normal human emotion for which no damages can be awarded. Those trapped in the crush at Hillsborough who were fortunate enough to escape without injury have no claim in respect of the distress they suffered in what must have been a truly terrifying experience. It follows that fear of impending death felt by the victim of a fatal injury before that injury is inflicted cannot by itself give rise to a cause of action which survives for the benefit of the victim's estate'.

1   [1992] 2 All ER 65, HL, a further case following the Hillsborough disaster.

[D103]   In the same case at Court of Appeal level[1], Parker LJ had said that, in resulting death cases, 'the last moments of mental agony and pain are in reality part of the death itself'.

1   [1992] PIQR P63.

Age of the claimant

[D104]   The age of the claimant may affect the appropriate level of award for PSLA. This can be seen in *Nutbrown v Sheffield Health Authority*[1], where the claimant was aged 72 and suffered severe brain damage. Potts J held that the correct approach to the assessment of general damages was to calculate the figure that would be appropriate for a man in the prime of his life. The next step would then be to reduce that figure in the light of all the particular circumstances of the case in question. In particular, the judge should give consideration to the state of health of the claimant before the accident and have regard to his age at the time of the injury. Potts J held that, if the claimant had been 30, the appropriate award would have been £50,000. However, as he was 72 the award should be halved to £25,000. A further example of this approach can be seen in *Laycock v William Morrison*[2], where Judge Cotton discounted the award by about one-third because the claimant was 79.

1   [1993] 4 Med LR 187. See also *Bird v Cocking* [1951] TLR 1260, CA, in which the award for PSLA was reduced simply by reason of the claimant's age.
2   [1991] CLY 1381.

[D105]   The thinking behind such a policy is plain to see: the young claimant will have to live with the effects of the injury for a greater length of time than the older claimant[1]. If a claimant has constant pain and suffering, he or she has to live with it for the rest of his or her life. Therefore, life expectancy has to be considered. Further, the loss of amenity suffered will cover a longer period for the younger claimant. Moreover, the younger claimant is likely to have been more active.

1   See eg *A v Powys Health Board* [2007] EWHC 2996 (QB), in which Lloyd Jones J awarded £225,000 for pain, suffering and loss of amenity to a 16-year-old female claimant suffering from cerebral palsy due to her long life expectancy and her degree of insight into her condition.

[D106]   Obviously, if the injury is totally cured then no such consideration of age needs to be given. Indeed, it may be the case that an older claimant in such a case may be awarded a greater sum, as the healing of the injury may take longer and the pain and discomfort be greater as a result of age. In *Frank v Cox* the claimant was a man of 77 and had suffered a hip injury. The same injury in a younger man could have been remedied by surgery; however, because of his age, this path was not open to this claimant. Sachs LJ stated[1]:

> 'I take the view myself that when one has a person in advancing years, in some respects an impairment of movement may perhaps be more serious than it is with a younger person. It is true … that [the claimant] has not got as many years before him through which he has to live with this discomfort, pain and impairment of movement. But it is important to bear in mind that as one advances in life one's pleasures and activities particularly do become more limited, and any substantial impairment in the limited amount of activity and movement which a person can undertake, in my view, becomes all the more serious on that account.'

1   (1967) 111 Sol Jo 670.

[D107]   This may have particular relevance where a claimant is at or nearing retirement age at the time of injury. The claimant may have been specifically looking forward to taking life easy and pursuing his or her leisure interests. For example, in *Spencer v ARCO*[1] the claimant had been retired for some years, and the judge found that the last few years of his life had been considerably blighted by reason of his injuries. Further, in *Sutton v Ling*[2] the claimant was aged 58 at the date she suffered a road traffic accident, and 61 at the date of trial. She suffered a whiplash injury to her neck, together with scalp muscle contraction, headaches, an adjustment disorder and an acute stress reaction. The claimant's ability to sail, sew, decorate, garden and keep house had been significantly impaired. The judge consequently held that the claimant's quality of retirement had been adversely affected by reason of her injuries, and took this into account when assessing the appropriate award for PSLA.

1   [1996] CLY 2240.
2   [1999] CLY 1550.

[D108]   It can, therefore, be seen that the argument concerning age is double-edged. On the one hand, young claimants are able to argue they have a greater length of time to suffer with the effects of the injury[1]. They can also put forward their previous active lifestyle and show how much they have lost. However, on the other hand, the alternative argument can be made by the elderly claimant. They are less resilient than the young and so suffer the recoverable injury for longer or perhaps for life. Further, the older claimant may have had extensive plans for their retirement. These valuable years have now been blighted by injury, and an award can be increased due to the claimant's limited prospects of any social interaction. The very fact that a claimant had only a limited ability to perform hobbies can be very telling if even that has now been removed. Therefore, Potts J's approach in *Nutbrown v Sheffield Health Authority*[2], of assessing a man in the prime of his life and then deducting for particular circumstances, may also apply in the opposite direction. If a circumstance means a man beyond the prime of his life suffers more, then the award should be increased.

1   See eg *Bayley v Bloomsbury Health Authority* in the context of a back injury to a 20-year-old woman, Henry J distinguishing a 'comparator' of £8,000 awarded to a 33-year-old saying: 'Well,

there is a world of difference, as has been pointed out to me by Mr May for the [claimant], between that happening to you at 33 and it happening to you at 20. In all these circumstances, I think the right figure for pain and suffering and loss of amenity is £10,000'.

2   [1993] 4 Med LR 187.

Sex of the claimant

[D109]   Generally speaking, the sex of the claimant is not relevant to the award of damages for PSLA, except in relation to cases involving scarring or disfigurement. In these cases, traditionally women have received larger awards because of the greater effect such injuries have upon them[1]. However, in the modern age of metrosexuals, such notions are potentially out-of-date and each case should be judged on its own facts. Take, for example, a male claimant who was particularly image and body conscious before suffering a disfiguring injury. It is discriminatory to suggest that he should be awarded less damages solely because of his sex where, due to his vanity, he has suffered as much or more distress and anxiety as a result of his altered body image than the average female.

1   This is recognised by the Judicial Studies Board Guidelines for the Assessment of General Damages in Personal Injury Cases. See also *Horman v Steel* [1979] CLY 690, in which it was said that the scar to a young man was not as serious a feature as it would be in the case of a young woman; and *Dimmock v Miles* (12 December 1969, unreported), referred to in *Kemp & Kemp* at D4–103, in which Phillimore J emphasised the importance of inquiring as to the claimant's own feelings with regard to any scarring.

The claimant's means

[D110]   The wealth or otherwise of the claimant is irrelevant to the assessment of damages for PSLA[1].

1   *Wise v Kaye* [1962] 1 QB 638; *Heil v Rankin* [2001] QB 272. In *Heil v Rankin* [2001] QB 272 at 296 and [33], Lord Woolf agreed with the defendant's submission that 'in making an award of damages the court is not concerned with whether the claimant is a pauper or a millionaire'. Cf the position where damages are claimed for death where, because compensation is a 'hard matter of pounds and pence', the relatives of a millionaire will recover more than those of a pauper.

Effect on others

[D111]   Although no general damages award is given for the actual effect on the claimant's family, in *Pickett v British Rail Engineering Ltd*[1] it was held that an award to the claimant can take into account the distress caused to the claimant who realises his family will be left without him due to early death. Lord Scarman stated[2]:

'The distress suffered by Mr Pickett knowing that his widow and children would be left without him to care for them was an element in his suffering for which I agree Mr Pickett was entitled to fair compensation.'

1   [1980] AC 136. See also *Cook v JL Kier & Co Ltd* [1970] 2 All ER 513, [1970] 1 WLR 774, CA, regarding the loss of sexual function, discussed at para **[D16]** above.
2   [1980] AC 136 at 171F.

The stoical or indomitable claimant

[D112] If a claimant redoubtably endures severe injury and makes the most of his or her remaining faculties, a court could be beguiled into under-compensating him or her. This risk was recognised by Kenneth Jones J at first instance in *Sully v Doggett*[1]:

> '... I am quite satisfied that she is a woman of indomitable courage and possessed of great reserves within herself. She does nothing to exaggerate that which she has suffered and, indeed, a real danger facing me in this case is that her reaction to her own injuries and her own sufferings might lead me to underrate them and to award to her less by way of damages than those to which she is truly and justly entitled ...'

[1]   (5 December 1984, unreported), CA. For other cases in which the claimant's stoical disposition was referred to, see *Osborn v Madgwick* [1994] CLY 1678; *Wright v Royal Doulton (UK) Ltd* [1997] CLY 1965; *Barnett v Lintern* [1998] CLY 1590; *Rutland v Ferguson* [1998] CLY 1643; *Brown v Owen* [2000] CLY 1595; *Evans v Silvery Lynz Products Ltd* [2001] CLY 1612; *Boyer v Everard* [2001] CLY 1621.

Inability to care for loved one

[D113] In *Rourke v Barton*[1], McCullough J took into account the inability of the wife, much as she would have wished to do so, to look after her husband terminally ill with cancer, particularly since the husband was looking to her for support.

[1]   (1982) Times, 23 June. See further *Lowe v Guise* [2002] EWCA Civ 197.

Inability to carry out domestic assistance

[D114] Where an award is not made for past pecuniary loss in respect of gratuitous assistance carrying out household chores that the claimant would otherwise have done himself or herself, it is permissible for the judge to increase the award in respect of PSLA to take account of this. In particular, in *Daly v General Steam Navigation Co Ltd*[1], Ormrod LJ said as follows[2]:

> 'So far as the approach to the loss of housekeeping ability is concerned, I would deprecate talking about "capacities" in this connection. The words "incapacity" and "capacity" are extraordinarily vague words upon which much can be built on rather insecure foundations. What we have to do is to look to see, so far as the pre-trial loss is concerned, the actual loss that has been sustained. It is perfectly true that the [claimant] is entitled to some compensation for the loss of her ability to do her housekeeping during that period, but I agree that properly the compensation is to be included in the estimated general damage.'

[1]   [1981] 1 WLR 120.
[2]   At 130. See also per Bridge LJ (as he then was) at 128.

[D115] Likewise, where the medical evidence suggests that the claimant is able to undertake domestic chores in the future but it may cause discomfort or take longer than it otherwise would have done in the absence of the injuries, the court may decide to make a higher award for PSLA rather than any separate allowance for paid assistance in the future[1].

[1]   *Ved v Caress* (9 April 2001, unreported), QBD, per HHJ Chapman.

Personality change

[D116]   There is no doubt that, when assessing the appropriate award of damages for PSLA on behalf of a claimant who suffers a change in his or her personality as a result of an injury (usually by reason of a traumatic head injury, chronic pain or alternatively a psychiatric injury), the court may take into account any reported changes from the pre-injury state, eg inappropriate behaviour, impulsiveness, anxiety, aggressiveness, irritability, fear of crowds, paranoia etc[1].

[1]   The Judicial Studies Board Guidelines specifically refer to impairment of personality in relation to several different categories, including brain injuries and severe back injuries.

[D117]   But what about personality changes which are severe enough to cause a claimant to start committing crimes? In *Meah v McCreamer*[1] the claimant was a passenger in a car driven by the defendant, who was drunk at the time. The car was involved in an accident, which was caused by the defendant's negligence, and the claimant sustained serious head injuries and brain damage which resulted in him undergoing a marked personality change. Prior to the accident the claimant had been convicted of various criminal offences such as theft and burglary, and had a poor employment record, but he had had a number of successful relationships with women and there was no evidence of his being violent towards women. In February 1982 the claimant sexually assaulted and maliciously wounded two women and, in September of that year, raped and maliciously wounded a third woman. He was sentenced to life imprisonment for those offences and was classed as a category A (ie highly dangerous) prisoner. The claimant claimed damages against the defendant on the grounds, amongst others, that but for the brain damage caused in the accident and the resulting personality change he would not have committed the offences for which he was imprisoned. Woolf J held that since, but for the injuries received in the accident and the resulting personality change, the claimant would not have committed the criminal acts for which he was serving a sentence of life imprisonment, he was entitled to damages to compensate him for being imprisoned[2]. However, in assessing those damages, it was necessary to take into account the claimant's previous criminal tendencies, which would probably have resulted in him spending periods in prison, and the fact that, having regard to his previous poor employment record and the free board he would receive in prison, there would be no continuing financial loss. In all the circumstances, the appropriate damages were a round figure of £60,000 to compensate the claimant for pain and suffering, his injuries including the physical after-effects of his brain injury, and his imprisonment. That figure would be reduced by 25% to take into account the claimant's contributory negligence in travelling as a passenger with a driver whom he knew to be drunk.

[1]   [1985] All ER 367.
[2]   It should be noted that the illegality defence was not raised in this case, and it is widely thought that had it been the claim would have been disallowed. See further the criticisms of this case in the Law Commission's Consultation Paper No 160 entitled 'The Illegality Defence in Tort' (2001). See also the doubt cast on the correctness of *Meah v McCreamer* [1985] All ER 367 by Beldam LJ in *Clunis v Camden and Islington Health Authority* [1998] QB 968 and *Worrall v British Rlys Board* [1999] CLY 1413, CA; and by the House of Lords in *Gray v Thames Trains Ltd v another* [2009] 3 WLR 167.

[D118] This case was re-incarnated as *Meah v McCreamer (No 2)*[1] when the claimant claimed against the defendant an indemnity against damages orders made against him arising out of two sex attacks. Woolf J ruled against the claim on the basis that it was too remote, since the claimant was not seeking to recover in respect of his own injuries or direct financial loss but in respect of the indirect loss he had suffered as a result of having to pay damages to third parties, who could not have sued him directly because he owed them no duty and the damage suffered by them at the [claimant's] hands was too remote vis-à-vis the driver, and if the claimant were to recover it would expose the defendant and other defendants in similar cases to an indefinite liability for an indefinite duration. Further, the claim was ruled to be against public policy, since it would be contrary to the public interest for the claimant to be indemnified for the consequences of his crimes by the defendant.

[1]   [1986] 1 All ER 943.

[D119] Subsequent cases have also taken a hard line in respect of claims which rely upon the claimant's criminal act(s) to establish a cause of action. For example, in *Clunis v Camden and Islington Health Authority*[1] the Court of Appeal doubted the correctness of the decision in *Meah v McCreamer* and held that considerations of public policy ('ex turpi causa non oritur actio') prevented a claimant who was convicted of manslaughter following discharge from hospital from claiming damages in respect of the hospital's negligence for failing to detain him or admit him for treatment. Likewise, in *Worrall v British Railways Board*[2] the Court of Appeal dismissed an appeal by a claimant who had suffered an electric shock during the course of his employment leading to personality changes. He claimed that, as a result of the personality changes, he committed two serious criminal offences for which he was imprisoned for six years. He sought damages for the lost earnings and pension rights arising out of his incarceration. The defendant successfully applied to strike out the claimant's claim as being contrary to public policy. The claimant's appeal was dismissed on the basis of illegality, since the court could not assist a claimant who pleads and relies upon his own criminal acts in order to establish his claim[3].

[1]   [1998] QB 968. See further *Hewison v Meridian Shipping PTE* [2002] EWCA Civ 1821.
[2]   [1999] CLY 1413, CA.
[3]   However, it should be noted that the point was taken that the claimant had never called psychiatric evidence or sought to argue in the criminal proceedings that he did not know that what he was doing was wrong. Since he had accepted that he had legal capacity and was responsible for committing the criminal offences, it was then difficult to argue in the civil claim that the criminal offences were caused solely as a result of the changes in his personality. The position might have been different (as per *Meah v McCreamer* [1985] All ER 367) if the claimant had shown that the injuries resulting from the defendant's wrongdoing rendered him incompetent and, but for the wrongdoing, the claimant would never have committed the offences; although see further the Law Commission's criticisms in their Consultation Paper No 160.

[D120] Most recently, the House of Lords has authoritatively re-affirmed the 'ex turpi causa non oritur actio' principle in *Gray v Thames Trains Ltd v another*[1]. This case involved a claimant who suffered post-traumatic stress disorder following a major railway accident. He subsequently killed a man and was convicted of manslaughter on the ground of diminished responsibility. He was detained in a hospital under ss 37 and 41 of the Mental Health Act 1983. His claims for general damages for his detention, conviction and damage to his reputation; claims for loss of earnings arising out of his detention; claims for an indemnity; and claims for damages for feelings of guilt and remorse consequent on the killing, were all rejected. Lord Hoffmann, giving the leading speech, explained that public policy prevented someone from being punished by the criminal courts for a particular act and, at the same time, being compensated by the civil courts for committing the same act. He distinguished between the narrow and wider principle[2]: the narrow principle prevents people from recovering damage which is the consequence of a sentence imposed as a result of a criminal act; the wider and simpler version is that you cannot recover for damage which is the consequence of your own criminal act. Lord Hoffmann explained that the original trial judge, Flaux J, had correctly applied both the narrow and wider principles, prohibiting any of the claims from succeeding. In the event, the House of Lords restored Flaux J's original decision and overturned the Court of Appeal's judgment, which had confusingly rejected the claims for general damages but had allowed a claim for ongoing loss of earnings.

[1]   [2009] 3 WLR 167.
[2]   Per Lord Hoffmann at para 32.

[D121]   What about personality changes which are beneficial? In some instances, personality changes resulting from an accident might make the claimant a nicer person to know. Paradoxically, the injuries sustained might also lead to an increase in the claimant's life expectancy, eg by causing a person who had previously led a life of crime and violence to settle down and take more responsibility. Can such advantages be offset against other claims? This is somewhat uncharted territory. It is not difficult to see that such an approach would be very controversial, since the claimant may have liked the way they were and dispute any suggested benefits resulting from the defendant's wrongdoing (especially since they did not ask to be changed in any way). In any event, it is submitted that any credit or offset which is allowed to take account of this element can only be on a like-for-like basis[1]. Therefore, whilst the award for PSLA might be reduced, past and future pecuniary expenses and losses should not be affected[2].

[1]   By analogy, see eg *Parry v Cleaver* [1970] AC 1, in which the House of Lords held that a pension received on account of injury is not to be taken into account against a claim for loss of earnings. See also the speech of Lord Hope in *Longden v British Coal Corpn* [1997] 3 WLR 1336 at 1347F–1348; and Dixon CJ in the High Court of Australia in *Espagne's case* (1961) 105 CLR 569.
[2]   See further at para **[D146]** regarding the overlap between general damages and other heads of loss.

Rape

[D122]   The circumstances and consequences of rape mean that it is placed in a different category of general personal injury cases[1]. In addition to an award for PSLA, the claimant may be entitled to an award for aggravated damages[2]. Separate awards may be less common now, following the Court of Appeal's decision in *Richardson v Howie*[3], encouraging global awards for general damages to include all tortious elements and the aggravation which the circumstances merit[4]. However, there is no hard and fast rule to this, and it is clear that separate awards may still be made for injury to feelings or aggravated damages in appropriate cases[5].

1   *Griffiths v Williams* (1995) Times, 24 November.

2   See eg *Parrington v Marriott* [1998] CLY 1509, in which HHJ Hall awarded the sum of £30,000 aggravated damages in addition to £25,000 general damages where the defendant had subjected the claimant to an 18-month campaign of sexual harassment and indecent assault. See also *B (a child) v D* [2001] CLY 1585, in which the claimant suffered a very serious and violent sexual assault involving vaginal rape and anal penetration. She was awarded £40,000 for PSLA and £20,000 for aggravated damages.

3   [2004] EWCA Civ 1127.

4   See further paras **[A150]–[A152]** and *Lawson v Glaves-Smith (Executor of the Estate of Christopher Dawes, Deceased)* [2006] EWHC 2865 (QB).

5   *Martins v Choudhary* [2007] EWCA Civ 1379; *Vento v Chief Constable of West Yorkshire Police (No 2)* [2003] IRLR 102; and *AT & others v Dulghieru* [2009] EWHC 225 (QB), in which Treacy J made awards of between £82,000 and £125,000 in respect of PSLA for each claimant and a further £30–£35,000 each in respect of aggravated damages.

(vii)   Heil v Rankin

The background

[D123]   There was a growing feeling among practitioners and the general public alike since the mid-1980s that awards for PSLA were too low, particularly in the larger cases where awards had not been keeping up with inflation. After consulting widely, the Law Commission recommended that all awards for PSLA over £2,000 should be increased[1]. In *Heil v Rankin*[2] the Court of Appeal heard a number of linked appeals regarding the sufficiency of awards for PSLA in the early part of 2000.

1   Law Commission Report No 257 'Damages for Personal Injury: Non-pecuniary Loss' (1998).

2   [2001] QB 272.

The decision

[D124]   The Court of Appeal decided that all awards over £10,000 should be increased by up to a third. However, the increase was tapered, so that awards of £10,000 received no increase, but what had been the largest awards received the greatest increase. A graph indicating the taper was attached to the Court of Appeal's judgment.

Updating awards

[D125]   Unfortunately, the graph that the Court of Appeal produced does not match the uplifts that were made in *Heil v Rankin*[1]. Probably the simplest method to calculate the *Heil v Rankin* increase is to use an electronic programme such as the one provided by Lawtel or www.picalculator.co.uk. Alternatively, awards may be updated manually using the table provided at para **[D127]** below. In order to calculate the present-day value of a pre-*Heil v Rankin* case, the award must first be updated using the RPI to March 2000, when the Court of Appeal's judgment was delivered. Then, by referring to the old award using the table, it is easy to read across to find its present-day value. Do not simply follow pre-2000 awards without both updating the award to its current figure and then applying the *Heil v Rankin* table.

1   [2001] QB 272.

Updated Judicial Studies Board Guidelines

[D126]　It should be noted that, following the *Heil v Rankin*[1] judgment, the Court of Appeal was very keen that an updated version of the Judicial Studies Board Guidelines was published as soon as possible. Another (fifth) edition of the Guidelines, which took into account the appropriate uplift in awards, was published shortly afterwards. These Guidelines have since been superseded by a number of further editions, which all take into account the appropriate uplift.

1　　[2001] QB 272.

Heil v Rankin table

[D127]　The following table can be used to manually uplift awards made before March 2000, as described in para [D125] above.

Pre-*Heil* (£)	Adjusted (£)	Pre-*Heil* (£)	Adjusted (£)	Pre-*Heil* (£)	Adjusted (£)
10,000	10,000	57,000	63,379	104,000	127,276
11,000	11,026	58,000	64,629	105,000	128,750
12,000	12,057	59,000	65,883	106,000	130,229
13,000	13,092	60,000	67,143	107,000	131,712
14,000	14,133	61,000	68,407	108,000	133,200
15,000	15,178	62,000	69,676	109,000	134,693
16,000	16,228	63,000	70,950	110,000	136,190
17,000	17,283	64,000	72,229	111,000	137,693
18,000	18,342	65,000	73,511	112,000	139,200
19,000	19,407	66,000	74,800	113,000	140,712
20,000	20,476	67,000	76,093	114,000	142,229
21,000	21,550	68,000	77,390	115,000	143,750
22,000	22,629	69,000	78,693	116,000	145,276
23,000	23,712	70,000	80,000	117,000	146,807
24,000	24,800	71,000	81,312	118,000	148,343
25,000	25,893	72,000	82,629	119,000	149,883
26,000	26,990	73,000	83,950	120,000	151,429
27,000	28,093	74,000	85,276	121,000	152,979
28,000	29,200	75,000	86,607	122,000	154,533
29,000	30,312	76,000	87,943	123,000	156,093
30,000	31,429	77,000	89,283	124,000	157,657

Pre-*Heil* (£)	Adjusted (£)	Pre-*Heil* (£)	Adjusted (£)	Pre-*Heil* (£)	Adjusted (£)
31,000	32,550	78,000	90,629	125,000	159,226
32,000	33,676	79,000	91,979	126,000	160,800
33,000	34,807	80,000	93,333	127,000	162,379
34,000	35,943	81,000	94,693	128,000	163,962
35,000	37,083	82,000	96,057	129,000	165,550
36,000	38,229	83,000	97,426	130,000	167,143
37,000	39,379	84,000	98,800	131,000	168,740
38,000	40,533	85,000	100,179	132,000	170,343
39,000	41,693	86,000	101,562	133,000	171,950
40,000	42,857	87,000	102,950	134,000	173,562
41,000	44,026	88,000	104,343	135,000	175,179
42,000	45,200	89,000	105,740	136,000	176,800
43,000	46,379	90,000	107,143	137,000	178,426
44,000	47,562	91,000	108,550	138,000	180,057
45,000	48,750	92,000	109,962	139,000	181,692
46,000	49,943	93,000	111,379	140,000	183,333
47,000	51,140	94,000	112,800	141,000	184,978
48,000	52,343	95,000	114,226	142,000	186,629
49,000	53,550	96,000	115,657	143,000	188,283
50,000	54,762	97,000	117,093	144,000	189,943
51,000	55,979	98,000	118,533	145,000	191,607
52,000	57,200	99,000	119,979	146,000	193,276
53,000	58,426	100,000	121,429	147,000	194,950
54,000	59,657	101,000	122,883	148,000	196,629
55,000	60,893	102,000	124,342	149,000	198,312
56,000	62,133	103,000	125,807	150,000	200,000

3   Other Heads of General Damages

[D128]   In many instances, the court will consider all the ways in which the injuries have affected the claimant in the award for PSLA. However, in some instances, it might be possible to persuade a judge to make a separate award under one or more of the following heads of claim.

(i)   Loss of Congenial Employment

History of the award

[D129]   If a claimant, owing to his or her injuries, has to give up work, then obviously the major award in respect of that will be the pecuniary damages for loss of earnings (either past, future or both). However, a claimant who is precluded from doing a job they enjoy suffers an additional loss, over and above the lost earnings, compared to another claimant who did not enjoy their work. In order to compensate for this loss, a separate head of damages emerged in the case law known as an award for 'loss of congenial employment'.

[D130]   Initially, the first loss of congenial employment awards were made in respect of people who were forced to give up a job they enjoyed in order to perform a job from which they derived little, if any, satisfaction[1]. One of the earlier examples of such an award can be seen in *Morris v Johnson*[2]. In this case, a man had been a skilled precious metal worker, but owing to his injuries he had to cease such work. The Court of Appeal increased his award for general damages by £1,000 (approximately £13,484 at 2009 prices) to give him 'something for the loss of a craft'. As Edmund Davies LJ pointed out, the claimant had to replace his craft with 'humdrum work'.

[1]   For a more in-depth look at the background to loss of congenial employment awards and a table of example cases, see further Piers Martin 'Loss of Congenial Employment – Can't get no (job satisfaction)?' [2002] JPIL, Issue 3/02 and Simon Allen 'Loss of Congenial Employment' [2009] JPIL Issue 2/09 pp 135–139.
[2]   (1967) 112 Sol Jo 32.

[D131]   Further, in *Hearnshaw v English Steel Corporation Ltd*[1] the claimant had enjoyed his work as a skilled coremaker. Following an accident, he worked as a stove attendant which, it was said, he found boring. Salmon LJ considered the deprivation of a job he enjoyed as part of the head of loss of amenity and increased the award accordingly. It could be said that a similar process was performed as had been done in *Morris v Johnson*[2]. That is, the court simply considered the loss of a pleasurable job as part of the loss of amenity and made no separate award.

[1]   (1971) 11 KIR 306.
[2]   (1967) 112 Sol Jo 32.

Applicability of the award

[D132]   It now seems clear that a claimant who is forced to give up work he or she enjoyed as a result of his or her injuries will be entitled to claim either an uplift in the award for general damages in respect of PSLA or, alternatively, a separate award for loss of congenial employment, even if the claimant has not had to change jobs to one which he or she finds less appealing[1].

[1]   See eg *Jones v Pandis* [1993] CLY 1590; *Rutland v Ferguson* [1998] CLY 1643; *Ellis v Liverpool City Council* [1998] CLY 1658; *Re Castle* [1998] CLY 1493; *Eardley v NW Anglia Health Care NHS Trust* [1998] CLY 1613; *Davies v Clarkson* [1999] CLY 1436; *Re Calvert* [2000] CLY 1539; *Re Goodall* [2000] CLY 1583; *Finnis v Caulfield* [2002] All ER (D) 353 (Oct).

[D133] Traditionally, awards for loss of congenial employment have in the main applied to the uniformed professions, eg doctors, nurses, firemen, the military etc. However, since the assessment of a person's loss is subjective, as long as the claimant derived a lot of job satisfaction from their pre-injury occupation, there does not seem to be any reason in principle why such awards cannot apply to other less publicly recognised forms of employment. In *Pratt v Smith*[1], David Foskett QC, who was considering the inability of an operations and IT director for a publishing house to continue with his pre-accident employment, carried out a review of the general principles relating to the assessment of damages for loss of congenial employment. He said[2]:

> 'Whilst I doubt that anyone would wish to deny the nurse, the firefighter or the police officer compensation for the disappointment associated with the loss of his or her employment, the other instances of awards (and, of course, there may be more in unreported cases) do suggest that the categories in which awards may be made are not closed. Equally, it would seem that considerations beyond merely the choice as a career of a vocational "public service" underpin this kind of award. If such an award is to be made in some cases, what logic or other policy consideration dictates that it should be restricted in this way? It does seem to me that endeavouring to justify the non-payment of an award in some cases by reference to the employment paying "a full commercial wage" is, if only in the practical sense, extremely difficult. Indeed why (other than where some obvious policy requirement dictates otherwise) should any form of employment be excluded provided that it can be demonstrated that the loss of that employment really means something to the person who, as the result of someone else's negligence, loses the ability to continue with it? Loss of employment can and often does connote direct financial loss. But the disappointment of not being able to continue with a chosen and, often, hard-fought for career is very real and, in some cases, quite overwhelming. This case is an example.'

[1]   (18 December 2002, unreported), QBD.
[2]   At [62].

[D134] The reasoning in this case was applied by Mr Leighton Williams QC, sitting as a Deputy High Court Judge in *Lane v Lake*[1], where he said at paras 21–22:

> 'The Claimant seeks an award under this head. Mr Gore says such a head of damage is in practice reserved for policemen, firemen and the like. Such awards are frequently made to policemen and firemen but that is because it has become almost a tradition to claim such an award in such cases. In my judgment such an award ought to be confined to those who truly have suffered a loss under this head and not be awarded merely by reference to the type of employment not automatically as an extra.
>
> The Claimant has always been a hard worker and enjoyed his work in the building industry. He told me with feeling that he loved his work, always wanted to be a carpenter and that when he was a lad he used to love going on to sites with his father. I suspect it is one of the things he misses most. I have no difficulty in considering an award of £5,000 appropriate under this head.'

[1]   LTL 31/7/2007, Document No AC0114378.

[D135] Indeed, this appears to have been the generally accepted approach taken by other first-instance judges, and awards for loss of congenial employment have been made in respect of a very diverse range of occupations, including a gas salesman[1], a beauty therapist[2], a florist[3], a manhole constructor[4], a secretary[5], a bricklayer[6], a self-employed builder and market stall holder[7], a naval pilot[8] and a kick-boxer[9].

1   *Gubbins v Bailie* [2001] CLY 1564.
2   *Swallow v Dwight* [2001] CLY 1626.
3   *Lower v Hagland* [1998] CLY 1526.
4   *Mulligan v McNicholas plc* (28 November 2000, unreported).
5   *Jacobs v Corniche Helicopters* [1999] CLY 1501.
6   *Rutland v Ferguson* [1998] CLY 1643.
7   *Noble v Owens* [2008] EWHC 359 (QB).
8   *Hanks v MOD* [2007] EWHC 966 (QB).
9   *Langford v Hebran* (26 October 1999, unreported), QBD. Note that this case was appealed (unsuccessfully) to the Court of Appeal, reported at [2001] EWCA Civ 361, but on grounds relating to other heads of loss.

[D136]   Of course, in order for an award under this head to be made, evidence will need to be called (usually from the claimant and/or the claimant's work colleagues) to prove how much they loved (or would have loved) their pre-injury occupation. Where the claimant had only been in the job a relatively short while before he or she became injured, it is unlikely that any significant award would be made for loss of congenial employment. For example, in *McCrae v Chase International Express Ltd*[1], the claimant had been working as a motorcycle courier for only seven weeks prior to the accident. Kennedy LJ stated:

'It might have been appropriate to make an award under this head if the claimant had been employed for a considerable length of time in this capacity and genuinely was a person who felt disadvantaged and aggrieved as a result of the loss of congenial employment. That could not possibly be said in relation to someone who had only been doing this work for some seven weeks or so. In those circumstances I, for my part, would not have made any award under this head, and I would set aside the award of £2,000 made by the judge.'

1   [2003] EWCA Civ 505.

[D137]   It should be that each case turns on its own facts, and the judge has a wide discretion in this area. Therefore, notwithstanding the comments of Kennedy LJ in *McCrae v Chase International Express Ltd*[1], there are numerous examples of awards made for loss of congenial employment where a young claimant who is a student or has just starting training for a particular job loses the ability to pursue their chosen career path[2]. Indeed, there are several examples of cases in which the claimant has received an award for loss of congenial employment before they have even started the job they claim they would have enjoyed[3]. Conversely, however, it may be difficult to persuade the court to make an award for loss of congenial employment where the claimant is at the end of his or her career and there is only a short period of loss[4].

1   [2003] EWCA Civ 505.
2   See eg *Cornbill v Tursoil* [1993] CLY 1540, involving an 18-year-old trainee electrical engineer in the Royal Navy at the time of the accident; *Kirk v Laine Theatre Arts* [1995] CLY 1712, involving a 17-year-old dance student at the date of injury who lost the ability to pursue her chosen career as a professional dancer; *Re Steadman* [2001] CLY 1611, involving a 19-year-old professional footballer at the date of injury; *Swallow v Dwight* [2001] CLY 1626, involving a 17-year-old beauty therapy student at the date of the accident; and *Goodman v Darby* [2001] CLY 1640, involving an 18-year-old trainee teacher at the time of injury.

3   See eg *Small v Somerville Roberts* [2000] CLY 1498, where the claimant lost the chance of enlisting in the Royal Navy; *Young v Black* [2001] CLY 1561, in which the claimant lost the opportunity of becoming a fire fighter; and *Willbye v Gibbons* [2003] EWCA Civ 372, involving a claimant who had hoped to pursue a career as a nursery nurse but at the date of the accident had not yet embarked on that career.

4   See eg *Limbu v MOD* LTL 17/7/2008.

Assessment of the award

[D138]   Although it can be encompassed in one overall figure for general damages, in *Hale v London Underground*[1], Otton J (as he then was) expressly stated that the loss of congenial employment is now well recognised as a separate head of damage[2]. In this case, the claimant had been a fireman and had taken a great deal of satisfaction and fulfilment from his work. Otton J awarded £5,000 for the loss of this job (being replaced with less challenging fire safety officer work). In *Byers v London Borough of Brent*[3] a talented musician was awarded £7,500 for the loss of his career and the lost pleasure of playing his double bass.

1   Although it should be noted that the Law Commission, in its Report No 257 entitled 'Damages for Personal Injury: Non-Pecuniary Loss' (1998), was of the opinion that there was no need for, nor advantage in, separating out new heads of non-pecuniary loss beyond the award for PSLA.

2   [1993] PIQR Q30.

3   [1998] CLY 1645.

[D139]   Arguably, when comparing awards from similar cases, the figures should be updated for inflation using the RPI[1] and possibly uplifted to take account of the *Heil v Rankin* factor[2]. However, the Court of Appeal's decision in *Willbye v Gibbons*[3] may limit the extent to which a claimant can contend for a significant uplift in previously decided cases to take account of inflation. Whilst the issue was not discussed in any great detail in his judgment, Kennedy LJ stated[4]:

'There is no complaint about the Recorder's award of £118,095.32 for future loss of earnings, calculated by reference to what the appellant could hope to have earned as a nursery nurse, less her average annual earnings over the last three years, nor is there any complaint about the award of £15,000 for handicap in the labour market, but the respondent asserts that the Recorder should not have awarded an extra £15,000 for loss of congenial employment. Mr Alldis tells us that so far as he has been able to ascertain the highest award to date under this head is £10,000, and in fact awards rarely exceed £5,000. In my judgment it is important to keep this head of damages in proportion. The appellant is being compensated for being unable to pursue a career she thought she would have enjoyed. She never actually embarked on that career, although she probably had the ability to obtain the qualifications required, and in financial terms she has been fully reimbursed, so this is really an award for a particular disappointment, which may or may not be prolonged. In my judgment the award in this case should not exceed £5,000, and I would substitute that sum for the sum awarded by the Recorder.'

1   See eg *Hale v London Underground Ltd* [1993] PIQR P30, in which Otton J, as he then was, in making an award of £5,000 under this head, appeared to take account of inflation on previous awards. Although see further Piers Martin 'Loss of Congenial Employment – Can't get no (job satisfaction)?' [2002] JPIL, Issue 3/02, which tends to suggest that awards for loss of congenial employment have not kept pace with inflation and tend to stay at a conventional level. The article notes, however, that there appear to be a number of categories where awards significantly in excess of the conventional level can be made, such as young claimants (eg *Small v Somerville Roberts*

[2000] CLY 1498); sportsmen or women (eg *Langford v Hebran* (26 October 1999, unreported), QBD); or claimants with exceptional promotion/career prospects (eg *Napier v Chief Constable of the Cambridgeshire Constabulary* (22 January 2001, unreported), QBD).

2   See further at paras **[D123]–[D126]**. Although cf *Pratt v Smith* (18 December 2002, unreported), QBD, in which David Foskett QC said that there was nothing in *Heil v Rankin* [2001] QB 272 which indicated that the Law Commission's suggested uplift was to apply to claims for loss of congenial employment; and that awards for loss of congenial employment were relatively modest, ie between £5,000 and £10,000. See further *Willbye v Gibbons* [2003] EWCA Civ 372, per Kennedy LJ.

3   [2003] EWCA Civ 372.

4   At [11], under the subheading 'Loss of congenial employment'.

[D140]   Although the above passage is often cited by defendants attempting to minimise awards for loss of congenial employment, Kennedy LJ's comments strictly only apply to such awards where the claimant has not yet started out on their intended career (and therefore the award is somewhat speculative, as the reality of the job may have been very different from the dream). In principle, despite the Law Commission's criticism of separate awards under this head of loss[1], there is no reason why these awards should not keep up with inflation; otherwise, the value of the award will be gradually eroded. For example, in *Appleton v Medhat Mohammed El Safty*[2], Christopher Clarke J awarded a professional footballer the sum of £25,000 for loss of congenial employment, which suggests that, on the right facts, the court may be persuaded to make a significant award under this head.

1   In its Report No 257 entitled 'Damages for Personal Injury: Non-pecuniary Loss' (1998), the Law Commission considered that damages for the loss of congenial employment should be considered as 'merely an aspect of pain, suffering and loss of amenity'. They saw no need for, or any advantage in, separating out new heads of non-pecuniary loss beyond PSLA.

2   [2007] EWHC 631 (QB).

(ii)   Loss of Job Security

[D141]   In *Ogden v Airedale HA*[1] the claimant was awarded a lump sum payment in order to represent loss of job security. Whilst the claimant still kept his job as a radiographer, by reason of the defendant's negligence there had been a dramatic change in his employment status and protection from termination of it. This is perhaps best seen as a variant of the more traditional award for handicap or disadvantage on the labour market.

1   [1996] 7 Med LR 153.

(iii)   Loss of Enjoyment of a Holiday

[D142]   Generally speaking, disruption to a claimant's holiday (including Christmas and New Year) caused by injuries will fall under the category 'loss of amenity' and therefore result in an uplift in the award for PSLA[1]. However, if a specific holiday trip has been ruined or had to be cancelled, a separate award for this loss can be made. For example, in *Ross v Bowbelle and Marchioness*[2] an award for £2,500 was made for a ruined European tour. Further, in *Davies v Phoenix Hotel*[3] the claimant was awarded general damages of £1,250 after she and 30 others suffered salmonella poisoning from eating improperly prepared turkey at her wedding reception. Her wedding day was ruined and her honeymoon blighted and cut short. The award for general damages made in 1982 was made up of £500 for PSLA and £750 for the embarrassment, distress and loss of happy memories.

1   See eg *Ichard v Frangoulis* [1977] 1 WLR 556, per Peter Pain J at 558d.
2   [1997] 1 WLR 1159.
3   [1982] CLY 874.

[D143]   However, it should be noted that the award in respect of a spoiled holiday is not necessarily equivalent to the cost of the holiday, but is based on the difference between the actual value to the claimant of the holiday in fact enjoyed and the value which it would have had if the claimant had not been injured[1]. Thus, in *Marson v Hall*[2] where, six months after a very serious and frightening car accident, the claimant went on a prearranged holiday to Florida with her family, the diminution in value of her enjoyment was assessed at £1,000 (the total price of the holiday being £6,000). The law in this area has recently been reviewed by the Court of Appeal who gave some authoritative guidance regarding the assessment of damages for ruined holidays in the case of *Milner v Carnival*[3]. This case confirms that damages may be claimed for the physical inconvenience, discomfort and mental distress of a ruined holiday but such damages must be kept in proportion to awards for psychiatric injury, awards for sex and race discrimination and damages for bereavement. Generally speaking a special occasion that is ruined such as a honeymoon will attract more damages than a run of the mill holiday. On the facts of *Milner* the judge's awards of £7,500 to each claimant for the distress and disappointment in respect of the ruined holiday of a lifetime were reduced to £4,000 for Mr Milner and £4,500 for Mrs Milner.

1   In calculating the loss of value, the court takes the lower discounted cost paid rather than the advertised cost of the holiday: *Milner v Carnival* [2010] EWCA Civ 239.
2   [1983] CLY 1046, per Webster J.
3   [2010] EWCA Civ 239.

(iv)   Loss of Leisure

[D144]   A claimant may recover an award to reflect loss of leisure time caused by a need to work longer hours to earn the same income[1]. But it should be noted that a defendant might not be able to argue the converse position for a reduction in the award of PSLA. For example, in *Arafa v Potter*[2] the defendant unsuccessfully sought to argue for a reduction in damages for PSLA on the basis that, although the income of the injured claimant in his new job was lower than his pre-accident income, he had to work less hard to earn it. Staughton LJ in the Court of Appeal held:

'In mitigation he has sought another job. He was, in a sense, obliged to do that; it is not that there would have been any sanction if he had failed to look for another job, but he would just have failed to recover the damages to the full extent of his claim. He must give credit for the money he has earned elsewhere. But shorter hours are not money, and longer hours are not money. At first sight he does not have to give credit for them.

   If there had been two kinds of teaching job available, one with a 40 hour week, a 10–12 week holiday and a modest rate of pay, the other with a 75 hour week, 2 weeks' holiday and a handsome rate of pay, and if Mr Arafa had been physically capable of doing either job, it seems to me that for the purpose of calculating damages, one would have said that he ought to have taken the job which was more comparable to his previous life style.

As far as we know, there was no such choice available to him. There was no teaching job at 75 hours a week, 2 weeks' holiday and handsome pay which he could do despite his physical problems. He cannot be reproached for not mitigating his loss in that way, or at all events it is not proved that he could be. The defendant must be content if the [claimant] does the best he can and mitigates his loss. I would not allow any credit for the shorter hours or the longer holidays.'

On the same issue, Wall LJ said:

'... I find it very difficult to import into these two situations a calculation of intangible benefits brought about by the alleged improvement in the conditions of employment. By what objective standard is that improvement to be judged? On the facts of this case, Mr Ryan points to the shorter hours and the longer holidays. Again, speaking for myself, I am unable to quantify these in monetary terms, nor am I convinced that it is necessarily right in principle to do so.'

[1]   *Kernohan v Dartmouth* (1964, unreported), CA No 9; *Hearnshaw v English Steel Corpn* (1971) 11 KIR 306, CA; *Cram and Howland v Ryton Marine Ltd* (30 November 1976, unreported), CA; *Tindale v Dowsett Engineering Construction Ltd* (2 December 1980, unreported), per Mustill J; *Joseph Allen v Burnley, Pendle and Rossendale Health Authority* (4 March 1987, unreported), QBD; *Brewster v National Coal Board* (19 March 1987, unreported), QBD, Judge Mellor QC; *Forbes v Scott Ltd* [1998] CLY 1660; *Collett v Bean* [1999] CLY 1497.
[2]   [1994] PIQR Q73.

(v)   Loss of Marriage Prospects and Marriage Breakdown

[D145]   Where the claimant was engaged to be married at the time of the accident, it may be possible for him or her to sustain a claim for loss of marriage prospects, particularly if the marriage was broken off as a result of the injuries suffered. Damages may also be awarded where the claimant was not engaged but, owing to the injuries, may now find it harder to meet a partner[1]. There is also authority to justify a separate award of general damages where the claimant's marriage has broken down as a result of the injuries sustained by the defendant's negligence[2] and also to compensate for the expenses arising out of the subsequent divorce[3]. However, rather than making a separate award, the modern approach has generally been to take into account the loss of marriage prospects or the breakdown of a marriage when assessing the appropriate global award for PSLA[4].

[1]   *Harris v Harris* [1973] 1 Lloyd's Rep 445.
[2]   *Lampert v Eastern Omnibus Co* [1954] 1 WLR 1047; *Pietryga v Shannon* (1955, unreported); and *Noe v Nester* (1966, unreported).
[3]   *Jones v Jones* [1985] QB 704, CA; cf *Pritchard v Parrott* (1986) Times, 30 July.
[4]   See eg *Assinder v Griffin* (25 May 2001, unreported), QBD; *Edwards v Team Roofing* LTL 13/11/02, Lawtel Document No AC0101165; *Titolo v Labinjo* (1988) Aug HLMR 18.

4   Overlap Between General Damages and Other Heads of Loss

[D146]   Notwithstanding a few cases which would tend to suggest otherwise[1], it is doubtful that there can be any overlap between pecuniary loss and non-pecuniary loss. In particular, Lord Scarman was sceptical that there could be any such overlap in the leading case of *Lim Poh Choo v Camden and Islington*[2]. As seen above, the Court of Appeal in *Arafa v Potter*[3] refused to take into account the intangible benefit to the claimant of working shorter hours and longer holidays against his claim for loss of earnings[4]. It is submitted that this correctly states the position in English law that a perceived benefit can only be set off against a claim of the same type[5]. Therefore, non-pecuniary advantage should not be used to restrict pecuniary loss[6].

[1]   See eg *Harris v Harris* [1973] 1 Lloyd's Rep 445, CA, in which there was a claim for the lost chance of marriage prospects and starting a family, together with a full claim for loss of earnings. See also *Musmar v Kalala* [1999] CLY 1565, in which Recorder Digney held that the claim for loss of amenity in respect of the claimant's inability to drive, due to a phobic reaction, overlapped with the damages claim for loss of use. And in *Brown v Merton Health Authority (Teaching)* [1982] 1 All ER 650, CA, the claim for a greenhouse and raised flower beds was rejected on the basis that these costs were properly met out of the award for PSLA.

[2]   [1980] AC 174 at 192, where Lord Scarman stated: 'Upon the point of principle whether damages for non-pecuniary loss can properly be reduced to avoid an overlap with damages for pecuniary loss I express no final opinion. I confess, however, that I doubt the possibility of overlap: and I note the Pearson Commission (Cmnd 7054-I, para 759) considers it wrong in principle to reduce the one by reason of the size of the other'.

[3]   [1994] PIQR Q73.

[4]   See also the speech of Lord McCluskey in the Court of Session's decision in *McFarlane v Tayside Heath Board* 1998 SLT 307, where he said at 316: 'But not all the benefits that might accrue to the victim of a legal wrong are brought into account. We were offered the example of a coal miner who, while working in a deep pit, is rendered unfit to work by an accident, caused by his employer's fault, and resulting in the loss of an arm. He leaves the coal industry and becomes a park attendant at a lower wage. Instead of the dust, darkness and dangers of the pit, his environment becomes one of fresh air bird song and sweet smelling flowers. No-one would dream of suggesting that a price has to be put on such non-patrimonial benefits accruing to him as an incident of his working in a park rather than a pit, and that that price should be deducted either from his calculated wage loss or even from the money awarded by way of solatium given to mark the pain, suffering and deprivation flowing from the loss of the limb. It would be possible to multiply such examples'.

[5]   The general rule is that only like can be set off against like. See eg *Parry v Cleaver* [1970] AC 1, in which the House of Lords held that a pension received on account of injury is not to be taken into account against a claim for loss of earnings. In the same case, reported at [1968] 1 QB 195, Winn LJ said at 211: 'Damages for pain, loss of mobility or enjoyment of life are different in kind from damages for monetary loss; the two are not to be set off'. See also the speech of Lord Hope in *Longden v British Coal Corpn* [1997] 3 WLR 1336 at 1347F–1348; *Rialas v Mitchell* (1984) Times, 17 July, CA; and Dixon CJ in the High Court of Australia in *Espagne's case* (1961) 105 CLR 569. This principle is mirrored in the statutory framework for the deduction of benefits (see further Chapter J). A more recent example is provided by *Samuels v Benning* [2002] EWCA Civ 858, in which the trial judge had held that the claim for DIY costs in the future was to be equated with the loss of a rewarding hobby and was adequately compensated from within the award for PSLA. The Court of Appeal held that there had not been adequate compensation for this loss (particularly as the claim for past loss had been made out) and awarded an additional £5,000 (applying a multiplier of 10 to the claimed multiplicand of £500 per annum).

[6]   Cf the House of Lords' decision in *McFarlane v Tayside Health* [2000] 2 AC 59, where it was held that it was not just, fair and reasonable to hold a doctor responsible for the costs of bringing up a child born as a result of an unwanted pregnancy. The birth of a healthy child was considered to be a blessing. Since it was impossible to value the pleasure derived from the child's existence which would counteract the financial burden placed on the parents, the cost of upbringing was not a recoverable head of damages.

5   Novel and Unrecognised Heads of Non-Pecuniary Loss

(i)   Novel Heads of Non-Pecuniary Loss

[D147]   The relatively recent emergence of claims for loss of leisure time and loss of congenial employment would seem to indicate that the heads of non-pecuniary loss are not necessarily closed. In due course, it may be that other heads of general damages become recognised by the courts.

(ii)   Unrecognised Heads of Non-Pecuniary Loss

[D148]   It is clear that the trouble, anxiety and inconvenience involved in pursuing litigation, eg photocopying receipts and invoices, attending a solicitor and being examined by medical experts, is not something which sounds in damages[1]. Likewise, the time spent writing letters, attending medico-legal appointments and meetings with solicitors/barristers is a matter for costs rather than damages[2]. However, arguably, compensation for the time spent dealing with the consequences of the defendant's negligence, eg obtaining repair estimates (that would have been necessary in any event, notwithstanding any litigation), booking and attending treatment appointments, and the time spent picking up prescriptions etc, should be recoverable[3].

---

1   *Dimond v Lovell* [2002] 1 AC 384 at 400–403. See also *Taylor v Browne* [1995] CLY 1842.
2   *O'Brien-King v Phillips* [1997] CLY 1814.
3   *O'Brien-King v Phillips* [1997] CLY 1814; *Marley v Novak* [1996] CLY 2112; cf *Dimond v Lovell* [2001] 1 QB 216, in which Sir Richard Scott V-C said at 239 that damages were not recoverable for 'the worry and nuisance caused by the inconvenience of dealing with the accident'.

E Interest on Non-Pecuniary Loss (General Damages)

1 Entitlement to Interest

[E1] By virtue of s 35A of the Senior Courts Act 1981 and s 69 of the County Courts Act 1984, the claimant is entitled to receive simple interest 'at such rate as the court thinks fit or as may be prescribed, on all or any part of the debt for all or any part of the period between the date when the cause of action arose and the date of the payment'. The entitlement to interest has been held to be a remedy rather than a statutory right[1]. As such, whilst the rules require that a claim for interest must be pleaded[2], failure to do so should not mean that interest cannot be recovered[3].

---

[1] *Riches v Westminster Bank* [1934] 2 All ER 725; *Jefford v Gee* [1970] 2 QB 130; *Maher and Maher v Groupama Grand Est* [2009] EWCA Civ 1191.

[2] CPR, r 16.4(2).

[3] See further CPR, r 16.2(5) which permits the court to award a remedy to which the claimant is entitled, even if that remedy has not been specified in the claim form.

2 The Rate

[E2] The current rate of interest on general damages[1] is 2%[2]. The courts are generally obliged[3] to award simple interest on damages for personal injury or death which exceed £200[4].

---

[1] It appears that, once an item is considered to be general damage, the 2% rule applies. This includes all past heads of general damage, such as loss of congenial employment, loss of holiday, loss of use etc. However, it should be noted that future losses, such as handicap on the open labour market, do not attract interest: *Clarke v Rotax Aircraft Equipment Ltd* [1975] 1 WLR 1570.

[2] *Birkett v Hayes* [1982] 1 WLR 816; *Wright v British Railways Board* [1983] 2 AC 773; *Lawrence v Chief Constable of Staffordshire* [2000] PIQR Q349. Note that the applicable rate of interest on general damages remains at 2%, notwithstanding that the discount rate for calculating future losses might be higher: *Lawrence v Chief Constable of Staffordshire* [2000] PIQR Q349.

[3] In *Davies v Inman* [1999] PIQR Q26, Roch LJ referred to the 'presumption' that interest will be awarded on compensation arising from personal injuries.

[4] Senior Courts Act 1981, s 35A(2) and County Courts Act 1984, s 69(2) both refer to interest on judgments given for personal injuries 'which exceed £200'.

3 The Period

[E3] The period over which the rate of interest is payable was decided in *Jefford v Gee*[1] as being from the date of service (of the claim form) until trial[2].

1   [1970] 2 QB 130. Approved by the House of Lords in *Pickett v British Rail Engineering Ltd* [1980] AC 136.

2   Note that interest is usually calculated to the first day of the trial, but obviously where the trial lasts any length of time it will be more advantageous to the claimant to re-calculate interest to the last day of the trial.

4   The Theory

[E4]   The rate of interest has been the subject of controversy for some period of time. The statutory language of the rate of interest is 'such rate as the Court thinks fit'[1].

1   See Senior Courts Act 1981, s 35A and County Courts Act 1984, s 69.

[E5]   However, the amount of general damages is not fixed and is necessarily, to an extent, conventional. A calculated money value cannot be put on pain, suffering and loss of amenity. Guidelines for the amount of these damages were set by the decision of the Court of Appeal in *Heil v Rankin*[1]. Except in cases where the claimant has fully recovered from the consequences of the injury by the date of trial, general damages relate both to the period before trial and to the future. General damages are awarded in the currency value at the date of judgment. They are therefore increased above the amount which would have been awarded at the date when proceedings were started, to take account of depreciation in the value of the currency by inflation. Interest is intended to compensate the claimant for the fact that the damages are awarded at the date of judgment, when the claimant was (or might have been) notionally entitled to those damages at an earlier date. The award of interest, therefore, has conventionally been set at a rate which is substantially lower than a rate that the court would award on a debt or other judgment sum which was not calculated to take account of inflation to the date of judgment. For general damages, the theory is to exclude any inflationary element from the rate of interest and to limit it to a component referable only to delayed payment[2].

1   [2001] QB 272.

2   *Pickett v British Rail Engineering Ltd* [1980] AC 136; *Birkett v Hayes* [1982] 1 WLR 816; *Wright v British Railways Board* [1983] 2 AC 773; *Lawrence v Chief Constable of Staffordshire* [2000] PIQR Q349.

5   The History

[E6]   In *Cookson v Knowles*[1] the Court of Appeal issued guidelines suggesting that no interest should be awarded on general damages[2]. *Cookson v Knowles* was overruled by the House of Lords in *Pickett v British Rail Engineering Ltd*[3]. The reasoning of the House of Lords, which was unanimous, was that some award of interest was necessary in order to compensate the claimant for being kept out of his or her money. The next question was the rate of interest.

1   [1977] QB 913.

2   This position received support from the Royal Commission on Civil Liability and Compensation for Personal Injury (Cmnd 7054) in March 1978 (the 'Pearson Commission').

3   [1980] AC 136.

[E7]   The current guideline rate of 2% was set by the Court of Appeal in *Birkett v Hayes*[1]. Although invited to do so, the House of Lords was not prepared to vary the rate in *Wright v British Railways Board*[2]. The reasoning of Eveleigh LJ in *Birkett* was approved by the House and has been cited with approval ever since. Lord Justice Eveleigh considered the following to be relevant in discovering a rate of interest which will compensate the claimant for recognition of the fact that a sum of money in respect of general damages over a relevant period was existing for his or her benefit. He said[3]:

'On the other hand, the sums payable as interest will be relatively small and it will generally be undesirable to add to the expense of litigation by seeking to achieve a precise determination of the [claimant]'s actual loss. Most [claimants] will be paying tax at the basic rate. Some would not have invested the money at all. Others might have skilfully used it in interest free stock.

In awarding interest the judge is exercising a discretion. In the great majority of cases the [claimant] could have proceeded with greater dispatch; and yet it may well be wrong to deprive him of interest particularly as the defendant will have had the use of the money. I therefore think that we should approach this matter upon the basis that the court should arrive at a final figure which will be fair, generally speaking, to both parties.

It is not a fair basis upon which to award interest to assume that the defendant should have paid the proper sum (and this means the exact sum) at the moment of service of the writ. It is true that he must be paid some interest from that date because a sum of money was due to him. Unlike the case of a claim for a fixed money debt, no one can say exactly how much. The [claimant] does not have to quantify his demand and yet in most cases he is in the best position to evaluate his claim. The defendant may not have the material upon which to do so. He may not have had the necessary opportunity for medical examination. The [claimant] may not have given sufficient details of his injuries for anything like an estimate, as opposed to a guess, to be made of the value of the claim.

Moreover, in many cases the [claimant]'s condition will not have stabilised. We all know that the picture at the date of trial can be very different from that which was given at the date of writ. It is nobody's fault as a rule, but simply a reflection of the difficulty in forming an accurate medical opinion. There may be an unexpected change for the worse. In this case the interval after service of the writ will help to ensure a proper figure for damages which will be greater than that which the [claimant] would have obtained at the time of writ. On the other hand if his condition has improved and his award is less in consequence, this will mean that the defendant has been saved from the possibility of paying more than he should have done. These considerations show that, while it is right to regard the [claimant] as having been kept out of an award we should not regard it as necessarily resulting in a loss to him of 4 per cent of the judgment sum. I appreciate that against this argument it may be said that the judgment sum is the true figure to work on and that any lower figure, inflation apart, which might have been awarded at an earlier trial, would have been unfair to the [claimant] because, as we now know, the claim was really worth the sum now awarded. However, to award interest on this sum as though it were a debt is to call upon a defendant to pay interest upon a figure that was never demanded and which at the date of the writ is usually sheer guesswork. These considerations lead me to the conclusion that what I call the true earnings rate of interest, namely 4 per cent[4], if appropriate to a debt, is too high when applied to general damages.

Moreover, the recipient of interest at 4 per cent will generally pay tax of at least 30 per cent and therefore, after tax, the net interest is only 2.8 per cent.

As the [claimant] does not pay tax on the interest on general damages and as I regard 4 per cent gross as too high, we must look for a net figure below 2.8 per cent. There was evidence in this case that to very select bodies, such as pension funds, two recent government stock issues which are index linked had all been taken up. The actual interest rate which these produced of course fluctuates according to the figure at which the stock stands after issue but the evidence was that around 2 per cent was enough to attract investors. National savings index-linked certificates also produce only a very low rate of interest.

These considerations lead me to regard the figure of 2 per cent as appropriate for interest on an award of general damages.'

1   [1982] 1 WLR 816.
2   [1983] 2 AC 773. The House of Lords said that the guideline rate should be a matter for the Court of Appeal.
3   [1982] 1 WLR 816 at 823H.
4   This passage was referred to with approval in the opinion of Lord Diplock in *Wright v British Railways Board* [1983] 2 AC 773 at 784C. It appears that the interest rate of 4% to which Eveleigh LJ refers was the then current rate of interest on judgment debts.

[E8]   As stated above, the House of Lords in *Wright v British Railways Board*[1] refused to interfere with the guideline rate of 2%. However, Lord Diplock acknowledged that the purpose of the guideline was to promote predictability and so facilitate settlements and eliminate the expense of regularly calling expert economic evidence at trials on personal injury actions. The 2% guideline should continue to be followed for the time being, at any rate until the long-term trend of future inflation had become predictable with much more confidence. When that state of affairs was reached, it might be that the 2% guideline would call for re-examination in the light of fresh expert economic evidence.

1   [1983] 2 AC 773.

[E9]   The latter part of the 1990s showed a consistent inflation rate considerably lower than that extant at the time *Wright v British Railways Board*[1] was decided. This was recognised in relation to future losses in *Wells v Wells*[2] when the House of Lords reduced the conventional discount rate of interest, which was currently between 4% and 5%, to 3% to take into account the return which a prudent investor might obtain from Government Index Linked Stock. The rate set by *Wells v Wells* was 3%[3].

1   [1983] 2 AC 773.
2   [1999] 1 AC 345.
3   See further Chapter H, Future Expenses and Losses.

[E10]   Since the decision in *Wells v Wells*[1] a number of cases have considered the rate of interest on general damages[2]. In *Craig Burns v Joseph Davies*[3], Connell J awarded interest on general damages at 3%, and the same rate of interest on general damages was adopted by McKinnon J in *Sparks v Royal Hospitals NHS Trusts*[4]. However, in *Alayan v Northwick Park Hospital*[5], Alliott J awarded interest on general damages at 2%.

1   [1999] 1 AC 345.
2   Note that, at paras 2.56–2.57 of its Report No 257 entitled 'Damages for Personal Injury: Non-Pecuniary Loss' (1997), the Law Commission suggested that the decision in *Wells v Wells* [1999] 1 AC 345 might have altered the applicable rate of interest for non-pecuniary loss.

3   [1999] Lloyd's Rep Med 215.
4   (21 December 1998, unreported), QBD.
5   *Kemp & Kemp* at 16-014.

[E11]   In *Warren v Northern General Hospital Trust (No 2)*[1] the Court of Appeal, in relation to interest on past expenses and losses, refused to alter the discount rate set by the House of Lords in *Wells v Wells*[2]. It stated that it was for the Lord Chancellor, using his powers under the Damages Act 1996, to revise the rate of return from the then rate of 3% to take into account evidence which showed that the rate should be even lower.

1   [2000] 1 WLR 1404.
2   [1999] 1 AC 345.

[E12]   In *Lawrence v Chief Constable of Staffordshire*[1] the Court of Appeal refused to increase the guideline rate of interest for general damages for personal injury from 2% to 3% to take into account the decision of *Wells v Wells*[2]. The court once again approved of the reasoning of Eveleigh LJ in *Birkett v Hayes*[3], ie that a rigid mathematical approach to the calculation of interest is less appropriate in claims for interest on general damages than in an actuarial calculation of future loss for special damages.

1   [2000] PIQR Q349.
2   [1999] 1 AC 345.
3   [1982] 1 WLR 816.

6   The Lord Chancellor's Decision

[E13]   On 25 June 2001 the Lord Chancellor exercised his powers under s 1 of the Damages Act 1996 and set the rate of interest for damages for future loss at 2.5%[1]. Given the reasoning set out above and the most recent Court of Appeal decision of *Lawrence v Chief Constable of Staffordshire*[2], it is unlikely that any attempt to change the rate of interest for general damages will be successful.

1   By virtue of the Damages (Personal Injury) Order 2001, SI 2001/2301. See Chapter H.
2   [2000] PIQR Q349.

F   Past Expenses and Losses

1   Introduction

[F1]   In this chapter we look at recoverability of past pecuniary expenses and losses, ie those expenses and losses which have been incurred up to and including the date of trial.

[F2]   The fundamental principle in respect of recovery for pecuniary loss is that the claimant should, so far as possible, be put back into the financial position as if the defendant's wrongdoing had not occurred[1]. A claimant is therefore entitled to claim 100% of his or her net expenses or losses resulting from the injuries[2]. In respect of the recoverability and assessment of damages for past expenses and losses, there are a number of additional general principles which apply:

- To be recoverable, the expense/loss claimed must be recognised in law and not be prohibited by reasons of illegality[3] or public policy[4].
- The expense/loss must be the claimant's or, alternatively, must fall into one of the recognised exceptions for claiming on behalf of third parties (in which case, the damages are held on trust by the claimant for the benefit of that person)[5].
- The expense/loss claimed must be attributable to the defendant's wrongdoing[6].
- The defendant takes his or her victim as he or she finds them. As long as personal injury was a foreseeable outcome of the defendant's relevant breach of duty, the defendant will remain liable for the claimant's expense/loss notwithstanding the fact that it is out of proportion to the injuries sustained (the 'eggshell skull principle')[7].
- Both incurring an expense which is claimed and the amount of the expense must have been 'reasonable'[8] – but this is to be judged from the standpoint of the claimant, such that the test is effectively that the expense is one which it is not unreasonable to have claimed, nor claimed in an unreasonable amount.
- The claimant is entitled to recover only his or her 'net' loss following any relevant deductions[9].
- The expense/loss must actually have been incurred as opposed to being notional or hypothetical[10], but damages may be recovered for lost opportunities arising between the date of the defendant's wrongdoing and the date of trial as long as the lost chance was 'real' or 'substantial'[11].
- A claimant may recover reasonable expenses/losses incurred attempting to mitigate his or her injury, loss or damage, even if the cost of an attempt to mitigate adds to the overall loss, but the defendant is entitled to the benefit of any successful mitigation[12].
- Damages may not be recovered for expenses/losses which would have occurred in any event[13].

- Discounts may be made to take account of contingencies and the risk that the claimed expenses/losses might have occurred in any event[14].
- The amount recoverable may be reduced by reason of contributory negligence[15].
- Claimed expenses/losses may be reduced where the claimant has been guilty of deliberate exaggeration or malingering[16].
- Interest will be awarded on past expenses and losses in order to compensate the claimant for being kept out of his or her money[17].

[1] *Livingstone v Rawyards Coal Co* (1880) 5 App Cas 25; *Lim Poh Choo v Camden and Islington Health Authority* [1980] AC 174; *Hodgson v Trapp* [1989] AC 807; *Pickett v Pickett* [1980] AC 136; *Wells v Wells* [1999] AC 345.

[2] In *Wells v Wells* [1999] AC 345, Lord Steyn said at 382–383:

> 'The premise of the debate was that as a matter of law a victim of a tort is entitled to be compensated as nearly as possible in full for all pecuniary losses. For present purposes this mainly means compensation for loss of earnings and medical care, both past and future. Subject to the obvious qualification that perfection in the assessment of future compensation is unattainable, the 100 per cent principle is well established and based on high authority: *Livingstone v Rawyards Coal Co* (1880) 5 App Cas 25, 39; *Lim Poh Choo v Camden and Islington Area Health Authority* [1980] AC 174, 187E, per Lord Scarman'.

[3] See eg *Burns v Edman* [1970] 2 QB 541; *Hunter v Butler* [1996] RTR 396; *Clunis v Camden and Islington Area Health Authority* [1998] QB 978; *Worrall v BRB* [1999] CLY 1413, CA; *Hewison v Meridian Shipping* [2002] EWCA Civ 1821. See further Chapter A at para **[A105]**.

[4] See eg *McFarlane v Tayside Health Board* [2000] 2 AC 59 in respect of a claim arising out of the birth of an unwanted healthy baby; *Hunt v Severs* [1994] 2 AC 350 in respect of a claim for gratuitous care provided by the tortfeasor; and *Dimond v Lovell* [2001] 1 QB 216 in respect of a claim for the general inconvenience of completing insurance claim forms, instructing solicitors and obtaining repair estimates.

[5] *Best v Samuel Fox & Co* [1952] AC 176; *Buckley v Farrow* [1997] PIQR Q78; *Swain v LAS NHS Trust* [1999] All ER (D) 260; *Hunt v Severs* [1994] 2 AC 350. See further Chapter A at para **[A46]**.

[6] See further Chapter A at para **[A75]**.

[7] *Bourhill v Young* [1943] AC 92, per Lord Wright at 109–110: 'If the wrong is established the wrongdoer must take the victim as he finds him'. See also *Smith v Leech Brain* [1962] 2 QB 405.

[8] See further Chapter K, Counter-schedules. It should be noted that, where a decision to incur the expense/loss in question was reasonable but the amount claimed is unreasonable, the claimant will be limited to recovering a reasonable amount. For example, a claimant will not be entitled to recover the cost of hiring a Rolls Royce during the period when his Mini is being repaired following an accident, and any expenses over and above the cost of hiring a reasonable replacement vehicle will be disallowed: *Watson Norie v Shaw* (1967) 111 Sol Jo 117, CA.

[9] As stated by Lord Bridge in *Hodgson v Trapp* [1989] AC 807 at 819E: 'the basic rule is that it is the net consequential loss and expense which the court must measure'.

[10] A claimant will not, therefore, be able to claim for the notional cost of medical treatment if it was provided on the NHS for free: *Harris v Bright's Asphalt Contractors Ltd* [1953] 1 QB 617; see further *Hunt v Severs* [1994] 2 AC 350, per Lord Bridge at 360–361. Likewise, a claimant who owns a sports car which is damaged in an accident and hires a more modest vehicle whilst his or her car is being repaired can only recover the hire charges spent on hiring the more modest vehicle and not the notional hire charges of a replacement sports car: *Clark v Tull* [2002] EWCA Civ 510 (upheld in *Lagden v O'Connor* [2003] UKHL 64). But this does not mean to say that assessment of hypothetical or notional loss will never be relevant. For example, if a claimant was unemployed at the date of his or her accident, he or she may have obtained work but for his or her injuries and, as long there was a real or substantial as opposed to a speculative or fanciful chance of obtaining employment, a claim can be brought for the lost chance of such hypothetical earnings.

[11] *Domsalla v Barr* [1969] 1 WLR 630; *Mallett v McMonagle* [1970] AC 166; *Davies v Taylor* [1974] AC 207; *Anderson v Davis* [1993] PIQR Q87; *Allied Maples v Simmons & Simmons* [1995] WLR 1602; *Doyle v Wallace* [1998] PIQR Q146; *Langford v Hebran* [2001] EWCA Civ 361; *Warrilow v Norfolk and Norwich Hospitals NHS Trust* [2006] EWHC 801 (QB). As HHJ Grenfell said in *Finnis v Caulfield* [2002] All ER (D) 353 at [10]:

'It is sometimes erroneously thought that all findings of fact on which a claim for past loss is based should be made on the balance of probabilities, namely to consider whether a particular fact was more likely than not to have occurred and then to treat it as a certainty, whereas if it was less likely to have occurred to ignore it completely. Although *Mallett v McMonagle* was a Fatal Accident Act case, the principle stated by Lord Diplock is in logic applicable to ordinary personal injury claims. He said at p 176:

"The role of the court in making an assessment of damages which depends upon its view as to what will be and what would have been is to be contrasted with its ordinary function in civil actions of determining what was. In determining what did happen in the past a court decides on the balance of probabilities. Anything that is more probable than not it treats as certain. But in assessing damages which depend upon its view as to what will happen in the future or would have happened in the future if something had not happened in the past, the court must make an estimate as to what are the chances that a particular thing will or would have happened and reflect those chances, whether they are more or less than even, in the amount of damages which it awards".'

12   *British Westinghouse Electric and Manufacturing Co Ltd v Underground Electric Railways Co of London Ltd* [1912] AC 673; *Bellingham v Dhillon* [1973] QB 304; *Birch v Aslam* [2001] CLY 1532; *Dimond v Lovell* [2002] 1 AC 384, cf *Woodrow v Whitbread plc* (10 December 2001, unreported), QBD, Rougier J, where the claimant retrained as a result of an accident and was thereby likely to receive more than he otherwise would in his pre-accident job.

13   *Barnett v Chelsea and Kensington Hospital Management Committee* [1969] 1 QB 428; *Jobling v Associated Dairies Ltd* [1982] AC 794; *Hotson v East Berkshire Health Authority* [1987] AC 750; *Kenth v Heimdale Hotel Investments Ltd* [2001] EWCA Civ 1283; *Morgan v Millett* [2001] EWCA Civ 1641.

14   See *Heil v Rankin & MIB* [2001] PIQR Q16..

15   See Chapter A at paras [A78]–[A79].

16   See further Chapter A at paras [A127]–[A129].

17   *Jefford v Gee* [1970] 2 QB 130.

[F3]   In practice, it is often the 'reasonableness' of the item claimed, both in terms of principle and cost, that leads to the most disputes between parties.

[F4]   Whilst there is an almost unlimited range of potential pecuniary expenses/ losses which might result from a personal injury, certain heads of loss commonly repeat themselves from case to case. Generally speaking, the two largest heads of loss will usually be loss of earnings and cost of care (whether professional or gratuitous). However, when attempting to quantify the value of a particular personal injury or clinical negligence claim, the practitioner should be mindful of the various different heads of loss that might be recovered and the relevant principles which apply to the assessment of them.

[F5]   The following main categories of loss/expense are discussed individually in more detail below:

- loss of earnings;
- pension loss;
- medical and treatment expenses;
- medication and prescription expenses;
- care (whether paid or gratuitous);
- aids, equipment and appliances;
- accommodation and housing expenses (either because of forced/necessary move or because of alterations, extension or adaptation);
- travel and transport expenses;

- damaged or destroyed clothing and property;
- inability to perform domestic tasks such as DIY, painting, decorating and gardening;
- increased household bills such as the additional heating costs whilst the claimant is recuperating and not out at work;
- inability to care for others;
- additional cost in respect of holidays;
- increased leisure costs;
- costs of relationship breakdown / divorce;
- costs of administering the claimant's affairs;
- education; and
- miscellaneous expenses.

2   Loss of Earnings

[F6]   As stated above, the general principle is that the claimant should be put in the position that he or she would have been in in the absence of the injuries. Thus, if a claimant has been earning prior to his or her injury (even if unemployed immediately prior to the injury), there will be, subject to the evidence, a claim for past loss of earnings. Care should be taken to evaluate with as much precision as possible the claimant's earnings and/or profits including fringe benefits that would have been received[1]. This head of damage is frequently the largest. There are many ways in which people earn or receive money. This chapter deals with the adult claimant who was either unemployed or working at the time of the injury. Where the claimant is an infant or child, the earnings will usually be future losses rather than past losses, and so the principles to be applied in such cases are dealt with elsewhere in this work[2].

[1]   See further Chapter C, Compiling the Evidence.
[2]   See further Chapter H, Future Expenses and Losses.

(i)   Adult Claimant Unemployed at the Date of the Injury

[F7]   A claimant who was not working at the time of injury may claim for the 'lost chance' of obtaining gainful employment in the absence of the defendant's wrongdoing. For example, in *Goodenough v Dunlop Ltd*[1] the claimant had been made redundant by the defendant employer. He was awarded full loss of earnings for the period of unemployment following his redundancy. Thereafter he received an award of £2,000 for the loss of a chance of employment during the 36 weeks to trial. A further example is *Oades v Park*[2] where the claimant, who was a student at the date of the negligence, recovered £3,500 for the lost chance of a year's earnings in the computer industry due to the fact that he had to defer his university entry by one year[3].

[1]   [1996] CLY 2243.
[2]   [1994] CLY 1623.
[3]   This is effectively the same as an award for damages in respect of disadvantage on the open labour market (see further Chapter H). Theoretically, where the claimant has spent a substantial amount of time recuperating from his or her injuries, consequently delaying his or her education and the commencement of his or her career, it is possible to claim the lost earnings attributable to that length

of time. The amount at which those earnings are assessed could be taken from the beginning, middle or end of the claimant's projected career. But the further away the loss, the greater is the discount that has to be applied in order to reflect uncertainties and accelerated receipt (see further Chapter A at para [A15]) and therefore, in cases of delayed education, it is usual to claim the lost chance of earnings at the level which would have applied during the first year(s) of work. However, where the claimant's earnings are progressive, we suggest that it might be appropriate for a lifetime average to be applied.

[F8]   So, what must be proved in order to succeed in a claim for the lost chance of obtaining paid employment? The burden is on the claimant to show that:

- The lost chance was 'real' or 'substantial' rather than merely 'speculative' or 'fanciful'[1].
- But for the defendant's wrongdoing, the claimant would probably have accepted, pursued or taken the opportunity in question, assuming it had materialised[2].
- The defendant's negligence was causative of the claimant's lost opportunity (and that the claimant would not have lost, or have been prevented from realising, the opportunity in any event, eg through ill-health)[3].
- The lost opportunity is not too remote from the defendant's negligence[4].
- There is sufficient evidence to evaluate the lost chance[5].
- The lost opportunity would have been profitable[6].

---

[1]   *Davies v Taylor* [1974] AC 207; *Allied Maples v Simmons & Simmons* [1995] WLR 1602. Although it is not clear what size a lost chance has to be before it is categorised as 'substantial', the courts have in analogous fields equated 'substantial' with 'not insubstantial' or 'more than merely minimal' (see *Kitchen v RAF* [1958] 2 All ER 241; *Bonnington Castings v Wardlow* [1956] AC 613). It appears that the Court of Appeal approved a claim in *Langford v Hebran* [2001] EWCA Civ 361 involving a lost chance of 14% (see further the case summary prepared by junior counsel in that case at pp 5–7 of [2001] Quantum, Issue 3/2001, 12 June). See also *Lloyds Bank v Parker Bullen* [2000] Lloyd's Rep PN 51, where a claim for a lost chance of 15% was allowed.

[2]   See eg *Assinder v Griffin* [2001] All ER (D) 356 (May), in which the trial judge held that the claimant had a 75% chance of becoming a partner but would have turned it down.

[3]   See eg *Edwards v Premier Brands (UK) Ltd* (3 December 1999, unreported), CA.

[4]   See eg *Edwards v Premier Brands (UK) Ltd* (3 December 1999, unreported), CA.

[5]   The claimant must prove his or her loss. Where there is insufficient evidence to support the claim, the claim must fail: *Domsalla v Barr* [1969] 1 WLR 630; *Ashcroft v Curtain* [1971] WLR 1731; and *Dureau v Evans* [1996] PIQR Q18. However, once the claimant has established that he or she has suffered some loss, the court must do its best to assess that loss: *Thompson v Smith Shiprepairers* [1984] QB 405. See also *Chaplin v Hicks* [1911] 2 KB 786, in which Vaughan Williams J stated: 'The fact that damages cannot be assessed with certainty does not relieve the wrongdoer of the necessity of paying damages'.

[6]   See eg *Dureau v Evans* [1996] PIQR Q18, in which the Court of Appeal held that the claimant was not entitled to an award for a lost chance of pursuing a business venture because the trial judge had held on the balance of probabilities that the venture would not have been profitable.

[F9]   A statement should be taken from the claimant detailing the reasons why he or she was unemployed at the time of the injury. His or her qualifications and work history should be set out in detail in the statement. The strength of a claim under this head of damage will depend upon answers to the following questions:

- How long has the claimant been unemployed?
- Why was the claimant unemployed?
- What steps, prior to the injury, had the claimant taken to obtain relevant employment?

- What qualifications and capacity did the claimant have prior to his or her injuries for this employment?
- What job offers did the claimant have prior to the injuries and when was any intended work due to start?
- What prospects did the claimant have of successfully obtaining paid employment but for his or her injuries?
- How much would the claimant probably have earned had he or she successfully obtained work in the absence of the injuries resulting from the defendant's wrongdoing?

[F10] It is necessary to form a view as to the period for which the claimant would have remained unemployed (ie the period of time it would have taken him or her to find a new job). This 'job search period' varies depending upon local labour market conditions (particularly given the current economic recession at the time of writing), the nature of the work sought and the motivation of the job-hunter. In many cases, it may be useful to instruct an employment consultant to give an opinion as to the reasonable job search period for the work which the claimant was seeking.

[F11] If the claimant is one of the long-term unemployed (unemployed for over two years) or has had periods of long-term unemployment in his or her employment history that cannot be reasonably explained, the court may require cogent evidence of earnings potential before making anything other than a nominal award under this head of damage[1]. If the claimant's period of unemployment falls within a reasonable job search period, then a claim under this head should not normally present any undue difficulty. The commencement of the claim for loss of earnings would start at the end of the reasonable job search period. Generally speaking, younger claimants will be regarded as more likely to realise their earnings potential and, if necessary, statistics or actuarial evidence can be used to help determine the level of the same[2]. It is unlikely that a person of working age would not have earned money at all during his or her lifetime, especially if he or she is young, fit and not lacking in intelligence.

---

[1]   See eg *Howarth v Whittaker* [2003] Lloyd's Rep Med 235, in which the claimant had a history of alcohol abuse and depression and had not worked for 13 years at the time of the material accident. Nonetheless, a claim was put forward for the lost opportunity of obtaining some sort of employment in the future (calculated using the earnings of an assembly worker for between four and five months a year at the rate of £4,500 per annum). Elias J held at [11] that 'The prospect of the claimant obtaining remunerative employment is too low and speculative to justify any award under this head'.

[2]   *Stefanovic v Carter* [2001] EWCA Civ 452; *Dorrington v Lawrence* [2001] All ER (D) 145 (Nov), Hooper J; *Stuart v Martin* [2001] All ER (D) 401 (Oct), Owen J; and *M (a child) v Leeds Health Authority* [2002] PIQR Q46, QBD, Sullivan J. See further Chapter C at para [C38].

(ii) Adult Claimant with a Steady Job

[F12] This presents the most straightforward claim for loss of earnings, which can be calculated by taking into account the claimant's basic salary, overtime, bonus payments and any other benefits or perks.

[F13] Details of wage loss should be obtained from the claimant's employer. To calculate the claimant's net loss of earnings, a representative period needs to be chosen as a reasonable example of the claimant's pre-injury earnings. Usually, the 13 weeks (ie three months) preceding the injury are taken to calculate this figure. But if, for any reason, this period is unrepresentative of the claimant's earning potential, then a longer or shorter period should be considered, and detailed reasons should be taken from the claimant in a statement to justify this change of approach from the usual. Where there are a number of different ways of presenting a claim for loss of earnings, it may be worthwhile finding the method which maximises the claimant's recovery (eg by taking an average of the claimant's earnings over the 6, 12, 24 or 36 months prior to the claimant's injuries and seeing which period results in the highest claim). A different approach may be justified, eg where the claimant was engaged in seasonal work or received a large bonus payment at a particular point each year. Where it is difficult to obtain the claimant's payslips for such an extended period, then if the claimant was paid by BACS directly into his or her bank account, obtaining copy bank statements can be very helpful to ascertain the claimant's net weekly or monthly receipts.

[F14]   There is a general presumption that, in the absence of his or her injuries, the claimant would have continued to earn at the same rate as at the date of the accident[1]. This may be rebutted where there is evidence that the claimant's salary would have increased. Therefore, whenever there is a claim for loss of earnings over an extended period, consideration should be given to whether or not the claimant might have been entitled to any salary increases (ie beyond inflation), profit-related pay or bonus payments between the date of the defendant's wrongdoing and the date of settlement/ trial. This information should be available directly from the claimant's employer. In the absence of any evidence regarding the likely level of any salary increases, it may be possible to argue that the claimant's salary would have increased in line with the Average Earnings Index[2]. However, often the best evidence regarding the level of earnings that the claimant would have received but for his or her injuries may be provided by one or more comparators, ie those people who continue to work in the same or similar job to the claimant's pre-injury position. Where possible, the person who took over the claimant's job during the relevant period of incapacity can provide useful information in respect of the level of earnings applicable to the post, including any applicable salary increases, bonuses etc which it may be assumed that the claimant would have enjoyed. For example, in *George v Stagecoach*[3], Mackay J had to assess the lost earnings of a claimant involved in 'knowledge management' (a new venture in the IT industry). He referred to the evidence that had been called on behalf of the claimant and said at [20]:

> 'I would have been better served by evidence from a human relations employee of either his present or another company. I would also have been served better by direct evidence of a specific comparator or comparators, particularly so where figures as high as those involved in this case are in play.'

[1]   *Roach v Yates* [1938] 1 KB 256.
[2]   *Smith v Rod Jenkins* [2003] EWHC 1356 (QB), cf *Cooke v United Bristol Health Care* [2003] EWCA Civ 1370 regarding future loss.
[3]   [2003] EWHC 2042 (QB).

[F15]   Instructions should also be taken in respect of any promotion prospects or career advancement opportunities that might have been available in the absence of the claimant's injuries. If possible, specific witness evidence should be sought confirming the claimant's skills, qualities, level of ability and prospects of being successfully selected for promotion if an opportunity had materialised. A claim for any such 'lost chance' need not be proved on the balance of probabilities. As long as there was a 'real' or 'substantial'[1] chance of such a promotion or career enhancement leading to an increase in salary, the claimant will be entitled to recover damages to reflect this lost opportunity[2]. For example, in *Anderson v Davis*[3] the claimant, who was a teacher prior to a road traffic accident, was found to have had a 66% chance of promotion to principal lecturer. He was therefore awarded 66% of the increased salary of this post. Further, in *Doyle v Wallace*[4] the claimant contended that, but for the accident, she would have trained to become a drama teacher. The trial judge concluded that she had a 50% chance of succeeding in this training. The Court of Appeal upheld the award regarding her loss of earnings, reflecting 50% of the difference between her earnings doing clerical work and her earnings as a drama teacher. Similar principles have been applied in other cases involving a single potential promotion associated with a significant pay rise[5] (although such an approach is not necessarily appropriate where the chances of promotion are almost certain or a 'reasonable career model' is taken[6]). They have also been applied to more complex cases where there are multiple potential career options resulting in significantly increased earnings, such as the kick-boxer case of *Langford v Hebran*[7] and the professional footballer cases of *Appleton v El Safty*[8] and *Collett v Smith*[9].

1   Ie not insubstantial.
2   *Domsalla v Barr* [1969] 1 WLR 630; *Mallett v McMonagle* [1970] AC 166; *Davies v Taylor* [1974] AC 207; *Anderson v Davis* [1993] PIQR Q87; *Allied Maples v Simmons & Simmons* [1995] WLR 1602; *Doyle v Wallace* [1998] PIQR Q146; *Langford v Hebran* [2001] EWCA Civ 361; *Appleton v El Safty* [2007] EWHC 631 (QB); *Collett v Smith* [2009] EWCA Civ 583.
3   [1993] PIQR Q87. See also *Williams v Green* [2001] EWCA Civ 1888.
4   [1998] PIQR Q146.
5   See eg *Williams v Green* [2001] EWCA Civ 1888; and *Crofts v Murton* LTL 10/9/2008, in which a 'loss of a chance' calculation was applied to both past and future loss.
6   *Herring v Ministry of Defence* [2003] EWCA Civ 528; *Brown v MOD* [2006] PIQR Q9, CA. See further para **[F16]** below.
7   *Langford v Hebran* [2001] EWCA Civ 361.
8   [2007] EWHC 631 (QB).
9   [2009] EWCA Civ 583. It should be noted that, although Swift J calculated loss of future earnings on the basis of loss of a chance, taking into account various percentage chances of increased earnings, the claimant's past loss of earnings were calculated on a balance of probabilities (and there was no appeal from her award in respect of past loss).

[F16]   However, where the claim concerns the loss of a career or a job involving a hierarchical promotion structure, it may be more appropriate to consider, on the balance of probabilities, the level that the claimant would have reached in the absence of his or her injuries. Where a 'reasonable career model' has been adopted, it may be possible to present a claim for full loss of earnings without any deduction for the loss of a chance[5]. As stated by Potter LJ in *Herring v MOD*[1], where there is sufficient evidence to adopt a 'reasonable career model', it is neither necessary nor appropriate to adopt the percentage based approach:

'In a case where the career model adopted by the judge has been chosen because it is itself the appropriate baseline and/or is one of a number of alternatives likely to give more or less similar results, then it is neither necessary nor appropriate to adopt the percentage chance approach in respect of the possibility that the particular career identified will not be followed after all.'

[1]   *Herring v Ministry of Defence* [2003] EWCA Civ 528, subsequently followed in *Dixon v Were* [2004] EWHC 2273 (QB), Gross J; *Rashid v Iqbal* [2004] EWHC 1148 (QB), Andrew Smith J; *Brown v MOD* [2006] PIQR Q9, CA; and *Leesmith v Evans* [2008] EWHC 134 (QB), Cooke J. See also *Lynham v The Morecambe Bay Hospitals NHS Trust* [2002] EWHC 823 (QB), Garland J, which pre-dates the decision in *Herring v MOD*. See further *McGregor on Damages* (18th edn), paras 8-072–8-078 and Theodore Huckle 'Damages for loss of earnings – reasonable model or loss of chance' 13 APIL Newsletter 7.

[F17]   Likewise, it is important that instructions are taken regarding the value of any lost perks, benefits or free/subsidised services that were associated with the claimant's employment. Care must be taken to ensure that all these losses are taken into account – they are frequently missed and may add up to a substantial amount. Common such perks and benefits include:

- loss of use of the company car (factors such as the type, engine size, how often renewed should be considered – a useful guide to which is the taxable benefit allowed by the Inland Revenue)[1];
- free fuel, servicing, insurance etc;
- concessionary fares;
- cheap loans;
- clothing allowance or free clothes[2];
- education allowance for children;
- gym or leisure club membership[3];
- private health insurance and/or life assuarance[4];
- dental care[5];
- critical illness cover;
- expense accounts;
- bonuses;
- tips;
- holiday pay;
- cheaper holidays[6];
- attendance bonuses;
- bonuses for living in certain parts of the country, eg a London living allowance[7];
- Christmas bonuses;
- free goods;
- free or subsidised food or meal tickets[8];
- share incentive schemes;
- travel concessions;
- free accommodation (eg service tied accommodation (police etc) – note that such benefit may also include household bills); and
- any other work-related benefits, eg directorships and share options[9].

[1]   See eg *Dixon v Were* [2004] EWHC 2273(QB).
[2]   See eg *Morgan v MOD* [2002] EWHC 2072 (QB), in which Andrew Collender QC allowed £800 pa for clothing (the claimant was given working clothes and a mess kit allowance).
[3]   See eg *Morgan v MOD* [2002] EWHC 2072 (QB), in which Andrew Collender QC allowed the claim for free access to sporting facilities, but deducted the claim in respect of the claimant's wife.
[4]   See eg *Dixon v Were* [2004] EWHC 2273(QB); *Morgan v MOD* [2002] EWHC 2072 (QB).

5   See eg *Morgan v MOD* [2002] EWHC 2072 (QB), where the claimant had the advantage of free and quickly available dental care in the Army, Andrew Collender QC allowed the cost of replacing that with an insurance scheme following the injury.

6   In *Morgan v MOD* [2002] EWHC 2072 (QB), a modest award of £1,000 was made because it was accepted that the claimant incurred lower holiday expenses when he was employed in the Army because he could often take his holiday where he was based and therefore did not incur the cost of flights.

7   See eg *Crofts v Murton* LTL 10/9/08, in which HHJ Collender QC sitting as a deputy judge of the High Court held that the claimant, who was employed as a Detective Chief Superintendent in the police, was entitled to claim London Allowance, a rent allowance, and Compensatory grant as part of his salary, even though he no longer lived in London because of his injuries (the defendant had argued that these items should be excluded from the loss of earnings calculations because they were only paid due to the higher costs of living in London which no longer applied).

8   See eg *Morgan v MOD* [2002] EWHC 2072 (QB), in which Andrew Collender QC allowed about £2,750 pa for food; *Hopkinson v MOD* [2008] EWHC 699 (QB) in which, at paras [57]–[59], Michael Harvey QC awarded the claimant £1,000 pa for 'free victuals'.

9   See eg *Collins v Jones* [2003] EWHC 187 (QB), in which Morland J awarded the claimant £300,000 in respect of the significant lost chance that the claimant would have been offered remunerative directorships or share options but for his injuries.

[F18]   In military claims, care should especially be taken to try to obtain evidence[1] to value the claimants' lost benefits, which may be extensive, including free medical and dental care, free gym access, reduced rent, enhanced service payments and private education etc[2].

1   In *Hanks v MOD* [2007] EWHC 966 (QB), Royce J refused to make an allowance to take account of increased payments to military personnel serving in Afghanistan and in Iraq without any evidence regarding the level of payments.

2   See eg *Morgan v MOD* [2002] EWHC 2072 (QB) regarding the assessment of lost benefits brought by a Major in the Royal Electrical and Mechanical Engineers.

[F19]   Generally speaking, a claimant will be restricted to claiming the earnings that can be supported by documentary evidence[1]. However, this is not necessarily so. For example, where the court accepts the claimant's evidence that their earnings were on average in excess of the incomplete payslips that have been obtained and the claimed amount is consistent with the national average earnings statistics, a higher figure may be awarded[2]. Indeed, the Annual Survey of Hours and Earnings, published by the Office for National Statistics, is a useful starting point for pleading a loss of earnings claim in the absence of other figures. The Court of Appeal approved the trial judge's use of this type of information in *Stefanovic v Carter*[3] to assess the earnings of a trainee accountant.

1   See further *Ashcroft v Curtin* [1971] 1 WLR 1731; and *Phillips v Holliday* [2001] EWCA Civ 1074.

2   *Froggatt v Chesterfield & North Derbyshire Royal Hospital NHS Trust* [2002] All ER (D) 218 (Dec). See also *McLaughlin v F & B Ltd* (7 February 2003, unreported), QBD.

3   [2001] EWCA Civ 452. See also *Dorrington v Lawrence* [2001] All ER (D) 145 (Nov), Hooper J; *Stuart v Martin* [2001] All ER (D) 401 (Oct), Owen J; and *M (a child) v Leeds Health Authority* [2002] PIQR Q46, QBD, Sullivan J.

[F20]   Even where there is very little documentary evidence of the loss of earnings sustained by the claimant, it may still be possible to maintain a claim under this head where there is an identifiable loss. For example, in *Eden v West & Co*[1] the trial judge rejected the claimant's claim for loss of earnings on the basis of the paucity of the evidence provided. However, the Court of Appeal held that the trial judge was not entitled to take such a robust approach. Pill LJ said[2]:

> 'In my judgment, however, on the material before the court there must be some award by way of damages for loss of earnings having regard to the agreed medical evidence and to the evidence that, plainly, during the months before his accident the appellant was working. It is not suggested by the defendants that he would have done other than continue to work for them, including work on the estate in question. The schedule claims net loss of earnings for one year in the sum of £11,500.
>
> In my judgment, this claim can only be approached on a global basis. I would award the sum of £5,000 for the period of six months during which the medical evidence shows that the appellant was unfit for work. I have regard to all the uncertainties which would arise thereafter. However, I would add to that sum, to cover the period of recuperation contemplated by the doctors in the second six months, the sum of £1,000.'

---

1   [2002] EWCA Civ 991, [2003] PIQR Q16.
2   [2002] EWCA Civ 991 at [24].

[F21]   Where the claimant alleges that he or she has missed the opportunity to perform paid overtime, it may be necessary to obtain supporting witness evidence from the claimant's employer about the overtime that would have been available. Calculations based upon the historic availability of overtime may not be accurate if the overtime was infrequent and only linked to a particular project or deadline which needed to be met. Additionally, where a loss of earnings claim is based upon the premise that the claimant is able to return to work but no longer has the stamina to do the same number of hours or overtime as before, this should, if possible, be supported by medical evidence and witness evidence of colleagues/managers at the claimant's place of work[1].

---

1   Although see *McMylor v Firth Rixson plc* [2002] EWCA Civ 1863, in which the trial judge accepted the claimant's evidence that this was the case when the medical evidence could not provide any reason for the claimant's continuing pain and inability to work overtime. It is noteworthy that no other cause apart from the material accident had been suggested for the ongoing symptoms. The Court of Appeal held that the trial judge was entitled to accept the claimant's own evidence of his inability to work overtime as a result of the accident.

[F22]   The annual figure used should be net of tax[1] and National Insurance[2] (the appropriate figures can be gleaned from the tables in the PNBA's publication 'Facts & Figures' if they are not readily available). It is up to the claimant to ensure that the correct net loss of earnings figure is claimed[3]. The claimant is deemed to lose that part of his or her earnings due to his or her injury that will be 'top sliced' when deducting tax[4]. Any tax rebate[5] must be taken into account if received as a result of the claimant's loss of wages. Credit must also be given for any tax saving or tax-free period the claimant enjoys upon return to work accruing by reason of the loss of earnings[6]. However, where the claimant is wealthy, the court may take account of steps that the claimant might have taken in order to minimise his or her tax liability in the absence of the injuries[7]. Further, where the claimant would have avoided paying tax or would have paid tax at a lower rate, eg working abroad[8] or due to spending long periods working on a ship sailing in foreign waters[9], then different tax calculations may need to be performed in order to put the claimant back into the position he or she would have been in had the injury not occurred. Likewise, it may be necessary to 'gross up' claims for loss of earnings which would become taxable on receipt in respect of claimants living in foreign jurisdictions, and therefore expert evidence may be required regarding the likely tax to be paid[10].

1   *British Transport Commission v Gourley* [1956] AC 185.
2   *Cooper v Firth Brown* [1963] 1 WLR 418.
3   *Phipps v Orthodox Unit Trusts* [1958] 1 QB 314, CA.
4   *Lyndale Fashion Manufacturers v Rich* [1973] 1 All ER 33, CA.
5   *Hartley v Sandholme Iron Co* [1975] QB 600.
6   *Brayson v Wilmot-Breedon* [1976] CLY 682.
7   *Beach v Reed Corrugated Cases Ltd* [1956] 2 All ER 656.
8   See eg *Biesheuval v Birrell* [1999] PIQR Q40.
9   See eg *Hopkinson v MOD and anor* [2008] EWHC 699 (QB).
10 See eg *Horton v (1) Evans and (2) Lloyds Pharmacy Ltd* [2007] EWHC 315 (QB). In this case, Keith J declared that the claimant was entitled to an indemnity for any tax that would be demanded by the US tax authorities upon receipt of the award for loss of earnings. However, it is doubted that the court had the power to order such an indemnity, and in other cases, unless an indemnity can be agreed, it may be safer to call expert evidence regarding the extent of the claimant's likely tax liability.

[F23]   Credit also needs to be given for expenses that would have been incurred whilst earning. An obvious example is childcare[1] or the cost of tools and materials. However, travel expenses are often ignored unless they would have been significant[2].

1   See eg *Warrilow v Norfolk and Norwich Hospitals NHS Trust* [2006] EWHC 801 (QB).
2   *Dews v National Coal Board* [1988] AC 1; *Warrilow v Norfolk and Norwich Hospitals NHS Trust* [2006] EWHC 801 (QB), cf *Sparks v Royal Hospitals NHS Trust* (21 December 1998, unreported); *Eagle v Chambers (No 2)* [2004] EWCA Civ 1033; and *Crofts v Murton* LTL 10/9/2008.

[F24]   If the employer is not a defendant, it is necessary to ascertain whether or not there is any contractual obligation to repay sick pay[1]. Where there is no such obligation or there is an agreement expressly excluding one, the claimant is not entitled to recover any sum in respect of the 'employer's outlay', since there would be no liability to repay this amount and the claimant would thereby benefit from double recovery[2]. The length of absence from work must be reasonable but, provided the claimant has not misled his or her medical advisers, he or she is entitled to remain off throughout the period of a valid sickness certificate[3].

1   If the claimant is under a contractual obligation to repay any sick pay, then the claimant is entitled to recover damages for the same: *Browning v War Office* [1963] 1 QB 750; *Davies v Inman* [1999] PIQR Q26. Even a moral obligation may impose an increase in damages: *Dennis v London Passenger Transport Board* [1948] 1 All ER 779. Where a voluntary payment is made with no expectation of reimbursement (either expressed or implied), such payment is not recoverable from the defendant but, likewise, is not to be set off against a claim for past loss of earnings: *Cunningham v Harrison* [1973] QB 942; *Bews v Scottish Hydro-Electric plc* 1992 SLT 749.
2   *Pratt v Smith* (18 December 2002, unreported), QBD.
3   *Port of London Authority v Payne* [1994] ICR 555, [1994] IRLR 9.

[F25]   Where the claimant had a patchy employment history prior to the defendant's wrongdoing, it may be that a discount will have to be made in order to reflect the time out of work that might have occurred in any event (assuming this has not already been taken into account when calculating the claimant's average net earnings). For example, such a discount might be made in cases where the claimant had a pre-existing illness which led to breaks between work[1] or had a history of low seasonal employment[2]. If possible, evidence should be obtained from work colleagues, close friends or relatives to show that the claimant had turned a corner prior to the injuries and was determined to make a fresh start.

[1]　See eg *Clenshaw v Tanner* [2002] EWHC 184 (QB), in which Silber J discounted the claim for past loss of earnings by 30% in order to take account of the time the claimant would have been out of work in any event (primarily due to his pre-existing psychiatric condition).

[2]　See eg *Brown v Berry* (14 October 1997, unreported), QBD, in which Mr Robert Seabrook QC sitting as a deputy judge of the High Court discounted the claim for past loss of earnings by 50% in order to take account of the claimant's lack of qualifications and driving licence and history of low seasonal employment.

[F26]　Other remunerative activities that the claimant has not been able to perform, such as roles in the Territorial Army, as a reserve fireman or a session musician, should be investigated and claimed for as appropriate.

[F27]　If the claimant has returned to work, credit must be given for any pay received against the loss of earnings claim. Where the claimant has not taken reasonable steps to seek alternative employment, he or she is at risk of being found to have failed to mitigate his or her loss. The burden is on the defendant to establish that the claimant has failed to take reasonable steps to find alternative work[1]. This may be achieved in a number of ways, such as establishing that the claimant could and should have returned to work sooner[2], could have performed a different job[3], or could have worked longer hours[4]. However, it may not necessarily be a failure to mitigate loss to resign before being pushed[5] or to take early retirement[6]. Likewise, a claimant will not necessarily be required to move his whole family to somewhere new, simply in order to increase his chances of finding work[7].

[1]　*Geest plc v Lansiquot* [2002] UKPC 48; *Froggatt v LEP International* [2002] EWCA Civ 600; *Eaton v Johnstone* [2008] UKPC 1.

[2]　See eg *McKeown v Ford Motor Company Ltd* [2006] EWCA Civ 336; *Hopkinson v MOD* [2008] EWHC 699 (QB).

[3]　See eg *Billingham v Hughes* [1949] 1 KB 643, where the Court of Appeal made allowance for the residuary earning capacity of a radiologist, where a GP who was qualified to be a radiologist could no longer pursue his career in general practice as a result of his injuries.

[4]　See eg *Butler & Anor v Thompson* [2005] EWCA Civ 864.

[5]　See eg *Morris v Richards* [2003] EWCA Civ 223.

[6]　See eg *McKeown v Ford Motor Company Ltd* [2006] EWCA Civ 336.

[7]　See eg *Limbu v MOD* LTL 17/7/2008.

(iii)　Reduced Hours

[F28]　Where a claimant has had to reduce his or her hours as a result of injury, it is important to establish that the reduction in hours was caused or contributed to by reason of the injury as opposed to simply being a matter of choice by the claimant and/or related to other factors. Expert opinion, even jointly instructed expert opinion, may not be determinative on this issue, where the claimant's evidence is accepted that it was the injury which caused the change in working practice. For example, in *Tucker v Watt*[1] an optometrist brought a claim for losses arising out of altering her working practice to using a laser instead of conventional optometric testing and reduced her working week from four days to three days following an accident. The defendant argued that the court was bound to accept the opinion of a jointly instructed orthopaedic expert that she was capable of working the same number of days as she did before the accident and the reduction in her hours was simply a matter of choice. However, the Court of Appeal held the trial judge was not bound to accept the expert evidence on this point, and upheld his decision that the reduction in the claimant's hours was caused by the accident.

[1]   [2005] EWCA Civ 1420.

(iv)   Retraining

[F29]   Where the claimant has spent money retraining or attending courses (which he or she would not otherwise have done), as long as such expenses have not been unreasonably incurred as a result of the injuries, they should usually be recoverable[1] as a cost of mitigation[2]. Likewise, any losses incurred during the period of retraining should usually be recoverable[3]. However, this is not always necessarily so, if, for example, the claimant decided to retrain when there was available work that he or she could have done without such retraining[4], or the case involves an acceleration of pre-existing symptoms, which would have necessitated the claimant incurring expenses to retrain in any event. Where a claimant has retrained or decided to pursue alternative work as a result of injuries sustained, the test to be applied is whether or not the claimant's actions were reasonable in all the circumstances[5]: if so, they will be disallowed at least to the extent that they are unreasonable. A failure to seek appropriate retraining may give rise to an argument that the claimant has failed to mitigate his loss. The burden is on the defendant to establish such an argument[6], which may be a difficult burden to discharge. A claimant is not necessarily required to retrain and undertake work in which he or she has no interest[7] and, in some circumstances, it may not be unreasonable for a claimant to notionally stay on a company's books where, even though he is no longer receiving any pay, he was getting a prospective pension benefit[8]. Where a claimant by retraining earns more money than he or she did before, the loss of earnings claim comes to an end. However, it has been held that, once the claimant's earnings catch up with his or her previous earnings, no credit needs to be given against the claim for past loss in respect of the increased level of future earnings[9].

[1]   See eg *Rowden v Clarke Chapman & Co* [1967] 3 All ER 608n.
[2]   The reasonable costs of steps taken by the claimant to mitigate his or her loss are recoverable from the tortfeasor: *Mattocks v Mann* [1973] RTR 13; *Candlewood Navigation Corporation Ltd v Mitsui OSK Lines Ltd* [1986] 1 AC 1; *Lagden v O'Connor* [2003] UKHL 64. See further Chapter A at para [A78].
[3]   *Rowden v Clarke Chapman &Co* [1967] 3 All ER 608; *Ronan v Sainsbury's Supermarkets Ltd* [2006] EWCA Civ 1074.
[4]   See eg *Luker v Chapman* (1970) 114 Sol Jo 788, in which the Court of Appeal declined to award the claimant, who had previously worked as a television engineer, his loss of earnings whilst retraining to be a teacher since he could have taken available clerical work. See also *Brown v Vosper Thornycroft* [2004] EWHC 400 (QB), where the judge held that the claimant was capable of performing a wide range of jobs which would have earned a comparable salary to that he would have enjoyed in the absence of the accident, and that it was unreasonable for the defendant to pay for the claimant's 'drastic change of direction' not only into a new field but into a higher level generally within the employment market.
[5]   *Woodrup v Nicol* [1992] PIQR Q104; and *Morris v Richards* [2003] EWCA Civ 223.

6   *Geest plc v Lansiquot* [2002] UKPC 48; *Eaton v Johnstone* [2008] UKPC 1.
7   *Woodrup v Nicol* [1992] PIQR Q104.
8   *Froggatt v LEP International* [2002] EWCA Civ 600.
9   *Woodrow v Whitbread plc* (10 December 2001, unreported), QBD, Rougier J. This case was
        subsequently mentioned with apparent approval by Sedley LJ in *Orthet Ltd v Vince-Cain* [2004]
        EWCA Civ 1613.

(v)   Adult Claimant Working 'On the Black'

[F30]   Difficulties can arise where the claimant is working 'on the black', that is, not paying tax or National Insurance on his or her income. Occasionally, claimants claim large losses of earnings when they have not been declaring their income to the appropriate authorities. Careful advice has to be given in this situation. This should cover the following four questions:

*   Is there sufficient evidence of the loss to make it worth claiming[1]?
*   Can the claimant be prosecuted if he or she makes such a claim against the defendant and the court finds out that he or she has not declared his or her income in the past?
*   Will the claimant (probably) be subject to a duty to pay capital, interest and/or penalties to the Inland Revenue (or other authority)? If so, will any success in the claim be self-defeating?
*   Were the claimant's actions such as to prevent the court from making an award under this head of damage for policy reasons (applying the maxim 'ex turpi causa non oritur actio' or otherwise)?

1   When the claimant is employed through a company, the starting point is the earnings disclosed
        in the accounts of that company, and it is illegitimate to go beyond the records of the company
        when seeking to assess what money the claimant was earning by way of salary or profits: *Phillips v
        Holliday* [2001] EWCA Civ 1074, per Waller LJ at [24].

[F31]   There is no doubt that the role of the claimant's lawyers is to advise him or her to make a declaration to the appropriate authorities immediately. This will inevitably mean that he or she will have to pay off past unpaid tax and National Insurance contributions. Provided that he or she informs the appropriate authorities immediately, it is perhaps unlikely that the court will refer the matter to the Director of Public Prosecutions with a view to bringing a prosecution for fraud. However, this cannot be guaranteed. The policy of the court when presented with this type of claim is to enable a claimant to recover under this head of damage. Otherwise, it would enable a tortfeasor to obtain a windfall to which he or she would not otherwise be entitled[1].

1   *Newman v Folkes & Dunlop Tyres Ltd* [2002] EWCA Civ 59; *Finnis v Caulfield* [2002] All ER (D)
        353; *Duller v South East Lincs Engineers* [1981] CLY 585; and *Le Bagge v Buses* [1958] NZLR
        630; cf *Hunter v Butler* [1996] RTR 396, which involved a fatal accident claim where the deceased
        had been working on the black at the same time as claiming state benefit; and *Burns v Edman*
        [1970] 2 QB 541, in which the claimant's income derived from criminal acts. In *Newman v Folkes
        & Dunlop Tyres Ltd* [2002] EWCA Civ 59, whilst the Court of Appeal was not concerned with
        this question, since there was no appeal about the trial judge's decision to award the claimant his
        earnings notwithstanding his failure to pay tax and National Insurance, nonetheless Ward LJ stated
        at [14] that, 'Quite correctly, in my view, there has been no appeal against that ruling'.

(vi)   Adult Self-employed Claimant

[F32]   If the claimant is self-employed, a claim for loss of profits as well as for loss of income can be made. Proof of earning capacity has to be obtained using accounts either prepared prior to the injury or by forensic accountants. The accounts will provide the foundation of any claim and, unless the accounts are unreliable[1], it will usually not be legitimate to go beyond the accounts or to prepare a claim on the basis of what the claimant could have been earning if he or she was being employed by someone else[2]. A helpful cross-check can be provided by comparing the business accounts with the Inland Revenue records. Loss of profit can be calculated on the same basis as in contract, ie profits actually made are deducted from profits that would have been made but for the accident. If the accounts are such that there is no proper basis for making a calculation in respect of lost earnings, the claim may be disallowed[3]. However, as long as there is at least some basis upon which to make a calculation, the court must do its best to assess the loss, even though it may be difficult[4]. Problems can arise where the claimant has no accounts or has not declared his or her income to the Inland Revenue[5]. Given the imponderables involved, the court may be inclined to make a single global award – known as a *Blamire* award[6] – encompassing lost profits and loss of future earning capacity[7]. Where the claimant's accounts show no loss over the relevant period of incapacity, it will be difficult to mount a claim for loss of earnings. Occasionally, it may be possible to argue that the claimant's business would have increased at a greater rate (and would have been more profitable) in the absence of his or her injuries. However, without solid evidence demonstrating what the increase in profits would have been, it will be difficult to establish that there has been any loss to the claimant[8]. Also, sometimes, the claimant's accounts are so unreliable that the court is unable to place any weight on them at all[9].

---

[1]   See eg *Crouch v King's Healthcare NHS Trust* [2004] EWCA Civ 853, in which the Court of Appeal upheld the judge's refusal to rely upon the claimant's accounts as evidence of his loss of earnings because they were unreliable. In the absence of any credible evidence regarding the claimant's loss, it was held that the trial judge was entitled to assess loss of earnings on the basis of a lump sum rather than using the conventional multiplier/multiplicand method.

[2]   *Phillips v Holliday* [2001] EWCA Civ 1074. Although it should be noted that occasionally, where there are good reasons for doing so, the court might be persuaded to go behind the claimant's accounts or tax returns. See eg *McLaughlin v F & B* (7 February 2003, unreported), QBD, in which Simon J, in assessing the loss of earnings sustained by a tunnel miner, was persuaded to make an award for loss of earnings in excess of the figure contained in the claimant's last tax return before his injury, since there was evidence that this was an underestimate of the claimant's earning potential.

[3]   *Ashcroft v Curtin* [1971] 1 WLR 1731. It should be noted that, just because the claimant's accounts do not show a loss of profit following the defendant's wrongdoing, it does not necessarily mean that no profit was in fact lost, assuming that evidence can be obtained which shows that even more profit could have been made but for the injuries. However, this is perhaps more appropriately described as a 'loss of business opportunity', which is discussed at para **[F36]**.

[4]   *Chaplin v Hicks* [1911] 2 KB 786 at 792; *The Mediana* [1900] AC 113 at 116–117; *Otter v Church* [1953] Ch 280; *Moeliker v A Reyrolle & Co Ltd* [1977] 1 WLR 132 at 141; and *Thompson v Smith Shiprepairers (North Shields)* [1984] QB 405. In *Chaplin v Hicks* [1911] 2 KB 786, Vaughan Williams LJ stated: 'The fact that damages cannot be assessed with certainty does not relieve the wrongdoer of the necessity of paying damages'. See also *Eden v West & Co* [2002] EWCA Civ 991.

[5]   See further at para **[F31]**.

[6]   After *Blamire v South Cumbria Health Authority* [1993] PIQR Q1. See further Chapter D at para **[D151]**.

7   See eg *Phillips v Holliday* [2001] EWCA Civ 1074; *Hannon v Pearce* (24 January 2001, unreported), QBD; *Willemse v Hesp* [2003] EWCA Civ 994. See also *Crouch v King's Healthcare NHS Trust* [2004] EWCA Civ 853, where Gage J (as he then was) said at [35]:

> 'Faced with the lack of credible evidence of earnings during what the judge rightly found was the crucial period post February 1997 but pre the accident to the arm, coupled with his conclusion that there had been a change of lifestyle, in my judgment the judge was quite entitled to reject the multiplier/multiplicand basis for assessment of past and future loss. Indeed, it is difficult to see how he could have approached the matter in any other way than to assess a global sum.'

8   See eg *Chang v Delgreco* [2004] EWCA Civ 407.
9   See eg *Horsley v Cascade Insulation Services and others* [2009] EWHC 2945 (QB).

(vii) Partnership

[F33] If the claimant was part of a partnership, then his or her loss will be his or her share of the profits. This will usually be easily calculated by looking at the partnership's accounts and tax returns. The usual situation will be equal partners with equal shares (ie 50:50 etc)[1]. The partner recovers his or her own real loss[2], even where it is a two-person, husband-and-wife partnership[3].

1   The presumption under Partnership Act 1890, s 24 is that, in the absence of a contrary agreement or evidence, a partnership is a partnership of equals.
2   *Lee v Sheard* [1956] 1 QB 192 at 196.
3   *Kent v British Railway Board* [1995] PIQR Q42, in which the Court of Appeal held that, where one member of a two-person partnership was injured, the injured person can only claim for losses to that partnership to the extent of that person's interest in it. The rule was applied even though the business in question was a husband-and-wife partnership in the running of a bed and breakfast property. This reasoning was subsequently applied in *Neal v Jones* [2002] EWCA Civ 1731, although Rix LJ said at [43]:

> '... it has to be said nevertheless that some of the reasoning in [*Ward v Newalls Insulation* [1998] 1 WLR 1722, CA] appears to go a certain length to undermine the logic of [applied in *Kent v British Railway Board* [1995] PIQR Q42]: for it seems that the extent of the recoverable loss turns not so much on what a claimant's real interest in his partnership is, but on the level of his partner's real contribution (see at 1730H/1731C). This Court has heard no submissions on these matters. As I have said, I will assume this Court to be bound by [*Kent v British Railway Board* [1995] PIQR Q42]. Nevertheless, it may be that in a family situation, where the partnership is between the husband and wife and all the earnings of the partnership go into the single family pot to support the family income, a schematic view of that partnership which leaves the injured person able to claim only 50 per cent of the established loss to the partnership is a result which can have unfortunate consequences.'

[F34] Where the wife or partner has contributed to the business, by way of capital or assisting the claimant, the reasoning in *Kent v British Railway Board*[1] is likely to be difficult to displace[2]. However, the presumption of equal shares may be rebutted where the wife or partner contributed little (if anything) to the running of the business and was merely included in the records as a tool for tax avoidance. For example, in *Ward v Newalls Insulation*[3], the partnership consisted of two working partners, but for the purposes of tax an agreement was made that both men's wives should be equal partners. It was held that the court should look at the reality of a situation and calculate the value of the claimant's contribution to the partnership. Only two of the four partners in *Ward* contributed and, therefore, these two were judged to receive a 50:50 split of profits. The wife's contribution was nil, and her inclusion in the partnership was simply a legal tool to reduce tax. The claimant therefore recovered his full 50% share of the lost profits.

1   [1995] PIQR Q42, CA.
2   See eg *Neal v Jones* [2002] EWCA Civ 1731, in which Rix LJ stated at [39]–[40]:
       'The facts, however, of this case are very striking. Two people, effectively husband and wife, were working together hand in hand in a business. They bought the business premises together; they fitted out those business premises together; they bought machinery together and spare parts with Miss De'Tedstone's capital; they held a bank account together; they represented themselves to their suppliers as trading together in the name of Matt's Engineering.
       In my view it was a partnership in the fullest sense of the term. The presumption of section 24 of the Partnership Act is that in the absence of a contrary agreement or evidence, a partnership is a partnership of equals, and in my judgment this was in every sense that. It is perfectly true, as Mr Cooksley has submitted, that it may be that it was Mr Neal's fame as an engineer that was the essential element (let me even put it that high) in the business as a whole. Nevertheless, that, in my judgment, does not undermine all the indicia of partnership to which I have referred. There is many a 50/50 partnership in which only one partner is the active partner and the other partner merely provides the capital. This partnership went very much further than that.'
3   [1998] 1 WLR 1722, CA.

[F35]   When assessing the claimant's loss of business profits, there may be many imponderables which prevent the court from making an accurate calculation using the conventional multiplier/multiplicand approach. In the circumstances, the court may be persuaded to award a global lump sum representing both past loss and loss of future earning capacity[1].

1   See eg *Neal v Jones* [2002] EWCA Civ 1731, in which the Court of Appeal made a lump sum award of £120,000 for his loss in business profits and loss of earning capacity for the remainder of his working life. See also *Hannon v Pearce* (24 January 2001, unreported), QBD.

(viii)   The Lost Chance of Pursuing a Business Opportunity

[F36]   There is no reason in principle why a claimant should not recover damages for the lost chance of pursuing a business venture[1]. However, the court applies a two-stage test as to recovery[2]. First, the claimant must show that, had the negligence not occurred, on the balance of probabilities, he or she would have entered into the postulated business venture, and it would have been profitable. Secondly, if persuaded that the business venture would probably have made a profit, the court must go on to consider how to evaluate that prospect. Often, since the quantification of the profits resulting from a business venture are more difficult to quantify than the benefits resulting from a particular job offer or promotion, it will be appropriate to make a broad brush lump sum award to reflect this head of loss[3]. However, sometimes it is possible to attempt a more accurate calculation. In *Horton v Evans and anor*[4], Keith J was required to assess the loss of value in a shareholding in a business venture. He held that the loss of value was to be assessed as at the date that the shareholding would have been sold but for the claimant's injuries. The value was calculated by taking a multiple of net annual profits before tax of the venture, less a small discount for the costs of disposing of the shares.

1   See eg *Bennett v Notley* [1999] CLY 1575; *Hannon v Pearce* (24 January 2001, unreported), QBD; *Finnis v Caulfield* [2002] All ER (D) 353. See also *Gleed v Set Scaffolding* (16 October 2001, unreported), QBD, in which the claimant was awarded 20% additional earnings on top of his claim based upon the salary of an employed scaffolder to reflect the chance that he might have set up his own business as supplier and erector of scaffolding equipment.

2   *Dureau v Evans* [1996] PIQR Q23.

3   See eg *Hannon v Pearce* (24 January 2001, unreported), QBD.

4   [2007] EWHC 315 (QB).

(ix)   Difficult Cases

[F37] In *Willemse v Hesp*[1] the claimant, who by occupation was a blacksmith and boat builder, had spent the years prior to the accident fulfilling his lifetime's dream of building a yacht. He had invested 8,000 hours in building what was recognised to be a magnificent craft. Consequently, his declared tax returns for the tax years in the four years prior to the accident showed very little profit. A number of different methods of assessment were put forward for calculating the claimant's claim for loss of past and future earnings, including the value of the boat (less materials) and using comparative rates in the field of boat building. At first instance, the trial judge had awarded the claimant £53,000 special damages for loss of earnings (taking into account post-accident receipts) and £110,000 for loss of future earnings. These figures were based upon an annual wage of £17,500 gross or £14,500 net. The defendant appealed, arguing that: (1) there was insufficient evidence for the judge to make any award at all for loss of earnings; and (2) the judge was wrong to have adopted a multiplier/multiplicand approach for the assessment of loss of earnings. The judgment of Potter LJ (with which Arden and Keene LJJ agreed) in respect of the calculation of past loss of earnings is salutary and deserves to be set out in some detail:

'Calculation of Past Loss

On the basis of the uncertain evidence which confronted him, the judge was faced with the difficult task of assessing the claim for loss of earnings in the period of 6 years 5 months between accident and trial. At paragraph 68 of his judgment, the judge rejected the justice or, indeed, the possibility, of calculating the pre-accident earnings loss on the orthodox basis of loss of actual earnings less post-accident receipts because the claimant had earned very little in the four years prior to the accident, being involved almost full-time in constructing his own large boat virtually single-handed. The judge accepted (at paragraph 73 of his judgment) that the claimant had the burden of proof of showing that he had suffered a loss of money which he would, but for the accident, otherwise have earned, but equally accepted that the absence of formal earnings was due to the creation of "a magnificent craft" of high capital value when completed. He further held that, had the claimant not been so engaged, he would have spent at least a large extent of the time undertaking other remunerative work. The end product would have been completion of a boat which would either have been sold to realise capital, if only to build another boat, or retained as a valuable asset. The judge concluded that not to recognise those facts would be unfair to the claimant and result in gross under-compensation.

In my view that was a legitimate approach. What the claimant had done in the four years or so prior to the accident was in effect to exchange income for future capital value so that his receipts and earnings in the four years of construction were not a fair reflection of his earning capacity and could not be used as an appropriate basis in which to calculate his post-accident loss.

It was the claimant's case that he had put in about 8000 hours' work on the boat over a period of about four years' actual production time. The judge's method of calculation involved a series of discounts from that starting point. First, he reduced the figure of 2000 hours per annum to 1500 (ie 6000 hours in total) because of the uncertainty as to the accuracy of the calculation and the amount of other labour involved. Second, he valued the 1500 hours work on the production of the boat over the 4 year period at a rate of £10 per hour which, on the evidence, was well below the " going" rate for such work. That produced a figure of roughly £15,000 per annum, to which the judge added the claimant's average receipts in earnings in the years prior to the accident namely £2,250 per annum, rounding it up to £17,500 to reflect "just over" 1500 hours per annum on the boat. He then netted that down to a sum of £14,500 per annum to allow for the incidence of tax. Finally, he made a further discount by applying a 5½ year multiplier rather than the 6½ years since the accident, to reflect the fact that the claimant would have sailed the vessel for a substantial period of time after completing it, even assuming that he thereafter sold it.

As I have already indicated, Miss Perry's primary submission is that the evidence as to the claimant's earnings was so unreliable that no award should have been made for past earnings loss. I would reject that submission. It was essentially a matter for the judge. Unless he was satisfied, and plainly he was not, that in the four years prior to the accident the claimant had concealed true earnings over and above the time which he spent on building his own boat, it was clear that compensation at the level of £2,250 per annum would be a gross injustice to the claimant who was well capable of sustained hard work and in respect of whom it was not suggested that, for four years prior to the accident, he was doing other than work hard upon a valuable capital project. In my view, the judge was right to consider that compensation at a realistic level was required in a situation where the accident had prevented final completion of his boat and the realisation of his plans and where, but for a year out allowed by the judge for the claimant's voyage once the boat was complete, he would have resumed working, whether on a new capital project or as the accomplished working blacksmith he was.

In this last connection, Miss Perry has placed weight upon the observation of the judge at paragraph 74 of his judgment (quoted at paragraph 6 above) that his finding as to the value of the work done on the boat "does not mean that it is appropriate to assume that from the date of the accident to date the claimant would have earned £17,500 each year. I do not believe he would have". However, it is plain from the sentence which follows that that remark referred not to the claimant's ability to earn at that rate but to the fact that he would have taken substantial time out to sail his boat once completed. In that respect the judge made a discount of one year from the period for which loss of earnings to trial was calculated. He also accepted that there would be other periods when the claimant did not earn during the pre-trial period; however for the purposes of calculating the annual rate of remuneration, he set off such periods of non-earning against periods of work in respect of which he was satisfied the claimant would have earned at a rate far higher than the £10 per hour underlying his £17,500 calculation (cf the Horrobin employment).

Miss Perry's alternative submission is that, in any event, the judge was wrong to take a multiplier/multiplicand approach even on the basis of £10 an hour for earnings loss in the light of the uncertainty as to the number of hours worked by the claimant upon the boat. She submits that the judge should simply have attempted a broad assessment on the lines approved by this court in *Blamire v South Cumbria Health Authority* [1993] PIQR/ Q1. The approach in *Blamire* was of course one which related to award of a global sum to assess as at trial the present value of the risk of *future* financial loss. However, to the extent that it represents an example of the necessity on occasion, in the light of uncertain circumstances, for the court to award a global (and somewhat impressionistic) sum, I accept that it affords Miss Perry some assistance in principle in relation to pre-trial loss. Had the judge decided that, on the general state of the evidence and his judgment of the claimant, a *Blamire* (ie round sum) award was all that was appropriate, I cannot think that this court would have interfered. Equally, however, the judge having felt able to take the approach he did as the just way of dealing with the difficult question of past-earnings loss, I do not think that this court should interfere with the sum awarded in that respect.'

1   [2003] EWCA Civ 994.

[F38]   Other examples of the assessment of loss of earnings in difficult cases include *Chang v Delgreco*[1], in which the claimant was a full-time medical practitioner who had reorganised his time following an accident to be more efficient, and *Pankhurst v (1) White and (2) MIB*[2], in which the claimant was a landlord before the accident, but sold his properties after the accident and claimed a loss of investment/rental income (he failed in his claim, because his sale of the property to fund expenses was premature at best, before the possibility of interim payments had been exhausted).

1   LTL, 11/2/04, CA.
2   [2009] EWHC 1117 (QB).

3   Pension Loss

[F39]   This will normally arise at some future time. For this reason, we deal with it under future loss (see further Chapter H).

[F40]   If someone of pensionable age is injured, this is unlikely to have any effect on receipt of pension. Where a claimant is injured whilst of working age, but reaches retirement age before trial, then he or she can claim any shortfall on pension receipts to the date of trial as part of special damage. It is also arguable that a self-employed person who is no longer able to contribute to a defined contribution-type pension by reason of the accident may be able to claim the tax relief on the payments he or she would have made into his or her pension up to the date of trial before he or she is in a position to take advantage of investing tax-free sums in a stakeholder pension[1].

1   See Chapter H, Future Expenses and Losses.

[F41]   A pension which is paid earlier than it otherwise would have been (eg an ill-health pension paid ten years before normal retirement age) is not deducted from the claim for loss of earnings[1]. The claimant may keep it, without giving the defendant credit for it, until normal retirement age. From that date on, the claimant must account for the pension actually received against any loss claimed in respect of pension entitlement under the same pension scheme[2]. In terms of past loss, it may not necessarily amount to a failure to mitigate loss not to pay into a private pension in order to obtain the tax advantage if the claimant's former pension was non-contributory and the financial prudence of such a course is not properly explored in evidence[3].

1   *Parry v Cleaver* [1970] AC 1; *Smoker v London Fire and Civil Defence Authority* [1991] 2 AC 502.
2   *Longden v British Coal Corpn* [1997] 3 WLR 1336.
3   *Morgan v MOD* [2002] EWHC 2072 (QB).

4 Medical and Treatment Expenses

(i) General Principles

'Reasonable' medical expenses

[F42] A claimant is entitled to recover any costs not unreasonably incurred in an attempt to mitigate loss, including any medical expenses[1]. The cost of past medical expenses and an estimate of future expenses should be included in the claimant's schedule of loss. This includes any expenditure which was – with the benefit of hindsight – either unnecessary or mistaken[2].

---

[1]   *Roberts v Roberts* (1960) Times, 11 March. It has been held reasonable for a Canadian, injured in France, to seek medical treatment in New York, despite the fact that the medical fees seemed to Streatfield J to be 'colossally high' by English standards: *Winkworth v Hubbard* [1960] 1 Lloyd's Rep 150. It is no bar to recovery, merely because the claimant has yet to pay the medical accounts: *Allen v Waters & Co* [1935] 1 KB 200, CA.

[2]   *Rubens v Walker* [1946] SC 215. See eg *Crofts v Murton* LTL 10/9/2008 regarding the cost of an upper arm prosthetic from Dorset Orthopaedics which was doomed to failure. See further Chapter A at para **[A36]**.

[F43] All reasonable medical and treatment expenses which are substantiated by medical evidence can be recovered, such as:

- bandages;
- physiotherapy;
- rehabilitation;
- dentistry;
- emergency treatment in hospital;
- psychotherapy;
- alternative medicines, such as acupuncture or treatment from a chiropractor (although these can sometimes be more problematic, as it may be difficult to obtain supporting evidence regarding the need for them)[1];
- speech therapy/occupational therapy/hydrotherapy/music and art therapy;
- future operation and hospitalisation costs[2];
- chiropody; and
- manicure and pedicure[3].

---

[1]   See further at para **[F53]**.

[2]   This may involve an absence from work for the duration of recuperation – and this should be allowed for unless there is also a total loss of earnings claim.

[3]   This expense was allowed by Eady J in *Biesheuval v Birrell* [1999] PIQR Q40 because, but for the accident, the claimant would have cut his own nails.

[F44] A course of treatment is likely to be regarded as 'reasonably' undertaken if it has been recommended by the claimant's doctor. Evidence of the efficacy of a new treatment will be relevant as to whether the cost of that treatment is reasonably incurred, but not conclusive[1]. If the medical expenses have been reasonably incurred, it does not matter if they later prove not to have been necessary.

---

[1]   See eg *Bishop v Hannaford* (22 March 1990, unreported), in which Otton J (as he then was) awarded the costs of the 'Somerset regime', a therapy devised by the British Society for the Brain Injured. This can be contrasted with *Duhelon v Carson* (18 July 1986, unreported), where the costs of the

'Philadelphia regime', a therapy devised by the British Institute of Brain Injured Children, were held by Stuart Smith LJ not to be reasonably necessary. See also *McMahon v Robert Brett & Sons* [2003] EWHC 2706 (QB) and para **[F53]**.

[F45]   The most important area, and therefore the starting point when assessing the 'reasonableness' of care, is the actual nature and severity of the injuries. It is for this reason that a medical report is of the utmost importance. The extent of injury will have a considerable impact on whether a particular regime is 'reasonable'. Obviously, the more grave and disabling the injury, the greater the care required: however, specific focus on certain injuries may be required.

[F46]   Medical expenses may be reasonably incurred even if there is a less expensive alternative available[1]. However, notwithstanding a defendant's acceptance regarding the reasonableness of a particular treatment, a claimant is under a duty to mitigate his or her loss. Therefore, if the claimant chooses to have that treatment privately, which is much more expensive than other treatments, or decides to obtain the same treatment but from a more expensive provider, he or she may not be able to recover the difference.

1   *Rialis v Mitchell* (1984) Times, 17 July.

Failure to make use of NHS services

[F47]   Law Reform (Personal Injuries) Act 1948, s 2(4) provides that[1]:

'In an action for damages for personal injuries ... there shall be disregarded, in determining the reasonableness of any expenses the possibility of avoiding those expenses or part of them by taking advantage of facilities available under the National Health Service.'

1   The Law Commission has recommended in its Report No 262 entitled 'Damages for Personal Injury: Medical, Nursing and other Expenses; Collateral Benefits' (November 1999) that this provision is kept without amendment. By contrast, the Chief Medical Officer in his report 'Making Amends' (1999) suggests it is removed, at least for claims against the NHS.

[F48]   In the circumstances, a claimant cannot be found to have failed to mitigate his or her loss by paying for treatment privately rather than making use of services which would have been freely available on the NHS.

[F49]   But can a claimant who makes use of the NHS claim for the notional costs of treatment had they paid for such treatment privately? The scope of s 2(4) of the 1948 Act was interpreted in *Harris v Brights Asphalt Contractors Ltd*[1]. Slade J said[2]:

'I think all that means is that, when an injured claimant in fact incurs expenses which are reasonable, that expenditure is not to be impeached on the ground that, if he had taken advantage of the facilities available under the National Health Service Act, 1946, those reasonable expenses might have been avoided. I do not understand section 2(4) to enact that a claimant shall be deemed to be entitled to recover expenses which in fact he will never incur.'

1   [1953] 1 QB 617.
2   At 635.

[F50] In *Woodrup v Nicol*[1] the court found that the claimant would probably pay for physiotherapy himself. Regular check-ups and emergency services were presently available within the NHS. Wright J at first instance found that there was a risk that, at some time in the future, the claimant might have to have recourse to his own resources if he was to have regular check-ups. He found that, overall, the claimant would fund half of his future medical expenses privately, and as to the other half rely on the NHS. On the basis of these findings, the Court of Appeal held that the claimant was only entitled to recover the 'private' half of those expenses. Russell LJ stated[2]:

> '... if, on the balance of probabilities, the claimant is going to use private medicine in the future as a matter of choice, the Defendant cannot contend that the claim should be disallowed because National Health Service facilities are available. On the other hand, if, on the balance of probabilities, private facilities are not going to be used, for whatever reason, the claimant is not entitled to claim for an expense which he is not going to incur.'

[1]   [1993] PIQR Q104.
[2]   At Q114.

[F51] The net result is that, in non-road traffic accident cases[1], if the claimant has not incurred and is not likely to incur medical expenses, because he or she makes unconditional use of the NHS or services provided free of charge by a local authority, the claimant cannot recover what would have been paid if he or she had had private treatment or care[2]. Depending upon the circumstances, if the evidence shows that the claimant is unlikely to incur such expenses because of NHS facilities, but the possibility remains that he or she might do so, he or she may claim a sum for the possibility that some such expenses may be incurred in the future[3]. The defendant cannot escape liability for paying private medical or treatment expenses merely by suggesting that there is no evidence that the services cannot be obtained on the NHS: the defendant must establish that (i) the services are available free of charge on the NHS or through social services; and (ii) the claimant would make use of the free service[4], assuming a choice of 'NHS or private' without financial constraint.

[1]   For road traffic accidents, see para **[F56]**.
[2]   *Harris v Bright's Asphalt Contractors Ltd* [1953] 1 QB 617; *Hunt v Severs* [1994] 2 AC 350, per Lord Bridge at 360–361.
[3]   *Cunningham v Harrison* [1973] QB 942. The facts in this case were that the claimant was unlikely to get the care he needed privately. This should not apply these days, where there is an abundance of private care professionals available at a price. In *Lim Poh Choo v Camden and Islington Area Health Authority* [1980] AC 174 at 190–192, the House of Lords agreed with the interpretation of s 2(4) adopted by Slade J, and by the Court of Appeal in *Cunningham*. See also *Housecroft v Burnett* [1986] 1 All ER 332 at 341 and, more recently, *Sowden v Lodge* [2004] EWCA Civ 1370, it which it was held that the claimant might have suffered no loss of accommodation where her needs were reasonably met by the provision of residential accommodation and care provided free of charge by the local authority and topped up by the defendant (although the matter was remitted back to the High Court for final determination of the factual issues).
[4]   *Eagle v Chambers (No 2)* [2004] EWCA Civ 1033.

[F52] The Government is considering whether any repeal or amendment is required to s 2(4) of the Law Reform (Personal Injuries) Act 1948 following its consultation on the Law of Damages[1]. Misleadingly, though, its initial consultation paper appears not to have recognised that the costs of non-NHS treatment will only be recoverable if the injured party would probably have such treatment.

¹   Response to consultation on the Law of Damages, published by the Ministry of Justice on 1 July 2009, p 54.

Alternative treatment and remedies

[F53]   Debate often arises as to whether unconventional treatment expenses can be recovered. Examples include (cranial) osteopathy, chiropractic treatment, acupuncture, reflexology, the Alexander Technique, Chinese herbal medicine, Reiki, healing, spa treatments and massage. There are no hard and fast rules regarding the recovery of such expenses although, generally speaking, the courts will be sceptical about treatment and remedies undergone without proven scientific benefit. What is reasonable in one case may not be considered reasonable in another. For example, it is more likely to be reasonable for a claimant to try alternative treatment and remedies if: they have been specifically recommended by his or her GP or other treating health professional (such as a physiotherapist); he or she is reluctant to accept conventional medicine[1]; or they have exhausted without success all the treatment modalities which conventional medicine has to offer[2]. A test which is commonly applied to the recovery of past expenditure on alternative treatment and remedies is whether or not the treatment has given any relief to the claimant from his or her symptoms: if relief has been obtained, the expense in question will be considered a reasonable expense incurred in the mitigation of the claimant's loss[3]. For example, in *Noble v Owens*[4], Field J allowed a significant claim for past and future hydrotherapy/acupuncture, even though the orthopaedic surgeons in their joint statement agreed that there was no good scientific evidence to support its use. At para 53 of the judgment he said:

> 'At the suggestion of his physiotherapist, Mr Noble has been attending hydrotherapy and acupuncture treatment on a weekly basis. I accept his evidence that these treatments make him feel better, improve the pain, and improve his sleeping and help with his constipation. The defendant submits that it ought not to have to pay for these treatments because in their joint report the orthopaedic experts say that there is no good scientific evidence to justify regular and formal physiotherapy/hydrotherapy/acupuncture. I disagree. In my opinion these treatments are reasonably required. I accept Mr Noble's evidence that his weekly hydrotherapy and acupuncture sessions help with the pain and make him feel better generally. I also note that Mr Noble was advised at St George's Hospital to continue with hydrotherapy and his treating physiotherapist has given him the same advice.'

¹   In *George v Stagecoach* [2003] EWHC 2042 (QB), Mackay J said at [57]: 'Acupuncture and Chinese herbs. The claimant has some evident reluctance to accept conventional medicine, though, paradoxically, uses non-prescribed specifics such as Neurofen to help her when she needs it. She has documented evidence that she has taken this Chinese treatment to date, and I allow it to date at the agreed sum of £3,700'.

²   See eg *Warrilow v Norfolk and Norwich Hospitals NHS Trust* [2006] EWHC 801 (QB), in which Langstaff J made awards for alternative treatment including acupuncture and Reiki, as the claimant had reasonably turned to such methods when conventional therapy did not assist.

³   See eg *O'Brien v Harris* (22 February 2001, unreported), QBD, in which Pitchford J allowed the cost of herbal remedies because 'relief was obtained from the same'. See also *McMahon v Robert Brett & Sons* [2003] EWHC 2706 (QB), in which Cox J allowed the cost of aromatherapy

treatment, despite the absence of medical evidence to support a medical benefit, because it had been recommended as part of the claimant's pain management therapy and she said it has been helpful to overcome her pain. See also *Cannon v Cannon* [2005] EWHC 1310 (QB), in which the claimant recovered £17,992.89 in respect of past medical and complementary treatments.

4 [2008] EWHC 359 (QB).

Hydrotherapy pools

[F54] One of the most controversial heads of loss that arises in catastrophic injury claims is for the construction of a private hydrotherapy pool at the claimant's home. Whether or not such a claim will succeed will depend upon the facts of the case and the availability of suitable hydrotherapy pools in the local area. Medical and physiotherapy evidence is usually required to support the therapeutic need for hydrotherapy, eg to control spasms, to prevent contractures or to provide cardiovascular exercise. Whilst the pool itself may not be particularly expensive, the building or extension required to house the pool will be costly to construct and maintain, as well as there being additional equipment, running and maintenance costs (including heating and water treatment etc)[1]. Sometimes, the benefits of hydrotherapy can be achieved through alternative, cheaper forms of activity or exercise, in which case it may not be proportionate to allow the costs of a home pool. However, in some instances it can be demonstrated that, having tried other methods, hydrotherapy alone provides the necessary relief from symptoms and there are no pools in the local area or the ones that are available have inadequate changing facilities, no hoist, are too cold, too noisy or cannot be hired (a disabled claimant may feel self-conscious about using a public pool unless it can be hired for a private session). Claims which have succeeded and failed are listed in the following table.

Successful	Unsuccessful
• *Haines v Airedale NHS Trust (unreported, 2 May 2000, QBD)*	• *Cassell v Hammersmith and Fulham HA* [1992] PIQR Q1
• *Hart v Pretty (unreported, 18 April 2005, HHJ Taylor)*	• *Iqbal v Whipps Cross University Hospital NHS Trust* [2006] EWHC 3111(QB)
• *Lewis v Shrewsbury Hospital NHS Trust (HHJ MacDuff, QB, 29.1.07)*	• *Sarwar v (1) Ali and (2) MIB* [2007] LS Medical 375
• *Wakeling v McDonagh and MIB* [2007] EWHC 1201 (QB)	• *Smith v East and North Hertfordshire Hospitals NHS Trust* [2008] EWHC 2234 (QB)
• *Burton v Kingsbury* [2007] EWHC 2091 (QB)[2]	
• *Morgan v Phillips* LTL 29/9/08	

1 However, it should not necessarily be assumed that the costs of a home pool are necessarily always more expensive than attending a local pool. Sometimes, the cost of hiring a pool, say, 3 times a week, together with travel costs and any additional carer costs, can amount to more over a lifetime than the total costs of providing a pool at home.

2 Note that the claim in this case was linked to the accommodation claim, ie that the house that was purchased was suitable for the claimant's needs and it happened to have a pool. See also *Willett v North Bedfordshire HA* [1993] PIQR Q166.

(ii)   Services Provided by the NHS

[F55]   Generally speaking, as recognised by the National Health Service Act 1977, treatment provided by the NHS will be provided free of charge and there can be no recoupment from the defendant[1]. However, s 1(2) of the 1977 Act provides that this is so 'except insofar as the making and recovering of charges is expressly provided for by or under any enactment'. Various statutory powers exist which allow health authorities and trusts to make charges where certain conditions are met, such as an undertaking being made by the patient who is in receipt of accommodation, treatment or care[2]. Thus, provided the authority responsible for caring for a claimant is a health authority or a trust, these provisions can be used to reach an agreement with it so that the claimant can recover his or her past and/or future care costs from the defendant[3].

[1]   Although the Law Commission recommended in its Report No 262 entitled 'Damages for Personal Injury: Medical, Nursing and other Expenses; Collateral Benefits' (November 1999) that, subject to a cost-benefit analysis, the exception applying to road traffic accidents should be extended so that the NHS could recoup their charges from other tortfeasors whose tort results in the NHS providing care or treatment to the claimant.

[2]   A detailed analysis of the statutory framework is beyond the scope of this work, and the position should be checked with the relevant treatment or care provider in each case.

[3]   See eg National Health Service and Community Care Act 1990, Sch 2, para 14.

(iii)   Road Traffic Cases

[F56]   In respect of accidents occurring before 29 January 2007, the Road Traffic (NHS Charges) Act 1999, as amended, creates an exception to the general rule that the NHS can neither charge the claimant for the treatment provided, nor recoup from the defendant tortfeasor the cost that it has incurred in treating the injured claimant[1]. The Act replaces former provisions regarding such recoupment under ss 157 and 158 of the Road Traffic Act 1988[2]. In summary, an obligation arises on the defendant to pay NHS charges where a compensation payment is made in respect of the death or injury of any person arising from the use of a motor vehicle, by an authorised insurer pursuant to a properly issued policy[3]. Liability under the Act is therefore based on fault, although the obligation arises regardless of whether or not liability is admitted[4]. The Act also extends liability to include compensation paid by the Motor Insurers' Bureau (MIB)[5]. A tariff system is set out in the regulations accompanying the Act, which details the sums payable by the defendant[6]. When a claim is settled or a compensation payment is made, the defendant must apply to the Secretary of State for a 'certificate of NHS charges'[7]. The system is similar to recoupment of DWP benefits and is administered by the same body, ie the Compensation Recovery Unit. However, there is no provision for offsetting the amounts paid for NHS charges, since the claimant is not entitled to damages for the cost of NHS care. The defendant may apply for the certificate either before or after settlement[8]. In the event of disagreement about the level of charges, a review and appeal procedure is available[9].

[1]   The Road Traffic (NHS Charges) Act 1999 came into force on 5 April 1999 and applies to accidents occurring on or after 2 July 1997. See further the Road Traffic (NHS Charges) Regulations 1999, SI 1999/785, and the Road Traffic (NHS Charges) Act 1999 (Commencement No 1) Order 1999, SI 1999/1075, and subsequent amendment regulations.

[2]   Although ss 157 and 158 of the Road Traffic Act 1988 still apply to non-NHS not-for-profit hospitals and GPs (the latter of whom can recover the emergency treatment fee): see further para 2.8 of the

Law Commission's Report No 262 'Damages for Personal Injury: Medical, Nursing and Other Expenses; Collateral Benefits' (November 1999).

3   Road Traffic (NHS Charges) Act 1999, s 1(2) which makes a person making a 'compensation payment' to a 'traffic casualty' liable to pay the appropriate NHS charges to the Secretary of State in respect of the treatment.

4   Road Traffic (NHS Charges) Act 1999, s 1(9).

5   Road Traffic (NHS Charges) Act 1999, s 1(3)(d).

6   See further the Road Traffic (NHS Charges) Regulations 1999, SI 1999/785, and subsequent amendment regulations.

7   Road Traffic (NHS Charges) Act 1999, s 2.

8   See further para 2.11 and 2.14 of the Law Commission's Report No 262 'Damages for Personal Injury: Medical, Nursing and Other Expenses; Collateral Benefits' (November 1999).

9   See further the Road Traffic (NHS Charges) (Reviews and Appeals) Regulations 1999, SI 1999/786.

[F57]   For accidents occurring on or after 29 January 2007, there is a similar system to the above for recovery of NHS charges, but the governing statute is now the Health and Social Care (Community Health and Standards) Act 2003[1]. The Act applies where a compensation payment is made to or in respect of an injured person in consequence of a physical or psychological injury suffered by that person and NHS services were provided to that person. The compensator applies to the CRU for a certificate of NHS charges (this can be applied before making a payment or, alternatively, must be applied for within 14 days of making the payment)[2]. The amount of charges payable is specified by regulations which are amended regularly and is reduced by the same proportion of any deduction for contributory negligence. Again, the certificate may be reviewed or appealed much like a CRU certificate.

1   This Act was brought into force by the Health and Social Care (Community Health and Standards) Act 2003 (Commencement) (No 11) Order 2006 (SI 2006/3397), art 2, which repealed the Road Traffic (NHS Charges) Act 1999.

2   Health and Social Care (Community Health and Standards) Act 2003, s 151.

5   Medication and Prescription Expenses

[F58]   The same principles which govern the recoverability of medical and treatment expenses apply to medication and prescription expenses. In summary:

*   The claimant will be entitled to recover reasonable expenses incurred in an attempt to mitigate loss, eg by taking painkillers in order to relieve his or her symptoms.
*   The claim should be supported by the medical evidence.
*   Generally speaking, the medication or prescriptions taken should have been recommended by a health professional and have a proven scientific benefit[1].
*   The recoverability of alternative medications and remedies is problematic but not an absolute bar to recovery[2].
*   The amount claimed should be reasonable and supported by documentary evidence[3].
*   Credit should be given for any medication or prescription expenses which would have been incurred in any event.

1   In *Biesheuval v Birrell* [1999] PIQR Q40, a claim for Viagra was disallowed; cf *Re McCarthy* [2001] 6 CL 172, in which Blofeld J awarded the claimant £37,500 for Viagra treatment.

²   See eg *George v Stagecoach* [2003] EWHC 2042 (QB), in which an award of £3,700 was made for acupuncture and Chinese herbal medicine; *O'Brien v Harris* (22 February 2001, unreported), QBD, in which Pitchford J allowed the cost of herbal remedies because 'relief was obtained from the same'; and *McMahon v Robert Brett & Sons* [2003] EWHC 2706 (QB), in which Cox J made an award for aromatherapy treatment.

³   See eg the first instance judgment of Leveson J in *Hesp v Willemse* [2002] EWHC 1256 (QB), where, in the absence of supporting documentary evidence, £500 was allowed in respect of a claim for past medication in the sum of £750. Where past expenditure on prescriptions has been significant, it may be argued that the claimant should have availed him or herself of an annual pre-paid prescription certificate. However, if the cost of such a pre-paid certificate was beyond the claimant's means, the claimant's impecuniosity should not be used against him or her when assessing the question of reasonableness: *Lagden v O'Connor* [2003] UKHL 64.

6 Care and Case Management

(i) Commercial Care

[F59] If the claimant has been cared for by a paid carer, then, provided this is supported by medical evidence as reasonable and necessary, the expense can be recovered upon production of the receipts.

[F60] There are numerous possible commercial care regimes that can be implemented depending on the circumstances of the case. In any case where the care element is likely to be significant, specific evidence should be sought from a care expert. However, the following is provided as a rough guide of the main types of care that can be provided. The advantages and disadvantages of each are discussed. Of course, each case must be decided on its own facts, and a care package which is appropriate to meet the reasonable needs of one claimant might not be suitable for another[1]. Importantly, it should be noted that the different types of care package described below are not mutually exclusive, and it is not unusual for different elements to be combined as a package in order to best meet the claimant's needs.

¹   See further *Sowden v Lodge* [2004] EWCA Civ 1370 and *Crookdake v Drury* (jointly reported).

Different types of private care regime

(1) SINGLE CARER

[F61] Probably the cheapest form of care (beyond taking advantage of the services of friends, relatives and spouses) is to employ a single carer to attend to the claimant. In this way, one person is employed to meet all of the claimant's care needs. As well as cost, this approach has a number of beneficial points. In particular, a single carer may well become a friendlier sight than several shift workers (especially those employed by an agency who may have no permanence in their roles). However, there are some negative points.

[F62] A live-in carer requires his or her own accommodation, which must be of a relatively high standard. More importantly, if the injuries are particularly severe, a single residential carer would simply be unable to care effectively for the claimant. Thus, if the claimant requires constant supervision, two or more carers are needed and the regime of daily carers is more efficient. Also, if the claimant needs to be moved manually, it may be obligatory to have more than one person doing it[1]. To this end, it is often useful to obtain a risk assessment from a specialist manual handling assessor.

[1]   Manual Handling Operations Regulations 1992, SI 1992/2793; see further *A v B Hospitals NHS Trust* [2006] EWHC 1178 (QB); *A v Powys Local Health Board* [2007] EWHC 2996 (QB); and *XXX v A Strategic Health Authority* [2008] EWHC 2727 (QB).

[F63]   Furthermore, whilst live-in care packages are commonly used in cases where ad hoc care is required throughout the day, such packages are arguably in breach of the Working Time Regulations 1998 and therefore unlawful[1]. Whilst it is currently possible for UK employees to opt out of the 48-hour maximum week, there is no opt-out from other provisions, in particular regulation 10 which requires workers to have a minimum of 11 hours of consecutive hours of rest in each 24-hour period. European case law is to the effect that, where workers are on site and 'on-call' at night, eg in case of emergency, this still counts as 'working time' and therefore does not count towards the necessary rest period[2]. There have been moves on a number of occasions to seek to alter the effect of the Working Time Directive but, so far, these have not come to anything. Negotiations between the European Council and the European Parliament broke down following the failure of conciliation which concluded on 27 April 2009. One of the stumbling blocks has been the UK's opt-out in relation to the maximum working week of 48 hours. Even if there were developments regarding the approach to 'on-call' work, especially in the context of live-in carers, any amendment may be at the expense of the opt-out in respect of the 48-hour maximum working week, thus also rendering the provision of live-in care unlawful but for different reasons.

[1]   *Iqbal v Whipps Cross University Hospital NHS Trust* [2006] EWHC 3111 (QB); *Corbett v South Yorkshire Strategic Health Authority* [2007] LS Law Medical 430; *and A v Powys Health Board* [2007] EWHC 2996. See further 'The Single Resident Carer – an Endangered Species?' [2006] JPIL Issue 3/06.

[2]   *SIMAP* (C-303/98) [2000] ECJ; *Dellas* (C-14/04) [2005] ECJ; *Jaegar* (C-151/02) [2003] ECJ.

(2)   CARERS WORKING SHIFTS

[F64]   These are more expensive than a live-in carer, owing mainly to the fact that the cost is that of hours worked. Therefore, where night supervision is necessary, the cost is 24 hours a day. Although it is easier to find such carers, the mere fact that they are shift workers means that the injured claimant may see a variety of different people and not be limited to a familiar carer(s). In many situations, for a variety of reasons[1], it may not be feasible for the claimant to remain at home.

[1]   The most obvious being the extent of injuries, but others include the inability to adapt accommodation, the unavailability of care workers or even, simply, the wishes of the claimant.

[F65]   However, in some instances, directly employed carers working shifts can be the preferable option (despite the increased costs)[1]. Such a system will provide continuity of care and ensure that the claimant's needs are always met by a carer who is not overly tired from working too many hours. Further, such a system is unlikely to fall foul of the Working Time Regulations 1998, but can sometimes be considered too onerous by claimants who are not keen on having the responsibility of being employers.

[1]   See eg *Lynham v The Morecambe Bay Hospitals NHS Trust* [2002] EWHC 823 (QB).

[F66]   It should be noted that, where the claimant is responsible for directly employing professional carers, there are a number of additional costs which need to be factored into the calculations, including[1]:

- Training[2], eg on manual handling[3], epilepsy and challenging behaviour.
- Changeover hours or days[4].
- Holiday and sickness pay[5].
- Bank holidays[6].
- Respite care[7].
- Accommodation and furnishings (if the carers are to live in)[8].
- Recruitment, eg the costs of advertisement and interviewing prospective carers[9].
- Insurance[10].
- Medical or (neuro-)psychological input to devise and comment upon appropriate care programmes[11].
- Payroll expenses.
- Criminal Records Bureau checks for new carers.
- Travel costs[12].
- Contingency or emergency relief[13].
- ERNIC (Earnings Related National Insurance Contributions)[14].
- Shift overlap / handovers[15].
- Team meetings / liaison[16].
- Team leader[17].
- Manual handling risk assessments[18].
- Cleaning[19].
- Double-up care[20].
- Pension contributions[21].
- Food and expenses for outings[22].
- An allowance for eating out[23].

[1]   See eg *Dorrington v Lawrence* [2001] All ER (D) 145 (Nov), in which Mrs Sargent's evidence regarding the cost of professional care was preferred over that of Tessa Gough because of her greater experience and the fact that she had taken into account many of the above listed factors when making her assessment of the cost of meeting the claimant's care needs.

[2]   See eg *Stuart v Martin* [2001] All ER (D) 401 (Oct), in which Owen J preferred the evidence of Maggie Sargent to that of Mrs Welsch and allowed £500 per annum for training. See also *Lynham v The Morecambe Bay Hospitals NHS Trust* [2002] EWHC 823 (QB), in which Garland J accepted Mrs Sargent's evidence that an allowance for two weeks' training per year was necessary.

[3]   As an employer, the claimant may owe duties to any carers under the Manual Handling Operations Regulations 1992, SI 1992/2793. See further *A v B Hospitals NHS Trust* [2006] EWHC 1178 (QB); *Sarwar v (1) Ali and (2) MIB* [2007] EWHC 1255 (QB); *Massey v Tameside & Glossop Acute Services NHS Trust* [2007] EWHC 317 (QB); *Wakeling v McDonagh and MIB* [2007] EWHC 1201 (QB); *A v Powys Local Health Board* [2007] EWHC 2996 (QB); and *XXX v A Strategic Health Authority* [2008] EWHC 2727 (QB).

[4]   See eg *Taylor v Weston AHA* [2003] All ER (D) 50 (Dec).

[5]   See eg *Taylor v Weston AHA* [2003] All ER (D) 50 (Dec).

[6]   See eg *Lynham v The Morecambe Bay Hospitals NHS Trust* [2002] EWHC 823 (QB), in which Garland J accepted Mrs Sargent's evidence that an allowance should be made for two weeks' sick leave and four weeks' holiday per year. Four weeks' paid holiday per year is obligatory under the Working Time Regulations 1998, SI 1998/1833.

[7]   See *Evans v Pontypridd Roofing Ltd* [2001] EWCA Civ 1657, per May LJ at [39] and [40].

8　　See eg *Biesheuval v Birrell* [1999] PIQR Q40.
9　　See eg *Stuart v Martin* [2001] All ER (D) 401 (Oct), in which the care experts agreed and Owen J awarded the sum of £400 per annum for recruitment; and *XXX v A Strategic Health Authority* [2008] EWHC 2727 (QB) in which the sum of £1,000 pa was allowed for advertising.
10　See eg *Stuart v Martin* [2001] All ER (D) 401 (Oct), in which the care experts agreed and Owen J awarded the sum of £300 per annum for insurance.
11　See eg *Lynham v The Morecambe Bay Hospitals NHS Trust* [2002] EWHC 823 (QB), in which Garland J accepted Mrs Sargent's evidence that an allowance should be made for additional neuropsychological input in order to devise care programmes. See also *Howarth v Whittaker* [2003] Lloyd's Rep Med 235, in which Elias J accepted Mrs Sargent's evidence on the same point.
12　See eg *Taylor v Weston AHA* [2003] All ER (D) 50 (Dec).
13　See eg the contingency sum awarded in *A v B Hospitals NHS Trust* [2006] EWHC 1178 (QB) to cover times when the claimant's parents would be unable to provide the care required. Although this will not necessarily be allowed where an agency is contracted, since it is not right to assume that the carers will, in breach of contract, fail to supply care: *Taylor v Weston AHA* [2003] All ER (D) 50 (Dec).
14　As to the correct approach to calculating ERNIC, see further *A v B Hospitals NHS Trust* [2006] EWHC 1178 (QB); *Iqbal v Whipps Cross University* [2007] LS Law Medical 97; *Wakeling v McDonagh and MIB* [2007] EWHC 1201 (QB); and *Noble v Owens* [2008] EWHC 359 (QB).
15　See eg *Massey v Tameside & Glossop Acute Services NHS Trust* [2007] EWHC 317 (QB); however, note that staff handovers were not allowed in *XXX v A Strategic Health Authority* [2008] EWHC 2727 (QB).
16　In *XXX v A Strategic Health Authority* [2008] EWHC 2727 (QB), Jack J allowed team meeting of 1.5 hours every 4 months.
17　See eg *Massey v Tameside & Glossop Acute Services NHS Trust* [2007] EWHC 317 (QB); *XXX v A Strategic Health Authority* [2008] EWHC 2727 (QB).
18　See eg *Massey v Tameside & Glossop Acute Services NHS Trust* [2007] EWHC 317 (QB).
19　Cleaning in addition to a full care regime was allowed in the following cases: *Sarwar v (1) Ali and (2) MIB* [2007] EWHC 1255 (QB); *Massey v Tameside & Glossop Acute Services NHS Trust* [2007] EWHC 317 (QB); *XXX v A Strategic Health Authority* [2008] EWHC 2727 (QB); and *Huntley v Simmonds* [2009] EWHC 405 (QB).
20　See eg *A v B Hospitals NHS Trust* [2006] EWHC 1178 (QB); *Sarwar v (1) Ali and (2) MIB* [2007] EWHC 1255 (QB); *Massey v Tameside & Glossop Acute Services NHS Trust* [2007] EWHC 317 (QB); *Wakeling v McDonagh and MIB* [2007] EWHC 1201 (QB); *A v Powys Local Health Board* [2007] EWHC 2996 (QB); and *XXX v A Strategic Health Authority* [2008] EWHC 2727 (QB).
21　From 2012, pension contributions for employees will become compulsory under the Pensions Act 2008: see further *XXX v A Strategic Health Authority* [2008] EWHC 2727 (QB).
22　£25 per week was allowed for carers' food and expenses in *Iqbal v Whipps Cross University* [2007] LS Law Medical 97; and £50 per week was allowed for carers' food and expenses in *XXX v A Strategic Health Authority* [2008] EWHC 2727 (QB).
23　Such a claim was rejected on the facts in *XXX v A Strategic Health Authority* [2008] EWHC 2727 (QB), since it was held that the allowance for food and outings of £50 pa was sufficient to cover meals out.

(3) AGENCY CARE

[F67] Agency care is the one of the most flexible forms of care arrangements. The agency supplies the necessary number and type of carers to meet the claimant's care need at any given time. The main advantage of the agency is that alternative carers can be provided during times of illness or holiday. Further, the agency will be responsible for training the carers and ensuring that the claimant's needs are always met. However, the main drawbacks with agency care are the lack of continuity between carers and (arguably) the lower quality of care that is provided as a result. In addition, the agency will usually charge an uplift on the normal hourly rates for care in order to meet its costs.

(4)   RESIDENTIAL CARE

[F68]   There is a wide range of care homes from nursing homes to specialist units. Obviously, the more complex the care the claimant needs, the more specialised a unit is necessary, and this will be reflected in the cost. It is therefore necessary, when residential care is claimed, to show that the level is reasonable in all the circumstances. It should also be noted that, if a claim for future loss of earnings is made, a deduction will have to be made for the cost of feeding and housing, as this is provided for by the cost of future care[1].

1   *Lim Poh Choo v Camden and Islington Area Health Authority* [1980] AC 174 at 191–192.

(5)   SHELTERED ACCOMMODATION

[F69]   In cases where the claimant does not need full-time care, it may be that his or her care needs are best met by some form of sheltered accommodation. This promotes independence, whilst at the same time offering the claimant a degree of back-up and support. Where such accommodation is not available in the claimant's locality, as an alternative, it might be possible to cost the same on the basis that the claimant remains at home, but part-time professional support/care is bought in[1].

1   *Goldfinch v Scannell* [1993] PIQR Q143.

(6)   RESPITE CARE

[F70]   Respite care is the care provided to a claimant when his or her main carers take a break. It is not healthy for anyone to work non-stop without a holiday, and respite care allows either full-time professional carers or gratuitous carers to relax and recharge their batteries. Respite care covers any of the above forms of care, so that the claimant may be placed in residential care for a short while, different professional carers may be employed to take over for a few weeks, or an agency might be used to provide the necessary care. The need for respite care was challenged by the defendant in *Evans v Pontypridd Roofing Ltd*[1]. As can be seen in the following extract of May LJ's judgment, the Court of Appeal took the opportunity to emphasise the importance of respite care notwithstanding the views of the care provider[2]:

> 'I have already set out earlier in this judgment the passage in the summary of the judgment in which the judge held that allowance should be made for 8 weeks' respite for Mrs Evans. The defendants submit that the judge was wrong to allow any additional amount for respite care. Since the rate taken for respite care and the commercial rate taken as the starting point for future care generally are the same, this submission only goes to the amount of the discount for the period of respite care. The defendants' submission is that an enhanced allowance for respite care was against the evidence. Mrs Evans was quite determined that she was going to be the only provider of care because the claimant would accept no one else. He would not even accept care services from his parents. That there was no basis for the finding that 1/6th of the future care would be provided commercially, other than a recommendation by the claimant's care expert. It was contrary to Mrs Evans' own evidence.
>
>   In my judgment, the judge was entitled to make the finding which he did on the evidence. Not only did Mrs MacLean strongly recommend that provision should be made for Mrs Evans to have two half days off each week to recharge her batteries,

during which Mr Evans could be cared for by a suitably qualified and appropriate carer. She also recommended a respite break of one week three times a year to allow both Mr and Mrs Evans some relief. In addition, a psychiatric report on Mrs Evans based a conclusion, that she was unlikely to suffer a psychiatric illness which would seriously affect her or her ability to look after her husband, on a proviso that she was allowed to have her therapeutic breaks from the home. Although Mrs Evans' own evidence was that only she would and could care for her husband, the judge was, in my view, entitled to conclude as a matter of common sense that this simply could not continue without respite throughout the many years which were the subject of his assessment. I would reject the defendants' contention here.'

1   [2001] EWCA Civ 1657.
2   At [39]–[40].

Reasonableness of past care regime

[F71]   When considering a claim for past care, the court will consider whether or not the regime implemented was reasonable and the claimed expenses are reasonably incurred. The general principles regarding mitigation of loss will be relevant[1]. The test for judging the claimant's actions is not high[2], and will be judged objectively[3], taking into account only matters known at the time and ignoring the benefit of hindsight[4]. Furthermore, it is trite law that the reasonable course of action is not necessarily the cheapest, especially where the regime adopted by the claimant has significant advantages over a cheaper alternative[5].

1   See further Chapter A at paras **[A80]–[A87]**.
2   The claimant's conduct ought not to be weighed in nice scales at the instance of the party which has occasioned the difficulty: *Melia v Key Terrain Ltd* (1969) No 155B; *Morris v Richards* [2003] EWCA Civ 232.
3   *Morgan v T Wallis* [1974] 1 Lloyd's Rep 165.
4   See eg *Rubens v Walker* [1946] SC 215. See also *Morris v Richards* [2003] EWCA Civ 232.
5   *Rialis v Mitchell* (1984) Times, 17 July, CA; *Sowden v Lodge* [2004] EWCA Civ 1370. See also *Cunningham v Kensington, Chelsea and Westminster* [1998] CLY 1480, in which the care home selected for the claimant was held to be reasonable, despite the availability of a significantly cheaper alternative, which was found to be less advantageous.

[F72]   When considering the reasonableness of a claim for past commercial care, consideration must be given to the following matters:

* The nature and severity of the claimant's injuries (including any special needs or challenging behaviour).
* The suitability of the care regime to the claimant's needs.
* Whether the claimant has been shown to benefit from the care regime in question.
* Whether there were any cheaper alternatives which would have adequately met the claimant's needs.
* Whether there has been any overlap in the care provided to the claimant[1].
* Whether the care regime was instituted on the advice of treating health professionals.
* The claimant's background, culture and religion[2].

1   Whilst it might be contended in some cases that the different components of the care claim overlap with each other, the appearance of overlap might be deceptive, as was the case in *Thomas v Wignall* [1987] 1 All ER 1185, [1987] 2 WLR 930, per Nicholls LJ at 1191h, 937f–938b:

'Second, two of the items in the judge's costing were "(c) Night cover: 10 hours per night, for 7 nights per week, and for 52 weeks, at £2.80 per hour … £10,192," and "(e) Holiday care: £300 per week for 4 weeks plus £300 for contingencies … £1,500." It was submitted that there was duplication in these two items to the extent that the cost of night cover is included for every night in the year even though the four weeks' holiday care allowance would include the cost of night cover in the holiday periods, when the plaintiff would be away from her house. I cannot accept this. There was evidence that the cost of specialist holidays varied from £100 to £260 per week, plus the cost of attendance. Furthermore if, as the defendants contended, holiday care includes night cover, the consequences would be that exclusive of night cover normally costing £28 per night, which equals £196 per week, holiday care would cost some £104 per week. This is a far lower sum than the regular weekly cost of care exclusive of night cover, the regular cost being £175 per week for the housekeepers and £100 for nursing relief. It seems improbable that this can be right. The defendants have not satisfied me that the cost of holiday care allowed by the judge included the cost of night cover …'

2   See eg *Ahsan v University Hospitals Leicester NHS Trust* [2006] EWHC 2624 (QB).

[F73]   In *Ellis v Denton*[1], Rougier J had to decide upon the reasonableness of a care regime which was more expensive than a less effective alternative. In making his decision, he asked himself the following questions:

- What are the chances of organising and maintaining the proposed optimum scheme?
- What are the chances of this scheme having the optimum result?
- What are the chances of successfully adopting the next best alternative?
- What are the likely effects of adopting the next best alternative, and in terms of amenities of life, what is the gap between the two possible schemes?
- What is the cost difference?

1   (30 June 1989, unreported), QBD.

[F74]   More recently, in *Burns v The Personal Representatives of Derek Wilding Deceased*[1], Newman J had to consider the reasonableness of a care regime provided by the Brain Injury Rehabilitation Trust (BIRT). The defendant challenged this regime on the basis that the level of care being provided to the claimant was excessive and the charges were unreasonable. In a detailed judgment, it was held that (i) the BIRT scheme was flexible, subtle and persuasive; (ii) the claimant had benefited from the structure of the scheme; and (iii) the scheme was and would be for the future the appropriate regime for the care of the claimant. The allegations in relation to the charges were held not to have any foundation and were not capable of demonstrating an excessive margin given the quality of care provided.

1   (12 December 2001, unreported), QBD.

[F75]   The question of a particular care regime being reasonable must, therefore, be assessed on the individual facts. This is based not only on the scheme itself but also on the alternatives available. The claimant and his or her advisers must be prudent not to set up an expensive private scheme when a cheaper alternative is available which, in effect, produces a similar result for the amenities of life[1].

1   See eg *C v Dixon* [2009] EWHC 708 (QB); *Huntley v Simmonds* [2009] EWHC 405 (QB).

[F76] It may be reasonable for a severely injured claimant to be cared for in the family home, and the defendant be liable in damages for the reasonable cost of caring for the claimant there, even though he or she could be cared for substantially more cheaply in a private institution[1]. Where the costs of caring for the claimant are substantially greater at home rather than in an institution, the burden of proving that it is reasonable for the claimant to be cared for at home is (in practical terms) on the claimant[2]. Expert evidence is vital.

[1]   See *Cunningham v Harrison* [1973] QB 942, where the court declined, when considering the claimant's nursing expenses, to take into account the fact that the claimant's personality was such that he would not fit well with others in a home for the disabled. The court was probably heavily influenced by (i) the finding that the claimant would not be able to obtain the help he needed privately; and (ii) the hope that the Chronically Sick and Disabled Persons Act 1970 would ensure a substitute at public expense. It directly contradicts the eggshell skull principle and is of questionable authority on this point. See also *Rialis v Mitchell* (1984) Times, 17 July, CA; *Lim Poh Choo v Camden and Islington Area Health Authority* [1980] AC 174; *Ashan v University Hospitals Leicester NHS Trust* [2007] PIQR P19; *Rowe v Dolman* LTL 14/10/2008; and *Willett v North Bedfordshire Health Authority* [1993] PIQR Q166, in which Hobhouse J rejected the alternatives of institutional care and full-time care by the claimant parents assisted by one professional, in favour of care at home by two professionals, although the amount awarded reflected the likelihood that the claimant would in any case have to spend some time in an institution.

[2]   *Rialis v Mitchell* (1984) Times, 17 July, CA.

[F77] Tactically, where possible, the claimant should seek an interim payment in order to put in place (and test) the care regime contended for[1]. Once in place, assuming the regime is satisfactory, both expert and witness evidence can be prepared in order to address the benefits of the regime and support its continuance. Whilst defendants will be mindful that the 'level playing field'[2] might be prejudiced by the claimant taking such action, assuming the care regime is set up properly and is shown to be working well and meeting the claimant's needs as at the date of trial, there is no doubt that this is helpful evidence to establish the reasonableness of future costs. In particular, implementing a care regime and carrying out the relevant risk assessments may flag up important issues concerning the likely costs for the future, such as the number of carers required for transfers[3]. However, on occasions, courts have still been prepared retrospectively to criticise care regimes that have been set up and to disallow some elements of expenditure[4]. There can be particular problems in brain injury cases, where attempting to implement a care regime using an interim payment highlights problems which are likely to prevent a care regime from ever working smoothly, such as the claimant not getting on with his carers and trying to sack them[5]. In such circumstances, it may be that additional case management or deputyship costs will be incurred to cater for the high turnover of staff.

[1]   See eg *Havenhand v Jeffrey* (24 February 1997, unreported), CA, in which Otton LJ stated: 'The level of day and night care was not in place before, or at the time of, trial. The level of actual provision fell well below that, notwithstanding an interim payment and the undoubted availability of further interim payments if required. More significantly, the regime has not even now been put into effect. The explanation given is that the claimant wished to be cautious in view of the impending appeal. I regret that I cannot accept this as the sole explanation …

It is never a pleasurable task to reduce a claimant's damages, particularly for a person of indomitable spirit who has coped so courageously with the disastrous effects of an accident. However, it was most unfortunate, in my view, that the magnitude of the claimant's claim for future care was only made apparent in the last few weeks before trial. The defendant showed an admirable sense of responsibility by not seeking an adjournment in view of the claimant's advancing years.

Even so, it behoved the Judge to scrutinise closely this aspect of the claim, and not to accept without question the premise upon which the claim was advanced.'

2   See further *Campbell v Mylchreest* [1999] PIQR Q17, CA.

3   See eg *A v B Hospitals NHS Trust* [2006] EWHC 1178 (QB); *A v Powys Local Health Board* [2007] EWHC 2996 (QB); and *XXX v A Strategic Health Authority* [2008] EWHC 2727 (QB).

4   See eg *Palmese v Reboul* [2007] EWHC (QB); *C v Dixon* [2009] EWHC 708 (QB); *Huntley v Simmonds* [2009] EWHC 405 (QB).

5   See eg *Huntley v Simmonds* [2009] EWHC 405 (QB).

(ii)   Care Provided by Local Authorities

[F78]   It is trite law that, where a claimant has received free past care from the NHS or a local authority (as opposed to gratuitously from a friend or relative), damages for the cost of that care may not be recovered from the defendant (eg for the notional costs of providing the same) because the claimant has suffered no loss[1].

1   *Harris v Bright's Asphalt Contractors Ltd* [1953] 1 QB 617; *Cunningham v Harrison* [1973] 3 All ER 463; *Taylor v Bristol Omnibus* [1975] 2 All ER 1107; *Woodrup v Nicol* [1993] PIQR Q104; *Hunt v Severs* [1994] 2 AC 350, per Lord Bridge at 360–361; *Firth v Geo Ackroyd Jnr Ltd* [2000] Lloyd's Law Rep Med 312; *Sowden v Lodge* [2004] EWCA Civ 1370. As regards the state's obligations to provide care to vulnerable people, see further *R v North and East Devon Health Authority, ex p Coughlan* [1999] Lloyd's Rep 306; *R v Manchester CC, ex p Stennett* [2002] UKHL 34; and *R v North and East Devon HA* [2002] 2 WLR 622, CA, and Peter Carlin 'Wrongfully Charged Patients' Personal Injury Journal, March 2004.

[F79]   Where a local authority does make charges in respect of past care, these would fall to be assessed under ordinary general common law principles, ie (i) it must have been reasonable for the claimant to incur the charges; (ii) the charges themselves must be reasonable; and (iii) the claimant must have acted reasonably and not failed to have mitigated his or her loss, eg by turning down a cheaper but equally appropriate regime.

[F80]   However, a difficulty arises in the situation where, as a result of his or her injuries, the claimant has received care (or accommodation) from his or her local authority prior to trial/settlement and no charge has been made in respect of it, but there is a possibility that a claim will be made for charges in the future in respect of the past or ongoing care needs. Such a position may arise either because of a change in the applicable law relating to the local authority's power to recoup its charges from the claimant or, alternatively, by reason that the damages award received by the claimant means that the local authority is then entitled to recoup its charges because the claimant is considered to have the means to pay the charges. It should be noted that it is unlikely that the local authority would have a viable claim to recover any expenses incurred directly against the tortfeasor, because the tortfeasor will not owe the local authority a duty of care, leaving the claimant as the only potential source for recoupment of fees incurred[1].

1   *Islington BC v University College London Hospital NHS Trust* [2005] EWCA Civ 596.

[F81]   Under s 17 of the Health and Social Services and Social Security Adjudications Act 1983, a local authority is entitled to recover such charge (if any) as the authority considers reasonable from the recipient of services provided under various statutory provisions (such as the National Assistance Act 1948, s 29). If the recipient satisfies the local authority that his or her means are insufficient for it to be reasonably practicable to pay the amount which would otherwise have been charged, the authority may not charge more than the sum which is reasonably practicable[1]. In *Avon County Council v Hooper*[2], the Court of Appeal held that 'means' for these purposes includes the existence of a contractual indemnity obliging a defendant to pay any such charges.

[1] Provisions which are slightly different in detail, but similar in terms of the relevance of means, are contained in Children Act 1989, s 17, in relation to services provided to disabled children and other children in need. See also Chronically Sick and Disabled Persons Act 1970, s 2, as interpreted by Popplewell J in *R v Powys County Council, ex p Hambridge* (1997) Times, 5 November.

[2] [1997] 1 WLR 1605.

[F82] In *Avon County Council v Hooper*[1] a settlement had been made which included provision by way of the defendant indemnifying the claimant in respect of any charges which might be made by the county council. The county council proceeded to make such a claim and succeeded because the indemnity provided the claimant with 'the means' to pay. Therefore, in effect, the claimant would not lose anything. The following is an example of the type of indemnity that was commonly sought in settlements after *Avon County Council v Hooper*:

> 'The Defendant and/or his insurers, [ ], agree to indemnify the claimant against any claim(s) brought by a local authority for the recovery of the costs of services and/or equipment provided to or for the benefit of the claimant up to and including [date]. In return for such indemnity, the claimant agrees:
> (i) to notify the Defendant and/or his insurers if any claim is intimated against him by such local authority and if any proceedings are served upon him by such local authority;
> (ii) not to compromise or to make any admission in relation to any claim (indicated in (i)), without the written consent of the Defendant or his insurers;
> (iii) to co-operate fully with the Defendant and/or his insurers in the defence or compromise of any claim made, and to take such action as the Defendant's insurers reasonably request with regard to the Defence dispute or settlement of any such claim;
> (iv) to be represented in connection with any such claim by such solicitors and counsel as the Defendant or his insurers shall reasonably specify.'

[1] [1997] 1 WLR 1605.

[F83] Since *Avon County Council v Hooper*[1], there has been a significant change in the statutory framework governing the provision of residential care for people over 18[2]. In many cases, an *Avon County Council v Hooper* indemnity is not needed (and the claimant is not entitled to one) because the local authority has no general power to seek reimbursement from the claimant in most circumstances relevant to an injury claimant[3]. The applicable statutory or regulatory provisions do not take into account the claimant's award of damages when assessing the claimant's means to pay and he or she has no other relevant source of income or capital[4]. Each case must be decided on its own facts, and the local authority concerned should be invited to confirm at an early stage whether or not it intends to seek reimbursement of its accommodation or care costs. If there is any doubt as to a potential claim for reimbursement on behalf of the local authority, it is suggested that an application should be made under CPR, r 19.3 in order to join the local authority as a party to the main proceedings[5]. The recommendation of the Master of the Rolls' Structured Settlements Working Party, chaired by Brian Langstaff QC, was to allow the court to grant an indemnity against potential future loss which is uncertain in occurrence or amount, eg charges levied by third parties[6]. However, no such power exists at present[7] and, unless a change in the law is reasonably to be anticipated as opposed to speculative, no award of damages can be made to compensate the claimant for the risk that the law might change in the future leading to a recoupment of the local authority's charges[8]. But indemnities and undertakings can be given by consent and, if agreement can be reached as to the wording, they may be an effective way of avoiding the risk of double recovery[9].

[1]   [1997] 1 WLR 1605.
[2]   For a detailed analysis of this subject, see *Halsbury's Laws*, *Kemp & Kemp* and articles in JPIL.
[3]   See *Thrul v Ray* [2000] PIQR Q44; and *Kidd v Plymouth Health Authority* [2001] Lloyd's Rep Med 165. See further *Firth v Geo Ackroyd Jnr Ltd* [2000] Lloyd's Law Rep Med 312, *Bell v Todd* [2002] Lloyd's Law Rep Med 12, and *Ryan v Liverpool Health Authority* [2002] Lloyd's Law Rep Med 23, where it was held in all three cases that an award of damages for personal injuries and any income generated by a fund administered by the Court of Protection are to be disregarded in determining the liability of a patient to pay the local authority's costs of residential care provided under the National Assistance Act 1948. The position has also since been regularised by the National Assistance (Assessment of Resources) (Amendment) (No 2) (England) Regulations 2002, SI 2002/2531, which has the effect that income received from trusts whose funds derive from personal injury payments to a resident, from an annuity purchased with such funds, and those received by virtue of any agreement or court order to make personal injury payments to the resident in local authority accommodation, are disregarded in their entirety when intended and used for any item which was not taken into account when the standard rate was fixed for the accommodation provided (otherwise, £20 of all such income will be disregarded).
[4]   See eg *Firth v Geo Ackroyd Jnr Ltd* [2000] Lloyd's Law Rep Med 312, in which HHJ Taylor decided that the local authority was not entitled to seek reimbursement of its care and accommodation costs provided under the National Assistance Act 1948, as amended by the National Health Service and Community Care Act 1990. HHJ Taylor also refused to grant the claimant an indemnity regarding any liability to pay accommodation or care charges in the future due to a potential change in the law or, in the alternative, an award of damages to reflect the chance that the claimant might become so liable in the future.
[5]   This was the approach taken in *Firth v Geo Ackroyd Jnr Ltd* [2000] Lloyd's Rep Med 312. The local authority was also joined as a party in *Crofton v NHSLA* [2007] EWCA Civ 71 and *Peters v East Midlands Strategic HA* [2009] EWCA Civ 145.
[6]   Report of the Master of the Rolls' Working Party on Structured Settlements, chaired by Brian Langstaff QC (9 August 2002), together with the addendum dated 9 October 2002.
[7]   *Iqbal v Whipps Cross University* [2007] LS Law Medical 97. Likewise, the court has no power to order a party to give an undertaking to account for monies received from the state: see *XXX v A Strategic Health Authority* [2008] EWHC 2727 (QB).
[8]   *Firth v Geo Ackroyd Jnr Ltd* [2000] Lloyd's Rep Med 312.
[9]   *Peters v East Midlands Strategic HA* [2009] EWCA Civ 145.

[F84]   Local authorities are under a statutory duty[1] to make an assessment of the patient's needs in respect of (a) accommodation – which includes ancillary care; and (b) domiciliary care. As described above, where such an assessment is undertaken and the claimant is provided with accommodation or domiciliary care, or alternatively direct payments to pay for the same, no claim can be brought unless charges are made for these services. If the claimant is happy with the state-funded services and wishes them to continue in the future, an assessment will be required regarding the extent of any likely provision in the future. This may involve a reduction to the multiplier to reflect the uncertainty of future provision[2]. But, where the claimant decides (or, if the claimant lacks capacity, the claimant's deputy decides) that he or she does not wish to rely upon state funding, there is no obligation upon him or her to do so. The Court of Appeal held in *Peters v East Midlands Strategic HA*[3] that a claimant was entitled as a matter of right to opt for self-funding and damages in preference to reliance on the statutory obligations of a public authority. Provided there is no real risk of double recovery, there is no reason why a claimant should give up his or her right to damages to meet her wish to pay for his or her care needs rather than becoming dependent on the state[4]. In *Peters* the claimant's deputy offered an undertaking (which has since become known as a '*Peters* undertaking') to notify the defendant of any attempt to apply for state funding, and this was approved by the court as an effective way of dealing with the risk of double recovery. However, such an undertaking may not be required where the court finds as a fact that the possibility of double recovery is effectively eliminated by making the defendant pay for the claimant's private costs of care and accommodation[5].

[1]   National Health Service and Community Care Act 1990, s 47.
[2]   *Crofton v NHSLA* [2007] EWCA Civ 71.
[3]   [2009] EWCA Civ 145.
[4]   Para [56].
[5]   *Freeman v Lockett* [2006] EWHC 102 (QB).

(iii)   Gratuitous Care

[F85]   The majority of people who are injured do not have sufficient funds to pay for professional nursing care, and are therefore reliant upon friends and relatives in order to meet their care needs[1]. The law recognises that a claimant is able to recover damages for the value of nursing services provided gratuitously by a friend or relative[2]. However, the assessment of the appropriate award is not without its difficulties, and below we set out the relevant principles governing recovery under this head of loss.

[1]   This is borne out by the empirical research carried out by the Law Commission: see further the Law Commission's Report No 262 'Damages for Personal Injury: Medical, Nursing and other Expenses; Collateral Benefits' (November 1999), para 2.15.
[2]   *Hunt v Severs* [1994] 2 AC 350. For a history of the law relating to gratuitous care claims, see further *Lowe v Guise* [2002] EWCA Civ 197; [2002] PIQR Q9; and *Evans v Pontypridd Roofing Ltd* [2001] EWCA Civ 1657.

Who can claim?

[F86]   The House of Lords in *Hunt v Severs*[1] held that, where care was provided gratuitously to an injured claimant, the loss belongs to the carer and not to the claimant. Although there can be no direct claim by the carer (who is unlikely to be owed a duty of care by the defendant in any event), the claimant is entitled to recover compensation on the carer's behalf. Any damages recovered in respect of the care provided are held on trust by the claimant for the benefit of the carer[2] or the carer's estate[3].

[1]   [1994] 2 AC 350. In this regard, the House of Lords overruled its previous decision in *Donnelly v Joyce* [1974] QB 454, preferring the obiter reasoning of Denning MR in *Cunningham v Harrison* [1973] QB 942 at 952.

²   *Hunt v Severs* [1994] 2 AC 350. The consequences of this decision may be quite far reaching. See further *ATH v MS* [2002] EWCA Civ 792; [2003] QB 965 and 'Did *Hunt v Severs* Create a Real Trust?' [2003] JPIL Issue 2/03.

³   In the event of the carer's death, the damages are held on trust for the benefit of the carer's estate: *Hughes v Gerard Lloyd and anor* LTL 10/1/2008.

Care provided by defendant

[F87] As the claimant holds the damages, representing the cost of gratuitously provided care, in trust for the provider of that care, it logically follows that no damages should be recoverable, where the carer is the defendant, for the claimant would be recovering damages from the defendant only to hold them on trust for the defendant. In addition, there is strong countervailing policy argument that a tortfeasor should not be able to benefit from his or her wrongdoing, as he would do where the liability is in effect paid for by an insurer. Under the present law, therefore, no damages can be recovered for gratuitous care provided by the tortfeasor[1].

¹   *Hunt v Severs* [1994] 2 AC 350 at 363–364.

Proposals for change

[F88] The Law Commission has recommended that this rule in *Hunt v Severs*[1] should be legislatively reversed, and that as a matter of policy all claimants should be able to recover in full, even where the defendant has personally provided services gratuitously[2]. The Ministry of Justice issued a consultation paper entitled 'The Law of Damages' on 4 May 2007 suggesting that, instead of a trust, there should be a personal obligation to account. In the Government's response published on 1 July 2009, the Government confirmed that it considered that a more flexible 'personal obligation to account' should replace the current method of holding damages on trust. Clause 7 of the draft Civil Law Reform Bill published in December 2009 provides the proposed legislative framework to bring these recommendations into effect. At clause 7(3) of the draft Bill, it is proposed that the court must not refuse to award damages which have been gratuitously provided merely because the person providing the services is the defendant. The thinking behind this was to avoid the unnecessary costs of commercial care where there was a tortfeasor who was willing and able to provide the care gratuitously[3].

¹   [1994] 2 AC 350.

²   See further the Law Commission's Report No 262 'Damages for Personal Injury: Medical, Nursing and other Expenses; Collateral Benefits' (November 1999), para 3.76.

³   See further Ministry of Justice – The Law of Damages, Response to consultation, published 1 July 2009, pp 52–53.

Threshold tests for recovery?

(1) Mills v BRE

[F89] Following *Mills v British Rail Engineering Ltd*[1], it was argued that care claims were limited to 'very serious cases' where the care provided went 'well beyond the ordinary call of duty'. However, the Court of Appeal clarified the position in *Giambrone v JMC Holidays Ltd*[2], which involved a claim brought on behalf of numerous claimants for food poisoning. Giving the lead judgment of the court (with which Mance LJ and Park J agreed), Brooke LJ said[3]:

> 'I reject the contention that *Mills* presents any binding authority for the proposition that such awards are reserved for "very serious cases". This was not a point which had to be decided in *Mills*, which was on any showing a very serious case, and a proposition like this would be very difficult to police. Where is the borderline between the case in which no award is made at all (unless, for example, a working mother incurs actual cost in hiring someone to look after her sick child when she was at work) and the case in which a full award of reasonable recompense is made? An arbitrary dividing line, which would be likely to differ from case to case, and from judge to judge, would be likely to bring the law into disrepute ...
>
> In my judgment the judge was correct in principle to make an award for the cost of care in each of these cases. Anyone who has had responsibility for the care of a child with gastro-enteritis of the severity experienced by these children will know that they require care which goes distinctly beyond that which is part of the ordinary regime of family life. The fact that one of these mothers had a child who had suffered in this way on previous occasions provides no good reason for concluding that an award of some sort is not appropriate if there is an identifiable tortfeasor to blame'.

Therefore, there is no threshold test for recovery as long as the care provided goes 'distinctly beyond that which is part of the ordinary regime of family life'[4]. This approach ties in with the Court of Appeal's earlier decision in *Evans v Pontypridd Roofing Ltd*[5], which made no mention of the need to surpass a threshold test. Indeed, as detailed below, Evans LJ specifically took the opportunity in that case to emphasise that judges at first instance should not be put in a strait-jacket when assessing proper recompense for carers[6]. In passing, it is noteworthy that this approach also accords with the view of the Law Commission, which considered that there should not be any limits on the recovery of gratuitous care claims[7].

---

[1]   [1992] PIQR Q130.

[2]   [2004] EWCA Civ 158.

[3]   At paras [26] and [31].

[4]   Since *Giambrone v JMC Holidays Ltd* [2004] EWCA Civ 158, it is unusual to find a claim for care where this test is not satisfied; however, one example is the decision of HHJ Seymour in *Palmer v Kitley* [2008] EWHC 2819 (QB).

[5]   [2001] EWCA Civ 1657.

[6]   See para **[F93]** below.

[7]   At para 3.79 of its Report No 262 entitled 'Damages for Personal Injury: Medical, Nursing and other Expenses; Collateral Benefits' (November 1999), the Law Commission stated that: 'In accordance with our provision recommendation and the views of all our consultees who responded on this issue, we therefore recommend that no limits, either in the form of ceilings or thresholds, should be introduced on damages awarded for gratuitous care'.

(2)   THE CLAIMANT MUST INTEND TO REPAY THE MONEY TO THE CARE PROVIDER

[F90]   As seen above, the claimant will hold any damages he or she receives by way of gratuitous care for the person who provided that care[1]. Where there are reasons which prevent the claimant from being able to repay the money to his or her gratuitous care providers – eg if the care providers have died since providing the care or the claimant is no longer in contact with them – the court may be disinclined to make such an award. In *ATH v MS*[2], Kennedy LJ, in considering a claim for service dependency under the Fatal Accidents Act 1976, said at [19]:

> 'The simple underlying truth is that in justice the claimant should not be compensated for the cost of services already provided gratuitously if that compensation is not going to find its way to the service provider.'

In an extreme case where the care provider is still alive but the court has considerable doubts as to whether or not the money received will be paid to the carer, the court may direct that the damages are to be paid into court and the administration of the monies (including any application for payments out) should be dealt with by the Master[3]. But what happens where the care provider has since passed away? In *Hughes v Gerard Lloyd and anor*[4], HHJ Hodge QC (sitting as a judge of the High Court) held that damages recovered in respect of gratuitous care are held on trust for the deceased's estate.

1   *Hunt v Severs* [1994] 2 AC 350.
2   [2002] EWCA Civ 792, [2003] PIQR Q1.
3   This was the approach taken in *ATH v MS* [2002] EWCA Civ 792, [2003] PIQR Q1 – see further the judgment of Kennedy LJ at paras [40] and [41].
4   LTL 10/1/2008.

For what services are damages recoverable?

[F91]   In *Evans v Pontypridd Roofing Ltd*[1] the claimant fell off a roof and suffered severe injuries to his right arm and elbow. He required a great deal of physical care and assistance from his wife on a daily basis. In addition, he developed severe clinical depression and had historically been at risk of suicide at night. He relied upon his wife heavily for emotional support. At first instance, the judge made an award for gratuitous care based upon his wife providing 24-hour care per day. On appeal, the defendant submitted that it was wrong to include in the assessment of care those activities which were not strictly required by reason of the claimant's physical injuries. It was suggested that the claim for care should have been limited to the physical nursing care (including assistance with mobility and assistance with washing, dressing etc), without allowing anything for the companionship, emotional and psychological support that was provided. In addition, it was argued that no account should have been taken of the normal household chores which the claimant's wife would have performed in any event or of the time when she was asleep (and was therefore not providing physical care). The Court of Appeal unanimously rejected this interpretation of the assessment of care. May LJ stated at [30]:

> 'Any determination of the services for which the court has to assess proper recompense will obviously depend on the circumstances of each case. There will be many cases in which the care services provided will be limited to a few hours each day. The services should not exceed those which are properly determined to be care services consequent upon the claimant's injuries, but they do not, in my view, have to be limited in every case to a stop-watch calculation of actual nursing or physical assistance. Nor, as Mr Purchas' submissions appeared to suggest, must they be limited in every case to care which is the subject of medical prescription. Persons, who need physical assistance for everything they do, do not literally receive that assistance during every minute of the day. But their condition may be so severe that the presence of a full time carer really is

necessary to provide whatever assistance is necessary at whatever time unpredictably it is required. It is obviously necessary for judges to ensure that awards on this basis are properly justified on the facts, and not to be misled into findings that a gratuitous carer is undertaking full time care simply because they are for other reasons there all or most of the time.'

May LJ continued at [31]:

'In the present case, I am not persuaded that the judge made an over-assessment of the services provided by Mrs Evans to her husband as a result of his injuries. He concluded that there was no doubt that the claimant requires 24 hour care and he said that the evidence was overwhelming. In my view, the evidence to which we have been directed justified the judge's conclusion and justifies the conclusion that the services which Mrs Evans provides are those of a full time carer. The fact that for some of the time she does things which she would have done if her husband had not been injured does not detract from this conclusion. It is neither necessary nor to be expected that a full time carer should spend every hour of the day and night engaged in providing physical services. In substance, on the judge's finding Mrs Evans does provide the services of a full time carer and her proper recompense should be assessed on that basis.'

[1]   [2001] EWCA Civ 1657.

[F92]   In summary, under the present law, damages may be recovered for, but are not necessarily limited to, the following types of gratuitously rendered services (as long as the same are supported by the medical evidence as being reasonably necessary as a result of the claimant's injuries and the claimant would not have needed such assistance in any event):

- Physical nursing care and attendance – such as washing, dressing, undressing, brushing teeth, combing/brushing hair, changing bandages, administering medication etc.
- Assistance with mobility – such as assisting the claimant on and off the lavatory or commode, helping with wheelchair transfers, helping the claimant get in and out of vehicles, acting as a support when walking, being there in case of falls etc.
- Taking the claimant to and from hospital appointments, treatment appointments, X-rays etc.
- Making sure that the claimant does not injure him or herself.
- Prompting and organising a brain-injured claimant[1].
- Cutting up food for an injured claimant who is unable to do it him or herself[2].
- Offering emotional support and reassurance (particularly where there is a recognised psychological injury or risk of suicide)[3].
- Helping to manage the claimant's affairs and finances[4].
- Attending a sick child[5].
- Babysitting/child minding a healthy child who otherwise would have been looked after by the claimant[6].
- Performing domestic chores such as cooking, cleaning, washing, ironing, shopping etc[7].
- Performing DIY or home maintenance activities – such as painting, decorating, gardening and car servicing[8].
- Providing care and assistance to family members or friends which the claimant would otherwise have provided[9].

- Feeding and looking after pets and animals – such as mucking out horses, dog walking, taking sick animals to the vet[10].
- Case management, ie liaising with treating medical staff and therapists, liaising with the claimant's school and/or employers, corresponding with the local authority, local education authority or social services, helping to find suitable alternative accommodation etc[11].

However, it should be noted that, in the absence of an expressed or implied contract, care provided voluntarily to assist the claimant's business is not recoverable[12]. Further, in relation to services provided which do not amount to 'nursing care', it is arguable that the decision in *Daly v General Steam Navigation Co Ltd*[13] prevents an award for past loss over and above an uplift in the award for general damages in respect of pain, suffering and loss of amenity, save where the claimant has either spent money or where the services were provided gratuitously by someone who had to forgo paid employment in order to provide them. This distinction may seem somewhat illogical and arbitrary. Indeed, to the extent that there remains a rule following *Hunt v Severs*[14] that past and future non-care gratuitous services are to be treated differently (which is uncertain), the courts have in practice tended to ignore it[15]. The Law Commission has criticised any such difference in treatment and has recommended that the law permits a claimant to recover damages for the cost of work done where the work has been or will reasonably be done gratuitously by a relative or friend[16].

[1]   *Pratt v Smith* (18 December 2002, unreported), QBD, in which David Foskett QC said:
    'I accept that one must approach this kind of claim with circumspection and endeavour to exclude from consideration those aspects of what one member of a married partnership would do for the other without even thinking that it constituted something outside the ordinary incidents of married life. However, in this case the Claimant has sustained brain damage which requires him to need prompting and organising (and occasional sustained emotional support during depressed periods and when he becomes angry). If his wife was not there, someone would have to take her place to do this. She also has to help him cut up his food from time to time and doubtless there are other aspects of everyday life which now she has to help him with which she never had to before. All these things do take time that, but for the accident, would have been spent doing other things. I do not think it is sufficient simply to say that the family dynamics have changed and that the attention that the Claimant's wife now gives him is simply part of something that was there already. As she said, the accident has affected everything they do.
    The Claimant is very reluctant to acknowledge that he needs this help, but my impression is that he is beginning to recognise how much he is dependent on others, albeit in fairly subtle ways, to carry on his life. I noticed him nodding during that part of the submissions of Mr Purchas when Mr Purchas averred that the Claimant will have learned a lot about himself during the trial. He said that he needed help, though not of the "group therapy" nature that he had been offered hitherto. If, as I am confident he will, he does seek the kind of one to one counselling advocated by the psychologists, he may come to recognise this even more and possibly seek to relieve his wife of some of the burden of the additional support she has been giving him by employing someone occasionally to help. If his wife is no longer willing or able to provide the help, he will be forced to do this in any event.
    The claim is, in my judgment, presented in a fairly modest way and, subject to slight modification, I propose to accede to it in principle. As to the first six months, I will allow the full amount claimed to 30 June, 1997 as provided for in Ms Watkins' report, subject to a deduction of 25% to reflect the gratuitous element (see *Evans v Pontypridd Roofing* [2002] PIQR Q5, CA). That yields £1,679. The same approach will apply to the date of trial, yielding a figure of £3,463. The total past loss on this account is, therefore, £5,142.'
[2]   *Pratt v Smith* (18 December 2002, unreported), QBD.

3   *Evans v Pontypridd Roofing Ltd* [2001] EWCA Civ 1657.

4   By analogy, see eg the allowances made for paid care in respect of these services in *O'Brien v Harris* (22 February 2001, unreported), QBD.

5   *Giambrone v JMC Holidays Ltd* [2004] EWCA Civ 158.

6   See eg *Froggatt v Chesterfield & North Derbyshire Royal Hospital NHS Trust* [2002] All ER (D) 218 (Dec), in which £945 was awarded for the past cost of childcare provided gratuitously by the children's grandmother.

7   *Daly v General Steam Navigation Co Ltd* [1981] 1 WLR 120. See further at paras **[F167]–[F170]**.

8   See eg *Hoffman v Sofaer* [1982] 1 WLR 1350; *Assinder v Griffin* [2001] All ER (D) 356 (May); *Tagg v Countess of Chester Hospital Foundation NHS Trust* [2007] EWHC 509 (QB); and *Smith v East and North Hertfordshire Hospitals NHS Trust* [2008] EWHC 2234 (QB). See further at paras **[F167]–[F170]**.

9   *Lowe v Guise* [2002] EWCA Civ 197, [2002] PIQR Q9.

10   Whilst such services might be considered a little more controversial than others, there is no reason in principle why such services should not be recoverable. The claimant owes a duty to his or her pets to ensure that they are properly fed and looked after. Any services in this regard may be considered equally onerous and valuable as other services provided gratuitously, and there is also a commercial market for valuing the same: see further *Dennison v Dennison & anor* LTL 24/7/2008, in which a claim for future dog walking was allowed at £11 per hour for 14 hours per week.

11   In *Massey v Tameside & Glossop Acute Services NHS Trust* [2007] EWHC 317 (QB), Teare J awarded £8,750 for past gratuitous case management. Similar awards have been subsequently agreed in other cases, such as *A v Powys Local Health Board* [2007] EWHC 2996 (QB) and *Noble v Owens* [2008] EWHC 359 (QB).

12   *Hardwick v Hudson* [1999] 1 WLR 1770, [1999] PIQR Q202.

13   [1981] 1 WLR 120. See further *Lowe v Guise* [2002] EWCA Civ 197, [2002] PIQR Q9.

14   [1994] 2 AC 350.

15   See eg *Blair v Michelin Tyre plc* (25 January 2002, unreported), QBD; *Assinder v Griffin* [2001] All ER (D) 356 (May); *Froggatt v Chesterfield & North Derbyshire Royal Hospital NHS Trust* [2002] All ER (D) 218 (Dec), QBD; *Tagg v Countess of Chester Hospital Foundation NHS Trust* [2007] EWHC 509 (QB); *Smith v East and North Hertfordshire Hospitals NHS Trust* [2008] EWHC 2234 (QB).

16   See paras 3.87–3.93***[AQ please check]*** of its report No 262 entitled 'Damages for Personal Injury: Medical, Nursing and other Expenses; Collateral Benefits' (November 1999).

The quantum of damages

(1) THE OBJECT OF THE AWARD

[F93]   The object of an award for gratuitous care is 'to enable the voluntary carer to receive proper recompense for his or her services'[1]. There is, however, no conventional way or ways of quantifying this loss, which is essentially a jury question for the judge to decide[2]. As May LJ stated in *Evans v Pontypridd Roofing Ltd*[3]:

'In my judgment, this court should avoid putting first instance judges into too restrictive a straight-jacket, such as might happen if it was said that the means of assessing a proper recompense for services provided gratuitously by a family carer had to be assessed in a particular way or ways. Circumstances vary enormously and what is appropriate and just in one case may not be so in another. If a caring relation has given up remunerative employment to care for the claimant gratuitously, it may well be appropriate to assess the proper recompense for the services provided by reference to the carer's lost earnings. If the carer has not given up gainful employment, the task remains to assess proper recompense for the services provided. As O'Connor LJ said in *Housecroft v Burnett*[4], regard may be had to what it would cost to provide the services on the open market. But the services are not in fact being bought in the open market, so that adjustments will probably need to be made. Since, however, any such adjustments are no more than an element in a single assessment, it would not in my view be appropriate to bind first instance judges to a conventional formalised calculation. The assessment is of an amount as a whole. The means of reaching the assessment must depend on what is appropriate to the individual case. If it is appropriate, as I think it is in the present case, to have regard to what it would cost to buy the services which Mrs Evans provides in the open market, it may well also be appropriate to scale them down. But I do not think that this can be done by means of a conventional percentage, since the appropriate extent of the scaling down and the reasons for it may vary from case to case.'

1   *Hunt v Severs* [1994] 2 AC 350, per Lord Bridge at 363A; *Evans v Pontypridd Roofing Ltd* [2001] EWCA Civ 1657, per May LJ at [36]. See also *Housecroft v Burnett* [1986] 1 All ER 332, in which O'Connor LJ at 334 referred to the need to provide 'a capital sum ... sufficient ... to make recompense to the relative'.
2   *Spittle v Bunney* [1988] 1 WLR 847.
3   [2001] EWCA Civ 1657.
4   [1986] 1 All ER 332.

(2)   THE 'CEILING PRINCIPLE'

[F94]   In *Housecroft v Burnett*[1], O'Connor LJ stated at 343D:

'Once it is understood that this [that is, this element of compensation] is an element in the award to the claimant to provide for the reasonable and proper care of the claimant and that a capital sum is to be available for that purpose, the court should look at it as a whole and consider whether, on the facts of the case, it is sufficient to enable the claimant among other things to make reasonable recompense to the relative, so in cases where the relative has given up gainful employment to look after the claimant I would regard it as natural that the claimant would not wish the relative to be the loser and the court will award sufficient to enable the claimant to achieve that result. The ceiling would be the commercial rate.'

1   [1986] 1 All ER 332. See further *Fitzgerald v Ford* [1996] PIQR Q72.

[F95]   The last sentence of the above passage has become known as the 'ceiling principle', ie that the ceiling of any claim for gratuitous care should be limited to the commercial rate. In other words, the maximum award that can be made in respect of gratuitous care should be limited to the cost of obtaining those services professionally. However, in *Lamey v Wirral Health Authority*[1], Morland J expressly regarded the ceiling as a guideline rather than as a binding rule of law. He stated:

'In my judgment fair recompense for the parents' care of their disabled child should be assessed not only quantitatively, but also qualitatively. It is not only the number of hours wholly or partly devoted to the disabled child but at the standard of that care that has to be assessed in deciding what is fair recompense.'

Further, in the fatal accident case of *Mehmet v Perry*[2], Brian Neill QC sitting as a deputy judge held that it was reasonable that the claimant had given up full-time employment to care for his children on the basis of medical advice following his wife's death. His children had a rare blood disorder, requiring daily injections and periodical blood transfusions. In the circumstances, the damages for the loss of his wife's services were assessed by reference to the claimant's loss of wages and not by the reference to the reasonable cost of employing a housekeeper.

1   [1993] CLY 1437. Cf *Woodrup v Nicol* [1993] PIQR Q104; *Bell v Gateshead Area Health Authority* (22 October 1986, unreported); *Abdul-Hosn v Trustees of The Italian Hospital* (10 July 1987, unreported), QBD, summarised in *Kemp & Kemp* at B2-006. See also *A v National Blood Authority* [2001] Lloyd's Rep Med 187, in which Burton J said at 231:

> 'In the absence of any special evidence of any exceptional circumstances, I conclude that the proper recompense for gratuitous services in these cases will normally be commercial cost, less a deduction to allow at least for tax and national insurance which in this case is conceded to be no more than 25%; and that *it is not appropriate to allow recovery in respect of loss of the gratuitous carer's earnings or benefits of more than that amount*' (emphasis added).

2   [1997] 2 All ER 529.

[F96]   Also, as seen above, it is noteworthy that May LJ in *Evans v Pontypridd Roofing Ltd*[1], having cited the above passage from O'Connor LJ's judgment in *Housecroft v Burnett*[2], explained that judges at first instance should not be put in too restrictive a strait-jacket such as might happen if it was said that the means of assessing a proper recompense for services provided gratuitously by a family carer had to be assessed in a particular way or ways. In particular, he did not expressly refer to the ceiling principle as placing any fixed limit on the court's ability to award proper recompense for the gratuitous services provided[3].

1   [2001] EWCA Civ 1657.
2   [1986] 1 All ER 332.
3   See also the view of the Law Commission expressed in its Report No 262 'Damages for Personal Injury: Medical, Nursing and other Expenses; Collateral Benefits' (November 1999) to the effect that there should not be any thresholds or artificial ceilings placed upon awards for gratuitous care. Although note that in *Bell v Gateshead Area Health Authority* (22 October 1986, unreported), *Abdul-Hosn v Trustees of The Italian Hospital* (10 July 1987, unreported), QBD, summarised in *Kemp & Kemp* at B2-006, and *A v National Blood Authority* [2001] Lloyd's Rep Med 187, the judges considered themselves to be bound by the ceiling principle as expressed by O'Connor LJ in *Housecroft v Burnett* [1986] 1 All ER 332. See also the Court of Appeal's judgment in *Woodrup v Nicol* [1993] PIQR Q104.

(3)   THE DIFFERENT APPROACHES IN PRACTICE

[F97]   The two leading cases in relation to the quantification of damages for gratuitous care are the Court of Appeal decisions in *Housecroft v Burnett*[1] and *Evans v Pontypridd Roofing Ltd*[2]. As explained above, the law does not lay down any dogmatic rules regarding the assessment of this head of loss, and judges are given a very wide discretion to select the method of calculation most appropriate to the facts of the case. In practice, however, the approach adopted by the court largely depends upon whether or not the care provider has had to give up paid employment in order to look after the claimant.

1   [1986] 1 All ER 332.
2   [2001] EWCA Civ 1657.

(i)   Where the carer gives up paid employment

[F98]   Where employment is forgone in order to care for a claimant, then the loss which may be claimed is prima facie the loss of the net income to have been expected from that employment[1]. However, this may not be all. Where the employment that the carer carried out prior to the claimant's injuries was part-time or not very well paid, the voluntary carer may be entitled to recover more than the total amount of his or her net loss of earnings. For example, in *Fish v Wilcox*[2] the carer gave up a job earning £4,000 per annum to look after a seriously disabled child. The judge assessed the value of that care at £5,000 per annum. Further, in *Hogg v Doyle*[3] the Court of Appeal upheld an award of one-and-a-half times the claimant's wife's earnings. The wife was a nurse who was found to have been providing the level of care of two full-time nurses (and was on the verge of a nervous breakdown).

[1]   *Housecroft v Burnett* [1986] 1 All ER 332. See also *Fitzgerald v Ford* [1996] PIQR Q72 and *Evans v Pontypridd Roofing Ltd* [2001] EWCA Civ 1657, in which May LJ stated at [25] that: 'If a caring relation has given up remunerative employment to care for the claimant gratuitously, it may well be appropriate to assess the proper recompense for the services provided by reference to the carer's lost earnings'.

[2]   [1994] 5 Med LR 230.

[3]   (1989, unreported), CA. Although see further the comments in relation to this case in *Fitzgerald v Ford* [1996] PIQR Q72. In summary, Stuart-Smith LJ referred to *Hogg v Doyle* as being a decision on its own facts which created no new principle, in particular, there was no principle that, where a member of the family who was working eight hours a day for five days a week gives up their employment to care for the claimant 24 hours a day, they should be paid 1.5 times of their earnings or, indeed, any more than their loss of earnings.

[F99]   The position may be different, however, where the gratuitous carer gives up a well-paid job to look after the claimant. Under the present law, arguably the maximum that can be recovered is the professional costs of providing the care following the 'ceiling principle' in *Housecroft v Burnett*[1]. For example, in *Woodrup v Nicol*[2] the Court of Appeal reduced the damages awarded by Wright J at first instance in relation to the care provided by the claimant's father. These damages consisted of the father's estimated loss of earnings for the period in question, amounting to twice the commercial cost of his services, although the sum awarded by the Court of Appeal still exceeded the commercial rate.

[1]   [1986] 1 All ER 332. See further at para **[F94]**.

[2]   [1993] PIQR Q104. See also eg *Bell v Gateshead Area Health Authority* (22 October 1986, unreported), in which the claimant's mother had given up plans to return to work. Alliott J took her lost earnings as the starting point to value her services, past and future, but applied the commercial ceiling. In *Abdul-Hosn v Trustees of The Italian Hospital* (10 July 1987, unreported), QBD, summarised in *Kemp & Kemp* at B2-006, Hirst J found he was bound by the ceiling principle to award the commercial rate where the claimant's father had given up his job and both parents had made a huge commitment to provide the necessary care in what was a grinding regime. See further Burton J's judgment in *A v National Blood Authority* [2001] Lloyd's Rep Med 187 at 231.

[F100]   This has been criticised by the Law Commission, which recommended that the courts should be more willing to award damages to compensate carers for their loss of earnings, even though these exceed the commercial cost of care[1].

[1]   See further para 3.86 of the Law Commission's Report No 262 'Damages for Personal Injury: Medical, Nursing and other Expenses; Collateral Benefits' (November 1999).

(ii)   Where the care provider does not give up paid employment

[F101]   In *Housecroft v Burnett*, O'Connor LJ referred to 'two extreme solutions'[1] in resolving the problem of assessing the 'proper and reasonable cost' of supplying the claimant's needs where care is provided by a relative or friend gratuitously. The first was to assess the carer's contribution at the full commercial rate for the services provided by the carer. The second was to assess the cost as nil, just as it is where the claimant is treated under the NHS. O'Connor LJ concluded that neither of the extreme solutions was correct, and that any assessment should be somewhere between the two, depending on the facts of the case. The award would have to be[2]:

> '... sufficient to enable the claimant, among other things, to make reasonable recompense to the relative. So, in cases where the relative has given up gainful employment to look after the claimant, I would regard it as natural that the claimant would not wish the relative to be the loser and the court would award sufficient to enable the claimant to achieve that result. The ceiling would be the commercial rate.'

[1]   [1986] 1 All ER 332, CA, at 342.
[2]   [1986] 1 All ER 332, CA, at 343.

[F102]   In cases where there has been no loss of earnings as such, courts have tended to calculate damages for care by relatives by taking the commercial rate[1] and applying a discount to it[2]. A 'conventional' discount in the writers' experience has been about 25%, but there are good reasons today for taking the starting point at 20% (25% represents a figure more appropriate to days of higher taxation: nowadays, a higher percentage of the gross 'commercial rate' would actually end up in the pocket of the commercial carer). Much depends on the nature of the services provided. If they are usually performed by skilled workers (eg accountancy services, painting and decorating, plumbing and tiling), then to pay a carer unskilled in such tasks the 'skilled' rate is to over-compensate. On the other hand, many domestic services are perhaps qualitatively better performed by those caring for their own home rather than for another's, and require little experience to do well, and basic caring/nursing services are likely to be performed just as well if not better by a close relative than by a paid stranger. In these latter cases, there seems to be no reason why a friend or relative providing gratuitous services should not be paid the full commercial rate, subject only to the deduction of a sum to represent the likely impact of tax and National Insurance[3]. If, therefore, a commercial rate is £8 per hour, and tax and National Insurance are taken as being 20% (a broad approximation including an element for the effect of the tax-free personal allowance[4]), the commercial carer would actually receive £6.40 net per hour. There seems good reason why a gratuitous carer should receive the same – and this, of course, equates to the commercial rate less a discount of 20%.

[1]   See further at paras **[F105]–[F107]**.
[2]   See further at para **[F109]**.
[3]   See eg *Hassell v Abnoof & Anor* (6 July 2001), QBD, Lawtel Document No AC0101866, where Gage J (as he then was) only applied a discount of 15% in relation to the past gratuitous care claim which was made up of cleaning services, on the basis that a professional cleaner would not pay tax and National Insurance of more than this.
[4]   At the time of writing, the standard personal tax allowance stands at £6,475, although higher rates apply to people aged between 65 and 74, and those aged over 75.

[F103]   The discount may be reduced if the claimant can show a likely future need for commercial care[1]. It may also be reduced if the quality of the care required from the carers is of a particularly high level. In exceptional cases, courts have refrained from making a discount at all[2], and in one case the Court of Appeal upheld an award based on one-and-a-half times the earnings which the claimant's mother, a qualified nurse, would have earned, on the basis that the mother was doing the work of two nurses who would otherwise have been needed to provide the care[3].

1   In *Maylen v Morris* (21 January 1988, unreported), it was anticipated that future care would be by the claimant's mother and two other relatives, but it was anticipated that the mother might later become unable to cope because of old age. She was already, at the date of trial, unable to do the heavy work involved. The Court of Appeal refused to discount further the 25% discount set by Mann J.

2   See further at para **[F113]**, to reflect the 'gratuitous element'.

3   *Hogg v Doyle* (6 March 1991, unreported). See *Kemp & Kemp* at paras 13–10 to 13–11. See further at para **[F98]**.

[F104]   Care provided commercially will be paid for at an overtime rate during weekends, during 'long' shifts and may involve on-call or sleep-over charges when no work is actually done but the carer is not free to enjoy the time as his or her own. Thus, payment even at a discount no greater than the 20%, which broadly approximates to the impact of tax and National Insurance contributions, may under-compensate the spouse or parent who is ready to help at all hours of the day, night and week. On this basis, it can be argued that there should be no – or only a minimal – discount as against the gross commercial rate, especially if 'flat' commercial rates (ie with no uplift for care provided at unsociable hours) have been used to assess the care provided[1].

1   *Newman v Folkes* [2002] EWCA Civ 591; *A v B Hospitals NHS Trust* [2006] EWHC 1178 (QB); *Warrilow v Norfolk and Norwich Hospitals NHS Trust* [2006] EWHC 801 (QB). See further at para **[F113]**.

(4)   ASSESSMENT OF THE COMMERCIAL RATES

[F105]   There are numerous different commercial pay scales for nursing care provided by different bodies including the National Joint Council for Local Government Services (known as the 'National Joint Council rates'), the Crossroads rates, the Whitely rates and the British Nursing Association rates (the 'BNA rates')[1]. Within the different pay scales, there are different rates which depend upon the grade of carer, the nature of the services provided, as well as how and when that care is provided (ie whether the care is provided by the hour, by the day or by the week, and whether the care is provided during the day or during the evening, at night or at the weekend). The rates have historically tended to increase either annually or bi-annually at a rate outstripping inflation, as recorded by the RPI; and, following the European Working Time Directive[2], even agency workers are entitled to take annual holiday or payment in lieu of holiday.

1   The applicable rates can either be found in *Personal Injury Damages Statistics* by Rodney Nelson-Jones, in 'Facts & Figures' produced by the Professional Negligence Bar Association, or by contacting the relevant bodies directly.

2   Council Directive 93/104/EC.

[F106]   Where significant care has been provided over an extensive period, it is both prudent and proportionate to instruct a care expert to value the commercial cost of these services. Although there is no nationally accepted or approved rate for assessing past gratuitous care, it is common for care experts to use Spine Point 8 of the

NJCLGS (NJC) rates, ie the rates applicable to home helps or companions[1]. However, following the Court of Appeal's decision in *Thompstone*[2], which confirmed that ASHE (6115) was the correct measure for the indexation of future care costs, it may be argued that ASHE (6115) should be used for assessing past gratuitous care as well. In 2010, the Civil Justice Council issued a consultation regarding the standardisation of care costs. It remains to be seen whether a single rate could be agreed for past gratuitous care, which would reduce disputes regarding the appropriate hourly rate and save costs.

[1] See further Jacqueline Webb 'One claimant – two opposing views about the cost of care' [2003] Quantum, Issue 4/2003. The job description for this post/Spine Point is as follows: 'The duties will include: domestic duties (for example, cleaning, cooking and washing), physical tasks approximating to home care (for example, dressing, washing and feeding clients) and social duties (for example talking with clients to maintain contact with family, friends and community, assisting with shopping and recreation) aimed at creating a supportive homely atmosphere where clients can achieve maximum independence.'

[2] *Thameside & Glossop v Thompstone and ors* [2008] 1 WLR 2207, [2008] EWCA Civ 5.

[F107]   Whilst the applicable hourly rate remains open for debate, care should be taken to ensure that the correct rate is applied to the service that has been provided. For example, where a family member has been trained how to carry out certain procedures such as administer medicine or provide therapy, it might be possible to claim care at a higher rate. The best evidence is quotes or estimates from local providers. It may be that the hourly rate for directly employing support workers is significantly higher than Spine Point 8 of the NJC rates (which is often demonstrated once carers have been employed). Also, it will often be more expensive to employ someone to carry out tasks such as home maintenance (including painting and decorating) and gardening than it would be to employ someone to carry out domestic tasks such as hoovering and cleaning. In the absence of local rates, appropriate average figures may be gleaned from the annual publication produced by the Royal Institute of Chartered Surveyors entitled the 'Building Maintenance Price Book' (the applicable rates usually being attributed to 'building craft operators' or 'labourers')[1].

[1] A copy of this book can be obtained from Building Maintenance Information, 3 Cadogan Gate, London SW1X 0AS (tel 020 7695 1500) or the Building Cost Information Service Ltd & Building Maintenance Information website: www.bcis.co.uk/index.html. It should be noted that the costs of maintenance have also shown a substantial increase over and above the rate of inflation in recent years.

(5) AGGREGATE OR FLAT RATES

[F108]   Often, care is provided by friends and relatives during anti-social hours such as evenings, weekends, bank holidays etc. A home help employed on NJC Spine Point 8 would receive various enhancements for working unsociable hours, which forms part of the commercial rate. When assessing past gratuitous care, the following reasons may suggest that, save in exceptional circumstances[1], aggregate rates should generally be preferred over the flat or basic rate:

•   The provision of gratuitous care is not limited to normal working hours. More often than not, care is provided by family members before or after they return from work, during weekends and other holiday periods such as bank holidays, Christmas and Easter. Further, a gratuitous carer may have given up well-paid employment to provide the necessary care, and their loss may far exceed the NJC hourly rate.

- The NJC basic hourly rate does not reflect the actual package that the carer receives. In particular, NJC carers are entitled to benefits such as sick pay, holiday pay and maternity leave. They are also entitled to join the Local Government Pension Scheme, which is a generous final salary pension scheme. This is a benefit that should not be under-estimated. A gratuitous carer giving up paid employment to provide gratuitous care would be significantly under-compensated if he or she was only rewarded at flat NJC rates for ongoing care, when in fact he or she has not only lost employment but also employer contributions towards a pension (which all workers earning over £5,035 will be entitled to from 2012 as a result of the Pension Act 2008). In reality, local government carers are content to accept the low hourly rates of pay because of the additional benefits that they receive.

- Although it is often used as a measure for assessing past nursing care, the basic NJC rate is invariably less than the agreed cost for employing private carers. In any catastrophic injury case, this can readily be seen by comparing the NJC rate allowed for ongoing care with the rate being paid to carers in a private regime and/or the rates suggested for future care (which, in and around London, are often as much as £12 or £14 per hour, particularly for care provided at the weekend). Where care is being provided in part by the family and in part by paid support workers, it is not uncommon to see (defendant) care experts value the gratuitous care at basic NJC rates, which are 30–40% lower than the actual rates being paid to support workers for carrying out exactly the same tasks.

- Although the basic NJC rate (currently £6.84 per hour) is often used to measure past assistance with domestic tasks, the rate is usually significantly less than it costs to employ a private cleaner (circa £8–10 per hour).

- Although it is often used to assess other types of past gratuitous assistance, the basic NJC rate is usually significantly below what would need to be paid for other tasks such as childcare, gardening and DIY.

- NJC carers also enjoy the possibility of career advancement and obtaining higher levels of pay, eg if they take on any managerial responsibility.

As such, arguably the basic NJC rate may not provide 'proper recompense'[2] for the care provided, since it falls far short of the actual commercial cost of the care. It is noteworthy that the care rates published in 'Facts & Figures' are the aggregate hourly rates[3]. Such rates have been awarded or agreed in a number of cases, particularly where there has been a significant element of night care[4]. An alternative to assessing care at the aggregate rate is to value past care using a flat rate, but without any discount to reflect 'the gratuitous element'[5]. However, there are some judges who have declined to award any uplift on the standard rates, to take account of the care provided during unsociable hours because the care was provided gratuitously, and still applied a 25% discount[6].

---

[1]   For example, where all the care has been provided between 9 am and 5 pm on weekdays.

[2]   *Hunt v Severs* [1994] 2 AC 350, per Lord Bridge at 363A; *Evans v Pontypridd Roofing Ltd* [2001] EWCA Civ 1657, per May LJ at [36]. See also *Housecroft v Burnett* [1986] 1 All ER 332, in which O'Connor LJ at 334 referred to the need to provide 'a capital sum ... sufficient ... to make recompense to the relative'.

3   See pp 289–291 of the 2009/2010 edition.

4   *Massey v Tameside and Glossop Acute Services NHS Trust* [2007] EWHC 317 (QB); *Smith v East and North Hertfordshire Hospitals NHS Trust* [2008] EWHC 2234 (QB). Aggregate rates were also agreed in *Pankhurst v (1) White and (2) MIB* [2009] EWHC 1117 (QB). It also appears they were used in *Crofts v Murton* LTL 10/9/2008 and *Beesley v New Century Group* [2008] EWHC 3033 (QB).

5   See eg *Newman v Folkes* [2002] EWCA Civ 591; *A v B Hospitals NHS Trust* [2006] EWHC 1178 (QB); *Warrilow v Norfolk and Norwich Hospitals NHS Trust* [2006] EWHC 801 (QB).

6   *Fairhurst v St Helens and Knowsley Health Authority* [1995] PIQR Q1; *Noble v Owens* [2008] EWHC 359 (QB); *Willisford v (1) Jones and (2) MIB* LTL 11/6/2009.

(6)   Discount to reflect the 'gratuitous element'

[F109]   As seen above, when calculating the claim for gratuitous care, a discount is commonly applied to the commercial rate. The rationale for this discount is fourfold, in order to take account of[1]:

- Tax that the commercial carer would pay.
- National Insurance that the commercial carer would pay.
- Travel expenses that the commercial carer would have incurred[2].
- The fact that the quality of the care provided might be lower than that available professionally[3].

1   See *Evans v Pontypridd Roofing Ltd* [2001] EWCA Civ 1657, per May LJ at [36]: 'It is necessary, I think, to consider why a discount or scaling down is under consideration. The assessment is to determine the proper recompense to the carer for the gratuitous services provided. If the starting point is a reasonable commercial rate for those services, an appropriate scaling down will usually be necessary because that amount is not in fact being paid or received. The payment is by way of damages, which are not subject to tax. It is accepted, I think, that, if the rates under consideration in the present case were paid to a professional carer, they would be subject to tax and National Insurance contributions of about 20%. Mr Purchas submits that there should be additional deductions because a professional carer would have expenses of travel and clothing and other matters resulting from the fact that they are working away from home. He submits that 25% as a total deduction is too little and that Mrs Evans' services in the present case were not specialist services such as justified the deduction of only 25% in *Fairhurst*'.

      Further, in *A v National Blood Authority* [2001] Lloyd's Rep Med 187, Burton J said at 230iii):
      'The justification for the discount is substantially the saving of tax and national insurance (although there may be additional justification for discounts, if, for example, the level of care is inevitably less than a commercial cost because of the absence of special qualifications possessed by a commercial carer). If such discount is not allowed for, then the recipient is receiving, by way of a gross sum including provision for tax and national insurance for which he or she will not in fact have to account to the Revenue, that amount *more* than the cost of commercial care.'

2   Of course, if the gratuitous carer is a friend or relative who does not live with the claimant and has to incur expenses getting to and from the claimant's home in order to provide their services, then this reason for deduction does not apply.

3   However, in many cases it might be argued that, given their love and devotion to the claimant, a gratuitous carer who learns the necessary skills for looking after the claimant may actually provide better care than could be obtained professionally. But, as stated by Burton J in *A v National Blood Authority* [2001] Lloyd's Rep Med 187 at 230ii: 'There is no authority ... that simply giving to a claimant the same services, but with greater affection, would justify payment over and above commercial cost'. Sed quaere: see per Watkins J in *Regan v Williamson* (a fatal claim, but one in which the fatality makes no difference in principle) [1976] 2 All ER 241 at 244e–245a, where he recognised the particular value which a mother's services could have over and above that which could be provided by a commercial carer.

[F110]   Whilst discounts of up to 35% are not unknown[1] in order to take account of these factors, at today's rates of tax and National Insurance, as seen above, the common discount is more likely to be in the region of 20–25%. However, there is no conventional percentage discount, and each case must be decided on its own facts[2]. In *Evans v Pontypridd Roofing Ltd*[3] the defendant argued that the discount made by the judge of 25% was too low and should be increased to 33.33%. As explained by May LJ at [37] and [38] in *Evans v Pontypridd Roofing Ltd*:

'In my judgment, there is no scientific basis for a strictly mathematical answer to this question. Nor is the exercise upon which the court is engaged amenable to such an answer. The assessment has to be a broad one, and what in the end is required is a single broad assessment to achieve a fair result in the particular case. I appreciate that a conventional discount would be convenient and might remove one variable from practical settlement negotiations. But I do not consider that one possible element of a single broad assessment should be required to be a conventional figure. On the contrary, it seems to me that first instance judges should have a latitude to achieve a fair result. For instance, if the gratuitous carer provides specialist care services, that might be reflected in the commercial rates rather than a discount to scale them down. On the other hand, I do not consider that the judge in *Fairhurst* was wrong to allow this element of his assessment to take effect through his discount. Although there may well be elements such as tax and National Insurance contributions which would normally feature as to contributing to a discount, there may in particular cases be other elements which can properly be reflected by a greater or lesser discount. One possibility might be if it were necessary for the assessment for future care to take account of the possibility that the services of the gratuitous carer may not be available for the entire period upon which the assessment is based. That is not to say that this consideration has got to be reflected in an adjustment to a discount; only that in an appropriate case it may be one possibility. That consideration does not arise in the present case on either party's submissionIn my judgment Mr Purchas' submissions do not persuade me that the judge's assessed discount in the present case of 25% was wrong. I am not persuaded that the reasons for making a discount which may be regarded as normal should result in a deduction greater than 25%. There were no grounds in the present case for making a discount which was greater or less than normal. I would uphold this part of the judge's assessment for both past and future care.'

1   See eg *Bordin v St Mary's NHS Trust* [2000] Lloyd's Rep Med 6(287).
2   *Evans v Pontypridd Roofing Ltd* [2001] EWCA Civ 1657. Approved and followed in *Newman v Folkes* [2002] EWCA Civ 591 in which Ward LJ stated at [40]: 'There is, therefore, no conventional discount. Each case depends upon its own facts. In this case there was such a broad margin of matters to take into account that the matter had to be looked at in the round. That is what the judge did. I can see no error of principle, nor did the exercise of his judgment produce a figure which can be said to be plainly wrong. I would, therefore, dismiss the appeal against that head of damages'.
3   [2001] EWCA Civ 1657.

[F111]   While the Court of Appeal was not obviously influenced by the Law Commission's view (which was not expressly referred to in May LJ's judgment), it is perhaps interesting to note that the Law Commission had previously considered that a discount of one-third from that rate to account for tax and other commercial expenses was too high in the economic conditions prevailing in 1999, and that, given the potential infinite factual variations, judges should be left sufficient flexibility to deal with the situation in each case[1].

1   See further paras 3.85 and 3.86 of its Report No 262 'Damages for Personal Injury: Medical, Nursing and other Expenses; Collateral Benefits' (November 1999).

[F112]   In the circumstances, it is perhaps not a particularly worthwhile exercise examining each case where a discount has been applied to the claim for gratuitous care. Notwithstanding May LJ referring to a 25% discount as 'normal' in *Evans v Pontypridd Roofing Ltd*[1], there is clearly no set formula. However, the table at para **[F115]** provides a breakdown of the discounts that have been applied to take account of the 'gratuitous element' in recent cases, which practitioners may wish to follow up if contending for an especially high or low discount in a given case.

1   [2001] EWCA Civ 1657.

[F113]   As one commentator has pointed out, it seems unfair that a discount as much as a third should be allowed against the claim for gratuitous care, bearing in mind that, although the care provider may not pay tax and National Insurance, likewise the carer does not benefit from any of the security of employment such as sick pay, holiday pay, pension, maternity leave etc[1]. Where the professional carer would be on a low wage (eg the national minimum wage), the discount for tax and National Insurance is very unlikely to be as much as 25% or 33.3% (see at paras **[F97]**–**[F99]**). Indeed, it should be noted that there have been a number of cases in which no discount in respect of the 'gratuitous element' has been allowed against the full commercial rate at all. Instances where no discount would be appropriate may include the following factual situations:

*   Where the care provider has given up well-paid employment in order to care for the claimant[2].
*   Where no allowance has been made when calculating the commercial rate of care for services during unsociable hours, ie evenings, nights, weekends and public holidays[3].
*   Where the commercial rates claimed by the claimant are at a lower rate than probably would be charged for the care involved, eg charging at the rates for a 'home help' when the services would have been more appropriately provided by a specialist carer[4].
*   Where the care provided was of extremely high quality[5].
*   Where the care provided is modest and the amount of damages received does not exceed the personal annual tax allowance[6].
*   Where the defendant accepts on the basis of full information the care claim advanced on behalf of the claimant in its counter-schedule without any discount[7].
*   Where the carer, who receives the award for gratuitous care, will actually have to pay tax and National Insurance on the money received[8].

1   See further Jacqueline Webb 'One claimant – two opposing views about the cost of care' [2003] Quantum, Issue 4/2003.

2   See eg *Hogg v Doyle* (6 March 1991, unreported); *Fish v Wilcox* [1994] 5 Med LR 230; *Abdul-Hosn v Trustees of The Italian Hospital* (10 July 1987, unreported), QBD, summarised in *Kemp & Kemp* at B2-006.

3   *Newman v Folkes* [2002] EWCA Civ 591; *A v B Hospitals NHS Trust* [2006] EWHC 1178 (QB); *Warrilow v Norfolk and Norwich Hospitals NHS Trust* [2006] EWHC 801 (QB).

4   *Parry v NW Surrey Health Authority* (29 November 1999, unreported), QBD.

5   *Lamey v Wirral Health Authority* [1993] CLY 1437 in which Morland J held that gratuitous services needed to be assessed 'not only quantitatively but also qualitatively'. Further, in *A v National Blood Authority* [2001] Lloyd's Rep Med 187 at 230, Burton J held that it was 'plainly right that the services must be valued qualitatively as well as quantitatively'. See also *Wells v Wells* [1997] 1 WLR 652, in which the Court of Appeal refused to overturn the original judgment of Dyson J in *Page v Sheerness Steel Co plc* [1996] PIQR Q26 in applying *no* discount for tax and National Insurance. And, more recently, *Brown v King's Lynn and Wisbech NHS Hospitals Trust* (20 December 2000, unreported), in which Gage J also declined to apply a discount in order to reflect the 'gratuitous element' because of the remarkable quality of the care provided, notwithstanding that the full commercial rate had been applied throughout, including an uplift for weekend rates etc.

6   See further *Lane v Lake (Deceased)* LTL 31/7/2007. The personal tax allowance for 2010/11 is £6,475 (although higher rates apply to people aged over 65 and other categories).

7   *Parkhouse v North Devon Healthcare NHS Trust* [2002] Lloyd's Rep Med 100.

8   It is unclear that a gratuitous carer would need to pay tax on payments received for gratuitous care in the UK (see *Lane v Lake (Deceased)* LTL 31/7/2007), but it could happen where the claimant and care provider live abroad.

[F114] Where the care provider has received state benefits or increased payments in respect of the care provided, such benefits or payments should be offset against the calculation of gratuitous care in order to avoid double recovery, in accordance with the principle in *Hodgson v Trapp*[1]. For example, credit has been given for Carer's Allowance[2], Jobseeker's Allowance[3] and Foster payments[4] which would not otherwise have been received but for the claimant's injury. This brings the law into line with the procedure in Scotland where, by virtue of s 8 of the Administration of Justice Act 1982, a pursuer may recover 'reasonable remuneration for those services and repayment of reasonable expenses'; but, under s 10 of the 1982 Act, Scots law provides that account should be taken of any benefit payable from public funds designed to secure to the injured person, or any relative of his or hers, a minimum level of subsistence[5]. However, if a deduction is to be contended for, the point should be raised promptly[6] and credit need not be given for Incapacity Benefit which results from the gratuitous carer's ill-health looking after the claimant[6].

1   [1989] 1 AC 807.

2   *Warrilow v Norfolk and Norwich Hospitals NHS Trust* [2006] EWHC 801 (QB); *Morgan v Phillips* LTL 29/9/2008; *Massey v Tameside & Glossop Acute Services NHS Trust* [2007] EWHC 317 (QB); *Noble v Owens* [2008] EWHC 359 (QB).

3   *Noble v Owens* [2008] EWHC 359 (QB).

4   See eg *Whyte v Barber* (18 February 2003, unreported), QBD. This was an approval hearing of a settlement in which a gratuitous care claim in respect of past care was brought, notwithstanding the fact that the voluntary carers had received foster payments from the local authority. Credit was given as against the past gratuitous care claim for the payment of £15 per week which was specifically attributable to the claimant's disability, but no credit was given for the remainder of the payment which the carers would have received in any event. See further William Norris QC and John Pickering 'Claims for Catastrophic Injury' [2004] JPIL, Issue 1/04.

5   See further Simon Lindsay 'The Cost of Gratuitous Care: Who Cares Who Pays' [2003] JPIL Issue 2/03.

6   See eg *Huntley v Simmonds* [2009] EWHC 405 (QB).

7   *Noble v Owens* [2008] EWHC 359 (QB).

[F115] The following discounts have been applied to gratuitous care claims (court awards):

Case	Judge	Discount (%)
Housecroft v Burnett [1986] 1 All ER 332	Brown J (upheld by CA)	18
Abdul-Hosn v Trustees of The Italian Hospital (10 July 1987, unreported), QBD, summarised in *Kemp & Kemp* at B2-006	Hirst J	0
Maylen v Morris (21 January 1988, unreported)	Mann J (upheld by CA)	25
McCamley v Cammell Laird Shipbuilders Ltd [1990] 1 All ER 854	Caulfield J (upheld by CA)	14
Lamey v Wirral Health Authority (22 September 1993, unreported)	Morland J	0
Nash v Southmead Health Authority [1993] PIQR Q156	Alliot J	33.33
Fairhurst v St. Helens and Knowsley Health Authority [1995] PIQR Q1	HHJ Clark QC	25
Brown v Berry (14 October 1997, unreported), QBD	Robert Seabrook QC sitting as a deputy judge of the High Court	33.33
Sparks v Royal Hospitals NHS Trust (21 December 1998, unreported)	McKinnon J	20
Burns v Davies [1999] Lloyd's Rep Med 215	Connell J	20
Parry v NW Surrey Health Authority (29 November 1999, unreported), QBD	Penry-Davey J	0
Biesheuvel v Birrell [1999] PIQR Q68	Eady J	25
Hardman v Amin [2000] Lloyd's Rep Med 498	Henriques J	25
Barry v Ablerex Construction (Midlands) Ltd [2000] PIQR Q263	Latham J	30
Taylor v Shropshire Health Authority (No 2) [2000] Lloyd's Rep Med 6(96)	Nicholl J	25
Bordin v St. Amry's NHS Trust [2000] Lloyds Rep Med 6(287)	Crane J	35
Brown v King's Lynn and Wisbech NHS Hospitals Trust (20 December 2000, unreported)	Gage J	0*

Case	Judge	Discount (%)
Dorrington v Lawrence (9 November 2001, unreported)	Hooper J	20
O'Brien v Harris (22 February 2001, unreported), QBD	Pitchford J	25
Hassell v Abnoof & Anor (QBD, 6 July 2001, Lawtel Document No AC0101866)	Gage J	15
Evans v Pontypridd Roofing [2001] EWCA Civ 1657	HHJ Prosser QC (upheld by CA)	25
A v National Blood Authority [2001] Lloyd's Rep Med 187	Burton J	25
Parkhouse v Northern Devon Healthcare NHS Trust [2002] Lloyd's Rep Med 100	Gage J	0
Owen v Brown [2002] EWHC 1135 (QB)	Silber J	25
Newman v Folkes [2002] EWCA Civ 591	Garland J (upheld by CA)	0
Pratt v Smith (18 December 2002, unreported), QBD	David Foskett QC	25
Finnis v Caulfield [2002] All ER (D) 353	HHJ Grenfell sitting as a judge of the High Court	25
Taylor v Weston AHA (3 December 2003, QBD, Lawtel Document No AC0106195)	Pitchers J	25
Hart v Pretty (unreported, 18 April 2005)	HHJ Taylor sitting as a judge of the High Court	20
Cannon v Cannon [2005] EWHC 1310 (QB)	Forbes J	25
Warrilow v Norfolk and Norwich Hospitals NHS Trust [2006] EWHC 801 (QB)	Langstaff J	0
A v B Hospitals NHS Trust [2006] EWHC 1178 (QB)	Lloyd-Jones J	0
Tinsley v Sarkar [2006] PIQR Q1	Leveson J	25
Tagg v Countess of Chester Hospital Foundation NHS Trust [2007] EWHC 509 (QB)	McCombe J	25
Burton v Kingsbury [2007] EWHC 2091 (QB)	Flaux J	25

Case	Judge	Discount (%)[1]
Massey v Tameside & Glossop Acute Services NHS Trust [2007] EWHC 317 (QB)	Teare J	20*
Noble v Owens [2008] EWHC 359 (QB)	Field J	25
Smith v East and North Hertfordshire Hospitals NHS Trust [2008] EWHC 2234 (QB)	Penry-Davey J	25*
C v Dixon [2009] EWHC 708 (QB)	King J	25

* Aggregate rates used

(7) THE NATIONAL MINIMUM WAGE

[F116] Presumably, the bottom limit to the quantification of a claim for gratuitous care would now be the national minimum wage[1] adjusted for tax and National Insurance, the effects of which are likely to be minimal at such a low level of wage.

[1]   National Minimum Wage Regulations 1999, SI 1999/584, as amended. The applicable rates from 1 October 2009 are £5.80 for those over 22, or £4.83 per hour for those aged between 18 and 21.

Lump sum award

[F117] Generally speaking, as seen above, where the carer has given up work to care for the claimant, the appropriate award for gratuitous care is usually determined by reference to the care provider's lost earnings (subject to the ceiling principle). Where the carer has not had to give up paid employment, the care claim is calculated by working out the number of hours of care provided per day or week, applying the commercial hourly cost to the same and then discounting the total to reflect the savings made by reason of the fact that the care was provided gratuitously.

[F118] If the facts of a particular case merit such an approach, the court may instead decide to make a broad brush assessment of the care gratuitously provided. This involves the court making an assessment in the round of the value of the voluntary services provided, and awarding one global lump sum reflecting reasonable recompense for the same. For example, in *Giambrone v JMC Holidays*[1], HHJ MacDuff QC adopted this method of assessment and made awards for six claimants, who had suffered from the effects of food poisoning whilst on holiday, of between £120 and £275 for the services provided.

[1]   [2004] EWCA Civ 158 (this judgment was subsequently upheld by the Court of Appeal: [2004] EWCA Civ 158). See also *Collins v Jones* [2003] EWHC 187 (QB), in which Morland J awarded the claimant the global sum of £2,500 in respect of the past care provided by the claimant's wife in the first two years after the accident.

[F119] However, a broad brush assessment is not necessarily limited to trivial or minor cases of injury involving a relatively brief period of care. Such an approach may also be appropriate where it is difficult actually to assess the total number of hours of care provided, or the calculation is hampered by many changes of rate over an extended period. For example, in *Pollitt v Oxfordshire Health Authority*[1], Daniel Brennan QC made a lump sum award of £10,000 for past gratuitous care.

[1]   (16 July 1998, unreported), QBD. See also *Woodrup v Nicol* [1993] PIQR Q104, in which the Court of Appeal awarded the global sum of £3,500 for past care.

Care provided during hospital visits

[F120]   It may be considered that a claimant should not be entitled to recover damages for gratuitous care during the period when the claimant is in hospital receiving treatment from trained professionals. However, compensation for such care provided by friends/relatives during the period of the claimant's hospitalisation will be recoverable, assuming the same is an aid to the claimant's recovery rather than facilitating ordinary social contact which would have occurred in any event[1]. As Beldam LJ stated in *Havenhand v Jeffrey*[2]:

'There is one further matter to which it is necessary to refer. It is a small part of the amount awarded by the Judge, but in his judgment, after paying tribute (as anybody would) to the care which the family gave to their mother when she was in hospital, considered the extent of the claim made on their behalf for payment for assistance given to their mother whilst she was actually in hospital. The appellants argued that it would be wrong to take the entire estimated period during which they were visiting their mother in hospital because, for a large part of the time, they would simply be chatting with her and generally improving her outlook on life, making her feel that her family cared for her and that she was not, as it were, abandoned alone in the hospital. In short, the majority of the hours which were taken up by these hospital visits were the normal hospital visits arising from family affection, and not given for the purpose of providing services which the hospital did not provide.

The Judge clearly accepted that there were occasions on which the family did perform services for the respondent, and the real question was: for how many hours should an award be made and at what rate? The Judge estimated the number of hours during which this family were administering to the respondent in hospital at 400 hours, and Mr Douthwaite says that this is a gross over-estimate of the period. He submits that a figure of 100 hours would be much closer when it is borne in mind that these services consisted, for example, of taking the respondent down to X-ray or for physiotherapy, and going with her when she had to go somewhere about the hospital. They helped to feed the claimant until she was able to feed herself, and they took her for walks in a wheelchair while they were visiting hospital. But Mr Douthwaite says, taking all those factors into account, 100 hours at a rate which the Judge decided should be GBP3.75 per hour was an appropriate award for those services.

I agree with Mr Douthwaite's submission. Though it is a very small amount and involves a reduction in the sum awarded of no more than GBP1,125, nevertheless, the submission was valid and I would accept the 100 hours' figure which Mr Douthwaite puts forward.'

[1]   See eg *Owen v Brown* [2002] EWHC 1135 (QB), in which Silber J allowed 12 hours' gratuitous care per day even though the claimant was in hospital; and *Warrilow v Norfolk and Norwich Hospitals NHS Trust* [2006] EWHC 801 (QB).

[2]   (24 February 1997, unreported), CA. Although it should be noted that this decision now needs to be read in light of the Court of Appeal's more recent decision in *Evans v Pontypridd Roofing Ltd* [2001] EWCA Civ 1657, which applied a less restrictive definition in relation to what constituted 'care'.

[F121] A further example is provided by *O'Brien v Harris*[1], in which Pitchford J awarded the sum claimed of £1,865 for the claimant's wife's attendance at hospital which was considered to be 'essential to the claimant's recovery'. Likewise, in *Warrilow v Warrilow*[2], Langstaff J rejected the argument that *Havenhand v Jeffrey* laid down any principle that 'companionship cannot amount to care'. He distinguished the facts of *Havenhand*, which involved an old lady who may have had various relatives going to visit her in any event. But, where a claimant reasonably requires companionship for psychological or psychiatric stability, it may be recoverable provided the relative would not otherwise have done any similar act[3].

[1]   (22 February 2001, unreported), QBD.
[2]   [2006] EWHC 801 (QB).
[3]   Per Langstaff J at para [159]: 'Care is not only physical labour: time has its cost, and if time is devoted which would not otherwise be, and meets the reasonable needs of an injured party, it deserves recompense'.

[F122] Unfortunately, the decisions in *Owen v Brown, O'Brien v Harris* and *Warrilow v Warrilow* do not appear to have been brought to the attention of Underhill J in the more recent case of *Huntley v Simmonds*[1]. In this case, Underhill J rejected the entire claim for time spent by family members visiting the claimant whilst he was in hospital, accepting the defendant's submission based upon *Havenhand* that no allowance should be made for 'normal hospital visits arising from family affection and not [made] for the purposes of providing services which the hospital did not provide'[2]. The claimant's care expert had justified some allowance for care during hospital visits, on the basis that the family needed to be present in order to 'provide information and support to the clinicians as required' and because 'they were concerned about his safety'. Although these justifications might seem objectively reasonable, no direct evidence was called on this aspect and the claimant had been in a coma for much of the period he was in hospital. Interestingly, when disallowing the claim under this head, Underhill J purportedly relied upon the endorsement of *Havenhand* in *Evans v Pontypridd Roofing Ltd*[3]. However, in *Evans* it was the defendant's counsel, Christopher Purchas QC, who was relying upon *Havenhand* to support his submissions, and there was no express endorsement of a principle arising from *Havenhand* to the effect contended. Indeed, May LJ (with whom Rix and Ward LLJ agreed), specifically held at paras 30–31 that that care did not have to be limited to a stop-watch calculation of actual nursing or physical assistance[4].

[1]   [2009] EWHC 405 (QB). See also *Morgan v Phillips* LTL 29/9/2008.
[2]   It should be noted that, even in *Havenhand*, some allowance was made for services provided; it was just that the award was reduced by the level of ordinary social contact which would have occurred anyway.
[3]   [2001] EWCA Civ 1657.
[4]   See above the reasoning of Langstaff J in *Warrilow v Norfolk and Norwich Hospitals NHS Trust* [2006] EWHC 801 (QB) which, it is submitted, is to be preferred on this point.

(iv)   Deductions to Avoid Double Recovery

Payments received in relation to past care

[F123] Generally speaking, any payments made in respect of past care which are not taken into account under the statutory scheme of recoupment fall to be assessed

at common law in accordance with the principles laid down in *Hodgson v Trapp*[1].
For example, in *Dorrington v Lawrence*[2] the claimant received payments from the
independent living fund. Hooper J stated[3]:

'The independent living fund, a Government funded organisation, has made payments
of £66,524.70 to assist the family to buy in the services of paid carers. These sums are
not repayable. It is agreed that the money has been used for paid carers. The defendant
submits that the claimant should give credit for this money ... It seems to me that,
applying *Hodgson v Trapp*, these sums are deductible and I so decide.'

Applying the same principle, any benefits received by gratuitous carers in respect
of the care they provide, eg by way of Carer's Allowance or Jobseeker's Allowance
which they would not otherwise have received but for the claimant's injury, fall to be
deducted[4]. However, the benefits received need to be considered carefully, since not
all of them may be deducted. For example, in *Noble v Owens*[5] the claimant's partner,
his main carer up to the date of trial, gave up work to care for the claimant and was in
receipt of Carer's Allowance, Jobseeker's Allowance and Incapacity Benefit. Credit
was given in respect of the first two benefits, but not Incapacity Benefit which was only
received because the claimant's partner had suffered ill-health as a result of looking
after him[6]. Where it is suspected that benefits have been received by gratuitous care
providers, it is sensible for the defendant to raise the question of deduction at an early
stage, since the court may not be inclined to discount the claim for past care in respect
of benefits received if the point is not raised promptly and there is no evidence at trial
regarding what the appropriate deduction should be[7].

[1]   [1989] AC 807. See further Chapter J, Recovery of State and Collateral Benefits.
[2]   [2001] All ER (D) 145 (Nov).
[3]   At [35].
[4]   *Warrilow v Norfolk and Norwich Hospitals NHS Trust* [2006] EWHC 801 (QB); *Morgan v Phillips*
       LTL 29/9/2008; *Massey v Tameside & Glossop Acute Services NHS Trust* [2007] EWHC 317 (QB);
       Noble v Owens [2008] EWHC 359 (QB).
[5]   [2008] EWHC 359 (QB).
[6]   The benefit was paid to the claimant's partner not as compensation for looking after him but as
       compensation for her injuries – it would have been unfair to the claimant's partner to make her give
       any credit for this benefit received when she had no right of action to pursue a claim for the injuries
       she had suffered.
[7]   See eg *Huntley v Simmonds* [2009] EWHC 405 (QB).

The domestic element

[F124]   The ordinary living expenses that the claimant would have incurred had
the injury not occurred are deducted from the cost of staying in a private hospital
or home so as not to over-compensate the claimant[1]. This is known as the 'domestic
element'. It includes such expenses as the cost of food, heating and board and lodging,
provided they are not trifling. Evidence has to be adduced to show what proportion
of the hospital expenses are attributable to board and lodging. The court should not
make any deduction in the absence of such evidence[2], unless this can reasonably be
estimated. Thus, the court can take into account savings on food, as this is essentially
a jury question. Useful evidence of the expenses saved may be found in the Family
Earnings Survey[3].

¹   *Lim Poh Choo v Camden and Islington Area Health Authority* [1980] AC 174 at 191–192. See also *Shearman v Folland* [1950] 2 KB 43, in which the expenses that the claimant would have incurred on board and lodging in any event were offset against the claim for private nursing home fees.

²   *Shearman v Folland* [1950] 2 KB 43.

³   See further *Fairhurst v St Helens and Knowsley Health Authority* [1995] PIQR Q1 at Q8–Q9.

[F125] The Administration of Justice Act 1982, s 5 provides that any saving to the injured person which is attributable to his or her maintenance, either wholly or partly, at public expense in a hospital, nursing home or other institution is to be set off against loss of earnings.

Deductions to take account of pre-existing and normal parental care

[F126] In accordance with normal tortious principles, a claimant may only recover for the additional care which has been provided over and above that which would have been provided in any event. But, where care would otherwise have been provided at no cost to the claimant due to pre-existing injuries, it may not be appropriate to deduct a notional allowance to reflect the value of such care¹. Further, when assessing future loss in respect of a severely injured child, it may not be appropriate to deduct 'normal parental care' from the costs of the future paid care where a 24-hour care regime is required². It remains a moot point whether or not the parental care that would have been provided in any event should always be deducted from past gratuitous care. For example, it may be argued that time which would have been spent performing enjoyable activities, such as playing football in the park or supervising games or homework, should not be used to offset the demanding one-to-one physical nursing care required to look after a severely brain-damaged child. In other words, the 'care' that is now required may be of a very different nature and not truly comparable to the care (or, more usually, supervision) that may have been required before. Also, parents with multiple (uninjured) children may be able to supervise them all at the same time without difficulty and/or carry out a number of activities at the same time, eg supervise children whilst cooking or cleaning. However, a severely disabled child may need constant attention, and to deduct the whole time that would have been spent looking after the child whilst looking after other children and/or performing other activities at the same time might be considered to be unfair.

¹   *Sklair v Haycock* [2009] EWHC 3328 (QB).

²   *Stephens v Doncaster Health Authority* [1996] Med LR 357; *Iqbal v Whipps Cross University* [2007] LS Law Medical 97.

(v)   Case Managers¹

[F127] In more serious cases, it may be necessary to appoint a case manager, whose duties might include:

- implementation and management of the claimant's care regime;
- the hiring, firing and disciplining of carers;
- arranging contracts for cares and organising payroll;
- carrying out CRB and background checks on potential carers;
- carrying out risk assessments;

- helping to draw up job descriptions, staff rotas and information packs;
- helping to select an appropriate care agency and then liaising between the claimant and the claimant's care manager at the agency (if care is sourced through an agency);
- liaising between the claimant and different healthcare professionals (such as medical experts, physiotherapists, special and language therapists, carers, occupational therapists etc);
- ensuring that the claimant's care needs are being met and recommending any changes to the existing system;
- managing the claimant's financial affairs and ensuring entitlement to state benefits;
- helping to plan appropriate holidays;
- dealing with accommodation issues, including helping to find suitable alternative accommodation and assisting with locating suitable architects and builders with a view to carrying out necessary adaptations;
- ensuring that the claimant is adequately insured;
- helping to source aids and equipment (with or without the assistance of an occupational therapist); and
- attending multi-disciplinary team meetings.

[1]　The Case Management Society of America defines case management as follows:
　　　'Case Management is a collaborative process which assesses, plans, implements, co-ordinates, monitors and evaluates options and services to meet an individual's health needs through communications and available resources to promote quality cost effective outcomes.'

[F128]　The more structured the claimant's environment – such as residential accommodation – the less likely it is that a case manager will be justified[1]. Further, an eye should be kept on the cost of any case management, to ensure that the same is reasonable and accords with any previous estimate given[2].

[1]　See eg *Thrul v Ray* [2000] PIQR Q44, in which Burton J held that a case manager was not necessary, given the provision of assistance to the claimant by staff at her residential home and the local authority care manager.
[2]　See eg *O'Brien v Harris* (22 February 2001, unreported), QBD, in which Pitchford J limited the amount claimed for past rehabilitation and case management costs because the sums claimed significantly exceeded the estimates given without adequate explanation. See also *Hart v Pretty* (unreported, 18 April 2005).

[F129]　Where case management has been provided gratuitously, there is no reason why this should not be recovered and held on trust for the person providing the services in the usual way[1].

[1]　In *Massey v Tameside & Glossop Acute Services NHS Trust* [2007] EWHC 317 (QB), Teare J awarded £8,750 for past gratuitous case management. Similar awards have been subsequently agreed in other cases such as *A v Powys Local Health Board* [2007] EWHC 2996 (QB) and *Noble v Owens* [2008] EWHC 359 (QB).

(vi)　Other Types of Care/Supervision

[F130]　In appropriate cases, it may be reasonable for the claimant to have paid for other types of care/supervision. For example, in head injury cases it is not uncommon for a buddy or coach to be involved in order to supervise the claimant's outings, to ensure that the claimant takes their medication, and to make sure that the claimant's behaviour is kept under control[1]. Alternatively, a professional mentor might be useful to encourage the claimant in his or her rehabilitation and return to work, a personal assistant might be required in order to help with the claimant's business needs, and a banking service can be used to assist the claimant with his or her finances[2].

[1] See eg *Goldfinch v Scannell* [1993] PIQR Q143, in which the trial judge found that the claimant required daily supervision to ensure that she behaved herself reasonably, took her medication regularly and to help with cooking, finances and general household management.

[2] In *O'Brien v Harris* (22 February 2001, unreported), QBD, claims were made for a personal assistant and 'a premier banking service'. Pitchford J awarded the claimant the sum of £1,822, although this was discounted to take account of the periods in which the assistance was not necessary as a result of the claimant's disability. See also *A v Powys Local Health Board* [2007] EWHC 2996 (QB).

7 Aids, Equipment and Appliances

[F131] Traditionally, the expenses for aids and appliances which the claimant incurred were taken into account in the loss of amenity award. Since 1980, however, different expenses have been allowed separately on a case-by-case basis. There nevertheless remains a danger of overlap between the expense and the loss of amenity award[1].

[1] As regards the question of overlap between pecuniary and non-pecuniary loss, see further Chapters A, General Principles, and D, General Damages.

[F132] As a general rule, if the expense can be shown to have arisen out of a genuine medical or therapeutic need and it was reasonably necessary for the claimant, the cost of the item will be recoverable. Care should be taken to consider the following questions:

- Is the claim for the aid, appliance or item of equipment supported by the medical evidence[1]?
- Does the claimant have the necessary capacity to use and benefit from the aid, appliance or item of equipment claimed[2]?
- Does the claimant and/or the litigation friend understand the need for and actually want the aid, appliance or item of equipment claimed[3]?
- Might the aid, appliance or item of equipment claimed have been purchased by the claimant in any event[4]?
- Is the expense of the aid, appliance or item of equipment unreasonably disproportionate to the anticipated benefit that it will bring?
- Are there less expensive alternatives, and could the claimant make do with something he or she already has?

[1] See eg *Cottrell v Redbridge Healthcare NHS Trust* (2001) 61 BMLR 72, in which the claim for the past cost of a reclining chair was disallowed on the basis that the medical experts in their joint report had agreed that such a chair was unnecessary.

[2] See eg *Dorrington v Lawrence* [2001] All ER (D) 145 (Nov), in which Hooper J disallowed a claim for a computer and £600-worth of software because the claimant already had a computer which he did not use, and it was unclear whether the claimant had the capacity to make use of the software that was recommended.

³   See eg in *Blair v Michelin Tyre* (25 January 2002, unreported), HHJ Marr-Johnson sitting as a judge of the QBD, the trial judge rejected the claim for a second wheelchair because the claimant did not seem keen on it and it 'might seldom, if ever, be used'.

⁴   Some items such as TVs, videos, mobile phones, cookers, washing machines and dishwashers may be considered normal everyday household items which the claimant may well have bought in any event. See eg *Parkhouse v North Devon Healthcare NHS Trust* [2002] Lloyd's Rep Med 100, in which Gage J disallowed the claims for a microwave, a dishwasher, TV, video and lawnmower, since these were 'everyday household items' and were not attributable to the claimant's injuries. In *O'Brien v Harris* (22 February 2001, unreported), QBD, Pitchford J disallowed claims for a Walkman, radio, computer, scanner, software and stylewriter because the same were either purchases for recreation and hobbies, which would have been incurred in an alternative form in any event, or purchases which would have been made irrespective of the accident. See also *Ved v Caress* (9 April 2001, unreported), QBD, where HHJ Chapman disallowed the cost of an automatic transmission because he held that the claimant, who was a professional woman, would probably have bought an automatic car in any event. A laptop was disallowed in *Huntley v Simmonds* [2009] EWHC 405 (QB) because it was held that the claimant would have bought one in any event.

[F133]   Once it is anticipated that the claimant might benefit from specialist equipment, consideration should be given to obtaining a care report from an occupational therapist or a nurse with special experience in providing such reports. Experience has shown that care reports in serious cases will put forward a large number of appliances that should be considered in the claim. It is impossible to set out an exhaustive list of the appliances and aids that may be appropriate in this work. However, in appropriate cases in addition to instructing an expert in occupational therapy, thought should also be given to instructing a separate expert in relation to prosthetics[1], information technology[2] and bespoke footwear / orthotics[3].

¹   See eg *Sparks v Royal Hospitals NHS Trust* (21 December 1998, unreported); *Pinnington v Crossleigh Construction* [2003] EWCA Civ 1684.

²   See eg *Burton v Kingsbury* [2007] EWHC 2091 (QB); and *Noble v Owens* [2008] EWHC 359 (QB).

³   See eg *Cannon v Cannon* [2005] EWHC 1310 (QB).

[F134]   It should be noted that, as long as it was reasonable to purchase the same, it is not necessarily relevant that the aid, appliance or item of equipment claimed may have been available on the NHS[1]. Also, as regards some items of aids and equipment, such as prosthetics, it is often the case that the most sophisticated and life-like limbs are not available on the NHS[2]. When items are purchased privately, an allowance may be required to cover delivery and/or shipping charges[3].

¹   *Bishop v Hannaford* (21 December 1988, unreported), Otton J (as he then was); and *Parkhouse v North Devon Healthcare NHS Trust* [2002] Lloyd's Rep Med 100. See further Law Reform (Personal Injuries) Act 1948, s 2(4) which provides that '... there shall be disregarded, in determining the reasonableness of any expenses the possibility of avoiding those expenses or part of them by taking advantage of facilities available under the National Health Service'. See also *Eagle v Chambers (No 2)* [2004] EWCA Civ 1033; and *Pinnington v Crossleigh Construction* [2003] EWCA Civ 1684 regarding a claim for prosthetics.

²   See eg *Sparks v Royal Hospitals NHS Trust* (21 December 1998, unreported), in which McKinnon J allowed the costs of prosthetics from Dorset Orthopaedics because their silicone cosmetic covers were the most life-like limbs available on the market at the time and, 'all things being equal', the claimant was entitled to say she wanted the most life-like limb.

³   *A v Powys Local Health Board* [2007] EWHC 2996 (QB).

[F135]   In general, however, the item of equipment may be ancillary to care needs, or the educational and/or working needs of the claimant. Each aspect of his or her life has to be thought through to decide whether equipment is available which is reasonably necessary to help the claimant. Only equipment that is reasonably necessary for the individual claimant will be recoverable. The claimant may need the use of various aids and appliances to enable him or her to live as conventional a life as possible. These may vary in cost and sophistication, up to and including technologically advanced computer systems giving the claimant the ability to communicate and to control his or her home environment[1], and, especially in the case of visually handicapped people, guide dogs or other trained animals. Also, in the case of amputees there might be a range of prosthetic devices which may allow the claimant to mobilise again. Claims for such prosthetics may run into several hundred thousand pounds (particularly the future costs), since it may be necessary for the claimant to have several different types, eg everyday prosthetics, sports prosthetics and spare prosthetics[2].

[1]   However, in *Leon Seng Tan v Bunnage* (23 July 1986, unreported), Gatehouse J refused to award the cost of a computer because he found that the claimant, who had been studying with a view to a possible career in electronics, would have bought one anyway. With the increasingly widespread purchase of computers for personal use, the difficulty in recovering damages in respect of at least a conventional computer is likely to increase.

[2]   See eg *DT v Dr Rohatgi* (21 July 2004), Lawtel Document No AM0200647, in which £215,000 was claimed for prosthetics; *A v B NHS Hospitals Trust* (17 June 2004), Lawtel Document No AM0200683, in which the claimant recovered prosthetics costs of £265,300; and *Re P* (March 2004), Lawtel Document No AM0200602, in which the claimant was awarded £484,755 for prosthetics.

[F136]   The issues concerning equipment claims usually relate to:

* the need for appropriateness, cost and replacement intervals of the equipment;
* the provision of some items – such as wheelchairs at public expense – and also as to the adequacy of this equipment; and
* an allowance for eg computers and washing machines, on the basis that the claimant would have bought them anyway, and would have used them less frequently and to a less expensive specification and without the specialist hardware and software tailored to the claimant's disability.

[F137]   Like certain other past losses, expenses for aids and appliances can be divided into 'wasting assets' and 'appreciating assets'. Wasting assets wear out from time to time and need to be replaced, whereas an appreciating asset does not. Even where particular items can be treated as capital expenditure because they do not recur on a regular basis, they may still recur in the future when the equipment wears out, and damages should be assessed accordingly. The calculation of the loss is different depending on the type of asset in question. In the case of a wasting asset, the annual cost of the item needs to be calculated and this usually involves the following:

* the initial capital cost of the item;
* any duplicate costs (eg if the item of equipment is needed at home and at school, work or a relative's house[1]);
* its reasonable life expectancy;
* its replacement cost (usually the same as its initial capital cost);
* the maintenance or running costs; and
* costs of special adaptations, if any.

[1]   See further the award for aids and equipment in *A v Powys Local Health Board* [2007] EWHC 2996 (QB).

[F138]   For example, a claimant may require a motorised wheelchair:

- The initial cost of purchasing the wheelchair is, say, £10,000 and it will need replacing every ten years. However, beyond this, there is the cost of maintaining this chair (insurance, batteries, repairs etc) of £500 per year.
- Therefore, although the initial cost is only £10,000, there needs to be compensation in respect of the future cost of replacement. This is £500 per year maintenance and £1,000 per year (£10,000 divided by the ten-year life expectancy) for replacement. If the life multiplier is 10, then the total damages in respect of the wheelchair amount to £25,000.

[F139]   Where there is a dispute between the parties concerning the reasonableness or cost of a particular item, it may be of assistance for a claimant to pray in aid the decision in *Rialis*[1]. In *A v Powys Local Health Board*[2], Lloyd-Jones J held that the *Rialis* principle, which applies to care needs, applies equally to aids and equipment. Lloyd-Jones J stated at para [94]:

> 'The claimant is entitled to damages to meet her reasonable requirements and reasonable needs arising from her injuries. In deciding what is reasonable it is necessary to consider first whether the provision chosen and claimed is reasonable and not whether, objectively, it is reasonable or whether other provision would be reasonable. Accordingly, if the treatment claimed by the claimant is reasonable it is no answer for the defendant to point to cheaper treatment which is also reasonable. *Rialis* and *Sowden* were concerned with the appropriate care regime. However, the principles stated in those cases apply equally to the assessment of damages in respect of aids and equipment. In determining what is required to meet the claimant's reasonable needs it is necessary to make findings as to the nature and extent of the claimant's needs and then to consider whether what is proposed by the claimant is reasonable having regard to those needs'.

[1]   6 July 1984 (CA), as approved in *Sowden v Lodge* [2005] 1 WLR 2129.
[2]   [2007] EWHC 2996 (QB).

[F140]   Applying this reasoning, Lloyd-Jones J went on to hold that it was irrelevant that the defendant's occupational therapy expert had suggested a cheaper bed, even thought it met the claimant's needs, since the bed claimed for by the claimant was reasonable[1]. Some may argue that this conclusion goes too far and that, where there is a cheaper item which meets the claimant's needs, then it cannot be irrelevant and the judge should be restricted to awarding the lesser sum[2]. More often than not, however, there will be a difference in quality between the more expensive and the cheaper item, and there may be a range of pros and cons which need to be weighed up. This is evident in other parts of Lloyd-Jones J's judgment, for example, where he compares the relative merits and demerits of the portable hoist and the bath suggested by each party's respective expert. If there is in reality no difference between the item being claimed on behalf of the claimant and the item allowed by the defendant save for the cost, assuming they both reasonably meet the claimant's needs, then the claimant should be restricted to claiming the cheaper item. However, on the basis that you usually 'get what you pay for', there are often distinct advantages or benefits associated with purchase of the more expensive item and, when assessing the question of reasonableness, the court may consider proportionality, ie whether the additional benefits are worth the extra cost. If the two versions of the disputed item are similar but each with different advantages and disadvantages, it is submitted that the judge has a wide discretion. Assuming both items reasonably meet the claimant's needs and are not disproportionate, then a generous judge might allow the more expensive item, and the mean judge might allow the cheaper item. However, it is unlikely that the aggrieved party in either case would be able to launch a successful appeal.

[1]   6 July 1984 (CA), as approved in *Sowden v Lodge* [2005] 1 WLR 2129.
[2]   See further James Rowley QC 'Serious Personal Injury Litigation – a Quantum Update' [2008] JPIL 109.

8   Accommodation and Housing Expenses

(i)   The Claimant's Home

[F141]   The claimant's home may need to be altered and adapted. Typical alterations include: installation of ramps or lifts for a wheelchair; alterations in the internal layout of the premises; installation of a hoist and any strengthening of the structure which this might necessitate; constructing a tarmac drive; and creation of extra storage space to accommodate wheelchairs and other aids and appliances. In very serious cases, it may be necessary to create living accommodation for carers. The claimant's existing home may well be unsuitable to be adapted for wheelchair access in this way, especially if it is on multiple levels, and it may therefore be reasonable to move to more suitable accommodation[1]. By the time of trial, accommodation may have been purchased. If so, the following form part of the claim for past loss:

*   The cost of acquisition (or extension) of the new house and sale of the old[2].
*   The cost of any necessary alterations[3].
*   The cost of providing accommodation for the claimant's carer(s)[4].
*   The cost of providing any necessary additional furnishings and fittings (eg carpets and curtains and fitting out a room for a full-time carer)[5].

[1]   What is to be regarded as suitable accommodation is usually a matter for expert evidence. Rented accommodation is usually not appropriate because of the difficulty of finding rented accommodation which meets the claimant's needs and/or where the landlord is happy to permit alterations. There is some authority to suggest that factors other than purely functional factors will be taken into consideration, eg the desire to live near to family and friends: *Biesheuval v Birrell* [1999] PIQR Q40. See also *M (a child) v Leeds Health Authority* [2002] PIQR Q4.
[2]   In *George v Pinnock* [1973] 1 WLR 118, Orr LJ stated (at 125) that the claimant would 'have been entitled to claim the expenses of a move to a new home imposed by her condition and the expense of any new items of furniture required because of that condition'. See also *Parkhouse v North Devon Healthcare NHS Trust* [2002] Lloyd's Rep Med 100 as regards the costs of the claimant's parents moving house. In *Warrilow v Norfolk and Norwich Hospitals NHS Trust* [2006] EWHC 801 (QB), Langstaff J allowed the costs of moving from Norwich to the north-west because these costs were caused or contributed to by the need to move there in respect of care.
[3]   *Roberts v Johnstone* [1989] QB 878; *Willett v North Bedfordshire Health Authority* [1993] PIQR Q166; *Campbell v Mylchreest* [1999] PIQR Q17. See also *Taylor v (1) Chesworth and (2) MIB* [2007] EWHC 1001 (QB), in which it was accepted that the claimant required a larger home than he otherwise would have needed due to the need to provide accommodation for a support worker.
[4]   See eg *Fitzgerald v Ford* [1996] PIQR Q72 at Q83, in which the Court of Appeal upheld the trial judge's decision that each of two carers would require their own room.
[5]   *George v Pinnock* [1973] 1 WLR 118.

[F142]   The purchase cost, as distinct from the costs of agents, solicitors etc, does not form part of the recoverable loss on a pound-for-pound basis. A *'Roberts v Johnstone'* calculation has to be made (detailed in Chapter H), since it involves calculating the difference in capital value between old and new properties[1] and applying a notional 2.5% interest rate[2] to the resulting sum, and then multiplying the interest figure produced by the multiplier appropriate to the lifetime of the claimant. If, however, the property is extended or acquired before trial, then the 2.5% rate per annum (simple interest) will be applied to the capital spent (including any enhancement to value), or the capital difference between the sale and purchase prices of the old and new properties (taking into account any enhancement in value)[3]. The question of whether the alterations are reasonable will be judged by reference to the appropriate care regime[4]. Generally speaking, it is usually recognised that it is reasonable for a live-in carer to have his or her own room in the claimant's new accommodation[5]. Furthermore, when judging the issue of reasonableness, the claimant's background, culture and religion may be relevant[6].

[1]   Although it should be noted that, if new accommodation needs to be bought for the claimant but the old property is kept, eg for the claimant's partner and children who are unable to live together with the claimant, then it might not be necessary to give any credit for the equity in the old home: *Crookdake v Drury* [2003] EWHC 1938 (QB).

[2]   See further *Willett v North Bedfordshire Health Authority* [1993] PIQR Q166; *Almond v Leeds Western Health Authority* [1990] 1 Med LR 370; and Chapter H at para **[H251]**.

[3]   In accordance with the Lord Chancellor's decision to set the discount rate at 2.5%.

[4]   *Campbell v Mylchreest* [1999] PIQR Q17.

[5]   See eg *Fitzgerald v Ford* [1996] PIQR Q72 at Q83, in which the Court of Appeal accepted that it was reasonable and necessary for two carers each to have separate rooms in the claimant's new accommodation.

[6]   See eg *Ahsan v University Hospitals Leicester NHS Trust* [2006] EWHC 2624 (QB).

[F143]   It should be noted that, in some cases where the local authority provides the claimant with adequate accommodation, he or she might be held to have suffered no loss. It will not be possible to claim the costs of re-housing the claimant privately if his or her needs are already being met. It all depends upon the facts of the case and whether or not the local authority's provision of accommodation reasonably meets the claimant's needs[1]. The guiding principle is 'reasonableness'[2]. The reasonable course of action is not necessarily the cheapest and is a question of fact in each case[3]. For example, it may be reasonable to purchase a property at greater expense than expected if the claimant undertook a significant search and there were no other suitable properties in the area[4], particularly if he or she relied upon expert advice when purchasing the relevant property[5]. Evidence must be produced to show that it was reasonably necessary for the past accommodation costs to have been incurred[6]. However, as long as this can be done, it will be no defence to say, for example, that the claimant should have been cared for in an institution as opposed to at home[7]. In the event that the local authority does provide an injured claimant with new accommodation under its statutory obligations, the associated costs are unlikely to be recoverable directly from the defendant, because the defendant will probably not owe the local authority a duty of care[8]. But a claimant who acts with unnecessary haste, and purchases a house without proper consideration for the results of the survey, may be found to have acted imprudently and therefore unreasonably[9].

[1]   Compare *Sowden v Lodge* [2004] EWCA Civ 1370 with *Crookdake v Drury* [2003] EWHC 1938 (QB) (upheld in *Sowden v Lodge* [2004] EWCA Civ 1370). See also the comments of Lord Denning MR in *Cunningham v Harrison* [1973] QB 942 at 952, where account was taken of suitable state

accommodation that would have been available to the claimant within two years. See further William Norris QC and John Pickering 'Claims for Compensation and entitlement to the provision of services from public funds: some issues arising in *Whyte v Barber*' [2003] JPIL, Issue 3/03, at 183–198.

2   *Cunningham v Harrison* [1973] QB 942, where Lord Denning MR emphasised that accommodation and nursing claims must be kept to 'reasonable limits'; and *Rialis v Mitchell* (1984) Times, 17 July. See also *O'Brien v Harris* (22 February 2001, unreported), QBD, in which Pitchford J disallowed the costs of moving to the 'dream house' of the claimant's parents over and above the reasonable costs of accommodation which were directly attributable to the claimant's injuries. See also *Pankhurst v (1) White and (2) MIB* [2009] EWHC 1117 (QB).

3   *Rialis v Mitchell* (1984) Times, 17 July.

4   See eg *Sarwar v (1) Ali and (2) MIB* [2007] EWHC 1255 (QB); *Smith v East and North Hertfordshire Hospitals NHS Trust* [2008] EWHC 2234 (QB).

5   See eg *Sarwar v (1) Ali and (2) MIB* [2007] EWHC 1255 (QB).

6   *Cunningham v Harrison* [1973] QB 942; *George v Pinnock* [1973] 1 WLR 118.

7   *Rialis v Mitchell* (1984) Times, 17 July; *Peters v East Midlands Strategic HA* [2009] EWCA Civ 145.

8   *Mayor & Burgess of Islington London Borough v University College London Hospital* [2004] EWHC 1754 (QB).

9   *Pankhurst v (1) White and (2) MIB* [2009] EWHC 1117 (QB).

[F144]   Credit must be given for any accommodation expenses that the claimant would have incurred in any event[1] assuming the same were not speculative[2]. Although where, in the absence of the injuries, the claimant might reasonably have been expected to purchase accommodation jointly with a partner, credit should only be given for 50% of the equity in the property that would have been purchased in any event[3].

1   See eg the first instance judgment of Collins J in *Thomas v Brighton Health Authority* [1996] PIQR 30; *Biesheuval v Birrell* [1999] PIQR Q40; and *Lynham v The Morecambe Bay Hospitals NHS Trust* [2002] EWHC 823 (QB). See also the Court of Appeal's decision in *Evans v Pontypridd Roofing Ltd* [2001] EWCA Civ 1657, where the claimant's notional rent costs were offset against the *Roberts v Johnstone* accommodation claim. Although note that, where the old property is kept on, eg for the claimant's partner and children (who cannot live together with the claimant), then it might not be necessary to give credit for these expenses against the *Roberts v Johnstone* calculation if a whole new property has to be bought in order to house the claimant: *Crookdake v Drury* [2003] EWHC 1938 (QB).

2   *Parkhouse v North Devon Healthcare NHS Trust* [2002] Lloyd's Rep Med 100.

3   *M (a child) v Leeds Health Authority* [2002] PIQR Q4; *Iqbal v Whipps Cross University* [2007] LS Law Medical 97; *Sarwar v (1) Ali and (2) MIB* [2007] EWHC 1255 (QB). Although, arguably, if the claimant had bought a property with a friend or partner, he or she would have bought a more expensive property.

[F145]   But no credit is to be given to reflect the benefit that the claimant's parents might receive of living rent free in new accommodation purchased as a result of the claimant's injuries, because it is a benefit to the parents not to the claimant due to the considerable extra love and support the parents are likely to provide to the claimant[1]. Likewise, if the claimant is living rent free in his partner's property as at the time of the accident, there is no need to give credit for the 'notional costs' of his accommodation or his partner's accommodation costs[2]. Any benefit to the claimant's partner being able to live rent free in the claimant's property is a benefit to the partner, and is not to be offset against the claimant's claim, in the same way that the partner is unable to claim for any losses that he or she has suffered.

1   *Parkhouse v North Devon Healthcare NHS Trust* [2002] Lloyd's Rep Med 100; *M (a child) v Leeds Health Authority* [2002] PIQR Q4; *Iqbal v Whipps Cross University* [2007] LS Law Medical 97; cf *Lewis v Shrewsbury NHS Trust* (29 January 2007).
2   *Noble v Owens* [2008] EWHC 359 (QB).

[F146] It is unclear whether the claimant should have to give any credit for a windfall profit due to the increase in house prices following a property purchase as a result of the claimant's injuries (eg using an interim payment)[1].

1   See further *O'Brien v Harris* (22 February 2001, unreported), QBD, in which Pitchford J was alive to this argument but, on the facts of the case, did not have to decide the same. Although cf *Edward Maxim Parry v North West Area Health Authority* (2000) Times, 5 January, regarding the treatment of interim payments, in which Penry-Davey J held that credit interest did not have to be given for an interim payment after judgment had been entered. Also, if account could be taken of a windfall profit arising out of the advantageous use of an interim payment, it would seem to offend against the principle that the court is not concerned with what the claimant spends his or her money on: see further *Wells v Wells* [1999] AC 345, per Lord Clyde at 394H; and Chapter A at para **[A110]**; and it would imply the converse – if money had to be spent on more expensive accommodation than would otherwise be the case and property values fell, there would on this principle arguably be a loss – yet this does not appear to be the law.

(ii) The Claimant's Parents' Home

[F147] In *Biesheuval v Birrell*, the defendant objected to the claim for past adaptations to the claimant's parents' house in order to facilitate regular visits from the claimant. As regards past adaptations, Eady J stated[1]:

'I agree that the family was very close prior to the accident, although naturally the [claimant] could not have been such a frequent visitor had he continued to live in the United Kingdom. Further, as I have already recognised, the ready availability of their home and personal support was invaluable to him over the last few years in coming to terms with his difficulties, as I am sure it will continue to be in the future.

I have come to the conclusion that these heads of expenditure are reasonably recoverable as part of the compensation exercise and I therefore award the sum of 114,611 guilders.'

Where it is reasonable for adaptations to be made for the claimant to make regular visits, it may also be appropriate for there to be necessary equipment (such as special toilets and air conditioning) in both homes[2].

1   [1999] PIQR Q40 at Q44. See also *Noble v Owens* [2008] EWHC 359 (QB), in which Field J allowed the one-off sum of £10,000 for adaptations to houses of friends and family.
2   See further the award for aids and equipment in *A v Powys Local Health Board* [2007] EWHC 2996 (QB).

[F148] Further, in *Parkhouse v North Devon Healthcare NHS Trust*[1], Gage J allowed the costs of the claimant's parents purchasing a house because the costs were incurred on behalf of the claimant and it was speculative that they would have moved in any event. Following the decision in *Hunt v Severs*[2], any damages recovered by the claimant for costs incurred by his or her parents will be held in trust for them.

1   [2002] Lloyd's Rep Med 100.
2   [1994] 2 AC 350.

(iii) Increased Household Expenses

[F149] Where, by reason of the adaptations carried out to the claimant's existing accommodation or, alternatively, the purchase of new accommodation resulting from the claimant's injuries, it might be the case that additional running costs are incurred over and above those the claimant could have expected in any event. For example, claims can be made for the increased amounts of council tax, building insurance[1], maintenance, heating[2], etc actually paid. The claimant might also incur increased DIY, gardening or decorating bills, eg repairing damage caused by wheelchair use[3].

---

[1]   In *Parkhouse v North Devon Healthcare NHS Trust* [2002] Lloyd's Rep Med 100, Gage J allowed the excess council tax and increased building insurance incurred by the claimant living in a larger property, although allowed some discount against the claim for increased insurance to reflect the chance that the claimant might have bought his own accommodation in any event.

[2]   In *Warrilow v Norfolk and Norwich Hospitals NHS Trust* [2006] EWHC 801 (QB), Langstaff J allowed the claim for past and future heating on the basis that, but for her injuries, the claimant would not have spent so much time in her house.

[3]   *Owen v Brown* [2002] EWHC 1135 (QB).

(iv) Proposal for the Future

[F150] In its consultation paper 'The Law of Damages' published on 4 May 2007, the Ministry of Justice sought views on possible alternatives to the *Roberts v Johnstone* method of assessment. There was a lack of consensus in the answers to the consultation. The Government indicated an intention to ask the Civil Justice Council's Serious Injury Committee to review the area and consider the merits of the various suggestions made. A working party has also been set up to consider the issue of accommodation and periodical payments, particularly in cases involving short life expectancy. It remains to be seen what, if anything, will come of these initiatives.

9 Travel and Transport Costs

(i) Generally

[F151] The claimant is entitled to reimbursement in respect of any travel expenses reasonably incurred as a result of his or her injuries. Such expenses include the cost of getting from A to B, as well as any associated costs such as parking. Common additional travel expenses incurred as a result of injuries include those:

- Attending the hospital and doctor's appointments.
- Attending treatment and therapy appointments, eg physiotherapy.
- Attending the police, repair garage or purchasing replacement chattels.
- Fulfilling duties that the claimant would otherwise have done.
- Collecting prescriptions.
- Flying back early from holiday or cancelling a planned trip.
- Getting the train to work because the motor vehicle usually used is being repaired following the accident.
- Using a taxi to go to the shops or visit friends when otherwise the claimant would have walked, used public transport or a company car[1].

- Hiring a vehicle during the period of time that the claimant's car is being repaired.
- Travelling further than was previously required to get to and from an alternative job[2].

---

[1]   See eg *Dixon v Were* [2004] EWHC 2273 (QB); *Warrilow v Norfolk and Norwich Hospitals NHS Trust* [2006] EWHC 801 (QB); *Garth v (1) Grant and (2) MIB*, QBD, LTL 17/7/2007; *Huntley v Simmonds* [2009] EWHC 405 (QB).

[2]   See eg *Morgan v MOD* [2002] EWHC 2072 (QB).

(ii)   Costs of Attending Legal and Medico-legal Appointments

[F152]   Travel costs incurred attending medico-legal appointments with experts and lawyers are not recoverable as damages. Technically, such expenses are, strictly speaking, costs and are not claimable as damages, since they arise out of the litigation rather than the injuries[1].

---

[1]   *O'Brien-King v Phillips* [1997] CLY 1814; *Lane v Lake (Deceased)* LTL 31/7/2007; *Van Wees v (1) Karkour and (2) Walsh* [2007] EWHC 165 (QB); *Tagg v Countess of Chester Hospital Foundation NHS Trust* [2007] EWHC 509 (QB).

(iii)   Assessment of Travel Expenses

[F153]   Generally speaking, the assessment of travel expenses does not pose any difficulties. The claimant will be entitled to recover the expenses/losses incurred as long as the sums claimed are reasonable. Where the claimant has personally incurred the cost of a train ticket, for instance, it will be difficult to challenge the cost of the same unless, say, it was unreasonable for the claimant to have travelled first class or before 9.30 am when the ticket might have been more expensive. However, the cost of mileage claimed often leads to dispute. Claimants often tend to claim mileage at the rates allowed by the HMRC or the Legal Services Commission (at 40 pence per mile or more). Although these higher rates are sometimes allowed[1], unless the claimant has had to purchase a vehicle as a result of his or her injuries, he or she should, in theory, probably be restricted to claiming the running charges as set out by the AA or RAC (and listed in 'Personal Injury Damages Statistics' by Rodney Nelson-Jones and in 'Facts & Figures' produced by the Professional Negligence Bar Association)[2]. However, it should be noted that these tables do not appear to allow for depreciation caused by driving additional miles and, therefore, where the additional mileage is significant, reliance upon them without adjustment is likely to produce an underestimate of the true cost.

---

[1]   See eg *Newman v Folkes* [2002] PIQR Q2, in which 30 pence per mile was allowed by the trial judge (this case was subsequently appealed to the Court of Appeal but not on this point); 35 pence per mile was allowed in *Burton v Kingsbury* [2007] EWHC 2091 (QB); 36 pence per mile was allowed in *Tagg v Countess of Chester Hospital Foundation NHS Trust* [2007] EWHC 509 (QB); and 40 pence per mile was accepted as appropriate in *Cannon v Cannon* [2005] EWHC 1310 (QB).

[2]   *Haines v Airedale NHS Trust* (2 May 2000, unreported), QBD, per Bell J, who allowed 12 pence per mile. See also *Eagle v Chambers (No 2)* [2003] EWHC 3135 (QB), in which Cooke J allowed 7.5 pence per mile (although this case was subsequently appealed to the Court of Appeal, this point was not in issue on appeal).

(iv) Transport and Increased Running Expenses

[F154] The claimant's condition may make it reasonable for him or her to purchase or adapt a car or other vehicle. These days, most claimants, if they had not been injured, would have owned a car in any event which they would probably have paid for out of their earnings. Therefore, care should be taken to ensure that only the extra transport needs or costs arising from the injuries are claimed for.

[F155] Allowance may need to be made for the following:

* the need to drive a larger vehicle;
* more miles are likely to be covered, since the disabled person may not be able to walk, or to use public transport, both of which are cheaper;
* the need for regular replacement, because a premium has to be placed on reliability, which, of course, diminishes with age (and also potential greater use of the vehicle);
* increased insurance costs be incurred, eg for carers to drive; and
* increased servicing and maintenance costs (especially if the claimant previously undertook this work).

[F156] A car is, of course, a considerable financial asset, but in *Woodrup v Nicol*[1] the Court of Appeal held that a car ought to be treated as a wasting asset, in the same way as a piece of equipment such as a special bed, which might be expected to wear out periodically. Therefore, the correct approach was to assess a figure which would purchase the car (the purchase price – plus adaptation expenses less any money that would have been spent in any event), and add to that a surplus which, when invested, would enable the claimant to replace the car as many times as necessary (which may require expert evidence) within the period to be covered (usually the claimant's life expectancy), taking into account the likely 'trade-in' value of the car[2]. However, the same approach is not necessarily appropriate to any adaptations to the claimant's vehicle. These may not have any resale value, and may in fact devalue the vehicle because they might need to be removed before resale[3]. Common adaptations include automatic transmission, hand controls[4], hoists and accelerator pedals. In the most serious cases, it may be necessary for the claimant to drive whilst remaining seated in his wheelchair, and ramped access may be required, eg to a Chrysler Voyager[5]. However, before the court will award the additional costs of a self-drive car, it is important for the claimant to obtain properly admissible evidence to prove that he or she will be able to drive (with any necessary adaptations) and will be to obtain the necessary insurance to drive despite his or her injuries[6].

---

[1] [1993] PIQR Q104. See also *Goldfinch v Scannell* [1993] PIQR Q143; and *Taylor v Weston AHA* [2003] All ER (D) 50 (Dec).

[2] Of course, the calculations must take account of the particular situation. For example, the trade-in price will probably be reduced by any special adaptations made to the car to suit it to the claimant's needs, and a disabled claimant's car may be expected to depreciate more quickly than other cars because of factors such as decreasing reliability, greater mileage and greater than usual wear and tear. See P Noble, E Fanshawe and B Hellyer *Special Damages for Disability* (2nd edn, 1988), pp 22–25.

[3] See eg *Sarwar v (1) Ali and (2) MIB* [2007] EWHC 1255 (QB); *A v Powys Local Health Board* [2007] EWHC 2996 (QB).

4   See eg *Sarwar v (1) Ali and (2) MIB* [2007] EWHC 1255 (QB); *Noble v Owens* [2008] EWHC 359 (QB).

5   See eg *Sarwar v (1) Ali and (2) MIB* [2007] EWHC 1255 (QB); *A v Powys Local Health Board* [2007] EWHC 2996 (QB); *Noble v Owens* [2008] EWHC 359 (QB).

6   See eg *Owen v Brown* [2002] EWHC 1135 (QB), in which Silber J refused to attach any weight to the 'Fish fax'.

[F157]   A claimant with injuries which have caused a severe disability is vulnerable if the car breaks down, thus the court is likely to allow for the car to be changed more frequently than for an able-bodied person, to provide for breakdown recovery insurance[1] and to provide for a mobile phone for the claimant's use in cases of emergency. The reasonable replacement period will depend upon the annual mileage driven[2]. Claimants who have not driven for some time by reason of the accident may have lost confidence on the road as a result. In this scenario, a claim may reasonably be made for refresher driving lessons. Likewise, claimants who have to learn to drive again using special aids and equipment may claim for the cost of attending special mobility centres where they are given expert training suited to their individual needs. The increased cost of insuring the claimant's vehicle for his or her carers may also be recoverable[3].

1   Cf *Biesheuval v Birrell* [1999] PIQR Q40 at Q79, where Eady J did not accept on the facts that the rescue recovery service was specifically related to the claimant's disability. Likewise, this item was not recovered in *Sarwar v (1) Ali and (2) MIB* [2007] EWHC 1255 (QB) because it would have been required anyway. However, in *Noble v Owens* [2008] EWHC 359 (QB), the claimant used to undertake his own servicing and repairs, and a claim for breakdown cover was conceded until age 70.

2   *Sarwar v (1) Ali and (2) MIB* [2007] EWHC 1255 (QB).

3   *Biesheuval v Birrell* [1999] PIQR Q40; *Sarwar v (1) Ali and (2) MIB* [2007] EWHC 1255 (QB); *A v Powys Local Health Board* [2007] EWHC 2996 (QB); *Burton v Kingsbury* [2007] EWHC 2091 (QB); *Smith v East and North Hertfordshire Hospitals NHS Trust* [2008] EWHC 2234 (QB); *Noble v Owens* [2008] EWHC 359 (QB).

[F158]   In addition to the damages associated with the capital cost of a car, the claimant may also be entitled to damages in respect of the annual running costs, insofar as these exceed the costs which the claimant would have incurred but for the injury. The annual running cost is generally calculated by estimating the annual mileage[1] and applying to it a figure representing cost per mile[2]. There are likely to be two separate additional costs: first, the additional mileage over and above the mileage that would have been driven but for the injuries and, secondly, the increased costs of driving a larger, more expensive vehicle[3]. Automatic transmission (which many disabled drivers need) may also increase running costs.

1   See *Woodrup v Nicol* [1993] PIQR Q104 at Q109–Q110; *Sarwar v (1) Ali and (2) MIB* [2007] EWHC 1255 (QB); *A v Powys Local Health Board* [2007] EWHC 2996 (QB).

2   The tables of motoring expenses produced by the AA are commonly used for these calculations (these tables are reproduced in PNBA's 'Facts & Figures'). However, they divide into two parts: fixed (or standing) costs, such as road fund licence, depreciation etc; and running costs, petrol, oil, servicing, tyres, batteries, exhausts etc. The running costs will depend on the mileage done. The fixed costs will involve a comparison of depreciation between the old and the new car.

3   See eg *Haines v Airedale NHS Trust* (2 May 2000, unreported), QBD; *Sarwar v (1) Ali and (2) MIB* [2007] EWHC 1255 (QB); *A v Powys Local Health Board* [2007] EWHC 2996 (QB); *Smith v East and North Hertfordshire Hospitals NHS Trust* [2008] EWHC 2234 (QB); and *Noble v Owens* [2008] EWH

[F159] A different approach is required where the claimant has made use of the Motability lease scheme. Use of the scheme is not compulsory, and many claimants opt for private provision which they are entitled to do without it being held against them[1]. When used, the scheme enables a disabled person to obtain a new car every three years by paying a deposit and then using the mobility component of his disability living allowance as the lease instalments. The claim is likely to be limited to the difference between the deposit paid under the scheme and the deposit a claimant would, if not disabled, have paid, less frequently and for a smaller car under a hire-purchase agreement. However, arguably the claimant may also recover the disability living allowance surrendered as part of the Motability scheme which, unless included in the claim, will be offset against the past travel and transport costs in any event[2].

[1]   *Eagle v Chambers (No 2)* [2004] EWCA Civ 1033.
[2]   See further Chapter J.

[F160] Where the claimant was a keen or regular motorcyclist, allowance has to be made for the difference in travel cost per mile as between a motorcycle of the size he or she used – but a judgment also has to be made as to how long he or she would have continued to use a motorbike in preference to a car[1].

[1]   See eg *O'Brien v Harris* (22 February 2001, unreported), QBD, in which Pitchford J accepted that the claimant should be entitled to claim the increased running costs of running a Fiesta and a Mercedes over and above the cost of running a motorcycle. Further, this claim was allowed into the future because, at the time of the accident, the claimant was already in his forties and the trial judge did not see why the claimant would change the habit of a lifetime without good reason.

[F161] Further, where the claimant previously undertook the servicing and maintenance of his or her own vehicles but is unable to do so by reason of injuries sustained, any additional costs paying a garage to carry out the same work will be recoverable[1]. However, the claimant will only be entitled to recover the losses associated with servicing and maintaining his own car, as opposed to the losses for servicing and maintaining cars of family and friends[2].

[1]   *Noble v Owens* [2008] EWHC 359 (QB).
[2]   *Swain v London Ambulance Service NHS Trust* [1999] All ER (D) 260; *Noble v Owens* [2008] EWHC 359 (QB).

(v) Evidence

[F162] Where possible, claims for travel expenses should be supported by documentary evidence. Assuming the claimant receives early advice about the need to keep a record of expenses, it should be possible to produce copy taxi receipts, train tickets and receipts for petrol etc. In the absence of such evidence, unless the loss can be inferred from the evidence[1], the court may be forced to make a conservative estimate of the loss or, alternatively, make no award at all[2].

[1]   See eg *Bygrave v Thomas Cook Tour Operations Ltd* [2004] EWCA Civ 1631, in which the Court of Appeal upheld the trial judge's allowance for additional expenditure on taxis. See also *Pratt v Smith* (18 December 2002, unreported), QBD, in which David Foskett QC awarded £1,000 for past travel expenses when the claimant had attended a lot of medical appointments but there was no clear evidence regarding the travel expenses that had been incurred.
[2]   *Hughes (Gordon Clifford) v Addis (John)* (23 March 2000, unreported), CA.

(vi)   Hospital Visits

Travel and associated expenses

[F163]   Generally speaking, the reasonable costs incurred by the claimant's family and friends (except the tortfeasor) visiting the claimant in hospital will be recoverable as damages[1]. Such costs would include travel expenses to and from hospital, and associated costs such as car parking, accommodation costs and increased expenditure on food and drink etc. It is submitted that, in relation to the recoverability of such expenses, there is a three-stage test[2]:

- It must have been reasonably necessary for the costs to have been incurred, eg it would not be reasonably necessary for a long-lost aunt to fly over to visit the claimant from abroad on learning that the claimant had twisted an ankle which required no hospital treatment.
- The out-of-pocket expenses incurred by the friends/relatives must be reasonable, eg it would be unreasonable to claim the costs of 5-star hotel accommodation for a month when the claimant made a good recovery from his or her injuries within a matter of days.
- The claimant will hold any damages recovered under this head on trust for the person who incurred them, and therefore it must still be possible to honour that trust by contacting the relevant person and/or repay them their out-of-of-pocket expenses[3].

---

[1]   *Kirkham v Boughey* [1958] 2 QB 338; *Schneider v Eisovitch* [1960] 2 QB 430; *Bordin v St Mary's NHS Trust* [2000] Lloyd's Rep Med 287. See further para 2.36 of the Law Commission's Report No 262 'Damages for Personal Injury: Medical, Nursing and other Expenses; Collateral Benefits' (November 1999).

[2]   This test is largely based upon the test set out by Paull J in *Schneider v Eisovitch* [1960] 2 QB 430 in respect of gratuitous services provided by family/friends.

[3]   *Hunt v Severs* [1994] 2 AC 350; *ATH v MS* [2002] EWCA Civ 792.

[F164]   Following the decision in *Hunt v Severs*[1], no damages will be recoverable for expenses incurred by the tortfeasor making hospital visits.

---

[1]   [1994] 2 AC 350.

Recovery versus social contact

[F165]   Sometimes a distinction is drawn between travel costs incurred by reason of a hospital visit, which can be said to be a real aid in the claimant's recovery, and travel costs incurred by maintaining ordinary social contact. In *Kirkham v Boughey*[1], Diplock J stated:

'Mr Harington has, however, pressed upon me two matters. First he says it is well known that husbands are frequently awarded, as part of their damages for injuries to their wives, the cost of visiting the wife in hospital, and such damages have been claimed, and, indeed, agreed, in this case. As I have said, I do not know how the agreed figure of special damage was made up. It was done at my urging to save costs and it would be quite wrong to regard this agreement as conceding that the cost of a husband's visit to hospital was recoverable in law. But I see no difficulty in reconciling the recovery of this item with the principle which I have already discussed. Visits by a spouse may well be a factor in the recovery of a patient, and a visit to a wife in hospital may thus be a proper step in mitigating the damage sustained by loss of consortium by reducing the period during which the consortium is lost. But if the sole justification for the visit is the comfort or pleasure which it gives to the wife, then I think it is not recoverable.'

1   [1958] 2 QB 338.

[F166]   Further, as seen above, when considering the question of gratuitous care provided to the claimant during a period of hospitalisation in *Havenhand v Jeffrey*[1], Beldam LJ took account of the nature of the services provided and made a distinction between care and 'normal hospital visits arising from family visits'. By analogy, the same principles will apply to recovery of travel expenses incurred by relatives making hospital visits. Of course, a claimant may only recover the true costs attributable to his or her injuries. Therefore, where a friend or family member would have incurred travel expenses visiting the claimant to maintain ordinary social contact in any event, the claimant may only claim the extra travel costs which have been incurred as a result of his or her injuries[2].

1   (24 February 1997, unreported), CA. See also *O'Brien v Harris* (22 February 2001, unreported), QBD; *Owen v Brown* [2002] EWHC 1135 (QB); *Warrilow v Norfolk and Norwich Hospitals NHS Trust* [2006] EWHC 801 (QB); and *Huntley v Simmonds* [2009] EWHC 405 (QB).
2   *Bordin v St Mary's NHS Trust* [2000] Lloyd's Rep Med 287. See further at para **[F168]**.

Loss of earnings

[F167]   Any earnings forgone by visiting relatives will not be recoverable, even where the visits are reasonable[1]. The damages are said to be too remote and not sufficiently attributable to the accident. These are decisions of the High Court which may be distinguishable by a case with sufficiently strong facts[2]. Certainly the rule is harsh.

1   *Kirkham v Boughey* [1958] 2 QB 338, per Diplock J; *Walker v Mullen* (1984) Times, 19 January, per Comyn J.
2   It should be noted that both of these cases were decided prior to *Hunt v Severs* [1994] 2 AC 350, and may be decided differently today.

(vii)   Travel Expenses Which Would Have Been Incurred In Any Event

[F168]   No claim can be made in respect of travel expenses which would have been incurred in any event. This means that an allowance has to be made to take account of the costs that would have been incurred in the absence of the defendant's wrongdoing (such as the costs of travelling to work). These costs are usually offset against the claim for loss of earnings[1] or, alternatively, the claim for increased travel costs. However, in practice, unless these costs were significant and there is specific evidence as to their value, the court is unlikely to inquire into them too deeply[2].

1   *Lim Poh Choo v Camden and Islington Area Health Authority* [1980] AC 174 at 191–192.
2   See the speech of Lord Griffiths in *Dews v National Coal Board* [1988] AC 1 at 14, and *Warrilow v Norfolk and Norwich Hospitals NHS Trust* [2006] EWHC 801 (QB), although cf *Eagle v Chambers (No 2)* [2004] EWCA Civ 1033, in which the Court of Appeal upheld the trial judge's discount of 15% from the claim for past loss of earnings to reflect the claimant's travel expenses, and *Sparks v*

Royal Hospitals NHS Trust (21 December 1998, unreported), in which McKinnon J deducted £3 per week for travel costs; and *Crofts v Murton* LTL 10/9/08 where £50 per week was deducted for travel expenses.

(viii)   Travel Expenses Incurred Fulfilling Duties to Others

[F169]   Arguably, on the basis of the Court of Appeal's decision in *Lowe v Guise*[1], a claimant would be able to recover increased travel costs incurred by reason of his or her injuries preventing the fulfilment of a legal or moral duty to another. For example, if the claimant paid someone to collect his or her children from school or paid for a taxi to take his or her grandparents to the shops, damages might be recoverable in respect of these expenses (assuming they are related to the claimant's injuries and inability to fulfil these tasks). However, in *O'Brien v Harris*[2], Pitchford J refused to make an award for £150 in respect of a claim for the costs of a driver who was hired by the claimant to take his daughter to university. The cost was held to be disproportionate and, since his daughter could have travelled by bus or train, the claim was disallowed[3].

[1]   [2002] EWCA Civ 197.
[2]   (22 February 2001, unreported), QBD, at [237].
[3]   Although, arguably, if the increased travel costs of taking the claimant's daughter to university were recoverable as a matter of principle, the trial judge should have made an award under this head but restricted the same to the reasonable cost of the relevant bus or train journey.

10   Damaged or Destroyed Clothing and Property

(i)   General Principles

[F170]   In *Voaden v Champion*[1] the Court of Appeal had occasion to carry out a detailed review of the principles relating to damages arising from damaged or destroyed chattels. Rix LJ, delivering the lead judgment (with which Hale and Schiemann LJJ agreed), said[2]:

'In the light of these authorities and the principles discussed in them, I would draw the following conclusions.

(1) Unless the parties are taken to have agreed otherwise, it is difficult to see that in the normal case of damage to or destruction of a chattel, it should make any difference whether the loss is caused by breach of contract or of tortious duty. The question remains, as Lord Blackburn said in *Livingstone v Rawyards Coal Co* (1880) 5 App Cas 25 at 39, to find

"that sum of money which will put the party who has been injured, or has suffered, in the same position as he would have been in if he had not sustained the wrong for which he is now getting his compensation or reparation."

As Lord Lloyd emphasised in *Ruxley v Forsyth* at 366B, after citing a similar statement of principle from Viscount Haldane LC in *Westinghouse Electric and Manufacturing Co Ltd v Underground Electric Railways Co of London Ltd* [1912] AC 673 at 689

"Note that Lord Haldane does not say that the plaintiff is always to be placed in the same situation physically as if the contract had been performed, but in as good a position financially, so far as money can do it. This necessarily involves measuring the pecuniary loss which the plaintiff has in fact sustained."

(2) It follows that cases where a claimant recovers *more than* he has lost, as will happen where betterment occurs without a new for old deduction, ought as a matter of principle to be exceptional. Recognised examples of such exceptions, again whether in contract or in tort does not seem to matter, are cases of the repair of chattels (*The Gazelle, Bacon v Cooper Metals Ltd* [1982] 1 All ER 397) and also the destruction of buildings provided that a replacement building is necessary to prevent the collapse of a business or loss of profits (*Harbutt's Plasticine, Dominion Mosaics v Trafalgar Trucking*). It may well be, therefore, that the distinction between repair and total loss relied on by the judge is not definitive, and that the exceptions are to be explained on a more fact sensitive basis. A factor mentioned in some of these exceptional authorities is that otherwise the claimant is exposed to an inconvenience or burden or the expenditure of money from which the law ought to protect him. I suspect, however, that the true principle is that in the relevant cases the betterment has conferred no corresponding advantage on the claimant. Take the ordinary case of the repair of some part of a machine. Where only a new part can be fitted or is available, the betterment is likely to be purely nominal: for unless it can be posited that the machine will outlast the life left in the damaged part just before it was damaged, the betterment gives the claimant no advantage; and in most cases any such benefit is likely to be entirely speculative. So in the case of replacement buildings: the building may be new, but buildings are such potentially long-lived objects that the mere newness of a building may be entirely by the way. Of much more importance to a business owner is whether the replacement answers the needs of his business. Even where the replacement is of a moderately bigger size (*Dominion Mosaics v Trafalgar Trucking*), in the absence of any reason for thinking that the bigger size is of direct benefit to the claimant, he has merely mitigated as best he can. If, however, it were to be shown that the bigger size (or some other aspect of betterment) were of real pecuniary advantage to the claimant, as where, for instance, he was able to sublet the 20% extra floor space he had obtained in his replacement building, I do not see why that should not have to be taken into account. It is after all a basic principle that where mitigation has brought measurable benefits to a claimant, he must give credit for them: see *British Westinghouse v Underground Electric Railways*, where defective machines were replaced by new machines of superior efficiency.

(3) Where in the case of a second-hand chattel there is no market to replace what has been lost, a problem of betterment will often arise because there is no automatic market mechanism for measuring the loss. In physical terms, the only way to replace the loss is to buy new. But the basic principle is not physically to replace what the claimant has lost but to replace it financially, to make him whole in financial terms. If he is given the price of a new chattel, he will be made more than whole. (The problem of the wrongly constructed swimming-pool is different, but analogous: the claimant is not entitled to specific performance, but to financial compensation for what he has lost.) The authorities suggest that prima facie such a case is not within the range of exceptional situations where betterment is ignored. On the contrary, the proper approach appears to be to make a fact specific review of what the claimant has lost and then attempt to put a financial figure on it as best one can: *The Harmonides* approved in *The Liesbosch; Sealace Shipping v Oceanvoice* approved in *Ruxley v Forsyth*.

(4) It is in any event an error to think in terms of the correct answer lying only at the extremes, such as, at one end, the cost of replacement from new. Several of the cases, even those which have on appeal been driven by the way in which the case has been

argued to select the answer from a limited choice, have commented on this factor: The *Harmonides, Dominion Mosaics v Trafalgar Trucking* and *Ruxley v Forsyth* itself.

(5) In such circumstances the test of reasonableness has an important role to play. This role goes further than the proposition that replacement from new has to be absurd for it to be rejected as the measure of loss. The loss has to be measured, and where what is lost is old and second-hand and coming towards the end of its life, it is not prima facie to be measured by the cost of a brand-new chattel, even where the market cannot supply a closer replica of what has been lost; and where such a measure would not be a reasonable assessment of what has been lost, it should not be used. As May J said in *Taylor v Hepworths*, cited with approval in *Dominion Mosaics v Trafalgar Trucking* and (at 356G and 369G) in *Ruxley v Forsyth*, damages ought to be reasonable as between claimant and defendant. I do not see why in the realm above all of remedies the common law cannot mould its principles flexibly to the needs of the situation, and as so often the test of reasonableness lies to hand as a useful tool. It may also be possible to speak in terms of proportionality, a closely analogous but not necessarily identical test: see Lord Lloyd in *Ruxley v Forsyth* at 367B and 369H.'

1   [2002] EWCA Civ 89.
2   At [83]–[88].

[F171]   Generally speaking, where the claimant's clothing or possessions have been damaged in an accident, the appropriate measure of damages is the diminution in their value which is usually measured by the cost of repair[1]. Where clothing or possessions have been destroyed or damaged beyond economical repair, the claimant is entitled to recover the market value of the item as at the date of the accident (less any salvage value of the destroyed item)[2]. Exceptionally, where an item is unique or has a high salvage value, it may be appropriate to adjourn the trial so that the item can be put on the market and/or sold in order to obtain evidence to assist with the assessment of the diminution in value[3]. Where a replacement item has been bought, the claimant may need to give credit for betterment, to take account of the fact that the item in question was second hand, but the replacement item may have been bought new and is a better or more valuable item. However, in some instances no credit needs to be given for betterment, for example where there is no second hand market readily available for the items in question, so they had to be bought new[4].

1   *Darbishire v Warran* [1963] 1 WLR 1067.
2   *The Clyde* (1856) Swab 23. See further chapter 32 of *McGregor on Damages* (18th edn).
3   *Constantine v Totalfinaelf UK Ltd* [2003] EWHC 428 (QB).
4   *Harbutt's Plastircine v Wayne Tank & Pump Co* [1970] 1 QB 447; and *Barkin Construction Ltd v Re-Source America International Ltd* [2005] EWCA Civ 97.

[F172]   It should be noted that, where a claimant receives the full value of a damaged or destroyed chattel, eg where a defendant insurer writes a cheque for the pre-accident value of the claimant's car, there can be no further claim for loss of use, since the claimant can reasonably be expected to purchase a replacement vehicle with the money provided. Further, where a claimant is awarded the full cost of a lost or damaged chattel at trial, no additional claim can be brought for loss of use derived from that chattel, because the same is covered in the award of interest[1].

1   *Voaden v Champion* [2002] EWCA Civ 89.

(ii) Clothing / footwear

[F173] Increased clothing expenses are often incurred following injuries as follows:

- damage to clothing at the scene of an accident;
- clothing cut off or removed at hospital;
- additional clothing bought for use in hospital, such as night garments and slippers etc;
- the need to buy a replacement wardrobe due to significant weight gain or loss;
- the need to buy specialist footwear or orthotics[1];
- the need to buy replacement clothing due to incontinence and the need to wash clothes more frequently;
- the need to replace clothes more frequently because they catch on medical devices (such as external fixators[2]) or the claimant's wheelchair[3];
- the need to buy special clothing such as loose fitting clothing[4], clothes without zips, specially made trousers[5] or shoes with Velcro.

[1] Such claims may be significant: see eg *Cannon v Cannon* [2005] EWHC 1310 (QB), in which the claimant recovered £328,728.48 for the future costs of bespoke footwear and Wellington Boots.
[2] See eg *Cannon v Cannon* [2005] EWHC 1310 (QB).
[3] See eg *Owen v Brown* [2002] EWHC 1135 (QB).
[4] See eg *Tagg v Countess of Chester Hospital Foundation Trust* [2007] EWHC 509 (QB).
[5] See eg *Owen v Brown* [2002] EWHC 1135 (QB); and *Burton v Kingsbury* [2007] EWHC 2091 (QB).

(iii) Vehicle Damage

[F174] When a motor vehicle is damaged, there may be a number of ancillary or related costs. It is important not to overlook the potential associated expenses/losses which may include:

- loss of insurance excess;
- loss of no claims bonus;
- cost of repairs or replacement (less salvage)[1];
- replacement hire and insurance[2];
- delivery and collection charges[3];
- recovery costs such as towage and storage;
- pro rata period of the claimant's insurance or AA or RAC subscriptions whilst the car is being repaired/off the road (insurers, the AA or RAC should surrender the unexpired period if the car is a write-off);
- engineer's fee for valuation purposes;
- loss of petrol if the vehicle is a write off; and
- loss of the use of the vehicle, if a replacement is not hired.

[1] The claimant is entitled to recover the cost of repairs, whether or not they have been paid by the claimant or a third party, and whether or not they have been carried out in accordance with an enforceable credit hire agreement, since this is the measure of the claimant's loss: *Lagden v O'Connor* [2003] UKHL 64; *Jones v Stroud District Council* [1986] 1 WLR 1141. As the Court of Appeal explained:

> 'In our judgment a fundamental distinction must be drawn, for present purposes, between repair costs and hire charges. When a vehicle is damaged by the negligence of a third party,

the owner suffers an immediate loss representing the diminution in value of the vehicle. As a general rule, the measure of that damage is the cost of carrying out the repairs necessary to restore the vehicle to its pre-accident condition.'

2   The claimant is entitled to go to the nearest local hirer and claim for the full hire charges whilst his or her car is being repaired unless the defendant can show there has been a supervening event or a failure to mitigate loss: *Clark v Tull* [2002] EWCA Civ 510 (upheld in *Lagden v O'Connor* [2003] UKHL 64). At [147] of its joint judgment, the Court of Appeal said:

'The fundamental principle is that a person whose car has been damaged is entitled to compensation for the loss caused. In a case where such loss includes loss of use and he establishes a need for a replacement, he is entitled to the cost of hiring a replacement car. He can go round to the nearest car hire company and is prima facie entitled to recover the amount charged whether or not the charge is at the top of the range of car hire rates. However the basic principle is qualified by the duty to take reasonable steps to mitigate the loss. What is reasonable will depend on the particular circumstances.'

3   These are recoverable in principle: *Clark v Tull* [2002] EWCA Civ 510 (upheld in *Lagden v O'Connor* [2003] UKHL 64).

(iv)   Loss of Use

[F175]   Damages may be awarded for the use of any items damaged in the accident. The most common example of this type of claim relates to damaged vehicles following road traffic accidents, but is certainly not limited to the same[1]. Where the claimant has hired a replacement vehicle, the claim for loss of use will usually be restricted to the cost of hire[2]. Unless the claimant is impecunious[3], he or she will be restricted to recovering the spot hire rate, ie the average rate of hire for an appropriate replacement vehicle without any enhancement for deferred payment or additional services[4]. The spot hire rate need not be the rate for hiring an exact replacement car but is the rate of hire for a broadly similar type of vehicle[5]. Sometimes, free replacement vehicles are offered by the defendant's insurers. In these circumstances, it is not unreasonable (and therefore not a failure to mitigate) for a claimant to reject or ignore an offer from a defendant (or his insurers) which does not make clear the cost of hire to the defendant for the purpose of enabling the claimant to make a realistic comparison with the cost which he or she is incurring or about to incur[6]. Where the claimant does unreasonably reject or ignore a defendant's offer of a replacement car, the claimant is entitled to recover at least the cost which the defendant can show he would reasonably have incurred: the claim for damages is not forfeited in its entirety[7].

1   See eg *Cunliffe v Murrell* [1994] CLY 1724 involving a claim for the loss of use of a horse.
2   *Mattocks v Mann* [1993] RTR 13.
3   *Dimond v Lovell* [2002] 1 AC 384. The claimant will be able to recover the full cost of the spot hire rate charged by a hire company provided by his or her insurers (assuming it is reasonable), even if there is an additional undisclosed payment made by the claimant's insurers to the hire company: *Bee v Jenson* [2007] EWCA Civ 923.
4   *Lagden v O'Connor* [2003] UKHL 64. Where there is no evidence regarding the exact spot hire rate at the time, the spot hire rate a year or so later is likely to throw considerable light on what the spot rate would have been at the time: *Bent v (1) Highways and Utilities Construction Ltd and (2) Allianz Insurance Plc* [2010] EWCA Civ 292.
5   See *Bent v (1) Highways and Utilities Construction Ltd and (2) Allianz Insurance Plc* [2010] EWCA Civ 292, in which Jacob LJ said at para [9]: 'one must not be hypnotised by any supposed need to find an exact spot rate for an almost exactly comparable car. Normally, the replacement need be no more than in the same broad range of quality and nature as the damaged car. There may be a bracket of spot rates for cars rather "better" and rather "worse". A Judge who considered that bracket and aimed for some sort of reasonable average would not be going wrong'.

6   *Copley v Lawn and others* [2009] EWCA Civ 580.
7   This was the obiter conclusion of the Court of Appeal in *Copley v Lawn and others* [2009] EWCA Civ 580, in reliance upon *Strutt v Whitnell* [1975] 1 WLR 870.

[F176]   Where a replacement car has not been hired, the following factors are likely to influence the value of the claim for loss of use:

- the make, model, age and value of the damaged vehicle;
- the frequency with which the claimant (and/or his or her family) used the vehicle, eg to travel to work, to the shops, to visit friends and/or relatives, to go to church etc;
- the availability and convenience of local public transport;
- the cost incurred using alternative means of transport;
- any additional journey time to and from work caused by using alternative means of transport;
- the claimant's locality – in particular, whether the claimant lives in a rural or suburban area;
- the effect on social or sporting activities;
- any planned trips or holidays that had to be cancelled; and
- the time of year (loss of use in winter months will generally attract higher awards than loss of use in summer months).

[F177]   It should be noted that, where a claimant receives the full value of a damaged or destroyed chattel, eg where a defendant insurer writes a cheque for the pre-accident value of the claimant's car, there can be no further claim for loss of use, since the claimant can reasonably be expected to purchase a replacement vehicle with the money provided. Further, where a claimant is awarded the full cost of a lost or damaged chattel at trial, no additional claim can be brought for loss of use derived from that chattel because the same is covered in the award of interest[1]. Likewise, where a claimant has a car or possession which has not been damaged but he or she is unable to use or enjoy it because of injury, this is likely to be viewed as a claim for loss of amenity and compensated by way of the award in respect of general damages for pain, suffering and loss of amenity, rather than attracting any separate award for pecuniary loss. For example, a claimant who has not been able to play tennis since an accident is unlikely to be able to recover damages for 'loss of use' of his or her tennis racket. The fact is that the claimant still has the tennis racket and could lend or hire it out to someone else until he or she has sufficiently recovered to use it. The real loss is the claimant's inability to play tennis, and this is already covered by the award for loss of amenity.

1   *Voaden v Champion* [2002] EWCA Civ 89.

(v)   Profit-earning Chattels

[F178]   Damage will not infrequently be caused to a profit-earning chattel such as a boat, taxi, lorry or bus. In such circumstances, it will be usual to claim the replacement cost of hiring an alternative chattel so that the claimant's business can continue (and indeed the claimant is obliged to mitigate his or her loss by hiring such a replacement). In rare situations where the chattel is irreplaceable, a claim may be brought for the resulting profit loss whilst the chattel is being repaired or rebuilt[1].

[1]   See further chapter 32 of *McGregor on Damages* (18th edn).

11   Inability to Perform Domestic Activities

[F179]   The claimant may well be able to recover for the past costs incurred in respect of the loss of his or her ability to do work in the home, such as DIY, decorating or gardening. The first case to recognise that the lost ability to carry out household tasks should be a separate head of damage from loss of amenity was *Daly v General Steam Navigation Co Ltd*[1]. The services whose loss would fall within this head include housekeeping, home maintenance[2] and gardening. However, it should be recognised that past and future loss of the ability to undertake housekeeping etc are treated in different ways.

[1]   [1981] 1 WLR 120. See further John Snell 'Damages for DIY and gardening' [2002] JPIL, Issue 4/02 at 385–391.
[2]   See eg *Hoffman v Sofaer* [1982] 1 WLR 1350, in which a claimant recovered the cost of maintenance and decoration work which the claimant would have done himself but for the accident.

[F180]   Prior to trial, only expenses actually incurred by the claimant performing tasks that he or she would otherwise have done, but for injuries, can be recovered, such as:

• payments made for domestic services, eg cooking, cleaning, washing, ironing, vacuuming etc;
• payments made in respect of painting, decorating, DIY and home maintenance;
• payments made for gardening, clearing rubbish, laying patios, building fences etc;
• payments made in respect of vehicle servicing, maintaining and valeting; and
• the cost of eating out where the injury prevents food preparation at home or makes it more difficult.

[F181]   Where the claimant has not actually expended any money on such services, the position is less clear. Certainly, if the claimant struggles to perform domestic tasks which he or she did prior to the accident without requiring any assistance from a third party, but, by reason of the injuries, it takes longer or causes pain and discomfort, this may result in an increased award in respect of general damages for pain, suffering and loss of amenity[1]. However, where the claimant has required the services of a third party, on face value, the Court of Appeal's decision in *Daly v General Steam Navigation Co Ltd*[2] prohibits recovery for pecuniary loss reflecting the notional cost of providing those services commercially, unless the provider of the services has had to give up paid employment in order to provide the services. It is noteworthy, however, that this decision was made before the House of Lords clarified the basis upon which gratuitous care claims could be recovered in *Hunt v Severs*[3]. To the extent that there remains any difference in treatment between past and future claims for gratuitous services which do not fall into the category of nursing care, this has been criticised by the Law Commission[4]. Indeed, this point rarely arises in practice, and courts often tend to award damages for the reasonable provision of gratuitous services such as childminding, painting, decorating and gardening in the same way as if the services had been the provision of nursing care[5]. By analogy with the principles concerning the provision of gratuitous nursing care, any such damages recovered for these services are held on trust by the claimant for the benefit of the voluntary carer[6].

[1]   *Daly v General Steam Navigation Co Ltd* [1981] 1 WLR 120.
[2]   [1981] 1 WLR 120. See also *Lowe v Guise* [2002] EWCA Civ 197.
[3]   [1994] 2 AC 350.
[4]   See paras 3.87 to 2.93 of its Report No 262 'Damages for Personal Injury: Medical, Nursing and other Expenses; Collateral Benefits' (November 1999).
[5]   See eg *Blair v Michelin Tyre plc* (25 January 2002, unreported), QBD, in which HHJ Marr-Johnson (sitting as a judge of the High Court) made an award for past services carried out by the claimant's son and son-in-law, including tasks such as 'window cleaning, painting and decorating, routine maintenance and normal household shopping'; *Assinder v Griffin* [2001] All ER (D) 356 (May), in which HHJ Peter Clark awarded the claimant £1,053 representing 301 hours spent by two friends who stayed at the claimant's home for two weeks without charge and, in return, carried out jobs about the house and garden; and *Froggatt v Chesterfield & North Derbyshire Royal Hospital NHS Trust* [2002] All ER (D) 218 (Dec), QBD, in which £945 was awarded for the past cost of childcare provided gratuitously by the children's grandmother. See also *Tagg v Countess of Chester Hospital Foundation NHS Trust* [2007] EWHC 509 (QB), and *Smith v East and North Hertfordshire Hospitals NHS Trust* [2008] EWHC 2234 (QB), in which Penry-Davey J awarded £4,000 (400 hours at £10 per hour) for past gratuitous DIY.
[6]   *Hunt v Severs* [1994] 2 AC 350. See further at para **[F86]**.

[F182]   In respect of quantum, it should be noted that only the labour costs may be recovered in respect of any work done, since, even if the claimant had done the work him or herself, the cost of any tools or materials would have been incurred in any event. Further, any claim should be supported by the medical evidence in order to counter the argument that the claimant might not have been able to manage the domestic services, painting, decorating, DIY etc and would have paid someone else to perform the work anyway[1]. However, it may be possible to bring a claim, eg for assistance with domestic chores, where the claimant is physically able to do the chores but is too exhausted by reason of his or her injuries to carry out such chores after a full day's work[2].

[1]   It should be noted that the courts recognise that a person's capacity to perform physical activities, including DIY, tends to deteriorate with age: *Smith v McCrae* [2003] EWCA Civ 505. See also *Blair v Michelin Tyre* (25 January 2002, unreported), HHJ Marr-Johnson sitting as a judge of the QBD, in which the trial judge refused to allow anything for decorating because it was doubted that the claimant would have been doing much at his age in any event.
[2]   *Bygrave v Thomas Cook Tour Operations Ltd* [2004] EWCA Civ 1631. In this case, the Court of Appeal upheld the trial judge's decision that it was reasonable for the claimant to have taken a full-time job which then gave rise to her tiredness problems (and inability to carry out domestic chores), because she had taken this job in mitigation of her loss.

12   Inability to Care for Others

[F183]   In *Lowe v Guise*[1] the claimant was injured in a road traffic accident. Prior to the accident, the claimant was the full-time carer of his brother who suffered from Down's Syndrome. As a result of the accident, the claimant was unable to provide the same level of care for his brother, and the claimant's mother had to meet the shortfall in the care provided. The question of whether or not the claimant could recover damages to represent his inability to provide the pre-accident level of care to his brother was tried as a preliminary issue. At first instance, the trial judge held that he was bound by the decision in *Swain v LAS*[2], which prevented him from making an award of damages to compensate a claimant for the reduction in his ability to provide the services to another. The claimant was successful on appeal. Rix LJ said[3]:

> 'In my judgement [the claimant] is entitled to claim in respect of the loss of his ability to look after his brother. Since he will maintain his state allowance, he has suffered no loss so far as that allowance is itself concerned. But he has suffered a loss nevertheless because, even though his care was provided gratuitously, it can and ought as a matter of policy to be measured in money's worth. To the extent that his mother has by her own additional care mitigated the appellant's loss, it may be that the appellant would hold that recovery in trust for his mother ... a person [in the claimant's] position has suffered a real loss when he is forced by his injuries to give up the value of work which he has previously donated to his brother's care, work which although carrying no income because gratuitously given nevertheless in principle has and as a matter of policy should have a real value attached to it. The common law should not, and need not, leave the question "Am I my brother's keeper?" with the wrong answer.'

[1]   [2002] EWCA Civ 197, [2002] PIQR Q9.
[2]   [1999] All ER (D) 260.
[3]   At [38].

[F184]   Interestingly, Potter LJ, who was a member of the two-man Court of Appeal in the earlier *Swain v LAS*[1] decision, reviewed his judgment in that case and made it clear that he was only intending to limit a claim made in respect of the performance of a gratuitous service for a spouse in relation to property used exclusively for that spouse's own benefit, rather than the performance of a task which benefited a household or family. But this leaves the law in a state of confusion. Does this mean that, if the claimant's brother in *Lowe v Guise*[2] had lived separately and was not part of the same household so that the claimant had to travel in order to provide the necessary care, the claim would not have succeeded? What if the care provider is a neighbour with no family tie? Such an arbitrary distinction would seem contrary to the general principles expressed in *Hunt v Severs*[3] regarding the recoverability of compensation in respect of gratuitous services and would lead to unfair results. It is submitted that the better view is to determine the question of recoverability by reference to the nature of and reasonableness of the pre-injury services which were provided. If, as a result of the defendant's negligence, the claimant is rendered unable to provide valuable services to another, such that the person reasonably requires assistance from others, the claimant should be entitled to recover 'reasonable recompense' on behalf of the substitute carer. However, this line of argument was not accepted in *Morgan v MOD*[4], where the services in question were domestic activities such as making the bed, taking children to school, putting out the bins and doing the washing etc. Andrew Collender QC held that these matters did not go 'beyond the ordinary interaction of members of a household' rather than being a particular service which sounded properly in damages[5].

[1]   [2002] EWCA Civ 197, [2002] PIQR Q9.
[2]   [1999] All ER (D) 260.

[F185]   Further, whilst the Court of Appeal in *Lowe v Guise*[1] was not dealing with the issue of quantum, some obiter remarks were made regarding the assessment of damages in respect of the past and future loss suffered by the claimant. In particular, Potter LJ expressed the view that the decision in *Daly v Steam Navigation Co*[2] would operate so as to bar any claim for past loss if no actual expense had been incurred by the claimant. However, with respect to Potter LJ, the application of the principle which was applied in *Daly* to the claimant's inability to carry out domestic tasks may perhaps be considered a little incongruous in the context of a claim regarding the inability to carry out services involving physical nursing care (in relation to which, historically, no distinction has been drawn in principle between the assessment of past and future loss)[3]. Unfortunately, it is understood that the claim in *Lowe v Guise* settled before there could be any authoritative ruling in relation to the appropriate assessment of quantum.

1   [2002] EWCA Civ 197, [2002] PIQR Q9.
2   [1981] 1 WLR 120. See further at paras **[F167]**–**[F170]**.
3   See further at para **[F92]**.

13   Increased Household Bills

[F186]   These might include:

- additional clothing expenses, owing to a need for special clothing and/or increased wear and tear[1];
- additional heating expenses[2];
- additional wear and tear on carpets and floors (eg because of wheelchair use);
- increased laundry expenses;
- additional use of telephone[3];
- additional child care;
- additional home or contents insurance; and
- additional expenditure on food, owing to a need for a special diet and/or a reduced ability to cook, leading to a reliance on more expensive ready-prepared foods[4].

1   *Brown v Berry* [2003] All ER (D) 50 (Dec), in which £500 was awarded for increased wear and tear. Although in *Ellis v Denton* (30 June 1989, unreported), QBD, Rougier J refused to take increased wear and tear into account because he found it to be offset by a reduction in the variety and quality of the clothes needed by the claimant.
2   See eg *Taylor v Weston AHA* [2003] All ER (D) 50 (Dec); *Dixon v Were* [2004] EWHC 2273 (QB); *Warrilow v Norfolk and Norwich Hospitals NHS Trust* [2006] EWHC 801 (QB).
3   See eg *Brown v Berry* [2003] All ER (D) 50 (Dec), in which £5 per month additional usage of the telephone was considered to be reasonable; and *Cannon v Cannon* [2005] EWHC 1310 (QB), in which £2,000 was awarded for past additional telephone use. See also *Dixon v Were* [2004] EWHC 2273 (QB), and *Kidd v Plymouth Health Authority* [2001] Lloyd's Law Rep Med 165, in which Kay J (at 173) accepted that the claim for increased telephone use had a therapeutic basis, and in its extent, was substantially attributable to the claimant's condition. However, in *Huntley v Simmonds* [2009] EWHC 405 (QB), although Underhill J accepted the claim in principle, in the absence of any proof, he refused to 'pluck a figure from the air'.

4   In *Owen v Brown* [2002] EWHC 1135 (QB), Silber J allowed £475 for the additional cost of buying
        ready cooked food. See also the Scottish decision of *Duffy v Shaw* 1995 SLT 602.

[F187]   It should be noted that, in the absence of sufficient evidence, it is unlikely
that the increased costs of the claimant being at home more as a result of their
incapacity (as opposed to work) will result in anything other than a modest award[1].

1   *Smith v Rod Jenkins* [2003] EWHC 1356 (QB). On a similar point, see further *Hughes (Gordon
        Clifford) v Addis (John)* (23 March 2000, unreported), CA.

14   Increased Holiday Expenses

[F188]   A disabling condition will mean that a claimant will probably have to spend
more money on holidays than he or she would otherwise have done, since cheaper
types of transport and accommodation may no longer be suitable[1], and in serious
cases it may be necessary for the claimant to be accompanied by carers who will
attend to his or her needs[2]. Further, disabled people often incur additional expenses,
such as extra baggage charges for the equipment they need to take with them,
additional hire charges for larger vehicles, and additional insurance. If the claimant
has incurred any extra cost over and above what he or she would normally have paid,
this may be claimed assuming it is reasonably related to his or her injuries and is
reasonable in amount. What is reasonable or not will depend upon the facts of the
case and the claimant's previous holiday profile. A claimant who previously enjoyed
holidaying in Skegness will not be able to claim the additional costs of a 5-star trip
to Las Vegas!

1   For example, a claimant may need the greater space of Business Class on travel or need to stay in
        a hotel with a lift rather than a guesthouse without. Camping or caravanning may no longer offer
        sufficient comfort.
2   When a carer accompanies a claimant on holiday, this necessarily involves extra travel expenses (eg
        an extra flight, train ticket or connection charge) and additional accommodation. For an example of
        the additional holiday costs allowed by reason of injuries, see *Taylor v Weston AHA* [2003] All ER
        (D) 50 (Dec), where an award of £920 per annum was made for the additional costs of needing to go
        to a specially designed resort. See also *Burton v Kingsbury* [2007] EWHC 2091 (QB), and *Huntley v
        Simmonds* [2009] EWHC 405 (QB), in which £500 was awarded for past holiday costs to allow the
        claimant's support worker to accompany him.

[F189]   The key question when assessing any claim for increased holiday expenses
will be, 'What are the additional costs of putting the claimant back into the position
he or she would have been in but for his or her injuries?'. Therefore, if the claimant
has incurred additional expenses, eg undertaking the Hadj or pilgrimage to Islamic
holy sites, these should be recoverable[1]. It is submitted that the approach of Field
J in *Noble v Owens*[2] should be treated with caution. It matters not that there might
be reasonable holiday destinations in Europe that the claimant could travel to. If
the claimant had previously enjoyed holidaying in the Bahamas and, as a result of
injuries, incurs significant additional expense enjoying similar holidays, those costs
should be recoverable as long as the additional costs themselves are not unreasonable.
Where possible, it is important to prove by evidence the difference between the cost
of holidays previously enjoyed and the additional cost of holidays arising from the
claimant's injuries[3].

1   Although such a claim for the additional costs of undertaking the Hadj in the future were recognised in principle in *Rahman v West Pennine HA* LTL 13/5/2003, on the facts of the case they were not allowed, as the claimant failed to prove that he would have undertaken the pilgrimage but for his injuries.

2   [2008] EWHC 359 (QB).

3   See *Cornes v Southwood* [2008] EWHC 369 (QB), in which the claim for increased holiday costs failed for want of proof. It is understood that this case was appealed but subsequently settled.

15   Increased Leisure Costs

[F190]   An injured claimant may require special equipment or adaptations to allow him or her to participate in previous (or new replacement) sporting and leisure activities. An obvious example is that of a sports wheelchair. However, claims can also be made for other additional expenses, such as adaptations required to existing chattels, eg alterations to a summer home or to a sailing boat to allow better access. Increased costs may also be incurred by needing to pay for carers or support workers to attend events such as football matches[1], going to concerts, the theatre or the cinema[2], or going to the gym[3]. A claimant who used to play football in the park for free with his friends may be restricted to more expensive leisure activities following injury, particularly if he or she is confined to the home. Further, a claimant who used to be at work all day may need to spend more on leisure activities to occupy his or her time[4]. When calculating the additional expenditure, credit needs to be given for the expenses which would have been incurred in any event[5].

1   See eg *Sarwar v (1) Ali and (2) MIB* [2007] EWHC 1255 (QB).

2   In *Dixon v Were* [2004] EWHC 2273 (QB), Gross J awarded £30 per week for support workers to go on outings to the cinema, swimming, meals in a public house and for the support worker's food in the home. In *XXX v A Strategic Health Authority* [2008] EWHC 2727 (QB), £50 per week was agreed by the care experts as being a reasonable allowance for food and expenses (and Jack J held that this would be sufficient for the support workers to eat out as well).

3   In *Dixon v Were* [2004] EWHC 2273 (QB), Gross J awarded £750 pa so that support workers could accompany the claimant to the gym.

4   See eg *Owen v Brown* [2002] EWHC 1135 (QB), in which Silber J allowed £4,000 for past leisure activities, £4,352 for computer equipment (the claimant had no previous interest in computers) and £500 for satellite TV; cf *Lewis v Shrewsbury NHS Trust* (29 January 2007), in which no award was made for satellite TV. See also *Burton v Kingsbury* [2007] EWHC 2091 (QB), in which Flaux J awarded £6,000 against a claim for past hospital expenses of £6,740.59, including a claim for 194 DVDs at £2,520.

5   See eg *Owen v Brown* [2002] EWHC 1135 (QB).

16   Costs of Relationship Breakdown and Divorce

[F191]   It is sometimes possible to prove that the injuries suffered by the claimant have led to him or her becoming divorced. The claimant might need to instruct solicitors and incur financial losses as a result, eg running two houses or paying legal fees. Further, the financial arrangements which are ordered by the court, or agreed by the spouses, as a result of the divorce may well represent a loss to the claimant[1].

1   Including lump sums and periodical payments under Matrimonial Causes Act 1973, s 22A and property adjustment orders under Matrimonial Causes Act 1973, s 23A, as inserted by Family Law Act 1996, s 15.

[F192]   There are two conflicting decisions of the Court of Appeal. *Pritchard v J H Cobden Ltd*[1] decided that the claimant would not be entitled to recover damages for his loss. In refusing to award damages under this head, the Court of Appeal declined to follow its earlier decision in *Jones v Jones*[2], in which a claimant had recovered the loss represented by a lump sum payment to enable his wife to live in a separate establishment. The court distinguished *Jones*, as the principle of the recovery of such payments had not been argued by the advocates in *Jones*[3] (thus making *Pritchard* the more authoritative decision).

1   [1987] 1 All ER 300, [1988] Fam 22. The applications in the matrimonial proceedings were heard together with the claimant's claim for damages. Note that the Law Commission analysed the recoverability of damages consequent on divorce in its Report No 262 'Damages for Personal Injury: Medical, Nursing and other Expenses; Collateral Benefits' (November 1999) and concluded that the law should not be reformed to allow claimants to recover damages for losses, whether pecuniary or non-pecuniary, arising out of a divorce foreseeably consequent on an actionable personal injury.
2   [1985] QB 704.
3   See [1988] Fam 22, per O'Connor and Croom-Johnson LJJ (joint judgment) at 40; and per Sir Roger Ormrod at 49.

[F193]   The Court of Appeal in *Pritchard* relied on three principal arguments. First, it took the view that the lump sum did not represent a genuine loss to the claimant at all, but merely a redistribution of the spouses' assets. Secondly, it was considered that to allow compensation for this sort of loss would produce 'infinite regress' in deciding on the orders to be made after divorce. Any award of damages would itself be part of the total assets to be taken into account in making an order for (eg) a lump sum in the matrimonial proceedings[1] and the lump sum would then be paid out of those assets. However, if the lump sum were to be regarded as a loss to the claimant, recoverable as part of the claimant's damages, it would have to be reckoned as part of the matrimonial assets, which would necessitate a fresh calculation of the lump sum, which would in turn lead to a reassessment of the damages, and so on. If the assessment of the damages and the orders for ancillary relief were treated as entirely independent matters, so omitting the cost of the divorce from the claimant's damages, the infinite regress could, in the Court of Appeal's view, be avoided.

1   See eg *Daubney v Daubney* [1976] Fam 267; and *Wagstaff v Wagstaff* [1992] 1 All ER 275.

[F194]   The third argument was that the court deciding the quantum of damages in the personal injury case would be involved in an inappropriate exercise of predicting, and applying, the likely outcome of future court proceedings conducted for wholly different purposes.

[F195]   Other arguments included the contention: that an award of damages under this head would lead to 'abuse', meaning, presumably, divorces deliberately contrived by collusion between the spouses with a view to obtaining damages under this head; that it would act as an incentive to divorce sooner rather than later; and that there was difficulty and expense in quantifying claims.

[F196]   These arguments were fully reviewed by the Law Commission in their report entitled 'Medical, Nursing and Other Expenses' (Law Com No 262) published in 1999. They agreed with some of the principled objections to allowing such losses as set out in *Pritchard v J H Cobden Ltd*[1]. It was concluded that the current state of the law did not allow recovery of pecuniary or non-pecuniary losses arising out of foreseeable divorce (or relationship breakdown) following an actionable injury, and they recommended that the law should not be reformed to permit such recovery[2].

1   [1987] 1 All ER 300, [1988] Fam 22.
2   Para 6.34. See further *Kemp & Kemp*, chapter 19.

[F197]   Note, however, that a claimant may recover indirectly for the breakdown of his or her marriage. He or she may have to rely on expert professional carers rather than his or her spouse[1]. The lack of any ability to do domestic tasks will require recompense as well, and at a commercial rate[2]. There may also be increased accommodation costs as a result of the need to live independently, and/or additional running, maintenance and DIY costs[3]. Thus, breakdown of marriage may add to the value of the claim where there is a clear causal link between the breakdown and the accident, albeit that increased expenses which are directly incurred, such as the legal costs of divorce, are irrecoverable for policy reasons.

1   See eg *Tame v Professional Cycle Marketing Ltd* 19/12/2006; *Crofts v Murton* LTL 10/9/2008.
2   Such a claim was recently awarded in *Warrilow v Norfolk and Norwich Hospitals NHS Trust* [2006] EWHC 801 (QB).
3   See eg *Edwards v Martin* [2010] EWHC 570 (QB), in which such claims succeeded, but the running costs were reduced by half because these would have been shared had the couple stayed together. See also *Crookdake v Drury* [2004] EWCA Civ 1370 at para [48], where the claimant recovered the costs of private accommodation and a care regime in a bungalow in close proximity to his wife's home.

[F198]   Where there is any possibility of divorce, it is important that any judgment or settlement sets out the sums paid under the various heads of damage. This is so that the claimant's care costs can be 'ring fenced' in any future matrimonial proceedings. The matrimonial court is unlikely to order that small sums of money paid specifically for pain and suffering should be paid to the other spouse or greater sums that have been paid to compensate the claimant for his or her loss of amenity, care costs etc[1].

1   Per Butler-Sloss LJ in *Wagstaff v Wagstaff* [1992] 1 All ER 275 at 280E–280F.

17   Costs of Administering the Claimant's Affairs

(i)   Court of Protection and Deputyship Fees

[F199]   Where the claimant is not able to manage his or her own affairs, additional expenses may be incurred in managing any award of damages that is received. The incapacity may be pre-existing or result from the injuries sustained, eg a serious brain injury. If the claimant is not already under the jurisdiction of the Court of Protection, an application will need to be made, supported by a doctor[1], that the claimant is incapable of managing or administering his or her own affairs[2]. Fees are likely to be charged by the Office of the Public Guardian (OPG)[3] and any deputy[4] appointed, in order to manage the claimant's affairs. These fees are recoverable from the defendant[5] as long as the court is satisfied, on the balance of probabilities, that the claimant is incapable of managing his or her own affairs and the disability results from the injuries sustained as opposed to any pre-existing disability[6]. In addition, there may be solicitors' costs, which may be fixed or taxed, and disbursements (eg the cost of obtaining the medical report to support the initial application), which are again recoverable from the defendant as long as they are reasonable[7]. It may also be necessary to incur additional professional charges, eg accountancy fees to prepare annual income and expenditure accounts for the Court of Protection[8]. However, it should be noted that all such charges will be subject to a reduction by reason of a finding of contributory negligence on the part of the claimant[9].

[1]   It should be noted that the medical evidence should usually come from a (neuro)psychiatrist rather than a neuropsychologist, since the latter may not necessarily be medically qualified.
[2]   For a definition of incapacity, see further the Mental Health Act 1983 and *Masterman-Lister v Brutton & Co* [2003] PIQR P310.
[3]   The administrative arm of the Court of Protection and part of the Ministry of Justice. Established on 1 April 2001 and based in North London, the PGO is responsible for providing the mental health functions previously undertaken by the Public Trustee Office (which included the work of the Court Funds Office and Trust Division). The PGO offers financial protection services for people who are unable to manage their own affairs through mental incapacity. The current fees charged are governed by the Court of Protection (Amendment) Rules 2004, SI 2004/1291. See further Heywood and Massey *Court of Protection Practice* (13th edn, looseleaf).
[4]   Anyone can be appointed deputy as long as they can demonstrate their suitability to the Court of Protection. Generally speaking, the deputy will usually be a professional deputy, eg a solicitor specialising in private client work or a family member. As a last resort, the PGO may act as deputy through its Chief Executive where the Court of Protection can find no one else willing or suitable to become the deputy. When the Court of Protection appoints the Chief Executive of the PGO as deputy, the claimant's affairs will be assigned to a specific named official in the PGO's deputyship division called a 'case worker'. The case worker has delegated responsibility from the Court of Protection to deal with the claimant's day-to-day affairs.
[5]   *Futej v Lewandowski* (1980) 124 Sol Jo 777, approved by the Court of Appeal in *Rialis v Mitchell* (1984) Times, 17 July. See further paras 2.47 to 2.54 of the Law Commission's Report No 262 'Damages for Personal Injury: Medical, Nursing and other Expenses; Collateral Benefits' (November 1999).
[6]   *Smith v Rod Jenkins* [2003] EWHC 1356 (QB).
[7]   In *Hodgson v Trapp* [1988] 1 FLR 69, Taylor J awarded past but not future costs under this head, which was not directly challenged in the subsequent appeals to the Court of Appeal and House of Lords. See also *Wells v Wells* [1997] 1 WLR 652, in which the Court of Appeal awarded the reasonable solicitors' costs to be incurred in the future by the claimant's daughter in her capacity as the claimant's deputy. And in *Willbye v Gibbons* [2003] EWCA Civ 372, where the claimant's solicitor acted as deputy, the Court of Appeal awarded costs of deputyship in the annual sum of £2,848.75 (subject to a deduction for contributory negligence).
[8]   *Parry v North West Surrey Health Authority* (29 November 1999, unreported), QBD.
[9]   *Willbye v Gibbons* [2003] EWCA Civ 372. See also *Cassel v Riverside Health Authority* [1994] PIQR Q168.

[F200]   The OPG's annual fees are governed by the Mental Capacity Act 2005 and Public Guardian (Fees etc) Regulations 2007 (as amended). Guidance regarding the current fees can be downloaded from the OPG's website at www.publicguardian. gov.uk. Different types of annual supervision charges apply as well as various other charges including fees in relation to the appointment of a deputy, making paper and oral applications and the assessment of fees.

[F201]   As regards deputyship fees, the reasonableness of the sums claimed will depend upon the facts of the case including the type of work carried out, the amount of work carried out, the complexity or difficulty of the work, the rate charged and the location of the claimant/deputy. In *Eagle v Chambers (No 2)*[1], Master Lush gave evidence that the costs of a professional deputy were likely to exceed £3,500 per annum (plus VAT). However, following the implementation of the Mental Capacity Act 2005, experience has been that professional deputyship costs often tend to be significantly in excess of that sum[2]. In any case where a professional deputy has been or is likely to be instructed, it is sensible to obtain evidence in the form of an admissible witness statement from a suitably qualified and experienced practitioner who can advise upon the likely costs that will be incurred[3]. Where possible, the best evidence regarding future loss will be based upon assessed bills of fees already incurred.

1	[2004] EWCA Civ 1033.
2	See eg the awards made in *Iqbal v Whipps Cross University* [2007] LS Law Medical 97; *Smith v East and North Hertfordshire Hospitals NHS Trust* [2008] EWHC 2234 (QB); and *Huntley v Simmonds* [2009] EWHC 405 (QB), in which past losses under this head were agreed at £35,579 and future loss at £321,003.
3	See eg *Peters v East Midlands Strategic HA* [2008] EWHC 778 (QB), in which the claimant called her deputy, Mrs Miles, to give evidence about the likely future costs of professional deputyship fees and, on her unchallenged evidence, Butterfield J awarded £5,000 pa as claimed.

(ii) Transaction and Investment Charges

[F202]   As well as the above expenses, separate fees will often be charged on each transaction made involving the claimant's assets. The claimant may also incur further annual investment and brokerage charges. Despite there being some evidence of judges previously being prepared to consider awards for these types of charges[1], it is now clear that any such charges stemming from the investment of the damages received will not be recoverable[2]. In *Page v Plymouth Hospitals NHS Trust*[3], Davis J carried out a thorough review of the authorities and arguments for and against such claims, and concluded that the costs of investment advice (including transaction charges) were not recoverable in principle, because they had already been taken into account by the Lord Chancellor when fixing the discount rate at the rate he had[4]. The attempt to claim investment advice as a separate head of damages was seen as an impermissible attack on the discount rate[5]. This reasoning was approved by the Court of Appeal in *Eagle v Chambers (No 2)*[6] and found to be equally applicable to claimants who lacked capacity and were under the jurisdiction of the Court of Protection, even though they had no control over how their money was managed or invested.

1	*Duller v South East Lincs Engineers* [1981] CLY 585; *Cassel v Hammersmith and Fulham Health Authority* [1992] PIQR Q168; *Anderson v Davies* [1993] PIQR Q87; *Ejvet v AID Pallets* (11 March 2002, unreported), QBD, and related article by Matthias Kelly QC 'Are Broker's Fees Recoverable' [2002] Quantum, Issue 2/2002, 27 March.
2	*Webster v Hammersmith Hospitals NHS Trust* [2002] All ER (D) 397; *Anderson v Blackpool, Wyre & Fylde Community Health Services NHS Trust* (unreported); *Page v Plymouth Hospitals NHS Trust* [2004] EWHC 1154 (QB). See further William Norris QC and Douglas Hall 'Claims for the Cost of Investment Management' [2004] JPIL, Issue 3/04, at 214–224; and Edward Duckworth 'The End of the Line for Claims for Investment Management Charges? – *Page v Plymouth Hospitals NHS Trust* and *Eagle v Chambers (No 2)*' [2004] Quantum, Issue 6/2004, 1 November.
3	[2004] EWHC 1154 (QB).
4	Davis J said at [52]:
	'Moreover, I find it difficult to think that the Lord Chancellor, in making these observations, could or would have overlooked the attendant costs involved in seeking investment advice in setting the discount rate as he did. It is true that the Lord Chancellor does not expressly

say that he had taken them into the account (and Mr Spink told me that the point seems not to have been explicitly raised in the preceding consultation process). But in my judgment it is inherent in the Lord Chancellor's reasoning: and that is of a pattern with the observations of Lord Hope and Lord Clyde in *Wells v Wells*. Thus when, in the course of his reasons, the Lord Chancellor refers to the position about investment on mixed asset portfolios, I think it likely that he was there referring to a real rate of return "comfortably" exceeding 2.5% as connoting a return net not only of tax but also of investment costs.'

[5]   Which was blocked by cases such as *Warriner v Warriner* [2002] 1 WLR 1703 and *Cooke v United Bristol Health Care* [2003] EWCA Civ 1370.

[6]   [2004] EWCA Civ 1033.

(iii)   Trust Fees where Claimant is Competent

[F203]   Where the claimant has capacity, there may still be a number of reasons why the claimant wishes to have a trust. First, a trust protects the claimant from losing means-tested benefits[1]. Secondly, a trust may prevent a local authority from taking into account lump sum payments when assessing means for statutory assistance[2]. Thirdly, a trust will provide professional assistance to those who need assistance managing their finances, and a layer of protection for those who are vulnerable to exploitation. Although, to our knowledge, there is no decided case regarding the first category, the court may consider that the costs of setting up and running the trust are more than offset by the advantage of keeping means-tested benefits. Therefore, despite s 17 of the Social Security (Recovery of Benefits) Act 1997 obliging the court to disregard any listed benefits paid after the relevant period[2], a court may be reluctant to award the claimant's costs of setting up and running purely to keep this advantage (which may be considered a matter of personal choice). However, there are some cases in which claims in the second category have been agreed, especially where the claimant has suffered a brain injury and, whilst he or she meets the test for legal capacity, there are some concerns about the claimant's ability to manage money[4]. Although, in *A v Powys Local Health Board*[5], Lloyd-Jones J considered the claim for setting up and running a trust in relation to a competent 17-year-old girl with cerebral palsy resulting in severe dysarthria. Lloyd-Jones disallowed the claim on the basis that the proposed assistance was not required because, although her speech was difficult to understand, those who knew her could understand her well, she had a protective family, a case manager who could help with organising carers and occupational therapy input to assist with equipment. But he was persuaded that she would benefit from a premier banking service, and allowed an annual sum of €500 to cover this. It remains to be seen whether such a claim could succeed where the claimant does not suffer from lack of capacity due to a brain injury, but nonetheless requires assistance with managing his or her own financial affairs due to severe communication or physical disabilities. In principle, where such assistance is reasonably required, there seems to be no good reason why it should not be recovered, just as such assistance would be recovered for care, or assistance with domestic tasks and DIY etc.

[1]   Although note that there is a 52-week disregard period by virtue of Income Support (General) Regulations 1987, Sch 10, para 12A. See further David Coldrick and Lynne Bradey 'Personal Injury Trusts and the New Temporary Disregard for Personal Injury Awards' [2006] JPIL Issue 4/2006, pp 354–360.

[2]   Such a trust may therefore have considerable advantages to a defendant. Prior to the Court of Appeal's decision in *Peters v East Midlands Strategic HA* [2009] EWCA Civ 145, this led some

defendants to attempt to argue that failure to set up such a trust and apply for local authority funding amounted to a failure to mitigate loss.

3   Under Social Security (Recovery of Benefits) Act 1997, s 3(1), the 'relevant period' is defined as five years from the day upon which the accident or injury in question occurred or, in a disease case, five years from the date upon which the claimant first claims a listed benefit in consequence of the disease.

4   See eg *S v L* (settlement in May 2006, reported in PI Focus, Volume 16, Issue 5, September 2006); *Sarwar v (1) Ali and (2) MIB* [2007] EWHC 1255 (QB); and *Ure v Ure* (unreported, QBD, settlement 13 July 2007).

5   [2007] EWHC 2996 (QB). See also *Owen v Brown* [2002] EWHC 1135 (QB), in which Silber J rejected the suggestion that a trust could protect the claimant because it could be wound up by the claimant at any time.

(iv)   Accountancy Fees where Claimant is Competent

[F204]   Where the claimant lacks capacity, accountancy fees are often recovered as part of the administration costs of managing his or her money. Accountancy fees may take the form of assistance with compiling accounts, completing annual tax returns and/or checking the annual uprating of periodical payments. Such claims are usually allowed if the claimant was able to manage his or her own finances prior to the injury, since the need for assistance flows from the injury and would not have been required otherwise[1]. But might it also be reasonable for a competent claimant to claim such assistance? Prior to injury, most claimants are employed on a PAYE basis and are not responsible for preparing their own accounts or filing tax returns. Further, those claimants who are self-employed are able to set off any accountancy fees against tax. In *A v Powys Local Health Board*[2], Lloyd-Jones J held that accountancy fees fall into the same category as investment advice, because such costs flow from the decision not to invest in gilts. However, this may not be entirely correct where there is a large sum of damages, because the claimant may need to complete an annual tax return when otherwise this would not have been necessary whatever he or she invests in, and this need only arises by reason of the injury suffered. Therefore, if by reason of a large award of damages the claimant is now required to complete accounts and tax returns, and wishes to have some assistance in this regard, especially if he or she suffers from memory and concentration problems falling short of incompetence, it may be reasonable for the claimant to recover such costs[3].

1   *Rialis v Mitchell* (1984) Times, 17 July.
2   [2007] EWHC 2996 (QB).
3   See eg *Noble v Owens* [2008] EWHC 359 (QB), in which this claim was settled for £7,500.

18   Education

[F205]   Claims for the increased cost of education may arise in a number of ways. Where the claimant is a child, costs may be incurred paying for private schooling because there are no suitable state schools for people with the claimant's injuries[1], or paying legal fees forcing the local education authority to make adequate provision, eg appealing the claimant's statement of educational needs[2]. Additional costs may also be incurred in respect of home tutoring or paying for a one-to-one classroom assistant where this is required but is not funded by the state[3]. If the claimant would probably have gone to private school anyway, only the additional costs of any special or residential school can be claimed compared to the costs that would have been incurred[4]. Where the claimant is an adult, claims may be made for the costs of retraining or further education in order to help realise any residual earning capacity. Claims may also be made for the loss of benefit of private schooling for the claimant's family where this was a perk of a job which has been lost by reason of injuries sustained[5].

[1]   See eg *O'Brien v Wharton* LTLPI 1/11/2004, Lawtel Document No AM0200671.
[2]   In *Iqbal v Whipps Cross University* [2007] LS Law Medical 97 the claimant recovered the (agreed) sum of £10,429 for past education costs and an indemnity in respect of future education costs.
[3]   See eg *Haines v Airedale NHS Trust* (2 May 2000, unreported), QBD.
[4]   This point was rightly conceded in *Ryan-Ndegwa v Kings College Hospital NHS Trust* LTLPI 28/11/2002, Lawtel Document No AM0900575.
[5]   This head of loss was recognised in principle but not awarded on the facts in *Morgan v MOD* [2002] EWHC 2072 (QB), since the benefit only related to boarding school and was not an educational allowance as such.

19   Miscellaneous Expenses

[F206]   We have already seen examples of increased household expenditure on items such as food, clothing and heating (at paras **[F174]–[F176]**). Further examples of miscellaneous 'one-off' and ongoing expenses which might be incurred as a result of the claimant's injuries include:

- Loss of insurance no claims bonus.
- Loss of value on investment or insurance polices[1].
- Delivery charges for food and other purchases[2].
- Special food or dietary requirements[3].
- Gym fees[4].
- Overdraft fees or debt interest[5].
- Postage, photographic expenses, telephone calls, stationery, faxing and photocopying[6].
- Additional cigarettes wasted/destroyed by reason of a head/brain injury[7].
- Costs of bespoke footwear and orthotics[8].
- Legal fees incurred appealing a statement of special educational needs (SEN)[9].
- Relationship counselling due to problems in relationship caused by the claimant's injuries[10].
- Increased cost of hairdressing[11].
- Dog walking[12].
- Legal fees incurred pursuing an employment tribunal claim caused by the claimant's injuries[13].
- Videoconferencing[14].
- Additional tax levied as a result of the claimant's residence in a foreign country[15].
- Increased cost of life insurance, critical illness cover, permanent health insurance, private medical insurance, mortgage protection, travel insurance and pension benefits[16].
- Lost rental income due to the inability to rent the family home whilst abroad on business[17].
- Increased washing machine usage and cleaning[18].

- Carpet cleaning[19].
- The need to wear spectacles[20].
- Additional expenditure on toiletries, disinfectant, washing powder and cleaning materials[21] etc.
- Expenditure on incontinency materials such as nappies[22], disposable gloves, wipes, creams etc.
- Sundry expenses incurred during stay in hospital such as cost of television, food for family and friends, magazines etc[23].
- Cleaning / domestic assistance[24].
- Car washing / cleaning / valeting[25].
- Furnishings for carers.
- Bed linen and towels (eg for carers or because of the need to replace more frequently because of incontinence).
- Increased cost of toys[26].
- Tips paid to taxi drivers for bringing in groceries[27].
- Livery charges[28].
- Delivery and/or shipping charges in respect of items of aids and equipment purchased[29].
- Repairs to accommodation to rectify wheelchair damage[30].

[1] In some cases, the claimant might have been forced to sell off investments or insurance policies which would otherwise have matured to advantage. In these circumstances, there may well be a recoverable loss which is likely to require expert evidence in order to properly assess/value. However, the claimant will need to demonstrate that, but for his or her injuries, the investment would have been sold at a different time at a different value, thus giving rise to the loss; a claim arising out of the sale of investment properties failed in *Pankhurst v (1) White and (2) MIB* [2009] EWHC 1117 (QB), where the court held, inter alia, that there had been no loss since the value of the investment had not changed, but had merely been converted into cash.

[2] See eg *Assinder v Griffin* [2001] All ER (D) 356 (May), in which HHJ Peter Clark awarded the claimant £5 per week for the additional expense of ordering her food on the Internet.

[3] For example, in *Biesheuval v Birrell* [1999] PIQR Q40, Eady J allowed the cost of an orange juicer (but not the costs of cranberry juice and vitamin tablets as well).

[4] See eg *Assinder v Griffin* [2001] All ER (D) 356 (May), in which HHJ Peter Clark awarded the claimant £868 for the costs of joining a gym on medical advice following the accident, having never been a member of a gym or fitness centre before, notwithstanding the savings made in respect of hobbies she previously enjoyed. See also *Huntley v Simmonds* [2009] EWHC 405 (QB).

[5] See eg *Kidd v Plymouth Health Authority* [2001] Lloyd's Law Rep Med 165, in which Kay J at 173 said that the defendant's counsel had rightly conceded that the claim for an overdraft fee of £506 was appropriate (given that the fee was incurred at a time when the defendant would not consent to an application for an interim payment).

[6] Technically, any expenses incurred as a result of pursuing the litigation (as opposed to, say, arranging treatment appointments) are costs and are not recoverable as damages: *O'Brien-King v Phillips* [1997] CLY 1814. However, it is not uncommon for a modest sum to be awarded under this head, especially if unchallenged by the defendant.

[7] In *Eagle v Chambers (No 2)* [2004] EWCA Civ 1033, the Court of Appeal upheld the trial judge's award for past loss relating to cigarettes destroyed rather than additional cigarettes smoked resulting from a brain injury.

[8] See eg *Cannon v Cannon* [2005] EWHC 1310 (QB).

[9] *Haines v Airedale NHS Trust* (2 May 2000, unreported), QBD, per Bell J.

[10] *Taylor v Weston AHA* [2003] All ER (D) 50 (Dec); cf *Smith v East and North Hertfordshire Hospitals NHS Trust* [2008] EWHC 2234 (QB), in which family counselling was disallowed because the parents were not parties to the action.

[11] *Dennison v Dennison & anor* LTL 24/7/2008, where a claim for past and future hairdressing was agreed in the sum of £12,000.

[12]   *Dennison v Dennison & anor* LTL 24/7/2008.

[13]   *Assinder v Griffin* [2001] All ER (D) 356 (May). Note that the claimant should give credit for the net compensation received as a result of any claim, ie the damages received less any reasonable legal costs incurred in obtaining the damages.

[14]   *Patel v Patel* [2005] EWHC 347 (QB).

[15]   In some cases, it may be necessary to 'gross up' some claims if they are taxed when received by the claimant living in a foreign jurisdiction: *Horton v (1) Evans and (2) Lloyds Pharmacy Ltd* [2007] EWHC 315 (QB).

[16]   It may be possible to show that, by reason of the claimant's injuries, such products are now more expensive to purchase: see further *A v National Blood Authority* [2001] Lloyd's Rep Med 187.

[17]   See eg *Morgan v MOD* [2002] EWHC 2072 (QB), in which Andrew Collender QC allowed £3,000 pa in respect of this claim.

[18]   See eg *Warrilow v Norfolk and Norwich Hospitals NHS Trust* [2006] EWHC 801 (QB), where increased washing machine usage and cleaning was allowed due to the effects of excessive morphine use; and *A v Powys Local Health Board* [2007] EWHC 2996 (QB), in which £55 pa was allowed for increased washing machine and dryer usage due to incontinence.

[19]   See eg *Smith v East and North Hertfordshire Hospitals NHS Trust* [2008] EWHC 2234 (QB).

[20]   See eg *Cannon v Cannon* [2005] EWHC 1310 (QB), in which Forbes J awarded £328,728.48 in respect of the future costs of bespoke footwear and Wellington Boots.

[21]   See eg *Smith v East and North Hertfordshire Hospitals NHS Trust* [2008] EWHC 2234 (QB).

[22]   See eg *Smith v East and North Hertfordshire Hospitals NHS Trust* [2008] EWHC 2234 (QB).

[23]   See eg *Burton v Kingsbury* [2007] EWHC 2091 (QB), in which Flaux J awarded £6,000 against a claim for past hospital expenses of £6,740.59, including a claim for 194 DVDs at £2,520.

[24]   See eg *Massey v Tameside & Glossop Acute Services NHS Trust* [2007] EWHC 317 (QB).

[25]   See eg *Crofts v Murton* LTL 10/9/2008.

[26]   See eg *Lewis v Shrewsbury NHS Trust* (29 January 2007).

[27]   See eg *Garth v (1) Grant and (2) MIB*, QBD, LTL 17/7/2007.

[28]   See eg *A v Powys Local Health Board* [2007] EWHC 2996 (QB).

[29]   See eg *A v Powys Local Health Board* [2007] EWHC 2996 (QB).

[30]   See eg *Owen v Brown* [2002] EWHC 1135 (QB).

G Interest on Past Expenses and Losses

1 Introduction

[G1] Up to the date of the final assessment of quantum, the claimant may have incurred a number of pre-trial expenses and losses (known as 'past expenses and losses' or 'special damages'). Despite the laudable aims of the CPR to speed up the litigation process, once proceedings have been issued it may still take a number of months or years before judgment is finally entered and the claimant receives compensation for the items claimed. By this time, there might be a significant period between when the item of expense or loss was incurred and when damages are recovered for the same. If the final sum awarded were to remain the same as the amount of the expenses/losses incurred, the claimant would be under-compensated in times of inflation. Therefore, it is usually necessary for interest to be added to the final figure in order to compensate the claimant for not being reimbursed at the time of the loss[1].

---

[1] In the Employment Tribunal, interest on past special damages is calculated in the same way as at common law: Industrial Tribunals (Interest on Awards in Discrimination Cases) Regulations 1996, SI 1996/2803.

2 Requirements under the CPR

[G2] Under CPR, r 16.4(1)(b), if the claimant is seeking interest, the particulars of claim must include a statement to that effect and set out the details contained in CPR, r 16.4(2), which reads as follows:

'If the claimant is seeking interest he must:
(a) State whether he is doing so:
    (i) under the terms of a contract;
    (ii) under an enactment and if so which; or
    (iii) on some other basis and if so what that basis is; and
(b) if the claim is for a specified amount of money, state:
    (i) the percentage rate at which interest is claimed;
    (ii) the date from which it is claimed;
    (iii) the date to which it is calculated, which must not be later than the date on which the claim form is issued;
    (iv) the total amount of interest claimed to the date of calculation; and
    (v) the daily rate at which interest accrues after that date.'

[G3] Since the claim for interest in personal injury cases is rarely, if ever, for a specified amount of money, it is unlikely that it will ever be necessary to set out the details listed in CPR, r 16.4(2)(b) above regarding the percentage rate, the date from which interest runs and the date to which interest is calculated etc in the particulars of claim. Therefore, practitioners often end particulars of claim by stating something along the lines of 'The Claimant is further entitled to and claims interest pursuant to [s 69 of the County Courts Act 1984 or s 35A of the Senior Courts Act 1981[1]] on the amount found to be due to the Claimant at such rate and for such period as the Court thinks fit'. However, it is becoming more common practice, particularly for substantial claims, to set out in the particulars of claim the basis upon which interest is claimed, the dates and rates of interest claimed, and the total amount of interest claimed on past losses and expenses. This has the advantage of putting the whole claim before the court, and may therefore identify at an early stage any disputes between the parties regarding the calculation of interest. However, the entitlement to interest has been held to be a remedy rather than a statutory right[2], and thus a failure to plead a claim for interest should not necessarily mean that no interest can be recovered[3].

[1]   Depending upon whether the claim is issued in the county court or the High Court.
[2]   *Riches v Westminster Bank* [1934] 2 All ER 725; *Jefford v Gee* [1970] 2 QB 130; *Maher and Maher v Groupama Grand Est* [2009] EWCA Civ 1191.
[3]   See further CPR, r 16.2(5), which permits the court to award a remedy to which the claimant is entitled, even if that remedy has not been specified in the claim form.

[G4]   CPR, r 40.8 reads as follows:

'(1)   Where interest is payable on a judgment pursuant to section 17 of the Judgments Act 1838 or section 74 of the County Courts Act 1984, the interest shall begin to run from the date that judgment is given unless:
    (a)   a rule in another Part or a practice direction makes different provision; or
    (b)   the court orders otherwise.
(2)   The court may order that interest shall begin to run from a date before the date that judgment is given.'

3   The General Principle

(i)   The Presumption

[G5]   There is a general presumption that, by virtue of s 69 of the County Courts Act 1984 or s 35A of the Senior Courts Act 1981, interest will be payable on all awards for personal injury which exceed £200[1]. However, the court has a discretion not to order interest where it is satisfied that there are special reasons for displacing the presumption[2].

[1]   *Davies v Inman* [1999] PIQR Q26.
[2]   For example, where the claimant has issued prematurely in breach of the Personal Injury Pre-action Protocol or where the claimant has been guilty of gross delay in pursuing the claim. See further at para **[G29]** and Chapter K, Counter-schedules.

(ii)   The Calculation

[G6]   The general rule concerning the assessment of interest on special damages was stated in *Jefford v Gee*[1]: interest on special damages is calculated at half the special account rate on the total amount of special damages over the period commencing on the date of the accident and concluding on the date of trial. This general rule is for convenience of calculation, and can be rebutted in appropriate cases[2].

---

[1]   [1970] 2 QB 130, [1970] 1 All ER 1202.

[2]   *Prokop v Department of Health and Social Security* [1985] CLY 1037, CA; *Ichard v Frangoulis* [1977] 2 All ER 461, [1977] 1 WLR 556; *Hobin v Douglas* (1998) 143 Sol Jo LB 21, CA. See below at para **[G9]**.

(iii)   The Special Account Rate

[G7]   The special account rate is set by the Court Funds Office[1] following a direction from the Lord Chancellor[2]. The rate varies from time to time and there is no way of predicting when the rate will change. The Lord Chancellor periodically meets with officials from the Bank of England to decide whether the rate needs to be changed and what the new rate should be. The details of any new rate changes are published in the *New Law Journal* and *The Times*. From 1 July 2009 the special account rate has been 0.5%. The following table sets out the rates from 1988 onwards.

Date of rate change	Full special account rate	Half special account rate
	(%)	(%)
01/11/88	12.25	6.125
01/01/89	13	6.5
01/11/89	14.25	7.125
01/04/91	12	6
01/10/91	10.25	5.125
01/02/93	8	4
01/08/99	7	3.5
01/02/02	6	3
01/02/09	3	1.5
01/05/09	1.5	0.75
01/07/09	0.5	0.25

---

[1]   The Court Funds Office can be contacted at 22 Kingsway, London WC2B 6LE, DX: 149780 Kingsway 5. Customer Service Helpline: 0845 223 8500; Court Funds Office: general enquiries email: enquiries@courtfunds.gsi.gov.uk.

[2]   Note that the rate is not set by way of statutory instrument. Further information and the latest rate can be checked by checking the Court Funds Office website: www.officialsolicitor.gov.uk/cfo/cfo. htm.

(iv)   The Future Rate

[G8]   In February 2004 the Law Commission published a report on pre-judgment interest on debts and claims, recommending that there should be one specified rate of interest on past losses set each year at 1% above the Bank of England Base Rate[1]. The current Labour Government agreed that the relevant legislation should be amended, to give the Lord Chancellor power to prescribe a pre-judgment interest rate which would be set by reference to the Bank of England base rate[2]. Likewise, it was thought that there was a case for amending s 17 of the Judgments Act 1838 so that the post-judgment interest rate can also be set by reference to the Bank of England base rate. On 15 December 2009, the Ministry of Justice published a draft Bill[3] setting out the proposed changes, providing the Lord Chancellor with a power to set the appropriate rate of interest on damages together with a consultation paper. The consultation closes on 9 February 2010 and it remains to be seen what any subsequent Government decides to do and what, if anything, happens to the proposed Bill.

[1]　Law Commission's Report No 287 'Pre-judgment Interest on Debts and Damages' (2004).
[2]　The Government's response to the Law Commission report: 'Pre-judgment interest on debts and damages' 19 September 2008 available from the Ministry of Justice website at www.justice.gov.uk.
[3]　Civil Law Reform Bill, reference CP53/09, available from the Ministry of Justice website at www. justice.gov.uk.

(v)　Compound or Simple Interest

[G9]　The Law Commission also recommended that the court should have the power to award interest on a compound basis, and that there should be a rebuttable presumption that interest will be awarded on a compound basis for cases worth more than £15,000[1]. However, in its response the Government rejected this idea, which was described as a major step which would require further consultation and a more detailed and quantified impact assessment[2]. It is noteworthy that the Law Commission estimated that their proposal would add between £20 and £25 million to the cost of clinical negligence claims each year[3]. The draft Civil Law Reform Bill published by the Ministry of Justice suggests that, where damages are awarded in a currency other than sterling, the court should give consideration as to whether or not simple or compound interest is awarded[4]. Furthermore, where damages are awarded in sterling, it is proposed that the Lord Chancellor will determine whether or not the interest is to be compound or simple when making an order setting the appropriate rate of interest[5].

[1]　Law Commission's Report No 287 'Pre-judgment Interest on Debts and Damages' (2004).
[2]　The Government's response to the Law Commission report: 'Pre-judgment interest on debts and damages' 19 September 2008 available from the Ministry of Justice website at www.justice.gov.uk.
[3]　See para 1.23.
[4]　See clause 11(6) of the draft Civil Law Reform Bill, reference CP53/09, available from the Ministry of Justice website at www.justice.gov.uk.
[5]　See clause 11(4) of the draft Civil Law Reform Bill, reference CP53/09, available from the Ministry of Justice website at www.justice.gov.uk.

4　Methods of Calculation

[G10]　In practice, there are essentially two methods of calculating the interest due on past losses. These can be illustrated by the cases of *Prokop v Department of Health and Social Security*[1] and *Dexter v Courtaulds Ltd*[2]. The former authority was not cited in the latter case, and the two cases represent two different approaches to the calculation of interest upon special damages approved at Court of Appeal level.

¹   [1985] CLY 1037, CA.
²   [1984] 1 All ER 70, [1984] 1 WLR 372.

(i)   Prokop

[G11]   In *Prokop v Department of Health and Social Security*¹ the Court of Appeal decided that a claimant who incurs his or her special damage loss at the beginning of the period of accrual of interest should receive interest at the full rate from the mid-date of incurring those expenses. Thus, take, for example, a straightforward road traffic accident where a claimant has to incur 28 days' car hire for a replacement vehicle. No other continuing expenses are incurred until the date of trial. He should receive interest at the full rate from half-way through the period (ie 14 days) of incurring the car hire expenses, up until the date of trial.

¹   [1985] CLY 1037, CA. The full special account rate from the date that the loss was incurred was also awarded in *Ichard v Frangoulis* [1977] 1 WLR 556 and *Hobin v Douglas* (1998) 143 Sol Jo LB 21, CA.

(ii)   Dexter

[G12]   In *Dexter*¹, the Court of Appeal, for policy reasons, applied the general approach of *Jefford v Gee*². In a typical personal injury case, where the expenses such as loss of earnings and care are incurred continuously over a period up until the date of trial or thereabouts, it would, as a matter of policy, be less tedious to calculate the interest on behalf of the claimant by halving the full interest rate from the date of the accident until trial. The reasons for this are clear enough to see. Such a practice avoids having to calculate interest on each item from when it was incurred at the various special account rates over the duration of the loss.

¹   [1984] 1 All ER 70, [1984] 1 WLR 372.
²   [1970] 2 QB 130, [1970] 1 All ER 1202.

5   Choosing the Appropriate Method of Calculation

[G13]   The two authorities are not necessarily incompatible. (Although, on its facts, one would have expected the court in *Dexter*¹ to apply the *Prokop*² method of calculation.) The cases seek to deal with different situations. In *Dexter*, the Court of Appeal acknowledged that there may be 'occasional' cases where it would be appropriate and fairer to the claimant to award interest at the full rate, and warned of the need in such cases to plead special circumstances for the calculation of interest.

¹   [1984] 1 All ER 70, [1984] 1 WLR 372.
²   [1985] CLY 1037, CA.

[G14]   It would be absurd if the method of quantification of interest in a particular case depended upon whether it was a 'typical' or 'occasional' personal injury case. The principle must be that, if the claimant would be more than minimally under-compensated by applying the general rule (*Jefford*[1] or *Dexter*[2]), then *Prokop*[3] should be applied. *Prokop* was followed in an unreported decision of Mars-Jones J, *Singh (Mengha) v C & D Smith Foundries Ltd*[4]. The court in that case, having considered arguments based upon *Dexter* and *Prokop*, preferred to apply the latter to the particular circumstances of the case. This was because the special damages were not incurred continuously up until the date of trial or thereabouts.

[1]   [1970] 2 QB 130, [1970] 1 All ER 1202.
[2]   [1984] 1 All ER 70, [1984] 1 WLR 372.
[3]   [1985] CLY 1037, CA.
[4]   (17 July 1985, unreported).

[G15]   In its report regarding personal injury damages, published in 1999, the Law Commission recommended[1] that interest should be awarded on discrete losses at full rate from the date of the loss until trial, whereas any loss spread over time should accrue interest at half rate from the mid-point of loss. Since an award of interest is discretionary, a judge can properly award interest on the Law Commission approach (which essentially prefers *Prokop*[2] to *Dexter*[3]). In summary, the Law Commission recommended that interest on past expenses and losses be calculated as follows:

- Interest on damages for pre-trial pecuniary loss should continue to be awarded only if claimed.
- Interest on damages for a non-recurring pre-trial pecuniary loss should be awarded at the full average rate from the date of the loss to the date of trial.
- Interest on damages for a recurring pre-trial pecuniary loss should be awarded at the full average rate from the midpoint of the specific period during which the loss was suffered to the date of trial.
- Either of the parties may establish (provided the details have been specifically pleaded) that a different method of calculating interest is more appropriate.
- The court should retain a discretion to refuse interest, or to award interest on a different basis.

[1]   Law Commission Report No 262 'Damages for Personal Injury: Medical, Nursing and Other Expenses; Collateral Benefits' (November 1999).
[2]   [1985] CLY 1037, CA.
[3]   [1984] 1 All ER 70, [1984] 1 WLR 372.

[G16]   Thus, it can be seen that the court will apply the method of calculation which is most suitable to the expenses/losses incurred in the particular case. If the expenses/losses are continuous from the date of the accident to the trial, then the *Dexter*[1] method would be preferred. Such a case would be continuous loss of earnings or cost of care. However, on a significant head of loss where the loss does not start until a later date, interest may not be awarded until the loss starts, eg when the claimant losses his or her job following an injury[2]. Also, where particular losses occur for only a short period (especially near the start of the period), the court may be persuaded to adopt an approach akin to *Prokop*[3].

[1]   [1984] 1 All ER 70, [1984] 1 WLR 372.

See eg *Van Wees v (1) Karkour and (2) Walsh* [2007] EWHC 165 (QB), in which Langstaff J
     awarded interest at half the special account rate on the claimant's award for past loss of earnings, but
     from the date that the claimant ceased work with her employer rather than the date of the accident as
     claimed; and *Horton v (1) Evans and (2) Lloyds Pharmacy Ltd* [2007] EWHC 315 (QB).
³   [1985] CLY 1037, CA.

6   The Effect of Interim Payments

(i)   General Principles

[G17]   The calculation of interest on special damages is obviously based on the
fact that the claimant has been denied access to the money which was rightly judged
to have been his or hers over the relevant period. Therefore, if an interim payment
is ordered by the court, the claimant will, in fact, have received compensation for at
least a partial amount of the losses they have suffered to date. Therefore, the question
then arises as to how the court should take account of these payments in the final
interest calculation. With regard to the total damages, the court assesses a final figure
and can simply set off the amount paid by way of interim payments. However, the
interest has not been suffered on the global sum for the entire period, as the interim
payments have, in effect, partially paid off the total at times prior to final assessment.

[G18]   The parties in *Bristow v Judd*[1] argued two different approaches to interest
credit in cases involving interim payments. Both parties argued that the correct
approach would be to award interest on the global amount of damages on the
conventional basis, but there should then be deducted from this an amount of interest
on the interim payments calculated from the date of such payments. Where the parties
differed is that the defendant argued that the rate of interest should be at the full rate,
whereas the claimant argued it should be at half the full rate, so as to keep in line with
the interest on the global figure.

¹   [1993] PIQR Q117.

[G19]   The judge at first instance adopted the approach of the claimant, stating that
he had considered the general fairness of the case and that the basis suggested by
the claimant was right. However, the Court of Appeal adopted an entirely different
approach from either of the two approaches suggested by the parties. Beldam LJ,
in giving judgment, however, expressed his view that the Court of Appeal was
not giving general guidance for an interest calculation in a case involving interim
payments. Instead, he emphasised the fact that the court was considering the facts
of the particular case and, since the facts of cases often differ widely, it is within the
discretion of the judge in awarding interest to decide each case on its own particular
facts. However, that said, the approach adopted by the Court of Appeal would
obviously influence the courts in following cases.

[G20]   Beldam LJ set out the principles of interim awards and interest calculations
that the Court of Appeal accepted, as follows[1]:

'I would accept in principle that the payment of an interim award should be taken to be
compensation first of all for loss and expense incurred until the date of payment of the
interim award. Until an interim payment reduces the amount due for special damage,

a claimant is entitled to interest at one half of the special account rate on the amount outstanding. Where an interim payment is made which exceeds the amount of special damages due on the date it is paid, I see no reason why the balance should not be taken to have been paid in diminution of the compensation payable as general damages. Thereafter the claimant would be entitled to interest at one-half the special account rate on special damage accruing between the date of payment of the interim payment and the date of trial and 2% on the outstanding amount of general damages.'

Therefore, although the Court of Appeal stated it was not setting any guidance, it has set out the principles that can be accepted as applicable.

¹   [1993] PIQR Q117 at Q130.

[G21]   The approach is, therefore, to calculate the interest over set periods between accident and interim payment(s), and interim payment(s) and trial. The court should calculate how much loss has accrued from accident to interim payment, and then calculate the interest on the loss over that period at one-half of the special rate (unless the full rate is claimed). The loss accrued is then reduced by the amount of the interim payment, and interest is again calculated on this sum combined with that accrued until the next relevant date (be it a further interim payment or trial). If the interim payment is greater than the amount of special damages, then the excess should be deducted from the general damages in respect of the interest calculation. That is, the general damages interest is calculated at 2% on the full amount until the interim payment, and thereafter on the reduced sum until trial.

Example

Accident occurs on 01/01/08. The claimant suffers loss at a rate of £2,000 per annum and is awarded £5,000 in general damages. Proceedings were issued on 01/06/08.

The court orders the following interim payments:

£1,000 on 31/12/08; and

£5,000 on 31/12/09.

Trial is on 30/06/10.

The interest is therefore calculated on the damages as follows:

SPECIAL DAMAGES

Interest at one-half rate on the £2,000 loss accrued to 31/12/08 for the period of 01/01/08 to 31/12/08; plus

Interest at one-half rate on £3,000 (the £2,000 for 2009 less £1,000 interim, plus £2,000 for 2009) for the period of 01/01/09 to 31/12/09;

but no further interest in respect of the loss to trial (£5,000 interim covers the £3,000 loss to 31/12/09 and £1,000 more to 30/06/10).

GENERAL DAMAGES

Interest at 2% per annum, on £5,000 from date of the claim form (01/06/08) to 31/12/09; plus

Interest at 2% per annum on £4,000 (the original general damages is reduced by £1,000 being the excess over special damages accrued up until the £5,000 interim payment) from 31/12/09 to trial on 30/06/10.

[G22] It can be seen that the correct approach is to work out the amount of special damages due to the claimant immediately prior to the interim payment, and calculate interest at one-half rate on this figure over the relevant period, the relevant figure being that from a preceding relevant date (accident or previous interim payment).

(ii) Interest Earned on Interim Payments

[G23] In a first-instance judgment on 29 November 1999, Penry-Davey J held that interest accrued on interim payments from the date of judgment should not be set off against the final sums awarded[1]. Judgment had been entered for the claimant, and the defendants had made three interim payments totalling £950,000. The claimant's mother and litigation friend gave evidence that the money had been invested in a high-interest account and had earned 8% per annum gross. The defendant sought credit for the interest earned from the final sums due. Penry-Davey J held that, once an interim payment had been made, it was up to the claimant to do with it as he or she pleased. As a matter of principle, no account of interest accrued on interim payments should be taken[2]. An exercise to trace the money earned on the interim payments would be time-consuming, complicated and an exercise fraught with difficulties. Although these practical considerations were not determinative of the argument in principle, they did fortify the conclusion reached. In effect, the court held that, once an interim payment was paid, it stopped interest running on that element of the damages, but no further account was taken of sums earned on the interim payment which involved an impermissible investigation into what the claimant did with the interim payment after it was made. However, Penry-Davey J did allude to the fact that, if there was overpayment by way of interim payment, then the court had the power to deal with that and to take account of the interest that the defendant has lost as a result.

[1]   *Edward Maxim Parry v North West Area Health Authority* (2000) Times, 5 January.
[2]   Applying the principles in *Wells v Wells* [1999] AC 345 and *Stringman (a minor) v McArdle* [1994] 1 WLR 1653.

(iii) A Different Approach

[G24] Notwithstanding the approach taken by the Court of Appeal in *Bristow v Judd*[1] and by Penry-Davey J in *Maxim Parry v North West Area Health Authority*[2], there have been several cases where the court has adopted a different approach. Where there have been numerous interim payments received, it may be difficult or time consuming to carry out the calculations as set out by Beldam LJ in *Bristow v Judd*. Likewise, where past losses are largely made up of recurring expenses, or interim payments have been made which significantly exceed the award for past loss, it may be thought that a different approach is required. In the first-instance case of *Massey v Tameside & Glossop Acute Services NHS Trust*[3], Teare J awarded interest to the claimant at half the special account rate on losses accruing from the date of injury, giving credit for interest on the single interim payment of £60,024 received at half the special account rate from the date of the payment. At para 56 of his judgment, he held on the facts of that particular case, since almost all of the past losses had consisted of recurring expenditure on which interest was awarded at half rate, that the fair approach was to give credit on the interim payment at the half rate, as contended by the claimant. However, in the earlier case of *Warrilow v Norfolk and Norwich Hospitals NHS Trust*[4], Langstaff J held that when calculating the interest due on past losses, credit would need to be given on interim payments at the full rate on each such payment from the date it was paid[5]. Such a decision may be viewed as the reverse of awarding interest at the full rate on significant items of specific, one-off loss, such as bereavement damages under the Fatal Accidents Act 1976.

[1]   [1993] PIQR Q117.
[2]   (2000) Times, 5 January.
[3]   [2007] EWHC 317 (QB).
[4]   [2006] EWHC 801 (QB).
[5]   At para 177.

7   Payments Received Prior to the Commencement of Proceedings

[G25]   Care must be taken to ensure that any payments received for items of expense or loss prior to the commencement of proceedings include an allowance for interest. The court only has power to award interest on the judgment sum[1]. Therefore, where payments are received in respect of specific items of expense or loss, the court may be prevented from later awarding interest on any such payments, notwithstanding the unfairness of the position. Likewise, since s 35A of the Senior Courts Act 1981 envisages payment by the defendant, if the claimant accepts payment from a third party this may mean that the claimant loses his or her entitlement to interest[2]. In order to get round these problems, instead of accepting payments in order to satisfy specific heads of loss, it may be considered prudent to only accept general payments on account from the defendant (or his or her agent), thus leaving the whole judgment sum (and entitlement to interest thereon) intact.

[1]   *IM Properties plc v Cape & Dalgleish (a firm)* [1999] QB 297, [1998] 3 All ER 203.
[2]   *IM Properties plc v Cape & Dalgleish (a firm)* [1999] QB 297, per Waller LJ at 306D–E.

8   Subrogated Claims

[G26]   Where the claimant is pursuing a subrogated claim on behalf of a third party, the claimant may claim interest on the amount of the subrogated claim, but any interest that is awarded is held on trust by the claimant for the third party (in the same way that an award for gratuitous care is held on trust by the claimant for the care provider). For example, in *Davies v Inman*[1] the claimant's employer continued to pay the claimant for the 13 weeks he was off work as a result of an accident, on the undertaking that such payments would be refunded from any award of damages received. The employer's outlay was included as part of the claim, and the claimant sought interest on the sum recovered in respect of this head of loss. The defendant objected to interest being paid on this item because the claimant had not been kept out of his money and, therefore, the rationale behind the award of interest did not apply. On appeal, the Court of Appeal held that the claimant's employer was in the same position as a volunteer who had been deprived of money, and so there was no special reason for not awarding interest on the amount recovered for loss of earnings, which was held on trust by the claimant for his employer in accordance with the principles in *Roberts v Johnstone*[2]. Logically, the reasoning of this case would seem to apply to other subrogated claims, such as the outlay of a vehicle insurer or the outlay incurred by a private healthcare insurer for medical expenses.

[1]   [1999] PIQR Q26.
[2]   [1989] QB 878, [1988] 3 WLR 1247.

9   Social Security (Recovery of Benefits) Act 1997

[G27]   Interest is payable on the full amount of special damage before allowing for recoupment: benefits received do *not*, therefore, reduce the interest payable[1].

[1]   *Wadey v Surrey County Council* [2000] 2 All ER 545, [2000] 1 WLR 820.

[G28]   However, an award of interest on damages for past losses of earnings does fall within the expression 'compensation for earnings lost' in Sch 2 to the Social Security (Recovery of Benefits) Act 1997, and is therefore subject to reduction, on account of payments by the tortfeasor to the Secretary of State, to reimburse benefits paid to the claimant as a result of the tortfeasor's wrong[1]. Therefore, if the total amount of recoupment is greater than and extinguishes any particular head of damage, the claimant must continue to give credit for any outstanding benefits against the award of interest in relation to that head of damage.

[1]   *Griffiths v British Coal Corpn* [2001] EWCA Civ 336, [2001] 1 WLR 1493.

10   Part 20 Claims

[G29]   When does interest start to run in the situation where a claimant sues a defendant, the defendant brings a Part 20 claim against a third party, and the claimant then joins the third party as a second defendant? In this case, interest is likely to run against the second defendant from the date of the Part 20 notice because, up to that time, it cannot be said that the second defendant had kept the claimant out of his or her money[1].

[1]   See further *Slater v Hughes* [1971] 3 All ER 1287, [1971] 1 WLR 1438. Although this case is pre-CPR, the court's reasoning on this point should be equally valid under the CPR.

11   Gratuitous Care

[G30]   Interest on damages awarded in respect of past gratuitous care and attendance is awarded in accordance with the principles for the assessment of pecuniary, as opposed to non-pecuniary, loss[1].

[1]   *Roberts v Johnstone* [1987] QB 878, [1988] 3 WLR 1247.

12   Hire Charges

[G31]   Where there are no rights of subrogation and the claimant has not been kept out of his or her money, no interest can be claimed on hire charges[1]. Likewise, no interest can be claimed on credit repair charges where there is no subrogated claim, the charges were incurred at no cost to the claimant, and the reality is that the claimant has not been kept out of his or her money[2].

[1]   *Giles v Thompson* [1994] 1 AC 142, [1993] 3 All ER 321. However, the position may be different where the hire company has an interest in proceedings and/or a subrogated claim: *Clark v Tull* [2002] EWCA Civ 510.
[2]   *Clark v Tull* [2002] EWCA Civ 510.

13   Delay

[G32]   The court may diminish the rate or period of interest awarded where the claimant has been guilty of gross delay in prosecuting the claim[1]. The court has a wide discretion in this regard[2]. What amounts to a culpable period of delay will depend upon a number of factors including: the complexity of the claim; the length of time one would normally expect a case involving similar issues to reach trial; the reasons, if any, provided for the delay; and whether the defendant has been pushing forwards for a trial. However, under the CPR, judges may well be more inclined to mark their disapproval of delay in advancing proceedings by reducing the amount of interest payable (because of the duty imposed by the overriding objective)[3].

[1]   See *Spittle v Bunney* [1988] 3 All ER 1031, [1988] 1 WLR 847; *Cresswell v Eaton* [1991] 1 All ER 484, [1991] 1 WLR 1113; *Nash v Southmead Health Authority* [1993] PIQR Q156, CA; *Read v Harries (No 2)* [1995] PIQR Q34; *Derby Resources AG v Blue Corinth Marine Co Ltd (No 2)* [1998] 2 Lloyd's Rep 425; *Barry v Ablerex* [2000] PIQR Q263; and *Eagle v Chambers (No 2)* [2004] EWCA Civ 1033.
[2]   See *Adcock v Co-operative Insurance Society* [2000] Lloyd's Rep IR 657, in which the Court of Appeal refused to interfere with the first-instance judge's decision to limit the award of interest made to the claimant.
[3]   See *Beahan v Stoneham* (19 January 2001, unreported), per Buckley J.

H Future Expenses and Losses

I Introduction[1]

[H1] The general and overriding principle with regard to damages for personal injury is to put the claimant in the position, so far as is practicable, that he or she would have been in but for the accident[2]. Quite clearly, when a loss is not financial but physical, then the calculation can never be perfect. Likewise, when a loss is destined to occur in the future, given the uncertainties involved, the amount has to be estimated as closely as possible.

[1] See further Chapter A at paras **[A15]–[A21]**.
[2] See further Chapter A at paras **[A23]–[A28]**.

[H2] Traditionally, as with other heads of loss such as general damages and past expenses and losses, future expenses and losses have been awarded as a single lump sum. However, since 1 April 2005, awards for future loss may take the form wholly or partly of periodical payments (PPs). In the case of future pecuniary loss, the court has the power to make, or alternatively the parties may agree, a variable or non-variable periodical payment order to cover any anticipated expenses or losses.

[H3] This represented a fundamental change in the assessment of damages for future loss, and the parties will have to consider carefully in each case the most appropriate vehicle for compensating the claimant. A number of considerations need to be taken into account, and the parties may well need to take financial advice regarding the most appropriate option. The reader is referred to Chapter O for a detailed explanation and discussion of PPs.

[H4] When deciding how to present the schedule of loss, it may be necessary to include calculations on the basis of both a lump sum and PPs. In this chapter we deal with the traditional assessment of future loss, as a lump sum. Lord Oliver of Aylmerton expressed the theory behind a lump sum payment in *Hodgson v Trapp*[1] as follows:

> 'Essentially what the court has to do is to calculate as best it can the sum of money which will on the one hand be adequate, by its capital and income, to provide annually for the injured person a sum equal to his estimated annual loss over the whole of the period during which that loss is likely to continue, but which, on the other hand, will not, at the end of that period, leave him in a better financial position than he would have been apart from the accident.'

[1] [1989] AC 807 at 826D.

[H5] In effect, the court compensates future loss by assuming an annuity which will pay for all the losses for the period over which they are predicted to arise. The assumed annuity is designed to expire on the very last day of loss (often, at the expiry of the claimant's life). The lump sum awarded is the sum which will notionally produce that annuity. To calculate that sum requires assumptions to be made about the rate of return on the capital sum, over and above inflation, and as to the likely life expectancy of the claimant, as well as the continuing cost of the items comprising his or her future loss claim. Given that the claimant is receiving money to compensate him or her for an expense or loss that will not occur until some time in the future, the court has to adopt a method of calculating the appropriate lump sum which takes into account the fact that the claimant is receiving the money earlier than he or she needs it (otherwise known as 'accelerated receipt') and can invest that money to earn further income.

2 One-off Future Expenses and Losses

[H6] The calculation of one-off expenses/losses is perhaps the most straightforward of future loss calculations. Assuming that the claimant is able to show that there is a 'real' or 'substantial', as opposed to a 'speculative or 'fanciful', chance that an item of expense/loss will be incurred[1], the assessment of that expense or loss will be performed in three stages. First, the amount of the expense/loss must be ascertained. This will usually be the present day value of the expense or loss, unless there is good evidence to suggest that the expense or loss will increase at a rate faster than ordinary inflation as measured by the Retail Price Index (RPI)[2]. Secondly, the expense or loss is discounted to reflect early receipt by applying a discount factor calculated at the prevailing discount rate[3]. And lastly, the expense/loss is discounted for uncertainty, ie to reflect the chance that the expense/loss might not be incurred[4]. A common claim for a one-off future loss is for the cost of a future medical operation. Take, for example, the case of a claimant who suffers a knee fracture leading to risk of degenerative changes and the possible need for a knee replacement operation in the future. The medical evidence is that the claimant has a 50% chance of requiring a knee replacement operation ten years from the date of trial, the private cost of which is £10,000 at current rates. Using a discount rate of 2.5%, the calculation is as follows:

$$£10,000 \times 0.7812^5 \times 0.50^6 = £3,906$$

Thus, the appropriate present day award to reflect a 50% chance of incurring medical treatment costs of £10,000 at a point ten years in the future is £3,096[7].

---

[1] *Davies v Taylor* [1974] AC 207; *Allied Maples v Simmons & Simmons* [1995] WLR 1602; and *Doyle v Wallace* [1998] PIQR Q146. Although it is not clear what size a lost chance has to be before it is categorised as 'substantial', the courts have in analogous fields equated 'substantial' with 'not insubstantial' or 'more than merely minimal' (see *Kitchen v RAF* [1958] 2 All ER 241; *Bonnington Castings v Wardlow* [1956] AC 613). It appears that the Court of Appeal approved a claim in *Langford v Hebran* [2001] EWCA Civ 361 involving a lost chance of 14% (see further the case summary prepared by junior counsel in that case at [2001] Quantum, Issue 3/2001, 12 June, pp 5–7). See also *Lloyds Bank v Parker Bullen* [2000] Lloyd's Rep PN 51, where a claim for a lost chance of 15% was allowed. For examples of claims which were considered too speculative for an award to be made, see *Howarth v Whittaker* [2003] Lloyd's Rep Med 235; *Parkhouse v North Devon Healthcare NHS Trust* [2002] Lloyd's Rep Med 100; and *D and D v Donald* [2001] PIQR Q44.

[2] Section 1(2) of the Damages Act 1996 gives the court the power to use a different discount rate, which would potentially be able to take account of inflation at a rate slower or faster than the RPI,

but this has been narrowly interpreted so as to apply only in exceptional circumstances: *Warriner v Warriner* [2002] 1 WLR 1703.

[3] The discount rate is currently fixed by the Lord Chancellor at 2.5%: Damages (Personal Injury) Order 2001, SI 2001/2301. However, the court may adopt a different rate of return under Damages Act 1996, s 1(2) if it is 'more appropriate' in the case in question. See further at paras **[H25]**–**[H35]**.

[4] See further Chapter A at paras **[A60]** and **[A61]**.

[5] The discount factor to be applied for accelerated receipt of ten years at a discount rate of 2.5% (Table 27 of the Ogden Tables).

[6] The chance that the surgery will be required.

[7] For examples of similar claims in real cases, see *Newman v Folkes* [2002] PIQR Q2 and *Garth v (1) Grant and (2) MIB*, QBD, LTL 17/7/2007.

3 Ongoing Future Expenses and Losses

(i) The Theory

[H7]   The conventional means by which the courts assess ongoing future loss is known as the multiplier/multiplicand method. This approach was examined by the Court of Appeal in the test cases of *Cooke v United Bristol Health Care*[1]. As Dyson LJ said in that case, the assessment of future loss 'is not an exact science' and there 'will always be cases where some claimants who receive lump sum payments will, as things turn out, be under-compensated, and others will be over-compensated'. Laws LJ set out the background and principles behind the conventional assessment as follows[2]:

'*FUTURE LOSS: CONVENTIONAL MEANS OF ASSESSMENT*

Damages for personal injuries have long taken the form of a single lump sum payment assessed at the date of trial. (We are not on these appeals concerned with other models, such as that of the structured settlement constituted by an order for periodical payments.) Thus the single lump sum must include compensation both for the claimant's pre-trial losses (and of course general damages for pain, suffering and loss of amenity) and the losses which he will sustain in the future, notably represented in cases like these by the cost of future care. In fixing the lump sum, the trial judge must follow a basic principle, namely that it should represent "as nearly as possible *full* compensation for the injury which the plaintiff has suffered": *Wells v Wells* [1999] 1 AC 345, 363F *per* Lord Lloyd of Berwick (my emphasis). Lord Lloyd added at 364 A–B:

"The purpose of the award is to put the plaintiff in the same position, financially, as if he had not been injured. The sum should be calculated as accurately as possible, making just allowance, where this is appropriate, for contingencies. But once the calculation is done, ... there is no room for a judicial scaling down."

There are other no less emphatic references in the books to the principle of full compensation. Although this principle has been a central pillar of the appellants' arguments, I need not set out any further learning. There is no suggestion by the respondents to these appeals that the principle should be called into question, nor, they would submit, has it been called into question by virtue of the orders made in the courts below.

How is the element of future loss contained in the single lump sum payment to be arrived at? Suppose that at prices current at the date of trial the loss is proved or agreed to amount to £1,000 per annum. Assume further that the claimant's life expectancy is taken to be 20 years. It would obviously be possible simply to award the product of these two factors: £1,000 x 20 = £20,000. But that would leave out of account two important matters. The first is that the claimant does not receive his money as and when he suffers the loss, that is, over the 20 year period, but now and all at once. So he can invest the cash, thus ultimately getting more (maybe a lot more) than £20,000. The second is that the calculation of the annual loss at current prices (£1,000) leaves out of account the possibility, or rather (now and for many years past) the certainty, of future inflation. It will be plain that the first of these two circumstances may tend to lead to the claimant being over-compensated, and the second to his being under-compensated. Accordingly some adjustment has to be made either to the "multiplicand" – the £1,000, or the "multiplier" – the figure of 20, or both. As I shall show it has been well settled for many years that the adjustment is to be made to the multiplier alone.

In *Hodgson v Trapp* [1989] AC 807, Lord Oliver said this (826–827):

> "Essentially what the court has to do is to calculate as best it can the sum of money which will on the one hand be adequate, by its capital and income, to provide annually for the injured person a sum equal to his estimated annual loss over the whole of the period during which that loss is likely to continue, but which, on the other hand, will not, at the end of that period, leave him in a better financial position than he would have been apart from the accident. Hence the conventional approach is to assess the amount notionally acquired to be laid out in the purchase of an annuity which will provide the annual amount needed for the whole period of loss. The process cannot, I think, be better described than it was in the speech of Lord Diplock in *Cookson v Knowles* [1979] AC 556. He was there concerned with a claim under the Fatal Accidents Act 1846–1959 ... but his description of the approach to and method of assessment of damages is equally applicable to claims for future loss of earnings and future expenses by the injured party himself. Lord Diplock said, at pages 567–568:
>
> > 'When the first Fatal Accidents Act was passed in 1846, its purpose was to put the dependants of the deceased, who had been the bread-winner of the family, in the same position financially as if he had lived his natural span of life. In times of steady money values, wages levels and interest rates this could be achieved in the case of the ordinary working man by awarding to his dependants the capital sum required to purchase an annuity of an amount equal to the annual value of the benefits with which he had provided them while he lived, and for such period as it could reasonably be estimated they would have continued to enjoy them but for his premature death. Although this does not represent the way in which it is calculated such a capital sum may be expressed as the product of multiplying an annual sum which represents the "dependency" by a number of years' purchase. This latter figure is less than the number of years which represents the period for which it is estimated that the dependants would have continued to enjoy the benefit of the dependency, since the capital sum will not be exhausted until the end of that period and in the meantime so much of it as is not yet exhausted in each year will earn interest from which the dependency for that year could in part be met.
> >
> > The number of years' purchase to be used in order to calculate the capital value of an annuity for a given period of years thus depends upon the rate of interest which it is assumed that money would earn, during the period. The higher the rate of interest, the lower the number of years' purchase...'"

As is no doubt obvious the "dependency" referred to by Lord Diplock is the multiplicand, and the "number of years' purchase" is the multiplier. It is I think useful to cite certain further passages from *Cookson v Knowles*. First, at 571G–572A Lord Diplock said this:

> "The conventional method of calculating [future loss] has been to apply to what is found upon the evidence to be a sum representing 'the dependency', a multiplier representing what the judge considers in the circumstances particular to the deceased to be the appropriate number of years' purchase. In times of stable currency the multipliers that were used by judges were appropriate to interest rates of 4% to 5% whether the judges using them where conscious of this or not. For the reasons I have given I adhere to the opinion Lord Pearson and I had previously expressed …, that the likelihood of continuing inflation after the date of trial should not affect either the figure of the dependency or the multiplier used. Inflation is taken care of in a rough and ready way by the higher rates of interest obtainable as one of the consequences of it, and no other practical basis of calculation has been suggested that is capable of dealing with so conjectural a factor with greater precision."

As will be apparent, it is implicit in this reasoning that the two contingencies to which I have earlier referred, that is the effect of accelerated payment and the effect of inflation, are both accommodated by treating the multiplier not simply as a number representing the claimant's life expectancy, but rather as a number which (when applied to the multiplicand) will represent the cost of buying an appropriate annuity to meet the relevant future loss over the predicted period. Thus the multiplicand remains the figure proved as representing the loss at current prices at the date of trial. Inflation and acceleration are built into the multiplier, and the mechanism for doing that requires that a rate of interest be arrived at as the notional return to be earned on the lump sum over the period in question. This rate of interest is what is known as "the discount rate"; and as I will shortly show this concept of the discount rate is at the core of these appeals. The fact that the multiplicand remains fixed at current prices is confirmed by Lord Diplock's statement in *Cookson* at 573C–D, that "[f]or the purpose of calculating the future loss, the 'dependency' used as the multiplicand should be the figure to which it is estimated the annual dependency would have amounted by the date of trial." And Lord Fraser of Tullybelton said this at 575G–H:

> "For the period after the date of trial, the proper multiplicand is, in my opinion, based upon the rate of wages for the job at the date of trial. The reason is that that is the latest available information …"

Two points about this approach to the assessment of damages are I think worth noticing at this stage. The first – plain enough – is that an appropriate discount rate will depend upon prevailing economic conditions, and so is likely to shift from time to time. The second is that if a *single* discount rate is set for all cases, whether by the courts or by statute (or executive decision taken under statute), the full compensation principle will only be achieved in a rough and ready way, since actual rates of inflation will differ between different sectors. Thus wages are prone to rise at a faster rate in some sectors than others; and prices likewise.'

1   [2003] EWCA Civ 1370.
2   At [7]–[12].

(ii)   The Multiplicand

[H8]   The multiplicand is simply the amount calculated to be needed every year, be it lost earnings, cost of care or general expenses. Once the figures have been ascertained, they only need to be added up or averaged if the loss occurs over an extended period[1]. Generally speaking, the multiplicand will remain fixed at current prices as at the date of trial, and the court will be mindful of any attempt to use an increasing or stepped multiplicand in order to take account of future inflation[2]. This works both ways, so that a claimant is unable to argue that the multiplicand for certain heads of loss should be increased to take account of alleged inflation above the assumed level of the RPI[3], and the defendant is unable to argue that the multiplicand for heads of loss should be reduced to take account of inflation below the RPI[4]. However, in appropriate cases, the court might be justified in using different multiplicands for different periods. For example, where there is evidence that, but for the claimant's injuries, his earnings would have increased at certain ages, a different multiplicand can be used and the multiplier split so as more accurately to reflect the claimant's loss[5].

---

[1]   See eg *Brown v Berry* (14 October 1997, unreported), QBD, in which Robert Seabrook QC applied an average for case management expenses of £3,000 per annum, taking into account the fact that the claimant's parents would wish themselves to be involved in the management in the early years, but his case management needs were likely to escalate in the future.

[2]   *Cooke v United Bristol Health Care* [2003] EWCA Civ 1370, in which Laws LJ said at [30]:
'In the end, the central issue in these appeals falls to be resolved upon what, I have to say, seems to me to be a very straightforward basis. Once it is accepted that the discount rate is intended in any given personal injury case to be the *only* factor (in the equation ultimately yielding the claimant's lump sum payment) to allow for any future inflation relevant to the case, then the multiplicand cannot be taken as allowing for the same thing, or any part of it, without usurping the basis on which the multiplier has been fixed. And it must be accepted that the discount rate was so intended: by the House in *Wells*, by Parliament in the Act of 1996, and by the Lord Chancellor in making his order under the Act. Mr Hogg's attempt to treat his calculation of the multiplicand as a "separate issue" from the discount rate, and counsel's submissions supporting that position, are in the end nothing but smoke and mirrors. It follows that the substance of these appeals constitutes an illegitimate assault on the Lord Chancellor's discount rate, and on the efficacy of the 1996 Act itself, and (subject to Mr Hogarth's point on s 1(2)) they must in my judgment be dismissed.'

[3]   *Cooke v United Bristol Health Care* [2003] EWCA Civ 1370.

[4]   See eg *Patel v Patel* [2005] EWHC 347 (QB), in which the judge, Treacy J, made an allowance for videoconferencing. The defendant argued that it was likely that the costs for this technology would decrease in the future (but did not call any evidence to establish this). Applying *Cooke v United Bristol Health Care* [2003] EWCA Civ 1370, Treacy J held that the multiplicand should remain fixed at current prices as at the date of trial.

[5]   See eg *Winwood v Bird* (9 November 1986, unreported), QBD; and *Parry v North West Surrey Health Authority* (29 November 1999, unreported), QBD. See also *Potts v Buckley* (21 December 1992, unreported), QBD, in which Tuckey J accepted the argument that the claimant's wife was unlikely to be able to care for her husband after he reached the age of 65, and he should receive an allowance for 24-hour care costed on a commercial basis from 65 onwards. Further, in *C (a patient: severe head injuries) v Crisp* [2001] Current Law, March, the court split the lifetime multiplier into two periods in respect of the provision of future care. For guidance as to how to split the multiplier into different periods, see further paras 23–24 of the guidance notes to the Ogden Tables (6th edn).

(iii)   The Multiplier

[H9]   The multiplier is the figure by which it is appropriate to multiply the multiplicand, in order to arrive at a lump sum which is adequate for the number of years that the loss is to cover and no more. The calculation of the multiplier needs specifically to take into account the interest likely to be earned on the lump sum awarded. The greater the real rate of return is taken to be on an investment, the lower the lump sum needs to be to produce enough money, year on year, to meet the total loss over a lifetime, such that it notionally runs out the moment the claimant dies. Thus, if one assumes a real rate of return (ie an interest rate over and above the rate of inflation) of 4%, the multiplier will be less than if one assumes a 2.5% return. Multipliers were traditionally assessed using a discount rate of 4–5%. Lord Diplock explained it in *Cookson v Knowles*[1]:

'In times of stable currency the multipliers that were used by judges were appropriate to interest rates of 4 per cent to 5 per cent whether the judges using them were conscious of this or not.'

[1]   [1979] AC 556 at 571G.

[H10]   The 'rule of thumb' method used by those unable to calculate a figure mathematically was to take the relevant period for which the multiplier was to be assessed (say ten years of future care), halve it and add one (resulting in a multiplier of 6), with a greater proportionate reduction where longer periods of loss were involved. This crude method has been refined in tables[1] which used to be cross-referenced to arrive at a multiplier, though on rare occasions it might be exceeded.

[1]   First set out in the Pearson Commission Report of 1969.

[H11]   The multiplier would, in practice, be further restricted by two judicial practices. The first was that the judge would generally discount further due to 'unforeseen circumstances' or 'contingencies', and the second was that the judiciary generally believed a ceiling of 18 was appropriate for a whole of life multiplier.

(iv)   Wells v Wells

[H12]   The judicial practices were challenged in the linked cases of *Wells v Wells*, *Thomas v Brighton Health Authority* and *Page v Sheerness*[1]. In this landmark House of Lords decision, it was held that the multiplier should be calculated on the assumption that the claimant would invest in Index-Linked Government Securities (ILGS), and therefore a discount rate of 3% was appropriate. The importance of the decision can be clearly illustrated by the damages awarded in each case. The decision to use a discount rate of 3% instead of 4.5% increased the awards in each case, roughly, by the following amounts:

* Wells: £108,000
* Thomas: £300,000
* Page: £186,000.

The main policy consideration behind the decision in *Wells* was that investment in ILGS was the most appropriate to the claimant in a personal injury case. It was stated that, although an ILGS investment is not entirely risk free, it is much more secure than investment in equities etc. If bought in the short term, ILGSs may result in a simple gain or loss in capital. However, in the long term, particularly if held to the redemption date, a return is produced which is both inflation proof and can be relied upon.

¹   [1999] 1 AC 345.

[H13]   Although it was argued that a prudent investor can achieve much more than a 3% rise, the test of a prudent investor was not appropriate. It was held that a claimant is in an entirely different position from that of a prudent investor. As Lord Steyn stated[1]:

> 'The premise that the claimants, who have perhaps been very seriously injured, are in the same position as ordinary investors is not one that I can accept. Such claimants have not chosen to invest: the tort and its consequences compel them to do so.'

Lord Steyn went on to express the specific differences of a claimant investor[2]:

> 'Typically, by investing in equities an ordinary investor takes a calculated risk which he can bear in order to improve his financial position. On the other hand, the typical claimant requires the return from an award of damages to provide the necessities of life.'

The Court of Appeal had assumed that claimants invested in equities etc. However, this was not the finding of the Law Commission[3]. Their research revealed that the majority of claimants invest securely in banks etc.

¹   [1999] 1 AC 345 at 353D.
²   [1999] 1 AC 345 at 353F.
³   Law Commission Report No 225 'Personal Injury Compensation: How much is enough?' (1994).

[H14]   Lord Lloyd, further, looked at the policy of the Court of Protection[1]. Its fund managers invested in equities and therefore produced a rate of return closer to 5%. Lord Lloyd felt the Court of Appeal was overly influenced by this policy. The reasoning behind such investment was that the managers were obliged to take risks in order to achieve the 4–5% interest imposed by the method of compensation awarded[2]:

> 'As for the Court of Protection's current policy, it may be that they feel obliged to invest in equities so long as the sums available for investment are calculated on the basis of a 4.5 per cent return. In spite of the risks, it may be the only way of making the money go around.'

¹   [1999] 1 AC 345 at 337.
²   [1999] 1 AC 345 at 337E.

[H15]   In short, their Lordships held that it would be unfair to calculate the multiplier on the basis that a claimant has a duty to run an element of risk in his or her investment. A claimant cannot be under a duty to invest in higher risk equities etc, as if the prices go down, the claimant has lost more than his or her savings: he or she has lost the money needed to provide for necessary care. Claimants may not be in a position to weather the storm or hope for an increase in share prices. A claimant needs a set income from any investment to expire at a set date, and it was held by the House of Lords that the ILGS provided the best form of risk-free investment. The Lords took an average return of 3.8% and held that the appropriate rate was 3% net of tax. However, it was stated that this rate was not set in stone and could be departed from if, in the words of Lord Steyn, there had been a 'very considerable', or, in the words of Lord Hutton, 'marked', change in economic circumstances. An acknowledged exception to the 3% discount rate applied in the case where the claimant is subject to higher tax (eg because of the size of the award or because of the operation of a different tax regime from the United Kingdom's) and, arguably, a lower discount rate is appropriate[1].

1   [1999] 1 AC 345 at 355G. Lord Steyn expressed the view that the position regarding higher tax should remain as stated by Lord Oliver in *Hodgson v Trapp* [1989] AC 807 at 835B. That position is that the claimant should be free to argue for a lower rate if, by way of higher taxation, the income earned on the award will be lower: see eg *Biescheuval v Birrell* [1999] PIQR Q40 regarding the higher tax rates in the Netherlands. However, this is not universally applicable, and is likely only to apply to awards for catastrophic injury at the highest level: *Van Oudenhaven v Griffin Inns Ltd* [2000] 1 WLR 1413. After the exercise of the statutory power to fix a discount rate which was exercised by the Lord Chancellor in setting it at 2.5%, it may be difficult, even in a very high value claim with tax implications for the claimant, given the size of his or her fund, to persuade a court to adopt a different rate: *Warriner v Warriner* [2002] 1 WLR 1703.

[H16]   The courts have since construed the circumstances which are sufficient to justify a significant change in economic circumstances very narrowly. Following *Wells v Wells*[1] the average rate of return on ILGS has consistently fallen, such that the average current rate is nearer to 1 or ½%[2]. This prompted many commentators, including Sir Michael Ogden QC, to argue that the discount rate should be reduced accordingly. This argument was run on behalf of the claimant in *Warren v Northern General Hospital NHS Trust (No 2)*[3]. However, the Court of Appeal stated that the drop in the rate of return complained of did not constitute such a serious change in economic circumstances, as envisaged by the House of Lords in *Wells*, to disturb the 3% discount rate. It was stated that no other court than the House of Lords had the power to change the discount rate, and that the applicable rate would stay at 3% until the Lord Chancellor exercised his power under the Damages Act 1996 to set a different rate[4].

1   [1999] 1 AC 345.
2   See further Rowland Hogg 'The discount rate – a reappraisal' [2001] Quantum, Issue 6/2001; the introduction to Facts & Figures 2009/2010; and 'Fair Compensation Needs Actuaries' by Chris Daykin [2009] JPIL Issue 1/09 pp 48–65. See also *Helmont v Simon* (Royal Court of Guernsey, judgment handed down on 14/1/10), in which, unencumbered by the discount rate set at 2.5% by the Lord Chancellor under the Damages (Personal Injury) Order 2001, SI 2001/2301, the Deputy Bailiff used a discount rate for future losses of 1%.
3   [2000] PIQR Q284.
4   The Lord Chancellor has now exercised his power under Damages Act 1996, s 1, and has fixed the discount rate at 2.5%. See further at paras **[H25]–[H32]**.

(v)   The Consequences of Wells v Wells[1]

Judicial discount

[H17]   The practice of a judicial discount being made because of unforeseen contingencies has now been severely limited. Lord Lloyd of Berwick stated[2]:

'Mr Havers conceded that there is room for a judicial discount when calculating the loss of future earnings, when contingencies may indeed affect the result. But there is no room for any discount in the case of a whole life multiplier with an agreed expectation of life. In the case of loss of earnings the contingencies can work in only one direction – in favour of the defendant. But in the case of life expectancy, the contingency can work in either direction. The claimant may exceed the normal expectation of life, or he may fall short of it.'

There is no purpose in the courts making as accurate a prediction as they can of the claimant's future needs, if the resulting sum is arbitrarily reduced for no better reason than that the prediction might be wrong. A prediction remains a prediction. Contingencies should be taken into account where they work in one direction, but not where they cancel out. There is no more logic or justice in reducing the whole life multiplier by 15% or 20% on an agreed expectation of life than there would be in increasing it by the same amount.

1   See also Maggie Young 'Practical Implications of the House of Lords' decision in *Wells v Wells*' (1999) 5(1) Clinical Risk 231; Rodney Nelson-Jones *Multipliers* (Butterworths, 1998); and the various articles in 1999 Quantum magazine and JPIL.
2   *Wells v Wells* [1999] 1 AC 345 at 346B.

[H18]   Therefore, it is clear that a judge can no longer discount the multiplier because of the possibility of early death. This is already taken into consideration in working out life expectancies in the tables and should therefore not be considered again. Lord Lloyd accepts that a figure reached by the calculation may be wrong, but there is no use in reducing or increasing it because of this, as the revised figure has just as much chance of being wrong. However, a reduction in the multiplier may still be made in relation to loss of future earnings. It is still open to the judge to conclude there was a chance of certain contingencies materialising, if the accident had not occurred, which would have shortened the claimant's working life (eg a risky work environment, potential illness, high chance of redundancy, leaving work etc).

Certainty

[H19]   One fundamental principle is that the claimant can now be relatively certain of his or her potential award. As the difference in the three cases has shown, the effect of the discount rate change can be substantial. Therefore, the present situation eliminates areas of uncertainty and prevents any judicial reduction being made to the whole life multiplier. The only outstanding areas of dispute are likely to relate to the multiplier for loss of future earnings (and loss of pension), but the explanatory notes to the Ogden Tables provide suggested discounts based upon the claimant's level of educational attainment and whether or not the claimant is disabled under the Disability Discrimination Act[1].

1   See further Tables A–D regarding deductions other than for mortality in the Introduction to the Ogden Tables (6th edn). Paragraph 30 of the guidance notes states that the same tables do not specifically apply to pension loss calculations. Different considerations may apply to pension loss, such as greater uncertainty in the level of pension payment, and also the fact that an ill-health pension payment may have been payable in any event, had the claimant suffered from an injury or illness. These discounts are open to the objection that they seek to apply a generalised approach to the circumstances which are necessarily individual, but they afford at least a good starting point, and are a useful check as to the appropriateness of the size of any more individually tailored discount.

Actuarial tables

[H20]　The Ogden Tables were given judicial backing by the House of Lords (per Lord Lloyd of Berwick)[1]:

> 'I do not suggest that the judges should be a slave to the tables. There may well be special factors in particular cases. But the tables should now be regarded as the starting-point, rather than a check. A judge should be slow to depart from the relevant actuarial multiplier on impressionistic grounds, or by reference to "a spread of multipliers in comparable cases" especially when the multipliers were fixed before actuarial tables were widely used.'

It can therefore be seen that the first point of call in deciding upon a multiplier is now the Ogden Tables[2].

---

[1]　*Wells v Wells* [1999] 1 AC 345 at 346b (this was in relation to a whole-life multiplier).

[2]　The Ogden Tables (6th edn) are based upon projected mortality figures. The court has repeatedly emphasised that the tables based upon projected mortality should be used as opposed to the tables based upon historical data. See further *Worrall v Powergen plc* [1999] PIQR Q103; *Biesheuval v Birrell* [1999] PIQR Q40; *Jenkins v Groscott and Hoyte* [2000] PIQR Q17; *Barry v Ablerex* [2000] PIQR Q263; and *Ved v Caress* (9 April 2001, unreported), QBD, HHJ Chapman.

[H21]　In practice, the Ogden Tables are now commonly admitted into evidence without the need for a supporting statement from someone at the Government Actuary's Department. Section 10 of the Civil Evidence Act 1995 was drafted to give this practice a more formal basis. However, notwithstanding the Government indicating an intention to implement this provision[1], as at the time of writing, s 10 of the Civil Evidence Act 1995 continues not to be in force.

---

[1]　See eg para 17 of the Lord Chancellor's consultation paper entitled 'The Discount Rate and Alternatives to Lump Sum Payments' (March 2000), available from the Lord Chancellor's website at www.dca.gov.uk/consult/general/damagesfr.htm. The GAD.'s website, however, appears to express approval of the Ogden Tables.

Roberts v Johnstone[1]

[H22]　The House of Lords expressly stated that the correct approach in housing cost claims is that adopted by the Court of Appeal in *Roberts v Johnstone*[2]. However, the conventional rate of discount of 2% was increased to 3%, to put it in line with the discount rate for future loss. It was also stated that, as this is now in line with the discount rate for future loss, then any exercise by the Lord Chancellor of the power under s 1 of the Damages Act 1996 would also apply to a *Roberts v Johnstone* award; and, therefore, the applicable rate for these claims is currently 2.5%.

---

[1]　See further at paras **[H248]–[H260]**.

[2]　[1989] QB 878.

General damages[1]

[H23]　Although *Wells v Wells*[2] did not expressly concern the interest to be applied to general damages, it was originally argued that the rate of interest should follow the decision in *Wells* and be set at a rate of 3%. This argument was favourably received on a number of occasions at first instance[3]. However, the subsequent decision in *Lawrence v Chief Constable of Staffordshire*[4] confirmed that the interest rate on general damages remained at 2%.

1   See further Chapter E, Interest on General Damages.
2   [1999] 1 AC 345.
3   See eg *Burns v Davies* [1999] PIQR P222; and *Sparks v Royal Hospitals NHS Trusts* (21 December 1998, unreported).
4   [2000] PIQR Q349.

How the claimant actually spends his or her award[1]

[H24]   It should be noted that, although the decision in *Wells* meant the claimant no longer has to invest in equities, it was held that how the money was actually invested was irrelevant. Therefore, a claimant is free to invest in higher risk shares etc, even though this may result in his or her receipt in practice of a sum higher than that needed to compensate him or her exactly. It is up to the claimant whether or not to accept this risk, because he or she has to bear the consequences if the share prices fall.

1   See further para **[A110]**.

Criticisms of the multiplier/multiplicand method of assessment: a structural flaw

[H25]   Lord Steyn in *Wells v Wells* expressed a view, obiter, that the system of lump sum payments was structurally flawed. He stated that the system of a lump sum to provide an annual income brought about an inevitable failure to provide 100% compensation. By its very nature, the amount finally payable will be more or less than that judged sufficient. With a 3% discount rate, he suggested that the usual situation will be over-compensation, but this has to be preferred to general under-compensation. Lord Steyn stated that the solution is relatively straightforward[1]:

> 'The court ought to be given the power of its own motion to make an award for periodic payments rather than a lump sum in appropriate cases. Such a power is perfectly consistent with the principle of full compensation for pecuniary loss. Except perhaps for the distaste of personal injury lawyers for change to a familiar system, I can think of no substantial argument to the contrary.'

1   [1999] 1 AC 345 at 383c–d. See also *Cooke v United Bristol Health Care* [2003] EWCA Civ 1370, per Dyson LJ at [45].

[H26]   In March 2002 the Lord Chancellor's Department issued a consultation paper entitled 'Damages for Future Loss: Giving the Courts the Power to Order Periodical Payments for Future Loss and Care Costs in Personal Injury Cases'. Subsequent provisions in the Courts Act 2003 now give the court the power to impose PPs upon the parties[1]. When introducing the power to award PPs, the Government stated that it hoped they would become the norm in high-value cases and would be a fairer way of compensating the catastrophically injured[2].

1   Courts Act 2003, ss 100 and 101, amending Damages Act 1996, s 2, came into force on 1 April 2005.
2   See further Chapter O.

(vi)   The Lord Chancellor's Power to Set the Discount Rate
The Damages Act 1996

[H27]   Under Damages Act 1996, s 1 the Lord Chancellor was given the power to set the appropriate discount rate to be applied by the courts to future pecuniary loss claims in personal injury cases. Once set, the discount rate remains fixed at that amount and applies to all cases unless, on the facts of a particular case, one of the parties is able to persuade the court that adopting a different rate would be more appropriate. Section 1 reads as follows:

'(1) In determining the return to be expected from the investment of a sum awarded as damages for future pecuniary loss in an action for personal injury the court shall, subject to and in accordance with rules of court made for the purposes of this section, take into account such rate of return (if any) as may from time to time be prescribed by an order made by the Lord Chancellor.

(2) Subsection (1) above shall not however prevent the court taking a different rate of return into account if any party to the proceedings shows that it is more appropriate in the case in question[1].

(3) An order under subsection (1) above may prescribe different rates of return for different classes of case.

(4) Before making an order under subsection (1) above the Lord Chancellor shall consult the Government Actuary and the Treasury; and any order under that subsection shall be made by statutory instrument subject to annulment in pursuance of a resolution of either House of Parliament.

(5) In the application of this section to Scotland for references to the Lord Chancellor there shall be substituted references to the Secretary of State.'

[1]   See further *Warriner v Warriner* [2002] 1 WLR 1703 regarding the interpretation of Damages Act 1996, s 1(2). The defendant successfully appealed a case management decision allowing the claimant permission to call expert accountancy evidence to show that a different discount rate should be applied, given the claimant's long life expectancy and the size of the award (over £2 million). Dyson LJ said at 1710A–C:
'We are told that this is the first time that this court has had to consider the 1996 Act, and that guidance is needed as to the meaning of "more appropriate in the case in question" in section 1(2). The phrase "more appropriate", if considered in isolation, is open-textured. It prompts the question: by what criteria is the court to judge whether a different rate of return is more appropriate in the case in question? But the phrase must be interpreted in its proper context which is that the Lord Chancellor has prescribed a rate pursuant to section 1(1) and has given very detailed reasons explaining what factors he took into account in arriving at the rate that he has prescribed. I would hold that in deciding whether a different rate is more appropriate in the case in question, the court must have regard to those reasons. If the case in question falls into a category that the Lord Chancellor did not take into account and/or there are special features of the case which (a) are material to the choice of rate of return and (b) are shown from an examination of the Lord Chancellor's reasons not to have been taken into account, then a different rate of return may be "more appropriate". [In] my judgment the Lord Chancellor must have meant by "exceptional circumstances" no more than special circumstances not taken into account by him in fixing the rate of 2.5%. If "exceptional circumstances" is understood in that way, the phrase is, in my view, a helpful explanation of the meaning of the subsection.'

The consultation process

[H28]   Following a number of cases and criticism from leading commentators, there was mounting pressure on the Lord Chancellor to exercise his power under the Damages Act 1996 to fix the discount rate[1]. By virtue of s 1(4) of the Damages Act 1996, the Lord Chancellor was obliged to consult the Government Actuary and the Treasury before setting the appropriate rate. In March 2000 the Lord Chancellor issued a consultation paper entitled 'The Discount Rate and Alternatives to Lump Sum Payments' which requested responses to a number of specific questions by 31 May 2000.

[1]   For example, *Wells v Wells* [1999] 1 AC 345; *Warren v Northern General Hospital NHS Trust (No 2)* [2000] PIQR Q284; and letters printed in *The Times* written by Sir Michael Ogden QC.

The decision

[H29]   On 25 June 2001, the Lord Chancellor issued a notice on his website stating that it was his responsibility to set a discount rate under s 1 of the Damages Act 1996 and, in light of the responses he had received from the consultation process, he decided to fix the rate at 2.5%[1].

[1]   The rate was fixed at 2.5% by virtue of the Damages (Personal Injury) Order 2001, SI 2001/2301.

The responsibility

[H30]   In his notice accompanying the Damages (Personal Injury) Order 2001 made on 25 June 2001, the Lord Chancellor stated:

'I also consider that it is highly desirable to exercise my powers under the Act so as to produce a situation in which claimants and defendants may have a reasonably clear idea about the impact of the discount upon their cases, so as to facilitate negotiation of settlements and the presentation of cases in court. In order to promote this objective, I have concluded that I should:

a.   set a single rate to cover all cases. This accords with the solution adopted by the House of Lords which was considered to be appropriate in *Wells v Wells* [1999] 1 AC 345. It will eliminate scope for uncertainty and argument about the applicable rate. Similarly, I consider it is preferable to have a fixed rate, which promotes certainty and which avoids the complexity and extra costs that a formula would entail;

b.   set a rate which is easy for all parties and their lawyers to apply in practice. For this reason, I consider it appropriate to set the discount rate to the nearest half per cent, so as to ensure that the figure will be suitable for use in conjunction with the Ogden Tables, which are a ready means for parties to take into account actuarial factors in computing the quantum of damages;

c.   set a rate which should obtain for the foreseeable future. I consider it would be very detrimental to the reasonable certainty which is necessary to promote the just and efficient resolution of disputes (by settlement as well as by hearing in court) to make frequent changes to the discount rate. Therefore, whilst I will remain ready to review the discount rate whenever I find there is a significant and established change in the relevant real rates of return to be expected, I do not propose to tinker with the rate frequently to take account of every transient shift in market conditions.'

The reasons for setting the rate at 2.5%

[H31]   In the introduction to his notice, the Lord Chancellor referred to the average gross redemption yield on Index-Linked Government Stock for the three years leading up to 8 June 2001 as being 2.61%. On the basis of this figure, after an adjustment for tax, the Lord Chancellor stated that it would be appropriate to fix the discount rate at between 2 and 2.5%. Following a number of criticisms of the Lord Chancellor's reasoning behind fixing the discount rate at 2.5%, the Lord Chancellor decided to revisit his decision. On 27 July 2001 a detailed statement of reasons was produced, stating that the Lord Chancellor had considered the matter 'completely afresh'. Whilst the Lord Chancellor admitted to some 'limited inaccuracies', he confirmed that the rate would remain at 2.5%. In summary, the Lord Chancellor relied upon the following reasons for leaving the discount rate at 2.5%:

- The real rate of return to be expected from ILGS tends to be higher the lower the rate of inflation is assumed to be, and the Government has been successful in keeping the rate of inflation low. In recent years, inflation has been kept close to or below the 2.5% target. This low rate of inflation looks likely to continue for the foreseeable future.
- The current rate of return on ILGS is distorted so as to produce an artificially low figure, given the continuing high demand for the stock but the scarcity of its supply.
- The Court of Protection continues to invest in multi-asset portfolios and no family of the patients has chosen to invest in ILGS since *Wells v Wells*[1] despite being given that option[2].
- Claimants who receive large awards of damages and reasonably seek investment advice are unlikely to invest solely or primarily in ILGS. No one who responded to the consultation paper knew of a case where this had happened. The financial experts who responded to the consultation process suggested that a mixed portfolio was usually more suitable to fulfil the objectives sought by investment of the damages.
- It remains possible under s 1(2) of the Damages Act 1996 for the courts to adopt a different discount rate in any particular case if there are exceptional circumstances which justify such a departure from the fixed rate of 2.5%.

[1]   [1999] 1 AC 345.
[2]   Although this may not be correct. See further Rowland Hogg 'The discount rate – a reappraisal' [2001] Quantum, Issue 6/2001, 27 November, which stated that the Court of Protection had discontinued its policy of equity investment for all substantial damages cases.

[H32]   In March 2002 the Lord Chancellor published an analysis of the impact of the prescribed discount rate of 2.5%. The National Health Service Litigation Service (NHSLA) were reported as estimating that the cash cost of reducing the discount rate from 3% to 2.5% was £100 million. The total additional cost to insurers (including Lloyds motor insurance, MDU, MPS and the insurance industry) was estimated at £254 million.

The future

[H33]   The Lord Chancellor's decision to fix the discount rate at 2.5% has not gone without criticism[1]. However, it appears that the discount rate is likely to remain at

2.5% for the foreseeable future. It is conceivable that the Lord Chancellor could be persuaded by political pressure to adopt a different rate or be amenable to judicial review[2]. However, as long as the rate has been fixed by the Lord Chancellor, the courts will not allow it to be subverted or undermined[3].

[1]   See eg Rowland Hogg 'The discount rate – a reappraisal' [2001] Quantum, Issue 6/2001, 27 November.
[2]   *Cooke v United Bristol Health Care* [2003] EWCA Civ 1370, per Laws LJ at [32], although it should be noted that Laws LJ specifically said that he was encouraging nothing as regards the possibility of judicial review.
[3]   *Cooke v United Bristol Health Care* [2003] EWCA Civ 1370, per Laws LJ at [32].

(vii)   Damages Act 1996, s 1(2): Warriner v Warriner[1]

[H34]   Under s 1(2) of the Damages Act 1996, the court has the power to apply a different rate of return if a party shows that 'it is more appropriate in the case in question'.

[1]   [2002] 1 WLR 1703.

[H35]   In *Warriner v Warriner*[1] an attempt was made to call expert evidence in order to argue that a different discount rate should be applied because of the claimant's long life expectancy and the size of the award (in excess of £2 million). At a case management hearing, the Master granted the claimant permission to call expert accountancy evidence from Rowland Hogg in order to explain why a discount rate of 2.5% would be inappropriate on the facts of the case. The defendant successfully appealed this order. The Court of Appeal held that such accountancy evidence should not be allowed. Dyson LJ stated that, if the case in question falls into a category that the Lord Chancellor did not take into account and/or there are special features of the case which (a) are material to the choice of rate of return and (b) are shown from an examination of the Lord Chancellor's reasons not to have been taken into account, then a different rate of return may be 'more appropriate'. Although the phrase 'exceptional circumstances' does not appear in the Damages Act 1996, if by 'exceptional circumstances' what is meant is no more than special circumstances not taken into account by the Lord Chancellor when fixing the rate of 2.5%, this phrase was a helpful explanation of the subsection. Since the combination of a life expectancy of between 30 and 50 years and a claim worth between £2 and £3 million was not particularly uncommon, it was held that there was nothing within the particular facts of the case in order to justify applying a lower rate than 2.5%. A similar argument raised by the claimant was dispatched by the Court of Appeal in *Cooke v United Bristol Health Care*[2].

[1]   [2002] 1 WLR 1703.
[2]   [2003] EWCA Civ 1370.

[H36]   In the circumstances, the court's power to adopt a different discount rate to that set by the Lord Chancellor is likely to be used sparingly. One situation in which the court might be persuaded to adopt an alternative discount is where the claimant will be subjected to unusually high or low tax on his or her damages award[1].

[1]   See further *Hodgson v Trapp* [1989] AC 807; *Wells v Wells* [1999] 1 AC 345; and *Biescheuval v Birrell* [1999] PIQR Q40, cf *Van Oudenhaven v Griffin Inns Ltd* [2000] 1 WLR 1413.

(viii)   Investment Advice

[H37]   Following the decision of the House of Lords in *Wells v Wells*[1] and the Lord Chancellor's decision to set the discount rate at 2.5%, it is clear that there is no longer any entitlement to claim damages to cover expenses arising out of the investment of the award[2]. In *Page v Plymouth Hospitals NHS Trust*[3], Davis J held that the costs of investment advice were not recoverable in principle, because they had already been taken into account by the Lord Chancellor when fixing the discount rate at the rate he had[4]. The attempt to claim investment advice as a separate head of damages was seen as an impermissible attack on the discount rate[5]. This reasoning has been approved by the Court of Appeal and held to be equally applicable to cases involving patients[6].

[1]   [1999] 1 AC 345.
[2]   *Webster v Hammersmith Hospitals NHS Trust* [2002] All ER (D) 397; *Anderson v Blackpool, Wyre & Fylde Community Health Services NHS Trust* (unreported); *Page v Plymouth Hospitals NHS Trust* [2004] EWHC 1154 (QB). See further William Norris QC and Douglas Hall 'Claims for the Cost of Investment Management' [2004] JPIL, Issue 3/04 at 214–224; and Edward Duckworth 'The End of the Line for Claims for Investment Management Charges? – *Page v Plymouth Hospitals NHS Trust* and *Eagle v Chambers*' [2004] Quantum, Issue 6/2004, 1 November.
[3]   [2004] EWHC 1154 (QB), which was approved by the Court of Appeal in *Eagle v Chambers (No 2)* [2004] EWCA Civ 1033.
[4]   Davis J said at [52]:
'Moreover, I find it difficult to think that the Lord Chancellor, in making these observations, could or would have overlooked the attendant costs involved in seeking investment advice in setting the discount rate as he did. It is true that the Lord Chancellor does not expressly say that he had taken them into the account (and Mr Spink told me that the point seems not to have been explicitly raised in the preceding consultation process). But in my judgment it is inherent in the Lord Chancellor's reasoning: and that is of a pattern with the observations of Lord Hope and Lord Clyde in *Wells v Wells*. Thus when, in the course of his reasons, the Lord Chancellor refers to the position about investment on mixed asset portfolios, I think it likely that he was there referring to a real rate of return "comfortably" exceeding 2.5% as connoting a return net not only of tax but also of investment costs.'
[5]   Which was blocked by cases such as *Warriner v Warriner* [2002] 1 WLR 1703 and *Cooke v United Bristol Health Care* [2003] EWCA Civ 1370.
[6]   *Eagle v Chambers (No 2)* [2004] EWCA Civ 1033.

(ix)   Specific Multipliers

Multipliers for loss of earnings

[H38]   The multiplier will be initially calculated by reference to the claimant's prospective retirement age (the starting point will be that calculated from the Ogden Tables with a discount rate of 2.5%). However, as stated, the judge will be free to discount further in consideration of the following:

* The claimant's job history (eg periods of unemployment).
* The nature of the work (physically arduous work attracts a larger discount).
* Job prospects/opportunities (but for the accident).
* The claimant's health (but for the accident).
* The risk of redundancy.

[H39]   The discount to take account of these factors is known as the 'discount for contingencies other than mortality'[1]. The starting point for the calculation of the relevant discount factor will be Tables A–D of the Introduction to the Ogden Tables[2].

A further adjustment may then be made to take account of the specific facts of the case if there are good reasons to suspect that the suggested adjustment is too high or too low[3].

1   See further at paras **[H185]–[H191]**.
2   *Herring v Ministry of Defence* [2003] EWCA Civ 528.
3   See further paras 19 and 26 to 42 of the explanatory notes to the Ogden Tables (6th edn); *Conner v Bradman* [2007] EWHC 2789 (QB) (Coulson QC) at paras 72–73, relying on paras 31 to 32 of the introduction to the Ogden Tables (6th edn); and 'Discretion in the Application of the New Ogden Six Multipliers: The Case of *Conner v Bradman and Company*' [2008] JPIL 2 pp 154–163).

[H40]   The courts may have to provide for prospects of promotion or increased pay progression etc and, as such, apply a split multiplier to more than one multiplicand. In such a situation, the calculation becomes increasingly elaborate. See further the explanation and examples set out at paras 22 to 23 of the explanatory notes to the Ogden Tables (6th edn).

Multipliers in respect of claims for care / assistance / DIY / gardening etc

[H41]   *Wells*[1] makes it clear that, once the Ogden multiplier has been calculated based on the expected life expectancy, there is no room for any additional discount. However, the position may be different with regard to domestic help, DIY, gardening etc. The court must consider the pattern of such work that was undertaken by the claimant before the accident and the actual reality of the claimant undertaking, say, heavy gardening or DIY work beyond, say, 65. The courts recognise that, even in the absence of injury, a claimant's capacity to carry out the heavier domestic chores is likely to decline with age[2]. Thus, claims in respect of domestic assistance, painting, decorating, home maintenance, DIY and gardening etc usually tend to be limited to the claimant's working life[3] or until the claimant reaches the age of 70 or 75[4]. This may mean that it will be difficult to persuade a court that the claimant would have been doing much DIY or gardening work once he or she has reached a certain age in any event[5]. It may, however, be emphasised that early retirement is for many a period when they engage in practical occupations such as gardening, decorating and DIY, since they then have the time for it. The work may take a little longer, perhaps, but the total value of it might be expected to increase. This argument suggests that claims for gardening, decorating and DIY should not diminish beyond 65, though increased physical difficulty may suggest a lessening at a later age. The anticipated extension of normal retirement age to 70 or 75 emphasises these points, and suggests that the current assumptions as to what would, but for the accident, have been the case may be too pessimistic so far as a claimant is concerned. Perhaps a fairer way to assess the loss under this head would be to apply a full multiplicand up to age 70 or 75 and thereafter a reduced multiplicand[6].

1   [1999] 1 AC 345.
2   See eg *Smith v McCrae* [2003] EWCA Civ 505. Although cf *Hassell v Abnoof* (6 July 2001), QBD, Lawtel Document No AC0101866, in which Gage J applied a whole life multiplier to the claim for assistance with cleaning.
3   See further the Court of Appeal's decision in *Wells v Wells* [1997] 1 WLR 652, in which the claimant's working life multiplier was applied to the claim for DIY. See also *Assinder v Griffin* [2001] All ER (D) 356 (May), in which HHJ Peter Clark allowed a claim for DIY and decorating of £1,250 per annum with a multiplier to age 65; and *Smith v East and North Hertfordshire Hospitals*

NHS Trust [2008] EWHC 2234 (QB), in which Penry-Davey J awarded £2,290 per annum from age 19 to 65.

4   See eg *Pratt v Smith* (18 December 2002, unreported), QBD, in which David Foskett QC allowed a claim for DIY in the sum of £500 per annum.

5   See eg *Blair v Michelin Tyre plc* (25 January 2002, unreported), QBD.

6   See eg *Crofts v Murton* LTL 10/9/2008, in which Andrew Collender QC at para [203] applied a multiplicand of £1,500 to age 70 and a multiplicand of £1,095 from age 70.

Other reduced multipliers

[H42] Instances where multipliers for particular heads of loss have been reduced also include:

(i) *Thomas v Bath District Health Authority*[1]: the prospect of an operation in the future which will alleviate the disabilities should be considered (the multiplier in that case was reduced from 12 to 10 owing to a reduction of 10% in respect of the anticipated disability).

(ii) *Vernon v Bosley*[2]: the prospect of marriage may reduce a claim for domestic help (the multiplier was reduced from 7 to 3).

(iii) *Sklair v Haycock*[3]: in which Edwards-Stuart J reduced the multiplier for future care and case management from 20.8 to 18 to take account of the likelihood that the claimant would spend the last few years of his life looked after in accommodation provided by the local authority.

1   [1995] PIQR Q19.

2   [1997] PIQR P255.

3   [2009] EWHC 3328 (QB).

[H43] It can therefore be seen that, although *Wells*[1] stated that no judicial discount can be applied to a whole life multiplier, the 'starting point' of the Ogden multiplier can still be manipulated in relevant instances where the loss will not extend for the whole of the claimant's life. A distinction always has to be made between 'loss of earnings multipliers' and 'cost of care multipliers', as the contingencies that must be considered differ greatly[2]: in the latter, it is frequently only death which is a relevant risk. In the former, a discount must be made for contingencies other than mortality[3].

1   [1999] 1 AC 345.

2   *O'Brien's Curator Bonis v British Steel* 1991 SLT 477 at 481.

3   The starting point for calculating the relevant discount factor will be the discount factors set out in the Introduction to the Ogden Tables: *Herring v Ministry of Defence* [2003] EWCA Civ 528. See further at para **[H185]**.

[H44] Where the claimant's life expectancy has been reduced by reason of his or her injuries, special principles apply. Evidence will be required regarding the extent of the claimant's shortened life. There then may be arguments as to how the multiplier is calculated and whether Table 1 or 2 of the Ogden Tables is used as opposed to Table 28 (fixed term multiplier) – see further paras **[H45]–[H68]** below.

4 Life Expectancy

[H45] Where there are ongoing expenses and losses, the claimant's life expectancy is likely to have a significant impact upon the appropriate multiplier, particularly as regards those items of expense or loss which are claimed throughout the claimant's lifetime, such as care and aids and equipment. Statistically, people are living longer and longer. Given the technological advances that have been made in relation to rehabilitation, treatment and care, even those who have been catastrophically injured may now sometimes be capable of achieving a normal or near normal life expectancy[1].

> 1   See further Julian Chamberlayne 'Who wants to live forever?' [2002] PILJ, September, at 2–5; Bill Braithwaite QC 'Professor Strauss on life expectancy in cerebral palsy babies' [2003] Quantum, Issue 5/2003, although cf Professor Strauss 'Longer Life' [2003] PILJ, February, at 2–5; and Professor Barnes 'Life Expectancy for People with Disabilities' [2004] JPIL, Issue 2/04, at 131–155.

(i) The Presumption of Normal Life Expectancy

[H46]   A claimant will be (rebuttably) presumed to have a normal life expectancy[1]. Normal life expectancy is the average number of additional years that a person will live, calculated by reference to statistical information collected from population studies. The most up-to-date information regarding 'normal' life expectancy can be obtained from the Office of National Statistics (ONS)[2]. Data is also available from 'life expectancy tables'[3] or can be downloaded from the Government Actuary's website[4]. Alternatively, a crude assessment of 'normal' life expectancy can be ascertained by using the 0% discount rate column of Table 1 (for a man) or Table 2 (for a woman) of the Ogden Tables. However, it should be noted that there is often a time lag between the latest edition of the Ogden Tables and the most up-to-date projected mortality figures[5]. For example, at the time of writing the Ogden Tables (6th edn) are calculated by reference to 2004-based population data, whereas the ONS has recently published life expectancy projections based upon 2008 data.

> 1   *Rowley v London and North Western Railway* (1873) LR 8 Ex 221.
> 2   See further www.statistics.gov.uk.
> 3   These tables are reproduced in 'Personal Injury Damages Statistics' by Rodney Nelson-Jones, and 'Facts & Figures' produced by the Professional Negligence Bar Association.
> 4   www.gad.gov.uk.
> 5   Tables 1 and 2 are calculated by reference to projected mortality figures, as opposed to historical data, in accordance with the decisions in *Worrall v Powergen plc* [1999] PIQR Q103; *Biesheuval v Birrell* [1999] PIQR Q40; *Jenkins v Groscott and Hoyte* [2000] PIQR Q17; *Barry v Ablerex* [2000] PIQR Q263; and *Ved v Caress* (9 April 2001, unreported), QBD, HHJ Chapman.

[H47]   The presumption of normal life expectancy may be rebutted if sufficient evidence is adduced to show that an individual claimant has a shorter or longer life expectancy than normal. However, permission should be sought sooner rather than later in order to call the necessary evidence[1]. In particular, a court may not be particularly receptive to late applications to call such evidence[2].

> 1   Note that, once a decision has been taken regarding the admissibility of life expectancy evidence at a case management level or on appeal, it will be difficult to entertain a second tier appeal in respect of the same issue: *Rawlinson v Cooper* [2002] EWCA Civ 392.
> 2   *Parkin & Parkin v Bromley Hospitals NHS Trust* [2002] EWCA Civ 478; cf *Hanley v Stage & Catwalk Ltd* [2001] EWCA Civ 1739.

(ii) Factors Affecting Life Expectancy

Sex of the claimant

[H48] There are different tables for men and women. On average, women are expected to live about three years longer than males of a similar age. It is, therefore, important to use the correct table!

Medical factors

[H49] There are a number of medical factors which may impact upon life expectancy. In some instances, there may have been a pre-existing condition such as ischemic heart disease, diabetes or cancer which would have reduced life expectancy from the norm in any event. In other instances, the claimant's injuries will be severe enough to shorten life expectancy over and above any reduction in life expectancy due to a pre-existing condition. For example, it is important to assess the claimant's degree of mobility following a catastrophic brain or spinal cord injury. The more sedentary the claimant, the more likely it is that he or she will develop respiratory difficulties, pressure sores and other potential complications which can be life threatening. Other relevant factors include the risk of infection, epilepsy and the state of his or her mental health. How the claimant has progressed from the date of injury will be important, especially following discharge from hospital.

[H50] Where the potential reduction in life expectancy is due to a medical or psychiatric condition, expert evidence will be required to ascertain what the claimant's likely actual life expectancy will be, whether the condition was pre-existing or developed only as a result of the injuries which are the subject matter of the claim. Although the ability to award periodical payments has reduced the need for such evidence, it is unusual for all heads of future loss to be awarded by way of periodical payments. Therefore, the chances are that it will not be possible to avoid obtaining appropriate expert evidence regarding life expectancy where there are medical or psychiatric reasons for suspecting that it is not normal.

Quality of care and favourable economics

[H51] Common sense implies that a claimant who receives a large award of damages and can pay for high-quality care, private medical treatment, suitable accommodation and necessary equipment may be in a more favourable position when compared to a similar person who suffers the same injuries without access to the same amenities. Examples include the spinally injured patient who has good-quality care, such that pressure sores are likely to be avoided or will be picked up at the earliest opportunity[1], and a claimant with epilepsy who has 24-hour private care, so that there is always someone on hand in case he or she has a fit[2]. The courts have generally accepted the force of this common sense argument and, where appropriate, have applied an uplift to the statistical data regarding the life expectancy of a cohort of people, with a mixture of financial backgrounds, to reflect the position of a claimant who will benefit from receipt of substantial compensation in order to meet his or her needs[3]. In *Pankhurst v (1) White and (2) MIB*[4], MacDuff J said:[5]

'[The claimant] will have the benefit of a first class care package. This high level of care is likely to improve his prospects of survival... This helps to guard against the risks responsible for producing the reduction in life expectation, but also ensures that early warnings systems are in place, and prompt treatment is given in an emergency.'

1   See further Krause et al 'Health Status, community integration and economic risk factors for mortality after spinal cord injury' Arch Phys Med Rehabil 2004;85:1764–1773; although see D. Strauss, M. DeVivo, R. Shavelle, J. Brooks, D. Paculdo 'Economic Factors and Longevity in Spinal Cord Injury: A Reappraisal' Arch Phys Med Rehabil Vol 89, Issue 3, pp 572–574, and *Burton v Kingsbury* [2007] EWHC 2091 (QB).

2   See further *Lewis v Shrewsbury NHS Trust* LTL 14/6/2007, in which HHJ MacDuff (at paras 144–146) increased the claimant's life expectancy by 3 years above the statistical average to account for her well above average care package.

3   See eg *Owen v Brown* [2002] EWHC 1135 (QB); *Sarwar v (1) Ali and (2) MIB (No 1)* [2007] EWHC 274 (QB); *Lewis v Shrewsbury NHS Trust* LTL 14/6/2007; *Burton v Kingsbury* [2007] EWHC 2091 (QB); *Pankhurst v (1) White and (2) MIB* [2009] EWHC 1117 (QB).

4   [2009] EWHC 1117 (QB). The same judge made similar comments in *Lewis v Shrewsbury NHS Trust* LTL 14/6/2007 at paras [144]–[145].

5   At para [7.17].

Psychiatric factors

[H52]   Claimants who suffer from clinical depression as a result of their injuries and the loss of their pre-injury job and quality of life may be exposed to a higher risk of suicide than would otherwise be the case. It will be the claimant's psychiatric state as at the date of trial or assessment of damages which is important.

Lifestyle factors

[H53]   There are also a number of lifestyle factors which may or may not be relevant to life expectancy. Examples include smoking, obesity, hypertension, alcohol intake and exercise. These factors do not necessarily cause a reduction in life expectancy themselves, but give rise to the risk that the claimant *may* develop a condition which *may* in turn shorten life. The relevance of a 'lifestyle factor' is two-fold: (1) it may lower the starting point from what would be expected for the uninjured claimant, before further reducing it for the after-effects of the injury suffered, such that, where loss of earnings is calculated by years of shortening, ie by deducting the 'years less' from the normal to be expected [as in the formula N (normal) years – X (deducted years)], it will lower the value of N and hence the result; and (2) it may interact with the actual injuries to further reduce life expectancy. The calculation in (1) may be of particular importance when considering 'lost years'[1]. Although evidence as to factors tending to reduce life expectancy is admissible in theory in any case in which a life-long loss is contended for, there are sound practical reasons (including cost-benefit) for the courts not readily entertaining attempts to reduce, or augment, the statistically normal figure of life expectancy in individual cases. These reasons (expanded below) mean that the courts are generally unwilling to apply other than statistical life expectancy for a claimant of a given age and gender, where there is no suggestion that the injuries which have been suffered are such as to lessen lifespan. Where there is such a suggestion, the approach tends to be different.

1   See Chapter 1.

(1) Relevance of lifestyle factors when no reduction in life expectancy due to injuries

[H54] Where claimants have suffered injuries which have no effect on their life expectancy, eg a whiplash injury, it is a moot point whether or not either party should be allowed to adduce evidence regarding lifestyle factors to increase or reduce life expectancy. The main purpose of the Ogden Tables is to provide a set of tables which can be used in the vast majority of cases based upon average population statistics. This avoids the need to call life expectancy evidence in the vast majority of cases, reduces costs and increases settlement because respective parties can value cases with relative ease and certainty.

[H55] However, there have been several recent attempts, especially on behalf of defendant insurers, to obtain permission to adduce expert evidence to suggest that a claimant's life expectancy should be reduced because he or she is a smoker, overweight and/or drinks too much. Of course, it needs to be recognised that the life expectancy tables are based upon averages and so already contain a number of people with a similar profile. To date, courts have generally been reluctant to grant permission to adduce expert evidence relating simply to pre-existing lifestyle factors, for the following reasons[1]:

- The tables are based upon averages which already take into account such factors.
- If defendants were able to call evidence to show that smokers have a reduced life expectancy, claimants would be able to call evidence to establish how non-smokers compared to the average (which includes smokers and non-smokers).
- If such applications were permitted, life expectancy evidence would need to be called in the majority of cases, vastly increasing the costs and uncertainty of litigation (which the use of the average tables was largely designed to be avoided).
- If such arguments were permitted, it would be difficult to know where to draw the line, and it may well be possible to argue for different life expectancy figures based upon different geographical location, race or socio-economic class, which might be considered discriminatory.

[1] See further Dr Simon Fox 'Life Expectancy – Issues and Evidence' [2005] JPIL Issue 4/05, citing *Vickers v Parniak* (unreported, 14/6/2005, DJ Asokan, Birmingham CC); *Titley v Caddick* (unreported, 2/8/2004, High Court, Birmingham District Registry, DJ Lettal); *Broderick v Royal Wolverhampton Hospitals NHS Trust* (unreported, 15/1/2008, HHJ McKenna sitting as a judge of the High Court); *Edwards v Martin* [2010] EWHC 570 (QB); although cf *Tinsley v Sarkar* [2006] PIQR Q1, in which Leveson J appeared to accept a reduction in life expectancy of 10 years due to a pre-existing smoking habit. Arguably, however, *Tinsley v Sarkar* [2006] PIQR Q1 is distinguishable, because the judge was performing an individual or bespoke assessment of life expectancy which took into account both pre- and post-injury factors.

(2) Relevance of lifestyle factors when life expectancy is reduced due to injuries

[H56] Where a claimant's life expectancy is shortened by reason of injury, expert evidence will be required to perform an individual or bespoke assessment of life expectancy. In order to be as accurate as possible, it is submitted that this assessment should take account of positive and negative factors relating to *both* pre- and post-injury status. Therefore, when assessing the life expectancy of a claimant who suffers from a brain injury resulting in poorly controlled epilepsy causing a reduction in life expectancy of 4 years, instead of simply taking 4 years off the figure for 'normal' life expectancy, it should be considered whether or not there were any other reasons why the claimant might die sooner than normal. In order words, once it becomes necessary to assess a claimant's life expectancy by reason of injury, both positive and negative lifestyle factors which may not otherwise have been relevant, arguably, should be taken into account when attempting to make the best prediction of the claimant's remaining years of life[1].

[1]   It is submitted that this is why the claimant's smoking or non-smoking status may become relevant to the assessment of his or her life expectancy, as can be seen in cases such as *Sarwar v (1) Ali and (2) MIB (No 1)* [2007] EWHC 274 (QB); *Tinsley v Sarkar* [2006] PIQR Q1; and *Pankhurst v (1) White and (2) MIB* [2009] EWHC 1117 (QB).

Other factors

[H57]   Other potential factors which might influence life expectancy include race, place of birth/residence and socio-economic status. It is submitted that the approach to these factors should be similar to lifestyle factors above, ie that unless the claimant's injury alters the claimant's life expectancy such that a bespoke assessment is required, any other factors should be ignored, except where it can reasonably be suggested they make a significant impact – examples might be those of a chronic alcoholic, an '80-a-day' smoker, or arguably a regular hang-gliding pilot. A court is likely to take a cautious approach before allowing lifestyle factors to become the subject of significant debate. One reason for an approach which seeks to identify remarkable and significant cases is that, otherwise, it would in principle be open to a claimant to argue that, because he (for example) never smoked, or drank, regularly exercised, and was naturally risk-averse, the life expectancy figure in his case should be higher than statistically normal. However, there may be exceptions, eg where it can be shown that the claimant is a foreign national who was injured whilst on holiday and returns to his place of residence, where different life tables might apply.

(iii)   The Assessment of Life Expectancy

General principles

[H58]   Where a claimant's life expectancy is in issue, it is a matter for the court to determine with regard to all the circumstances and available evidence. The assessment is essentially a medical or clinical issue[1]. In each case, the court has to make the best estimate it can of the claimant's individual life expectancy, based primarily upon the opinions of medical expert witnesses, but also taking into account relevant statistical material as might be available in relation to other similar cases[2]. Where there is a dispute between medical experts regarding the claimant's life expectancy, the court must make an assessment regarding whose expert evidence is to be preferred and the likely life expectancy, taking into account all relevant factors including any medical or statistical literature relied upon[3].

[1]   *RVI v B (a child)* [2002] PIQR Q137, per Tuckey LJ at para 20, and Sir Anthony Evans at para 39; *Arden v Malcolm* [2007] EWHC 404 (QB); and *Sarwar v (1) Ali and (2) MIB (No 1)* [2007] EWHC 274 (QB).

2   *RVI v B (a child)* [2002] PIQR Q137, per Sir Anthony Evans at paras 30, 145 and 39, Q147.
3   See eg *Owen v Brown* [2002] EWHC 1135 (QB); *Sarwar v (1) Ali and (2) MIB (No 1)* [2007]
      EWHC 274 (QB); *Lewis v Shrewsbury NHS Trust* LTL 14/6/2007; *Burton v Kingsbury* [2007]
      EWHC 2091 (QB); *Pankhurst v (1) White and (2) MIB* [2009] EWHC 1117 (QB).

[H59]   Where a range of life expectancy is provided by the medical evidence, it
will not necessarily be wrong for the court to take a figure other than the mean of
the range, assuming the same is supported by the evidence[1]. Likewise, the court may
find that neither the claimant's nor the defendant's expert evidence regarding life
expectancy is entirely correct and, based upon all the evidence, a figure somewhere
between the two positions is appropriate[2].

1   See eg *George v Pinnock* [1973] 1 WLR 118, in which the Court of Appeal upheld the trial judge's
      decision to adopt a life expectancy of 13 years for the claimant when the medical evidence supported
      a range of life expectancy between 10 and 15 years.
2   See eg *Patel v Patel* [2005] EWHC 347 (QB); *Rowe v Dolman* [2007] EWHC 2799; *Pankhurst v (1)
      White and (2) MIB* [2009] EWHC 1117 (QB).

Medical evidence

[H60]   There needs to be clear evidence before the court will depart from the ordinary
Ogden Tables[1]. Generally speaking, it will be necessary to adduce appropriate expert
evidence in respect of life expectancy[2]. The expert should set out clearly the factors
which lead them to think that life expectancy will be less or, as the case may be,
more than usual. It is not possible to generalise by saying, for instance, that in most
run-of-the-mill cases the relevant medical expert to give an opinion in respect of
the claimant's life expectancy will be a physician or a cardiologist, though this may
often be true. Much depends on the particular claimant. One suffering from a risk of
urinary infection will need a urologist's advice; a woman in her nineties will need a
geriatrician; someone who has incurred a cancer will need an oncologist etc. Where
the claimant has suffered injuries of a specific nature, such as a head injury or a spinal
cord injury, it may be appropriate to seek the opinion of an expert in the relevant field,
eg neurology or spinal cord injury and rehabilitation. Once obtained, life expectancy
should be updated periodically in order to take account of developments, such as
publication of up-to-date projected mortality data, new statistical evidence regarding
the effect of injuries, the claimant's increased survival since injury, and any significant
medical history including infections, pressure sores and seizures etc.

1   See para 5 of the explanatory notes to the Ogden Tables (6th edn).
2   See eg *Lane v Lake (Deceased)* LTL 31/7/2007, in which John Leighton Williams QC sitting as a
      deputy judge of the High Court refused to discount the multiplier due to hypertension and a family
      history of ischaemic heart disease, without medical evidence regarding the effect on life expectancy.

Statistical evidence and life expectancy databases

[H61]   Statistical evidence is necessarily general, whereas the life the length of
which has to be assessed is that of the individual claimant. In *RVI v B (a child)*[1], a case
in which the defendants tried (and failed) to persuade the Court of Appeal that the
judge should necessarily have been bound by statistical evidence, Tuckey LJ said[2]:

'This is not, I emphasise, to say that Professor Strauss's evidence or the evidence of any other statistician or actuary is inadmissible. In an appropriate case such evidence may well provide a useful starting point for the judge, but if it is to serve this purpose Professor Strauss or any other such expert should be required to give evidence if his report is not agreed. Such evidence, together with medical evidence, should provide a satisfactory inter-disciplinary approach to the resolution of issues of the kind which arose in this case.'

Statistical evidence cannot be used to usurp the function of the medical expert or the court. As Sir Anthony Evans said in the same case[3]:

'... the court must still rely primarily, in my judgment, on expert medical witnesses before reaching a conclusion in the particular case. It would be wrong to allow a statistician, or an actuary, to do more than inform the opinions of the medical witnesses and the decision of the court, on what is essentially a medical, or clinical, issue.'

Whilst statistical evidence is a useful starting point[4], the normal or primary route through which statistical evidence is put before the court is through medical experts, and only if there is disagreement between them on a statistical matter is the evidence of a statistician likely to be required[5].

[1]   [2002] PIQR Q10.
[2]   At para 20, Q143. See also at para 36, Q146, where Sir Anthony Evans said 'the evidence of a statistician is both relevant and admissible, and the judge must take account of all evidence, including this, when deciding what assumption he should make as to the future life span of the claimant'.
[3]   At para 39.
[4]   See eg *Lewis v Shrewsbury NHS Trust* LTL 14/6/2007 at para 101; and *Sarwar v (1) Ali and (2) MIB (No 1)* [2007] EWHC 274 (QB), where Lloyd-Jones J said at para 15: 'Although I have addressed in some detail the arguments advanced before me in relation to the application of the statistics contained in the published studies, I emphasise that the use of such statistics is no more than a starting point. The court is not engaged in a mechanical exercise and what matters is the clinical judgment of the experts on the facts of this particular case'.
[5]   *Arden v Malcom* [2007] EWHC 404 (QB), per Tugendhat J at para 36.

DEALE methodology

[H62]   There has been an increase in recent years of defendant insurers relying upon experts who use DEALE methodology to assess life expectancy. This methodology is used by the insurance industry to assess risks and appropriate 'loading' when calculating insurance premiums. Experts are often requested to produce desktop reports suggesting that a claimant's life expectancy has been compromised by reason of various factors including smoking, obesity, alcohol intake etc. This approach was recently rejected in *Edwards v Martin*[1]. David Clarke J refused to reduce the life multiplier on the basis of Dr Walker's evidence suggesting discounts due to smoking (which the claimant had taken up since his injury) and recurring episodes of depression. He preferred the evidence of the claimant's actuarial expert, Mr Patel, finding that it was essentially a statistical question and it was unconventional to take account of lifestyle factors in the typical case.

[1]   [2010] EWHC 570 (QB).

A worked example

[H63] In *C (a patient: severe head injuries) v Crisp*[1] the judge had to evaluate the life expectancy of a male claimant who had suffered a devastating and diffuse brain injury. The claimant was aged 17 at the date of the road traffic accident and 24 at the date of trial. The normal life expectancy for someone of his age was said to be 75.5 years. The judge deducted 13 years from this figure representing the risk factors: namely 5 years for the risks of immobility, 4 years for the risk of incontinence, 2 years for the risks associated with swallowing, and 2 additional years for other matters. The judge therefore assessed the claimant's life expectancy to be 62.5 years, which resulted in a lifetime multiplier of 22.48.

[1]   Current Law, March 2001.

(iv)   Agreed Life Expectancy

[H64]   Where the medical evidence provides for an agreed life expectancy, Table 28 of the Ogden Tables is used in order to calculate the applicable lifetime multiplier without further discount[1]. Arguably, however, a distinction can be drawn between agreement of a claimant's life expectancy to a particular age, and an agreement of an 'average' life expectancy which takes into account a range of life expectancy figures[2]. It remains to be seen whether an additional discount can be sought to reflect the fact that, statistically, the impact of a claimant who dies earlier than his or her agreed life expectancy figure has a greater effect on the multiplier than a claimant who dies the same amount of time after his or her agreed life expectancy, as suggested by paragraph 20 of the explanatory notes to the Ogden Tables (6th edn)[3]. The argument is that this phenomenon underpins the difference between Tables 1 and 2 (representing life multipliers) on the one hand, and Table 28 (representing fixed term multipliers) on the other, thus making it incorrect to use a fixed term multiplier in this situation. The difficulty is that this argument was run in the Court of Appeal case of *RVI v B (a child)*[4] and rejected. It may well have been that the argument was not properly understood by the court. But whether or not a differently constituted court would endorse the application of an additional discount is a moot point. There are considerable practical advantages to making assessments more straightforward for the trial judge who has to apply them, particularly if he or she is not very familiar with the principles involved. Uplifts to the life multiplier are not routinely applied to take account of the fact that injured victims do not smoke, drink, exercise well or have good diets[5]. Further, the court has been very dismissive of attempts by claimants to adjust the applicable multipliers by arguing for more favourable discount rates or increased multiplicands[6]. The courts have historically not been very interested in these sorts of technical arguments, and it may not seem fair when assessing future loss claims if discounts were always applied to the benefit of the defendant, but no account taken of the possible uplifts which could be applied to redress the balance. It must be remembered that the life expectancy figures being used are only averages, and it is not possible to make specific predictions of the exact date of death of any given individual using the tables. Using statistical arguments to challenge the average figures may undermine their utility, which avoids the need to obtain expensive bespoke life expectancy calculations in individual cases[7].

1   *Thomas v Brighton Health Authority (reported as Wells v Wells)* [1999] 1 AC 345; *Brown v King's Lynn and Wisbech NHS Hospitals Trust* (20 December 2000, unreported); *RVI v B (a child)* [2002] PIQR Q137. In *Wells v Wells* [1999] 1 AC 345, Lord Lloyd said at 378: 'Mr Havers conceded that there is room for a judicial discount when calculating the loss of future earnings, when contingencies may indeed affect the result. But there is no room for any discount in the case of a whole life multiplier with an agreed expectation of life. In the case of loss of earnings the contingencies can work only in one direction – in favour of the defendant. But in the case of life expectancy, the contingency can work in either direction. The [claimant] may exceed his normal expectation of life, or he may fall short of it'. See further Elizabeth-Anne Gumbel QC 'Calculating life expectation, periodical payments and developments since *Royal Victoria Infirmary & Associated Hospitals NHS Trust v B (a child)*' Clinical Risk 2008; 14; 133–139.

2   See further the papers delivered to the Professional Negligence Bar Association's Annual Clinical Negligence Weekend in 2004 by Professor Strauss and Nicholas Stallworthy.

3   This result arises because there is a greater discount to reflect accelerated receipt the further away in time the loss occurs.

4   [2002] PIQR Q137.

5   Of course, the tables are based upon averages which include people who smoke, drink, eat badly and do not exercise, as well as the converse.

6   *Warriner v Warriner* [2002] 1 WLR 1703; *Cooke v United Bristol Health Care* [2003] EWCA Civ 1370.

7   There are services run by Professor Strauss and others, providing individualised assessments of life expectancy and appropriate multipliers in certain categories of cases. Whilst they can be useful in certain high-value cases, their use in run-of-the-mill cases is likely to significantly increase the costs of litigation.

[H65]   The tendency to date has been that, in cerebral palsy cases[1] and spinal injury cases[2], where the experts agree life expectancy to a particular age or the court decides that the claimant will live to a certain age, Table 28 tends to be used rather than Table 1 or 2. The reason for this is that usually an individual or bespoke clinical assessment regarding life expectancy takes into account all factors, including published statistical data and all relevant pre- and post-injury factors, and therefore, if Table 1 or 2 were to be used, this would result in a double discount for mortality risks. However, the position may be different where, instead of the experts expressing a clinical assessment regarding the likely age to which the claimant will live, the claimant is expressed to have a normal life expectancy less a certain number of years due to a particular condition, eg epilepsy[3].

1   *RVI v B (a child)* [2002] PIQR Q137.

2   See eg *Sarwar v (1) Ali and (2) MIB (No 1)* [2007] EWHC 274 (QB); *Burton v Kingsbury* [2007] EWHC 2091; and *Davies v Bradshaw* [2008] EWHC 740 (QB).

3   See below para [H66].

(v)   Agreed Reduction of Years

[H66]   Where the medical evidence is expressed as an agreed reduction in the claimant's life expectancy – eg by reason of the claimant's injuries, it is agreed that he or she is likely to live five years less than would have been the case in the absence of the injuries – it is generally permissible to select an appropriate lifetime multiplier from Table 1 (if the claimant is male) or Table 2 (if the claimant is female) of the Ogden Tables, but treat the claimant as if he or she were five years older[1]. The 'addition of years' method will provide a rough estimate of the applicable multiplier, which will be good enough for most cases. However, where the agreed reduction in life expectancy is substantial, adopting such an approach will lead to inaccurate results, and it would be prudent either to instruct an actuary or to ask the doctors to provide an actual figure for life expectancy, so that Table 28 of the Ogden Tables can be used instead[2].

[1]   See eg *Tinsley v Sarkar* [2006] PIQR Q1; *Crofts v Murton* LTL 10/9/2008; *Smith v LC Window Fashions Ltd* [2009] EWHC 1532 (QB). In *RVI v B (a child)* [2002] PIQR Q137, Thorpe LJ said at para 45, Q148: '... in the majority of personal injury cases, where the claimant is not left with significant permanent disability, life expectancy is established by the use of life tables produced by the Government Actuaries Department, conveniently found in the tables for the calculation of damages compiled by the members of the Professional Negligence Bar Association. Equally where the claimant has a partial permanent disability it will be conventional to make use of the same tables with appropriate adjustment to reflect the disability factor. No doubt the judge in making that adjustment will depend upon expert medical advice specific to the claimant'. See further paragraph 20 of the explanatory notes to the Ogden Tables (6th edn), although see also Richard Hermer and John Pickering 'Future Loss Multipliers' [2002] JPIL, Issue 4/02, at 377–384.

[2]   In *RVI v B (a child)* [2002] PIQR Q137, Thorpe LJ said at para 44, Q148: 'However in cases such as the present where the defendant's negligence has resulted in massive permanent disability the life tables have nothing to offer.'

(vi)   Assessment of Lifetime Multiplier in the Absence of Agreement

[H67]   Where the presumption of normal life expectancy is not rebutted, the appropriate lifetime multiplier can be gleaned from Table 1, if the claimant is a man, or Table 2, if the claimant is a woman, of the Ogden Tables[1] at a discount rate of 2.5%[2].

[1]   Tables 1 and 2 are based on projected mortality figures, which are to be preferred to historical mortality figures: *Worrall v Powergen plc* [1999] PIQR Q103; *Biesheuval v Birrell* [1999] PIQR Q40; *Jenkins v Groscott and Hoyte* [2000] PIQR Q17; *Barry v Ablerex* [2000] PIQR Q263; and *Ved v Caress* (9 April 2001, unreported), QBD, HHJ Chapman.

[2]   The discount rate is currently fixed by the Lord Chancellor at 2.5%: Damages (Personal Injury) Order 2001, SI 2001/2301. However, the court may adopt a different rate of return under Damages Act 1996, s 1(2) if it is 'more appropriate' in the case in question. See further at paras [H25]–[H35].

[H68]   Where the presumption of normal life expectancy is rebutted and the court makes a determination of the claimant's actual life expectancy, there is no difference in principle between assessing the appropriate multiplier in respect of this determined life expectancy as opposed to an agreed life expectancy[1]. Following *Wells v Wells*[2], actuarial tables should be regarded as the starting point rather than a check. Therefore, once the claimant's life expectancy has been assessed by the judge, Table 28 of the Ogden Tables at a discount rate of 2.5% should be used in order to calculate the appropriate multiplier for the remaining fixed term without further discount[3].

[1]   *RVI v B (a child)* [2002] PIQR Q137, per Tuckey LJ at Q144: 'There is no difference in principle between an agreed expectation of life and one determined by the judge'.

[2]   [1999] 1 AC 345.

[3]   *Thomas v Brighton Health Authority* [1999] 1 AC 345; *RVI v B (a child)* [2002] PIQR Q137.

5   Periodical Expenses and Losses

[H69]   There are three main ways of calculating periodical expenses and losses, ie those expenses and losses which are not annual or continuous but occur at intervals.

(i)   The Averaging Method

[H70]   The first method of assessment, known as the averaging method, is the easiest to carry out but only provides a rough estimate of the loss. The cost of the claimed item is divided by the number of years of the replacement period so as to obtain an average annual multiplicand. The relevant multiplier for the whole duration of the loss is then applied to the average multiplicand. Take, for example, a claimant who as a result of his injuries requires an electric wheelchair at a cost of £5,000 which needs replacing every ten years. The claimant is aged 53 at the date of trial and has an agreed life expectancy of 27 years. Where the claimant does not already have an electric wheelchair as at the date of trial, the calculation using the averaging method is as follows:

£5,000[1] plus (£500[2] × 19.19[3]) = £14,595

[1]   Immediate capital outlay.
[2]   The average annual cost of the wheelchair, ie £5,000 divided by 10.
[3]   This is the appropriate fixed term multiplier for a period of 26 years taken from Table 28 of the Ogden Tables at a discount rate of 2.5%. The multiplier is calculated by reference to a period of 26 years instead of 27, because of the assumed capital purchase made in the first year.

[H71]   Where the claimant does already have an electric wheelchair as at the date of trial, the calculation is a little more straightforward, as follows:

£500[1] × 19.71[2] = £9,855

[1]   The average annual cost of the wheelchair, ie £5,000 divided by 10.
[2]   This is the appropriate fixed term multiplier for a period of 27 years taken from Table 38 of the Ogden Tables at a discount rate of 2.5%.

[H72]   As might be anticipated, this method of assessment does not lend itself very well to items of expense/loss which occur at irregular intervals. In order to be able to calculate the average annual loss easily, such a loss should occur at regular intervals, preferably measured in whole years[1]. Arguably, in the era of periodical payments and following the Court of Appeal's decision in *Eeles v Cobham Hire Services Ltd*[2], the averaged annualised method of assessing future loss is more appropriate than other more sophisticated methods, since it allows easy conversion between lump sums and PPs. It also assumes that the claimant will incur the expense of replacement. But, if he dies in the ninth year of use of an asset which requires renewal only every 10 years, he has been over-compensated by paying him 90% of the cost of an item he will never in fact buy.

[1]   For an example of an averaged annualised loss calculation, see *Morgan v Phillips* LTL 29/9/08 at paras 256–257.
[2]   [2009] EWCA Civ 204, in which the Court of Appeal held that, for the purposes of assessing whether an interim payment was a reasonable proportion of the likely capital award at trial, the only future losses that the court could assume would not be paid by way of periodical payments were future accommodation costs.

(ii)   Periodic Multiplier

[H73]   An alternative to the averaging method is to use a periodic multiplier derived from the tables contained in publications such as 'Personal Injury Damages Statistics' by Rodney Nelson-Jones, and 'Facts & Figures' produced by the Professional Negligence Bar Association or from a computer program such as Computing Personal Injury Damages or the Personal Injury Toolkit[1]. These tables and programs are based upon the same arithmetic as is used by the Government Actuary's Department to formulate the Ogden Tables. Inputting the facts of the above wheelchair example, where the claimant does not already have a wheelchair at the date of trial, into such a program may produce the following calculation:£5,000[2] x 2.731[3] = £13,655

[1]	For more examples of periodic multipliers in action, see the notes in Facts & Figures; *A v Powys Local Health Board* [2007] EWHC 2996 (QB); and *Willisford v (1) Jones and (2) MIB* LTL 11/6/2009.
[2]	Cost of the wheelchair.
[3]	Periodic multiplier calculated by reference to a period of purchase of 27 years, with a frequency of purchase every 10 years at a discount rate of 2.5%, including immediate purchase of the item.

[H74] Where no immediate purchase is necessary at the date of trial, the periodic multiplier will be reduced by 1, so the calculation becomes:

£5,000[1] × 1.731[2] = £8,655

| [1] | Cost of the wheelchair. |
| [2] | Periodic multiplier calculated by reference to a period of purchase of 27 years with a frequency of purchase every 10 years at a discount rate of 2.5% without immediate purchase of the item. |

(iii) Applying the Individual Discount Factors

[H75] Arguably, the most accurate method of assessment is provided by calculating the relevant discount factors for each replacement period, and applying the same to the cost of the item in question. The relevant discount factors can be gleaned from Table 27 of the Ogden Tables. Using the above electric wheelchair example, where the claimant does not have such a wheelchair as at the date of trial, the calculation would be as follows:

£5,000[1] + (£5,000 x 0.7621[2]) + (£5,000 x 0.5954[3]) = £11,787.50

Where the claimant already has a wheelchair at the time of the accident, the calculation will depend upon when that wheelchair was bought and when exactly it is likely to need replacing again.

[1]	The immediate capital outlay.
[2]	The discount factor for a term certain of 11 years (Table 27 of the Ogden Tables at a discount rate of 2.5%). The period taken is 11 years, to account for the fact that, if the item is bought straight away, it will not need to be replaced until the eleventh year.
[3]	The discount factor for a term certain of 21 years (Table 27 of the Ogden Tables at a discount rate of 2.5%). Twenty-one years is taken because, if the item is bought straight away, it will not need to be replaced for the second time until the twenty-first year.

[H76] However, we have used the expression 'arguably' here. Whilst at first blush this method of assessment, though somewhat laborious, particularly where there are many items of loss occurring at different periods, may seem sound in principle[1], the example given above demonstrates the importance of the assumptions built into it, all of which may in practice be questionable. First, there is an assumption as to the life expectancy of the claimant. Secondly, there is an assumption as to the length of time for which a wheelchair will last without the need for replacement. Thus, if the claimant in fact survives beyond the agreed age of 80 by three years, and the frequency of need for replacement is correct, he will just have purchased his final wheelchair before his actual death. Alternatively, if the frequency of replacement is actually nine instead of ten years, the same may occur with no alteration to projected life expectancy. There is an argument, sound in principle, that a claimant is entitled to be compensated for the risk that he might incur a given expense. The easiest way of compensating for that risk is by the averaging method, which would provide for seven years of loss towards the third wheelchair (assuming ten-yearly replacements) – the most accurate way of recompensing the claimant for the chance that he might live longer than a statistical average life expectancy, or the chances that the replacement period might be shorter than originally anticipated.

[1]   This method can also cater for irregular payments and variations in the cost of items over time.

6   Delayed Recurrent Expenses and Losses

[H77]   Where an item of expense/loss may not occur for some time but, when it does, will recur on either a regular or irregular basis, the calculation of that loss is performed in the same way as for ongoing or periodic items of expense/loss, but an additional discount is made in respect of accelerated receipt for the period before the loss starts. The classic example of such a loss is the loss of pension. Where, as a result of an accident, the claimant loses earnings which will ultimately reduce the value of his or her pension, that loss will not actually occur until the claimant reaches retirement age. Therefore, a discount needs to be made to reflect the accelerated receipt between the age of the claimant as at the date of trial and his or her intended retirement age. Tables 15–26 of the Ogden Tables (6th edn) provide tables for calculating pension loss multipliers which already take into account this additional element of accelerated receipt[1]. But, where the loss is other than a pension loss or falls outside the relevant tables, the calculation has to be performed manually or by using a computer program such as Computing Personal Injury Damages or the Personal Injury Toolkit.

[1]   See further *Phipps v Brooks Dry Cleaning* [1996] PIQR Q100.

[H78]   An example of this type of calculation is provided by considering a female claimant who has suffered a knee injury which will deteriorate to such an extent that, after ten years, she will need to wear a custom-made knee support costing £500. The knee support will need replacing annually for the rest of her life. If the claimant is aged 27 at the date of trial, the calculation is as follows:

$$£500^1 \times 27.26^2 \times 0.7812^3 = 10,647.76$$

[1]   Cost of the custom-made knee support.
[2]   This is the lifetime multiplier for a female aged 37, ie the time at which the loss will start, taken from Table 20 of the Ogden Tables at a discount rate of 2.5%.
[3]   This is the appropriate discount factor for a fixed term of ten years, taken from Table 37 of the Ogden Tables at a discount rate of 2.5%.

[H79] Where the delayed loss is irregular or varies in amount, a periodic multiplier or the exact discount factors can be applied, instead of using an adjusted whole life multiplier[1].

1   See further at paras **[H69]** and **[H72]**.

7   Broad Brush or Global Assessments

[H80] Where there are too many imponderables for the court to make an accurate assessment of the claimant's loss on a multiplier/multiplicand basis, the court may be inclined to make a broad brush or global assessment by considering matters in the round and awarding one lump sum which is considered sufficient compensation for the loss in question. A common example of such an assessment is the *Blamire* award, which is a type of hybrid award combining both loss of earnings and disadvantage on the labour market[1]. However, in principle there is no reason why a broad brush assessment cannot be made in respect of any head of loss where there is sufficient evidence to show that there is a loss but insufficient evidence to calculate that loss accurately on the conventional basis and examples.

1   Named after *Blamire v South Cumbria Health Authority* [1993] PIQR Q1: This method of assessment is commonly applied when assessing the lost chance of pursuing a business opportunity or in difficult cases. See further Chapter F at paras **[F31]** and **[F32]**.

8   Contingency Awards[1]

[H81] Where there is a risk that the claimant's loss will increase due to some event or deterioration in his or her condition in the future, a claim may be made for provisional damages if the relevant statutory criteria are made out[2]. In the alternative, the assessment of the relevant head of loss may be adjourned until a future date[3], or a contingency award may be sought. Contingency awards are usually made where the ongoing loss is readily identifiable, eg the ongoing cost of providing gratuitous care, but there is a risk that the amount of this loss will increase, eg due to the gratuitous care provider no longer being able to provide the necessary care, so that professional carers have to be bought in. For example, in *Bristow v Judd*[4] the Court of Appeal awarded the claimant an additional £15,000 on top of the claim for care, to reflect the chance that his girlfriend would not be able to continue providing housekeeping services. Further, in *Stuart v Martin*[5] the trial judge awarded a head-injured claimant £100,000 in respect of 'contingencies' to reflect the chance that he would suffer from further episodes of depression, and that his marriage might break down, thus requiring a greater level of guidance and support. The court has to assess the chances of the contingency occurring and its effect on the future costs incurred by the claimant[6]. However, such an award will not necessarily be appropriate where the evidence suggests that the contingency, such as a marriage breakdown, is likely to occur; in such a case, the court should be invited to make a finding regarding when the contingency is likely to occur, and the claim should be valued on that basis[7].

1   See further Chapter A at paras **[A20]**–**[A21]**.
2   See further Chapter A at paras **[A135]**–**[139]**.
3   See further Chapter A at paras **[A141]**–**[142]**.

9   Individual Heads of Future Loss and Expense

(i)   Loss of Earnings

General principles

[H82]   Once the claimant's net annual earnings have been calculated to the date of trial or to the date of settlement, a calculated estimate has to be made of the likely loss of earnings that the claimant will sustain for the remainder of his or her working life. This requires the court to evaluate the chances of events happening in the future, including the possibility of the event happening, and taking into account other imponderables which, by definition, cannot be estimated.

[H83]   Save in exceptional circumstances[1], the court will adopt the conventional multiplier and multiplicand method of calculating the loss. Where the claimant is already working at the time of injury, unless the court hears evidence to the contrary, it will assume that the claimant will continue to suffer the same ongoing net loss as at the date of trial. Thus, the claimant requires evidence of any potential increase in his or her net earnings post-trial. This usually takes the form of future promotion prospects or an increase in wages that is in the pipeline. This type of evidence should be obtained from the claimant's employers. If this is not forthcoming, an application for disclosure against a non-party can be made or, alternatively, if the tortfeasor is also the claimant's employer, an application can be made for pre-action disclosure or for further information under CPR, Pt 18 regarding comparable earners. Expert evidence may be necessary from an expert familiar with the type of work profile that the claimant was anticipating.

1   Where there are too many imponderables to calculate the loss using a multiplier and multiplicand, it may be appropriate to award a lump sum: see further below at paras **[H186]–[H189]**.

Employment consultant's evidence

[H84]   In certain situations, evidence may be obtained from an employment consultant (as discussed in Chapter C). The evidence can be used to help estimate the earning potential of the claimant if the accident had never occurred. Alternatively, the defendant may wish to instruct a consultant to prove that the labour market of the claimant had deteriorated in any event and, even if the accident had not occurred, the claimant would have been likely to lose his or her job or be earning less than before the accident. However, the parties should restrict the use of employment consultants to cases in which it is necessary.

[H85]   An expert can only really predict or describe the generalities of a particular market. It is impossible for an expert to give an accurate prediction of promotion, redundancy etc in a particular case. Such subjective considerations are assessments to be made relying on the evidence of witnesses and should therefore be left to the judge[1].

[1]   In *Larby v Thurgood* [1993] PIQR P218, May J held that the issue of the willingness of the claimant to seek better-paid employment, and his ability to obtain such, are matters of fact that the judge can evaluate.

[H86]   It is, therefore, often unnecessary for an employment consultant to be used. What is more important is the evidence of the claimant (and other witnesses) and the weight which the judge decides to attach to this. The use of an employment consultant should be limited to cases in which the actual job market is being evaluated, not the job seeker (see, in particular, Chapter C at paras **[C52]**–**[C55]**).

[H87]   In respect of the length of the job search period, post-recovery, the judge is entitled to treat the expert's opinion as no more than a starting point in determining the reasonable time[1].

[1]   *Singh v Garwood* (7 December 1998, unreported), CA.

Residual earning potential of the claimant

[H88]   If the claimant is capable of doing work in the future, the specific work that he or she is capable (or incapable) of doing must be identified by the medical experts. If any adaptations need to be made to accommodate the claimant's disabilities in the normal workplace, these should be identified. Once this evidence has been obtained, the opinion of an employment consultant may again be sought as regards the claimant's residual earning capacity, in particular following any period of retraining or requalification.

[H89]   Careful thought needs to be given to the type and amount of work that the claimant is likely to be able to undertake in view of his or her injuries. Realism is key here. It may be that the claimant is no longer able to carry out heavy manual work and is restricted to light or sedentary employment. The claimant may also be limited to a part-time role or a job which does not involve too much stress or pressure or contact with the general public. Often, flexible working hours or understanding employers are required to allow the claimant time off to attend medical and treatment appointments or to take time off due to flare-ups. If possible, the claimant's residual earning capacity should be tested before trial. It may be that, whilst in theory the claimant has a residual earning capacity, in practice it may be difficult for the claimant to exploit it, and the chances of actually finding and sustaining alternative employment are slim at best.

[H90]   Another factor is the difference in the likely retirement age doing the work the claimant now can, compared with that he or she could have done pre-injury. As will be seen below, the methodology used in the Ogden Tables (6th edn) ('Ogden VI') for calculating loss of earnings applies different discount factors to pre-injury earnings and post-injury earnings where the claimant is disabled. Where the claimant is disabled within the meaning of the Disability Discrimination Act 1995 and this affects the kind or amount of work they can do, the discount factors applied to residual earnings take into account the risk of periods of non-employment and absence from the workforce. This includes a risk that the claimant might retire earlier than he or she would have done in the absence of injury. However, in some cases it is necessary to take account of a lower multiplier for residual earnings, eg where the medical evidence suggests that the claimant is unlikely to work beyond a certain age[1].

[1]   See eg *Assinder v Griffin* [2001] All ER (D) 356 (May); and *O'Brien v Harris* (22 February 2001, unreported), QBD.

Discounts for contingencies other than mortality

[H91]   Following *Wells v Wells*[1], actuarial tables are to be used as the starting point rather than as a check for calculating future loss multipliers. However, when assessing the appropriate multiplier for loss of future earnings, the court needs to discount the starting point multiplier obtained for 'contingencies other than mortality'. As Lord Lloyd said in *Wells v Wells*[2]:

'Mr Havers conceded that there is room for a judicial discount when calculating the loss of future earnings, when contingencies may indeed affect the result ... In the case of loss of earnings the contingencies can work only in one direction – in favour of the defendant.'

[1]   [1999] 1 AC 345.
[2]   At 378.

[H92]   The types of risk that might apply to future earnings include:

* periods of unemployment;
* redundancy;
* illness;
* retiring early; and
* deciding to work shorter hours.

[H93]   Traditionally, a higher discount for such contingencies has been applied to women of childbearing age in order to take account of the chance that, but for the claimant's injuries, she would have taken time off to bring up and raise children. However, research carried out by the Equal Opportunities Commission suggests that two out of every three women returned to employment after childbirth. This has been helped by the compulsory maternity leave benefits which now apply, and by the effects of age discrimination legislation. In addition, various studies have been carried out showing that there is a trend for people to work longer, given the problem of inadequate pension provision (which is not helped by the problems with endowment mortgages), increased general health, a greater appreciation by employers of the value of experienced staff, and the lessening emphasis generally on set retirement ages.

[H94]   When assessing the appropriate discount for contingencies other than mortality, the starting point should be Tables A–D of the Introduction to the Ogden Tables. In *Herring v Ministry of Defence*[1], Potter LJ said in relation to the Ogden Tables (5th edn):

'... statistics, or at any rate guidance based upon research, are now available in the Notes to the Ogden Tables which demonstrate that so far as the level of any "arbitrary" or generally applied level of discount is concerned, a figure of 25% is a gross departure from that appropriate simply in respect of future illness and unemployment. In order to justify a substantially higher discount by reason of additional future contingencies, there should in my view be tangible reasons relating to the personality or likely future circumstances of the claimant going beyond the purely speculative.'

1   [2003] EWCA Civ 528.

[H95]   The discount made should be individual to the claimant, and consideration must be given to the specific risk factors involved in the case[1]. Therefore, where possible, specific evidence should be called in relation to the relevant risk factors in order to show that they are or are not present.

1   See eg *Pearce v Linfield* [2003] EWCA Civ 647, in which Kay LJ said at [21]: 'Mr Bate-Williams argues that against that evidence the judge should have concluded that there was at least an identifiable chance that the claimant would have retired before the age of 60 even if she had not had the three accidents. He submits the judge should therefore have gone on to make an allowance, albeit a relatively small one, for that chance in determining the appropriate multiplier in calculating her loss of earnings. The fallacy in that argument is that the judge was not assessing when any teacher might retire but was instead directing his mind as to when the claimant was likely to retire. He had to consider her as an individual and not merely as one of a class of people. He heard evidence from her that she wanted to go on working until the age of 60. I find it impossible to see how, without even hearing such evidence, this court could conclude that that was not a finding of fact open to the judge'.

[H96]   In some instances, there might be factors which the claimant would wish to highlight in order to minimise the applicable discount for contingencies, including:

- The claimant's good working history.
- The claimant's skills, qualifications and experience (and the ease he or she would have had finding alternative employment but for the injuries).
- The prospects of promotion or career advancement (assuming this has not already been taken into account in the calculation of the claimant's loss).
- The prospects of salary increase (assuming this has not already been taken into account in the calculation of the claimant's loss).
- The absence of any pre-existing illnesses or congenital problems.
- The possibility of working beyond normal retirement age.
- Any economic pressure to continue to work, eg where the date of expiry of a mortgage is later rather than earlier; or the likely date when children will finally leave full-time education and become self-supporting argues for a fuller working life, etc.

There might, on the other hand, be particular features which a defendant can point to which would suggest an earlier retirement date (eg where the claimant's spouse is significantly older, and they may wish to enjoy a joint retirement).

[H97]   Following *Wells v Wells*[1] the actuarial tables are the starting point not just a check. The scope for high judicial discounts purely on impressionist grounds has gone. The upshot is that discounts for 'contingencies' are not as high as they used to be and they are tailored to the facts of the individual case.

1   [1999] 1 AC 345.

Calculating the loss: Ogden VI methodology[1]

[H98]   The sixth edition of the Ogden Tables provided a new way of assessing claims for future loss of earnings. Research by Professor Verrall, Professor Haberman and Mr Zoltan Butt of City University, and by Dr Victoria Wass of Cardiff University, showed that people with disabilities spent more time out of employment than earlier research had suggested. The research, which was based upon data from the Labour Force Survey collected between 1998 and 2003, demonstrated that the factors other than gender that had the most effect on a person's future employment are: (i) whether the person was employed or unemployed at the outset; (ii) whether the person is disabled or not; and (iii) the educational attainment of the person.

[1]   For a worked example, see further the explanatory notes to Ogden VI. See further Dr Wass 'Discretion in the Application of the New Ogden Six Multipliers: The Case of *Conner v Bradman and Company*' [2008] JPIL 2/08 pp 154–163; Christopher Melton QC 'Ogden Six – Adjustments to Working Life Multipliers' [2009] JPIL Issue 1/09 at p 66; and Derek O'Sullivan in 'The 6th Edition of the Ogden Tables: The Story so far' Kemp News, Issue 1&2, July 10, 2009.

[H99]   Paragraphs 33 to 42 of the explanatory notes to Ogden VI set out the methodology to be applied when calculating a claim for future loss of earnings. It is essentially a three-stage process. The first stage is to calculate the claimant's 'but for' earnings by taking the annual loss (the multiplicand calculated by reference to the claimant's net annual pre-injury earnings) and applying a multiplier to normal retirement age (taken from Tables 3 to 14 of the Ogden Tables). The multiplier is discounted for contingencies other than mortality by applying a factor from Table A (for men) or Table C (for women). The discount factor to be applied depends upon the claimant's age as at the date of trial, and his or her educational attainment (category 'O' if he or she had no qualifications or GCSEs below grade C; category 'GE-A' if the claimant has GCSE grades A to C, or up to A-level or equivalent; and category 'D' for degree or equivalent). Where the claimant was likely to have been promoted or would have earned different amounts at different stages, the multiplier may be split to allow for variable future earnings (see further the example at paragraph 23 of the explanatory notes).

[H100]   The second stage is to calculate the claimant's future residual earnings by taking the multiplicand for residual earnings (the claimant's likely net post-injury earnings) and applying a multiplier discounted by a factor taken from Table B (for men) or Table D (for women). The starting point multiplier is often the same actuarial multiplier to normal retirement age used in the first stage of the calculation. However, the multiplier may be curtailed if there is medical evidence to suggest that the claimant will probably have to retire earlier because of his or her injuries. Again, the multiplier can be split where the evidence suggests that the claimant's residual earning capacity is likely to be more or less in the future.

[H101]   The third and final stage is to deduct the figure for residual earnings (the second stage) from the figure for 'but for' earnings (the first stage). The resultant figure is the net loss which can be claimed.

[H102]   There have been a number of cases which have applied the explanatory notes, and these are discussed under various factors below which may have an influence on the calculations.

(1)   DISABLED OR NOT DISABLED?

[H103]   Before a claimant is able to apply the lower discounts in Tables B and D to his or her residual earnings capacity, it must be established that (i) the claimant is disabled under the meaning of the Disability Discrimination Act 1995[1], and (ii) his or her condition affects either the kind or the amount of work that he or she can do.

1   See further para 35 of the explanatory notes to Ogden VI, and the 'Disability Discrimination Act 1995 Code of Practice: Employment and Occupation' (2004), published by the Disability Rights Commission and available from the Equality and Human Rights Commission website: www. equalityhumanrights.com.

[H104]   *Conner v Bradman & Co*[1] was one of the first cases to consider the meaning of disability within the context of Ogden VI. HHJ Peter Coulson QC (as he then was) considered the definition of disability in the Disability Discrimination Act 1995 and the guidance notes published by the Secretary of State. On the facts of the case, he held that the claimant, who had suffered a knee injury requiring surgery, was disabled. The claimant had been prevented from continuing to work as a mechanic by reason of his injuries. The judge went on to consider the appropriate discount for contingencies to be applied for residual earning capacity and, in particular, para 32 of the guidance notes, which states:

'The suggestions which follow are intended as a 'ready reckoner' which provides an initial adjustment to the multipliers according to the employment status, disability status and educational attainment of the claimant when calculating awards for loss of earnings and for any mitigation of this loss in respect of potential future post-injury earnings. Such a ready reckoner cannot take into account all circumstances and it may be appropriate to argue for higher or lower adjustments in particular cases. In particular, it can be difficult to place a value on the possible mitigating income when considering the potential range of disabilities and their effect on post work capability, even within the interpretation of disability set out in paragraph 35. However, the methodology does offer a framework for consideration of a range of possible figures with the maximum being effectively provided by the post injury multiplier assuming the claimant was not disabled and the minimum being the case where there is no realistic prospect of post injury employment.'

1   [2007] EWHC 2789 (QB).

[H105]   The medical evidence was that the claimant could probably work as a minicab driver until normal retirement age. The judge refused to apply the full discount allowed by the tables for the claimant's residual earning capacity of 0.49. Instead, he applied a midpoint discount for contingencies of 0.655 (which is the midpoint discount between someone who is disabled and someone who is not disabled). The discount factor was reduced because the judge considered that the claimant was less disabled than the average[1]. However, importantly, no reasons were given for suggesting the claimant was less disabled than the average, and the adjustment he made was significantly more than the adjustment to reflect educational attainment, ie whether or not the claimant had a degree. This decision has been criticised because there was no express basis for adjustment and, if anything, the adjustment should have been the other way, because the claimant was unable to make use of any of his previous qualifications or skills as a mechanic in light of his injuries[2].

1   See also the Scottish case of *McGhee v Diageo Plc* [2008] CSOH 74, in which Lord Malcolm held that an award claimed in accordance with Ogden VI was excessive, presumably because the tables were based upon some average disability of greater severity than that which afflicted the pursuer. In the event, the court decided to make a *Blamire* award rather than using the tables.

2   See further Dr Wass 'Discretion in the Application of the New Ogden Six Multipliers: The Case of *Conner v Bradman and Company*' [2008] JPIL 2/08 pp 154–163.

[H106]   In *Garth v (1) Grant and (2) MIB*[1], HHJ Hickinbottom (sitting as an additional judge of the High Court) had to decide whether a morbidly obese claimant was disabled as at the time of the accident so as to justify a higher discount to her potential future earnings. At the time of the accident, the claimant weighed 28–30 stones and accepted that she had a 'long and tortuous fight against obesity'. However, she gave evidence that she used to play tennis and do water aquaerobics, and her weight had never affected her work. The judge accepted that she was not significantly functionally disabled by her weight, and therefore applied Table C as opposed to Table D. He went on to apply an unadjusted discount for contingencies, derived directly from Table C, of 0.87.

1   LTL 17/7/2007.

[H107]   In *Leesmith v Evans*[1] the parties' respective employment consultants agreed that the claimant had a residual earning capacity of £10,000 net pa. The defendant argued that this multiplicand already took into account the degree of disability of the claimant, and therefore to apply the Table B discount factor of 0.54 was unjust. The judge said that he partly agreed with the submission, and reduced the discount to 0.60.

1   [2008] EWHC 134 (QB).

[H108]   The authors would caution that the modern approach of the Equality and Human Rights Commission stresses that persons are not 'disabled', as if there were one class sharing common features, but rather individuals may 'suffer from a disability'. Disabilities can be many and various, and it is entirely possible to be disabled within the meaning of the 1995 Act, yet be able to function every bit as well as formerly at a pre-accident job: for instance, an investment banker whose leg is amputated will be disabled, in that the amputation has a significant permanent effect on his day–to-day activities, yet be perfectly as able as before to continue his work, subject only to transport to it, and assuming the availability of lifts. It can thus be misleading to think in terms of applying discount factors as though they were analogous to 'one size fits all' figures.

(2)   PRE-EXISTING DISABILITY

[H109]   Paragraph 38 of the explanatory notes to Ogden VI suggests that Tables B and D should be used for those who were already disabled at the time of the accident. However, where a claimant's level of disability has been significantly worsened by reason of the defendant's negligence, this does not provide a satisfactory answer. In these circumstances, it may be necessary to fall back on a lump sum *Smith v Manchester* or *Blamire* award (see below).

(3) EMPLOYED OR NOT EMPLOYED

[H110] In the Northern Irish case of *Hunter v MOD*[1], Stephens J assessed the future loss of earnings for a Corporal in the Royal Irish Regiment in accordance with Ogden VI. The main live issue concerned the appropriate discount to the multiplier for the claimant's residual earning capacity. Since the claimant was unemployed and disabled as at the date of trial, Table B suggested a discount of 80%. However, if he was in employment and disabled, the discount would have been 61%. The judge held, on the basis of the medical evidence, that there was no reason why the claimant should not be in employment, and therefore approached the assessment on the basis that the claimant was employed. At para 13 of his judgment he held that:

> 'in arriving at the appropriate reduction to the multiplier, the court is required to consider the degree of the plaintiff's disability and where the plaintiff falls in the range of potential reductions to the multiplier.'

[1]   [2007] NIQB 43.

[H111] In the circumstances, a discount of 40% was held to be appropriate (ie half of the discount that would otherwise have been expected from a straightforward application of the tables).

[H112] In *Huntley v Simmonds*[1] there was an issue regarding whether or not the claimant should be treated as employed or non-employed as at the date of the accident. Prior to the accident, he had worked as a ground-worker. He had been in and out of work a good deal in the two years before the accident and, whilst the claimant argued that he should be treated as 'employed', giving a discount of 0.89, the defendant argued that he should be treated as 'unemployed', resulting in a discount of 0.82. In the circumstances, Underhill J preferred the defendant's approach, but this was influenced by a number of other case-specific factors, including the claimant's drug and alcohol use (he regularly got 'paralytic' at the weekends) and his brushes with the law.

[1]   [2009] EWHC 405 (QB).

(4) RETRAINING / POTENTIAL HIGHER EARNINGS

[H113] Paragraph 44 of the explanatory notes states that it is assumed that there will be no change in the claimant's educational status in the future. But where the claimant is retraining at the time of trial, it may be necessary to take into account any change of such status in the future. Where there are a number of imponderables regarding the claimant likely future earnings following a period of retraining, it may appropriate for the court to make a lump sum *Blamire* award instead[1].

[1]   See eg *McGhee v Diageo Plc* [2008] CSOH 74.

(5) INABILITY TO MAKE USE OF EDUCATIONAL STATUS

[H114] Where a claimant who has skills or qualifications in a particular field is prevented by reason of injury from using those skills or qualifications in the future, arguably he or she should be treated as not having those skills for the purposes of assessing the residual earnings discount factors[1].

[1]   'Discretion in the Application of the New Ogden Six Multipliers: The Case of *Conner v Bradman and Company*' [2008] JPIL 2 (154–163).

(6)   CHILD CLAIMANTS

[H115]   What if the claimant is a child as at the date of injury and was not employed? Should the claimant be treated as employed or unemployed? The answer to this lies in paragraph 41 of the guidance notes, which states:

> 'In the case of those aged under 16 at the date of the accident, the relevant factor from the tables would be chosen on the basis of the level of education the child would have been expected to have attained, had the injury not occurred, together with an assessment as to whether the child would have become employed or not. The relevant factor for 16 would be chosen using the assessed employment status and educational status likely to be ultimately attained, discounted by the appropriate factor from Table 27 for the number of years from the age at the date of trial to the age of 16.'

[H116]   In *A v Powys Health Board*[1], Lloyd-Jones J rejected a submission from the defendant that the claimant should be treated as unemployed, or that a higher discount should be applied to take account of the uncertainty that the claimant would complete her education and become employed, and he applied the ordinary Table C discount of 0.87.

[1]   [2007] EWHC 2996 (QB).

[H117]   That said, there is perhaps still an argument left open to a defendant in respect of a claimant who was aged less than 16 prior to injury, but is aged between 16 and 19 or between 20 and 24 as at the date of trial. Acting for a claimant, one would seek to minimise the reduction for contingencies, eg by arguing that the appropriate discount is the one to apply as at the date the claimant would have started employment (often age 21 if the claimant would have gone to university). Using the Tables, there is a small difference between the discounts to be applied between the different age groups (and the discount for the 20–24 age group is 2% less than the 16–19 age group). The reason for this discrepancy is uncertain from the guidance notes. However, a defendant could argue that the lower discount for those aged 16–19 should apply, because a higher discount is appropriate for someone who has not yet completed his or her education, compared to someone who has completed further education and started work, ie an additional small discount might apply to reflect the risk of dropping out of further education and not achieving the claimant's full educational potential.

(7)   TIME OFF TO HAVE CHILDREN OR BRING UP CHILDREN

[H118]   It should be noted that paragraph 40 of the explanatory notes to Ogden VI makes it clear that the suggested discounts in Tables A to D of the Ogden Tables already take into account time off for bringing up children and caring for dependants. This can be seen by comparing the discount factors between Tables A and C. Whilst the recommended discount factors for women of child-bearing age are significantly less than those for men (ie the suggested discounts are higher), for older claimants the discount factors are significantly higher (ie the discounts are less, since the factor is used to multiply the annual figure for loss). In *A v Powys Health Board*[1] the judge refused to apply a discount over and above that already allowed for in the tables, notwithstanding the expert employment evidence in the case which suggested that the many women take between 5 and 10 years off work to bring up children, and most would return on a part-time basis. The award made for loss of earnings was a little over £620,000, including about £9,000 for earnings from age 16–21.

[1]   [2007] EWHC 2996 (QB).

[H119]   Unfortunately, the decision in *A v Powys Health Board*[1] was not brought to the attention of Penry-Davey J in *Smith v East and North Hertfordshire Hospitals NHS Trust*[2]. Instead of making a discount in accordance with Table C of about 13%, Penry-Davey J discounted future earnings by 40%. This was said to be justified by taking into account the costs of working, career breaks and an element of overlap, as identified by Griffiths LJ in *Croke v Wiseman*[3]. This reasoning is not understood, bearing in mind that the explanatory notes already take account of career breaks, and the purported overlap with living expenses was not applicable, given that the judge made a finding that it was reasonable for the claimant to live independently rather than in an institution. Furthermore, whilst some discount may be appropriate to take account of travel costs, these would not have been significant on the facts of the case (a teacher living in the local community) and may well have been more than offset by perks and benefits associated with employment over and above salary and pension, eg access to leisure facilities, access to a library, free teas and coffees, free or discounted food, the ability to borrow equipment etc. The award made for loss of earnings was a shade under £220,000.

[1]   [2007] EWHC 2996 (QB).
[2]   [2008] EWHC 2234 (QB).
[3]   [1982] 1 WLR 71 at 83b–c.

(8)   PRE-ACCIDENT EMPLOYMENT HISTORY

[H120]   Paragraph 31 of the explanatory notes to Ogden VI makes it clear that the tables do not take account of 'pre-accident employment history'. The suggested discounts may not be appropriate where the claimant has a particularly secure or weak employment history. An upward or downward adjustment may be justified on the facts of a given case, in order to reflect the claimant's particular industry and/or the risk he or she would have had more time out of work than the average but for his or her injuries.

(i)   Earnings history

[H121]   In *Hopkinson v MOD*[1], Michael Harvey QC (sitting as a deputy judge of the High Court) increased the discount factor for contingencies (ie reduced the discount) for pre-accident earnings derived from Table A of 0.81 to 0.9. He justified the increase on the basis that the claimant had been consistently in work throughout his career. The suggested Table A discount to the multiplier was equivalent to reducing the multiplicand by up to 60% by age 65, which he considered too pessimistic on the facts of the case. Likewise, in *Fleet v Fleet*[2], Mackay J declined to apply the suggested discount factor from Table A lower than 0.8 (ie exceeding 20%). On the facts of the case, involving a claimant with a long history of employment with the same employer, the judge held that the reduction should be no more than 10%.

[1]   [2008] EWHC 699 (QB).
[2]   [2009] EWHC 3166 (QB).

(ii)   Family background

[H122]   It may be appropriate in some cases for the trial judge to adjust the multiplier or multiplicand to take account of good family background, eg where the claimant's family background can be shown to have been particularly impressive and would have instilled a strong work ethic and desire to earn a good living[1]. Conversely, it may be appropriate for the trial judge to increase the discount for contingencies other than mortality to reflect the claimant's troubled family background. For example, in *Peters v East Midlands Strategic Health Authority*[2], the appropriate discount for contingencies was 32% according to the explanatory notes to Ogden VI. However, Butterfield J increased the discount to 40% (pre-trial) and 50% (post-trial) to take account of the claimant's family background, which suggested a culture which relied upon benefits where the incentive to find and keep employment was not strong.

[1]   See eg *M (A Child) v Leeds HA* [2002] PIQR Q46; and *A v Powys Health Board* [2007] EWHC 2996 (QB).
[2]   [2008] EWHC 778 (QB).

(9)   OLDER CLAIMANTS

[H123]   Tables A to D are for people aged up to 54. Where claimants are aged 55 or older, paragraph 42 of the explanatory notes to Ogden VI states that the likely future course of employment will be particularly dependent upon individual circumstances, so that the use of factors based on averages would not be appropriate. It is therefore important to obtain witness evidence from (former) work colleagues, managers and/ or the human resources department regarding relevant factors such as the average retirement age in the claimant's industry, the long-term availability of work and whether the claimant could change to less physical work if required. Where it is accepted that the risks might be higher when the claimant is older, one way of dealing with this is to calculate the losses using the same discount factor as set out in the tables, but with a lower retirement age, eg to age 65 rather than 70[1].

[1]   This method was accepted by Cranston J in *Smith v LC Windows* [2009] EWHC 1532 (QB).

(10)   DIFFERENT RETIREMENT AGES

[H124]   The data from which the discount factors in Tables A to D were derived were based upon Labour Force Survey data for working males between the ages of 16 and 64 and working females between the ages of 16 and 59. However, paragraph 43 of the explanatory notes suggests that, where the retirement age is different from age 65 for men and 60 for women, this should be ignored unless the retirement age is close to the age of the claimant at the date of trial. Again, when faced with a case involving a claimant close to retirement, it is sensible to obtain supporting witness evidence regarding the claimant's likely retirement age and whether or not he or she was at less or more risk than that suggested by the tables of not being able to work up to normal retirement age.

(11)   ADJUSTMENTS TO THE SUGGESTED DISCOUNT FACTORS

[H125]   Although paragraph 32 of the explanatory notes to Ogden VI suggests that Tables A to D are intended to be used as a 'ready reckoner', and it may be appropriate to argue for higher or lower adjustments in particular cases, the approach of some judges to make adjustments to the recommended figures without sound reasons has been criticised by a number of commentators, most notably the leading labour economist, Dr Wass[1]. The great advantage of using the tables based upon statistical averages is that they reduce costs and provide a measure of certainty. If the tables become too easy to challenge or adjust, it becomes very difficult to predict the outcome at trial, which is of no assistance to either side. The research suggests that, in fact, the vast majority of people fall close to the average. Any adjustments which are made must reflect the fact that the data show that the main factors which affect employment are educational attainment, employment status and disability. Therefore, to adjust the relevant discount factor by more than that for the difference in educational attainment would require some compelling reasons. Care needs to be taken when dealing with those who have disabilities. There is no data concerning the extent of injuries suffered by people who fulfil the criteria for being disabled under the Disability Discrimination Act 1995, such that it may be arguable that there is no obvious reason for adjusting the discount factors up or down on the basis that the judge considers the claimant to be more or less disabled than the average. It should be noted that, where claimants who are disabled return to employment, they are being compared against other people who have returned to work and, therefore, there is less scope for increasing the discount on the basis that they are less disabled than the average, since the 'employed' rather than 'non-employed' factor will, to a large extent, already reflect this.

[1]   Dr Wass 'Discretion in the Application of the New Ogden Six Multipliers: The Case of *Conner v Bradman and Company*' [2008] JPIL 2/08 pp 154–163. See also Christopher Melton QC 'Ogden Six – Adjustments to Working Life Multipliers' [2009] JPIL Issue 1/09 at p 66.

[H126]   When considering the ease with which parties should be able to challenge the suggested discount factors in Tables A to D, Dr Wass raises the example of the life expectancy tables. The Ogden Tables are based upon broad averages of life expectancy; however, in individual cases, these vary significantly. For reasons of efficiency and certainty, the courts do not generally entertain arguments that multipliers should be adjusted, for example, to reflect the fact that someone smokes or lives in a particular geographical location (on average, people living in the affluent South West of England live far longer than those living in rundown parts of Glasgow). Were the court to accept such challenges more readily, it is likely that costs would proliferate, as experts would need to be instructed in most cases. It remains to be seen how the courts will react to similar arguments in relation to Ogden VI. Certainly, higher court guidance would be welcomed in order to minimise the inconsistent application of the tables.

[H127]   Another point to consider is, if an adjustment is to be made, what, if any, refinement should be made to reflect the recent recession. The discount factors in Tables A to D are based upon data from the Labour Force Survey between 1998 and 2003. It may be a while before further research charts the impact of the recession, which has been reported as hitting disabled people worse than their able-bodied counter-parts[1]; but, again, the exact nature of the disability in question may be highly relevant.

[1]   See 'Disabled workers "worst hit by cuts in recession"' (2009) Independent, 28 December.

Claimants of different ages

[H128]   Proving future losses for certain age groups can be fraught with difficulty. This section seeks to set out as many as possible of the various factual situations that commonly occur, so that the reader may apply the relevant principles to less obvious cases. The subject is dealt with chronologically, from birth to retirement.

(1)   THE CHILD CLAIMANT

[H129]   Evidence should be obtained with a view to clarifying the following points:

*   When would the child have been expected to start work?
*   What qualifications would the child have obtained[1]?
*   What work would the child have been able to do, but for the injuries suffered?
*   What physical disability has the child sustained as a result of the injury?
*   What qualifications might the child be expected to obtain with these injuries?
*   What work can the child be expected to do with the injuries suffered?
*   Has the working life expectancy of the child diminished as a result of the injuries? If so, by how much?

These factors will be considered in turn for each potential child claimant. Where possible, specific evidence should be obtained in order to support a claim for loss of earnings above the average[2].

[1]   In *McKeown v Munday* [2002] EWHC 725 (QB), HHJ Philip Price QC was persuaded that the claimant would have gone on to university but for her injuries, and therefore used the higher National Average Earnings Statistics for groups 1, 2, 3, producing a gross annual loss of £25,462.
[2]   See *M (a child) v Leeds Health Authority* [2002] PIQR Q46; *McKeown v Munday* [2002] EWHC 725 (QB); and *A v Powys Local Health Board* [2007] EWHC 2996 (QB).

(i)   Baby claimant – catastrophic injuries

[H130]   There is a large element of speculation in this assessment. The older the child is and the more that he or she has been able to demonstrate a working capacity, the easier this estimate becomes. In the case of an injured baby, the court will inevitably have to look at the social, educational and employment background of the parents and siblings. These matters must be investigated and appropriate statements prepared. The statements should contain details of the educational and any employment history. The siblings' school results should be obtained. An educational psychologist may be instructed to obtain the IQs of the parents and siblings. These are a useful indication of the baby's potential.

[H131] Once this information is available, it will often be possible to consider average earnings statistics to predict what the claimant may have earned[1]. In practice, the courts usually assume that a child will follow in the footsteps of its parents, in order to reach some assessment of the baby's future earning potential. Thus, in *Cassel v Hammersmith and Fulham Health Authority*[2] the claimant suffered from cerebral palsy caused at birth. He came from a middle class family and was expected to be educated at Eton and move on to university. The courts, therefore, had no difficulty in finding that he would probably have taken up a professional career in either accountancy or as a lawyer.

[1]   See eg *M (a child) v Leeds Health Authority* [2002] PIQR Q46, QBD, Sullivan J; *A v Powys Local Health Board* [2007] EWHC 2996 (QB); and *Smith v East and North Hertfordshire Hospitals NHS Trust* [2008] EWHC 2234 (QB).

[2]   [1992] PIQR Q168.

[H132] The broad brush approach of selecting a single averaged life time multiplicand has since been followed a number of other cases where the claimant had not yet entered employment as at the date of injury or assessment[1]. Whilst people tend to earn less than the average when they start out in their careers, they also tend to earn more than the average between 40 and 50. Attempting to map out a young claimant's earnings at different stages of his or her career might give an air of precision to the loss of earnings calculation that is difficult to justify. In short, it is impossible to know exactly what a child claimant would have earned at different stages and, therefore, adopting an average multiplicand based upon broad statistical data of average earnings may be considered the fairest way to approach the assessment of the claimant's loss. For example, in *Sarwar v (1) Ali and (2) MIB*[2], Lloyd-Jones J expressly rejected the defendant's stepped multiplicand in preference for a single averaged lifetime multiplicand, saying at para [19]:

> 'I am persuaded that the more appropriate course is to adopt a single multiplicand based upon average earnings across the whole of the Claimant's working life. In coming to this conclusion, I am influenced by the following considerations. First, we are concerned with a Claimant who at the time of his injury had not embarked on a career. As a result, the calculation of loss of future earnings will, in the nature of things, have to be assessed on a rather general basis. The calculations proposed by the Second Defendant suggest a degree of precision which may not be obtainable. Secondly, I consider that the use of the stepped multiplicands suggested by the Second Defendant may be unfair to the Claimant in that they take account of lower earnings in the early years while limiting the Claimant to an average figure for the remaining years, without taking account of the likelihood of higher than average earnings towards the end of a career. While people tend to earn less when they first start working, and possibly towards the very end of their career, there may well be a phase where they earn an above-average wage. The approach of the Second Defendant is to deny the Claimant the full benefit of the average figures. I consider that the use of a single multiplicand is fair to both parties provided that it is a realistic average of the likely wage throughout the Claimant's career.'

[1]   *Sarwar v (1) Ali and (2) MIB* [2007] EWHC 1255 (QB); *A v Powys Local Health Board* [2007] EWHC 2996 (QB); *Massey v Tameside & Glossop Acute Services NHS Trust* [2007] EWHC 317 (QB). In *Massey*, Teare J said at para 106: 'On behalf of the Defendant it is said that a lesser figure should be used for the years until 30 on the grounds that Joseph would not reach average earnings (or £25,500) until about that age. An "average" earnings figure can be expected to take into account the earnings of all working age groups. It would not therefore be appropriate to use a figure lower

than the average for the years to 30 whilst not using a figure higher than the average for the later years. For this reason it seems to me appropriate to use the figure of £25,500 alone'.

2   [2007] EWHC 1255 (QB).

(ii) Baby claimant – injuries not totally disabling from work

[H133]   If the claimant's injuries do not totally disable him or her from work, the position becomes more complicated. Medical evidence should be obtained to clarify the type of employment that the claimant could physically be expected to undertake despite his or her injuries. Thereafter, an employment consultant is likely to assist with evaluating the current market with respect to such work. Then, it is quite a straightforward calculation to evaluate the claimant's net loss of earnings. The claimant's pre-accident earnings potential (net) should have deducted from it the post-accident earnings potential (net), applying different discount factors as provided by Ogden VI.

(2)   CLAIMANT IN FULL-TIME EDUCATION

[H134]   As the claimant progresses through the education system, from nursery school to university/professional examinations, it should be increasingly possible to predict his or her potential field of work with growing confidence.

[H135]   Reliance upon the claimant's family for comparison should reduce as the claimant develops his or her own potential. If there are reasonable grounds for believing that the claimant has not at the time of injury reached his or her potential for whatever reason (illness, frequent moves etc), then this evidence may still be useful. Detailed evidence will be required to prove the reasons for his or her lack of achievement. However, the court is more likely to attach weight to the claimant's conventional educational history (in nursery, junior and secondary school) in assessing the prospects of further potential development in post-school education. Evidence should be obtained from the claimant's school records. His or her class teacher should be asked to provide a statement of the claimant's progress and expected level of achievement.

[H136]   Damages can potentially be claimed for the loss of opportunity to obtain better exam results and/or a delayed start into the open labour market as a result of having to 'catch up'. Claims under this head are less obvious, and therefore more difficult, as the severity of the injuries suffered decreases[1].

1   *Oades v Park* [1994] CLY 1488.

[H137]   Evidence should be obtained of the impact of the injuries upon the claimant's personality. This will usually include evidence from the claimant's close family.

[H138]   In cases where children have particular sporting, musical or artistic, perhaps, rather than academic abilities, a more specialist and subtle employment consultant's report may be required in order to explain whether there is a potential loss of earnings and, if so, the extent of it.

(3) CLAIMANT UNDERGOING PROFESSIONAL TRAINING OR AN APPRENTICESHIP WITH A VIEW TO
FULL-TIME EMPLOYMENT

[H139] In these cases, evidence should be obtained from the claimant's instructors
with respect to his or her ability to do the job required and potential to be taken on
full time, as well as any likely promotion profile.

(4) UNEMPLOYED CLAIMANT

[H140] Applying Ogden VI, the calculation would be performed in the usual way,
but using the 'unemployed' columns of Tables A to D.

(5) CLAIMANT IN EMPLOYMENT

[H141] Where the earnings of the claimant are expected to fluctuate over his or
her working life, then the court can use three distinct methods of assessing the loss,
depending on the circumstances:

(a) If the court accepts that the level of earning can be estimated at set rates over
set periods, a multiplier/multiplicand approach may be used. The multiplier can
be split and applied to the different levels of earning[1]. However, the multiplier
should not be split into two equal parts, since the later periods will attract a
greater discount for accelerated receipt than the earlier periods. See further the
example at paragraph 23 of the explanatory notes to Ogden VI.

(b) If the fluctuation of the claimant's potential earnings is less predictable but, on
the balance of probabilities, he or she would have been promoted, then the court
can attempt to ascertain an 'average' multiplicand. The judge has to evaluate
the fluctuating wage and decide upon an average to apply to the whole of the
multiplier[2]. Assistance can sometimes be obtained from accountants in order to
provide a weighted average. Such an average tends to be more accurate, because
it takes account of the respective amounts of time that the claimant will be
earning different levels of salary.

(c) If a court finds that a particular case simply has too many imponderables, then
it may discard the multiplier/multiplicand approach and simply award a lump
sum to reflect the claimant's loss[3]. Such a lump sum reflects an assessment of the
claimant's loss of earnings, loss of earning capacity and/or loss of a chance of
future earnings. Where a lost chance of promotion is claimed, it must be proved
and pleaded[4]. However, the court does not have to be satisfied on a balance of
probabilities. It is enough that the court is satisfied that the claimant has lost a
reasonable chance of promotion[5]. Therefore, the use of a lump sum is appropriate
when a court finds that an increase in salary, although not certain, is reasonably
possible. The lump sum can be reduced in order to compensate for the extent of
the likelihood.

---

[1] For example, *Malone v Rowan* [1984] 3 All ER 402; and *Brittain v Gardner* (1989) Times, 17
February.

[2] For example, *Housecroft v Burnett* [1986] 1 All ER 332; *Brightman v Johnson* (1985) Times,
17 December; and *Brown v King's Lynn and Wisbech NHS Hospitals Trust* (20 December 2000,
unreported), per Gage J.

[3] In *Blamire v South Cumbria Health Authority* [1993] PIQR Q1 the Court of Appeal upheld a
'broad brush' approach of awarding a single lump sum for loss of earnings where there were so

many imponderables that the multiplier/multiplicand approach was inappropriate. This decision was followed in *Goldborough v Thompson* [1996] PIQR Q86 and *Hannon v Pearce* (24 January 2001, unreported), QBD. See also *Rees v Dewhirst plc* [2002] EWCA Civ 871; and *Crouch v King's Healthcare NHS Trust* [2004] EWCA Civ 853, but cf *Cornell v Green* [1998] CLY 1485, CA.

4   *Domesalla v Barr* [1969] 1 WLR 630; *Turnbull v Waugh* (6 May 1999, unreported), CA.

5   *Davies v Taylor* [1974] AC 207; *Kitchen v Royal Air Force* [1958] 1 WLR 563; *Allied Maples v Simmons & Simmons* [1995] 1 WLR 1602; *Doyle v Wallace* [1998] PIQR Q146; *Langford v Hebran* [2001] EWCA Civ 361; *Appleton v El Safty* [2007] EWHC 631 (QB); *Collett v Smith* [2009] EWCA Civ 583.

[H142]   The claimant may be able to sustain a claim for the lost ability to work overtime as a result of his or her injuries, even though the same basic salary is still received[1].

1   See eg *McMylor v Firth Rixon plc* [2002] EWCA Civ 1863.

[H143]   In addition, where there is specific evidence that, as a result of the claimant's injuries, he or she will probably have to retire early, this can either be compensated by way of a lump sum award for handicap on the labour market[1] or ,alternatively, by using a multiplier/multiplicand method discounted for accelerated receipt[2]. It is perhaps now more relevant than ever to consider this risk, given the fact that many people are extending their retirement ages in order to meet the shortfall in their pension provision[3].

1   See, by analogy, *Herring v Ministry of Defence* [2003] EWCA Civ 528, in which the Court of Appeal awarded the claimant an additional lump sum of £5,000 in respect of his handicap on the open labour market on retiring from the police force aged 55.

2   See further at para **[H74]**. See also *Smith v Adye* (19 April 2000, unreported), CA, in which the Court of Appeal upheld the trial judge's finding to the effect that there was a 70% chance that the claimant would retire five years earlier than he otherwise would have done. Stuart-Smith LJ said that: 'In my judgment the judge was entitled to consider the wearing and ageing effect of pain, coupled with anxiety that must be caused by short term memory loss in a highly responsible job gave rise to a substantial risk of early retirement.'

3   See further Doug Hall 'Live long and prosper' [2002] PILJ, November/December, at 6–8.

(6)   THE RETIRED CLAIMANT

[H144]   Although a claimant might be retired from their full-time job, some people continue to work on a part-time basis well into their seventies and beyond. Some have the opportunity of consultant work, or self-employment, or may plan to become involved in a part-time business (perhaps utilising their capital to produce income, but nonetheless requiring some work). Where such an opportunity has been lost by reason of an injury, it may be compensated. Investigations should be made to ensure that there has been no lost opportunity to earn such an income.

Female earnings

[H145]   When considering the claim for loss of future earnings on behalf of a female claimant, arguably the court should take the average loss of earnings figure for men and women or the higher earnings of men, instead of limiting the claimant to the lower rates applicable to women. In particular, by only using the average earnings for women without taking into account the higher earnings of men, the court would fail to recognise the advances that have been made in female earnings, would fail to recognise that the law entitles women to equal pay for work which is the same or of equal value to that done by men (Equal Pay Act 1970), and would condone the discrimination in levels of pay outlawed by equal pay legislation. In *Van Wees v (1) Karkour and (2) Walsh*[1], Langstaff J said:[2]

'... I should acknowledge that the claimant would, at present, be disadvantaged in the salaried market because she is female (and, therefore, would earn less than the average or median Insead graduate, if it is assumed that it is the male Insead graduates who receive the higher salaries currently paid). However, the court must be entitled to take note of the fact that throughout the professions greater numbers of woman are achieving high positions, and with them commensurate salaries; that equal pay claims have been prominent in the recent past, particularly in the professions and amongst high earners in the city; and that the future is one in which the gap is narrowing. It must take account of the fact that in those positions in which men and women are doing equal work, a woman may not be paid a lesser salary without her having a claim for the shortfall against her employer (the contract of every woman includes a term to that effect, inserted by the Equal Pay Act 1970, section 1). Accordingly, I think it right to reflect in the sum which I shall award the fact that the claimant has (at present) the lower salary expectations of a woman, but within a few years should earn commensurately with a man. To take any other approach would be to enshrine current differences in pay which are gender based, rather than recognise their continuing and gradual attrition.'

Further, in *A v Powys Health Board*[3], when assessing a female claimant's lifetime loss of earnings based upon the evidence of an expert employment consultant using average female earnings, Lloyd-Jones J said:[4]

'I consider that some allowance should be made for the likelihood that remuneration of females in these categories is likely to move closer to that of males.'

[1]   [2007] EWHC 165 (QB). See further *Clark v Powell*, LTL 13/7/04, Lawtel Document No AM0900740.
[2]   At para [139].
[3]   [2007] EWHC 2996 (QB).
[4]   At para 39(5).

Loss of the chance of a specific job opportunity or career[1]

[H146]   Following *Allied Maples v Simmons & Simmons*[2], if the claimant's loss depends on the hypothetical actions of an independent third party, that claimant must show that he or she had a not insubstantial chance of reaching a specific goal. Therefore, in the situation of a prospective career, the third party is the hypothetical employer, and the claimant must show a chance of gaining the specific employment. Once a chance is shown, it is for the courts to assess its value. This can be done by awarding a simple lump sum[3].

[1]   See further Anthony Seys Llewellyn 'Damages – Loss of a Chance Future Earnings' [2002] JPIL, Issue 1–2/02, at 49–53; Chris Hough 'What might have been' [2002] PILJ, November/December, at 2–5; Hugh James 'Loss of chance? – no chance' [2003] PILJ, June /July, at 2–4; and Theodore Huckle 'Damages for loss of earnings – reasonable model or loss of chance' [2003] 13 APIL Newsletter 7, pp 16–20.
[2]   [1995] 1 WLR 1602.

³   For example, *Doyle v Wallace* [1998] PIQR Q146, in which there was evidence that the claimant
    had a 'not less than 50%' chance of qualifying and being employed as a teacher. Failing this, the
    claimant would have obtained clerical or administrative work. The trial judge's assessment of taking
    the mid-figure between the two contrasting salaries was upheld by the Court of Appeal. See also
    Williams v Green [2001] EWCA Civ 1888; but cf *Herring v Ministry of Defence* [2003] EWCA Civ
    528 and *Brown v MOD* [2006] PIQR Q9, CA, where the claims were advanced on the basis of a
    'reasonable career model'.

[H147]   The 'substantial' chance mentioned in *Allied* need not necessarily be as
high as 50%. The chance must merely be more than 'speculative'. In this respect,
it echoes the law's approach to questions of substance and materiality generally – a
chance is thought to be material, or substantial, unless it can be dismissed as merely
insubstantial, or de minimis¹. Beyond this, the question is not one of establishing a
chance but one of the quantification of the damage².

¹   It appears that the Court of Appeal approved a claim in *Langford v Hebran* [2001] EWCA Civ 361
    involving a lost chance of 14% (see further the case summary prepared by junior counsel in that
    case at pp 5–7 of [2001] Quantum, Issue 3, 12 June). See also *Lloyds Bank v Parker Bullen* [2000]
    Lloyd's Rep PN 51, where a claim for a lost chance of 15% was allowed.
²   *Allied Maples v Simmons & Simmons* [1995] 1 WLR 1602, per Stuart-Smith LJ at 1611. See also
    the assessment of future loss of earnings in cases of sex discrimination, in cases such as *Ministry of
    Defence v Cannock* [1995] 2 All ER 449.

[H148]   In *Langford v Hebran and Nynex Cablecomm*¹, the Court of Appeal
approved the loss of chance approach to calculate loss of earnings where there had
been multiple different career opportunities open to the claimant. The claimant was a
kick-boxer. He had won several competitions as an amateur kick-boxer and had won
his first fight as a professional. As a result of a road traffic accident, he was no longer
able to pursue his chosen career. A basic claim was advanced on the ground that the
claimant would continue with no more success than at the time of the accident. Four
alternative scenarios were then advanced, based upon increasing levels of success
with different percentage chances attached to each. The Court of Appeal held that it
was necessary for the judge to consider each different career scenario and to assess the
prospect of that particular career scenario succeeding. The 'additional value' method
was applied to ascertain the value of each additional career scenario over and above
the others². Thereafter, a discount of 20% was applied to allow for the possibility that
none of the four scenarios may have happened. In the event, although the judge at
first instance had applied the wrong methodology to the assessment of damages, the
difference between the resulting figures was too small to justify the Court of Appeal
interfering with the award. A similar 'lost chance' method of assessment has also
been used when calculating the loss of earnings of professional footballers³.

¹   [2001] EWCA Civ 361. See also *McKeown v Munday* [2002] EWHC 725 (QB); and Anthony Seys
    Llewellyn 'Damages – Loss of a Chance Future Earnings' [2002] JPIL Issue 1–2/02, at 49–53.
²   For an explanation of the different methods of assessment, see further the helpful case summary
    prepared by junior counsel at pp 5–7 of [2001] Quantum, Issue 3, 12 June.
³   *Appleton v El Safty* [2007] EWHC 631 (QB); and *Collett v Smith* [2009] EWCA Civ 583.

[H149]   No discount need necessarily be made, however, to reflect the 'loss of a
chance' where the court accepts a baseline career model for the calculation of future
loss and there is evidence that the claimant could have earned a similar salary doing
another job in any event¹. Another way of looking at this is that the court accepts

that the loss of a chance is 100% and therefore no discount should be made[2]. Such a situation might apply where one is considering the loss of earnings of a claimant who is a policeman or member of the armed services, where there is a hierarchical promotion structure, and it is necessary to assess which grade or level the claimant would have reached in the absence of his or her injuries. *Herring v Ministry of Defence*[3] would suggest that it is unnecessary to assess such losses on the basis of the loss of a chance and, as long as a 'reasonable career model' is taken, damages can be assessed by the trial judge on the balance of probabilities.

[1]   *Herring v Ministry of Defence* [2003] EWCA Civ 528; followed and applied in *Brown v MOD* [2006] PIQR Q9, CA.
[2]   In an employment context, the EAT has accepted that a lost chance of pursuing a career may be assessed at 100%: *Ministry of Defence v Hunt* [1996] ICR 554. However, the assessment of the lost chance depends upon the evidence presented to the court or tribunal, and the facts may have to be exceptional in order to justify a finding of a 100% lost chance, particularly over a prolonged period of employment: *Ministry of Defence v Nathan* (1996) Times, 13 February.
[3]   [2003] EWCA Civ 528. See further Theodore Huckle 'Damages for loss of earnings – reasonable model or loss of chance' [2003] 13 APIL Newsletter 7, pp 16–20.

[H150]   The assessment of the lost chance is a question of fact to be decided by the trial judge[1]. In the leading case of *Davies v Taylor*[2], Lord Reid said that the 'value of the prospect, chance or probability can be estimated by taking all significant factors into account'. Of course, what is significant will depend upon the particular circumstances of the case. However, as the burden is upon the claimant to prove his or her loss, he or she should adduce as much factual witness evidence as possible in order to substantiate the existence and value of the lost chance[3].

[1]   The claimant's ability to obtain better paid employment in terms of both his or her motivation to do so and the present state of the job market are questions of fact, to be determined by the judge rather than by expert opinion from an employment consultant: *Larby v Thurgood* [1993] PIQR 128.
[2]   [1974] AC 207 at 212c.
[3]   Note that the argument that witness evidence regarding the claimant's prospects of promotion is inadmissible opinion evidence is usually rejected by the court; however, there is a need for proportionality in the number of witnesses called giving similar evidence: see eg *Konopka v Boam* reported in [2002] 12 APIL Newsletter 1, February.

[H151]   Where the court is able to make a finding regarding the percentage of the lost chance, this figure is applied to the difference between the lost gain and the actual gain (if any)[1]. Take, for example, a claimant who brings a claim for the lost chance of pursuing a 22-year career in the Army, during which time he or she would have earned an average salary of £25,000 net per annum. By reason of the defendant's negligence, the claimant is no longer able to pursue his or her chosen career and has to settle for administrative work paying an average of £15,000 net per annum. The multiplier for future loss is agreed at 15. If the lost chance is assessed at 60%, the calculation would be as follows:

$$(£25,000 - £15,000) \times 15 \times 0.60 = £90,000$$

[1]   It has been held unfair to first apply the percentage chance to the lost gain and then to deduct from the resulting figure the actual gain: *Ministry of Defence v Wheeler* [1998] 1 WLR 639; and *Hartle v Laceys (a firm)* [1999] Lloyd's Rep PN 315.

[H152]   Where the court feels unable to specify actual percentage sums, it is legitimate to adopt a broad brush approach dealing with the matter in general terms[1].

In this way, if the court considers that there are simply too many imponderables to calculate the lost chance accurately using the traditional multiplier/multiplicand method, the court may award a single lump sum to reflect the relevant loss[2]. Of course, when assessing the value of a lost chance that would not have occurred for some time in the future, it is important to discount any award in order to take account of accelerated receipt, and this must be reflected in the size of any lump sum.

[1]   *Afedua-Amonoo v Grant Seifert and Grower* [2001] EWCA Civ 150.
[2]   *Doughty v Stena Offshore Ltd* (10 November 1997, unreported), CA. See also *Blamire v South Cumbria Health Authority* [1993] PIQR Q1; and *Goldborough v Thompson* [1996] PIQR Q86.

The lost chance of a promotion or career advancement

[H153]   It is a question of fact as to whether or not the claimant had a real or substantial, as opposed to speculative or fanciful, chance of obtaining promotion or career advancement but for his or her injuries. If there was such an opportunity, damages may be awarded to compensate for its loss, but a discount will be applied to reflect the chance that the opportunity would not have materialised to the claimant's advantage[1]. When considering such a claim, evidence regarding the following points is likely to be relevant:

- The general ability and aptitude of the claimant.
- The ambition/motivation of the claimant.
- The claimant's suitability for the job or position in question.
- Whether the claimant would have been likely to apply for the job or position.
- The strength of the other applicants that would have been competing for the same job or position.
- The application process and/or selection criteria that would have been used.
- The experience of previous holders of the claimant's post in relation to decisions regarding promotion.
- The statistical chance that the claimant would have been promoted[2].

[1]   *Anderson v Davis* [1993] PIQR Q87; *Doyle v Wallace* [1998] PIQR Q146. See eg *Williams v Green* [2001] EWCA Civ 1888, in which the Court of Appeal applied a 40% discount to the loss of earnings claim because the judge had held that the claimant, a teacher, had a 60% chance of promotion to the post of head teacher.
[2]   Statistical evidence may often be a useful 'starting point': see *Ministry of Defence v Cannock* [1994] ICR 918. To this end, the evidence of an employment consultant can sometimes be helpful to determine 'average' career prospects within a particular industry. However, the assessment of the chance that an individual claimant would have been promoted is ultimately a question of fact for the trial judge to decide, and the evidence of an employment consultant may not be considered reasonable or necessary to determine this issue: *Larby v Thurgood* [1993] PIQR P128.

[H154]   Where a loss of a chance claim is to be advanced, it must be pleaded[1]. A stark example of this is *Turnbull v Waugh*[2], in which the claimant claimed loss of earnings as an off-shore, as opposed to an in-shore, diver. Since the claim was not pleaded or argued on the basis of a loss of a chance, and the trial judge found that the claimant did not establish he would have progressed to being an off-shore diver on the balance of probabilities, Auld LJ held that he did not have to consider any questions arising out of the case law concerning claims for loss of a chance.

[1]   *Domsalla v Barr* [1969] 1 WLR 630.
[2]   (6 May 1999, unreported), CA.

Retirement ages – the Pensions Act 2007

[H155] In May 2006 the Government published a White Paper entitled 'Security in Retirement, Towards a New Pension System' which recommended increasing the state retirement age. These recommendations are to be implemented by the Pensions Act 2007 from 2024, with new retirement ages as set out in Schedule 3 to the Act (to a new maximum state retirement age of 68). Schedule 3 to the Pensions Act 2007 sets out the new retirement ages depending upon sex and date of birth. However, an easier way to calculate this for an individual claimant is to use the Pension Service's retirement age calculator which can be found at: www.thepensionservice.gov.uk/ state-pension/age-calculator.asp.

[H156] In both *Sarwar v (1) Ali and (2) MIB*[1] and *A v Powys Health Board*[2], Lloyd-Jones J accepted a retirement age of 68 for the respective young male and female claimants.

[1]   [2007] LS Medical 375.
[2]   [2007] EWHC 2996 (QB).

(ii)   Loss of Earning Capacity / Handicap on the Labour Market

[H157]   Traditionally, where a claimant suffered injuries which left him or her at a disadvantage on the open labour market, it was appropriate to bring a separate claim in respect of the claimant's loss of earning capacity. A separate lump sum was often awarded by the court to reflect the claimant's handicap on the labour market, otherwise known as a *Smith v Manchester* award. However, since the publication of the 6th edition of the Ogden Tables on 3 May 2007, such awards have become less common. Any ongoing risk to the claimant's employment and disadvantage on the open labour market is already taken into account by the discount factors applied to the claimant's residual earning capacity. But paragraph 14 of the explanatory notes recognise that there may be some cases in which the *Smith v Manchester* award may still be appropriate. Instances where such an approach might still be appropriate include cases where:

*   The claimant meets the technical definition of 'disability' under the terms of the Disability Discrimination Act 1995 but the effect on his or her level of work is very slight.
*   The claimant is at disadvantage on the labour market but fails to fulfil the definition of 'disabled' under the Disability Discrimination Act 1995.
*   The claimant was already disabled but has become more disabled (and disadvantaged on the open labour market) as a result of injuries sustained.

The relevant principles regarding the assessment of this head of loss are set out below.

General principles

[H158]   Although termed a *Smith v Manchester* award after *Smith v Manchester Corpn*[1], this head of loss is more fully discussed in the leading case of *Moeliker v A Reyrolle & Co Ltd*[2]. The principle was expressed by Browne LJ in *Moeliker*[3]:

'I do not think one can say more by way of principle than this. The consideration of this head of damages should be made in two stages. 1. Is there a "substantial" or "real" risk that a claimant will lose his present job at some time before the estimated end of his working life? 2. If there is (but not otherwise), the court must assess and quantify the present value of the risk of the financial damage which the claimant will suffer if that risk materialises, having regard to the degree of the risk, the time when it may materialise, and the factors, both favourable and unfavourable, which in a particular case will, or may, affect the claimant's chances of getting a job at all, or an equally well paid job.'

1	(1974) 17 KIR 1.
2	[1977] 1 WLR 132.
3	At 142A.

Identifying the risk

[H159]   Although the court is dealing with a loss which is based on the possibility of unemployment (as opposed to the lack of employment itself), Scarman LJ in *Smith v Manchester* said it is incorrect to describe this sort of loss of earning capacity as a 'possible loss'[1]:

'... it is an existing loss: the [claimant] is clearly weakened to that extent, though fortunately she is protected for the time being against suffering any financial damage because she does not, at present, have to go into the labour market.'

Therefore, although the claimant has suffered no financial loss, the actual loss being compensated is that of earning capacity, and this will be already in existence at the time of trial.

1	(1974) 17 KIR 1 at 7–8.

[H160]   The usual situation in which a *Smith v Manchester* award is made will be when the claimant is in work at the time of trial. Therefore, as earnings are continuing there is no obvious claim for loss of future earnings. However, if there is a chance that the claimant may, in the future, be out of work because of the injury, then not to compensate for this is unjust. It should also be noted that it is permissible for a loss of future earnings to be awarded at the same time as an award for a loss of earning capacity is made[1]. For example, if a claimant returns to work after an accident and receives less by way of earnings than he or she did previously, he or she will be entitled to claim the difference in earnings as a pecuniary loss, since the same is readily identifiable. But, if there is also a risk of time off work or unemployment in the future, and thereafter a handicap on the labour market, this too deserves to be compensated by way of a *Smith v Manchester* award. In short, an award for loss of future earnings can be made at the same time as an award for handicap on the labour market, because the two awards are designed to cover different aspects of the claimant's loss[2].

1	See *Frost v Palmer* [1993] PIQR Q14 at Q22; *Brown* [1982] CLY 814.
2	However, it should be noted that, occasionally, there will be overlap between the two, in which case it is permissible for the court to make one lump sum award called a *Blamire* award to cover both: *Blamire v South Cumbria Health Authority* [1993] PIQR Q1; *Goldborough v Thompson* [1996]

PIQR Q86; and *Hannon v Pearce* (24 January 2001, unreported), QBD. See further at paras **[D151]**–**[D153]**.

[H161] If the claimant is in work, then the initial question is: 'what is the risk that he will, at some time before the end of his working life, lose that job and be thrown on the labour market?'[1]. Browne LJ in *Moeliker* discussed this risk. He held that the question was whether the risk is 'substantial' as opposed to 'speculative' or 'fanciful'. In deciding whether the risk is 'substantial' or 'real'[2], all sorts of factors need to be considered by the courts. These include:

- the nature and prospects of the employer's business;
- the claimant's age and qualifications;
- length of service;
- length of remaining working life;
- the nature of the disabilities;
- any statement of intention by the employer; and
- any chance that the claimant will (for good reason) voluntarily come onto the labour market[3].

[1] *Moeliker v A Reyrolle & Co Ltd* [1977] 1 WLR 132 at 141B, CA.
[2] As per Scarman LJ in *Smith v Manchester* (1974) 17 KIR 1.
[3] *Drummond v J Hewitt & Son (Fenton) Ltd* (21 November 1978, unreported), CA, per Brown LJ.

[H162] If the court holds that there is no risk, then no damages will be awarded. However, if a 'real' or 'substantial' risk is identified, then it is for the court to quantify it in damages. The meaning of 'real' or 'substantial' risk was considered in *Robson v Liverpool City Council*[1]. It was stated[2] that there can be a 'real' risk, even if it is unlikely. That is, as long as there is an identifiable risk, then it is 'real'. Further, 'substantial' does not mean that the risk needs to be likely on the balance of probabilities. Even if the 'real' risk is relatively small, a *Smith v Manchester* award may still be appropriate[3].

[1] [1993] PIQR Q78. See further *Davies v Taylor* [1974] AC 207.
[2] By Neill LJ at Q82.
[3] *Booth v Hayward* (17 June 1998, unreported), CA.

[H163] It should be noted that the risk of being thrown onto the labour market does not necessarily have to be related to the injuries (only the subsequent disadvantage once on the labour market). For example, there might be a risk of redundancy following a downturn in the economic climate. As highlighted in *Robson v Liverpool City Council*[1], there may also be a number of reasons why a claimant might reasonably choose to leave work voluntarily. One possible reason might be that the claimant needs to move out of the locality, because his or her partner accepts a job in a different part of the country or to look after relatives who have fallen ill. As envisaged by Kennedy LJ, when discussing the award for disadvantage on the labour market relating to a pilot who worked for British Midland, in *Underwood v Foreman*[2]:

'There are other ways in which he could find himself back on the labour market. He might, for reasons of his own choice, find that he was in a position where he was no longer employed or no longer wished to be employed by British Midland. It could be a question of redundancy. His employers might amalgamate or be taken over. Those are the sort of risks which can occur over quite a lengthy period. It could also be that there would be some clash of personalities or something of that kind. Those are all the sorts of matters to which the judge was entitled to have regard in coming to the conclusion that here there was a real risk of the [claimant] losing his position with British Midland.'

1   [1993] PIQR Q78.
2   (29 July 1996, unreported), CA.

[H164]   Furthermore, since the risk of losing employment is a recognised vicissitude of life, it is not necessarily fatal to recovering an award under this head that there is no specific evidence that the claimant is at a real or significant risk of losing his or her job[1].

1   *Evans v Tarmac Central Ltd* [2005] EWCA Civ 1820.

Assessment of the appropriate level of award

[H165]   The quantification of the award for handicap on the labour market is problematic. Not only are there a large number of factors to be considered, but also the loss may not occur until an uncertain point in the future. *Page v Enfield and Haringey Area Health Authority*[1] is authority that the courts accept there is no set formula for the assessment of a *Smith v Manchester* award. Any such assessment is 'essentially an imprecise and speculative exercise'[2], and it is for the courts to make as accurate a calculation as possible, taking into account all the relevant circumstances of a given case.

1   (1986) Times, 7 November.
2   *Foster v Tyne and Wear County Council* [1986] 1 All ER 567, per Lord Lloyd at 570h.

[H166]   Given the imponderables involved, it is conventional for a lump sum to be awarded under this head. Whilst damages for prospective loss are usually awarded on a multiplier/multiplicand basis, in *Smith v Manchester*[1] it was said that this approach was inappropriate. However, Browne LJ in *Moeliker* interpreted this as not meaning that a court should have no regard to the amount of earnings lost or period over which they will be lost. Instead, the multiplier/multiplicand, simply, cannot provide a complete answer because of the huge number of uncertainties[2].

1   (1974) 17 KIR 1.
2   [1977] 1 WLR 132 at 141. See also *Gunter v Nicholas & Sons* [1993] PIQR P67, in which the Court of Appeal accepted the multiplier/multiplicand method as commonplace.

[H167]   The starting point for assessing the appropriate award of damages for a *Smith v Manchester* claim is the claimant's current net salary, if the claimant is working, or the net salary that he or she would be likely to obtain in the future if not currently working. With regard to this level of salary, the court looks at a number of factors before determining the appropriate lump sum to award. Depending upon the individual risks in the case, the judge will then often award a lump sum representing the claimant's level of disadvantage on the labour market, which is usually equivalent to a multiple of the claimant's net earnings[1].

1   Whilst it is not possible to lay down any hard and fast rules (and the courts have consistently declined to lay down any detailed guidance as to the method for calculating the exact award of

damages under this head), awards for handicap on the labour market are commonly made for sums of between six months' and three years' worth of net earnings. It is uncommon for the award to be less than about three months' net earnings, since the claimant would not necessarily pass the threshold of being at a significant risk of being thrown onto the open labour market in the future. At the other end of the spectrum, claims for over three years' worth of net earnings are relatively infrequent, because the chance of the claimant losing work and being unable to find alternative work will probably be large enough to justify a claim for loss of future earnings on a multiplier/ multiplicand basis.

[H168]   So, what factors are taken into account when assessing the appropriate lump sum award? In *Moeliker v A Reyrolle & Co Ltd*[1], Browne LJ stated that, once a risk of being thrown onto the labour market in the future is established, it is necessary to go on to consider the following:

- How great is the risk?
- When is the risk likely to materialise[2]?
- How far would the claimant be handicapped by his or her disability on the labour market?
- What are the claimant's chances of getting a job, and an equally well-paid job?

[1]   [1977] 1 WLR 132.
[2]   It should be noted that this is relevant because the award is calculated as at the date of trial. All future loss must be discounted in order to take account of accelerated receipt. Therefore, the further away the claimant is likely to find him or herself on the labour market, the greater the discount for accelerated receipt that will need to be given.

[H169]   The principles of assessment under this head of loss were also discussed in *Foster v Tyne and Wear County Council*[1], in which it was held that the risks to be quantified were twofold. First, whether the claimant would be more likely to lose his or her present job on account of the disability and, secondly, whether the claimant would be less likely to get another job on account of his or her disability should he or she have lost his or her present job. This would also, no doubt, include future jobs.

[1]   [1986] 1 All ER 567.

[H170]   The judge has to take into account a wide range of factors (many of which involve complex uncertainties) and identify a compensatory amount. Since the judge cannot accurately say when, if or for how long a claimant may be out of work in the future, the award under this head is very difficult to predict with any degree of accuracy. Thus the assessment, although made with skill, experience and judgment, can be little more than educated guesswork. Indeed, as Megaw LJ said[1] in *Eaton v Concrete (Northern) Ltd*[2], the assessment of damages under this head usually involves 'nothing more than a guess'.

[1]   [1979] CA Transcript 30. This quote of Megaw LJ was referred to by Auld LJ in *Dhaliwal v Personal Representatives of Hunt (deceased)* [1995] PIQR Q56 at 59, when he said:
  '... a multiplier/multiplicand approach may be an appropriate method, but so may the method of assessing a lump sum. In their different ways, they are almost equally speculative, certainly in a case where so much lies in the future and it is impossible to say what Amanpreet would and could have done but for the accident, and what she will want and be able to do now. As Megaw LJ said in *Eaton v Concrete (Northern) Ltd* [1979] CA Transcript 30, the assessment of damages under this head usually involves "nothing more than a guess".'
[2]   [1995] PIQR Q56.

Evidence

[H171] Generally speaking, when pursuing a claim for disadvantage on the open labour market, it is worthwhile supporting the claim with evidence. The more evidence that can be produced, the greater the chance that the court will be persuaded to make an award at the level contended for. The main types of evidence to consider are as follows:

- payslips and earnings details showing net salary (including any salary increases or bonus payments up to the date of trial);
- witness evidence detailing the difficulties experienced at work by reason of the claimant's injuries, and any related or unrelated risk that the claimant might be forced on to the open labour market and, if possible, when such an eventuality might occur;
- medical evidence specifically dealing with the effect of the injuries on the claimant's capacity to work, including any risk of deterioration in the claimant's condition or need to retire early;
- the claimant's occupational health file and personnel records (especially if these contain a job description, appraisals detailing how the claimant manages to cope with their injuries, adjustments made and the risk of redundancy or retirement on grounds of ill-health); and
- evidence from an employment consultant regarding the claimant's disadvantage on the labour market, the availability of suitable work in the claimant's locality and the likely length of any job-search period.

[H172] It should be noted that, whilst the above evidence is desirable, it is not necessarily fatal to such a claim if the same is not obtained. It is for the judge to assess the risk of unemployment in the future and, provided the court is in a position to evaluate the chance, this is enough[1]. In *Watson v Mitcham Cardboards Ltd*, O'Connor LJ said[2]:

> 'The fact that no evidence was called does not seem to me to matter. Here was a man who was in employment and the learned Judge had the evidence of the injury which he had sustained; he saw the man's hand. I think he was entitled on that evidence to come to the conclusion that, were he to lose his employment with these defendants, there was some slight risk of him suffering financially in gaining other employment. The fact that he assessed it in the sum of £200 shows that he regarded it as very small.'

[H173] Likewise, a claimant may still be entitled to recover an award for disadvantage on the labour market, even if there is no specific evidence that the claimant will lose her or her job, since losing employment is one of the vicissitudes of life[3].

[1]   *Patel v Edwards* [1970] RTR 425.
[2]   [1982] CLY 78, CA.
[3]   *Evans v Tarmac Central Ltd* [2005] EWCA Civ 1820; see further *Drummond v J Hewitt & Son (Fenton) Ltd*, Court of Appeal, 21 November 1978; *Watson v Mitcham Cardboards Ltd*, Court of Appeal, 5 March 1981.

The duty to plead

[H174] The claim for a handicap in the labour market should, as a matter of practice, be pleaded in an action[1]. However, since it is an item of general damage it need not necessarily be so. In *Thorn v Powergen plc*[2], the defendant attempted to avoid liability for a *Smith v Manchester* award where the claim had not been specifically pleaded. It was held that, if the risk of losing employment is made clear in the pleadings, then it is not fatal that it is not specifically identified as a *Smith v Manchester* or handicap in the labour market claim.

1   *Chan Wai Tong v Li Ping Sum* [1985] AC 446, PC.
2   [1997] PIQR Q71. See also *Crouch v King's Healthcare NHS Trust* [2004] EWCA Civ 853, in which the judge made a lump sum award representing the claimant's loss of earning capacity when only a claim for future loss of earnings had been pleaded.

The claimant in a superior (better paid) employment

[H175]   In the unreported case of *Stubbington v Stubbington, Wheatley (Wickham) Ltd and Crompton Engineering Ltd*[1], the judge accepted that, owing to the accident, the claimant was in a better position than before. Of course, the award for handicap on the labour market is to cover the risk that, at some time in the future working life of the claimant, he or she will lose employment and then suffer financial loss because of his or her disadvantage finding suitable work by reason of his or her injuries. Therefore, it was still necessary to assess the risk of a future loss caused by his or her handicap on the labour market where the claimant, because of the accident, has better work but there is a risk that the new job will be lost in the future.

1   (16 October 1989, unreported). See also *Chan Wai Tong v Li Ping Sum* [1985] AC 446; and *Lau Ho Wah v Yau Chi Biu* [1985] 1 WLR 1203.

One-man business

[H176]   If the claimant is in effect a one-man business then, following *Ashcroft v Curtin*[1], a claim for loss of earning capacity can still be brought. In this case, Edmund Davies LJ stated[2]:

> 'His capacity to engage himself outside the company, finding the sort of work for which he has been trained since he was a boy of 14, has been virtually extinguished. I agree that the risk of his being placed in such a predicament is not great. But it does exist, and I think it justifies some award being made in respect of it. Doing the best I can, and fully realising that I too am rendering myself liable to be attacked for simply "plucking a figure from the air", I think the proper compensation under this head is £2,500.'

This approach was also adopted in *Dureau v Evans*[3] and *Morgan v UPS Ltd*[4], where the claimant had given up employment voluntarily with the defendant employer and had aspirations to set up as a mechanic.

1   [1971] 1 WLR 1731, CA.
2   [1971] 1 WLR 1731 at 1738H, CA.
3   [1996] PIQR Q18.
4   [2008] EWCA Civ 375.

Claimant unemployed at date of trial

[H177]   Assuming that the claimant had some prospect of obtaining work in the future but for their injuries, it is not necessarily a bar to recovery that the claimant was not actually employed at the time of the defendant's wrongdoing or the time of assessment[1]. As it was put in *Cook v Consolidated Fisheries Ltd*[2]:

> 'it does not make any difference in the circumstances of this case that the [claimant] was not actually in work at the time of trial.'

1 *Dhaliwal v Personal Representatives of Hunt (deceased)* [1995] PIQR Q56; *Cook v Consolidated Fisheries Ltd* [1977] ICR 635, CA.
2 [1977] ICR 635, CA. See also *Morgan v UPS Ltd* [2008] EWCA Civ 375.

Claimant already at a disadvantage on the open labour market

[H178] In *Morgan v Millett*[1] the Court of Appeal had to deal with the situation where the claimant was already at a significant disadvantage on the open labour market prior to the defendant's negligence, due to pre-existing degenerative changes in her shoulder and lower back. In evidence, the claimant admitted that she would have been prevented from working in her pre-accident job as a carer in any event, due to her shoulder problem. Nevertheless, the trial judge awarded the claimant loss of earnings for four years and a *Smith v Manchester* award in the sum of £7,500. The defendant successfully appealed against these awards. Thorpe LJ stated:

> 'There seems to me to be an obvious flaw in an award against these defendants in relation to a period beyond the date at which natural degenerative changes, unattributable to the accident, prevented her from returning to the only work for which she was cut out. I would accordingly reduce the period during which special damages are recoverable for loss of earnings from four to two years.
>
> For similar reasons, it seems to me difficult to sustain a *Smith v Manchester* award. Of course, the way the case was presented and argued resulted in neither counsel having made any suggestion that a *Smith v Manchester* award was appropriate …
>
> I find some fundamental difficulty in seeing how the *Smith v Manchester* award would be appropriate in a case where the non-attributable degenerative changes would have in any event prevented her from resuming her career. Furthermore, because of the way in which the case was run, there was no evidence to justify the premise that removal from the established workplace and work during her forties had damaged her employability …
>
> So for those reasons I would allow this appeal and make those two adjustments to the component parts of the judge's award.'

1 [2001] EWCA Civ 1641.

[H179] But on different facts, it is submitted that a pre-existing injury giving rise to a pre-existing handicap on the labour market would not necessarily bar a claim under this head. A person who already had some difficulty finding suitable employment should be entitled to claim for any increased disadvantage on the open labour market resulting from their injuries. In order for damages to be recovered under this head, it would need to be shown that the claimant had more than a purely fanciful or speculative chance of finding suitable employment but for the defendant's negligence[1] and, of course, the award of damages would be limited to the extent of the proven exacerbation of their handicap[2].

Moeliker v A Reyrolle & Co Ltd [1977] 1 WLR 132 at 141B, CA; *Davies v Taylor* [1974] AC 207.
Page v Smith (No 2) [1996] 1 WLR 855; *Vernon v Bosley* [1997] PIQR P255.

Effect of the Disability Discrimination Act 1995

[H180]   Some commentators have sought to argue that the implementation of the Disability Discrimination Act 1995 (DDA 1995) effectively removes the need for a *Smith v Manchester* award[1]. The DDA 1995 came into force on 2 December 1996 and makes it unlawful for an employer to discriminate against a person suffering a long-term, substantial disability. Discrimination is now unlawful as against not only a present employee but also a prospective employee and, therefore, it is possible to argue that, if an employer cannot discriminate due to disability, then a claimant can suffer no loss of earning capacity.

1   See Simon Allen 'The Disability Discrimination Act 1995' (1998) 14 P&MILL 1.

[H181]   However, there are a number of points to be noted about this legislation. First, the legislation only applies to companies with more than 15 employees, which excludes many small businesses. Secondly, employers would not be acting unlawfully under the DDA 1995 if their actions are reasonable in the circumstances. Therefore, if a person is not capable of performing the job on offer, the employer will not be classified as discriminating if it fails to consider the claimant as an able-bodied applicant. For example, an obvious case would be a typist who had lost the use of a hand. It would be reasonable to consider this as restricting the key functions of the job and, as such, the claimant would not be protected by the Act. A reasonable adjustment could not be made to accommodate his or her needs. Lastly, notwithstanding the implementation of the DDA 1995, various research and studies have shown that employers still discriminate against disabled employees. An example of this, often quoted by employment consultants, is that the unemployment rate for disabled people is generally 2.5 times that for the non-disabled.

[H182]   It can, therefore, be seen that, although the Act may limit certain minor *Smith v Manchester* claims, it will have little, if any, effect on the majority of cases where the disability has made it impossible for the claimant to continue to perform the key functions of a job and so is left outside the protection of the Act. In practice, it does not seem that the courts consider that the DDA 1995 has effectively stamped out discrimination in the workplace, thus making such awards obsolete. Given the competitive nature of the current workplace, it seems probable that discrimination against those with disability will continue for the foreseeable future, notwithstanding the laudable legislative attempts to curb the same.

Continuing partial loss of earnings

[H183]   The Court of Appeal in *Cornell v Green*[1] addressed the question of when it would be appropriate for the court to calculate a loss on a *Smith v Manchester* basis as opposed to a straight loss of earnings. The claimant was 25 at the date of the accident (29 at trial) and ran two insurance businesses. Owing to the accident, the claimant suffered brain injuries and now worked on a commission basis from home. The court at first instance awarded £30,000 on a *Smith v Manchester* basis and none for future loss of earnings. The Court of Appeal held that this was an incorrect approach in such a case. It stated that a *Smith v Manchester* award is aimed at the situation where the claimant can return to the same or similar job but, due to the accident, had a greater chance of being unable to find work if, for whatever reason, they had to leave employment. It is not meant to cover continuing partial loss of earnings. The Court of Appeal stressed the point that all the circumstances should be considered and a route to justice found. The court applied a standard multiplier/multiplicand approach, and the award was increased to £220,000.

¹　[1998] CLY 1485. See also *Tait v Pearson* [1996] PIQR Q92; *Coates v Cury* (1997) Times, August 22; *Williams v Green* [2001] EWCA Civ 1888; and *Stefanovic v Carter* [2001] EWCA Civ 452.

[H184]　However, in the absence of sufficient evidence, the court may well be forced into making a lump sum award for disadvantage on the labour market or loss of earning capacity, instead of using the traditional multiplier/multiplicand method¹. This generally results in the claimant receiving considerably less than they otherwise would have done².

¹　*Ashcroft v Curtin* [1971] 1 WLR 1731, CA; *Dureau v Evans* [1996] PIQR Q18; *Smith v McCrae* [2003] EWCA Civ 505, in which Kennedy LJ stated at [6], [8] and [14]: 'The first matter still in dispute is the award made in respect of future loss of earnings. The judge had before him in relation to this issue practically no evidence ... In order to calculate on the multiplier/multiplicand basis, it was necessary for the judge to have before him reliable evidence as to the claimant's pre-accident earning capacity and as to his post-accident earning capacity ... The claimant here simply had not laid before the court the materials which might well, had they been laid before the court, have enabled the judge to adopt the approach he did [ie a calculation on the multiplier/multiplicand basis]. But the materials were not there. In the absence of those materials it was not appropriate to attempt to use figures which were patently, for the reasons I have endeavoured to explain, unreliable'.

²　See eg *Rees v Dewhirst Plc & anor* [2002] EWCA Civ 871; *Willemse v Hesp* [2003] EWCA Civ 994.

[H185]　Sometimes, there is such a paucity of reliable evidence that it is difficult to know where to start in quantifying the claimant's loss. However, assuming there has been a real loss, the lack of credible supporting evidence does not absolve the court from its duty to quantify the same¹. For example, in *Hoath v Cripps Harries Hall²*, Kennedy LJ stated:

'... I accept that it is the duty of a claimant to prove his consequential loss of earnings and to do so in accordance with the rules by serving a schedule of loss supported so far as possible by documentary evidence. If a claimant fails to comply with the rules there are sanctions available which will be used ... this claimant did serve a schedule and gave evidence to support it. His misfortune was that his evidence was not found to be acceptable. That, however, did not mean that the judge was entitled to make no award in respect of loss of earnings. Plainly the claimant's earning capacity was impaired as a result of the tortious activation of his cervical spondylosis. What the judge had to do was arrive at an acceptable conclusion as to the measure of the claimant's loss on the basis of such evidence as there was which he found to be reliable. That, as Mr Russell pointed out, is trite law (see, for example *Ashcroft v Curtin* [1971] 1 WLR 1731 at 1737H) and it is also good sense.'

¹　*Chaplin v Hicks* [1911] 2 KB 786 at 792; *The Mediana* [1900] AC 113 at 116–117; *Otter v Church* [1953] Ch 280; *Moeliker v A Reyrolle & Co Ltd* [1977] 1 WLR 132 at 141; and *Thompson v Smith Shiprepairers (North Shields)* [1984] QB 405. In *Chaplin v Hicks* [1911] 2 KB 786, Vaughan

Williams LJ stated: 'The fact that damages cannot be assessed with certainty does not relieve the wrongdoer of the necessity of paying damages'. See also *Eden v West & Co* [2002] EWCA Civ 991.
²   (11 April 2000, unreported), CA.

(iii)   The Blamire Award

[H186]   Where there are a number of imponderables, the court may decide to make one broad brush lump sum award in respect of loss of earnings, or a combination of loss of earnings and handicap on the labour market[1]. This award is known as a *Blamire* award after *Blamire v South Cumbria Health Authority*[2]. Such an award should only be made where the uncertainties are so many or so great that there is insufficient evidence for a reasoned calculation to be made using the conventional multiplier/multiplicand method[3]. In *Bullock v Atlas Ward Structures Ltd*[4], Keene LJ stated[5]:

> 'Merely because there are uncertainties about the future does not of itself justify a departure from that well-established method [i.e. the multiplier/multiplicand method]. Judges therefore should be slow to resort to the broad-brush *Blamire* approach, unless they really have no alternative'.

¹   In *Ronan v Sainsbury's Supermarkets Ltd* [2006] EWCA Civ 1074, Hughes LJ stated that, although a *Blamire* award and a claim for *Smith v Manchester* may be combined, they are quite distinct: the former being a continuing loss where there are too many uncertainties to adopt a multiplier/ multiplicand method of assessment, and the latter an award for a contingent future loss in the event of the claimant losing his future job. However, it is submitted that loss of earnings and loss of earning capacity often overlap and can be difficult to distinguish. Further, loss of earning capacity is not restricted only to circumstances in which the claimant loses a job. The claimant may in the future be restricted in the type of work he or she can do, the number of hours he or she can undertake, or may suffer a disadvantage in terms of promotion prospects which are difficult to assess on a multiplier/ multiplicand basis. It is noteworthy that, in *Blamire* itself, a single award was made for loss of wages, loss of earning capacity and loss of pension.
²   [1993] PIQR Q1.
³   *Cornell v Green* [1998] CLY 1485; *Tait v Pearson* [1996] PIQR Q92; *Stefanovic v Carter* [2001] EWCA Civ 452; *Bullock v Atlas Ward Structures Ltd* [2008] EWCA Civ 194; and *Limbu v MOD* LTL 17/7/2008. See also *Coates v Curry* (1997) Times, 22 August.
⁴   [2008] EWCA Civ 194.
⁵   At para [21].

[H187]   The facts of *Blamire v South Cumbria Health Authority*[1] involved a 22-year-old female nurse who injured her lower back in a lifting accident at work, rendering her permanently vulnerable to further injury. She was forced to take various periods off work and was transferred to lighter duties, but was ultimately forced to give up her job as a nurse to take up part-time work at a residential home. At first instance, the judge found that, in the absence of negligence, the claimant would have pursued a lifelong career in nursing. As a result of the accident, she would now probably have to work as a secretary and she would be at a significant disadvantage obtaining such work due to her back problem. The judge rejected the multiplier/multiplicand approach in assessing future loss of earnings, and awarded the claimant £25,000 for future losses of wages, pension and earning capacity. The Court of Appeal upheld the trial judge's approach, given the number of imponderables, including the claimant's likely pattern of work if she had not been injured and the likely pattern of her actual future earnings. In the circumstances, it was held that there was no perfect arithmetical way of calculating compensation, and the judge was bound to look at the matter globally in his assessment of the present value of the claimant's future loss. The approach adopted in *Blamire* has been applied in a number of subsequent cases[2]. As in *Hannon v Pearce*[3] – where the claimant ran a horse-racing business – this method of assessment particularly lends itself to cases involving self-employed claimants, where it is extremely difficult to predict the claimant's level of earnings but for his or her injuries.

[1]   [1993] PIQR Q1.
[2]   *Goldborough v Thompson* [1996] PIQR Q86; *Michael v Ashdown* (2 December 1998, unreported), CA; *Hannon v Pearce* (24 January 2001, unreported), QBD; *Willemse v Hesp* [2003] EWCA Civ 994. See also *Crouch v King's Healthcare NHS Trust* [2004] EWCA Civ 853, in which Gage J (as he then was) said at [35]:
       'Faced with the lack of credible evidence of earnings during what the judge rightly found was the crucial period post February 1997 but pre the accident to the arm, coupled with his conclusion that there had been a change of lifestyle, in my judgment the judge was quite entitled to reject the multiplier/multiplicand basis for assessment of past and future loss. Indeed, it is difficult to see how he could have approached the matter in any other way than to assess a global sum.'
[3]   (24 January 2001, unreported), QBD.

[H188]   Although the sixth edition of the Ogden Tables has provided discount factors which take into account a number of imponderables which a *Blamire* award might attempt to value, paragraph 14 of the explanatory notes expressly states that there may be appropriate cases in which the *Blamire* approach remains appropriate. Such awards have been made in a number of recent cases[1], although this approach was rejected by Cooke J in *Leesmith v Evans*[2] when considering the claim for future loss of earnings of a relatively young claimant who was seeking to embark upon a career as a lighting engineer.

[1]   *Van Wees v (1) Karkour and (2) Walsh* [2007] EWHC 165 (QB); *Smale v Ball (MIB)*, QBD, LTL 6/6/07 and *Palmer v Kitley* [2008] EWHC 2819 (QB).
[2]   [2008] EWHC 134 (QB).

[H189]   An alternative to adopting a broad brush approach has been to take a lesser multiplier for future loss (ie apply a higher discount for contingencies other than mortality in respect of the future loss multiplier)[1], but it must be remembered always that the purpose of the exercise is to provide as accurate an assessment of the total future loss of earnings as can be made on the basis of current evidence.

[1]   *Newman v Folkes* [2002] EWCA Civ 591.

(iv)   Pension Loss

Introduction[1]

[H190]   If a claimant, owing to injury, is forced to retire earlier than planned, a claim for loss of pension rights may arise. In addition to loss of earnings, the claimant will be unable to continue to contribute to his or her pension and it will, therefore, be worth less on retirement. In an action for personal injuries, this loss is recoverable. However, the calculation of it is complex.

¹   See also C Bennett 'Pension Loss Claims' Parts 1 and 2 (1998) 17 Lit 2 at 55 and (1998) 17 Lit 4 at 138; Doug Hall 'PI damages: a practical approach to calculating pension loss' [1998] SJ, 25 September, at 16; Doug Hall and Keith Carter 'Dynamics of retirement in PI Claims' [1998] SJ, 16 April, at 363–364; James Rowley 'Incapacity Pension – to Deduct or not to Deduct' [1998] Quantum, Issue 1, 16 March, at 1–3; Richard Burns 'Calculating the *Longden* Set-off' [1998] Quantum, Issue 2, 19 May; Tim Sture 'Calculated loss' [2003] PILJ, June/July; Nick Munton 'Claiming Loss of Pension in PI and Fatal Accident Cases' [2004] JPIL Issue 2/04 at 156–161; James Rowley QC 'Pension loss calculation – improve your game', available from www.byromstreet.com.

[H191]   Pensions may be of two types: (a) 'final salary' or 'defined benefit' schemes where, by contract, the pension is calculated as a percentage of the last year (or sometimes three years) of service, multiplied by the total years of service (eg '1/80th for each year of service up to a maximum of 40'); or (b) 'money purchase' or 'defined contribution' schemes, where a pension fund personal to the claimant is built up by the contributions of the claimant and his or her employer over the claimant's years of service. The first type of pension is usually applicable to employed people who have a pension arranged through their employer, and the second type of pension is generally applicable to self-employed people or people who make their own pension provision.

[H192]   The calculation depends on the type of scheme and its terms. In particular, it is important to know in a 'defined benefit' scheme whether there is a pension for the surviving spouse and/or children.

Money purchase or defined contribution pensions

[H193]   In a 'money purchase' scheme, the loss may seem simply to be the value of the lost annual contributions by the employer to the fund¹. This will, however, understate the loss: pension funds have a double tax advantage. First, contributions to them are free of basic-rate tax, so a £500 gross annual payment by an employer to the claimant's pension fund is a £500 net loss to the claimant where he loses that employment. Secondly, the fund will roll up on a basis which is tax efficient. Although pension funds now pay tax on income, the rate is a composite one lower than standard rate taxation (and thereby a considerable advantage to the higher rate taxpayer). Quite apart from these advantages, the fund will provide a lump sum which is tax free (at retirement) in addition to the annual instalments of pension for life.

¹   Such claims may become much more common in light of the Pensions Act 2008, which obliges employers to make a contribution of 3% of gross annual earnings above qualifying earnings towards a pension. At the time of writing, qualifying earnings are defined as between £5,035 and £33,540. The exact start date of the legislation is unclear, but is expected to be from 2012.

[H194]   How does a court allow for these tax advantages? Traditionally, the answer was to take the annual payment (say, £500 gross) and treat it as a net loss; and then to add an estimate (say, 5%) for the advantages of taxation and professional investment which has historically produced a good return. However, given the recent economic conditions, it may be difficult to persuade the court to add any additional element to account for gains arising from professional investment, and any tax advantages may need to be proved by expert forensic accountancy evidence. Any such additional figure that can be proved may then be added to the 'loss of wages' figure. No separate calculation was done for receipts after retirement age for two reasons: (1) the fund accrued pre-accident in any event will produce a pension; and (2) the extent to which that pension is lower than would otherwise have been the case is directly related to the amount by which the fund itself is less – which is shown by the calculation outlined above. Likewise, where a claimant claims he or she would have made additional voluntary contributions (AVCs) to his or her fund, the capital comes from the claimant's income, and to claim for that would be to allow double recovery.

[H195]   Since the introduction of stakeholder pensions on 6 April 2001, the claim for lost tax relief on defined contribution pensions may no longer be a valid claim[1]. This is because an individual with no earnings can invest up to £3,600 per annum gross (using their damages award) and receive tax relief on the amount invested. Therefore, unless a claimant was regularly contributing in excess of £3,600 gross per annum into their pension pre-accident, they are not able to show any loss post-accident[2].

[1]   See further Tim Sture 'Calculated loss' [2003] PILJ, June/July.
[2]   However, arguably a claim may still be made where the claimant can show that he or she has suffered loss by way of a diminished pension fund as a result of earlier drawdown due to the injuries: see further *Smith v Adye* (19 April 2000, unreported), CA.

[H196]   In the rare case where a claim is pursued on the basis of lost tax relief over and above the limit that can be invested in a stakeholder pension, care should be taken regarding the predicted rates of return published by insurance companies: they may still be available otherwise, even if only as the return on a bond or ISA, and they are only quoted so as to facilitate comparison between financial providers rather than as a genuine pre-estimate of precise returns.

Final salary or defined benefit pensions

[H197]   So far as 'defined benefit' schemes are concerned, the leading case is *Auty v National Coal Board*[1]. This case has been criticised, yet has stood as good law for over 20 years and therefore must be the guide.

[1]   [1985] 1 WLR 784.

[H198]   The conventional approach preferred by the Court of Appeal in *Auty*[1] assesses damages net of tax and takes no direct account of inflation. The court assesses the prospective loss of lump sum (what would have been lost on today's salary less what will be lost on the basis of accrued entitlement) and adds it to the annual net loss of pension receipts. For the latter element, a multiplicand/multiplier approach is adopted. Following the Lord Chancellor's decision to exercise his powers under s 1 of the Damages Act 1996, the multiplier is calculated on the basis of a 2.5% discount rate. However, a further discount is generally applied to take account of life's manifold contingencies[2].

[1]   [1985] 1 WLR 784.
[2]   *Hunt v Severs* [1994] 2WLR 602 at 613H. This further discount has survived *Wells v Wells* [1999] 1 AC 345; see further at paras **[H208]**–**[H211]**.

[H199]   The loss is calculated and paid as a lump sum (as are other heads of damage, such as loss of earnings). However, the loss that is being compensated is not due to start until retirement age, and this can be a considerable time away in the case of a young claimant. Therefore, a further discount has to be made to take account of the accelerated receipt (although this discount is now already catered for when selecting the appropriate multiplier from the pension loss tables set out in the Ogden Tables[1]).

¹   See further *Phipps v Brooks Dry Cleaning Service Ltd* [1996] PIQR Q100.

Evidence of pension loss

[H200]   To evaluate the value of the claim, evidence is needed to identify the size of the loss, the period over which the loss is expected to be suffered, and the length of time to the start of this period. Of course, the first question to ask is whether or not the claimant already had a pension at the time of his or her injuries, and if not, whether there was a realistic chance that he or she would benefit from one in the future. Where the claimant had not made any such pension provision as at the time of his or her injuries, and there is no hard evidence to show that the claimant had a real chance of benefiting from such provision in the future, it is likely that a claim for pension loss will be held to be too speculative to calculate[1].

¹   *Finnis v Caulfield* [2002] All ER (D) 353. See also *D and D v Donald* [2001] PIQR Q44, although compare the position in relation to potential lost employer pension contributions, which are set to become obligatory under the Pensions Act 2008 from some time after 2012, at the rate of 3% on qualifying earnings (currently defined as earnings between £5,035 and £33,540).

[H201]   The claimant's life expectancy is important. This can be calculated from the most recent English Life Tables[1] or, in an appropriate case – where the tables are not applicable (eg shorter than average life expectancy) – from medical evidence. The life expectancy must be calculated as at the date of calculation and not at some future, theoretical date[2]. Further, information is needed from the claimant as to the expected date of retirement and the expected job title and position at retirement had the accident not occurred. (These will usually be pre-established by the investigation into loss of earnings.) Also, it has to be established whether the claimant would have exercised any option to commute part of the pension to a tax-free sum at retirement. It is known that most people do commute (ie ask for a lump sum payment rather than periodical payments) as much as possible under the terms of their pension, as it is tax free, and the loss will be less if they do not do so.

¹   It is important to use the most recent table (as life expectancies continue to change), which can be downloaded from the website of the Office for National Statistics (www.statistics.gov.uk) or the Government Actuary's Department (www.gad.gov.uk).
²   *Auty v National Coal Board* [1985] 1 WLR 784.

[H202]   More detailed information is required about the pension itself. This information can usually be obtained from a trustee of the pension fund, who can supply a copy of the full terms of the scheme. Specific information is required concerning the value of the loss. The question to be answered is what annual sum and/or lump sum would he or she expect to receive if there had been no injury and the employment had continued (using salary rates current at the date of trial)? Secondly, the annual and lump sums which he or she will receive, even despite the injury, must be established, again on the basis of the position current at trial. The loss of lump sum is prima facie the difference between the two lump sums. Annual loss of net pension is the gross difference, less applicable tax. Once all of this information is acquired, the basic calculation can be made.

The calculation

[H203]   The loss attributable to the accident is the net loss suffered due to the shortened period of contribution. Therefore, if a claimant would have received £10,000 per annum if he or she had continued working until 65, but instead will only receive £5,000 at 65, then the net loss is £5,000 per annum. The £5,000 per annum would then be increased by a multiplier which is worked out for the period from the date of retirement to expected death, based on a discount rate of 2.5%. Once the total has been calculated, then the entire figure must be discounted due to the early receipt of the amount prior to retirement age[1]. In addition to this, a discount may be applied for contingencies (see further at paras **[H208]-[H211]**). The calculation is made with figures 'net' of tax[2]. It must be remembered that the pension will almost all be taxable (it will represent a top slice of earnings over and above the old age state pension). In addition to this, if the claimant would have received a £20,000 lump sum tax free payment at 65 but will now only receive £10,000, then a lump sum value of £10,000 is lost. However, this lump sum has to be adjusted where a pension has been paid at an earlier age than would otherwise have been the case, although the annual payments of pension in advance of the scheme normal pension age are to be ignored in calculating losses[3]. The annual sum obtainable is calculated after tax, whereas the lump sum is tax free.

[1]   Unless the multiplier has already taken into account accelerated receipt (eg Tables 15–26 of the Ogden Tables, 6th edn): *Phipps v Brooks Dry Cleaning Service Ltd* [1996] PIQR Q100.
[2]   It is important that the net figures are used, following the principles laid down in *British Transport Commission v Gourley* [1956] AC 185; see further Chapter A at paras **[A93]–[A95]** and Chapter F.
[3]   *Parry v Cleaver* [1970] AC 1; *Smoker v LFCDA* [1991] 2 WLR 1052, HL; *Longden v British Coal Corpn* [1997] 3 WLR 1336.

Multipliers

[H204]   The pension loss is a loss that begins at retirement age[1]. The multiplier for the annual net loss of pension is a multiplier[2] for the years of pension loss after retirement age. There are three ways of calculating this. The first method is to calculate the multiplier from the claimant's normal retirement age and discount that multiplier for early receipt (using Table 27).

[1]   See further the Pensions Act 2007 regarding state retirement ages.
[2]   Further to the Lord Chancellor's decision to exercise his powers under s 1 of the Damages Act 1996, the multiplier must be discounted by using a discount rate of 2.5%.

[H205]   The second method is to take the claimant's life multiplier (Table 1 or 2) and deduct the earnings multiplier to normal retirement age (derived from Tables 3 to 14). Obviously, this method does not work where the claimant has already retired and is in receipt of a pension as at the date of assessment.

[H206] The third method is to apply tables for pension loss (Tables 15 to 26 of the Ogden Tables) at the relevant pension age (60, 65 or 70) for a person of the age and gender of the claimant. The multipliers obtained from these tables are already discounted for accelerated receipt, and no further discount is required[1]. However, when this second method is adopted, the loss of lump sum has nonetheless still to be discounted for acceleration.

1   *Phipps v Brooks Dry Cleaning Services Ltd* [1996] PIQR Q100.

[H207]   Where the claimant has a partner who is likely to outlive him or her, it may be necessary to adjust the multiplier to take account of any additional lost pension that the partner would have been entitled to. For example, many final salary schemes provide a partner's pension of 50%. It is important to establish the number of years by which the spouse (usually the wife) is likely to outlive the claimant, and to adjust the multiplier accordingly. Having used the life tables to calculate the number of years by which the spouse will outlive the claimant, an appropriate multiplier may be derived for this period. This multiplier then needs to be discounted for the proportion of the pension that the spouse is entitled to receive (eg if the spouse is entitled to 50% of the pension, the additional element of the multiplier must be reduced by 50%). The additional discounted multiplier is then added to the claimant's multiplier to produce an overall multiplier, which is finally discounted to take account of accelerated receipt in advance of normal retirement age (unless the pension loss tables are used, which already allow for a discount for accelerated receipt).

Discount for contingencies

[H208]   It was stated in *Wells v Wells*[1] that there should be no judicial discount in the whole life multiplier. However, following *Auty*[2], the amount may be 'adjusted for further eventualities'. The term 'discount for contingencies' is often used, but is in fact incorrect. The adjustment may go either way. In *Auty*, a downward adjustment was made on the facts. The eventualities were said to be the risk of voluntary wastage, redundancy, dismissal, supervening ill-health, disablement or death before 65. *Auty* does not mean an adjustment need always be made, nor that it must be in a downward direction. The discount applied in *Auty* was 10%. The discounts for contingencies other than mortality in respect of earnings set out in Tables A–D of the explanatory notes to the Ogden Tables do not apply to pension loss[3]. It may be that a lower discount can be contended for on the basis that, had the claimant had to retire due to ill-health, he or she might have benefited from an ill-health retirement pension. However, equally, a higher discount might be appropriate where the claimant enjoyed a final salary pension scheme with a particular employer, but was at risk of losing his job and may have struggled to find a similar benefit with other employers in the same industry.

1   [1999] 1 AC 345.
2   [1985] 1 WLR 784.
3   See paragraph 30.

[H209]   Although many upward tending factors may affect the calculation at the multiplier/multiplicand stage, the judge should look to the claimant's specific situation in working out any overall adjustment. Account can be taken of the following:

- The work history of the claimant (ie unemployed periods, multiple employer changes etc).
- The pre-accident health of the claimant.
- The chances of promotion/advancement or, alternatively, the chances of losing the job.

[H210]   Once all the features have been considered, the judge would then apply an adjustment in the appropriate measure.

[H211]   In practice, discounts are rarely less than 10%, but rarely over 20% (and that would tend to be for a youngish person with little chance of promotion in a risky occupation). Arguments have been accepted, as in *Wells*[1], that further to discount for the chances of early death is incorrect, as the multiplier has been calculated with regard to the risks of death. See eg *Pratt v Smith*[2], in which the same 15% discount was applied to both the future loss of earnings claim and the claim for future loss of pension.

[1]   [1999] 1 AC 345.
[2]   (18 December 2002, unreported), QBD.

Effect of other pensions

(1)   ADDITIONAL PENSIONS

[H212]   In *Auty*[1], it was accepted that, if the claimant is able to work in his years before retirement (ie has a residual pension-earning capacity), then any additional pension receivable should be offset. The value of the new pension is calculated in exactly the same way as the loss of pension. However, the situation is reversed, in the sense that it is the claimant who will be attempting to keep the value as low as possible and highlight eventualities that would produce a discount in the value.

[1]   [1985] 1 WLR 784.

(2)   PERSONAL PENSIONS

[H213]   Any losses under a personal pension plan are difficult to establish. The value at pensionable age cannot easily be assessed, but, more importantly, the claimant has arguably lost nothing. The plan is contribution based, and the contributions were made from the claimant's wages pre-accident. As the claimant can recover any loss of earnings, he or she is recovering the money that would have gone into the pension fund. A separate issue may be the loss of tax relief. The amount, if proved, can be added to the loss of earnings figure. However, where an employer makes a contribution to a pension in addition to salary[1], the amount of this additional contribution may be claimed, and multiplied by the same multiplier as that applicable to the claimant's loss of earnings.

[1]   As all employers will be obliged to make following implementation of the Pensions Act 2008, based upon 3% of gross annual earnings above qualifying earnings (currently defined as earnings between £5,035 and £33,540). The exact date for implementation is unclear but is expected to be from 2012.

Early receipt of pension and lump sums

[H214] In a case involving personal injuries, the claimant may be entitled to early pension payments (ie payments made before the actual date of planned retirement). If the claimant is able to exercise some form of early retirement option, how is such payment to be taken into account? The claimant may receive a lump sum and/or periodic payments just as he or she would at normal retirement age. The claimant does not have to give any credit for those payments. The House of Lords dealt with the situation in *Parry v Cleaver*[1]. In short, three propositions can be taken from *Parry v Cleaver* regarding early pension payments:

- Any receipts of pension should not be deducted from other heads of damages/loss.
- Credit must be given for any pension payment received after the date of normal retirement. The actual name given to such payments is irrelevant. It is the nature of the payments that makes them a pension.
- Prior to the normal date of retirement, no credit is to be given for payments.

These principles were reviewed, and upheld, in the House of Lords' case of *Smoker v LFCDA*[2], in which their Lordships declined an invitation to depart from their earlier decision.

[1]   [1970] AC 1.
[2]   [1991] 2 WLR 1052, HL.

[H215] The House of Lords reviewed the principles relating to pension loss in *Longden v British Coal Corpn*[1]. The defendant argued that, although pension payments could not be offset against earnings lost during the period of payment prior to retirement age, they should nonetheless be deducted from the final loss of pension award (on the 'deduct like from like' principle apparently endorsed in *Parry v Cleaver*[2] and *Smoker v LFCDA*[3]). A further point raised (which was not considered in *Parry*) was the status of a lump sum payment made prior to original retirement age.

[1]   [1997] 3 WLR 1336.
[2]   [1970] AC 1.
[3]   [1991] 2 WLR 1052, HL.

(1)   EARLY RECEIPT OF PENSION

[H216] As regards prior payments, the House of Lords in *Longden* upheld the decision in *Parry v Cleaver*. Lord Hope (delivering the only speech) said[1]:

> 'He [the claimant] cannot reasonably be expected to set aside the sums received as incapacity pension during this period in order to make good his loss of pension after normal retirement age. I think that it would, to adopt Lord Reid's approach in *Parry v Cleaver*[2], strike the ordinary man as unjust if the claimant's claim for loss of pension after his normal retirement age were to be extinguished by capitalising sums paid to him before that age as an incapacity pension to assist him during his disability. On the other hand there can be no injustice in setting off the sums received by way of incapacity pension against the sums lost by way of retirement pension arising in the same period.'

The situation is now, therefore, clear. Any additional pension payments made prior to normal pension age are not to be brought into account. Only the payments made in the same period as the loss claimed should be offset. This is common sense: a claimant cannot claim a loss of pension from the age of 65 whilst receiving a pension without expecting payments by way of pension received after 65 to be included in the calculation.

---

¹   [1997] 3 WLR 1336 at 1348A.
²   [1970] AC 1.

(2)   LUMP SUMS

[H217]   The House of Lords in *Longden*[1] held that a lump sum represents a commuted payment in respect of the whole of the pension. Therefore, part represents a commutation in respect of pension actually paid during the years that would have fallen (but for the accident) pre-retirement, and the other part represents the period after normal retirement age. It was held that the proportion that represents pre-retirement age is not to be brought into account, whereas that representing post-retirement is to be offset. For example:

> If a claimant has a whole life multiplier of 15 and at retirement age a multiplier of 10, then 15 less 10 (ie 5) divided by 15 is the proportion to be ignored: namely $5/15 = 1/3$. Thus 2/3 of the lump sum is to be offset, and 1/3 ignored.

---

¹   [1997] 3 WLR 1336.

Shortened life expectancy

[H218]   In some cases, the life expectancy of a claimant has been so affected by an injury that medical evidence suggests that the claimant will die short of retirement age. If *Auty*[1] were applied to such a situation, the outcome would obviously result in no loss[2]. However, the medical evidence may be such that it does not rule out the chance of the claimant reaching and surpassing his or her expected normal retirement age. This has to be compensated in some form. The most appropriate method would be to obtain detailed medical evidence of the longest life expectancy in realistic terms. This can then be used to calculate loss as per the usual method. However, the resultant sum will, appropriately, be discounted in accordance with the likelihood of earlier death, as set out in the medical evidence.

---

¹   [1985] 1 WLR 784.
²   The multiplier in such a situation being zero.

Too many imponderables: lump sum calculation

[H219]   Although the conventional approach to the calculation of pension loss is to use the multiplier/multiplicand method of assessment, where there are numerous imponderables preventing such an assessment, it may be appropriate to adopt a broad brush lump sum valuation[1].

---

¹   See eg *Van Wees v (1) Karkour and (2) Walsh* [2007] EWHC 165 (QB), in which Langstaff J awarded £100,000 in respect of pension loss.

(v)   Future Medical Treatment and Therapy Expenses

[H220]   The general principles regarding the recovery of past medical and treatment expenses apply equally to claims for future medical and treatment expenses[1].

1   See further Chapter F at paras **[F36]–[F48]**.

[H221]   Where treatment has been undergone, it is no bar to recovery that the treatment has not yet been paid for (assuming that the claimant remains liable to pay)[1].

1   *Allen v Waters & Co* [1935] 1 KB 200, CA.

[H222]   Where the medical expenses in question are claimed for the future, there will inevitably have to be difficult decisions made as to the claimant's likely needs[1]. It is especially difficult to cater for possible future changes in the claimant's condition, for better or worse. For example, in *Cassel v Hammersmith and Fulham Health Authority*[2], Rose J rejected the argument that, on the evidence before the court, likely improvements in the sleeping patterns of the child claimant would enable his parents to negotiate reduced rates of pay with the claimant's night carers, as they would have been required to be present in any event.

1   See eg *Leon Seng Tan v Bunnage* (23 July 1986, unreported), in which Gatehouse J awarded the cost of a housekeeper and helper, but refused the cost of assistance at night to turn the claimant over in bed, as this could be carried out by an electric turning bed.
2   [1992] PIQR Q1 at Q8.

[H223]   Furthermore, it is foreseeable that, even though a medical condition remains stable, a particular claimant's needs may well change during the course of his or her life. This is especially the case with a claimant who is a young child, where care needs will have to be projected for his or her childhood, adolescence and adulthood[1]. Different multiplicands may apply for different periods of time. The multiplier will then be split proportionately to take into account these periods. Where there are numerous imponderables regarding the likely cost of future medical or treatment expenses, it may be appropriate for a single lump sum to be awarded. For example, in *Seepersad v (1) Persad and (2) Capital Insurance*[2], in delivering the joint opinion of the Privy Council, Lord Carswell said as follows[3]:

'It is not possible to form an accurate and verifiable estimate of the future cost of medical treatment and medication, because so much depends on how the appellant progresses in the future. It was not challenged that he had incurred such expense in the past, as is shown by the inclusion in the agreed special damage of a significant sum for medical treatment and medication. It does appear that there is likely to be some continuing expense, even if he improves significantly as time goes on. In their Lordships' opinion the most appropriate way to deal with this item is to allow a figure which will reflect the possibility of his incurring future expense of this type, on similar lines to the well-established approach to valuing loss of employment capacity: cf such cases as *Smith v Manchester Corporation* (1974) 17 KIR 1 and *Moeliker v Reyrolle & Co Ltd* [1976] ICR 253. The appropriate figure in their view is $100,000 and they would include that in the damages awarded.' [Author's note: instead of '*cf* such cases as *Smith v Manchester Corporation* ...' it is believed this should read '*see* such cases as *Smith v Manchester Corporation* ...' since these cases, by analogy, support the award of similar lump sums

1   See eg *Willett v North Bedfordshire Health Authority* [1993] PIQR Q166.
2   [2004] UKPC 19.
3   At [22].

[H224]   Where there are uncertainties regarding the claimant's need for future medical expenses in the future and/or difficulties assessing the likely expenditure that will be incurred, it may be reasonable to award a lump sum for these losses[1]. Alternatively, the court may apply a discount to the claim to reflect the risk that the treatment costs might not be incurred[2].

1   See eg *Seepsersad v (1) Persad and (2) Capital Insurance Ltd* [2004] UKPC 19, in which the Pricy Council awarded a lump sum of $100,000 to reflect the possibility of the claimant incurring medical expenses in the future.
2   See eg *Lane v Lake (Deceased)* LTL 31/7/2007, in which claim for future treatment was discounted by 10%; and *Crofts v Murton* LTL 10/9/08, in which a discount of 35% was applied to the claim for the costs of future surgery.

[H225]   The recoverability of future therapies (usually supported by adducing the evidence of various experts) is assessed in accordance with the same principles applying to medical treatment. Therefore, it does not matter that the therapies may be available on the NHS if, on the balance of probabilities, the claimant will incur such costs privately[1]. Further, the court may not be persuaded that carers can be taught how to perform such therapies, or that provision for such therapies could be added to a claimant's statement of educational needs[2].

1   Law Reform (Personal Injuries) Act 1948, s 2(4). See further Chapter F at paras **[F47]–[F52]**.
2   See eg *Haines v Airedale NHS Trust* (unreported, 2 May 2000, QBD).

[H226]   The recoverability of alternative and complementary therapies is a grey area and is fact-sensitive. It may have been reasonable for a claimant to have tried various forms of alternative therapy in the past, particularly if conventional medicine was unable to provide adequate relief from symptoms. However, whether or not ongoing claims for such therapies or treatment including hydrotherapy, acupuncture and herbal remedies are recoverable will depend upon the available witness and expert evidence; whether such treatment or therapy is recommended by the claimant's treating doctors; and whether or not such treatment is of benefit to the claimant[1]. Claims for the provision of a home hydrotherapy pool are particularly contentious, but a number of these claims have succeeded where there is sufficient supporting evidence[2].

1   Significant claims for ongoing alternative treatment/therapies were allowed in *O'Brien v Harris* (22 February 2001, unreported), QBD (hydrotherapy); *McMahon v Robert Brett & Sons* [2003] EWHC 2706 (QB) (aromatherapy); *Cannon v Cannon* [2005] EWHC 1310 (QB) (osteopathy, massage and physical therapy); and *Noble v Owens* [2008] EWHC 359 (QB) (hydrotherapy and acupuncture). See further Chapter F at para **[F53]**.
2   See further Chapter F at para **[F54]**.

(vi)   Future Fertility, Reproductive and Sexual Costs

[H227]   Where the claimant is unable to bear children without assistance, there have been a number of cases in which the claimant has recovered the costs of fertility treatment[1]. The court has to make an assessment regarding the number of children that the claimant wishes to conceive, when the treatment is likely to be required and the likely costs involved[2]. A discount may be applied to reflect uncertainty as regards the amount of fertility treatment that will be required and the costs involved, eg if there is uncertainty about how many children the claimant will try for[3]. Although the costs of assisted conception or IVF may be recovered, as a matter of law, the costs of surrogacy using donor eggs are not recoverable because it does not provide the claimant with the same thing he or she would have had (ie a child made up of his or her own genetic material) and therefore is not reasonable[4]. Likewise, it is debatable whether the court would award the costs of 'sexual gratification' in respect of someone who is brain injured[5].

[1] See eg *Owen v Brown* [2002] EWHC 1135 (QB), in which Silber J awarded £23,899 for fertility treatment; *Patel v Patel* [2005] EWHC 347 (QB), in which £17,500 was awarded by Treacy J; and *Burton v Kingsbury* [2007] EWHC 2091 (QB), in which £20,000 was awarded by Flaux J.

[2] See eg the approach of Treacy J in *Patel v Patel* [2005] EWHC 347 (QB).

[3] See eg *Owen v Brown* [2002] EWHC 1135 (QB), in which Silber J discounted the agreed costs of £29,873 by 20%.

[4] *Briody v St Helens* [2001] EWCA Civ 1010, [2001] 2 FLR 481.

[5] There have been reports of settled cases where the costs of the claimant visiting prostitutes has been claimed in circumstances where the claimant suffers from a personality disorder arising from a severe brain injury, and such costs are argued to be reasonably necessary to replace a lost amenity and to prevent the claimant from becoming aggressive and a danger to women.

(vii) Future Medication and Prescription Expenses

[H228] There is little to note in respect of future medication and prescription expenses, over and above the general principles applying to the recovery of past medication and prescription expenses. However, practitioners may wish to bear in mind the following:

- Any ongoing claim should be supported by medical evidence, including evidence as to the claimant's prognosis and the length of time that any medication or prescriptions will be required.
- A deterioration in the claimant's condition in the future might lead to an increase in the amount of medication and/or prescription costs.
- The claimant must give credit for the medication and prescription expenses he or she would have incurred in any event.
- Where numerous prescriptions are required, it may be cheaper for the claimant to purchase a pre-paid annual prescription card.
- Prescriptions are free of charge for those over the age of 60.

(viii) Future Care and Case Management

[H229] The cost of future care costs will primarily depend upon the available expert medical evidence and any expert care evidence which is obtained. In catastrophic injury claims, the claim for future care and case management will usually be the highest value claim. Given the sums involved, future care and case management will not infrequently be the only head of loss in dispute[1].

[1] See eg *A v B Hospitals NHS Trust* [2006] EWHC 1178 (QB); *XXX v A Strategic Health Authority* [2008] EWHC 2727 (QB); and *C v Dixon* [2009] EWHC 708 (QB).

Lump sum or periodical payments?

[H230]   Whilst it is generally recognised that the annual cost of providing private nursing care has been increasing at a rate outstripping inflation (as measured by the RPI), the courts have rejected an argument that a different discount rate should be applied[1]. Likewise, the courts have resisted an argument that the multiplicand should be adjusted in order to take account of this factor[2]. That is why, in larger claims, future care and case management costs are often awarded by way of PPs, since there is a significant advantage that such PPs can be up-rated annually by reference to a more appropriate earnings-based measure, ASHE (6115), which is more likely to keep pace with inflation of those costs[3].

[1]   *Warriner v Warriner* [2002] 1 WLR 1703; *Cooke v United Bristol Health Care* [2003] EWCA Civ 1370, cf *Moran v Miller Construction Ltd* (6 June 2003), Document No AM0200500.

[2]   In *Cooke v United Bristol Health Care* [2003] EWCA Civ 1370 at [30], Laws LJ described Rowland Hogg's attempt to do this as 'nothing but smoke and mirrors'.

[3]   *Thameside & Glossop v Thompstone and others* [2008] 1 WLR 2207, [2008] EWCA Civ 5. See further Chapter O.

Recovery in principle

(1)   REASONABLENESS

[H231]   As regards whether or not certain heads of loss are recoverable, and if so, the extent of the loss that is recoverable, the test is reasonableness. The claimant is entitled to damages to meet his 'reasonable requirements' or 'reasonable needs' arising from his injuries[1]. However, it is important to note that there may be a range of 'reasonable' options to meet the claimant's needs, and the item or package claimed does not need to be the cheapest available[2]:

> 'What the [claimant] here claims has been spent, is being spent and will be spent on his care may be looked at as mitigation of the injury and damage done to him by the defendant's negligence or as a natural result of them. In either case the question is: is it reasonable? For if it is reasonable it is a reasonably foreseeable consequence of the wrong done (sic) the [claimant] and the defendant cannot complain that it requires payment of a very large sum of money. The court must not react to dreadful injuries by considering that nothing is too good for the boy which will ameliorate his condition and increase pathetically little enjoyment of life which is all that is left to him; that would lead to making the defendant pay more than a fair and reasonable compensation. But the court must not put the standard of reasonableness too high when considering what is being done to improve a [claimant's] condition or increase his enjoyment of life… I think, the right question is: what is it reasonable to do for this injured boy? Mr Fricker gives the wrong answer in submitting that it would be reasonable to give him the less expensive care and treatment which other parents might prefer to give him or which these parents, if restricted by their own means without the defendant or insurers to look to, might or would have given him. **That may be the answer in some cases, but what has to be first considered by the court is not whether other treatment is reasonable but whether the treatment chosen and claimed for is reasonable**. There is here the complication that because of his injuries the injured person cannot himself choose his treatment or make known his choice, and the choice has to be made for him by his parents. But that does not alter the principle that the defendant is answerable for what is

reasonable human conduct and if their choice is reasonable he is no less answerable for it if he is able to point to cheaper treatment which is also reasonable'. [emphasis added]

1   *Sowden v Lodge* [2004] EWCA Civ 1370.
2   *Rialis v Mitchell* (1984) Times, 17 July, per Stephenson LJ at pp 24–26 of the transcript.

(2) A SUBJECTIVE OR OBJECTIVE TEST?

[H232]   In a clutch of recent cases[1], first instance courts have accepted, often without dispute, a submission based upon the above extract from *Rialis*[2], as approved in *Sowden*[3], that the test for assessing the award for future care is whether the claim for care as advanced by the claimant is reasonable, ie it is a subjective rather than objective test. For example, in *Taylor v (1) Chesworth and (2) MIB*, Ramsay J said[4]:

> 'I accept that the test therefore, as submitted by Mr Sephton, is to consider what course the claimant proposes to adopt and to consider whether it is reasonable having regard to the nature and extent of the claimant's needs, not to consider objectively what approach is reasonable. However, the logical way of approaching the issue must, in my judgement, be to make findings as to the nature and extent of the claimant's needs and then to consider whether what is proposed by the claimant is reasonable having regard to those needs'.

Similarly, in *Wakeling v (1) McDonagh and (2) MIB*[5], His Honour Judge Mackie QC said[6]:

> 'The legal approach is not in dispute having been restated by the House of Lords in *Wells v Wells* [1999] AC 345 carried through by the Court of Appeal in *Sowden v Lodge* and *Crookdake v Drury* [2005] 1 WLR 2129. The Court of Appeal in effect reiterated the principle that the court is first concerned not with whether other identified treatment is reasonable but whether that chosen by the Claimant is reasonable recognising that a Claimant or those looking after him are entitled to make a choice. This is an aspect of the basic principle that a Defendant is obliged to put the Claimant back so far as money can, into the position he would have been in but for the negligence'.

1   *Taylor v (1) Chesworth and (2) MIB* [2007] EWHC 1001 (QB); *Wakeling v (1) McDonagh and (2) MIB* [2007] EWHC 1201 (QB); *Massey v Tameside & Glossop Acute Services NHS Trust* [2007] EWHC 317 (QB); *Smith v East and North Hertfordshire Hospitals NHS Trust* [2008] EWHC 2234 (QB); *XXX v A Strategic Health Authority* [2008] EWHC 2727 (QB); *Smith v LC Fashion Windows* [2009] EWHC 1532 (QB); cf *Iqbal v Whipps Cross University Hospital NHS Trust* [2006] EWHC 3111(QB), in which Sir Rodger Bell rejected such a submission.
2   (1984) Times, 17 July.
3   [2004] EWCA Civ 1370.
4   [2007] EWHC 1001 (QB), at para 84.
5   [2007] EWHC 1201 (QB).
6   At para [45].

[H233]   Further, in *Massey v Tameside & Glossop Acute Services NHS Trust*[1], Teare J stated at para 59:

> 'In resolving the differences of opinion on these matters I have sought to apply the principles stated and explained in *Sowden v Lodge* [2004] EWCA Civ 1370 and [2005] 1 WLR 2129 which were in turn derived from *Rialis v Mitchell* (unreported 6 July 1984). In the former case Pill LJ approved statements of Stephenson LJ and O'Connor LJ in the latter case to the effect **that the claimant was entitled to the reasonable cost**

of caring for him in the manner chosen by him, or by those with responsibility for the claimant, so long as that choice was reasonable. A lesser sum would only be payable if the claimant's choice of care was unreasonable and another form of care was reasonable; see paragraphs 10–11 and 38. Longmore LJ agreed with Pill LJ that the correct question to be addressed in relation to care was "What is required to meet the claimant's reasonable needs?"; see paragraph 94. Scott Baker LJ agreed with both judgments; see paragraph 101.' [emphasis added]

Further, he went on to say at para 91[2]:

'The care regime suggested by Mrs. Bingham is clearly cheaper; but that, on the authorities, is not the test. The Defendant needs to show that Mrs. Daykin's care regime is unreasonable. I do not consider that the Defendant can show this.'

---

[1]   [2007] EWHC 317 (QB).

[2]   It might be thought that Teare J reverses the burden of proof here. However, a proper analysis might be that the claimant has a loss, which gives rise to a need for care and appliances; he chooses a method of satisfying that need which actually meets it; he is thus entitled to payment in the sum incurred or to be incurred, unless he is failing to mitigate his loss properly in this respect. As to that, it is for the defendant to show that the claimant's choice is unreasonable, and not for him to establish that it IS reasonable. If this were not the case, then Stephenson LJ would arguably have had to require the claimant in *Rialis* to justify why he was not taking the cheaper option.

[H234]   These decisions have been criticised because it is said they elide the principles of mitigation of loss and the assessment of compensatory damages[1]. However, it is submitted that it is quite clear that both *Rialis* and *Sowden* were dealing with the assessment of damages (see, for example, Sir Denys Buckley's judgment in *Rialis* and the references in *Sowden* at paras 10–12 under the heading 'damages at common law'). Therefore, as statements of principle they are binding guidance upon lower courts. That said, it is arguable that *Rialis*[2] and *Sowden*[3] are distinguishable from cases where both parties are putting forward costings based upon private care regimes. *Rialis* and *Sowden* both involved cases where the defendant was suggesting that there would be no future care costs, because the claimant would be looked after in residential care paid for by the state. These arguments were rejected but, once a decision had been taken in those cases that it was reasonable for the claimant to set up a private regime, the costs of care in an institution were no longer strictly relevant. The court did not go on to consider the relevant principles where there were competing 'reasonable' private care regimes put forward by the parties.

---

[1]   See further James Rowley QC 'Serious Personal Injury Litigation – a Quantum Update' [2008] JPIL 109.

[2]   *Rialis v Mitchell* (1984) Times, 17 July.

[3]   *Sowden v Lodge* [2004] EWCA Civ 1370.

[H235]   Here it is submitted that the court retains a large discretion to assess the loss as accurately as it can. In its simplest form, the court's job is to award a sufficient level of damages to meet the claimant's reasonable needs. But, it is submitted, there is, or ought to be, a three-stage approach to the assessment process, which combines a subjective and objective approach as follows:

(i)   What are the claimant's needs (including long-term needs resulting from any change in prognosis)?

(ii) Is the model of care chosen by the claimant reasonable (ie choosing a private care regime at home rather than a residential regime, or a directly employed model over an agency model)?

(iii) What are the reasonable costs of meeting the claimant's needs?

[H236] Clearly, the claimant's care needs will depend heavily upon the nature and extent of the injuries, as described in the medical and witness evidence. The second stage of the assessment has a large subjective element. The claimant (or his or her litigation friend or deputy, where the claimant lacks capacity) is likely to have a strong say in how the care should be provided, ie what form it should take (and not be coerced into accepting a form of care which is not desired[1]). However, the final stage of the assessment is objective and, it is submitted, may incorporate an element of proportionality. Here it is conceded that the costings and figures put forward by the defendant may well be relevant, eg if the defendant can prove that it is possible to meet the claimant's requirements by paying carers less per hour or working fewer hours

[1]   See further *Rialis v Mitchell* (1984) Times, 17 July and *Sowden v Lodge* [2004] EWCA Civ 1370 regarding the preference for a private care regime.

[2]   See eg *Huntley v Simmonds* [2009] EWHC 405 (QB); and *C v Dixon* [2009] EWHC 708 (QB).

[H237] It is submitted that, in the recent first instance cases, where judges have been asking themselves the question 'is the claimant's claim reasonable?', this is merely shorthand for the above three-stage test. The burden of proof is not reversed as such. Comments to that effect by Teare J in *Massey v Tameside & Glossop Acute Services NHS Trust*[1] may overstep the mark (but see the note above), though much will depend upon the evidence called at trial. In practice, often it will be possible to show that the defendant's care regime is defective in some way, does not fully meet the claimant's needs, or that there are significant advantages to the claimant's regime which justify an increased cost[2]. But, likewise, the defendant may be able to show that the claimant's care regime provides for more than is reasonably required[3].

[1]   [2007] EWHC 317 (QB).

[2]   See, for example, *Iqbal v Whipps Cross University Hospital NHS Trust* [2006] EWHC 3111(QB); *Sarwar v (1) Ali and (2) MIB* [2007] LS Medical 375; *A v Powys Health Board* [2007] EWHC 2996 (QB); and *Edwards v Martin* [2010] EWHC 570 (QB).

[3]   See, for example, *Huntley v Simmonds* [2009] EWHC 405 (QB); and *C v Dixon* [2009] EWHC 708 (QB).

[H238] In the unlikely event that the parties' respective regimes are identical in quality and the ability to meet the claimant's needs, the claimant is likely to struggle to recover the extra costs of the more expensive regime if there is no discernable benefit to him or her.

[H239] Where, however, there are advantages and disadvantages of both regimes and it is not possible to make a straight comparison, but both regimes are considered to be objectively reasonable, it is unlikely that any higher court will impose further guidance on the assessment process. A generous judge may award the claimant's care regime because it is reasonable, notwithstanding that there might also be a reasonable model suggested by the defendant, provided he is satisfied that the costs of it are likely to be incurred. A mean judge may restrict the claimant to recovering the cheaper regime since it meets the claimant's reasonable needs. The unsatisfied party in either scenario will find it difficult to appeal. The decision is likely to be considered a question of fact for the trial judge.

Calculating the appropriate lump sum

[H240]   The following points should be kept in mind when considering future care claims:

- Whilst care might have been provided gratuitously by friends and family members up to the date of trial, it may be reasonable for future care to be bought in, in which case no discount from the professional rates should be made[1]. There is no legal duty upon a voluntary carer to continue providing ongoing care into the future, and a gratuitous carer cannot be compelled to be part of the claimant's care team[2].
- Although there may have been some gratuitous care or care provided free by the state as a result of pre-existing injuries, it may not be appropriate to discount the claim for future professional care to reflect the notional cost of the pre-existing care provided (which would have been at no cost to the claimant)[3].
- Likewise, it may not be appropriate to discount the costs of providing a full professional 24-hour care package to a catastrophically injured child by the level of 'normal' parental care which would have been given in any event, especially where the parents will continue to live with the child and provide a similar level of care and attention in any event[4].
- As the claimant gets older, the costs of care may well increase as a result of the ageing process or because his or her condition deteriorates, eg by reason of osteoarthritis[5].
- The claimant may have periods of increased care needs following surgery or treatment[6].
- There may be a risk that the claimant's current gratuitous carers, even though they want to continue providing care for as long as possible, will not be able to continue providing care for as long as the claimant needs it[7]. Ongoing care by the same provider may be prevented by reason of age, ill-health, death or voluntary decision of the carer. Where necessary, a medical report should be obtained in respect of the care provider's health and life expectancy.
- The claimant's condition may deteriorate to such an extent that he or she will need to be looked after in long-term residential accommodation[8]. Where the state is likely to provide such accommodation or care, the claimant's claim may be reduced accordingly[9]. However, the claimant has a right to choose private provision over state-funded provision, and it is unlikely to be held an unreasonable failure to mitigate loss to opt for the former[10].
- The claimant may require increased assistance if he or she has children in the future[11]. It need not be proved that the claimant will, on the balance of probabilities, have children. So long as there is a real rather than a speculative chance that the claimant will have children, the court should make an award reflecting the likely increased costs of childcare[12]. However, it may be that additional costs will not be required on top of the proposed care package if it is sufficient to deal with this eventuality already[13].

- In order to attract good quality committed carers who are happy to provide care on a long-term basis, it is likely to be necessary to ensure that the carers are paid at or above the going rate and are provided with suitable accommodation and facilities.

- Past care and case management costs may be used as a guide in order to calculate the likely future costs[14].

- Where the claimant is of school age, consideration has to be given to the likely educational establishment that the claimant will attend in the future (whether residential or non-residential) and what effect this will have on the likely care costs[15].

- Where there is a chance that the claimant will attend state-funded day centres or play schemes in the future for at least some of his or her time, consideration needs to be given as to whether the costs of professional care should be reduced to reflect this chance[16].

- The burden is upon the defendant to prove[17] that the extent of any state-funded care that it says will be available to the claimant before any discount will be made to the claim for future loss, and that may be very difficult to establish, given the uncertainties of local authority funding and trying to predict the likely position many years into the future[18].

- It may be appropriate to discount the claim for future care where there is a chance that the proposed scheme will not be implemented[19] or there are risks that the claimant will not receive care at the level suggested because the regime will break down[20].

- It may be appropriate to reduce the allowances for support worker expenses in later years[21]. Likewise, there may be a diminishing need for case management over time[22].

- A discount may be appropriate if there is a prospect of the claimant moving abroad, where care costs are cheaper[23].

[1] See eg *Biesheuval v Birrell* [1999] PIQR Q40; although cf *Evans v Pontypridd Roofing* [2001] EWCA Civ 1657, in which the Court of Appeal upheld the trial judge's discount of 25% to both the past and future gratuitous care claim (presumably on the basis that the gratuitous care regime would continue for the foreseeable future).

[2] *Biesheuval v Birrell* [1999] PIQR Q40; *Duffield v Cumbria & Lancashire Strategic Health Authority* [2005] EWHC 1986 (QB); *Iqbal v Whipps Cross University* [2007] LS Law Medical 97; *Massey v Tameside & Glossop Acute Services NHS Trust* [2007] EWHC 317 (QB); *Noble v Owens* [2008] EWHC 359 (QB). In *Noble v Owens* [2008] EWHC 359 (QB), Field J said at para [88]: 'Mr Noble has been most fortunate as I am sure he appreciates in having been cared for Mrs Stanton. However, Mrs Stanton does not wish to continue to be his carer. She is exhausted and wants to get on with other aspects of her life. She is of course perfectly entitled to adopt this attitude. The consequence is that Mr Noble's future care needs must be met by outside support workers'.

[3] *Sklair v Haycock* [2009] EWHC 3328 (QB).

[4] *Stephens v Doncaster Health Authority* [1996] Med LR 357; *Iqbal v Whipps Cross University* [2007] LS Law Medical 97.

[5] See eg *Blair v Michelin Tyre plc* (25 January 2002, unreported), QBD; *Whyte v Barber* (February 2003, unreported), QBD, Smith J; and *Garth v (1) Grant and (2) MIB*, QBD, LTL 17/7/2007.

[6] *Garth v (1) Grant and (2) MIB*, QBD, LTL 17/7/2007.

[7] See eg *Tame v Professional Cycle Marketing Ltd* [2006] EWHC 3751 (QB), in which the judge found that the claimant's marriage would only last another year. Where there are risks, but not a likelihood, that gratuitous care will come to an end requiring professional care, it is often sensible to claim a contingency award: see eg *Potts v Buckley* (21 December 1992, unreported), QBD, Tuckey J; *Bristow v Judd* [1993] PIQR Q117; *Stuart v Martin* [2001] All ER (D) 401 (Oct); *Finnis v Caulfield* [2002] All ER (D) 353.

8   *Kidd v Plymouth Health Authority* [2001] Lloyds Law Rep Med 165.
9   *Mitchell v Mulholland (No 2)* [1972] 1 QB 65, CA; see also *Sklair v Haycock* [2009] EWHC 3328
      (QB), in which Edwards-Stuart J reduced the multiplier for future care and case management from
      20.8 to 18, to take account of the likelihood that the claimant would spend the last few years of his
      life looked after in accommodation provided by the local authority.
10   *Peters v East Midlands Strategic HA* [2009] EWCA Civ 145; see also *Freeman v Lockett* [2006]
      EWHC 102 (QB); *Sklair v Haycock* [2009] EWHC 3328 (QB).
11   *Dixon v Were* [2004] EWHC 2273 (QB); *A v Powys Local Health Board* [2007] EWHC 2996 (QB).
12   See eg *A v Powys Local Health Board* [2007] EWHC 2996 (QB), in which Lloyd-Jones J awarded
      the claimant the costs of a full-time nanny for 7 years and a part-time nanny for a further 11 years,
      discounted by 50% for contingencies.
13   See eg *C v Dixon* [2009] EWHC 708 (QB), in which King J declined to make an award for the
      increased cost of training support workers in respect of childcare.
14   *Stuart v Martin* [2001] All ER (D) 401 (Oct).
15   *Iqbal v Whipps Cross University* [2007] LS Law Medical 97.
16   Contrast *Iqbal v Whipps Cross University* [2007] LS Law Medical 97 and *Massey v Tameside &
      Glossop Acute Services NHS Trust* [2007] EWHC 317 (QB) with *Lewis v Shrewsbury NHS Trust*
      LTL 14/6/2007.
17   *Sowden v Lodge* [2004] EWCA Civ 1370.
18   See eg *Tinsley v Sarkar* [2006] PIQR Q1; *Godbold v Mahmood* [2006] PIQR Q5; *Freeman v Lockett*
      [2006] EWHC 102 (QB); and *A v B Hospitals NHS Trust* [2006] EWHC 1178 (QB); 1370 *Iqbal v
      Whipps Cross University* [2007] LS Law Medical 97. Further see *Peters v East Midlands Strategic
      HA* [2009] EWCA Civ 145 regarding the claimant's right to choose private provision.
19   See eg *Lane v Lake (Deceased)* LTL 31/7/2007, in which John Leighton Williams QC discounted
      the future care claim by 10% to reflect the chance that it would not be implemented.
20   *Huntley v Simmonds* [2009] EWHC 405 (QB). However, it should be noted that, if the claimant
      regularly fires his support workers, there may well be increased recruitment and case management
      costs and/or periods where two carers are being paid for, as the former carer works out his or her
      notice period.
21   See eg *Lane v Lake (Deceased)* LTL 31/7/2007, in which John Leighton Williams QC reduced the
      multiplier for support worker expenses.
21   See eg *Cannon v Cannon* [2005] EWHC 1310 (QB).
22   See eg *Lindsay v Wood* [2007] EWHC 3141 (Fam).
23   See eg *Lindsay v Wood* [2007] EWHC 3141 (Fam)

Notional weeks per annum

[H241] When assessing the costs of a private directly employed care regime, the court will usually take into account additional weeks for holidays, sickness and training etc. Under the Working Time Regulations 1998 (as amended), a worker is entitled to 4 weeks' paid holiday in any year, plus the usual statutory holidays – a total of 5.6 weeks per annum or 28 days a year. Sickness provision has to be made: the usual average period is up to 8 days per year (1.6 paid weeks), as has time for appropriate training. Whereas, previously, courts had been deciding cases on the basis of 58[1] or 59[2] weeks per annum, following *XXX v A Strategic Health Authority*[3] more recent cases have been compromised on the basis of 60 notional weeks per annum, ie an allowance of 8 additional weeks per annum to cover holidays, sickness and training etc.

1   See eg *A v B Hospitals NHS Trust* [2006] EWHC 1178 (QB); *Iqbal v Whipps Cross University
      Hospital NHS Trust* [2006] EWHC 3111(QB); and *Sarwar v (1) Ali and (2) MIB* [2007] LS Medical
      375.
2   *Lynham v The Morecambe Bay Hospitals NHS Trust* (Garland J, 25 March 2002); *Crofton v NHSLA*
      (first instance decision of HHJ Reid QC, QBD, 19 January 2006); *Lewis v Shrewsbury Hospital NHS*

Trust (HHJ MacDuff, QB, 29 January 2007); *A v Powys Health Board* [2007] EWHC 2996 (QB); *Smith v East and North Hertfordshire Hospitals NHS Trust* [2008] EWHC 2234 (QB); and *Huntley v Simmonds* [2009] EWHC 405 (QB).

3   [2008] EWHC 2727 (QB).

(ix)   Future Aids, Equipment and Appliances

[H242]   When the annual cost of aids and appliances has been calculated, the appropriate multiplier should be applied, allowing for accelerated receipt. It should be noted that most items of equipment, aids or appliance require replacement at regular intervals rather than annually. Therefore, using a periodic multiplier which takes account of the appropriate discount factors in respect of each of the replacement periods will usually provide a more accurate method of assessment than applying a lifetime multiplier to an annual multiplicand calculated on an average basis[1]. However, the advantage of calculating aids and equipment claims on the basis of averaged annualised loss is that it is easier to convert the claim to periodical payments if so required[2].

1   See further at paras **[H74]–[H76]**.
2   In *Eeles v Cobham Hire Services Ltd* [2009] EWCA Civ 204 the Court of Appeal held that, for the purposes of assessing whether an interim payment was a reasonable proportion of the likely capital award at trial, the only future losses that the court could assume would not be paid by way of periodical payments were future accommodation costs.

[H243]   Where there was a dispute regarding the likely costs of aids and equipment in *A v Powys Health Board*[1], Lloyd-Jones J applied the *Rialis*[2] principle to the effect that it did not matter that the defendant could identify a cheaper alternative, so long as the item being claimed was reasonable. However, the suggestion that the cost of the alternative item is irrelevant, where the item claimed is reasonable, may be taking the point too far, and much will depend upon the relative pros and cons of the respective items[2].

1   [2007] EWHC 2996 (QB).
2   Court of Appeal, 6 July 1984, as approved in *Sowden v Lodge* [2005] 1 WLR 2129.
3   See further Chapter F at paras **[F139]–[F140]**.

[H244]   In catastrophic injury cases, it may be appropriate to instruct a number of different experts to consider the need for and likely costs of various aids and appliances, including wheelchairs and hoists (usually covered by occupational therapists); exercise equipment (usually covered by physiotherapists); communication aids (usually covered by speech and language therapists or information technology experts); and environmental controls (usually covered by information technology experts). Such claims can be quite extensive. The idea is to put the claimant back into the position he or she would have been but for the injury. Therefore, any item of equipment which assists the claimant to performs functions previously taken for granted, eg to open doors and windows, should be awarded[1]. As Flaux J stated in *Burton v Kinsbury*[2], such items of equipment were claimed in order to 'assist the claimant to lead a life as normal as possible' and were still recoverable, whether or not a carer could perform the task for him[3]:

'If such technology is available to give the Claimant a level of independence so that he does not have to summon a carer or his wife to switch on a light or a piece of equipment or to draw a curtain or blind, it seems to me that he should be entitled to it and to recover its cost from the Defendant.'

1   See eg *Sarwar v (1) Ali and (2) MIB* [2007] EWHC 1255 (QB); *Burton v Kingsbury* [2007] EWHC 2091 (QB); *A v Powys Local Health Board* [2007] EWHC 2996 (QB); although cf *Owen v Brown* [2002] EWHC 1135 (QB), in which Silber J disallowed the claim for automatic garage doors and gates because the claimant would always have a carer with him; and *Iqbal v Whipps Cross University* [2007] LS Law Medical 97, in which Sir Rodger Bell refused to award the costs of a step lift to allow access to the grassy area of the claimant's garden, because the areas to which the claimant already had access were enough to make his accommodation suitable for his needs.
2   [2007] EWHC 2091 (QB).
3   At para [152]. See also *Noble v Owens* [2008] EWHC 359 (QB), in which Field J accepted the evidence of Steve Martin, saying at para [144]: 'In my judgement, all these recommendations are needed to allow Mr Noble a level of independence and function that will approximate to that he enjoyed before the accident'.

[H245]   It is not necessarily fatal to a claim that the equipment, aids or appliances are available from the state[1]. The defendant must do more than merely establish that the claimed items might be available on the NHS or through social services: the defendant must show that (i) the items are available free of charge on the NHS or though social services; and (ii) on the balance of probabilities, the claimant would make use of the free service to obtain the item in question[2]. However, a claimant will not be entitled to claim compensation in respect of ordinary household items which he or she would probably have purchased irrespective of his or her injuries, such as televisions, video recorders, mobile phones, cookers, microwaves, computers, lawn mowers etc[3]. But, where an item is more expensive than would otherwise have been bought, the extra cost attributable to the claimant's injuries can be claimed from the defendant.

1   *Parkhouse v North Devon Healthcare NHS Trust* [2002] Lloyd's Rep Med 100. See further Law Reform (Personal Injuries) Act 1948, s 2(4), which provides that 'there shall be disregarded, in determining the reasonableness of any expenses the possibility of avoiding those expenses or part of them by taking advantage of facilities available under the National Health Service'.
2   *Eagle v Chambers (No 2)* [2004] EWCA Civ 1033.
3   See further Chapter F at para **[F132]**.

[H246]   When assessing a claim for future loss, consideration has to be given to how the claimant's needs are likely to change over time. It may be that the claimant will become more disabled, and his or her need for aids and equipment will increase. Furthermore, additional items of equipment may be needed to assist with future events such as childcare. Conversely, as a claimant ages, he or she may no longer have any need for certain items of equipment, and a discount may be required[1].

1   In *Smith v East and North Hertfordshire Hospitals NHS Trust* [2008] EWHC 2234 (QB), Penry-Davey J applied a 25% discount to the claim for future aids and equipment on the basis that, as the claimant aged, particular items of equipment may no longer be of use to her.

[H247]   Consideration also needs to be given to whether or not certain items of equipment might need duplication, eg at the claimant's school, place of work or at the houses of friends and family. For example, in *A v Powys Local Health Board*[1], awards were made in respect of the long-term provision of equipment both at the claimant's own home and the parental home including a special bath, Clos-o-mat toilet, body drier and air conditioning.

¹   [2007] EWHC 2996 (QB).

(x)   Future Accommodation

Principles regarding lump sum assessment

[H248]   The acquisition of more suitable and, generally, larger and more expensive accommodation will involve expense on the claimant's part. If the courts were to award the total purchase price of the property, less the proceeds from the sale of the existing property, the claimant would be over-compensated, because the capital value of the property would remain intact on the claimant's death and represent a windfall to his or her estate. The solution developed by the courts to this problem is to treat the loss to the claimant, not as a straightforward capital loss, but as the loss of an annual sum representing either the loss of the income on the capital expended[1], or the cost of borrowing the capital expended. This requires a rate of interest to turn the capital expenditure into an annual figure which, since the decision by the Lord Chancellor to exercise his powers under s 1 of the Damages Act 1996, has been fixed at 2.5%.

¹   That is to say, the cost of a new house less the proceeds of sale from the old one, if any.

[H249]   If the claimant requires specialist adaptations to a property, such as a chair lift, which do not increase the value of the property, the cost of those items can be recovered in full (ie capital purchase costs plus running expenses)[1]. If the special adaptations do add to the value of the property or the claimant has to acquire a property (ie gains an asset), the claimant will only be able to claim for the expenditure involved over and above the enhancement of the value of the property[2]. There are several methods of calculating the damages recoverable for such expenditure. Each case depends upon its own facts. Sometimes, the damages will cover the extra mortgage which will be paid for the new accommodation[3]. At other times, the court will award damages based upon the wasted capital expenditure, ie the open market diminution in value of the property.

¹   *Roberts v Johnstone* [1989] QB 878; *Willett v North Bedfordshire Health Authority* [1993] PIQR Q166; *Campbell v Mylchreest* [1999] PIQR Q17. See also *George v Pinnock* [1973] 1 WLR 118, in which the cost of providing furnishings and fittings in respect of a room for a full-time carer was held to be recoverable.

²   *Willett v North Bedfordshire Health Authority* [1993] PIQR Q166.

³   *Fowler v Grace* (1970) 114 Sol Jo 193. In respect of how this might work with periodical payments, see further Robert Weir 'Accommodating Periodical Payments Orders into Housing Claims' [2008] JPIL Issue 4/08, p 147.

[H250]   If the claimant has had to purchase special accommodation, the Court of Appeal has set out a formula to calculate the claimant's loss. The annual additional cost of such accommodation should be taken as 2.5% of the difference between the capital cost of the new accommodation and the net proceeds of sale of the claimant's previous accommodation. This multiplicand is multiplied by the same multiplier as for other lifetime losses. A typical example of such a calculation (a *Roberts v Johnstone* calculation) is:

	Cost of new house:	£750,000
	Value added by extension:	£30,000
	Less value of existing house (if any):	(£200,000)
Therefore:	Additional capital cost:	£580,000
	Annual cost @ 2.5% per annum:	£14,500
	× a lifetime multiplier of 18	
	Subtotal	**£261,000**
	Plus cost of extension and adaptations:	£250,000
	Less value added	(£30,000)
	Subtotal	**£220,000**
	Therefore total loss:	**£481,000**

[H251]   In *Roberts v Johnstone*[1] the Court of Appeal took the total cost of alterations (£38,284), and deducted from that a figure representing the part of the expenditure that increased the value of the property (£10,000). It then added the net figure (£28,284) onto the damages awarded for the cost of acquiring the new property (£21,920). However, in *Willett v North Bedfordshire Health Authority*[2], Hobhouse J treated the cost of alterations to the property to provide a second bedroom, in which a carer would live, as part of the capital cost of the property, and therefore to be taken into account in the interest calculations. Hobhouse J said:

> 'It was drawn to my attention that in *Roberts v Johnstone* a similar item was not included in the capital value allowance of the property. The matter does not appear to have been the subject of argument, and indeed the smallness of the figures that result from this method of assessment for marginal items of capital expenditure amply explains why they should not often be the subject of the attention that they have received in the present case. But notwithstanding the way the figure was treated in *Roberts v Johnstone*, I consider there is no escape from the logical and proper approach of treating appropriate capital expenditure which is incurred after the purchase which enhances the value of the house in the same way as expenditure which is incurred in the acquisition of the house itself. Any other approach produces not only mathematically and logically inaccurate results but also an unjust result.'

[1]   [1989] QB 878, per Stocker LJ at 893.
[2]   [1993] PIQR Q166. See also *Almond v Leeds Western Health Authority* [1990] 1 Med LR 370.

[H252]   Where the alterations do not enhance the market value of the property (they may even reduce it), the cost of the works will simply be added to the damages. Where there is a *reduction* in value, the amount of that reduction can arguably (in the absence of authority) be added to the cost of the alterations, but then the figure to be used in the *Roberts v Johnstone*[1] calculation should be the reduced value of the altered property, rather than the higher figure of the acquisition cost.

[1]   [1989] QB 878.

[H253]   Where the proposed alterations have not been undertaken as at the date of the trial, it is sensible to build into the costings a contingency sum, since building projects almost invariably involve additional costs due to unexpected matters[1]. The appropriate level of contingency will depend upon all the circumstances including the age of the property, the extent of the proposed works and scope for things to go wrong. Expert evidence will be helpful regarding the appropriate level of contingency in any given case.

[1]   In *Iqbal v Whipps Cross University* [2007] LS Law Medical 97, Sir Rodger Bell allowed a contingency of 5% to the proposed works.

[H254]   Other extra costs likely to be incurred over time may be converted into capital sums and added to the damages, eg higher council tax payments, increased insurance premiums and enlarged maintenance costs[1]. The same would apply to additional heating expenses, incurred if the claimant's injuries mean that the home needs to be heated when it would not otherwise have been, such as if the claimant would, but for the accident, have been at work. Similarly, additional wear and tear may be caused to the property, eg where a wheelchair user damages carpets and paintwork (it is, after all, analogous to the repeated wheeling in of a bicycle across the floor, whatever the weather or ground conditions outside).

[1]   *Goldfinch v Scannell* [1993] PIQR Q143.

[H255]   These sums are in addition to the anticipated costs of acquisition of a new property, such as:

- stamp duty;
- solicitor's fees on both sale and purchase;
- estate agent's commission;
- architect's appraisal (if any);
- removal expenses; and
- inherent re-furnishing costs (less any element of betterment, as where a new carpet replaces a worn-out one).

[H256]   Where the 'new' property has not yet been purchased, some allowance will have to be made for the fact that the loss will be suffered at a date later than the date of trial. This adjustment involves calculating the total anticipated loss and reducing it by 2.5% per annum to allow for accelerated receipt. Where a property has already been purchased with an interim payment award, the court may be slow to allow the claimant to have a second bite of the cherry if that accommodation does not prove satisfactory[1]. However, each case must be decided on its facts and, in some instances, it might not be unreasonable for a claimant to have moved to one property which turned out to be a bad move and then to claim the costs of a second move[2].

[1]   *Brown v Berry* (14 October 1997, unreported), QBD.
[2]   *Tame v Professional Cycle Marketing Ltd* [2006] EWHC 3751 (QB).

[H257]   The conversion into a capital figure of the annual sum ascertained by the *Roberts v Johnstone* interest calculation will require the use of a multiplier based on the period of the anticipated loss. The principle on which this multiplier is assessed is broadly similar to that governing multipliers for other types of expenditure, although the accommodation multiplier may be adjusted in certain cases according to factors specific to the claimant's accommodation needs. For example, the fact that a room to accommodate a resident carer will not be required until some time in the future may justify a reduction in the multiplier. Similarly, the multiplier will, in appropriate cases, take account of the likely date when the claimant would have bought a house in any event but for the injury[1]. Although, where the claimant might otherwise have been expected to purchase a property jointly with a partner, credit should only be given for a half or two-thirds of the equity in the property that would have been bought[2]. Further, no credit should be given to reflect the benefit that the claimant's parents might receive by living rent-free in the new accommodation because of the considerable extra love and support that they are likely to provide to the claimant[3]. Equally, if the claimant is living rent-free in his partner's property as at the time of the accident, there is no need to give credit for the 'notional costs' of his accommodation or his partner's accommodation costs[4].

[1]   See eg the judgment of Collins J at first instance in *Thomas v Brighton Health Authority* [1996] PIQR 30; *Biesheuval v Birrell* [1999] PIQR Q40; *Lynham v The Morecambe Bay Hospitals NHS Trust* [2002] EWHC 823 (QB).

[2]   *M (a child) v Leeds Health Authority* [2002] PIQR Q44; *Iqbal v Whipps Cross University* [2007] LS Law Medical 97; *Sarwar v (1) Ali and (2) MIB* [2007] EWHC 1255 (QB). Although it should be noted that, arguably, a claimant would have bought a more expensive home if he or she bought it with a partner rather than on his or her own. To this end, it is worth looking at the claimant's earnings (or earnings he or she would have received in the absence of the injuries) to gauge the likely borrowing potential.

[3]   *Parkhouse v North Devon Healthcare NHS Trust* [2002] Lloyd's Rep Med 100; *M (a child) v Leeds Health Authority* [2002] PIQR Q4; *Iqbal v Whipps Cross University* [2007] LS Law Medical 97; cf *Lewis v Shrewsbury NHS Trust* LTL 14/6/2007.

[4]   Any benefit to the claimant's partner being able to live rent-free in the claimant's property is a benefit to the partner and is not to be offset against the claimant's claim, in the same way that the partner is unable to claim for any losses that he or she has suffered: *Noble v Owens* [2008] EWHC 359 (QB).

[H258]   Where the claimant would otherwise have been renting instead of buying a property, the notional costs of rent may be offset against the *Roberts v Johnstone* claim[1].

[1]   *Evans v Pontypridd Roofing Ltd* [2001] EWCA Civ 1657.

[H259]   As with other types of expense, the touchstone of recoverability in relation to housing costs is reasonableness. It may, for example, be reasonable for the claimant to move house more than once during the period for which the damages are being awarded[1]. A common example of this is where it is reasonable for the claimant's parents to purchase and adapt new accommodation to house the family, and thereafter for the claimant to purchase and adapt suitable accommodation to live independently in the future[2]. Reasonableness will also be relevant to the type and location of the property acquired: and the court will not necessarily discount damages merely because the quality of the accommodation goes beyond that which is strictly necessary for the claimant's needs, as long as the price of the property falls within the range of sums which it is reasonable for a person in the claimant's position to spend on a property[3]. But, where the claimant has acted unreasonably in purchasing a particular property, the court may be compelled to assess future losses on the basis of a notional or hypothetical property which the court considers more closely resembles what the claimant could and should have reasonably bought[4]. Likewise, the assessment of future loss may also need to be based upon a notional or hypothetical property where the claimant has not purchased a house as at the date of trial, but the claimant's accommodation evidence is rejected as being greater than his needs[5].

1   See *Willett v North Bedfordshire Health Authority* [1993] PIQR Q166; and *Tame v Professional Cycle Marketing Ltd* [2006] EWHC 3751 (QB).
2   See eg *A v Powys Local Health Board* [2007] EWHC 2996 (QB), which was compromised on this basis.
3   See *Willett v North Bedfordshire Health Authority* [1993] PIQR Q166, where the property included a swimming pool, which was not necessary to the claimant's needs. The cost of buying that property was nevertheless held to be reasonable and recoverable. Cf *Cassel v Riverside Health Authority* [1992] PIQR Q1. See also *Biesheuval v Birrell* [1999] PIQR Q40; and *M (a child) v Leeds Health Authority* [2002] PIQR Q46, which suggest that factors other than the purely functional will be taken into consideration when assessing the reasonableness of an accommodation claim, eg the desire to live near to family and friends.
4   *O'Brien v Harris* (22 February 2001, unreported), QBD; *Pankhurst v (1) White and (2) MIB* [2009] EWHC 1117 (QB).
5   *Noble v Owens* [2008] EWHC 359 (QB).

[H260]   Where the claimant is already housed in local authority accommodation, additional considerations might apply. In particular, it may be argued by the defendant that the claimant's current accommodation is adequate or the state will provide him or her with suitable accommodation, in which case the claimant has suffered no loss[1]. As mentioned above, the guiding principle in each case is reasonableness, and individual cases will be decided on their own facts. However, following *Peters*[2], it is now clear that the claimant has a right to choose private over state-funded provision, and it is unlikely to be a failure to mitigate loss to opt for the former.

1   See eg the comments of Lord Denning MR in *Cunningham v Harrison* [1973] QB 942 at 952; and *Sowden v Lodge* [2004] EWCA Civ 1370.
2   *Peters v East Midlands Strategic HA* [2009] EWCA Civ 145. See also *Rialis v Mitchell* (1984) Times, 17 July, and *Sowden v Lodge* [2004] EWCA Civ 1370.

Cases involving short life expectancy

[H261]   Where the claimant has a shortened life expectancy, there can be considerable difficulties funding the costs of moving to suitable accommodation. In most ordinary cases, there will be a shortfall from the *Roberts v Johnstone*[1] calculation, which means that damages from other heads of loss will need to be 'borrowed' in order to provide the missing funds to allow for the initial capital purchase and adaptation. However, these problems are magnified in cases involving short life expectancy as a result of the reduced lifetime multiplier, and there may not be sufficient funds from other heads of loss to meet the shortfall. One solution might be to claim the increased costs of a suitable rental property. But landlords can be reluctant to allow adaptations to be performed which may devalue or alter the aesthetics of the building. Also, it can be difficult to secure long rental periods, meaning that the claimant may have to move regularly. Innovative ideas might need to be considered, eg with the defendant buying a suitable property and holding it on trust for the benefit of the claimant during his or her lifetime or using periodical payments to fund a mortgage[2]. An ad hoc working party with claimant and defendant representatives has been set up to explore possible alternatives. Various proposals are being considered including the possibility of the defendant purchasing the property and holding on trust for the claimant during his or her lifetime and the possibility of the claimant taking out an interest only mortgage which the defendant would guarantee and pay for by way of periodical payments.

¹   [1989] QB 878.
²   See further Robert Weir 'Accommodating Periodical Payments Orders into Housing Claims' [2008] JPIL Issue 4/08, p 147; and Peter Miller 'An Alternative to *Roberts v Johnstone*' [2008] JPIL Issue 4/08, p 291.

Handicap on the accommodation market

[H262]   Where it is difficult to provide precise costings as to the claimant's likely increased accommodation expenses in the future, it may be possible to seek a lump sum to cover such expenses. In particular, the claimant may need certain adaptations in the future as a result of his or her injuries but it is difficult to predict the exact nature of the adaptations required or when they will become necessary. Likewise, the claimant may have had suitable alterations to his or her existing home but further adaptations will be required when the claimant moves house, and it is difficult to anticipate when exactly that might be. It is submitted that, in such circumstances, it would not be inappropriate for the court to assess this head of loss on a broad-brush basis by awarding a lump sum, taking into account uncertainties and accelerated receipt to cover such pecuniary losses as and when they occur. In effect, such an award would be compensating the claimant for 'handicap on the accommodation market'.

The future

[H263]   The Law Commission has recommended that, as an alternative, the defendant should provide the purchase price in return for a charge on the claimant's property, increasing in value in accordance with local property values¹. The Government is currently considering what, if any, changes to the law are required².

¹   Law Commission Report No 262 'Damages for Personal Injury: Medical, Nursing and other expenses' (November 1999), para 4.13.
²   See further Chapter F at para **[F150]**.

(xi)   Future Travel and Transport Expenses

[H264]   There is no difference in principle between the assessment of past travel and transport expenses and future travel and transport expenses. As long as the travel expenses are reasonably related to the claimant's injuries and reasonable in amount, they should be recoverable. However, the claimant may only claim for the extra travel expenses attributable to his or her injuries, and credit must be given for those expenses which would have been incurred in any event.

[H265]   More common ongoing transport and travel claims include:

- Any increased purchase and replacement costs associated with a suitably adapted vehicle (which is more expensive, has higher standing costs and depreciates faster than the vehicle which the claimant otherwise would have bought)¹.
- Costs of replacing the claimant's vehicle more frequently because of the greater need for reliability.
- Costs of converting to an automatic and/or the increased costs of driving an automatic in the future².

- An allowance for the replacement of a company car (and any other associated benefits, such as free MOT, insurance and fuel)[3].
- Replacement adaptations, such as handcontrols[4].
- Increased running costs due to driving a larger more expensive vehicle and/or incurring greater mileage, eg attending medical and therapy appointments or simply being more reliant upon a vehicle as opposed to walking and using public transport[5].
- An allowance for increased usage of taxis[6].
- An allowance for the deposits incurred in making use of the Motability Scheme[7].
- Increased insurance due to driving a larger vehicle or insuring carers to drive[8].
- Costs of undertaking special driving lessons[9].
- Costs of car washing / valeting.
- Costs of car servicing / maintenance[10].
- Costs of breakdow

---

[1]   See eg *Woodrup v Nicol* [1993] PIQR Q104; *Goldfinch v Scannell* [1993] PIQR Q143; and *Taylor v Weston AHA* [2003] All ER (D) 50 (Dec); *Sarwar v (1) Ali and (2) MIB* [2007] EWHC 1255 (QB); *A v Powys Local Health Board* [2007] EWHC 2996 (QB); *Noble v Owens* [2008] EWHC 359 (QB).

[2]   Automatic cars are generally a little more expensive than manual cars: see further 'Facts & Figures'. However, the court may not award the difference if the claimant may have driven an automatic car in any event: *Cannon v Cannon* [2005] EWHC 1310 (QB).

[3]   See eg *Dixon v Were* [2004] EWHC 2273 (QB).

[4]   See eg *Sarwar v (1) Ali and (2) MIB* [2007] EWHC 1255 (QB). Note that such adaptations may not have any resale value, and therefore it may be possible to claim the whole costs thrown away each time the vehicle is replaced: *Sarwar v (1) Ali and (2) MIB* [2007] EWHC 1255 (QB); *A v Powys Local Health Board* [2007] EWHC 2996 (QB).

[5]   See eg *Haines v Airedale NHS Trust* (2 May 2000, unreported), QBD; *O'Brien v Harris* (22 February 2001, unreported), QBD; *Sarwar v (1) Ali and (2) MIB* [2007] EWHC 1255 (QB); *A v Powys Local Health Board* [2007] EWHC 2996 (QB); *Noble v Owens* [2008] EWHC 359 (QB).

[6]   See eg *Dixon v Were* [2004] EWHC 2273 (QB); *Warrilow v Norfolk and Norwich Hospitals NHS Trust* [2006] EWHC 801 (QB); *Garth v (1) Grant and (2) MIB*, QBD, LTL 17/7/2007; *Huntley v Simmonds* [2009] EWHC 405 (QB).

[7]   However, note that the claimant is under no obligation to make use of the Motability Scheme: *Eagle v Chambers (No 2)* [2004] EWCA Civ 1033.

[8]   *Biesheuval v Birrell* [1999] PIQR Q40; *Sarwar v (1) Ali and (2) MIB* [2007] EWHC 1255 (QB); *A v Powys Local Health Board* [2007] EWHC 2996 (QB); *Burton v Kingsbury* [2007] EWHC 2091 (QB); *Smith v East and North Hertfordshire Hospitals NHS Trust* [2008] EWHC 2234 (QB); *Noble v Owens* [2008] EWHC 359 (QB).

[9]   *Sarwar v (1) Ali and (2) MIB* [2007] EWHC 1255 (QB).

[10]   *Noble v Owens* [2008] EWHC 359 (QB).

[11]   This is often considered to be a cost that the claimant might have incurred in any event: see eg *Biesheuval v Birrell* [1999] PIQR Q40 at Q79; *Sarwar v (1) Ali and (2) MIB* [2007] EWHC 1255 (QB) at para [71]. However, where the claimant used to undertake all his own servicing and was not a member of a breakdown service, such a claim may be recoverable: see eg *Noble v Owens* [2008] EWHC 359 (QB) at para [142]. Further, such a claim may be successful on behalf of a child before the claimant would have bought a car in any event and/or it may be reasonable to claim for the difference between the cost of blue badge premium cover, including home start and roadside relay etc, and the cost of ordinary cover without the extra benefits.

[H266]   As regards the frequency of replacing any vehicle purchased, much depends upon the claimant's annual mileage. In *Sarwar v (1) Ali and (2) MIB*[1] the defendant's occupational therapy expert accepted that it was reasonable to replace the claimant's car after 80,000 miles. Since the claimant was driving in excess of 20,000 miles per annum, a replacement period of every 4 years was held to be reasonable. However, each case is different and the following table shows that there is not much consistency between the replacement periods allowed.

Case	Judge	Type of Vehicle	Replacement Period (No of Years)
Owen v Brown [2002] EWHC 1135 (QB)	Silber J	VW Sharan	7
Taylor v Weston AHA (3 December 2003, QBD, Lawtel Document No AC0106195)	Pitchers J	Mercedes Sprinter	6
Lewis v Shrewsbury NHS Trust LTL 14/6/2007	HHJ MacDuff	VW Caravelle	5
Sarwar v (1) Ali and (2) MIB [2007] EWHC 1255 (QB)	Lloyd-Jones J	Chrysler Voyager	4
Burton v Kingsbury [2007] EWHC 2091 (QB)	Flaux J	Chrysler Voyager	6
A v Powys Local Health Board [2007] EWHC 2996 (QB)	Lloyd-Jones J	Chrysler Voyager	5
Noble v Owens [2008] EWHC 359 (QB)	Field J	Chrysler Voyager	5
Morgan v Phillips LTL 29/9/08	HHJ Seymour	Fiat Multipla	5
Smith v East and North Hertfordshire Hospitals NHS Trust [2008] EWHC 2234 (QB)	Penry-Davey J	? (7 seater vehicle)	6.5

¹   [2007] EWHC 1255 (QB).

(xii)   Future Clothing and Property

[H267]   The reasonable cost of future repairs in respect of damaged clothing and chattels will be recoverable¹. Since the repair costs are prima facie the measure of damage, these will be recoverable notwithstanding the fact that they have yet to be incurred². Save where the repair costs are significant and it might pay to obtain a number of repair estimates, it will usually be considered reasonable for the claimant to attend his or her nearest local repairers³.

¹   See further *Voaden v Champion* [2002] EWCA Civ 89.
²   *Jones v Stroud District Council* [1986] 1 WLR 1141; *Lagden v O'Connor* [2003] UKHL 64.
³   A similar argument was accepted in relation to obtaining a replacement hire vehicle in *Clark v Tull* [2002] EWCA Civ 510 (upheld in *Lagden v O'Connor* [2003] UKHL 64).

[H268]   In some cases, it may be that the claimant's injuries require him or her to wear special clothes. Alternatively, clothing may become worn more quickly, eg due to being caught on an external fixator or as a result of soiling from incontinence. In such cases, a claim may be made for the additional cost of clothing. Extra clothing may also have to be bought for the claimant where he or she gains or loses a lot of weight as a result of the injuries and their pre-injury wardrobe no longer fits. In this instance, credit must be given for the clothes that would probably have been bought in any event[1] (and, arguably, for the second-hand value of any clothes that are no longer used which could be sold). Wear and tear may be caused to carpets by reason of the claimant using a wheelchair, or items such as washing machines may have a reduced lifespan due to increased use[2]. Where the losses are thought to be significant, an appropriate expert (usually an expert in the field of accommodation, care or occupational therapy) should be asked to assess the same.

1   See eg *Owen v Brown* [2002] EWHC 1135 (QB), in which credit was given for the claimant's work clothes.
2   See eg *Owen v Brown* [2002] EWHC 1135 (QB), in which Silber J allowed £115.53 for additional washing and replacement of a washing machine; and *A v Powys Local Health Board* [2007] EWHC 2996 (QB), in which Lloyd-Jones J awarded £55 per annum for the increased costs of replacement of washing machines and tumble driers.

(xiii)   Inability to Perform Domestic Chores, Painting, Decorating, Home Maintenance and DIY etc[1]

[H269]   The case law on domestic skills[2] indicates that, where a claimant's ability to carry out housework is impaired, he or she may recover damages in respect of future work which will need to be done, based on the cost of having the work done on a commercial basis by a third party. This is treated as a pecuniary loss. It is immaterial whether the claimant actually intends to engage a housekeeper or persevere with the housekeeping on his or her own and spend the money on luxuries.

1   See further John Snell 'Damages for DIY and Gardening' [2002] JPIL, Issue 4/02.
2   *Daly v General Steam Navigation Co Ltd* [1981] 1 WLR 120. See also *Hoffman v Sofaer* [1982] 1 WLR 1350, in which a claimant recovered the cost of maintenance and decoration work which the claimant would have done himself but for the accident.

[H270]   It should be noted that it is not necessarily relevant that the claimant enjoyed performing the activities he or she can no longer perform, such as DIY and gardening. In *Samuels v Benning*[1] the judge at first instance made an award in respect of past DIY jobs in the sum of £1,500 (which had been accepted by the defendant), but awarded nothing for future loss because the loss was viewed as equating to the loss of a rewarding hobby which was adequately compensated by the award in respect of general damages for pain, suffering and loss of amenity. The Court of Appeal rejected this reasoning and made an award of £500 per annum to cover the costs of the work the claimant would otherwise have done himself but for his injuries.

1   [2002] EWCA Civ 858.

[H271]   Where future DIY, redecoration and home maintenance costs are involved, it is sensible to support the case by obtaining either a report from a care or occupational therapy expert familiar with valuing such services, or to obtain estimates from local painters/gardeners/handymen, or both. Only the labour costs may be claimed, because the claimant would have needed to buy the tools and materials had he or she done the work. Specific instructions should be taken regarding the jobs that the claimant would have done him or herself but for the injuries. Photographic evidence can be useful in this regard, eg to show a patio that the claimant may have laid or a kitchen that the claimant may have installed. In addition, activities such as painting and decorating, gutter clearance, hedge trimming, window cleaning, lawn mowing, car servicing and valeting can all add up. This is even more so where the claimant had specific skills prior to the injuries, such as being a carpenter or a garage mechanic.

[H272]   Where estimates are not obtained, the court may be willing to assess this loss, either by awarding a conventional annual sum in line with other cases or, alternatively, by taking judicial notice of the typical costs of performing such work. Examples include:

- *Larence v Osborn*[1] – in which May J allowed £750 per annum for DIY.
- *Wells v Wells*[2] – the Court of Appeal made an allowance of £1,000 per annum for DIY.
- *Assinder v Griffin*[3] – HHJ Peter Clark allowed a claim for £1,250 per annum, with a multiplier of 18 to age 65 for DIY and decorating.
- *Parkhouse v North Devon Healthcare NHS Trust*[4] – Gage J awarded the claimant £800 per annum for DIY.
- *Samuels v Benning*[5] – the Court of Appeal applied a multiplier of 10 to a multiplicand for DIY of £500 per annum.
- *Smith v McCrae*[6] – the Court of Appeal accepted the trial judge's multiplicand of £250 per annum for DIY, but applied a lower multiplier to take account of the likelihood that the claimant would have been performing less heavy work as he got older in any event.
- *Pratt v Smith*[7] – David Foskett QC allowed an award for DIY in the sum of £500 per annum to age 70.
- *Hart v Pretty*[8] – HHJ Taylor awarded £3,500 per annum for gardening and DIY for a lady with extensive needs and a large house and garden.
- *Crofts v Murton*[9] – HHJ Collender QC (sitting as a deputy judge of the High Court) allowed an award for DIY and gardening in the sum of £1,500 up to age 70 and £1,095 from age 70.
- *Smith v East and North Hertfordshire Hospitals NHS Trust*[10] – Penry-Davey J awarded £2,290 per annum from age 19 to 65.
- *Beesley v New Century Group*[11] – Hamblen J awarded £2,000 per annum to age 75 for DIY and maintenance where the deceased was a builder and decorator who had done considerable work on his own home in the past.

[1]   (7 November 1997, unreported), QBD.
[2]   [1997] 1 WLR 652.
[3]   [2001] All ER (D) 356 (May).
[4]   [2002] Lloyd's Rep Med 100.
[5]   [2002] EWCA Civ 858.
[6]   [2003] EWCA Civ 505.
[7]   (18 December 2002, unreported), QBD.
[8]   (Unreported, 18 April 2005, HHJ Taylor).
[9]   LTL 10/9/2008.

[10]   [2008] EWHC 2234 (QB).

[11]   [2008] EWHC 3033 (QB). Note that this was a Fatal Accidents Act case, but the principles are similar. See also *Fleet v Fleet* [2009] EWHC 3166 (QB), another Fatal Accidents Act case, in which Mackay J awarded £1,500 per annum for DIY, decorating and gardening.

[H273]   Occasionally, the court may allow nothing under this head if it is thought that the claimant's carers / support workers / buddies will carry out the necessary DIY and gardening work[1].

[1]   In *Noble v Owens* [2008] EWHC 359 (QB), Field J allowed nothing for DIY and gardening on top of making an allowance for buddies at 6 hours per day; however, it should be noted that the buddies were to assist the claimant carrying out various DIY and other projects.

(xiv)   Inability to Care for Others

[H274]   There is no reason in principle why the claimant cannot recover the future costs of providing care to a third party which he or she is no longer able to do him or himself as a result of the injuries[1]. In accordance with the principles in *Lowe v Guise*[2], recovery of such expenses should be permitted as long as they are reasonable. Indeed, if anything, the claimant will only receive compensation in respect of the future costs, because the past costs may be caught by the rule in *Daly v Steam Navigation Co*[3].

[1]   *Lowe v Guise* [2002] EWCA Civ 197, [2002] PIQR Q9; cf *Swain v London Ambulance Service NHS Trust* [1999] All ER (D) 260. See further Chapter F at para **[F171]**.

[2]   [2002] EWCA Civ 197.

[3]   [1981] 1 WLR 120. In particular, see *Lowe v Guise* [2002] EWCA Civ 197, [2002] PIQR Q9, per Potter LJ.

(xv)   Future Increased Household Bills

[H275]   Claims for increased household expenditure usually relate to the additional time the claimant spends at home as a result of his or her injuries, and the rise in household bills such as gas, electricity because of increased heating costs as a result of staying in more or the need to heat a larger house with additional people in it[1], and increased telephone expenses because of the need to use the telephone more, eg to make medical and therapy appointments and to keep in touch with family and friends who otherwise would have been visited regularly[2]. A claim can only be brought for the extra costs arising out of the claimant's injuries. Therefore, generally speaking, such a claim might be limited to the claimant's working life, since he or she may well have spent more time at home following his or her retirement in any event.

[1]   See eg *Dixon v Were* [2004] EWHC 2273 (QB), in which £500 per annum was awarded for additional heating costs; and *Taylor v Weston AHA* [2003] All ER (D) 50 (Dec).

[2]   See eg *Owen v Brown* [2002] EWHC 1135 (QB), in which Silber J allowed £108.12 per annum for additional telephone costs; *Dixon v Were* [2004] EWHC 2273 (QB), in which £600 per annum was awarded for additional telephone costs; and *Cannon v Cannon* [2005] EWHC 1310 (QB), in which £150 per annum was awarded for additional telephone costs.

(xvi)   Future Holidays

Recovery in principle

[H276]   In *Heil v Rankin*[1], Lord Woolf said[2]:

'... over recent years, as a result of greater sophistication in the production of claims for pecuniary loss, many items which in the past would have been considered to be appropriately regarded as general damages are now compensated for by way of special damages. It may, for example, not be possible for a claimant to go on an ordinary holiday, but possible for the claimant to go on holiday if special arrangements are made. Quite reasonably the costs of those arrangements can be included in the schedules of pecuniary loss.'

1   [2001] QB 272.
2   At [96], p 311.

[H277]   It is submitted that recovery under this head of loss, as with all other heads of pecuniary loss, is to be guided by the 100% principle, ie that the claimant should be awarded damages for additional holiday costs so as to put him back, so far as possible, as he would have been in but for the injuries[1]. Therefore, the fact that the claimant used to holiday regularly in the Caribbean prior to an accident, assuming he or she still wishes to go back there, means that the claimant ought to be entitled to claim the additional costs of holidaying there as before. To the extent that judges restrict the claimant to recovery of 'reasonable' alternative holiday costs, eg in Europe as opposed to the Caribbean, it is submitted that this is a breach of the fundamental principle and is wrong in law[2]. It would be the equivalent of not compensating a previously high earning claimant with his loss of high earnings, but with a lower, more 'reasonable' amount. Importantly, damages under this head as well as others are not to be measured objectively in accordance with the expenditure that a reasonable person might be expected to spend on holidays[3]. Whilst there may be an objective element, in the sense that the *additional* costs must be reasonable, as regards the nature and type of holiday, the idea is to restore the claimant as far as possible to the position he or she previously enjoyed. Therefore, claimants who used to enjoy expensive holidays such as skiing, going on safari or visiting friends in Australia should be entitled to recover the additional costs of pursuing similar holidays in the future, assuming it is still possible for them to enjoy such holidays notwithstanding their injuries. The size of the award when totalled up, or the impact upon the defendant of paying the award, is irrelevant[4].

1   *Livingstone v Rawyards Coal Co* (1880) 5 App Cas 25; *Lim Poh Choo v Camden and Islington Area Health Authority* [1980] AC 174; *Wells v Wells* [1999] 1 AC 345.
2   In *Noble v Owens* [2008] EWHC 359 (QB), when assessing a holiday claim for a claimant who previously enjoyed cruising in the Caribbean and sought the additional costs of such holidays in the future, Field J said at para [117]: 'In my opinion the principle that a person negligently injured by another is entitled by way of damages to be put in the same position he was before the injury does not mean that he should be able as closely as possible to take holidays of the same type and in the same location as before the accident. In my view, the law takes a broader view of the measure of recovery than that implicit in Mr Noble's claim. Thus I think that Mr Noble should be put in the position that allows him at no material additional cost to travel once a year to a warm and scenic location and stay there for a couple of weeks. Mr Noble cannot fly but he can travel by TGV to the south of Europe where the weather is warm and there is a wide choice of scenic, relaxing and pleasurable locations'.
3   In *Rialis v Mitchell* (1984) Times, 17 July, Sir Denys Buckley rejected the notion that damages should be assessed 'objectively' by reference to 'what a reasonable person would spend who did not have access to exceptional financial resources'.
4   *Lim Poh Choo v Camden and Islington Area Health Authority* [1980] AC 174; *Wells v Wells* [1999] 1 AC 345, per Lord Lloyd of Berwick at 373. In *Lim Poh Choo v Camden and Islington Area Health*

Authority [1980] AC 174, Lord Scarman said at 187e-f: 'There is no room here for considering the consequences of a high award upon the wrongdoer or those who finance him. And, if there were room for any such consideration, upon what principle, or by what criterion, is the judge to determine the extent to which he is to diminish upon this ground the compensation payable?'.

[H278] However, to be entitled to recover damages under this head, the evidence needs to show that the claimant actually wishes to go on holiday in the future. This may be difficult for some claimants with brain injury, who may be unwilling to interrupt their routines so as to enjoy a holiday[1].

[1]   *Howarth v Whittaker* [2003] Lloyd's Rep Med 235.

The multiplicand

[H279]   There are a number of elements to considering the multiplicand for future holiday expenses. The main items that ought to be considered are the claimant's additional holiday costs, any additional holiday expenses for carers / support workers, and the number of weeks' holiday allowed each year.

(1) THE CLAIMANT'S INCREASED HOLIDAY COSTS

[H280]   Increased costs that the claimant might incur include:

- Increased cost of accommodation – wheelchair accessible accommodation, with suitable groundfloor accommodation or a wheelchair accessible lift is often more centrally located and may be 4 or 5* as opposed to 2 or 3*; and the claimant may need a larger room with a wet room.
- Additional fees for upgraded seats or flights (the claimant might require more leg room when flying or travelling by coach).
- Increased vehicle hire (the claimant may no longer be able to hire a small vehicle and may need a larger vehicle to carry equipment and/or one which is wheelchair accessible).
- Increased taxis fares (the claimant may be more reliant upon taxis if his or her walking distance is limited).
- Porterage fees.
- Additional fees in respect of increased baggage allowances.
- Hire of equipment.
- Increased cost of car parking (the claimant might previously have used a long stay car park, with a bus to get to and from the airport, but now is unable to use the bus and requires more expensive parking near to the airport or valet parking).
- Increased travel insurance (some travel insurers charge higher premiums when a person suffers from a condition such as epilepsy, which increases the chance that medical treatment will be needed whilst away).

[H281]   Where the claimant used to enjoy irregular long haul flights, eg to visit friends or relatives, the additional costs can be averaged out to provide an annual loss. Where a claimant had a pre-existing holiday home, it may be reasonable to claim the costs of necessary adaptation to allow him or her to use it (although this is likely to be claimed under the accommodation). Further special equipment might be required, such as a travel commode, overlay mattress or portable hoist (although these costs are usually claimed under the aids and equipment).

(2)   INCREASED COST OF CARERS / SUPPORT WORKERS

[H282]   Often, the most expensive part of any claim for increased holiday costs will be the increased expenses related to taking away professional carers or support workers to look after the claimant whilst on holiday. The carers' pay will usually be allowed for in the care costs. However, increased expenses relating to carers or support workers might include:

- Travel costs – any train, bus, coach or flight tickets (including any transfers to and from the airport).
- Accommodation expenses.
- Any additional food, subsistence or activity costs (over and above that already allowed for in the care claim).
- Any visa requirements.
- Travel insurance.

[H283]   The extent of the additional costs will depend heavily on the number of additional carers or support workers who are required to accompany the claimant on holiday. If the claimant has extensive care needs, it may be necessary for three, four or more carers to accompany the claimant, so that each carer gets sufficient breaks. Sometimes, if the claimant is likely to be away on holiday for any extended period, it may be more economical to consider employing local agency carers, and appropriate evidence should be obtained regarding the likely cost. However, save in exceptional circumstances, the claimant is likely to wish to be cared for by his or her existing carers who are tried and tested, and any savings made in terms of hourly rate are likely to be offset by additional recruitment costs whilst away and the stress and hassle of interviewing and finding such carers as opposed to enjoying the holiday.

(3)   NUMBER OF WEEKS' HOLIDAY PER ANNUM

[H284]   Claims are often made for an annual one- or two-week holiday. Much depends upon the claimant's pre-injury holiday pattern and the amount of holiday actually taken. However, it should be noted that, under the Working Time Regulations 1998 (as amended), from 1 April 2009, workers (including part-timers and most agency and freelance workers) have had the right to 5.6 weeks' paid leave each year (28 days). Indeed, many workers are entitled to contractual leave in excess of the minimum requirement.

(4)   WEEKEND BREAKS AND SPECIAL EVENTS

[H285]   In addition to traditional annual holidays in summer, winter and at Easter, the claimant may previously have enjoyed weekend breaks, eg visiting friends and relatives, looking around new places, visiting shows/fairs or attending weddings, parties and reunions etc. Whereas, previously, the claimant could have stayed at the houses of friends and family or in relatively low-cost B&B accommodation, this may no longer be possible. Wheelchair accessible accommodation (with a wheelchair accessible lift) tends to be more readily found in larger, more centrally located hotels, which are often more expensive due to the extra facilities they offer. Further accommodation, travel and food for carers may also need to be provided. In *Noble v Owens*[1], Field J awarded £1,500 per annum for weekend breaks (3 weekends x

[1]   [2008] EWHC 359 (QB).

(5)   EVIDENCE AND PRE-TRIAL COSTS

[H286]   Care or occupational therapy experts will usually estimate the additional holiday costs that are likely to be incurred. However, courts will not always be impressed by these estimated costs[1] and, where possible, it is better to adduce factual witness evidence regarding the actual costs based upon detailed research. Often, the best guide to the assessment of future increased holiday costs will come from the costs that have already been incurred by the claimant since the accident[2]. If possible, the claimant should be encouraged to go on holiday using monies from an interim payment. Where a case manager is instructed, he or she can be helpful in terms of investigating various holiday options and detailing the likely costs compared to the holidays the claimant would otherwise have taken.

[1]   In *Cornes v Southwood* [2008] EWHC 369 (QB), HHJ Seymour refused to make any award for the costs of support workers accompanying the claimant on holiday because the claim failed 'for want of proof'.
[2]   This is what led Lloyd-Jones J to award £10,000 per annum for increased holiday costs in *Sarwar v (1) Ali and (2) MIB* [2007] EWHC 1255 (QB).

The multiplier

[H287]   Often, one of the main arguments regarding future holiday costs will be whether a full life multiplier should be applied or a reduced multiplier. Some judges have been persuaded to apply a discounted multiplier to future holiday costs, on the basis that the claimant's wish to go on holidays may reduce as he or she ages[1]. However, other judges have taken the view that a claimant's desire or need to go on holiday may not reduce at all, and a full lifetime multiplier is appropriate[2]. To this end, it is noted that over time the nature and type of holidays that the claimant takes may change, eg involving less foreign travel, but that does not mean that the claimant will not go away as much or will not incur similar increased costs of a different type[3] (indeed, many retired people travel more than they did whilst working). Furthermore, the courts have rejected arguments that the multiplier should be reduced to reflect the possibility that the claimant may have the benefit of free holidays provided by friends[4], or that the sum recoverable in respect of each holiday should be reduced because some of the care required by the claimant may be provided by members of the family, or friends, who will be paying for their own holiday[5].

[1]   In *Cornes v Southwood* [2008] EWHC 369 (QB), HHJ Seymour refused to make any award for the costs of support workers accompanying the claimant on holiday because the claim failed 'for want of proof'.
[2]   See eg *Huntley v Simmonds* [2009] EWHC 405 (QB).
[3]   In *A v Powys Local Health Board* [2007] EWHC 2996 (QB), Lloyd-Jones J said at para [150]: 'On behalf of the Defendant it was submitted that the award for additional cost of holidays should be

made on the basis of two thirds of the full life multiplier. However, I consider that the whole life multiplier should be applied. As long as A takes holidays with her parents, there is no reason why they should be required to act as her carers during the holiday. Moreover, I do not accept that people stop taking holidays later in life, although the character of the holidays may change. A will have a reasonable need for holidays for the rest of her life'.

4 *Leon Seng Tan v Bunnage* (23 July 1986, unreported), Gatehouse J.

5 *Brittain v Gardner* (1989) Times, 17 February. The damages recoverable under this sub-head will obviously include the costs of travelling and accommodation and other incidental costs, but the cost of care itself, whether professionally or free of charge, may well have been already included in the award for nursing and care expenses.

Examples of awards made

[H288] Some recent examples of awards for increased holiday costs are set out in the following table.

Case	Judge	No of Weeks	Multiplicand	Multiplier
Lynham v The Morecambe Bay Hospitals NHS Trust [2002] EWHC 823 (QB)	Garland J	4	£800 pa	Full lifetime multiplier
Taylor v Weston AHA (3 December 2003, QBD, Lawtel Document No AC0106195)	Pitchers J	?	£920 pa	Full lifetime multiplier
Dixon v Were [2004] EWHC 2273 (QB)	Gross J	3	£2,250 pa	Full lifetime multiplier
Hart v Pretty (unreported, 18 April 2005)	HHJ Taylor	?	£6,000 pa	Full lifetime multiplier
Tinsley v Sarkar [2005] EWHC 192 (QB)	Leveson J	?	£2,000 pa (agreed)	Full lifetime multiplier
Lewis v Shrewsbury NHS Trust LTL 14/6/2007	HHJ MacDuff	?	£1,250 pa	? Full lifetime multiplier
Sarwar v (1) Ali and (2) MIB [2007] EWHC 1255 (QB)	Lloyd-Jones J	1–2	£10,000 pa	Full lifetime multiplier
A v Powys Local Health Board [2007] EWHC 2996 (QB)	Lloyd-Jones J	?	£5,000 pa	Full lifetime multiplier
Noble v Owens [2008] EWHC 359 (QB)	Field J	2	£4,750 pa	Full lifetime multiplier

Morgan v Phillips LTL 29/9/08	HHJ Seymour	2	£4,000 pa	Full lifetime multiplier
Smith v East and North Hertfordshire Hospitals NHS Trust [2008] EWHC 2234 (QB)	Penry-Davey J	1–2?	£3,000 pa	Full lifetime multiplier
Huntley v Simmonds [2009] EWHC 405 (QB)	Underhill J	3	£1,500 pa	Lifetime discounted by approximately 10%

[H289] Where there are too many uncertainties regarding the likely ongoing increased annual costs of holidays to justify a conventional multiplicand/multiplier assessment, the court may decide to award a lump sum instead[1].

1   See eg *Pankhurst v (1) White and (2) MIB* [2009] EWHC 1117 (QB), in which MacDuff J awarded £160,000 for future increased holiday costs (equivalent to about £11,000 pa); and *Edwards v Martin* [2010] EWHC 570 (QB), in which Clarke J awarded a lump sum of £10,000 to reflect future additional holiday costs.

[H290] It should finally be noted that, to be entitled to recover damages for increased holiday costs, the evidence needs to show that the claimant would be willing to interrupt his or her post-injury routine so as to enjoy a holiday and is likely to benefit from the same[1]. As regards the calculation of the claim for future additional holiday costs, the courts have rejected arguments that the multiplier should be reduced to reflect the possibility that the claimant may have free holidays provided because of his disabilities.

1   *Howarth v Whittaker* [2003] Lloyd's Rep Med 235.

(xvii)   Increased Leisure Expenses

[H291] Where a claimant has to spend more on leisure pursuits and entertainment – whether because of the costs of access, eg of a former walker to the countryside, who now needs motorised transport, or because additional support or appliances are needed, eg where a paraplegic engages in waterskiing, or wheelchair rugby, or because he merely wishes to enjoy that which he did before but finds the costs greater by reason of his injuries, the annual costs will form part of the multiplicand, but an estimate may have to be made of those more active pursuits which the claimant is likely only to enjoy for a proportion of his remaining lifespan, such that either the cost is averaged across a lifetime or a separate (and lesser) multiplier adopted for the particular costs.

(xviii)   Cost of Managing the Claimant's Affairs
The Court of Protection and deputyship fees

[H292] Claimants are presumed to have capacity unless the contrary is proved[1]. In difficult cases, it will be necessary to obtain evidence from a suitably qualified expert, such as a neurologist, psychiatrist or neuropsychiatrist[2]. Where the claimant is unable to manage his or her property and affairs[3], various additional costs are likely to be incurred, particularly where the Court of Protection has become involved. Such costs will be recoverable from the defendant[4] as long as they can be shown to be reasonably related to the claimant's injuries[5]. Likewise, where it has been reasonable for the claimant to employ the services of a professional deputy, the deputy's reasonable costs will be recoverable from the defendant[6]. However, the losses recoverable under this head will be reduced, as with all other losses, by the extent of any contributory negligence[7].

[1] Mental Capacity Act 2005, s 1(2). See further *Masterman-Lister v Brutton & Co* [2002] EWCA Civ 1889.
[2] Note that a neuropsychologist is usually not an appropriate expert because they are rarely medically qualified.
[3] The test for capacity is now set out in Mental Capacity Act 2005, s 3.
[4] *Futej v Lewandowski* (1980) 124 Sol Jo 777, approved by the Court of Appeal in *Rialis v Mitchell* (1984) Times, 17 July. See further paras 2.47–2.54 of the Law Commission's Report No 262 'Damages for Personal Injury: Medical, Nursing and other Expenses; Collateral Benefits' (November 1999).
[5] See eg *Smith v Rod Jenkins* [2003] EWHC 1356 (QB), in which the claim for Court of Protection fees was disallowed because the judge did not accept that the claimant had proved that any costs incurred in connection with the Court of Protection flowed from the claimant's injuries. Indeed, the judge was far from satisfied that the claimant was incapable of managing his own affairs in accordance with the test laid down in *Masterman-Lister v Brutton & Co* [2003] PIQR P310.
[6] *Cassel v Riverside Health Authority* [1994] PIQR Q168; *Willbye v Gibbons* [2003] EWCA Civ 372; *Hodgson v Trapp* [1988] 1 FLR 69; *Crookdake v Drury* [2003] EWHC 1938 (QB), where Owen J awarded £80,000 for future costs of receivership; and *Dorrington v Lawrence* [2001] All ER (D) 145 (Nov).
[7] *Cassel v Riverside Health Authority* [1994] PIQR Q168; *Willbye v Gibbons* [2003] EWCA Civ 372.

[H293] Apart from the initial set-up costs, the major item of expense will be the annual fee. The claimant may also be entitled to recover the accountancy fees in respect of preparing the annual income and expenditure accounts which are required by the Court of Protection[1].

[1] See eg *Parry v North West Surrey Health Authority* (29 November 1999, unreported), QBD, in which £750 + VAT was recovered in respect of annual accountancy fees for providing income and expenditure accounts.

[H294] In addition to the fees of the Court of Protection and of the deputy, the claimant will be able to recover the cost of instructing his or her own solicitor in relation to the application to the Court of Protection, and in relation to the claimant's continuing dealings with the Court of Protection, but only if the incurring of those fees is found to be reasonable[1]. Alternatively, where permission is obtained from the Court of Protection to administer the claimant's damages by way of a trust, the claimant's reasonable costs in setting up and administering the trust should be recoverable as damages in the same way as Court of Protection fees. When acting for a claimant, it is sensible to adduce evidence from a solicitor specialising in professional deputyship / trusteeship work, who can advise upon the likely future costs that will be incurred[2]. Such evidence should be disclosed in good time, ie at the appropriate time for serving other witness statements of fact, or at the time of serving the schedule and supporting documents[3]. When acting for a defendant, consideration needs to be given to whether or not to challenge the evidence adduced the claimant[4].

[1]   In *Hodgson v Trapp* [1988] 1 FLR 69, Taylor J awarded past costs but not future costs under this
      head. This part of the award was not challenged on direct appeal to the House of Lords. In *Crookdake
      v Drury* [2003] EWHC 1938 (QB), Owen J awarded £80,000 for future costs of receivership. See
      further *Dorrington v Lawrence* [2001] All ER (D) 145 (Nov), Hooper J, for a detailed analysis of the
      reasonableness of an ongoing claim for professional receivership fees and solicitor's costs.

[2]   The costs of administering a claimant's award who lacks capacity can be substantial – see eg *Smith v
      East and North Hertfordshire Hospitals NHS Trust* [2008] EWHC 2234 (QB); *Huntley v Simmonds*
      [2009] EWHC 405 (QB); and *Edwards v Martin* [2010] EWHC 570 (QB).

[3]   See eg *Lewis v Shrewsbury NHS Trust* LTL 14/6/2007, where HHJ MacDuff was critical of the late
      service of evidence supporting the claim for Court of Protection costs.

[4]   See eg *Peters v East Midlands Strategic HA* [2008] EWHC 778 (QB), in which Butterfield J
      accepted the unchallenged evidence of the claimant's deputy, Mrs Miles, regarding the likely future
      costs and, in the absence of any evidence from the defendant, held that the annual sum claimed of
      £5,000 was 'reasonable, proportionate and appropriate'.

[H295]   Where the claimant's affairs are being looked after by a lay deputy as at the
date of trial or settlement, consideration needs to be given to whether or not the lay
deputy is likely to continue in the future. Often, following resolution of the claim,
the burden of administering the claimant's finances and affairs become more onerous
once the full award of damages had been received and any accommodation and/
or care regime needs to be set up. Further, sometimes whilst the claimant's partner
may have been willing to act as deputy up to the date of trial, he or she may no
longer be willing to do this in the future, and it is necessary to cost for a professional
replacement[1]. But, equally, the court might consider that, where the claimant's affairs
are being administered by a professional deputy as at the date of trial and there is a
chance that a family member will take over in the future, the multiplier for assessing
damages under this head should be discounted accordingly[2].

[1]   See eg *Crofts v Murton* LTL 10/9/2008, in which it was held that the claimant's wife would continue
      to be his lay deputy for the next four years after trial, after which it was reasonable to allow the costs
      of a professional deputy.

[2]   See eg *Lewis v Shrewsbury NHS Trust* LTL 14/6/2007, in which HHJ MacDuff reduced the
      multiplier for Court of Protection and receivership fees by one third.

[H296]   Sometimes, there may be evidence that the claimant is likely to regain
capacity following treatment. In this scenario, the court may restrict any award under
this head to a limited period of time[1].

[1]   See eg *Warrilow v Norfolk and Norwich Hospitals NHS Trust* [2006] EWHC 801 (QB), in which
      Langstaff J restricted the claim for Court of Protection costs to a period of two years after trial, after
      which the claimant should regain capacity.

[H297]   Where the claimant is competent, the position is more complicated. Whilst
it is not inconceivable that there might be circumstances in which professional
assistance to assist the claimant managing his or her affairs will be recoverable, even
though in law the claimant is considered able to manage his or her affairs, unless this
head of loss is agreed[1], judges have been more cautious about allowing the ongoing
costs of running a personal injury trust[2]. It may also be possible to claim accountancy
input to assist a competent claimant to complete an annual tax return[3] and/or to check
the annual up-rating of periodical payments which would not otherwise have been
necessary in the absence of injury, but this head of loss remains relatively contentious,
despite the fact that there appears to be no difficulty recovering similar accountancy
assistance where the claimant lacks capacity[4]. It may, however, be possible to claim

other reasonable costs to assist with the management of financial matters, such as those of a personal assistant or a premier banking service[5].

1   See eg *S v L* (settlement in May 2006, reported in PI Focus, Volume 16, Issue 5, September 2006); *Sarwar v (1) Ali and (2) MIB* [2007] EWHC 1255 (QB); and *Ure v Ure* (unreported, QBD, settlement 13.7.2007).
2   See eg *Owen v Brown* [2002] EWHC 1135 (QB) and *A v Powys Local Health Board* [2007] EWHC 2996 (QB). See further Chapter F at paras **[F203]–[F204]**.
3   See eg *Noble v Owens* [2008] EWHC 359 (QB), in which £500 pa was agreed for such assistance.
4   See eg *Parry v North West Surrey Health Authority* (29 November 1999, unreported), QBD, in which £750 + VAT was recovered in respect of annual accountancy fees for providing income and expenditure accounts.
5   See eg *O'Brien v Harris* (22 February 2001, unreported), QBD, and *A v Powys Local Health Board* [2007] EWHC 2996 (QB).

Financial advice

[H298]   One of the consequences of the decision of the House of Lords in *Wells v Wells*[1] and the Lord Chancellor setting the discount rate at 2.5% is that the claimant, who is assumed to adopt the risk-free investment of ILGS, will not be able to claim the costs of future investment advice[2]. Therefore, cases such as *Anderson v Davis*[3] (where the deputy judge, R Bell QC, treated such costs as analogous to Court of Protection fees) may no longer be good authority on this point[4].

1   [1999] 1 AC 345.
2   *Webster v Hammersmith Hospitals NHS Trust* [2002] All ER (D) 397; *Anderson v Blackpool, Wyre & Fylde Community Health Services NHS Trust* (unreported); *Page v Plymouth Hospitals NHS Trust* [2004] EWHC 1154 (QB). See further Edward Duckworth 'The End of the Line for Claims for Investment Management Charges? – *Page v Plymouth Hospitals NHS Trust* and *Eagle v Chambers*' [2004] Issue 6/2004, Quantum.
3   [1993] PIQR Q87.
4   Although it is worth noting that, in his notice entitled 'Setting the Discount Rate: Lord Chancellor's Reasons' dated 27 June 2001, the Lord Chancellor accepted that it was reasonable to expect a real claimant with a large award of damages to seek investment advice and to instruct advisers as regards particular investment objectives which the advisers needed to fulfil.

[H299]   As it was stated in *Wells*[1], the court is not concerned with how the award is actually invested. If the claimant so desires, he or she may seek the aid of a financial adviser in order to attempt to achieve a high rate of interest on the lump sum (or may opt for periodical payments, thus avoiding the need for financial advice by placing the investment risk all on to the party subject to the order). However, it is obvious that claimants cannot be compensated at a level assuming low risk investment and then claim more because they will, in fact, seek to invest in a higher risk area[2]. In *Page v Plymouth Hospitals NHS Trust*[3], Davis J had to consider the recoverability of investment advice and fund management charges. He reviewed the relevant authorities and concluded that such costs were not recoverable in principle, because they had already been taken into account by the Lord Chancellor when fixing the discount rate at the rate he had[4]. At para [52] of his judgment, he said:

'Moreover, I find it difficult to think that the Lord Chancellor, in making these observations, could or would have overlooked the attendant costs involved in seeking investment advice in setting the discount rate as he did. It is true that the Lord Chancellor does not expressly say that he had taken them into the account (and Mr Spink told me that the point seems not to have been explicitly raised in the preceding consultation process). But in my judgment it is inherent in the Lord Chancellor's reasoning: and that is of a pattern with the observations of Lord Hope and Lord Clyde in *Wells v Wells*. Thus when, in the course of his reasons, the Lord Chancellor refers to the position about investment on mixed asset portfolios, I think it likely that he was there referring to a real rate of return "comfortably" exceeding 2.5% as connoting a return net not only of tax but also of investment costs.'

This reasoning was subsequently approved by the Court of Appeal in *Eagle v Chambers (No 2)*[5], and applied to disallow the recovery of panel broker's fees incurred by a patient when the Court of Protection invested his damages (even though the claimant lacked capacity and had no choice as to how his damages were to be invested).

[1]   [1999] 1 AC 345.
[2]   *Webster v Hammersmith Hospitals NHS Trust* [2002] All ER (D) 397.
[3]   [2004] EWHC 1154 (QB), which was approved by the Court of Appeal in *Eagle v Chambers (No 2)* [2004] EWCA Civ 1033.
[4]   This was held to constitute an indirect attack on the discount rate which was blocked by cases such as *Warriner v Warriner* [2002] 1 WLR 1703 and *Cooke v United Bristol Health Care* [2003] EWCA Civ 1370.
[5]   [2004] EWCA Civ 1033.

[H300]   Although *Page v Plymouth Hospitals NHS Trust*[1] did not concern the recoverability of actual transaction charges, and arguably a distinction can be drawn between the cost of investment advice and transaction charges, the reasoning of Davis J is probably equally applicable. Therefore, the correctness of previous decisions that permitted recovery of transaction charges or broker's fees is doubtful[2].

[1]   [2004] EWHC 1154 (QB).
[2]   See further 'Are Broker's Fees Recoverable?' Quantum Issue 2, March 27 2002 and the appendixed case report of *Ejvet v Aid Pallets* (11 March 2002, unreported), Cooke J.

(xix)   Costs Resulting from Relationship Breakdown and Divorce

[H301]   The case of *Pritchard v J H Cobden Ltd*[1] may prevent recovery of losses directly attributable to divorce (and, logically, the breakdown of a similar common law marriage or civil relationship). However, there may be indirect ongoing costs which are reoverable[2]. Examples might include the costs of professional care as opposed to gratuitous care[3], increased running and maintenance costs as a result of the need to live independently[4], and increased DIY costs[5]. Where there is a risk of relationship breakdown potentially causing an increase in care costs, such a situation may justify the making of a separate 'contingency' award to reflect the chance of the additional costs being incurred[6].

[1]   [1987] 1 All ER 300, [1988] Fam 22.
[2]   See further Chapter F at paras **[F191]–[F198]**.
[3]   See eg *Tame v Professional Cycle Marketing Ltd* 19/12/2006; *Crofts v Murton* LTL 10/9/2008.
[4]   See eg *Edwards v Martin* [2010] EWHC 570 (QB), in which such claims succeeded, but the running costs were reduced by half because these would have been shared had the couple stayed together. See also *Crookdake v Drury* [2004] EWCA Civ 1370 at para [48], where the claimant recovered the costs of private accommodation and a care regime in a bungalow in close proximity to his wife's home.

5   See eg *Warrilow v Norfolk and Norwich Hospitals NHS Trust* [2006] EWHC 801 (QB).
6   See eg *Potts v Buckley* (21 December 1992, unreported), QBD, Tuckey J; *Bristow v Judd* [1993] PIQR Q117; *Stuart v Martin* [2001] All ER (D) 401 (Oct); *Finnis v Caulfield* [2002] All ER (D) 353; *Smith v LC Fashion Windows* [2009] EWHC 1532 (QB). See further Chapter A at para **[A20]**, and Chapter H at para **[H78]**.

(xx)   Future Education Costs

[H302]   Various additional education costs can arise, as referred to in Chapter F[1]. In terms of future loss, the most common example of possible increased education costs relates to legal costs incurred relating to the possible need to challenge and appeal the statement of educational needs for a catastrophically injured child. There are several different ways of dealing with this head of loss, bearing in mind that, as at the date of trial or settlement, such costs are uncertain:

- Award a lump sum to reflect the likely costs that will be incurred, giving appropriate discounts to reflect accelerated receipt and the chance that the costs will not be incurred[2].
- To agree an indemnity with the defendant that they pay for any such costs as and when they are incurred in the future (note that the court does not have the power to award such an indemnity in the absence of agreement)[3].
- To adjourn this head of loss for determination at a later point and/or give the claimant liberty to apply for a trial in relation to the costs incurred in relation to education, if agreement cannot be reached[4].

1   See para **[F205]**.
2   See eg *Haines v Airedale NHS Trust* (unreported, 2 May 2000, QBD), in which Bell J awarded £4,600 to reflect approximately half the shortfall if the claimant was required to meet the costs of the classroom assistant at one rate, rather than the rate that was being paid; and one third of the costs of paying for a one–to–one classroom assistant in case the facility provided by Bradford LEA was withdrawn.
3   See eg *Iqbal v Whipps Cross University* [2007] LS Law Medical 97.
4   See eg *Smith v East and North Hertfordshire Hospitals NHS Trust* [2008] EWHC 2234 (QB).

(xxi)   Future Increased Tax Liabilities

[H303]   Foreign claimants may find that awards for personal injuries made in this jurisdiction are taxed on receipt in their country of residence. In particular, there might not be statutory exceptions for personal injury awards for loss of earnings. In these circumstances, it is necessary to obtain expert advice regarding any additional tax liabilities, and either gross up the award to take account of the likely additional tax that will be levied, claim a separate sum for the additional tax in the schedule of loss, or seek an indemnity for the additional tax[1].

1   See eg *Horton v (1) Evans and (2) Lloyds Pharmacy Ltd* [2007] EWHC 315 (QB).

(xxii)   Future Increased Insurance

[H304]   As a result of injury, the claimant may find it more difficult and more expensive to obtain insurance such as life insurance, private healthcare insurance and travel insurance. Alternatively, the claimant may have lost a job which provided such insurance as part of a salary package but, as a result of injuries, the claimant is forced to give up his or her employment and has to purchase replacement insurance privately. The best way of proving any loss under this head is to obtain quotes regarding the additional cost of obtaining equivalent insurance cover and claim the difference[1]. Where it is uncertain whether or not such increased costs will be incurred as at the date of trial, it might be possible to adjourn this head of loss, especially if both parties agree to the adjournment

[1]   See eg *Dixon v Were* [2004] EWHC 2273 (QB); *Morgan v MOD* [2002] EWHC 2072 (QB).
[2]   See eg *A v National Blood Authority* [2001] Lloyd's Rep Med 187.

(xxiii)   Future Miscellaneous Expenses/Losses

[H305]   Any future miscellaneous expenses/losses which are reasonably related to the claimant's injuries will be recoverable in the same way as past miscellaneous expenses/losses – see further Chapter F. Therefore, if the claimant can show an ongoing need for home delivery of shopping, gym fees or dog walking, he or she should be able to recover an award in respect of the same. However, when calculating the appropriate award for future loss, the court must take into account:

- the length of time such items are likely to be reasonably necessary;
- any uncertainty regarding the future provision of such items; and
- the possibility that the claimant might have incurred the same or similar expenses/ losses in any event.

I The Claim for Lost Years

1 Introduction

[I1] We are concerned in this chapter with the situation where a defendant's tortious act reduces a living[1] claimant's life expectancy. As a result of his or her shortened life, a claimant may suffer financial losses in addition to the anxiety and distress caused by the knowledge that his or her lifespan will be diminished[2]. Take, for example, the case of an employee who develops mesothelioma as a result of his employer's failure to put in place proper safeguards with regard to his working with asbestos. In the absence of the tort, the claimant would have probably worked to a retirement age of 65 and would have had a normal life expectancy to age 85. If, as a result of the defendant's negligence, his life expectancy is reduced to age 50, he has suffered a loss of years in which he can earn a salary and thereafter receive a pension. Can a claim be made whilst the claimant is still alive for losses which will arise as a result of his loss of earnings and pension after his death, during the so-called 'lost years'? The short answer is yes: the House of Lords confirmed in *Pickett v BRE*[3] that an adult[4] claimant can recover damages for loss of financial expectations[5] during the 'lost years'[6]. We therefore set out the principles in relation to the assessment of this head of loss and attempt to provide some practical guidance regarding the calculations that need to be performed.

---

[1] Although it used to be possible to bring 'lost years' claims on behalf of an injured person's estate, such claims may no longer be brought in cases where the death occurred on or after 1 January 1983 (Administration of Justice Act 1982, s 4(2)).

[2] Historically, it used to be possible to claim an award for loss of expectation of life. However, this was removed by Administration of Justice Act 1982, s 1 for all claims whose cause of action accrued on or after 1 January 1983. By virtue of s 1(1)(b) of the 1982 Act, if the claimant's expectation of life has been reduced by the injuries, the court when assessing the appropriate award for pain and suffering must take into account any suffering which has been or is likely to be caused to the claimant by reason of his or her awareness that his or her life expectancy has been reduced.

[3] [1980] AC 136.

[4] Claims of this type for children are a good deal more contentious, as expanded upon in the following section.

[5] *Pickett v BRE* [1980] AC 136, per Lord Scarman at 170. 'Lost years' claims are therefore not just restricted to claims for loss of earnings and pension. See at paras **[I3]–[I9]**.

[6] This brought the law into line with the recommendation of the Law Commission. In particular, para 90 of the Law Commission report on Personal Injury Litigation Assessment of Damages (Law Com No 56, 1973) had stated: 'We are also of the opinion that, in line with the reasoning of the Australian High Court in *Skelton v Collins* [(1966) 115 CLR 94], the [claimant] should be entitled to compensation for other kinds of economic loss referable to the lost period, no less than he would lose his earnings capacity.'

2   The Rationale behind 'Lost Years' Claims

[I2] Logically and philosophically, there were initially some difficulties understanding how a person whose life had been shortened by a tortious act could suffer a loss recoverable in damages after their death, when he or she would not be around to make use of the claimed pecuniary benefit which would have otherwise occurred. However, in *Pickett v BRE*[1] the House of Lords held that such losses were pecuniary losses[2] which did have a genuine value to the claimant, because he or she would be deprived of the opportunity to employ the income in the way he or she desired, eg spending it upon him or herself (had he or she lived), providing for his or her dependants, or giving it away to charities[3]. The unfairness to dependants by not allowing recovery for income during the 'lost years' was noted to be the principal social reason for permitting recovery of such claims[4]. This injustice is thought to outweigh the potential problem of over-compensation to dependants who might not have benefited in the absence of the defendant's tortious act[5]. Furthermore, it reduces the phenomenon that someone who is more gravely injured such that his life expectancy is shortened receives less compensation than someone whose life expectancy is not reduced[6]. But, notwithstanding the seemingly clear statement of the law given in *Pickett*, this principle permitting recovery for lost years claims has continued to be questioned. Lord Denning in a dissenting judgment in *Croke v Wiseman*[7] made it clear he could not find for such a claim, commenting that the damages would do the injured person '… no good at all. He is dead'. Lord Phillips of Worth Matravers has also questioned the rationale in regarding lost years claims as a different species of claim from that made by dependants under the Fatal Accidents Act 1976[8]:

> 'It seems to me that this right is a poor substitute for the right of the claimant's dependants[9] to make full recovery for loss of dependency if and when the claimant dies prematurely. It would be much better if the claimant had no right to recover for such loss of earnings and the dependants' right to claim under section 1(1) of the Fatal Accidents Act 1976 subsisted despite the claimant's recovery of damages for his injury. I am not persuaded that this result could not be achieved by a purposive construction of that section.'

It should not be thought that the loss will amount to the same annual sum as it would in the case of a claimant whose injuries prevented him or her permanently from working but did not shorten his or her life expectancy. Such a 'full life' claimant receives his or her full loss of earnings, but has to pay out of them sums needed to meet his or her usual expenses of life such as food, housing and clothing etc. By definition, someone who is dead no longer has to meet the expenses of the living. The earnings loss of the claimant who expects imminent death will thus consist of his loss of earnings on a full basis, up until his probable date of death, and that loss less the sums needed to maintain him in life thereafter. The underlying principle, that of full compensation for the loss to the claimant and his or her estate, is the same: but it will be obvious that the loss per year in numerical terms is very much less for the 'lost years' than for the 'living years'. The reader thus should not assume that losses of the types described below are calculated in the same way as they are for a claimant with full life expectancy. This assessment involves some difficulty and is not without controversy[10].

¹   [1980] AC 136.

²   In holding that the loss was the claimant's own pecuniary loss, the House of Lords approved two previous Australian decisions of *Skelton v Collins* 115 CL 94 and *Pope v D. Murphy & Son Ltd* [1961] 1 QB 222.

³   See per Lord Wilberforce at 149 where he said: 'To the argument that "they are of no value because you will not be there to enjoy them" can he not reply, "yes they are: what is of value to me is not only my opportunity to spend them enjoyably, but to use such part of them as I do not need for my dependants, or for other persons or causes which I wish to support. If I cannot do this, I have been deprived of something on which a value – a present value – can be placed"?' See further per Lord Scarman at 170: 'The [claimant] has lost the earnings and the opportunity, which, while he was living, he valued, of employing them as he would have thought best. Whether a man's ambition be to build up a fortune, to provide for his family, or to spend his money upon good causes or merely a pleasurable existence, loss of the means to do so is a genuine financial loss. The logical and philosophical difficulties of compensating a man for a loss arising after his death emerge only if one treats the loss as a non-pecuniary loss – which to some extent it is. But it is also a pecuniary loss – the money would have been his to deal with as he chose, had he lived'.

⁴   Per Lord Scarman at 170.

⁵   See per Lord Scarman at 170–171.

⁶   [1982] 1 WLR 71 at 76B.

⁷   In *Pickett v BRE* [1980] AC 136, Lord Edmund-Davies referred to the following passage by Taylor J in the Australian case of *Skelton v Collins* 115 CLR 94: 'I need scarcely mention the anomaly that would arise if *Oliver v Ashman* [1962] 2 QB 210 is taken to have been correctly decided. An incapacitated [claimant] whose life expectation has not been diminished would be entitled to the full measure of the economic loss arising from his lost or diminished capacity. But an incapacitated [claimant] whose life expectancy has been diminished would not'.

⁸   *Gregg v Scott* [2005] 2 AC 176 at 182; note this has also been the long-held view of *McGregor on Damages* (15th, 16th, 17th and 18th edns). It has, however, been roundly rejected by Langstaff J in *Thompson v Arnold* [2008] PIQR P1, and appears inconsistent with *Reader v Molesworths Bright Clegg Solicitors* [2007] EWCA Civ 169, [2007] 1 WLR 1082, which is appellate authority for the contrary.

⁹   It should be noted that Lord Phillips was only looking at the position of dependants here, and did not make reference to the fact that such claims are only valid on behalf of living claimants without dependants – see further **[I3]** below, in particular note 2.

¹⁰   See paras **[I16]–[I43]** below.

[I3]   It is important to keep in mind that *Pickett* held that these losses are considered to be those of the claimant for which he has a claim in his own right¹. The recovery of claims for 'lost years' therefore applies regardless of the existence, or likelihood of existence, of dependants². Once the loss is considered to be pecuniary in nature, the law dictates that there should be full recovery of that loss and, therefore, an assessment of the extent of the loss has to be made, no matter how difficult the assessment might be³. The only qualification is that the loss must not be too remote to be measurable⁴. It is also important to remember that a claim under the Fatal Accidents Act cannot be pursued if a final award of damages has already been made prior to death, even if that claim did not include a claim for the lost years⁵. Discontinuance of the personal injury action after death will only end the estate's claim⁶, and so the dependency claim could still be pursued unless expressly abandoned on discontinuance.

¹   *Pickett v BRE* [1980] AC 136, per Lord Wilberforce at 149H–150B, Lord Salmon at 154A–C, Lord Edmund-Davies at 162C–H, and Lord Scarman at 169D–171A, essentially preferring the reasoning in *Pope v D Murphy & Son Ltd* [1961] 1 QB 222 to that in *Oliver v Ashman* [1962] 2 QB 210. In particular, the following passage by Streatfield J in *Pope* was expressly approved in *Pickett* by Lord Edmund-Davies at 161B–D and Lord Scarman at 169C–D: 'the proper approach to this question of loss of earning capacity is to compensate the [claimant], who is alive now, for what he has in fact lost. What he has lost is the prospect of earning whatever it was he did earn from his business over

the period of time that he might otherwise, apart from the accident, have reasonably expected to earn it'.

2   See *Pickett v BRE* [1980] AC 136, per Lord Wilberforce at 150A–B, Lord Salmon at 154B and Lord Scarman at 170A–C. Also see the comments of Gage LJ in *Iqbal v Whipps Cross University NHS Trust* [2007] EWCA Civ 1190 at 34–35, that *Gammel v Wilson* [1982] AC 27 made it clear that neither the age of the victim nor lack of dependants were factors that could defeat a lost years claim.

3   Per Lord Scarman at 168. See further Chapter A at para **[A26]**.

4   Per Lord Scarman at 171: 'I conclude, therefore, that damages for loss of future earnings (and future expectations) during the lost years are recoverable, where the facts are such that the loss is not too remote to be measurable'.

5   *Read v Great Eastern Railway Co* (1867–68) LR 3 QB 555 and *Thompson v Arnold* LTL 14/8/2007, (2008) PIQR P1, (2008) LS Law Medical 78.

6   *Reader & Others v Molesworths Bright Clegg Solicitors* [2007] EWCA Civ 169, [2007] 1 WLR 1082.

[I4]   In *Gammell v Wilson*[1], Lord Scarman stated[2]:

'The correct approach in law to the assessment of damages in these cases presents, my Lords, no difficulty, though the assessment itself often will. The principle must be that the damages should be fair compensation for the loss suffered by the deceased in his lifetime. The appellant in Gammell's case was disposed to argue by analogy with damages for loss of expectation of life, that, in the absence of cogent evidence of loss, the award should be a modest conventional sum. There is no room for a 'conventional' award in a case of alleged loss of earnings of the lost years. The loss is pecuniary. As such, it must be shown, on the facts found, to be at least capable of being estimated. If sufficient facts are established to enable the court to avoid the fancies of speculation, even though not enabling it to reach mathematical certainty, the court must make the best estimate it can. In civil litigation it is the balance of probabilities which matters. In the case of a young child, the lost years of earning capacity will ordinarily be so distant that assessment is mere speculation. No estimate being possible, no award – not even a 'conventional' award – should ordinarily be made. Even so, there will be exceptions: a child television star, cut short in her prime at the age of five, might have a claim: it would depend on the evidence. A teenager boy or girl, however, as in Gammell's case may well be able to show either actual employment or real prospects, in either of which situations there will be an assessable claim. In the case of a young man, already in employment (as was young Mr. Furness), one would expect to find evidence upon which a fair estimate of loss can be made. A man, well established in life, like Mr Pickett, will have no difficulty. But in all cases it is a matter of evidence and a reasonable estimate based upon it.'

1   [1982] AC 27. See also *Connolly v Camden and Islington AHA* [1981] 3 All ER 250, in which Comyn J held that there was 'insufficient evidence' to award a five-year-old boy damages for loss of earnings during the 'lost years'.

2   At 78.

[I5]   However, in the same year, in *Croke v Wiseman*[1], Griffiths LJ made the following statement[2] which suggested a claim for 'lost years' could never succeed on behalf of a child claimant with no dependants:

'If it could be shown that part of the deceased's income was available to be spent on his dependants, then a claim for that part of the income was available to cover the lost years of working life. In the case of a child, however, there are no dependants, and if a child is dead there can never be any dependants and, if the injuries are catastrophic, equally there will never be any dependants. It is the child that will be dependent. In such circumstances, it seems to me entirely right that the court should refuse to speculate whether in the future there might be dependants for the purpose of providing a fund of money for persons who will in fact never exist.'

1   [1982] 1 WLR 71.
2   At 82G.

[I6]   In 2007 in both *Massey v Tameside & Glossop Acute Services NHS Trust*[1] and *Lewis v Royal Shrewsbury Hospital NHS Trust*[2], claims for the lost years for children were disallowed, following *Croke v Wiseman*[3]. In contrast, Mrs Justice Cox in *Neale v Queen Mary's Sidcup NHS Trust*[4], when faced with a 6-year-old claimant with a life expectancy to 19, took the view that the lost years claim was no more remote than the loss of earnings claim between 18 and 19 and, notwithstanding *Croke*, she held there would be no logic in allowing one but not the other, hence she allowed both claims. Sir Roger Bell in *Iqbal v Whipps Cross University NHS Trust*[5] was of a similar mind. He considered the issues of assessment were ones that could be overcome now that the approach of the courts to the assessment of loss in personal injury cases had moved on, following the House of Lords' decision in *Wells v Wells*[6] and with the Ogden Tables now regarded as the 'starting point' rather than a check[7]. Accordingly, he allowed a lost years claim for a claimant who was aged 9 at trial. *Iqbal* then proceeded to the Court of Appeal[8], which found that the House of Lords in *Pickett* specifically did not restrict claims for the lost years to those who had dependants or might use their earnings for other purposes[9]. Gage LJ in *Iqbal* commented that[10]:

'Gammell makes quite clear, what might be said to be less clear from *Pickett*, that the age of a victim is not as a matter of principle relevant to the issue of whether or not a claim can be made for the lost years. Further, the lack of dependants cannot be a factor which defeats a claim for damages for loss of earnings in the lost years.'

Whilst he went on to find that the decision in *Croke* was inconsistent with the decisions of the House of Lords in *Pickett* and *Gammell*, the doctrine of stare decisis[11] meant that the Court of Appeal on this occasion was obliged to follow *Croke* and disallow the claim. Any error could only be corrected by the House of Lords. Permission to appeal was granted, but the defendant settled the claim before the petition could be heard.

1   [2007] EWHC 317 (QB).
2   29 January 2007 (unreported).
3   [1982] 1 WLR 71.
4   [2003] EWHC 1471 (QB).
5   [2006] EWHC 3111 (QB).
6   [1999] 1 AC 345.
7   Per Lord Lloyd of Berwick at 346b.
8   [2007] EWCA Civ 1190.
9   [1980] AC 136, per Lord Wilberforce at 150A–B, Lord Salmon at 154B and Lord Scarman at 170A–C.
10   [2006] EWHC 3111 (QB) at para 35.
11   As *Pickett* had been cited in *Croke*.

[I7]   Until another claim advances to the House of Lords, *Croke* remains binding authority against lost years claims for children. However, the comments of the Court of Appeal in *Iqbal* are sufficient encouragement to justify the continued pursuit of such claims, many of which will be settled in the claimant's favour. We tend to agree that the courts should recognise claims on behalf of children[1]. Just because a child's loss occurs further in the distance does not mean it is any less real than the loss suffered by an adult. Methods of calculation now exist which enable reasonably accurate calculations of loss, albeit that the loss in question does not arise until many years in the future[2]. Where a pecuniary loss is shown to exist, the principle of full compensation requires the court to do its best to assess the value of that loss with as much precision as possible[3]. Now that appropriate tools exist to assist courts and practitioners to perform assessments of future losses more accurately, the fact that a child's 'lost years' claim may not occur for many years is no longer a sufficient argument for preventing a court from undertaking this assessment. If, for example, a child claimant has a life expectancy reduced to the age of 30 by catastrophic injury, he may claim in principle for a loss of the earnings between adulthood at 18, and death at 30. It is difficult to understand by what principle losses beyond 30 are any more speculative and should not be recoverable for the rest of the anticipated working lifespan of the claimant.

[1]   See also Matthias Kelly QC 'The Lost Years Claim' [2000] JPIL, Issue 2–3/00; and William Norris QC and John Pickering 'Claims for Catastrophic Injury' [2004] JPIL, Issue 1/04 at 56–57.

[2]   In *Iqbal* LJ, Rimmer said at 82: 'In short, the techniques of assessment had moved on since *Pickett* and *Gammell,* and there was no reason to shy away from the assessment of the claim in respect of the lost years merely because of the extreme youth of the claimant. In principle, I would not fault that approach.'

[3]   In *Wells v Wells* [1999] 1 AC 345, Lord Steyn said at 382–383:
      'The premise of the debate was that as a matter of law a victim of a tort is entitled to be compensated as nearly as possible in full for all pecuniary losses. For present purposes this mainly means compensation for loss of earnings and medical care, both past and future. Subject to the obvious qualification that perfection in the assessment of future compensation is unattainable, the 100 per cent. principle is well established and based on high authority: *Livingstone v Rawyards Coal Co* (1880) 5 App Cas 25, 39; *Lim Poh Choo v Camden and Islington Area Health Authority* [1980] AC 174, 187E, per Lord Scarman.'

3   Types of Claim

(i)   Limited to Pecuniary Loss

[I8]   Although the House of Lords was dealing only with claims for loss of earnings in *Pickett v BRE*[1], the obiter remarks of their Lordships made it clear that claims for 'lost years' were not necessarily limited to loss of earnings, and such claims could be brought in relation to all forms of lost pecuniary benefits[2].

[1]   [1980] AC 136.

[2]   Lord Scarman used the phrase 'loss of financial expectations'. As he put it at 170: 'For myself, as at present advised (for the point does not arise for decision and has not been argued), I would allow a [claimant] to recover damages for the loss of his financial expectations during the lost years provided always the loss was not too remote'. See further *Adsett v West* [1983] QB 826; *Marley v MOD* (30 July 1984, unreported), QBD; *Phipps v Brooks Dry Cleaning Services Ltd* [1996] PIQR Q100; and *West v Versil & others* (4 March 1998, unreported), CA.

(ii)   Recognised Claims

[I9]   Common claims which have succeeded for 'lost years' include: loss of earnings[1], loss of pension[2] and loss of inheritance[3]. However, the categories of possible claims are not necessarily closed, and it may be that damages for other pecuniary benefits during the lost years will be recoverable. For example, in *Pickett v BRE*[4], Lord Scarman said that he agreed with the following passage from the Law Commission's report No 56[5]:

'There seems to be no justification in principle for discrimination between deprivation of earning capacity and deprivation of the capacity otherwise to receive economic benefits. The loss must be regarded as a loss of the [claimant]; and it is a loss caused by the tort even though it relates to monies which the injured person will not receive because of his premature death. No question of the remoteness of damage arises other than the application of the ordinary foreseeability test.'

[1]   *Pickett v BRE* [1980] AC 136; *Harris v Empress Motors Ltd* [1984] 1 WLR 212, CA; and *Phipps v Brooks Dry Cleaning Services Ltd* [1996] PIQR Q100.

[2]   *Marley v MOD* (QBD, unreported, 30 July 1984); *Phipps v Brooks Dry Cleaning Services Ltd* [1996] PIQR Q100; *West v Versil* (CA, unreported, 4 March 1998); and *Jeffrey v Cape Insulation Ltd* [1999] CLY 1536. It should be noted that a claimant's pension loss during the 'lost years' might include entitlement to a state pension. See further *Whyte v Barber* (18 February 2003, unreported), QBD, and the article by William Norris QC and John Pickering 'Claims for Catastrophic Injury' [2004] JPIL, Issue 1/04 at 56–57. In *Sarwar v (1) Ali and (2) MIB (No.2)* [2007] EWHC 1255 (Admin), the multiplier for loss of earnings was increased by 0.5 to allow for loss of pension during the lost years.

[3]   *Pickett v BRE* [1980] AC 136; *Adsett v West* [1983] QB 826.

[4]   [1980] AC 136.

[5]   At 170.

[I10]   An example of an award for a less common pecuniary benefit is provided by the first instance decision of *Kent v Wakefield Metal Traders*[1], in which the claimant recovered £10,000 representing the loss of a company car during the 'lost years'. In addition to allowing a lost years claim for a company car and petrol, in *Shanks v Swan Hunter Group PLC*[2] an allowance was made for an element of saving due to the loss of use of company accommodation.

[1]   [1990] CLY 1637.

[2]   [2007] EWHC 1807 (QB).

[I11]   However, a claim for funeral expenses was not accepted in *Watson v Cakebread Robey Ltd*[1] on the basis that the provisions in the Fatal Accidents Act 1976 and Law Reform (Miscellaneous Provisions) Act 1934 (LR(MP)A 1934) were specific to claims post death, and to allow such claims for a living claimant would open the floodgates to all claimants with impaired life expectancy advancing such a claim. It was suggested in *Watson* that, post death, the estate would have a separate cause of action in this regard under LR(MP)A 1934, s 1(2)(c), a position which ought to be expressly reserved in cases where the life expectancy is short.

[1]   [2009] EWHC 1695 (QB).

(iii)   The Chance of Income during the Lost Years

[I12]   Theoretically, as long as there is a real as opposed to a speculative chance that the claimant will have a shortened life expectancy by reason of the defendant's tortious act or omission, a claim may be made for the lost chance of enjoying a pecuniary benefit, even where, although the chance of future loss could be established, it was more likely than not that there would be no such loss (ie it would lie below a 50% chance). However, in *Gregg v Scott*[1], Lord Phillips of Worth Matravers was troubled by the unconventional nature of the lost years claim advanced[2] and, whilst he[3] suggested that he may have allowed a more restricted and conventional claim[4], he was not prepared to extend the law, on the complex facts of this clinical negligence case, to a loss of the chance of a cure and consequently achieving earnings in the lost years.

[1]   [2005] 2 AC 176.
[2]   Lord Phillips of Worth Matravers at 190: 'Awarding damages for the reduction of the prospect of a cure, when the long term result of treatment is still uncertain, is not a satisfactory exercise'.
[3]   It would appear that he was supported by Baroness Hale in this respect, at 207.
[4]   Lord Phillips of Worth Matravers at 183: 'It seems to me that this right is a poor substitute for the right of the claimant's dependants to make full recovery for loss of dependency if and when the claimant dies prematurely. It would be much better if the claimant had no right to recover for such loss of earnings and the dependants' right to claim under section 1(1) of the Fatal Accidents Act 1976 subsisted despite the claimant's recovery of damages for his injury. I am not persuaded that this result could not be achieved by a purposive construction of that section'.

(iv)   Income Earned on Investments

[I13]   In *Adsett v West*[1] a claim was rejected for income on investments during the lost years. The reason for this is that the income is not actually lost, and the claimant's dependants may still benefit from the income, assuming that adequate testamentary provision is made for them. As McCullough J put it[2]:

'By dying, a man loses the opportunity to provide for his dependants and others out of future earnings from work, but he does not lose the opportunity to provide for them out of income earned by capital of which he dies possessed. This he can achieve by suitable testamentary disposition, if this is required. The only opportunity which has gone is the opportunity to change his will – or to make one if he has not done so already ... Once dead it would no longer be open to a victim to deal as he chose with the income which accrued after his death from the capital of which he died possessed, but he could, before, choose how he wished it to be used after his death.'

[1]   [1983] QB 826.
[2]   At 842 and 845.

(v)   DIY/Decorating/Gardening

[I14]   The Court of Appeal in *Phipps v Brooks Dry Cleaning Services Ltd*[1] held that a claim cannot be made for the loss of performing unpaid services such as gardening, DIY and decorating during the 'lost years'. As Stuart-Smith LJ stated[2]:

'The [claimant] has not lost anything of value in performing work which would save him expense which he will never incur ... If it could be established that the primary victim was in the habit of selling vegetables or being paid for DIY work done for others, this would found a claim for loss of earnings. The fact that it cannot be so recovered does not justify awarding it on some other unspecified basis ... insofar as anything can be recovered in respect of inability to do DIY in the future during the lost years, this is a

loss of amenity and falls to be taken into account in general damages to a modest extent
and not on a multiplier/multiplicand basis.'

The reasoning of this judgment has been questioned[3] and it does not sit comfortably
with *Lowe v Guise*[4] in relation to loss of ability to perform gratuitous care
claims. If, post death, the widow will have to pay for someone else to perform these
services, does that not further reduce the 'available surplus' in real terms? However,
as the law stands, this decision is one of the examples of the anomalies between the
court's approach to claims for lost years when contrasted with claims for losses, either
during the claimant's lifetime, or if made after his death under the Fatal Accidents
Act.

1   *Phipps v Brooks Dry Cleaning Services Ltd* [1996] PIQR Q100.
2   [1996] PIQR Q100 at Q107.
3   Fisher & Johnson 'Reform to lost years damages in mesothelioma claims' APIL PI Focus, vol 18,
    issue 9.
4   [2002] EWCA Civ 197, [2002] PIQR Q9, as discussed further in the following section.

(vi)   Providing Gratuitous Care to Others

[I15]   To the authors' knowledge, there is no direct authority on the point, but, by
analogy with the case of *Lowe v Guise*[1], where a living claimant is providing gratuitous
services to a third party living in the same household[2] who is then forced to replace
those lost services due to the claimant's injuries, it may be possible to claim the value
of these services during any 'lost years'. Lord Justice Rix, quoting favourably from
the Pearson report[3], viewed these losses as being the claimant's[4]. He also expressed a
clear desire to ensure equal treatment of claimants, when commenting[5]:

> 'if public policy and the law's transparent recognition of the special ties of family life,
> as it has done (*Hunt v Severs*), a mechanism which enables it to value in pecuniary
> terms the gratuitous care thus provided, then there is, in my judgment, no difficulty
> in valuing in pecuniary terms the gratuitous care provided by a claimant to his or her
> family household'.

In the same way that the inability to provide these services during the claimant's
lifetime is treated as the claimant's loss to be measured in money's worth, it may be
arguable that, if the third party is forced to incur the cost of professional carers to
replace services during the 'lost years', this should also be treated as pecuniary loss to
the claimant. Of course, any damages recovered under this head (suitably discounted
for accelerated receipt) would be held on trust by the claimant for the benefit of the
third party[6]. See further at paras **[F171]–[F173]**. There is one reported settlement,
Crowther v Jones[7], of a significant lost years claim for gratuitously provided case
management services, where in the alternative it was proposed in the schedule that
this aspect be adjourned for determination post death under the Fatal Accidents Act.
It would appear that strategy overcame the defendant's opposing arguments which
were based on *Phipps*[8]. It is unfortunate that the Government did not include this
issue in their consultation on the Law of Damages in 2007, although their response
did endorse the concept that there ought to be no difference between the position of
personal injury claims brought by living claimants and claims brought by dependants
under the Fatal Accidents Act[9].

[1]   [2002] EWCA Civ 197, [2002] PIQR Q9.

[2]   Note that Rix LJ states (at para 41) that this decision was predicated on the fact of the carer and cared living in the same household, and it is uncertain whether this would be followed in a less closely connected familial scenario.

[3]   The Pearson Report 'Royal Commission on Civil Liability, and Compensation for Personal Injury', Cmnd 7054-1.

[4]   Rix LJ said at para 38: 'In my judgment [the claimant] is entitled to claim in respect of the loss of his ability to look after his brother. Since he will maintain his state allowance, he has suffered no loss so far as that allowance is itself concerned. But he has suffered a loss nevertheless because, even though his care was provided gratuitously, it can and ought as a matter of policy to be measured in money's worth. To the extent that his mother has by her own additional care mitigated the claimant's loss, it may be that the claimant would hold that recovery in trust for his mother ... a person [in the claimant's] position has suffered a real loss when he is forced by his injuries to give up the value of work which he has previously donated to his brother's care, work which although carrying no income because gratuitously given nevertheless in principle has and as a matter of policy should have a real value attached to it. The common law should not, and need not, leave the question "Am I my brother's keeper?" with the wrong answer.'

[5]   At para 27.

[6]   *Hunt v Severs* [1994] 2 AC 350.

[7]   LTLPI 22/4/09.

[8]   *Phipps v Brooks Dry Cleaning Services Ltd* [1996] PIQR Q100.

[9]   Ministry of Justice, The Law of Damages – Response to consultation CP(R) 907, 1 July 2009.

5   Principles of Assessment

(i)   General Principles

[I16]   The assessment of the claim for lost years is carried out in much the same way as any assessment for pecuniary loss. The principle of full compensation requires the claimant to be placed back into the position had he or she not been injured. Thus, the court must do its best to assess the appropriate level of financial compensation as precisely as possible[1]. The question is: what loss has the claimant suffered, calculated now, in respect of the years during which he or she would, but for the defendant's tort, have expected to be alive and now will not be? This is transparently not the same as the loss which would exist in respect of the same period of time for an injured claimant who has a full life expectancy. The award in each case depends upon the facts. There is no conventional award. As Lord Salmon said in *Pickett v BRE*[2]:

> 'Damages for the loss of earnings during the "lost years" should be assessed justly and with moderation. There can be no question of these damages being fixed at any conventional figure because damages for pecuniary loss, unlike damages for pain and suffering, can be naturally measured in money. The amount awarded will depend upon the facts of each particular case. They may vary greatly from case to case. At one end of the scale, the claim may be made on behalf of a young child or his estate. In such a case, the lost earnings are so unpredictable and speculative that only a minimal sum could properly be awarded. At the other end of the scale, the claim may be made by a man in the prime of life or, if he dies, on behalf of his estate; if he has been in good employment for years with every prospect of continuing to earn a good living until he reaches the age of retirement, after all the relevant factors have been taken into account, the damages recoverable from the defendant are likely to be substantial. The amount will, of course, vary, sometimes greatly, according to the particular facts of the case under consideration.'

¹   In *Pickett v BRE* [1980] AC 136, Lord Scarman said at 168: '… when a judge is assessing damages for pecuniary loss, the principle of full compensation can properly be applied … Though arithmetical precision is not always possible, though in estimating future pecuniary loss a judge must make certain assumptions (based upon the evidence) and certain adjustments, he is seeking to estimate a financial compensation for a financial loss. It makes sense in this context to speak of full compensation as the object of the law …'.

²   [1980] AC 136 at 153.

(ii)   Deduction for Living Expenses

[117]   It is clear that, although a claimant is entitled to recover the full extent of his or her pecuniary loss during the lost years, that loss will be less than if the claimant had a full life expectancy. For example, when considering the claim for loss of earnings and/or pension, a deduction must be made to reflect the claimant's living expenses, ie the amount that the claimant would have spent on him or herself (which would not have accrued to his or her estate/dependants in any event). In *Pickett v BRE*[1], their Lordships each expressed it slightly differently as follows:

- Lord Wilberforce[2] described the calculation as 'the amount to be recovered in respect of earnings in the "lost" years should be after deduction of an estimated sum to represent the victim's probable living expenses during those years'.
- Lord Salmon[3] described the position as follows: 'I think that in assessing those damages, there should be deducted the [claimant's] own living expenses which he would have expended during the lost years because they clearly can never constitute a part of his estate'.
- Lord Edmund-Davies[4] said: 'The only guidance I can proffer is that, in reaching their final figure, the court should make what it regards as a suitable deduction for the total sum which [the claimant] would have been likely to expend upon himself during the "lost years"'.
- Lord Scarman[5] put it as follows: 'A [claimant], or his estate, should not recover more than that which would have remained at his disposal after meeting his own living expenses'.

¹   [1980] AC 136.
²   At 151a.
³   At 154c.
⁴   At 163d.
⁵   At 171b.

(iii)   The Definition of Living Expenses

[118]   Unfortunately, in *Pickett v BRE*[1] their Lordships declined to give any assistance regarding the meaning of 'living expenses' or the detailed calculation of claims for 'lost years'. This issue was left to the lower courts to address. As Lord Wilberforce put it[2]:

'We are not called upon in this appeal to lay down any rules as to the manner in which such damages should be calculated – this must be left to the courts to work out conformably with established principles.'

¹   [1980] AC 136.
²   At 151.

[I19] In *Harris v Empress Motors*[1] the Court of Appeal grappled with the constituent ingredients of 'living expenses' for the purposes of a 'lost years' calculation. O'Connor LJ stated[2]:

> 'In my judgment three principles emerge: 1. The ingredients that go to make up "living expenses" are the same whether the victim to be young or old, single or married, with or without dependants. 2. The sum to be deducted as living expenses is the proportion of the victim's net earnings that he spends to maintain himself at the standard of life appropriate to his case. 3. Any sums expended to maintain or benefit others do not form part of the victim's living expenses and are not to be deducted from the net earnings.'

[1]   [1984] 1 WLR 212.
[2]   At 228.

6   Methods of Assessment

(i)   Two Main Methods of Assessment

[I20] Where the court is persuaded that the claim is not too remote, there are two main accepted methods of assessment for loss of earnings during the lost years: (1) applying a separate multiplier and multiplicand; and (2) adjusting the existing multiplier. The claim for loss of pension during the lost years is usually dealt with by way of its own multiplier and multiplicand, since the calculation will often be based upon different figures. As regards other types of loss, such as the lost chance of benefiting from an inheritance during the lost years, this will often have to be calculated on a one-off basis by making an appropriate discount for early receipt and uncertainty[1].

[1]   See further Chapter H at para **[H2]**.

(ii)   Separate Multiplier and Multiplicand

Calculation of the multiplier

[I21] The calculation of the appropriate multiplier is usually a relatively straightforward process involving consideration of three elements[1]:

- The appropriate starting point multiplier for the period of the loss in question.
- A discount for accelerated receipt[2].
- A discount for contingencies[3].

In *Iqbal v Whipps Cross University NHS Trust*[4], Gage LJ suggested obiter that discounts for contingencies applied to multipliers for lost years may be greater than for claims for loss of earnings during the claimant's lifetime. His comments were primarily concerned with difficulties assessing the available surplus after deduction for living expenses and keeping claims in moderation. However, as long as a separate discount is made to reflect the claimant's likely living expenses, there appears to be little reason in principle why the similar discount factors as set out in the Ogden Tables, to take account of contingencies other than mortality such as redundancy, ill-health and periods out of work etc when calculating loss of earnings claims, should not be used as a starting point for assessing damages in respect of lost years claims.

Indeed, in practice the same discount factor for contingencies other than mortality is often applied to both the claim for loss of earnings and lost years, which is perhaps unsurprising given that these discount factors represent the risks that would have applied had the claimant's working life not been reduced by the defendant's negligence[5].

1   See further Chapter F, Delayed Recurrent Expenses and Losses at paras **[H74]**–**[H76]**.
2   See further Chapter H at para **[H2]**.
3   See further Chapter A at para **[A96]**; paras **[H113]**–**[H121]**; and paras **[K199]**–**[K204]**. The discounts for contingencies other than mortality in section B of the Ogden Tables (6th edn) are derived from data for whole of working lifetimes (see paragraphs 43 and 44), and hence it would require actuarial evidence to attempt to split them for pre- and post-death periods. This is unlikely to be warranted save in exceptional cases. In *Watson v Cakebread* [2009] EWHC 1695 (QB), just one factor was derived for both pre- and post-death loss of earnings.
4   [2007] EWCA Civ 1190 at para [72].
5   See, for example, *Watson v Cakebread* [2009] EWHC 1695 (QB).

Calculation of the multiplicand

(1) Three different approaches

[I22] Historically, courts at first instance had adopted three different approaches to the assessment of claims for the 'lost years' as follows:

- Fatal Accidents Act approach – the most generous of the three approaches involves deducting the same amount from the claimant's net earnings that would be deducted from the deceased's net earnings when considering a claim for dependency under the Fatal Accidents Act 1976, ie 75% where there is a dependent wife/husband as well as dependent children; and 67% where there is a wife/husband but no dependent children[1].
- The available surplus approach – the 'lost years' claim has also been assessed by reference to such surplus as remained after deducting from the net earnings the cost of maintaining the claimant in his station in life[2].
- The savings approach[3]. Adopting this least generous approach restricted the loss of income claimed to such sums as the victim would have saved during the lost years (including mortgage repayments). Typically, this reduced the claim to 15% or so of the average claimant's income.

1   See *Benson v Biggs Wall & Co Ltd* [1982] 3 All ER 300, [1983] 1 WLR 72n; *Warwick v Jeffrey* (1983) Times, 21 June. As regards the calculation to be performed in dependency claims, see further Chapters L and M.
2   See *White v London Transport Executive* [1982] QB 489, [1982] 1 All ER 410, per Webster J.
3   *Sullivan v West Yorkshire Passenger Transport Executive* (17 December 1980, unreported), cited by McCowan J at first instance in *Harris v Empress Motors Ltd* [1982] 3 All ER 306 at 309.

(2) Harris v Empress: the available surplus

[I23] Although the Court of Appeal in *Harris v Empress Motors*[1] refused to give any firm guidance as regards the percentage deduction to be applied in each case[2], the court endorsed the available surplus method of assessment preferred by Webster J in *White v London Transport Executive*[3]. Thus, the multiplicand in respect of a claim for loss of earnings or pension during the 'lost years' is calculated by deducting the proportion of the claimant's net earnings that he or she spends to maintain him or herself at his or her station of life, not including any savings or sums spent exclusively for the maintenance or benefit of others[4]. Where the claimant's living expenses are shared with others[5], only a 'pro rata' proportion of those expenses is to be deducted. Although the appropriate percentage discount for living expenses is likely to vary from case to case, generally speaking, the discount will be higher than that applied when calculating dependency claims under the Fatal Accidents Act 1976[6]. A useful starting point, which may have to be adjusted in the light of the particular circumstances of the claimant, is 50% of the net earnings loss which a claimant of full life expectancy would incur during the 'lost years'[7].

[1]   [1984] 1 WLR 212.
[2]   O'Connor LJ stated at 231:
     'We were asked by Mr Ogden and Mr Whitby to give guidance, if we could, as to what proportion of the net earnings in the lost years should be deducted for the purpose of the Law Reform claim. Regretfully, I find it impossible to do this because so much depends upon the amount of the joint expenditure and the number of persons among whom it is to be divided; but in general, according to the circumstances it seems to me that the proportion will be greater than the percentage used for calculating the dependency under the Fatal Accidents Act.'
[3]   [1982] QB 489.
[4]   Although the Court of Appeal in *Wilson v Stag* (1986) Times, 27 November, held that no account should be taken of the deceased's expenditure on entertaining his girlfriend when calculating the deduction for living expenses from his net income, because such expenditure did not fall within the category of 'living expenses'.
[5]   O'Connor LJ stated at 229: 'Items of living expenses which are shared in practice will be found to be limited to the cost of housing, that is to say rent or mortgage interest, rates, heating electricity and gas; the cost of running a motor car, the telephone and I suppose the television licence'.
[6]   O'Connor LJ stated at 231: '... in general, according to the circumstances it seems to me that the proportion will be greater than the percentage used for calculating the dependency under the Fatal Accidents Act'.
[7]   See further *Phipps v Brooks Dry Cleaning Services Ltd* [1996] PIQR Q100.

(3)   CHALLENGE TO HARRIS V EMPRESS

[I24]   A number of leading commentators have criticised the adoption of the 'available surplus' method of calculating the multiplicand for 'lost years' claims[1]. It also appears to be inconsistent with Lord Wilberforce's comments in *Pickett*[2] that 'there is the additional merit of bringing awards under this head into line with what could be recovered under the Fatal Accidents Act'. It should be noted that, at the time the Court of Appeal reached its decision in *Harris v Empress Motors*[3], it was still possible for a lost years claim to be brought on behalf of the estate of a person killed by reason of another's tort[4]. These anomalous claims gave rise to the prospect of double recovery for dependants who might benefit from both a claim for 'lost years' on behalf of the deceased's estate as well as a dependency claim for themselves under the Fatal Accidents Act 1976 (FAA 1976)[5]. The courts were therefore keen to moderate awards for lost years, and this may have influenced the Court of Appeal to suggest a method of calculation which was less generous than the approach taken when calculating a dependency claim. Given that, in many cases, a claim by a living claimant for lost years will be less advantageous than a claim for dependency brought under the FAA 1976, interested parties may be encouraged to delay proceedings until after the victim's death. Such delay is clearly not in the interests of the parties, nor does it do credit to the civil justice system[6]. There is much to be said in policy terms for harmonising the assessment of 'lost years' claims with dependency claims. In

Shanks v Swan Hunter Group PLC[7], HHJ Higginbottom (as he was) described the difference in the court's approach to these two similar classes of case as 'curious and difficult to justify rationally'. Until this happens, lost years claims should, in the alternative, be pleaded so as to be adjourned, following a substantial interim payment[8], for determination under the Fatal Accidents Act post death[9].

[1]   See eg *McGregor on Damages* (15th, 16th, 17th and 18th edns); Matthias Kelly 'The Lost Years Claim' [2000] JPIL, Issue 2–3/00; and Richard Hermer and John Pickering 'Future Loss Multipliers – The Quantification of Damages for Catastrophic Injuries' [2002] JPIL, Issue 4/02 at 381–383.

[2]   [1980] AC 136 at 151. Cf *Phipps v Brooks Dry Cleaning Services Ltd* [1996] PIQR Q100.

[3]   [1984] 1 WLR 212.

[4]   By virtue of Administration of Justice Act 1982, s 4(2), such claims may no longer be brought in cases where the death occurred on or after 1 January 1983.

[5]   In the circumstances, cases pre-dating the coming into force of Administration of Justice Act 1982, s 4(2) may not necessarily be considered as authoritative as those cases which post-date this change in the law, such as *Phipps v Brooks Dry Cleaning Services Ltd* [1996] PIQR Q100. See further Matthias Kelly 'The Lost Years Claim' [2000] JPIL, Issue 2–3/00.

[6]   Examples of the disparity between results of these alternative claims are given in Fisher & Johnson 'Reform to lost years damages in mesothelioma claims' APIL PI Focus, vol 18, issue 9.

[7]   [2007] EWHC 1807 (QB), at para 35.

[8]   See further *Murray v Shuter* [1972] 1 Ll Rep 6, CA, and *Thompson v Arnold* LTL 14/8/2007, [2008] PIQR P1, [2008] LS Law Medical 78, per Langstaff J at para 28.

[9]   A tactic that resulted in a pre-death settlement in *Crowther v Jones* LTLPI 22/4/09, although its practical application may be limited to claims where the remaining life expectancy is predicted to be short.

[125]   However, whilst there is force in the submission that the calculation of awards for lost years should be brought into line with the calculation of dependency claims, it is by no means certain that the higher courts could be persuaded to revisit this issue. In *Pickett v BRE*[1], Lord Edmund-Davies referred to the calculation of lost years claims being 'similar' to the task of assessing claims under the Fatal Accidents Act 1976, thereby implying that there were differences between the two assessments[2]. Further, in *Phipps v Brooks Dry Cleaning Services Ltd*[3], some of the above arguments were raised by the claimant's representatives in the Court of Appeal. Dismissing the suggestion that lost years claims should be brought into line with dependency calculations under the Fatal Accidents Act 1976, Stuart-Smith LJ stated[4]:

> 'it is not surprising that there is a difference in approach to assessing dependency under the Fatal Accidents Act and the primary victim's loss whether it be on his own behalf or on behalf of his estate. The jurisprudential bases of the claims are quite separate and distinct; it is this difference that gives rise to the different approach to valuing different losses.'

[1]   [1980] AC 136.

[2]   At 163.

[3]   [1996] PIQR Q100.

[4]   At [Q105].

(iii)   An Alternative Method of Assessment: Adjustment to the Existing Multiplier

[126]   A simpler, less accurate method of assessment for earnings during the lost years claims has traditionally been adopted in cases where the loss is some distance away[1]. Instead of calculating a separate multiplier and multiplicand, a modest adjustment is made to the existing multiplier for loss of earnings[2]. For example, in *Hunt v Severs*[3] the Court of Appeal upheld the trial judge's calculation of lost years, by adding 0.5 to the existing multiplier for loss of earnings and the full multiplicand[4]. This approach has been adopted in a number of other such cases[5]. Generally speaking, when the loss is more proximate, this broad brush approach tends to find less favour[6] with modern judges, who tend to attempt to calculate each head of the claimant's losses with as much precision as possible[7]. See at paras **[I12]–[I13]**.

[1]   In *Housecroft v Burnett* [1986] 1 All ER 332, O'Connor LJ said:
'The lost years, because of their remoteness in time, are highly speculative and I think are better dealt with by some small adjustment in the multiplier, such as a factor of one, or even half, as applied to the full multiplicand, rather than trying to speculate what proportion of notional earnings 30 years hence would not form part of the [claimant's] then living expenses.'

[2]   However, more recently, some judges, such as Mrs Justice Cox in *Neale v Queen Mary's Sidcup NHS Trust* [2003] EWHC 1471 (QB) and Sir Roger Bell in *Iqbal v Whipps Cross NHS Trust* [2006] EWHC 3111 (QB) (although note, as above, that this decision was overturned by the Court of Appeal for a different reason) have gone further and applied the available surplus method even for child claimants.

[3]   [1993] QB 815, CA.

[4]   It should be noted that (1) this decision was not altered on appeal to the House of Lords; but (2) the prevailing discount rate at the time of 4.5% was much higher than the current discount rate of 2.5%, and therefore the discount for accelerated receipt was greater.

[5]   See eg *Lay v SW Surrey Health Authority* (26 June 1989, unreported); *Almond v Leeds HA* [1990] 1 Med LR 370; *O'Donnell v South Beds HA* [1990] CLY 1578; *Biesheuval v Birrell* [1999] PIQR Q40, in which Eady J added 0.5 to the loss of earnings multiplier; and *Brown v King's Lynn and Wisbech NHS Hospitals Trust* (20 December 2000, unreported), QBD, in which Gage J added 2 to the multiplier for loss of earnings without any deduction to take account of the 'available surplus'. In *Sarwar v (1) Ali and (2) MIB* [2007] EWHC 1255 (Admin), the multiplier for loss of earnings was increased by 0.5 to allow for loss of pension during the lost years. See further William Norris QC and John Pickering 'Claims for Catastrophic Injury' [2004] JPIL, Issue 1/04 at 56–57.

[6]   Given the greater reliance on actuarial tables following the House of Lords' decision in *Wells v Wells* [1999] 1 AC 345.

[7]   See eg *Phipps v Brooks Dry Cleaning Services Ltd* [1996] PIQR Q100; *Warren v Northern General Hospital NHS Trust (No 2)* [2000] 1 WLR 1404; *Jeffrey v Cape Insulation Ltd* [1999] CLY 1536; *Eagle v Chambers* [2003] EWHC 3135 (QB); and *Neale v Queen Mary's Sidcup NHS Trust* [2003] EWHC 1471 (QB).

7   The Calculation

(i)   Does it Matter Whether the Victim is Young or Old?

[I27]   Apart from the scenario in which the claimant is a young child and, arguably, the claim for 'lost years' is too speculative to be assessed[1], the age of the claimant is irrelevant to the principle of the calculation of available surplus following deduction of living expenses. As O'Connor LJ said in *Harris v Empress Motors*[2]:

'The ingredients that go to make up "living expenses" are the same whether the victim be young or old, single or married, with or without dependants.'

[1]   See at paras **[I4]–[I6]**.

[2]   [1984] 1 WLR 212 at 228.

[I28]   However, the practical application of those principles has in the past often seen greater deductions for young claimants without dependants. An example of an assessment of a lost years claim for a young victim that now appears overly harsh is that of *Lolley v Keylock*[1]. The deceased, aged 21 at death, was a junior technician in the Royal Air Force. The estate recovered £6,310 in respect of 'lost years' – calculated on the basis of the surplus being 12% of net income. On appeal, Watkins LJ held that 12% was not demonstrably wrong, taking into account that the deceased was living up to the limit of his pay; the award was possibly on the generous side. A more modern and equitable approach to a young claimant was adopted in *Eagle v Chambers*[2], in which Cooke J awarded the claimant, who was aged 17 at the time of the accident and over 30 at the time of assessment, £11,352 (£9,082 per annum × a multiplier of 2.5 × 0.50 deduction for living expenses) for loss of earnings during the lost years; and £13,982 (£4,237 per annum × a multiplier of 6.6 × 0.50 deduction for living expenses) for loss of pension during the lost years. Mrs Justice Cox in *Neale v Queen Mary's Sidcup NHS Trust*[3] was not minded to apply more the 0.50 deduction, which is common for adults, to the less common scenario of a 6-year-old child claimant[4]. In *Iqbal v Whipps Cross University Hospital*[5], although the assessment of the lost years claim did not arise for consideration since the claim was rejected, Gage LJ said he would have allowed the cross appeal but, at para 72, suggested there were a number of reasons why lost years claims on behalf of children may be discounted more heavily than claims for loss of earnings. Had the claim succeeded, he would have allowed the cross appeal, permitting an agreed discount of 10% for contingencies under the Ogden Tables (6th edn), as opposed to the 20% which had been applied by the trial judge.

[1]   (1984) 128 Sol Jo 471, CA.
[2]   [2003] EWHC 3135 (QB). Note that, whilst this case was appealed to the Court of Appeal at [2004] EWCA Civ 1033, the calculation of this item of loss does not appear to have been challenged by either party.
[3]   [2003] EWHC 1471 (QB).
[4]   This decision preceded *Iqbal* in the Court of Appeal, and so it is unlikely to be followed on the wider point of principle concerning lost years claims for children, pending a case proceeding to the House of Lords.
[5]   [2007] EWCA Civ 1190.

(ii)   Is the Income and Standard of Living of the Victim Relevant?

[I29]   Yes: 'the sum to be deducted as living expenses is the proportion of the victim's net earnings that he spends to maintain himself at the standard of life appropriate to his case'[1]. The expenses of living attributable to the claimant alone will occupy a larger proportion of his earnings when the claimant's income is low (eg where the claimant is living on a state pension), and a smaller proportion where significant living expenses, such as housing or utility bills, are shared with another, eg where expenses are shared with a spouse.

[1]   *Harris v Empress Motors Ltd* [1984] 1 WLR 212, CA, per O'Connor LJ at 228.

(iii)   What is Not Included in Living Expenses?

[I30]   In *Harris v Empress Motors Ltd*[1], O'Connor LJ made it clear that any expenditure spent on the exclusive maintenance or benefit of others does not form part of a claimant's living expenses. An additional dimension is added by *Wilson* *v Stag*[2], where the Court of Appeal held that, in assessing the damages recoverable by the estate for loss of future earnings, the fact that the deceased spent all his disposable income on entertaining his girlfriend was to be disregarded in determining the estimated living expenses to be deducted from his future earnings, because such expenditure did not fall within the category of 'living expenses'.

---

1 [1984] 1 WLR 212, CA. O'Connor LJ stated at 229: 'I think one can say in relation to a man's net earnings that any proportion thereof that he saves or spends exclusively for the maintenance or benefit of others does not form part of his living expenses'.

2 (1986) Times, 27 November.

(iv) What are 'Living Expenses'?

[I31] In *Harris v Empress Motors*, O'Connor LJ defined living expenses as 'the proportion of the victim's net earnings that he spends to maintain himself at the standard of life appropriate to his case'[1]. He went on to say that any proportion of the claimant's net earnings which are spent exclusively upon him or herself count as living expenses[2]. Thus, in *Cole v Crown Poultry Packers*[3], living expenses were assessed at 25% where the deceased cohabited as a stable family unit with two adult children, and spent most of his time at home. More recently, in *Shanks v Swan Hunter Group PLC*[4], a 40% deduction was made for a claimant with a wife and dependent grandchildren.

---

1 [1984] 1 WLR 212 at 228.

2 At 229.

3 (1983) 133 NLJ 400.

4 [2007] EWHC 1807 (QB).

(v) How is the Problem of Shared Expenses Tackled?

What are shared expenses?

[I32] 'The items of living expenses which are shared in practice will be found to be limited to the cost of housing, that is to say rent or mortgage interest, rates, heating, electricity and gas, the cost of running a motor car, television and I suppose the television licence'[1].

---

1 *Harris v Empress Motors Ltd* [1984] 1 WLR 212, per O'Connor LJ at 229, CA.

How are shared expenses apportioned?

[I33] 'In cases where there is a proportion of the earnings expended on what may conveniently be called shared living expenses, a pro rata part of that proportion should be allocated for deduction'[1].

---

1 *Harris v Empress Motors Ltd* [1984] 1 WLR 212, per O'Connor LJ at 229, CA.

(vi) How are the Words 'Pro Rata' to be Applied in Practice?

[I34] In *Harris v Empress Motors Ltd*[1], O'Connor LJ said[2]:

'It seems to me that as the numbers of persons provided for out of the victim's net earnings increase, so must the amounts to be allocated as being his share of those items fall. Therefore in the present case, where the household consisted of four persons, a quarter of the cost of the joint items should be deducted. In practice this may result in the total deduction not being very much greater than that made for the purpose of the Fatal Accidents Act.'

1   [1984] 1 WLR 212, CA.
2   At 249.

8   Practical Considerations

(i)   Married Person with No Children – Application of Harris

[I35]   In the case of a married man with no children, the following calculation can be advanced for an average earner. As in a fatal accident claim, one may take 33% as the percentage of the net income which represents what the *Pickett* claimant would have spent exclusively on him or herself during the lost years. Since, on such a basis, the joint living expenses will also be 33%, the claimant's share thereof (where there are only husband and wife in the family) is 33% divided by 2 = 16.5%. Thus, the deduction for the claimant's living expenses may be taken as 33% + 16.5% = (to all intents and purposes) 50%[1]. Naturally, if the claimant's income or expenditure varied significantly from the average then, providing the evidence proves the point, these figures should be adjusted to fit the facts of the case.

1   See eg *Phipps v Brooks Dry Cleaning Services Ltd* [1996] PIQR Q100, in which the trial judge held that the claimant (who was aged 51 at the date of trial and recently married to his second wife) would split his net earnings equally between himself and his wife.

(ii)   Married Person with Children – Application of Harris

[I36]   In the event that the claimant is married with, say, three children, the calculation may be undertaken as follows. The claimant's own exclusive living expenses during the lost years are to be taken as 25% (as in a fatal accident case). The amount of joint living expenses (mortgage, heating etc) would in a fatal case be 25% (the division approximates to one quarter for 'him', one quarter for 'her' one quarter for 'the children' and one quarter for 'them all'). If this same approach is taken to a Law Reform Act or "lost years" claim, the claimant's share of the joint 'them all' expenses is 25% divided by 5 = 5%. Thus, the total living expenses attributable to the claimant are 25% + 5% = 30%. However, in *Crofts v Murton*[1], HHJ Collender QC (sitting as a judge of the High Court) applied a discount of 40% for living expenses for a 48-year-old married man with two children still at home. The 'divide by 5' example is open to criticism, since it may assume that the cost of expenditure purely on the married claimant alone is actually one fifth of the joint expenses. This may be unrealistic: has it actually decreased in amount since the claimant had one child (divide by 3), or two children (by 4) such that, from the moment of birth, the claimant is to be taken to spend less on himself alone? A court may thus be inclined to find that the amount of money attributable purely to the claimant himself may be less than a calculation such as that done above may suggest. However, some allowance will still have to be made for the fact that such a claimant will be paying expenses which are greater than they would have been had he had fewer children, or none – such as paying for a larger home, higher costs for holidays and travel, increased weekly shopping bills etc. Having children necessarily reduces the amount he can (and, therefore, should be taken to) spend on himself. The difficult question is putting a precise figure on the percentage to be attributed to him. Perhaps the key to the likely answer is that the court may focus not so much on a percentage to be attributed to the claimant's expenditure purely on himself, but upon the likely level of the money left over which he does not require to spend simply to live reasonably but has available for uses of his choice.

[1]   LTL 10.9.08.

(iii)   Young Married Person – Application of Harris

[137]   In the event of a young married couple, where the claimant's life is curtailed, the calculation may take a hybrid form – namely, living expenses on the basis of there being only husband and wife for x years, and living expenses on the basis of there also being children for y years thereafter[1].

[1]   Although cf the cases involving Fatal Accident Act claims where, if the dependant is not already pregnant at the time of the deceased's death, the court will not take account of the dependant's intended greater reliance upon the deceased's earnings, since it must assess the dependency as at the time of death: *Higgs v Drinkwater* (1956) CA No 129a; followed in *Malone v Rowan* [1984] 3 All ER 402. Arguably, however, the position in relation to a 'lost years' claim is different to a Fatal Accidents Act claim especially where, although there has been a reduction in the claimant's life expectancy, there is still a chance of him or her conceiving children in the future. In the circumstances, every case must be determined on its own facts.

(iv)   Unmarried Person – Application of Harris

[138]   In the case of a young unmarried person, the court is faced with imponderables, in that allowance has to be made for the contingency that he or she may never marry, or never save or never support anyone. Such factors may justify a high percentage deduction in respect of living expenses, postulated in *White v London Transport Executive*[1] and *Gammell v Wilson*[2]. In such circumstances, the decision of Webster J in the *White* case appears to meet the approval of the Court of Appeal in *Harris* (even if his approach was via a different route). That case is authority for the proposition that a young man living at home with his parents may be regarded as having living expenses of 67% of his net earnings but that, upon his leaving home, and getting a flat, such living expenses rise to 75%[3]. However, in a number of recent cases, a figure closer to 50% has been taken as the appropriate deduction for living expenses in respect of an unmarried person[4]. This may be a reflection of the courts today taking a more detailed and generous approach to the assessment of these claims[5], or alternatively the fact that, when considering the position of a young unmarried person, some account has to be taken of the chances that, in the absence of his or her injuries, the claimant would have married and/or had children (thus reducing the proportion of net earnings spent exclusively on him or herself), or simply proportionally saved more as he aged and his earnings increased.

1   [1982] QB 489, [1982] 1 All ER 410.

2   [1982] AC 27, [1981] 1 All ER 578, HL.

3   See also *Smith v Cape* [1991] CLY 1409, in which the claimant lived alone, and the trial judge found that he would have spent 80% of his pension on his own living expenses. Further, in *Lolley v Keylock* (1984) 128 Sol Jo 471 the Court of Appeal held that Talbot J was not demonstrably wrong in adopting 12% as the available surplus after date of death where the deceased (aged 21 at death) was living up to the limit of his pay.

4   See *Warren v Northern General Hospital NHS Trust* [2000] 1 WLR 1404, in which Robert Smith QC deducted 60% in respect of living expenses; and both *Eagle v Chambers* [2003] EWHC 3135 (QB) and *Neale v Queen Mary's Sidcup NHS Trust* [2003] EWHC 1471(QB), in which Cooke J and Cox J each deducted 50% for living expenses.

5   See further at para **[I22]**.

(v)   Claimants on Low Income

[I39]   The lower a claimant's income, the greater the proportion of it which is likely to be spent on the expenses of keeping alive. Conversely, the higher the claimant's income, the more likely it will be that the expenses of living are a smaller proportion. In the former case, therefore, the percentage of the earnings (and, in particular, pension loss) which will be recovered is lower than the latter.

(vi)   Investigations into Expenditure

[I40]   When assessing individual and shared living expenses, assistance may be derived from the chart set out at para **[I45]**. It may be that evidence can be obtained to support an argument for a different percentage discount than would usually be applied in light of the claimant's level of income and family situation. In particular, where the evidence shows that the claimant was either saving significant sums or spending money exclusively on others, the applicable deduction for 'living expenses' may be less than it would have been otherwise. In practice, situations in which a more detailed examination of the claimant's expenditure might be required involve claimants with high or low earnings, or those with numerous dependants. The court is likely to require a reasonably high degree of proof, in the form of witness statements, bank statements, credit card statements, receipts/invoices etc, before being persuaded to depart from the standard percentage discounts for living expenses indicated by the case law[1].

1   Such an approach has been adopted successfully in a number of fatal accident claims where the deceased was a high earner: *Farmer v Rolls Royce Industrial Power* LTL 27/5/2003 and *Williams v Welsh Ambulance Services NHS Trust and Anr* [2008] EWCA Civ 81. See further Chapter L.

9   Worked Examples

(i)   Example I

[I41]   The claimant is a married man with two children. He was aged 35 at the date of the defendant's negligence and is aged 40 at the date of trial. He has been unable to work post accident. He had a degree and was employed at the date of the accident. His life expectancy has been reduced from normal to 50 by reason of the negligence. At the date of trial, but for his injuries, he would have been earning £40,000 net per annum and would have been entitled to a net pension of £10,000 per annum from his expected retirement age of 65[1].

[1]   See further Chapter H regarding claims for later retirement ages.

Loss of earnings during the lost years

[I42]   Starting with the loss of earnings to 50, the multiplier is 8.78 (Table 3 of the Ogden Tables). The multiplier must be discounted for contingencies other than mortality by applying a discount of 0.88 (see further Tables A–D set out in section B of the explanatory notes to the Ogden Tables). Therefore, this multiplier reduces to 7.73; with a multiplicand of £40,000, the loss prior to death is £309,200. The claim for the lost years is then derived by taking the multiplier to age 65 (Table 9) of 18.01 × 0.88 = 15.85, then deducting the preceding multiplier of 7.73 = 8.12. On the basis of *Harris v Empress Motors Ltd*[1], the appropriate discount in this case is likely to be 25% plus 6.25% (25% divided by 4) = 31.25%[2]. Therefore, the multiplicand is £40,000 × 68.75% = £27,500. Therefore, the lost years claim is £27,500 × 8.12 = £223,300.

[1]   [1984] 1 WLR 212, CA.
[2]   Although it may be argued by the defendant that, by the time the claimant's loss occurs, one or both of his children may have left home and, therefore, the deduction should be greater, ie in the region of 50%. Likewise, the claimant may seek to argue that the deduction should be brought into line with dependency claims, resulting in a discount of only 25% whilst the children are dependent and 33% thereafter.

Loss of pension during the lost years

[I43]   The appropriate starting point pension loss multiplier for a 40-year-old man commencing at age 65[1] is 7.78 (Table 21). No additional discount needs to be applied for accelerated receipt, since this has already been taken into account by using the appropriate Ogden table[2]. Applying, say, a 10% discount for contingencies other than mortality[3] gives a final multiplier of 7. Applying a 50% discount for living expenses, on the assumption that his children have by then left home, means the multiplicand is £5,834. Therefore, the loss under this head is £5,834 × 7 = £40,838[4].

[1]   See further Chapter H regarding claims for later retirement ages.
[2]   See *Phipps v Brooks Dry Cleaning Services Ltd* [1996] PIQR Q100.
[3]   See explanatory notes 3 and 30 to the Ogden Tables. See also Chapter H regarding pension loss.
[4]   The modest figures derived by this example demonstrate why a small adjustment to the loss of earnings multiplier can achieve a similar result. See further at para **[I26]**.

(ii)   Example 2

[I44]   The claimant is an unmarried female aged 20 at the date of trial, who was working pre-accident. Her life expectancy has been reduced from normal to age 60 by reason of the defendant's negligence. But for her injuries, the claimant would have continued earning an average of £30,000 net per annum, up to an expected retirement age of 70. The loss of earnings multiplier to age 60 is 25.18 (Table 18). The multiplier must be discounted for contingencies other than mortality by applying a discount of

0.82[1]. Therefore, the multiplier reduces to 20.65. With a multiplicand of £30,000, the loss prior to death is £619,500. The claim for the lost years is then derived by taking the multiplier to age 70 (Table 12) of 28.26 × 0.82 = 23.17, then deducting the preceding multiplier of 20.65 = 2.52. Allowing 50% for expenses, on the basis that it is impossible to accurately predict how many dependants the claimant will have, results in a lost years claim of £30,000 × 50% × 2.52 = £37,800. Due to her youth, it is impossible to predict what pension provision the claimant would have had, but the multiplier should be increased by a small increment, in this example rounding it up to a multiplier of 3 (adding nearly 0.5, to take account of the fact that, by reason of her injuries, the claimant has a reduced life expectancy. This adds a further £7,200 to the lost years claim.

[1]   Assuming she was employed at the date of the accident and had a GE-A educational background, applying Table C. However, see also explanatory notes 43 and 44 to the Ogden Tables, as the statistics behind these tables are based on a state female retirement age of 60.

Chart for the Assistance of Calculating Living Expenses

[I45]

I	Items which benefited the family as a whole:	
(i)	Cost of maintaining family home (assessed on annual basis):	
	(a) Mortgage/rent	£
	(b) General rates/water rates	£
	(c) Gas	£
	(d) Electricity	£
	(e) Coal	£
	(f) TV licence/rental/HP	£
	(g) Decorations	£
	(h) Repairs	£
	(i) Gardener	£
	(j) Window cleaning	£
	(k) Central heating maintenance	£
	(l) Furniture	£
	(m) Carpets etc	£
(ii)	Annual cost of maintaining family motor car:	
	(a) Petrol	£
	(b) Motor insurance	£
	(c) Vehicle excise licence	£
	(d) Motor repairs	£
	(e) Annual capital costs of vehicle	£

2	Cost of benefiting the spouse, the claimant and the children as individuals (assuming 2 children):				
Items of expense:		*Spouse*	*Claimant*	*Child (1)*	*Child (2) etc*
1	Holidays				
2	Clothing				
3	School fees				
4	Insurances				
5	Gifts				
6	Tobacco				
7	Food				
8	Entertaining and dining out				
9	Public Transport				
10	Newspapers				
11	Hairdressing				
12	School meals				
13	Private lessons (music etc)				
14	Incidentals				
15	Second motor vehicle etc (adopting the items of cost recited under (ii) above)				

J   Recovery of State and Collateral Benefits

1   Introduction

[J1] Following an accident or incident resulting in a personal injury claim, it is more than likely that the claimant will receive some form of benefit whether from the state, his or her employer, an insurer or gratuitously from a third party. It is often the case that the injury leads to time off work, when the claimant would be entitled to benefits such as sick pay, disability benefits, incapacity benefits and other income-related support. Further, if a person requires special care, then an attendance allowance etc might be claimed. If a person is disabled, either permanently or for a specified period, then mobility allowance or disability living allowance may be an option. However, a claimant will be entitled to claim equivalent losses as part of the personal injury claim. To take the obvious example, a claimant who, owing to his injuries, has to take time off work will be entitled to claim loss of earnings. Therefore, unless credit is given for the benefits received, there is a danger of double recovery. In this section we look at the principles relating to the recoupment of statutory benefits, and the deductions that are made to take account of other collateral benefits received.

2   Recovery of State Benefits

(i)   Background

[J2] The Social Security Act 1989 set up the Compensation Recovery Unit (CRU). This body calculates the amount of benefits claimed in consequence of an injury. Where a payment is made in respect of any accident, injury or disease, the court must consider which of these benefits are recoupable, ie can be offset against the claims made. The system of recoupment is governed by the Social Security (Recovery of Benefits) Act 1997[1]. Hale LJ (as she then was) in *Lowther v Chatwin*[2] described the aims of this legislation as follows:

> 'The scheme of the 1997 Act serves two objectives. The first is to ensure that a defendant who is liable to compensate a claimant for an accident, injury or disease reimburses the state for certain state benefits paid to the claimant in respect of that accident, injury or disease. The second is to ensure that the benefits recouped from the defendant are offset against the sums received by the claimant so that the claimant does not obtain a double recovery. But there are important qualifications to that second principle. Under the previous scheme, first enacted in the Social Security Act 1989, the compensator was entitled to deduct the sums paid to the state from the total award of damages. If those sums were more than the sums awarded in special damages, the victim might lose some

of her general damages as well. Under the 1997 Act, the sums paid to the state to recoup certain benefits can only be deducted from the equivalent head of damages awarded. The object is to "ring fence" the general damages for pain, suffering, loss of amenity, or for loss of congenial employment, or the like, while enabling the state to recoup its expenditure on benefits paid in respect of loss of earnings, the cost of care and loss of mobility. Another important qualification is that the state can only recover benefits paid, and accordingly such benefits can only be deducted from the damages, for the "relevant period", which is a maximum of five years.'

[1]   The Act was brought fully into force on 6 October 1997 by SI 1997/2085 and applies to all claims not settled as of that date. Therefore, all existing claims are covered. See also the Social Security (Recovery of Benefits) Regulations 1997, SI 1997/2205.

[2]   [2003] EWCA Civ 729 at [3].

(ii)   Applicability

[J3]   The Social Security (Recovery of Benefits) Act 1997 applies where:

(a)   a person makes a payment to any other person in consequence of an accident, injury or disease suffered by the other; and

(b)   any listed benefits have been, or are likely to be, paid to the other during the relevant period in respect of the accident, injury or disease.

[J4]   The reference to a payment in consequence of any accident, injury or disease is to a payment made:

(a)   by or on behalf of a person who is, or is alleged to be, liable to any extent in respect of the accident, injury or disease; or

(b)   in pursuance of a compensation scheme for motor accidents;

but does not include a payment mentioned in Sch 1, Pt I (Exempted payments).

[J5]   The Act applies to all cases where a payment is made by one party because of an accident etc, and where the person receiving the payment has been paid a specified benefit[1] as a consequence of the accident during the relevant period[2].

[1]   See Social Security (Recovery of Benefits) Act 1997, Sch 2.

[2]   See at para **[J7]**.

[J6]   It should be noted that s 1(1)(b) of the 1997 Act indicates that it is not just benefits that *have* been paid, but those *likely* to be paid for the relevant period. Therefore, difficulties could arise in the possible situation where a benefits decision has rejected a claim but an appeal is lodged. If the appeal is yet to be concluded when a compensatory payment is made, what would be the standing of the potential benefit payments? If the appeal is ultimately successful, the payments would be paid in relation to the relevant period, and therefore should have been deducted. However, at the time of the compensation payment, the benefits cannot be said to be 'likely to be paid'.

(iii)   The Relevant Period

[J7]   By s 3(1) of the 1997 Act, 'the relevant period' has the following meanings:

(i) Subject to (iii) below, if it is a case of accident or injury, the relevant period is a period of five years immediately following the day upon which the accident or injury in question occurred.

(ii) Subject to (iii) below, if it is a case of disease, the relevant period is the period of five years beginning with the date on which the claimant first claims a listed benefit in consequence of the disease.

(iii) If at any time before the end of the period referred to in (i) or (ii):

    (a) a person makes a compensation payment in final discharge of any claim made by the claimant arising out of the accident, injury or disease; or

    (b) an agreement is made under which an earlier compensation payment is treated as having been made in final discharge of any such claim,

the relevant period ends at that time.

[J8] The relevant period for benefit recovery is therefore a maximum of five years. Usually, this time period will begin on the day of the accident or injury in question. However, it is more difficult with a disease. In such a case, the relevant period begins only when the victim claims a specified benefit. The relevant period can be less than five years if the claim is fully discharged by way of compensation payment etc. In such a case, the relevant period ends on the date of the payment of compensation. As the calculation of deductible and recoupable benefit concerns the relevant period only (see ss 1 and 8 of the Social Security (Recovery of Benefits) Act 1997), then if a compensation payment is made prior to the five-year period the claimant gains any further benefits. They are not taken into account in assessing the damages. The same applies to any listed benefits which are received after the relevant period. Ordinarily, such benefits would fall to be taken into account by reason of the common law principles expressed in *Hodgson v Trapp*[1]. However, by reason of s 17 of the 1997 Act[2], any listed benefits paid after the relevant period are to be disregarded when assessing the claimant's award of damages[3].

[1]   [1989] AC 807, [1988] 3 All ER 870.

[2]   Social Security (Recovery of Benefits) Act 1997, s 17 reads as follows: 'In assessing damages in respect of any accident, injury or disease, the amount of any listed benefits paid or likely to be paid is to be disregarded'.

[3]   See further *Eagle v Chambers (No 2)* [2004] EWCA Civ 1033 regarding the application of this provision.

(iv) Certificate of Recoverable Benefits

[J9] Before making any payment for compensation, a defendant is under a duty to apply to the Secretary of State for a certificate of recoverable benefits[1], commonly referred to as a 'CRU certificate'. Once the certificate is received, it remains in force for the period specified within it. The defendant may apply for further certificates or, if it runs out, the Secretary of State may issue a new certificate without application. More detail of each recoverable benefit is necessary because of the way recoupment works[2].

[1]   Social Security (Recovery of Benefits) Act 1997, s 4(1). Also see Social Security (Recovery of Benefits) Regulations 1997, SI 1997/2205, reg 8 and para 10 of the PD to CPR, Pt 36.

[2]   See further at paras **[J13]–[J18]**.

(v)   Liability of the Compensator

[J10]   A person who makes a compensation payment in any case is liable after 14 days to pay to the Secretary of State an amount equal to the total amount of the recoverable benefits. This liability arises immediately before the compensation payment or, if there is more than one payment, before the first of them is made[1].

[1]   Social Security (Recovery of Benefits) Act 1997, s 6.

[J11]   The effect of s 6 constituted a major change in the law. It has considerable consequences for defendants, in that the person paying the compensation is liable to pay the whole of the amount deemed recoverable on the CRU certificate. This is a surprising burden in some cases, as liability may extend beyond the figure of compensation, and so more than the compensation figure may need to be paid. It also puts the burden on the defendant to argue that any benefits on the certificate are not relevant.

[J12]   As Hale LJ explained in *Lowther v Chatwin*[1]:

> 'It will thus be apparent that there are circumstances in which the operation of the Act means that a claimant will receive, or a defendant will have to pay, more than the court has awarded in damages. First, if there is a finding of contributory negligence, the total of the benefits recouped and the damages paid to the claimant will be more than the judge's order; the defendant has to pay out more than the claimant receives from the court, although not more than the claimant has received overall as a result of the accident. Secondly, benefits paid for longer than five years are neither recouped nor offset, and so the claimant achieves more in total than the court has awarded; the defendant does not have to pay but there is an element of double recovery. Thirdly, and perhaps more relevantly to this case, benefits may be paid as a result of an accident even though there is little or no loss of earnings for which damages may be claimed; once again, the defendant has to pay a total of more than the claimant can achieve in damages, although not more than the claimant has received overall as a result of the accident.'

[1]   [2003] EWCA Civ 729 at [7].

(vi)   Reduction of Compensation Payment

[J13]   Section 8 applies in relation to any head of compensation listed in column 1 of Sch 2 (see below) where:

(a)   any of the compensation payment is attributable to that head; and
(b)   any recoverable benefit is shown against that head in column 2 of Sch 2.

In such a case, any claim of a person to receive the compensation payment is to be treated for all purposes as discharged if:

(a)   he or she is paid the amount (if any) of the compensation payment calculated in accordance with s 8; and
(b)   the amount of the compensation payment so calculated is nil, and he or she is given a statement saying so by the person who (apart from s 8) would have paid the gross amount of the compensation payment[1].

[1]   Social Security (Recovery of Benefits) Act 1997, s 8(2).

[J14]　In respect of each head of compensation listed in column 1 of Sch 2, so much of the gross amount of the compensation payment as is attributable to that head is to be reduced (to nil, if the benefits equal or exceed the head of compensation) by deducting the amount of the recoverable benefit or, as the case may be, the aggregate amount of the recoverable benefits shown against it in column 2[1].

[1]　Social Security (Recovery of Benefits) Act 1997, s 8(3).

[J15]　Thus, the amount of the compensation payment calculated in accordance with s 8 is:

(a)　the gross amount of the compensation payment; less
(b)　the sum of the reductions made under s 8(3) – the amount may be nil.

[J16]　It should be noted that special provisions apply to the calculation of recoupment in complex cases[1], cases involving structured settlements[2], and those involving periodical payments[3]. In these cases, where recoupment has already been made from interim payments, this is taken into account when calculating the final payment to be made. Where a settlement is reached including periodical payments, the defendant is treated as having made a single compensation payment on the day of settlement, and the total of the periodical payments due to be made under the agreement are taken to be a compensation payment for the purposes of the 1997 Act[4].

[1]　Social Security (Recovery of Benefits) Act 1997, ss 18 and 19; Social Security (Recovery of Benefits) Regulations 1997, SI 1997/2205, reg 9.
[2]　Social Security (Recovery of Benefits) Act 1997, ss 18 and 19; Social Security (Recovery of Benefits) Regulations 1997, SI 1997/2205, reg 10. See also the Social Security Amendment (Personal Payments) Regulations 2002, SI 2002/2442.
[3]　Social Security (Recovery of Benefits) (Lump Sum Payments) Regulations 2008, reg 18.
[4]　Social Security (Recovery of Benefits) (Lump Sum Payments) Regulations 2008, reg 18. There is no guidance as to how this works in practice, given that it is unknown how many periodical payments will be due under a particular agreement, because this depends upon life expectancy. However, presumably the payments would be limited to those payments due in respect of heads of loss such as earnings, care and mobility/transport during the 'relevant period' – see further para **[J7]** above for a definition.

(vii)　Schedule 2

[J17]　The Social Security (Recovery of Benefits) Act 1997, Sch 2 provides:

(1)	*(2)*
Head of compensation	*Benefit*
1.　Compensation for earnings lost[1] during the relevant period	Disability working allowance
	Disability pension payable under section 103 of the 1992 Act[2]
	Incapacity benefit
	Income support
	Invalidity pension and allowance
	Jobseeker's allowance

(1)	(2)
Head of compensation	Benefit
	Severe disablement allowance Sickness benefit Statutory sick pay[3] Unemployability supplement Unemployment benefit
2. Compensation for cost of care[4] incurred during the relevant period	Attendance allowance Care component of disability living allowance Disablement pension increase payable under section 104 or section 105 of the 1992 Act[2]
3. Compensation for loss of mobility during the relevant period	Mobility allowance Mobility component of disability living allowance

[1]   'Compensation for earnings lost' includes an award of interest on damages for past loss of earnings: *Griffiths v British Coal Corpn* [2001] EWCA Civ 336, [2001] 1 WLR 1493. It also includes a rent liability in respect of business premises for a self-employed individual: *Lowther v Chatwin* [2003] EWCA Civ 729. Further, it has been held that loss of pension contributions, which otherwise would have been deducted from the claimant's monthly wages had he worked during the relevant period, amounted to 'compensation for earnings lost': *Nizami v London Clubs Management Ltd* [2004] EWHC 2577 (QB).

[2]   Social Security Contributions and Benefits Act 1992.

[3]   For this purpose, statutory sick pay includes only 80% of payments made between 6 April 1991 and 5 April 1994, and does not include any payments made on or after 6 April 1994.

[4]   'Cost of care' in column 1 includes gratuitous care provided by friends and family: *Griffiths v British Coal Corpn* [2001] EWCA Civ 336, [2001] 1 WLR 1493.

[J18]   Section 8 is clearly the most important reform of the 1997 Act, and imposes limits on which benefits can be recouped against certain heads of compensation. Because of the splitting of the heads of compensation and benefits, the certificate of recoverable benefits needs to be detailed in full. More important still, any final settlement or order needs also to be specific and, if necessary, a statement needs to be provided by the defendant as to why no compensation payment has been made under the relevant head.

(viii)   When the Court Decides

[J19]   Section 15 applies where a court makes an order for a compensation payment to be made, unless the order is made with the consent of the injured person and the person by whom the payment is to be made. If the court decides, it must (in the case of each head of compensation listed in column 1 of Sch 2 to which any of the compensation payments is attributable) specify in the order the amount of the compensation payable which is attributable to that head[1].

[1]   Social Security (Recovery of Benefits) Act 1997, s 15(2).

[J20]   The defendant must be fully aware of the benefits he or she may deduct from the compensation payment in considering a settlement offer. It is clear from the exhaustive list contained in Sch 2 that the damages awarded for pain, suffering and loss of amenity are not subject to recoupment. They are entirely safe from the deductions and, therefore, the claimant will always recover what is deemed to be appropriate for his or her injuries and their physical/mental consequences, so far as they are non-pecuniary.

[J21]   The Act does restrict certain claims, however. For example, if a claim for loss of earnings would be less than the benefits deductible for the relevant benefits, then there would be little point in claiming these. It would be an exercise (pointless as far as the claimant was concerned) of bringing an action for the benefit of the DWP. However, it may not be an abuse of process: in *McCaffery v Datta*[1], the claimant incurred no cost penalties, despite the fact that the value to himself was no more than the £2,500 paid into court.

[1]   [1997] 2 All ER 586. See further at paras **[J58]–[J65]**.

[J22]   In light of the protection now offered to the damages for pain and suffering, the successful claimant will normally always receive something.

[J23]   Difficulties, however, are inevitable with regard to negotiated settlements. The claimant will want to maximise the damages payable for pain, suffering and loss of amenity, as these cannot be deducted, while the defendant will want to minimise such damages in order to reduce any overall payout.

Example (assuming the damages are loss of earnings and pain and suffering)

If the certificate of recoverable benefits for the specified period stands at £20,000 and a settlement is in negotiation, then this figure will be paid by the defendant whatever the final settlement. If the defendant's offer is £30,000, then the apportionment of this figure would be of huge significance. If the general damages are £10,000, then the total payable is £30,000 (£20,000 to CRU and £10,000 to the claimant). However, if the claimant argues for £20,000 as general damages, the defendant would still have to pay £20,000 to the CRU but would only offset £10,000 against the settlement. Therefore, the total payment would be £40,000 (£20,000 to CRU and £20,000 to the claimant).

[J24]   For a detailed example of a breakdown:

A compensation order is made in the order of £10,000. The order is broken down as follows:

* £5,000 for general damages;
* £3,000 for loss of earnings; and
* £2,000 for cost of care.

The CRU certificate states that the recoverable benefit is £7,000, which is broken down as follows:

* £3,500 for incapacity benefit;

- £1,500 for attendance allowance;
- £1,000 for mobility allowance; and
- £1,000 for the mobility component of disability living allowance.

[J25] As a compensation payment is made, the Act obviously applies and the defendant must pay the CRU the £7,000. However, the problem is what he or she must pay the claimant. It is not now a question of paying the £3,000 balance, but of setting off 'like for like' items. The £5,000 general damages cannot be touched, but the £3,000 loss of earnings is totally exhausted by the incapacity benefit. The £2,000 cost of care is reduced by the £1,500 attendance allowance, but the remaining £500 goes to the claimant. The £1,000 for mobility allowance and the £1,000 for the mobility component have no 'like for like' damages. Therefore, the claimant receives £5,500, yet the defendant has to pay a total of £12,500.

[J26] One anomaly that may arise is a claimant not bringing a claim under a specific head of damages (having calculated that he or she would receive nothing). In the above example, the claimant could be aware that his or her £3,000 loss of earnings was going to be exhausted by the benefit of recoupment. Also, if the attendance allowance had totalled £2,000, again, the claim for cost of care would have been extinguished. The CRU certificate would stand at £7,500 (the extra £500 being for attendance allowance) but, if the claimant decided to claim only general damages, the court order would be £5,000. The defendant would have to pay the claimant £5,000 and the £7,500 in total, and so will be no worse off: but the DSS has, in this case, gained at the expense of the claimant.

[J27] Under s 9 of the Act, a person making a compensation payment in accordance with s 8 must inform the person receiving payment of the following:

(a) how the payment has been calculated (ie by way of s 8 deductions); and
(b) the relevant date of calculation.

If the amount of payment calculated is nil (because of total benefit set-off), then the official date of payment is the day on which the above statement is given specifying the nil payment.

(ix) Review and Appeals Regarding the Certificates of Recoverable Benefits

Review

[J28] By s 10 the Secretary of State may review any certificate of recoverable benefits if he is satisfied:

(a) that it was issued in ignorance of, or was based on a mistake as to, a material fact; or
(b) that a mistake (whether in computation or otherwise) has occurred in its preparation.

On a review under s 10 the Secretary of State may either:

(a) confirm the certificate; or

(b) issue a fresh certificate containing such variations as he considers appropriate.

[J29]   The Secretary of State may not vary the certificate so as to increase the total amount of the recoverable benefits, unless it appears that the variation is required as a result of the person who applied for the certificate supplying incorrect or insufficient information.

Appeals[1]

[J30]   By s 11(1) an appeal against a certificate of recoverable benefits may be made on the grounds:

(a) that any amount, rate or period specified in the certificate is incorrect; or

(b) that listed benefits which have been, or are likely to be, paid otherwise than in respect of the accident, injury or disease in question have been brought into account.

[1]   See further Robert Hetherington's article in [2002] JPIL, Issue 2/02 at 146 with regard to appealing CRU certificates; and Mark Barnett's article 'CRU Appeals – Lessons from Case Law and a Reminder of the Procedure' [2004] Quantum, Issue 4/2004, 8 July.

[J31]   An appeal may be made by:

(a) the person who applied for the certificate of recoverable benefits; or

(b) (where the compensation payment has been reduced) the injured person or other person to whom the payment is made[1].

[1]   Social Security (Recovery of Benefits) Act 1997, s 11(2).

[J32]   No appeal may be made under s 11 until:

(a) the claim giving rise to the compensation payment has been finally disposed of[1]; and

(b) the liability of the compensator has been discharged[2].

[1]   If an award of provisional damages has been made, the payment is treated as having been finally disposed of.
[2]   Social Security (Recovery of Benefits) Act 1997, s 11(3).

[J33]   Thus, it will be seen that a review is made by the Secretary of State only where there was a mistake as to a material fact or as to the calculation. This may be done at any time after the issue of the certificate. However, an appeal is based on an argument by a relevant party that the certificate was in any way wrong. Generally speaking, under s 11 of the Social Security (Recovery of Benefits) Act 1997 the claimant will be entitled to a return of some monies repaid in consequence of a successful appeal of a CRU certificate. Thus, it is important that the defendant takes care to draft any notices of payment into court to make sure that any offer made to the claimant is correctly expressed to reflect the defendant's intention[1].

[1]   See further *Williams v Devon County Council* [2003] EWCA Civ 365; *Hilton International Hotels Ltd v Smith* [2001] PIQR P197, discussed further at paras **[J46]–[J56]**; and *Bruce v Genesis Fast Food Ltd* [2003] EWHC 788, [2004] PIQR P9.

[J34] A point worthy of specific note is the mandatory reference to a medical appeal tribunal, where there is a question of an appeal under s 11 concerning the amount in the certificate and whether the benefits have been, or are likely to be, paid 'otherwise than in consequence of the accident, injury or disease'[1]. A further point is that, whilst a review of the certificate under s 10 can take place at any time, an appeal can only take place under s 11 after the claim has been disposed of and liability discharged. This may well be a useful avenue to pursue for the defendant where the claimant is found to be a malingerer and has received benefits to which he or she was not entitled.

[1]   Social Security (Recovery of Benefits) Act 1997, s 12(1), (2).

(x) Payments Into Court

General principles

[J35] These are covered by reg 8 of the Social Security (Recovery of Benefits) Regulations 1997[1], as specified by s 16 of the 1997 Act.

[1]   SI 1997/2205.

[J36] By reg 8, where a party to an action makes a payment into court which would have constituted a compensation payment:

(a) the making of that payment is treated for the purposes of the 1997 Act as the making of a compensation payment;
(b) a current certificate of recoverable benefits[1] must be lodged with the payment; and
(c) where the payment is calculated under s 8, the compensator must give the relevant party the information specified in s 9 (see above), instead of the person to whom the payment is made.

[1]   Ie one that is in force: see Social Security (Recovery of Benefits) Regulations 1997, SI 1997/2205, reg 4(4).

[J37] The liability under reg 6(1) to pay an amount equal to the total amount of the recoverable benefits does not arise until the person making the payment into court has been notified that the payment into court has been paid out of court to the relevant party[1].

[1]   Social Security (Recovery of Benefits) Regulations 1997, SI 1997/2205, reg 8(2).

[J38] Where a payment into court is accepted either within 21 days or by consent between the parties, the relevant period will end, if it has not done so already, on the date on which application to the court for the payment out is made[1].

[1]   Social Security (Recovery of Benefits) Regulations 1997, SI 1997/2205, reg 8(3), (4).

[J39] In the absence of consent, where, after the expiry of the initial (21 days) period, payment out of court is made wholly or partly to or for the relevant party in accordance with an order of the court and in satisfaction of the claim, the relevant period will end, if it has not done so already, on the date of that order[1].

[1]   Social Security (Recovery of Benefits) Regulations 1997, SI 1997/2205, reg 8(5).

[J40] In summary, if the payment in is accepted within 21 days, the 'relevant period' will end on the day the payment in was actually made. However, where the payment in is accepted by consent (reg 8(4)) or where the court orders payment out (reg 8(5)), then the 'relevant period' ends on those specific days. The consequences of this are serious to the defendant. Take, for example, a defendant who wishes to offer £30,000. All benefits are deductible, and total £15,000. The defendant pays in £15,000 and holds back £15,000. This payment in is not accepted within 21 days, and so benefits continue to accrue at a rate of £200 per week. If, one year later, the claimant applies to take money out of court (by consent or on notice) then, unless the court orders otherwise, the £15,000 goes to the claimant but the defendant has to pay the £15,000 to the CRU, plus the further year's benefit of £10,400. Therefore, the total paid is not the £30,000 first intended, but £40,400. This will have the obvious consequence of defendants contesting claimants' late applications to accept a payment into court[1].

[1]   See further *McCarthy v Recticel Ltd* [2000] PIQR Q74 regarding the prejudice caused to the defendant due to delay on behalf of the claimant, which is discussed further at paras **[J46]–[J56]**.

[J41]   As discussed below, defendants have to be extremely careful about what they specify on the notice of the payment into court, especially where there is an allegation of contributory negligence[1].

[1]   *Williams v Devon County Council* [2003] EWCA Civ 365; *Hilton International Hotels Ltd v Smith* [2001] PIQR P14; and *Bruce v Genesis Fast Food Ltd* [2003] EWHC 788, [2004] PIQR P9. See further at paras **[J46]–[J56]**.

Requirements of the CPR

[J42]   Under CPR, r 36.2(2), a Part 36 offer must:

'(a)   be in writing;
(b)   state on its face that it is intended to have the consequences of Part 36;
(c)   specify a period of not less than 21 days within which the defendant will be liable for the claimant's costs in accordance with rule 36.10 if the offer is accepted;
(d)   state whether it relates to the whole of the claim or to part of it or to an issue that arises in it and if so to which part or issue; and
(e)   state whether it takes into account any counterclaim.'

[J43]   More details of the requirements regarding notice of CRU recoupment when making payments into court are found in CPR, r 36.15. A defendant who makes a Part 36 offer should state whether the offer is made without regard to any liability for recoverable amounts or that it is intended to include any deductible benefits[1]. Before making an offer, the defendant must apply for a CRU certificate[2], and the offer must state the gross amount of the compensation, the name and amount by which the gross amount has been reduced, and the net amount of the compensation[3]. Where an offer is made at the time that a CRU certificate has been requested but not yet provided, the defendant must provide the necessary information within seven days of receipt of the CRU certificate[4].

[1]   CPR, r 36.15(3).
[2]   CPR, r 36.15(5).
[3]   CPR, r 36.15(6).
[4]   CPR, r 36.15(7).

[J44] If the claimant accepts the offer, the claim (or relevant part thereof) is stayed, and the defendant must pay the agreed sum net of recoverable benefits within 14 days of the acceptance[1]. When the court decides whether or not the defendant has obtained a more advantageous result than their Part 36 offer, the court bases its decision on the net sum specified in the Part 36 offer[2].

[1]   CPR, r 36.11(6).
[2]   CPR, r 36.15(8).

[J45] Where further deductible amounts have accrued since the Part 36 offer was made and the relevant period for accepting the offer has expired, the court's permission is required before the claimant will be allowed to accept the offer out of time[1]. If the court does give permission to allow the offer to be accepted after the relevant period has expired, the court may direct that the offer is reduced by a sum equivalent to the further deductible benefits which have accrued since the offer was made[2].

[1]   CPR, r 36.9(6).
[2]   CPR, r 36.15(9).

Case law

(1) Pre-CPR case law

[J46] *Rees v West Glamorgan County Council*[1] is authority for the proposition that, where the parties intend to reach settlement without taking into account the statutory deduction (ie a net figure for the claimant 'in their pocket'), then the same has to be agreed expressly. The general presumption is that recoupment will apply unless agreed otherwise. Therefore, on the facts, an agreement to settle the claimant's claim for £33,000 without mentioning anything in relation to the benefits position was a gross settlement, and the defendant was entitled to deduct the recoverable benefits from the settlement figure in accordance with the statutory scheme.

[1]   [1993] NLJR 814, [1993] PIQR P37. See also *Houghton v British Coal Corpn* (1997) 35 BMLR 33, CA; and *Hi-Group plc and Mallinson v Wright* [1997] CLY 1817.

[J47] In *Black v Doncaster Metropolitan Borough Council*[1], the defendants paid into court a sum of £2,500 in March 1997 (at this time, the old law applied and such a sum was outside the recoupment scheme). The claim was for £150,000 and the small payment in was a protection against a small award in respect of general damages. The payment in was not accepted and trial was fixed for 27 October 1997. This was only 21 days after the Social Security (Recovery of Benefits) Act 1997 came into force (ie 6 October 1997). On 22 October 1997 the claimant issued a notice of acceptance of payment in, which would mean the defendant having to pay £15,247.15 to the CRU. The Court of Appeal held that the payment in could not be accepted as it would lead to injustice to the defendant. There had been a complete change in circumstances because of the 1997 Act, and the claimant had had ample opportunity to accept prior to 6 October 1997.

[1]   [1998] 3 All ER 631.

[J48] In *McCarthy v Recticel Ltd*[1] the argument in *Black*[2] was taken further, and it was held that the claimant's delay had caused the defendant substantial prejudice. In this case, the defendant had again paid £2,500 into court under the old scheme. Due to the delay and the introduction of the 1997 Act, the defendant faced an increased liability for recoupment which it was unable to off-set against general damages. Daniel Brennan QC held that delay by the claimant had caused sufficient prejudice for the claim to be struck out.

[1]   [2000] PIQR Q74.
[2]   [1998] 3 All ER 631.

[J49] In *Houghton v British Coal Corpn*[1], the defendant paid in £15,800 but made it clear that £9,000 was being held back in accordance with the Regulations. The claimant's solicitors misinterpreted the notice and believed the payment in was to be repaid on top of the relevant benefits (ie £24,800) and the claimant accepted under such an assumption. The Court of Appeal refused to allow the claimant to rescind the acceptance. The notice of payment in was clear enough. Although this case was decided under the 1989 Act, it is an indication of the potential problems which have only been heightened by the greater detail required under the 1997 Act.

[1]   (1997) 35 BMLR 33, CA.

[J50] In *Spence v Wilson (No 2)*[1], Wilson lodged £40,000 with the court in 1995. In 1998, Spence was awarded £10,085 and Wilson sought his costs from the 1995 payment in. The court held that, following the 1997 Act, the parties needed to agree precisely where the obligation to repay the benefit lay. Further, any tender that is unclear as to this obligation and, therefore, the sum the claimant will receive is invalid after 6 October 1997 (the date of the commencement of the Act). Thus, a payment in is only likely to be effective if it details the breakdown of the settlement (ie how much is being retained for recoupment).

[1]   1998 SLT 959, OH.

[J51] In *Al-Amiry v Manchester City Council*[1], the defendants made a payment in of £12,500 21 days before the trial. The certificate of total benefit stood at £5,000 to be recovered and, as such, the total value of the settlement was intended to be £17,500. However, the actual wording of the payment in indicated that the value was £12,500 less the recoverable amount (ie £7,500 to the claimant). At the trial, the claimant was awarded £9,000 and, relying on the payment in, the defendant sought costs. Realising the false indication given by the notice of the payment in, the City Council had sent a letter to the claimant clarifying the fact that the total value was £17,500. It was held, however, that it is the notice of payment in itself that must be clear and, even though the letter clarified the matter, the notice remained unchanged and so not effective. This decision indicates the importance and weight attached to the wording of the payment in. However, the harsh result was mitigated by the court using its discretion and not ordering costs to either side from the date of the letter (approximately 12 days before trial).

[1]   [1998] CLY 444.

(2) Post-CPR case law

[J52]   In *Bajwa v British Airways plc*[1], the Court of Appeal rejected appeals from three claimants who had beaten payments into court made prior to the enactment of the 1997 Act. At the time the offers were made, they had been reasonable estimates of the likely damages. However, by reason of the 1997 Act coming into force, the claimants, despite losing all the major evidential disputes at trial, were able to beat the payments into court. The Court of Appeal held that had the claimants given serious consideration to the offers made they could have asked the defendants to renegotiate the offers in light of the 1997 Act. The claimants had chosen not to do this and had contested all issues at trial. Since they had lost all of these issues at trial, it was not appropriate to award the claimants their costs, and the defendants were awarded their costs from the dates of their offers.

[1]   [1999] PIQR Q152, CA.

[J53]   In *McCann v Wimpey Construction (UK) Ltd*[1], the Court of Appeal upheld the decision of the judge at first instance not to strike out the claimant's claim following an inordinate and inexcusable delay of at least three years, which had led to the defendant's liability in damages in a substantial case being increased under the 1997 Act by about 10%. The court held that notwithstanding the delay it was still possible to have a fair trial, and that any injustice caused to the defendant could be adequately taken into account when the court considered the payment into court that had been made prior to the 1997 Act coming into force and the question of costs. This is an example of the greater flexibility that the court now has when dealing with these matters under the CPR. It was indicated that, had the defendant made a genuine attempt at settlement prior to the 1997 Act coming into force which was in the right region of damages, it would be likely that the court would exercise its discretion in favour of the defendant and award costs from that point (as the court did in *Bajwa v British Airways plc*[2]).

[1]   (11 November 1999, unreported), CA.
[2]   [1999] PIQR Q152, CA.

[J54]   In *Hilton International Hotels Ltd v Smith*[1], Pitchford J dismissed the defendant's appeal from a decision of the judge below, ordering the defendant to repay to the claimant the sum of £40,124. The defendant had made a payment into court with a notice stating that the gross compensation payable was £46,124. The CRU certificate stood at £40,124, leaving £6,000 for general damages. The defendant's intention was not to pay the claimant any more than the £6,000 he deserved since, on the medical evidence, his claim for loss of earnings was not related to the accident. The claimant accepted the payment into court. Both parties then appealed the CRU certificate. The CRU certificate was reassessed at nil, and the Secretary of State repaid £40,124 to the defendant. The claimant sought recovery of that money. It was held that, under s 11 of the Social Security (Recovery of Benefits) Act 1997, the claimant was entitled to the repayment, and the claimant could not be fixed with knowledge that the notice of payment into court meant anything other than what it appeared to. There were no exceptional circumstances which meant that the claimant had taken unfair advantage of the defendant. If the defendant had made a mistake, it was fixed with it because a means had been chosen to express the offer which was unequivocal in its terms[2].

1   [2001] PIQR P14.
2   Pitchford J suggested that there were two ways in which the defendant could have achieved its desired object: either they could have specified the gross compensation payment in the notice of payment in as nil or, alternatively, a *Calderbank* letter could have been sent which made its intention clear. Part 36 has been amended since this decision, and CPR, r 36.15(6) now requires a defendant to state the amount of the gross compensation, the name and amount of any deductible amount by which the gross amount is reduced, and the net amount of the compensation.

[J55] A similar scenario arose in *Bruce v Genesis Fast Food Ltd*[1], where the defendant successfully appealed the CRU certificate, having already agreed settlement of a claim including terms as to the repayment of recoverable benefits. A second CRU certificate was issued, which was £39,540.82 less than the first certificate, and the claimant requested payment of the outstanding sum. It was held that the settlement created a binding agreement between the parties who could not contract out of the 1997 recoupment scheme. A proper construction of the statutory framework demonstrated that the claimant was entitled to repayment of the additional £39,540.82 with interest[2]. Although the defendant sought rectification as a remedy, it was held not to be an appropriate remedy since the situation arose out of a unilateral mistake on the part of the defendant as to statutory interpretation, which was not the responsibility of the claimant or his advisers[3].

1   [2003] EWHC 788 (QB), [2004] PIQR P9.
2   *Hilton International Hotels Ltd v Smith* [2001] PIQR P14 and *Wisely v John Fulton (Plumbers) Ltd* [2000] 1 WLR 820, HL, applied.
3   One way round this, in an appropriate case, is for the claimant to assign his rights to the benefit of any subsequent CRU appeal or review to the defendant as part of any compromise agreement reached.

[J56] Defendants must also be careful regarding the drafting of a Part 36 payment/ offer where contributory negligence is alleged or it is argued that the claimant is not entitled to loss of earnings for the whole period claimed. The Social Security (Recovery of Benefits) Act 1997 does not make provision for either situation, and the defendant therefore remains liable to meet the full amount of the recoverable benefits. This can lead to the defendant becoming liable after trial to pay a total sum in excess of what the claimant was awarded by way of damages and, unless the Part 36 notice is worded appropriately, may result in an impingement upon the claimant's award of general damages for pain, suffering and loss of amenity, which is supposed to be ring-fenced under the statutory scheme.

[J57] Such a situation occurred in *Williams v Devon County Council*[1] where the judge at first instance awarded the claimant damages on a full liability basis of £34,587.58, which were reduced to £23,058.39 in order to reflect a finding of one-third contributory negligence. The defendant had paid £10,000 into court which, together with CRU of £15,669.91, made a total of £25,669.91. The trial judge awarded the defendant's costs from the last date the claimant could have accepted the payment, since he had not bettered the Part 36 payment. However, the claimant would have actually received £15,738.91 under the judge's order, because the recoupable benefits could only be set off against the claim for loss of earnings and not against the remaining claims for general damages, home maintenance, travel expenses etc. In the event, the Court of Appeal overturned the judge's decision on contributory negligence, so that the costs point did not arise for consideration, but Latham LJ took the opportunity to give some helpful guidance. The touchstone was said to be that the claimant is entitled to the full value of his or her general damages claim for pain, suffering and loss of amenity (as intended by Parliament). It is not appropriate for the claimant to make up any shortfall in damages by appealing the CRU certificate. CPR, r 36.23(3)(b) [as it then was] required the payment into court notice to state 'the name and amount of any benefit by which the gross amount is reduced in accordance with Section 8 and Schedule 2 of the 1997 Act'[2]. In order to comply with this provision, the defendant had to make a calculation in accordance with s 8, ie the amount by which the gross sum is reduced must be no more than the amount appropriate for the head of damages against which the benefits can be offset[3]. Therefore, unless the defendant made a proper assessment of the award for general damages and made it clear how the gross amount had been reduced in accordance with s 8, the notice will not be proper and effective (unless suitable clarification has been obtained pursuant to a request under CPR, r 36.9). Alternatively, the court may proceed to deal with all matters, except for the question of costs which could be deferred until any appeal of the CRU certificate has been heard. However, this solution involving inevitable delay and further expense was not considered to be the preferred option.

[1] [2003] EWCA Civ 365.
[2] This rule has since been replaced by CPR, r 36.15(6) which requires a defendant who makes a Part 36 offer to state the amount of the gross compensation, the name and amount of any deductible amount by which the gross amount is reduced, and the net amount of compensation.
[3] It is likely that similar considerations to those which arose in *Williams v Devon County Council* [2003] EWCA Civ 365 will apply under the new rules when there is a finding of contributory negligence.

(xi) Exempted Payments

Payments exempted by primary legislation

[J58] These are dealt with by Sch 1 to the Social Security (Recovery of Benefits) Act 1997:

'1. Any small payment specified by Regulation: there are currently no such regulations in force.
2. Any payment made as a compensation order against a convicted person.
3. Any payment made in the exercise of a discretion out of property held subject to a trust in a case where no more than 50% by value of the capital contributed to the trust was directly or indirectly provided by persons who are, or are alleged to be, liable in respect of –
    (a) the accident, injury or disease suffered by the injured person; or
    (b) the same or any connected accident, injury or disease suffered by another.
4. Any payment made out of property held for the purposes of any prescribed trust (whether the payment also falls within para 3 or not).
5. Any insurance payment resulting from the injury.
6. Any redundancy payment taken into account in the assessment of damages.
7. So much of any payment as is referable to costs.
8. Any prescribed payment.

PART II POWER TO DISREGARD SMALL PAYMENTS

9. (1) Regulations may make provision for compensation payments to be disregarded for the purposes of ss 6 and 8 in prescribed cases where the amount of the compensation payment, or the aggregate amount of two or more connected compensation payments, does not exceed the prescribed sum.

(2) A compensation payment disregarded by virtue of this paragraph is referred to in para 1 as a 'small payment'.

(3) For the purposes of this paragraph –

(a) two or more compensation payments are 'connected' if each is made to or in respect of the same injured person and in respect of the same accident, injury or disease; and

(b) any reference to a compensation payment is a reference to a payment which would be such a payment apart from para 1.'

Payments exempted by secondary legislation

[J59] By virtue of reg 2(2) of the Social Security (Recovery of Benefits) Regulations 1997 the following payments are 'prescribed payments' under para 8 of Sch 1 to the 1997 Act and are therefore also exempt from payment:

- Fatal Accident Act 1976 payments.
- Payments under the Vaccine Damages Payments Act 1979.
- Criminal Injuries Compensation Board (CICB) and Criminal Injuries Compensation Authority (CICA) awards[1].
- Any payment made by British Coal in accordance with the NCB Pneumoconiosis Compensation Scheme[2].
- Deafness payments in respect of sensorineural hearing loss where the loss is less than 50dB in either ear.
- Any contractual amount paid to an employee by an employer in respect of the claimant's incapacity to work.
- Any payment under the NHS (Injury Benefits) Regulations 1995.
- Any payment under the Secretary of State's scheme established on 24 April 1992.

[1]   See *Oldham v Sharples* [1997] PIQR Q82.
[2]   See *Ballantine v Newalls Insulation Co Ltd* [2000] PIQR Q57.

The small payment exception

[J60] Under the old statutory recoupment scheme, there was a small payments exemption of £2,500. Although the power has been granted under Pt II of Sch 1 to the 1997 Act to enable a similar small payment to become disregarded, currently no such regulation has been, or is currently expected to be, imposed. There is, therefore, less threat of claimants being persuaded to accept less than an appropriate amount of compensation.

[J61] In *MacCaffrey v Datta*[1] the defendants paid into court £2,500 in a case where £25,000 was due for recoupment. The claimant rejected the payment but was finally awarded only £22,000. As this sum effectively meant the claimant would receive nothing, the defendant argued that the claimants had not beaten the payment in. The Court of Appeal held that, in considering whether a payment in has been beaten, the court should look at the total award, not at what a claimant actually receives.

[1]   [1997] 2 All ER 586, [1997] 1 WLR 870 (decided under the 1989 Act).

[J62]   Although this was under the previous regime, the principle is still sound. Under the 1997 Act, to beat a payment in, it is the total award, not the sum the claimant takes home, that is relevant, ie the payment inclusive of any sum recouped against the money the defendant has had to pay back to the CRU.

Example

The defendant values a claim at £20,000 but as a safety net calls it £22,000. The CRU certificate shows benefits of £10,000 capable of being set off against earnings, and so the defendant makes an offer of £22,000 gross, £12,000 net. At trial, the claimant recovers £20,000 and so the defendant believes he has succeeded on costs. However, if the award is made up as follows:

£10,000 general damages;
£3,000 special damages (property); and
£7,000 loss of earnings,

the claimant recovers £20,000 – £7,000, ie £13,000 and the defendant still has to pay the £10,000 benefits. Even though he can set the £10,000 off against the loss of earnings, the offer is arguably[1] beaten. £3,000 of the benefits has to be paid to the DWP in addition to the claimant's award.

[1]   The court retains a discretion, where a Part 36 offer has only been beaten by a small margin, to disallow the claimant's costs and/or order him to pay the defendant's costs as the real victor: see further *Carver v BAA* [2008] EWCA Civ 412, [2009] 1 WLR 113, in which the Court of Appeal held that CPR, r 36.14(1)(a) permitted a more wide-ranging review of all the facts and circumstances of the case in deciding whether the judgment, which was the fruit of the litigation, was worth the fight, and money was no longer the sole governing criterion. See also *Nizami v London Clubs Management Ltd* [2004] EWHC 2577 (QB).

[J63]   This is clearly quite confusing, as the defendant seemed to have exceeded the damages with his Part 36 offer. The situation is even more confusing if the claimant decides not to proceed with his loss of earnings claim as it will be exhausted by benefits. In such a case, the award is reduced to £13,000, yet the payment in of £12,000 is still beaten.

[J64]   The simple solution is to break down exactly the elements of a payment in. Instead of globally retaining the benefits to be repaid, the defendant should only retain the sum that may be recouped from the claimant's award by way of repayment to the DWP.

[J65]   Under the CPR, there is now much more flexibility, especially where costs are concerned. Of course, Pt 36 of the CPR requires the court to consider awards made against the gross sum of payments into court[1]. But it may be that the court would be more likely to award costs against a claimant where the actual benefits to the claimant are not proportionate to the costs involved[2].

1 CPR, Pt 36, PD, para 10.5. See further *Williams v Devon County Council* [2003] EWCA Civ 365.
2 See further *Bajwa v British Airways plc* [1999] PIQR Q152, [1999] All ER (D) 558.

(xii) Interest

[J66] Section 103 of the Social Security Contributions and Benefits Act 1992 made specific provision for the deduction of relevant benefits before interest was calculated on the award of damages. However, the 1997 Act makes no such provision and, thus, the House of Lords in *Wadey v Surrey County Council*[1] held that the amount of any benefits paid or likely to be paid during the relevant period was to be disregarded in the assessment of special damages and the calculation of interest on those damages. Therefore, interest on the various heads of damages awarded is to be assessed prior to making any deduction for recoupable benefits.

1 [2000] 2 All ER 545, [2000] 1 WLR 820.

[J67] However, an award of interest on damages for past losses of earnings does fall within the expression 'compensation for earnings lost' in Sch 2 to the Social Security (Recovery of Benefits) Act 1997[1]. Therefore, a claimant must give credit to the defendant for any award of interest on heads of damage that have been extinguished by recoupable benefits under the 1997 Act.

1 *Griffiths v British Coal Corpn* [2001] EWCA Civ 336, [2001] 1 WLR 1493.

(xiii) Benefits Not Caught by the Statutory Recoupment Scheme

[J68] As detailed above, the statutory scheme for the recoupment only applies to specified benefits[1]. The following are not within the statutory scheme:

* Christmas bonus for pensioners.
* Widow's payment.
* Widowed mother's allowance.
* Widow's pension.
* Child's special allowance.
* Guardian's allowance.
* Invalid care allowance.
* State maternity allowance.
* Statutory maternity pay.
* Child benefit.
* Housing benefit[2].
* Community charge / Council tax benefit[3].
* Reliefs available to the disabled from public transport charges.
* Parking charges and Vehicle Excise Duty.
* Payments out of the social fund.
* Foreign state benefits[4].
* Payments from the Independent Living (1993) Fund and the Independent Living (Extension) Fund.

1   As set out in column 2 of Sch 2 to the Social Security (Recovery of Benefits) Act 1997.
2   See *Clenshaw v Tanner* [2002] EWHC, [2002] All ER (D) 412 (Nov), QB.
3   See *Smith v Jenkins (trading as Rod Jenkins Marine)* [2003] EWHC 1356 (QB), [2003] All ER (D) 159 (Jun).
4   See para **[J111]** below.

[J69]   The recoverability of these benefits therefore depends upon the position at common law and the principles laid down in *Hodgson v Trapp*[1]. Likewise, the statutory recoupment scheme does not apply to payments made to a claimant under the Pneumoconiosis (Workers' Compensation) Act 1979[2] or to claims for economic loss following the birth of a handicapped child[3]. The common law will also determine whether or not any tax benefits enjoyed by the claimant – such as working tax credit or child tax credit – should be taken into account.

1   [1989] AC 807, [1988] 3 All ER 870. See further at paras **[J101]**–**[J105]**.
2   *Ballantine v Newalls Insulation Co Ltd* [2000] PIQR Q57. See further at para **[J58]**.
3   *Rand v East Dorset Health Authority (Deduction of Benefits)* [2001] PIQR Q1, [2000] Lloyd's Rep Med 377.

3   Collateral Benefits

[J70]   The term 'collateral benefit' in this context means a gain which, although it would not have been received but for the injury, is ignored for the purpose of damages because it is so coincidental to the claimant or so indirectly related to the injury. This term was adopted by the Law Commission[1]. However, the reference to matters 'collateral' has been previously extensively considered. In *British Transport Commission v Gourley*[2], Lord Reid stated, 'I do not think that it is possible to formulate any principle by which it can be determined what is and what is not too remote'.

1   Law Commission Report No 262 'Damages for Personal Injury: Medical, Nursing and Other Expenses; Collateral Benefits' (November 1999).
2   [1956] AC 185 at 214–215.

[J71]   The leading case regarding collateral benefits is *Parry v Cleaver*[1], in which Lord Wilberforce considered judges' tasks in the assessment of damages:

> 'They have to grapple with each type of benefit as it arises, and they have done so sometimes by setting themselves to ascertain what is "fair" sometimes by attempting to squeeze the appropriate answer from, or to explain the answer arrived at by reference to, such words as "compensatory", "loss", "collateral" or "caused".'

In that case, it was held, by a majority, that disablement pensions were 'collateral' to the injury. In deciding what was 'just', 'reasonable' and in line with 'public policy', the House of Lords decided it was good law to ignore benevolence and insurance in the assessment of damages. Thus, by analogy to insurance, disablement pensions should also be ignored.

1   [1970] AC 1 at 39.

[J72]   There is no single test for determining whether collateral benefits are to be deducted or not. However, prima facie the rule is that benefits should be deducted, since the fundamental principle is that the claimant is entitled to recovery of his or her *net* loss[1]. As Lord Reid pointed out in *Parry v Cleaver*[2]:

> 'Two questions can arise. First, what did the [claimant] lose as a result of the accident? What are the sums which he would have received but for the accident but which by reason of the accident he can no longer get? And secondly, what are the sums which he did in fact receive as a result of the accident but which he would not have received if there had been no accident? And then the question arises whether the latter sums must be deducted from the former in assessing the damages.'

[1]   See further Chapter A at paras **[A97]–[A99]**.
[2]   [1970] AC 1 at 13.

[J73]   Generally speaking, there are only two recognised exceptions to the rule that credit must be given: (i) acts of charity or benevolence; and (ii) insurance payments[1]. However, it is necessary to look separately at the treatment afforded to each of the main types of benefit that could be described as being of a collateral nature. These are dealt with below.

[1]   In *Gaca v Pirellis General plc* [2004] EWCA Civ 373, Dyson LJ put it as follows at [10]: 'It has also been stated on a number of occasions that there are two classes of payment to a claimant as a result of an accident which are not required to be brought into account in the assessment of damages. These are often referred to as the two exceptions against the rule against double recovery of damages. They are (i) payments made gratuitously to the claimant by others as a mark of sympathy ("the benevolence exception"); and (ii) insurance monies ("the insurance exception")'.

(i) Charitable Payments

[J74]   In *Redpath v Belfast and County Down Rly*[1], it was established that payments of a benevolent nature should be ignored in assessing damages. The basis for this is very simple. The reason behind the payment is not the tort itself but the generosity of the contributor[2]. In *Parry v Cleaver*[3], the court stated that benevolence by, for example, the employer should be disregarded in the assessment of damages in personal injury cases. This was followed in *Cunningham v Harrison*[4], in which the Court of Appeal refused to take account of an ex gratia payment by an employer of £828 per annum for life. Lord Denning MR said of the payment simply[5]: 'It is voluntary. He gets it and it is not to be taken into account'.

[1]   [1947] NI 167. See also *Liffen v Watson* [1940] 1 KB 556; *Connolly v Tesco Stores plc* (2 May 1989, unreported), QBD; *Chan v Butcher* [1984] 4 WWR 363.
[2]   Lord Reid in *Parry v Cleaver* [1970] AC 1 at 14: 'It would be revolting to the ordinary man's sense of justice, and therefore contrary to public policy, that the sufferer should have his damages reduced so that he would gain nothing from the benevolence of his friends or relations or of the public at large, and that the only gainer would be the wrongdoer'.
[3]   [1970] AC 1.
[4]   [1973] QB 942, [1973] 3 All ER 463, CA.
[5]   [1973] QB 942 at 951.

[J75]   There is some dispute over the status of an ex gratia payment made by an employer who is also the tortfeasor. In *Hussain v New Taplow Paper Mills Ltd*[1], Lloyd LJ indicated obiter that ex gratia payments by employers to employees injured in the course of their employment should also be taken into account, when the employer is the tortfeasor[2].

¹   [1987] 1 All ER 417; affirmed [1988] AC 514. Also see *Williams v BOC Gases* [2000] PIQR Q253, where an ex gratia payment made by an employer defendant was held to be deductible from the damages, not only because the gift had been made by the wrongdoer himself but also because he had said in terms, at the time the gift was made, that it was to be treated as an advance against any damages he might have to pay the claimant.

²   [1987] 1 All ER 417 at 428.

[J76] Subsequently, in *McCamley v Cammell Laird Shipbuilders Ltd*¹ a payment made by an employer pursuant to a personal accident insurance policy was not an advance in respect of any particular head of damage, but had been provided by the benevolence of the employer and should, therefore, be ignored. O'Connor LJ distinguished *Hussain*'s case², stating that the payment was not an ex gratia act following the accident. The whole idea of the policy was to make the benefit payable as an act of benevolence whenever a qualifying injury took place. Significance was placed on the fact that what the policy provided was a lump sum payable, regardless of fault, and that it was in no way part of a contractual scheme.

¹   [1990] 1 All ER 854, [1990] 1 WLR 963.

²   *Hussain v New Taplow Paper Mills Ltd* [1987] 1 All ER 417.

[J77] However, the Court of Appeal carried out a detailed analysis of this area of the law in *Gaca v Pirellis General Plc & others*¹. The court held that *McCamley*² was wrongly decided and should not be followed. A proper interpretation of the authorities, including *Parry v Cleaver*³, *Hodgson v Trapp*⁴, *Hunt v Severs*⁵, *Hussain v New Taplow Paper Mills Ltd*⁶, *Williams v BOC Gases*⁷, indicated that there was no good policy reason why account should not be taken of ex gratia payments made by a tortfeasor which would, in effect, require the tortfeasor to compensate his or her victim twice over. Indeed, there was an important policy consideration which militated against treating ex gratia payments by tortfeasors as falling within the benevolence exception: employers should be encouraged to make such payments to their employees when injured in the course of their employment⁸. Dyson LJ, who gave the lead judgment of the court, concluded⁹:

> 'As a matter of principle, therefore, and on the basis of the authorities (apart from *McCamley*) I would hold that ex gratia payments made to victims by tortfeasors do not normally fall within the benevolence exception, even if it can be shown that they are made from motives of benevolence. I say "normally" because it would be possible, in theory at least, and so long as there is nothing in his insurance policy to put his cover at risk if he takes such a course, for the tortfeasor to make an ex gratia payment, and to spell out explicitly that the payment is a gift made on the basis that it should not be deducted from any damages that may be awarded to the employee if litigation ensues. In that exceptional situation, the position may be different.'

He went on to say¹⁰:

> 'In my judgment, *McCamley* was wrongly decided for two principal reasons. First, the payment in that case manifestly was not analogous to a payment within the classic benevolence exception. There is a fundamental difference between (i) payments made by an employer to his employees to compensate them for the consequences of injuries suffered in an accident (whether or not caused by the employer's fault, and whether or not the payments are made directly or indirectly by means of an insurance policy as in *McCamley* and the present case), and (ii) payments made to victims of accidents

by third parties out of sympathy for their plight. As I have said earlier, different public policy considerations apply in the two cases. Moreover, it is unreal to treat the payment of benefits under an insurance policy as equivalent, or even analogous, to payments made by third parties out of sympathy. Such benefits are made available by employers to their employees not (or, at least, not principally) out of sympathy or charity, but in order to promote good relations with their employees and the trade unions to their mutual advantage. In other words, they are essentially management arrangements. The judgment in *McCamley* does not explain why, despite the obvious differences, it is right to classify ex gratia payments by an employer in the same way as ex gratia payments by third parties.

The second principal reason why I consider *McCamley* to have been wrongly decided is that, for the reasons I have given earlier, ex gratia payments made to employees by their employer tortfeasors do not normally fall within the benevolence exception, even if it can be shown that they are made from motives of benevolence. It is worthy of note that in *McCamley* the court cited, with apparent approval, the passage from the judgment of Lloyd LJ in *Hussain,* in which he said that (i) public policy considerations required ex gratia payments by tortfeasors to fall outside the benevolence exception, and (ii) the fact that the payment by the tortfeasor was one which he had contracted to pay in advance should make no difference. And yet the court did not explain why the payments fell within the benevolence exception although they had been made by the tortfeasor, or why it made a difference that the defendant had contracted to make the payments in advance.

In *Williams*, Brooke LJ said that *McCamley* should be treated as a case turning on its own facts, ie for what the court, deciding the issue as a jury question, thought was just, reasonable and in accordance with public policy on the facts of that case. I prefer to hold that *McCamley* was wrongly decided and should not be followed. As I have explained, the question whether a payment falls within one of the two classic exceptions is not a jury question to be determined in some vaguely Solomonic way according to the judge's sense of what is just and reasonable and what is therefore required by public policy. A payment should only be treated as analogous to a benevolent payment by a third party if the case for doing so is clearly made out, having regard to the rationale for the existence of the benevolence exception. As the Law Commission has said, when referring to *McCamley*, (Law Com No 262 para 10.14), the law in relation to charity by tortfeasors is unclear. For the reasons that I have given, there is no case for generally extending the scope of the benevolence exception to include payments made by tortfeasors to their victims.'

1   [2004] EWCA Civ 373. See further the helpful article 'Deductions of Receipts from Damages: *Pirelli v Gaca*' by Andrew Ritchie and Oliver Millington [2005] JPIL Issue 1/05 at 51–58.
2   [1990] 1 All ER 854, [1990] 1 WLR 963.
3   [1970] AC 1.
4   [1989] 1 AC 807.
5   [1994] 2 AC 350.
6   [1987] 1 All ER 417.
7   [2000] PIQR Q253.
8   See further *Hunt v Severs*, per Lord Bridge; *Hussain v New Taplow Paper Mills Ltd* [1987] 1 All ER 417, per Lord Lloyd; and *Williams v BOC Gases* [2000] PIQR Q253, per Brooke LJ.
9   At [31].
10   At [35]–[37].

[J78] In summary, true benevolence or charity by a third party can be ignored. However, generally speaking, credit will have to be given for an ex gratia payment by an employer who also happens to be the tortfeasor[1]. Indeed, given the compelling analysis of the law set out in *Gaca v Pirellis General Plc & others*[2], is it likely that credit must be given for an ex gratia payment made by a tortfeasor, irrespective of whether or not the tortfeasor also happens to be the claimant's employer.

[1]   *Hussain v New Taplow Paper Mills Ltd* [1987] 1 All ER 417, *Williams v BOC Gases* [2000] PIQR Q253 and *Gaca v Pirellis General Plc & others* [2004] EWCA Civ 373 are likely to be followed in preference to *McCamley v Cammell Laird Shipbuilders Ltd* [1990] 1 WLR 963.
[2]   [2004] EWCA Civ 373.

(ii) Insurance Payments

[J79]   *Bradburn v Great Western Rly Co*[1] established the general rule that insurance payments should not be taken into account in the assessment of damages. This decision has been followed on a regular basis. In *Parry v Cleaver*, Lord Reid stated[2]:

> 'As regards money coming to the claimant under a contract of insurance, I think that the real and substantial reason for disregarding them is that the claimant has bought them and that it would be unjust and unreasonable to hold that the money which he prudently spent on premiums and the benefit from it should enure to the benefit of the tortfeasor.'

It was clearly the thinking that the reason for the payment was the contract of insurance and not the accident. Although it is the accident that activates the pay-out, the prudence of the insured enables it.

[1]   (1874) LR 10 Exch 1.
[2]   [1970] AC 1 at 14.

[J80]   It should be noted that the authorities suggest that an insurance payment should only be ignored if the claimant actually paid or contributed to the insurance[1]. Lord Reid (as above) specified the unfairness of deducting insurance 'if the claimant has bought [the premium]'. In *Page v Sheerness Steel plc*, Dyson J (as he then was) said[2]:

> 'It seems to me that it is an essential requirement of the insurance exception that the cost of the insurance be borne wholly or at least in part by the [claimant].'

[1]   *Page v Sheerness Steel plc* [1996] PIQR Q26; and *Gaca v Pirellis General Plc* [2004] EWCA Civ 373.
[2]   [1996] PIQR Q26 at Q34.

[J81]   From time to time, a suggestion has been made that 'contribution' could be construed to mean a non-financial method, such as working for an employer who pays the premiums. The premiums then are paid because of the work performed by the claimant. Until recently, there was little guidance on this in the English cases[1]. However, in *Gaca v Pirellis General Plc*[2] this point was raised, and it was held that there needed to be evidence that the claimant paid or contributed to the cost of the insurance policy before the insurance exception can be said to apply. On the facts of the case, Dyson LJ concluded[3]:

> 'Turning to the facts of the present case, Mr Foy cannot identify any evidence which shows that the claimant paid or contributed to the cost of the insurance policy. All he can point to is the fact that the fruits of the claimant's labour enabled the defendants to pay for the insurance. But for the reasons that I have given, that is not enough to avoid the deduction of the benefits from his damages.'

1   However, there was some Canadian authority which addressed the issue; see eg *Cunningham v Wheeler* (1994) 113 DLR (4th) 1.
2   [2004] EWCA Civ 373; see in particular at [41]–[59].
3   At [59].

[J82]   The indemnity insurer has the unique right to take over the claimant's claim by subrogation, in order to recover the value of the insurance payments made[1].

1   Indemnity insurance is that taken to cover a specific head of loss, as opposed to the payment of a sum of money on a specified event.

(iii)   Sick Pay

[J83]   Sick pay can be contractual (based upon the statutory requirement or a more generous allowance) or voluntary/additional to any contractual terms, and can be paid in a variety of ways. The most common, however, is in the form similar to the claimant's wages.

[J84]   *Parry v Cleaver*[1] held that sick pay is in the same form as wages, so that, if a claimant receives sick pay, this is the same as receiving a like sum in wages. Therefore, unlike charity and insurance payments, sick pay is deductible. This means that, if the claimant receives sick pay in the same amount as his or her wages, no loss has been suffered and no damages can be brought for loss of earnings (which have been replaced by sick pay). However, the position is different where there is a contractual right for the claimant's employer to seek recovery of sick pay paid to the claimant in the event of a valid claim against a third party tortfeasor. In this scenario, the claimant is entitled to seek recovery of the 'employer's outlay' from the defendant[2], unless the employer has agreed to waive all rights to such recovery[3].

1   [1970] AC 1. See also *Palfrey v GLC* [1985] ICR 437; *Turner v MOD* (1969) 113 SJ 585; and *Hensman v Goodsall* (unreported, January 23 1997), QBD.
2   If the claimant is under a contractual obligation to repay any sick pay, then the claimant is entitled to recover damages for the same: *Browning v War Office* [1963] 1 QB 750, CA; *Davies v Inman* [1999] PIQR Q26. Even a moral obligation may impose an increase in damages: *Dennis v London Passenger Transport Board* [1948] 1 All ER 779. Where a voluntary payment is made with no expectation of reimbursement (either expressed or implied), then such payment is not recoverable from the defendant but, likewise, is not to be set off against a claim for past loss of earnings: *Cunningham v Harrison* [1973] QB 942; *Bews v Scottish Hydro-Electric plc* 1992 SLT 749.
3   *Pratt v Smith* (18 December 2002, unreported), QBD.

[J85]   *Hussain v New Taplow Paper Mills Ltd*[1] followed suit. The court held that personal incapacity payments restoring pay to full levels during a period of ill-health absence are essentially sick pay in lieu of wages, and as such should be deducted from loss of earnings. Lord Bridge stated[2]:

'It positively offends my sense of justice that a claimant, who has certainly paid no insurance premiums as such, should receive full wages during a period of incapacity from two different sources, her employers and the tortfeasor. It would seem to me still more unjust and anomalous where, as here, the employer and the tortfeasor are one and the same.'

1   [1987] 1 All ER 541.
2   At 548.

[J86] An employer has no claim against a tortfeasor to recover payments made to an employee which meet losses resulting from a tort. In *Metropolitan Police District Receiver v Croydon Corpn*[1], Lord Goddard CJ specified that the only loss suffered by an employer is the loss of services. The sick pay is such that the equivalent would have been paid, with or without the accident. The accident causes the employee to be unable to work, but no extra costs are incurred regarding the wages of that employee. An exception to the general rule can be seen in *Dennis v London Passenger Transport Board*[2], in which sick pay was ignored. The employer had a right to recover sick pay from the employee and, therefore, to deduct sums equivalent to sick pay from the damages which would potentially leave a shortfall. Thus, if an employee's contractual terms allow for such recoupment by the employer resulting in a shortfall of earnings, the shortfall may be recovered from the tortfeasor as a loss caused by the injuries (this is sometimes referred to as the 'employer's outlay').

[1]   [1957] 2 QB 154.
[2]   [1948] 1 All ER 779.

(iv)   Permanent Health Insurance

[J87] In *Page v Sheerness Steel plc*[1] the claimant contributed 4.5% of his earnings to an occupational pension plan which entitled the claimant to permanent health insurance. The trial judge held that, since there was no contract between the claimant and the health insurance company, and the claimant did not pay the premiums for the payments he received under the scheme which corresponded to wages and had the character of sick pay, applying *Hussain v New Taplow Paper Mills Ltd*[2], the benefits under the pension scheme were deductible from the claimant's claim for loss of earnings. This decision was subsequently upheld on appeals to the Court of Appeal and House of Lords[3].

[1]   [1996] PIQR Q26.
[2]   [1987] 1 All ER 417.
[3]   [1997] 1 WLR 652; [1999] 1 AC 345. See also *Gaca v Pirellis General Plc & others* [2004] EWCA Civ 373.

(v)   Tribunal or Court Awards

[J88] Where a claimant is dismissed unfairly or discriminated against by reason of his or her injuries and brings a claim for compensation in the Employment Tribunal (or civil court), the claimant must give credit for any award received[1]. Credit is given for the net compensation received, ie the gross amount of the compensation minus any irrecoverable costs incurred obtaining the same, such as legal fees (which, by virtue of r 12 of the Employment Tribunal Rules of Procedure, are unlikely to be recoverable).

[1]   *Assinder v Griffin* [2001] All ER (D) 356 (May).

(vi)   Pensions

Disablement pension[1]

[J89] The principle derived from *Parry v Cleaver*[2] is that disability pensions should be ignored in the assessment of damages for loss of earnings[3]. This was recently followed in *Smoker v London Fire and Civil Defence Authority*[4], in which Lord Templeman accepted that the pension was 'the fruit, through insurance, of all the money which was set aside in the past in respect of his past work'[5]. Lord Templeman then went on to state that this 'fruit cannot be appropriated by the tortfeasor'. The same point arose in relation to the calculation and was upheld in *Longden v British Coal Corporation*[6].

1   Also known as incapacity pensions, ie when a person is retired on grounds of ill-health, as opposed to reaching his or her normal retirement age.
2   [1970] AC 1.
3   Per Lord Reid at 15 and 16, and Lord Pearce at 42.
4   [1991] 2 AC 502.
5   Per Lord Reid in *Parry v Cleaver* [1970] AC 1 at 16.
6   [1997] 3 WLR 1336, HL.

[J90]   In effect, a disablement pension is a form of insurance and, as such, should be ignored in terms of calculating any loss of earnings.

[J91]   However, as regards a claim for loss arising out of reduced retirement pension due to injury, whilst the defendant cannot offset the amount of the annual disablement/ incapacity pension received before (intended) retirement age, the claimant must give credit (i) for the post-retirement disablement/incapacity benefit payments against the claim for annual pension loss; and (ii) for the post-retirement element of any lump sum received[1].

1   *Longden v British Coal Corporation* [1997] 3 WLR 1336, HL. See further at para **[H149]**.

Retirement pension

[J92]   The *Parry*[1] and *Smoker*[2] cases were relied on in *Hopkins v Norcros plc*[3]. In this case, it was held that, if a claimant had claimed a retirement pension before his usual retirement age, then this too should be ignored as it has been paid for by his previous work. Further, in *Hewson v Downs*[4] it was held that the pension payable should not be brought into account to reduce the apparent loss, even though the claimant was of retirement age. He had intended to carry on work until 70 and, therefore, had lost his wages up until that age plus the extra pension he would have been entitled to had he not been injured.

1   [1970] AC 1.
2   [1991] 2 AC 502.
3   [1994] ICR 11.
4   [1970] 1 QB 73. See also *Longden v British Coal Corporation* [1997] 3 WLR 1336, HL.

[J93]   *Parry v Cleaver*[1] considered that, before normal retirement age, to compare earnings and incapacity pension was not to compare like with like. However, after normal retirement age, the comparison of incapacity pension and retirement pension was to compare like with like.

1   [1970] AC 1.

Other pensions

[J94] As a general rule, state retirement pensions[1] and ex gratia pensions[2] will also not be deductible from claims in respect of loss of earnings, for the reasons expressed in *Parry v Cleaver*[3].

1   *Hewson v Downs* [1970] 1 QB 73.
2   *Cunningham v Harrison* [1973] QB 942; *Bews v Scottish Hydro-Electric plc* 1992 SLT 749, OH.
3   [1970] AC 1.

(vii)   Redundancy Payments

[J95] These are payments to which certain employees are entitled on the termination of their employment[1]. The essential criterion for eligibility is that the relevant employee has been dismissed, not because of factors individual to the employee, such as an inability to do the job, but because the requirements of the employer for an employee to do the job at all (or to do it in the same place) had ceased or diminished[2]. The amount of payment is calculated according to a set formula laid down by statute. The amount of payment is based on length of service, but the total may be increased under terms in the contract of employment. Another reason for a superficially increased payment can be if the employee has, in effect, volunteered for redundancy. The case law (set out below) is not conclusive on whether redundancy payments should be deducted from the loss claimed in a personal injury action.

1   Employment Rights Act 1996, s 162.
2   See Employment Relations Act 1999, s 139.

[J96] In *Wilson v National Coal Board*[1] the House of Lords said that only in exceptional circumstances should redundancy payments be deducted from the loss of earnings. This stemmed from the 'like for like' argument. The redundancy payment is not compensation for loss of earnings but for the loss of a settled job[2]. However, their Lordships went on to say that the payment should be deducted where redundancy would never otherwise have occurred, as for instance where a claimant would have continued to retirement age in the same job.

1   1981 SLT 67, HL.
2   Their Lordships relied on *Hindle v Percival Boats Ltd* [1969] 1 All ER 836, [1969] 1 WLR 174, CA.

[J97] The defendants must establish that the redundancy has been caused by the claimant's injury, and this is not easy to do. As Heilbron J stated in *Mills v Hassalls*[1]:

> 'There is no evidence, and no justifiable inference, in my judgment, to be drawn from the evidence such as has been called in this case, that Mr Mills would not have been dismissed at all for the purposes of the Employment Protection (Consolidation) Act 1978 but for the very incapacity to which his claim for loss of earnings relates.'

Heilbron J had earlier specified that only in exceptional circumstances would the redundancy payment be deducted. Following such argument, a redundancy payment, by its very nature, cannot be said to entirely flow from the injury. The whole point is that the employee is dismissed not because of incapacity etc, but because the employer has decided that his job no longer exists.

1   [1983] ICR 330 at 341.

[J98]   The Court of Appeal rejected such an approach in *Colledge v Bass Mitchells & Butlers Ltd*, in which a redundancy payment was deducted from the loss of earnings. If there had been no injury, the claimant would have been unlikely to accept redundancy. Sir John Donaldson rejected a plea to ignore redundancy payments in computing the loss[1]:

> 'The only way in which, as it seems to me, this argument can be put is that the claimant suffered a head of damage which one can describe as "loss of the job" and that the redundancy payment was exclusively designed and intended to compensate him for this head of damage. Loss of future earnings was something distinct and fell to be compensated separately. So far so good, but if this is correct every workman who loses his job in consequence of an accident, but is not redundant, should receive damages for "loss of the job", the measure presumably being the amount which he would have received if he had been made redundant. This does not happen ... I have also considered whether any different result could be achieved by regarding the claimant as claiming a "loss of redundancy rights". This may be slightly more promising, in that he would not have lost those rights but for the accident. However, it grinds to a halt because exactly the same could have been said by the claimant in *Wilson v National Coal Board*[2].'

[1]   [1988] 1 All ER 536, CA.
[2]   1981 SLT 67, HL.

[J99]   The law is, therefore, in some disarray. On the one hand, *Wilson*[1] is saying that only in exceptional cases would redundancy payments be deducted. On the other, *Colledge*[2] is saying the opposite, namely that only in rare cases should it be ignored. The conflict is essentially one of interpretation. Sir John Donaldson in *Colledge* specifies the rare case as 'where the claimant would have been made redundant regardless of the accident', while *Wilson* accepted that payment should be deducted if the tort was the cause of the redundancy. In effect, the courts come to the same conclusion, but from opposite starting points. A redundancy payment will be deducted if the accident has caused the claimant to accept or suffer redundancy. Clarity is necessary regarding what is the cause of the claimant's redundancy. If a claimant is made redundant, and if not caused by his or her injury, then he or she will have no claim for future loss of earnings from that particular job.

[1]   1981 SLT 67, HL.
[2]   [1988] 1 All ER 536.

(viii)   Tax Rebates and Savings

[J100]   If the claimant receives a tax rebate as a result of his or her injuries and consequent time off work, the same falls to be deducted from any claim for loss of earnings[1]. Likewise, credit must be given for any tax savings as a result of the injuries[2]. This may have particular relevance to the Government's tax credit schemes, such as working tax credit and child tax credit.

[1]   *Hartley v Sandholme Iron Co* [1975] QB 600.
[2]   *Brayson v Wilmot-Breedon* [1976] CLY 682.

(ix)　Social Security Benefits Outside the Statutory Recoupment Scheme

Benefits received as a result of the injuries sustained

[J101]　As seen above, the statutory provisions for the recoupment of state benefits apply only to specified benefits[1], and there are a number of benefits which fall outside the statutory scheme[2]. The recovery of such unlisted benefits falls to be determined under the common law.

1　The recoupable benefits are listed in column 2 of Sch 2 to the Social Security (Recovery of Benefits) Act 1997: see para **[J17]**.
2　See at paras **[J68]**, **[J69]**.

[J102]　The leading case on the recoupment of unlisted benefits is *Hodgson v Trapp*[1], in which it was held that if, in the absence of an express indication by Parliament, the benefit was in addition to tort damage, then past and future payments of the benefit should be deducted to avoid any double recovery. This case was decided before the recoupment scheme, and concerned mobility and attendance allowances. These are now listed in the relevant section of the 1997 Act, and are therefore subject to recoupment. However, the speech of Lord Bridge is helpful in relation to any other relevant benefit not covered by recoupment[2]:

> 'My Lords, it cannot be emphasised too often when considering the assessment of damages for negligence that they are intended to be purely compensatory. Where the damages claimed are essentially financial in character, being the measure on the one hand of the injured claimant's consequential loss of earnings, profits or other gains which he would have made if not injured, or on the other hand, of consequential expenses to which he has been and will be put which, if not injured, he would not have needed to incur, the basic rule is that it is the net consequential loss and expense which the court must measure. If, in consequence of the injuries sustained, the claimant has enjoyed receipts to which he would not otherwise have been entitled, prima facie, those receipts are to be set against the aggregate of the claimant's losses and expenses in arriving at the measure of his damages. All this is elementary and has been said over and over again. To this basic rule there are, of course, certain well established, though not always precisely defined and delineated exceptions. But the courts are, I think, sometimes in danger, in seeking to explore the rationale of the exceptions, of forgetting that they are exceptions. It is the rule which is fundamental and axiomatic and the exceptions to it which are only to be admitted on grounds which clearly justify their treatment as such.'

Lord Bridge went on to refer to the following obiter remarks by Lord Reid in *Parry v Cleaver*[3]:

> '... We do not have to decide in this case whether these considerations also apply to public benevolence in the shape of various uncovenanted benefits from the welfare state, but it may be thought that Parliament did not intend them to be for the benefit of the wrongdoer.'

He then continued:

> '... when I turn to consider statutory benefits for the relief of various forms of need which are payable as of right to those who fulfil the qualifying conditions, I find the concept

of "the intent of the person conferring the benefit" a somewhat elusive one. Statutory benefits of the kind in question come either directly from the pocket of the taxpayer or from some fund to which various classes of citizens make compulsory contributions. The legislation providing for the benefits is prompted by humanitarian considerations directed to meeting certain minimum needs of the disadvantaged, irrespective of their cause. It is, of course, always open to Parliament to provide expressly that particular statutory benefits shall be disregarded, in whole or in part, and s 2 of the Law Reform (Personal Injuries) Act 1948 is the most familiar instance where it has done so. But in the absence of any such express provision, where statutory benefits are payable to one whose circumstances of qualifying need arise in consequence of a tort of which he was the victim, I can certainly discern no general principle to support Lord Reid's tentative opinion "that Parliament did not intend them to be for the benefit of the wrongdoer".'

Lord Bridge referred in his judgment to *Parsons v BNM Laboratories Ltd*[4] in which it was held that unemployment benefit is taken into account as mitigation of loss of earnings occasioned by wrongful dismissal before concluding that credit should be given in full for both the attendance and mobility allowances received by the claimant:

'In the end the issue in these cases is not so much one of statutory construction as of public policy. If we have regard to the realities, awards of damages for personal injuries are met from the insurance premiums payable by motorists, employers, occupiers of property, professional men and others. Statutory benefits payable to those in need by reason of impecuniosity or disability are met by the taxpayer. In this context to ask whether the taxpayer, as the "benevolent donor," intends to benefit "the wrongdoer" as represented by the insurer who meets the claim at the expense of the appropriate class of policy holders, seems to me entirely artificial. There could hardly be a clearer case than that of the attendance allowance payable under section 35 of the Act of 1975 where the statutory benefit and the special damages claimed for cost of care are designed to meet the identical expenses. To allow double recovery in such a case at the expense of both taxpayers and insurers seems to me incapable of justification on any rational ground. It could only add to the enormous disparity, to which the advocates of a "no-fault" system of compensation constantly draw attention, between the position of those who are able to establish a third party's fault as the cause of their injury and the position of those who are not.'

---

1   [1989] 1 AC 807. See also *Clarke v South Yorkshire Transport Ltd* [1988] PIQR Q104, in which Mantell LJ stated: 'On ordinary principles the [claimant] must give credit for sums received from a source other than the defendant in respect of the same damage'.

2   At 819E.

3   [1970] AC 1.

4   [1964] 1 QB 95; affirmed by the House of Lords in *Westwood v Secretary of State for Employment* [1985] AC 20.

[J103] The principles in *Hodson v Trapp*[1] have since been applied to a number of unlisted benefits, including:

- Housing benefit[2].
- Council tax[3].
- Payments received from the Independent Living Fund[4].
- Payments made under the Pneumoconiosis (Workers' Compensation) Act 1979[5].

---

1   [1989] 1 AC 807.

2   *Clenshaw v Tanner* [2002] EWHC 184 (QB), in which Silber J said: 'So applying those principles to the Housing Allowance on the facts of this particular case, its purpose was to compensate the Claimant for the fact that he did not have means to pay rent or, put in another way, his earnings deficiency. That absence of income is encompassed in the loss of earnings claim, which seeks compensation for this loss. In other words, it seems to me that there is a sufficient correlation, because the sums that have been received as Housing Benefit are in respect of the same damage, namely loss of income. To adopt MacGregor's test, the Housing Benefit in this case covers the earnings loss and so is deductible. If this were not the case, the Claimant would be in a position of being substantially better off, as he would receive both compensation for loss of income and as a result of the housing benefits reduced level of expenditure to which the income would have been put, and that would mean that the Claimant would be compensated twice. I do not consider that to be correct and in accordance with general principles. If two men who were both renting accommodation were both injured in an accident and both lost their jobs in consequence, but only one is entitled to receive Housing Benefit because of his impecuniosity, then it would be strange if he could retain the Housing Benefit without giving credit for it in the loss of earnings claim while the other did not have that particular benefit. I do not consider that that would be in accordance with established principles. Mr. Allison disputes whether the Housing Benefit was paid in consequence of the injuries sustained. To my mind even that is a requirement, it was satisfied in the case here, because if the injury had not been sustained the Claimant would not have been entitled to Housing Benefit for the period during which he would have been working. Thus, bearing in mind that this is a fact-sensitive decision, part of the Housing Benefit is deductible, save in respect of the proportion that would have been paid anyway, which is 30%'. See further Nicholas Davies 'Housing Benefit and the Special Needs Trust' [2004] Quantum, Issue 4/2004, 8 July.

3   *Smith v Rod Jenkins* [2003] EWHC 1356 (QB), in which under the subheading 'Credit for Council Tax Benefit' Gibbs J said: 'Whilst the issue was not conceded by Mr de Wilde, no argument was advanced against the proposition that credit should be given for this benefit; accordingly credit is given in the undisputed sum of: £4392.98'.

4   *Dorrington v Lawrence* [2001] All ER (D) 145 (Nov), in which Hooper J said: 'The independent living fund, a Government funded organisation, has made payments of £66,524.70 to assist the family to buy in the services of paid carers. These sums are not repayable. It is agreed that the money has been used for paid carers. The defendant submits that the claimant should give credit for this money ... It seems to me that, applying *Hodgson v Trapp*, these sums are deductible and I so decide'.

5   *Ballantine v Newalls Insulation Co Ltd* [2000] PIQR Q57.

[J104]   When considering whether credit needs to be given for an unlisted benefit, it is important to bear in mind that 'like may only be offset against like'[1]. Therefore, if the benefit received relates to an aspect of damages which is not claimed or which the claimant is in law prevented from recovering[2], no credit need be given for the same. It is also important to consider whether or not there will be any liability to repay the benefit in question if damages are awarded, because this is likely to avoid the problem of double recovery and therefore militate against deduction[3].

1   *Parry v Cleaver* [1970] AC 1; *Clarke v South Yorkshire Transport Ltd* [1998] PIQR Q104; *Cresswell v Eaton* [1991] 1 WLR 1113 at 1125.

2   See eg *Rand and Rand v East Dorset Health Authority* [2001] PIQR Q1.

3   See eg *Berriello v Felixstowe Dock & Railway Co* [1989] 1 WLR 695.

Benefits that would have been received in any event

[J105]   To be recoupable, the benefits must be related to the injury or disability caused by the defendant's wrongdoing. If the claimant would have been entitled to the benefit in question or a proportion of it, notwithstanding the injuries sustained, no credit need be given for the same[1]. This principle applies irrespective of the fact that the title of the benefit might have changed following the defendant's wrongdoing, as long as the substance and amount of the benefit remains the same[2].

[1] See eg *Clenshaw v Tanner* [2002] EWHC 184 (QB), in which Silber J only gave credit for 70% of the amount of housing benefit received by the claimant, because 30% would have been received irrespective of the defendant's negligence.

[2] *Hassall and Pether v Secretary of State for Social Security* [1995] PIQR P292.

(x) Future Statutory Benefits

Listed statutory benefits

[J106] By virtue of s 17 of the Social Security (Recovery of Benefits) Act 1997, any listed benefits paid after the relevant period[1] are to be disregarded when assessing the claimant's award of damages. In *Eagle v Chambers (No 2)*[2] the Court of Appeal held that this section should be given a wide meaning. Therefore, it was held that, on the facts of the case, the defendant could not offset the claimant's future mobility allowance against the claim for future transport/mobility.

[1] Under Social Security (Recovery of Benefits) Act 1997, s 3(1) the 'relevant period' is defined as five years from the day upon which the accident or injury in question occurred or, in a disease case, five years from the date upon which the claimant first claims a listed benefit in consequence of the disease.

[2] [2004] EWCA Civ 1033.

Unlisted benefits

[J107] As seen above, any unlisted benefits fall to be assessed in accordance with the common law principles as set out in *Hodgson v Trapp*[1]. Therefore, unless the unlisted benefit would have been received in any event, future receipt as well as past receipt of unlisted benefits will be recouped on a 'like for like' basis. For example, in *Smith v Salford Health Authority*[2], Potter J held that the claimant had to give credit for future receipt of disability living allowance.

[1] [1989] 1 AC 807.

[2] (4 August 1995, unreported).

[J108] However, this does not necessarily mean that the multiplier adopted for the deduction of future benefits has to be the same as that used in order to calculate the head of loss in question. For example, in *Lay v SW Surrey Health Authority*[1], Phillips J applied a multiplier of only 9 to the multiplicand representing future attendance, but a multiplier of 18 to the multiplicand for future care, since there were likely to be some stages where the claimant was not entitled to the benefit. This decision was followed by Potter J, in *Smith v Salford*[2], who reduced the multiplier of 15 which had been applied to the future care claim to 10 when calculating the amount to be offset in respect of future disability living allowance. It was held that it would be unjust to apply the same multiplier when there was an obvious risk that the benefits rules might change in the future.

[1] (26 June 1989, unreported), referred to in *Kemp & Kemp* at A4-025.

[2] (4 August 1995, unreported).

[J109] In rare cases, the court might even take a higher multiplier to calculate the deduction for receipt of future benefits than used to calculate the head of loss in question. Such a situation arose in *Soper v Criminal Injuries Compensation Appeals Panel*[1], in which the applicant suffered from a pre-existing disability which might have given rise to the need for care in any event, but may not have triggered the entitlement to the benefit now received as a result of the injuries. On the facts, the Court of Appeal held that it was not irrational, illogical or unlawful of the Criminal Injuries Compensation Board to use a higher multiplier to take account of the likely receipt of future social security benefits than the multiplier used to calculate the award for future care.

[1]   [2002] EWCA Civ 1803.

(xi) CICB/CICA Awards

[J110] The claimant need not give credit for an award received from the Criminal Injuries Compensation Authority/Board. In *Oldham v Sharples*[1] the claimant brought a claim against her employer for failing to inform her about the dangerous nature of a man she was guarding. The man escaped from the claimant's custody, inflicting a needlestick injury to her during the process. She claimed to have suffered from post-traumatic stress disorder as a result. During the civil claim, it was revealed that the claimant had made a claim to the Criminal Injuries Compensation Board (CICB) and had received the sum of £3,000. At first instance, although the claimant won on liability, causation and contributory negligence, the judge rejected her medical evidence and awarded her the sum of £886.76. Given that she had recovered less than the amount she had received from the CICB, the judge made no order as to costs. The Court of Appeal held that the CICB award was not to be taken into account when assessing an award of damages if it has preceded the court action[2]. There was a public interest in the tortfeasor repaying money paid by the state to the claimant in compensation. In the circumstances, the Court of Appeal applied the reasoning in *McCafferty v Datta*[3], finding that the claimant had obtained a judgment of value and ordered that the defendant pay the claimant's costs on the old scale 1[4]. Most recently, in *AT & others v Dulghieru*[5], Treacy J refused to reduce the claimant's damages in a civil claim to take account of a CICA claim, holding that it 'would be contrary to notions of restorative justice to permit a Defendant to place any great weight on a payment which he did not make and has not offered to pay back to the CICA'[6].

[1]   [1997] PIQR Q82.
[2]   But the injured party cannot be awarded twice over and the claimant must repay the CICA/B award in full up to the amount of the civil award – see para 49 of the 1996 and 2001 schemes (which apply to claims made after 1 April 2001).
[3]   [1997] 1 WLR 870.
[4]   The Court of Appeal's reasoning in relation to costs in this case may have to be reconsidered in the light of the CPR and the principle of proportionality.
[5]   [2009] EWHC 225 (QB). See also *A v Hoare* [2008] EWHC 1573.
[6]   [2009] EWHC 225 (QB) at para [53].

(xii)   Foreign State Benefits

[J111]   If the claimant receives foreign state benefits which would not otherwise have been received in the absence of an injury, past and future sums are likely to be deducted in accordance with the principles laid down in *Hodgson v Trapp*[1]. However, if it is established that the claimant will have to repay the foreign state benefits upon receipt of his damages, then there is no danger of double recovery and therefore no need to give credit for such benefits[2].

1   [1989] 1 AC 807, [1989] 1 AC 807.
2   See eg *Berriello v Felixstowe Dock & Railway Co* [1989] 1 WLR 695.

(xiii)   Accounting Devices

[J112]   If the claimant receives money from a company for services as a shareholder or company secretary by way of an accounting device, as long as the payment(s) did not arise by reason of the claimant's injuries and would have arisen in any event, no credit needs to be given for such payment(s)[1].

1   *Ved v Caress* (9 April 2001, unreported), QBD, HHJ Chapman.

(xiv)   Summary of Collateral Benefits

[J113]

- Charitable payments are ignored in the assessment of damages, although there is some uncertainty as to whether it makes a difference if the benefactor is the tortfeasor.
- Insurance is ignored in the assessment of damages; however, there needs to be evidence that the claimant has either paid for or contributed to the insurance.
- Sick pay is deducted from damages for loss of earnings, however, it may be possible to reclaim sick pay on behalf of the claimant's employer, especially if there are specific contractual terms of employment which allow for this.
- Disablement pensions are ignored in the assessment of damages for loss of earnings, but after retirement age they are taken into account in the assessment of damages for loss of pension rights. The rule is the same whether or not the provider of the pension is the tortfeasor.
- Retirement pensions are ignored in the assessment of damages for loss of earnings. The rule is the same whether or not the provider of the pension is the tortfeasor. However, they are taken into account in the assessment of loss of pension (see further Chapter H).
- Redundancy payments (where injury has caused the redundancy) are deducted from damages for loss of earnings.
- Social security benefits are deductible as per the recoupment scheme.
- Credit is not given in any civil claim for a previous CICB/CICA award made in relation to the same injuries.
- Credit is not given for payments received by way of an accounting device that are not linked to the claimant's injuries.

K   Counter-schedules

I   Introduction

[K1]   The drafting of a counter-schedule involves a skill separate and distinct from that which is required in order to draft a schedule of loss. Of course, the drafter has to be familiar with the relevant legal and procedural framework in the same way that the drafter of the schedule of loss has to be. However, a counter-schedule involves much more than simply applying these principles in reverse. Although the counter-schedule is responding to the schedule of loss, the drafter of the counter-schedule is not bound by the same format, layout or style of the schedule of loss. The counter-schedule is the defendant's opportunity to present its own detailed case, both as to causation and as to the value of the claim. It is a key document – together with the skeleton argument, it is often a judge's starting point in considering a defendant's case on quantum – and time spent crafting a carefully constructed and reasonable case will often reap considerable benefits.

[K2]   Of course, it is trite law that the principle of compensation in tort is to put the claimant back into the position that he or she would have been in but for the negligence of the defendant[1]. However, the claimant is not entitled to be put into a better position[2]. This is particularly important with future losses and, as Lord Hope said in *Wells v Wells*[3]:

> '... the object of the award of damages for future expenditure is to place the injured party as nearly as possible in the same financial position he or she would have been in but for the accident. The aim is to award such a sum of money as will amount to no more, and at the same time no less, than the net loss.'

[1]   *Livingstone v Rawyards Coal Co* (1880) 5 App Cas 25.
[2]   *Thrul v Ray* [2000] PIQR Q44, per Burton J at Q47: 'It is therefore important in assessing the [claimant's] claim for compensation to bear in mind that it is not the purpose of this court to make allowance for anything which would, as it was put on various occasions by, I think, all the witnesses called by the [claimant], improve her "quality of life". It is not the test that the defendant should be required to pay by way of damages to the [claimant] consequent upon the unfortunate injuries resulting from the accident any sum which will simply make the [claimant] happier or more comfortable ... the provision must be one which is reasonably necessary to compensate for what she has lost, but also no more than is reasonably likely to be expended on her behalf in providing her with the substitute for what she has lost'.
[3]   [1999] 1 AC 345 at 390A–B.

[K3]   In the same way that the drafter of the schedule of loss will require evidence (often expert evidence) and access to supporting documentary materials before the schedule can be drafted, the drafter of the counter-schedule will also require source material in order to inform any challenges to the sums claimed. The general principle

493

is that he who asserts must prove[1]. As a result, where the counter-schedule puts forward a positive case – eg that the claimant has failed to mitigate his or her losses – that allegation must be supported by admissible evidence and cogent legal argument.

[1]   See further Chapter A, General Principles at para **[A50]**, chapter 45 of *McGregor on Damages* (18th edn), and *Phipson on Evidence* regarding the burden of proof.

[K4]   Given the flexibility of the rules relating to costs under the CPR, the incentive for defendants to challenge spurious or exaggerated claims is probably greater than it has ever been before. If a claimant exaggerates his claim, and recovers significantly less damages than the amount claimed, he may not be regarded as the successful party, and may be at serious risk of costs sanctions, even if he recovers more than the defendant's Part 36 offer.[1]

[1]   Under CPR, Pt 44.3 the court may make awards relating to the costs of arguing particular issues or points and must take into account the conduct of the parties, including whether a claimant has exaggerated his or her claim in whole or in part. See *Painting v University of Oxford* [2005] EWCA Civ 161; *Carver v BAA Plc* [2008] EWCA Civ 412.

[K5]   However, following the decision of the House of Lords in *Wells v Wells*[1], the scope for challenging claims has narrowed. Given the greater reliance upon actuarial tables, it is now much more difficult to obtain discounts for general contingencies or simply because the overall award appears too high. As Lord Lloyd alludes to in *Wells v Wells*, the drafter of the modern counter-schedule has to be much more imaginative in the way that claims are attacked and, given the decreasing level of applicable discount rate, must focus upon the individual multiplicands for each head of loss[2]:

'In my view the Court of Appeal was right to scrutinise the individual items which went to make up the multiplicand. Since the effect of reducing the rate of discount will be to increase the multiplier in every case, it is all the more important to keep firm control of the multiplicand. [Claimants] are entitled to a reasonable standard of care to meet their requirements, but that is all.'

[1]   [1999] 1 AC 345.
[2]   [1999] 1 AC 345 at 377E. Note that the attempt by claimants to get round the discount rate, by applying a stepped multiplicand, was rejected by the Court of Appeal in *Cooke v United Bristol Health Care* [2003] EWCA Civ 1370. This argument propounded by Rowland Hogg was described by Laws LJ at [30] as being 'in the end nothing but smoke and mirrors'.

[K6]   Ultimately, the object of the counter-schedule is to commend itself to the judge as an aid to quantifying the claim over and above the schedule of loss. In order for the defendant's approach to quantification to be preferred, the points taken and counter offers made must be well argued and reasonable. The schedule which takes every point regardless of merit is unlikely to find favour with the tribunal. If the sums claimed are genuine and reasonable, they should be agreed, or agreed subject to the production of documents evidencing the expenditure, particularly insofar as the relatively small items of past loss are concerned (which can be agreed without prejudice to a defendant's arguments as to principle or the future losses). A judge is much more likely to look sympathetically upon a defendant's case if he seeks to limit the scope of the dispute to the principal issues. Any arguments relating to quantum should be restricted to points that can be properly and fairly made and substantiated by evidence. Where a defendant wishes to claim that the claimant is malingering or exaggerating, he should plead any such case in the counter-schedule, but such claims should not be made lightly[1]. Obtaining the right balance between vigorously protecting the interests of the defendant and making reasonable concessions[2] where appropriate will often take considerable time and careful planning.

[1] The drafter of a counter-schedule who alleges fraud without credible evidence may be liable for wasted costs. Wasted costs may be awarded as against any solicitor or counsel involved in the case. Although such material does not necessarily have to be admissible, it must be of such character as to lead responsible counsel to conclude that serious allegations could be based upon it: *Medcalf v Mardell* [2002] UKHL 27.

[2] Note that concessions in counter-schedules should be made with care, because it may be difficult to resile from them at a later stage. See eg *Gleed v Set Scaffolding* (16 October 2001, unreported), QBD; and *Parkhouse v North Devon Healthcare NHS Trust* [2002] Lloyd's Rep Med 100. See further paras **[K232]–[K233]**.

[K7] With that in mind, in this chapter we look at the procedural requirements relating to counter-schedules, before going through the general principles applicable to the majority of schedules. By necessity, when dealing with the general principles there is some overlap here with other sections in the book and apologies are made for any repetition which the reader finds irksome. Finally, we look at some common heads of loss in detail, and highlight some of the considerations to be borne in mind when responding to these particular claims.

2   Requirements of the CPR

(i)   The Need for a Counter-schedule

[K8] By virtue of para 12.2 of the PD to CPR, Pt 16, a counter-schedule is needed where the claim is for personal injuries and the claimant has included a schedule of past and future expenses and losses.

(ii)   Format of the Counter-schedule

[K9] The counter-schedule may be included as part of the defence or be attached separately to the defence[1]. Generally speaking, it is sensible to prepare a separate counter-schedule for anything other than a small claim. This is because it makes it a lot easier to compare the two documents against each other, and to amend it if needed. It would appear from the terms of CPR, Pt 16 (entitled statements of case), and para 12.2 of the PD thereto, that a counter-schedule forms part of the defendant's defence, and hence is a statement of case, which would also be consistent with the requirement that a counter-schedule be verified by a statement of truth[2].

[1] CPR, PD 16, para 12.2.
[2] CPR, PD 22, para 1.4(3).

(iii)   Layout of the Counter-schedule

[K10] There are no specific requirements laid down by the CPR in relation to the style, layout or presentation of the counter-schedule[1].

[1] See further para **[K17]** et seq.

(iv)   Contents of the Counter-schedule

[K11]   Under para 12.2(1) of the PD to CPR, Pt 16 the defendant must state in the counter-schedule which items in the schedule of loss he or she:

(a) agrees;
(b) disputes; or
(c) neither agrees nor disputes, but has no knowledge of.

[K12]   By virtue of para 12.2(2) of the PD to CPR, Pt 16, where any items are disputed, the defendant must supply alternative figures where appropriate.

[K13]   A counter-schedule must be also verified by a statement of truth[1].

[1]   CPR, PD 22, para 1.4(3).

(v)   Timing of the Counter-schedule

[K14]   Since the counter-schedule must be included in the defence or attached to the defence, the counter-schedule must be served in compliance with CPR, r 15.4(1), which reads as follows:

'The general rule is that the period for filing a defence is—
(a)   14 days after service of the particulars of claim; or
(b)   if the defendant files an acknowledgement of service under Part 10, 28 days after service of the particulars of claim.'

[K15]   This period may be extended by agreement with the claimant by a period up to 28 days under CPR, r 15.5. The court must be notified of any such agreement[1].

[1]   CPR, r 15.5(2).

(vi)   Who Must be Served With a Copy of the Counter-schedule?

[K16]   Under CPR, r 15.6 a copy of the defence must be served on every other party to the proceedings. Although this rule does not specifically refer to the counter-schedule, on the assumption that the counter-schedule must be either included in the defence or attached to it, the counter-schedule must also be served on every other party.

3   The Aims, Layout and Style of the Counter-schedule

(i)   The Aims of the Counter-schedule

[K17]   A counter-schedule should be designed to be:

- attractive to the court which is to read it;
- user friendly;
- clear;
- logical;

- flexible enough to incorporate amendments, additions, deletions and new information;
- compendious; and
- persuasive enough to the claimant to make him or her moderate or abandon some or all of the claims made.

(ii)   The Layout of the Counter-schedule

[K18]   The layout of any counter-schedule is a matter of personal style, but it is generally sensible to cover a number of matters of principle at the start of a counter-schedule, before turning to the response to each individual head of claim. The following suggested structure may be adapted according to the requirements of each particular case.

(1)   Introduction

A counter-schedule should contain an introduction covering any or all of the following matters:

- A summary of any abbreviations adopted in the counter-schedule.
- If necessary, a statement to the effect that any admissions made in the counter-schedule are made subject to any issues of liability.
- If the counter-schedule is provisional, a statement to that effect, and a summary of the further evidential steps which will be necessary (in terms of a final schedule of loss, further information and disclosure which is required, outstanding factual and expert witness evidence etc) before the defendant will be in a position to finalise his counter-schedule. In particular, it is often sensible to list any further categories of disclosure which the defendant requires the claimant to give, or which need to be obtained from third parties (eg educational records, medical records, employment files, personnel and occupational health records, earnings and tax documentation, benefits files etc).

(2)   Relevant data and information

- Generally speaking, it is useful for the counter-schedule to contain a section setting out all relevant data and information (eg all dates and ages relevant to the claims in question) at or near the beginning (particularly if this is not included in the schedule of loss).

(3)   Multipliers (and life expectancy)

- A section setting out the defendant's case as to the various multipliers, or at least the starting point multipliers (before discounting for further contingencies), which he contends are appropriate in respect of life, earnings, pension, etc.
- If there is an issue as to life expectancy, the defendant should set out his case on that issue in justifying the life multiplier for which he contends.

(4)   Periodical payments

- In any case where it is appropriate to do so, the defendant should state whether he considers that periodical payments or a lump sum is the more appropriate form of award for all or part of an award of damages, and should provide relevant particulars of the circumstances relied upon in support of his stance (see CPR, rr 41.5, 41.7).

(5) The defendant's case in outline
- In more complex claims, a defendant should consider setting out his case on (i) causation, and (ii) any arguments of principle. It may also be helpful, and tactically desirable, in a complex claim, to preface this summary with a summary of the claimant's case in outline by way of contrast.
- It is often helpful, in the course of this exercise, to summarise the relevant expert (and possibly other) evidence on which the defendant relies in support of his case.
- In terms of causation, a simple structure is to summarise: (i) the relevant features of the claimant's life – what is relevant will depend on what is being claimed – before and at the time of the accident (eg any relevant educational, occupational, medical, and family or social history); (ii) how the claimant's life would probably have progressed but for the accident, whether medically (eg would he have developed some disabling condition in any event and, if so, what impact would that have had on his life?), educationally, occupationally (eg would he have remained in continuous or the same employment but for the accident?); (iii) the injuries and disabilities which the claimant sustained as a result of the accident, and the consequences of the same, including, where appropriate, any medical prognosis for an improvement in the claimant's condition; and (iv) the defendant's case in principle on issues of causation in terms of the various claims advanced (eg which losses are not attributable to injuries he sustained in the accident, and would have been incurred in any event?), including any failure by the claimant to mitigate his losses.
- In addition, any further arguments of principle, should be particularised.
- Any allegation that the claimant is malingering should be identified.
- If a defendant challenges an allegation that the claimant does not have mental capacity, this should be identified.
- If a defendant is going to contend that, for example, there are so many imponderables surrounding the claimant's claim for loss of earnings that only a *Blamire* award is appropriate, then this argument, and a summary of the imponderables, should be identified at this stage.

[K19]   The counter-schedule should then proceed to a summary of the defendant's responses to the various heads of claim, outlining the differences in the subtotals and final total between the parties. In order to be user friendly, it is often better to split the counter-schedule into its component parts, namely:

(1) general damages;
(2) past expenses and losses;
(3) interest on past expenses and losses; and
(4) future expenses and losses.

Within each section, each head of loss should be covered under a separate subheading. In many instances, it will be convenient to follow the layout of the schedule of loss. However, the drafter of the counter-schedule should not feel constrained to adopt the same order if there is no logical structure to it, or if there is a better way of presenting the information to the reader.

[K20]   Whatever the precise form in which the response is laid out, the counter-schedule should aim to identify, in respect of each head of loss:

(a)   the name of the head of loss;
(b)   the amount claimed by the claimant and, in respect of larger heads of claim, a summary of the factual assumptions made by the claimant in advancing that claim;
(c)   the amount allowed by the defendant and, in respect of larger heads of claim, a summary of any positive case raised in response to the main factual assumptions made by the claimant in advancing his claim; and
(d)   if not already covered by the above, the reasons for any dispute.

[K21]   It is helpful to the court, and therefore invariably sensible, to append to the counter-schedule, or to conclude with it, a summary in the form of a spreadsheet which sets out, in respect of each head of claim, the sums claimed by the claimant, and the sums agreed or offered by the defendant in response. In that way, the court is able to identify at a glance the main areas of dispute.

(iii)   The Style of the Counter-schedule

[K22]   Styles of counter-schedule differ from the extremely bullish and aggressive to the more reasonable and open-minded. Although styles will often change with the particular drafter, it is suggested that thought should specifically be given to the nature of the individual case and the message that the defence is attempting to convey. This will often turn on the perceived credibility of the claimant. On the one hand, if the claimant's evidence is unreliable or tainted with deceit, there is often scope to challenge heads of claim in their entirety. On the other hand, if the claimant is likely to be found by the court to be a credible witness, it may be futile to deny the claimant's entitlement to various heads of claim in principle (unless they are unsustainable in law, or not caused by the injuries in question). In this scenario, it is likely to be more fruitful to concentrate on challenging the reasonableness of the sums claimed and/or the duration of the claim.

[K23]   There is no strict requirement for the drafter to refer to any specific rule or case law in support of his or her arguments[1]. The danger of citing any specific rule or case is that the law may change before the case is heard and/or the claimant's advisers may be able more readily to anticipate and prepare for certain lines of attack. However, it may be that, in a particular case, express reference to a certain rule or case would serve to narrow the issues between the parties and curtail the length of any hearing, or may alert the claimant to a line of case law about which he or she appears to have been ignorant, and thus reduce the claim to a level at which it might settle.

---

[1]   There is a general discretion to refer to any point of law relied upon under CPR, PD 16, para 13.3(1).

4   General Principles

[K24]   The following principles should always be borne in mind when drafting a counter-schedule.

(i)   The Claimant Must Prove His or Her Loss

[K25]   At all times, it must be remembered that the burden of proof rests upon the claimant to establish the extent of his or her loss and the fact that he or she is entitled to recover substantial rather than nominal damages[1]. The court is only able to assess the appropriate amount of damages to be awarded if there is sufficient evidence[2]. If the claimant fails to provide sufficient evidence in support of the various claims made, those claims are likely to fail[3].

[1]   See further chapter 45 of *McGregor on Damages* (18th edn).

[2]   *Harrison v Leake* (1989) Times, 12 October, CA.

[3]   See eg *Ashcroft v Curtin* [1971] 1 WLR 1731, CA, where it was held that it was impossible accurately to quantify the claimant's claim for loss of earnings in the absence of reliable accounts and therefore the claim must fail. For a more recent example, see *Hughes (Gordon Clifford) v Addis (John)* (23 March 2000, unreported), CA, involving a claim for increased fuel costs arising out of the claimant's car phobia. The appeal was rejected because of the claimant's failure to provide evidence in support of the claim. Also, in *Cottrell v Redbridge Healthcare NHS Trust* (2001) 61 BMLR 72, the claimant was restricted to claiming the amounts allowed by the defendant in respect of past gratuitous care where the judge had rejected the evidence of the claimant and his witnesses.

[K26]   However, it should be noted that, assuming that the claimant is able to show that he or she suffered some type of loss, it will be no defence that the loss is too difficult to quantify. The court must do its best to assess the extent of the loss[1]. Also, certain loss can be inferred or presumed from the facts[2]. Take, for example, the common situation where, following an accident, the claimant has attended numerous sessions of physiotherapy. The claimant drove to the physiotherapist using a vehicle that he or she already had. The claimant is able to produce the receipts for treatment and the records from the physiotherapist to prove that he or she had the number of physiotherapy sessions claimed, but is unable to produce the petrol or parking receipts for each of the trips. Here, there is a definite loss of the cost of travel that has been sustained, and most judges would be content to award a reasonable estimate of the likely costs incurred.

[1]   *Thompson v Smith Shiprepairers (North Shields)* [1984] QB 405. See also *Chaplin v Hicks* [1911] 2 KB 786, in which Vaughan Williams LJ stated, 'The fact that damages cannot be assessed with certainty does not relieve the wrongdoer of the necessity of paying damages'.

[2]   See further chapter 45 of *McGregor on Damages* (18th edn). See also *Bygrave v Thomas Cook Tour Operations Ltd* [2003] EWCA Civ 1631, where the Court of Appeal held that it was reasonable for the trial judge to draw an inference from the evidence that the claimant would spend more on taxis in the future because of her injuries; and *Huntley v Simmonds* [2009] EWHC 405 (QB), where Underhill J, in the face of a complete absence of appropriate evidence as to the cost of the accommodation which the claimant (i) would have rented and purchased but for the accident, and (ii) required now given his additional needs, but was satisfied that there would be a loss, estimated the likely costs differential on a conservative basis.

[K27]   The degree of proof required depends on the nature and type of loss claimed. Certainly, under the CPR, proportionality is the key. It would not necessarily be reasonable to expect a claimant to detail every single item of expenditure to the nearest penny – although the larger the claim, the greater the need for evidence to establish its value.

[K28]   Often, the defendant will be forced to respond to a claim before any documentary evidence has been provided in support or full disclosure has taken place.

In such a case, the defendant is likely to be unable properly to respond to the claim and this should be made clear in the counter-schedule. If the claim appears genuine and reasonable, it is often sensible to admit the claim 'subject to the production of documentation evidencing the expenditure alleged'.

(ii) Failure to Plead a Head of Loss

[K29]   Technically, the court has the power to grant any remedy to the claimant to which he or she is entitled, even if that remedy is not specified in the claim form[1]. However, it is incumbent on a claimant who wishes to recover damages under a particular head of loss to make the defendant aware of the claim as early as possible[2].

[1]   CPR, r 16.2(5).
[2]   See eg *Harding v Watts Tyre & Rubber Co* (8 December 1986, unreported).

[K30]   Given the modern 'cards on the table' approach to litigation, it is likely to be difficult for a claimant to recover damages for heads of loss which are not specifically set out in the claimant's statement of case or schedule of loss. Under para 4.2 of the PD to CPR, Pt 16 the claimant is required to attach to his or her particulars of claim a schedule of 'details of any past and future expenses and losses which he claims'[1]. This becomes most apparent when, on the basis of the claims set out in the schedule of loss, the defendant has properly taken steps to protect him or herself as to costs by making a Part 36 offer or payment into court.

[1]   This may cast some doubt on the decision of *Thorn v Powergen* [1997] PIQR Q71, decided under the old law, in which it was held that, although it was good practice to plead a claim for handicap on the labour market, it was not strictly necessary if such a claim was disclosed on the face of the medical evidence. *Chan Wai Tong v Li Ping Sum* [1985] AC 446 is Privy Council authority to the same effect – there is no rule inherent in the common law that requires such a claim to be pleaded, though it is obviously desirable that it should be. However, it is worth noting that CPR, r 16.2(5) states that the court may grant any remedy to which the claimant is entitled, even if that remedy is not specified in the claim form. See also *Crouch v King's Healthcare NHS Trust* [2004] EWCA Civ 853, where the Court of Appeal upheld the lump sum award made by the trial judge of £20,000 for loss of earning capacity, even though a claim had only been pleaded for future loss of earnings.

[K31]   These considerations are highly relevant in smaller cases which are swiftly propelled towards a trial once proceedings have begun. In *Taylor v Brock*[1], the claimant applied to adjourn a disposal hearing, in order to obtain updated medical evidence and more information regarding the claim for special damages (particularly loss of earnings) and to investigate a claim in respect of handicap on the labour market. Tuckey LJ stated[2]:

'The procedure demands, as one would expect, that defendants to such claims should be given ample notice of what claims they face ... This was a case which had been allocated to the fast track. The fast track means what it says. The adherence to a fixed timetable is all-important. The Practice Direction makes it clear that in such cases "litigants and lawyers must be in no doubt that the court will regard the postponement of a trial as an order of last resort".'

[1]   [2001] CP Rep 11.
[2]   At [17], [18].

(iii)   Financial Limit on Claims

[K32]   If a claimant has limited the claim to a particular amount, eg £5,000, the court may be reluctant to allow the claimant to recover more than that amount without applying to extend the limit[1]. The nearer the case is to trial, the more difficult it will be for the claimant to extend the limit. This is particularly relevant in fast track (or small claims track) cases, where the interests of justice and the interests of the administration of justice often do not favour an adjournment[2].

[1]   Although note that technically CPR, r 16.3(7) does not limit the power of the court to give judgment for the amount which it finds the claimant is entitled to.

[2]   See *Dunn v Lewisham* [2001] 5 CL 70, in which *Taylor v Brock* [2001] CP Rep 11 and *Gregory v Bartlett* (3 May 2000, unreported) were applied. See further *Maguire v Molin* [2002] EWCA Civ 1083, [2003] 1 WLR 644.

(iv)   Duty to Plead a Positive Case

[K33]   The CPR created a sea-change in the way that defendants were expected to deal with claims. Under the old law, a defendant could deny liability without giving reasons and simply put the claimant to strict proof of his or her losses. Although there were a number of specific allegations that had to be pleaded[1], many procedural and legal arguments could be left to the start of the trial.

[1]   For example, contributory negligence, novus actus, limitation and fraud.

[K34]   The CPR requires a defendant to state whether or not the sums claimed in the schedule of loss are agreed, not agreed or disputed, and obliges the defendant to supply alternative figures where appropriate. Technically, there is no requirement to state why the sums are not agreed or disputed. However, in the experience of the authors, judges have tended to interpret Pt 16 as requiring a defendant who intends to raise a positive case at trial to set out that case in the defence. This is certainly the obligation under CPR, r 16.5(2), which requires a defendant who denies an allegation in the particulars of claim to state his or her reasons for so doing, and to state an alternative version of events if the intention is to rely upon an alternative version of events at trial. In theory, there is no reason why the obligation upon a defendant to plead a positive case on liability should be any different from the obligation to plead a positive case on quantum.

[K35]   This obligation has specific ramifications for certain defences or counter-schedules of a complex nature, such as responses to claims for credit hire (where, usually, quantum is the only issue). It is not uncommon for such counter-schedules to run to numerous pages, setting out the various legal arguments that are relied upon.

(v)   Reasonableness

[K36]   Any claim must represent a real loss. Where it is for some benefit which is not a replacement of something lost (such as a salary or damaged clothing), the yardstick against which any claim must be measured is 'reasonableness'. The reasonableness of the claim usually falls to be considered in two principal ways: first, the reasonableness of making the claim at all; and secondly, the reasonableness of the amount claimed.

Reasonableness of the claim

[K37] As regards the first category of reasonableness, it is for the claimant to establish that the item claimed is a reasonable expense or loss required in order to put the claimant back into the position that he or she would have been in but for the accident. The following principles should be borne in mind:

- The claimant is entitled to damages to meet his reasonable requirements or reasonable needs arising from his injuries[1].
- What is reasonable is to be judged not only by reference to what is reasonably necessary as a result of the injuries a claimant has sustained, but also as to the sort of lifestyle the claimant would have enjoyed but for the accident[2].
- It is not necessarily enough for a defendant merely to identify a cheaper alternative to that which is claimed: he must show that what is being claimed goes beyond what is reasonably necessary[3].
- Although it has been suggested[4] that the issue as to whether this is a question of compensation for loss sustained, or one of mitigation of loss, is immaterial, as the test is the same (namely, in either case the question is 'is it reasonable?'), it is submitted that there is a difference at least in terms of the burden of proof, which only falls on the defendant where he asserts a failure to mitigate.
- In determining what is required to meet the claimant's needs, it is first necessary to make findings as to the nature and extent of those needs to consider whether what is proposed by the claimant is reasonable, having regard to those needs[5].
- A defendant should therefore challenge the reasonableness of any claim by reference to the claimant's reasonable needs.

---

[1] *Sowden v Lodge* [2005] 1 WLR 2129.

[2] See *Huntley v Simmonds* [2009] EWHC 405 (QB), where the claim for the cost of a claimant's rented accommodation in a marina by a claimant who had grown up on a council estate was reduced because it included a premium 'for features which are not in any sense necessary', including 'a balcony with a marina view' (see para 89).

[3] This principle was summarised in the judgment of Stephenson LJ in *Rialis v Mitchell* (1984) Times, 17 July: 'The court must not react to dreadful injuries by considering that nothing is too good for the boy which will ameliorate his condition and increase pathetically little enjoyment of life which is all that is left to him; that would lead to making the defendant pay more than a fair and reasonable compensation. But the court must not put the standard of reasonableness too high when considering what is being done to improve a plaintiff's condition or increase his enjoyment of life ... the defendant is answerable for what is reasonable human conduct and if their choice is reasonable he is no less answerable for it if he is able to point to cheaper treatment which is also reasonable'. Cf *Smith v LC Window Fashions Ltd* [2009] EWHC 1532 (QB) per Cranston J: 'So long as the proposals of his professional advisers are reasonable, he is entitled to the reasonable costs of effecting them. There is no need to approve the least cost option unless any other option would be unreasonable'.

[4] Stephenson LJ in *Rialis v Mitchell* (1984) Times, 17 July.

[5] See *A v Powys Local Health Board* [2007] EWHC 2996 (QB), per Lloyd Jones J at para 94, following *Massey v Tameside and Glossop Acute Services NHS Trust* [2007] EWHC 317 (QB), per Teare J at para 59; and *Taylor v Chesworth and MIB* [2007] EWHC 1001 (QB), per Ramsay J at para 84.

[K38]   Examples of unreasonable claims include:

- A claim for the hire of a replacement vehicle when the claimant already had access to an alternative car[1] (although not taking up an offer of a replacement car via the claimant's own insurance policy will not amount to a failure to mitigate[2]).
- A claimant seeking to recover the costs of private healthcare treatment where, on the balance of probabilities, the claimant is likely to avail him or herself of treatment on the NHS[3].
- A claim for a hydrotherapy pool at home, where it would be beneficial for the claimant to integrate with her surroundings as much as possible, and thereby attend the local swimming pool with family or carers (and where her sensitivity to noise was surmountable by taking her at quieter times of the day)[4].
- Claims for a quad bike in order to take a dog for a country walk where the claimant did not own a dog at the date of the trial, and for the purchase of a golf buggy where the claimant only played golf a few times a year (when he could hire one)[5].
- Claiming for the cost of aids or equipment for which there is no support in the expert evidence[6].
- Claiming for the cost of items which are desirable but not reasonably necessary[7].
- A claim for the cost of a case manager when the claimant has sufficient intellectual capacity to manage and control his or her own affairs[8].
- A claim for the cost of an orange juicer as well as cranberry juice and vitamins[9].
- A claim for the cost of a new drug for which there is no proven data regarding its long-term efficacy or possible side-effects[10].

[1]   See *Whitworths v Crenoon* [2006] LTL 11.8.2006, Lawtel Document No AC0111618.
[2]   See *Trevor Rose v The Cooperative Group* [2005] LTL 21.3.2005, Lawtel Document No AC0108490.
[3]   See eg *Woodrup v Nicol* [1993] PIQR Q104, CA.
[4]   *Smith v East & North Hertfordshire Hospitals NHS Trust* [2008] EWHC 2234 (QB).
[5]   *Morgan v MOD* [2002] EWHC 2072 (QB).
[6]   See eg *Cottrell v Redbridge Healthcare NHS Trust* (2001) 61 BMLR 72, where the claim for the past cost of a reclining chair was disallowed on the basis that the medical experts in their joint report agreed that such a chair was unnecessary.
[7]   See eg *Duhelon v Carson* (18 July 1986, unreported) where Stuart Smith J refused to award the cost of the 'Philadelphia Programme' which had been recommended by the British Institute of Brain Injured Children. See also *Biesheuval v Birrell* [1999] PIQR Q40, where Eady J refused the claim for skin treatment and massage because there was no 'pressing need' for these treatments.
[8]   *Page v Sheerness Steel plc* [1996] PIQR Q26.
[9]   *Biesheuval v Birrell* [1999] PIQR Q40 (although Eady J did allow the cost of a bath and a shower because it was reasonable to allow the claimant to have the choice of how to wash).
[10]   In *Biesheuval v Birrell* [1999] PIQR Q40 the claim for Viagra was disallowed; cf *Re McCarthy* [2001] 6 CL 172, in which Blofeld J awarded the claimant £37,500 for Viagra treatment.

Reasonableness of amount claimed

[K39]   The claim will not be allowed if it is excessive or exaggerated. The claim will be denied or, alternatively, reduced to the level that is reasonably recoverable. For example:

- It is not reasonable for a claimant to claim the cost of hiring a Rolls Royce for the duration that the claimant's Mini is being repaired[1].

- It would be unreasonable to claim the running and standing costs of travelling to hospital appointments when the claimant already had the vehicle used for the journeys and the purchase of the vehicle was not related to the accident[2].
- The claimant will not be entitled to claim the cost of care provided by a State Registered Nurse where the care required could reasonably be provided by a nursing auxiliary or someone less qualified (and therefore cheaper)[3].
- Claiming for a powered wheelchair when the medical evidence supports the view that a manual wheelchair would be sufficient for the claimant's needs.
- It would be unreasonable to claim for the cost of a hydrotherapy pool where the medical evidence did not support the need for a hydrotherapy pool at the claimant's home[4].
- Where a baby is brain damaged at birth by reason of the defendant's negligence, it would be unreasonable to recover the whole cost of the baby's care[5].
- The purchase and adaptation of a property which went far in excess of what had originally been recommended by the accommodation experts, to which the claim was confined[6].

[1]   See eg *Watson Norie v Shaw* (1967) 111 Sol Jo 117, CA.
[2]   In this scenario, the claimant would be restricted to only claiming the running costs, because the standing costs (such as tax, insurance etc) would have been incurred in any event.
[3]   See eg *Radford v Jones* (1973, unreported). Also see *Leon Seng Tan v Bunnage* (23 July 1986, unreported), in which Gatehouse J disallowed the cost of a night-time carer because the job of turning the claimant could just as easily have been done by an electric bed with a timer set to operate every four hours. It was held that 'it would be quite unreasonable for the defendants to have to pay a capital sum of over £130,000 for this additional care assistant to carry out no more than about 10 minutes' work per night'.
[4]   See eg *Cassel v Riverside Health Authority* [1992] PIQR Q1; and *Smith v East & North Hertfordshire Hospitals NHS Trust* [2008] EWHC 2234 (QB). Cf *Haines v Airedale NHS Trust* (2 May 2000, unreported), QBD, per Bell J, where the evidence did support the need for a hydrotherapy pool at the claimant's home; and *Willett v North Bedfordshire Health Authority* [1993] PIQR Q166, where the property included a swimming pool, which was not necessary to the claimant's needs. The cost of buying that property was nevertheless held to be reasonable and recoverable.
[5]   Babies require a lot of care in any event, and the claimant is only entitled to claim for the additional amount of care that is required by reason of the defendant's negligence.
[6]   See *Pankhurst v White & others* [2009] EWHC 1117 (QB).

(vi)   Claimant's Duty to Mitigate Loss

Introduction

[K40]   The claimant is under an obligation to take reasonable steps to mitigate the loss to him or her consequent on the defendant's wrongdoing. Failure by the claimant to take reasonable steps to minimise his or her loss will prevent recovery for the loss that could have been avoided. However, a failure to mitigate has to be raised by the defendant, upon whom the burden of proof lies to show such a failure.

The duty to plead

[K41]   As a consequence of the burden of proof resting upon the defendant, if the defendant seeks to argue that the claimant has failed to mitigate his or her loss, this should be expressly pleaded in the defence or counter-schedule[1]. Likewise, the claimant must specifically plead any facts relating to mitigation of loss or damage on which he or she wishes to rely at trial[2].

1   See further para **[K33]**. In *Geest plc v Lansiquot* [2002] UKPC 48, Lord Bingham said at [16]: 'It should be clearly understood that if a defendant intends to contend that a [claimant] has failed to mitigate his or her damage, notice of such contention should be clearly given to the [claimant] long enough before the hearing to enable the [claimant] to prepare to meet it. If there are no pleadings, notice should be given by letter'.
2   CPR, PD 16, para 8.2(8).

The burden of proof

[K42]   The onus of proving that the claimant has failed to mitigate his or her loss rests on the defendant[1].

1   *Roper v Johnson* (1873) LR 8 CP 167; *Garnac Grain Co v Faure & Fairclough* [1968] AC 1130; *Geest plc v Lansiquot* [2002] UKPC 48; *Froggatt v LEP International* [2002] EWCA Civ 600. See further Chapter A, General Principles at paras **[A80]**–**[A87]**, and chapter 7 of *McGregor on Damages* (18th edn).

A question of fact or law?

[K43]   Whether or not the claimant has failed to mitigate his or her loss is a question of fact and not law[1].

1   *Payzu v Saunders* [1919] 2 KB 581, CA; and *The Solholt* [1983] 1 Lloyd's Rep 605, CA.

The standard to be expected

[K44]   The claimant need only avoid acting unreasonably, and the standard of reasonableness is not high[1]. A claimant is not expected to take undue risks to their health or financial stability in protecting the defendant's interests. A claimant need only go so far. For example, it does not amount to a failure to mitigate loss for a woman to refuse to undergo an abortion to end an unwanted pregnancy[2].

1   See further chapter 7 of *McGregor on Damages* (18th edn). The following words of Sachs LJ in *Melia v Key Terrain Ltd* (1969) No 155B were cited with approval by the Court of Appeal in *Morris v Richards* [2003] EWCA Civ 232: 'As between a claimant and a tortfeasor the onus is on the latter to show that the former has unreasonably neglected to mitigate the damages. The standard of reasonable conduct required must take into account that a claimant in such circumstances is not to be unduly pressed at the instance of the tortfeasor. To adopt the words of Lord Macmillan in the well-known *Waterlow* case, the claimant's conduct ought not to be weighed in nice scales at the instance of the party which has occasioned the difficulty'.
2   *Emeh v Kensington Area Health Authority* [1985] QB 1012, CA.

The benefit of mitigation

[K45]   Assuming that the claimant does take successful steps in order to limit his or her loss, the defendant is entitled to the benefit of the mitigation and is only liable for the reduced amount of the loss[1]. For example, in *Bellingham v Dhillon*[2] the claimant, who owned and ran a driving school, sustained a back injury in a car accident. He claimed the lost profits that he would have made if he had been able to buy an electronic driving simulator. At the time of the accident, he was in negotiations to buy such a simulator, but as a result of his injuries these negotiations fell through. Over three years later, the claimant was able to buy a simulator at a much cheaper price. Forbes J held that the claimant had to give credit for the saving that he made by buying the cheaper simulator against his claim for lost profits. This reduced his claim for financial loss to nil.

¹   *British Westinghouse Electric and Manufacturing Co Ltd v Underground Electric Railways Co of London Ltd* [1912] AC 673.
²   [1973] QB 304.

Worsening of condition

[K46]   If a claimant takes reasonable actions to mitigate his or her loss which actually increase the extent of the damage, the defendant is liable for the increased damage¹. Therefore if, for example, a claimant with a back injury is advised by his or her treating doctor to undergo a certain form of treatment and this treatment actually makes the condition worse, the defendant will be liable for the resulting deterioration in the claimant's condition. The only qualifications to this rule are that the claimant's actions must not have been unreasonable and the chain of causation must not be broken (eg by the treatment being performed negligently²).

¹   *Hoffberger v Ascot* (1976) 120 Sol Jo 130, CA – although this was a claim in contract, the principle applies equally in tort.
²   See para **[K73]**.

Expenses incurred during attempts to mitigate loss

[K47]   The claimant is entitled to recover all reasonable expenses incurred in taking steps to mitigate his or her loss. The most common example in personal injury cases is the cost of obtaining medical treatment or rehabilitation. However, in order to satisfy the court that such treatment is reasonable, it will usually be necessary to show that the treatment has been recommended by a qualified medical practitioner and is shown to have some proven benefit. Thus, the cost of new drugs whose long-term efficacy and side-effects are unknown may not be recoverable¹. Likewise, it may be difficult for the claimant to recover compensation for alternative therapies and remedies not approved by conventional (Western) medicine².

¹   See eg *Biesheuval v Birrell* [1999] PIQR Q40, in which Eady J disallowed the claim for Viagra; cf *Re McCarthy* [2001] 6 CL 172.
²   This is a very grey area in terms of what is recoverable and what is not. In the authors' experience, reasonable claims for osteopathy, chiropractic treatment and acupuncture are often upheld (albeit not necessarily for life), whereas claims for massage (but not sports massage), spa treatment, aromatherapy and herbal remedies are more difficult. See further para **[K167]** and Chapter F, Past Expenses and Losses at para **[F46]**.

Impecuniosity

[K48]   It is trite law that a defendant must take his or her victim as they find them. Therefore, a claimant ordinarily should not be prejudiced by reason of impecuniosity for not being able to take reasonable steps to mitigate his or her loss[1]. *Liesbosch Dredger v SS Edison*[2] has been distinguished numerous times on this point, especially since the decision in that case was based on the remoteness rather than the measure of damage. For example, in *Martindale v Duncan*[3] the Court of Appeal held that the claimant's impecuniosity justified his delay in carrying out repairs to his taxi, causing an increased claim for loss of profits. Further, in *Lagden v O'Connor*[4] the House of Lords held that *Liesbosch* could no longer be regarded as authoritative and had been overtaken by subsequent developments in the law.

1   *Alcoa Minerals of Jamaica plc v Broderick* [2000] 3 WLR 23, PC; *Robbins of Putney v Meek* [1971] RTR 345; *Clippens Oil Co v Edinburgh and District Water Trustees* [1907] AC 291; *Lagden v O'Connor* [2003] UKHL 64.
2   [1933] AC 449.
3   [1973] 1 WLR 574, CA.
4   [2003] UKHL 64.

Common examples of failure to mitigate loss

(1)   FAILURE TO SHOP AROUND

[K49]   It may not be reasonable for a claimant to plump for the first estimate or quotation regardless of the price. Although it may be too burdensome to expect the claimant to spend a considerable amount of time obtaining and comparing numerous different quotes or estimates, the claimant must establish that the price quoted is reasonable[1]. A touch of common sense is required here. For example, if the claimant has a particular type of car and, when damaged, always takes it to the same dealership garage because it always does a good, professional job, the court is likely to allow the claim in full. On the other hand, if a claim is advanced himself, for extensive painting and decorating work that, but for the accident, the claimant would have done, it may be reasonable to expect the claimant to obtain more than one quote. However, it should be noted that, if the defendant wishes to challenge the reasonableness of a particular quotation, it will be prudent to obtain evidence in support of this contention in the form of other more competitive quotes.

1   In *Clark v Tull* [2002] EWCA Civ 510 (upheld in *Lagden v O'Connor* [2003] UKHL 64), it was held that a claimant was not under a duty to get competitive tenders. A claimant is entitled to go to his or her nearest car hire company and was entitled to recover the amount charged. Thereafter, the evidential burden falls upon the defendant to show that the claimant's conduct was unreasonable, and that he or she failed to mitigate his or her loss. Unreasonableness in opting for credit hire without making any enquiries as to alternatives was found in *McLaren v Hastings Direct* [2009] LTL 5.10.2009, Lawtel Document No AC0122216 .

[K50]   In passing, it is also worth noting that the Vice-Chancellor in *Dimond v Lovell*[1] (at the Court of Appeal level) stated (obiter) that it was eminently reasonable in that case for the claimant to rely upon the broker's recommendation regarding the choice of hire firm. He went on to say[2]:

'A broker is more likely to have a knowledge of the services on offer than an individual could acquire even after a tedious hour or so with Yellow Pages and a telephone. It cannot be the law that a [claimant] who asks for the advice of a broker and does not herself telephone around to test the market is failing to take reasonable steps to mitigate her damage. The broker was, of course, her agent. Should he have tested the car hire market in order to advise her whom she should approach for a replacement vehicle? There was no evidence from the broker, so what, if any, thought he gave to ordinary car hire firms one cannot tell. But it seems to me that he was entitled to take the view that a firm like 1st Automotive, which would provide Mrs Dimond with a suitable vehicle and relieve her from the worry of having to argue with Mr Lovell's insurers about recovery and from the worry of any necessary litigation, would provide a service that she could reasonably decide to take.'

1   [2000] 1 QB 216, [1999] 3 All ER 1. This case went to the House of Lords, where Lord Hoffmann also referred to the prima facie reasonableness of the claimant's reliance upon her broker's recommendation: [2002] 1 AC 384 at 401E.
2   [2000] 1 QB 216 at 235.

(2)   FAILURE TO UNDERGO MEDICAL TREATMENT

[K51] In taking all reasonable steps to mitigate loss, a claimant is expected to undergo all reasonable recommended treatment that is expected to be of benefit[1]. Failure to undergo that treatment will restrict the claimant to recovering the level of damages that the claimant would reasonably expect to recover if the treatment had been pursued[2].

1   There must be a proven benefit on the balance of probabilities: *Morgan v T Wallis* [1974] 1 Lloyd's Rep 165.
2   *Morgan v T Wallis* [1974] 1 Lloyd's Rep 165.

[K52] The burden of proving that the claimant has failed to mitigate his or her loss by not taking up certain treatment rests on the defendant[1]. The test of reasonableness is an objective test, and the defendant must show that the reasonable man or woman in the claimant's position would not refuse to undergo the treatment[2]. Evidence is required to prove that a refusal to have certain medical treatment is unreasonable[3]. Such evidence can usually be provided by finding an express indication in the claimant's medical notes or records to such effect, or by obtaining a recommendation from one of the experts in the case that certain treatment should be taken up. It is not necessarily conclusive that the claimant's treating expert recommends that the claimant should have certain treatment. The claimant is entitled to take into account all the circumstances when making his or her decision, including medical advice against the treatment[4]. Where the medical opinion is divided regarding the suggested benefits of a particular treatment, it is unlikely that a court would find the claimant acted unreasonably in adopting the medical view which advocated against the treatment in question[5].

1   *Richardson v Redpath Brown & Co* [1944] AC 62; *Steele v Robert George & Co* [1942] AC 497; *Froggatt v LEP International* [2002] EWCA Civ 600; *Geest plc v Lansiquot* [2002] UKPC 48; cf *Selvanayagam v University of the West Indies* [1983] 1 WLR 585.
2   *Morgan v T Wallis Ltd* [1974] 1 Lloyd's Rep 165.
3   *Gee v Bayes* (20 October 1999, unreported), QBD, a decision of Garland J which is referred to in *Butterworths Personal Injury Litigation Practice* at para I[84.1].
4   *Richardson v Redpath Brown & Co* [1944] AC 62, in particular per Lord Scarman at 72.
5   *McAuley v London Transport Executive* [1957] 2 Lloyd's Rep 500.

[K53] In deciding whether a decision to refuse particular treatment is reasonable or not, a court is likely to have regard to all the circumstances, including:

- The nature of the treatment (and, in particular, whether or not it involves any invasive procedure[1]).
- The likely duration of the treatment.
- The pain and discomfort involved in the suggested procedure.
- The risks associated with the procedure.
- Whether the treatment is conventional or experimental.
- The inconvenience involved in undergoing the treatment (is it something which can be done at home, or does the claimant have to have in-patient treatment in hospital, and will the claimant be likely to lose his or her job by submitting him or herself to the treatment?).
- The likely outcome of the procedure (and whether the potential benefits outweigh the risks).
- The likely rehabilitation period following the treatment.
- The timing of the treatment[2].
- The cost of the treatment, if it is not available on the NHS and no interim payment is available to cover it.

[1]   A refusal to undergo physiotherapy is much more likely to be held to be unreasonable than a refusal to undergo an operation under general anaesthetic which carries with it inherent risks of significant injury.

[2]   Refusal of a procedure at one time may not be unreasonable, but could later become unreasonable. See eg *Thomas v Bath District Health Authority* [1995] PIQR Q19, in which all parties accepted it was not unreasonable for the claimant to refuse to undergo major back surgery while she was bringing up children, but that her view regarding the surgery might change in the future when her children had grown up.

(3)   FAILURE TO SATISFY EARNING CAPACITY

[K54]   This situation arises in a number of different contexts. For example, it may simply be the case that the claimant could and should have returned to work sooner[1]. Alternatively, it might be argued that the claimant should have returned to more lucrative employment[2] or a different type of employment that he or she was capable of doing[3]. Further, it might be alleged that the claimant could have worked longer hours[4].

[1]   See eg *Stafford v Antwerp Steamship Co* [1965] 2 Lloyd's Rep 104; *Morgan v Dorman Long (Steel) Ltd* (1966), CA No 267; and *Ireson v Wilkinson* (1970, unreported), CA No 155B, per Danckwerts and Phillimore LJJ. See further *Kemp & Kemp* at 13-005.

[2]   See eg *Dooley v Board of Governors at the United Liverpool Hospitals* (1967, unreported), CA No 44A.

[3]   See eg *Billingham v Hughes* [1949] 1 KB 643, where the Court of Appeal made allowance for the residuary earning capacity of a radiologist, where a GP who was qualified to be a radiologist could no longer pursue his career in general practice as a result of his injuries.

[4]   See eg *Butler & Anor v Thompson* [2005] EWCA Civ 864.

[K55]   Where the claimant has returned to some form of work but is unsuited to that work, and is either fired or resigns on the basis that it is better to jump before being pushed, it may be difficult to establish that the claimant has failed to mitigate his or her loss[1]. Where a claimant reasonably leaves his post-accident employment to study and qualify for an alternative (but less well-paid) career for reasons attributable to his injuries, a decision subsequently not to abandon that course and return to his former employment cannot be characterised as an unreasonable failure to mitigate his loss[2]. However, where the claimant could have returned to a wide variety of jobs paying a comparable wage to that which he or she was earning prior to the tortious act, the defendant may not be responsible for paying for the costs of retraining, and any loss of earnings during the retraining period, where such retraining was the voluntary choice of the claimant seeking a change of direction in his or her career[3].

[1]   *Morris v Richards* [2003] EWCA Civ 232, CA.

[2]   *Ronan v Sainsbury's Supermarkets Ltd & Anor* [2006] EWCA Civ 1074.

[3]   See further *Brown v Vosper Thornycroft* [2004] EWHC 400 (QB), in which HHJ Price QC said at [51]: 'While it may well be a reasonable choice for the claimant to make in the long-term to obtain a degree and to move into, in my judgment, a much different market with much greater potential future earnings, the question for me is whether the defendant should be required to pay for it. In my judgment, they should not. I accept the defendant's submissions that this claimant is capable of a wide range of jobs which would earn him a comparable salary to that which he would have enjoyed if the accident had not occurred. There is limited impact of the injuries upon his activity and his employability, and in my judgment it is unreasonable to expect the defendants to pay for this drastic change of direction, not only to a new field, but at a higher level generally speaking within the employment market as a whole'.

[K56] In order successfully to reduce the claim for loss of earnings on the basis of a failure to pursue a residual earning capacity, it will usually be necessary for the defendant to call specific evidence and to challenge the claimant in cross-examination[1]. Such evidence usually takes three forms. First, medical evidence will usually be required to show what physical and mental capacity the claimant has for work. Secondly, evidence from an employment consultant or someone at the claimant's local job centre might be useful in respect of any need for retraining and the availability of suitable employment in the claimant's locality. Lastly, evidence should be obtained which indicates the likely level of earnings if the claimant were able to find employment[2].

[1]   In *Froggatt v LEP International* [2002] EWCA Civ 600, Pill LJ said: 'Where in circumstances such as the present defendants are seeking to show unreasonableness in the claimant, it is customary to produce evidence, in one way or another, as to alternative employments which are open to him and for which he could have applied. There is a conspicuous lack of any such evidence in this case ...'.

[2]   In the absence of expert evidence from an employment consultant, a defendant should rely upon the National Average Earnings Statistics, as contained in the Annual Survey of Hours and Earnings (ASHE) which is accessible online at www.statistics.gov.uk. Alternative sources of earnings information are contained within 'Personal Injury Damages Statistics' by Rodney Nelson-Jones, and 'Facts & Figures' produced by the Professional Negligence Bar Association: see further *Stefanovic v Carter* [2001] EWCA Civ 452 and Chapter C, Compiling the Evidence at paras **[C38]** and **[C39]**.

(4) Failing to repair

[K57] Generally speaking, if a damaged item can be repaired, it is usually cheaper to repair that item than to buy a replacement. It would, therefore, be a failure of the claimant's duty to mitigate his or her loss not to investigate the possibility of repair. However, in order to restrict the claimant to the value of repair, evidence would be required to show the difference in cost (including any charge for hire while the damaged item is being repaired).

(5) FAILING TO REPLACE WHEN REPAIR IS TOO EXPENSIVE

[K58] It may be unreasonable for a claimant to claim the cost of repair where it would be cheaper to replace the damaged article. For example, in *Darbishire v Warran*[1] the claimant's car was damaged in an accident and he had it repaired at a cost in excess of the market value of the car. The court held that he had failed to mitigate his loss by purchasing a replacement car of the same value. It should be noted, however, that this argument does not apply to unique objects, for which there may be no comparable substitute[2].

[1]   [1963] 1 WLR 1067.
[2]   *O'Grady v Westminster Scaffolding* [1962] 2 Lloyd's Rep 238.

(6) FAILURE TO PROGRESS CLAIM

[K59] Where the claimant is suffering from compensation or litigation neurosis, and there is evidence that the claimant's condition is aggravated by the litigation process, it is likely to be unreasonable for the claimant not to progress his or her claim with all due expedition[1].

[1]   See eg *James v Woodall Duckham Construction Co* [1969] 1 WLR 903, CA, where the claimant's claim for loss of earnings was restricted to three of the six-and-a-quarter years claimed. The remaining years were held to have been caused by the claimant's delay progressing the claim, and it was held that the claimant had failed reasonably to mitigate his loss by not bringing the claim to trial sooner.

(vii) Double Recovery and Overlapping Heads of Loss

[K60] Care should be taken to ensure that the claimant has not claimed the same loss under separate heads of damage. Examples include claiming:

*   Gratuitous care at the same time as claiming the carer's loss of earnings[1].
*   The cost of paid help to prepare meals and the cost of buying pre-cooked meals[2].
*   The cost of an orange juicer as well as cranberry juice and vitamin tablets[3].
*   Skin treatment and massage[4].
*   The cost of additional heating charges and double glazing[5].

There is often duplication in respect of claims, quantified by accommodation and care/occupational therapy experts respectively, in respect of (i) aids and equipment in a claimant's home (eg stairlifts; showers etc), and/or (ii) increased accommodation expenses (eg electricity, heating etc).

[1]   *Fish v Wilcox* [1994] 5 Med LR 230.
[2]   *Osborne v Oetegenn* (10 April 1997, unreported), CA.
[3]   *Biesheuval v Birrell* [1999] PIQR Q40.
[4]   *Biesheuval v Birrell* [1999] PIQR Q40.
[5]   Example provided by Goldrein, de Haas and Frenkel in *Personal Injury Major Claims Handling: Cost-Effective Case Management* (Butterworths, 2000).

[K61] It is unusual for non-pecuniary losses to overlap with pecuniary losses. However, an example of this is provided by *Brown v Merton, Sutton and Wandsworth Area Health Authority (Teaching)*[1], where the cost of a greenhouse and raised flower beds was claimed in order to maintain the claimant's interest and activity. Here, it was accepted that the sums claimed ought properly to be financed out of the award provided for loss of amenity.

¹   [1982] 1 All ER 650, CA. See also *Musmar v Kalala* [1999] CLY 1565. See further Chapter A, General Principles at para **[A12]** and Chapter D, General Damages at para **[D146]**.

[K62]   In addition, save for the two recognised exceptions of insurance and the benevolence of third parties, the claimant must give credit against his or her loss for any money or benefits in kind which he or she would not have received but for his or her injuries¹. Therefore, a claimant who receives state benefits not covered by the statutory recoupment scheme must give credit for the same. For example, credit must be given for any housing benefit² or council tax benefit³ or working or child tax credits that the claimant would not otherwise have received but for his or her injuries.

¹   *Hodgson v Trapp* [1989] 1 AC 807. See also *Parry v Cleaver* [1970] AC 1 at 14. See further Chapter J, Recovery of State and Collateral Benefits.
²   *Clenshaw v Tanner* [2002] EWCA Civ 1848; and *Huntley v Simmonds* [2009] EWHC 405 (QB), per Underhill J at para 124.
³   *Smith v Rod Jenkins* [2003] EWHC 1356 (QB).

(viii)   Betterment

[K63]   The claimant is entitled only to be put into the position he or she would have been in but for the accident. The court therefore discounts for what Alliot J in *Roberts v Johnstone*¹ called the 'Rolls Royce' element, ie an allowance for the fact that what the claimant may be claiming is better than he or she would have had in any event. This commonly occurs in claims for damage to possessions and clothes. Claimants often claim the replacement costs of these items on a new-for-old basis. However, the claimant is only entitled to recover the market value of the clothes or possessions damaged at the time of the accident, and an allowance should be made for the element of 'betterment'². As regards the test for proving an element of betterment, Lord Hope said in *Lagden v O'Connor*³:

> 'It is for the defendant who seeks a deduction from expenditure in mitigation on the ground of betterment to make out his case for doing so. It is not enough that an element of betterment can be identified. It has to be shown that the claimant had a choice, and that he would have been able to mitigate his loss at less cost. The wrongdoer is not entitled to demand of the injured party that he incur a loss, bear a burden or make unreasonable sacrifices in the mitigation of his damages. He is entitled to demand that, where there are choices to be made, the least expensive route which will achieve mitigation must be selected. So if the evidence shows that the claimant had a choice, and that the route to mitigation which he chose was more costly than an alternative that was open to him, then a case will have been made out for a deduction. But if it shows that the claimant had no other choice available to him, the betterment must be seen as incidental to the step which he was entitled to take in the mitigation of his loss and there will be no ground for it to be deducted.'

¹   [1989] QB 878, CA.
²   See further chapter 32 of *McGregor on Damages* (18th edn).
³   [2003] UKHL 64 at [34].

(ix) Malingering[1]

[K64] As Judge LJ acknowledged in *Ford v GKR Construction Ltd*[2], sometimes claimants do 'lie, embellish or fantasise'. It is important that defendants are alive to this issue and, if necessary, ready to take appropriate steps in order to protect their position.

1   See further Chapter A, General Principles at paras **[A124]–[A129]**.
2   [2000] 1 WLR 1397.

The duty to plead

[K65] Although there is a duty upon a claimant to specify any particulars of fraud in his or her particulars of claim, by virtue of para 8.2 of the Practice Direction to CPR, Part 16, there is no corresponding duty upon a defendant to set out details of fraud relied upon in his or her defence, over and above the general duty to provide reasons for disputing the claim required by CPR, r 16.5. However, if fraud is alleged, there is authority to the effect that it must be particularised and should be pleaded, so that the party against whom fraud is alleged knows the case they have to meet[1]. Logically, the same principles would apply to any allegation that the claimant was malingering to any significant extent, which is tantamount to a serious criminal offence. In a recent case concerning a low velocity impact it was held that a defendant does not necessarily have to plead fraud or malingering, and it will be sufficient for the purposes of CPR, r 16.5 to set out fully any facts from which the defendant will invite the court to draw the inference that the claimant had not in fact suffered the injuries he alleged[2]. It is therefore suggested that if the evidence is cogent enough to support an allegation of fraud or malingering, then that should be pleaded. But if the evidence falls short of that, a defendant who wishes to run such arguments should plead the essential facts and evidence on which he will rely to invite the court (i) to draw an inference of fraud or malingering or (ii) to conclude that the claimant cannot prove his case.

1   *Jonesco v Beard* [1930] AC 298; *Cooper v P&O Stena Line Ltd Ferries* [1999] Lloyd's Rep 734; *Scruton v Bone* (20 November 2001, unreported); *Pickering v JA McConville* [2003] EWCA Civ 554; and *Noble v Owens* [2010] EWCA Civ 224. In *Scruton v Bone* (20 November 2001, unreported), Sir Andrew Morritt held that allegations of dishonesty must be pleaded clearly and with particularity, and are not to be left to inference alone.
2   *Kearsley v Klarfeld* [2005] EWCA Civ 1510. Although this case concerned low velocity impact litigation, there is no reason why this principle is not of general application.

Evidence

[K66] As such an allegation is tantamount to alleging fraud[1], credible evidence is required before such an allegation may be pleaded[2], and a high degree of proof is needed before the allegation can be made out[3]. Often, although the defendant may have suspicions regarding the veracity of the claimant's evidence, unless there is clear evidence of malingering – by way of surveillance video or otherwise[4] – it will be difficult to establish that the claimant has deliberately concocted the claim and/ or consciously exaggerated its value. Where a claimant is guilty of conduct aimed at preventing a fair trial (eg the forgery of documents), and his conduct puts the fairness of any trial in jeopardy or prevents the court from doing justice, he may lose the right to continue participating in the proceedings, and the claim may be determined against him[5]. But where a fair trial remains possible, there is no general rule of law, whether in contract or in tort, that the dishonest exaggeration of a genuine claim would result in the dismissal of the whole claim: the invariable rule is that the judge awards the limited damages which are appropriate to his findings as to any genuine part of the claim. A claimant's credibility may be so damaged that he fails to prove any part of his loss, but if he proves some entitlement to damages he will not be deprived of the damages to which he is entitled because he has fraudulently attempted to obtain more than his entitlement[6]. If the matter proceeds to trial and the judge makes findings of fact regarding dishonesty, it is likely that the court will refer the matter to the Director of Public Prosecutions, for consideration as to whether the claimant should be charged with criminal proceedings[7]. In such a scenario, it is likely that the defendant should be able to recover the full costs of defending the action, particularly where the claimant has failed to beat a Part 36 offer or payment into court[8]; but even where the claimant has beaten a Part 36 offer, he may still incur costs penalties where there has been exaggeration[9]. Furthermore, if the matter does not proceed to trial because, after revelation of a fraud, the claimant seeks to discontinue his claim, or compromises it on terms favourable to the defendant, the Attorney General or the defendant may thereafter bring proceedings for contempt of court pursuant to CPR, r 32.14[10].

[1]   *Stojalowski v Imperial Smelting Corp (NSC)* (1976) 121 SJ 118, CA; and *Cooper v P&O Stena Line Ltd* [1999] 1 Lloyd's Rep 734.

[2]   Although such material does not necessarily have to be admissible, it must be of such character as to lead responsible counsel to conclude that serious allegations could be based upon it: *Medcalf v Mardell* [2002] UKHL 27. The claimant's representatives may be liable for wasted costs where reasonable investigations would have discovered that the claim was tainted by fraud: *Ali v Ali and Provident Insurance* (7 March 2003, unreported). An allegation of professional negligence on the part of a solicitor may be difficult to establish because it should be approached in an untechnical way and, where there is a conflict of medical evidence, it is not for the claimant's lawyers to decide that conflict of evidence before the trial: *Afzal v Chubb Guarding Services Ltd & another* [2003] EWHC 822 (TCC).

[3]   *Hornal v Neuberger Products Ltd* [1957] 1 QB 247; *Re Dellow's Wills Trusts* [1964] 1 WLR 451; and *Blyth v Blyth* [1966] 1 All ER 524, HL, which all approved the following passage in *Bater v Bater* [1951] P 35, per Lord Denning at 37: 'The degree [of probability] depends on the subject-matter. A civil court when considering a charge of fraud will naturally require for itself a higher degree of probability than that which it would require when asking if negligence is established. It does not adopt so high a degree as a criminal court even when considering a charge of a criminal nature; but still it does require a degree of probability which is commensurate with the occasion'.

[4]   Note that, in order for any Part 36 offer to be effective, any such evidence should be obtained and disclosed promptly to the other side: *Ford v GKR Construction Ltd* [2000] 1 WLR 1397. However, it may be possible to justify delaying service of obtained video evidence until the claimant has committed him or herself to their witness statement and/or schedule of loss: *Uttley v Uttley* [2002] PIQR P123; and *Booth v Britannia Hotels Ltd* [2002] EWCA Civ 579. See further Chapters A and C.

[5]   *Arrow Nominees v Blackledge* [2000] 2 BCLC 167. This case, however, is not authority for the proposition that, where the trial has taken place and the court has been able, despite some dishonesty on the part of a claimant, to reach reliable findings, that court has jurisdiction to strike out any genuine claim: see *Shah v (1) Ul-Haq, (2) Khatoon and (3) Parveen* [2009] EWCA Civ 542.

[6]   See *Shah v (1) Ul-Haq, (2) Khatoon and (3) Parveen* [2009] EWCA Civ 542, in which the Court of Appeal indicated that the comments made by Laws LJ in *Molloy v Shell UK Ltd* [2001] EWCA Civ 1272, which suggested that the court might have jurisdiction to dismiss an entire claim merely

because it was dishonestly exaggerated, had been little more than 'wishful thinking'; cf *Churchill Car Insurance v Kelly* [2006] EWHC 18 (QB).

7   See eg *Cottrell v Redbridge Healthcare NHS Trust* (2001) 61 BMLR 72; and *Hussein v William Hill Group* [2004] EWHC 208 (QB).

8   *Molloy v Shell UK Ltd* [2001] EWCA Civ 1272 (although see the comments in *Shah v (1) Ul-Haq, (2) Khatoon and (3) Parveen* [2009] EWCA Civ 542, and *Widlake v BAA Ltd* [2009] EWCA Civ 1256 about this case); *Painting v University of Oxford* [2005] EWCA Civ 161. Alternatively, the claimant may be restricted to claiming costs appropriate to the small claims or fast track: *Devine v Franklin* [2002] EWHC 1846 (QB). See also *Booth v Britannia Hotels Ltd* [2002] EWCA Civ 529, in which Jonathan Parker LJ stated: 'In my judgment, a claimant who pursues an exaggerated and inflated claim for damages must expect to bear the consequences when his costs come to be assessed'.

9   Under CPR, r 44.3(5)(d), when considering costs the court takes into account the conduct of the parties and whether or not the claimant has exaggerated his or her claim. See further *Carver v BAA Plc* [2008] EWCA Civ 412 and *Widlake v BAA Ltd* [2009] EWCA Civ 1256.

10   See *Walton v Kirk* [2009] EWHC 703 (QB); *Caerphilly County Borough Council v Hughes and Others* (QB) LTL17.3.2006, Lawtel Document No AC0110415.

Assessment and costs

[K67]   Where a claimant has been caught consciously exaggerating his or her symptoms, the judge must attempt to separate out the elements of conscious and unconscious exaggeration, and award the claimant those sums to which he or she would have been entitled in the absence of conscious exaggeration/malingering[1]. Where the claimant would only have been entitled to a modest award but for the deliberate exaggeration, the claimant may be restricted to claiming fixed costs in accordance with the small claims track[2]. In *Booth v Britannia Hotels Ltd*[3], Jonathan Parker LJ stated:

'In my judgment, a claimant who pursues an exaggerated and inflated claim for damages must expect to bear the consequences when his costs come to be assessed.'

1   *Bracknell District Council* (17 October 1987, unreported), QBD; *Smith v Rod Jenkins* [2003] EWHC 1356 (QB); *Shah v (1) Ul-Haq, (2) Khatoon and (3) Parveen* [2009] EWCA Civ 542.

2   *Devine v Franklin* [2002] EWHC 1846 (QB).

3   [2002] EWCA Civ 529. See also *Molloy v Shell UK Ltd* [2001] EWCA Civ 1272, CA; *Painting v University of Oxford* [2005] EWCA Civ 161; *Carver v BAA Plc* [2008] EWCA Civ 412; and *Widlake v BAA Ltd* [2009] EWCA Civ 1256.

Anxiety/litigation/compensation neurosis

[K68]   Where there is evidence of exaggeration of symptoms, but this is due to an unconscious psychological reaction, the claimant will be entitled to recover the full extent of his or her losses[1]. It is therefore important to obtain specific evidence from an appropriate expert (usually a consultant psychiatrist) regarding whether or not the symptoms are being consciously (and deliberately) exaggerated or whether the exaggeration is unconscious. At the same time, it is also useful to ask the expert to confirm whether or not the claimant's condition is likely to improve once the case has been resolved[2].

1   *Digby v Essex County Council* [1994] PIQR P53.

2   In which case, there is a duty to ensure that the claim is resolved as quickly as possible. See further *Blyth Valley Borough Council v Henderson* [1996] PIQR P64.

Failure of the claimant's legal representatives properly to investigate

[K69] Where there are clear signs that a claim might be fraudulent, the claimant's solicitors are under a duty to take reasonable steps to investigate the matter. In rare circumstances, a failure to take such reasonable steps may permit the defendant successfully to recover his or her wasted costs from the claimant's legal representatives[1]. However, it should be noted that an allegation of professional negligence on the part of a solicitor should be approached in an untechnical way and, where there is a conflict of medical evidence, it is not for the claimant's lawyers to decide that conflict of evidence before the trial[2].

[1]   See eg *Ali v Ali and Provident Insurance* (7 March 2003), Lawtel Document No AC0104915.
[2]   *Afzal v Chubb Guarding Services Ltd* [2003] EWHC 822 (TCC).

No finding of malingering

[K70] Where a defendant who has pleaded malingering fails to establish it at trial, he or she is unlikely to recover the costs in relation to this issue. But where a claimant fails to beat a Part 36 offer, the normal costs rule will still apply to costs other than those relating to the issue of malingering, ie the claimant will be liable to pay the defendant's costs from the last day he or she could have accepted the offer, notwithstanding the fact that an allegation of malingering was incorrectly levelled at the claimant[1].

[1]   *Burgess v British Steel* [2000] PIQR Q240.

(x)   Causation

Introduction

[K71]   Although a detailed exposition of the law regarding causation is beyond the scope of this book[1], there are a number of arguments that the drafter of a counter-schedule should be familiar with. In approaching issues of causation, however, it is helpful to bear the following features of any particular case in mind:

*   In cases concerning multiple tortfeasors, consider whether they are concurrent (responsible for different torts but which caused the same damage) or independent (responsible for different torts which caused different damage).
*   Distinguish between cases where the injury or damage caused is divisible (ie cumulative, and related to the level of exposure, such that a greater level of exposure causes a greater level of injury) or indivisible (where the injury and the level of symptoms do not depend on the level of exposure).

[1]   See further chapter 2 of *Clerk & Lindsell on Torts*; chapter 5 of *Charlesworth & Percy on Negligence*; chapter 6 of *McGregor on Damages* (18th edn); chapter 5 of Michael A Jones *Medical Negligence*; and I Kennedy and A Grubb *Principles of Medical Law*.

The tests for causation of injury

[K72]   It is important to note that no liability *can* be established at all for the tort of negligence unless some loss has, on the balance of probabilities, been suffered in consequence of the fault alleged – but that once *some* loss is established, quantification of that loss does not involve the question as to whether the loss was more probable than not, but rather the likelihood in percentage or 'chance' terms of that loss being suffered[1]. First, then, the claimant has to prove causation of some injury, and the general rule is that, if the claimant proves on the balance of probabilities that, but for the defendant's negligence he would not have suffered the injury, loss or damage complained of, then causation is established; and it is usually sufficient to apply the 'but for' test in order to determine the extent of the defendant's liability. That general rule, however, is subject to two other tests of causation, which will apply in certain circumstances, namely (1) where the claimant proves that the negligence made a material contribution to the injury or damage in question, and (2) where the claimant proves that the negligence made a material contribution to the risk that he would sustain the injury or damage in question. As to which test should be applied, the following is intended only as a brief summary; and, for a more detailed analysis, regard should be had to the publications referred to in para **[K71]** above.

(i)   Where the medical evidence is sufficient to show that an injury or condition results from the cumulative (as opposed to alternative) causes, some negligent and some non-negligent, the position may be summarised as follows[2].

  •   If the medical evidence shows on a balance of probabilities that the injury would have occurred at the same time as a result of the non-tortious cause or causes in any event, the claimant will fail to show that the tortious cause materially contributed to the injury, and fail to satisfy the 'but for' test, and the claim will fail[3].

  •   If the medical evidence shows that, but for the contribution of the tortious cause, the injury would probably not have occurred, the claimant will have established causation: the 'but for' test is satisfied.

  •   However, in a case where the defendant's breach of duty was one of a number of cumulative causes of the claimant's injury, and the claimant can establish that the breach made a material (ie more than minimal) contribution towards the injury, the severity of the injury or the time of onset of the injury, the claimant succeeds[4].

  •   Where a claimant succeeds on the grounds that the negligence made a material contribution to his damage, in cases of cumulative damage and a divisible injury, such as industrial disease, damages are apportioned, and the claimant only recovers for that part of the injury caused by the negligent exposure or cause[5].

  •   Where a claimant succeeds on the grounds that the defendant's breach of duty made a material contribution to his damage, then if that damage is cumulatively caused but it cannot be established if, or to what extent, the breach has distinctly contributed to the damage (ie the damage cannot easily be divided into the portion caused by the tort, and that part not so caused), the defendant will be liable to the full extent of the damage suffered[6].

(ii) Where the injury does not result from cumulative causes, and the medical evidence can only show that the negligence of one or more defendants caused or materially contributed to the risk of injury, but cannot show that such negligence actually caused or materially contributed to the injury itself, the claim will succeed[7], and this is so even though the injury might in fact have been caused by some non-negligent factor[8], provided that the claimant proves that his injury was in fact caused by the same agency that resulted from the defendant's negligence, or at least by an agency which operated in substantially the same way. Although this principle has been applied to a variety of industrial disease cases[9], it appears that its scope beyond such cases is very limited. It appears to be inapplicable to a personal injury claim arising from a single incident with a single defendant[10], and to claims where there is no crucial lack of scientific knowledge[11]. Nor will it be extended to cases where there are a number of different agents or causes of the injury: in such a case, the claimant must prove, on a balance of probabilities, which agent did cause his injury[12].

(iii) If, however, the defendant's negligence has more than doubled the risk of injury which would have existed in any event, the claimant will succeed, because he will have shown that it is more likely than not that the negligence caused his injury[13].

[1]   See *Davies v Taylor (No 2)* [1973] 1 All ER 959, HL.
[2]   See the summary in *Bailey v Ministry of Defence* [2008] EWCA Civ 883, per Waller LJ at paras 46–7.
[3]   See *Hotson v East Berkshire Health Authority* [1987] 1 AC 750, HL. See also *Gregg v Scott* [2005] UKHL 2, [2005] 2 AC 176: where, but for the negligence, a claimant would in any event have had a less than 50% chance of survival, he cannot claim damages for the loss of a chance of a better outcome, as he fails to satisfy the 'but for' test.
[4]   See *Bonnington Castings Ltd v Wardlaw* [1956] AC 613. For applications of this principle in the context of clinical negligence cases, see *Bailey v Ministry of Defence* [2008] EWCA Civ 883; *Boustead v North West SHA* [2008] EWHC 2375 (QB); and *Canning-Kishver v Sandwell and West Birmingham Hospitals NHS Trust* [2008] EWHC 2384 (QB). And for an application of this principle in the context of a case concerning multiple road traffic accidents, where each materially contributed to the claimant's chronic pain, see *Pearce v Lindfield & Others* [2003] EWCA Civ 647; and, in the field of psychiatric injury, see *Page v Smith (No 2)* [1996] 1 WLR 855 (CA).
[5]   See eg *Thompson v Smiths Shiprepairers Ltd* [1984] QB 405; *Holtby v Brigham Cowan (Hull) Ltd* [2000] 3 All ER 421. This situation may also apply in cases of psychiatric injury: see *Hatton v Sunderland* [2002] EWCA Civ 76, per Hale LJ. Note, however, that in 'Causation: the search for principle' [2009] JPIL Issue 2/09 pp 101–113, Janet Smith LJ has doubted that psychiatric injury is divisible, and that damages for such injury can be apportioned, because psychiatrists are not usually able to quantify the contributions towards a psychiatric illness which different stressors or factors have made. See also her remarks to similar effect, obiter, in *Dickins v O2* [2008] EWCA Civ 1144. Note that, where the injury is indivisible, then no question of apportionment can arise (see below).
[6]   *Bonnington Castings Ltd v Wardlaw* [1956] AC 613; *Nicholson v Atlas* [1957] 1 WLR 613, HL.
[7]   See *McGhee v National Coal Board* [1973] 1 WLR 1; and *Fairchild v Glenhaven Funeral Services Ltd* [2003] 1 AC 32.
[8]   See *Barker v Corus (UK) Ltd* [2006] 2 AC 572.
[9]   See eg *Transco v Griggs* [2003] EWCA Civ 564 (a case involving palmar arch disease); *McGhee* supra (dermatitis); and *Fairchild* supra (mesothelioma).
[10]   See *Clough v First Choice Holidays and Flights Limited* [2006] EWCA Civ 15.
[11]   See *Hull v Sanderson* [2008] EWCA Civ 1211.
[12]   See *Wilsher v Essex Area Health Authority* [1988] AC 1074.
[13]   See *Novartis Grimsby Ltd v Cookson* [2007] EWCA 1261; cf *Shortell v Bical Construction Limited* Lawtel 4.6.2008 (unreported elsewhere); and the observations of Janet Smith LJ in 'Causation: the search for principle' [2009] JPIL Issue 2/09 pp 101–113.

Factual causation

[K73]   Causation arguments that may be employed to bar or limit recovery of loss include the following:

- The whole or part of the claimant's injuries, loss or damage would have been sustained in any event, whether due to a condition which pre-existed the defendant's negligence and would have become symptomatic in any event, or due to some subsequent event or other injury[1].
- The causal link between the defendant's negligence and the claimant's injury, loss or damage has been broken by a supervening event constituting a 'novus actus interveniens' (a new and supervening cause)[2].
- The causal link between the defendant's negligence and the injury, loss or damage complained of has been broken by the claimant's unreasonable behaviour[3].
- The injury, loss or damage resulted from a voluntary decision on the part of the claimant rather than anything arising out of the defendant's negligence[4].
- Where there are a number of distinct possible causes (some negligent and others not) for the injury, loss or damage complained of, the claimant must show on the balance of probabilities that it was the defendant's negligence which caused or materially contributed to the injury, loss or damage claimed[5].
- Where there are multiple torts by different defendants, but the injury or damage caused by each defendant is separate and distinct, each defendant is liable for the injury, loss or damage arising out of their tortious conduct (and the degree of blameworthiness of each defendant is not relevant)[6].
- Where the injury is divisible[7], then each tortfeasor will only be responsible for the percentage of his contribution to the injury or damage[8].
- But if the injury is indivisible[7]: where there are concurrent tortfeasors (different torts materially contributing to the same damage), they will usually each be jointly and severally liable for the whole of the damage[9]; but in the event that the *Fairchild* principles apply (material contribution to the risk of damage), then each tortfeasor is only liable for their proportionate share of the damages, as reflected by the proportion of his contribution to the risk[10].

[1]   This argument is commonly used in back injury cases, where there are pre-existing problems which would have generated symptoms in any event. The Court of Appeal has recently endorsed the 'acceleration period' approach where this is supported by the medical evidence: *Kenth v Heimdale Hotel Investments Ltd* [2001] EWCA Civ 1283; *Morgan v Millett* [2001] EWCA Civ 1641; and *Environment Agency v Ellis* [2008] EWCA Civ 1117, [2009] PIQR P5. Thus, where the evidence suggests that, but for the accident, the claimant's symptoms would have developed in five years in any event, the claimant will be restricted to a five-year period for injury, loss and damage. Where the medical evidence is disputed on the issue of the acceleration period, it is open to the trial judge to examine the claimant's life and work and make his or her own assessment of the likely acceleration period: *Skerman v H Bollman Manufacturers Ltd* [2002] EWCA Civ 919. See also *Jobling v Associated Dairies Ltd* [1982] AC 794, in which the claimant's claim for loss of earnings was disallowed because, following the accident caused by the defendant's negligence, the claimant suffered from a disease which would have prevented him from working in any event. For a more recent example, see *Gardner v R P Winder (Wholesale Meats) Ltd* [2002] EWCA Civ 1777, in which the claimant's loss of earnings as a farmer were held to be due to the foot and mouth outbreak and his pre-existing shoulder condition, as opposed to his injuries.

[2]   For example, see *West v Versil Ltd* (1996) Times, 31 August, CA, in which the Court of Appeal held that the claimant's decision to exercise an option early, which reduced his pension, amounted to a novus actus for the consequences of which the defendant could not be liable. In passing, it is worth noting that, if the novus actus point is taken, it must be pleaded: *Weait v Jayanbee Joinery* [1963] 1 QB 239. This approach may be subject to the impact of changing attitudes with changing times.

[3]   See eg *McKew v Holland & Hannen & Cubitts* [1969] 3 All ER 1621, in which the House of Lords held that it was unreasonable for the claimant, who had a weakened ankle by reason of the defendant's negligence, to have jumped down some stairs, thereby sustaining further injury. Also

see *Sabri-Tabrizi v Lothian Health Board* (1997) 43 BMLR 190, in which the claimant, who had terminated an unwanted pregnancy following a failed sterilisation, then became pregnant again: the Outer House held that it was unreasonable for her not to have taken sufficient precautions to protect herself against pregnancy, once she already knew that there was a risk she could become pregnant. A similar decision was reached by Kennedy J, in *Richardson v LRC Products Ltd* [2000] PIQR Q164, who held that the claimant had failed to act reasonably in not taking the morning-after pill when a condom her husband was using failed, resulting in her falling pregnant. Although note *Emeh v Kensington and Chelsea and Westminster Health Authority* [1984] 3 All ER 1044, where Slade LJ stated that it would only be in the most exceptional circumstances that a court would declare it unreasonable for a claimant to decline to have an abortion where there were no medical or psychiatric grounds for terminating the pregnancy. Where a deceased's suicide was attributable to disabling mental injury foreseeably caused by the defendant's negligence some years earlier, that suicide did not break the chain of causation between the defendant's tort and the loss attributable to the deceased's death: see *Corr v IBC Vehicles Ltd* [2008] 2 WLR 499, HL.

4   This argument is commonly used when the claimant has accepted voluntary redundancy or has decided not to follow up their residual earning capacity. For example, see *Carter v British India Steam Navigation Co Ltd* [1974] 1 Lloyd's Rep 419, in which the court held the claimant could not recover loss of earnings where he had chosen to undertake voluntary work following the accident rather than to do paid work. Also see *Jeffries v Mills Scaffold Co* (1963), CA No 115, Guardian, 27 April, in which it was held that the claimant had made a rational decision to pursue a less lucrative job following the accident.

5   *Wilsher v Essex Area Health Authority* [1988] AC 1074.

6   *Rahman v (1) Arearose Ltd and (2) University College London NHS Trust* [2001] QB 351.

7   See para **[K71]**.

8   See *Thompson v Smiths Shiprepairers Ltd* [1984] QB 405; and *Holtby v Brigham and Cowan (Hull) Limited* [2000] ICR 1086; *Allen v British Rail Engineering* [2001] EWCA Civ 242, [2001] ICR 942.

9   See eg *Dingle v Associated Newspapers* [1962] 3 WLR 229; *Thompson v Smiths Shiprepairers Ltd* [1984] QB 405.

10   See *Barker v Corus UK Limited* [2006] 2 AC 572; but note that, in relation to mesothelioma, this position has since been reversed by Compensation Act 2006, s 3.

[K74]   It is worth noting that, where the claimant had pre-existing injuries which made him or her more vulnerable to further injury, it will be no defence to rely upon the pre-existing injuries. This principle known as the 'egg-shell skull principle'[1] means that defendants must take claimants as they find them, and are liable for the full extent of the aggravation or exacerbation of their pre-existing conditions[2]. Perhaps the most famous example of this principle is *Smith v Leech Brain*[3], in which the claimant's husband was struck by a piece of molten metal and suffered a small burn on his lip. Thereafter, because of a predisposition to cancerous cells, he developed cancer and died. The defendant was held liable for the death. In such a case, however, a defendant should explore whether it is arguable that, given the claimant's egg-shell skull, on a balance of probabilities, but for the material accident, some other event would have triggered a similar injury in any event: if such a case is arguable, then in reality the claim may be confined to an acceleration case[4].

1   There is no difference in principle between an egg-shell skull and an egg-shell personality: *Malcolm v Broadhurst* [1970] 3 All ER 508.

2   *Bourhill v Young* [1943] AC 92, per Lord Wright at 109–110: 'If the wrong is established the wrongdoer must take the victim as he finds him'.

3   [1962] 2 QB 405.

4   See para **[K73]**, footnote 1, and para **[K75]**.

[K75]   Where the claimant claims that his or her pre-existing injuries were aggravated or exacerbated by the defendant's wrongdoing, the defendant will only be liable for the extent of the aggravation/exacerbation[1]. Further, if the claimant would have suffered similar symptoms in any event, he or she will be restricted to claiming expenses and loss arising from the acceleration period, ie the period of time by which the symptoms have been brought forward by reason of the defendant's wrongdoing[2].

[1]   *Page v Smith (No 2)* [1996] 1 WLR 855; *Vernon v Bosley* [1997] PIQR P255.
[2]   *Kenth v Heimdale Hotel Investments Ltd* [2001] EWCA Civ 1283. See also *Morgan v Millett* [2001] EWCA Civ 1641; *Skerman v H Bollman Manufacturers Ltd* [2002] EWCA Civ 919; and *Environment Agency v Ellis* [2008] EWCA Civ 1117, [2009] PIQR P5.

[K76]   Further, a subsequent supervening event may not always break the chain of causation, even if that event is tortious. The most common example of this in personal injury cases is where a claimant suffers an accident caused by the negligence of the first defendant, but then is negligently treated by a doctor or surgeon. For example, in *Webb v Barclay's Bank plc*[1] the claimant tripped over a protruding stone in the forecourt of her employer's premises. She was treated with physiotherapy and bracing of the knee. Thereafter, when her symptoms did not resolve because of complications relating to her pre-existing condition of polio, she was negligently advised to undergo an above-knee amputation of the leg. Henry LJ relied upon the Australian case of *Mahoney v Kruschick (Demolitions) Pty Ltd*[2] and approved the following passage in *Clerk & Lindsell on Torts*[3]:

'... only medical treatment so grossly negligent as to be a completely inappropriate response to the injury inflicted by the defendant should operate to break the chain of causation.'

On the facts, the Court of Appeal held that the doctor's negligence was not grossly negligent and did not eclipse the first defendant's negligence in failing to properly maintain their forecourt. However, the Trust, which was vicariously liable for the actions of the doctor, was held to be much more responsible for the amputation and all that went with it. In the circumstances, liability was apportioned 25% against the bank and 75% against the Trust.

[1]   [2001] EWCA Civ 1141. But see also *Robinson v Post Office* [1974] 1 WLR 1176, CA; *Rothwell v Caverswall & Co* [1944] 2 All ER 350, CA; and *Hogan v Bentinck Collieries* [1949] 1 All ER 588, HL, per Lord Normand at 596: 'I start from the proposition which seems to me to be axiomatic, that if a surgeon, by lack of skill or failure in reasonable care, causes additional injury or aggravates an existing injury and so renders himself liable in damages, the reasonable conclusion must be that his intervention is a new cause, and that the additional injury or the aggravation of the existing injury should be attributed to it and not to the original accident. On the other hand, an operation prudently advised and carefully carried out should not be treated as a new cause, whatever its consequences may be'.
[2]   (1985) 156 CLR 522.
[3]   18th edition at para 2-55.

[K77]   Also, it is possible that a defendant who is liable for causing injuries in a first accident may be liable for subsequent injuries sustained in a second accident arising out of the claimant's disabilities caused by the first accident. For example, in *Wieland v Cyril Lord Carpets*[1], the claimant suffered a whiplash injury in the first accident for which the defendant was responsible. As part of her treatment for the whiplash injury, she was required to wear a neck collar. Whilst wearing the collar, she fell down some stairs and sustained further injuries. Eveleigh J held the defendant responsible for the injuries arising out of the second accident because he said it was 'foreseeable that that one injury may affect a person's ability to cope with the vicissitudes of life and thereby cause another injury'[2]. However, this case must be contrasted with *McKew v Holland & Hannen & Cubitts*[3], which also involved two accidents, but where the House of Lords held that the second accident was caused by the claimant's behaviour in taking an unreasonable risk by jumping down some stairs with a weak ankle rather than by the disabilities left by the first accident.

[1] [1969] 3 All ER 1006, followed in *Pyne v Wilkenfeld* (1981) 26 SASR 441.
[2] [1969] 3 All ER 1006 at 1010.
[3] [1969] 3 All ER 1621, HL, which has been applied in *Sabri-Tabrizi v Lothian Health Board* (1998) 43 BMLR 190.

Legal causation (remoteness)

[K78] A claimant must show that the loss complained of was reasonably foreseeable[1]. He or she must do so, not only to establish culpability, but also to establish that the loss was consequent upon the breach of duty alleged. If the type of loss is not so reasonably foreseeable, it will be held to be too remote and not recoverable. For our purposes, the only type of loss that has to be foreseeable is personal injury, and it matters not whether this is physical or psychiatric[2].

[1] *The Wagon Mound* [1961] AC 388.
[2] *Page v Smith* [1996] AC 155. Although note the restrictions placed upon 'primary victims' of psychiatric injury discussed in Chapter D, General Damages. See now also *Cross v Highland and Islands Enterprise Board* [2001] IRLR 336.

[K79] Examples of damage held to be too remote (and therefore irrecoverable) include:

- Side-effects occurring in consequence of a drug prescribed for injuries[1].
- The cost of investment advice[2].
- The cost of future nursing on the basis that there was a 5–10% risk of developing malignant tumours[3].
- An exacerbation of injuries caused by the claimant's neurotic mother[4].
- Lost earnings of a father who stayed in this country to look after his injured son rather than going abroad where he could have earned a substantial salary[5].
- A dependency claim based upon the presumption that the deceased infant would have cared for his parents when older[6].
- A dependency claim based upon the deceased's pension which was a matter of sheer speculation[7].

[1] *Alston v Marine and Trade Insurance Co* 1964 (4) SA.
[2] *Routledge v Mackenzie* [1994] PIQR Q49.
[3] *Barker v Roberts* [1997] CLY 1946.
[4] *McLaren v Bradstreet* (1969) 113 Sol Jo 471, CA.
[5] *Walker v Mullen* (1984) Times, 19 January.
[6] *Barnett v Cohen* [1921] All ER Rep 528.
[7] *D and D v Donald* [2001] PIQR Q44.

[K80] On the other hand, it has been held that compensation for time spent in prison[1], and loss caused by the claimant's wife leaving[2] following a personality change due to the injuries sustained, is not too remote. The former of these two decisions is questionable: see the Law Commission consultation paper on the Illegality Defence in Tort[3]. *Meah v McCreamer*[4] represents possibly the only case in which a litigant has been compensated for his own wrong – so that, as the Law Commission comment, one court of justice is punishing the claimant for what he has done, whilst another is rewarding him for having done it.

[1]   *Meah v McCreamer* [1985] 1 All ER 367. Although note that the 'illegality' defence was not argued.
[2]   *Oakley v Walker* (1977) 121 Sol Jo 619.
[3]   Consultation Paper No 160 (2001).
[4]   [1985] 1 All ER 367.

[K81]   In passing, it is worth noting that there are conflicting authorities regarding which party bears the onus of proof in relation to remoteness of damage. Certainly, the claimant must prove on a balance of probabilities that he or she has suffered some loss; and, once he or she has done that, need not prove the exact extent of that loss on the balance of probabilities test (otherwise a person with, say, a 10% chance of promotion would be more likely than not to fail to be promoted and would thus receive nothing for it, whereas it is well established that he or she receives 10%). It is unclear, however, whether each head of loss must be shown to exist on a balance of probabilities test, or whether it is sufficient simply to produce some evidence that that loss has resulted from the breach of duty alleged.

(xi)   Evaluating Chances and Discounting for Contingencies

General

[K82]   Whenever a court makes an assessment as to what is likely to happen in the future, or what would have happened but for the defendant's negligence in the past, this assessment involves evaluating a chance. Common examples include:

- The chance that the claimant's condition will improve or deteriorate in time.
- The chance that particular sequelae will develop, eg osteo-arthritis or epilepsy.
- The chance that the claimant will need particular treatment or surgery in the future.
- The chance that the claimant would have obtained a promotion, but for the injuries sustained[1].
- The chance that the claimant's symptoms would have developed at some stage, even if the defendant had not committed the tort[2].
- The chance that the claimant is now at risk on the open labour market as a result of his or her injuries[3].
- The chance in Fatal Accidents Act 1976 cases that the dependency would have ceased, eg due to the breakdown of marriage[4].

[1]   See eg *Anderson v Davis* [1993] PIQR Q87. Note that a claim can only be made to reflect the 'lost chance' of such a promotion, and a discount must be applied to take account of the fact that the claimant might not have been promoted in the absence of the injuries: *Williams v Green* [2001] EWCA Civ 1888.
[2]   *Kenth v Heimdale Hotel Investments Ltd* [2001] EWCA Civ 1283; *Morgan v Millett* [2001] EWCA Civ 1641.

³   See further Chapter H.
⁴   *Owen v Martin* [1992] PIQR Q151; *Stanley v Saddique* [1992] QB 1, CA; and *D and D v Donald*
    [2001] PIQR Q44.

[K83]   Whether or not the claimant is allowed full recovery for the particular head of loss claimed will depend upon a number of factors. In particular, it is important to distinguish between heads of loss dependent upon certain events in the past, hypothetical events, events dependent upon the actions of third parties, and future events.

[K84]   In *Allied Maples v Simmons & Simmons*[1], Stuart-Smith LJ distinguished between three categories of cases: (i) cases in which the defendant's negligence consists in some positive act or misfeasance and the question of causation is one of historical fact; (ii) cases in which the defendant's negligence consists of omission[2], where causation depends not upon a question of historical fact but upon the answer to the hypothetical question of what the claimant would have done if there had been no negligence; and (iii) cases in which the claimant's loss depends upon the hypothetical action of a third party. In categories (i) and (ii), the balance of probabilities will prevail, ie if the claimant is able to establish that there was a 51% or more chance of the particular event happening, it is deemed to have happened. In category (iii) cases, the claimant need only show that there was a 'substantial' as opposed to a 'speculative' chance that the event would have happened in order to recover. Once the claimant has established that there is a substantial chance, recovery is limited to the extent of the chance, eg in a solicitor's negligence case where, due to the defendant's negligence, a claim which had a 30% chance of succeeding is struck out, the claimant is restricted to claiming a maximum of 30% of the recoverable damages.

¹   [1995] 1 WLR 1602.
²   It should be noted that there is a compelling argument that there should be no distinction between
    acts or omissions depending upon hypothetical questions as to what the claimant would have done –
    see further Chapter 8 of *McGregor on Damages* (18th edn).

Certain events in the past

[K85]   Where the claimant is claiming that a particular event in the past would have resulted in his or her benefit, it is important to put him or her to proof of (a) the fact that the event would have happened; and (b) that it would have been to his or her benefit[1]. Failure to prove, on the balance of probabilities, that a particular event occurred in the past will lead a judge to find as a fact that the event did not occur. All attempts to argue such a claim on the basis of a lost chance should be strongly resisted because, as McGregor says, '[w]hen we are looking at past events we are necessarily in the realm of causation; the test is the balance of probabilities and chances do not matter'[2]. Where the claimant avers that an event which did not occur would have occurred (eg success in a promotion interview) but for the injury, then (conversely) the chance approach is appropriate.

¹   Alternatively, this allegation may be denied if there is evidence to suggest that the particular event
    would not have occurred.
²   *McGregor on Damages* (18th edn) Chapter 8, para 8-037.

Hypothetical events dependent upon the claimant's actions alone

[K86]   Again, where the damage alleged in the claim is that, but for the defendant's negligence, he or she would have taken a particular course (eg going back to college to retake exams), the claimant must prove what they would have done on the balance of probabilities[1]. Therefore, it is important to put the claimant to strict proof about his or her purported actions. This insistence on proof on the balance of probabilities, which is necessary to show that there is a claim, needs to be carefully distinguished from the quality of the evidence needed to quantify the extent of an injury or loss once it has been established that, on balance, some loss has been occasioned.

[1]   Although it may not be necessary for the claimant actually to give evidence of what he or she would have done, assuming that there is other evidence that the judge can draw conclusions from: see eg *Webb v Barclays Bank plc and Portsmouth Hospitals NHS Trust* [2001] EWCA Civ 1141, in the context of whether or not the claimant would have accepted advice to undergo certain medical treatment.

[K87]   Efforts should be made to obtain evidence to challenge the contentions of the claimant who is putting forward his or her case with the benefit of hindsight. It may be possible to obtain evidence from relatives, friends, colleagues or associates of the claimant which tends to cast doubt on the likelihood of the version of events that he or she contends for; or, alternatively, from other records pre-dating the accident.

[K88]   A common example of this situation in personal injury actions arises in relation to intended retirement dates. Often, the claimant will contend that, but for the accident (leaving other factors such as redundancy and/or illness aside), he or she would have chosen to continue working until the age of 65 or, as is becoming more and more common, the age of 70. However, it may well be that the claimant had never really given his or her intended retirement date much thought, particularly if still young. The claimant's medical records, employer's personnel file and/or personal details may reveal stated intentions which conflict with the claimant's sworn evidence. The claimant may have a partner who has already retired with whom he or she would like to spend time, or an elderly relative who requires looking after. Further, it may be possible to obtain statistical evidence from an employment consultant to show that, on average, people in the claimant's line of work tend to retire earlier than most (eg in physically demanding or high-risk manual jobs, such as tunnel mining).

Hypothetical events dependent upon the actions of third parties

[K89]   When dealing with events that: (i) may happen in the future; or (ii) which might have happened, whether in the future or in the past, if circumstances had not intervened to prevent them, the court cannot decide the matter on a simple balance of probabilities but must assess the chances of their happening[1]. In a case where the claimant suggests that, but for the accident, an event would have happened in his or her favour that was not entirely dependent upon their own actions (eg training to be a barrister), it is necessary to assess the chances of that event actually occurring. For example, in *Doyle v Wallace*[2] the Court of Appeal upheld the trial judge's decision to award the claimant loss of earnings on the basis of the mid-point between the salary of a clerical/administrative worker and the salary of a drama teacher because, on the facts, he found there was a 50% chance that the claimant would become a drama teacher. Although the Court of Appeal reduced the multiplier for earnings as a drama teacher, because the assumption that the claimant would have continued as a full-time drama teacher was not justified by the evidence, the trial judge's approach to the assessment of quantum was not criticised. It was held that the case fell within category (iii) of Stuart-Smith LJ's categories in *Allied Maples v Simmons & Simmons*[2] and, therefore, the assessing of the claimant's loss by way of a lost chance was justified.

[1]   See *Mallet v McMonagle* [1970] AC 166 per Lord Diplock at 176, and *Davies v Taylor* [1974] AC 207, per Lord Reid at 212H–213A.
[2]   [1998] PIQR Q146.
[3]   [1995] 1 WLR 1602. But see *Herring v Ministry of Defence* [2003] EWCA Civ 528.

[K90]   Where one is concerned with a career path, the proper approach is to adopt a career model as the basis for the assessment of loss of future earnings and pension; the prospects of enhanced or reduced earnings resulting from the ordinary chances of life (eg promotion) can be allowed for by adjustments to the multiplicand and multiplier as appropriate; and it is only when the court has to consider the possible effects of an unusual turn of events (eg a career change), that would have a significant effect on earnings or pension rights, that it is necessary to assess the chances of such events occurring and to assess their financial consequences[1]. In passing, however, it is worth noting that the decision in *Doyle v Wallace*[1] has been the subject of academic criticism, and its applicability to almost every personal injury case where the claimant's future employment is in issue is doubtful[2]. However, in the authors' experience, what tends to happen is that, rather than conducting a detailed analysis of the exact career path and pay structure that the claimant would have received but for the defendant's negligence, the court will take a more broad-brush approach[3] and may decide the most likely type of work that the claimant would have embarked upon, and thereafter make a deduction for the risks of not succeeding in obtaining or persevering with that job[4]. Where 'a reasonable career model is taken', there is no need to assess damages on a lost chance basis[5]. In other cases where there are difficulties ascertaining the applicable level of earnings for certain types of work, recourse may be had to the National Earnings Statistics[6], or the Annual Survey of Hours and Earnings[7].

[1]   See *Herring v Ministry of Defence* [2003] EWCA Civ 528; *Doyle v Wallace* [1998] PIQR Q146; and *Langford v Hebran* [2001] EWCA Civ 361.
[2]   See further the strong criticism of this case in Chapter 8 of *McGregor on Damages* (18th edn), in particular at para 8-073.
[3]   For an example of the broad-brush approach, see *Doughty v Stena Offshore* (10 November 1997, unreported), CA, where the Court of Appeal awarded the claimant a single lump sum in order to represent the chance that the claimant would have moved into more profitable work.
[4]   See eg *Biesheuval v Birrell* [1999] PIQR Q40, in which Eady J approached the claimant's claim for loss of earnings on the basis that the claimant would most likely embark upon a career in management consultancy, but applied a conservative approach in order to take account of the fact that the claimant might not have made partner level. See also *Vernon v Bosley* [1997] PIQR P255, where the Court of Appeal held that the claimant had established on the balance of probabilities that he would have sought alternative employment, but discounted the award of the trial judge by 20% to reflect the intervals between jobs and the difficulty he would find obtaining fresh jobs. More recently, see *Herring v Ministry of Defence* [2003] EWCA Civ 528.

5 *Herring v Ministry of Defence* [2003] EWCA Civ 528; and cf *Dixon v Were* [2004] EWHC 2273 (QB). See further Theodore Huckle 'Damages for loss of earnings – reasonable model or loss of chance' [2003] 13 APIL Newsletter 7, pp 16–20.

6 Lady Justice Hale approved the use of these figures by the trial judge to reach an assessment of the claimant's likely future earnings in *Stefanovic v Carter* [2001] EWCA Civ 452, [2001] PIQR Q55.

7 Available online at www.statistics.gov.uk.

[K91] The upshot of *Doyle v Wallace*[1] for defendants is that, whenever a claim is put forward for loss of a chance, the facts of the claim must be carefully considered. If the claim is a true category (iii) type case, the loss may be recovered on a lost chance basis[2]; if not, the claim must be assessed on what probably would have happened. In both instances, however, it is in the defendant's interests to obtain as much evidence as possible to emphasise the risks associated with the suggested form of employment and the chances that the suggested career path would not have been successful[3]. It is important, when considering this aspect of the claim, to take into account the nature of the proposed employment and the area where the claimant lives.

1 [1998] PIQR Q146, CA.

2 It should be noted that the 'lost chance' basis of assessment is not always disadvantageous to the defendant, since a discount is applied for the chance that the claimant would not have succeeded which might not apply if the claim is assessed on the balance of probabilities. See eg *Williams v Green* [2001] EWCA Civ 1888, in which the Court of Appeal applied a 40% discount to the loss of earnings claim because the judge had held that the claimant, a teacher, had a 60% chance of promotion to the post of head teacher.

3 Where appropriate, it is permissible to deal with the lost chance in general terms and award a lump sum without actually specifying percentage discounts: *Ata-Amonoo v Grant* [2001] EWCA Civ 150.

The chance of better treatment

[K92] At present, the commonly accepted view is that, in order to succeed in a claim arising out of alleged negligent medical treatment, the claimant must show on the balance of probabilities that the treatment he or she should have received would have made a measurable difference to his or her condition[1]. A claim for a lost chance of treatment with a success rate of 50% or less is therefore not recoverable. As stated by Otton LJ in *Tahir v Haringey Health Authority*[2]:

> 'A [claimant] cannot recover damages for the loss of a chance of a complete or better recovery.'

1 *Hotson v East Berkshire Health Authority* [1987] AC 750; *Tahir v Haringey Health Authority* [1998] Lloyd's Rep Med 104 at 108; *Pearman v North Essex HA* [2000] Lloyd's Rep Med 174; *Hardaker v Newcastle HA* [2001] Lloyd's Rep Med 512; *Gregg v Scott* [2005] UKHL 2, cf *Smith v NHSLA* [2001] Lloyd's Rep Med 512.

2 [1998] Lloyd's Rep Med 104 at 108.

[K93] A good example of this rule is provided by the well-known case of *Hotson v East Berkshire Area Health Authority*[1], in which the claimant was a young boy who fell out of a tree and fractured his left femoral epiphysis. He was taken to hospital but, owing to negligence, his injury was not diagnosed for five days. The claimant developed avascular necrosis. Had the injury been diagnosed promptly and proper treatment given, the claimant would have had a 25% chance of preventing the avascular necrosis. However, as a result of the defendant's negligence, the chance of preventing the avascular necrosis was nil and there was a 100% chance that it would occur, as in fact it did. The claimant claimed for the 25% loss of a chance of avoiding the avascular necrosis. The House of Lords held that the action failed because the claimant had not satisfied the court, on the balance of probabilities, that he could have avoided the injury that he in fact suffered, had he been given prompt and proper treatment.

1   [1987] AC 750, HL.

[K94] In *Gregg v Scott*[1] the House of Lords was given the opportunity to review the law in this area and decide whether or not claims for clinical negligence should be brought into line with other types of claim for professional negligence, eg solicitors' negligence where claims for the loss of a chance are recognised. By a majority of 3:2, their Lordships held that the lost chance of a better medical outcome is not recoverable. However, the judgments bear close scrutiny, since the appeal was finely balanced and a number of different arguments were advanced for not developing the law to allow such claims.

1   [2005] UKHL 2.

Discounting for contingencies

[K95] In the same way that a claimant may contend for an increase in the measure of damages to be awarded because of the prospect of a favourable occurrence in the future – eg a promotion – the defendant may contend for a reduction in order to take account of unfavourable contingencies[1].

1   See *Mallet v McMonagle* [1970] AC 166, per Lord Diplock at 176.

[K96] It is important to note that a discount for the contingency that a given event may happen – or may have happened, at least where past history does not itself determine the issue – may be made, even if the defendant does not prove that the event is likely to occur on the balance of probabilities. For example, in *Heil v Rankin MIB*[1], the Court of Appeal upheld the decision of Daniel Brennan QC to discount the claimant's claim for past and future loss of earnings on the basis of possible future supervening events. In that case, the claimant, who was a police officer, suffered from pre-existing post-traumatic stress disorder. It was held that, quite apart from the defendant's tortious act, a further trigger event may have occurred in any event which would have caused exactly the same exacerbation of the pre-existing condition that was complained of. The trial judge discounted the claims for past and future losses by 50% to reflect this contingency. On appeal, the discount was reduced to 25%.

1   [2001] PIQR Q16, CA (note this is not the same hearing that dealt with the Law Commission's recommended increase in awards for general damages).

[K97] A further example is provided by *Thomas v Bath District Health Authority*[1]. In this case, the Court of Appeal upheld the trial judge's decision to reduce the claimant's general damages by a factor of 10% in order to reflect the chance that the claimant might undergo a successful back operation in five to six years after the trial.

The trial judge's reduction in the multiplier for future losses from 12 to 10, to reflect the same possibility of a successful operation, was also upheld.

¹   [1995] PIQR Q19, CA.

[K98]   Discounts for contingencies tend to be most prevalent in claims brought under the Fatal Accidents Act 1976[1]. In particular, discounts are often made to reflect the following possibilities:

•   That the deceased would have died before the date of trial in any event[2].
•   The prospect that the deceased would have retired early.
•   That the relationship of dependency would have come to an end (eg infidelity leading to a divorce).
•   That the deceased would have married.
•   That a dependent widow will remarry.
•   That the dependant will return to work.

¹   See further Chapter L.
²   Allowance is normally made for this in the multiplier for the dependency which, in a fatal accident case, runs from the date of death and not from the date of trial: *Cookson v Knowles* [1979] AC 556. See further *Wilkins v William Press Ltd* (30 November 2000, unreported), QBD; *White v ESAB Group UK* [2002] PIQR Q76; *ATH v MS* [2002] 3 WLR 1179.

(xii)   The 'Domestic Element'

[K99]   The claimant must give credit for any savings made as a result of the defendant's wrongdoing. Thus the House of Lords in *Lim Poh Choo v Camden and Islington Area Health Authority*[1] held that, where claims were advanced for both lost earnings and care, an element should be deducted from the lost earnings to reflect the living expenses of the claimant[2]. Also, a deduction for the 'domestic element' should be made when dealing with a claim for dependency under the Fatal Accidents Act 1976[3] or a claim for 'lost years'[4]. (This is conventionally achieved in the course of calculation of the dependency itself, with a normal starting assumption that, in the case of a deceased husband, where there was a stable marriage but no dependent children, the dependency on earned income would be 66% of the net income; where there were dependent children, it would be 75%.) A discount should also be made under statute where the claimant has been maintained at public expense in a hospital[5]. Technically, a further deduction should be made in respect of a claim for lost earnings to reflect all expenses that would have been incurred to obtain the earnings, eg travel and clothing expenses, and the cost of tools. However, unless these claims are considerable it is unusual for the cost of travel expenses to be calculated and deducted[6]. The claim will, however, be considerable if the claimant travels a long way to work, or works away from home during the week.

¹   [1980] AC 174, HL.
²   See also *Donovan v Cammell Laird* (1949) 82 LIL Rep 642, where a widower was prevented from doing domestic work in his house for 12 months. Had he been working, he would have had to pay for domestic assistance out of his earnings. The court therefore deducted this amount from his claim for loss of earnings. See further *Jenkins v Groscott* [2000] PIQR Q17, where the claimant was receiving a notional wage from his rehabilitation unit, and the total future loss of earnings claim was deducted from the total future cost of care claim.

3   *Harris v Empress Motors* [1984] 1 WLR 212; and *Phipps v Dry Docks* [1996] PIQR Q100.
4   *Pickett v British Rail Engineering* [1980] AC 136.
5   Administration of Justice Act 1982, s 5. See para **[K138]**.
6   *Dews v National Coal Board* [1988] AC 1, per Lord Griffiths; cf *Sparks v Royal Hospitals NHS Trust* (21 December 1998, unreported), where McKinnon J deducted the travel costs of £3 per week; and *Eagle v Chambers (No 2)* [2004] EWCA Civ 1033, where the Court of Appeal upheld the trial judge's deduction of 15%, to reflect travel expenses, from the claim for past loss of earnings.

(xiii)   Accelerated Receipt

[K100]   A claim for a specific item of expenditure in the future must be reduced to reflect the fact that the claimant has the benefit of the money earlier than he or she otherwise would. Following the Lord Chancellor's decision to exercise his powers under the Damages Act 1996, the applicable discount rate is 2.5%[1]. A common application of this principle relates to the costs of future medical treatment.

Example

The medical evidence indicates that the claimant is likely to require a hip replacement in ten years' time. The current cost of the operation (including all surgical, anaesthetist and hospital fees) is £10,000. This figure should be discounted by a factor of 0.7812 (Table 27 of the Ogden Tables at 2.5% discount rate), giving a figure of £7,812.

1   See further Chapter H, Future Expenses and Losses at paras **[H25]**–**[H32]**.

(xiv)   No Entitlement to Claim in Law

[K101]   There are a number of distinct claims to which the claimant has no entitlement in law, and these should be denied in their entirety. For example:

*   Costs of raising and caring for a healthy baby[1].
*   Surrogacy treatment[2].
*   A claim by a child, for the loss of services provided by his or her mother, arising out of injuries caused to the mother by the defendant[3].
*   The general inconvenience of completing insurance claim forms, instructing solicitors and obtaining repair estimates[4].
*   Gratuitous services rendered by the tortfeasor[5].
*   Damages for the risk that the law might change in the future, making the claimant liable to account for the assistance provided by a local authority[6].

1   *McFarlane v Tayside Health Board* [2000] 2 AC 59, which was applied in *Greenfield v Flather* [2001] EWCA Civ 113, (2001) 59 BMLR 43 and *A v East Kent NHS Trust* [2002] EWCA Civ 1872 to bar claims arising out of the birth of healthy babies. A claim over and above a conventional award of £15,000 is also prohibited where, by reason of the defendant's negligence, a healthy baby is born but additional costs are incurred because of the claimant's disability: *Rees v Darlington Memorial Hospital NHS Trust* [2003] UKHL 52. Cf the position in respect of a disabled child, where the additional costs of bringing up the child may be recoverable: *Groom v Selby* [2001] Lloyd's Rep Med 39; *McLelland v Greater Glasgow Health Board* 2001 SLT 446; *Lee v Taunton and Somerset NHS Trust* [2001] 1 FLR 419; *Parkinson v St James and Seacroft University Hospital NHS Trust* [2001] EWCA Civ 530, [2001] 3 All ER 97, CA; *Taylor v Shropshire Health Authority* [2000]

Lloyd's LR Med 96; *Hardman v Amin* [2000] Lloyd's Rep Med 498; and *Rand v East Dorset Health Authority* [2000] Lloyd's Rep Med 181.

2　*Briody v St Helen's & Knowsley AHA* [2001] EWCA Civ 1010, [2001] 2 FLR 481.

3　*Buckley v Farrow* [1997] PIQR Q78. But a claimant can recover damages in respect of gratuitous care or services which he is no longer able to provide to members of his family living as part of the same household, if the same goes beyond 'the ordinary interaction of members of a household': see *Lowe v Guise* [2002] 3 All ER 454 (CA), discussed at para **[K173]**.

4　*Dimond v Lovell* [2001] 1 QB 216. See also *Morris v Johnson Matthey* (1967) 112 SJ 32; *Taylor v Browne* CLY [1995] 1842; and *O'Brien-King v Phillips* [1997] CLY 1814.

5　*Hunt v Severs* [1994] 2 AC 350.

6　*Firth v Ackroyd* [2000] Lloyd's Rep Med 312. See further Chapter F, Past Expenses and Losses at paras **[F69]–[F75]**.

(xv)　Illegality ('ex turpi causa non oritur actio')

[K102]　As a general rule, for policy reasons, the court will not allow a claimant to benefit from his or her own criminal actions. Therefore, if a claimant earned his or her living by stealing prior to an accident, the court would not allow the claimant to recover any compensation for loss of earnings[1]. The position, however, is less clear-cut where the claimant's earnings are derived from a lawful source, but the claimant has not declared his or her earnings for the purposes of tax and National Insurance[2].

1　*Burns v Edman* [1970] 2 QB 541.

2　Compare *Finnis v Caulfied* [2002] All ER (D) 353 (Oct); *Newman v Folkes & Dunlop Tyres Ltd* [2002] PIQR Q2, QBD, Garland J – appealed to the Court of Appeal but not on this point; *Duller v SE Lincs Engineering* [1981] CLY 585; *Bagge v Buses* [1958] NZLR 630; with *Hunter v Butler* [1996] RTR 396. See further Chapter F, Past Expenses and Losses at paras **[F25]** and **[F26]**. See *Enfield Technical Services Ltd v Ray Payne: BF Components Ltd v Ian Grace* [2008] EWCA Civ 393, [2008] ICR 1423 for a recent review of the principles: where a claimant acting in good faith participates in arrangements made by his employer to trial him as self-employed, but was later held to be an employer, he has not unlawfully performed the contract of employment so as to be disentitled to compensation for unfair dismissal from employment.

[K103]　The principle of illegality is extremely wide and will prevent any damages being awarded which would be an affront to the public conscience[1]. This includes immoral as well as criminal conduct. The policy may apply to defeat just one head of damages without defeating the rest of the claim such that, where a claimant lies to get a job, eg by hiding his or her condition of epilepsy from his or her employer, thereby committing the offence of obtaining pecuniary advantage by deception, he or she will not be able to claim for loss of earnings[2]. There is a useful review of the present law in the Law Commission consultation paper on the illegality defence generally, including the defence in tort[3].

1　See eg *Clunis v Camden and Islington Health Authority* [1998] QB 978, in which the claimant, who was convicted of manslaughter, sued the health authority that treated him for failing properly to treat his mental condition and prevent him from committing the offence. See also *Gray v Thames Trains Ltd & another* [2007] EWHC 1558 (QB); *Pickering v JA McConville* [2003] EWCA Civ 554; *Wilson v Coulson* [2002] PIQR P22; *Edgar v Rayson* [2001] CLY 5349; *Birkett v Acorn Business Machines Ltd* [1999] 2 All ER (Comm) 429; *Worrall v BRB* [1999] CLY 1413.

2　*Hewison v Meridian Shipping Services* [2002] EWCA Civ 1821, cf where the defendant has put the claimant in the position of needing to lie: *Major v Ministry of Defence* [2003] EWCA Civ 1433.

3　Consultation Paper No 189 (2009).

[K104]   Where the defence of illegality is advanced, it should be pleaded, since it is contrary to the concepts of English jurisprudence for the court either to take a point of illegality of its own motion or to act on such evidence unless it was satisfied that the whole of the relevant circumstances were before it[1]. When pleading the defence, the claimant should be given sufficient details, particularly where dishonesty or fraud is alleged[2].

1   *Pickering v JA McConville* [2003] EWCA Civ 554.
2   *Jonesco v Beard* [1930] AC 298; *Scruton v Bone* (20 November 2001, unreported); and *Noble v Owens* [2010] EWCA Civ 224. In *Noble v Owens* [2010] EWCA Civ 224, Elias LJ said at para [37]: '... where allegations of fraud are made they should be particularised and established to the appropriate standard of proof. This is a hallowed principle of law which has been repeated by the courts on many occasions'.

(xvi)   Limitation of Actions[1]

[K105]   Claimants will generally have three years from their 'date of knowledge' in which to bring a claim for personal injuries[2]. This will usually commence when the accident or injury is sustained, but may be delayed due to lack of symptoms, the relevant knowledge[3], disability[4] or deliberate concealment[5]. Of course, if the limitation period has expired and the court does not exercise its power to extend the limitation period[6], the defendant has a complete defence to the claim and no damages are recoverable. Where additional time is considered desirable in order to reach a settlement without issuing proceedings, a defendant may agree to waive any limitation defence. However, before a claimant can rely upon such an agreement, there must have been a 'clear, unequivocal, unambiguous and unconditional promise' to this effect[7].

1   For a full discussion of this topic, see further David Oughton *Limitation of Actions* (LLP, 1998); Andrew McGee *Limitation Periods* (Sweet & Maxwell, 2002); Michael Jones *Limitation Periods in Personal Injury Actions* (Blackstone Press, 2002); and Rodney Nelson-Jones *Personal Injury Limitation Law* (Butterworths, 1994).
2   Limitation Act 1980, s 11.
3   Limitation Act 1980, s 14.
4   Limitation Act 1980, s 28.
5   Limitation Act 1980, s 32.
6   By reason of the power under Limitation Act 1980, s 33.
7   *Surendranath Seechurn v ACE Insurance SA-NV* [2002] EWCA Civ 67.

[K106]   If a limitation defence is taken, it must be expressly pleaded[1].

1   CPR, PD 16, para 13.1.

(xvii)   Damage Arising Before the Cause of Action Arose

[K107]   The defendant cannot be liable for damage prior to the existence of the claimant's claim. Although this may sound obvious, it has important ramifications for claims involving industrial diseases, where the claimant's injuries may have been contributed to by a number of different employers[1].

1   See further Chapter 9 of *McGregor on Damages* (18th edn).

(xviii)   Contributory Negligence

[K108]   Of course, if the claimant is found to have contributed to the accident, the claimant's award will be reduced by the extent of his or her contribution. In passing, it is worth noting that there was some authority which suggested that a finding of contributory negligence could be as much as 100%[1]. However, this view is logically unsupportable after the Law Reform (Contributory Negligence) Act 1945, and the better view is that, in order for the claimant to 'contribute' to any blame, the defendant must already be at least 1% to blame, ie contributory negligence is only a partial defence[2], at least in any common law claim. In a claim for breach of statutory duty, however, contributory negligence may itself be a breach of duty which disentitles the claimant to an award of damages[3]. But such a finding is perhaps more consistent with an argument that the sole cause of the claimant's injuries was the fault of the claimant, as opposed to saying that the claimant was 100% to blame[4]. As Sedley LJ stated in *Anderson v Newham College of Further Education*[5]:

> 'The relevant principles are straightforward. Whether the claim is in negligence or for breach of statutory duty, if the evidence, once it has been appraised as the law requires, shows the entire fault to lie with the claimant there is no liability on the defendant. If not, then the court will consider to what extent, if any, the claimant's share in the responsibility for the damage makes it just and equitable to reduce his damages. The phrase "100 per cent contributory negligence", while expressive, is unhelpful, because it invites the court to treat a statutory qualification of the measure of damages as if it were a secondary or surrogate approach to liability, which it is not. If there is liability, contributory negligence can reduce its monetary quantification, but it cannot legally or logically nullify it.'

1   *Jayes v IMI* [1985] ICR 155; *Marshall v Lincolnshire Roadcar Co Ltd* (7 December 2000, unreported), CA.
2   *Boyle v Kodack* [1969] 1 WLR 661; *Pitts v Hunt* [1991] 1 QB 24; *Lunnun v Singh* [1999] CPLR 587; and *Anderson v Newham College of Further Education* [2002] EWCA Civ 505. See further Chapter A, General Principles at paras **[A78]** and **[A79]**.
3   See further *Jayes v IMI* [1985] ICR 155, although cf *Anderson v Newham College of Further Education* [2002] EWCA Civ 505.
4   See eg *Wallis v Balfour Beatty Rail Maintenance Ltd* [2003] EWCA Civ 72. See further in *Pitts v Hunt* [1991] 1 QB 24, per Beldam LJ at 48; and *Anderson v Newham College of Further Education* [2002] EWCA Civ 505, per Sedley LJ at [18].
5   [2002] EWCA Civ 505 at [18].

[K109]   The following points should also be noted about the operation of contributory negligence:

- The defence should be pleaded[1].
- In order for there to be a finding of contributory negligence, fault on the part of the claimant is not enough – it must be shown that the claimant's alleged negligent act or omission was causative of the injuries, ie the claimant's negligent act or omission must have either caused or materially contributed to his or her injuries[2].
- Documents in support of the allegations of contributory negligence should be disclosed[3].
- If the claimant is found to have been partly to blame for his or her injuries, the extent of this responsibility will depend upon the degree of causative potency and blameworthiness of each party's actions or inactions[4].

- When a finding of contributory negligence is made, the relevant proportion should be deducted from the claimant's total award of damages before any apportionment is carried out as between joint torfeasors[5].
- A finding of contributory negligence will apply equally to all aspects of the claim, including eg costs arising from management of the claimant's affairs by the Court of Protection[6].

1   *Fookes v Slaytor* [1978] 1 WLR 1293, CA.
2   See eg *Toole v Bolton Metropolitan Borough Council* [2002] EWCA Civ 588.
3   Personal Injury Pre-action Protocol (PIPAP), para 3.12.
4   *Davies v Swan Motor Co* [1949] 2 KB 291; *Stapley v Gypsum Mines Ltd* [1953] AC 663; *Baker v Willoughby* [1970] AC 497; *Froom v Butcher* [1976] QB 286; *Madden v Quirke* [1989] 1 WLR 702; *Fitzgerald v Lane* [1989] AC 328; *Jones v Wilkins* [2001] RTR 283; *Cleminson v John Addley Ltd* (11 May 1999, unreported), CA; and *Eagle v Chambers* [2003] EWCA Civ 1107.
5   *Fitzgerald v Lane* [1989] AC 328. See also *Sharpe v Michael Addison* [2003] EWCA Civ 1189 in relation to the approach as regards contributory negligence in a professional negligence claim arising out of a personal injury case.
6   *Willbye v Gibbons* [2003] EWCA Civ 372. See also *Cassel v Riverside Health Authority* [1994] PIQR Q168.

[K110] In some instances, it may be tempting to argue, by analogy with cases such as *Woodrup v Nicol*[1], that, because of the practical effect of the deduction for contributory negligence, the claimant will not be able to purchase some of the items of expense/loss claimed. In which case, arguably, the claimant should be entitled to an even lower sum because he or she is unlikely to incur the cost of these items. However, it is submitted that such an argument is contrary to public policy and established legal principles, and was rejected by the Court of Appeal in *Sowden v Lodge*[2]. It was held that, when assessing damages, the court calculates the claimant's entitlement to damages on a 100% basis, and shuts its eyes to contributory negligence at that stage. This was supported by the wording of s 1(2) of the Law Reform (Contributory Negligence) Act 1945. The reduction for contributory negligence takes account of share of responsibility for the damage but not how the damages are likely to be spent. Therefore, the finding of contributory negligence has no bearing upon the manner of the assessment of damages in any given case.

1   [1993] PIQR Q104, CA.
2   [2004] EWCA Civ 1370. See further Chapter A, General Principles at para **[A79]**.

(xix) Rehabilitation

[K111] In 1995, a working party made up of claimant and defendant lawyers, insurers and various charitable organisations was formed to consider the need for early intervention for injured claimants. In 1999, the Code of Best Practice on Rehabilitation was drawn up.

[K112] There is a duty upon every claimant solicitor to consider in consultation with the claimant, and/or the claimant's family, whether it is likely or possible that early intervention, rehabilitation or medical treatment would improve their present and/or long-term physical or mental well being[1]. Likewise, there is a duty on the insurer to consider, in any appropriate case, whether it is likely that the claimant will benefit, in the immediate, medium or longer term, from further medical treatment, rehabilitation or early intervention[2]. Unless the need for such intervention or treatment has already been identified by medical reports obtained by either side and disclosed, the need for, and extent of, such intervention, rehabilitation or treatment will be examined by means of an independent assessment[3]. It is important to note, however, that any assessment report, and any notes or correspondence prepared in relation to it, are covered by legal professional privilege and are not to be disclosed in any legal proceedings unless both parties agree[4].

[1]   Code of Best Practice on Rehabilitation, para 2.1.
[2]   Code of Best Practice on Rehabilitation, para 3.1.
[3]   Code of Best Practice on Rehabilitation, para 4.1.
[4]   Code of Best Practice on Rehabilitation, paras 6.2, 6.3.

[K113]   It remains to be seen whether a defendant will be able to request that proceedings should be stayed if the claimant refuses to undergo a rehabilitation programme. Much will depend upon the individual facts of the case, including the type of injury, the nature of the suggested rehabilitation, and the suggested benefits that the rehabilitation could bring. However, given the duties upon the parties to rehabilitate the claimant, and by analogy with cases involving failure to undergo treatment, perhaps we may see more of these types of application being successful[1].

[1]   See further at paras **[K40]–[K59]** and *Laycock v Lagoe* [1997] PIQR P518.

(xx)   The Rule in Henderson v Henderson[1]

[K114]   The rule in *Henderson v Henderson*[2] provides that a claimant is barred from litigating a claim that has already been adjudicated upon, or could and should have been brought before the court in earlier proceedings arising out of the same facts[3]. It is clear that the rule applies to personal injury actions[4]. However, the rule has undergone considerable modification in recent times, following the decision of the House of Lords in *Johnson v Gorewood*[5]. In essence, the rule in *Henderson v Henderson* is to be seen as part of the court's wider jurisdiction for striking claims out as an abuse of process. It is not possible to formulate a comprehensive list of all the possible forms of abuse. There are no hard and fast rules. In each case, a merits-based judgment has to be made, taking account of all the public and private interests involved, as well as the facts that give rise to the particular claim[6].

[1]   For a detailed exposition of the relevant law, see Spencer Bower 'The Doctrine of Res Judicata', and the 'Doctrine of Res Judicata and Issue Estoppel' in *Halsbury's Laws*.
[2]   (1843) 3 Hare 100.
[3]   This rule will also apply to claims where there has been a settlement rather than a judgment or a consent order: *Johnson v Gorewood* [2002] AC 1, [2001] 1 All ER 481. What is important is whether or not the settlement was intended to cover the subsequent claim – see further *Phipson on Evidence* (16th edn).
[4]   *Talbot v Berkshire County Council* [1994] QB 290.
[5]   [2002] AC 1.
[6]   *Johnson v Gorewood* [2002] AC 1, [2001] 1 All ER 481.

(xxi)   De Minimis

[K115]   Some claims may be disallowed because they are 'de minimis', ie too small or trivial to calculate. Whether an injury is too small or trivial is a matter of degree[1]. In

Rothwell v Chemical & Insulating Co Ltd[2] the House of Lords held that pleural plaques were not sufficiently serious to amount to an actionable injury, even if associated with a psychiatric injury resulting from anxiety regarding the contemplation of developing future illness, since they were symptomless.

1   *Rothwell v Chemical & Insulating Co Ltd* [2008] 1 AC 281, per Lord Hoffmann at 289E.
2   [2008] 1 AC 281.

5   General Damages

[K116]   Generally speaking, it is unusual for a counter-schedule to deal with claims for general damages, because such claims are not ordinarily claimed in the schedule of loss. Technically, there is no requirement for such claims to be set out in the schedule of loss, and many practitioners leave these heads of loss – which, by their very nature, are not capable of precise quantification – to be assessed by the judge following evidence. However, sometimes sums will be claimed for heads of general damage in the schedule of loss, in which case, if the defendant wishes to raise a positive defence to the claim in its entirety or alternatively disputes the amount claimed, a section of the counter-schedule should be devoted to these heads of claim.

(i)   Pain, Suffering and Loss of Amenity ('PSLA')

[K117]   Schedules of loss will often set out a narrative describing the claimant's injuries and the effect of those injuries on the claimant's life, including work, domestic, leisure and social activities. This narrative should be carefully read in order to assess whether or not the description matches the medical reports and witness evidence and can be reasonably related to the negligence of the defendant. In most cases, the full nature and extent of the injuries will not be in the knowledge of the defendant until he has obtained his own medical evidence, pending which the claimant should be required to prove the matters set out in the schedule.

[K118]   When responding to the pleaded details of injury in the schedule of loss, it is often helpful to highlight the positive features of the medical reports and, where appropriate, to emphasise the recovery made (or that should, with reasonable effort, have been made) by the claimant, and the period over which he was disabled, or the prognosis for the future. For convenience, the court's attention can be drawn to the relevant mitigating features of the injuries by way of bullet points. Where there is any serious dispute regarding the nature or extent of the injuries, or as to the cause of those injuries (or other injuries or conditions which would have had an impact on the claimant's life), reference should be made to the specific medical records or medical reports which support the defendant's case. It should be noted that any pre-existing injury or disability may operate to reduce the appropriate level of award for PSLA, especially where there is an overlap between the appropriate category of the JSB Guidelines and the disability which would have been present in any event due to an unrelated or pre-existing condition. In this instance, it is usually appropriate to discount the appropriate award to reflect the disability that is not attributable to the defendant's conduct[1]. Occasionally, however, a pre-existing condition will make the consequences of the claimant's injuries worse, in which case a higher award might be justified[2].

[1]   *Taylor v Weston AHA* [2003] All ER (D) 50 (Dec).
[2]   See eg *Smith v Leech Brain* [1962] 2 QB 405, [1961] 3 All ER 1159; *Mustard v Morris* [1982] 1 CLY 11; *Savory v Burningham* [1996] CLY 2362; and *Brown v Vosper Thornycroft* [2004] EWHC 400 (QB).

[K119]   Where a sum has been put forward for PSLA, it is usually appropriate to respond either by (i) agreeing the sum claimed (if it is reasonable), or (ii) making a counter-proposal; but, if the claimant's condition is not settled, or the medical evidence has not been finalised, it is prudent to advance a sum on a provisional basis. There are often factors regarding the claimant's condition and prognosis which are liable to change, especially if further treatment or surgery is pending; and, even in the most severe cases, the claimant's ability to cope with his or her disabilities tends to improve with time, as the claimant adjusts his or her lifestyle to its new parameters.

(ii)   Loss of Congenial Employment

[K120]   Technically, an award for loss of congenial employment is part of the lump sum award for PSLA. It may apply to any job which the claimant particularly enjoyed and which he or she is no longer able to do by reason of the defendant's negligence. However, a cursory look through the reported quantum summaries in Butterworths Personal Injury Litigation Service and *Kemp & Kemp* indicate that awards for loss of congenial employment tend to be reserved for cases involving the loss of a professional job such as a fireman, a nurse or an army officer, or those with unusual features such as the actor's 'smell of greasepaint and the roar of the crowd'[1]. It may be harder for a manual worker to convince a court that he or she has suffered a similar loss of job satisfaction to someone who had spent many years training to do a job that they had always wanted to pursue, but such a worker is not precluded from such an award, because the award is not confined to reference to any particular type of employment: it is not to be regarded as an 'automatic extra' but it is available to any claimant who has truly suffered such a loss[2]. Further, it may be inappropriate for a claimant who has only been in a job for a very short period of time to receive such an award[2].

[1]   An observation made by Waite J in the course of argument in *Pape v Cumbria County Council* [1992] 3 All ER 211.
[2]   See *Lane v The Personal Representatives of Deborah Lake (Deceased)* (18 July 2007, unreported (QB)), Lawtel 31.7.2007, where an award was made in respect of a carpenter who had worked in the construction industry and who had loved his work; and see also *Noble v Owens* [2008] EWHC 359 (QB) involving a builder who was also developing a plant stall business.
[3]   See eg *Smith v McCrae* [2003] EWCA Civ 505, in which the Court of Appeal allowed an appeal against an award for loss of congenial employment for a claimant who, at the time of the accident, had been working as a motorcycle courier for some seven weeks or so.

[K121]   As regards the assessment of damages for loss of congenial employment, a conventional lump sum will be awarded. These sums are kept at a modest level and rarely exceed £5,000[1]. As Kennedy LJ said in *Willbye v Gibbons*[2]:

'Loss of congenial employment

There is no complaint about the Recorder's award of £118,095.32 for future loss of earnings, calculated by reference to what the appellant could hope to have earned as a nursery nurse, less her average annual earnings over the last three years, nor is there any complaint about the award of £15,000 for handicap in the labour market, but the respondent asserts that the Recorder should not have awarded an extra £15,000 for loss of congenial employment. Mr Alldis tells us that so far as he has been able to ascertain the highest award to date under this head is £10,000, and in fact awards rarely exceed £5,000. In my judgment it is important to keep this head of damages in proportion. The appellant is being compensated for being unable to pursue a career she thought she would have enjoyed. She never actually embarked on that career, although she probably had the ability to obtain the qualifications required, and in financial terms she has been fully reimbursed, so this is really an award for a particular disappointment, which may or may not be prolonged. In my judgment the award in this case should not exceed £5,000, and I would substitute that sum for the sum awarded by the Recorder.'

1   But see *Hanks v MOD* [2007] EWHC 966 (QB), where an award of £9,000 was made to a naval pilot; and *Appleton v Medhat Mohammed El Safty* [2007] EWHC 631 (QB), in which £25,000 was awarded to a professional footballer. There is nothing to suggest that a *Heil v Rankin* [2001] QB 272 uplift should be applied: *Pratt v Smith* (18 December 2002, unreported), QBD. In any event, awards below £10,000 would not be subject to any such increase. See further Chapter D, General Damages at paras **[D129]–[D140]**.

2   [2003] EWCA Civ 372 at [11]. See also *Pratt v Smith* (18 December 2002, unreported), QBD.

[K122]   It is worth noting that the Law Commission, in its Paper No 257 'Damages for Personal Injury: Non-pecuniary Loss', was of the view that damages for the loss of congenial employment were 'merely an aspect of pain, suffering and loss of amenity' and did not believe that there was any need for, or any advantage in, separating out new heads of non-pecuniary loss beyond pain and suffering and loss of amenity[1].

1   Although the Court of Appeal made no mention of this recommendation in *Heil v Rankin* [2001] QB 272.

(iii)   Handicap on the Labour Market

[K123]   A *Smith v Manchester*[1] award is distinct from a *Blamire* award: the former is an award for a contingent future loss in the event of a claimant who is employed at the time of trial losing his current job, and thereafter being at a handicap on the open labour market as a result of his injuries; whereas the latter is appropriate where there is a continuing loss of earnings at the time of trial, but there are too many uncertainties to adopt the conventional multiplier/multiplicand approach to its quantification[2]. A claimant is not entitled to an award for disadvantage on the labour market in the following situations:

- Where a full loss of earnings claim is awarded on a multiplier/multiplicand basis, the claimant being deemed to have no residual earning capacity whatsoever.
- Where a loss of earnings claim is awarded on a multiplier/multiplicand basis, and the multipliers are calculated in accordance with the methodology suggested in the Ogden Tables (6th edn). This is because the future contingencies arising out of the claimant's disability or handicap on the open labour market are already

factored into the discount which is applied to the multiplier for the claimant's residual future earning capacity.

- Where there is a 'speculative' or 'fanciful' risk (as opposed to a 'substantial' or 'real' risk) that the claimant will be put onto the open labour market in the future[3].

- Where the medical evidence does not support that the claimant will be disadvantaged at work (especially in relation to the claimant's pre-accident occupation) because of his or her injuries.

- Where the claimant would have been at a disadvantage on the open labour market in any event, due to his or her pre-existing condition[4]. But where a claimant is more handicapped than he would have been in any event by reason of an additional injury, then he remains entitled to an award.

[1]   (1974) 17 KIR 1.
[2]   See *Ronan v Sainsbury's Supermarkets Ltd & Anor* [2006] EWCA Civ 1074. Although note that, in *Blamire v South Cumbria Health Authority* [1993] PIQR Q1, a single lump sum award was made reflecting both handicap on the labour market and loss of earnings without making any distinction between the two and, whilst theoretically possible, it may be difficult and somewhat artificial to attempt to calculate the losses attributable to each separate element.
[3]   *Moeliker v Reyrole* [1976] ICR 253; *Wren v North Eastern Electricity Board,* unreported, 14 November 1978 (CA).
[4]   See eg *Morgan v Millett* [2001] EWCA Civ 1641.

[K124]   It is important to note that, whereas (as has already been observed) any assessment of a claimant's future loss of earnings which adopts the methodology contained within the Ogden Tables (6th edn) will preclude a *Smith v Manchester* award, the Ogden Tables themselves recognise that the methodology will not be appropriate for all cases, and that in some cases *Smith v Manchester* or *Blamire* awards will remain more appropriate[1]. Defendants should therefore be ready to identify all such cases, and to contend that a *Smith* (or *Blamire*) award is a more appropriate form of award than an award for loss of earnings which adopts the methodology of the Ogden Tables (6th edn)[2].

[1]   See the Ogden Tables (6th edn), Explanatory Notes, para 31.
[2]   See further discussion at paras **[K200]–[K203]**.

[K125]   Where an award for disadvantage on the labour market is applicable, general arguments to reduce the level of the award include the following:

- The risk that the claimant will lose his or her current job and be thrown onto the open labour market is a low one[1].

- The risk that the claimant may lose his or her current employment is unlikely to materialise for a considerable time in the future (and should therefore be subject to a considerable discount to take account of accelerated receipt).

- There is a buoyant job market in the claimant's area and, notwithstanding the claimant's injuries, he or she should have no difficulty securing alternative employment[2].

- Despite the claimant's injuries, (i) his disabilities have little or no impact on the type of employment in question, and/or (ii) his or her skills, qualifications and experience continue to make him or her attractive to employers. This is particularly so where the claimant has, despite his injuries, obtained and/or changed employment since the accident with relative ease and speed.

- The claimant has been or is likely to be promoted to a management level, where manual work is not required and his or her injuries will not be a bar to employment.
- The claimant's pre-existing injuries would have placed him or her at a disadvantage on the labour market in any event.

---

1   The claimant's personnel file should be obtained and/or evidence from the claimant's current employer regarding the security of his or her current position.
2   In appropriate cases, it may be useful to obtain expert evidence from an employment consultant in order to support this argument.

(iv) Loss of Marriage Prospects and Marriage Breakdown

[K126]   Where the claimant was engaged to be married at the time of the accident, it may be possible for him or her to sustain a claim for loss of marriage prospects, particularly if the engagement was broken off as a result of the injuries suffered[1]. Damages may also be awarded where the claimant was not engaged but, owing to the injuries, may now find it harder to meet a partner[2]. Such claims should be scrutinised with regard to the age and sex of the claimant and the nature of the injuries. It is also worth noting that, if a claim for loss of marriage prospects succeeds, it is likely to reduce the multiplier for loss of earnings for a female claimant who may have taken time off work to have children and may have given up work altogether[3]; and defendants might like to argue that a man who is married may well for that reason wish to retire before normal retirement age to enjoy the benefits of retirement with his partner, so that the multiplier for future loss of earnings should be reduced a little below that applicable to a single man.

---

1   *Aloni v National Westminster Bank* (20 May 1982, unreported), referred to in *Kemp & Kemp* at 19-022.
2   *Harris v Harris* [1973] 1 Lloyd's Rep 445. Notwithstanding the fact that such contingencies are now already accounted for within Tables C and D of the Ogden Tables (6th edn), there seems to be no reason why a defendant could not, by analogy, argue for a greater discount to the multiplier than that stipulated by these Tables.
3   *Moriarty v McCarthy* [1978] 1 WLR 155; and *Housecroft v Burnet* [1986] 1 All ER 332.

[K127]   There is authority to justify a separate award of general damages where the claimant's marriage has broken down as a result of the injuries sustained by the defendant's negligence[1] and also to compensate for the expenses arising out of the subsequent divorce[2]. It is unlikely that a claimant would be able to recover damages under this head unless the relationship is one of marriage or de facto marriage. Further, it is a sad fact of life that a high proportion of marriages fail, and it may be difficult for the claimant to persuade the court that it was their injuries which led to the marriage breakdown[3]. Even if the claimant can establish the causal link, it is open for the defendant to argue that an award should be discounted in order to reflect the risk that the marriage might have failed in any event[4].

---

1   *Lampert v Eastern Omnibus Co* [1954] 1 WLR 1047; *Pietryga v Shannon* (1955, unreported); and *Noe v Nester* (1966, unreported).
2   *Jones v Jones* [1985] QB 704, CA; cf *Pritchard v Parrott* (1996) Times, 30 July.

3   See eg *Lampert v Eastern Omnibus Co* [1954] 1 WLR 1047 where, although Hilbery J accepted the claim in principle, it was held that the claim had not been made out on the facts.

4   See eg *Noe v Nester* (1966, unreported), in which Sachs J held that there was a 50% chance that the marriage would not have broken up but for her injuries.

(v)   Loss of Enjoyment

[K128]   Claims are often advanced for an award of general damages in respect of the loss of enjoyment of a holiday (or leisure activity) by reason of the injuries which a claimant has sustained. Where the claimant suffers his injuries during a holiday, as a result of some breach of contract for a holiday (eg by a tour operator), general damages for loss of enjoyment are recoverable because the primary purpose of the contract is to provide enjoyment[1]. But where a claimant suffers his injuries before going on the holiday or activity, as a result of some tortious act of the defendant, the better view, and the argument any defendant should advance, is that general damages for loss of enjoyment (a form of mental distress) are not recoverable as a separate head of damage in tort, but are recoverable as a loss of amenity and should therefore only be taken into consideration in assessing the appropriate level of award for PSLA[2]. Such awards will tend to be higher when made by way of a separate award for loss of enjoyment rather than an additional element within the damages awarded for PSLA, and in either case they are usually kept within modest limits[3]. The factors which may influence the size of the award will include:

- The cost of the holiday.
- The type of holiday (special occasions will attract more damages than regular holidays).
- The holiday destination.
- The degree to which the claimant was looking forward to going on the holiday.
- Whether the claimant had to miss the holiday entirely, or was able to go but was restricted in his or her activities.

1   See *Jarvis v Swan Tours* [1973] QB 233; and *Jackson v Horizon Holidays* [1975] 1 WLR 1468.

2   See *Ichard v Frangoulis* [1977] 1 WLR 556.

3   It is impossible to give much guidance on the assessment of this head of loss, because so much depends upon the individual facts of the case. By analogy, there is something to be gained from looking at the awards made in ruined holiday cases. Awards rarely exceed £1,000.

(vi)   Loss of Use[1]

General

[K129]   This claim most commonly arises in respect of damaged vehicles following road traffic accidents. Where the claimant has hired a replacement vehicle, the claim for loss of use will usually be restricted to the cost of hire[2]. However, where the claimant has not hired a replacement vehicle, he or she will not be able to pursue a claim for loss of use in any of the following situations:

- Where the claimant's vehicle is still roadworthy.
- Where the claimant had the use of another vehicle (eg a second car, a car loaned by a friend or a courtesy car).

- Where the claimant has not lost the use of the vehicle because he would not have been able to use, or would not have used, the car but for the accident, eg by reason of the injuries he sustained.
- Where it was obvious from the start that the claimant's car was a write-off and he or she had sufficient funds to replace it.

---

[1] See further the following articles: Malcolm Johnson 'Off the Road' [1996] SJ, 26 November, at 1156; Alec Samuels 'Damages for Loss of Use of a Vehicle' [1995] Road Law at 492; Irvine Marr and Paul Coppin 'Vehicle accident damage: loss of use and hire costs' [1993] SJ, 29 October, at 1072; and N Yell 'Damages for loss of use of a motor vehicle' (1992) 2 Litigation 3. Also, see generally the review of the law regarding loss of use of chattels in *Lagden v O'Connor* [2003] UKHL 64.

[2] *Mattocks v Mann* [1993] RTR 13.

[K130] Assuming that none of the above situations apply, the following points will be relevant when considering the award for loss of use:

- The make, model, age and value of the damaged vehicle[1].
- The frequency with which the claimant (and/or his or her family) used the vehicle, eg to travel to work, to the shops, to visit friends and/or relatives, to go to church etc.
- The availability and convenience of local public transport.
- The cost incurred using alternative means of transport.
- Any additional journey time to and from work caused by using alternative means of transport.
- The claimant's locality – in particular, whether the claimant lives in a rural or suburban area.
- The effect on social or sporting activities.
- Any planned trips or holidays that had to be cancelled.
- The time of year (loss of use in winter months will generally attract higher awards than loss of use in summer months).
- The extent to which the claimant has been able to adapt to life without his or her vehicle.

---

[1] Although it is conceivable that, where the claimant owned a particularly expensive and comfortable vehicle but mitigated his or her losses by hiring a much smaller (and cheaper) alternative, a claim for loss of use could be made in order to reflect the difference in comfort.

[K131] Depending upon the duration of the claim for loss of use, judges will usually award damages on a daily, weekly or monthly basis. Generally speaking, the rate will gradually decrease as time goes by and the claimant gets more used to life without his or her vehicle. If the claim persists for any significant length of time, it is possible for a lump sum to be awarded on a 'broad brush' or 'global' basis[1].

---

[1] See eg *Bailey v Munns* (15 October 1997, unreported).

Hire of alternative vehicles

[K132] Where the claimant claims the cost of hiring an alternative vehicle, the following points should be considered:

- Was it reasonable to hire an alternative vehicle? The need to hire a replacement car is not 'self-proving'[1]. Such a need will be disproved if, inter alia, the claimant would have been unable to make use of a vehicle (eg through illness or being out of the country), if he already had access to an alternative car, or if he could easily have used public transport for a few days. However, a failure by the claimant to accept a courtesy car through his own insurance policy will not generally constitute a failure to mitigate[2].

- Was the make and model of hire vehicle reasonable? The presumption is that a claimant is entitled to hire a like-for-like car (which need not be the exact same make and model as his own)[3] and that, if he does so, the defendant will not generally be able to show any failure to mitigate. While he will not be entitled to recover for hiring a car superior to his own, neither will he be expected to hire a make or model that is inferior[4]. However, if the claimant hires an inferior car and expresses satisfaction with such a vehicle, his loss is limited to the cost of hiring the inferior car[5].

- Was the rate charged reasonable[6]?

- Was the duration of the hire period reasonable[7]?

[1] *Giles v Thompson* [1994] 1 AC 142, per Lord Mustill at 167.
[2] *Trevor Rose v The Cooperative Group* (2005) Lawtel 21.3.2005 (unreported elsewhere).
[3] *Clark v Ardington Electrical Services* [2002] EWCA Civ 510, per Aldous LJ at paras 132–133; *Lagden v O'Connor* [2003] UKHL 64, per Lord Hope at para 27; cf *Brain v Yorkshire Rider Ltd* (2007) Lawtel 19.4.2007, unreported elsewhere.
[4] *Brain v Yorkshire Rider Ltd* (2007) Lawtel 19.4.2007, unreported elsewhere.
[5] *Clark v Ardington Electrical Services* (supra).
[6] Generally speaking, if the claimant knows that he or she may have to hire a vehicle for a while, it is likely to be cheaper to hire a replacement vehicle on a weekly or monthly basis than it is to hire the vehicle on a daily basis. If the rate of hire is challenged as unreasonable, the defendant should obtain a list of cheaper quotes for similar vehicles in the claimant's locality. The relevant issue is whether the quotes show, on a balance of probabilities, that a better price could have been obtained: see *Standard Chartered Bank v Pakistan Nation Shipping* [2001] EWCA Civ 55, per Potter LJ at para 41.
[7] Note that it may be reasonable for a claimant to continue hiring a replacement vehicle until his or her own insurers have looked at his or her vehicle and have authorised any repairs to be carried out (or have confirmed that it is a write-off). The claimant will also be entitled to recover for the period during which any repairs are carried out. If that period is lengthened due to the failings of the repairing garage (or, indeed, the failings of any person other than the claimant or any person for whose actions the claimant is, in law, responsible), the defendant cannot seek to reduce the period by pointing to the amount of time it ought to have taken to repair the vehicle: see *Clark v Ardington* [2002] EWCA Civ 510, per Aldous LJ at paras 115–121. Contribution proceedings against the person responsible for the delay might be possible. If the claimant's car is a total loss, it is arguable there comes a point at which continuing to incur hire charges that greatly outstrip the pre-accident value of the car constitutes a failure to mitigate: see eg *Ayub v Somerfield* [2007] LTL 6.6.2007, Lawtel Document No AC0113617.

Credit hire

[K133]   The law of credit hire is beyond the scope of this book. All the points made above at para **[K132]** are relevant in credit hire situations, and indeed many of the cases cited there involve the credit hiring of vehicles. The following additional points can be made:

- The defendant should check whether hire was on a credit basis, and whether the terms of the agreement comply with the principles set out in *Dimond v Lovell*[1] and subsequent cases.
- If the agreement is enforceable and the hire charges are therefore enforceable against the defendant, the rate and period of hire claimed should be examined in detail.
- The claimant will only be entitled to recover the credit hire rate if he is impecunious[2].
- If the claimant is not impecunious, he will only be entitled to what it would have cost to hire a car at the 'spot' rate in his locality. The defendant should provide sufficient spot rate evidence to allow the court to make a judgment, on the balance of probabilities, as to the appropriate rate. It is arguable that the defendant need not show that a particular car would have been available in the claimant's locality at the time of hire[3]. Defendants would be wise, however, to provide sufficient evidence to allow the court to reach a conclusion as to the availability of a suitable car, and its rate, on the balance of probabilities.
- If the defendant has made an offer to the claimant of a replacement car prior to entering into the credit hire agreement, the refusal of such an offer might amount to a failure to mitigate, provided the defendant has made clear how much it would cost to provide that replacement car. Even in those circumstances, however, the claimant's claim would not be extinguished: the claimant would be entitled to recover at least the cost which the defendant could show it would reasonably have incurred in supplying the replacement car[4].
- Statutory interest is not recoverable on credit hire charges[5]. Likewise, contractual interest, if the hire agreement allows for it, is arguably not recoverable[6].

[1]   [2002] 1 AC 384.
[2]   *Lagden v O'Connor* [2003] UKHL 64.
[3]   *Bransgrove v Vermorel* (2008) Colchester CC, 27.7.2008, HHJ Dedman (unreported).
[4]   *Copley v Lawn; Malden v Haller* [2009] EWCA Civ 580. Note that this case may be subject to an appeal.
[5]   *Clark v Ardington* (supra), per Aldous LJ at paras 157–162.
[6]   *Corbett v Gaskin* [2008] LTL 20.6.2008, Lawtel Document No AC0117410.

Company cars

[K134] Theoretically, it is possible for a company to claim for the loss of use of a vehicle. However, the number of vehicles at the company's disposal should be checked. For example, if the vehicle was a 'pool' vehicle and there were other spare vehicles that could have been used as a substitute, it is unlikely to be reasonable for the company to hire a replacement vehicle. In *Watson Norie v Shaw*[1] it was held that it was unreasonable for a company to hire a replacement prestige car for the managing director when it could have hired a much less expensive vehicle. It is doubtful, however, that this decision has much applicability, in light of more recent case law establishing the principle that the starting point is that the claimant is entitled to hire an equivalent vehicle to the one damaged[2].

[1]   (1967) 111 Sol Jo 117, CA.
[2]   *Brain v Yorkshire Rider* (supra), reviewing *Lagden v O'Connor* (supra) and *Giles v Thompson* (supra).

Profit-earning vehicles

[K135]   Of course, if the damaged vehicle was a profit-earning vehicle, eg a taxi or a bus, a claim may be made for loss of profits during the period that the claimant was without it. The claimant should be put to strict proof regarding the amount of the lost earnings, and disclosure sought of all relevant supporting documentation. The claimant is restricted to claiming the profits had the vehicle not been damaged: therefore, if the claimant incurs expenses in hiring an alternative vehicle that outweigh the claim for loss of profits, the claimant is restricted to claiming the loss of profits[1]. Also, if it can be shown that the claimant was in fact able to make a greater profit than he or she would have done if his or her chattel had not been damaged, the additional profit must be set off against his or her loss[2].

[1]   See *Clerk & Lindsell on Torts* (19th edn, 2009), Ch 27.
[2]   *The World Beauty* [1969] P 12.

6   Specific Heads of Pecuniary Loss

(i)   Loss of Earnings

General

[K136]   The issue of multipliers is dealt with separately in paras **[K197]–[K215]**. When considering the mutliplicands in respect of claims for loss of earnings, the following matters should be borne in mind, although in some instances imponderables surrounding some of the matters listed can be applied, insofar as they relate to future losses, to discount the multiplier rather than the multiplicand:

- The amounts claimed must be net of tax[1], National Insurance contributions[2] and the claimant's own (as opposed to the employer's) pension contributions[3].
- Credit must be given for any tax rebate as a result of the injuries[4] and any tax saved as a result of the injuries[5].
- Credit must be given for any sick pay received[6].
- Credit must be given for any ex gratia payment made by a tortfeasor (especially if the tortfeasor also happens to be the claimant's employer)[7].
- Credit must be given for any redundancy payments arising from the injuries, except where the redundancy was on the cards in any event[8].
- Credit must be given for any deductible benefits, eg compensation under the Pneumoconiosis (Workers' Compensation) Act 1979[9].
- Credit must be given for any significant expenses that would have been incurred earning the money, eg childminding expenses, clothing for work, and travel expenses[10]. If a claimant (eg a contract labourer) works away from home during the week, these expenses will probably include other accommodation, living, and travel expenses (eg regular travel to and from work and home).
- Credit should be given for any failure to pursue any residual earning capacity[11].
- Credit may have to be given for an award made by an employment tribunal that would not otherwise have been received but for the claimant's injuries[12].
- Credit should be given for any benefits received by the claimant which he would not have received but for his injuries, and which fall outside the statutory

recovery of benefits scheme (the Social Security (Recovery of Benefits) Act 1997, eg housing benefit[13], council tax benefits, and tax credits such as working or child tax credits). Some of these may no longer apply to future loss, bearing in mind that the claimant may not be eligible for such benefits after his award of damages, unless the claimant holds his damages in a trust such that his right to claim means-tested benefits will continue.

- Where a claimant now lives abroad and receives foreign welfare benefits which he would not otherwise have received but for his injuries, credit should be given for such benefits.
- Where a claimant wishes to claim for the lost chance of increased earnings or pursuing a business venture, the claim must be pleaded[14].
- Where a claimant claims periodical payments in respect of a future loss of earnings, a percentage discount should be applied to the multiplicand to account for the contingencies other than death which would normally be applied to the multiplier.
- But if the claimant lives abroad, and there is no appropriate earnings index or series [equivalent to ASHE] measuring the relevant earnings in that country, to which periodical payments could be appropriately pegged, then an order for periodical payments is unlikely to be made[15].

1   *British Transport Commission v Gourley* [1956] AC 185.
2   *Cooper v Firth Brown* [1963] 1 WLR 418.
3   *Dews v National Coal Board* [1988] AC 1. See also *Pratt v Smith* (18 December 2002, unreported), QBD, in which David Foskett QC sitting as a deputy High Court judge found that the claimant would have contributed 2.5% from his basic salary to his pension.
4   *Hartley v Sandholme Iron Co* [1975] QB 600.
5   *Brayson v Wilmot-Breedon* [1976] CLY 682. Arguably, a claimant would also have to give credit for any tax credits received as a result of his or her injuries.
6   *Parry v Cleaver* [1970] AC 1; *Hussain v New Taplow Paper Mills Ltd* [1988] AC 514.
7   *Hussain v New Taplow Paper Mills Ltd* [1987] 1 All ER 417; *Williams v BOC Gases Ltd* [2000] PIQR Q253, CA; *Gaca v Pirellis General Plc & others* [2004] EWCA Civ 373. But an annual injury disability pension and a lump sum injury gratuity payment paid to a police officer pursuant to the Police Pensions Regulations 1987 under non-contributory schemes cannot be offset against a claim for past or future loss of earnings, because only benefits of a like nature can be taken into account, and a pension is distinct from earnings: see *Crofts v Murton* [2009] EWHC 3538 (QB) (HHJ Collender QC sitting as a High Court judge), following *Parry v Cleaver*. See further Chapter J.
8   *Parry v Cleaver* [1970] AC 1; and *Colledge v Bass Mitchell & Butlers Ltd* [1988] 1 All ER 536 (CA).
9   *Ballantine v Newalls Insulation Co Ltd* [2000] PIQR Q57. See further Chapter J, Recovery of State and Collateral Benefits at paras **[J59]** and **[J69]**.
10 See para **[K99]** and *Eagle v Chambers (No 2)* [2004] EWCA Civ 1033, in which the Court of Appeal upheld the trial judge's discount of 15% from the claim for past loss of earnings to reflect the claimant's travel expenses. See also *Sparks v Royal Hospitals NHS Trust* (21 December 1998, unreported), in which McKinnon J deducted £3 per week for travel costs.
11 See further at para **[K40]**. See also *Brown v Vosper Thorneycroft* [2004] EWHC 400 (QB), where the costs of retraining were disallowed because the claimant was capable of performing a wide range of jobs and the decision to retrain was a voluntary decision of the claimant to make a drastic change of direction.
12 *Assinder v Griffin* [2001] All ER (D) 356 (May).
13 *Clenshaw v Tanner* [2002] EWHC 184 (QB).
14 *Domsalla v Barr* [1969] 1 WLR 630; *Turnbull v Waugh* (6 May 1999, unreported), CA. Assuming that the claim has been correctly pleaded, a discount must be applied to take account of the lost chance, eg to reflect the chance that the claimant might not have been promoted in the absence of the injuries: *Williams v Green* [2001] EWCA Civ 1888.

15   See *A v Powys Local Health Board* [2007] EWHC 2996 (QB), in relation to a periodical payments
order in respect of care, where there was no foreign equivalent of ASHE 6115 in respect of carers'
earnings. The same principle is likely to apply in respect of any claim for loss of earnings.

[K137]   It should be remembered that the claimant bears the burden of proving that
his or her injuries have caused the lost earnings. In the absence of such evidence, no
award for loss of earnings will be made[1]. Likewise, no award will be made under this
head where the loss would have incurred in any event, eg due to a pre-existing injury[2].

1   See eg *Raitt v Lunn* (22 October 2003, unreported), CA, in which the claimant, a professional golfer,
failed to establish that the loss of his fingertip had affected his ability to play golf professionally; cf
Ashcroft v Curtin [1971] 1 WLR 1731, CA.
2   See eg *Gardner v R P Winder (Wholesale Meats) Ltd* [2002] EWCA Civ 1777, in which the
claimant's loss of earnings as a farmer was held to be due to the foot and mouth outbreak and his
pre-existing shoulder condition, as opposed to his injuries.

[K138]   Further, if the claimant has spent any time in hospital, credit must be given
in respect of the expenses saved. Section 5 of the Administration of Justice Act 1982
provides:

'In an action under the law of England and Wales or the law of Northern Ireland for
damages for personal injuries (including any such action arising out of a contract) any
saving to the injured person which is attributable to his maintenance wholly or partly
at public expense in a hospital, nursing home or other institution shall be set off against
any income lost by him as a result of his injuries.'

Methods of calculation

[K139]   The usual method of calculating the claimant's lost earnings is to take
the average net pay for the 13-week period prior to the injuries being sustained.
However, the defendant should be alive to the possibility that this may over-estimate
the claimant's actual loss (eg if a bonus falls within that period). Therefore, it is
generally worth considering the claimant's level of earnings for a longer period, to
check for seasonal and other variations. Which period it is most appropriate to take as
the baiss for calculating the claimant's average net earnings at the time of the accident
will depend on the facts of each case, and any pay rises within that period should be
taken into account. Consideration should be given to the claimant's employment and
earnings history (over as long a period as can reasonably be justified) prior to the
injuries: this may have an important bearing on the appropriate multiplicand (eg in a
case of fluctuating earnings where there is no fixed employment or career pattern) or
on the appropriate discount to be applied to any multiplier under the Ogden Tables
(6th edn), eg where a claimant has had regular periods of unemployment. It may well
be that a discount should be applied to the multiplicand, the multiplier or the claim
globally, to take account of the time out of work the claimant might have had in any
event[1].

1   See eg *Clenshaw v Tanner* [2002] EWHC 184 (QB), in which a 30% discount was applied as against
past expenses and losses. See also *Brown v Berry* (14 October 1997, unreported), QBD, in which
a 50% discount was applied to the claim for past loss of earnings, to reflect the claimant's lack of
qualifications and driving licence and history of low seasonal employment.

[K140]   Future loss of earnings claims may be pleaded in many different ways. Where it is alleged that the claimant's earnings would have increased by way of promotion or advancement, this may be presented by using a split multiplier, a multiplicand which adopts a weighted average, or a loss of a chance. Different methods of calculating and presenting the loss may be experimented with in order to assess the most appropriate way of responding to a claim. It is often worth considering what potentially negative events might have occurred such as to reduce the multiplicand: it can then be argued that the claimant's alleged prospects of promotion or increased earnings can be set off against the prospects of, for example, redundancy.

[K141]   It is important, when responding to a claim where a split multiplier has been used, that adjustments are made to the multipliers to reflect the fact that the claimant is more likely to survive to the end of the earlier periods than the later periods, and that earlier periods of future loss, though numerically equal to the later periods (eg ten-year periods), are appropriately represented by higher multipliers than are the later ones[1].

[1]   See further para **[K213]**.

The unemployed claimant

[K142]   No claim can be brought for loss of earnings where the prospect of the claimant obtaining remunerative employment but for the injuries was speculative[1].

[1]   *Howarth v Whittaker* [2003] Lloyd's Rep Med 235.

The self-employed claimant

[K143]   Whenever a claim is brought for loss of profits by a self-employed claimant, it is important to obtain as much documentary evidence regarding the claimant's business as possible. Sources of information will include daily accounting books such as ledgers of receipts and expenses, accountancy reports, profit and loss accounts, tax returns and bank statements. If business accounts are available, the court will not look behind these documents unless there are compelling reasons to do so[1].

[1]   *Phillips v Holliday* [2001] EWCA Civ 1074.

[K144]   Once received, the documents should be carefully scrutinised. Of course, it is for the claimant to prove his or her loss, and if the accounts are in a terrible state it may be that the loss of earnings claim will be disallowed in its entirety[1].

[1]   *Ashcroft v Curtin* [1971] 1 WLR 1731.

[K145]   It should be remembered that often the 'net' loss claimed by a business is the total receipts less the expenses incurred. However, account must also be taken of the tax that the claimant would have to pay. This can usually be worked out using tax tables such as those provided in the Professional Negligence Bar Association's 'Facts & Figures' book, although sometimes it is necessary to employ an accountant to calculate the true value of the net loss of earnings. Where the accounts do not show any drop in net profits, it will usually be difficult for the claimant to show that there has been any loss of earnings (ie to prove that he or she would have earned increased profits but for the injuries)[1].

1   See eg *Chang v Delgreco* [2004] EWCA Civ 407.

[K146]   When considering the expenses that would have been saved by not running the business, consideration must be given to all possibilities such as wages, electricity, water, gas, rates and raw materials.

[K147]   Where the business was new or developing – eg an internet start-up – consideration should be given to the current financial climate and the chance that that business would not have succeeded. In such a case, it may be appropriate to instruct a business analyst, an employment consultant, or an accountant who regularly acts for clients trading in the sector in question, to explain what has happened to that particular industry and the average failure rate of start-up businesses. The same approach may also be warranted when assessing businesses which are cyclical and heavily dependent upon the economy, such as the building industry. If it can be shown that, following the accident, the industry has taken a particular downturn, an accountant may be instructed to work out the consequent effect on the claimant's loss of profits.

[K148]   Where there are too many imponderables, it may be most appropriate to take a 'broad brush' approach to loss of profits, and award a lump sum rather than to calculate the loss on a multiplicand/multiplier basis[1].

1   See eg *Hannon v Pearce* (24 January 2001, unreported), QBD, where the judge awarded a lump sum of £50,000 for loss of profits, following *Blamire v South Cumbria Area Health Authority* [1993] PIQR Q1.

The fraudulent claimant

[K149]   Where there is evidence that the claimant has been working when he or she says that he or she has been unable to work, or that a loss of profits claim has been concocted by the claimant, the claimant may have difficulty recovering anything at all for loss of earnings. For example, in *Cottrell v Redbridge Healthcare NHS Trust*[1] the claimant advanced a claim for past and future loss of profits arising out of his parents' company totalling £332,079. However, the judge was satisfied that no loss of profits had actually been incurred by reason of the claimant's injuries. He concluded that the claimant had conspired with his family to defraud the defendant, and therefore disallowed any damages under this head of loss. He further directed that the defendant refer its papers to the Director of Public Prosecutions for consideration as to whether prosecution was appropriate.

1   (2001) 61 BMLR 72.

[K150]   It may be possible to argue that a fraudulent claim for loss of earnings should be struck out, but the scope for this is now probably very limited[1].

1   See further *Shah v (1) Ul-Haq, (2) Khatoon and (3) Parveen* [2009] EWCA Civ 542 and the discussion at para **[K66]**.

Earnings from illegal sources

[K151] Public policy will prevent a claimant from recovering any damages in respect of money that would have been earned from criminal or immoral acts[1]. Further, account should also be taken of any time that the claimant has spent in prison and the free board that would have been provided there[2].

[1]   *Burns v Edman* [1970] 2 QB 541.
[2]   *Meah v McCreamer* [1985] 1 All ER 367.

Working 'on the black'

[K152] Where the claimant has not been declaring his or her earnings for the purposes of tax and National Insurance, it may be possible to argue that the claimant should be debarred from pursuing a claim for past and future loss of earnings. Traditionally, however, the courts have generally been willing to entertain such claims as long as the earnings were not derived from criminal or immoral acts, subject, of course, to the relevant deductions being made to the claim for the tax and National Insurance that should have been paid[1]. The position may be different where the claimant has been claiming state benefits at the same time as working and not paying tax or National Insurance[2].

[1]   *Finnis v Caulfield* [2002] All ER (D) 353; *Newman v Folkes & Dunlop Tyres Ltd* [2002] PIQR Q2, QBD, Garland J – appealed to the Court of Appeal but not on this point; *Duller v South East Lincs Engineers* [1981] CLY 585; and *Bagge v Buses* [1958] NZLR 630.
[2]   *Hunter v Butler* [1996] RTR 396; and *Kanu v Kashif* [2002] EWCA Civ 1620.

The Blamire *award*[1]

[K153] Where there is sufficient evidence to justify an award for past and future loss of earnings, but there are too many imponderables accurately to calculate the loss on a multiplier/multiplicand basis, it will often suit the defendant for a single lump sum to be awarded to cover both past and future loss of earnings as well as loss of future earning capacity. This is known as a *Blamire* award after *Blamire v South Cumbria Health Authority*[2]. Generally speaking, a single lump sum award will often be significantly less than what the claimant could expect by adopting a multiplier/multiplicand approach: indeed, whilst there is no limit to the level of these awards, they often fail to exceed £50,000. Whilst judges have been encouraged to be slow to to resort to the *Blamire* approach, given that all personal injury claims involve some degree of uncertainty which can be reflected within the multiplicand or the multiplier[4], defendants should be quick to identify those cases where there are genuine and considerable imponderables as to: (i) how the claimant's employment and earnings would have progressed but for his injuries; and (ii) how the claimant's employment and earnings will in fact now progress, such that it can be said to be inappropriate to adopt a mathematical approach. In any case where that can be said, a defendant should contend for a *Blamire* approach. The Ogden Tables (6th edn) expressly recognise that there will still be cases where a *Blamire* approach will be more appropriate[5], and the courts have of late proved ready to accede to such an approach in the face of, and as an alternative to, a large claim formulated on the basis of a multiplicand and multipliers from Ogden Tables (6th edn)[6].

1   See further Chapter H.
2   [1993] PIQR Q1. See also *Dureau v Evans* [1996] PIQR Q18, CA; *Goldborough v Thompson* [1996] PIQR Q86; *Hannon v Pearce* (24 January 2001, unreported), QBD; *Rees v Dewhirst plc* [2002] EWCA Civ 871; *Willemse v Hesp* [2003] EWCA Civ 994; *Crouch v King's Healthcare NHS Trust* [2004] EWCA Civ 853; *Van Wees v (1) Karkour and (2) Walsh* [2007] EWHC 165 (QB); *Smale v (1) Ball and (2) MIB* LTL 6/6/07; *Palmer v Kitley* [2008] EWHC 2819 (QB).
3   See eg *Rees v Dewhirst plc* [2002] EWCA Civ 871, in which a 'conventional' lump sum of £45,000 was substituted for an original award made by the trial judge of £89,352 for loss of future earnings/earning capacity on a multiplier/multiplicand basis.
4   *Bullock v Atlas Ward Structures Ltd* [2008] EWCA Civ 194, per Keene LJ at paras 19–21.
5   See the Ogden Tables (6th edn), Guidance Notes, para 31.
6   See eg *McGhee v Diageo* [2008] CSOH 74 (a decision of Lord Malcolm in the Outer House of the Court of Session); and *Palmer v Kitley* [2008] EWHC 2819 (QB).

(ii) Pension Loss

[K154]   A detailed analysis of the approaches to be adopted in respect of pension loss claims is outside the scope of this book[1]. It is important to establish at the outset in what type of pension scheme a claimant participated at the time of the accident. There are two basic types of pension – (i) a personal pension plan or money purchase scheme; and (ii) a final salary scheme (now fast becoming a thing of the past) – and, whilst there are some principles of quantification which are of general application to both types of scheme, the two schemes lead to very different methods of quantification. The *Auty* calculation applies to final salary schemes but not to money purchase schemes.

1   For a more detailed analysis, see Chapter 12 of the *PIBA Personal Injury Handbook* (Jordans, 3rd edn).

Principles of general application

[K155]   When challenging claims for pension loss, the following general points should be borne in mind:

- The loss may be too remote or speculative to quantify if the claimant did not have a pension at the time he or she sustained the injuries[1] or the claimant was still a child[2].
- Any calculations should be made net of tax[3].

1   See eg *Finnis v Caulfield* [2002] All ER (D) 353. See also *D and D v Donald* [2001] PIQR Q44.
2   See eg *M (a child) v Leeds Health Authority* [2002] PIQR Q4.
3   *British Transport Commission v Gourley* [1956] AC 185.

Money purchase schemes

[K156]   Where the claimant participates in a money purchase scheme, he and/or his employer make contributions into such a scheme and the following principles will apply.

- To the extent that the claimant personally contributes to such a plan, there is no loss beyond his claim for loss of earnings, because the claimant pays his contributions out of those earnings, and he can continue to pay into such a scheme once he is compensated for his lost earnings. The claimant will, however, have lost tax relief on his earnings in respect of his pension contributions, and is entitled to tax relief in the calculation of his loss of earnings. The appropriate way to calculate this loss is (i) to deduct the value of the claimant's personal contributions from his gross annual earnings before deducting tax, and then (ii) to add the value of his pension contributions back onto his annual net loss of earnings.
- Where the employer was contributing to the claimant's pension, the claimant is entitled to claim the lost value of the employer's contributions, which will usually be a set percentage of the claimant's gross salary, or may match whatever contributions the claimant makes personally.
- The multiplier to adopt is the loss of earnings multiplier, discounted as appropriate, because any contributions are contingent upon employment and earnings, so the applicable contingencies other than death are the same as the contingencies in respect of earnings.
- In either case, no claim lies in respect of a projected loss of pension based on any assumed growth in the capital fund which accrues, because such a claim depends on the future performance of any given fund and is entirely speculative.
- Where the claimant has a residual earning capacity, but has not yet returned to employment, the defendant should claim credit for the pension benefits which he is likely to achieve from any such employment: these will almost certainly be future employer's contributions under a money purchase scheme.

Final salary schemes

[K157] Where there is a final salary scheme, a more complicated *Auty*[1] calculation will be necessary.

- Before this calculation can be done, a defendant first needs to formulate his case as to what promotions and/or salary increments, if any, the claimant would have achieved prior to retirement, but for the accident. He will then have established the claimant's final salary at the date of retirement (at present-day values, of course). Thereafter, he needs to establish the answers to two essential questions from the employer or the pension fund trustees:
  - (1) Assuming the defendant's case as to the claimant's final position and salary at the time of retirement, what would the claimant have received by way of annual pension and lump sum if the accident had not occurred and the claimant had continued through to his normal retirement age?
  - (2) What annual pension and lump sum will the claimant now receive as a result of the accident?
- The loss in annual pension is the difference between the two figures, after allowing for tax. To that figure the appropriate multiplier for pension loss taken from the Ogden Tables is applied. An *Auty* discount for contingencies other than death must be applied to the resulting loss[2].
- The loss of lump sum is similarly calculated but, where the lump sum is received early by way of ill-health pension, credit must be given for that part of the

lump sum which represents the commutation of the post-retirement periodical pension[3]. Where the claimant makes a claim for a reduced potential lump sum in the future, this lump sum should be reduced for accelerated receipt and the chance that the claimant would have died before receiving the lump sum.

- The quantification of the pension in question may have to be discounted to reflect percentage chances that the claimant, at any particular stage in her career (i) would have ceased employment at that stage, and/or (ii) ceased her employment at a rank or level of earnings lower than that contended for[4].

1	*Auty v National Coal Board* [1985] 1 WLR 784. See further the pension loss examples in Chapter Q, precedents **[Q20]–[Q25]**.
2	See para **[K158]** below.
3	[1998] AC 653.
4	See *Brown v Ministry of Defence* [2006] EWCA Civ 546, applying the principle in *Davies in Taylor (No 1)* [1974] AC 207 to a claim for pension loss.

[K158] As regards the correct level of discount for contingencies, each case must be assessed on its own facts. In *Auty v National Coal Board*[1] the judge made a discount of 27% for contingencies including voluntary wastage, redundancy, dismissal, supervening ill-health, disablement and death before 65. Such a high reduction is unlikely to be sustainable now, given the decision of the House of Lords in *Wells v Wells*[2] and the fact that the Ogden Tables already take into account the risk of mortality. In *Page v Sheerness*[3] the House of Lords upheld the trial judge's discount of 10% for contingencies. In *Phipps v Brooks Dry Cleaning Services Ltd*[4] a discount of 5% was applied by the trial judge and, although thought to be a bit on the low side, it was not challenged on appeal. The level of discount to be applied will vary, depending on the particular facts of each case and, bearing in mind that the principal contingency is any future inability to remain in pensionable employment, regard should be had to the following factors:

- The nature of the claimant's work and employment, and the likelihood of redundancy or early retirement.
- The claimant's health, and the likelihood that ill-health would have disabled him from such work in due course in any event.
- The availability to the claimant of an ill-health pension in the event that he would have become disabled in any event.
- The claimant's pre-accident employment pattern: frequent changes in employment (eg within or between employment sectors, where some employers are unlikely to offer a pension scheme) and/or periods of unemployment will tend to have a negative effect on the value of a pension fund.

1	[1985] 1 WLR 784.
2	[1999] 1 AC 345.
3	[1996] PIQR Q26, which was upheld on appeal regarding this point: [1999] 1 AC 345 at 381G.
4	[1996] PIQR Q100.

(iii) Accommodation

[K159] *Roberts v Johnstone*[1] claims quantify the additional annual cost over a claimant's lifetime of the capital which he will have to invest in accommodation as a result of his injuries, the additional cost being the difference between the capital he would have invested in a home but for his injuries, and the capital he will now have to invest in it as a result of his injuries. The purchase of the property is deemed to be an investment secured against inflation, and a rate of return of 2.5% is therefore applicable, that being the current discount rate. There will usually be other related claims, such as alteration costs, the additional costs of moving, the higher running costs which will be incurred in respect of a larger property, and the like. When considering claims for accommodation costs, the following points should be borne in mind.

- The claim for new or adapted accommodation must be shown to be reasonable and necessary. The accommodation claimed must be shown on the medical evidence to be reasonably necessary by reason of the claimant's injuries[2]. But the reasonableness of any claim will also be judged by reference to the sort of lifestyle and accommodation that the claimant would have had but for the accident[3].

- If a claimant buys and/or adapts a property significantly in excess of what the accommodation experts had originally envisaged or recommended, then unless such increased expenditure can be justified a defendant should contend that such expenditure is unreasonable, and that the claim should be quantified by reference to the original recommendations of the experts[4].

- Certain aspects of a housing claim may improve the claimant's quality of life but may not be reasonably necessary by reason of the claimant's disability, eg a greenhouse[5], a conservatory, a swimming pool[6], and a hydrotherapy pool[7].

- Accommodation for carers only has to be reasonable and does not have to be the best available.

- Where the claimant is already a homeowner but the property is jointly owned, the claimant may only be entitled to advance a claim for accommodation based upon the proportion of his or her share in the house.

- Credit should be given for any increase in value provided by adaptations and extensions[8]. This element of betterment should be deducted from the claim for the cost of alterations, and added to the claim for capital costs to which the *Roberts v Johnstone* formula is applied.

- Where the claimant is not already a house owner, credit must be given for the property that the claimant probably would have bought in any event[9].

- Where the claimant would have been renting but for his or her injuries, the cost of rent that would otherwise have been paid can be offset against the accommodation claim[10]. Where a claimant is to rent his future accommodation, his loss is the difference between the rental and council tax payments he would have incurred in any event and the increased costs he will or should incur now, the claim being confined to what is reasonably necessary, given his injuries[11].

- Where the claimant would otherwise have married and made contributions to the capital cost of the matrimonial home, a discount should be given for the extent of the contributions[12].

- Where the claimant is a child and new accommodation is purchased by the claimant's parents, credit should be given for the housing expenses that would have been incurred by the claimant[13].

- Where the claimant's parents had rented their house prior to the claimant's injury and paid for that rent with housing benefit, but then lived rent-free with the claimant in a property subsequently bought for him with the claimant's funds, no allowance is likely to be made against the claim for accommodation to reflect the rent which the parents would otherwise have paid (or housing benefit they would otherwise have received), because there is no failure to mitigate his loss by a claimant in failing to demand rent from his parents[14].

- Where the claimant had previously lived with his parents in their own property, but they subsequently live in a property purchased in the claimant's name with his funds, no credit may need to be given for the value of the parents' equity in their former home (or for the sale or rental income therefrom)[15].

- No award may be appropriate where the claimant would probably have left home and acquired his or her own similar accommodation by the relevant date[16].

- Unless the medical evidence justifies a further move, it will usually be presumed that the claimant will continue to live in the new or adapted accommodation for the rest of his or her life[17].

- Where the claimant has already bought one property with his or her interim payment award, the court will not necessarily allow the claimant to have 'another bite of the cherry' if that property turned out to be unsuitable[18].

- Where the claimant bought a property with his or her interim payment which has increased in value, resulting in a windfall profit, the claimant may have to give credit for the same[19].

- Where the claimant is or will be housed in local authority accommodation, it may be argued that the claimant's accommodation is adequate to meet the claimant's needs, either on its own or with the provision of a 'top up' from the defendant[20], in which case the claimant has suffered no loss that can be recovered from the defendant[21]. But such cases are now likely to be rare, in the light of the decision in *Peters v East Midlands SHA & others*[22], in which the Court of Appeal held that a claimant is entitled as of right to choose to pursue the tortfeasor for damages to provide for his care or accommodation needs, rather than having to rely on a public authority providing for those needs pursuant to its statutory obligations, provided that there is no risk of double recovery.

- The claimant may not necessarily recover damages in respect of an accommodation claim which obviously does not accord with his or her wishes, eg it will not be possible to claim the costs for accommodation with accommodation on the ground floor if this is not what the claimant wants and he or she has already bought property which does not meet this specification[23].

- If a claimant chooses to sell an investment property in order to purchase alternative accommodation for himself, he has not suffered any loss of income caused by his injuries recoverable as damages: he has merely converted his investment or asset into another form and retained its value. Any claim for loss of rental income is a collateral attack on the *Roberts v Johnstone* formula. *Roberts v Johnstone* implicitly assumes that a claimant will have to borrow against other heads of claim (or another source) to make up the shortfall between the damages awarded for accommodation and the amount of capital outlay on the property purchased. A claimant cannot claim the difference between the annual amounts he would have received from his investment property and 2.5% of the capital sum tied up in the new property, just as he cannot claim the difference between 2.5% and the percentage payable on a loan taken out to fund the purchase[24].

- As against any claim, the claimant must give credit for any housing benefit and council tax benefit or relief to which he is entitled (and which he would not have received but for the accident)[25].

- Certain expenses associated with buying a property, such as surveyor's fees, legal fees, estate agent's commission etc, may have been incurred by the claimant in any event and, if so, should not be recoverable: only any additional cost over and above that which would have been incurred in any event is recoverable.

[1]   [1989] QB 878, CA.

[2]   See eg *Maylen v Morris* (21 January 1998, unreported), CA. See also *Parry v North West Surrey Health Authority* (29 November 1999, unreported), QBD, in which Penry-Davey J considered that the sum claimed for adaptations was unreasonable and excessive. See further *O'Brien v Harris* (22 February 2001, unreported), QBD, in which Pitchford J held that the claimant's family were not entitled to recover the full costs of their 'dream house' which exceeded the claimant's reasonable requirements.

[3]   See eg *Huntley v Simmonds* [2009] EWHC 405 (QB), where the claim for the cost of a claimant's rented accommodation in a marina by a claimant who had grown up on a council estate was reduced because it included a premium 'for features which are not in any sense necessary', including 'a balcony with a marina view' (see para 89).

[4]   For example, see *Pankhurst v White & others* [2009] EWHC 1117 (QB); and *Noble v Owens* [2008] EWHC 359 (QB).

[5]   See *Brown v Merton, Sutton and Wandsworth Area Health Authority (Teaching)* [1982] 1 All ER 650, CA, where the cost of a greenhouse and raised flowerbeds was disallowed because it overlapped with the claim for loss of amenity.

[6]   See eg *Cassel v Riverside Health Authority* [1992] PIQR Q1, where the cost of a swimming pool was not held to be reasonable; cf *Haines v Airedale NHS Trust* (2 May 2000, unreported), QBD, per Bell J; and *Willett v North Bedfordshire Health Authority* [1992] PIQR Q166, where the property included a swimming pool, which was not necessary to the claimant's needs. The cost of buying that property was nevertheless held to be reasonable and recoverable. See also *Sarwar v Ali* [2007] EWHC 1255; and *Lewis v Royal Shrewsbury NHS Trust* (QB) 29.10.2007 (unreported).

[7]   See eg *Smith v East & North Hertfordshire Hospitals NHS Trust* [2008] EWHC 2234 (QB).

[8]   *Willett v North Bedfordshire Health Authority* [1993] PIQR Q166; and *Almond v Leeds Western Health Authority* [1990] 1 Med LR 370.

[9]   See eg the judgment of Collins J at first instance in *Thomas v Brighton Health Authority* [1996] PIQR 30; *Biesheuval v Birrell* [1999] PIQR Q40; *Lynham v The Morecambe Bay Hospitals NHS Trust* [2002] EWHC 823. Although, where the claimant would probably have bought property jointly with a partner in the absence of the injuries, he or she may only have to give credit for his or her share in that property, ie 50%: *M (a child) v Leeds Health Authority* [2002] PIQR Q4. Although, arguably, if the claimant had bought a property with a friend or partner, he or she would have bought a more expensive property.

[10] *Evans v Pontypridd Roofing* [2001] EWCA Civ 1657.

[11] See *Huntley v Simmonds* [2009] EWHC 405 (QB), per Underhill J at paras 89–91.

[12] *Goldfinch v Scannell* [1993] PIQR Q143, QBD; and *Lamey v Wirrall Health Authority* [1993] CLY 1437, QBD.

[813] *Cummings v Clark* (1991, unreported), QBD.

[14] See *Iqbal v Whipps Cross University Hospital NHS Trust* [2006] EWHC 3111 (QB).

[15] See *M (a child) v Leeds Health Authority* [2002] PIQR Q4; and *Parkhouse v North Devon Healthcare NHS Trust* [2002] Lloyd's Law Reports (Medical) 100.

[16] *Dorrington v Lawrence* [2001] All ER (D) 145 (Nov), in which Hooper J said at [42]: 'Taking into account my conclusions on the earnings which the claimant would have recovered but for the accident I take the view that the defendants are right in their contention that the claimant would probably have left home by then and acquired his own accommodation. There will therefore be a nil award under this heading'.

[17] See eg *Knott v Newham Healthcare NHS Trust* [2002] EWHC 2091 (QB), in which Simon J disallowed a second accommodation claim brought on the basis that the claimant would need to move in ten years' time. This case was subsequently (unsuccessfully) appealed to the Court of

Appeal but not on this issue. But query whether some allowance might need to be made to cover the chance that a claimant may (like any full-bodied uninjured person) reasonably wish or need to move in the future, eg to live with a spouse who changes jobs, or ageing parents.

18   *Brown v Berry* (14 October 1997, unreported), QBD.

19   This issue was appreciated but not decided in *O'Brien v Harris* (22 February 2001, unreported), QBD. Although this should be contrasted with *Edward Maxim Parry v North West Area Health Authority* (2000) Times, 5 January. In the ordinary course of events, the court is not concerned with what the claimant spends his or her money on: *Lim Poh Choo v Camden and Islington Area Health Authority* [1980] AC 174, per Lord Scarman at 191; *Wells v Wells* [1999] AC 345; *Heil v Rankin* [2001] QB 272.

20   See eg *Sowden v Lodge* [2004] EWCA Civ 1370. See further William Norris QC and John Pickering 'Claims for Compensation and entitlement to the provision of services from public funds: some issues arising in *Whyte v Barber*' [2003] JPIL, Issue 3/03, at 183–198.

21   See eg the comments of Lord Denning MR in *Cunningham v Harrison* [1973] QB 942 at 952.

22   [2009] EWCA Civ 145.

23   See eg *Willbye v Gibbons* [2003] EWCA Civ 372, per Kennedy LJ at [17].

24   See *Pankhurst v White & others* [2009] EWHC 1117 (QB) at paras 8.10–8.12.

25   See *Clenshaw v Tanner* [2002] EWCA Civ 1848; cf *Huntley v Simmonds* [2009] EWHC 405 (QB), per Underhill J at para 124, where the argument was raised late and there was no evidence regarding the extent of the payments.

(iv)   Travel and Transport Expenses[1]

The claimant's travel expenses

[K160]   When considering claims for travel expenses on behalf of the claimant, the following points should be considered:

- Whether or not the claimed travel expenses can be reasonably related to the claimant's injuries or whether they would have been incurred in any event, as if often the case, for example, with claims for membership of a motoring or rescue organisation[2].

- The item or amount claimed must be reasonable and, since the claimant is required to mitigate his losses, if there was a cheaper means of transport available which the claimant could or should reasonably have used, he should be restricted to claiming the lower amount[3].

- Travel expenses incurred attending legal or medical appointments for the purposes of litigation are strictly costs not damages, and therefore should not be recoverable by way of judgment[4], but if contributory negligence is in issue it may be advantageous for a defendant to agree to deal with the matter as an item of damages and not costs.

- Where the claimant used a vehicle to travel which was not bought in consequence of his or her injuries, the claimant should be restricted to claiming mileage rates at the level of the running costs prescribed by the AA, which are set out in the PNBA's 'Facts & Figures'[5].

- Where a claimant is claiming the cost of purchasing a vehicle by reason of his or her injuries, credit should be given for the vehicle that the claimant may have had in any event, and only the additional costs of travel should be allowed[6].

- Where a claimant is claiming the cost of purchasing a vehicle with automatic transmission or power-assisted steering, whether or not the claimant would probably have bought a vehicle with such extras in any event[7].

- Where a claim is made for a specially adapted vehicle for the claimant to drive him or herself, the claim is unlikely to be allowed if the claimant would not be able to satisfy the DVLA regarding his or her fitness to drive or be able to obtain the necessary insurance[8].

- When a claimant finds a vehicle that suits him or her, he or she may not change that vehicle as often as an ordinary motorist might (eg every three years), and it might be appropriate, where the claimant is likely to only travel low mileage, to allow a longer replacement interval (eg every six years)[9]. In a claim where it is reasonable for a severely injured claimant to have a more reliable (eg new rather than second-hand) vehicle, replacement every five years is often considered reasonable[10].

- Claims for the additional cost of insurance (eg in respect of a larger or more expensive vehicle) should be supported by properly admissible evidence[11], but such claims are recoverable in principle.

- Claims for the additional cost of insurance based upon the increased cost of carers under the age of 25 driving the claimant's vehicle will not be allowed where the evidence establishes that the carers are likely to be at least 25 years old[12].

- Credit should be claimed for any similar travel or transport expenses which the claimant would have incurred but for his injuries, but will not now incur. So, for example, in a case where a claimant owned and rode one or more motorcycles before the accident, but no longer does so as a result of his injuries, the defendant should offset against any claim the costs he would have incurred in owning and replacing, insuring and running the motorcycle(s).

[1] See further Chapter F, Past Expenses and Losses at paras **[F144]–[F161]**.

[2] For example, in *Biesheuval v Birrell* [1999] PIQR Q40, Eady J held that the claim for the annual cost of a rescue service was not related to the claimant's disability. A similar decision was reached in *O'Brien v Harris* (22 February 2001, unreported), QBD, in which Pitchford J disallowed the claim for AA membership as he did not consider that it was related to the accident. But, in *A v Powys Local Health Board* [2007] EWHC 2996 (QB), Lloyd Jones J (at para 146) allowed the claim in respect of a young claimant between the ages of 18 and 23, whereafter he allowed nothing on the basis that the claimant would have joined such an organisation in any event.

[3] See eg *Brown v Berry* (14 October 1997, unreported), QBD, in which Mr Robert Seabrook QC, sitting as a deputy judge of the High Court, allowed the costs of a Vauxhall Vectra rather than a people carrier. See also *O'Brien v Harris* (22 February 2001, unreported), QBD, in which Pitchford J refused a make an award for £150 in respect of a claim for the costs of a driver who was hired by the claimant to take his daughter to university when she could have travelled by train or coach. Cf *A v Powys Local Health Board* [2007] EWHC 2996 (QB), in which Lloyd Jones J (at para 146) held that it was reasonable for the claimant to have a vehicle large enough for her, her carers, and one or two family members.

[4] *Morris v Johnson Matthey* (1967) 112 SJ 32.

[5] *Haines v Airedale NHS Trust* (2 May 2000, unreported), QBD, per Bell J who allowed 12 pence per mile (against a claim of 25 pence per mile). See also *Eagle v Chambers* [2003] EWHC 3135 (QB), in which Cooke J allowed 7.5 pence per mile against a claim of 30 pence per mile (appealed to the Court of Appeal but not on this point), but cf *Newman v Folkes & Dunlop Tyres Ltd* [2002] PIQR Q2, QBD, in which Garland J allowed the higher rate of 30 pence per mile (also appealed to the Court of Appeal but, again, not on this point).

[6] See eg *Goldfinch v Scannell* [1993] PIQR Q143; and *Taylor v Weston AHA* [2003] All ER (D) 50 (Dec). See also *Woodrup v Nicol* [1993] PIQR Q104 at Q109, CA. In *Parry v North West Surrey Health Authority* (29 November 1999, unreported), QBD, the claim for a second car was rejected by Penry-Davey J because the claimant's family was likely to have remained a two-car family in any event.

7   For example, in *Ved v Caress* (9 April 2001, unreported), QBD, HHJ Chapman disallowed the cost of automatic transmission because he held that the claimant, who was a professional woman, would probably have bought an automatic car in any event.

8   *Owen v Brown* [2002] EWHC 1135 (QB).

9   See eg *Taylor v Weston AHA* [2003] All ER (D) 50 (Dec).

10   See *A v Powys Local Health Board* [2007] EWHC 2996 (QB), per Lloyd Jones J at para 139.

11   See further *Owen v Brown* [2002] EWHC 1135 (QB) regarding the 'Fish fax' evidence. For cases where such claims have succeeded, see *Sarwar v Ali* [2007] EWHC 1255 (Lloyd Jones J); and *A v Powys Local Health Board* [2007] EWHC 2996 (QB), per Lloyd Jones J at para 147.

12   *Eagle v Chambers (No 2)* [2004] EWCA Civ 1033.

[K161]   The burden remains upon the claimant to establish the extent of his or her loss so that, if a claimant fails to provide copies of increased petrol receipts etc where increased travel expenses are claimed, the court may allow nothing under this head[1]. Further, a claimant may not be able to claim the significant travel costs which are likely to be incurred by attending medical or rehabilitation treatment at a centre far away from his or her home without any checks being made to see if such treatment could be obtained nearer[2].

1   *Hughes (Gordon Clifford) v Addis (John)* (23 March 2000, unreported), CA. Although cf *Bygrave v Thomas Cook Tour Operations Ltd* [2003] EWCA Civ 1631, where the Court of Appeal held that it was reasonable for the trial judge to draw an inference from the evidence that the claimant would spend more on taxis in the future because of her injuries.

2   *Dorrington v Lawrence* [2001] All ER (D) 145 (Nov).

Travel expenses of friends and relatives

[K162]   In order to claim the travel costs of friends and family, the claimant must prove that:

- The services provided by the friends and family members were reasonably necessary as a consequence of the injuries sustained.
- The out-of-pocket expenses of the friends or family members are reasonable, bearing in mind all the circumstances, including whether expenses would have been incurred had the friends not assisted.

[K163]   It should be borne in mind that the claimant is obliged to repay the sums awarded to the friends or family members who incurred them; therefore, where this is unlikely or impossible, the claimant may be prevented from recovering them[2]. Credit must be given to reflect the travel expenses which would have been incurred in any event. Further, no travel expenses can be recovered on behalf of the tortfeasor making hospital visits[3].

1   *Schneider v Eisovitch* [1960] 2 QB 430.

2   *ATH v MS* [2002] EWCA Civ 792. But see *H v S* [2003] QB 965 (Ch); and *Hughes v Lloyd* [2007] EWHC 3333 (Ch), in which it was held that the trust in favour of a former voluntary carer who had since died was enforceable by the estate of that carer.

3   *Hunt v Severs* [1994] 2 AC 350.

[K164]   It may be that the cost of international travel (including plane tickets) is recoverable. However, care should be taken to ensure that only the travel costs arising out of the defendant's negligence are claimed. Therefore, where travel costs are claimed in respect of gratuitous carers, any travel expenses which would have been incurred in any event by maintaining family or social contact should be disallowed[1]. Where the sole justification for visiting the claimant is the comfort or pleasure of the visiting person, as opposed to aiding the recovery of the claimant, damages will not be recoverable[2]. Further, the claimant's friends and family members are not entitled to claim for any loss of earnings in visiting the claimant, since they are considered too remote[3].

[1]   *Bordin v St Mary's NHS Trust* [2000] Lloyd's Rep Med 287.
[2]   *Kirkham v Boughey* [1958] 2 QB 338, per Diplock J; *Havenhand v Jeffrey* (24 February 1997, unreported), CA.
[3]   *Kirkham v Boughey* [1958] 2 QB 338, per Diplock J. *Walker v Mullen* (1984) Times, 19 January, per Comyn J.

(v) Medical Expenses and Treatment

General

[K165]   Section 2(4) of the Law Reform (Personal Injuries) Act 1948 provides as follows:

> 'In an action for damages for personal injuries (including any such action arising out of a contract), there shall be disregarded, in determining the reasonableness of any expenses, the possibility of avoiding those expenses or part of them by taking advantage of facilities available under the National Health Service Act 1977 or the National Health Service (Scotland) Act 1978 or any corresponding facilities in Northern Ireland.'

[K166]   When considering claims for medical expenses, the following points should be borne in mind:

- The treatment (and the amount of treatment claimed) must be reasonable and necessary, and should be supported by the medical evidence.
- The claimant must prove that he intends to undergo the proposed treatment. If there is any doubt in this regard, the claim should be put in issue.
- The cost of the treatment must be reasonable[1].
- The cost of proposed medical treatment should be discounted for accelerated receipt[2].
- The cost of proposed medical treatment should be discounted to take account of uncertainty and the fact that the claimant may not need the suggested treatment[3]; so where, for example, there is only a 10% chance that the claimant will undergo the treatment, he recovers only 10% of the cost.
- It may be unreasonable for the claimant to continue with treatment on a long-term basis if the same does not resolve his or her symptoms[4].
- It might be possible to train carers or family members to administer drugs, provide basic treatment or perform therapies[5].
- Where there are too many imponderables for a multiplier/multiplicand approach to future loss to be adopted, a lump sum may be awarded[6].

[1]   For an example of a case where the treatment costs were held to be unreasonable, see *Roberts v Roberts* (1960) Times, 11 March.
[2]   See at para **[K100]**. See eg the first instance decision of *Newman v Folkes and Dunlop Tyres* [2002] PIQR Q2, in which Garland J awarded the claimant £1,500 for the 35–40% chance that the claimant would require a hip replacement operation in 15 years' time. Although this case was appealed, this point was not taken on appeal.

3   *Thomas v Bath District Health Authority* [1995] PIQR Q19.

4   This argument will usually depend upon the available medical evidence and the facts of a particular
     case. For example, many orthopaedic experts will not support the long-term use of physiotherapy.
     But, where such treatment provides regular albeit temporary relief from the claimant's symptoms, it
     may be viewed in a similar way to painkilling medication, ie the cost of painkillers is not disallowed
     just because they fail to provide any long-term relief or provide a cure for the claimant's symptoms.
     Some medical experts may be willing to support an annual allowance for maintenance physiotherapy
     to cover times of flare-up. Others may consider it reasonable for the claimant to recover the costs of
     any treatment which provides some relief from the symptoms, including alternative remedies such
     as herbal medicine: see eg *O'Brien v Harris* (22 February 2001, unreported), QBD; and *McMahon v
     Robert Brett & Sons* [2003] EWHC 2706 (QB).

5   An example of this is the regular carers being trained to provide a claimant with cerebral palsy
     with maintenance therapy, therefore only needing occasional input from a skilled physiotherapist.
     However, it should be noted that running this sort of argument may have undesired consequences in
     other areas, eg the possibility of the claimant arguing for a higher care rate to take into account the
     additional training/services.

6   *Seepersad v (1) Persad and (2) Capital Insurance* [2004] UKPC 19.

Treatments without proven benefit

[K167]   Claims in respect of alternative treatments such as reflexology may
be disallowed on the basis that the claimant is unable to prove that the suggested
treatment provides a medicinal benefit. Treatments which tend to be susceptible to
challenge include acupuncture, aromatherapy[1], spa treatment, massage and herbal
remedies[2]. If a defendant wishes to challenge the reasonableness of the claimed
treatment, it is useful to obtain specific medical evidence dealing with the need for
such treatment. Claims for new or experimental treatments, where the efficacy of the
treatment has not yet been proved, may also be challenged on the same basis[3].

1   Although see *McMahon v Robert Brett & Sons* [2003] EWHC 2706 (QB), in which Cox J allowed
     a claim for aromatherapy where the claimant had been recommended to take such therapy as part of
     her treating pain management team, and it was the claimant's evidence that the treatment had helped
     her overcome her pain, even though the expert medical evidence indicated that it was of no medical
     benefit to her.

2   Although see *George v Stagecoach* [2003] EWHC 2042, in which an award was made for
     acupuncture and Chinese herbs. See also *O'Brien v Harris* (22 February 2001, unreported), QBD, in
     which the cost of herbal remedies was allowed because 'relief was obtained from the same'.

3   See eg *Biesheuval v Birrell* [1999] PIQR Q40, in which Eady J disallowed the claim for Viagra; cf
     Re McCarthy [2001] 6 CL 172.

NHS/Private

[K168]   Where, on the balance of probabilities, the claimant will have treatment on
the NHS rather than pay for it privately, no claim for private medical treatment can be
sustained[1] (save, arguably, to the extent that the claimant shows that there is a chance,
even though less than 50%, of his or her having such treatment). Further, a discount in
the cost of providing care and future medical treatment may be contended for where
there is a possibility that the claimant's condition will deteriorate to such an extent
that long-term admission to an NHS hospital is warranted[2].

1   *Woodrup v Nicol* [1993] PIQR Q104, CA.

2   *Mitchell v Mullholland (No 2)* [1972] 1 QB 65, CA.

(vi)   Care

[K169]   First consider the question of causation: a claim for care cannot be sustained where the claimant would have needed the same amount of care by reason of pre-existing injuries in any event[1]. Usually, however, the principal consideration when assessing a claim for the cost of care is that it is for the claimant to prove, on the basis of the expert evidence, that the care claimed is both reasonable and necessary[2]. This includes the duration, rate and amount of care claimed. Where the issue of care is not specifically covered by the expert evidence, and it is not possible to draw reasonable inferences about the need for care from the facts, the claim is likely to be disallowed.

[1]   *Ford v GKR* [2000] 1 WLR 1397, CA.
[2]   See generally paras **[K37]–[K38]**.

[K170]   Where the care claimed is significant (ie in excess of, say, £20,000), it is usually appropriate to instruct a care expert, either individually or on a joint basis[1]. This expert will probably have to meet and interview the claimant at his or her home in order to make a proper assessment of the claimant's care needs. It will usually be necessary for the expert to interview the people who have been providing the care to date, or at least consider their witness statements, in order to assess the amount of care that has been given and to work out how much care will be required in the future. Defendants should be alert to potential discrepancies between the amount of hours estimated by the carers in their witness statements and the amount of hours quantified by any expert.

[1]   See further Chapter C.

Paid care

[K171]   In respect of claims for paid care, the following points should be noted:

- The claimant may not reasonably require full residential care and/or the numbers of carers and/or the number of hours put forward by the claimant[1]. A defendant should therefore investigate closely whether the proposed regime goes beyond what is reasonably necessary to meet the claimant's care needs. In this context, it is useful to contrast the costs incurred to date with what is being claimed into the future, while bearing in mind whether there is any suggestion that the care to date has been inadequate or unsatisfactory.
- A claimant may claim for a night carer when only a night sleeper is reasonably necessary; or may claim for a night sleeper when none is necessary.
- An overprotective regime may not be necessary and may promote dependence rather than independence; but it may be necessary to ensure the claimant's condition does not deteriorate as a result of destabilising events; and, if the claimant's injuries present him with risks then, if the consequences of those risks are potentially catastrophic, he is entitled to adequate protection from such risks, even if they are small[2].
- Bear in mind that some support may be capable of being provided by telephone (with a support worker on call) and this arrangement may be desirable, to provide a claimant with privacy and space and some independence. If so, the hourly rate payable during such periods will probably be less[3].

- The care required might be properly provided more cheaply by a lower grade of carer[4].
- If agency care is being claimed, regard should be had to whether it would be more appropriate for the claimant to employ the carers directly. The advantages of direct employment include (i) the cost of care will be cheaper (but case management costs will increase, as more case management will be necessary), (ii) the claimant has more control over the staff employed, and (iii) there is often more continuity in the staff employed.
- The quantification of what paid care the claimant reasonably needs may be reduced to reflect the chances that he might not in fact receive such care ,whether because (i) he will not accept that level of care, (ii) he may be convicted of a criminal offence, resulting in a custodial sentence, or (iii) he may be committed under the Mental Health Act[5]. There may be other reasons.
- The care provided might be provided more cheaply by a machine[6].
- There may be breaks in the care needed, in order to allow the claimant to attend day centres, rehabilitation units, medical appointments[7], or therapeutic employment (unless, of course, the claimant requires to be accompanied by a carer during these times).
- There may be times when the claimant's family would voluntarily want to dispense with paid care, eg to take the claimant on holiday[8].
- Future care may, in fact, be provided gratuitously by friends and family members, in which case a discount should be applied to reflect the gratuitous element of the care[9].
- The cost of 24-hour care to a young catastrophically injured claimant is not to be reduced by the hours of normal parental care which his parents would have provided to him if uninjured, but by the hours which they would willingly take it upon themselves to become part of his care package and provide such care for him in the future[10]. The justification for this is that caring for a catastrophically injured child is very different to caring for an ordinary child.
- Where a young claimant requires a high level of care, there will often be no justification for reducing the amount of professional care which is reasonably necessary, on the assumption that some will continue to be provided by the parents: the parents are entitled to return to their role as parents and place disability-related care in the hands of the professionals[11].
- In the long term, the claimant may need to be institutionalised, when the care may be free[12].
- Once aids and equipment (often recommended by an occupational therapist) have been provided in order to help the claimant perform his or her daily activities, it may be that the claimant's care needs might reduce accordingly.
- Over time, certain repetitive tasks which are usually performed by trained professionals may be learnt and performed by the claimant's family (or support workers) with minimal input from skilled (and more expensive) individuals.
- The claimant might have required some care due to disability arising from an unrelated or pre-existing condition in any event[13].
- Claims for support worker expenses must be properly proved. Absent any evidence as to the likely destination for any holidays, and the likely costs of travel thereto, and accommodation and food there, the claim for support workers' expenses whilst accompanying the claimant on holiday may fail for want of proof[14].

- In addition, following the principles laid down in *Hodgson v Trapp*[15], the claimant must give credit for any payments received from the state to assist with the cost of paid carers, eg by the Independent Living Fund[16].

- Where there is a claim for periodical payments, if the claimant lives abroad, and there is no appropriate earnings index or series (equivalent to ASHE 6115) measuring the earnings of carers in that country to which a periodical payments order in respect of care could be appropriately pegged, then such an order is unlikely to be made[17].

- Where the court is considering an order for periodical payments in respect of the future care costs, but there is uncertainty surrounding the precise amount of fluctuating care which the claimant will receive in the future, the court may make an order for periodical payments in respect of the minimum level of care which the claimant is certain to receive, and a lump sum award in respect of the uncertain balance of the care awarded[18].

[1] See eg *Bristow v Judd* [1993] PIQR Q117, where the trial judge was satisfied that there was no need for full-time residential care, nor any need for someone to sleep in the claimant's house if he was alone. See also *Goldfinch v Scannell* [1993] PIQR Q143, in which the Court of Appeal overturned the trial judge's assessment of care on the basis of a full-time carer living with the claimant. Instead, the care costs were calculated on the basis that the claimant's mother would provide the necessary supervision, with part-time assistance and allowances for holidays and for when the claimant's mother might not be able to help in the future.

[2] See eg *C v Dixon* [2009] EWHC 708 (QB) at para 35.

[3] See eg *C v Dixon* [2009] EWHC 708 (QB) at paras 95–98. King J allowed for such time (2.5 hours per day) by enhancing the hourly rate of the support worker when he was on direct support duty by 9.5%, and allowing nothing for the hours on call, except for periods when he had to attend the claimant's home during the on-call period. This on-call charging structure is in line with a Department of Health publication entitled 'Agenda for Change'.

[4] See eg *Radford v Jones* (1973, unreported), where care was awarded at the rates of a nursing auxiliary rather than the full rate of a State Registered Nurse.

[5] See *Huntley v Simmonds* [2009] EWHC 405 (QB), per Underhill J at para 111: the multiplicands were reduced to reflect such contingencies. This decision was subsequently upheld on appeal: [2010] EWCA Civ 54.

[6] See eg *Leon Seng Tan v Bunnage* (23 July 1986, unreported), in which Gatehouse J disallowed the cost of a night-time carer because the job of turning the claimant could just as easily have been done by an electric bed with a timer set to operate every four hours. It was held that 'it would be quite unreasonable for the defendants to have to pay a capital sum of over £130,000 for this additional care assistant to carry out no more than about 10 minutes' work per night'.

[7] For example, see *Barry v Ablerex* [2000] PIQR Q263.

[8] See eg *Biesheuval v Birrell* [1999] PIQR Q40.

[9] *Bordin v St Mary's NHS Trust* [2000] Lloyd's Rep Med 287; *Evans v Pontypridd Roofing Ltd* [2001] EWCA Civ 1657; although cf *Biesheuval v Birrell* [1999] PIQR Q40, where Eady J said there was no right to expect friends and family to continue providing voluntary services.

[10] *See Iqbal v Whipps Cross University Hospital NHS Trust* [2006] EWHC 3111 (QB). The parents are entitled to be reimbursed for their time, but this will be at a (lower) rate that reflects the voluntary nature of the arrangement. See also *Stephens v Doncaster HA* [1996] Med LR 357.

[11] See *A v Powys Local Health Board* [2007] EWHC 2996 (QB), per Lloyd Jones J at para 57; *Massey v Tameside & Glossop Acute Services NHS Trust* [2007] EWHC 317 (QB).

[12] *Mitchell v Mulholland (No 2)* [1972] 1 QB 65, CA.

[13] See eg *Taylor v Weston AHA* [2003] All ER (D) 50 (Dec), in which the claim for past and future care was reduced to take account of the care that the claimant would have required in any event due to her pre-existing Crohn's disease.

[14] See eg *Cornes v Southwood* [2008] EWHC 369 (QB).

[15] [1989] 1 AC 807.

16   *Dorrington v Lawrence* [2001] All ER (D) 145 (Nov).
17   *A v Powys Local Health Board* [2007] EWHC 2996 (QB).
18   See *Huntley v Simmonds* [2009] EWHC 405 (QB), per Underhill J at para 114. This decision was upheld on appeal: [2010] EWCA Civ 54.

State provision

[K172]   It may be that, in some cases, the claimant has suffered no loss because the claimant's care needs have been and will continue to be adequately met by the state at no cost to the claimant[1].

- Such cases are now likely to be rare, in the light of the decision in *Peters v East Midlands SHA & others*[2], in which the Court of Appeal held that a claimant is entitled as of right to choose to pursue the tortfeasor for damages to provide for his care or accommodation needs, rather than having to rely on a public authority providing for those needs pursuant to its statutory obligations, provided that there is no risk of double recovery; and that an effective of way of preventing the risk of double recovery, where a claimant's affairs are administered by the Court of Protection, is to provide that court with a copy of the judgment of the personal injury claim and seek an order that (i) no application for public funding of the claimant's care should be made without further order, and (ii) the defendant must be notified of any application for permission to apply for public funding.
- Where, however, a court decides that direct payments will be made to the claimant by the local authority in respect of his care needs, such payments must be taken into account in calculating damages: see *Crofton v NHSLA*[3], in which the uncertainty as to whether the direct payments would continue was reflected in a reduction to the multiplier.
- Alternatively, credit can be given for direct payment by a claimant agreeing to provide the defendant with a reverse indemnity, whereby the claimant receives his full award of damages without any reduction, but in return undertakes to use his best endeavours, at the defendant's expense, to obtain the maximum payment by way of funding for care from the local authority (and reimburse the defendant to the extent that such funding is obtained). The court does not have the power to order such an arrangement where the parties do not agree it: see *Burton v Kingsbury*[4]. In that case, where a periodical payments order was made in respect of care, Flaux J ordered that the amount of the periodical payments awarded should be reduced annually by the actual amount of direct payments which the claimant received in any given year. But this produced the consequence that, because the variation in the periodical payments did not occur as a result of a change in the claimant's health, the payments were not eligible for tax relief, and the order did not comply with the requirements of the Damages Act 1996, and this case is unlikely to be followed.

1   By analogy, see *Sowden v Lodge* [2004] EWCA Civ 1370. See further Chapter F, Past Expenses and Losses at paras **[F69]–[F75]**.
2   [2009] EWCA Civ 145.
3   [2007] EWCA Civ 71, per Dyson LJ at para 87.
4   [2007] EWHC 2091 (QB), per Flaux J at para 107.

Gratuitous care

[K173]   Whenever claims for gratuitous care are considered, the following points should be borne in mind:

- The care or assistance provided must be 'well beyond the call of duty'[1].
- The rate claimed must be reasonable for the type of care provided and the claimant's locality[2].
- Gratuitous carers may not be allowed to claim the higher weekend rates that professional carers charge for working weekends and bank holidays[3]. A defendant will usually wish to argue that the basic rate, as opposed to the enhanced or aggregate hourly rate (which includes allowances for care given at antisocial hours, eg evenings and weekends), is appropriate[4]. Alternatively, a defendant will wish to argue that, if the aggregate rate is adopted, then a one-third (rather than 25%) discount is appropriate.
- Where a care provider has given up a job to look after the claimant, the claimant may not recover the carer's loss of income as well as the care provided[5] and will be restricted by the 'ceiling principle' to, at the most, claiming the cost of a professional carer[6].
- A discount should be made to reflect the 'gratuitous element' of the care provided and the fact that a professional carer would have to pay tax and National Insurance[7].
- Where gratuitous care was already being provided prior to the injuries sustained, or would have been required in any event by reason of some other constitutional condition, the claimant may only recover the additional extent of the care due to the injuries[8].
- Care should be taken to avoid any overlap between gratuitous care, paid care, and care provided during the claimant's stay in hospital[9]. Although it may be arguable that no care is recoverable in respect of a period when the claimant was an in-patient in hospital, it may be tactically sensible to make some concession in this regard.
- It may be more appropriate to award a lump sum for past gratuitous care rather than to apply a multiplier/multiplicand approach[10].
- A claimant is not entitled to recover the costs of care on behalf of the tortfeasor[11].
- No damages are likely to be recoverable where the claimant is unable or unwilling to give the money to the actual care provider[12].
- A claim for gratuitous care does not extend to assistance with the claimant's business[13].
- A claimant is unable to recover for gratuitous services he or she rendered to third parties[14]. But a claimant can recover damages in respect of gratuitous care or services which he is no longer able to provide to members of his family living as part of the same household, if the same goes beyond 'the ordinary interaction of members of a household'[15].
- A claimant is unable to recover, in their own right, for gratuitous care provided by a third party who sustains injuries as a result of the defendant's negligence[16].
- Where a gratuitous care provider receives (increased) state benefits in respect of the care provided to the claimant, account should be taken of the same in order to avoid double recovery[17]. In cases where the carer, usually a spouse or partner, has

been or is receiving Carer's Allowance, the defendant should offset the amount of such payments against any claim and call for disclosure of the amount of such payments, or seek further information in that regard.

- A claimant's care needs might reduce following provision of equipment, aids and appliances in order to assist him or her with the performance of daily activities.

- Loss of earnings incurred by friends and family members visiting the claimant in hospital are not recoverable, because they are too remote[18].

[1] *Mills v British Rail Engineering Ltd* [1992] PIQR Q130, CA. Although it should be noted that *Mills* did not lay down any new principle, and gratuitous care claims are not limited to 'very serious cases': *Giambrone v JMC Holidays Ltd* [2004] EWCA Civ 158. There is no arbitrary threshold for recovery. 'Well beyond the ordinary call of duty' means that the claimant's illness or injury is sufficiently serious to give rise to a need for care and attendance significantly over and above that which would be given anyway in the ordinary course of family life. See further Chapter F, Past Expenses and Losses at paras **[F80]–[F84]**.

[2] The rates of care vary widely, depending upon the type of care required and the geographical region and, in any significant claim, it will usually be necessary to obtain evidence from a nursing expert regarding the applicable rates.

[3] *Fairhurst v St Helen's and Knowsley Health Authority* [1995] PIQR Q1.

[4] See *A v B Hospitals NHS Trust* [2006] EWHC 1178 (QB), in which the basic hourly rate was adopted, despite the care being intensive and given at antisocial hours. There are, however, other cases in which the level of care has been intensive and often given at antisocial hours and weekends, and an enhanced rate has been considered appropriate: see eg *Massey v Tameside & Glossop Acute Services NHS Trust* [2007] EWHC 317 (QB); and *Smith v East & North Hertfordshire Hospitals NHS Trust* [2008] EWHC 2234 (QB).

[5] *Fish v Wilcox* [1994] 5 Med LR 230.

[6] *Housecroft v Burnett* [1986] 1 All ER 332, CA. Where a carer gives up employment to provide the care, the conventional approach is that the claimant may recover the commercial or discounted cost of the care provided and not the carer's loss of earnings. See *Batt v Highgate Private Hospital* [2004] EWHC 707 (Ch), in which a widower had given up work in order to look after his young child following the death of his wife. The court valued the claim in terms of the commercial cost of the care less the usual discount, distinguishing *Mehmet v Perry* [1977] 2 All ER 529, in which the court allowed the widower's loss of earnings as the correct basis for the calculation of the loss of the deceased's mother's care.

[7] The discount may be applied equally to past and future care: *Evans v Pontypridd Roofing Ltd* [2001] EWCA Civ 1657. The level of discount to be applied usually varies between 20% and 35%, and in *Evans* it was suggested that '25% may be regarded as normal'. Note, though, that one rationalisation of the discount is that it represents the net payment after tax and other costs of employment (or those borne by an employee upon receiving a net sum). A gratuitous carer will not usually pay tax etc. 25% represented an average deduction for tax and other deductions in days of higher basic rates of income tax – such that nowadays a discount of 20% (or less) is arguably more appropriate. See further Chapter F, Past Expenses and Losses at paras **[F104]–[F110]**. To the authors' knowledge, the highest reported discount was 35% which was applied by Crane J in *Bordin v St Mary's NHS Trust* [2000] Lloyd's Rep Med 287. However, there are cases in which no discount has been made. It should be noted that, if a claim does not include allowance for weekend and overtime rates, that fact itself represents a discount element which may justify a court not accepting any further discount because the care is gratuitous: *Newman v Folkes* [2002] EWCA Civ 591.

[8] *Thrul v Ray* [2000] PIQR Q44. An example of this is where a baby is injured. Notwithstanding the baby's injuries, he or she would have required a considerable amount of care in any event, and damages can only be recovered for the additional care attributable to the claimant's injuries.

[9] As regards hospital visits, see further *Havenhaud v Jeffrey* (24 February 1997, unreported), CA, [endorsed by the CA in *Evans v Pontypridd Roofing Ltd* [2001] EWCA Civ 1657], where Beldam LJ distinguished between care and 'normal hospital visits arising from family affection and not for the purposes of providing services which the hospital did not provide'. Any claim should therefore be limited to what can properly be described as the provision of care.

10   See eg *Pollitt v Oxfordshire Health Authority* (16 July 1998, unreported), QBD, referred to in *Kemp & Kemp* at C1-012, where Daniel Brennan awarded the sum of £10,000 for past gratuitous care. See also *Woodrup v Nicol* [1993] PIQR Q104, in which the Court of Appeal awarded the global sum of £3,500 for past care.

11   *Hunt v Severs* [1994] 2 AC 350.

12   This is because, technically, following *Hunt v Severs* [1994] 2 AC 350, the claimant holds the money on trust for the care provider; so, where it is not possible for the money to be given to that person, the object of the trust is thwarted. See *ATH v MS* [2002] EWCA Civ 792. But see also the decisions in *H v S* [2003] QB 965, in which the Court of Appeal held that damages were only awarded on the basis that the money would be used to reimburse the voluntary carer, and that the court would enforce the trust if necessary; and *Hughes v Lloyd* [2007] EWHC 3333 (Ch), in which it was held that, where the voluntary carer has died before damages were awarded, his estate remains entitled to the award of damages, and the trust in favour of the estate was enforceable at law.

13   *Hardwick v Hudson* [1999] 1 WLR 1770, CA.

14   *London Ambulance Service National Healthcare Service Trust v Swain* (12 March 1999, unreported) CA.

15   See *Lowe v Guise* [2002] 3 All ER 454 (CA). Before the accident, the claimant provided gratuitous care and services to his disabled brother, and after the accident he provided much reduced services to his brother, the shortfall being made up by his mother. On a trial of a preliminary point as to whether the claimant could recover damages in respect of such a loss, the Court of Appeal held that in principle such a claim is sustainable, but (per Rix LJ at 469E) 'where the care is to a relative ... – to which I would add a spouse or partner – ... living as part of the same household *and goes beyond the ordinary interaction of members of a household*'. Cf *Morgan v MOD* [2002] EWHC 2072 (QB), in which the claimant had to work away from home for 4.5 days per week as a result of his injuries. He claimed 1 hour a day in respect of lost domestic services he no longer did as a result of his being away, and his wife not wanting him to do too much on the days he was at home. The domestic support in question was said to be making the beds, doing school runs, putting out the bins, doing the washing etc. The claimant still, however, performed 40% of the domestic tasks at home. The claim failed on the basis that it was not sustainable at law because it was in respect of matters which involved the ordinary interaction of members of a household (see paras 47–52).

16   *Buckley v Farrow* [1997] PIQR Q78.

17   For example, in *Whyte v Barber* (18 February 2003, unreported), QBD, credit was given as against the past gratuitous care claim for £15 per week which reflected the increase in foster payments from the local authority that were specifically attributable to the claimant's disability. See further Simon Lindsay 'The Cost of Gratuitous Care: Who Cares Who Pays' [2003] JPIL, Issue 2/03; and Chapter F, Past Expenses and Losses at para **[F109]**.

18   *Kirkham v Boughey* [1958] 2 QB 338, per Diplock J; *Walker v Mullen* (1984) Times, 19 January, per Comyn J.

[K174]   The correct rate of discount (if any) to be applied to the claim for gratuitous care will depend on a number of factors. The justification for the discount principally reflects the saving of tax and National Insurance contributions; however, the discount may also reflect the fact that a carer who lives in the same household as the claimant will not incur the expenses (eg travel) which a commercial carer would incur; and also the nature and quality of care provided and the fact that the care provider has no relevant qualifications[1]. But there are cases where the cost of care has been increased because of the specialist knowledge and number of hours worked by the carer. For example, in *Hogg v Doyle*[2] the Court of Appeal upheld the trial judge's decision to award the claim for the care provided by the claimant's wife, who was a trained nurse, at one-and-a-half times her salary. However, there is no strict rule regarding the discount or increase to be applied, and each case must be decided on its own facts[3].

1   *A v National Blood Authority* [2001] Lloyd's Rep Med 187 at 273.

2   (6 March 1991, unreported), CA, referred to in *Kemp & Kemp* at A2-005.

3   *Fitzgerald v Ford* [1996] PIQR Q72, CA.

[K175]   It is worth noting that the Law Commission recommended in their report 'Damages for Personal Injury: Medical, Nursing and Other Expenses'[1] that damages should not be allowed for past or future gratuitous care or assistance unless the claimant satisfies the court that he or she would otherwise employ someone to do the work. Instead, they argued that an additional amount should be allowed for general damages to reflect this loss.

[1]   Law Com No 262 (November 1999).

Domestic assistance

[K176]   Following the Court of Appeal's decision in *Giambrone v JMC Holidays Ltd*[1], it may be difficult to contest even relatively modest claims for domestic assistance where the assistance is significantly over and above that which would ordinarily have been provided in the course of family life. However, any claim for such assistance should still be scrutinised, as they are often overstated or nor supported by the evidence. Arguments against such awards may be raised as follows:

- The claim for domestic assistance is not made out as reasonable and necessary on the basis of the medical evidence.
- No allowance should be made for past domestic assistance, unless actual expenses have been incurred[2].
- The claim should be limited to the services required to carry out the proportion of housework that could properly be regarded as the claimant's share in the absence of the accident[3].
- Where the domestic assistance has been provided gratuitously, a discount should be applied for the 'gratuitous element', ie to take account of the fact that tax and National Insurance are not paid, and travel expenses are unlikely to have been incurred.
- The claimant would have probably paid for domestic assistance in any event (and therefore the claim cannot be attributed to the defendant's negligence)[4]. In all cases concerning claimants who lived busy professional and social lives, and in particular those where there is also a working spouse, a defendant should scrutinise the claimant's pre-accident lifestyle and expenditure closely.
- Where the medical evidence suggests that the claimant is able to perform household chores but thereby suffers an aggravation of pain or discomfort, assistance is not reasonably required and the award for PSLA can be uplifted to take account of any increase in discomfort[5].
- The claimant's carers will carry out any cleaning/domestic assistance tasks that need to be done[6].

[1]   [2004] EWCA Civ 158.
[2]   *Daly v General Steam Navigation Co Ltd* [1981] 1 WLR 120 (although note that this authority may have been overtaken by developments in the law, in particular *Hunt v Severs* [1994] 2 AC 350).
[3]   *Shaw v Wirral HA* [1993] 4 Med LR 275.
[4]   *Mills v British Rail Engineering Ltd* [1992] PIQR Q130, CA.
[5]   *Ved v Caress* (9 April 2001, unreported), QBD, per HHJ Chapman.
[6]   See eg *Eagle v Chambers (No 2)* [2004] EWCA Civ 1033.

[K177]   Where claims are properly made in respect of the need for domestic assistance, it should be checked that the rates claimed are reasonable. Generally speaking, the rates for domestic assistance are significantly lower than the rates charged by professional carers because the work is unskilled and requires no qualifications. Further, the applicable rates vary from place to place, and it is important to check that the claimant is claiming at the appropriate rates for his or her locality.

Case managers

[K178] Case managers are expensive. Before the cost of a case manager will be recoverable, the claimant must demonstrate the reasonable need for such a person. Usually, the need for a case manager will be restricted to cases of brain or other catastrophic injuries, where there is a need to (i) liaise with various treating professionals from different specialities; (ii) supervise and arrange the employment and training (whether directly or through an agency) of care providers, to ensure that the current care regime is meeting the claimant's needs; and (iii) manage and control the claimant's financial affairs and state benefits.

[K179] In *Thrul v Ray*, Burton J stated[1]:

'[A]n individual case manager is not necessary, given the present involvement at the residential home and its dedicated and caring staff, particularly Mrs Chu, and the occasional, though rare and restricted, assistance of the local authority care manager. I entirely accept the fact that the assistance of the care manager will be irregular, but it can be called upon if necessary. The primary care and responsibility will obviously lie at the doors of Mrs Chu and the Home, but, albeit that I respect entirely the concern of the Home that they should not take on any more responsibility than they presently have, I do not believe that by the course which I propose much if any additional responsibility or time will be in fact imposed. Mrs Chu and her successors in any event have the responsibility for the overall care and control of the [claimant] and her programme, and appear to me to be fulfilling to date admirably. What I aim to do is to do my best to ensure, within the limits of reasonableness, that the additional money which I am ordering the Defendant to pay by way of damages for an additional carer can be spent, rather than lie unspent in the hands of the Court of Protection, for the intended benefit of the [claimant] to give her extra outings; but that the manner of such expenditure should not so far as possible impose any unreasonable additional burden upon Mrs Chu and her successors. I conclude that in any event there would be no gain to the [claimant] from the simple introduction of yet another layer of supervision and involvement; certainly none which would justify the expenditure of the money required.'

[1]   [2000] PIQR Q44.

[K180] The medical evidence must show that the costs of case management are reasonably necessary[1]. Therefore, where the evidence shows that the claimant has sufficient intellectual capacity to manage his or her own affairs, the costs of a case manager will not be recoverable[2]. It may also be argued that, where the claimant's family take over the care of the claimant, they would also be able to take over the handling of the claimant's affairs[3]. Further, whilst significant input of a case manager might be reasonable when a new care regime is set up, over time the need for a case manager may lessen, such that only a modest maintenance allowance is required[4].

[1]   See the first-instance decision in *Hesp v Willemse* [2002] EWHC 1256, in which the costs of case management were not considered reasonably necessary.

2   *Page v Sheerness Steel plc* [1995] PIQR Q26.
3   In which case, a discount for the 'gratuitous element' should be applied. See further Chapter F, Past Expenses and Losses at paras **[F104]–[F110]**.
4   See eg *O'Brien v Harris* (22 February 2001, unreported), QBD.

(vii)   Destroyed or Damaged Clothes and Possessions

[K181]   The following points should be borne in mind when defending claims for the cost of damaged or destroyed possessions:

- The claimant is only entitled to the market value of destroyed or ruined clothes or possessions at the time of the accident, and any claim for new replacements should be discounted to take account of the element of betterment[1].
- Where a damaged chattel is repairable, the normal measure of damage is the cost of repair[2].
- The cost of repair will not be recoverable where the claimant was already required to repair the chattel prior to the defendant's tort[3].
- The cost of repair will also not be recoverable where it would have been cheaper to buy a replacement[4].
- A claimant may only recover the hire costs he or she actually paid, and not the notional costs of hiring an equivalent chattel of the same value[5].
- Where the claimant is awarded the full replacement cost in respect of a chattel which is damaged or destroyed, no additional claim can be brought for loss of personal use of the chattel, because this is already taken into account by the award of interest and saved expenses[6].
- Where a claim is made for the cost of clothing in the future, credit should be provided for the clothes that the claimant would have bought in any event.

1   See further chapter 32 of *McGregor on Damages* (18th edn); and *Voaden v Champion* [2002] EWCA Civ 89.
2   *Darbishire v Warran* [1963] 1 WLR 1067, CA. See further *Jones v Stroud* [1986] 1 WLR 1141; and *Lagden v O'Connor* [2003] UKHL 64.
3   *Performance Cars v Abraham* [1962] 1 QB 33, CA.
4   *Darbishire v Warran* [1963] 1 WLR 1067, CA.
5   *Harris v Bright's Asphalt Contractors Ltd* [1953] 1 QB 617; *Hunt v Severs* [1994] 2 AC 350, per Lord Bridge at 360–361; *Lagden v O'Connor* [2003] UKHL 64.
6   *Voaden v Champion* [2002] EWCA Civ 89.

(viii)   Aids and Equipment

[K182]   When defending claims for aids and equipment, the following matters should be considered:

- Whether the claim is reasonable and necessary on the basis of the medical evidence[1].
- Whether the expense of the item claimed is disproportionate to the benefit that it would bring.
- Whether any of the items claimed are available on the NHS or through social services, eg wheelchairs, crutches etc[2].
- Whether the claimant has the intellectual or physical capacity to make use of the items claimed[3].

- Whether the claimed price and replacement intervals are reasonable[4].
- Whether the item claimed is a common household appliance such as a mobile telephone, television, video, fridge, freezer, washing machine, lawn mower etc that the claimant might have bought in any event[5].
- Whether the claimant (or litigation friend) understands the need for, and actually wants and will buy or make use of, the item claimed[6]. Where the equipment has been recommended some time before trial, but not yet purchased despite the availability of funds (eg by way of an interim payment), the defendant should put the claim in issue.
- Whether a discount should be applied to the claim on the basis that, over time, the claimant's needs will change with age, such that some of the items will no longer be of use[7].
- Whether credit should be given for similar items which would have been bought in any event.
- Whether credit should be given for any resale or residual value of the item claimed when it is replaced.
- Whether the claimant is likely to make use of items provided free by the state, charity or friends/relatives[8].
- Whether the claimant might have needed the item(s) claimed by reason of an unrelated or pre-existing condition in any event[9].

[1]   In *A v Powys Local Health Board* [2007] EWHC 2996 (QB), Lloyd Jones J held (at para 94: following *Massey v Tameside and Glossop Acute Services NHS Trust* [2007] EWHC 317 (QB)) that, in determining what is required to meet the claimant's needs, it is necessary to make findings as to the nature and extent of those needs and then to consider whether what is proposed is reasonable having regard to those needs. See eg *Cottrell v Redbridge Healthcare NHS Trust* (2001) 61 BMLR 72, where the claim for the past cost of a reclining chair was disallowed on the basis that the medical experts in their joint report agreed that such a chair was unnecessary. See also *Cassel v Riverside Health Authority* [1992] PIQR Q1, in which the cost of a swimming pool was disallowed.

[2]   Although see *Eagle v Chambers (No 2)* [2004] EWCA Civ 1033, in which the Court of Appeal held that the defendant must do more than merely show that the items might be available free of charge on the NHS: it must be shown that: (i) the item in question would be available on the NHS or through social services; and (ii) the claimant would make use of the free service. See also *Parkhouse v North Devon Healthcare NHS Trust* [2002] Lloyd's Rep Med 100, in which it was held to be not necessarily relevant that the claimant could have obtained such items on the NHS.

[3]   Where there is doubt about this, it is worth considering instructing an expert psychiatrist/ psychologist to prepare a report. See eg *Dorrington v Lawrence* [2001] All ER (D) 145 (Nov), in which the claimant was not allowed to recover damages for a computer and software, where the claimant already had a computer he did not use, and it was doubtful whether he could make use of the proposed software.

[4]   To this end, it is often worth checking the manufacturer's specifications for the items in question.

[5]   See eg *Parkhouse v North Devon Healthcare NHS Trust* [2002] Lloyd's Rep Med 100, in which Gage J disallowed the claims for a cooker, a TV and a microwave, since these were 'everyday household items'. In *O'Brien v Harris* (22 February 2001, unreported), QBD, Pitchford J disallowed claims for a Walkman, radio, computer, scanner, software and stylewriter, because the same were either purchases for recreation and hobbies which would have been incurred in an alternative form in any event, or purchases which would have been made irrespective of the accident. A laptop was disallowed as a standard item not related to the claimant's injuries in *Knott v Newham Healthcare NHS Trust* [2002] EWHC 2091 (QB) (this case was subsequently appealed to the Court of Appeal but not on this issue); and also in *Huntley v Simmonds* [2009] EWHC 406 (QB). In *Dorrington v Lawrence* [2001] All ER (D) 145 (Nov), Hooper J disallowed the following items which were normal pieces of household equipment, and the need for the same was not attributable to the claimant's injuries: a lawnmower, a microwave, a dishwasher, a TV and video. In *Parry v North*

West Surrey Health Authority (29 November 1999, unreported), QBD, Penry-Davey J disallowed the cost of a mobile telephone, since the claimant probably would have had one in any event; and cf *Morgan v MOD* [2002] EWHC 2072 (QB) at para 62, where it was held that mobile phone use is now so common that it would have been incurred in any event. See also *Ved v Caress* (9 April 2001, unreported), QBD, where HHJ Chapman disallowed the cost of a car with automatic transmission because he held that the claimant, who was a professional woman, would probably have bought an automatic car in any event.

6   See eg in *Blair v Michelin Tyre* (25 January 2002, unreported), HHJ Marr-Johnson sitting as a judge of the QBD rejected the claim for a second wheelchair because the claimant did not seem keen on it and it 'might seldom, if ever, be used'. See also *O'Brien v Harris* (22 February 2001, unreported), QBD, in which Pitchford J refused to allow the cost of shoe inserts because he did not think that the claimant would make use of them.

7   See *Smith v East & North Hertfordshire Hospitals NHS Trust* [2008] EWHC 2234 (QB), in which Penry-Davey J applied a 25% discount to the claim on this basis.

8   In this case, there would be no loss: see *Woodrup v Nicol* [1993] PIQR Q104, CA.

9   See eg *Taylor v Weston AHA* [2003] All ER (D) 50 (Dec), in which the claimant suffered from pre-existing Crohn's disease before the defendant's negligence, and Pitchers J held that the claimant had not established that a manual wheelchair would not have been needed in any event.

(ix) DIY, Decorating, Car Maintenance, Car Valeting and Gardening

[K183]   Before recovering damages under this head, the claimant must show that:

- he or she would have performed these services in the absence of their injuries[1], in which case close regard should be had to the claimant's pre-accident lifestyle;
- by reason of the injuries, he or she is now prevented from performing these services[2]; and
- it is reasonable to rely upon someone else to perform these services[3].

1   See eg *Blair v Michelin Tyre* (25 January 2002, unreported), QBD, in which nothing was awarded for decorating because it was doubted that the claimant would have been doing much at his age (68) in any event.

2   This is an issue which should be covered in the medical evidence. Where the claimant is able still to perform household activities but they take longer or cause pain and discomfort, this is covered by the award for general damages in respect of PSLA: see further *Daly v General Steam Navigation Co Ltd* [1981] 1 WLR 120; and *Ved v Caress* (9 April 2001, unreported), QBD.

3   The Law Commission has recommended that no award should be made for the cost of future domestic activities including DIY, gardening etc unless the claimant actually intends to employ a professional to do the work: see further their Report No 262 'Damages for Personal Injury: Medical, Nursing and other Expenses; Collateral Benefits' (November 1999), para 3.91.

[K184]   Generally speaking, it is necessary for the medical evidence to support the need for someone else to perform these services, unless the same can reasonably be inferred from the nature of the injuries. Further, relying upon *Daly v General Steam Navigation Co Ltd*[1], it may be possible to resist paying damages in respect of past domestic activities unless the claimant paid for the work to be done or a friend/family member gave up paid work to carry out the chores. However, where the claimant enjoyed performing DIY activities such that he or she has lost a hobby as a result of the defendant's wrongdoing, the claimant will not usually be adequately compensated by way of general damages for PSLA, and an award should be made for the cost of paying someone else to perform the activities that the claimant would have done him or herself but for the injuries[2].

1   [1981] 1 WLR 120. Note that it is uncertain how this case is affected by the House of Lords' decision in *Hunt v Severs* [1994] 2 AC 350 as regards gratuitous care. Certainly, there have been a number of cases in which the claimant has recovered damages on behalf of friends and family members for the provision of household activities including DIY, gardening, painting and decorating etc up to the date of trial: see eg *Blair v Michelin Tyre plc* (25 January 2002, unreported), QBD; and *Assinder v Griffin* [2001] All ER (D) 356 (May).

2   *Samuels v Benning* [2002] EWCA Civ 858.

[K185]   As regards the amount claimed, it is up to the claimant to prove the value of the lost ability to perform the services claimed. This is often now quantified by the care or occupational therapy experts. Where no evidence has been put forward to establish the sum claimed, the amount is often susceptible to challenge. For example, in *Cottrell v Redbridge Healthcare NHS Trust*[1], £750 per annum was claimed as the 'conventional' figure awarded under this head of loss. No evidence was put forward as to the nature and extent of the claimant's inability to do DIY. HHJ Richard Seymour QC said that it was for the claimant to prove the value of such a claim. The judge said that, but for the fact that the Trust agreed the annual figure of £325 per year, he would have been inclined to award £51 a year, which was also the agreed figure for window cleaning.

1   (2001) 61 BMLR 72.

[K186]   In respect of a claim for expenditure on DIY, decorating, gardening etc, the claimant is only entitled to claim the labour costs of the work involved and not the costs of materials which would have been incurred in any event. Where necessary, a defendant should challenge the hourly or yearly rates claimed. A defendant should also contend that a claimant is likely to have required such assistance in any event from the age of 65 or 70[1].

1   See eg *Wells v Wells* [1999] 1 AC 345, in which the Court of Appeal allowed a claim for DIY to the age of 65; and *Smith v East & North Hertfordshire Hospitals NHS Trust* [2008] EWHC 2234 (QB), in which Penry-Davey J only allowed the claims to the age of 65.

[K187]   In cases where there are a number of factors making the calculation of this head of loss difficult, a lump sum may be awarded instead of using the traditional multiplier/multiplicand approach[1].

1   See eg *Worrall v Powergen plc* [1999] PIQR Q103.

(x)   Holidays and Leisure Activities

[K188]   Of course, the claimant is only entitled to recover the additional cost of holidays caused by his or her injuries. Claims are often made for: (i) the increased costs of travelling business class (where there is additional legroom); (ii) the increased costs of accommodation suitable for the disabled claimant and/or his carer(s); and (iii) the additional travel costs of the carer(s) needed to look after the claimant and/ or the need to hire a vehicle suitable for a disabled claimant whilst on holiday. Such claims need to be supported by the medical and/or care evidence.

•   In respect of claims for the cost of holidays or leisure activities or equipment, be ready to dispute: (i) expenditure that would have been incurred in any event;

or (ii) expenditure that can be offset against other expenditure on similar items, which the claimant would have incurred on holidays and leisure but for the accident, but will not now incur.

- Where there are significant imponderables surrounding the holidays which a claimant would take in the future, and the extent to which carers would in fact accompany the claimant on such holidays, the court may award a lump sum in place of a conventional award on the basis of a multiplicand and multiplier[1].

[1] See *Pankhurst v White & others* [2009] EWHC 1117 (QB).

[K189] In order to determine the true extent of the claim, consideration must be given to the type and amount of holidays that the claimant took prior to the tort. It may be that the claimant was not used to taking holidays every year, in which case an annual claim should be resisted[1]. Also the claimant may not have been used to taking holidays abroad. However, in the case of a young claimant, a court may be willing to accept that, as time went on, and earnings increased, he or she would have taken more expensive holidays further afield. The relevance of past holidays is that they are the best indicator of the sort of holiday which it would be reasonable to allow for: but they are no more than indicative of what is reasonable.

[1] *Sparks v Royal Hospitals NHS Trust* (21 December 1998, unreported). See also *Parry v North West Surrey Health Authority* (29 November 1999, unreported), QBD, in which the claim for holiday costs was considered to be unreasonable and excessive.

[K190] When defending claims for increased holiday costs, defendants should investigate whether or not the claimant has gone on holiday since the tortious event. If the claimant has gone on such a holiday, disclosure should be sought regarding the travel expenses involved, in order to determine whether any additional expense has in fact been incurred. If, for example, the claimant is claiming the costs of travelling business class but has in fact been able to travel in an ordinary seat before the date of the trial, such a claim may be challenged. As stated by Burton J in *Thrul v Ray*[1]:

> 'It is not the test that the Defendant should be required to pay by way of damages to the [claimant] consequent upon the unfortunate injuries resulting from the accident any sum which will simply make the [claimant] happier or more comfortable … the provision must be one which is reasonably necessary to compensate for what she has lost, but also no more than is reasonably likely to be expended on her behalf in providing her with the substitute for what she has lost.'

[1] [2000] PIQR Q44.

[K191] Similar considerations apply to the claimant's leisure activities. If the claimant spent money on leisure activities before the injuries, he or she is only entitled to claim the reasonable difference (if any) in expenditure as a result of the injuries[1]. Thus, where the claimant spends the same or similar amount on leisure activities after the injuries as he or she spent before the injuries (albeit in respect of different activities), no award under this head may be recovered[2].

[1] *Owen v Brown* [2002] EWHC 1135 (QB).
[2] *Dorrington v Lawrence* [2001] All ER (D) 145 (Nov).

(xi) Court of Protection Costs

[K192]   In order to be able to recover damages under this head, the claimant must show that he or she is incapable of dealing with his or her affairs (and, in particular, managing his award of damages) in accordance with the definition of mental incapacity contained within the Mental Capacity Act 2005[1], and that his or her incapacity is related to his or her injuries as opposed to any pre-existing disability[2]. It is important to bear in mind that, by section 1 of the Mental Capacity Act 2005, a person must be assumed to have mental capacity unless it is established, on the balance of probabilities, that he lacks capacity; the burden of proof will therefore fall on the claimant who alleges incapacity. Where a claimant is properly regarded as a protected beneficiary (ie he lacks capacity to manage a fund of damages) by reason of the defendant's negligence, although Court of Protection expenses (eg the first application to the Court of Protection, preparation and lodgment of accounts, annual fixed fees etc) will be claimable, these need to be differentiated from investment advice and transaction charges (eg panel broker's fees). Fees/expenses arising out of the investment of the claimant's damages will not be recoverable as a separate head of damages, as they are covered by the prevailing discount rate set by the Lord Chancellor[3]. Any recoverable fees will be subject to a deduction for contributory negligence in the usual way[4].

[1]   See Mental Capacity Act 2005, ss 2 and 3. By s 2, 'a person lacks capacity in relation to a matter if at the material time he is unable to make a decision for himself in relation to the matter because of an impairment of, or a disturbance in, the functioning of the mind or brain'.
[2]   *Smith v Rod Jenkins* [2003] EWHC 1356.
[3]   *Eagle v Chambers (No 2)* [2004] EWCA Civ 1033; and *Page v Plymouth Hospitals NHS Trust* [2004] 3 All ER 367.
[4]   *Willbye v Gibbons* [2003] EWCA Civ 372.

(xii) Deputyship Fees

[K193]   Where a claimant is unable to manage his or her own affairs, sometimes a professional deputy (usually a solicitor) is appointed under the Mental Capacity Act 2005. When resisting such claims, consideration should be given to the following matters:

- Whether the claimant actually requires a professional deputy or whether there is a suitable member of his or her family who could adequately perform the tasks involved[1], possibly with some assistance from a professional deputy if necessary.
- Whether the claimant will always require a professional deputy, or if a professional might only be needed in the first year or two (when matters might be more complicated, eg arranging accommodation and setting up a care regime), and thereafter it would be appropriate for a family member to take over[2].
- Whether the costs claimed are reasonable[3].
- Whether account has been taken of the likely decrease in the deputy's involvement over time[4].
- Whether the routine work may be carried out by someone less senior.
- Whether the professional deputy suggested on behalf of the claimant has the necessary experience and is a suitable person to act as deputy[5].

- Whether there is a finding of contributory negligence which should reduce the claim in line with other heads of loss[6]. In cases where there is a finding of contributory negligence, it is probable that the fund will be exhausted at some point during the claimant's lifetime, such that the need for a professional deputy will cease.

[1]   See eg *Eagle v Chambers (No 2)* [2004] EWCA Civ 1033, in which the Court of Appeal upheld the trial judge's decision that the claimant's mother could act as deputy.

[2]   There are no hard and fast rules in this regard. See further Master Lush's evidence to the Court of Appeal in *Eagle v Chambers (No 2)* [2004] EWCA Civ 1033.

[3]   In *Eagle v Chambers (No 2)* [2004] EWCA Civ 1033, Master Lush gave evidence that the costs of a professional deputy were likely to exceed £3,500 per annum (plus VAT). Claims under the new Mental Capacity Act regime are often advanced for annual costs considerably in excess of this amount. When challenging such claims, it is sensible to obtain evidence (usually in the form of witness statements or expert reports from experienced solicitors/professional deputies in the field) supporting lower figures.

[4]   After a while, much of a deputy's work may be routine. For example, the claimant's accommodation has been sorted out, the care regime set up and direct debits arranged, and there may be a lot less work for the deputy to carry out on a day-to-day basis.

[5]   See eg *Eagle v Chambers (No 2)* [2004] EWCA Civ 1033, in which the Court of Appeal upheld the trial judge's decision that the claimant's instructing solicitor was not a suitable person to act as deputy.

[6]   *Willbye v Gibbons* [2003] EWCA Civ 372.

[K194]   Where the claimant has mental capacity and is not a protected beneficiary, but is severely physically disabled, the costs of a professional trustee (whose duties would be very similar to those of a professional deputy or a court-appointed deputy under the Mental Capacity Act 2005) to assist with administrative tasks such as paying carers and dealing with employment disputes; the preparation of annual accounts and tax returns; and to help negotiate contracts and protect the claimant from unscrupulous individuals, are unlikely to be recoverable. Such tasks are likely to be responsibility of the case manager[1].

[1]   See *A v Powys Local Health Board* [2007] EWHC 2996 (QB), per Lloyd Jones J at paras 158–9. But note that, in this case, the costs of a private banking service (estimated at €500 p.a.) was recovered, as the claimant was unable to handle cash, use bank cards, or write cheques.

(xiii)   Investment Advice

[K195]   Historically, although there were a few cases in which additional damages was awarded to cover the costs of investment advice[1], such claims were often disallowed, on the basis that they arose out of the administration of the compensation received and not the defendant's negligence[2], or that the damage was too remote[3]. Following the decision of the House of Lords in *Wells v Wells*[4] and the Lord Chancellor's decision to set the discount rate at 2.5%, it is clear that, if there ever was, there is no longer any entitlement to claim damages to cover such expenses[5]. The entitlement to claim the costs of investment advice (including transaction charges) was heard as a preliminary issue in *Page v Plymouth Hospitals NHS Trust*[6]. Following a thorough review of the authorities and arguments for and against such claims, Davis J concluded that the costs of investment advice were not recoverable in principle, because they had already been taken into account by the Lord Chancellor when fixing the discount rate at the rate he had[7]. The attempt to claim investment advice as a separate head of damages was seen as an impermissible attack on the discount rate[8]. This reasoning has now been held to be equally applicable to cases involving patients as well as competent adults[9].

[1]   *Duller v South East Lincs Engineers* [1981] CLY 585; *Cassel v Hammersmith and Fulham Health Authority* [1992] PIQR Q1; *Anderson v Davies* [1993] PIQR Q87; and *Ejvet v Aid Pallets* (11 March 2002, unreported), Cooke J.

[2]   *Francis v Bostock* (1985) Times, 9 November; *Cunningham v Camberwell Health Authority* (21 July 1988, unreported), QBD; and *Blackburn v Newcastle Area Health Authority* (1 August, unreported), QBD.

[3]   *Routledge v Mackenzie* [1994] PIQR Q49.

[4]   [1999] AC 345.

[5]   *Webster v Hammersmith Hospitals NHS Trust* [2002] All ER (D) 397; *Anderson v Blackpool, Wyre & Fylde Community Health Services NHS Trust* (unreported); *Page v Plymouth Hospitals NHS Trust* [2004] EWHC 1154 (QB). See further William Norris QC and Douglas Hall 'Claims for the Cost of Investment Management' [2004] JPIL, Issue 3/04, at 214–224; and Edward Duckworth 'The End of the Line for Claims for Investment Management Charges? – *Page v Plymouth Hospitals NHS Trust* and *Eagle v Chambers*' [2004] Quantum, Issue 6/2004, 1 November.

[6]   [2004] EWHC 1154 (QB), which was approved by the Court of Appeal in *Eagle v Chambers (No 2)* [2004] EWCA Civ 1033.

[7]   At [52] David J said: 'Moreover, I find it difficult to think that the Lord Chancellor, in making these observations, could or would have overlooked the attendant costs involved in seeking investment advice in setting the discount rate as he did. It is true that the Lord Chancellor does not expressly say that he had taken them into the account (and Mr Spink told me that the point seems not to have been explicitly raised in the preceding consultation process). But in my judgment it is inherent in the Lord Chancellor's reasoning: and that is of a pattern with the observations of Lord Hope and Lord Clyde in *Wells v Wells*. Thus when, in the course of his reasons, the Lord Chancellor refers to the position about investment on mixed asset portfolios, I think it likely that he was there referring to a real rate of return "comfortably" exceeding 2.5% as connoting a return net not only of tax but also of investment costs'.

[8]   Which was blocked by cases such as *Warriner v Warriner* [2002] 1 WLR 1703 and *Cooke v United Bristol Health Care* [2003] EWCA Civ 1370.

[9]   *Eagle v Chambers (No 2)* [2004] EWCA Civ 1033.

(xiv)   Miscellaneous Expenses

[K196]   Often, claims are made for postage, stationery, telephone calls, faxes etc that the claimant has incurred pursuing the claim. These are technically costs and not allowable[1]. As long as the sums claimed are modest, the claim is usually unobjectionable (though there should be no overlap with the costs ultimately claimed). However, where larger sums are claimed, supporting evidence should be requested.

[1]   *O'Brien-King v Phillips* [1997] CLY 1814. See also *Morris v Johnson Matthey* (1967) 112 SJ 32, in which it was held that damages for the travel expenses attending appointments with solicitors and experts were not recoverable as damages.

7   Future Loss: Multipliers

[K197]   Following the House of Lords' decision in *Wells v Wells*[1], it has become difficult to chisel down future loss multipliers on the basis of general contingencies. Since the greatest risk of all – mortality – is already catered for in the Ogden Tables, it is necessary to consider other factors which may affect the longevity of the claim. It is important to appreciate the different factors at play in relation to each particular head of loss and the different arguments that may be applied.

¹   [1999] 1 AC 345. See further Chapter H, Future Expenses and Losses at paras **[H17]**–**[H24]**.

(i)   The Discount Rate

[K198]   The discount rate has been fixed by the Lord Chancellor at 2.5%¹. Whilst the court has the power to adopt a different discount rate if it considers it more appropriate in any particular case, the case must have special features which fall outside the reasons expressed by the Lord Chancellor for setting the discount rate at the rate he did². Further, any attempt to get round the discount rate, eg by adopting stepped multiplicands, is unlikely to find favour with the court³.

¹   See further Chapter H, Future Expenses and Losses at paras **[H25]**–**[H32]**.
²   *Warriner v Warriner* [2002] 1 WLR 1703. See further Chapter H, Future Expenses and Losses at paras **[H33]**–**[H35]**.
³   See further *Cooke v United Bristol Health Care* [2003] EWCA Civ 1370, in which Rowland Hogg's argument was described by Laws LJ at [30] as being 'in the end nothing but smoke and mirrors'.

(ii)   Life Expectancy

[K199]   The claimant's life expectancy is of particular relevance where he or she seeks a lump sum award, rather than periodical payments. It is almost always likely to be financially more advantageous for a defendant to seek a lump sum award, just as it is almost always an advantage for a claimant to opt for periodical payments. But many claimants prefer lump sums awards for a variety of reasons and, where this applies and future loss is substantial, evidence of life expectancy becomes critical. If there is any reason to think that the claimant does not have a normal life expectancy, appropriate expert evidence should be obtained in order to confirm how long the claimant is likely to live. Prima facie, this should be the evidence of a clinician or clinical expert, as permission to adduce statistical evidence on life expectancy will not generally be given unless there is disagreement between the clinical experts on a statistical matter¹. Often, the injuries sustained by reason of the defendant's negligence will shorten life, and a lower life multiplier may be contended for². In a catastrophic injury case, the first question to be answered, in settling upon an appropriate multiplier for future annual losses, is: what is the claimant's current life expectancy? There are two different methods of calculating the appropriate life multiplier where there is a reduction in life expectancy: which method is correct depends on the nature of the medical evidence, and the approach taken by the court to the reduction in question.

•   Where the medical evidence assesses, and the court decides, the issue of a claimant's life expectancy by reference to a reduction in years to the claimant's pre-morbid statistical life expectancy, the appropriate approach is to adopt Table 1 of the Ogden Tables, to increase the claimant's actual age at trial by the appropriate reduction in his life expectancy, and to apply the Table 1 multiplier to that assumed age³.

- Where, however, the medical evidence predicts, and the court decides, the claimant's overall expectation of life, ie for how many more years he will in fact live, then the appropriate approach is to take the appropriate multiplier from Table 28[4].

---

[1]   See *Arden v Malcolm* [2007] EWHC 404 (QB); cf *Royal Victoria Infirmary v B* [2002] Lloyds LR (Med) 282 (CA).

[2]   See eg *Barry v Ablerex* [2000] PIQR Q263.

[3]   See *Smith v LC Window Fashions Ltd* [2009] EWHC 1532 (QB), per Cranston J at paras 40–43, following *Crofts v Murton* [2009] EWHC 3538 (HHJ Collender QC, sitting as a deputy High Court judge, at paras 88–100). See also *Tinsley v Sarkar* [2005] EWHC 192 (QB).

[4]   Where the court has already taken into account, the chances of dying earlier or living longer than the predicted date, to take mortality further into account in deciding the multiplier, would amount to a double discount for mortality: *Royal Victoria Infirmary v B* [2002] Lloyds LR (Med) 282 (CA). See also *Sarwar v (1) Ali and (2) MIB* [2007] EWHC 274 (QB); *Burton v Kingsbury* [2007] EWHC 2091 (QB).

(iii) Specific Multipliers

Loss of earnings multipliers

[**K200**]   The Ogden Tables (6th edn) have ushered in an entirely new method for calculating future loss of earnings claims, and for reducing the multiplier to allow for contingencies other than mortality. For a detailed analysis as to the new methodology to be adopted, reference should be made to the explanatory notes to the Tables, and in particular to paras 26 to 42. In summary, however, the new methodology operates in the following way.

- Two calculations (and two multipliers) are now necessary: (1) the earnings which the claimant would have achieved but for his accident; and (2) the residual earnings he will now achieve given his disability (if any).
- In each case, the multiplier is to be reduced by the appropriate reduction factor taken from one of Tables A to D. The reduction factors allow for the risks of non-employment due to economic factors, sickness, employment breaks for parenthood and the like, by reference to three issues which are said to have the greatest bearing on a person's future employment status: (i) employment status; (ii) disability status; and (iii) educational attainment. This represents a fundamental change from previous editions of the Ogden Tables, in which the reduction factors depended on the type of occupation of the claimant and the region in which he lived.
- Insofar as the multiplier for the claimant's earnings but for the accident is concerned, the relevant status is the claimant's status at the time of the accident. So, the defendant must investigate whether, at the time of the accident, the claimant was (i) employed or unemployed, (ii) disabled or not, and (iii) what his educational and vocational attainments were.
- Insofar as the multiplier for the claimant's residual earnings is concerned, the relevant status is the claimant's status at the time of trial. So, the defendant must investigate (i) whether he is (or will become) employed; (ii) whether he is or will be disabled; and (iii) what educational or vocational attainment has now has (or will have after any retraining).

Disability status

[K201]   Issues of the claimant's employment and education status are relatively straightforward, and the reader is referred to paragraph 35 of the Explanatory Notes to the Ogden Tables, but the issue of disability status is likely to prove to be more contentious, and warrants separate consideration. In determining whether a claimant is disabled within the meaning of the Disability Discrimination Act 1995, the starting point is section 1(1) of the Act: a person has a disability 'if he has a physical or mental impairment which has a substantial and long-term adverse effect on his ability to carry out normal day-to-day activities ...'. The following matters should be borne in mind when assessing disability status:

- Regard must also be had to Schedule 1 to the Act and the Guidance Notes thereto. In particular:
  - (i) Consideration has to be given to the time taken to carry out an activity, the way in which the activity is carried out and so on: see Section B of the Guidance Notes.
  - (ii) Paragraph 6 of Schedule 1, and paragraphs B11 to B12 of the Guidance Notes make clear that, where an impairment has been the subject of medical treatment or correction, that treatment or correction is to be disregarded even if it has resulted in the effect being completely under control or not apparent[1].
  - (iii) Paragraph D11of the Guidance Notes make clear that, where an impairment does not prevent someone from doing a daily activity, but causes him pain or fatigue such that it has a substantial adverse long-term effect on how they do it, or the period of time over which they can do it, that may amount to a disability.
- If a claimant is disabled, the extent to which the claimant is disabled, given the nature of his particular work, may justify adjustments to the reduction factors suggested in the Ogden Tables.
- Paragraphs 31 and 32 of the Explanatory Notes to the Tables (cf paras 12 and 15) make clear that:
  - (i) The Tables provide a 'ready reckoner' which provide an initial adjustment to the multipliers.
  - (ii) In many cases, it will be appropriate to increase or reduce the discounts suggested in the Tables to take account of (i) the nature of a particular claimant's disabilities, (ii) his pre-accident employment history, and (iii) other material circumstances. A defendant should contend that the relatively low threshold required to qualify as disabled will often result in a need for potentially significant adjustment, depending on the extent of the claimant's disabilities[2].
  - (iii) In some cases, lump sum awards pursuant to (i) *Smith v Manchester* or (ii) *Blamire* principles will be more appropriate[3]. Defendants should be alert to spot those cases where the imponderables are such that a powerful case can be advanced for a lump sum award, as the size of any such award is likely to be very considerably less than a conventional award[4].
- Paragraph 44 of the Explanatory Notes to the Tables makes clear that the Tables assume that there will be no change in disability status or educational

achievement after the date of the accident. Further adjustments will, therefore, be necessary in any case where that assumption cannot be made.

¹ See *Conner v Bradman* [2007] EWHC 2789 (QB), per HHJ Coulson QC (now Coulson J) at paras 33 and 39.

² See *Conner v Bradman* [2007] EWHC 2789 (QB), per HHJ Coulson QC (now Coulson J) at para 72. But Dr Wass has argued that, as the reduction factors are averages for the defined group in question (according to age, sex, disability status, educational attainment and employment status), statistically most members of that group will lie close to the average, so that, once a claimant falls within a certain group, any adjustment to the reduction factor should be small: see 'Discretion in the Application of the New Ogden Six Multipliers: The case of *Conner v Bradman and Co*' [2008] JPIL Issue 2/08, pp 154–163.

³ See *McGhee v Diageo* [2008] CSOH 74 (a decision of Lord Malcolm in the Outer House of the Court of Session); and *Palmer v Kitley* [2008] EWHC 2819 (QB).

⁴ See further *Blamire* awards at para **[K153]**.

The multiplier for the claimant's earnings but for the injury

[K202] In assessing the multiplier appropriate for the claimant's earnings but for his injury, the following matters must be borne in mind.

- It is plainly open to a defendant to argue for a greater reduction factor to the multiplier than the starting point stipulated in the Tables, on a variety of grounds.
- Employment status and history: where a claimant was employed at the date of the injury, a defendant may be able to argue that he should be regarded as unemployed or that a further reduction should be applied to the reduction factor for an employed person if, for example:
  - (i) the claimant, although employed at the time of the accident, has had long periods of unemployment immediately prior thereto and/or no clear pattern of employment/earnings[1]; or
  - (ii) the claimant's employment was insecure, whether because his personnel files reveal that he was at risk of dismissal or he was at risk of redundancy for wider economic reasons[2].
- Medical history and disability: even where a claimant was not already disabled at the time of injury, a defendant may be able to argue that he should be regarded as disabled, or that a significant further reduction should be applied to the reduction factor, where medical records reveal a likelihood or chance that C would have become disabled in the near future in any event, for example:
  - (i) where, as a result of the accident, the claimant has sustained an acceleration of symptoms attributable to a degenerative condition from which he would have suffered within a short period in any event; or
  - (ii) where the claimant already suffered from some unrelated degenerative condition which would have resulted in a future disability in any event.
- In the case of young female claimants: a defendant may be able to contend for a significant further discount to the reduction factor, to reflect the contingencies of career breaks, part-time working, work-related expenses etc:
  - (i) In *Smith v East & North Hertfordshire Hospitals NHS Trust*[3] a reduction factor of 0.60 (40%) was applied to the claim for loss of earnings (and pension) in respect of a claimant who would have worked from age 25 onwards as a primary school teacher, to reflect (i) the costs associated with

work, (ii) the contingencies of life, including likelihood of significant career breaks due to maternity, and (iii) the element of overlap between this claim and the other claims for future living (see *Croke v Wiseman*[4]).

(ii) In *Peters v East Midlands Strategic Health Authority*[5] a reduction factor of 0.50 (50%) was held to be appropriate for a female who was 20 years old at trial, who would have been of low average intelligence and capable only of unskilled or semi-skilled work, and who had been born into a family which was dysfunctional – her mother was educationally subnormal, her family had been known to social services for many years owing to poor childcare and allegations of sexual abuse by family members against the children, and long before trial the claimant and her two sisters were all the subject of a Full Care Order granted to the local authority; and her family relied on state benefits and had a poor work ethic – and who would only have held sporadic employment.

(iii) But in *A v Powys Local Health Board*[6], it was held that no further discount to the reduction factor of 0.87 – appropriate for someone who would have attained a degree and been employed – was appropriate in respect of a 16 year-old girl whose parents were both hard-working professionals; who, despite her severe impairments, had since the accident obtained good grades in a range of Junior Certificate Examinations (ranging from A to D), and who but for the injury would have gone to university and pursued a professional career, earning £40,000 gross p.a. on average. The judge held that Table C already makes allowances for interruptions due to child-raising and caring for other dependants.

• It may be appropriate to argue for a higher reduction factor to reflect the fact that a claimant's earnings would have reduced over time (as he got older) in any event[7].

[1]   See eg *Huntley v Simmonds* [2009] EWHC 405 (QB). A young male claimant who, prior to the accident, had received no schooling since being expelled at the age of 12, had regularly abused alcohol and drugs, had suffered from behavioural problems, had been in trouble with the police (with convictions for violence and drink-driving, but no custodial sentences), but had begun to settle down to some extent before the accident. He had been in and out of work as a labourer a good deal in the year or two before the accident. The judge held that it would be wrong if the size of the multiplier depended on whether or not the claimant was in or out of work on the actual day of the accident; that the risk that the claimant would not have been in continuous employment and working all the year round was significantly greater than the average risk; and that the appropriate reduction factor was 0.82, ie that which applied to someone unemployed at the time of the accident.

[2]   See eg *Smith v LC Window Fashions Ltd* [2009] EWHC 1532 (QB). Although the claimant had some periods off work prior to the accident, and would have been made redundant in any event after the accident at the age of 54, the judge rejected the defendant's suggestion that he would thereafter not have been in work. Despite the known high unemployment rates in South Wales, he had always had work when he wanted it. His health problems had never stopped him working but had restricted only his choice of work; and his drinking habit had never had any effect on his employment in the past. The judge appears to have allowed the claimant his full loss of earnings multiplier to 65 rather than 70, appearing to offset the chance of his working beyond 65 against the chance that he might not have been in full-time employment prior thereto, for the contingencies relied upon by the defendant.

[3]   [2008] EWHC 2234 (QB). Although it should be noted that para 40 of the Introductory Notes to the Ogden Tables (6th edn) and the decision in *A v Powys Local Health Board* [2007] EWHC 2996 (QB) were not brought to the judge's attention.

[4]   1 WLR 71 (at 83b–c).

⁵   [2008] EWHC 778 (QB) (appealed to the Court of Appeal, but not on this point).
⁶   [2007] EWHC 2996 (QB).
⁷   See *Newman v Folkes* [2002] PIQR Q2 at Q31, para 51, but bear in mind that this was a decision
      made under the former edition of the Ogden Tables.

The multiplier for the claimant's residual earnings

[K203] In assessing the multiplier appropriate for the claimant's residual earnings, the following matters must be borne in mind:

- Disability status. It will be important to examine the degree to which the claimant's injuries really disable him in his working life, bearing in mind the nature of his employment. If the claimant is not very disabled in terms of the actual work he will be doing, the court may increase the reduction factor suggested by the Ogden Tables[1].
- Employment status. If a claimant could and should, but for his failure to mitigate, have been in alternative employment by the time of trial, then he should be regarded as employed for the purposes of the Ogden Tables and the starting point for the reduction factor[2]. A similar approach should prevail if a claimant is fit or will soon become fit for work (after any necessary rehabilitation and/or retraining), and will probably find employment soon after trial[3].
- It may be possible to argue for an adjustment to the reduction factor if there is a real prospect that the claimant will achieve promotion, or his level of earnings will increase, in the future; alternatively, this may be factored into the multiplicand(s).

¹   See *Conner v Bradman* [2007] EWHC 2789 (QB), and *Hunter v Ministry of Defence* [2007] NIQB
      43, in both of which cases the reduction factor adopted was mid-way between those suggested for a
      disabled person and an able-bodied person respectively. But cf *Leesmith v Evans* [2008] EWHC 134
      (QB), where the appropriate reduction factor for a disabled person was only increased marginally
      from 0.54 to 0.60.
²   See *Hunter v Ministry of Defence* [2007] NIQB 43.
³   See *McGhee v Diageo* [2008] CSOH 74 (a decision of Lord Malcolm in the Outer House of the
      Court of Session) where, after allowing for a period for rehabilitation, re-education and retraining,
      the court only allowed a modest lump-sum *Blamire* award on the grounds that, thereafter, the
      claimant would regain the same earning capacity as he would have had in any event, in sedentary
      employment in which his residual physical disabilities would have relatively less impact.

Contingencies other than mortality

[K204] The following contingencies and risk factors are of general applicability, and should be borne in mind when assessing the appropriateness of the reduction factor in each particular case, but the reader should bear in mind that the case law referred to below pre-dates the Ogden Tables (6th edn):

- Failing exams or training.
- Periods of unemployment (particularly in seasonal, manual or unskilled work where there is a high turnover of workforce or work)[1].
- The desire to 'have a break' or to go travelling.
- Redundancy.
- Marriage[2].

- Ill-health.
- Inability to cope with a physically demanding job.
- Non-tortious accidents and injuries (both domestic and, particularly, in employment or sport).
- Retiring early (particularly to be with an older partner who has already retired or where, financially, there is no longer any need to work)[3].
- High unemployment in the claimant's locality[4].
- Imprisonment[5].
- Choosing to work shorter hours (or in a less stressful position) in increasing age.

[1]   See eg *Vernon v Bosley* [1997] PIQR P255, where the Court of Appeal held that the claimant had established on the balance of probabilities that he would have sought alternative employment, but discounted the award of the trial judge by 20% to reflect the intervals between jobs and the difficulty he would find obtaining fresh jobs. Also see *Ved v Caress* (9 April 2001, unreported), QBD, where HHJ Chapman discounted the Ogden Table multiplier to allow for some breaks in employment and for maternity leave.

[2]   See eg *Harris v Harris* [1973] 1 Lloyd's Rep 445, CA.

[3]   In order to support this argument, it may be helpful to prove, using an employment consultant, that the majority of people within the claimant's industry retire earlier than the pleaded retirement age.

[4]   See eg *Hassall and Pether v Secretary of State for Social Security* [1995] 1 WLR 812, which was settled on the basis that the claimants would not have been able to find work even if they were fit to do it. See also *Brown v Berry* (14 October 1997, unreported), QBD, in which Mr Robert Seabrook QC sitting as a deputy judge of the High Court discounted the claim for future loss of earnings by 25% to take account of the high level of unemployment in the claimant's area and difficulties obtaining work in the building trade.

[5]   In *Meah v McCreamer* [1985] 1 All ER 367, it was held that the claimant's previous criminal tendencies, which would probably have resulted in his spending periods in prison, and his previous poor employment record could eliminate any continuing loss of earnings claim, when combined with the fact that the claimant would receive free board in prison.

[K205]   In order to prove the existence of the above contingencies and risks, it is important to obtain as much supporting evidence as possible. It is now of critical importance for a defendant to obtain as much information as possible about the claimant's (i) educational and vocational attainment, (ii) employment history (including, particularly in cases where the claimant has not settled employment, as long a history of employment and earnings as is possible), and (iii) medical history. A defendant faced with a significant claim for loss of earnings will usually want to obtain the claimant's medical, personnel and occupational health records; and income details (possibly from the Inland Revenue/HM Revenue and Customs if a longer period of pre-accident history is required). Additional information may also be gained from the claimant's former colleagues.

Pension loss multipliers

[K206]   The correct approach to adopt in fixing the multiplier will depend on the type of pension[1]. In the case of a money purchase scheme, the multiplier to adopt is the loss of earnings multiplier, discounted as appropriate, because any contributions are contingent upon employment and earnings, so the applicable contingencies other than death are the same as the contingencies in respect of earnings. In the case of a final salary scheme, the correct multiplier to adopt is the appropriate multiplier taken from Tables 15 to 26 of the Ogden Tables (6th edn), depending on the predicted retirement age. To that multiplier, however, one must then apply the *Auty* discount for contingencies other than mortality[2].

1   See further at paras **[K154]–[K158]**.
2   See further at paras **[K157]–[158]** for a fuller discussion of the *Auty* discount. Paragraph 30 of the Explanatory Notes to the Ogden Tables (6th edn) makes it clear that the discount factors do not apply to pension rights.

Care and domestic assistance multipliers

[K207] The scope for attacking future care and domestic assistance multipliers has been greatly reduced since the House of Lords' decision in *Wells v Wells*[1]. However, the following contingencies should be considered as possible reasons for reducing or rounding down the appropriate multiplier:

* Marriage[2].
* The chance that the claimant would have suffered the same or similar injuries in any event, giving rise to the same or a similar need for care[3].
* The chance that the claimant's condition will improve (particularly after planned treatment or surgery).
* The claimant's needs for care might reduce, eg once the claimant has retired and no longer requires a mentor at work or following withdrawal of support in the long term[4].
* The fact that the claimant's condition might deteriorate to such a point that he or she is taken into NHS long-term care[5].
* The fact that the claimant may have paid for someone to carry out his or her domestic chores later in life in any event[6].
* The fact that the claimant would not have been able to do the heavier domestic chores beyond a certain age in any event[7].
* The fact that the claimant may have moved to residential accommodation in any event, where there was a shared cleaner who carried out the domestic chores.

1   [1999] 1 AC 345. See further Chapter H, Future Expenses and Losses at paras **[H17]–[H24]**.
2   See eg *Vernon v Bosley* [1997] PIQR P255, where the multiplier for domestic assistance was reduced from 7 to 3.
3   *Heil v Rankin & MIB* [2000] PIQR Q16, CA.
4   *Hay v Konig & MIB* [2002] EWCA Civ 19.
5   *Mitchell v Mulholland (No 2)* [1972] 1 QB 65, CA. See also *Lamey v Wirral Health Authority* [1993] CLY 1437, in which the future care multiplier was scaled down from 18.5 to 18, in order to take account of the slight risk of prolonged hospitalisation due to injury, illness or terminal illness.
6   See eg *Ved v Caress* (9 April 2001, unreported), QBD, where HHJ Chapman held that the claimant, who worked full-time as a clinical psychologist, would have needed some help in the home and would have chosen to spend her income or part of her income in that way.
7   See eg *Smith v McCrae* [2003] EWCA Civ 505.

Aids and equipment multipliers

[K208] The correct multiplier to apply to the costs of aids and equipment aims to ensure that such aids are replaced when necessary, but not so often that there is any element of gain. This will heavily depend upon the evidence of an expert (such as an occupational therapist) regarding the recommended interval periods for the items claimed and the claimant's whole life multiplier taken from the Ogden Tables. The correct and more accurate method is to calculate the cumulative multiplier, by adding up the relevant periodic multipliers (from Ogden Table A5 adopting a discount rate of 2.5%: the method of calculation is set out in the Introductory Notes to Table A5) for the duration of the claimant's life expectancy, bearing in mind the frequency with which the item has to be replaced, but an alternative method often adopted by claimants is to calculate the loss by annualising the replacement costs – this is done by dividing the capital cost by the replacement period – and applying the life multiplier to that annual multiplicand. Which method is more advantageous to a defendant will depend on the circumstances. The smaller the cost of any particular item, and the shorter the replacement period, the less difference it will make. But where the item is expensive, and the replacement period longer, it is usually more advantageous to adopt the periodic multiplier. It is usually worth trying a number of different approaches in order to determine which method produces the most favourable result, at least in respect of the more expensive items[1]. In passing, it is important to remember that, whenever an item of equipment is claimed as an immediate cost and requires replacement annually, or alternatively an annual average has been calculated for the replacement of the item, the life multiplier should be reduced by one to take account of the fact that it is being claimed as an immediate item of expenditure cost and so will not be needed for the first year[2].

[1]   For a few worked examples, see further Chapter H, Future Expenses and Losses at paras **[H65]**–**[H73]**.
[2]   For an example of this in operation, see *Biesheuval v Birrell* [1999] PIQR Q40.

DIY, decorating, gardening, car maintenance multipliers

[K209]   The correct multiplier for DIY, decorating, gardening, window cleaning, car maintenance etc claims depends largely upon the claimant's evidence about what he or she says he or she would have done, and any supporting evidence from friends or family regarding the claimant's general level of fitness and inclination to do these tasks before he or she suffered the injuries.

[K210]   Often, it will be possible to argue that the multiplier for these claims should not be the whole life multiplier. This is because the court accepts that a person's capacity to undertake heavier domestic activities, such as DIY, deteriorates with age[1]. In *Wells v Wells*[2] the Court of Appeal applied a working life multiplier to age 65 to the claim for DIY. Much depends upon the nature and extent of the work the claimant did before the injuries and his or her intentions following retirement. It may be that the claimant could sustain a claim for DIY assistance until the age of 70 or 75, but this might not apply to certain physically demanding or hazardous jobs, such as clearing the guttering etc. Once the end date has been chosen, the correct multiplier to apply can then be obtained from using Table 28 of the Ogden Tables (6th edn) for a fixed term of years.

[1]   See eg *Smith v McCrae* [2003] EWCA Civ 505.
[2]   [1999] 1 AC 345. See also *Assinder v Griffin* [2001] All ER (D) 356 (May), in which HHJ Peter Clark allowed a claim for DIY and decorating of £1,250 per annum with a multiplier to age 65; and *Smith v East & North Hertfordshire Hospitals NHS Trust* [2008] EWHC 2234 (QB), in which claims

for DIY and gardening assistance were allowed to the age of 65. Although cf *Hassell v Abnoof & anor* (6 July 2001), QBD, Lawtel Document No AC0101866, where Gage J applied a full lifetime multiplier for a cleaner to provide domestic assistance.

[K211] Where there are numerous imponderables regarding this type of claim, it may be possible to dispense with the multiplier/multiplicand approach and simply award a modest lump sum[1].

1   See eg *Worrall v Powergen plc* [1999] PIQR Q103, in which a global sum of £4,000 was awarded for the loss of ability to carry out DIY.

Court of Protection multipliers

[K212] It should be noted that, since some of the Court of Protection's charges (especially as regards transaction fees) are proportionate to the size of the fund, over time the charges are likely to reduce in size as the fund is depleted. This may be taken into account by applying a discount to the multiplier, usually of between 25% and 50%.

(iv) Split Multipliers

[K213] Split multipliers are often used to separate various periods in the claimant's life, when he or she might be expected to earn more money or require more care because of deterioration in their condition. However, it is important to ensure that the multipliers are correctly split and apportioned because: (a) there is much more chance that a claimant will survive the early years rather than the later years; and (b) the discount for accelerated receipt must inevitably be greater for years which are further away in the future than those which are nearer. If this factor is not taken into account, the defendant may face a much larger claim because the multiplicand for the later years is generally greater than the multiplicand for the earlier years, whether the claim is for loss of earnings or for care. Worked examples of how to split multipliers in respect of variable future earnings or care costs are set out in the Explanatory Notes to the Ogden Tables (6th edn), at paragraphs 22 to 24.

(v) Inflation

[K214] It is trite law that no adjustment should be made to the multiplier to take account of inflation[1]. Now that the Lord Chancellor has set the discount rate at 2.5%, this effectively takes account of the problem of future inflation altogether[2].

1   *Cookson v Knowles* [1979] AC 556; *Lim Poh Choo v Camden and Islington Health Authority* [1980] AC 174; and *Auty v National Coal Board* [1985] 1 WLR 784.
2   See further Chapter H, Future Expenses and Losses at paras **[H25]–[H32]**.

(vi) Tax

[K215] The general presumption is that the tax rate will stay the same, and therefore no adjustment should be made to the multiplier[1]. It should be noted that the Ogden Tables assume that the injured claimant will pay a marginal rate of tax of 25%, and that this presumption may be displaced if either party can show that a different rate of tax is more appropriate. However, it is a difficult presumption to displace and a party – usually a claimant attempting to show that they will have to pay a higher rate of tax on a large award – faces an uphill struggle to persuade a court to adopt a different rate[2].

1   *Hodgson v Trapp* [1989] AC 807.
2   *Van Oudenhaven v Griffin Inns Ltd* [2000] 1 WLR 1413.

8   Interest

(i)   The Requirement to Plead

[K216]   Given that a claimant must plead that they are seeking interest if they wish to claim it[1], the presumption is that interest will not be awarded if it is not claimed in the claim form or particulars of claim. However, case law would suggest that the entitlement to interest is a remedy rather than a statutory right, and therefore need not be pleaded[2]. Furthermore, once classified as a remedy rather than a right, the CPR specifically allows the court to grant a remedy, even if that remedy is not specified in the claim form[3].

1   CPR, r 16.4(2).
2   *Riches v Westminster Bank* [1934] 2 All ER 725; *Jefford v Gee* [1970] 2 QB 130; *Maher and Maher v Groupama Grand Est* [2009] EWCA Civ 1191.
3   CPR, r 16.2(5).

(ii)   The Details of the Claim

[K217]   The claimant is obliged to set out the rate and period that is claimed where a claim is made for a specified sum of money. It is rare that claims for specified sums of money are made in personal injury actions, owing to the fact that a number of the heads of loss (not least PSLA) are, by their very nature, not capable of precise quantification and need to be assessed by the court. The eventual award is thus not certain, nor can it be presented as a claim for a definite liquidated sum.

(iii)   Loss/Expense Not Incurred Yet

[K218]   The claimant may not recover interest on items of expense or loss which have not yet been incurred[1]. Thus, no interest is payable on credit hire charges which have yet to be paid[2].

1   *Jefford v Gee* [1970] 2 QB 130, per Lord Denning MR at 147.
2   *Clark v Ardington Electrical Services & Helphire UK Ltd* [2001] EWCA Civ 585, per Aldous LJ at paras 157–162.

(iv)   Discretion

[K219]   Interest is awarded at the discretion of the court; however, there is a presumption that interest is to be awarded on compensation awarded for personal injuries[1], and a statutory requirement that interest be awarded in respect of general damages for PSLA[2].

1 *Davies v Inman* [1999] PIQR Q26.
2 *Wright v British Railways Board* [1983] 2 AC 773, HL.

(v) The Rate of Interest[1]

[K220] As regards general damages for PSLA, the appropriate rate of interest is 2% from the date of service of the claim form[2]. As regards special damages, the defendant should contend for interest to be awarded at half the special account rate[3] since the date of the accident but, if the majority of the losses are incurred closer to trial, the defendant should be ready to argue for a lesser rate. Inadvertently, some claimants may bind themselves to this approach by reason of their pleaded claim for interest which, in the absence of an abuse of process, the court is unable to circumvent[4].

1 For a full discussion of this topic, see Chapters E and G.
2 *Lawrence v Chief Constable of Staffordshire* [2000] PIQR Q349.
3 *Dexter v Courtaulds Ltd* [1984] 1 WLR 372.
4 *Headford v Bristol and District Health Authority* [1995] PIQR P180.

(vi) Interim Payments

[K221] Interim payments should be taken into account when calculating the award of interest on past losses and expenses; however, there is no set rule as to how this should be done[1]. A defendant should contend for interest to be credited back to him on each interim payment at the full rate from the date on which each payment was made.

1 *Bristow v Judd* [1993] PIQR Q117, in which the Court of Appeal declined to give general guidance on the correct method of calculation. See further Chapter G, Interest on Past Expenses and Losses at paras **[G15]–[G21]** for a detailed discussion of this topic and a worked example.
2 Langstaff J accepted this at para [177] of his judgment in *Warrilow v Norfolk and Norwich Hospitals NHS Trust* in [2006] EWHC 801 (QB); but cf *Massey v Tameside & Glossop Acute Services NHS Trust* [2007] EWHC 317 (QB), in which Teare J held that credit should be given at half the special account rate.

(vii) Voluntary Payments

[K222] In *Davies v Inman*[1] the Court of Appeal rejected the argument that the defendant should not be liable for interest on voluntary payments made by an employer, because the claimant had not been 'kept out of his money'. The interest paid to the claimant is to be on trust for the employer, which is similar to the position as regards a voluntary carer.

1 [1999] PIQR Q26.

(viii) State Benefits

[K223] Interest on the various heads of damages awarded is to be assessed prior to making any deduction for recoupable benefits[1], but a claimant must give credit to the defendant for any award of interest on heads of damage that have been extinguished by recoupable benefits under the Social Security (Recovery of Benefits) Act 1997[2].

[1]   *Wadey v Surrey County Council* [2000] 1 WLR 820.
[2]   *Griffiths v British Coal Corpn* [2001] EWCA Civ 336, [2001] 1 WLR 1493.

(ix)   Smith v Manchester Awards

[K224]   No interest is payable on damages for an award to reflect disadvantage on the open labour market, because it is a claim in order to reflect future loss of earning capacity[1].

[1]   *Clarke v Rotax Aircraft Equipment Ltd* [1975] 1 WLR 1570.

(x)   Delay[1]

[K225]   The court may diminish the rate or period of interest awarded where the claimant has been guilty of delay in prosecuting the claim[2]. The reduction applies equally to general and special damages[3]. Where there has been such delay, the payable interest should be limited up to the point when the case would have been heard but for the claimant's delay[4]. In *Birkett v Hayes*[5], Watkins LJ said[6]:

> '... Usually this period will run from the date of the writ to the date of trial, but the court may in its discretion abridge this period when it thinks it is just so to do. Far too often there is unjustifiable delay in bringing an action to trial. It is, in my view, wrong that interest should run during a time which can properly be called unjustifiable delay after the date of the [claim form]. During that time the [claimant] will have been kept out of the sum awarded to him by his own fault. The fact that the defendants have had the use of the sum during that time is no good reason for excusing that fault and allowing interest to run during that time ...'

Further, Morland J said in *Read v Harries (No 2)*[7]:

> 'In my judgment, insurers are entitled to expect to be able to close their books in respect of claims within a reasonable period of time, and they are prejudiced if they have to keep alive the outstanding claim, and inevitably it results in increased costs payable by them to their solicitors, which will not be recoverable from the [claimant].'

[1]   See further Chapter G, Interest on Past Expenses and Losses at para **[G29]**.
[2]   See *Nash v Southmead Health Authority* [1993] PIQR Q156, CA; *Read v Harries (No 2)* [1995] PIQR Q34; *Spittle v Bunney* [1988] 1 WLR 847; *Derby Resources AG v Blue Corinth Marine Co Ltd (No 2)* [1998] 2 Lloyd's Rep 425; and *Eagle v Chambers (No 2)* [2004] EWCA Civ 1033, in which interest for seven (out of 14) years since the accident was disallowed.
[3]   *Barry v Ablerex* [2000] PIQR Q263.
[4]   *Read v Harries (No 2)* [1995] PIQR Q34.
[5]   [1982] 1 WLR 816, CA.
[6]   At 825E–825F.
[7]   [1995] PIQR Q34 at Q35.

[K226]   Although each case will turn upon its own facts, it is likely that under the CPR the courts will be more willing to mark their disapproval of delay by reducing awards for interest[1].

[1]   See eg *Beahan v Stoneham* (19 January 2001, unreported), per Buckley J.

[K227] In order to support an application to limit the claimant's entitlement to interest, the defendant should set out any arguments relating to the delay (or more generally regarding the claimant's conduct) in the counter-schedule. Where appropriate, it would also be helpful to any such application if the defendant were able to point to specific references in the correspondence requesting that the claimant progressed his or her claim with due diligence. Of course, such an application may not find too much favour with the court, if the defendant is also guilty of delaying the progress of the claim!

9 Premature Issue of Proceedings

[K228] Where a claimant unnecessarily issues proceedings where liability is not contested, but the defendant has not yet had the chance properly to consider the medical evidence, the defendant may be successful in an application to recover the costs of the proceedings. In *Mongiardi v IBC Vehicles Ltd*[1] the defendant's insurers had admitted liability but the claimant issued proceedings without disclosing their medical evidence. Having considered the claimant's medical report, the defendant paid £3,699 into court. The claimant applied to accept the money outside the time period for acceptance. The Court of Appeal (consisting of Lord Woolf, Phillips LJ and Chadwick LJ) held that the claimant should pay to the defendant (i) the costs of and incidental to the preparation and service of the defence, and (ii) any costs incurred after the last date when the claimant could have accepted the payment into court.

---

[1]   Jointly reported with *Burrows v Vauxhall Motors Ltd* [1998] PIQR P48.

[K229] Paragraph 2.16 of the Personal Injury Pre-action Protocol reads as follows[1]:

' The parties should consider whether some form of alternative dispute resolution procedure would be more suitable than litigation….The Courts take the view that litigation should be a last resort, and that claims should not be issued prematurely when a settlement is still actively being explored. Parties are warned that if the protocol is not followed (including this paragraph) then the Court must have regard to such conduct when determining costs.'

---

[1]   See also para 2.11 of the Personal Injury Pre-Action Protocol, which recommends that a defendant be given three months to investigate and respond to a claim before proceedings are issued (unless limitation is a problem). This is mirrored by para 3.21 of the Pre-action Protocol for the Resolution of Clinical Disputes, which states that proceedings should not be issued until after three months from the letter of claim, unless there is a limitation problem and/or the patient's position needs to be protected by early issue.

[K230] In addition, para 2.22 of the Personal Injury Pre-action Protocol suggests that the parties may wish to carry out a 'stocktake' of the issues in dispute, and the evidence that the court is likely to need to decide those issues, before proceedings are started.

[K231] Since the introduction of the CPR, the court has a much wider discretion regarding costs. Under CPR, Pt 44 the court must take into account all the circumstances of the case, including the conduct of the parties[1]. Although the application of the

Personal Injury Pre-action Protocol and the wide use of pre-action Part 36 offers have greatly reduced the extent of the problem regarding premature issue of proceedings, it is clear that the arguments raised in *Mongiardi v IBC Vehicles Ltd*[2] under the old law are just as valid under the CPR.

¹   CPR, r 44.3(4)(a). This includes any breaches of relevant pre-action protocols.
²   Jointly reported with *Burrows v Vauxhall Motors Ltd* [1998] PIQR P48.

10   Making Concessions

[K232]   Whilst reasonable concessions should be made in a counter-schedule, save possibly where the defendant's case is that the claim is fraudulent or deliberately exaggerated, it is important that any such concessions have been carefully thought through, since it may be difficult for the defendant to resile from them at a later date. In *Parkhouse v North Devon Healthcare NHS Trust*[1] the defendant had agreed the claimant's claim for past gratuitous care without any discount. At trial, the defendant sought to withdraw from this agreement in order to argue that a 25% discount should be made against the claim in order to reflect the 'gratuitous element'[2]. This application was refused. Gage J said:

> 'In my judgment there should be no discount from the sum claimed and agreed by the defendant in its counter schedule. The whole purpose of such schedules is to define the issues and limit their scope. Where an admission is made by reason of wrong information provided by the other party, clearly it would not be proper to hold the parties to such an agreement, but where, as here, agreement was made on the basis of full information, it would defeat the object of providing schedules and counter schedules to allow the admission to be withdrawn.'

¹   [2002] Lloyd's Rep Med 100.
²   See further Chapter F, Past Expenses and Losses at paras **[F104]–[F110]**.

[K233]   Further, care should be taken before suggesting any figures under individual heads of loss. Such figures may be seen as tantamount to making an offer. Again, it may be difficult for the defendant to resile from these figures at a later date. For example, in *Gleed v Set Scaffolding*[1] the claimant advanced a claim in respect of the loss of earnings from playing in a jazz band (in addition to his loss of earnings as a scaffolder). The defendant had allowed £10,000 for this element of the claim in its counter-schedule. The trial judge awarded the claimant £10,000 offered under this head, notwithstanding the fact that she was not satisfied that the claimant had enjoyed any regular income from playing in jazz bands or that his income had materially exceeded his expenses.

¹   (16 October 2001, unreported), QBD. See also *Cottrell v Redbridge Healthcare NHS Trust* (2001) 61 BMLR 72.

L   Fatal Accident Claims

I   Introduction

[L1]   This chapter covers actions that arise following a death caused by some tortious act or omission. In some cases, death may be instantaneous whereas in others, notably asbestos related claims, it may follow decades after the act or omission that forms the basis of the claim.

[L2]   Claims arising out of a person's death are different from ordinary personal injury claims. The entitlement to claim is statutory, rather than based upon the common law. Whilst there are some overlapping principles with the assessment of damages in personal injury claims, in a fatal accident case the quantification of loss depends largely upon the relevant statutory provisions and the case law interpreting those provisions.

[L3]   The reader is referred to Chapter M with regard to deciding how best to present claims for the dying. Comparative illustrations are given, showing the differences in value between claims brought whilst still living and claims brought after death. It is crucial to keep in mind that the right to bring a fatal accident claim will be lost by final determination of the claim during the deceased's lifetime, even if that claim did not include a claim for the lost years[1], and even if there were concurrent tortfeasors, one of whom had not previously been pursued[2]. Discontinuance after death will only end the estate's claim[3], and so the dependency claim could still be pursued, unless expressly abandoned on discontinuance. Likewise, where a claim is brought by a living claimant who subsequently dies before the claim is concluded, his or her personal representatives and dependants may be substituted as claimants and continue the claim on behalf of the claimant's estate and in respect of their own losses[4]. In contrast, where the claim concluded post death was a preceding unrelated tort, the value of which is reduced by the second tort which causes the death, the lost differential can be claimed by the estate[5]. In addition, Chapter Q contains two example precedents for schedules airing out of death: one using the traditional approach to the calculation of the multiplier, and the other using the approach suggested by the Law Commission and the 4th and subsequent editions of the Ogden Tables (see paras **[L51]–[L65]** below).

---

[1]   *Read v Great Eastern Railway Co* (1867–68) LR 3 QB 555; *Reader & others v Molesworth Bright Clegg Sols* [2007] EWCA Civ 169; and *Thomson v Arnold* TL 14/8/2007; [2008] PIQR P1; [2008] LS Law Medical 78.

[2]   *Jameson v Central Electricity Generating Board* [2000] 1 AC 455.

[3]   *Reader & Others v Molesworths Bright Clegg Solicitors* [2007] EWCA Civ 169, [2007] 1 WLR 1082.

4   This is what happened in *Corr v IBC Vehicles Ltd* [2008] 1 AC 884.
5   *Singh v Aitken* [1998] PIQR Q37.

2   Types of Fatal Accident Claim: an Overview

(i)   Statutory Basis

[L4]   There are two types of fatal accident claim: the estate's claim on behalf of the deceased under the Law Reform (Miscellaneous Provisions) Act 1934 (LR(MP) A 1934), as amended by the Administration of Justice Act 1982; and a claim on behalf of the dependants of the deceased brought in their own right under the Fatal Accidents Act 1976 (FAA 1976), as amended by the Administration of Justice Act 1982[1]. There is also a third type of claim which, although not strictly speaking a fatal accident claim, arises out of a negligent stillbirth. In the following paragraphs, a brief overview of the three different types of claim is given, before the two types of pure fatal accident claim are discussed in more detail below.

> 1   Note that claims under each statute are not mutually exclusive, therefore claims are usually brought both on behalf of the deceased's estate under the LR(MP)A 1934 and on behalf of the deceased's dependants and relatives under FAA 1976.

(ii)   The Estate's Claim on Behalf of the Deceased

[L5]   Under LR(MP)A 1934, the deceased's estate has a claim for the damages that could otherwise have been claimed personally by the deceased. All causes of action (apart from defamation) survive the death of any person for the benefit of his or her estate[1]. Heads of loss may include:

- General damages for pre-death pain, suffering and loss of amenity.
- Pre-death special damages, ie past losses and expenses up to the date of death.
- Funeral expenses, if paid by the estate.

> 1   LR(MP)A 1934, s 1(1).

(iii)   The Relatives and Dependants' Claim in Their Own Right

[L6]   Under FAA 1976, s 1(1), the dependants may claim for their loss of dependency in circumstances where the deceased would have been able to bring a claim for damages for personal injury if the deceased had not died. By virtue of s 2(3), only one action may be brought in respect of the same subject matter. The claim is usually brought by the executor(s) or administrator(s) of the deceased's estate in conjunction with the LR(MP)A 1934 claim; but, if no such action is brought within six months of the death, a claim may be brought by and in the name of all or any of the dependants[1].

> 1   FAA 1976, s 2(2).

The relatives' claim

[L7] A limited and defined class of relatives can claim for a 'bereavement award', the amount of which is fixed by statute. There may also be a claim for damages for post-traumatic stress disorder or psychiatric injury, if the relative was either a primary victim or within the rules limiting claims for secondary victims, but this will be a personal claim to which the principles set out in Chapter D of this book apply[1].

1   It is possible to bring a claim for psychiatric injury at the same time as a claim under FAA 1976. However, care should be taken to bring all the claims before the court at the same time, in order to avoid the problems associated with the rule in *Henderson v Henderson* [1843] 3 Hare 100. See further *Toth v Ledger* (21 December 2000, CA), Lawtel Document No C840080.

The dependants' claim

[L8] Dependants may claim, providing they had a reasonable expectation of (i) a pecuniary benefit, (ii) arising from the dependent family relationship, and (iii) which would be derived from the continuance of life[1].

1   See further below. For a practical example showing how these criteria are applied to a particular head of loss, see *Batt v Highgate Private Hospital* [2005] PIQR Q1.

[L9] Claims brought on behalf of dependants may include the following heads of damage:

- Loss of financial support.
- Loss of other support and services (eg care, housekeeping etc).
- Funeral and other expenses, if paid for by the dependants.

(iv)   Summary Table of Main Types of Claim

[L10] The main types of claim under each statute are summarised in the following table:

LAW REFORM MISCELLANEOUS PROVISIONS ACT 1934 (AS AMENDED)	FATAL ACCIDENTS ACT 1976 (AS AMENDED)
(a) Pain, suffering and loss of amenity (from the date of injury up to the date of death)	(a) Funeral expenses[1]
	(b) Bereavement award – £11,800 (for causes of action accruing on or after 1 January 2008[2] but only for people who fall into categories listed in FAA 1976, s 1A(2))
(b) Special damages (from the date of injury up to the date of death):	
• Damage to clothing and possessions	(c) Past and future dependency on the deceased's earnings or income (NB including any promotions or career advancement opportunities that the deceased might have benefited from and any fringe benefits such as car allowance, private medical care etc)
• Loss of earnings	
• Medical expenses and treatment	
• Care (whether professional or gratuitous and whether provided by the deceased or needed by the deceased post-injury but pre-death)	
• Travelling expenses	(d) Dependency on gifts or luxury items (eg wedding money, birthday and Christmas presents)
(c) Funeral expenses[1]	(e) Past and future pension dependency
(d) Probate fees	(f) Past and future loss of services, eg:
(e) Miscellaneous one-off losses to the estate	• Child minding
(f) Interest on past expenses and losses	• Domestic chores
	• Bookkeeping and finances
	• Painting and decorating
	• Home maintenance
	• DIY
	• Gardening
	• Car servicing/valeting
	• Looking after pets/animals eg dog-walking, mucking out horses etc
	(g) Interest on past expenses and losses

---

[1]　Funeral expenses may be claimed under either statute; however, they are discussed further below under the estate's claim.

[2]　The award had been fixed at £10,000 since 1 April 2002 but, in the Ministry of Justice consultation on the Law of Damages of 4 April 2007, it was stated that the Government intended to increase these awards, by RPI up-rating, every three years. This point is repeated in the consultation (CP53/09) on the Civil Law Reform Bill.

(v)　A Further 'Fatal' Accident Claim

[L11]　One type of claim that may be brought is that in the case of a stillbirth caused by the tortfeasor. However, this is not strictly speaking a fatal accident, as the foetus is not considered legally to have lived, and the damages are related to the associated injury to the mother[1]. Such an action was considered in *Bagley v North Herts Health Authority*[2] by Simon Brown J, who stated:

> 'The hospital's negligence in the present case did not of course kill a live child; rather it caused the child to be born dead. That critical distinction here precludes any claim under the statute.'

Even though he disallowed a fatal accident claim, he then went on to consider three recoverable heads of damage:

* The loss of satisfaction of the mother bringing her pregnancy to a successful conclusion.
* The loss associated with the physical loss of the child.
* Damages for the physical illness brought on the claimant by her grave misfortune[3].

---

[1]   In *Kelly v Kelly* [1997] 2 FLR 822, it was held that there was no authority in existence that gave a foetus the status of legally living. Any pre-natal injuries to a baby are only actionable once the child is born alive.

[2]   (1986) 136 NLJ 1014.

[3]   See *Maria Davies v West Lancashire NHS Trust* [1998] 49 P&MILL vol 14 No 7. See also *Walters v North Glamorgan NHS Trust* [2002] EWCA Civ 1792.

3   The Estate's Claim on Behalf of the Deceased Under the Law Reform (Miscellaneous Provisions) Act 1934

[L12]   Section 1(1) of LR(MP)A 1934 provides as follows:

> 'Subject to the provisions of this section on the death of any person after the commencement of this Act all causes of action subsisting against or vested in him shall survive against, or, as the case may be, for the benefit of, his estate.'

[L13]   Certain claims that were deemed as entirely personal in nature were exempt[1]. However, the actions that may follow a tortious accident[2] are not exempt, and so a claim for the diminished value of a personal injury claim may be brought[3]. The claim, however, can be brought only by executors or administrators for the beneficiaries of the deceased estate. In short, the LR(MP)A 1934 allows the estate to act as the deceased 'as if' there had been no death. Therefore, aside from the exception of funeral expenses, in effect the estate steps into the shoes of the deceased, and can only claim for the losses that the deceased could have claimed for had he or she survived[4].

---

[1]   For example, libel and slander.

[2]   Including acts of clinical negligence.

[3]   This includes any prospective (uncompromised) claims for personal injury that existed at the time of the deceased's death: see eg *Singh v Aitken* [1998] PIQR Q37. In this case, it was held that the dependants were able to claim the reduction in the value of a personal injury claim arising out of the defendant's second and consecutive tort. HHJ Whitburn QC held that the defendants must take the victim as they find him and if, but for the defendants' negligence, the deceased would have been entitled to a much larger award of damages against the first tortfeasor, a proportion of which would have been spent on the dependants, the defendants must account to the dependants for that loss.

[4]   See further *McGregor on Damages* (18th edn), para 36-132.

(i) Pain, Suffering and Loss of Amenity

[L14] The estate can commence or continue a claim for pain, suffering and loss of amenity which the deceased endured before death. Following the Administration of Justice Act 1982, it is no longer possible to claim any damages for the deceased's loss of expectation of life[1]. Also, damages for loss of earnings in respect of the 'lost years' are no longer recoverable by the estate[2]. This is because similar losses can be claimed under FAA 1976, and so to allow a lost years claim as well would amount to double recovery[3].

1   LR(MP)A 1934, s 1(1)(b). See further Chapter I.
2   Cf the position where someone who is alive has a reduced life expectancy by reason of injury. In such a case, he or she has a claim for his or her losses during the years he or she was due to – but post injury will not – survive. See further Chapter I.
3   See further para **[I2]**, including the comments of several eminent judges and jurisprudential commentators to the effect that it would be preferable to prohibit lost years claims altogether, and instead allow a second action after the eventual death for the post-death earnings dependency.

[L15] Although the court will not award damages for the loss of expectation of life, it will still consider the deceased's awareness of a shortened life in the award for pain and suffering recoverable by the estate. A relevant factor is, therefore, the time which elapses between the injury suffered by the deceased and his or her eventual death. If the period is lengthy, considerable weight may be attached[1]. If short, then a smaller sum is appropriate. As in a living claimant's claim, no damages are awarded for pain and suffering, as opposed to loss of amenity[2], if the claimant is unconscious.

1   For instance, a general damages award of £72,000 was made in *Beesley v New Century Group* [2008] EWHC 3033 (QB). The deceased, who was 62 at death, underwent three cycles of chemotherapy and was in extreme pain for a period of 17 months, and was in need of continual care and diamorphine infusions before his death.
2   In *Doleman v Deakin* (Kemp and Kemp A5-005, January 1990), the Court of Appeal upheld an award of £1,500 for loss of amenity in circumstances where the deceased was unconscious for a period of six weeks until his death (current value about £2,650).

[L16] In *Hicks v Chief Constable of South Yorkshire Police*[1] (a case arising out of the Hillsborough disaster), it was held by the House of Lords that no damages would be recoverable where the deceased suffered for a matter of seconds before unconsciousness and, ultimately, death occurred. No actionable loss could be proved, as the small period of suffering was considered to be part and parcel of the actual death.

[L17] Further, fear of the impending death could not be considered as a separate head external to any injuries being suffered, since[2]:

'Fear of impending death felt by a victim of a fatal injury before that injury is inflicted, cannot, by itself, give rise to a cause of action which survives for the benefit of the victim's estate.'

1   [1992] 2 All ER 65.
2   Per Lord Bridge at 69e.

(ii) Deceased's Pre-death Loss of Earnings

[L18] The estate cannot claim loss of future earnings (as stated earlier). However, there can be a claim for the loss of earnings sustained by the deceased between injury and death. This award will be on a net basis after the relevant deductions generally associated with loss of earnings[1].

[1]   See Chapter F.

(iii) Loss of Expectation of Future Capital

[L19]   The estate can claim some lost future capital that the deceased would have received. For example, if a deceased who died at the age of 10 was to receive the capital held under a trust for his benefit when he reached the age of 18, such a loss is recoverable. It is subject to the appropriate discount due to accelerated receipt[1].

[1]   See *Gammell v Wilson* [1982] AC 27.

(iv) Damage to Clothing and Property

[L20]   If there was damage to the deceased's property in the accident, then the claim for special damages relating to this survives. The quantum remains the same as it would have been if the victim had survived (ie the cost of repair or the value if beyond economical repair).

(v) Travel Expenses

[L21]   Travel expenses incurred by the deceased before death will be recoverable. Travel expenses incurred by the deceased's family or friends providing gratuitous care will be recoverable, as long as three conditions are met:[1]

*   the services rendered were reasonably necessary as a consequence of the tort;
*   the out-of-pocket expenses of the friend or family member who rendered these services are reasonable, bearing in mind all the circumstances, including whether expenses would have been incurred had the friend or friends not assisted; and
*   the claimant undertakes to pay the sum awarded to the friend or friends[2].

[1]   *Schneider v Eisovitch* [1960] 2 QB 430.
[2]   This may be unnecessary now, since the decision in *Hunt v Severs* [1994] 2 AC 350, the principle of which is that, where expense in time or money by third parties is recoverable by a claimant, it is to be recoverable by a claimant, and it is to be held on trust for them by the claimant. There is no reason why this principle should not bind an estate as it does a living claimant. However, in the recent Ministry of Justice consultation paper and draft Civil Law Reform Bill, there is a proposal that the trust mechanism in gratuitous care cases be replaced by a personal legal obligation to account – it is unclear whether this is also to apply to other heads of loss, such as travel expenses.

[L22]   Travel expenses incurred by friends or family will be disallowed to the extent that they would have been incurred in any event maintaining social/family contact[1].

[1]   *Bordin v St Mary's NHS Trust* [2000] Lloyd's Rep Med 287.

(vi) Medical Expenses

[L23]   Any reasonable expenses incurred by the deceased prior to death will be recoverable in the normal way. It may be the case that some judges would be more receptive to claims for holistic therapies (particularly those aimed at pain relief) for a claimant who knew he was dying, than they might be for a living claimant[1]. Evidence (such as a witness statement, pain diary and/or video testimony) that the deceased believed them to be working would be helpful.

[1]   See further para **[F43]** regarding claims for alternative therapies.

(vii)   Care

[L24]   Likewise, the estate may make a claim to recover the pre-death costs of care, either paid or unpaid. Not only does this cover the claim for care that the deceased required, but also care that he provided to others[1], potentially subject to a notional discount for the gratuitous element, as applies in personal injury claims.

[1]   *Devoy v William Doxford & Sons Ltd* [2009] EWHC 1598 (QB), where the deceased's extensive past care for his wife, who had Parkinson's disease, was allowed, less a 25% deduction for the gratuitous element (see para 63).

(viii)   Funeral Expenses

[L25]   Under LR(MP)A 1934, s 1(2)(c) the funeral expenses may be recoverable by the estate. In some cases, there may be an advantage in the estate recovering rather than a dependant: that is the estate's claim will not be restricted by any contributory negligence on the part of the dependant[1]. In contrast, even where the death is predicted to occur in the near future, the common law does not allow for the recovery of funeral expenses by a live claimant.[2] This is a further example of the limitations of a 'lost years' claim and the potential monetary advantage to the action being brought post death. Against this must be balanced the understandable desire, in many cases, for the claimant to resolve the matter during his own lifetime. It is deeply unsatisfactory that the law forces fatally injured claimants into making such a decision.

[1]   See *Mulholland v McCrea* [1961] NI 135 (Northern Ireland CA).
[2]   *Watson v Cakebread & Robey Ltd* [2009] EWHC 1695 (QB).

[L26]   The expenses claimed must be 'reasonable in all the circumstances'. The relevant circumstances will include the deceased's station in life and his or her cultural origin[1]. What is reasonable will vary from case to case. In *Schneider v Eisovitch*[2], it was held that the expenses of friends who travelled to France to arrange for the return of the body were reasonable. Paull J ruled that the services provided by the friends had to be necessary and, as the expenses would have occurred in any event, they were reasonable. Other claims accepted as reasonable include the cost of a tombstone[3], a Buddhist renaming ceremony for the dead and payments for attendance of Buddhist monks[4], a reception[5] and embalming[6]. However, claims that have failed include the expenses for the cost of a wake[7], the cost of mourning clothes[8] and the cost of a monument[9].

[1]   *Quainoo v Brent & Harrow AHA* (1982) 132 NLJ 1100, an extreme case in which the deceased was a member of the Ghanaian Royal Family. See also *St George v Turner* (10 May 2003, unreported), Ch D, an exceptional case in which damages were recovered for a family Buddhist altar and fittings;

funeral costs; the cost of a Buddhist renaming ceremony for the dead; payments for attendance by Buddhist monks; a gravestone and works; a memorial day reception; and an anniversary reception.

2   [1960] 2 QB 430.

3   *Goldstein v Salvation Army Assurance Society* [1917] 2 KB 291.

4   *St George v Turner* (10 May 2003, unreported), Ch D. Note this decision has been criticised by *McGregor on Damages*, 18th Edition (2003), para 36-133.

5   *Sally Ann Smith v 'Marchioness'/'Bowbelle'* (27 January 1993), noted in [1993] NLJR 813. A claimant cannot ignore the social obligation to provide some refreshments to guests. Social decencies must be observed, and the £400 spent was recovered. See also *St George v Turner* (10 May 2003, unreported), Ch D, although cf *Gammell v Wilson* [1982] AC 27, CA.

6   *Hart v Griffiths Jones* [1948] 2 All ER 729.

7   *Quainoo v Brent & Harrow AHA* (1982) 132 NLJ 1100. See also *Gammell v Wilson* [1982] AC 27, CA, *and Jones v Royal Devon & Exeter NHS Foundation Trust* [2008] EWHC 558 (QB). In *Williams v Welsh Ambulance Services NHS Trust* [2008] EWCA Civ 81, LTL 15/2/2008, Hickinbottom HHJ indicated that, left to his own devices, he may well have allowed the costs of the wake, but in the absence of any supportive authorities in the 30 years since *Gammell* he would, with some reluctance, follow what he saw as the direction of the common law to disallow them. It is a shame that this point does not feature in the appeal of this case (as referred to below).

8   *Gammell v Wilson* (at first instance).

9   The Court of Appeal in *Gammell v Wilson* [1982] AC 27 approved the approach 'that there is a distinction between a headstone finishing off, describing and marking the grave, which is part of the funeral expense, and a memorial, which is not'.

(ix)   Probate Fees

[L27]   Since the sole statutory exception is for funeral expenses, the jurisprudential basis for claiming probate fees is not entirely clear. However, when there are modest sums involved, defendants will usually agree this head of loss, and they have been recovered in a number of cases[1]. It can be anticipated that, where there were substantial probate fees of a large estate[2], there may be a more substantial dispute and, consequently, a fully reasoned judgment may then follow. Further, where letters of administration and probate expenses have been incurred which would not otherwise have been necessary, it is common practice and widely recognised that these may be claimed as a cost of litigation at the end of the case[3].

1   See eg *Betney v Rowlands and Mallard* [1992] CLY 1786 (also reported in Kemp & Kemp at O3-030), where reference is made to the agreement of 'funeral expenses, probate etc'.

2   Note, in the £5 million settlement of *Paton v MOD*, LTLPI 13/3/2006, the claimant's solicitors estimated breakdown included £18,000 for the combination of funeral, probate and miscellaneous expenses.

3   There is an analogy here with the costs of representation at an inquest, which are also recoverable: *Stewart v Medway NHS Trust* (6 April 2004, unreported), Master O'Hare; *Gadd (deceased) v Milton Keynes NHS Trust* (13 May 2004, unreported), Master Gordon-Saker; and *Roach v Home Office* [2009] 3 All ER 510.

(x)   State Benefits

[L28]   As the claim for damages survives, so does the benefit recoupment. Any benefits paid to the deceased before death are recovered as per the recoupment scheme[1].

1   For a detailed discussion of this topic, see Chapter J.

(xi)   Miscellaneous One-off Expenses/Losses

[L29]   Occasionally, the deceased's estate will suffer some kind of loss linked to the deceased's death which does not fall into the above categories, but which may still be recoverable. For example, it may be that, by reason of the deceased's early death, the estate is exposed to an additional tax liability[1] or there was a missed opportunity to delay a tax liability[2], or perhaps even the acceleration of payment of tax[3]. Further, where the deceased's death results from a negligent operation performed on a private basis, it might be possible to recover the wasted fee in a claim for breach of contract[4].

[1]   See eg *Davies v Whiteways Cyder Co Ltd* [1975] QB 262, in which the dependants were able to claim for the additional estate duty (IHT) they had to pay on gifts from the deceased as a result of the deceased being killed less than seven years after the gifts were made, less a notional deduction of £500 for the remote chance that the deceased may not have survived the seven-year period for other reasons. It should be noted that this decision pre-dated the FAA 1976 and, whilst it is logical, logic does not always prevail in fatal accident claims and it is uncertain whether it would still be followed. There are no reported decisions in which the entire IHT liability to the estate has been recovered.

[2]   This potential head of loss was discussed in *Farmer & anor v Rolls Royce Industrial Power (India) Ltd* (26 February 2003), Lawtel Document No AC0105047 and AM0200488. In principle, it was accepted that such a CGT liability could be claimed by the estate but, on the facts of the case, the judge said he allowed for the claimed deferral in liability for capital gains tax when calculating the base capital figure.

[3]   The authors are unaware of any decision relating to the loss caused by early payment of IHT, with credit given for the later payment that would have been made at the date of the deceased's life expectancy had it not been for the accident. However, based on the above two cases, the point would appear to be arguable and, if the period of advancement of death was several decades and the sum on which IHT accrued substantial, then the acceleration claim could be sizeable. The likely counter-argument is that the claim is too speculative and the benefit (later payment of IHT) is not one they have suffered at the time of the death of the deceased. The claim would be further complicated if the deceased's life expectancy were longer than that of the dependants.

[4]   A similar claim failed in *Batt v Highgate Private Hospital* [2005] PIQR Q1, but it was brought in tort against the surgeon (the contract having been made between the deceased and the hospital). It was held that the cost of the operation did not flow from the negligence of the defendant surgeon, but from the promise of the deceased to pay the hospital for undertaking the surgical procedure. It was noted that the position may have been different in a claim brought for breach of contract against the hospital.

4   Claims Made by Relatives for Bereavement Awards Under the Fatal Accidents Act 1976

[L30]   A claim may be made by a limited list of relatives for their 'bereavement' suffered due to the death. A basic condition imposed by FAA 1976, s 1(1) is that the deceased must have been entitled to maintain an action in respect of the wrongful act of the defendant, had death not occurred.

[L31]   A bereavement award is an oddity in the law of damages. The fundamental principle in personal injury claims is that the claimant should be compensated for his or her loss. Therefore, a claimant needs to prove the loss, and an attempt to quantify it must be made. However, bereavement awards are subject to no such condition. Once the relative has proved he or she is within the specified class of claimant, and that the defendant is liable, then an award is made. There is no need to prove any actual loss suffered by the death of the relative; the court assumes certain people will inevitably be adversely affected by the death of a close relative. There is no right to seek to argue for any additional or higher sum in the event of extreme suffering[1]. This may seem an arbitrary approach to awarding damages, but the alternative has long been considered to be against public policy. If a judge had to assess damages based on the extent of loss suffered by the relative, then the bereaved claimant would have to give evidence of close ties etc and be cross-examined about it, which may be distressing[2].

[1]   Although it is not uncommon for sums to be recovered on an amicable basis, to fund counselling or other therapies for the bereaved.
[2]   Such an approach can be seen in the application of *Alcock v Chief Constable of South Yorkshire Police* [1992] 1 AC 310 in which, to qualify as a 'secondary' victim for psychiatric injury, the claimant must have sufficient 'close ties' with the 'primary' victim.

[L32]   Section 1A(2) of FAA 1976 provides that a claim for damages for bereavement shall only be for the benefit:

(a)   of the wife, husband or civil partner[1] of the deceased; and
(b)   where the deceased was a minor who was never married or a civil partner
    (i)   of his parents, if he or she was legitimate; and
    (ii)   of his mother, if he or she was illegitimate.

The restrictive nature of the list ultimately means a range of people, whom the general public would surely consider to be bereaved on a person's death, are excluded from claiming. The most notable absence is that of a child who loses one or both parents but is clearly not covered by the Act. These restrictions may arguably fall foul of the European Convention on Human Rights, Articles 6 (access to justice) and 8 (family life). Consequently, notwithstanding the clear limitations of the statute, claims are frequently advanced and settled for claimants who fall outside the strict criteria. In recognition of this issue, the Ministry of Justice sought views on this issue in their consultation on the Law of Damages in 2007. In their response published in 2009[2], they stated an intention to widen the class of beneficiaries of bereavement damages to include:

(a)   children under 18 on the death of a parent (and, if there is more than one child, for each to receive a payment of £5,900);
(b)   cohabitants of at least two years' duration; and
(c)   unmarried fathers with parental responsibility.

The draft Civil Law Reform Bill and accompanying consultation was published by the Ministry of Justice on 15 December 2009 but, with an impending election at the time of writing, whether and when this Bill will be passed is unclear.

[1]   As introduced by Civil Partnership Act 2004, s 83.
[2]   Ministry of Justice 'The Law of Damages – Response to consultation CP(R) 907', 1 July 2009.

[L33]   The FAA 1976 list restricts the claims to a current spouse or civil partner of the deceased, and therefore excludes any former spouse or civil partner from claiming. A person who, although not married to the deceased, was living in the same household with the deceased as his or her husband or wife[1] is also currently excluded from the FAA 1976 list. This restriction applies, no matter how long the relationship has been in place. As referred to above, it is now Government policy to extend the list to cohabitants of at least two years' duration. In the meantime, many such claims will no doubt be advanced and settled on human rights grounds.

[1]   Examples of cases where a settlement was achieved and court approved, including a bereavement award, on HRA grounds, to a co-habitant, include *Chivers v Metcalfe* [2005] CLY 3237; *W v Johnson* LTLPI 2/11/2006; and *W (Widower & Executor of the Estate of X, Deceased) v Oxford Radcliffe Hospitals NHS Trust*, Lawtel 8/6/07.

[L34]   FAA 1976 makes a distinction based on the legitimacy of the child. Unlike dependency, in which a reputed father of an illegitimate child is included[1], only the mother can claim for bereavement of an illegitimate child. As referred to above, the Government intends to pass legislation to extend the class to unmarried fathers with parental responsibility. The wording of FAA 1976 excludes adoptive parents or those bringing the child up as their own (eg grandparents). The Ministry of Justice response to the consultation on the Law of Damages recorded that, whilst three-quarters of the responses that they received were in favour of including step-parents and others acting as parents in the class of those eligible for a bereavement damages award, they were concerned that such a change would lead to disputes. Consequently, it appears that they will continue to be excluded. Whether this is contrary to the Human Rights Act is clearly arguable.

[1]   See at paras **[L37]**–**[L40]** regarding the entitlement to claim for dependency under FAA 1976, s 1(3)–(5) and a number of cases allowing dependency claims beyond the strict statutory list.

[L35]   FAA 1976 requires the child to be a minor and, therefore, strict application leads to results such as in *Doleman v Deakin*[1]. In this case, the claimant's son had died due to the negligence of the defendant. The son was unmarried but died less than a month after his eighteenth birthday. Therefore, the claim failed. As can be seen from the above, FAA 1976 is strictly applied[2]. The consultation on the Law of Damages considered an extension of the age of the deceased child, but the Ministry of Justice response was in favour of retaining the limitation that bereavement awards would not be available to the parents in the event that the deceased child was 18 or older, and the subsequent draft Civil Law Reform Bill, published on 15 December 2009, contains no proposed changes on this point.

[1]   (1990) Times, 30 January, CA.
[2]   See also *Martin v Grey* (1999) P&MILL vol 15(1).

[L36]   As stated earlier, the award is made as of right to the qualifying relatives without proof of loss. The award is a set figure prescribed in FAA 1976, s 1A(3). The Administration of Justice Act 1982 provided that the figure should be a fixed sum of £3,500. However, the Lord Chancellor is given the power to vary the conventional figure by statutory instrument[1]. This power was invoked by the then Lord Chancellor, in 1990, who set the award at £7,500 in respect of deaths occurring on or after 1 April 1991[2]. The applicable award was increased to £10,000 for deaths arising on or after 1 April 2002[3]. It was increased again, with effect from 1 January 2008, to £11,800[4], with reference to the Ministry of Justice consultation on the Law of Damages of 4 May 2007, which stated that the Government intended from then on to increase these awards, by RPI up-rating, every three years[5].

[1]   FAA 1976, s 1A(5).

2   Damages for Bereavement (Variation of Sum) (England and Wales) Order 1990, SI 1990/2575.

3   Damages for Bereavement (Variation of Sum) (England and Wales) Order 2002, SI 2002/644.

4   Damages for Bereavement (Variation of Sum) (England and Wales) Order 2007, SI 2007/3489.

5   This commitment was reiterated on 15 December 2009 in the consultation paper (CP/53) accompanying the draft Civil Law Reform Bill.

[L37] The claim for bereavement is a one-off payment. However, if there is only one defendant in an action, (s)he must pay the whole sum even if only held partially liable for death[1]. Interest on a bereavement award is calculated from the actual date of death[2] and is recoverable at the full special account rate[3]. Where there is a claim by two parents for the loss of a minor child, the award is split between them. The draft Civil Law Reform Bill proposes to extend bereavement awards to minor children who lose a parent, and indicates that, where there is more than one child, each child would receive an award at half the current full rate[4]. Accordingly, in a large family, this will add to the defendant's liability. For instance, if both parents were killed leaving four minor children, then the children would each be eligible for £5,900 per parent, a total of £47,200. This is, of course, still a very modest sum when compared to general damages in personal injury claims. It remains the case that, in England and Wales, it is cheaper to kill than to maim.

1   *Griffith v British Coal Corporation* [1999] P&MILL vol 15(1).

2   Not the date of any accident.

3   See eg *Prior v Hastie (Bernard and Co)* [1987] CLY 1219, followed in *Khan v Duncan* (9 March 1989, unreported), QBD.

4   Clause 5 of the draft Civil Law Reform Bill proposes amending FAA 1976, s 1A, adding sub-sections (2)(ab) and (3A) amongst other changes.

5 The Dependants' Claim Under the Fatal Accidents Act 1976

[L38] This is the most significant aspect of most fatal accident claims. The dependant can claim for the financial loss suffered because of the deceased's death. Again, who can be classified as a 'dependant' is contained in a statutory list, which extends to a greater range of claimants than those entitled to 'bereavement awards'.

(i) Who Can Claim?

[L39] The following relatives of the deceased are classified as 'dependants' in FAA 1976, s 1(3)–(5)[1]:

(a) The spouse/civil partner[2] or former spouse/civil partner[3].

(b) Cohabitants, provided they have been living with the deceased 'as husband and wife' and in the same household:
    (i)   immediately prior to the date of death[4], and;
    (ii) for at least two years prior to the date of death[5], and;
    (iii) for the whole of the two years prior to the date of death[6].

(c) The parents or other ascendants of the deceased.

(d) Any person who the deceased treated as a parent.

(e) The children or other descendants of the deceased.

(f) Any person who, not being the deceased's own child, by reason of marriage or civil partnership was treated by the deceased as a child of the family[7].

(g) The brother, sister, uncle or aunt (or any issue thereof) of the deceased.

[1]   It should be noted that the list of dependants under FAA 1976 has for many years been criticised by leading commentators, such as *McGregor on Damages*, and also the Law Commission in its Report No 263 entitled 'Claims for Wrongful Death' (1999), for being too restrictive. A number of other European countries such as France, Belgium and Switzerland operate a wider system of recovery that seems to work well, without needing an exhaustive list of possible dependants. The Ministry of Justice consultation on the Law of Damages addressed this issue and, on 15 December 2009, a draft Civil Law Reform Bill and related consultation was published, as further described below.

[2]   By Civil Partnership Act 2004, s 83.

[3]   A former spouse is expressly included and extends even to a person whose marriage had been annulled or declared void, as in *Martin v Grey* (1999) P&MILL vol 15(1). It also covers a person who has divorced and remarried: *Shepherd v Post Office* (1995) Times, 15 June, CA.

[4]   The courts will look at all the facts in deciding if the deceased was living in the same household: see further *Pounder v London Underground* [1995] PIQR P217; and *Kotke v Saffarini* [2005] EWCA Civ 221. In *Kotke v Saffarini* the Court of Appeal approved the trial judge's propositions extracted from the authorities as follows: (1) that each case is fact sensitive (ie dependent upon its peculiar facts); (2) the relevant word for consideration is 'household' and not 'house'; (3) 'living together' is the antithesis of living apart; (4) parties will be in the same household if they are tied by their relationship; (5) the tie of that relationship may be manifest by various elements, not simply living under the same roof, but the public and private acknowledgment of their mutual society and the mutual protection and support which binds them together, ie the whole of the consortium vitae. No one factor is necessarily more important than any other or determinative of the issue. It was also observed that the reasons why parties do not live together in a given case may be an important factor in deciding whether they live in the same household. Similarly, the reasons one party may have for not wishing to marry may be of importance.

[5]   Common sense indicates that a brief absence on the part of the deceased will not prevent a claimant being classified as a dependant. See further *Pounder v London Underground* [1995] PIQR P217; *Kotke v Saffarini* [2005] EWCA Civ 221; and the analogous Inheritance Act case of *Gully v Dix* [2004] EWCA Civ 139.

[6]   It follows, therefore, that the cohabitant is in a weaker position than that of the spouse. A spouse may have only recently married the deceased, only be married for a limited period before separation etc, and may even have left the marital home, whereas the cohabitant must have been in place for two years and not have left before the accident. Further, in cases involving couples living together as husband and wife but who were not actually married at the time of the deceased's death, by virtue of FAA 1976, s 3(4) the court is obliged to take account of the fact that the dependant had no enforceable right to financial support: see *Drew v Abassi* (24 May 1995, unreported), in which the Court of Appeal upheld a trial judge's decision to reduce the multiplier from 15 to 13, notwithstanding the fact that the relationship was of long standing and appeared happy and settled. As regards married couples where there is no evidence of pre-existing marital problems, the courts have been reluctant to reduce the multiplier to take account of the statistical chance of relationship breakdown: see eg *Wheatley v Cunningham* [1992] PIQR Q100.

[7]   In *Fretwell v Willi Betz* (unreported, but discussed in (2001) NLJ, 6 July), it was accepted that an individual treated as a child of a relationship between the deceased and a partner, where there was no marriage, should be considered as being a dependant for the purposes of FAA 1976. However, the court specifically said that, since there was no argument on the matter, the case could not be used as a precedent on the point. Arguably, the exclusion of such children as dependants offends against ECHR, Art 14: see further APIL Newsletter 2002, vol 12, Issue 1, p 11.

[L40]   A number of general rules also follow from FAA 1976, s 1(5):

*   A relationship of marriage is treated as a relationship of blood.
*   Any half relationship should be treated as a full one.
*   A stepchild is treated as a full child of the stepparent.

- An illegitimate child is treated as the child of not only his natural mother but also the child of his 'reputed' father.

[L41] Other rules come from other sources:

- By s 39 of the Adoption Act 1976, an adopted child is treated as legitimate to the adopters.
- An unborn child conceived before the accident is included[1].
- A dependant can still claim, even if the actual dependency arose after the accident or injury to the deceased[2].
- By s 83 of the Civil Partnership Act 2004, civil partners are given the same status as a married couple, and the same applies to any children of the civil partnership.

---

[1] *The George and Richard* (1871) LR 3 A&E 466; *Wheatley v Cunningham* [1992] PIQR Q100; and *Hymas v West* (1987, unreported). Note that some commentators, eg *McGregor on Damages* (18th edn), argue that a child conceived after injury but before the deceased's death should also be included. See further para **[L42]** below concerning the Government's plan to extend eligibility to children 'in utero' or conceived by IVF pre-death.

[2] In the Scottish case of *Phillips v Grampian Health Board (No 2)* 1992 SLT 659n, the claimant was successful, despite only marrying the deceased after it was inevitable he would die as a result of the defendant's negligence. This may also be argued, by analogy, as authority for an unborn child conceived after the cause of action arose being classed as a dependant.

[L42] Thus, the list of dependants is far wider than the list of 'bereavement' relatives. However, a number of classes of potential dependants are still left off the list, notably people who have been living together for less than two years, and a child who is not a child of the deceased but was treated by the deceased as a child of his family[1]. Arguably, these omissions fall foul of the Human Rights Act 1998, leading to a right to claim[2]. The Government recognised this issue in the consultation on the Law of Damages in 2007[3]. The draft Civil Law Reform Bill proposes to widen the class of dependants under the FAA to include 'any person who was being maintained by the deceased immediately before death'[4]. If and when the draft Civil Law Reform Bill is implemented, this new category is likely to cover most meritorious claimants that are currently excluded under FAA 1976, including cohabitants of less than two years' duration, providing actual dependency can be proved. The consultation on the Law of Damages in 2007 had considered eligibility to children 'in utero' or conceived by IVF pre-death, but the draft Civil Law Reform Bill is surprisingly silent on the issue. However, it is likely that claims will continue to be pursued on human rights grounds, many of which will settle on favourable terms[5].

---

[1] See further *Fretwell v Willi Betz* (unreported, but discussed in (2001) NLJ, 6 July).

[2] See further APIL Newsletter 2002, vol 12, Issue 1, p 11. In a different context, see also *Britton v Cardiff & Vale NHS Trust* (Lawtel Document No AM0200724) regarding a claim involving an alleged breach of the state's positive obligation to protect life under Art 2 of the European Convention on Human Rights.

[3] Ministry of Justice 'The Law of Damages – Response to consultation CP(R) 907', 1 July 2009.

[4] Clause 1(2) of the Civil Law Reform Bill, proposing amendment to FAA 1976, s 1(3).

[5] *W v Johnson* LTLPI 2/11/2006, where the claimant also received damages on behalf of her children, one of whom was conceived by artificial insemination posthumously and born approximately two years after her partner's death; *Chivers v Metcalfe* [2005] CLY 3237, where the judge approved an apportionment of £17,500 to a child of the deceased's co-habitant's former relationship, who had been treated by the deceased as a child of the relationship.

(ii) Entitlement to Claim

[L43]   FAA 1976, s 3(1) reads as follows:

'In the action such damages, other than damages for bereavement, may be awarded as are proportioned to the injury resulting from the death to the dependants respectively.'

Therefore, in order to recover damages, there must be an injury which results from the death. But, in this context, what needs to be proved to enable a dependant to recover damages?

[L44]   There is no statutory definition of the injury or loss which must be shown in order to recover damages. However, the courts have developed a test known as the 'reasonable expectation test', where claimants are entitled to recover damages if they can prove they (a) reasonably expected to receive a pecuniary benefit[1], (b) arising from the dependent family relationship[2], (c) but for the deceased's death. The pecuniary benefit may take many forms, as the following examples indicate[3]:

- loss of money brought into the family household by the deceased;
- loss of gratuitous services (eg housekeeping, childminding, gardening, decorating etc);
- loss of fringe benefits (eg company car);
- loss of one-off benefits (eg money to help pay for a wedding or help to buy a house); and
- loss of greater benefits had the deceased lived (eg estate duty paid on gifts received less than seven years after the gifts were made).

[1]   *Franklin v SE Railway* [1858] 3 H&M 211; *Dalton v The SE Railway* (1858) 4 CB(NS) 296; *Kassam v Kampala Aerated Water Co Ltd* [1965] 1 WLR 668; *Batt v Highgate Private Hospital* [2005] PIQR Q1. In *Auty v National Coal Board* [1985] 1 WLR 784, Oliver LJ stated that it was necessary to establish that the dependant has in fact suffered an injury (ie lost something) as a result of the death. If the dependant was claiming for loss of something which had been provided in any event (eg a widow's pension), there is no loss that can be claimed in law because there has been no injury.

[2]   In this context, business relationships are excluded: *Burgess v Florence Nightingale Hospital for Gentlewomen* [1955] 1 QB 349. See paras **[L46]–[L49]** below.

[3]   See further para 2.9 of the Law Commission's Paper No 263 'Claims for Wrongful Death' (1999). It should be noted that 'pecuniary' in this sense means money or money's worth, and therefore includes services that have a monetary value.

[L45]   The fact that a benefit had not been enjoyed prior to the deceased's death is not a bar to recovery, so long as there was a reasonable expectation of it being enjoyed in the future[1]. It should be noted that it is not necessary to prove, on the balance of probabilities, that the dependant would have received the benefit. All that must be shown is that the chance of receiving the benefit was 'substantial', ie more than a mere possibility or speculation[2]. But this principle has been held by the Court of Appeal not to apply to the situation where a female dependant, who was not pregnant at the time of the deceased's death, says that her dependency would have increased in the absence of death due to the intention to have a family and give up work to look after children[3].

[1]   See eg *Betney v Rowlands and Mallard* [1992] CLY 1786 (also reported in *Kemp & Kemp* at O3-030); *Piggott v Fancy Wood Products Ltd* (31 January 1985, unreported), noted in Kemp & Kemp at O4-42; and *Taff Vale Rly Co v Jenkins* [1913] AC 1.

2   *Franklin v SE Railway* [1858] 3 H&M 211; *Taff Vale Rly Co v Jenkins* [1913] AC 1; *Davies v Taylor* [1974] AC 207; *Davies v Bonner* (6 April 1995, unreported), CA.
3   *Higgs v Drinkwater* (1956) CA No 129a; followed in *Malone v Rowan* [1984] 3 All ER 402.

(iii)   Exclusion of Business Relationships

[L46]   Although a claimant may theoretically fall within the classes of people identified as dependants under FAA 1976, he or she may nevertheless fail in an action for the loss sustained. This is because a claim must be based on losses sustained due to a dependency relationship being terminated by the death of the deceased. Therefore, any loss suffered due to the death extinguishing a largely business relationship is not recoverable. An example of such a situation can be seen in *Burgess v Florence Nightingale Hospital for Gentlewomen*[1], in which the claimant was part of a successful professional dance act along with his wife. When his wife died, he claimed damages for the resultant loss of earnings he would have made along with his wife. It was held, however, that this claim did not satisfy the necessary family relationship. Although the point was strongly argued that the reason for the success of the dance act was the husband/wife combination, the courts found that the relationship in relation to the dance act was professional, and the fact of family ties was incidental. This case can be contrasted with cases in which the services, although partly in connection with a professional matter, were nevertheless rendered largely due to the family relationship.

1   [1955] 1 QB 349.

[L47]   In *Cookson v Knowles*[1], a widow could no longer perform her duties as a cleaner due, in part, to the inevitable removal of her husband's assistance in heavy lifting etc. It was held that, as the help had been given gratuitously out of the family relationship, the loss of earnings could be claimed. It must be noted, however, that the award was reduced due to the claimant's ability to continue some form of work (see below).

1   [1979] AC 556.

[L48]   Further, in *Malyon v Plummer*[1], a wife was paid a substantial salary by her husband's company in return for what amounted to part-time, casual work. When the husband died, the wife claimed loss of earnings. The court found largely in her favour on the grounds that the high wage was due to the family relationship, and therefore awarded a sum equal to the salary less the actual value of the work she did. The extra was the amount due to the family relationship.

1   [1964] 1 QB 330.

[L49]   In a similar vein, in *Williams v Welsh Ambulance Services NHS Trust*[1], Lady Justice Smith described an 'unusual dependency' where the deceased's widow and three adult children successfully continued the business in which two of the children and the widow had worked pre-death. On appeal, the defendant tried to argue this was a business relationship, as in *Burgess*. Lady Justice Smith made it clear they could not do so, having not raised the point before the judge, but in any event she commented that the family members were brought into what otherwise would have been the deceased's sole business, purely because they were family members and it was his intention that they benefit from it. This, in her view, underlined the correctness of the decision that they had an eligible dependency.

¹   [2008] EWCA Civ 81.

(iv)   No Entitlement to Injured Feelings or Pain, Suffering and Loss of Amenity

[L50]   Under FAA 1976, there is no entitlement for the dependants to damages for psychological loss, emotional distress[1] or pain, suffering and loss of amenity. The relatives will either be entitled to a bereavement award under s 1A of the Act or not. As regards the assessment of the lost dependency, this is purely a matter of pounds, shilling and pence[2]. Therefore, the mental suffering of losing a wife or husband does not sound in damages under FAA 1976 and cannot be taken into account when computing the value of the lost dependency[3]. However, if the dependant also has a claim for recognised psychiatric injuries in his or her own right, whether as a primary or secondary victim, then FAA 1976 does not prevent or restrict that claim[4], nor is the award for pain, suffering and loss of amenity reduced by the amount of the bereavement award[5].

¹   In *Thomas v Kwik Save Stores Ltd* (8 June 2000, unreported), CA, Lawtel Document No C8400690, Latham LJ said: 'It has to be remembered that the court is carrying out an exercise in determining the financial, not the emotional, dependency of the claimant on the deceased. That does not mean that the claimant has to show increased expenditure on the one hand or decreased income on the other. The loss of services which can be valued in money terms, even if not in fact replaced by an outside agency, will represent a loss for which the claimant can obtain compensation'.

²   *Davies v Powell Duffryn Collieries* [1942] AC 601, per Lord Wright at 617.

³   *Blake v Midland Ry* (1852) 18 QB 93.

⁴   For instance, see *Jones v Royal Devon & Exeter NHS Foundation Trust* [2008] EWHC 558 (QB), where King J awarded general damages of £20,000 for a pathological grief reaction sustained by a mother following the death of her daughter. This was in addition to a bereavement damages award.

⁵   *Vernon v Bosley (No 1)* [1997] PIQR P255, in particular per Evans LJ at P313–4.

(v)   Calculating the Loss

The objective

[L51]   It is important to recognise that, because of the operation of ss 3(2) and 4 of FAA 1976, benefits arising out of the deceased's death are ignored, so the dependants may actually be put into a better position financially than they otherwise would have been. This was recognised by Lord Diplock in the leading case of *Cookson v Knowles*[1]:

> 'Today the assessment of damages in fatal accident cases has become an artificial and conjectural exercise. Its purpose is no longer to put dependants, particularly widows, into the same economic position as they would have been in had their late husband lived. Section 4 of the Fatal Accidents Act 1976 requires the court in assessing damages to leave out of account any insurance money or benefit under national insurance or social security legislation or other pension or gratuity which becomes payable to the widow on her husband's death, while section 3 (2) forbids the court to take into account the re-marriage of the widow or her prospects of re-marriage.'

Lord Justice Buxton also observed in *Harland & Wolff Plc and Husbands Ltd v Mcintyre*[2] that double recovery is inherent in s 4 of FAA 1976.

[1]   [1979] AC 556 at 568.
[2]   [2006] 1 WLR 2577, [2007] 2 All ER 24, [2006] ICR 1222.

Method of assessment

[L52]   The task of assessing the loss of dependency was historically a question for the jury. There are no prescribed ways of assessing the loss. As long as some damage capable of being quantified in money terms is established, the court's task is to[1]:

> 'examine the particular facts of the case to determine whether or not any loss in money or in money's worth has been occasioned to the dependants and if it determines that it has, it must then use whatever material appears best to fit the facts of the particular case in order to determine the extent of that loss.'

[1]   Per Latham LJ in Cape *Distribution v O'Loughlin* [2001] EWCA Civ 178.

The general approach: an overview

[L53]   When the losses claimed by the dependant are identifiable and specific, the calculation is simply one of adding them up. However, problems arise when a continuing dependency is pleaded (as in most cases). Like all calculations involving future loss, the result is an estimate of potential loss and can never be precisely accurate. Awards under FAA 1976 are split into:

(i)   losses sustained in the period between the deceased's death and the date of trial; and

(ii) the future losses to be incurred post-trial.

Such a split is necessary, as the pre-trial losses will usually attract interest at half the special account rate between death and trial (see below), yet future losses will not.

[L54]   The Practice Direction to CPR, Part 16 states what must be included in the schedule for a FAA claim as follows:

> '5.1 In a fatal accident claim the claimant must state in his particulars of claim:
>   (1)   that it is brought under the Fatal Accidents Act 1976,
>   (2)   the dependants on whose behalf the claim is made,
>   (3)   the date of birth of each dependant, and
>   (4)   details of the nature of the dependency claim.
> 5.2 A fatal accident claim may include a claim for damages for bereavement.
> 5.3 In a fatal accident claim the claimant may also bring a claim under the Law Reform (Miscellaneous Provisions) Act 1934 on behalf of the estate of the deceased.'

The multiplicand

[L55]   The multiplicand will be the annual value of the pre-trial dependency. This is usually split between the annual loss of financial dependency and the annual loss of services habitually provided by the deceased. The financial dependency is usually expressed as a percentage of the deceased's loss of earnings[1]. The multiplicand for financial dependency (usually based on earnings or pension) is calculated net of tax, National Insurance and any significant expenses[2]. The lost services are often more difficult to calculate, but are usually assessed by looking at how the services have been subsequently provided and the cost (if any) thereby incurred[3]. The range of services that might have to be replaced includes childminding, housekeeping, domestic assistance, driving, bookkeeping, DIY, decorating, car maintenance, gardening and dog-walking.

[1]   See below and *Harris v Empress Motors* [1984] 1 WLR 212, per O'Connor LJ at 217.
[2]   This is consistent with the principles in *British Transport Commission v Gourley* [1956] AC 185; *Cooper v Firth Brown* [1963] 1 WLR 418; and *Dews v National Coal Board* [1988] AC 1. See further Chapters F and K.
[3]   See below and *Bordin v St Mary's NHS Trust* [2000] Lloyd's Rep Med 287.

[L56]   It is important to note that, although the multiplier is traditionally calculated as at the date of death (see below), the multiplicand continues to be assessed as at the date of trial[1]. Therefore, the award for financial dependency is calculated on the basis of what the deceased would have been earning at the date of trial had he or she survived. In this way, the dependant's award attracts a measure of protection against inflation[2], and avoids the unfairness of receiving an award for dependency which would otherwise be worth much less (or more) than the true value of the loss at current rates. Further, the multiplicand must also be adjusted to take into account any pre[3]- or post[4]-trial promotions or more than inflationary salary increases etc. If necessary, more than one multiplicand can be used to apply to different periods of loss; and this is often the case where there are differing levels of dependency, eg whilst there are still dependent children, and when the children have left home, leaving the surviving spouse as the only remaining dependant[5].

[1]   *Cookson v Knowles* [1979] AC 556, HL.
[2]   In other words, the court will take into account pre-trial inflation, even though post-trial inflation is ignored: *Cookson v Knowles* [1979] AC 556, HL. The same would apply to pre-trial deflation.
[3]   See eg *Malone v Rowan* [1984] 3 All ER 402; and *The Swynfleet* (1947) 81 Ll L Rep 116. See also para 2.18 of the Law Commission's Report No 263 'Claims for Wrongful Death' (1999).
[4]   In *Mallett v McMonagle* [1970] AC 166, Lord Diplock said that anticipated future variations in dependency were normally dealt with by an adjustment in the multiplicand. See further *Robertson v Lestrange* [1985] 1 All ER 950, in which salary increases due to the deceased's anticipated promotions were averaged over a 33-year period, leading to a higher multiplicand.
[5]   *Robertson v Lestrange* [1985] 1 All ER 950.

The multiplier

(1)   THE TRADITIONAL APPROACH

[L57]   Unlike for a living claimant, traditionally, the multiplier in a FAA 1976 claim has been calculated from the date of death and not from the date of trial[1]. The reason for this is that the deceased's death is considered to be the only certain event, and everything after that date remains uncertain[2]. The multiplier is therefore fixed once and for all at the date of death, and then the period from death to trial is deducted from the overall multiplier to give the multiplier to be adopted for future loss[3].

1   *Cookson v Knowles* [1979] AC 556, HL.

2   As Lord Fraser put it in *Cookson v Knowles* [1979] AC 556 at 57: 'In a personal injury case, if the injured person has survived until the date of trial, that is a known fact and the multiplier appropriate to the length of his future working life has to be ascertained as at the date of trial. But in a fatal accident case the multiplier must be selected once and for all as at the date of death, because everything that might have happened to the deceased after that date remains uncertain'.

3   For example, in *Cookson v Knowles* [1979] AC 556, HL, a final future loss multiplier of 8.5 was used. This was calculated as an initial multiplier of 11, and the trial was 2.5 years after death.

[L58]   Following the decision of the Lord Chancellor on 27 June 2001 to exercise his power under the Damages Act 1996, the multiplier will be calculated on the basis of a 2.5% discount rate[1].

1   See further at paras **[H25]–[H31]**.

[L59]   The method for calculating the multiplier was set out by Purchas LJ in *Corbett v Barking, Havering & Brentwood Health Authority*[1], where he said[2] that there are five essential elements in the calculation:

(a) The likelihood of the provider of the support continuing to exist.

(b) The likelihood of the dependant being alive to benefit from that support.

(c) The possibility of the providing capacity of the provider being affected by the changes and chances of life, either in a positive or negative manner.

(d) The possibility of the needs of the dependant being altered by the changes and chances of life, again in a positive or negative way.

(e) An actuarial discount to compensate: (i) for the immediate receipt of compensatory damages in advance of the date when the loss would in fact have been incurred; and (ii) the requirement that the capital should be exhausted at the end of the period of dependency.

1   [1991] 2 QB 408 at 421–431.

2   At 422F.

[L60]   Purchas LJ then went on to say that, as a general rule, certain steps need to be followed:

(i) consider the combined effects of (a) and (c) above in order to arrive at the number of years during which provision of support is likely to be available, if needed by the dependant;

(ii) consider the combined effects of (b) and (d) above in order to arrive at the number of years during which the dependant is likely to need the support; and

(iii) apply (e) to the lesser of (i) and (ii) above, with an added but usually minor discount to take account of an outside chance that the choice between (i) and (ii) might, in the event, prove to be wrong.

(2) CRITICISMS OF THE TRADITIONAL APPROACH

[L61]   The traditional approach to the assessment of the value of dependencies in FAA 1976 claims has been criticised by a number of leading commentators[1]. The Law Commission in their Paper No 263 entitled 'Claims for Wrongful Death', published in November 1999, recommended that the law in this area should be reformed. Criticisms of the traditional approach include:

- The traditional approach is too complicated, and a simpler method is needed.
- Following *Wells v Wells*[2] the starting point for calculating multipliers should be the Ogden Tables[3].
- It is wrong to apply a discount rate pre-trial, as the dependants have not yet received their damages, and hence are in no position to achieve the investment return it presumes.
- The contingencies post-death and pre-trial are, in most cases, very low and so do not justify applying a discount rate.
- The traditional approach is arbitrary and illogical, which can lead to absurd results.

[1]　See eg *Kemp & Kemp*; *McGregor on Damages* (18th edn); and David Kemp and Rowland Hogg 'How to Determine Multipliers in Assessing Damages under the Fatal Accidents Acts, Using the Revised "Ogden Tables"' [2000] JPIL, Issue 2–3/00 at 142–155 and also [1999] JPIL, Issue 1/99 at 42.

[2]　[1999] 1 AC 345.

[3]　See further Chapter H.

[L62]　*Corbett v Barking, Havering & Brentwood HA*[1] is a case which illustrates some of the difficulties of the traditional method of assessment. The dependent child's mother died following mismanagement of a caesarean section during his birth. There had been a long delay between the date of death and the date of trial, which did not come on until 11 years and six months after the date of death. The trial judge held that the boy would remain dependent until the age of 18, and the appropriate multiplier was 12 for the whole period. But, as the boy was aged 11½ at the date of trial, this only left him with a future dependency of 6 months. The Court of Appeal substituted an initial multiplier of 15 leaving 3½ years dependency. The reasoning was that the uncertainties concerning the dependants present at death had been reduced by the time of the trial, due to the passage of time.

[1]　[1991] 2 QB 408.

(3)　THE SUGGESTED APPROACH

[L63]　The Law Commission suggests using the Ogden Tables in order to calculate the multiplier from the date of trial, thus bringing the valuation of dependency claims in line with ordinary personal injury claims[1].

[1]　Law Commission Paper No 263 'Claims for Wrongful Death' (1999).

[L64]　The fourth edition of the Ogden Tables was especially drawn up to deal with the problem of fatal accident claims, following the Law Commission's recommendation that the Ogden Working Party should be reconvened to consider how the tables should be used in these cases. The fourth edition contained a specific introductory note on how the Ogden Tables should be used in FAA 1976 claims. The fourth edition has now been superseded by the fifth and sixth editions, which again contain useful notes and helpful examples on how the Ogden Tables may be used to calculate claims for dependency. There are now two alternative approaches: the first based on calculating the multipliers from the date of trial, and the second based on calculating multipliers from death, but utilising the 0% discount rate column for the pre-trial losses. These two alternatives tend to result in similar multipliers, which are higher than those derived from the traditional approach, particularly in cases where there is a lengthy pre-trial period.

[L65]   Unfortunately, to date, whilst recognising the force of the arguments supporting the new approaches, the lower courts and Court of Appeal have considered themselves bound, by *Cookson v Knowles*[1], to use the traditional approach of calculating the multiplier as at the date of death[2]. Notwithstanding this fact, most experienced claimant practitioners continue to draft their schedules using one or other of the alternative approaches, and often achieve favourable settlements on that basis[3]. It must, therefore, be left to the Supreme Court to consider, in an appropriate case, whether the time has come to follow the recommendations of the Law Commission and determine that dependency calculations should be brought into line with the assessment of personal injury claims. It is disappointing that the Government did not include this issue in their consultation on the Law of Damages.

---

[1]   [1979] AC 556, HL. See further Ian McLaren QC 'Multipliers in Fatal Accident Claims' (2001) NLJ 12, January, at 12–13.

[2]   *Wilkins v William Press* (30 November 2000, QBD, unreported); *White v ESAB* [2002] PIQR Q76; *ATH & anor v MS* [2002] EWCA Civ 792; and *A Train & Sons Ltd v Fletcher* [2008] 4 All ER 699.

[3]   It is believed that the appeal in *A Train & Sons Ltd v Fletcher* [2008] 4 All ER 699 settled on the basis of the approach of the claimant in accordance with a calculation under the Ogden Tables (4th edn) before the case could get to the House of

(vi)   Type of Loss

[L66]   The loss suffered by a dependant falls into two main categories: the loss of financial support, and the loss of services provided by the deceased. A deceased who seemingly provided little, if any, financial contribution can still provide significant services which must be quantified and included. Both categories can then, in turn, be split into the loss received before death and the projected loss that would have occurred in the future.

(vii)   Financial Dependency

Dependency on earnings

[L67]   The loss which is most common in a dependency claim will be that of the earnings of a spouse, partner or parent[1]. Such a loss can be calculated on the rate of earnings prior to death, and will be compensated up until the likely retirement age of the deceased or likely date that the dependency would have stopped[2]. Dependency after retirement can be relied upon if a spouse is entitled to a reduced pension because of the death, or it can be shown that other income has been lost[3]. In respect of a dependent child, the dependency claim will usually continue to the age of 18, or higher if there is evidence that the child was likely to have gone on to tertiary or higher education requiring continued financial support[4]. However, there is no fixed cut-off point and, for instance, in the case of a disabled child, the dependency claim could last much longer[5]. A further example of longer dependencies is in the case of high earners, where it is shown that income is being accumulated for the long-term benefit and ultimately inheritance of the remainder of the family[6].

[1]   In certain situations, it is possible for a dependant to be able to show a financial loss merely through the reduction of state benefits: see eg *Cox v Hockenhull* [2000] PIQR Q230. However, such situations are unusual, and the normal scenario will be that the dependant will be supported by the state to the same extent as he or she was previously, and is therefore unable to prove any loss has been suffered as a result of the death: see eg *Hunter v Butler* [1996] RTR 396.

[2]   Where it is extremely difficult to calculate the deceased's rate of earnings by using conventional methods, other methods may be used to calculate the lost financial dependency. For example, in *Cape Distribution v O'Loughlin* [2001] EWCA Civ 178, it was difficult to assess the value of the dependency, because all of the deceased's money was tied up in property (by the time of his death, he had built up a portfolio worth about £750,000). The Court of Appeal upheld the unconventional approach of the trial judge, which was to find that the claimants had lost the 'flair and business acumen' of the deceased and, consequently, to award the cost of replacing those services with another person who had the necessary skills to manage the deceased's property portfolio.

[3]   See para **[L88]**.

[4]   In *Spittle v Bunney* [1988] 1 WLR 847 the court held there was a dependency until the age of 22. See also *Martin v Grey* (1999) P&MILL vol 15(1); and *Laniyan v Barry May Haulage* [2002] PIQR Q35, in which Stuart Brown QC held that the evidence supported the child dependant was likely to progress to higher education and therefore would have been dependent until the age of 21, although his dependency would have diminished with time. In *Betney v Rowlands and Mallard* [1992] CLY 1786 (also reported in *Kemp & Kemp* at O3-30), one of the daughters recovered a dependency to age 28.

[5]   See eg *Turner & Turner v (1) Peach and (2) Derbyshire CC* (21 December 2001, unreported), in which one of the dependent children, who was aged nine at the date of his mother's death, had special needs, and a multiplier of 14 was used for the future. Although not involving a fatal accident claim, see also the first-instance decision of Morison J in *Nunnerley v Warrington and Liverpool Health Authority* [2000] PIQR Q69; and *Fish v Wilcox* [1994] Lloyd's Rep Med 12 regarding the recoverability of the costs of care beyond the age of majority, despite there being no legal duty to provide the care.

[6]   *Williams v Welsh Ambulance Services NHS Trust* [2008] EWCA Civ 81; and *Paton v MOD*, LTLPI 13/3/2006.

[L68]   The assessment of the lost dependency is a question of fact and will depend upon a number of factors, including:

- The deceased's historical level of earnings, and how reliant the dependant had been on them.
- How much the deceased was earning as at the date of his or her death, and how reliant the dependant was on these earnings.
- How much the deceased would have continued to earn but for his or her death, and the extent to which the dependant would have relied upon such earnings.
- The dependent's likely future earnings had it not been for the death.

(1)   THE USUAL DEPENDENCY PERCENTAGES

[L69]   The court can use two methods of calculating the loss to the family of the death of a main wage earner: the general rule of thumb method; or a more accurate calculation based upon the accounts of the deceased. The principle is to produce the sum which represents that which a spouse and children, if any, have lost by reason of the death. This involves assessing the net earnings of the deceased (just as one would if the deceased were a claimant in a personal injury claim), and making an allowance for any amount which the deceased would have spent on him or herself alone (since it is only the amount of the dependency to which the spouse and children are entitled).

[L70]   The general rule of thumb for couples with children is that the court will adopt as a starting point the assumption that 25% is spent on 'him', 25% on 'her', 25% on the children, and 25% on joint expenses (house etc) which are no less after the death than before, thus giving 75% as the combined dependency of a partner and dependent children. Where there are no dependent children[1], the corresponding proportions become thirds[2]. The proposition is that there was a joint purse. If more than one partner or member of the family was earning, and those earnings were in fact pooled, then all the earnings should be considered together before any calculation of dependency is considered. The simplest method would be to pool the earnings together, deduct the deceased's personal expenditure, and then deduct the survivor's proportion of the earnings. No detailed analysis of the family's outgoings is undertaken using this method.

Example 1

Where a husband dies, earning £31,000 net per annum, with a wife surviving but not earning nor anticipated to do so, and no dependent children, the approach is as follows:

Husband's earnings	£31,000
× two-thirds to work out the dependency =	£20,333
Annual dependency loss =	£20,333

Example 2

Where a husband dies, earning £31,000 net per annum, with a wife surviving, earning £29,000 net per annum, but no dependent children, the approach is as follows:

Husband's earnings	£31,000
Wife's earnings	£29,000
Joint earnings =	£60,000
× two-thirds to work out the dependency =	£40,000
Less surviving spouse's income	− £29,000
Annual dependency loss =	£11,000

[1]   *Harris v Empress Motors* [1984] 1 WLR 212.
[2]   This method was approved in *Coward v Comex Houlder Driving Ltd* (18 July 1988, CA), noted in *Kemp & Kemp* at O1-011.

Example 3

Where a husband dies, earning £31,000 net per annum, with a wife surviving earning £29,000 net per annum and two dependent children, the approach is as follows:

Husband's earnings	£31,000
Wife's earnings	£29,000
Joint earnings =	£60,000
× 75% to work out the dependency =	£45,000
Less surviving spouse's income	− £29,000
Annual dependency loss =	£16,000

(2) DISPLACING THE USUAL DEPENDENCY PERCENTAGES

[L71]   The general rule regarding the dependency factor may be displaced where there are good reasons to suspect that the usual percentage split is not appropriate in a particular case. For example, when:

* the deceased was supporting a number of young children;
* the deceased's income was very low[1] or high[2];
* there is age disparity and/or differing retirement ages[3];
* both parents die[4];
* the deceased is a high earner and dies a short time into a childless marriage[5]; or
* dependent children were never really wholly dependent upon the deceased's income[6].

[L72]   In these circumstances, the court may be invited to conduct a more detailed analysis of the family's finances (checking all income and outgoings, eg bank accounts, credit card statements, bills etc) to determine exactly what was spent by whom and on what[7]. Care needs to be taken to avoid treating investments (eg a valuable fine wine collection) or transfers of funds (eg payment of a credit card bill, where the components of it have already been brought into account) as expenditure. From such an analysis, it should hopefully be possible to assess whether or not the rule of thumb percentage dependency figures are appropriate or should be displaced, given the individual facts of the case. To this end, it is often relevant to assess how much the deceased spent on him or herself, eg whether or not he or she had any expensive hobbies or leisure interests, or spent most of any money earned on family expenses such as the mortgage and bills. Given that mortgage payments or rent, together with utility bills and council tax etc, tend to be the major expenses of families these days, it might be possible to show that a higher dependency factor should be applied.

[1]   For example, the Court of Appeal in *Cox v Hockenhull* [2000] PIQR Q230 held that calculating the dependency at two-thirds of relevant income was too high, because this took no account of the fact that some of the most significant expenses (such as rent, which was paid for by housing benefit) were joint expenses. The dependency was reduced to one-half of the relevant income.

[2]   See eg *Farmer v Rolls Royce Industrial Power (India) Ltd* (26 February 2003, unreported), QBD, Lawtel Document No AC0105047, and *Paton v MOD*, LTLPI 13/3/2006, in which a higher rate of percentage dependency of 85% was used for a higher-income family, and there were significant savings which benefited the dependants. See also *Williams v Welsh Ambulance Services NHS Trust* [2008] EWCA Civ 81, LTL 15/2/2008, where the combination of the high earnings and low expenditure of the deceased led to a 82.5% dependency rate to the age of 70, and 66% from 70 to 80.

[3]   In this scenario, it might be appropriate to split the multiplier: see further *Coward v Comex Houlder Driving Ltd* (18 July 1988, CA), noted in *Kemp & Kemp* at O1-011; and *Crabtree v Wilson* [1993] PIQR Q24.

[4]   In *Dhaliwal v Personal Representatives of Hunt (decd)* [1995] PIQR Q56, Auld LJ stated that, where both working parents die, the *Harris v Empress Motors* [1984] 1 WLR 212 percentage split should not be applied. A more subjective view of how much was spent by the parents on themselves should be undertaken. The result was a 50% allowance of the aggregate wages. Auld LJ (at Q61) held that the mortgage payments made by the parents were not made for the children but as an investment in property.

[5]   *Owen v Martin* [1992] PIQR Q151, CA.

[6]   *ATH v MS* [2002] EWCA Civ 792. Kennedy LJ stated at [32]: 'In my judgment in the peculiar circumstances of this case the judge was right to abandon the approach suggested in *Coward v Comex* and in the absence of satisfactory evidence as to the value of the benefits received by the infant dependants from the deceased he was bound to turn to the deceased's own net income as

a starting point. However, his conclusion seems to me to be unacceptable because it made no allowance at all for the contributions of AK and later of the father Paul and his wife. These children never were, and in reality were never likely to be wholly dependent upon what their mother could earn. I would therefore reduce the multiplicand from 75% to 60% of the deceased's earnings'.

7   See *Davies v Hawes*, a decision of Sir Michael Ogden QC, reported in *Kemp & Kemp* at O1-010 and commented on at 29-041; *Wheatley v Cunningham* [1992] PIQR Q100.

(3)   SURVIVING PARTNER'S EARNING CAPACITY

[L73]   When assessing the level of dependency upon the deceased's earnings, the dependant's own level of income and financial resources becomes relevant, since the more the dependant earns in his or her own right, the less he or she is likely to have been dependent upon the deceased's income had the deceased survived[1]. How does this work in practice? This very much depends upon the facts of the individual case and the intentions of the parties involved. In particular, it is important to establish whether or not the dependant was already working prior to the deceased's death, what his or her intentions were with regard to working in the future, and the prospects of the same. The principles relating to the main different factual scenarios and intentions which commonly arise in dependency situations are set out below.

1   A notable exception is where the dependency has been calculated by a detailed analysis of the deceased personal expenditure when contrasted with his earning capacity, as in *Williams v Welsh Ambulance Services NHS Trust* [2008] EWCA Civ 81. Consequently, in this case, the earnings of the dependants were irrelevant to the assessment of the deceased's earning capacity on which they were dependent.

[L74]   Where the surviving partner was working prior to the deceased's death and continues to work after his or her death, if the surviving partner had always intended to continue working and does in fact carry on working after the deceased's death, the partner's earnings and/or earning capacity must be taken into account and be deducted from the dependency element of the joint income[1]. This is because, if the dependant's earnings went into the family pool before the deceased's death, the dependant's earnings and/or earning capacity must be taken into account when assessing the loss to the family pool after the deceased's death[2]. Indeed, a dependant's earning capacity must still be taken into account where the dependant had a long-standing job but is subsequently made redundant following the deceased's death[3].

1   *Malyon v Plummer* [1964] 1 QB 330, CA; *Davies v Whiteways Cyder Co* [1975] QB 262 at 272F; *Coward v Comex Houlder Driving Ltd* (18 July 1988, CA), noted in *Kemp & Kemp* at O1-011; and *Crabtree v Wilson* [1993] PIQR Q24.
2   *Cookson v Knowles* [1977] QB 913.
3   *Edgson v Vickers Plc* [1994] ICR 510 at 527.

[L75]   Arguably, a different principle should apply where the surviving partner had always intended to give up work in any event, notwithstanding the deceased's death. Here, the dependant would have become more reliant upon the deceased's income but, as a result of the deceased's death, has no choice but to continue working in order to support him or herself and/or any other dependants. In this scenario, the court may be persuaded to take no account of the dependant's earnings or future earning capacity. For example, in *Howitt v Heads*[1] the deceased's wife had been earning £10 per week in the three weeks they had cohabited prior to his death. The judge did not take these earnings into account when assessing the value of the lost dependency, because he found that the dependant would have ceased work shortly thereafter and she would have relied upon the deceased to 'face the financial responsibilities they had as a family'[2]. Further, the judge refused to take into account the dependant's future earning capacity, even though it was probable that, after a few years, she would return to work and obtain a significant degree of financial independence. It should be noted, however, that the decision in *Howitt v Heads* was made over 30 years ago when the socio-economic circumstances were somewhat different than they are today. Now, many more women work and return to work after career breaks[3]. Therefore, save where the dependant can prove that he or she had no intention of continuing to work, it may be unrealistic not to take into account a dependant's future earnings or earning capacity. Further, the Court of Appeal in *Cookson v Knowles*[4] expressly doubted the correctness of the decision in *Howitt v Heads*. Lord Denning MR put it as follows[5]:

'The wife's earnings

Seeing that the husband helped the wife in her work, it was quite legitimate for the judge to regard them as conducting a joint operation. He took the combined earnings of husband and wife and calculated the dependency as two-thirds of the combined figure. He regarded that as completely lost by his death. He seems to have disregarded the future earning capacity of the wife. We do not think that was right. After his death, she retained her earning capacity. By his death the dependants were deprived of the contribution provided by the husband. But not of the contribution provided by the wife. It is true that she could no longer do her previous work as a cleaner after his death. But she could do other work, at any rate part-time work, whilst the children were at school, and full-time work later. Her prospects of remarriage are, of course, to be disregarded; but not her prospects of going out to work and earning money: see *Malyon v Plummer* by Pearson LJ. It is very different from those cases where the widow was not working at the time of his death, so that her earnings did not come into the family pool. In those cases it may be said that she is not bound to go out to work so as to reduce the award (see *Howitt v Heads*), although we are not so sure about this. She may prefer to go out to work rather than sit at home grieving over the loss of her husband. But, when her earnings before his death come into the family pool so also her earning capacity after his death must be taken into account.'

However, the more recent decision of the Court of Appeal, in *Williams v Welsh Ambulance Services NHS Trust*[6], suggests that *Howitt* was correctly decided after all, and that mitigation of loss has no part to play on this issue, as the dependency will be fixed by the intentions of the deceased and dependants at the time of death[7].

---

[1]   [1973] 1 QB 64.

[2]   In this regard, Cumming Bruce J followed the Australian cases of *Carroll v Purcell* (35 ALJR 384), *Goodger v Knapman* [1924] SASR 347 and *Usher v Williams* (1955) 60 WALR 69; and the New Zealand case of *Jamieson v Greene* [1957] NZLR 1154. Note that this approach may also accord with FAA 1976, s 4 which requires that any benefits accruing as a result of the deceased's death – which, arguably, includes the ability of the dependant to obtain work he or she would not otherwise have pursued – shall be disregarded.

[3]   See eg the research carried out by the Equal Opportunities Commission, the Policy Studies Institute and the CBI.

[4]   [1977] QB 913.

[5]   At 922.

[6]   [2008] EWCA Civ 81; see further at paras **[L78]** and **[L80]** below.

[7]   *Davies v Whiteways Cyder Co Ltd* [1975] QB 262 is also consistent with both *Howitt* and *Williams*, with the actual earnings post death ignored, on the grounds that they would not have been earned had it not been for the death.

[L76]   So far as *Howitt v Heads*[1] creates an exception to the usual rule, it does not necessarily apply to the situation where the dependant intended to take time off work to bring up children. Under the present law – unless the dependant was already pregnant at the time of the deceased's death[2] – the court will not take account of the dependant's intended greater reliance upon the deceased's earnings, since it must assess the dependency as at the time of death. The Court of Appeal so held in *Higgs v Drinkwater*[3]. However, it should be noted that this decision has received a fair degree of criticism from judges and commentators alike[4]. Arguably, if there was a substantial chance[5] that the dependant would have become more dependent upon the deceased's income but for his or her death, this chance should sound in damages[6]. The Law Commission also considered that s 4 of FAA 1976 (which was not in force at the time that *Higgs v Drinkwater* was decided) made it strongly arguable that a widow's earning capacity should be disregarded[7]. It is therefore possible that, with the right case, assuming the parties were willing to appeal to the Supreme Court and the amounts involved made it worthwhile, *Higgs v Drinkwater* could be overturned, and the prospect of a greater dependency but for the deceased's death, eg whilst the dependant intended to raise a family, could be taken into account.

1   [1973] 1 QB 64.
2   *Wheatley v Cunningham* [1992] PIQR Q100; *Hymas v West* (1987, unreported). In *Wheatley v Cunningham* the dependant was pregnant at the time of the deceased's death and, although an adjustment was made to reflect the dependant's earnings, this only took effect for a limited period up until the birth of the child.
3   (1956) CA No 129a; followed in *Malone v Rowan* [1984] 3 All ER 402.
4   See eg Pearson J's judgment in *Malone v Rowan* [1984] 3 All ER 402; Russell J's judgment in *Coward v Comex* (18 July 1988, CA), noted in *Kemp & Kemp* at O1-011.
5   In this context, 'substantial chance' means a chance which is more than 'speculative' or 'fanciful': *Allied Maples v Simmons & Simmons* [1995] WLR 1602; and *Davies v Taylor* [1974] AC 207. Although it is not clear what size a lost chance has to be before it is categorised as 'substantial', it appears that the Court of Appeal approved a claim in *Langford v Hebran* [2001] EWCA Civ 361 involving a lost chance of 14% (see further the case summary prepared by junior counsel in that case at pp 5–7 of (2001) Quantum, Issue 3, 12 June). See also *Lloyds Bank v Parker Bullen* [2000] Lloyd's Rep PN 51, where a claim for a lost chance of 15% was allowed.
6   *Taff Vale Rly Co v Jenkins* [1913] AC 1; *Davies v Taylor* [1974] AC 207.
7   See further para 2.51 of the Law Commission Report No 263 'Claims for Wrongful Death' (November 1999).

[L77]   Where the surviving partner was working prior to the accident but stops working following the accident, the court must take into account the dependant's earning capacity[1]. Assuming the dependant retains some earning capacity, albeit on a part-time basis, this rule applies even where the dependant was working together with the deceased at the time of his or her death and relied upon the deceased to help perform his or her duties (as on the facts which arose in *Cookson v Knowles*[2]).

1   *Cookson v Knowles* [1977] QB 913.
2   [1977] QB 913.

[L78]   Where the surviving partner was not working prior to the deceased's death, if the surviving partner never intended to work and only goes out to work after the deceased's death as a result of financial need to support themselves or other dependants (eg children of the family), then arguably, on the basis of *Howitt v Heads*[1], no credit should be given in respect of these earnings. This principle was reaffirmed in *Wolfe v*

Del'Innocenti[2], where the court was satisfied that had it not been for the accident the widow would not have worked, even though, following the accident, she was trying to continue her deceased husband's business. This decision is also consistent with *Williams v Welsh Ambulances NHS Trust*[3], where the increased hours and commitment to the deceased's business by the widow and adult children, which occurred after his death, were not treated as reducing the dependency. Lady Justice Smith succinctly summarised the important point of principle that a dependant cannot, by their conduct after the death of the deceased, affect the value of the dependency.

[1]   [1973] 1 QB 64. See also *Davies v Whiteways Cyder Co* [1975] QB 262 at 272H, where O'Connor
       J held that a widow's earnings following the death of her husband should not be taken into account,
       because those earnings reflected 'what her labours [were] worth [on] the open market'.
[2]   [2006] EWHC 2694 (QB), LTL 22/6/07.
[3]   [2008] EWCA Civ 81, LTL 15/2/2008.

[L79]   If the surviving partner had intended to return to work in any event, the dependant's earnings and/or earning capacity will be taken into account from the date he or she expected to return to work[1].

[1]   *Dodds v Dodds* [1978] QB 543.

(4)   NOTIONAL OR ACTUAL EARNINGS

[L80]   Applying the reasoning of Lady Justice Smith in *Williams v Welsh Ambulances NHS Trust*[1], that a dependant cannot by their conduct after the death of the deceased affect the value of the dependency, it would seem that the courts ought to calculate the dependency claim based on the notional earnings of the dependant, but for the death. Unless there was an issue regarding a failure to utilise full earning capacity[2], in several cases pre-dating *Williams*, it appeared that the surviving spouse's actual as opposed to notional earnings would usually be taken into account in order to calculate the appropriate multiplicand[3]. However, in *Beesley v New Century*[4], where the dependent wife did a small amount of casual work for the deceased but was paid at a rate in excess of her actual contribution, the court only applied a credit for half of her actual earnings when calculating the loss of dependency. The simple but forceful logic of *Williams* is likely to prevail in many circumstances, although there is scope for arguing exceptions where application of the rule creates manifest injustice[5], eg where a dependant has been unable to realise his or her presumed earning capacity due to bereavement following the death[6].

[1]   [2008] EWCA Civ 81, LTL 15/2/2008.
[2]   *Cookson v Knowles* [1979] AC 556, HL.
[3]   This would appear to be more consistent with the court's approach to the assessment of lost
       dependency in *Coward v Comex Houlder Driving Ltd* (Independent, 25 July 1988, CA), noted in
       Kemp & Kemp at para O1-011, and commented on at 29-041.
[4]   [2008] EWHC 3033 (QB).
[5]   The potential hardship and injustice of a rigid application of this rule can easily be seen, if you take
       example 3 from para **[L70]** above and then assume that, as a consequence of the death, the widow
       was unable to cope with caring for the children, her job and her grief, and hence gave up her work. If
       her notional earnings were factored in, not only would she have lost her own salary of £29,000 p.a,
       but she would only receive a dependency of £16,000, less than the widow in example 1 who had no
       children and had never worked.
[6]   *McGregor on Damages* (18th edn) at 36-044 comments that, whilst the merits of ignoring either
       potential or actual earnings can be questioned, it is at least sensible to have the same rule for both.

(5) Uplifts and discounts for contingencies

[L81] The court's job is to assess, as best it can, the value of the lost dependency. Therefore, account should be taken of any salary increases, promotions etc that would have increased the level of the dependency[1]. But, likewise, account should be taken of any risks or contingencies that might have operated to shorten or reduce the level of dependency[2].

1   *Malone v Rowan* [1984] 3 All ER 402; *The Swynfleet; Robertson v Lestrange* [1985] 1 All ER 950; *ATH & anor v MS* [2002] EWCA Civ 792.
2   See further Chapters A, H and K regarding discounting for contingencies.

(6) Two family households

[L82] The calculation of financial dependency on a parent can be complicated by the common situation of a separate parent being outside the family home. In such circumstances, the absent parent will usually contribute to the child's expenses and living costs. If it is the child's dependency on this absent parent that is to be evaluated, the situation is relatively clear, in that the court can calculate the amount the deceased paid or was likely to pay exclusively for the child, by reference to maintenance paid by court order or agreement, or likely to be paid pursuant to intervention of the Child Support Agency at the rates they would prescribe[1]. However, if the court has to assess a child's financial dependency on a parent where additional money was being contributed to the household by an absent parent, the calculation is complex. Such a calculation had to be made in *Martin v Grey*[2]. In this case, the court assessed how much of the household income was accounted for as expenses by the deceased, and found the lost dependency was the remainder. The court made it clear that, because of the various imponderables and variables, the assessment was an evaluation rather than simple calculation.

1   See further 'Pennies from Heaven – calculating fatal accident claims for loss of dependency in the non-nuclear family' by Warren Collins in APIL PI Focus Vol 19, Issue 8, which refers to *Conlon v Permasteelisa* (unreported, 2009), in which Master Roberts approved a settlement reached on this basis.
2   [1999] P&MILL vol 15(i).

(7) Fringe benefits

[L83] A significant amount of loss may be pleaded due to the very fact that the deceased's job provided more than the simple wage. The most obvious example is that of a company car. Not only have the dependants lost the earnings of the deceased, but also the use of the car provided by the employers. In *Clay v Pooler*[1], an award was allowed as compensation for the loss of a company car. The court did not award the full value of the car, as this would be clear over-compensation (the deceased used the car mainly for work). However, the proportion of the car's use for the benefit of the family was taken into account, along with reducing factors such as lower running costs, slower depreciation etc and an award made. The proportion depends on the facts of each case – in this case, it was £800 per annum.

1   [1982] 3 All ER 570.

(8) SUPPORT BY CHILDREN

[L84] If a child is working and contributing to the household expenses, a claim for the loss of this can clearly be brought. A sizeable figure was awarded for loss of a son's household contribution in *Dolbey v Goodwin*[1]. The court held, however, that the figure should be discounted, as the son would not be living at the family home for good. He would be expected to marry and, therefore, in having to support his new family, would be unable to continue to support his parents to the same extent[2]. It was held in *Hetherington v North Eastern Railway Company*[3] that occasional assistance was enough[4].

1	[1955] 1 WLR 553.
2	The figure was reduced from £3,000 to £1,500 (still approximately £25,000 at today's rates).
3	(1882) 9 QBD 160.
4	In this case, a father gave evidence that his son would have supported him if necessary, and this was enough to found a claim.

[L85] A loss of prospect of financial support, based on the notion that a child will help the parents when they grow old, may found a claim. However, the prospect must be 'substantial' and not simply possible or speculative[1]. If a child is young when he or she dies, and the parents are also in ill-health, it may be the case that it cannot be deemed any more than speculative that the parents will survive to a point where the child is in a position to support them. In such a case, a claim would fail[2]. If there are fewer uncertainties and a child was nearing an age where he or she could and would have supported his or her parents but for his or her death, a claim is likely to succeed[3].

1	*Davies v Taylor* [1972] 3 All ER 836.
2	*Barnett v Cohen* [1921] All ER 528.
3	*Taff Vale Railway v Jenkins* [1913] AC 1.

[L86] In *Kandalla v British European Airways Corporation*[1], two daughters died in an air crash. They had both been practising doctors in England. The claimants in the action were the mother and father of the two girls (both lived in Iraq). The father was a wealthy man but, on leaving Iraq (due to the change in circumstances associated with the country), he was unable to take his money out. It was held by Griffiths J that the parents had intended to live in England with their daughters and, although they would have tried to remove their wealth from Iraq, this would be extremely difficult. It was, therefore, probable that they would be supported by the daughters to a large degree. It was held one-quarter of the daughters' net income would be used for this, and an award was accordingly assessed on this basis.

1	[1980] 1 All ER 341.

(9) SUPPORT BY ESTRANGED PARTNER/SPOUSE

[L87] Where the deceased and the dependant were separated at the time of the death, whether or not a claim can be brought for dependency will depend upon whether or not there was a 'real' or 'substantial' chance of the dependant becoming dependent again on the support of the deceased, as opposed to a mere possibility or speculation that such support would have been provided[1].

1	*Davies v Taylor* [1974] AC 207; *Davies v Bonner* (6 April 1995, unreported), CA.

Dependency on pension

[L88] Dependency does not necessarily cease on retirement. A person may be dependent upon the deceased's pension in the same way that he or she could be dependent upon the deceased's earnings[1]. For example, where the deceased was the main breadwinner and had a pension, it may be reasonable for a spouse to have had a reasonable expectation of being dependent on the deceased's pension income (especially if the dependant had no separate pension provision of his or her own)[2]. Further, where the deceased was retired at the date of his or her death and was actually in receipt of a pension, there may have been some people, such as the surviving spouse, children and/or grandchildren, who were dependent upon the deceased's pension income. If so, the same principles applying to the calculation of dependency on loss of earnings apply to the calculation of dependency on the deceased's pension[3]. The position is different, though, where the deceased is not retired at the date of death. Where the dependant receives a lump sum or an allowance under the terms of the deceased's pension as a result of the death, this is regarded as a benefit under FAA 1976, s 4 which must be disregarded[4] and so no credit for the widow's pension need be given. However, if the claimant attempts to claim damages for the hypothetical lost chance of dependency on a widow's pension after retirement, notwithstanding the fact that she is in fact already in receipt of such a pension, she has suffered no loss and no dependency claim can be brought[5]. Arguably, depending on the terms of the scheme, a claim can be advanced for the balance of the widow's pension that would have been received less that actually received, limited to the period which the widow's life expectancy exceeds that of the deceased's immediately pre-injury/death life expectancy.

[1] For examples of pension loss awarded in FAA 1976 cases, see *Loader v Lucas* [1999] CLY 1620; and *Worrall v Powergen Plc* [1999] PIQR Q103.
[2] There must be a real expectation of dependency on pension. See eg *D and D v Donald* [2001] PIQR Q5, in which the trial judge, Moxon-Brown QC, held that it was a matter of sheer speculation as to the extent to which the claimant would have relied upon the deceased's pension and, therefore, no account was taken of it in the assessment of her dependency.
[3] See eg *Pidduck v Eastern Scottish Omnibuses Ltd* [1990] 1 WLR 993, where the dependency was assessed at two-thirds of the deceased's pension in the absence of any dependent children.
[4] *Pidduck v Eastern Scottish Omnibuses Ltd* [1990] 1 WLR 993. See further paras **[L103]–[L105]** below.
[5] *Auty v National Coal Board* [1985] 1 WLR 784. See further below.

The cost of replacing the deceased's entrepreneurial skills

[L89] In some cases, whilst it is clear that there was some dependence upon the deceased's finances, the value of that dependency is difficult to calculate, since the deceased may not have been in regular employment earning a predictable salary. Such cases may arise where the deceased lived on benefits[1], was self-employed or engaged in a new business venture. A number of these cases highlight an alternative method of valuing the dependency, by reference to the cost of replacing the deceased's skills. Examples of cases, which may provide some ideas as to how to value lost dependency in this sort of situation, include:

- *Cape Distribution v O'Loughlin*[2] – the deceased was a property investor with a property portfolio worth £750,000 at the time of his death. Damages were awarded on the basis of the loss of the deceased's 'flair, experience and entrepreneurial skills'. The value of these skills was, assessed by reference to the cost of replacing them, held to be £28,000 per annum. After a deduction of £5,000 per annum to take account of past and future costs, dependency was calculated using a multiplicand of £23,000. The Court of Appeal upheld the trial judge's approach, holding that there was no prescribed method for calculating the value of non-bereavement damages. It was a matter for the court how to use the available material to fit the facts of the particular case in order to establish the extent of the loss.

- *Farmer & anor v Rolls Royce Industrial Power (India) Ltd*[3] – in this case, the court had to assess the value of dependency on a successful businessman's income, capital and pension. The deceased had started a company from scratch with a partner which was eventually sold for over £30 million (split equally between him and his partner). The court had to assess the value of the financial dependency based upon the prospect that the deceased would have started up another successful business. A dependency factor of 85% was taken and applied to a loss of income dependency of over £2.2 million, and a further £4 million for a loss of capital dependency from the likely eventual proceeds of sale of the business that the deceased was developing at the time of his death.

- *Williams v Welsh Ambulance Services NHS Trust*[4] – the deceased was an entrepreneur, who started a successful building merchants business which generated profits of £384,000 in the year before his death. He had amassed a property portfolio worth £3.9 million and bought houses for his three adult children. In addition, he had a profitable sideline as a collector of steam engines and farm machinery. His widow and two of his children were employed in the business pre-accident and they, plus his third child, continued it successfully after his death. Notwithstanding strong defence contentions that there was no loss and/or their dependency was of an irrecoverable business type, the judge and the Court of Appeal allowed a dependency of just over £1.7 million, derived by calculating the cost of replacing the deceased's skills (as in *Cape*) assessed at a dependency ratio of 82.5% to age 70 and 66% thereafter, following careful analysis of the deceased's expenditure[5].

---

[1]   *Cox v Hockenhull* [2000] PIQR Q230 – in this case, it was possible to show that there was a loss by reason of a reduction in benefits following the death of the deceased.

[2]   [2001] EWCA Civ 178, [2001] PIQR Q8.

[3]   (26 February 2003), Lawtel Document No AC0105047 and AM0200488.

[4]   [2008] EWCA Civ 81, LTL 15/2/2008.

[5]   Note that the Court of Appeal judgment mistakenly refers to a reduction of 12.5% for personal expenditure. However, as their judgment was one of principle and they endorse the first instance calculations, it must follow that the dependency ratio was 82.5%.

(viii)   Dependency on Gifts, Holidays, Luxuries, Wedding Money etc

[L90]   A claim may be made in respect of the loss of holidays, gifts, clothes, luxuries etc. This can particularly be the case where a child has lost a parent who would have supported that child with more than the bare essentials. Such a claim can be quite significant if a parent is not living with the child (eg a divorced parent). In such circumstances, the absent parent is more likely to provide not only maintenance to the child but, in addition, possible expensive treats and gifts on the limited opportunity of contact ('quality time'). The court will require clear proof that such luxuries were provided prior to death. Evidence regarding the extent of the gifts, treats, holidays etc that were received in the past may then be used to assess the likely level of ongoing dependency.

[L91] *Betney v Rowlands and Mallard*[1] shows that the financial loss need not be on the basis of a proportion of income. In this case, three daughters lost their parents in an accident and succeeded in a claim for loss of prospective wedding cost contributions. Further, the daughter who was still living with her parents at the date of the accident succeeded in recovering the value of her keep (less the amount she contributed to the household) through to age 28.

[1]   [1992] CLY 1786.

(ix)   Claims for the Loss of Appreciating Assets

[L92] In *Batt v Highgate Private Hospital*[1], it was claimed that, but for the deceased's death, the deceased and her husband would have bought a property which would then have increased in value. At the time of the death, the couple had just agreed a sale price on a property and a claim was brought for the lost capital appreciation in the sum of £116,000. The trial judge rejected this head of loss as not being one which could be claimed under FAA 1976, s 3(1). Under s 3(1) of the Act, the court was permitted to award 'such damages … as are proportioned to the injury resulting from the death to the dependants respectively'. Case law had further restricted recovery to a loss containing each of the following elements: (a) pecuniary benefit; (b) arising from the relationship; and (c) which would be derived from the continuance of life. It was held that the claim for the loss of an appreciating asset, such as a house, did not satisfy these criteria, since it was a speculative loss based upon a notional gain. The loss also post-dated the death and the value of the dependency which was said to be 'freeze-framed' at the point of death and without the benefit of hindsight that a trial brings. In other words, at the time of death, the deceased's widow and family were not dependent upon the house purchase. Further, the house purchase had never been intended as an investment and, had it been, it would have fallen foul of the decision in *Burgess v Florence Nightingale Hospital for Gentlewomen*[2].

[1]   [2005] PIQR Q1.
[2]   [1955] 1 QB 349.

(x)   Service Dependency
The theory

[L93] A dependant need not receive any actual financial wages from the deceased to qualify for an award for loss of dependency. The mere fact that the deceased provided some form of service to the claimant, which is now absent, is enough. Indeed, it is sufficient to show that there was a prospect of a dependency on future services. Such a situation occurred in *Betney v Rowlands and Mallard*[1]. One of the daughters in the action gave evidence to the effect that her mother had agreed to give up work whenever the daughter had a child, and provide childminding. Further, a claim was made that the deceased grandparent would provide baby-sitting services and this was now lost. The claims succeeded, but were reduced due to the speculative nature of the claim, not least because, at the time of the accident, no children existed[2]. Services of the father rendered before his death were also awarded[3].

1   [1992] CLY 1786.
2   Although the daughter had a child at the time of trial and was again pregnant.
3   The father had provided DIY, car maintenance and gardening services prior to death.

[L94] It can be seen from the *Betney* case that the services which can be claimed as losses are wide ranging. The services rendered by a wife around the home may also be claimed[1], and it was held by Watkins J that the services of a wife are worth more than that of a housekeeper[2]. A wife may provide, in effect, 24-hour loving care for the husband and family, and the value is therefore greater.

1   *Berry v Humm & Co* [1915] 1 KB 627.
2   *Regan v Williamson* [1976] 1 WLR 305.

[L95] A common claim is for that of the dependency of the children on their mother. Naturally, the same principle could apply to the situation were a father/male partner[1] was the main carer and housekeeper although, as the cases predominantly concern mothers, the feminine is used below. This dependency is based on the services she provided and not any financial input into the household. Such a claim is notoriously difficult to quantify. In *Regan v Williamson*[2] it was expressed by Watkins J that not only are the services provided by the wife/mother undertaken over less restrictive hours than a nanny or housekeeper, but also the very fact of the services being performed by a mother increases the quality. A mother's services must be recognised as being performed with greater commitment and, although the love factor is present only in an award for bereavement, it will increase the value of ordinary nanny/housekeeper costs.

1   *Devoy v William Doxford & Sons Ltd* [2009] EWHC 1598 (QB).
2   [1976] 1 WLR 305.

[L96] Not only will the mother's services usually be of a higher quality, but there cannot really be a set employee who would fit the role. The mother would often perform many roles covering a broad spectrum of professions[1]. Obviously, the value cannot be that of each and every aspect calculated and an aggregate figure taken. The mother is not performing many of the tasks on a full-time (or even part-time) basis, and therefore any calculation using such would be inflated. Further, in *Spittle v Bunney*[2] it was held that the value of a mother's services varies as the child gets older. This is common sense. As a child becomes older and more independent, the reliance on the mother's services diminishes (even though the reliance on the parent's financial contribution remains and may increase!).

1   Including housekeeper, nanny, nurse, bookkeeper, chauffeur, homework checker/enforcer, cook, cleaner and gardener, just to mention a few.
2   [1988] 1 WLR 847.

[L97] Therefore, a calculation based on any particular professional (usually a nanny) is not entirely satisfactory, as this is not a realistic but practical comparison.

In *Stanley v Saddique*[1], it was held that the quality and continuity of the mother's services are a factor. However, in that case, the value of services was reduced because of the mother's unreliability as a mother[2]. Further, a multiplicand/multiplier method may be inappropriate in such a calculation (see below).

[1]   [1992] QB 1, CA.
[2]   See also *Hayden v Hayden* [1992] 1 WLR 986 at 993G, CA, in which the value is increased because of the 'quality and continuity of the services which this mother was likely to have provided'; and *R v CICB, ex p Kavanagh* (1998) Times, 25 August.

The calculation of lost services

[L98]   Generally, the starting point for evaluation of the lost services will be to look at services that have actually been provided and the cost of replacing those services, if any, following the death[1]. Thus, where a nanny or housekeeper has actually been employed, these costs will be recoverable, assuming they are reasonable[2]; likewise where a cleaner, carer, gardener and chiropodist were employed for a widower with Parkinson's disease who would have been cared for by the deceased[3]. However, where a person has given up work to provide the services the deceased performed, the norm would be to award the net loss of earnings[4]. But this must be reasonable, in the circumstances. It is not considered justifiable (except in exceptional circumstances) for the new carer to give up highly paid employment to provide services for which professional help would be cheaper[5]. Such exceptional circumstances arose, however, in *Mehmet v Perry*[6]. In this case, the claimant's wife died and, on medical advice, the claimant gave up a well-paid job to look after his five young children. The advice was that this was in the best interests of the children, especially as two had a rare blood disorder requiring constant care. Brian Neill QC (sitting as a deputy judge) held that this was reasonable in the circumstances. He said[7]:

> '[The father] discussed what he should do with Dr Modell who was well acquainted both with the family circumstances and the needs of the children. It is not suggested that any relative has been available to take charge of the household and I consider that the claimant was entitled to rely and act on the medical advice which he received.'

[1]   *Bordin v St Mary's NHS Trust* [2000] Lloyd's Rep Med 287.
[2]   *Bordin v St Mary's NHS Trust* [2000] Lloyd's Rep Med 287.
[3]   *Devoy v William Doxford & Sons Ltd* [2009] EWHC 1598 (QB).
[4]   See eg *Cresswell v Eaton* [1991] WLR 1113.
[5]   In *Martin v Grey* [1999] P&MILL vol 15(i), Bernard Livesey QC (sitting as a deputy High Court judge) had to evaluate a child's loss of service dependency on her mother. The claimant contended that the loss should be evaluated at the level of loss of earnings suffered by her stepmother in rejecting work. However, it was held that a more accurate calculation is made by considering that a jury would 'have had an eye to' the cost of employing a housekeeper. See also *Batt v Highgate Private Hospital* [2005] PIQR Q1.
[6]   [1977] 2 All ER 529.
[7]   [1977] 2 All ER 529 at 535.

[L99]   Where no nanny or housekeeper has actually been employed and no one has given up paid employment to care for the children, the starting point for evaluating the lost services remains the commercial cost for employing someone to perform the missing services[1]. The assessment has to be realistic (a 'jury question' it was said in *Spittle v Bunney*[2], where it was recognised that the cost of a nanny might provide a guide when bereaved children were young, but less and less so as they grew older, went to school, became less dependent and had a need for rather different parenting skills). It may be difficult to persuade a court to assess the loss by reference to a nanny, where a nanny would never in fact be used. Alternative measures can be the National Joint Council rates paid to home helps, the payments made to foster parents by local authorities, or the cost of employing a housekeeper, childminder or guardian. It should be noted that, where the deceased's lost services have been replaced gratuitously, any payment to the claimant in respect of these services is to be held on trust for the provider of the services[3]. The court must be satisfied that the claimant will actually pay the money to the care provider[4]. Therefore, where there are any concerns that the money might not be paid to the care provider, the court will take steps to ensure that the trust is fulfilled. An example of this is provided by *ATH v MS*[5], in which the Court of Appeal was concerned that the trust would not be enforced, and directed that the monies recovered would be placed in the Special Investment Account, to be held by the court in that account or otherwise dealt with as the court may direct (following an application to the Senior Master). This approach has been criticised, and the Ministry of Justice recently published a draft Civil Law Reform Bill for consultation which proposes that, instead of the money being held on trust, there is a personal obligation to account to the carer[6].

[1]   The commercial rate should be net of tax and National Insurance. For an example of the discount applied to the gratuitous services provided by grandparents, see *Bordin v St Mary's NHS Trust* [2000] Lloyd's Rep Med 287, in which Crane J applied a discount of 35%. Under LR(MP)A 1934, a 25% deduction was applied to the pre-death gratuitous care by the deceased in *Devoy v William Doxford & Sons Ltd* [2009] EWHC 1598 (QB). Also see further Chapter F.
[2]   [1988] 1 WLR 847.
[3]   By analogy with *Hunt v Severs* [1994] 2 AC 350. See further *ATH v MS* [2002] EWCA Civ 792.
[4]   *ATH v MS* [2002] EWCA Civ 792.
[5]   [2002] EWCA Civ 792.
[6]   Clause 8 of the Civil Law Reform Bill.

[L100]   Thus, it can be seen that a judge will look at the individual factors and circumstances of the case and make an informed decision as to the best form of quantifying the loss. The correct approach is not necessarily the broad brush approach, and the court should attempt to calculate each head of loss as accurately as possible[1]. Much will depend upon the ages of the dependants, how much care they require, and would continue to require in the future, and the extent of the services that were in fact provided by the deceased[2]. Travel expenses incurred in the provision of the services should also be recoverable[3]. Usually, a multiplier/multiplicand approach will be applied to the quantification of lost services in the same way as in the calculation of a dependant's financial dependency. In order to calculate the multiplicand, a report from a care expert may be appropriate. Occasionally, however, where there are numerous imponderables, a multiplier/multiplicand approach may not be justified, and a lump sum will be awarded to reflect the particular loss of services in question[4]. For example, in *ATH & anor v MS*[5] the Court of Appeal reduced the trial judge's award for loss of the mother's services from £150,000 to £37,500 without any explanation as to how this figure was arrived at, save that the original figure was said to be outside the bracket of other awards when properly adjusted. Another example is provided by *Thomas v Kwik Save Stores Ltd*[6], in which the deceased had provided housekeeping services prior to her death, but suffered from a number of physical disabilities which meant it was difficult to predict the length of the likely dependency and the extent of the services she would have provided had she survived. The Court of Appeal reduced the trial judge's award of £50,000 to £20,000. Latham LJ said[7]:

> 'Dealing first with the claim under the Fatal Accidents Act, I consider that this was a classic example of a case in which the multiplier/multiplicand approach was wholly inappropriate. The future progress of the claimant's wife's disabilities had the accident not happened was entirely unpredictable, save in so far as there was the certainty of deterioration. She may well have been able to continue to provide some assistance in the house, but on the other hand she may not, and indeed may have become a burden on the claimant rather than a benefit. How should the court provide appropriate compensation in such a case? It has to be remembered that the court is carrying out an exercise in determining the financial, not the emotional, dependency of the claimant on the deceased. That does not mean that the claimant has to show increased expenditure on the one hand or decreased income on the other. The loss of services which can be valued in money terms, even if not in fact replaced by an outside agency, will represent a loss for which the claimant can obtain compensation.'

[1]   *Bordin v St Mary's NHS Trust* [2000] Lloyd's Rep Med 287.
[2]   For an example of a case in which a great deal of care was required to look after a disabled child, see *E (A Child) v North Middlesex Hospital NHS Trust* (13 December 1999, unreported), QBD, a decision of Judge John Rogers QC noted in [2000] *Current Law*, August.
[3]   *Bordin v St Mary's NHS Trust* [2000] Lloyd's Rep Med 287.
[4]   See *Stanley v Saddique* [1992] QB 1, CA, in which the trial judge's award of £24,000 for loss of a mother's services (calculated using a multiplier and multiplicand) was reduced by the Court of Appeal (performing a 'jury' calculation) to a lump sum of £10,000. See also *Cox v Hockenhull* [2000] PIQR Q230, where a lump sum of £7,500 was awarded for loss of a wife's services; *Laniyan v Barry May Haulage* [2002] PIQR Q35, in which an award for services was claimed and allowed of £25,000; and *Thomas v Kwik Save Stores Ltd* (8 June 2000), CA, Lawtel Document No C8400690, where the lump sum to reflect lost services was reduced to £20,000.
[5]   [2002] EWCA Civ 792.
[6]   (8 June 2000), CA, Lawtel Document No C8400690.
[7]   At paras [15]–[17].

[L101]   Although the larger claims for lost services will usually involve the death of a mother who provided housekeeping, childminding and domestic services, claims should not be forgotten for other services such as DIY, gardening, car washing, window cleaning etc. Awards are often made for between £500 and £3,000[1] per annum in order to cover these services. Much depends upon the nature and extent of the services that it is claimed would have been provided. If the deceased was skilled or trained (eg a builder or carpenter), the loss might be significant. On the other hand, if the deceased was a busy working professional who used to pay labourers to carry out most domestic and home maintenance tasks, the loss is likely to be less. Examples of awards made by the courts include:

*   *Robertson v Lestrange*[2] – a sum for services was recovered of £750 per annum (updated to 2009 prices = approximately £1,680 per annum).
*   *Crabtree v Wilson*[3] – in which the Court of Appeal allowed £1,500 per annum (updated to 2009 prices = approximately £2,270 per annum) for work on the family home.
*   *Loader v Lucas*[4] – an award of £750 per annum (updated to 2009 prices = approximately £965 per annum) was made for DIY, home and car maintenance services.

- *Wolfe v Del'Innocenti*[5] – £1,500 per annum (updated to 2009 prices = approximately £1,545 per annum) for the loss of services of an inveterate handyman.
- *Williams v Welsh Ambulance Services NHS Trust*[6] – £1,950 per annum for loss of gardening and DIY to age 80 for the family of an indefatigable entrepreneur.
- *Beesley v New Century Group*[7] – £2,000 per annum to age 75 was allowed for DIY and maintenance where the deceased was a builder and decorator who had done considerable work on his own home in the past. This was in addition to a £2,000 award for loss of intangible benefits.
- *Kirk v VIC Hallam Holdings Ltd*[8] – £2,000 per annum each for two daughters for their loss of child care services by the deceased to his grand children.

[1] A figure of about £3,400 p.a appears to have been achieved for loss of services in the 'lost years' in the settlement of *Hammill v FPA Pitchmastic Ltd & Briggs Roofing & Cladding Ltd*, LTLPI2/2/07.
[2] [1985] 1 All ER 950.
[3] [1993] PIQR Q24, CA.
[4] [1999] CLY 1620.
[5] [2006] EWHC 2694 (QB), LTL 22/6/2007. £1,500 per annum was also awarded on similar grounds in *Fleet v Fleet* [2009] EWHC 3166 (QB).
[6] [2008] EWCA Civ 81, LTL 15/2/2008.
[7] [2008] EWHC 3033 (QB), LTL 23/12/2008.
[8] [2008] EWHC 2969 (QB), LTL 9/12/2008.

[L102] It is arguable that all of the above awards are well below the real value of the deceased's services. An alternative measure that exposes the low value of most awards under this heading is the Office of National Statistics survey from 2000 on the value of unpaid labour[1]. That survey concluded that the average value of unpaid household labour in UK by men was £8,411 and by women £17,418[2].

[1] Francis & Tiwana 'Unpaid household production in the UK, 1995–2000', Economic Trends 2004, available at www.statistics.gov.uk/articles/economic_trends/ET602Perry.pdf.
[2] Based on an average of £12,104 per individual per year, and split by gender time spent of 59% females and 41% males.

[L103] In passing, it should be noted that, as alluded to above, unlike claims for lost services in a personal injury action[1], it is strongly arguable that damages are recoverable for the lost dependency on services prior to trial (together with interest), even though those services have not actually been replaced[2]. The reason is that the intention in a fatal accident case is to value the lost dependency. Often, the most appropriate way to assess the value of the lost dependency on the deceased's services is to consider the cost of employing a third party to perform the services, but this is used only as a measure of the value of the services as opposed to being a requirement for recovery[3]. Of course, where money has been spent on employing a third party, the reasonable costs will be recoverable from the defendant. As noted above, any damages recovered on behalf of a third party for gratuitous services will be held on trust for the provider of the services under the principles laid down in *Hunt v Severs*[4]. However, where the claimant is impecunious and has not been able to replace the lost services, this does not mean that he or she has not lost something of value. The loss still needs to be quantified.

[1] See further Chapter F. It should be noted that, whilst *Daly v General Steam Navigation Co Ltd* [1981] 1 WLR 120 may technically bind the lower courts not to award damages for past loss of

domestic services, DIY etc unless money has actually been spent, it was criticised by the Law Commission in its Report No 262 'Damages for Personal Injury: Medical, Nursing and other Expenses; Collateral Benefits' (November 1999) and may well have been overtaken by developments in the law, particularly by the House of Lords' decision in *Hunt v Severs* [1994] 2 AC 350. In any event, the decision in *Daly* is often ignored in practice by judges, and awards are often made for the gratuitous provision of services such as DIY, decorating and gardening, even though the claimant has incurred no monetary loss: see eg *Blair v Michelin Tyre plc* (25 January 2002, unreported), QBD; *Assinder v Griffin* [2001] All ER (D) 356 (May); *Froggatt v Chesterfield & North Derbyshire Royal Hospital NHS Trust* [2002] All ER (D) 218 (Dec); and *Beesley v New Century Group* [2008] EWHC 3033 (QB), LTL 23/12/2008.

[2]   *Williams v Welsh Ambulance Services NHS Trust* [2008] EWCA Civ 81; Lady Justice Smith's reasoning, that a dependant cannot by their conduct after the death of the deceased affect the value of the dependency, is potentially relevant to this issue.

[3]   See further paras 2.26–2.28 of the Law Commission's Report No 263 'Claims for Wrongful Death' (1999). See also *Loader v Lucas* [1999] CLY 1620, in which £750 per annum was awarded for dependency on DIY, home maintenance and car maintenance during the pre- and post-trial periods; and *Beesley v New Century Group* [2008] EWHC 3033 (QB), in which £2,000 was awarded for pre- and post-trial loss of services.

[4]   [1994] 2 AC 350. See further *ATH v MS* [2002] EWCA Civ 792. Although note that the Ministry of Justice has recently published a consultation paper and draft Civil Law Reform Bill, which proposes that the trust mechanism in gratuitous care cases be replaced by a personal legal obligation to account to the carer.

[L104]   A defendant may argue that the best way of valuing the lost services up to the date of trial is not necessarily by using the same multiplicand for the ongoing loss of services, but is most appropriately reflected by the cost of putting the claimant/ dependant back into the position he or she would have been in had the deceased been able to provide those services. Take, for example, the case of a deceased who used to look after his family's garden. At the date of trial, the annual value of the deceased's services is calculated to be £1,500 per annum. If a number of years have passed between the date of death and the date of trial, the simplest method of assessing the lost dependency is to apply to same multiplicand of £1,500 to pre- and post-death periods[1]. However, where the lost services have not been replaced, instead of calculating the lost dependency on gardening services using the multiplicand of £1,500 per annum, an alternative would be to award a one-off fee that it would cost to pay a gardener to put the family garden back into the position it would have been in had the deceased survived[2]. However, this alternative fails to recognise the loss to the dependants of the good maintenance of the garden during the pre-trial period.

[1]   See eg *Loader v Lucas* [1999] CLY 1620 and *Beesley v New Century Group* [2008] EWHC 3033 (QB).

[2]   The size of the one-off sum will be based on the available evidence, the best form of which is usually quotes from local tradesmen.

(xi)   Loss of Intangible Benefits

[L105]   In a number of cases[1], an additional lump sum has been awarded to dependants for the so-called *Regan v Williamson*[2] factor. This sum is said to reflect the special qualitative factor of the services provided by a parent or spouse over and above the level of services that can be provided by a replacement housekeeper or nanny. In *Devoy v William Doxford & Sons Ltd*[3] it was described as the loss of 'special attention and affection' that the deceased would have continued to provide when caring for his disabled wife, had it not been for his death. In *Beesley v New Century Group*[4], Hamblen J described the practice of making such awards as now being established, and saw no reason to distinguish between spouses and children in relation to the availability of such awards, although he endorsed an extract from *Kemp and Kemp*[5] that such awards will usually be lower where the deceased is the breadwinner. However, Mackay J in *Fleet v Fleet*[6] was of the view that the extension of these awards to spouses should not be automatic, but on the facts of the case awarded £2,500 to the widow because she was considerably older than the deceased and would have needed more care than usual as the years went by. Traditionally, the lump sum for the loss of these intangible benefits has been kept relatively modest, usually between £2,000 and £5,000, in order to avoid any overlap between this award and the awards for bereavement damages[7] and loss of defined services (eg DIY, gardening), as described in the preceding section.

[1] See eg *Mehmet v Perry* [1977] 2 All ER 529; *Topp v London Country Bus* [1993] 3 All ER 448; *Johnson v British Midlands Airways Ltd* [1996] PIQR Q8; *Bordin v St Mary's NHS Trust* [2000] Lloyd's Rep Med 287; *ATH v MS* [2002] EWCA Civ 792.

[2] [1976] 1 WLR 305.

[3] [2009] EWHC 1598 (QB), LTL 30/7/2009; £2,000 awarded.

[4] [2008] EWHC 3033 (QB), LTL 23/12/2008; £2,000 awarded.

[5] At para 29-047.

[6] *Fleet v Fleet* [2009] EWHC 3166 (QB).

[7] See further *McGregor on Damages* (18th edn).

[L106] The award under this head has, therefore, become a conventional figure which does not appear to have kept up with inflation[1]. *ATH v MS*[2] provides an example of the Court of Appeal keeping the applicable award within modest limits. In this case, the judge at first instance had made awards of £1,000, £5,000 and £7,000 to the deceased's three children who were aged 19, 11 and 8 respectively at the date of the deceased's death. The highest two awards were challenged by the defendant as being excessive. The Court of Appeal agreed, holding that the highest two awards fell outside the appropriate bracket. The awards were reduced to £3,500 and £4,500 respectively.

[1] *Batt v Highgate Private Hospital* [2005] PIQR Q1. Given that the award was a conventional sum more akin to a bereavement award than general damages (eg for pain, suffering and loss of amenity), the trial judge in this case awarded interest at the full special account rate on this element of the claim.

[2] [2002] EWCA Civ 792.

[L107] It should be noted that, although the awards under this head have traditionally been awarded for the loss of intangible benefits provided by a mother/wife, similar awards have also been made for the loss of intangible benefits provided by a father/husband[1]. Logically, there would seem to be no reason to distinguish between the two sexes. Likewise, there seems to be little reason in principle to discriminate against cohabitants simply because they are not married.

[1] See eg *O'Toole (deceased) v Iarnrod Eireann Irish Rail* [1999] CLY 1535; *Beesley v New Century Group* [2008] EWHC 3033 (QB); *Fleet v Fleet* [2009] EWHC 3166 (QB).

(xii)   Benefits Arising Out of Death in Dependency Cases

[L108]   Section 4 of FAA 1976 states as follows:

'In assessing damages in respect of a person's death in an action under this Act, benefits which have accrued or will or may accrue to any person from his estate or otherwise as a result of his death shall be disregarded.'

The section looks relatively straightforward. In assessing damages, any benefit a dependant receives because of the death is not considered[1]. The most obvious is that of a deceased bequeathing property to the dependant. In *Wood v Bentall Simplex Ltd*[2], a farmer died, leaving the farm to his family. The family also brought a claim for dependency on the farmer's earnings from the farm. It was held that the farmer's work, and therefore the benefit of the capital value of the farm, was not to be set off following s 4.

1   Note that a pecuniary payment made to a claimant under the Pneumoconiosis (Workers' Compensation) Act 1979 does fall to be deducted from the total damages awarded to the claimant: *Ballantine v Newalls Insulation Co Ltd* [2000] PIQR Q57; and *Cameron v Vinters Defence Systems Ltd* LTL 19/10/2007, [2008] PIQR P5. However, it is doubtful that these cases remain good law following *Arnup* (see further below). Also see Chapter J.
2   [1992] PIQR P332.

[L109]   The controversy caused by FAA 1976, s 4 is usually the question whether the receipt of the benefit negates any loss to such an extent that the loss does not arise in the first place. This has arisen in four main areas: pensions, replacement families, income from investment capital, and employment-related benefits. The recent Court of Appeal decision in *Arnup v M W White Ltd*[1] has brought welcome clarity to the application of ss 3 and 4 of FAA 1976. In a nutshell, if the receipt of the benefit was not caused by the death, then, pursuant to s 3 of FAA 1976, it is irrelevant to the assessment; or, if it was, then it is to be disregarded under s 4. Consequently, all, or virtually all[2], payments made as a result of death will not feature in the calculation of loss of dependency.

1   [2008] ICR 1064; (2008) Times, 25 June.
2   It is unlikely that the reasoning of the pneumoconiosis scheme cases of *Ballantine v Newalls Insulation Co Ltd* [2000] PIQR Q57 and *Cameron v Vinters Defence Systems Ltd* LTL 19/10/2007, [2008] PIQR P5 survives *Arnup*.

Pensions

[L110]   Two situations can arise regarding the calculation of loss of pensions in a fatal accident claim. The dependant may claim they are or would have been dependent on the deceased's pension. In other words:

(i)   the deceased was claiming a pension and, out of such, the dependant was supported; or

(ii)   the deceased was not of pensionable age, but on reaching that, they would have received a pension and contributed to the dependant's expenses.

The obvious example of such a dependant is a spouse of the deceased. The loss is recoverable in both cases, calculated in the same form as loss of earnings. That is, the loss the claimant has actually suffered. The value of the pension can be calculated in the same form as in a standard personal injury case[1].

[1] See further Chapter H regarding pension loss. For examples of pension loss awarded in FAA 1976 cases, see *Loader v Lucas* [1999] CLY 1620; and *Worrall v Powergen Plc* [1999] PIQR Q103. Note also *D and D v Donald* [2001] PIQR Q5, in which the trial judge, Moxon-Brown QC, held that it was a matter of sheer speculation as to the extent to which the claimant would have relied upon the deceased's pension and, therefore, no account was taken of it in the assessment of her dependency.

[L111] However, the question arises, what is the standing of the pension a widow receives because of the death of the deceased? Is this a benefit and therefore irrelevant to the question of damages? Generally speaking, the answer to this question is 'yes'. Therefore, when calculating the dependant's lost dependency on the deceased's pension, any lump sum or benefit received from the deceased's pension providers as a result of the deceased's death will be regarded as a benefit and is to be disregarded from the dependency calculation[1]. However, in *Auty v National Coal Board*[2], Mrs Popow, who received a widow's pension after the death of her husband, claimed she was entitled to an award for the lost chance of dependency on a widow's pension she would have received in the event that the deceased had lived to retirement age but had then died thereafter. In other words, in addition to claiming damages for dependency on the deceased's pension, she was also seeking to claim damages on the widow's pension that would have been paid contingent on the deceased's death following retirement. It was argued on her behalf that FAA 1976, s 4 meant that the actual widow's pension she received should be ignored. The Court of Appeal rejected this argument, holding that she had suffered no loss because she was already in receipt of a widow's pension. Therefore, she could not claim for the hypothetical loss of a widow's pension when she was in fact already in receipt of one.

[1] *Auty v National Coal Board* [1985] 1 WLR 784; *Pidduck v Eastern Scottish Omnibuses Ltd* [1990] 1 WLR 993.
[2] [1985] 1 WLR 784.

[L112] Where the claim is for loss of a dependency on a pension which is being paid at the time of the accident, and the claimant then becomes entitled to an allowance as a result of the deceased's death, the position is much more straightforward. Assuming the allowance is only payable as a result of the death, it is considered to be a benefit covered by s 4 and can therefore be disregarded. This was the position in *Pidduck v Eastern Scottish Omnibuses Ltd*[1], in which the Court of Appeal held that a sum which became payable directly to the deceased's wife, when the deceased died within five years of retirement, was a benefit arising out of the deceased's death and was therefore to be disregarded when assessing the wife's dependency under FAA 1976. Interestingly, it did not matter that the dependant in this case was already in receipt of payments from a widow's annuity fund prior to the deceased's death and carried on receiving these payments. Having regard to the wording of the pension policy, the important point was that the right to a widow's allowance only came into existence upon the death of the deceased. Accordingly, the benefit accrued to the claimant 'as a result of' the deceased's death and was therefore disregarded.

[L113] A similar result on different facts was arrived at in *McIntyre v Harland & Wolff plc*[2]. In this case, the deceased had elected, following diagnosis of mesothelioma, to stop working, and he consequently received payment for termination of service under his employer's provident fund scheme. Had it not been for the tort, he would have continued working to retirement age and then been eligible for a termination of service payment under the same scheme. His widow successfully recovered a dependency for the payment that would have been due on retirement and, pursuant to s 4 of the FAA 1976, did not have to give credit for the moneys she ultimately received, via her husband's estate, for the earlier payments for termination of service.

1   [1990] 1 WLR 993.
2   [2006] 1 WLR 2577, CA.

Replacement families

[L114]   As stated earlier, a claim may be made on behalf of a child for the loss of his or her mother's services (see above). The question of FAA 1976, s 4 arises again here if the child is subsequently provided with a replacement carer, providing similar or at least equally good 'services'. Such a replacement may be a family member, such as an aunt and uncle, or it may be a stepmother.

[L115]   In *Stanley v Saddique*[1], the claimant's mother died in a car accident. At the time, the mother and father were separated and the child had been living with the mother. After the accident, the claimant went to live with his father, stepmother and stepsiblings. It was held that FAA 1976, s 4 applied not only to financial benefit but also to substitute services provided. Purchas LJ said[2]:

'... the Judge was correct in his decision that the benefits accruing to the claimant as a result of his absorption into the family unit consisting of his father and stepmother and siblings should be wholly disregarded for the purposes of assessing damages.'

Ralph Gibson LJ[3] expressed the view that, although he had come to the same conclusion as Purchas LJ, in that the effects of remarriage should be ignored, he was not sure as to whether this was Parliament's intention.

1   [1992] QB 1, CA.
2   [1992] QB 1 at 14A.
3   [1992] QB 1 at 20A.

[L116]   In *Hayden v Hayden*[1], a four-year-old infant girl was living with her parents and older siblings. Her mother was killed in an accident for which her father was liable. The father then gave up work to look after the claimant. The judge at trial awarded a sum for dependency on the mother, but took the services provided by the father into consideration. The Court of Appeal affirmed this decision, yet held itself bound by *Stanley v Saddique*. McCowan LJ, dissenting, and Sir David Croom-Johnson both held that the effects of introduction into a family are 'benefits' under s 4. However, they differed in their interpretation of the application of *Stanley v Saddique*.

1   [1992] 1 WLR 986.

[L117]   Sir David Croom-Johnson considered that the courts should ask two questions:

(i)   Has the claimant suffered loss?
(ii) If so, has the claimant accrued a benefit as a result of the death?

Sir David answered the former in the affirmative. Therefore, how did he reconcile *Stanley v Saddique*? He stated[1]:

> 'The facts in the instant case, however, are wholly different from those in *Stanley v Saddique*. The claimant remained in the family home with her father and, for a time, with her older brothers and sisters until they left home. She continued to be looked after by him. No reasonable Judge or jury would regard the defendant, in doing what he did, as doing other than discharge his parental duties, many of which he had been carrying out in any event, and would be expected to continue to do. The reasoning of the trial Judge in the instant case seems to be that he was making the first of Diplock LJ's two estimates, that is, of the initial loss to the claimant caused by the death of the mother. Whether that is so or not, the continuing services of the father are not a benefit which has accrued as a result of the death. In the end, what is a "benefit" must be a question of fact.'

[1]   [1992] 1 WLR 986 at 999H.

[L118]   Sir David Croom-Johnson did not consider the fact that the claimant was receiving more care from the father than before as a benefit. McCowan LJ simply interpreted *Stanley v Saddique* as meaning that extra family care was a benefit. Parker LJ's judgment, however, makes the application difficult. He agreed in the result with Sir David Croom-Johnson, but not for the same reasons. Parker LJ held[1] that he was following the earlier pre-s 4 case of *Hay v Hughes*[2], which stated that gratuitous services of a relative are not a benefit resulting from the death of the deceased.

[1]   [1992] 1 WLR 986 at 1003H.
[2]   [1975] QB 790.

[L119]   These two cases of *Stanley v Saddique* and *Hayden v Hayden* are arguably in conflict and inconsistent with each other. However, the law has subsequently been clarified in *R v CICB, ex p K*[1]. The mother was murdered by the father, and the children went to live with their aunt and uncle. Brooke LJ reviewed the law relating to the 'benefits' of inclusion in a near family in fatal cases. He rejected Parker LJ's following of *Hay v Hughes*[2] and found the court bound by *Stanley v Saddique*[3], and also expressed the opinion that Parker LJ was influenced by the fact that the tortfeasor in *Hayden* was the supplier of services.

[1]   [1998] 2 FLR 107.
[2]   [1975] QB 790.
[3]   Two members of the court in *Hayden* held *Stanley v Saddique* was to be followed.

[L120]   Rougier J clarified the point. He stated that the court in *Hayden v Hayden* accepted that *Stanley v Saddique* was binding. The reason they reached a contrary decision was that they distinguished *Hayden's* case on two counts:

(i)   the tortfeasor was the person providing the replacement services; and
(ii) the father had been providing the services before the death by way of parental duty, and so the services provided after death did not accrue as a result of that death.

[L121]   Following this interpretation, the correct approach may be inferred by asking the two questions:

(i)   has there been a loss? (If the answer is no, then there is no claim.) If so, then;

(ii) have any benefits been accrued as a result of the mother's death? If so, these will be disregarded.

[L122]   Although a relative may provide replacement parenting, a claim for the loss of parental services can still be maintained. The replacement services provided by a family member can be a benefit, and the only case in which *Hayden* should be considered is where the service provider already has a parental duty or is the tortfeasor. *Stanley v Saddique* has since been followed in several other cases, including *Laniyan v Barry May Haulage*[1] and *ATH v MS*[2]. In *ATH v MS*, giving the lead judgment of the court (with which Tuckey LJ and Jackson J agreed), Kennedy LJ said[3]:

> 'In my judgment, in the light of the authorities, the position is reasonably clear. Where, as here, infant children are living with and are dependent on one parent, with no support being provided by the other parent, in circumstances where the provision of such support in the future seems unlikely, and the parent with whom they are living is killed, in circumstances giving rise to liability under the Fatal Accidents Act, after which the other parent (who is not the tortfeasor) houses and takes responsibility for the children, the support which they enjoy after the accident is a benefit which has accrued as a result of the death and, pursuant to section 4 of the 1976 Act, it must be disregarded, both in the assessment of loss and in the calculation of damages.'

But he went on to say at [30]:

> 'However, such damages can only be awarded on the basis that they are used to reimburse the voluntary carer for services already rendered, and are available to pay for such services in the future. In the words used by Lord Bridge in *Hunt v Severs* damages are held on trust and if the terms of the trust seem unlikely to be fulfilled then the court awarding damages must take steps to avoid that outcome. Contrary to what was said by Crane J in *Bordin* I believe that the trust is one which the court can, and in an appropriate case should enforce. It is not sufficient to leave the matter for further litigation in another division. I will return to that matter at the end of this judgment.'

---

[1]   [2002] PIQR Q3. Although Stuart Brown QC, sitting as a deputy High Court judge, said in this case that the situation would have been entirely different if the parents had been living together before the death, as in *Hayden v Hayden* [1975] QB 790 or *Martin v Grey* (13 May 1998, unreported), there had been a financial order or actual support in place before the death.
[2]   [2002] EWCA Civ 792.
[3]   At [29].

Income from investment capital

[L123]   The third specific situation in which FAA 1976, s 4 comes into play concerns the treatment of income from investment capital, including property, stocks, shares, bonds, savings etc. Where the capital passes to the dependants under the terms of the deceased's will or the rules of intestacy, the capital itself is likely to be seen as a benefit and is therefore disregarded under s 4[1]. As regards the income derived from the capital, such as rent, interest and dividends, much depends upon the individual facts of the case. The general starting point is that, if there was a dependency upon income derived from the deceased's capital prior to the deceased's death, assuming that the capital passes to the dependants after the death, there is arguably no loss because the dependants can continue to benefit from the income from the capital[2].

However, there are cases in which the dependants still suffer some loss, eg where the deceased had a particular flair for investment and it is argued that the capital (and the income from the capital) would have grown, but for the deceased's death. It may also be that the management of the capital requires a degree of skill or experience not possessed by the dependants, and it may be possible to claim a dependency based upon the cost of replacing the deceased's services. An example of this can be seen in *Cape Distribution v O'Loughlin*[3], in which the deceased was a property developer with a large portfolio. The Court of Appeal upheld a dependency calculation based upon a multiplicand of £23,000, which was found to be the net cost of replacing the deceased's skills after expenses.

[1]   See eg *Wood v Bentall Simplex Ltd* [1992] PIQR P332.

[2]   See Oliver LJ's judgment in *Auty v National Coal Board* [1985] 1 WLR 784; and Sir David Croom-Johnson's judgment in *Hayden v Hayden* [1992] 1 WLR 986.

[3]   [2001] EWCA Civ 178. See also *Farmer v Rolls Royce Industrial Power (India) Ltd* (26 February 2003), Lawtel Document No AC0105047 and AM0200488; and *Williams v Welsh Ambulance Services NHS Trust* [2008] EWCA Civ 81.

Employment-related benefits

[L124]   The fourth type of post-death benefits that have been disregarded are employment-related benefits that are paid as a result of death. In *Arnup v M W White Ltd*[1] the dependants received £129,600 from the defendant employer's death in service scheme, and a further £100,000 from a trust fund set up by the defendant employer. The defendant sought a credit for these payments against the dependency claim. The claimant's response was disarmingly simple and compelling: if these payments were not caused by the death then, pursuant to s 3 of FAA 1976, they were irrelevant to the assessment; or, if they were, then they were to be disregarded under s 4. The Court of Appeal agreed, with Lady Justice Smith commenting that, consequently, the issue of causation was no longer of any great importance on this point. It was argued that this would make it impossible for employer defendants from making such payments and seeking credit for them in any future claim. The court disagreed, and stated that all such benefits were to be disregarded under s 4, unless they were expressly conditional on credit for them being given in any claim.

[1]   [2008] ICR 1064, (2008) Times, 25 June.

(xiii)   Other Factors in the Calculation of Dependency

Length of the dependency

[L125]   Certain elements concerning the deceased will be taken into account when calculating the value of the lost dependency. The pre-injury health of the deceased is of utmost importance. If he or she had a shortened life expectancy, the dependency would have been for a limited period and, as such, the multiplier would have to be reduced. Likewise, if the dependant has died before the date of trial, this is something which can properly be taken into account[1]. Also, the likely retirement age of the deceased will, of course, impact upon the amount of dependency, as will potential likely increases or decreases in earnings. Another factor is the health of the dependant.

If the dependant's life expectancy is reduced on account of illness, then account must be taken for this in the multiplier. In relation to children, the court will need to form a view on the evidence as to the likely duration of the dependency, which will vary from case to case[2].

[L126]   The above-mentioned response by the Ministry of Justice to their consultation on the Law of Damages[3] and the subsequent draft Civil Law Reform Bill[4] make several proposals relating to what factors can be taken into account concerning marriage, relationships and dependency:

- the prospects of divorce or dissolution of a civil partnership, but only if a petition for divorce, judicial separation, dissolution or nullity has actually been made;
- the prospects of the breakdown of a dependent relationship, but only if evidenced by the couple no longer living together; or
- the fact but not prospects of post-death remarriage, entry into a civil partnership or financially supportive co-habitation of at least two years' duration.

[L127]   It is to be hoped that legislation is passed to give effect to these sensible proposals, which will add clarity and limit intrusive enquiries into a couple's personal background which are clearly unwelcome when the surviving partner is already going through the grief of their loss. If and when the draft Civil Law Reform Bill is passed, many of the cases referred to below will be consigned to history.

1   *Williamson v Thornycroft* [1940] 2 KB 658, CA.
2   See para **[L67]** for further details of the duration of child dependencies.
3   Ministry of Justice 'The Law of Damages – Response to consultation CP(R) 907', 1 July 2009.
4   Published on 15 December 2009, with related consultation CP 53/09.

Whether or not there was an enforceable right to support

[L128]   Where the dependant was merely cohabiting with the deceased as opposed to being married, by virtue of FAA 1976, s 3(4), the court must take into account the fact that the dependant had no enforceable right to financial support by the deceased as a result of their living together. In *Drew v Abassi*[1], notwithstanding the evidence that the claimant and deceased were in a happy and settled relationship of long standing, the trial judge reduced the multiplier from 15 to 13. This reduction of approximately 13% was upheld on appeal to the Court of Appeal. Whether such a distinction between marriage and long-term co-habitation would be taken today is debatable.

1   24 May 1995, unreported, CA.

Prospects of divorce

[L129]   In some cases, the length of the dependency and assessment of the multiplicand will be affected by the risk that the relationship giving rise to the dependency would have failed in any event.

[L130]   A reduction to the applicable multiplier will often be appropriate in cases where there is a history of previous adulterous behaviour. For example, in *Owen v Martin*[1] it was held by the Court of Appeal that the prospects of a divorce should be taken into account given: (i) the possibility of divorce as shown by marriage statistics; (ii) the claimant and the deceased had only been married for one year prior to his death; and (iii) the deceased had a previous history of adultery which did not easily lend itself to the probability of the marriage lasting the natural life of the deceased. In the circumstances, the multiplier for future dependency was reduced from 15 to 11, ie a reduction of 27%. However, the fact that the claimant had actually remarried and her new husband was a higher earner than the deceased did not defeat the claim[2]. Another example is provided by *D and D v Donald*[3], in which the deceased suffered injuries resulting in his death whilst out with his mistress. The trial judge, Moxon-Brown QC, said:

> 'It is a hard thing to penalise a widow in damages who is herself entirely blameless, but who faces evidence that during their short marriage her husband strayed. But I cannot ignore that evidence … In the case of a man who could behave like that and who might have behaved like that again, there must have been a substantial chance that the marriage would have failed.'

[1]   [1992] PIQR Q151.
[2]   Consequent to FAA 1976, s 3(3); see further below.
[3]   [2001] PIQR Q5.

[L131]   A similar conclusion was reached in *Stanley v Saddique*[1], in which the court took account of the fact that the deceased was an unreliable mother and may have left the family at some point[2].

[1]   [1992] QB 1, CA.
[2]   See also *Bordin v St Mary's NHS Trust* [2000] PIQR Q230, where Crane J held that the multiplier had to be adjusted downwards in order to reflect the possibility of something happening to the claimant, his mother or his parents' marriage.

[L132]   It is a moot point, however, whether statistical evidence regarding divorce – which tends to suggest that 45% or more marriages end in divorce – might of itself be sufficient to reduce the dependency multiplier. If the evidence points to a strong, happy pre-death relationship, to what extent should a judge speculate whether or not the marriage in question would have failed? Can judicial notice be taken of the high national divorce rate and the possibility that the dependency would have ended? It is submitted that a degree of caution must be exercised before reducing the dependency multiplier on this basis alone. First, the statistics in question need to be put before the court and properly assessed, since it is often argued that a few people skew the figures by marrying and divorcing numerous times. Secondly, just because the relationship ends docs not necessarily bring an end to the dependency, especially where the dependant is not working or has taken time off to raise a family. Lastly, it involves the court speculating whether or not the relationship in question would have become one of the unfortunate statistics or would have survived. In this regard, Tudor Evans J rejected a similar argument in *Wheatley v Cunningham*[1]. He reasoned as follows:

> 'As to the risk of the break down of the marriage, I have to evaluate all future changes (save the chances of future children). In *Davies v Taylor (No 1)* [1974] AC 207, the claimant widow had deserted the husband before he died and she resisted all his offers to return. He had started divorce proceedings. In proceedings under the Fatal Accidents Act, the claimant claimed a dependency on the deceased. The claim failed. Lord Reid at 212 of the report said:

"He wanted her to come back but she was unwilling to come. But she says that there was a prospect or chance or probability that she might have returned to him later and it is only in that event that she would have benefited from his survival. To my mind the issue and the sole issue is whether that chance or probability was substantial. If it was it must be evaluated. If it was a mere possibility it must be ignored. Many different words could be and have been used to indicate the dividing line. I can think of none better than 'substantial' on the one hand, or 'speculative' on the other. It must be left to the good sense of the tribunal to decide on broad lines, without regard to legal niceties, but on a consideration of all the facts in proper perspective."

Applying this test and bearing in mind the evidence that the claimant and her husband were very happy together, I refuse to take mere statistics into account and so reduce the multiplier. It is pure speculation whether this marriage would have fallen into the 40 per cent assuming that these statistics will prevail in the future.'

In practice, defendants rarely seem to attempt such an argument unless there is clear case of specific evidence pointing to an unstable marriage.

---

[1]   [1992] PIQR Q100.

Prospects of marriage/remarriage

(1)   Widow's remarriage

[L133]   Under FAA 1976, s 3(3) the prospects of a dependent widow remarrying are not taken into account in the assessment of her lost dependency[1].

---

[1]   Before Parliament intervened, a widow's remarriage before trial had been taken into account when assessing her dependency: *Lloyds Bank and Mellows v Railway Executive* [1952] 1 TLR 1207; *Mead v Clarke Chapman* [1956] 1 WLR 76.

(2)   Widower's remarriage

[L134]   The position remains a little unclear in relation to dependent widowers. In s 3(3) of the Act, reference is only made to the prospects of remarriage of widows as opposed to widowers. Arguably, the application of s 6 of the Interpretation Act 1978 might result in reading 'widow' so as to include the masculine gender.

[L135]   However, in *Khan v Duncan*[1] it appears that Popplewell J did take into account the prospect of the dependent widower remarrying[2]. This may be seen as inconsistent with the proper interpretation of ss 3(3) and 4 of FAA 1976. In contrast, in *Topp v London County Bus (SW) Ltd*[3], May J dismissed a claim for damages under FAA 1976 due to a failure to establish liability, but he gave a judgment regarding quantum in case his decision on liability was successfully appealed[4]. The parties agreed that the trial judge was bound by the Court of Appeal decision of *Stanley v Saddique*[5] to ignore the effect of Mr Topp's possible remarriage[6].

---

[1]   9 March 1989, unreported, QBD.
[2]   He said: 'I have to take into account, of course, in looking at the multiplier all the usual risks in relation to Mr Khan and the possibility (to put it no higher) of his re-marrying. Mr Khan says presently he does not contemplate that at all but it is a factor that I have to take into account'. See also para 2.33 of the Law Commission's Report No 263 'Claims for Wrongful Death' (1999).

3   See further the first-instance decision of May J, reported together with the Court of Appeal's judgment, at [1993] 3 All ER 448.
4   The appeal on liability subsequently failed: [1993] 3 All ER 448.
5   [1991] 1 All ER 529.
6   Although the defendants reserved their right to argue this point in a higher court.

(3)   COHABITANTS AND CHILDREN

[L136]   Historically, prior to the introduction of s 4 of FAA 1976 by the Administration of Justice Act 1982, the court had taken into account the prospects of remarriage in relation to a claim brought on behalf of children[1]. However, if following *Stanley v Saddique*[2] the correct interpretation of s 4 is that the court must disregard the mothering services provided to children where the deceased's former co-habitant marries, then, logically, the benefits consequent on the prospects of the widow or widower forming a new relationship or remarrying should also be disregarded[3]. Arguably, discrimination between these groups may lead to human rights issues. Having said that, there is one recognised category of cases where marriage prospects are properly taken into account. Where the dependant is a parent and the claim is that the deceased child would have provided support, account must be taken of the prospects that the deceased would have married, thus decreasing the amount of support[4]. In this scenario, s 4 of the Act is unlikely to apply, because the prospects of marriage would have been present in any event and cannot be said to result from the death of the deceased.

1   See eg *Thompson v Price* [1973] 1 QB 838; *Goodburn v Thomas Cotton Ltd* [1968] 1 QB 845.
2   [1991] 1 All ER 529.
3   Cf para 2.33 of the Law Commission's Report No 263 'Claims for Wrongful Death' (1999), although it should be noted that the Law Commission does not appear to have considered the effect of s 4 in this context. It is arguable that the concession made in *Topp v London County Bus (SW) Ltd* [1993] 3 All ER 448 equally applies here.
4   See eg *Dolbey v Goodwin* [1995] 1 WLR 553; *Wathen v Vernon* [1970] RTR 471.

Adoption

[L137]   In *Watson v Willmott*[1], both the mother and father of a child died following an accident[2]. However, the claimant was later adopted, and it was held that an adoptive parent has a legal obligation to care and that the claimant was legally treated as the child of the adopters. The claim in relation to the loss of a mother's services thereby failed, although dependency on the father's financial input survived, albeit reduced by the adoptive father's contribution. It is difficult to reconcile the court's approach to s 4 of FAA 1976 in this case with that taken in *Stanley v Saddique*[3].

1   [1991] 1 All ER 473.
2   The father suffered depression and committed suicide as a direct result of the accident.
3   [1991] 1 All ER 529.

Reconciliation

[L138]   A remote possibility of reconciliation between separated spouses was ignored in *Davies v Taylor*[1].

1   [1974] AC 207, [1972] 3 All ER 836.

Illegality of the source

[L139] In *Burns v Edman*[1], the court inferred that the deceased had received an income solely through crime and that the claimant must have known this. The court therefore held that the claimant was entitled to no loss of dependency claim. Such a rule would probably not apply to minor infringements, or where earnings were undeclared as to tax etc[2].

[1] [1970] 1 All ER 886. Also see *Hunter v Butler* [1996] RTR 396.
[2] See Chapter F.

(xiv) Apportionment

The need to apportion

[L140] By virtue of FAA 1976, s 2(3), only one action may be brought under FAA 1976 on behalf of all dependants[1]. Therefore, after an award has been made (either by way of agreement or trial), the full amount has to be split and apportioned between relevant parties (eg between surviving spouse and children). Section 3(2) of the Act states as follows:

> 'After deducting the costs not recovered from the defendant any amount recovered otherwise than as damages for bereavement shall be divided among the dependants in such shares as may be directed.'

[1] However, this does not necessarily bar dependants from pursuing a claim where earlier proceedings have been issued but not served: see further *Cachia v Faluyi* [2001] EWCA Civ 998. Despite the wording of s 2(3) of FAA 1976, the European Convention on Human Rights gives dependants a right of access to a court. The Human Rights Act 1998 required the court to interpret primary legislation so as to give effect to Convention rights, and it was possible to interpret 'action' in s 2(3) as meaning 'served process'.

[L141] The award for bereavement will be split equally amongst the qualifying individuals. Damages recovered on behalf of the estate will be distributed in accordance with the deceased's will or the intestacy rules, as applicable (although some expenses may be held on trust for the person who incurred the expense, eg funeral expenses and travel expenses). However, it may be much more difficult to apportion damages for lost dependency on the deceased's income and services, particularly where there are multiple dependants. Where children are involved by virtue of para 7 of the Practice Direction to CPR, Part 21, it is necessary to seek approval of any apportionment from the court.

Method of apportionment

[L142] The Act itself contains no guidance as to how damages should be apportioned between dependants. The court retains a discretion to apportion damages in the most appropriate way, depending upon the facts of the individual case. In practice, however, much depends upon whether or not there is a need to apportion between a surviving spouse and children, and if there is any reason to doubt that the surviving spouse will continue to provide for the children.

Apportionment between surviving spouses and children

[L143]   Generally, two main methods of apportionment have emerged from the case law as regards the apportionment between surviving spouses and children.

(1)   PRAGMATIC APPROACH

[L144]   The first method of apportionment is known as the pragmatic approach, which involves giving the bulk of the damages to the surviving spouse. This method of apportionment is the most commonly used, particularly where there is a stable family background[1]. Although this pragmatic approach has been attacked by some commentators as having no sound basis in principle (see eg *McGregor on Damages* (18th edn)), it is usually considered appropriate for the lion's share of the damages to be paid to the remaining spouse[2]. The reasoning behind this is largely twofold: (i) the period of the widow or widower's loss is likely to be greater than the children's loss; and (ii) it will be assumed that the widow or widower will use any money received not only for their own benefit but also, in accordance with his or her parental duty, to continue maintaining the children whilst they remain dependent, eg in terms of providing accommodation, care, food, clothing etc. It is therefore uncommon for courts to require a detailed breakdown of the estimated dependency on behalf of each dependant, since the surviving spouse can be trusted to ensure that the money is spent to the benefit of all the dependants (as intended). This method of assessment also avoids the very real practical difficulties of attempting to apportion the level of the dependency on the deceased's income or services between a number of different individuals over an extended period of time, and thereafter the need to apply that calculation to the award of damages, which may be complicated by way of a reduction from the full value of the claim to take account of contributory negligence or a discount to take account of litigation risks.

[L145]   A variant on the pragmatic approach, involving a greater apportionment to the children, is to divide the dependency award along the lines of the ratio applied for the periods during and after the children are deemed dependent. By way of example, 67/75ths of the award (89%) be apportioned to the widow for the period during the children's period of dependency, and the remaining 11% be divided between the children in proportions relating to their years of remaining dependency. By way of example, if the loss of earnings to retirement, in what would have been 20 years post death, results in a net multiplicand of £30,000[3] and the deceased leaves a widow and two children of ages 5 and 10 who are each expected to go into higher education to age 23 then:

Dependency at 75% for 18 years = £30,000 × 75% × 14.53 = £326,925

Apportionment to children = 11% × £326,925 = £35,961.75

Apportionment between the children = £35,961.75 /(13 + 18 years) = £1,160.06 per year of dependency, that is:

£15,080 for the 10–year-old and £20,881 for the 5-year-old.

The balance of £290,964, plus the ongoing dependency at 67% for the two years to retirement age, would be apportioned to the widow.

1 In *R v CICB, ex p Barrett* [1994] PIQR Q47, Latham J stated: 'the approach to the apportionment of the overall figure has essentially been pragmatic; the courts have sought to provide as much money in free cash terms for the parent who is caring for the child as is sensible in all the circumstances, so that there can be ready access for that parent to the fund representing the lost dependency. The bulk has therefore been apportioned to the parent'.

2 See eg *Thompson v Price* [1973] 1 QB 838, in which Boreham J held that the children's apportionment should be limited to their loss of dependency over and above the cost of their keep. The remaining spouse has parental responsibility to provide for the children, and so should be given an appropriately sufficient sum. The courts will consider the needs of each individual child in evaluating apportionment: *Yelland v Powell Duffryn Associated Colleries Ltd (No 2)* [1941] 1 All ER 278.

3 After adjusting for employment contingencies (Ogden Tables A–D), and for the risk of alternative death pre-trial (Ogden Tables E, F).

(2) DETAILED CALCULATION OF EACH DEPENDENCY

[L146] The second, less common, method of apportionment is to attempt to calculate each dependant's actual entitlement to damages as accurately as possible by reference to the extent of their lost dependency. This method of apportionment may be considered more appropriate if: (i) there are any reasons to doubt that the surviving spouse will continue to look after the children and apply the money to their benefit as well as his or her own[1]; (ii) the family circumstances have changed and there is a new family unit[2]; (iii) the children are very young and the dependency very long; and (iv) by adopting the usual pragmatic approach to apportionment, due to the impact of insurance monies, the result would be contrary to the rationale behind the wording of FAA 1976 which requires the children to recover damages for their loss of support and care[3]. In *Robertson v Lestrange*[4], Webster J outlined five factors to be taken into account as follows:

(a) the relevant proportions of the loss suffered, that is to say the respective interests of the dependants in the dependency;

(b) the possibility that if the funds are left in the [surviving spouse's] hands they might, because of a series of accidents, devolve in such a way that they would not inure to the benefit of the children;

(c) the fact that any funds apportioned to the children should be administered on the basis that they were to be spent on their care, maintenance and education and exhausted by the end of the dependency;

(d) the obligation of the [surviving spouse] to care for the children, and the likelihood of [him or her] doing so responsibly; and

(e) the possible windfall effect of the apportionment which may impact upon the dependant[5].

1 See eg the concerns raised in *ATH v MS* [2002] EWCA Civ 792 regarding fulfilment of the trust.

2 In *Goodburn v Thomas Cotton* [1968] 1 QB 845, CA, it was recognised that there might be circumstances in which a widow's remarriage might have an adverse effect on her children's financial future.

3 *R v CICB, ex p Barrett* [1994] PIQR Q47.

4 [1985] 1 All ER 950.

5 This factor is no longer relevant since, by virtue of s 4(2) of the Administration of Justice Act 1982, it is no longer possible to bring 'lost years' claims on behalf of an injured person's estate where the death occurred on or after 1 January 1983.

[L147]   It should be noted that there are no set ways of attempting to carry out a more accurate apportionment between dependants. Given the numerous uncertainties that beset calculations for lost dependency in the first place, a broad brush assessment is almost inevitable. However, some damages may fall outside this assessment where it is clear that compensation for a particular head of loss is payable to a particular dependant rather than another, eg the bereavement award paid to the surviving spouse, and past special damages, past gratuitous care/services[1] and future services or intangible losses that are calculated by reference to individual dependants. In some cases, the widow may prefer to apportion a larger share to dependent children for familial or tax planning reasons. It is good practice for the recipients of a large award of dependency to meet with an experienced financial adviser to consider such issues before the apportionment takes place.

1   The award for past dependency on services, where the children have been looked after gratuitously by a friend or relative, is held on trust for the person who actually provided the care, following the principles laid down in *Hunt v Severs* [1994] 2 AC 350: *ATH v MS* [2002] EWCA Civ 792. However, on 15 December 2009, the Ministry of Justice published a consultation paper and draft Civil Law Reform Bill, which proposes that the trust mechanism in gratuitous care cases be replaced by a personal legal obligation to account to the carer.

[L148]   Following the court's decision in *R v CICB, ex p Barrett*[1] it may be that some judges will prefer to reach an apportionment, having carried out a more detailed assessment of each dependant's loss. Indeed, this was the approach adopted in *Baden-Powell v Central Manchester Healthcare NHS Trust*[2] and *ATH v MS*[3]. However, unless there are particular reasons to depart from the pragmatic approach on the facts of a given case, it may well be that, in the majority of cases, the bulk of the damages awarded will continue to be paid to the surviving spouse.

1   [1994] PIQR Q47. See also *Wells v Wells* [1999] AC 345 regarding use of the Ogden Tables as a starting point rather than a check, and moving away from judicial discounts for 'contingencies'.
2   [2002] 8 AVMA Medical & Legal Journal 4, July, at 160–161.
3   [2002] EWCA Civ 792.

Apportionment between children

[L149]   Although a younger child's claim might be more valuable in terms of greater dependency than an older child's claim, unless the age gap between the children is substantial, many courts tend to apportion damages between children equally[1]. This avoids potential difficulties that might develop between siblings if differing awards were made. For example, if one child receives less than another, when they reach the age of majority and receive their awards, they might be left with the feeling 'did my mother not love me as much as my brother?' or 'was my brother a better child than me?'. Providing the majority of damages have been apportioned to the surviving spouse, it may inherently follow that the younger sibling receives a secondary benefit from those sums for a longer period, and hence to a greater extent, than the elder sibling(s). If, however, a more substantial sum is to be apportioned to the children, it is then logical to divide their proportion by reference to the remaining years of their likely dependency[2].

1   This is demonstrated by the table set out in *Kemp & Kemp* at O1. See para **[L146]** above concerning *Robertson v Lestrange* [1985] All ER 950 (also reported in *Kemp & Kemp* at O1-006), where the

apportionment issue was considered in some detail, and three children aged between two and eight-and-a-half each received £21,883; *Loader v Lucas* (1999) 99(5) QR 8 in *Kemp & Kemp* at O1-003, in which £15,750 was apportioned to each of two children (age 10 and 12 at the hearing date) from a total dependency of £233,524.

2 See the example at para **[L145]** above and *T (A Child) v Lewisham Hospital NHS Trust* [2004] 1 QR 20 (also reported in *Kemp & Kemp* at O3-001), where slightly differing sums were apportioned to each of four children based on the length of dependency for each, on the basis that parity would have been contrary to principle.

(xv) Apportionment under the Civil Procedure Rules

[L150] If an award or settlement is reached for a single sum of money, an application can be made to the court for apportionment[1]. Such an application must be made, for both approval of the settlement[2] and apportionment, where there are child dependants (or adults lacking capacity)[3]. The Practice Direction to CPR 21 states:

'Apportionment under the Fatal Accidents Act 1976

7.1 A judgment on or settlement in respect of a claim under the Fatal Accidents Act 1976 must be apportioned between the persons by or on whose behalf the claim has been brought.

7.2 Where a claim is brought on behalf of a dependent child or children, any settlement (including an agreement on a sum to be apportioned to a dependent child under the Fatal Accidents Act 1976) must be approved by the court.

7.3 The money apportioned to any dependent child must be invested on the child's behalf in accordance with rules 21.10 and 21.11 and paragraphs 8 and 9 below.

7.4 In order to approve an apportionment of money to a dependent child, the court will require the following information:
(1) the matters set out in paragraphs 5.1(2) and (3), and
(2) in respect of the deceased –
(a) where death was caused by an accident, the matters set out in paragraphs 5.1(6)(a), (b) and (c), and
(b) his future loss of earnings, and
(3) the extent and nature of the dependency.'

If all the dependants are of full capacity, it is not strictly necessary for there to be an apportionment if they all agree[4]. Apportionment would need to be approached with considerable care in any claim involving periodical payments[5].

1 CPR, r 41.3A.
2 CPR, r 21.10.1.
3 CPR, rr 21.11 and 41.3A(3)(a).
4 *Williams v Welsh Ambulance Services NHS Trust* [2008] EWCA Civ 81.
5 See para **[L152]** below.

(xvi) Contributory Negligence

[L151] By s 5 of FAA 1976 and s 1(1) of the Law Reform (Contributory Negligence) Act 1945, any damages recoverable shall be reduced according to the deceased's own contributory negligence. This does not affect the claim by a dependant for their own personal injuries[1]. A dependant's own contributory negligence is to be taken into account, insofar as it is causative of the death. However, the negligence of one dependant does not adversely impact the claim of another dependant[2].

1   *Watson v Willmott* [1991] 1 All ER 473.
2   *Dodds v Dodds* [1978] QB 543, where a dependent child's claim succeeded without reduction, even though the dependent surviving spouse was negligent.

(xvii)   Inheritance Tax

[L152]   Claims brought under FAA 1976 are brought by the deceased's dependants as a result of the death, and do not form part of the deceased's estate, therefore any damages received should be free of inheritance tax.

(xviii)   Payments Received From the Deceased's Estate

[L153]   Historically, credit had to be given against the claim for dependency under FAA 1976 for any monies or payments received by the dependants from the executors of the deceased's estate[1]. For example, if a dependant were to receive the award for pain, suffering and loss of amenity or special damages under LR(MP)A 1934, these sums would have been deducted from the value of the lost dependency. However, following the introduction of FAA 1976, s 4 by the Administration of Justice Act 1982, all benefits as a result of the death must be disregarded. Indeed, s 4 specifically refers to benefits which have accrued, or will or may accrue, from the deceased's estate.

1   *Davies v Powell Duffryn Collieries* [1942] AC 601.

(xix)   Evidence

[L154]   The details needed for a fatal accident action are extensive. The calculation of loss is based on the details of a person who can clearly no longer participate in the litigation. Therefore, as much information as possible is required from the claimants accurately to predict likely quantum:

*   Personal details of the deceased, including name, date of birth and death, relationship with the claimant and a list of dependants giving ages and relationships to the deceased. Family photos can help personalise the claim.
*   Details of the death, accident and surrounding administration matters. These include date of an inquest, details of any will, death certificate, claims for personal injuries before death, hospital details and full particulars of the accident and surrounding circumstances (including witnesses).
*   Details of the actual dependency. In particular, full information of the deceased's earnings and, for each dependant, the amount spent on the living costs and the proportion of which related to the deceased. Full details also need to be obtained regarding any lost services that the deceased provided to his dependants, how those services have been replaced, and the cost (if any) thereby incurred.

[L155]   In appropriate cases, it may be necessary to instruct experts to assist with the calculation of a particular head of loss. Although they are no substitute for detailed witness evidence, care experts can be helpful to help evaluate the cost of replacing lost services, including housekeeping, childminding, DIY, decorating and gardening. An employment consultant's report may be required to prove the likely career path or expansion of a business. Likewise, it may be necessary to instruct an accountant to report on the likely level of dependency from a business venture or to analyse a deceased's accounts with a view to displacing the usual dependency factors[1]. However, in the majority of cases, permission is unlikely to be granted to instruct an actuary[2] to assist the court regarding the appropriate multiplier to adopt, since the Ogden Tables will usually suffice[3].

[1]   Guidance regarding the usual dependency factors can be gleaned from *Harris v Empress Motors* [1984] 1 WLR 212 and *Coward v Comex Houlder Driving Ltd* (18 July 1988, CA), noted in *Kemp & Kemp* at para O1-011. See para **[L72]**.

[2]   *Prigmore v Welbourne* [2003] EWCA Civ 1687. See also *Auty v National Coal Board* [1985] 1 WLR 784, in which Oliver LJ stated: 'Actuarial evidence is no doubt of the greatest assistance where one is seeking to value interests in a fund of ascertained amount for the purposes of purchase, sale or exchange. Indeed, such valuations are the foundation of virtually all schemes propounded under the Variation of Trusts Act 1958. But as a method of providing a reliable guide to individual behaviour patterns, or to future economic and political events, the predictions of an actuary can be only a little more likely to be accurate (and will almost certainly be less entertaining) than those of an astrologer'.

[3]   However, Explanatory Note 66 to the Ogden Tables (6th edn) states that it may be advisable to obtain a report from an actuary in very large claims.

[L156]   It should be noted that, although there are a number of helpful surveys, such as the Legal & General's 'Value of a Mum', each case is fact sensitive. There is no short cut to investigating thoroughly the level of services that the deceased provided. Although surveys may be admissible in evidence, they are technically hearsay, and it may be that little or no weight will attach to them[1].

[1]   See eg *Stothard (Widower & Administrator of the Estate of Christine Stothard, Deceased) v Gateshead Health Authority* (18 April 2002, unreported), QBD, HHJ Walton, Lawtel Document No AM0200402.

(xx)   Summary of Relevant Factors, Traps and Pitfalls

Summary of relevant factors

[L157]   The factors to be taken into account when calculating the value of a dependency:

- The eligibility of the dependant under the Act or alternative HRA arguments.
- The level of the deceased's earnings and earnings-related benefits.
- The type, conditions and level of the deceased's pension.
- The type, quality and amount of unpaid services provided by the deceased to each dependant.
- The health of the deceased and dependants.
- The likely retirement age of the deceased, and whether a secondary career may have been pursued.
- The earning capacity of the dependant.
- The prospects of the deceased marrying (especially if a child providing support to his or her parents).

- The prospect that a child dependant will go on to tertiary or higher education.
- The prospects of a divorce, separation or desertion, had it not been for the injury and death.
- The source of the dependency.
- The length of time to trial.
- Contributory negligence of the deceased or dependant.
- The appropriateness of periodical payments.

[L158]   However, the following are ignored in the calculation:

- Benefits accruing as a result of the death.
- Post-death actions of the dependants.
- A prospect of, or actual, marriage of a widow.
- An intention for the deceased and widow to have children in the future.
- A remote or speculative chance of an event occurring.
- Post-trial inflation.
- Taxation of the award.
- Recoupment (CRU does not apply to cases under FAA 1976).

Traps and pitfalls to avoid

[L159]   Some of the main points to be wary of, when calculating damages for a loss of dependency and preparing a schedule of loss, are as follows:

- Not fully investigating the claim for financial loss so as to include dependency on fringe benefits (eg company car, private healthcare etc).
- Not fully investigating the claim for dependency on pension loss (including private and state pensions).
- Failing to take account of pre-trial inflation.
- Failing to take account of lost chances of promotion or career enhancement when calculating the multiplicand.
- Not fully investigating and pleading the claim for loss of services (eg DIY, domestic chores, gardening, decorating).
- Giving credit for benefits when it was not necessary to do so.
- Failing to consider periodical payments.

6 Interest

[L160]   The general rules governing rates of interest in personal injury actions apply to fatal cases. Applying these principles may mean that the claimant is entitled to different rates of interest on different heads of loss.

(i)   Interest on claims under the Law Reform (Miscellaneous Provisions) Act 1934

[L161]   In LR(MP)A 1934 claims, where the deceased died reasonably soon after his or her injury, most of the items will be one-off expenses and therefore, arguably, the full special account rate should apply[1]. Where, however, the deceased survived for a period of time before death with ongoing expenses (eg medical expenses and care), the appropriate rate is half the special account rate up to the date of death. From death onwards, arguably the full special account rate should apply, since the damage crystallised at that point. Therefore, different interest calculations may have to be made to the pre- and post-death periods. On general damages, interest will accrue at 2% from the service of the claim form[2].

---

[1]   See Chapter G.
[2]   See further Chapter E.

(ii)   Interest on claims under the Fatal Accidents Act 1976

[L162]   In FAA 1976 claims, past dependency is classed as special damages, but future dependency clearly carries no interest[1]. The Court of Appeal in *A Train & Sons v Fletcher*[2] rejected a novel attempt to ameliorate the deficiencies in the multiplier by seeking interest on the pre-trial losses at the full special account rate rather than at half rate. Whilst Sir Mark Potter agreed that 'time was ripe for reconsideration of the position' of applying the discount rate to multipliers from the date of death, he was not at all convinced that a departure from the normal principles relating to interest on pre-trial losses was the appropriate way of doing it.

[L163]   Bereavement is a set sum awarded on death and, therefore, interest is awarded at the full special account rates from the date of death[3]. As regards the claim for past dependency, assuming that the dependency is ongoing, the appropriate rate will be half the special account rate[4]. But what should the rate of interest be on a *Regan v Williamson*[5] award for the loss of intangible benefits? At first blush, it might be thought that this head of loss falls into the category of general damages, since the amount claimed is not a set amount, but one which falls to be assessed by the court. Therefore, interest should be payable at the rate of 2% pa from the date of service of the claim form[6]. However, to the knowledge of the authors, the only reported case which has expressly dealt with the rate of interest on this type of award is *Batt v Highgate Private Hospital*[7], in which HHJ Darlow considered that interest should run at the full special account rate. He said[8]:

> 'In my judgment, interest should run at the full rate. Unlike an award in general damages, there has been no real attempt to update this award in line with inflation. Had there been any such attempt one sees that the figure in *Mehmet* would have a present day value of in excess of £12,000. It is a modest conventional award fixed and fixable at the point of death. In my judgment it is more akin to bereavement than to the principles that apply to general damages and that is why I award interest at the full rate.'

---

[1]   No interest is payable on future losses: *Jefford v Gee* [1970] 2 QB 130; *Cookson v Knowles* [1979] AC 556, HL.
[2]   [2008] 4 All ER 699.
[3]   *Prior v Hastie (Bernard and Co)* [1987] CLY 1219; followed in *Khan v Duncan* (9 March 1989, unreported), QBD.
[4]   See further Chapter G. See also *A Train & Sons Ltd v Fletcher* [2008] 4 All ER 699.
[5]   [1976] 1 WLR 305.
[6]   See further Chapter E.
[7]   [2005] PIQR Q1.
[8]   At [78].

(iii)   Proposals to Change Interest Calculations

[L164]   The Law Commission recommended that the court should have the power to award interest on a compound basis, and that there should be a rebuttable presumption that interest will be awarded on a compound basis for cases worth more than £15,000[1]. The Government rejected this proposal applicable to all claims, but the draft Civil Law Reform Bill, published on 15 December 2009 by the Ministry of Justice, suggests that, where damages are awarded in a currency other than sterling, the court should give consideration as to whether or not simple or compound interest is awarded[2]. Also, where damages are awarded in sterling, it is proposed that the Lord Chancellor will determine whether or not the interest is to be compound or simple when making an order setting the appropriate rate of interest[3].

---

[1]   Law Commission's Report No 287 'Pre-judgment Interest on Debts and Damages' (2004). See further at para **[G9]**.

[2]   See clause 11(6) of the draft Civil Law Reform Bill, reference CP53/09, available at www.justice. gov.uk.

[3]   See clause 11(4) of the draft Civil Law Reform Bill, reference CP53/09.

7   Periodical Payments and Structured Settlements

[L165]   It should be noted that, by virtue of s 7(1) of the Damages Act 1996, claims for 'personal injury' include claims brought under the LR(MP)A 1934 and FAA 1976. Therefore, under s 2 of the Damages Act 1996 (as inserted by ss 100 and 101 of the Courts Act 2003) the court has the power to award periodical payments in cases involving fatal accidents. These powers are now set out in the Civil Procedure Rules[1]. It is perhaps surprising that, at the date of writing, there have been no reported awards or settlements of a fatal accident claim on a periodical payment (PP) basis[2]. Pending a case proceeding to the House of Lords to overturn the traditional approach to the calculation of multipliers from death, periodical payments offer an effective way around this problem. They also avoid the interlinked problems of the discount rate being set well above the return on index linked government securities (ILGS) and on an assumption of RPI inflation, whereas PPs for an earning dependency can be indexed to an appropriate measure of earnings inflation[3]. They have the advantages of being tax-free and relieve the dependants from the risk, worry and responsibility of managing a large lump sum investment over many years. In most cases, it would be hard to argue that they were not an appropriate way of replicating what has been lost by the dependants; a regular income stream from the deceased. Careful wording of the PPO would be necessary to ensure that child dependants continued to receive the PPs up to the date of the deceased's likely retirement (or other dependency period), even if the widow were to die. In this regard, it is likely to be necessary to define distinct entitlements to PPs for each dependant. However, the provisions relating to the variation of PPs[4] only provide for variation in relation to worsening or improvement of pre-defined medical conditions caused by the tort. It may be necessary for these provisions to be revisited, to ensure that they do justice for dependants under FAA 1976. The reader is referred to Chapter Q for a detailed discussion of the relevant principles.

1   CPR, rr 41.3A, 41.8(2).
2   The point is very briefly considered in *Wolfe v Del'Innocenti* [2006] EWHC 2694 (QB), LTL 22/6/07.
3   Chris Daykin 'Fair Compensation needs actuaries' [2009] JPIL C48–66, and Robin de Wilde QC in the Preface to the 14th Edition of the PNBA 'Facts & Figures'.
4   Damages (Variation of Periodical Payments) Order 2004.

M Damages for the Dying

I Introduction

[M1] Most personal injury claims are not fatal. Many of those that are involve instantaneous death in an accident. In some cases, however, there may be a period of weeks, months or even years between the start of the injury and eventual death.

[M2] If the tort does not cause the death, such cases become straightforward claims for past loss to the injured person's estate under the Law Reform (Miscellaneous Provisions) Act 1934. Where the tort leads to and causes the death, more complex issues involving both past and future loss are apt to arise; they form the subject matter of this chapter.

[M3] Initially, it is necessary to establish how to value and present such claims. However, the problems do not stop there. The combined effect of the cases of *Pickett v British Rail Engineering Ltd*[1], *Harris v Empress Motors Ltd*[2], *Coward v Comex Houlder Driving Ltd*[3] and *Phipps v Brooks Dry Cleaning Services Ltd*[4] is that the value of any claim of this type will differ according to whether it is completed during the sufferer's life or concluded after his or her death. Consequently, it is also necessary to compare the values of any claim on a living and on a fatal basis.

[1]   [1980] AC 136.
[2]   [1982] 3 All ER 306.
[3]   (18 July 1988, CA) noted in *Kemp & Kemp* at O1-011.
[4]   [1996] PIQR Q100.

[M4] This is because a choice has to be made. Section 1 of the Fatal Accidents Act 1976 provides a right of action to dependants where the tort would, if death had not ensued, 'have entitled the person injured to maintain an action and recover damages in respect thereof'. An injured person who has settled his case can no longer maintain an action. Therefore, damages can be recovered on a living basis or on a fatal basis, but not on both in succession[1].

[1]   *Read v The Great Eastern Railway Company* (1868) LR 3 QB 555; subsequently affirmed in *Reader & others v Molesworth Bright Clegg Sols* [2007] EWCA Civ 169.

[M5] This principle was confirmed in the clinical negligence case of *Thompson v Arnold*[1], in which a breast cancer sufferer's case was settled for £120,000 before her death. Striking out her dependants' subsequent action under the Fatal Accidents Act, Langstaff J held that the above principle did not infringe Article 6 or 8 of the European Convention on Human Rights.

[1]   [2007] EWHC 1875 (QB).

[M6] In modern times, the largest single category of claims by the dying stems from the asbestos-related tumour of mesothelioma which, therefore, is used as an example. Nevertheless, the principles set out apply equally to all other cases where the tort causes a period of injury leading to death.

2 Preparing the Schedule

(i) Overview

[M7] This section may be read in conjunction with the specimen schedule in Chapter Q at **[Q27]**. It is helpful to start with a front page containing the title of the action and a paginated index to the rest of the claim. The index should identify the main heads of loss: general damages, past expenses and losses, future loss during life, and future loss after death.

[M8] The second page may then set out key facts. These include not only the claimant's name and date of birth but also, for the purpose of evaluating the lost years element, his or her marital status, and the name(s) and date(s) of birth of anyone living with him or her. It is also relevant to state, where applicable, the date on which he or she ceased work due to the tort, and the date on which he or she would have retired but for the disease. If possible, an estimated date of death should be inserted in order to establish the dividing line between pre-death and post-death loss.

(ii) General Damages

[M9] These will largely depend on the nature and duration of the pain, suffering and loss of amenities, together with any awareness of approaching death.

[M10] The following guidance for the asbestos-related tumours of mesothelioma and lung cancer is to be found in the 9th edition of the Judicial Studies Board Guidelines for the Assessment of General Damages in Personal Injury Cases[1]:

'(a) Mesothelioma causing severe pain and impairment of both function and quality of life. This may be of the pleura (the lung lining) or of the peritoneum (the lining of the abdominal cavity); the latter being typically more painful. The duration of pain and suffering accounts for variations within this bracket. For periods of up to 18 months, awards in the bottom half of the bracket may be appropriate; for longer periods of four years or more, an award at the top end. In cases of unusually short periods of pain and suffering lasting three months or so, an award in the region of £25,000 may be appropriate ... **£52,500 to £81,500**

(b) Lung cancer, again a disease proving fatal in most cases, the symptoms of which may not be as painful as those of mesothelioma, but more protracted ... **£50,000 to £64,250**'

[1] See 9th edn, p 22.

[M11] The final sentence in guideline (a) has attracted little judicial support. An authoritative analysis of the issues is contained in the Senior Master's judgment in *Smith v Bolton Copper Ltd*, where he awarded £55,000 general damages for a 2 to

3-month period of rapidly deteriorating and increasingly intense pain and suffering resulting from peritoneal mesothelioma.

(iii)   Past Expenses and Losses

[M12]   The principles governing these are the same as in any other personal injury claim. In practice, certain items arise with increased frequency in cases of injuries leading to death. A non-exhaustive list is set out below:

- Earnings loss, ie loss of net earnings.
- Loss of associated perks, eg free board and lodging, pension premiums.
- Care and assistance, either from paid professionals or unpaid family/friends.
- Home help, eg to free partner to care for claimant.
- Aids and appliances, eg stairlift or recliner chair.
- Bedding, eg sheets, pillows and pillow cases.
- Medical fees, eg for private care or complementary therapy.
- Prescriptions or prescription certificates.
- Other drugs, lotions or ointments.
- Travel to hospital(s) by the claimant for treatment.
- Travel to hospital(s) by relatives to visit the claimant.
- Hospital parking fees.
- Accommodation near hospital, whilst the claimant is an in-patient.
- Cab fares, when the claimant is no longer able to use public transport.
- Clothes for hospital, eg dressing gown, pyjamas, slippers etc.
- Extra clothes, due to significant increase or decrease in size.
- Extra heating, due to the claimant feeling cold or being indoors more often.
- Extra telephoning, eg to doctors, nurses, social workers, relatives etc.
- Extra telephone, eg if the claimant is confined to his or her bedroom.
- Special foods and drinks, in order to keep the claimant nourished.
- Heaters or fans, to warm or cool the claimant.
- Radio or TV, if the claimant is confined to his or her bedroom.
- Adaptations to home, eg installation of non-slip shower with seat.
- Tradesmen's fees, for performing tasks that the claimant would otherwise have carried out him or herself.

(iv)   Future Loss During Life

[M13]   The general principles governing future loss apply to these cases. The only difference is that the period of loss is reduced by premature death.

[M14]   In practice, it is essential to estimate the probable date of death. This is not only because most items of loss cease then; it is also because special rules govern the calculation of loss of earnings (and loss of pension) during the lost years of life.

[M15]   All the items that have formed part of the claim for past expenses and losses will, insofar as they are expected to continue or recur, form part of the claim for future loss until death. Some items may arise for the first time during this final period; others, such as care and assistance, will often increase in cost and frequency.

(v)   Future Loss After Death

[M16]   Inevitably, death terminates all claims for expenses, including care and assistance. This means that, in most cases, damages for the period after death are limited to the loss of the earnings and pension(s) that the claimant would have received during the lost years of life.

[M17]   In *Pickett v British Rail Engineering Ltd*[1], where the House of Lords allowed this head of damage for the first time, it was held that the loss was subject to deduction of the claimant's probable living expenses during the lost years.

[1]   [1980] AC 136.

[M18]   In *White v London Transport Executive*[1], Webster J proposed an 'available surplus' solution to the problem of defining the net loss: the claimant's prospective net income minus the cost of maintaining him or herself. In the cost of maintenance are included not only the expenses of housing, heating, food, clothing, necessary travel and insurances, but also a short holiday, modest amount of entertainment and social activity and, depending on the claimant's particular circumstances, a car.

[1]   [1982] QB 489.

[M19]   In *Harris v Empress Motors Ltd*[1], the Court of Appeal endorsed the 'available surplus' approach and held that, in a standard case of a husband and wife living together, one-third of the claimant's net income would be attributable to his own exclusive living expenses, one-third to his wife's expenses, and one-third to joint expenses such as the costs of their home. The joint expenses should be divided according to the number of members of the household.

[1]   [1982] 3 All ER 306.

[M20]   Consequently, the following standard percentages have emerged from the case law:

*   *Claimant living with wife and two children.* Living expenses deduction 33⅓% for claimant alone plus quarter of 33⅓% joint expenses = total deduction of 42% living expenses. *Claimant recovers 58% of lost income.*
*   *Claimant living with wife alone.* Living expenses deduction 33⅓% for claimant alone plus half of 33⅓% joint expenses = total deduction of 50% living expenses. *Claimant recovers 50%.*
*   *Claimant living with parents.* No dependants but good available surplus. *Claimant recovers 33%.*
*   *Claimant living alone.* The cases of *White v London Transport Executive*[1] and *Smith v Cape plc*[2] indicate higher living expenses. *Claimant recovers 20–25%.*

[1]   [1982] 1 QB 489.
[2]   [1991] CLY 1409.

[M21]   It must be stressed that these percentages are only starting points applicable to standard cases in each category. There may be variations in either direction. For instance, only 25% of a high-earning husband's income might be devoted to his living expenses, in which case he would recover 75%. Whereas it might be argued that, with a single man living alone off income support, all his income is needed for his living expenses, so that he is not entitled to recover anything under this head.

[M22] There are two valid approaches to selection of the appropriate multiplier for the period after death:

* The first is to take from Table 28 of the Ogden Tables the multiplier for the period by which the tort has accelerated death (eg 12.54 for 15 years) and then discount it by the remaining period of reduced life (eg 0.9756 for 1 year): 12.54 × 0.9756 = 12.23.

* The second is to take the appropriate multiplier for the whole period of future loss, both before and after death (eg 13.22 for 16 years) and deduct the multiplier for the remaining period of life (eg 0.99 for 1 year): 13.22 – 0.99 = 12.23.

[M23] Whichever approach is used, it is necessary to note that any deduction from the multiplier for contingencies in the earnings loss claim should be added back on to the multiplier in the pensions loss claim. The shorter the working life, the longer the retirement from it.

[M24] Apart from loss of income, the main potential head of damages relates to services that the claimant would have performed during the lost years of his life. In most cases, no damages can be recovered for these. This is because, as seen in Chapter I at para **[I15]**, the Court of Appeal has ruled in *Phipps v Brooks Dry Cleaning Services Ltd*[1] that a claimant cannot recover damages for the cost or value of unpaid painting, decorating and gardening services that he would have carried out during the rest of his or her natural life span.

[1]   [1996] PIQR Q100.

[M25] This principle may be qualified, however, by the Court of Appeal decision in *Lowe v Guise*[1], discussed in Chapter F at paras **[F171]–[F173]**. The claimant's primary responsibility was the gratuitous care of his severely disabled brother, to which he devoted 77 hours per week. As a result of an accident, the claimant could only provide 35 hours per week of care and claimed for the value of the remaining 42 hours per week care, probably to be provided by his mother in the first instance. The Court of Appeal upheld this claim on the basis that, even though the claimant's care was provided gratuitously, it ought as a matter of policy to be measured in money's worth. This principle was confined to the assumed facts of the case: where the care was to a relative, spouse or partner living as part of the same household, and going beyond the ordinary interaction of members of the household.

[M26] It remains to be seen whether this principle will be extended to comparable care which a claimant would have provided during the last years of his or her life. In *Crowther v Jones*[1], a claimant whose life expectancy was much reduced due to recurrent breast cancer had a severely disabled son for whom there was a 24-hour care regime in place. She had managed the carers, in effect performing the role of a case manager. Her settlement damages of £445,000, approved on a global basis with no agreed breakdown, included a sum for her son's case management after her death, which was estimated by her solicitors at £200,000. Perhaps significantly, she had reserved the right to apply at trial for an interim payment and a stay of proceedings designed to defer assessment of damages until after her death: a pressure which probably induced the defendants to include a *Lowe v Guise*[2] case management element in the damages, despite the lack of decided authority for allowing this during the lost years of life.

[1]   LTLPI 22/4/09.
[2]   [2002] EWCA Civ 197, [2002] PIQR Q9.

[M27]   Pragmatically, a claimant's position may well be strengthened by paying for the services that he or she is no longer able to perform. In *Dennison v Cape Insulation Ltd*,[1] the dying claimant paid his daughter £2,000 for having looked after his disabled wife for him for 20 weeks, and agreed to pay her £100 per week for the rest of his life. It is interesting to speculate whether such a claim would be further strengthened by the bequest of a sum to cover continued care after a claimant's death. A far simpler solution, certainly, would be for the courts to allow damages under the *Lowe v Guise*[2] principle to be paid in respect of the lost years.

[1]   Unreported; settled 18 July 2009.
[2]   [2002] EWCA Civ 197, [2002] PIQR Q9.

[M28]   The balance of case law is to the effect that funeral expenses are not recoverable in living cases. After conflicting court decisions in the 1990s (*Smith v Cape plc*[1] and *Bateman v Hydro Agri (UK) Ltd*[2]), the issue received careful consideration in the recent case of *Watson v Cakebread Robey Ltd*[3]. Section 1(2)(c) of the Law Reform (Miscellaneous Provisions) Act 1934 provides that damages recoverable for the benefit of the estate of the deceased 'where the death of that person has been caused by the act or omission which gives rise to the cause of action, shall be calculated without reference to any loss or gain to his estate consequent on his death, except that a sum in respect of funeral expenses may be included'. Mr Satinder Hunjan QC sitting as a deputy judge of the High Court took the view that, by providing for an exception in respect of funeral expenses, this created to that extent a new cause of action which could only arise on death. He observed that to hold otherwise would mean that, in every personal injury case in which the claimant's life expectancy is to some extent reduced, he would be entitled to recover prospective funeral expenses, subject only to a deduction for accelerated receipt – neither an appealing nor a practical prospect. He concluded that the claim for funeral expenses in a live claimant's case was wrong in principle and could not be allowed.

[1]   [1991] CLY 1409.
[2]   Unreported, 15 September 1995.
[3]   [2009] EWHC 1695 (QB).

3   Defendants' Arguments

[M29]   The specimen schedule is a claimant's document. Confronted by such claims, defendants are apt to deploy some of the counter-arguments below.

[M30]   In earnings loss claims, defendants should almost always argue for a discount for contingencies if none has been included. Few claimants are 100% certain of undiminished earnings on an uninterrupted basis up to their proposed retirement ages. Where allowance has already been made for a discount, defendants may argue for a larger one[1].

¹ See generally Chapter H at paras **[H114]–[H121]** and Chapter K at paras **[K200]–[K205]**.

[M31] In earnings and pension loss claims, defendants often seek a larger deduction for living expenses during the last years of life. Where a claimant's income is low, they argue that a higher proportion of it is devoted to living expenses. Where a claimant's spouse has a significant income in his or her own right, some defendants plead that the same calculation should be performed as in *Coward v Comex Houlder Driving Ltd*[1]. There is no reported authority for the application of the *Coward* principle to a non-fatal case, however, and understandably defendants do not advance the argument in a case where the surviving spouse has little or no income and the *Coward v Comex* formula would operate unfavourably for them.

¹ (18 July 1988, CA) noted in *Kemp & Kemp* at O1-011.

[M32] In care claims, customary defences are that:

(a) not all the proposed care and assistance will be needed, since the dying claimant may spend part of the rest of his or her life in hospitals or a hospice; and

(b) the value of gratuitous care should be discounted by up to about one-third, to take account of the tax, National Insurance and travel expenses that a commercial carer would pay[1]. The high-water mark for such deductions is the 35% discount on commercial rates applied by Crane J in *Bordin v St Mary's NHS Trust*[2].

¹ See further Chapter F at paras **[F104]–[F110]**.
² [2000] PIQR 230.

[M33] In equipment claims, defendants often argue that:

(a) not all the claimed equipment will be purchased, especially as some of it may be supplied by the social services; and

(b) those items that are purchased may have a resale value after death.

4 The Comparative Calculation

(i) Major Factors

[M34] Perhaps unfortunately, the value of the claim of an injured person who is dying differs according to whether it is concluded during his or her life or after his or her death. There are five main reasons for this.

[M35] The first, arising from the Court of Appeal decision in *Harris v Empress Motors Ltd*[1], concerns their earnings loss. During their life, they are entitled to their loss of net income minus their living expenses. After their death, their dependants are entitled to the extent of their dependency. The difference may be illustrated by the traditional case of an injured husband living alone with a non-earning wife. In normal circumstances, he will recover half his loss when living, whereas she will recover two-thirds of it after his death.

¹ [1982] 3 All ER 306.

[M36] The second stems from the entitlement to bereavement damages, introduced by s 1A of the Fatal Accidents Act 1976, as amended by the Administration of Justice Act 1982. From 1 April 2002, the value of this was £10,000[1]. Since 1 January 2008 it has been £11,800[2].

1   Damages for Bereavement (Variation of Sum) (England and Wales) Order 2002, SI 2002/644.
2   Damages for Bereavement (Variation of Sum) (England and Wales) Order 2007, SI 2007/3489.

[M37] The third results from the Court of Appeal decision in *Phipps v Brooks Dry Cleaning Services Ltd*[1], that a dying claimant cannot recover the value of his unpaid DIY and other services during the lost years of life[2]. However, his widow and other dependants can recover this after his death.

1   [1996] PIQR Q100.
2   But see the discussion regarding *Lowe v Guise* [2002] EWCA Civ 197, [2002] PIQR Q9 in Chapter F at paras **[F171]**–**[F173]** and at paras **[M25]**–**[M27]**.

[M38] The fourth factor is the growing tendency in recent years to make an award to dependants in fatal cases for the loss of the intangible services of the deceased[1]. Damages under this head often fall within the bracket of between £2,000 and £5,000.

1   See the discussion of *Mehmet v Perry* [1977] 2 All ER 529 and other cases in Chapter L.

[M39] The fifth is that funeral expenses are awarded in fatal cases, whether under the Law Reform (Miscellaneous Provisions) Act 1934 or the Fatal Accidents Act 1976, but not in cases brought by living claimants (*Watson v Cakebread Robey Ltd*[1]).

1   [2009] EWHC 1695 (QB).

[M40] The second, third, fourth and fifth factors, where they apply at all, always serve to produce higher damages on a fatal than on a living basis. The first factor will often do so as well but, due to the impact of the Court of Appeal decision in *Coward v Comex Houlder Diving Ltd*[1], will not always do so. In certain cases, a dying claimant with a higher-earning spouse may recover more rather than less in his or her lifetime for earnings loss during the lost years of his or her life.

1   (18 July 1988, CA) noted in *Kemp & Kemp* at O1-011.

[M41] Consequently, there is no simple rule of thumb that a fatal claim will always be worth more than a living one on the same facts. Instead, it is necessary in each case to calculate at the outset the approximate worth of the claim on each basis.

[M42] Three examples of these comparative calculations are set out below. For the sake of convenience, references to events occurring at a certain age (eg 50) may be construed as referring to the first day of that age (eg 50th birthday). For the sake of simplicity, interest and contingency discounts are disregarded as being basically neutral items. It is assumed that the case would have been heard on the day before the claimant's death, on a living basis, or on the day after it, on a fatal basis.

Example 1 – Husband with non-earning wife

[M43]   H contracts mesothelioma at age of 48¾

He earns £18,000 per annum net

He retires prematurely at age of 49

Death at age 50

He would have retired at age 65

He would have received pensions of £7,500 per annum net

He would have had standard life expectancy

W is same age

She had no income

She will receive state pension at age 65.

LIVING CLAIM

General damages			£67,500
Earnings loss	£7,500		
Care and equipment	£12,500		
Other expenses	£2,500		
Special damages			£22,500
Annual earnings	£18,000		
50% living expenses	× 50%		
Earnings multiplicand		£9,000	
Earnings multiplier		× 12	
Future earnings loss			£108,000
Annual pensions	£7,500		
50% living expenses	× 50%		
Pensions multiplicand		£3,750	
Pensions multiplier		× 8.8	
Future pensions loss			£33,000
TOTAL DAMAGES			**£231,000**

FATAL CLAIM

General damages (as above)			£67,500
Special damages (as above)		£22,500	
Plus funeral expenses, say		£2,500	
			£25,000
Bereavement damages			£11,800
H's earnings	£18,000 pa		
W's dependency	× 2/3		
Earnings multiplicand		£12,000	
Earnings multiplier		× 12	
Earnings dependency			£144,000
H's specific services	£750 pa		
Services multiplier	× 10		
Specific services	£7,500		
Intangible services	£3,500		
Services dependency			£11,000
H's pensions	£7,500 pa		
W's pension	£3,000 pa		
Joint pensions	£10,500 pa		
Dependency ratio	× 2/3		
Joint dependency	£7,000 pa		
W's pension	− £3,000 pa		
Pensions multiplicand		£4,000	
Pensions multiplier		× 8.8	
Pensions dependency			£35,200
TOTAL DAMAGES			**£294,500**

DISCUSSION

In this example, the claim is worth an extra £63,500 (about 25%) if pursued on a fatal basis. The main reasons are:

- The earnings dependency is much higher, since two-thirds rather than one-half of the net earnings are recovered.
- Bereavement damages of £11,800 are added.
- A services dependency of £11,000 is added.
- Funeral expenses of £2,500 are added.

It is notable, however, that the difference in respect of the pensions loss/dependency claims is relatively slight. This is because the wife receives a pension too. The transforming effect of a wife's income is shown in the example below.

Example 2 – Husband with earning wife

[M44]   Facts as in Example 1, save that W earns £27,000 pa net and will receive pensions of £7,500 at age 65.

LIVING CLAIM

As in Example 1

TOTAL DAMAGES	**£231,000**

FATAL CLAIM

General damages (as above)		£67,500
Special damages (as above)	£22,500	
Plus funeral expenses	£2,500	
		£25,000
Bereavement damages		£11,800
H's earnings	£18,000 pa	
W's earnings	£27,000 pa	
Joint earnings	£45,000 pa	
Dependency ratio	× 2/3	
Joint dependency	£30,000 pa	
W's earnings	− £27,000 pa	
Earnings multiplicand	− £3,000	
Earnings multiplier	× 12	
Earnings dependency		£36,000
H's specific services	£750 pa	
Services multiplier	× 10	
Specific services dependency	£7,500	
Intangible services	£3,500	
		£11,000
H's pensions	£7,500 pa	
W's pensions	£7,500 pa	
Joint pensions	£15,000 pa	
Dependency ratio	× 2/3	
Joint dependency	£10,000 pa	
W's pensions	− £7,500 pa	
Pensions multiplicand	£2,500	
Pensions multiplier	× 8.8	
Pensions dependency		£22,000
TOTAL DAMAGES		**£173,300**

Discussion

In this example, the claim is worth £57,700 (about 25%) less when pursued on a fatal basis. The reason is the impact of the wife's income on the earnings and pensions dependency. It is worth noting that, in a typical two-thirds dependency case:

- Where the incomes of the deceased spouse and surviving spouse were equal, the survivor's dependency is a mere one-sixth of the deceased's income.
- Where the income of the surviving spouse was, and would have continued to be, at least twice as much as that of the deceased spouse, there is no income dependency at all.

Example 3 – Single man, living alone

[M45]   Same facts as in Example 1, save that he has no wife, partner or dependant.

Living claim

General damages			£67,500
Special damages			£22,500
Annual earnings	£18,000		
80% living expenses	– £14,400		
Earnings multiplicand		£3,600	
Earnings multiplier		× 12	
Future earnings loss			£43,200
Annual pensions	£7,500		
80% living expenses	– £6,000		
Pensions multiplicand		£1,500	
Pensions multiplier		× 8.8	
Future pensions loss			£13,200
TOTAL DAMAGES			**£146,400**

Fatal claim

General damages			£67,500
Special damages (as above)	£22,500		–
Plus funeral expenses	£2,500		
			£25,000
TOTAL DAMAGES			**£92,500**

DISCUSSION

In this example, the claim is worth £53,900 (about 37%) less when pursued on a fatal basis. The reason is that there is no dependency. Consequently, the moral is that, in the case of a single man living alone – whether as a bachelor, divorcee or widower – there is usually a large premium attached to concluding his claim before his death.

(ii) Minor Factors

[M46]   The following minor factors can also enter into the equation:

* If swayed by sympathy, some judges may award slightly higher general damages to a living claimant.
* The future care claim may be higher on a living basis, since a successful claimant can purchase care that may be unaffordable by a sufferer who has not recovered damages.

5   Practical Considerations

[M47]   The comparative values of a claim on a living and on a fatal basis are not conclusive in determining how quickly it should be pursued. This is not only because the wishes of the claimant, suitably advised, must be paramount. It is also because other factors apart from quantum need to be considered. These include whether:

* Liability is in dispute since, if it is, it may be invaluable for the claimant to give instructions and evidence, comment on the defendant's arguments and counter their evidence.
* The claimant is needed to give instructions and evidence about quantum, eg in the case of a self-employed sole trader running his or her own business.
* A signed statement by the claimant will, due to the effects of the disease or his or her personal qualities, represent better evidence than he or she will ever provide in court.
* These matters can be resolved by a preliminary trial on liability and/or an interim payment, leaving quantum to be determined after death.
* If the above approach is attempted, the court in the exercise of its case management powers will require the case to be pressed on to its conclusion.

[M48]   In general, where the value of a case will be significantly higher after a claimant's impending death, courts can be expected to grant an adjournment to enable it to be concluded on a fatal basis. Historically, the leading case has been *Murray v Shuter*[1] in which the Court of Appeal allowed an eight-month adjournment for this purpose, with Stephenson LJ observing: 'Delay usually defeats justice; but there are cases ... where expedition may work injustice'.

[1]   [1972] 1 Lloyd's Rep 6.

[M49]   The principle has been applied in more modern times by Senior Master Whitaker in the live mesothelioma case of *Boden v Crown House Maintenance Ltd*[1]. He observed that, under CPR Part 3, the court possessed a wide discretion to further the overriding objective of dealing with cases justly. Adding that it was in the interests of all concerned that liability and its investigation be dealt with during the claimant's life, he pointed out that a policy of refusing requests to defer assessment of damages in such cases would encourage a situation in which claims would not be brought until after the death of the victim, a consequence which would be neither fair nor desirable. Accordingly, he rejected the defendants' argument that deferral of the hearing would be an abuse of process, entered judgment on liability, awarded the claimant an interim payment, and adjourned the assessment of quantum.

[1]   QBD (Master Whitaker) 24/5/2006, LTL 8/2/2008.

[M50]   Since damages, if unspent during life, form part of a deceased's estate, it is necessary also to consider the possible incidence of inheritance tax. None is payable when one spouse leaves all his property to the other. However, if the estate is bequeathed to other beneficiaries, they will be liable to inheritance tax above the tax-free limit (£325,000 in 2009/10). Insofar as damages form part of such an estate at this level, they are effectively taxed at 40%. Therefore, if, for example, a widower wishes to leave his estate to dependent children, it may be beneficial to them for him to defer conclusion of his claim until after his death, since no tax will be payable on their dependency damages.

[M51]   Such factors need to be weighed in the balance by the claimant's lawyer when advising him or her. It is usually kinder not to present the choice starkly in terms of whether he or she will be alive or dead when the case is concluded. Instead, it can be explained that, due to legal technicalities, the case will probably be worth rather more, or less as the case may be, if conducted on a speedy basis over several months than on a standard basis over two to three years. Once the claimant has some idea of the percentage or amount involved, he or she may proceed to make an informed choice.

[M52]   Where the case is worth more on a living basis, it is unnecessary to raise the issue, since it may safely be assumed that a claimant prefers his or her case to be concluded quickly if there is no financial loss attached to doing so.

6   Periodical Payments

[M53]   As noted in Chapter O at para **[O19]**, CPR, r 41.8(2) provides that a court may order part of the award to continue after the claimant's death for the benefit of the claimant's dependants. It remains to be seen how judges will exercise this power. If it is applied on a traditional basis, the differences in damages described above will continue, albeit partly in the form of periodical payments. However, there is perhaps now scope for judges to order periodical payments after a claimant's death on the 'bottom up' basis of dependants' needs, thereby reducing the gap between living and fatal compensation.

N Professional Negligence Claims

1 Introduction

[N1] This chapter considers the calculation of damages in claims which stem from the negligent conduct of personal injury claims by lawyers. Clinical negligence cases are included as personal injury claims for this purpose.

[N2] The majority of such claims result from time-related failures: to issue proceedings in time; to serve proceedings in time; or to avoid proceedings being struck out. A minority arise from under-settlement: failure to recover the proper value of the claim. In the former category, the loss is total. In the latter, it is partial.

[N3] So far as the lawyer's liability is concerned, this is determined on the traditional 'balance of probabilities' test. If the judge holds that the lawyer was probably liable, he is treated as if his liability was certain.

[N4] On quantum, however, such cases constitute claims for the loss of a chance: the opportunity of pursuing the personal injury claim to a successful conclusion. Therefore, the damages to be awarded are the benefit from the claim succeeding, discounted by the risk of failure[1]. In calculating these damages, it is recommended that the following seven-stage approach be adopted:

1. Decide the date on which the personal injury action ought to have been concluded if pursued with reasonable expedition.
2. Allowing for any contributory negligence, assess the damages (including interest) that would have been recovered on that date.
3. Deduct the Compensation Recovery Unit (CRU) entitlement that would have been offset against the damages, together with any interim or settlement payments that were in fact made.
4. Add interest to 2 minus 3 above, from the notional date of trial in 1 above.
5. Add any damages (eg costs of original action) due to the professional negligence.
6. Add interest due on the extra damages in 5 above.
7. Multiply the resultant net figure (2 − 3 + 4 + 5 + 6 above) by the percentage chance of success in the original action.

[N5] In principle, 2 and 7 above are separate steps to be applied at different stages. In practice, they may occasionally be elided: see *Sharpe v Addison* discussed in para **[N47]** below.

Each of the seven stages is considered in more detail below.

---

[1]   *Kitchen v Royal Air Force Association* [1958] 2 All ER 241.

2 Date of Conclusion

[N6] It is essential to determine at the outset the date on which the personal injury action should have been concluded by award or settlement, since the rest of the calculation flows from this. In the personal injury part of the schedule, this date defines the dividing line between special damages and future loss, and fixes the date on which damages were notionally assessed. In the professional negligence part, it marks the point from which judgment debt interest is to be added.

[N7] Usually, the date taken is the date on which the personal injury action should have come to trial, had it not been conducted negligently[1]. Since such negligence will seldom have crystallised within three to three-and-a-half years of the accident or other cause of action, it is often appropriate to adopt a date between four and five years after an accident.

---

[1] See eg *Charles v Hugh James Jones & Jenkins (a firm)* [2000] 1 WLR 1278 and *Harrison v Bloom Camillin* [2000] 1 WLR 1278.

[N8] In a case which would probably have been settled, it is permissible to substitute a slightly earlier date as being the date of settlement rather than trial. Nevertheless, except perhaps in small or simple claims, it is not valid to substitute a much earlier date, eg 15 months after an accident, on the basis that this is when the case would have settled had it been well conducted. The comparison is not with good conduct but with adequate conduct – the difference between negligence and its absence.

[N9] However, in the Canadian case of *Rose v Mitton*[1], a case of under-settlement, it was held that, since the negligence of the solicitor lay in settling the claim, it was at that point that the claim crystallised, and the date of settlement was the appropriate date for assessment of damages.

---

[1] (1994) 128 NSR (2d) 99.

[N10] Striking-out cases may be treated differently. In *Hunter v Earnshaw*[1], the accident occurred on 1 November 1984 and the claim was struck out on 15 July 1997. Garland J held that the claimant had lost a chose in action which should be valued at the moment of its loss. Accordingly, the personal injury damages fell to be assessed as at the date of the striking-out order in July 1997.

---

[1] [2001] PNLR 42.

3 Personal Injury Damages

[N11] It is necessary to decide whether the claimant would have succeeded in full in his or her personal injury action, or whether contributory negligence would have been found against him or her. If the latter, the appropriate percentage deduction must be applied.

[N12] The damages are to be determined on standard personal injury law principles, as at the notional date of conclusion.

[N13]   This means that:

* General damages are assessed according to the tariff applicable at this date, not at the later date of the professional negligence trial (see further Chapter D as regards the calculation of general damages).
* Past expenses and losses are awarded for financial loss and expenses up to this date (see further Chapter F as regards the calculation of past expenses and losses).
* Interest on general damages and past expenses and losses is calculated up to this date (see further Chapters E and G regarding the calculation of interest).
* All subsequent financial loss and expense counts as future loss from this date (see further Chapter H regarding the calculation of future expenses and losses).
* The relevant principles of law are those that applied on this date, regardless of subsequent reforms.

[N14]   In a case arising out of under-settlement, ie a case of partial loss, there should at this stage be deducted the damages that the claimant received through the settlement, eg the £50,000 paid in *Griffin v Kingsmill*[1]. Similarly, any interim payment(s) that the claimant received should be deducted at this stage.

[1]   [2001] EWCA Civ 934.

4   Subsequent Developments

[N15]   In general, the claimant's prognosis at the notional date must be taken, and subsequent progress or deterioration should be ignored. Similarly, the personal injury damages should be based on the evidence that was or could have been available then, and later evidence should not be admitted. These principles govern the majority of such cases.

[N16]   The issue of exceptions to these general principles was considered by the Court of Appeal in *Charles v Hugh James Jones & Jenkins*[1]. Swinton Thomas LJ, with whom the Vice Chancellor Sir Richard Scott and Robert Walker LJ, as they then were, agreed, said[2]:

> 'It is right, as Mr Jackson submits, that the judge's task is to assess damages that the claimant would have recovered at the notional trial date. However, in appropriate circumstances, in my view, a judge may well be assisted in coming to a view as to the damages which would have been awarded at the notional trial date by knowledge of what had in fact occurred. Although a judge at the notional trial date is making an assessment, it is to be hoped that it is an accurate assessment and evidential matters which would assist in that task are, to my mind, capable of being received in evidence. So far as the evidence of Dr Roberts is concerned, the point does not arise in an acute form in this case for reasons which I will explain in a moment. *I would be prepared to accept that if some entirely new condition which can be attributed to the accident, manifests itself for the first time after the notional trial date it may be that it has to be ignored. I would wish to reserve any final opinion in relation to that.* However, in contrast, if a condition has manifested itself prior to the notional date, in my judgment the judge is entitled to, and indeed should, take into account what has in fact occurred. As Mr Marshall, on behalf of the plaintiff, points out in his skeleton argument, it would be absurd, and

in my judgment wrong, if, for example, at the notional trial date the medical evidence indicated that there was a strong probability that the claimant would in future suffer some adverse medical consequence as a result of the injuries sustained in the accident, but it was shown as at the date of the actual hearing that there was no such risk, that the claimant should recover damages in respect of it. Similarly, if there was evidence as at the notional trial date that the probability was that the claimant would never work again, but at the actual trial date he or she had obtained remunerative employment, it would be wrong not to take that fact into account. Equally, if the evidence was less certain as to the claimant's prospects of obtaining employment at the notional trial date, but it was quite certain as at the actual trial date that she would be unable to go back to work again, that is a fact which can properly be considered by the judge. In my judgment, it would be absurd and wrong in principle to disregard such evidence.' (Emphasis added.)

1   [2000] 1 WLR 1278.
2   At 1290–1291.

[N17]   Following the decision of the High Court of Australia in *Johnson v Perez*[1], the Court of Appeal held in *Charles*[2] that it may well be appropriate to consider evidence that has emerged after a final judgment should have been obtained, provided that the evidence sheds light on the condition of the claimant at that time. A report from a dermatologist in November 1997 was admitted, to explain repeated breakdowns in the claimant's skin condition up to the date of the notional trial in January 1996.

1   (1988) 82 ALR 587.
2   [2000] 1 WLR 1278.

[N18]   Also, in *Snowdown v Thurston Hoskins & Partners*[1], David Foskett QC, sitting as a Recorder, allowed an application by the claimant to rely upon evidence to the effect that, after the agreed notional trial date, he had probably developed epilepsy attributable to the original accident.

1   (14 November 2002, unreported).

[N19]   The Court of Appeal has provided further clarification in *Dudarec v Andrews*[1]. In 1983 the claimant was diagnosed as having a false traumatic aneurysm of the left carotid artery, a condition which limited his capacity for work and for which it was reasonable for him to refuse to undergo surgery. In 1996 his action was struck out for want of prosecution. He subsequently sued his solicitors who admitted liability. In 2004, fresh medical evidence showed that he did not have a false aneurysm after all. The court held that the 2004 medical evidence was knowable before, and ought to have been available to the judge at, the notional trial in 1996. A court should not conjecture when it knew, so it was right to take it into account. Since it had to be treated as unknown until 1996, the claimant was entitled to his loss of earnings until then. He was further entitled to his loss until 2004, since the defendant solicitors could not rely on their own negligence to accelerate the notional discovery of the true condition. However, the damages awarded against them were reduced, to reflect the fact that there was no justifiable loss of earnings after 2004.

1   [2006] EWCA Civ 256, [2006] 1 WLR 3002.

[N20]   The Court of Appeal in *Dudarec*[1] confirmed the distinction drawn in *Charles*[2], between facts which were discoverable but unknown at the notional trial date, and facts which at that stage were both unknown and unknowable. Sedley LJ observed that facts which were unknowable may have to be ignored, but judgment on the status of this class of evidence remains reserved until a case which directly involves it.

1   [2006] EWCA Civ 256, [2006] 1 WLR 3002.
2   [2000] 1 WLR 1278.

[N21]   The Court of Appeal in *Charles v Hugh James Jones & Jenkins*[1] left open a different question, namely what should be done when, after the date of the notional trial, some entirely new event supervenes which, if taken into account in the later professional negligence claim, would have altered the damages compared to the award which the judge would have made in the original trial. The Court of Appeal considered this in *Whitehead v Searle & another*[2], in which the claimant committed suicide after the original case ought to have been heard but before the hearing of the professional negligence claim. The Court of Appeal endorsed the *Bwllfa* principle, derived from the following words on an arbitrator's duty in the *Bwllfa and Merthyr Dare Steam Collieries*[3] case[4]:

'Why should he listen to conjecture on a matter which has become an established fact? Why should he guess when he can calculate? With the light before him, why should he shut his eyes and grope in the dark?'

Consequently, the Court of Appeal held that the claimant's suicide should be taken into account, and upheld the defendant solicitors' appeal.

1   [2000] 1 WLR 1278.
2   [2009] 1 WLR 549.
3   *Bwllfa and Merthyr Dare Steam Collieries (1891) Limited v The Pontypridd Waterworks Company* [1903] AC 426.
4   [2009] 1 WLR 549 at 561G–H.

5   Social Security Benefits

[N22]   The position over deductibility of social security benefits is governed by the Social Security (Recovery of Benefits) Act 1997 and has been set out in Chapter J. Schedule 2, which lists the benefits that defendants are entitled to offset against each head of damages, is summarised in the table at para **[J17]**.

[N23]   Section 1 provides that the Act only applies to compensation payments directly due to personal injury. Thus, damages paid by a negligent lawyer, for loss of a chance to sue for that injury, do not result in repayment to the Compensation Recovery Unit. Nevertheless, it is clearly correct to deduct the offsettable benefits at this stage of the assessment exercise, since a claimant can only recover against his or her lawyers the net sum that he or she ought to have received in the original personal injury action.

[N24]   In *Wadey v Surrey County Council*[1], the House of Lords held that the effect of s 17 of the 1997 Act was that repayable benefit was to be disregarded in the assessment of past loss and in the calculation of interest on these damages. That is why stage 2 –

the assessment of the personal injury damages and calculation of interest thereon – is to be completed before the deduction of offsettable benefits under stage 3.

¹   [2000] 2 All ER 545.

6   Interest on Personal Injury Award

[N25]   Stages 1–3 above only establish the net damages up to the notional date of the personal injury trial. The claimant is entitled to additional interest on these damages up to the date of the conclusion of the professional negligence claim.

[N26]   The Court of Appeal considered the basis of this interest in *Pinnock v Wilkins & Sons*[1]. It noted that, so far as judgment debt interest under s 17 of the Judgments Act 1838 was concerned, the interest rate was fixed as at the date of judgment and could not vary thereafter. One option open to judges in a professional negligence action is to award interest at the fixed judgment rate as if the Judgments Act 1838 applied. The Court of Appeal declined to lay down any general guidelines governing the award of interest in professional negligence actions against lawyers. It held that trial judges are entitled to exercise their discretion in awarding interest. There are two other methods of doing so.

¹   (1990) Times, 29 January. See also para [58] of *Nicholson v Knox Ukiwa & another* [2007] EWHC 2430 (QB), HHJ Reddihough sitting as a judge of the High Court.

[N27]   The approach that the Court of Appeal (by a majority) adopted in *Pinnock*[1] is allowed by the fact that s 17 of the Judgments Act 1838 does not directly apply to legal negligence cases, since their very nature almost always means that no judgment has been obtained. Therefore, the majority of the court held that the appropriate rate in *Pinnock*'s case was the variable rate which 'over the relevant period was payable *from time to time* on judgment debts'. Over the period in question, from March 1983 until January 1989, this resulted in a period at 12% per annum followed by a period at 15% per annum.

¹   (1990) Times, 29 January.

[N28]   Since 1 April 1993 the judgment debt interest rate has been 8% per annum. This means that, for over a decade, the issue of applying fixed or variable interest rates has been a distinction without a difference. The rate has been 8% per annum on either basis[1].

¹   Although 8% remains the current rate at the time of writing, following a report from the Law Commission, the Government has proposed that s 17 of the Judgments Act 1838 be repealed and a power given to the Lord Chancellor to set the applicable rate of interest on judgment debts. On 15 December 2009 the Ministry of Justice published the draft Civil Law Reform Bill and a consultation paper suggesting that the Lord Chancellor be provided with a wide discretion to order fixed rates for pre- and post-judgment interest. It remains to be seen what will come out of the consultation process, and whether or not the draft Bill will be enacted by any subsequent Government – see further Chapter G.

[N29]   The last option is to use the interest rate payable on funds in the court special account. Currently, the special account produces a lower rate (0.5% per annum) than the judgment rate (8% per annum). The special account rate was adopted by Neuberger J in *Harrison v Bloom Camillin (No 2)*[1], when he observed that the judgment debt rate tends to be high and that there was no reason to penalise the defendants.

[1]   [2000] Lloyd's Rep PN 89.

7 Professional Negligence Damages

[N30]   So far as possible, a personal injury claimant is entitled to be placed in the same position as if the personal injury negligence had not occurred. Hence, the calculation of his or her net entitlement in the notional personal injury action. By the same principle, he or she is also entitled to be placed in the same position as if the professional negligence had not occurred. Consequently, he or she is entitled to recover in addition in the professional negligence action the extra damages that have resulted from his or her lawyers' delays or other negligence.

[N31]   The most obvious of these is costs. The failure of the original personal injury action may have left him or her with a liability for (a) his or her own legal costs, and (b) the defendant's legal costs. This was recognised by Salmon LJ in *Allen v Sir Alfred McAlpine & Sons Ltd*[1], when he said: 'The damages will be all the costs thrown away, together with the sum which the plaintiff would have recovered by way of damages against the defendants'. Despite an apparent finding to the contrary by the trial judge in *Mount v Barker Austin*[2], it is submitted that the claimant should only be awarded the lost costs of the personal injury action insofar as it is held that he should have succeeded in it, since, if the original action would have failed, he would have incurred these costs in any event.

[1]   [1968] 1 All ER 543.
[2]   [1998] PNLR 493.

[N32]   It is also now clear that, where the delay that inevitably results from failure of a personal injury action causes financial prejudice to a claimant, he or she can recover damages for the resultant financial loss and expenses. These may include interest on a new loan that he or she has to take out due to lack of the personal injury damages, or on an existing loan that he or she would have otherwise been able to repay out of them. Another example is the costs and interest of meeting a default judgment entered against him or her in respect of a debt that he or she would have repaid out of his or her damages, although not the debt itself which would have been repayable in any event. All such recoverability is subject to, and indeed based on, the general principle that a claimant must take reasonable steps to mitigate his or her loss.

[N33]   Former doubts as to the validity of such items, based on the 1933 House of Lords' decision in the *Liesbosch Dredger* case[1] that a claimant's impecuniosity could not be taken into account, have been laid to rest by the recent House of Lords' decision in *Lagden v O'Connor*[2], which stated that the *Liesbosch* principle had been overtaken by subsequent developments in the law[3]. Their Lordships held instead that a wrongdoer had to take his victim as he found him, and to pay for the consequences if it was reasonably foreseeable that the injured party would need to borrow money or incur some other expenditure to mitigate his damages.

1   *Liesbosch Dredger v SS Edison* [1933] AC 449.
2   [2003] UKHL 64.
3   See further Chapter A at paras **[A78]–[A83]**.

[N34]   In theory, a successful professional negligence claim will fully and directly compensate a claimant because, in almost every case, what he or she has lost is directly measurable in money. There is a complex minority of cases, however, where this does not entirely hold true. Such cases arise from the loss of provisions available to personal injury claimants that are not available in professional negligence actions.

[N35]   The first is the right to protect the damages by placing all or part of them into a personal injury trust. Paragraph 12 of Sch 10 (capital to be disregarded) to the Income Support (General) Regulations 1987[1] only applies 'where the funds of a trust are derived from a payment made in consequence of any personal injury to the claimant'. A personal injury trust is an important facility for those living off means-tested benefits whose entitlement to them will be removed by receipt of substantial lump sum damages. Here, at least, there is the opportunity of prima facie measurement of this head of loss in terms of the income support, housing or other benefit thus lost, although the lawyer defendants may respond by relying on the possibly more episodic payment of, and limited access to, damages held within a personal injury trust.

1   SI 1987/1967.

[N36]   The second is a personal injury claimant's entitlement to provisional damages under s 32A of the Senior Courts Act 1981 and s 51 of the County Courts Act 1984. These only apply to 'an action for damages for personal injuries'. Consequently, a claimant whose personal injury action has failed due to his or her lawyers' negligence may justly argue that they have deprived him or her of his or her right to return to court for a further award if the existing risk of serious illness or serious deterioration in condition caused by the defendant's negligence actually materialises. The difficulty in assessment is that final damages are in theory of equal value to provisional damages plus the right to return if the specified risks materialise, and in practice result in higher immediate payments. Nevertheless, the right to provisional damages can be a real benefit, for instance to a head injury sufferer with a risk of epilepsy or to an asbestosis victim with risks of lung cancer and mesothelioma. Since the value of this right is not precisely calculable, it is submitted that a moderate additional lump sum award is the correct method of compensating for its loss.

[N37]   The third arises out of a claimant's entitlement to periodic payments pursuant to s 2 of the Damages Act 1996. This forms the subject of Chapter O. In some cases, especially those of younger claimants with larger awards, periodical payments may be thought particularly appropriate and apt to provide better financial security than lump sum damages calculated by reference to retail price index inflation and adopting multipliers based on a discount rate of 2.5% pa. Such advantage is particularly pronounced in cases involving substantial damages for future care, following the endorsement of ASHE 6115 by the Court of Appeal in *Thompstone v Tameside Hospital NHS Foundation Trust*[1] (and related cases). However, quantification of the loss in the context of a professional negligence claim is an uncertain exercise, not least because the 100% principle applies equally to the assessment of damages in the form of a lump sum as it does to periodical payments[2]. Thus, as long as the lump sum was not an undervaluation, it may be difficult to establish that a claimant who was negligently advised to accept a lump sum rather than to consider periodical payments resulted in a recoverable loss. It is submitted that the correct course may be to formulate the claim on traditional grounds, and add a (sometimes substantial) sum for the loss of opportunity to recover the damages in the form of periodical payments. Evidence from financial experts would be required to establish, so far as possible, the alleged value of the lost benefit.

[1]   [2008] EWCA Civ 5, [2008] 1 WLR 2207.
[2]   *Flora v Wakom (Heathrow) Ltd* [2006] EWCA Civ 1103, [2007] 1 WLR 482; *Thompstone v Tameside and Glossop NHS Trust* [2008] EWCA Civ 5, [2008] 1 WLR 2207.

[N38]   A similar problem arises with structured settlements, which are also discussed in Chapter O on periodic payments. Section 5(1) of the Damages Act 1996 provides that the entitlement to a structured settlement only arises in personal injury claims, and not in professional negligence claims against lawyers. The combination of a lesser lump sum coupled with an annuity is, in theory, of equal value to receipt of all the damages in a single lump sum. It is submitted that the correct course is to assess the damages that would have been received on the latter basis and to add a modest further lump sum to compensate for the claimant's inability to enter into a structured settlement where he or she would or might well have done so in a personal injury action.

8   Interest on Professional Negligence Damages

[N39]   Interest on this aspect of the overall damages needs to be separately assessed for two main reasons.

[N40]   The first is that they arise over a different period. The personal injury damages crystallise as at the notional date of trial; interest on them accrues at full rate thereafter. In contrast, the professional negligence damages only start to arise after this notional date, since they are based on failure to recover the damages that ought to have been awarded then: interest on them accrues at half rate, since they are continuing rather than crystallised.

[N41]   The second reason is that different interest rates may be adopted. As seen above, the judgment debt interest rate is often applied to the notional personal injury judgment. As the additional professional negligence damages, arising later, would not have been incorporated in this judgment, it is submitted that the court special account rate should apply to them instead.

9   Chances of Success

[N42]   Some cases may be certain of success. In *Charles v Hugh James Jones & Jenkins*[1], where both the driver of a lorry which had caused a subsequent personal injury and the defendant solicitors in the professional negligence action had admitted liability, the Court of Appeal rejected the argument that in every case a discount should be made for the risks attendant on litigation. Where no discount is appropriate, the claimant is entitled to the full value of his or her claim.

1   [2000] 1 WLR 1278.

[N43] All other professional negligence cases are governed by the leading Court of Appeal authority of *Kitchen v Royal Air Force Association*. Lord Evershed MR stated[2]:

> 'what the court has to do (assuming that the plaintiff has established negligence) in a case such as the present is to determine what the plaintiff has by that negligence lost. The question is, has the plaintiff lost some right of value, some chose in action of reality and substance? In such a case, it may be that its value is not easy to determine, but it is the duty of the court to determine the value as best it can.'

Although regarding it as rather generous, the Court of Appeal upheld the trial judge's award of £2,000, as representing a two-thirds chance of recovering £3,000.

1   [1958] 2 All ER 241.
2   At 251.

[N44] One approach is to calculate the chances of success with arithmetical precision. This was adopted by Neuberger J in *Harrison v Bloom Camillin*[1], a case arising out of alleged negligence by accountants. He held that the claimants had a 65% chance of establishing negligence, combined with an 80% chance of winning on the issue of causation. Accordingly, he awarded them 52% (65 x 80%) of the full value of their initial claim.

1   [2000] Lloyd's Rep PN 89.

[N45]   In *Hanif v Middleweeks*[1], the Court of Appeal pointed out that the arithmetical approach is only valid when the issues to which the percentages are applied are separate and independent. If, on the other hand, the issues in question involve at least in part the same considerations, eg of honesty or credibility, then success on one could mean that success on another was more likely. In such cases, the arithmetical approach is invalid and a court needs to take a broader view of the chances of success. Accordingly, in *Hanif*, where the judge had assessed the prospects of success on three issues as 80%, 60% and 25% respectively, but all three issues involved the credibility of one witness in particular, the court rejected the arithmetical submission that 12% ($80 \times 60 \times 25\%$) should be taken, and substituted an overall figure of 20%.

1   [2000] Lloyd's Rep PN 920.

[N46]   Subjective factors may be taken into account, including attitudes towards settlement. In *Griffin v Kingsmill*[1], the Court of Appeal was inclined on objective grounds to value the loss of chance at 85%, on the basis of the likely outcome at a trial on the issues of primary liability and contributory negligence. However, they reduced this to 80% in view of the fact that the mother of the 12–year-old claimant was very cautious in her approach, so that an offer at this level would probably have been accepted.

1   [2001] EWCA Civ 934.

[N47]   Even if the original personal injury claim was weak, an award will be made in a professional negligence claim provided that it had more than negligible prospects of success. In *Sharpe v Addison*[1], the Court of Appeal concluded that there would have been a finding of 75% contributory negligence at a trial. Rix LJ assessed the chances of success on liability as 40%, leading to an award of a mere 10% of the claim's full value. Agreeing with him, Chadwick LJ added[2]:

> 'The greater the discount for contributory negligence, the greater the chance that the Claimant would have recovered that discounted amount ... there are of course other ways of reaching the same end figure. For example by discounting 70 per cent for contributory negligence and assessing the chance as one in three; or 80 per cent for contributory negligence and an evens chance. At the end of the day, the question is: what was the claim worth?'

[1]   [2003] EWCA Civ 1189, [2004] PNLR 23.
[2]   At para 50.

[N48]   Finally, there are cases that were almost bound to fail. In the Court of Appeal case of *Mount v Barker Austin*[1], Simon Brown LJ pointed out that, where the defendant lawyers had commenced court action on behalf of the claimant, the evidential burden lay on them to prove that the litigation was of no value and that this burden would be heavy if they had failed to advise the claimant of the hopelessness of his position. Nevertheless, mere nuisance value, unaccompanied by any merit, does not entitle a claimant to damages. In *McFarlane v Wilkinson*[2], Brooke LJ cited the statement from highly experienced counsel that he knew of 'no English case in which a court had been willing to award damages on the basis of the potential settlement value of a claim which was shown to be bound to fail as a matter of law'. As Lord Evershed MR stated in *Kitchen v RAF*[3], 'if it is made clear that the plaintiff never had a cause of action, that there was no case which the plaintiff could reasonably ever have formulated, then it is equally plain that the answer is that she can get nothing save nominal damages for the solicitors' negligence'.

[1]   [1998] PNLR 493.
[2]   [1997] 2 Lloyd's Rep 259.
[3]   [1958] 2 All ER 241.

[N49]   In summary, for the purposes of preparing the schedule of loss in a professional negligence claim, it is necessary:

- in a case that is certain of success, to take its full value on this basis;
- in a case with partial prospects of success, to apply to the full value the percentage chances of the original action succeeding, whether that chance is arithmetically calculated or broadly assessed.

In a case where the original action was devoid of merit, the claimant's only entitlement is to nominal damages.

10   Conclusion

[N50]   The operation of the above stages is summarised in the simple example below:

(i)   Personal injury action should have been tried on 1 October 2005.

(ii)   Personal injury damages (including interest) would have been £202,000 after 20% deduction for contributory negligence (ie full value £252,500).

(iii) Deduct offsettable social security benefits of £2,000.

(iv)   If the professional negligence case is concluded on 1 October 2009, judgment debt interest at 32% (8% per annum × 4) on £200,000 (2 – 3 above) is £64,000.

(v)   Add professional negligence damages of £20,000.

(vi)   Add interest thereon at half special account rate of 12% = £2,127.40.

(vii) 75% prospects of success on the grand total of £286,127.40 (2 – 3 + 4 + 5 + 6) produces a total award of £214,595.55.

O Periodical Payments

I Introduction

[O1] Sections 100 and 101 of the Courts Act 2003 inserted a new s 2 into the Damages Act 1996, enabling a court to order that damages for future pecuniary loss in respect of personal injury (including clinical negligence) should take the form wholly or partly of periodical payments ('PPs'). This came into effect on 1 April 2005. The ability to make a periodical payments order ('PPO'), ie to order that future loss should be paid by instalments, without any definite end date save for the date of the claimant's death (and, in some cases, such as fatal accidents, even beyond that), was a major development.

[O2] The power to order PPs applies to any case where there are claims for future loss, whenever begun[1].

[1]   Courts Act 2003 (Commencement No 9) Order 2005, SI 2005/547, art 13. However, the power to make a *variable* order only applies to proceedings begun after 1 April 2005.

[O3] The principle underlying compensation has always been that it should amount to full and fair compensation for that which a claimant has lost by reason of the wrong done to him or her. Until 1 April 2005, this was achieved by empowering the courts to award a lump sum which, once awarded, was final. It could not be re-opened, no matter how wrong were the assumptions which underpinned it, and it could be spent on whatever the claimant chose, no matter how he or she had justified the total sum which he or she was awarded. This had the virtue of finality, but also the vice of over-compensating in many cases and under-compensating in others, especially where the life expectancy of the claimant differed (in the event) from the length predicted at the time damages were assessed. Accordingly, Parliament made progressive inroads into the 'lump sum principle'. First, it allowed provisional damages to be claimed, where disease or deterioration might occur but at an unpredictable time and with unpredictable consequences in terms of cost to the claimant. Then, it supported the ability of parties to agree to receive damages spread over time (usually for the lifetime of the claimant), paid monthly, quarterly or yearly, under the terms of an annuity purchased by the defendant. Because the proceeds of the annuity represented part payments of the award of damages, and awards of damages are received net of income tax, payments under such an annuity were not taxable. Such arrangements, if made at the time of assessment of damages, so that they truly represented an award of damages rather than a commercial purchase made out of an award already received, were known as 'structured settlements'.

[O4] Continuing concern about the appropriateness of once and for all payments led to the courts requiring that, in every case involving patients or children, no claim could be settled without the parties demonstrating that they had at least considered whether or not to enter into a structured settlement[1]. Structured settlements could only be achieved by agreement between the parties, however, and were restricted by the availability of commercial products. They almost always took the form of the purchase of an annuity out of part of a lump sum calculated on conventional principles.

[1]   Practice Direction PD 21 (supplementing CPR Part 21) was amended in 2003 to reflect this, following a report, commissioned by the Master of the Rolls, from a working party chaired by Brian Langstaff QC.

[O5]   Eventually, Parliament amended the Damages Act 1996 by enacting provisions in the Courts Act 2003 which enable the court to order payment of future loss by regular instalments over a specified period – usually the lifetime of the claimant. These provisions came into force on 1 April 2005. Government guidance[1] regarding these provisions suggests that, where a claim includes a claim for future loss of earnings or for the future costs of care of a seriously injured claimant, it should ordinarily be satisfied by an award of PPs rather than by the formerly conventional lump sum award.

[1]   See para **[O12]** below.

[O6]   In addition to the court *ordering* such payments, the parties may *agree* (if they choose to do so) that damages for personal injury or clinical negligence other than those in respect of future loss (eg sums in respect of past loss, or in respect of non-pecuniary loss) should be paid periodically rather than as one lump sum. The court, however, has no power to order any part of a damages award other than that in respect of future loss to be paid in the form of PPs.

[O7]   PPs may appear superficially similar to payments made regularly under a 'structured settlement'. Structured settlements (introduced for the reasons set out above) were common since the late 1980s, in particular because of the mix of tax advantages, certainty and freedom from investment worry which they provided to a claimant. But they differ from PPs in particular because they represent an annuity, which is purchased by a lump sum payment (and are thus said to be 'top down' arrangements), because they can be provided only by agreement, and because they depend upon there being a market in which annuities on 'damaged lives' can readily be purchased. By contrast, PPOs do not depend on the consent of the parties (the needs of the claimant as opposed to the wishes of either party are determinative), nor require the calculation of a lump sum and its conversion into an annuity, but are designed simply to cope with annual needs as and when they arise (and are thus said to be 'bottom up' arrangements), and do not require the purchase of a commercially provided annuity product (though this remains one way in which an order for such payments may be met) by paying a capital lump sum, from the investment of which the annual payments are then derived (a 'top down' arrangement).

[O8]   The 'old' learning in relation to structured settlements is largely redundant – though it remains possible for lump sums to be converted into annuity products, and thus (somewhat confusingly) an award *can* theoretically result in a mix of lump sum, structured settlement-type annuity purchased by consent, and PPO.

2   Rationale

[O9]   The policy rationale underlying the introduction of the power to order PPs is, first, that the lump sum system can be unsatisfactory, because it is based upon predictions about the future life expectancy of a claimant which are inevitably uncertain and almost always lead to either over- or under-compensation. Secondly, with PPs, responsibility for and the risk of managing the investment of the award transfers from claimants to defendants, who are better able to bear it. A third rationale is that most future losses are periodic in nature (eg loss of future salary; payment of future care costs from month to month). Since the purpose of the law of compensation is to ensure that a victim of an accident is restored to the position in which he or she would have been if the accident had not occurred, so far as money can achieve it, it may be argued that to be placed in regular receipt of sums in respect of salary, or to cover the costs of care, more accurately replicates full restitution than does the payment of one lump sum which may be spent at any time and for any purpose. Waller LJ expressed it thus in *Tameside & Glossop v Thompstone and others* (at para 19):

> 'In 2002, the Master of the Rolls' Working Party published its report entitled "Structured Settlements". The disadvantages of a conventional lump sum award were summarised at paragraph 12 of the report: "The one thing which is certain about a once and for all lump sum award in respect of future loss is that it will inevitably either over-compensate or under-compensate. This will happen particularly where the claimant survives beyond the life expectancy estimated at the time of trial, or alternatively dies earlier. It will frequently be the case in practice that there is over-compensation in six figure sums, or, correspondingly, that a combination of increased life expectancy, the cost of care, and (it may be) the cost of new but necessary medical treatments is such that the sum needed exceeds anything that might have been awarded at the date of trial".
>
> 20. The Working Party therefore concluded at paragraph 21:
>
> " ... of the features we have identified that of accuracy is the most important. We are concerned that a consequence of a system of once and for all lump sum awards is that there will be under or over-compensation (in some cases considerable) and particularly concerned that a proportion of claimants whose life expectancy is uncertain, and who need significant continuing care, might be left with significant uncompensated need. It adds to our concern that this is likely to occur later in life when the consequences will be particularly hard to manage. It is also of concern that appreciation of this may give rise to excessive prudence and under expenditure in earlier years. Accordingly, we prefer a system that is better able to meet future needs as and when they arise. Such a system may also have its defects – as we shall go on to point out – but we believe the advantages outweigh them."
>
> 21. Following the report of the Working Party, amendments were made to the 1996 Act. As a result of these amendments, contained in the Courts Act 2003, it has since 1 April 2005 been open to a court to make an order for periodical payments whether or not the parties agree. Indeed, it is now mandatory, when a court is making an award of damages for future pecuniary loss in respect of personal injury, for it to consider whether the damages - or part of them – should be paid by way of periodical payments.'

[O10]   The 'Guidance on periodical payments' issued by the Department for Constitutional Affairs contains the following passage:

'The Government's policy intentions in introducing the provisions in the Courts Act 2003 were based on the belief that the existing system of compensation for future losses by way of lump sums is unsatisfactory, and that periodical payments are usually a much better and fairer way of compensating those facing long-term future loss and care needs'.

[O11] Paragraph 24 of the explanatory notes to the Courts Act 2003 states as follows:

'These sections aim to promote the widespread use of periodical payments as the means of paying compensation for future financial loss in personal injury cases. In principle, periodical payments made as the needs arise provide a more appropriate means of compensating claimants than lump sums.'

[Q12] In paragraphs 2 to 4 of the Regulatory Impact Assessment: 'Court's Bill: Power to Order Periodical Payments for Future Loss', published by the Lord Chancellor's Department, it was noted that the Government considered that it was 'generally preferable for claimants to receive periodical payments, rather than a lump sum for future care costs and loss of earnings'. The hope was expressed that an order for PPs would 'become the norm in larger cases'. The objective of introducing PPs was said to be:

'to make the system for compensating seriously injures accident victims more accurate in reflecting the amount and nature of the claimant's loss and so fairer as between claimants and defendants.'

[Q13] Lord Irvine of Lairg, the then Lord Chancellor, also made the following comments in the foreword to the consultation paper 'Damages for Future Loss: Giving the Courts the Power to Order Periodical Payments for Future Loss and Care Costs in Personal Injury cases', issued in March 2002, which resulted in the introduction of periodical payments:

'It is widely recognised that lump sum payments are not ideal. They are based on the predicted life expectancy of the claimant and they invariably provide under- or overcompensation, resulting in an injustice to either the claimant or the defendant.

The proposals set out in this paper will allow the courts to award periodical payments, in appropriate cases, either wholly or partly in place of a lump sum payment. This should help ensure that injured people receive the compensation to which they are entitled for so long as it is needed, without the worry of the award running out if they happen to live longer than was expected. Removing uncertainty should ensure that claimant are able to spend their money on providing the quality of life and the standard of care to which they are entitled.'

3 Procedural Provisions

[O14] Civil Procedure Rules 1998 (CPR), r 41.5 enables the parties to state in their statements of case whether they regard PPs or a lump sum as likely to be more appropriate for all or part of an award of damages in respect of future loss. Both claimants and defendants will need to consider whether to make such an indication. If they choose to do so, they should give brief reasons, or they may be asked to state them. They may have regard to the considerations which are expanded on later in this chapter.

[O15] However, if no view is expressed the court may order the parties to state one; and CPR, r 41.6 requires the court to consider, and to indicate to the parties as soon as practicable, whether an order for PPs or a lump sum is likely to be the more appropriate form for all or part of an award of damages. This may well be at the first case management conference.

[O16] Accordingly, it is necessary for all personal injury lawyers dealing with a claim for future loss – of whatever size – to have a working knowledge of the provisions which permit PPs to be ordered, and to be able to decide in any given case whether it is more appropriate to claim them, or conversely whether it is more appropriate to ask for a lump sum award.

[O17] This chapter distinguishes between *'non-variable'*[1] PPs and *'variable'* PPs, both of which may be ordered by a court. It distinguishes between *orders of a court*, and *agreements between the parties*, and deals with the need for schedules to take account of the possibility of PPs being ordered, applications for interim payments and how they may be affected by the possibility of a PPO being made at trial, appeals from an adverse decision in respect of such payments, and Part 36 offers. It will deal, in conclusion, with ways of providing for future loss other than by an order for PPs. This section will include a review of agreements to provide for future loss by annuities, as well as considering other possibilities.

[1]   This is entirely our own phrase, to distinguish such an order from one which is expressly variable, made under the terms of the Damages (Variation of Periodical Payments) Order 2005, SI 2005/841.

4   Agreements as to Form of Payment

[O18] The distinction between orders and agreements is important. Section 2(1) of the Damages Act 1996, inserted by Courts Act 2003, s 100, limits the power of a court when making an award of damages. In the absence of agreement, it may make a PPO (a) in respect of future pecuniary loss only (s 2(2)); moreover, (b) it may not make an order unless satisfied that continuity of payment under the order is reasonably secure (s 2(3)). Agreement may thus allow the parties to go further than a court is empowered to go.

[O19] It is unlikely that payments which remain level in numerical terms will ever prove satisfactory to a claimant, since the value of such payments will be eroded by inflation[1]. Under the Damages Act 1996 and the CPR, the default position for up-rating PPs is by reference to the RPI. Although, if it is left open to the court, following the cases of *Tameside & Glossop Acute Services NHS Trust v Thompstone & Ors*[2] and *Sarwar v Ali & the MIB*[3], indexation of PPs by reference to ASHE (6115)[4] for care and case management and a suitable earnings-based measure for loss of earnings is likely to be imposed, agreements to make periodical payments in cases other than clinical negligence claims are likely in practice to be limited to those which rise in line with the RPI (at any rate, where the claim is against a private person who is insured by a liability insurer). This is because the regulatory regime which controls the investments to be made by insurers effectively precludes any annuity which is designed by reference to an index other than the RPI. If this is seen as a problem in an individual case, it may be possible, however, for the parties to agree to provide for arrangements which better suit their wishes (see below). In recent clinical negligence cases, parties have routinely been agreeing indexation to ASHE 6115 by consent. Furthermore, parties have been agreeing PPOs with suitable indexation for other heads of loss, such as medical treatment and Court of Protection costs; but, in the absence of authoritative guidance relating to indexation of heads of loss other than care, the selection of relevant indices is less settled practice and the applicable index is essentially arguable.

1   See further paras **[O82]**–**[O88]** below.
2   [2008] 1 WLR 2207, [2008] EWCA Civ 5.
3   [2007] EWHC 1255 (Admin).
4   There has recently been a proposal to revise the index of which ASHE 6115 forms part: it should not, therefore, be assumed too readily that there is magic in the number.

[O20]   Agreement is normally possible as to any matter, where the claimant and defendant are of full age and capacity. In one respect, however, agreements are regulated by statutory instrument. If the parties agree that a claimant (or defendant) should be entitled to return to court to ask for the terms of the periodical payment agreement to be varied, then the agreement must comply with art 9(2) of the Damages (Variation of Periodical Payments) Order 2005[1], and the person permitted to apply for the terms to be varied must obtain the court's permission before making that application. This is a critical point which should be borne in mind by claimants' representatives making agreements which are variable in the light of future uncertain, but reasonably possible, events: contract alone will not carry an entitlement to return to the defendant to seek a variation – why else would the order require compliance with its terms?

1   SI 2005/841.

[O21]   Agreements by which the parties consent to an order for PPs have to take account of the provisions of CPR, r 41.8 (see para **[O44]**). If the parties wish the terms of a settlement to be embodied in a consent order made by the court, the requirements of that rule will also need to be satisfied. These are set out at paras **[O44]**–**[O56]**.

5   Why Ask for a Periodical Payment Order?

[O22]   The main advantages of a PPO over a lump sum award are (as summarised by Waller LJ in *Thompstone*[1]):

(i)   There is less risk of over- or under-compensation than with a lump sum system (which is based on predictions about life expectancy which are inevitably inaccurate) – actual life expectancy ceases to matter, since the payments will go on for the life of the claimant (and indeed, provision can be made for them to go on for longer).

(ii)   There is no tax to be paid upon the PPs when received (whereas income produced by a lump sum is taxable).

(iii)   PPs can be linked to a suitable index or measure, so that they more closely match the loss in question and keep pace with inflation, whereas lump sums are calculated by reference to the Ogden Tables which, in turn, are calculated by reference to the RPI, which may increase at a slower rate.

(iv)   Lump sums are calculated by reference to a discount rate of 2.5%, ie an assumed net investment return of 2.5% above inflation each year, which may be very difficult to achieve without taking considerable risk (this problem increases over time as the lump sum becomes smaller).

(v)   Any investment risk is borne by the provider of the payment.

(vi)   The time, trouble and effort of ensuring that a lump sum is invested so as to produce the required return is, again, borne by the provider of the periodical payment, and not by the injured claimant.

(vii)   Payment is guaranteed under the Financial Services Compensation Scheme or by the Government directly – by comparison, the payment of income from an invested lump sum is not guaranteed. This is important. One recent example of such exposure to the stock market is of lump sums invested in UK equities in 1999. The collapse of share values in the succeeding two years was severely damaging to such investments, possibly halving their value, yet without recompense. But an even more compelling example has been the fortune of the stock market, and investments linked to it, over the 2008–10 recession ('the global crash'), together with the sudden and unexpected drop in interest rates receivable on cash deposits. These two events demonstrate, within the last 12 years alone, how the uncertainties of investment in 'the market' can disrupt even the most careful of planning. Anyone with a PPO in their favour over the recent 'crunch' would have been blessing their advisers.

(viii) If the recipient should go bankrupt, sums in respect of his or her care needs remain payable to him or her, and are not property to which his or her trustee in bankruptcy is entitled (the position in respect of payments relating to future loss of income is different, however).

(ix)   Receipt of a periodical payment does not prejudice entitlement to free national or local authority provision in respect of state benefits, local authority residential care or local authority provided domiciliary care.

(x)   Any claimant who is vulnerable, but not so injured as to be a patient, is protected against unscrupulous third parties (or even well-meaning but irresponsible family and friends) – they might take a chunk of a lump sum, but cannot deprive the claimant of his or her right to go on receiving PPs.

(xi)   There is no need to engage in the difficulties which the Ogden Tables can give rise to, and lesser reliance on difficult (and often distressing) evidence as to life expectancy, because there is no need to determine what lump sum would be payable for the heads of future loss that take the form of PPs.

(xii)   Where a party has indicated a preference for PPs, it is easier to ask the court to make an interim PPO. (An interim payment order no longer has to be paid in one lump sum, since the provisions of s 2 of the Damages Act 1996, which allow for PPs, apply to interim payments as well[2].) This may be a considerable advantage, since an order can be made providing for specified (future)[3] losses to be paid until the date of trial at periodic intervals[4].

(xiii) It might further be added, though more speculatively, that it is less likely that the courts will permit the same scope for discounts in respect of heads of loss than the courts have historically done when assessing lump sum compensation.

The main disadvantages of a PPO, as opposed to a lump sum award, are:

(i)   The loss of flexibility: in particular, if the whole of provision for future loss is converted into PPs, there is no ability to meet large capital expenses or unexpected demands on income (eg for an urgent or new operation or treatment).

(ii)   Lump sum awards have certainty. Claimants in receipt of lump sum awards know exactly how much they have to spend. It is their money and they can spend it exactly how they want.

(iii) It may be possible to invest a lump sum in a way which produces a higher return than would be produced by any likely index such as RPI (though it is likely that the circumstances in which this will be so are limited, and may apply more where a claimant wishes to invest his or her award in the establishment of a business, purchase of property to let etc).

(iv) A lump sum award, though calculated such that every penny of future loss is used up at the exact moment when the claimant's life expires, has the potential of leaving funds for heirs and dependants. There is much less potential for this with PPs.

(v)   There is no clean break: the claimant has to prove he or she is alive each year before getting the next PP. Some claimants find the thought of a continuing relationship with the defendant or the defendant's insurers difficult to handle. Some also do not like the thought that the defendant keeps the money and they have to prove their continued existence every year.

(vi) There is a need to check the up-rating of payments to make sure that this has been done properly. Human error can lead to mistakes. It can be time consuming to correct errors and seek additional balancing payments and any interest due.

(vii) PPs do not sit well with accommodation claims in cases involving claimants with short life expectancies. Although short life expectancy cases are classic examples of those in which a PPO may be strongly desirable, eg for future care and case management, there may be difficulties reconciling this with the current system of assessing accommodation claims under *Roberts v Johnstone*[5]. In particular, if too many heads of loss are awarded by way of PPs, it may not be possible to raise the necessary capital to buy appropriate adapted accommodation.

[1]   *Thameside & Glossop v Thompstone and ors* [2008] 1 WLR 2207, [2008] EWCA Civ 5.

[2]   Damages Act 1996, s 2A(5).

[3]   In this respect, 'future' means future assessed as at the date of award, rather than as at the date of the final assessment of damages.

[4]   This can have a further advantage in relation to Claimant Part 36 Offers; see Julian Chamberlayne 'Claimant Part 36 Offers: Are they Working' JPIL 3/2009, p 240.

[5]   [1989] QB 878.

[O23]   A number of myths as to the advantages and disadvantages of periodical payment provision need to be debunked:

(i)   It is said that periodic payments afford '*No ability to raise capital*' – this is not so, since the presence of a guaranteed income stream of a guaranteed amount, rising with inflation, can be used to afford personal security for a loan, in the same way as mortgages are frequently granted on the expectation of continuing income. However, it is not possible to charge or assign the right to receive PPs without the express consent of the court (Damages Act 1996, s 2(6)), and lenders may be reluctant to enter into loans if their ultimate security depends on taking enforcement action against someone who is seriously disabled. It may not be something the disabled person wishes to embark upon.

(ii) *'There will be no money to leave to dependants'* – not so: CPR, r 41.8(2) provides that a court may order part of the award to continue after the claimant's death for the benefit of the claimant's dependants. The purpose is to permit payments to continue to dependants, particularly when they might otherwise have had a Fatal Accidents Act 1976 claim. This may, in particular, afford opportunities for those suffering from incurable cancers, such as mesothelioma, to secure provision during their lifetime with the security of their family, knowing that dependants will be provided for, whereas at present a lump sum award to a live claimant, who has only a 'lost years' claim for the period after his or her death, may afford less total compensation than the potential claim under the Fatal Accidents Act 1976 where the victim has a spouse, and more so where he or she has a spouse and dependent family[1].

(iii) *'Once ordered, the amount cannot be varied to meet future developments'* – true only in part, but no less so than a lump sum award, unless it is one of those comparatively rare awards which are of provisional damages. Any development which is anticipated at the date of trial/assessment of damages can be catered for within the PPO. For instance, payments in respect of loss of earnings can be ordered to cease being payable at the intended retirement age; additional payments for education, care or in the event of deterioration can be built in to the payment structure at the outset. Note that the ability to tailor an award to meet anticipated developments at or about the time that they are anticipated is to be distinguished from the making of a variable order, for which see below. An order which provides at the outset for increases of specified amounts on certain dates (and arguably contingent on certain future events) is not a 'variable order', but rather one which is anticipated.

(iv) *'A minimum sum is needed before PPs are appropriate'* – not so. There is no minimum limit in the legislation, and responses to the consultation paper which gave birth to the legislation showed that the majority of consultees rejected the idea that there should be. Everything will depend upon the circumstances. For instance, PPs may be more important to meet the needs of a person injured at the age of 90, where even a slight variation in life expectancy could affect the entire award, than they would be for a lifetime award for an injured victim aged 16, yet the total amount of future loss, if calculated conventionally, would be small.

(v) *'PPs are bad value because they are not linked to an appropriate index'* – true only in part. A lump sum is currently calculated upon assumptions as to the real return on investments (the Lord Chancellor's 'discount rate', reflected by the Ogden Tables, at 2.5%). The Lord Chancellor's discount rate assumes a real rate of return over and above inflation, as judged by the RPI. Lump sums are calculated on this basis. Thus, an RPI index-linked periodical payment should achieve at least the same overall financial result as that which is assumed for a lump sum award (there is no need to allow for the 'real' return, since this is used only to annuitise a lump sum, reducing the number of 'years' of payment because of the accelerated receipt of one large sum which may be invested. PPs may be paid for as long as the claimant lives, per year, without the claimant having to worry what lump sum is necessary at what investment rate). Current economic thinking is that the discount rate is too high[2], and thus the chance of a lump sum award meeting future expenses is poor, and hence even an RPI-indexed PP is likely to be better value and certainly less risky. The reality is that, if the RPI is an inappropriate index, both patterns of award (periodic or lump sum) suffer from the defect, and formal indexation is no reason for choosing one over the other. However, it is possible to seek an order from the court that the damages or part of them should be indexed by reference to a different index (CPR, r 41.8(1)(d); s 2(9) of the Damages Act 1996 – the court has a power to order that there should be a different index). This offers the opportunity of making the practical provision for future inflation in costs to which the claimant's unsuccessful argument in *Cooke v United Bristol Healthcare Trust*[3] was directed. The Court of Appeal in *Flora v Wakom (Heathrow) Limited*[4] established the principle that, if a PPO does not identify on its face the manner in which the amount of the payments is to vary in order to maintain their real value, the effect is that it is to be treated as providing for RPI indexation (Damages Act 1996, s 2(8)) unless the order identifies a more appropriate index (s 2(9)). It held that there was nothing in the language of those sub-sections to suggest that the power to make provision for some other index was only to be exercised in an exceptional case[5], as has been held in relation to attempts to depart from the discount rate for lump sums

(vi) '*An order for PPs won't pay for necessary accommodation*'. An order can only make provision for future pecuniary loss, unless the parties agree otherwise. It does not have to order that the entirety of future pecuniary loss be paid for periodically (thus, for example, the high cost of accommodation may be met by a capital payment, leaving a lower sum for the balance of future loss). There may, however, be problems with finding enough capital for housing in a case in which the overall damages are relatively low or the claimant's life expectancy is short[6].

(vii) '*A lump sum award offers a possibility of meeting expenses which a PPO cannot*' – possibly, but this is often said by reference to an award which is reduced to allow for contributory fault – then the one thing which is certain is that, if a claimant's needs are assessed at £x per year, the PPO will allow only for payment of the agreed percentage of £x, and no more. However, it is worth noting that this at least is certain and will (usually) continue for life. What is speculative is that a lump sum award will in fact produce enough income to meet the needs as and when they arise. There are three reasons at least to be sceptical of this, before considering any financial advice upon which ultimately a decision may depend. The first is that PPOs are liable to be calculated on a basis more favourable than a lump sum, since the former may adopt an index which more accurately maps the rise in the costs of care and earnings. There is, thus, ground to be made up by the holder of a lump sum award right from the start. Secondly, the lump sum is calculated using an assumed discount rate of 2.5%, ie a net return of 2.5% above inflation, which may be very difficult to achieve, particularly in the current investment climate. Thirdly, if and to the extent that a lump sum award does not produce enough income in any year to meet expenses, the only way to meet those expenses is to eat into the lump sum itself. Yet that is the income-producing asset, which will (by this manoeuvre) be reduced, thus inevitably becoming less able even to produce that amount of income. This process, if repeated, is termed capital attrition, and is a real risk if the claimant's returns on investments or the prevailing interest rates drop below those anticipated. It is worth noting that, in *Sarwar v Ali & the MIB*[7], Lloyd-Jones J held PPs to be appropriate, notwithstanding a 25% contributory negligence deduction.

1   See also Chapter M.
2   See eg Rowland Hogg in [2004] JPIL, Issue 3/04.
3   [2003] EWCA Civ 1370.
4   [2006] EWCA Civ 1103.
5   At para [10].
6   There are those who argue that PPs for the accommodation claim may be a realistic alternative; see Robert Weir 'Accommodating periodical payments orders into housing claims' [2008] JPIL, Vol 2, 146–153.
7   [2007] EWHC 1255 (Admin).

6   How Does the Court Decide Whether to Make an Award?

[O24]   A court is under a statutory obligation to consider whether or not to make an award in the form of PPs[1].

1   Damages Act 1996, s 2(1)(b).

[O25]   CPR, r 41.7 provides that the court, in considering whether to make such an order, 'shall have regard to all the circumstances of the case and in particular the form of award which best meets the claimant's needs, having regard to the factors set out in the Practice Direction'.

[O26]   The factors set out in paragraph 1 of Practice Direction PD41B 'include' (note this word: this is not a comprehensive list – the primary criterion is what best meets the claimant's[1] needs):

(1)   the scale of the annual payments, taking into account any deduction for contributory negligence;
(2)   the form of award preferred by the claimant, including (a) the reason for the claimant's preference, and (b) the nature of any financial advice received by the claimant when considering the form of award; and
(3)   the form of award preferred by the defendant, including the reasons for the defendant's preference.

1   Not the defendant's needs: the legislation here clearly prioritises the claimant.

[O27]   There is no provision that the claimant's preference is conclusive. Indeed, although this is important, the court will order PPs against the wishes of a competent adult claimant if it considers that PPs are more appropriate to meet future needs[1]. It is, therefore, all the more the case that the court will decline approval of a settlement for a child claimant, or a claimant who is a protected party, where it takes the view that the claimant's needs would be better served by such an order. It is his or her needs which the court must consider. 'Needs' is a phrase which has to be considered in a wide and general sense[2]. All future payments may be made subject to a PPO: but it is open to a judge to decide that only some of such payments will be paid periodically, and the rest paid by lump sum. This solution was, for instance, preferred by Flaux J in *Burton v Kingsbury*[3], where he drew a distinction based on the claimant's needs between payments for the future costs of care and case management (PPs) and other future costs (lump sum).

[1]   *Godbold v Mahmood* [2005] EWHC 1002 (QB), Mitting J; *Sarwar v (1) Ali and (2) MIB* [2007] EWHC 1255 (Admin), Lloyd-Jones J.

[2]   As the Court of Appeal held in *Tameside & Glossop NHA Trust* v *Thompstone* [2008] EWCA Civ 5 at para 107: '.. the claimant's needs are not limited to the provision of those things which are foreseeable necessities but must be considered in a wider and more general sense. The decision as to what form the order should take will be a balancing exercise of the various factors likely to affect the claimant's future life'.

[3]   [2007] EWHC 2091 (QB). See also a decision to similar effect by Ramsay J in *Taylor v Chesworth* [2007] EWHC 1053 (QB), where certain parts of a claim for care and case management costs were awarded as PPs, and part as a lump sum payment.

[O28]   There is a broad hint in the Practice Direction that, where there is a substantial deduction by reason of contributory negligence, an award of PPs may not be appropriate. This would be because the amount would never, in any year, match the need. 'Fifty per cent of a claimant's care needs', for example, will not come close to satisfying his or her requirements. The effect of a periodical payment in such an amount is to require him or her to subsidise current payments, under a PPO, from other resources (which he or she may not have). It is here that the flexibility provided by a lump sum may outweigh the benefits of the periodical payment arrangements set out above[1]. However, conversely, if contributory negligence is high (say, 80%), there may still be good reason for awarding a 20% periodical annual payment. Such sums may be regarded by the claimant as 'top-up' provision, in a world in which his or her basic care and accommodation needs are met, for instance, by the local authority. In such a case, the fact that PPs are tax-free, and do not affect entitlement to receive free provision from state or local authority sources, may tip the balance.

[1]   It was because the award was affected by a discount for contributory fault, coupled with the express wish of the claimant and the absence of any suggestion by financial advisers to the contrary, that Edwards-Stuart J declined to make a PPO in *Sklair v Haycock* [2009] EWHC 3328 (QB).

[O29]   In *A v B NHS Trust*[1], Lloyd-Jones J rejected a PPO in favour of a lump sum award, because he took the view that indexation by reference to RPI would not meet the costs of care, and the shortfall would be very substantial, whereas a lump sum would provide flexibility: but this should be viewed as an early decision, which may not fully have appreciated that, even when indexed against RPI, periodical payment awards are inherently likely to produce better financial returns over time than a lump sum (unless one assumes that the discount rate adopted by the Lord Chancellor is an accurate reflection of real investment returns available at low risk, after taking into account inflation and the deduction of tax from investment income), and in any event its reasoning can no longer stand since the acceptance by the Court of Appeal in *Thompstone*[2] that future care costs may be indexed by reference to ASHE 6115 (see below). In *Sarwar v Ali*[3], in the context of a 25% deduction, the same judge came to a conclusion in favour of PPs, having concluded that it was open to the court to index an award in this way. The award of an earnings PP in *Sarwar* was seen as a way of filling the contributory negligence shortfall in the care PP.

¹   [2006] EWHC 2833 (Admin)
²   [2008] 1 WLR 2207, [2008] EWCA Civ 5.
³   [2007] EWHC 1255 (Admin).

[O30]   In *Rowe v Dolman*[1], the Court of Appeal considered an appeal against a decision that there should be a lump sum award in a case in which a deduction of 20% from full damages had been agreed and approved (the claimant being a patient). The main reason for the claimant preferring a lump sum was that an 80% order would not fully cover the annual cost of continuing care and other needs; for the defendant, the main reason for preferring the opposite was uncertainty as to the claimant's life expectancy. The judge preferred the former view because, under an order for PPs, the claimant would never be able to live his life as he would wish to, with significant improvements mentioned by expert advisers, whereas with a lump sum he would be able to do so for at least a while. The court (May LJ, with Phillips LCJ and Hallett LJ agreeing) thought this a solid reason, and rejected a contention that it ignored evidence as to the ready availability of an equity release scheme, which could only fund the shortfall in damages for about three years.

¹   [2008] EWCA Civ 1040.

[O31]   In determining the scale of PPs under PD41B, the courts may also weigh up the amount of the annual payments and the period over which they are likely to be needed.

[O32]   Under paragraph 1(2)(b) of the PD, the description 'the nature of any financial advice' received by the claimant differs from an earlier version of the draft Practice Direction. The earlier version would have required the court to see the financial advice received by a claimant. The current form does not necessarily require this. Financial advice is likely to be privileged. In the regime which pre-dated the power to order periodical payments, the advice of a financial adviser in relation to a proposed infant settlement, for instance, was seen by the court but not by the defendant. In a 'lump sum' case, it still is. If, however, financial advice is to be relied upon by a claimant, in seeking to make an order which is resisted by a defendant, there seems to be no good reason why in principle the advice should not be treated like any other expert advice, and disclosed for the purpose of determining the method by which the payment is to be made. This leaves it open to a defendant to seek to put in contrary advice, particularly if the measure of indexation is contentious.

[O33]   Despite the suspicion that advice and counter-advice might lead to argument, appeals and thence to satellite litigation (just as costs regimes have done), there may be something to be welcomed in the provision of advice by or on behalf of a defendant, in that a claimant will have the benefit of advice which is honed in the knowledge that it may be contested, and will have the benefit of differing views as to how his or her future needs may best be accommodated. Once again, the emphasis in the rules that it is the needs of the claimant which are predominant may be of central importance: it is his or her needs, and how best to satisfy them, to which the advice of any financial adviser must be directed, whether instructed by the claimant or by the defendant.

7 Inter-relationship with Interim Payments

[O34] The award of an interim payment may affect the decision to make a PPO. It may mean that there is insufficient a lump sum left to be awarded as a means of meeting contingencies as and when they might arise, and thus render a PPO dangerously inflexible. Worse still, it may be at such a level that it 'eats into' the amount of the annual payments, thus ensuring that, although the claimant may need £x, he will receive less, since (in effect) the amount which would otherwise have provided for some PPs will have to be capitalised to meet the shortfall.

[O35] Whereas interim payments may themselves be made on a periodical basis – a very useful power, which is little used and may not be widely appreciated – such that care costs, loss of income and the like may be compensated pending trial as and when they arise, this does not of itself resolve the potential difficulties. First, if there is a live issue as to liability or contributory fault, the claimant is taking a risk that he does not enter into a settlement, or face a judgment, for less than 100% of the theoretical full value of his claim. If he receives 'too much' by way of periodical interims, the position is no different than if he had received a lump sum which ate significantly into his damages award. Second, one of the most common reasons for seeking an interim payment in a catastrophic injury claim is to fund the cost of accommodation. Whereas this can be achieved in part by mortgage, it is almost always likely to be more economically funded by a lump sum purchase. Depending on the proportions which the cost of the accommodation bears to the rest of the claim, the problem identified in the preceding paragraph may emerge.

[O36] Two particular issues arise: first, whether the court making an interim payment should have express regard to whether its award might fetter the freedom of the trial judge to award PPs; and, secondly, how the provision that any interim award must not exceed a reasonable proportion of the likely damages should be applied.

[O37] An early attempt to grapple with the first problem was made by HHJ MacDuff (as he then was) in *Dallow v Shrewsbury and Telford NHS Trust*[1] but, having suggested various relevant considerations (the likely size of the future award, the expressed intentions of the parties as to whether they would be seeking PPs, the likely heads of damages and the consequent availability of a PPs award, and evidence as to life expectancy), he concluded that all depended on the particular circumstances of the individual case, and that in *Dallow* itself there was no likelihood that the size of the interim payment requested would in any way fetter the discretion of the ultimate trial judge.

[1] High Court, Birmingham, 31 October 2005.

[O38] In *Mealing v Chelsea and Westminster NHS Trust*[1], Swift J also mentioned that there may be a need to take care not unduly to fetter a trial judge's freedom to allocate as large a proportion of an award to PPs as that judge considered appropriate. This was referred to in *Pitcher v Headstart Nursery Ltd & Ors*[2], where the court was faced with an application for a second interim payment, in the sum of £950,000. The case was one of catastrophic brain damage to a young child. The court took the view that, at trial, a judge was very likely to consider that some of the future losses, especially those of care and case management, should be paid by way of periodical payment, and in that light was asked to consider a defendant's submission (echoing *Mealing*) that the award of capital interim payment should not be so great a sum as would fetter the jurisdiction of the court when it came to consider whether to make such an order. Although the judge did not expressly found his decision – that the interim payment should be £320,000 – on this argument, but rather upon a consideration of the amounts of future awards likely to be capitalised (in that case, for accommodation, assistive technologies, therapies and equipment), he left unsaid whether he accepted it or not. In *Osunde v Guys and St. Thomas Hospital*[3] (a case not referred to in *Pitcher*), Calvert-Smith J observed that, if the sum applied for was well within the amount likely to be awarded, it would normally be awarded, unless perhaps it would make it impossible or extremely difficult for the trial judge to make a PPO, since there would not be sufficient left in the damages award to permit it[4]; but he too did not express a definitive view as to the significance of this question.

[1]   [2007] EWHC 3254 (QB).
[2]   [2008] EWHC 2681 (QB).
[3]   [2007] EWHC 2275 (QB).
[4]   Or it risked pre-judging issues which had to be left to trial.

[O39]   As to the second question referred to in para **[O36]** above, it is settled principle that an interim payment must not exceed a reasonable proportion of the likely final judgment. In *Braithwaite v Homerton University Hospitals NHS Foundation Trust*[1], Stanley Burnton J found it difficult to construe this expression as including the amount awarded by way of PPs, and considered whether to exercise his powers to award an interim payment of capital by reference to the capital lump sum which a court was likely to award as part of a larger award which also included sums paid periodically. Taking a different view, in *Brewis v Heatherwood and Wrexham Park Hospitals NHS Trust*[2], Coulson J thought that, when considering the proportionality of a proposed interim award to the amount of final damages, a court should identify the amounts likely to be awarded by way of capital lump sum, and should then predict the likely capitalisation of the future claims which might well be paid periodically. Thus, one judge would compare the proposed interim payment against only the capital element of any future award, ignoring the value of PPs; the other would include a notional capital value for the latter, even though they were extremely likely to be awarded.

[1]   [2008] EWHC 353 (QB).
[2]   [2008] EWHC 2526 (QB).

[O40]   A decision as to which was the correct approach to the making of an interim payment in a heavy personal injury claim, where the damages when finally assessed are likely to include one or more periodical payments orders, finally came before the Court of Appeal in *Eeles v Cobham Hire Services Ltd*[1]. An interim payment of £1.2 million was requested; likely damages were conservatively estimated by the first instance judge at £3.5 million. Notwithstanding his recognition that a trial judge might wish to make a PPO for some heads of damage, he made the order as requested. Both the questions raised in the cases mentioned above were answered by the Court of Appeal. On the second question, the court held that, in a case in which a PPO is made, the amount of the final judgment is the actual capital sum awarded. It does not include the notional capitalised value of the PPO, which sum is irrelevant for the purposes of determining an interim payment in a case of this kind. Thus, Stanley Burnton J's approach in *Braithwaite* was correct. In the days before PPOs, a judge would take the (conservatively estimated) full capital value of the claim as the basis for his consideration of an interim payment. In a case in which a lump sum award was to be made, that was the correct approach. However, in a case in which a PPO might be made, it was no longer correct. Further[2], Smith LJ emphasised that the judge should not normally begin to speculate about how the trial judge will allocate the damages. As a rule, he should stop at the figure which he is satisfied is likely to be awarded as a capital sum, in which he may reasonably include the likely award for general damages, past losses[3] and the capitalised value of future accommodation to be provided. He may award a reasonable proportion of that figure; indeed, it may be reasonable to award a high proportion of that figure, provided that the estimate has been a conservative one[4].

---

[1]   [2009] EWCA Civ 204.

[2]   At para [37].

[3]   Past losses are the losses incurred up to the date of trial, and therefore include anticipated losses between the date of the interim payment application and the date of trial: *Harris v Roy* LTL 8/3/2010.

[4]   However, see the qualification expressed at para 38: 'However there will be cases ... in which the judge at the interim payment stage will be able confidently to predict that the trial judge will capitalise additional elements of the future loss so as to produce a greater lump sum award. In such a case, a larger interim payment can be justified. Those will be cases in which the claimant can clearly demonstrate a need for an immediate capital sum, probably to fund the purchase of accommodation. In our view, before a judge at the interim payment stage encroaches on the trial judge's freedom to allocate, he should have a high degree of confidence that such a course is appropriate and that the trial judge will endorse the capitalisation undertaken'.

[O41]   As to the first question, it was important not to fetter the trial judge's freedom to allocate the heads of future loss. The fact that the capital sum ordered might be invested wisely and might be realised later missed the point about the importance of the trial judge's freedom to make an appropriate PPO. Smith LJ observed that[1]:

> 'A PPO has the potential to provide real security for a claimant for the whole of his life. Of course, there will be a tension between the claimant's need for an immediate capital sum and the desirability of the security of a substantial PPO. That tension cannot usually be properly resolved until the trial judge knows what sums are actually to be awarded under each head of damage and has financial advice available to him. At the interim payment stage, the judge does not have those materials. If the judge makes too large an interim payment, that sum is lost for all time for the purposes of founding a PPO. It cannot be put back into the pot from which the trial judge will allocate the damages.'

---

[1]   At para [32].

[O42]   For an example of the application of *Eeles*[1] in practice, see *Kirby v Ashford & St Peter's Hospital*[2], in which an interim payment was significantly reduced in amount by reference to the principles established in the Court of Appeal; although it should be noted that, in *FP v Taunton & Somerset NHS Trust*[3], Blair J, whilst applying the principles of *Eeles*, felt able to award an interim payment of £1.2 million, taking into account the claimant's pressing need for accommodation. It may be that a substantial interim payment is now only likely to be made if the claimant can demonstrate a 'real' or 'pressing need' for the interim payment requested, eg to fund the purchase of alternative accommodation[4]. An interesting question then arises as to whether or not the court may legitimately have a concern as to how money awarded by way of interim will be spent – if it does not, then there is a real risk that the power to award such a payment may indeed, in practical terms, fetter the choices available to the trial judge, yet the conventional position is that a claimant is free to spend his money as he likes[5], and this principle must normally include interim payments. In *FP v Taunton*, Blair J expressed concern about this problem, and the claimant's solicitor offered an undertaking to hold the interim payment in her firm's client account and to take reasonable steps before making payment out, to ensure that the payments were only made in respect of losses identified in the schedule of loss.

[1]   [2009] EWCA Civ 204.
[2]   [2008] EWHC 1320 (judgment 3 April 2009).
[3]   [2009] EWHC 1965 (QB).
[4]   Further, the claimant may struggle to obtain an interim payment in order to fund a private house purchase where there is likely to be a dispute regarding whether or not it is in the claimant's best interests to stay in publicly funded accommodation or move to adapted accommodation, and therefore whether private funded accommodation will be recoverable: see eg *Brown v Emery* [2010] EWHC 388 (QB).
[5]   *Lim Poh Choo v Camden and Islington Area Health Authority* [1980] AC 174, per Lord Scarman at 191; *Wells v Wells* [1999] 1 AC 345; *Heil v Rankin* [2001] QB 272. See also *Fitzgerald v Ford* [1996] PIQR Q72 at Q83, where the Court of Appeal refused an application from the defendant to see if the claimant, who had recovered damages on the basis of 75% liability, was spending damages in the way anticipated by the claimant's expert.

[O43]   Where there is substantial contributory fault, and the claimant has a clear preference for a lump sum award, a court may find that a PPO is unlikely in the final event, and thus calculate an interim award on the basis which was conventional prior to the possibility of PPOs: *Preston v City Electrical Factors Ltd*[1]. Likewise, the principles in *Eeles* will not apply where there is no scope for a PPO, because the defendant or his insurer is not secure, and/or in foreign cases where a lump sum is the only appropriate order because periodical payments are not recognised in the claimant's country of residence, are not exempt from tax, or there is no suitable index for the up-rating of future payments.

[1]   [2009] EWHC 2907 (QB).

8   Form of Order

[O44]   CPR, r 41.8(1) requires a court making an order for PPs to specify:

(a)   the annual amount awarded, how each payment is to be made during the year, and at what intervals;

(b)   the amount awarded for future:

   (i)   loss of earnings and other income; and

   (ii)   care and medical costs and other recurring or capital costs;

(c)   that the claimant's annual future pecuniary losses, as assessed by the court, are to be paid for the duration of the claimant's life, or such other period as the court orders; and

(d)   that the amount of the payments shall vary annually by reference to RPI, unless otherwise ordered.

[O45]   In addition:

(a)   where the court orders that any part of the award shall continue after the claimant's death, for the benefit of the claimant's dependants, the order must also specify the relevant amount and duration of the payments, and how each payment is to be made during the year and at what intervals (CPR, r 41.8(2));

(b)   where an amount in respect of future losses is to increase or decrease on a certain date, the order must also specify (i) the date on which the increase or decrease will take effect, and (ii) the amount of the increase or decrease at current value; and

(c)   where damages for substantial capital purchases are awarded under (b)(ii) above, the order must also specify (i) the amount of the payments at current value, (ii) when the payments are to be made, and (iii) that the amount of the payments shall be adjusted by reference to the RPI, unless otherwise ordered.

[O46]   The basic payment period is thus a year. It is a year by reference to which losses for the future are to be calculated. However, CPR, r 41.8(1)(a) permits an award, though expressed in terms of 'so much per year', actually to be paid at intervals of less than a year – eg half-yearly, quarterly, monthly or even weekly. The description as to 'how' a payment is to be made will presumably relate to whether by standing order, direct debit etc. There is no other specific guidance on the meaning of this[1].

---

[1]   It might mean the investment method chosen by the defendant: is it to be paid by the purchase of an annuity, out of free resources or reserves, or by some other satisfactory and secure arrangement?

[O47]   The distinction between future loss of earnings and other income, on the one hand, and care and medical and other costs, on the other, is important. First, it is likely that loss of earnings as such will be expressed to finish at notional retirement age. The authors suggest that the 'default' retirement age should nowadays be set at least at 68, though perhaps more likely 70, since the Government has indicated that: (a) there will be no distinction made between men and women as to normal retirement date; (b) the emphasis of anti-age discrimination is permitting people to continue to work despite their age; (c) increasing longevity has so attenuated pension provision as to make it necessary for workers to continue to work in order to enjoy a reasonable income in later life; (d) improvements in general health enable them physically to be able better to do so; and (e) the Pensions Act 2007 anticipates a steady increase in the youngest age at which state pension is to be payable to that of 68 years[1].

---

[1]   The Pensions Act 2007 gradually increases the state retirement age up to age 68 between 6 April 2024 and 5 April 2046. See further the comments of the Chairman of the Pensions Regulator, who believes people may have to work to age 70 (The Times, 8 August 2009).

[O48]   The courts will have to develop an approach to assessing annual loss of earnings which allows sufficiently for uncertainties. For instance, if the claimant had not been injured, would he or she have retired early? Or suffered an illness which resulted in time off work or loss of a job? Would the firm for which, or the market sector in which, the claimant worked have survived to his or her seventieth birthday? Would the claimant have slowed down at work, and done less overtime in later years? These factors can be 'broad brushed' into a generalised discount for employment risks, based on the suggested discount figures produced in the Ogden Tables[1]. They may be more scientifically, but possibly no less accurately, reflected by producing a template of employed earnings, which accommodates the different risks by attributing different salary levels for different years. The authors suspect that one advantage of the periodical payment regime may ultimately be future earnings claims designed to reflect an increase in annual earnings, as would have been expected with increasing seniority and possible promotion in post. The more care that is taken at the outset to reflect future losses, the better[2].

[1]   Although those figures were expressly calculated for application to lump sums and, as yet, there are no suggested discount factors for PPs.
[2]   See *Sarwar v (1) Ali and (2) MIB* [2007] EWHC 1255 (Admin).

[O49]   Although 'other recurring or capital costs' covers accommodation, damages for accommodation give rise to their own problems. Capital outlay is required to purchase a property. In the conventional lump sum order, the capital outlay is in part financed by a capitalisation of the annual payments made under the principle in *Roberts v Johnstone*[1]. This will no longer be possible if a PPO is made for the entirety of future loss. If, however, a court is to be invited to award damages in respect of loss of earnings, care and medical costs and other costs *apart from* accommodation, the value of accommodation over a lifetime must be capitalised in some form. This may require identification of whether evidence as to life expectancy is to be considered, thereby defeating one of the advantages of the periodical payment approach, which is that it operates 'bottom up' rather than 'top down' (see at paras **[O53]–[O58]**).

[1]   [1989] QB 878.

[O50]   In any case in which the amount of the lump sum and compensation for past earnings permits it (thus in large awards, such as in many cases of catastrophic injury), there will be the problem which, though still real, will be easier to accommodate, since a house may be purchased utilising the capital in respect of those past losses, and payment for the loss of use of the capital (which is the purpose of payments under *Roberts v Johnstone*) can then made in the usual way; however, this rarely amounts to the full capital cost, and the general damages and loss of earnings awards usually need to be drawn upon to make up the deficit.

[O51]   For example, if a case comes to trial six years after an accident, in respect of a claimant earning £40,000 per annum who has suffered catastrophic injuries, the value of past gratuitous care being, say, £50,000, it is not difficult for him to purchase a larger property (at, say, an additional cost of £200,000 over and above his present property). The alteration charges, moving expenses and the solicitors' and estate agents' costs of purchase and sale of the new and old properties are all one-off expenses in respect of which there will be a claim, which will not be periodicised. In such a case, the £200,000 additional cost will produce £5,000 per annum (at the conventional rate of 2.5%). (The claimant will possibly be better off making such an arrangement, because the amount of the payment for loss of use of his £200,000 capital will be index-linked, unless the defendant persuades the court otherwise: whereas, otherwise, it will be treated as a flat annual payment, by analogy with a mortgage payment.) One alternative, however, might be to consider whether a house might be held in trust for the claimant for life, with a reversionary interest to the paying party (or his or her insurer), on terms that provided for a periodical payment equivalent to a flat rate mortgage: such schemes have been proposed in the past, but thought unattractive, not least because of the administrative burden they impose on a defendant, and the difficulty such a defendant may have in ensuring vacant possession of a home which, when the claimant dies, may still be occupied by his or her partner or family. It still may be unattractive for such reasons under the new regime, but it seems open to the parties to take advantage of the fact that PPs may be payable for a lifetime at a pre-specified rate if they wish to do so[1].

[1]   See further Robert Weir 'Accommodating periodical payments orders into housing claims' [2008] JPIL, Vol 2, 146–153.

[O52]   The provision that the future pecuniary losses are to be paid for the duration of the claimant's life 'or such other period as the court orders' does not require one single period of time to be specified for all payments. Thus, future educational expenses may be ordered to be payable until the claimant reaches the age of 18 or 19 (or as may be); payment of salary until retirement age (see above); and accommodation costs until a hypothetical future date upon which, or by when, it is anticipated that the claimant will be in a residential home and will no longer need his or her own personal accommodation etc. Note that, under CPR, r 41.8(1), the period for which the losses are to be paid provides an end stop for any particular category of payment. Provision for the increase or decrease of a payment at different times within that period is provided for by CPR, r 41.8(3).

[O53]   The provision in CPR, r 41.8(3) for increasing or decreasing the amount of a payment operates by reference to date, and not to event. The authors' view in the previous edition, that 'certain date' means a calendar date, and not a date which can be made certain because it is expressed by reference to the happening of a particular event which, if and when it happens, will occur on a specific day, is borne out by *Burton v Kingsbury*[1]. Flaux J attempted to get round the problem which can be caused where it is possible that a local authority may make direct payments towards care or accommodation. His suggested solution was to make an order whereby the annual PP was reduced by the amount received from the local authority – however, this decision is questionable, since it was tantamount to a variable PPO, which can only be ordered if particular health-related conditions are met.

[1]   [2007] EWHC 2091 (QB).

[O54]   CPR, r 41.8(3)(a) and (b), providing for increase or decrease on a certain date in the future, is nonetheless of the greatest importance. It provides for a change in the amount to be paid under what we term a non-variable order. A variable order provides for variation upon the happening of a certain, limited class of future health-related events, and is distinct from a non-variable order, which in our definition is one in respect of which the future pattern of payment is fixed at the outset, at the date of the original order for PPs. More than one increase or decrease can be specified where a non-variable order is concerned. The design of a PPO is thus important. It should be tailor-made to fit as closely as possible to the needs of the claimant. As noted above, these needs include the need to be provided with the salary he or she would probably have enjoyed, and this can be stepped upwards or downwards to take account of anticipated changes in income, such as promotion (in early career) and consultancy etc (in later life).

[O55] Paragraph 2.2 of the Practice Direction (PD41B) gives examples of circumstances which might lead the court to order an increase or decrease on a future certain date. The list gives examples, and is not exclusive. It provides for the increase or decrease to take into account:

(i)   a change in the claimant's condition, leading to an increase or reduction in his or her need to incur care, medical or other recurring or capital costs (there may be different dates for different particular costs, eg the date of anticipated change from a manually operated to an electronically driven wheelchair);

(ii)   when gratuitous carers will no longer continue to provide care (note that this envisages an estimate being made of a future date on which parents or relatives will be unable to provide such care. It may also be possible, and occasionally preferable, to provide for this by insuring, say, the life of a principal gratuitous carer, or taking out critical illness cover, although the availability of this depends on market conditions);

(iii) when the claimant's educational circumstances will change;

(iv)   when the claimant would have received a promotional increase in pay (in some jobs, there may also be a decrease, as where the anticipated career plan would have provided for the claimant taking a consultancy, being less able to earn performance bonuses from hard physical work etc);

(v)   when the claimant will cease earning (this will normally lead to a reduction where the job is pensionable, to the anticipated level of pension);

(vi)   the need to add pension payments onto carers' wages from 2012, in accordance with the Pensions Act 2008[1].

---

[1]   See *XXX v A Strategic Health Authority* [2008] EWHC 2727 (QB).

[O56] Where a settlement is made, or order agreed between the parties, one provision of which is that the defendant is to be entitled to require the claimant to produce evidence in a form reasonably satisfactory to it that the claimant remains alive, as a precondition for making the next year's payments, it has been held that it should not include a paragraph which provides that the defendant shall reimburse the claimant for the reasonable costs of providing documentation[1]. It is, therefore, important to include any claim for providing such confirmation (eg by way of doctor's letter), and any financial expenses likely to be incurred checking the up-rating of annual periodical payment, as heads of damage in the schedule of loss if they are to be claimed. It is, however, arguable that they may be analogous to litigation costs, and thus need not be provided for – the time for awarding them being if and when an award is not properly up-rated, rather in anticipation that one party will not fulfil its legal responsibilities under the order. Any order contains an implied liberty to apply, unless excluded, and thus it is open to the claimant to return to court under this provision if he reasonably thinks he has been short-changed.

---

[1]   *Long v Norwich Union Insurance Ltd* [2009] EWHC 715 (QB), Mackay J.

9 Need to Consider Life Expectancy

[O57] The intention of the Government in introducing the power to order PPs was to lead to a culture change in the way in which payments were calculated, from a 'top down' approach to a 'bottom up' approach.

[O58] A top down approach is one in which a capital sum is calculated, out of which an annuity is purchased: the level of annual payment thus depends upon the size of the initial capital sum. Calculating that is as for a lump sum award: it requires a prediction to be made about the future life expectancy of the claimant. Using this method, the various heads of damages (earnings, care etc) are used to produce an annual multiplicand, which is then multiplied by a multiplier which is intended to accommodate both inflation, on the one hand, and real investment return, on the other, the exact numerical value of which is selected by reference to the estimated life expectancy of the claimant. Most structured settlements have in the past been worked out by converting a lump sum produced by such a method into an annuity. The annuity is purchased using the lump sum as a premium. The resulting payments are unlikely to match the original assessment of annual needs.

[O59] Such a system requires an agreement, or a finding of the court, as to the probable life expectancy of the claimant. One of the principal criticisms of the lump sum approach is that whatever figure is derived is unlikely to be right: it may, even, be wildly under- or over-stated.

[O60] By contrast, a bottom up approach requires no estimate of life expectancy, because it does not depend upon the calculation of an overall award. Instead, it is based upon the actual costs in each year as and when they arise. The various heads of damages produce an annual figure, as before. The order for PPs simply provides for the claimant to be paid that amount on an annual basis for the duration of the specific need to which the payment relates (usually life, though it may be less in respect of future earnings),m escalating in line with the RPI or an alternative index as specified by the court. (See at paras **[O78]–[O88]**, where the appropriate index is discussed.)

[O61] A further advantage of PPs over structured settlements for the defendant is that such payments may be funded in any way in which the defendant chooses, provided it meets the requirement of reasonable security as defined by the Courts Act 2003 (see at para **[O63]–[O74]**): a structured settlement requires the purchase of an annuity from a life office providing such a product.

[O62] However, it will only be if all the relevant future loss is made subject to a PPO[1] that life expectancy will cease to be of material importance in a quantum case. If part is calculated on a 'lump sum' basis, this will need life expectancy to be considered. It may, therefore, be particularly relevant if a house is paid for by lump sum award rather than by mortgage instalments provided for out of periodical income (a market which has yet to develop) – and thus payment by lump sum award will be a common case where the claimant is catastrophically injured. Also, save in rare cases, claimants will often be advised that it is sensible to have a 'contingency fund' made up of lump sum damages, in order to pay for unforeseen expenses as and when they occur. In practice, since the claimant's award for general damages will often be largely or wholly extinguished by the *Roberts v Johnstone* shortfall, this contingency award can only be realised by capitalising some heads of future loss, thus resulting in a continuing need in the majority of cases to obtain life expectancy evidence.

1   There have been no such cases yet reported in which PPs have extended beyond future care and earnings, although the authors know of a confidential settled case that also included PPs for medical treatment and therapies.

10   Security of Payments

[O63]   A court cannot order PPs unless it is satisfied that payment is reasonably secure (Damages Act 1996, s 2(3)). If the court is not satisfied of the security of the payments, it may either order a lump sum or require the party making the payment to use a method which is automatically considered to be reasonably secure by the terms of s 2(4) of the 1996 Act.

[O64]   Continuity of payment is automatically considered to be reasonably secure in three circumstances: (1) ministerial guarantee; (2) protection under the Financial Services Compensation Scheme (FSCS); and (3) where the source of the payment is a 'Government or health service body'[1]. We shall deal with each of these in turn. First, it is reasonably secure where it is protected by a **ministerial guarantee** under s 6 of the 1996 Act (no such guarantees have yet been given, but it is possible for this to be done on a case-by-case basis). This covers 'self-funded' payments made from public sector bodies – but note that Government or health service bodies named in the Damages (Government and Health Service Bodies) Order 2005[2] do not require to be specifically guaranteed under s 6.

1   Damages Act 1996, s 2(4).
2   SI 2005/474.

[O65]   *Protection under the Financial Services Compensation Scheme*   Secondly, by Damages Act 1996, s 2(4)(b), payment is automatically considered reasonably secure if it is protected by a scheme under s 213 of the Financial Services and Markets Act 2000 (ie which attracts statutory protection under the FSCS). This will apply to payments made by authorised insurers, whether they are self-funded, made directly by a liability insurer to the claimant or payments made by a life insurer under an annuity contract. It should be noted, however, that a defendant liability insurer providing aircraft or shipping insurance is not covered by the FSCS, and direct funding by such an insurer does not qualify as reasonably secure. Nor does the FSCS cover Lloyd's of London policies issued prior to 1 January 2004.

[O66]   The FSCS provides compensation to policyholders if they are insured by authorised insurance firms under contracts of insurance issued in the UK, or in some cases (but not all – please note) in the EEA, Channel Islands or Isle of Man. If an insurer is not issuing a policy in the UK, watch out[1]! The scheme covers compulsory, general and life insurance, and is triggered if an insurance firm goes out of business or into liquidation: continuity of PPs is protected to 100% under the scheme, although for the 'ordinary' uninjured insured policyholder the usual figure is 90%, except where insurance is compulsory, as in the case of employer's liability or motor insurance.

However, there may still be scope for some arrangement by which the FSCS is joined into the case, as happened in the case of Gibraltarian insurers in *Gleeson v Court* [2007] EWHC 2397 (QB); see para **[O75]** below.

[O67]   The FSCS protection stems not from the identity of the insurer handling the case but from the contract of insurance under which the insurer is indemnifying the defendant. The FSCS is governed by a set of rules in the COMP sourcebook, which in turn forms part of the FSA handbook.

To receive compensation through the FSCS, the following criteria must be satisfied (COMP 1.3.3G):

1.   the applicant must be an *eligible claimant* (COMP 4.2);
2.   the applicant must have a *protected claim* (COMP 5.2);
3.   the applicant must be claiming against a *relevant person* (COMP 6.2.1R); and
4.   that person must be *in default* (COMP 6.3).

Claimants in personal injury cases will be able to satisfy the first criterion. Clients will be able to satisfy the fourth criterion, essentially, if the relevant person is an insurer who goes bust. Potentially more difficult are the second and third criteria: where there are 'protected claims' made against a 'relevant person'. A claim under a protected contract of insurance will be a protected claim. A contract of insurance which it is compulsory by law to effect (eg motor insurance or employers' liability insurance) is a *protected contract of insurance*, subject to certain criteria being met¹. The vast majority of personal injury claims (other than those in respect of clinical negligence) involve such a type of insurance. This is likely, therefore, to be satisfied (but check the criteria in COMP, rather than simply assuming it).

A *relevant person* (as defined by COMP 6.2.1R) is (essentially²) a person who was, *at the time the act or omission giving rise to the claim against it took place*, a firm authorised by the FSA.

¹   COMP 5 sets out the scope of protected claims which are pegged to five different sub-schemes. According to COMP 5.4.2R, a protected contract is insurance is defined as being:
  'A contract of insurance issued after commencement (1 December 2001) which:
  1.   related to a protected risk or commitment;
  2.   is issued by the relevant person through an establishment in;
    a.   the United Kingdom; or ...
  3.   is a long-term contract of insurance or a relevant general insurance contract;
  4.   is not a reinsurance contract; and
  5.   if it is a contract of insurance entered into by a member (ie a Member of Lloyd's), was entered into on or after 1 January 2004.'
²   COMP 6.2.1R provides that a relevant person is 'a person who was, at the time the act or omission giving rise to the claim against it took place:
  1.   a participant firm; or
  2.   an appointed representative of a participant firm.'

[O68]   So, in short, a policy will have the backing of the FSCS providing:

1.   the contract was issued after 1 December 2001;
2.   the contract was issued by a firm which was authorised by the FSA or was a member of Lloyd's at the time of the accident/negligence relied on; and

3.   if it was issued by a member of Lloyd's, was a contract of insurance entered into after 1 January 2004.

[O69]   An unsubstantiated statement that the defendant is a secure funder should be treated with caution and, instead, the defendant should be asked, as early as possible, to answer a Part 18 request, which should include questions as to:

1.   the type of insurance;
2.   if a motor policy, confirmation of the country in which the vehicle was first registered as covered;
3.   the identity of the insurer that issued the policy;
4.   the date the policy was issued;
5.   if the insurer was a member of Lloyd's, the date on which the contract of insurance was entered into;
6.   whether or not the insurer was authorised by the FSA at the time the policy was issued;
7.   whether or not the insurer was authorised by the FSA at the time of the accident; and
8.   whether the policy of insurance has been assigned or novated and, if so, to provide full details of all insurers in the chain.

This issue of security of funding is one of the rare scenarios in which a court may force disclosure of the insurance policy[1].

[1]   *Harcourt v FEF Griffin & Others* [2007] EWHC 1500 (QB).

[O70]   A general insurer may prefer to fund payments directly from its own resources rather than purchase an annuity, or may wish to purchase an annuity in its own name and then contract to pass the PPs to the claimant. Defendants may find this latter possibility attractive if the payments stand to be varied downward at some later date, or if there is a chance of the reduction of the payments on appeal. Section 4 of the Damages Act 1996 provides for the extension of protection ordinarily afforded to uninjured policyholders to the recipients of PPs, even where the policyholder is, eg, the insurer, to 100%, and should be consulted if there is any doubt about security of payment.

[O71]   What is *not* specifically covered by s 2(4) of the Damages Act 1996, and therefore not reasonably secure under s 2(4)(b), are payments which are self-funded by Lloyd's insurers on policies issued prior to 1 January 2004, by the MIB, by the MDU, MPS, or other medical defence organisations, or by private defendants. Such payments do not obviously attract statutory protection. Another method of security must be used if such a defendant is to be ordered to provide PPs. However, in *Thacker v Steeples & MIB*[1], Cox J held that payments made by the MIB could be treated as secure. Foundation Trusts are also covered under the form of model order provided for in clinical negligence cases: see the appendix at para **[O139]**.

[1]   EWHC, 16 May 2005.

[O72]   *A Government or health service body*   Thirdly, under s 2(4)(c) of the Damages Act 1996, where the source of the payments is a Government or health service body named in the Damages (Government and Health Service Bodies) Order 2005[1], payment is automatically assumed to be reasonably secure. The Government bodies listed, as the list was amended with effect from 13 November 2009, are:

- Ministry of Justice
- Department for Culture, Media and Sport
- Ministry of Defence
- Office of the Deputy Prime Minister
- Department for Children, Schools and Families
- Department for Environment, Food and Rural Affairs
- Department of Health
- Home Office
- Foreign and Commonwealth Office
- Commissioners of Inland Revenue and Commissioners of Customs and Excise
- Department for International Development
- Northern Ireland Office
- Department for Business, Innovation and Skills
- Department for Transport
- HM Treasury
- Wales Office
- Department for Work and Pensions
- National Assembly for Wales
- Department of Health, Social Services and Public Safety (Northern Ireland).
- Department of Energy and Climate Change

The health services bodies listed in the 2005 Order are:

(i) National Health Service Litigation Authority
(ii) In Wales, NHS Trusts
(iii) In Wales, Local Health Boards
(iv) In Northern Ireland, Health and Social Services Boards
(v) In Northern Ireland, Health and Social Services Trusts
(vi) In Northern Ireland, Health and Personal Social Services Agencies and Special Agencies.

Note: health authorities and healthcare trusts in England are *not* designated bodies, so any PPO must be met by the NHSLA if it is to be reasonably secure: but the model directions in clinical negligence cases provide for the position of foundation trusts. Arrangements have been made and implemented between such bodies, the NHSLA and the Secretary of State which overcome any difficulty as to security of payments, by ensuring that the NHSLA is the effective source of the PPs to be made and that, therefore, the orders could be enforced against the NHSLA. This was recognised in *YM (a child) v Gloucestershire Hospitals NHS Foundation Trust & Anor*[2], which has as an appendix to the judgment a model form of order which ensures security in other similar cases, in accordance with the judgment – see particularly paragraphs 26–28 of the judgment: reference should be made to it before concluding such a case.

---

[1]   SI 2005/474.
[2]   [2006] EWHC 820 (QB).

[O73]   The list in s 2(4) of the Damages Act 1996 does not exclude consideration of other methods of funding. However, these must be scrutinised by a court, and a court must specify the alternative method of funding in its order. The criteria are set out in the Practice Direction (PD41B), but the court must be satisfied overall that the continuity of payment under the order is 'reasonably secure'. The criteria are:

(1)   that a method of funding provided for under s 2(4) of the 1996 Act is not possible or there are good reasons to justify an alternative method of funding;
(2)   the proposed method of funding can be maintained for the duration of the award or for the proposed duration of the method of funding; and
(3)   the proposed method of funding will meet the level of payment ordered by the court.

[O74]   What amounts to being 'reasonably secure' is not otherwise defined. However, it is likely in our view that the courts will take a restrictive view. This is because any appreciation of 'reasonableness' must take into account the view of Parliament that it is reasonable for a PPO to have the backing of the FSCS, not just to the extent of a 90% guarantee, as in the case of an ordinary insured policyholder, but as to 100%, and its decision that the bodies specified under the 2005 Order are departments of state, and no other public body is specified. Local authorities, which might constitute public bodies for the purposes of European law, are not themselves listed. This suggests that such bodies are not automatically to be regarded as reasonably secure. If so, the standard set is a high one.

[O75]   In *Gleeson v Court*[1], an agreement between the parties was adjourned into court for a decision as to the security of payments in a case in which the relevant insurers (Link Insurance Co Ltd, who transferred their rights and obligations to Zenith, and Zenith) were both registered in Gibraltar. In the subsequent hearing[2], the court came to the view that it would be necessary to join the FSCS as a party if any judgment to be made was to be binding upon it.

[1]   [2007] EWHC 2397 (QB), [2008] RTR 10.
[2]   Tugendhat J, QBD, 25 March 2009.

[O76]   An interesting test case might be to explore the extent to which a local authority which is self-insuring is held by a court to offer reasonable security. In the authors' view, this is likely to be on the borderline, though probably within 'reasonable security' depending upon the particular circumstances involved: the repercussions of a court declaring, for instance, that a local authority's promise to pay is not reasonably secure for the next 30 years are considerable!

[O77]   Another unresolved point concerns whether or not a defendant who is not a secure provider and cannot self-fund PPs can be forced by the court to buy an annuity which provides annual payments at the required level. The wording of the Act appears broad enough to give the court such power and, in the authors' experience, this point has been conceded in cases in which it has to date been raised. Potentially, this might be achieved in relation to RPI-linked periodical payments. The more difficult issue concerns the way that the court could replicate indexation to earnings-based measures such as ASHE (6115) because, at present, there are no annuity products which can be bought that track earnings-based measures. Whether or not the court could be persuaded to order that the defendant buy an annuity linked to RPI plus a fixed percentage in order to try to match a different index is a moot point, even if such a product were available (which at the time of writing is doubtful)[1]. However, in *Okeowo v Norton*[2] the court approved a settlement in respect of a pre-2004 Lloyd's syndicate insurer who was unable to self-fund a secure annuity but who agreed to purchase an annuity linked to RPI, in addition to making a lump sum payment of £1 million to represent the difference between annual payments increasing in line with RPI rather than ASHE (6115). If the stark choice is between a lump sum or a PP limited to RPI indexation, the latter, whilst not ideal, may still be more appropriate than the former.

[1]   See further paras **[O74]–[O80]**.
[2]   High Court (QBD), Swift J, 14 July 2008.

11   Security Beyond 2055

[O78]   Where a victim is likely to live beyond 2055, there may be a further problem with determining whether or not a PPO to which a defendant who is insured is a party offers reasonable security. This is because the Financial Services Authority regulates the long-term business funds of insurers who provide annuities. Put simply, an insurer must be able to purchase suitable matching assets to cover any liability to make annuity payments. In the case of an annuity linked to the RPI, matching assets are provided by purchasing index-linked Government stocks. At the time of writing, the longest dated stock of that type expires in 2055. At that stage, unless fresh stocks are issued, there will be no suitable matching asset. To continue to provide for an index-linked annuity beyond that date, significantly greater reserves would have to be tied up. Most life offices providing RPI-linked annuities incorporate a Limited Price Index clause into their policies, the effect of which is to provide that, if no suitable matching assets are available after 2055, the insurer will match the RPI up to a cap (typically within a range of 1% to 7%: the variation depends upon the age and health of the claimant, and varies from insurer to insurer).

[O79]   There is no possibility of close matching any index which is not used as the basis for an index-linked stock: and currently, the only linking is with RPI. Accordingly, it seems difficult to think that reasonable security can easily be assured for an award linked to another index and intended to be paid by an insurer (Government bodies are obviously immune from these problems).

[O80]   The problem may disappear if the Government issues index-linked securities which expire on a date after 2055. When the previous edition of this work was published in 2005, we anticipated that the Government would issue 50-year bonds, not least because, in his budget statement in March 2005, the Chancellor of the Exchequer had indicated such an intention, and have been proved right in the event. Since the availability of such stocks affects not just the relatively small market for injury victims, but also the much larger pensions market, and it is equally necessary to provide that insurers can 'close match' potential pension payments as it is that they can match injury payments, it seems likely that, as any later date approaches too closely to provide for certainty of future pension provision, the Government will once again issue longer-dated index-linked gilts. The potential problem here may thus be more theoretical than real – but it needs to be pointed out that it does depend on there being future Government action of the type mentioned.

[O81]   It may be that Government stocks are issued which are tied to some index other than the RPI. At the time of writing, however, this seems unlikely: and thus PCI, HCHS, NAE or ASHE indexation (see below) remains problematic and unlikely, except against secure self-funders including FSCS-backed insurers, public bodies or the NHSLA.

12   The Appropriate Index

[O82]   Section 2(8) of the Damages Act 1996 provides that an order for PPs 'shall be treated as providing for the amount of payments to vary by reference to the Retail Price Index (within the meaning of section 833(2) of the Income and Corporation Taxes Act 1988) at such times, and in such manner as may be determined by or in accordance with Civil Procedure Rules'. However, s 2(9) provides that an order made by a court for PPs may include provision 'disapplying sub-section (a) or (b) modifying the effect of sub-section (8)'.

[O83]   Thus, the 'default' index is RPI, which measures the cost of goods and services, and includes the cost of mortgages. It does not, however, directly measure any increase in average earnings.

[O84]   The CPR provide, similarly to the 1996 Act, that the amount of payments shall vary annually by reference to the RPI, unless the court orders otherwise. In guidance produced in respect of the power to impose PPs, the DCA noted that, during the passage of the Bill, ministers indicated[1] that it was expected that, as before, PPs would be linked to the RPI in the great majority of cases, but that it would remain open to the courts to adopt a different index (or none) in a particular case if there were exceptional circumstances which justified their doing so.

[1]   The debates took place in the House of Lords on 19 May 2003: see 648 HL Official Report (5th series) cols 536 and 537, 19 May 2003. See also the debate a week earlier at HL Official Report (5th series) col 57, 12 May 2003.

[O85]   Government guidance thus used the phrase 'exceptional circumstances', which echoed the phrase of the Lord Chancellor which, in *Warriner v Warriner*[1], was used to defeat an argument that a different discount rate should be applied in a particularly high-value case, since, although a high-value case was not the norm, it could not be said to be exceptional. Similarly, in *Cooke v United Bristol Health Care*[2] the court rejected a claim to calculate future loss by reference to a rate other than one which allowed for the RPI and impact of tax. Notwithstanding this, in *Flora v Wakom (Heathrow) Limited*[3] the Court of Appeal made it clear that an index other than RPI could be adopted in any case, where it was appropriate, and that case did not first have to be properly categorised as 'exceptional'. This gave the green light to arguments based on historical data to the effect that the cost of providing care had historically risen significantly faster than RPI inflation, and thus was likely to continue to do so. So it was that four first-instance decisions came before the Court of Appeal in *Tameside & Glossop NHS Trust v Thompstone & ors*[4], in which, on the basis of expert evidence, claimants had argued that a more appropriate index for continuing care costs would be a wage-related index, namely the 'Annual Survey of Hours and Earnings (ASHE) for the occupational group of care assistants and home carers (Standard Occupational Classification 6115)', produced by the Office of National Statistics (ONS): known more simply as ASHE 6115. In each case, the first instance judge had upheld the claimant's contentions. The Court of Appeal upheld their decisions. Also, in *Sarwar v Ali*[5], the trial judge (Lloyd-Jones J) thought that, for the young claimant with relatively high earning potential in the case before him, future earnings should be increased not by reference to RPI but by reference to the ASHE aggregate for male full-time employees at the 90th percentile.

[1]   [2002] 1 WLR 1703.
[2]   [2003] EWCA Civ 1370.
[3]   [2006] EWCA Civ 1103.
[4]   [2008] 1 WLR 2207, [2008] EWCA Civ 5.
[5]   [2007] EWHC 1255 (Admin).

[O86]   Since the court is concerned with the needs of the claimant, and with compensating as accurately as possible (two underlying reasons for adopting the power to provide for PPs), full restitution requires the identification of the most appropriate index. This, however, begs the question as to whether such an index can be identified as clearly more appropriate than the default index of RPI. In *Thompstone,* and the cases considered together with it, an answer was given, at least in cases where the defendant was a health authority and the claim involved continuing care costs to be provided by carers and care assistants. Although evidence may still be needed before a court is persuaded that another index is likely to produce more accurate figures over the lifetime of an award, and provide a more accurate picture of variation in costs so that neither claimant nor defendant is disadvantaged by the shift from RPI to such an index, one consequence of *Thompstone* was intended to be that it would give definitive guidance which should make repeated expert evidence unnecessary in practice[1]. It may be that expert evidence will still be required, but in the light of the observations of Brooke LJ in *Flora* (see footnote below) the party calling it should be prepared to justify the expense of doing so if any question of costs arises. Generally, though, it is likely to prove fruitless for defendants to contest indexation by reference to ASHE (6155) in cases where continuing care costs are largely those of paying for the labour of carers and care assistants. Likewise, since the accepted premise of the judgment in *Thompstone* was that earnings tend to rise faster than prices and it was inappropriate to up-rate the former by reference to the latter, save in exceptional circumstances, claims for loss of earnings are likely to be indexed to an appropriate earnings-based measure. This was the approach adopted by Lloyd-Jones J in *Sarwar v Ali*[2] (at first instance, too) when assessing the earnings of a claimant, albeit out of the ordinary mould. This approach is plainly correct if one considers the example of a claimant who worked as a carer / home help before an accident which leaves her catastrophically injured. If PPOs were made for care and loss of earnings, it would seem illogical if ASHE (6115) was used to up-rate her care PPO in order to closely match the earnings of carers doing a similar job to the one the claimant used to perform herself, but then not to use ASHE (6115) as the index to up-rate her loss of earnings. In short, earnings are different from prices and should be up-rated according to an appropriate earnings-based measure to ensure that they keep pace with inflation and that the 100% principle endorsed in *Flora v Wakom*[3] is met.

1   In the words of Brooke LJ in *Flora v Wakom Heathrow* [2006] EWCA Civ 1103, dealing with an argument that to permit any but exceptional cases to entertain departure from the RPI index would cause the repeated expenditure of time and costs involved in expert evidence being called, and anticipating that after a few first instance decisions: 'A group of appeals will then be brought to this court to enable it to give definitive guidance in the light of the findings of fact made by a number of trial judges. The armies of experts will then be able to strike their tents and return to the offices or academic groves from which they came' – the Court of Appeal in *Thompstone* considered it was dealing with such a group of appeals.

2   [2007] EWHC 1255 (Admin).

3   [2006] EWCA Civ 1103.

[O87]   The case of *RH*, one of those considered in *Thompstone*, subsequently came before Holland J for his approval of a form of order providing for indexation of care costs by reference to an index other than RPI (in that case, ASHE 6115) which might act as a model for other cases. This model form of order is annexed to this chapter (see para **[O139]**). Whilst PPs indexed to ASHE 6115 have become commonplace for future care awards in catastrophic injury cases, it is perhaps surprising that, at the time of writing, *Sarwar* still stands alone as the only reported case of a PP for loss of earnings with earnings-related indexation[1]. Pending further test cases, it also remains to be seen whether the court considers PPs appropriate for other heads of loss and how they might be indexed. Arguably, professional deputyship costs (which are largely earnings based) might also be to an earnings-based measure. However, there is no obvious measure for aids and equipment, travel and transport or holiday costs. It may be difficult to displace RPI as the default measure unless an obvious alternative is available, even though disability-related aids and equipment are not items that feature in the RPI basket. But, sometimes, even if there is a potentially suitable index, such as the HCHS[2] in respect of medical costs, practical difficulties regarding publication of the data, and the frequency of revisions to the data, may well arise. The guiding principles to consider when choosing an index or measure by which to up-rate a particular head of loss, as accepted by the first instance courts in each of the conjoined *Thompstone* cases, are the list of qualities put forward by Dr Wass (as largely agreed by the other economists and forensic accountants called in opposition to her evidence) as follows:

- accuracy of match of the particular data series to the loss or expenditure being compensated;
- authority of the collector of the data;
- statistical reliability;
- accessibility;
- consistency over time;
- reproducibility in the future; and
- simplicity and consistency in application.

1   Although the authors are aware of a number of settlements including earnings PPs.

2   The Hospital and Community Health Services index, which is used for the annual up-rating for the recovery of NHS costs following road traffic accidents.

[O88]   It has been suggested that, despite the 2055 problem, and the difficulties for bodies other than health service or public bodies in providing reasonable security for the continuity of PPs referenced to ASHE, the National Average Earnings (NAE) or Prices and Costs Index in the health service (PCI), a court could provide for indexation by reference to the RPI plus a fixed percentage uplift beyond it. It is likely that the courts would be hesitant to do this, since s 2(8) of the Damages Act 1996 and CPR, r 41.8 appear to envisage that the link will be to some index, or none, as opposed to a separate reference point (RPI plus) devised by the court itself. However, Baroness Scotland did say in Parliament during the passage of the Act that it would be open to a court to order that PPs should be linked to the RPI plus a percentage as a proxy for some other index[1]. A further alternative is that a non-secure insurer could make an additional lump sum payment in order to compensate for the difference between providing an annuity to RPI and a PPO linked to an earnings-based measure such as ASHE (6115)[2].

[1]   See generally W Norris QC 'Periodical Payments: Indexation, Variation, Protection and Practice' [2005] JPIL, Issue 1/05. Although whether or not such products are available depends upon the prevailing market conditions. At present, it is difficult to be able to purchase annuities linked to RPI, let alone annuities linked to RPI plus a fixed percentage.
[2]   *Okeowo v Norton*, approval hearing in the High Court (QBD), Swift J, 14 July 2008.

13   Variable Orders

[O89]   At the time when an order is made, provision may be made for the terms to be varied on the occurrence of some future health-related event. This is to be distinguished from a variation of the terms upon a certain future date (which is part of the design of a non-variable PPO). There is no power to order variation based on post-settlement social or economic changes.

[O90]   Note that the power to make a variable order may only be exercised in respect of proceedings commenced after 1 April 2005. It may be important, therefore, to check the date of issue of proceedings. Note, too, that an application for variation at a date after the original order can be made only if that order is expressly a variable one, and that an application may be made only once in respect of any specified deterioration or improvement in the claimant's condition.

[O91]   The Damages (Variation of Periodical Payments) Order 2005[1] provides that the court may, on the application of one party, with the agreement of all parties or of its own initiative, provide in an order for PPs that it may be varied if there is proved or admitted to be a chance that, at some definite or indefinite time in the future, the claimant will (a) as a result of the act or omission which gave rise to the cause of action, develop some serious disease or suffer some serious deterioration, or (b) enjoy some significant improvement in his or her physical or mental condition, where that condition had been adversely affected as a result of that act or omission[2].

[1]   SI 2005/841.
[2]   Article 2.

[O92]   In such a case, damages are to be assessed or agreed on the assumption that the disease, deterioration or improvement will not occur. The order: (a) must specify the disease or type of deterioration or improvement; (b) may (but does not have to) specify a period within which an application for variation may be made; (c) may (but does not have to) specify more than one disease or type of deterioration or improvement; and (d) may, in respect of each, specify a different period within which an application for variation in respect of it may be made.

[O93]   In addition, a variable order must provide that a party must obtain the court's permission to apply for it to be varied, unless the court otherwise orders. If the parties can agree a mechanism by which an application for variation can be facilitated, they might invite the court to exercise its power to order 'otherwise', for this would avoid the expense of one party going through the application for permission stage before a substantive hearing for a variation at some future date. Accordingly, claimants and defendants should consider whether an application for permission to apply is strictly necessary in their particular case: if not, they should apply to omit reference to permission in the original variable order at the time it is made.

[O94]   Where any period is specified within which an application for permission to vary may be made, an application to extend the period for applying may be made (such an application must, however, be made within the period originally stipulated).

[O95]   It is important to note that:

(i)   Only one application to vary may be made in respect of each specified disease or type of deterioration or improvement.
(ii)   There is no power to order unrestricted variation, eg because the money provided by the original order has proved insufficient, or because care costs have escalated over time beyond the rate of increase in the annual payments under the original order.
(iii) The case file documents must be preserved by the legal representatives of the parties, including barristers). (The documents will also be preserved by the court.)
(iv)   The parties may agree to settle a case upon terms that one will pay the other PPs which may be varied if there is agreed to be a chance that, at some definite or indefinite time in the future, the claimant will (a) as a result of the act or omission which gave rise to the cause of action, develop some serious disease or suffer some serious deterioration[1], or (b) enjoy some significant improvement in his or her physical or mental condition, where that condition had been adversely affected as a result of that act or omission. But note – the terms of such an agreement *must* comply with art 9(2) of the 2005 Order. The agreement, therefore: (a) must expressly state that a party to it may apply to the court for the terms of the variable agreement to be varied; (b) must specify the disease or type of deterioration or improvement; (c) may (but does not have to) specify a period within which an application for it to be varied may be made; and (d) may (but does not have to) specify more than one disease or type of deterioration or improvement and may, in respect of each, specify a different period within which an application for it to be varied may be made. The imperative suggests that, if an agreement is made which does not comply with art 9(2), it will not be enforceable.

---

[1]   Cf provisional damages.

[O96] Where an agreement provides that a party is permitted to apply for it to be varied, the party so permitted must nonetheless obtain the court's permission to apply for the variation. It is unclear whether the applicant is limited to one application per type of disease or deterioration: the safest course would be to assume that this is so, since in particular the applicant will have to ask the permission of the court to apply for a variation, and implicit in this is the possibility that the application might, for good reason, be refused. It is likely to be regarded as good reason that it is a second application where there is nothing express which permits it; and even if there is, that a consistent regime should apply as between variable orders and variable agreements.

[O97] There is an obvious overlap with the possibility of claiming an award of provisional damages under s 32A of the Senior Courts Act 1981 or s 51 of the County Courts Act 1984. The 2005 Order provides that a variable order may be made in addition to an order for an award of provisional damages.

[O98] Thus, in a situation in which there is uncertainty about whether an injured party will suffer further deterioration, or develop some further condition (eg epilepsy, syringomyelia, or immobility such that a wheelchair is necessary at all times), the parties may claim (or agree) one of five distinct possible forms of order:

(a) a lump sum award;
(b) a non-variable periodical payment order (if, for instance, deterioration to wheelchair status from partial mobility is anticipated, the consequent increase in financial need can be provided for by setting a fixed date at which the level of annual payment is to increase);
(c) a provisional damages award (subject to the restrictions envisaged in *Wilson v Ministry of Defence*[1] – inevitable deterioration does not qualify for an award of provisional damages);
(d) an award of provisional damages with a variable order (thus providing that, for instance, the order might be varied in the event that the claimant becomes wheelchair bound, but also being provisional, by asserting that the damages are to be assessed upon the footing that there will be no epilepsy, and no syringomyelia, or whatever); or
(e) a variable periodical payment order providing that the order for PPs may be varied upon the claimant suffering epilepsy, or developing syringomyelia, or becoming totally wheelchair bound (or whatever).

One of the comparatively rare cases yet to have considered a variable order, *Pankhurst v Lee White & MIB*[2], bore out the prediction (made in the last edition of this book) that syringomyelia might be a condition calling for such an order. It also demonstrated that there may be an overlap between the making of a variable order and the making of an order for provisional damages: both orders were made by the agreement of the parties. There is no conflict between them so as to require a choice only of one or the other, in suitable circumstances. Moreover, PPs will frequently only cover limited aspects of future losses.

---

[1]   [1991] 1 All ER 638, endorsed by the Court of Appeal per Roch LJ in *Curi v Colina* [1998] EWCA Civ 1326 and followed by Lloyd-Jones J in *Sarwar v Ali & Anor* [2007] EWHC 1255 (Admin). See also *Chewings v Williams* [2009] EWHC 2490 (QB), [2010] PIQR Q1 (Slade J). Note that the decision in *Davies v Bradshaw* [2008] EWHC 740 (QB) was successfully appealed by consent in

relation to this issue, and the judge's failure to make a provisional damages award to cover the risk of developing syringomyelia.

2   [2009] EWHC 1117 (QB) (MacDuff J).

[O99]   A principal use of the 'combination' of provisional damages and variable PPO may be to avoid the problems caused by the inability to claim provisional damages for progressive deterioration. The reasoning in *Wilson* (which denied a claim for provisional damages assessed on the footing that osteo-arthritis would not develop to certain specified levels of disability, when it was seen that such a progression was inevitable) arguably does not apply to prevent a variable agreement being made, despite the superficial similarity as to the circumstances in which such an order may be made when compared with the circumstances in which an order for provisional damages may be made.

[O100]   Note that variable orders may be made in respect of an improvement in the claimant's condition. It should not be thought that a deterioration will inevitably increase damages and an improvement inevitably decrease them. For instance, a claimant who is in a persistent vegetative state (PVS) and recovers a little from his coma is likely to need greater financial assistance than if he had remained in PVS, as would a claimant who recovers sufficiently from agoraphobia to wish to travel outside his home from time to time, thus requiring transport and company in which to do so. Likewise, someone who regains capacity will no longer incur Court of Protection or professional deputyship expenses. A deterioration may similarly reduce rather than increase costs: someone who is no longer able to care for him or herself in their own home is a case in point, since such a person might be more cheaply cared for in a residential setting, despite the fact that his overall physical state has deteriorated.

[O101]   The Government anticipates that variable orders may be little used[1]. Certainly, parties should think carefully before claiming such an order. There is very little clarity as to how the provisions will work in practice. Unlike orders for provisional damages, the defendant may apply for variation. This is likely to perpetuate the relationship between defendant and claimant: does it mean that, in practice, a defendant will occasionally employ surveillance techniques to see if a claimant has improved to the extent that such an application may be made? To what extent can a claimant be obliged to report to a defendant that his or her condition remains unchanged? Similar problems may be said to arise where pensions are payable – how does the insurer learn of the death of the pensioner? – but these have been overcome, largely by annual certification processes. But is a defendant insurer in the same position to demand such certification in respect not simply of life, but of condition, especially when there may be 'good days and bad days'[2]? Time alone will tell.

1   This claim is made in guidance produced for use with the legislation.
2   And, if so, a claim might need to be made in the schedule for the extra costs of such an annual medical examination, though it is arguable that, if the defendant is unwilling to bear the costs of an examination with a view to reducing the annual payments currently being made, the claimant may wish to exercise the implied liberty to apply which is contained in any court order unless excluded.

[O102]   The possibility of variation may create difficulties for an insurer in reserving to meet the liability. The liability is, however, that of the defendant and not his or her insurer directly. If the original order is variable, the defendant (or his or her insurer) will not normally be in a position to purchase an annuity providing for it. Hence, it is important to know what the prospective financial resources of the defendant – and possibly his or her insurer – may be. There is no statutory protection for the amount of any increased award in anticipation of its being made – so, if, between the date of the original variable order and the claimant returning to court to seek an increased payment, the insurer goes bust, the defendant will be left to provide for the increase him or herself. Hence, it is necessary to look at the defendant's financial position as well as that of his or her insurer. Article 3 of the Damages (Variation of Periodical Payments) Order 2005[1] thus requires the court to take into account the defendant's likely future financial resources (though, note, it does not have to do so where the defendant is insured in respect of the claim: art 3(a)).

[1]   SI 2005/841.

[O103]   We suggest that careful consideration be given to security for any increased payment, especially where the variable order is one made by consent – for, in this latter case, too, the court does not itself have to be concerned about the defendant's financial resources[1].

[1]   Legal advisers may wish to ensure that the court is not subsequently concerned with the making of such an order in an action for professional negligence if it should transpire that inadequate consideration was given to the financial ability of the defendant or his or her insurer to make future revisions in payment.

[O104]   In practice, defendants are unlikely to want to be saddled with a variable order – not least because it is unclear how they might budget for its coming into effect. There is one class of case, however, where the opposite may be true. This is where there is any real suspicion of malingering or overstatement by the claimant and/or there is psychological overlay related to the litigation and there is a real chance of improvement in the future. A defendant may secure a form of wording in a variable order which entitles an application to be made to the court if it should appear that the claimant has made a significant improvement in his or her condition. The exaggerating claimant is likely sooner or later to demonstrate such an improvement, and an application for downward variation may be made. However, in a serious case involving alleged fraud, the more appropriate route might be to bring fresh fraud proceedings to apply to set aside the original settlement or court award on the basis of fraud and/or appeal the original judgment, especially if the fraud is uncontested[1].

[1]   *Noble v Owens* [2010] EWCA Civ 224, where a novel solution was proposed by the court, permitting fraud allegations to be heard even if the evidence fell short of the incontrovertible, where it was suggested a personal injury claimant had wilfully overstated his injuries.

[O105]   Claimants too may prefer to build in uplifts to an award by making an order in 'non-variable' form, providing for increases in payment from time to time. It will nonetheless be a matter of judgment whether the defendant in any action may be persuaded to pay a premium for such an order to avoid the consequences of having a variable order hanging over it.

14   Assignment and Charge of Right to Receive Payments

[O106]   The right to receive PPs may not be assigned or charged, unless the court which made the original order is satisfied there are special circumstances which make this necessary. (This is intended to prevent claimants assigning their right to receive payments in return for a lump sum, and thereby bypassing the power to impose PPs.)

[O107]   CPR, r 41.10 requires the court to have regard to a number of factors in considering whether to permit an assignment or a charge. Those factors, which are identified in para 4 of the Practice Direction (PD41B), are:

(a) whether the capitalised value of the assignment or charge represents value for money;
(b) whether the assignment or charge is in the claimant's best interests, taking into account whether those interests can be met in some other way; and
(c) how the claimant would be financially supported following the assignment or charge.

[O108]   These provisions are not as restrictive as they might appear at first blush. They do not prohibit a loan being made to the recipient of PPs on personal security alone. If the recipient failed to repay, he or she could be sued, and the lender could recover out of the income stream provided for by the PPs. What the provisions do restrict, however, is the ability of a claimant to take out a loan which is secured upon the PPs rather than unsecured, such that the lender takes priority over other debtors. There is a link, here, with the insolvency provisions relating to PPs, which provide that PPs in respect of care may not be taken as property of the bankrupt recipient of such payments, although payments in respect of future loss of earnings may be. (This is partly why a distinction must be made in any award of PPs as between future earnings, on the one hand, and care and other recurring costs, on the other.)

15   Part 36 Offers

[O109]   Where both an offer and the award by the court are made in lump sum terms, CPR, Pt 36 operates as it always has done: a straightforward comparison may be made between the offer and the award. Where, however, the offer is in terms of a lump sum and the award is made in a PPO (or where there is a mixture of the two, or where the offer is to accept PPs and the award is a lump sum award), the simplicity of the Pt 36 regime will not apply.

[O110]   An offer may be made to pay (if made by a defendant) or to accept (if made by a claimant) (a) the whole or part of the damages for future pecuniary loss in the form of (i) either a lump sum or PPs or (ii) both a lump sum and PPs, and (b) the whole or part of any other damages in the form of a lump sum.

[O111]   Since a court only has a power to make a PPO in respect of future pecuniary loss, any claim for a lump sum in respect of pain, suffering and loss of amenity, and for past loss, must be made on a lump sum basis: however, such an offer does not require that the lump sum part of an offer stops there. It may provide that, so far as the future is concerned, payment will be made, or accepted, with a mixture of lump sum and periodical payment. Any permutation of capital and income is thus possible.

[O112] CPR, Pt 36 was significantly amended in 2007. CPR, r 36.5(4)(c) now provides, so far as concerns offers to settle personal injury claims in whole or in part by PPs, that the offer must state what part of it relates to damages for future pecuniary loss to be paid or accepted in the form of PPs, and must specify:

'(i) the amount and duration of the periodical payments;
(ii) the amount of any payments for substantial capital purchases and when they are to be made; and
(iii) that each amount is to vary by reference to the retail prices index (or to some other named index, or that it is not to vary by reference to any index)'.

Further, by CPR, r 36.5(4)(d), the offer 'must state either that any damages which take the form of periodical payments will be funded in a way which ensures that the continuity of payment is reasonably secure in accordance with section 2(4) of the Damages Act 1996 or how such damages are to be paid and how the continuity of their payment is to be secured'.

Note that the rule does not require that an offer contains all the details which are required to be set out in an order by CPR, r 41.8. If the parties wish the terms of a settlement to be embodied in a consent order made by the court, the requirements of that rule will also need to be satisfied.

[O113] Where the offeror makes a Part 36 offer which offers to pay or to accept damages in the form of both a lump sum and PPs, the offeree may only give notice of acceptance of the offer as a whole (CPR, r 36.5(6)). If he does accept, then by CPR, r 35.5(7) he must, within seven days of the date of acceptance, apply to the court for an order for an award of damages in the form of PPs under CPR, r 41.8(1)(a). If, before he accepts, he wishes to have more details of the offer by CPR, r 36.8(1) he may, within seven days of a Part 36 offer being made, request the offeror to clarify it.

[O114] By CPR, r 36.10(1), where a Part 36 offer is accepted within the relevant period the claimant will be entitled to the costs of the proceedings up to the date on which notice of acceptance was served on the offeror. If there is no such acceptance, and the case is fought to a conclusion, then where a periodical payment offer has been made under Pt 36, and the claimant fails to obtain a judgment which is 'more advantageous' than the Part 36 offer, then CPR, r 36.14 provides that a court will order a claimant to pay the defendant's costs incurred after the latest date on which the payment or offer could have been accepted, without needing the permission of the court. Similarly, if a judgment against a defendant is more advantageous to the claimant than the proposals contained in a periodical payment Part 36 offer, the court may order interest on the whole or part of the sum of money awarded to the claimant at a rate not exceeding 10% above base rate, for some or all of the period beginning with the latest date on which the defendant could have accepted the claimant's offer without needing permission of the court, and may order indemnity costs from the same date together with interest on those costs. If the recommendations of Lord Justice Jackson's Costs Review (published 2010) are implemented, then there may be a more significant uplift still.

[O115] No guidance is given by the rule as to when an offer will be considered 'more advantageous'. In particular, problems are likely to arise if a lump sum award is made where a periodical payment offer was advanced, or vice versa. Similarly, where a lump sum offer is made by a defendant, but PPs are awarded, it may be difficult to know whether the judgment is more or less advantageous than a defendant's Part 36 offer.

[O116] Considerable thought was given as to whether there should be more detailed guidance or provision by rule as to the costs consequences of Part 36 offers. So many and varied are the possibilities and permutations for which provision would have to be made to ensure the guillotine-like simplicity of the unamended Pt 36 provisions that it was decided best to leave the matter to the general discretion of the courts. In most cases it is thought that it will be clear whether a claimant has, or has not, done better or worse than a relevant Part 36 offer. In those cases where it is less clear, parties may seek to argue that it is necessary to establish what would have been the lump sum if the PPs are capitalised, taking into account the probable life expectancy of the claimant. However, this is to introduce evidence of life expectancy which an award of PPs is in part designed to avoid. The cases (referred to above) decided in relation to the inter-relationship of PPs and interim awards of damages are clear that the two payment regimes are chalk and cheese, such that one cannot simply be converted into the other by capitalising an income stream of PPs. It is not easy to circumvent a broad based application of discretion by the courts in determining whether or not a claimant has, or has not 'beaten' the payment in by, for instance, advancing two Part 36 offers in advance of trial, one consisting of a lump sum alone, the other consisting of a mix. This is because the mix of lump sum and periodical payment element may vary considerably. The two regimes for satisfying liability for future losses are regarded by the courts as quite distinct[1]. If this line of reasoning is followed where costs are concerned, then arguments based on capitalising PPs are unlikely to hold much weight.

[1]   See *Flora v Wakom (Heathrow) Limited* [2006] EWCA Civ 1103.

[O117] It is too early at the date of writing to know quite how the court will exercise its powers in difficult cases, but the rules allow a court not to make an order against a party where the court considers it unjust to do so. Part of the consideration of that injustice may be asking whether it was appropriate for the claimant or defendant to make an offer based on either lump sums or PPs. In particular, a defendant who ignores a claimant's stated preference for PPs when making a Part 36 offer may find it to be ineffective if the judgment ultimately includes PP terms. (The authors doubt that the costs of evidence as to life expectancy will be allowed if it is directed merely to a possible argument that a Part 36 offer has or has not been beaten.

[O118] The authors' provisional view is that the Court of Appeal is unlikely to be sympathetic to any appeal in respect of the award, or withholding of, Part 36 costs, taking the view that the matter is a discretion to be exercised by the trial judge, and should not involve satellite litigation to establish what the award would have been if the award had been differently composed. The general view is likely, we think, to be that litigants must expect to 'take the rough with the smooth' as part of the price for the introduction of the periodical payment system, and to accept the reduction in certainty and clarity which the previous operation of the Pt 36 regime has provided.

[O119] It remains a moot point as to how the court should approach the question of interest if the claimant betters his or her own Part 36 offer on periodical payments. Should the interest be added to the annual PP and, therefore, be subject to the same annual up-rating, eg by reference to ASHE (6115), or should the interest be capitalised[1]? In catastrophic injury cases, allowing enhanced interest on multi-million pound care claims where Part 36 offers have been bettered would result in significant additional sums being paid, and Court of Appeal guidance on the correct approach would be welcomed sooner rather than later[2]. The approach taken on this issue by the courts has tended to regard interest as, in principle, payable where a claimant is kept out of his money. Insofar as he claims for losses that he will suffer in the future, but has not yet incurred, he has not been kept out of his money. Thus, where a settlement offer is made by the claimant and rejected, yet bettered or equalled by the claimant, he will not have been kept out of his money (so the argument goes) because it is future loss, and because interest is normally receivable only on past loss payable by way of special damages, and on a compensatory lump sum for pain, suffering and loss of amenity: see per Tugendhat J. in *Andrews v Aylott*[3].

[1] For further thoughts on this issue, see Julian Chamberlayne 'Claimant Part 36 Offers: Are they Worth it?' JPIL 2009, 3, 237–241, and Julian Chamberlayne 'Claimant Part 36 Offers: Are they Working' JPIL 3/2009.

[2] See further the approach of MacDuff J in *Pankhurst v Lee White & MIB* [2010] EWHC 311 (QB), who refused to award interest on future losses including periodical payments for care and case management, although his reasoning did not appear to be expressly related to PPs – at the time of writing, this decision is currently the subject of an appeal.

[3] [2010] EWHC 597 (QB).

[O120] An offeror will need to state what recoverable benefits are to be deducted from his offer, so that the offeree knows precisely what sums will be available to him. Where a PPO is entered into, then whether it provides for no lump sum at all, or for a mix of lump sum and periodical provision, regulation 18 of the Social Security (Recovery of Benefits) (Lump Sum Payments) Regulations 2008[1] applies. The compensator is to be taken to have made a single compensation payment on the day of settlement (so that there is no deduction from PPs as and when made thereafter, nor any liability resting on the compensator to pay recoupment). The settlement or order is to be regarded as a single payment from which lump sum payments may be recovered under the Regulations. The amount of the single payment is the total of the payments due to be made under the periodical payment agreement. There is no recognition in the instrument of the difficulty of applying this provision – since no-one knows precisely how long the payments will go on being made if, as will be the usual case, they are to last for the claimant's lifetime, the calculation is thus impossible to do with accuracy. Nor will it be easy to apply if a PPO is made without a lump sum payment also being made. In practice, however, the authors do not expect there to be any real problem – since the amount of recovery will be slight in relation to the lump sum in almost every case in which a PPO is to be made, and the cases in which a PPO will be made on its own will be hard to envisage (though the Regulations themselves manage to envisage it!).

[1]   SI 2008/1596.

[O121]   Where a compensator purchases an annuity from a third party (such as an insurer), he nonetheless remains the compensator liable to make the payment to the Compensation Recovery Unit[1].

[1]   SI 2008/1596, reg 18.

16   Appeals

[O122]   No separate rule deals with appeals in respect of PPOs which are imposed against the wishes of one or both parties.

[O123]   Where there is a dispute as to whether a PPO should be made or a lump sum order instead, the 'default' position would appear to be that PPs should be preferred by the court. This follows from the policy background (set out, for instance, in the DCA guidance, and summarised above). It is incumbent upon the court to consider whether an award can be made in every case involving future pecuniary loss.

[O124]   The factors to which the rules, and the Practice Direction, refer are such that the decision whether to order PPs or a lump sum is one of discretion. Although it has been said that a judicial discretion must meet the requirements of relevance, reason, justice and fairness[1], this still makes it difficult for the exercise of a discretion to be faulted.

[1]   Per Mummery P in *Selkent Bus Company v Moore* [1996] ICR 836, EAT.

[O125]   Provided that the court has in mind that the central requirement is to meet the needs of the claimant, as opposed to adopt his or her wishes, it seems unlikely to the authors that many appeals will succeed.

[O126]   However, if an appeal is made, what happens to financial provision for the claimant in the meantime? The answer seems to be that it is effectively no different from any case in which there is an appeal against an award. Where PPs are ordered, there seems to be no good reason why, pending the determination of the appeal, any periodical payment falling due should not be paid (unless, that is, a stay is sought if, for instance, there is an appeal against liability). In the case of a lump sum order, again, there seems to be no reason why there should not be at least some payment pending the appeal. However, the principles are bound to be individual to each case. Moreover, defendants may wish to seek an early stay of payment if they intend to satisfy the requirement of reasonable security by purchasing an annuity from a life insurer. Such a purchase demands a lump sum outlay which, once paid, is likely to be irrecoverable.

17   Pros and Cons of the Periodical Payment System in Operation

[O127]   We have set out advantages and disadvantages of the system at the start of this chapter. These paragraphs concern the likely extent of take-up of such orders.

[O128]   Claimants may instinctively distrust the provisions which have not been around very long. A large lump sum may seem to be more attractive. This may be all the more so if the defendants seek a variable order, so that they might argue that the sums should be reduced because of some later improvement (or, for that matter, deterioration in condition which implies a lower cost).

[O129]   In general, however, a claimant will usually benefit more than he or she will lose from having a PPO. Certainly, those advising a claimant who is either a child or a patient will need to be careful to provide considered advice, usually supported by expert financial opinion, if the claimant proposes not to take advantage of a PPO. Other advisers who are not registered to provide financial advice must be careful to restrict their advice to the legal pros and cons. It is possible that the choice between whether to opt for PPs or a lump sum will be seen as tantamount to an investment decision. We doubt that in reality it is, but this position has yet to be determined authoritatively. It does not, however, need detailed or expert financial advice to appreciate that lump sum awards have to be managed carefully if they are to produce the income needed from time to time by a claimant, and that this is likely to be so where they are placed in investments the capital value of which may go down as well as up (the stock market during the 'credit crunch' of 2008–10 has been a classic example of this).

[O130]   Consideration should be given to the effect of applying for an interim payment. This will probably form part of the lump sum and, therefore, if it is large, it may reduce what would otherwise be the periodical payment award, since it may not be possible to fund it entirely from the lump sum award for pain, suffering and loss of amenity and/or from the award for past expenses and losses. Even if it were possible to do so, contingency planning suggests a need to retain a reasonable lump sum fund.

[O131]   Defendants, on the other hand, have probably on balance something to lose by having a PPO imposed. Although the ability to self-fund gives greater flexibility financially to the paying insurer or public body than the previous requisite purchase of an annuity to provide a structured settlement, the need to be able to provide reasonable continuity of payment into the future, whatever the life expectancy of the claimant, implies that the insurer will need to reserve[1] so as to cover the eventuality that the claimant will live to the greatest age which falls within a reasonable bracket of life expectancy. Over-reserving ties up funds. It seems likely that many general insurers will therefore prefer to purchase annuities (but, at the moment, there are few available on the open market) or will pay a premium by way of lump sum in order to avoid the difficulties of having to over-reserve. Time may tell whether or not this prediction is borne out.

---

[1]   This does not appear to be such an issue for self-funding bodies, such as the NHSLA and MIB.

18   Other Methods of Providing for Future Loss

[O132]   PPs need to be seen in context. They are one way of providing for future loss. Advisers need to consider whether other methods may be more appropriate. Some future losses may be covered by the ability to return to court where a provisional damages award is made. Some may be susceptible to insurance (eg life or critical illness insurance of a gratuitous carer[1], to provide for additional costs if he or she should be unable to provide the care anticipated as likely, though not certain, at the date of trial). Some may be provided in kind (eg, by agreement with a defendant insurer, rehabilitation paid for by the insurer may be available). Some may be capable of being covered by an indemnity (though this has to be agreed, and cannot in our view be ordered by a court). In addition, a trust may usefully be established, especially of a 'special needs' type which does not prejudice the continued receipt of free accommodation or care support. No adviser should therefore confine his or her consideration of a client's case (or of the other party's claim) to the simple question: 'Lump sum award or periodical payment order?'. Much may still be provided by agreement (despite the restrictions on such agreements where they deal with PPs if they are to be effective in conferring the tax advantages and the security of an order) which cannot be given by the courts, and advisers should always be alert to this.

[1]   Although cf *Crofts v Murton* LTL 10.9.08, in which HHJ Collender QC refused to allow a claim for health insurance to cover the claimant's partner to ensure she could be treated quickly in times of ill-health and therefore return to caring for the claimant as quickly as possible (unfortunately, the reasoning is scant and all is said is that this item was not reasonably related to the claimant's injuries).

19   Schedules

[O133]   The impact of the changes in compensation law to permit the ordering of PPs will change the format of schedules of damages.

[O134]   In a case in which the claimant has indicated, the parties have agreed or the court has taken the view at an early stage that compensation should consist of PPs for the future, then:

(i)   Life expectancy does not matter significantly, where the intention is to have all care costs (including appliances and equipment used for caring) and loss of earnings paid for periodically (subject to the *Roberts v Johnstone* difficulties discussed above).

(ii)   It may therefore be seen as a waste of money to obtain evidence as to life expectancy – but all will depend upon the particular facts of the case. There may be many in which it remains relevant, and a cost/benefit appraisal, evaluating the importance of the issue in relation to the amount of the claim, may need to be undertaken.

(iii)   There is no need to calculate lifetime multipliers, nor to discount future losses for accelerated receipt.

(iv)   It becomes necessary, instead, to calculate the annual loss, for the first year of loss identifying in particular any capital needs that are likely to arise in the first year, eg by the purchase for the first time of aids and equipment (these are better claimed as a lump).

(v)   Then the loss per year thereafter should be calculated, doing so separately for (a) future loss of earnings, (b) care, and (c) aids and equipment costs. In particular, provision should be made for any step up or down in earnings (eg employment so far as promotion is concerned), or drop from earned income to pension receipts; in care, where a wheelchair has to be provided, or a night carer becomes essential; and in education, where residential schooling stops and care at home begins.

(vi)   In each case, work out a rough career/lifetime profile. If the date at which a change is relatively certain can be identified, the financial impact of it is better provided for by a non-variable order. If it is very uncertain when a health change may occur, and even if it will, then a variable order might be better (and defendants in particular may wish one to be made, to take advantage of improvements in condition): but remember that the requirements of variable orders are demanding in practice.

(vii)   The career profile is relevant almost exclusively to loss of earnings. In this case, consider how to allow for discount (we suggest adopting the discount factors set out in the Ogden Tables and in Facts and Figures, for use in different risk classes of occupation and in differing geographical areas). In most cases, promotion will be uncertain as to both if and when, and even as to what position: broad judgments will have to be made, and the profile adjusted to cope with them.

(viii)   The care profile requires no discount, unless it is for risks of future deterioration which are specifically allowed for (eg whether a future operation is needed). It will, however, demand a degree of anticipation as to the time when events will occur (eg will X be wheelchair-bound by 50, or should it be 55?). Robust common sense is required in taking a broad view, where 'reasonably possible' is likely to be better than marginal changes from year to year, each of which will have to be explained to a court.

(ix)   Once the career and care profiles are set out, on what we suggest should be a broad rather than over-detailed basis, the annual sums for the years beginning with the prospective date of award can be set out. Consider at this stage how future accommodation losses are to be claimed (see above) and whether there is a sufficient capital reserve for contingencies.

The schedule thus comes to a sub-total for lump sum claims (pain, suffering, loss of amenity – if a figure is expressed at all – plus interest thereon; past loss plus interest thereon; future losses insofar as a lump sum is thought necessary), and an annual total for the first year (and on the two profiles for the years thereafter). There is no overall total figure.

[O135]   In practice, when the schedule is drafted, it will not be clear what view the defendant will take to whether there should be a lump sum or periodical award, whether as to the whole of the award or as to specific heads of it. Nor will it be clear which view the court will take – and, as the existing case-law demonstrates, a court may depart from the expressed wish of the claimant and impose its own view as to which better suits his needs. Thus, it is at present sensible to draft a schedule which provides equally for the preferred PPs, but also for the possibility of a lump sum award.

[O136]   If the claimant is uncertain as to whether to seek a PPO, or lump sum provision, then they may be claimed in the alternative. In this case, the lump sum calculation should be performed as described elsewhere in this work, and then a section be added which deals with future loss calculated on the basis of PPs. This should be approached, we suggest, in the same way as we have indicated above.

[O137]   In the case of either a claimant or defendant who seeks an award in one or other form (but not in the alternative), it is sensible to set out at the start of the schedule a paragraph which expresses the preference (eg 'The claimant seeks an order for periodical payments' or 'The claimant wishes a lump sum order'). Reasons for the choice should follow, where they have been formulated. Given that the court is to decide which form of provision best suits the claimant's needs, such an expression as 'the claimant prefers it' is unlikely to suffice. It would be preferable to say something[1] such as:

> 'The claimant anticipates that within the next five years he will have to replace X, involving him in significant capital expense, but he cannot say when this will be since the original X has not yet required replacement. He thus needs a ready reserve of capital. He has to allow for 25% contributory fault as well. The combined effect of these factors, and that of the payment so far of more money by way of interim payment than he will recover on his claim for past losses, means that any PPs he will recover can at best only meet a small proportion of his annual needs. He will thus inevitably have to meet continuing expenses as they fall due out of capital, to some extent, and the flexibility which a lump sum gives is in these circumstances the best way of making provision for his needs.'

[1]   Assuming the facts justify it!

[O138]   An example of a periodic payment schedule is provided in Chapter Q, at para **[Q28]**.

[O139]   Finally, as an appendix, we attach the form of order which was approved as a model by Holland J in considering the practical implementation of periodical payment regimes in *Thompstone et al* – see para **[O87]** above:

SCHEDULE TO THE ORDER

Part 1 of the Schedule to the order

Each sum payable under part(s) 2 and 3 of this schedule is a "periodical payment" subject to the conditions set out in paragraphs 1-8 of this part

1.   Unless specifically stated, all the periodical payments under part(s) 2 and 3 of this schedule will continue during the lifetime of the Claimant
2.   No minimum number of periodical payments under part(s) 2 and 3 of this schedule shall be made
3.   Payment of the periodical payments under part(s) 2 and 3 of this schedule will cease on the death of the Claimant
4.   The final periodical payment under part(s) 2 and 3 of this schedule will be pro-rated for so much of the final year that the Claimant had survived and any

balance owing to the NHSLA or its successor will be repayable to it out of the Claimant's estate, subject only to deduction by the Claimant's estate of such sums as the Claimant's estate may be liable for in respect of the termination of the employment of any persons employed to care for the Claimant

5.   The NHSLA shall be entitled to require the Claimant to produce evidence in a form reasonably satisfactory to the NHSLA that the Claimant remains alive before making any periodical payment

6.   The periodical payments under part(s) 2 and 3 of this schedule are to be made by BACS to the Court of Protection (or its successor) for the benefit of the Claimant under reference [*insert as appropriate*] (where applicable)

7.   At the time of each periodical payment under part(s) 2 and 3 of this schedule the NHSLA shall provide to the Claimant and/or the Deputy details in writing explaining how the periodical payment has been calculated

8.   The NHSLA shall pay the relevant annual sums set out in part[s] 2 and 3 of this schedule on 15 December of each year, save that:

8.1.   If the Office for National Statistics ['*ONS*'] does not publish by 17th November in the relevant year all the relevant data and as a result the NHSLA is unable to perform the relevant calculations under part(s) 2 and 3 to recalculate the periodical payment(s) due to the Claimant before 15 December of the relevant year, the NHSLA shall on 15 December of the relevant year make the periodical payment(s): (a) in the same sum as that paid in the previous year; or (b) in the increased/decreased sum recalculated in accordance with the relevant data for the previous year where in the relevant year the annual sum was due to be increased or decreased or commenced under the relevant sub-paragraph of paragraph 1 of part(s) 2 or 3.

8.2.   Any balancing payment due to the claimant or the NHSLA shall be made within 28 days after the publication of all the relevant data by the ONS.

8.3.   The NHSLA shall pay interest at the then applicable Judgment Act rate on any outstanding periodical payment or part of a periodical payment not paid on 15 December in any year from 16 December in that year until full payment is made, except that in the circumstances contemplated in paragraphs 8.1-2 interest due on any balancing payment shall only be payable by the NHSLA from 28 days after publication of all the relevant data until full payment is made.

9.   For the period from [the date when the future loss period accrues assuming periodical payments relate only to future loss] to [14 December of the relevant year when the periodical payments will commence] to represent the periodical payment under part(s) 2 and 3 of this schedule for that period the Defendant do pay the sum of [£] ( ) due as the balance of the periodical payment for the above period and that sum shall be paid 4.00 pm on the [ ].

Part 2: The RPI-Linked Periodical Payments

1.   The following present value annual sums as recalculated in accordance with paragraph 3 shall be paid in advance:

1.1   The annual sum of [£] ( ) payable on the 15th of December in each year from 15th December [ ] until 15th December [ ] inclusive, with the first such payment to be made on 15th December [ ]

1.2 The annual sum of [£] ( ) payable on the 15th of December in each year from 15th December [ ] until 15th December [ ] inclusive

1.3 The annual sum of [£] ( ) payable on 15th of December in each year from 15th December [ ]

The expiry of one period and the commencement of another period under the above sub-paragraphs constitutes a "step change" under this Schedule

2. The index to be applied is the United Kingdom General Index of Retail Prices for all items ['RPI'] published by the ONS (January 1987 = 100) or any equivalent or comparable measure which in the parties' reasonable opinion replaces such index from time to time. In the event of a dispute between the parties as to the appropriate alternative measure and/or the formulae to be applied in the event of a rebasing of RPI the same shall be determined by the court

3. Each periodical payment referred to in paragraph 1 *[1.1 to 1.3]* above shall be recalculated annually in November in each year prior to payment on 15th December of the same year from November [ ] in accordance with the following formula

$$PP = \frac{C \times NP}{A}$$

3.1 Where

3.1.1 *'PP'* = the amount payable by way of periodical payment in each year, the first *PP* being the payment made on 15th December [ ]

3.1.2 *'C'* = the relevant annual sum set out in paragraph 1 *[1.1 to 1.3]* above respectively

3.1.3 *'NP'* = the index applicable to September in the year in which the calculation is being carried out, the first NF being in respect of September [ ]

3.1.4 *'A'* = the index applicable to [the index applicable to three months prior to the date of settlement or judgment]

Part 3: The ASHE 6115-Linked Periodical Payments

1. The following present value annual sums as recalculated in accordance with paragraphs 3-10 shall be paid in advance

1.1 The annual sum of [£] ( ) payable on 15th December in each year from [ ] until 15th December [ ] inclusive, with the first such payment to be made on 15th December [ ]

1.2 The annual sum of [£] ( ) payable on 15th December in each year from [ ] until 15th December [ ] inclusive

1.3 The annual sum of [£] ( ) payable on 15th December in each year from [ ]

The expiry of one period and the commencement of another period under the above sub-paragraphs constitutes a "step change" under this Schedule

2. The relevant earnings data are the gross hourly pay for *"all"*2 employees given by the present Standard Occupational Category [*'SOC'*] for (Care assistants and home carers) [*'6115'*] at the relevant percentile shown below (currently in table 14.5a at the tab for *"all"* employees) of the Annual Survey of Hours and Earnings in the United Kingdom [*'ASHE'*] published by the ONS. The original relevant percentiles are:

2.1 [ ] percentile shall be applied to paragraphs [ ] above

2.2   [ ] percentile shall be applied to paragraphs [ ] above

First payment of periodical payments under each step

3.   Unless paragraphs 5-10 below apply, the annual periodical payments referred to in paragraph 1 *[1.1 to 1.3]* above shall be recalculated in November prior to payment on the 15th December of the same year from November [ ] in accordance with the following formula

$$PP = C \times \frac{NP}{A}$$

3.1   Where
3.1.1   *'PP'* = the amount payable by way of periodical payment in each year being calculated in November and paid on the 15th of December the first *'PP'* being the payment on the 15th of December [ ]
3.1.2   *'C'* = the relevant annual sum set out in paragraph 1 *[1.1 to 1.3]* above respectively
3.1.3   *'NP'* = the *"first release"* hourly gross wage rate published by the ONS for the relevant percentile of ASHE SOC 6115 for *"all"* employees for the year in which the calculation is being carried out, the first *NP* being the figure applicable to the year [ ] published in or around October [ ]
3.1.4   *'A'* = the *"revised"* hourly gross wage rate for the relevant percentile of ASHE SOC 6115 for all employees applicable to [ ] and published by the ONS in or around October [ ]. In the event of a correction by the ONS it will be the replacement *"revised"* figure issued by the ONS.

Subsequent payment of periodical payments under each step

4.   Unless paragraphs 5-10 below apply, the annual periodical payments referred to in paragraph 1 *[1.1 to 1.3]* above shall be recalculated annually in subsequent years in November in each year prior to payment on the 15th December of the same year from November [ ] in accordance with the following formula

$$PP = C \times \frac{NP + (NF - OP)}{A}$$

4.1   Where in addition to the definitions previously set out
4.1.1   *'NF'* = the *"revised"* hourly gross wage rate published by the ONS for the relevant percentile of ASHE SOC 6115 for *"all"* employees for the year prior to the year in which the calculation is being carried out, the first *NF* being that applicable to the year [ ] and published in or around October [ ]
4.1.2   *'OP'* = the *"first release"* hourly gross wage rate published by the ONS for the relevant percentile of ASHE SOC 6115 for *"all"* employees for the year prior to the year in which the calculation is being carried out, the first *OP* being the figure applicable to the year [ ] published in or around October [ ].

Payments upon reclassification of the SOC or a change of methodology by the ONS

5.   Reclassification for the purposes of paragraphs 6-9 below occurs when the ONS publishes for the same year *"revised"* hourly gross wage rates for both:

5.1   the previously applied SOC (for which the "*revised*" wage rate is defined as 'AF' in paragraph 6.1.1 below) and

5.2   for a new SOC (for which the "*revised*" wage rate is defined as '*AR*' in paragraph 7.1.4 below) that includes those currently defined as "*home carers*" in ASHE SOC 6115.

In that event the new SOC shall be applied.

6.   The relevant annual sum referable to the sums at paragraph 1 *[1.1 to 1.3]* above following reclassification shall be known as '*CR*' and shall be calculated only in the year of reclassification, in accordance with the following formula

$$CR = C \times \frac{AF}{A}$$

6.1   Where in addition to the definitions previously set out

6.1.1   '*AF*' = the final published "*revised*" hourly gross wage rate for the relevant percentile of the previously applied SOC for "*all*" employees

7.   When reclassification occurs the first payment only shall be

$$PPR = [CR \times \frac{NPR}{AR}] + [AF - \frac{OPF}{A}]$$

The second bracket of the above formula shall not apply where at the time of reclassification, either (a) there has been no periodical payment made in the previous year or (b) where at that time a step change in the annual sum is due under paragraph 1 above and in those circumstances the first payment shall be calculated in accordance with the following formula

$$PPR = \frac{CR \times NPR}{AR}$$

7.1   Where in addition to the definitions previously set out

7.1.1   '*PPR*' = the amount payable by way of periodical payment in each year following reclassification

7.1.2   '*NPR*' = the "*first release*" hourly gross wage rate published for the relevant percentile of the new SOC following reclassification for the year in which the calculation is being carried out

7.1.3   '*OPF*' = the final "*first release*" hourly gross wage rate published for the relevant percentile of the previously applied SOC for "*all*" employees

7.1.4   '*AR*' = the "*revised*" hourly gross wage rate for the relevant percentile of the new SOC, when first published, which is closest to *AF*, and the new percentile shall be the percentile to which *AR* corresponds

8.   Until further reclassification the formula for calculating subsequent values of *PPR* shall be

$$PPR = CR \times \frac{NPR + (NFR - OPR)}{AR}$$

8.1   Where in addition to the definitions previously set out

8.1.1   '*NFR*' = the "*revised*" hourly gross wage rate published for the relevant percentile of the new SOC following reclassification for the year prior to the year in which the calculation is being carried out

8.1.2   *'OPR'* = the *"first release"* hourly gross wage rate published for the relevant percentile in the new SOC following reclassification for the year prior to the year in which the calculation is being carried out

9.   Further reclassifications shall be dealt with in the same way by the application of paragraphs 5-8 above

10.   For the purposes of this part a change of methodology occurs when the ONS publishes two sets of data for the applied SOC. In that event, the same process as set out in paragraphs 6-9 above shall be undertaken. However, in these circumstances references to

10.1   *'reclassification'* shall be treated as being a reference to *'a change of methodology'*,

10.2   *'the new SOC'* shall be treated as being a reference to *'the existing SOC using the new methodology'*, and

10.3   *'the previously applied SOC'* shall be treated as being a reference to *'the existing SOC using the old methodology'*.

Miscellaneous

11.   In the event of a dispute between the parties arising out of the application of this Part, there be liberty to apply.

P Personal Injury Schedules in the Employment Tribunal

I Introduction

[P1] Since *Sheriff v Klyne Tugs (Lowestoft) Ltd*[1], it has been confirmed that the employment tribunal has jurisdiction to hear claims for damages in discrimination cases in which the damages include claims indistinguishable from personal injury claims.

1   [1999] ICR 1170.

[P2] The measure of damages is the same as it would be before an ordinary court[1], except that the employment tribunal can award damages for 'injury to feelings'[2]. Injury to feelings is not compensatable in the common law courts in the absence of personal injury. This chapter concentrates on how damages and interest differ between claims at common law and the employment tribunal.

1   Race Relations Act 1976 ('RRA'), s 56(1)(b); Sex Discrimination Act 1975 ('SDA'), s 65(1)(b); Disability Discrimination Act 1995 ('DDA'), s 8(3); Employment Equality (Religion or Belief) Regulations 2003 ('ROB Regs'); Employment Equality (Sexual Orientation) Regulations 2003 ('SO Regs'); Employment Equality (Age) Regulations 2006 ('Age Regs').
2   RRA, s 57(4); SDA, s 66(4); DDA, s 8(4); ROB Regs, reg 31(3); SO Regs, reg 31(3); Age Regs, reg 39.

[P3] The statutory cap on compensation in discrimination cases was removed following the European Court of Justice ruling in *Marshall v Southampton and South-West Hampshire Area Health Authority (No 2)*[1].

1   [1993] IRLR 445. Sex Discrimination and Equal Pay (Remedies) Regulations 1993, SI 1993/2798.

[P4] Thus, awards in the employment tribunal can be very high. In discrimination cases, the EAT has said that the remedies hearing should be carefully managed, and might well require proper directions and, possibly, the exchange of witness statements[1].

1   *Buxton v Equinox Design Ltd* [1999] IRLR 158, EAT. For the general management powers of employment tribunals, see the Employment Tribunals (Constitution and Rules of Procedure) Regulations 2004, SI 2004/1861 ('the 2004 Regulations'), Sch 1, para 10.

2 Compensation for Sex Discrimination

[P5] Compensation is to be assessed in the same way as damages for a statutory tort[1]. It is not to be assessed according to the tribunal's views as to what is 'just and equitable' – the standard which is appropriate to the calculation of a compensatory award in unfair dismissal. Compensation is to be awarded on the basis that 'as best as money can do it, the applicant must be put into the position she would have been in but for the unlawful conduct of [her employer]'[2]. It is the individual's own personal loss (or estimated loss) which is important, not any hypothetical loss calculated on the basis of how a 'reasonable employer' might have behaved[3].

[1]   *Hurley v Mustoe (No 2)* [1983] ICR 422, EAT.
[2]   *Ministry of Defence v Cannock* [1994] IRLR 509, EAT.
[3]   *Abbey National Plc v Formoso* [1999] IRLR 222, EAT.

[P6]   Morrison J said in *Ministry of Defence v Cannock*[1] that 'Tribunals [should] ... not simply make calculations under different heads, and then add them up. A sense of due proportion involves looking at the individual components of any award and then looking at the total to make sure that the total award seems a sensible and just reflection of the chances which have been assessed'. This view was endorsed by another division of the EAT in *Abbey National and Hopkins v Chagger*[2], where it was held to be permissible for tribunals to take account of the size of the overall award, and the extent to which it relates to the procedural default, when deciding the level of any uplift under the statutory dismissal and disciplinary procedures.

[1]   [1994] IRLR 509, [1994] ICR 918, EAT, at para 132.
[2]   [2009] IRLR 86.

[P7]   It is unlikely that there is a need to show that the loss in respect of which a claim is made was reasonably foreseeable as a consequence of breach of duty (cf negligence claims)[1].

[1]   Cases decided to this effect are under the RRA: *Sheriff v Klyne Tugs (Lowestoft) Ltd* [1999] IRLR 481; and *Essa v Laing Ltd* [2004] IRLR 313.

[P8]   Sexual discrimination may be either direct (either intentional or unintentional) or indirect (either intentional or unintentional or arising out of victimisation)[1]. For losses occurring before March 1996 the tribunal may not award any money compensation if the complaint is for indirect discrimination, unless it is shown that the respondent intended to discriminate on the grounds of sex or marital status[2]. For losses occurring after 25 March 1996, tribunals have the power, if they think it just and equitable to do so, to award compensation even where the respondent did not intend to treat the claimant unfavourably on the grounds of his or her sex or marital status[3].

[1]   SDA, s 1, as the Sex Discrimination (Indirect Discrimination and Burden of Proof) Regulations 2001, SI 2001/2660.
[2]   SDA, s 66(3); *Turton v McGregor Wallcoverings Ltd* [1977] IRLR 249.
[3]   Sex Discrimination and Equal Pay (Miscellaneous Amendments) Regulations 1996, SI 1996/438.

[P9]   The employment tribunal can only award compensation for loss caused by the specific acts of which complaint is made[1]. Thus, if discrimination is alleged to have occurred over a considerable period, the ET1 must specify the principal acts complained of in order to give a summary of the whole picture which is relied upon. In such cases, 'It is particularly important that the tribunal should not carve up the case into a series of specific incidents and try and measure the harm or detriment in relation to each'[2].

[1]   *Chapman v Simon* [1994] IRLR 124.
[2]   *Reed and Bull Information Systems Ltd v Stedman* [1999] IRLR 299, EAT.

[P10]   Where a dismissal is both an act of discrimination and unfair[1] dismissal, it may be important to choose which breach is relied upon. The recoupment provisions (see below) do not apply where the award is made under the SDA, but they do for unfair dismissal. Unfair dismissal awards are calculated to be what a tribunal considers to be 'just and equitable', whereas SDA claims are assessed as a tortious claim would be. In general, a claimant is more likely to profit from a claim based upon discrimination. A tribunal faced with a claim based upon unfair dismissal and discrimination should award compensation for loss, ignoring the upper limits fixed for compensatory awards in unfair dismissal claims[2].

[1]   Within the meaning of Employment Rights Act 1996 ('ERA'), s 94.
[2]   *D'Souza v London Borough of Lambeth* [1997] IRLR 677, EAT.

[P11]   Where the act of discrimination results in the loss of employment, the tribunal should calculate the future loss. In so doing, it will have to make decisions about the chances that employment would have continued had the discrimination not taken place. It is important that this is done by calculating the percentage probabilities, and not by deciding what would have happened, as a matter of fact, on a simple balance of probabilities[1].

[1]   *Vento v Chief Constable of West Yorkshire Police (No 2)* [2003] IRLR 102; *MOD v Cannock* [1994] ICR 918, EAT.

[P12]   Thus, if it is shown that a man has lost his job as a result of a sexually discriminatory dismissal, the tribunal has to decide what would have happened to him 'but for' the dismissal. This involves considerations of the chances that he would have lost his job in any event, making due discount for the vicissitudes of life. Statistical evidence may be helpful, but should be treated with caution as a guide to the future[1], especially in areas where cultural attitudes and behaviours are changing. The tribunal should estimate the percentage chance that he would have kept his job for a fixed period of time. It is a mistake for the tribunal to decide, as a fact, whether he would have kept his job and then to determine compensation on this basis.

[1]   *Ministry of Defence v Cannock* [1994] IRLR 509, EAT.

[P13]   In calculating loss of earnings, deduction should not be made for loss of pension benefits received, but should be made for loss of invalidity benefits[1].

[1]   *Chan v Hackney London Borough Council* [1997] ICR 1014, EAT; cf *Parry v Cleaver* [1970] AC 1; *Smoker v LFCDA* [1991] 2 AC 502.

[P14]   Although there is no equivalent to s 123(6) of the Employment Rights Act 1996 (the provision which allows for reduction of a compensatory award in unfair dismissal on the ground of the claimant's contribution to his dismissal), it has been held that, as a matter of principle, a reduction in compensation can be made in an award of compensation for sex (and other forms of unlawful) discrimination on the basis of contributory negligence[1]. This is because statute deems the wrong, which unlawful discrimination comprises, to be compensated as though it were a tort, and in tortious claims, a deduction for contributory negligence on the part of the claimant is permitted under the Law Reform (Contributory Negligence) Act 1945.

[1]   *Way v Crouch* [2005] IRLR 603, EAT.

3   Compensation for Race Discrimination

[P15]   There are some slight differences in the rules for compensation as between the SDA and the RRA.

[P16]   Race discrimination may be either direct (either intentional or unintentional) or indirect (either intentional or unintentional or arising out of victimisation). In cases of indirect discrimination[1], the tribunal cannot award any money compensation unless the respondent intended to discriminate on racial grounds[2]. The changes made under the SDA did not extend to indirect discrimination under the RRA.

[1]   RRA, ss 1 and 2, as amended.
[2]   RRA, ss 56(1)(b), 57(3); and *Orphanos v Queen Mary College* [1985] AC 761.

[P17]   The tribunal has to consider that it is just and equitable to make an order for compensation. However, once it decides to make such an order, it must award the same measure of damages as it would in respect of a claim in tort. There is no jurisdiction to award only such an amount as the tribunal considers just and equitable in the circumstances[1].

[1]   *Hurley v Mustoe (No 2)* [1983] ICR 422, EAT; cf unfair dismissal awards – ERA, s 123.

4   Compensation for Disability Discrimination

[P18]   There is no reason why the general principles enunciated in *Vento v Chief Constable of West Yorkshire Police (No 2)*[1] and other cases should not apply to disability discrimination cases. Where discrimination results in loss of employment, the compensation recoverable for future loss may arguably be even higher in disability cases than in other types of discrimination. Persons with disabilities face considerable problems in securing employment, and it is reasonable for this to be reflected in the level of awards.

[1]   [2003] IRLR 102 (see below).

5   Entitlement to Interest on Discrimination Awards

[P19]   The relevant regulations are the Industrial Tribunals (Interest on Awards in Discrimination Cases) Regulations 1996[1].

[1]   SI 1996/2803, in force 2 December 1996.

[P20] These regulations are different from the Employment Tribunals (Interest) Order 1990[1], in that the latter is solely concerned with the payment of interest on monetary awards that are paid late[2]. With respect to sex discrimination, the regulations have a wider impact than just discriminatory dismissals. They also apply to awards for arrears of remuneration, for damages under the Equal Pay Act 1970, and to all orders made under SDA, s 65(1)(b)[3].

[1]   SI 1990/479.
[2]   After 42 days.
[3]   Compensation for discrimination.

[P21] The power to award interest is discretionary. However, if a tribunal decides not to make an award, it must give reasons for not doing so[1]. Once the tribunal decides to make an award, there is no discretion as to the manner in which it is to be calculated. It will be calculated as simple interest accruing from day to day[2]. The rate is that from time to time prescribed for the special investment account under reg 27(1) of the Court Fund Rules 1987[3]. Where there is a variation in the rates over the period in respect of which interest is awarded, median or average rates may be applied[4].

[1]   SI 1996/2803, regs 2(1), 7(2).
[2]   SI 1996/2803, reg 3(1).
[3]   SI 1987/821.
[4]   SI 1996/2803, reg 3(3).

[P22] The 'relevant period' is the period beginning with the contravention or discriminatory act complained of[1] and ending with the day when the tribunal calculates the interest[2]. Interest is to be calculated on the whole of the sum at the applicable rate for the period from the mid-point date of the relevant period[3], unless the sum is a claim for injury to feelings, which attracts interest for the whole of the relevant period. The tribunal can, in exceptional circumstances and where serious injustice would be caused, change the relevant period for which interest is payable[4].

[1]   By way of example, in *Doshoki v Draeger* [2002] IRLR 340 the discriminatory act was taken as the second racial taunt.
[2]   SI 1996/2803, reg 5.
[3]   SI 1996/2803, regs 6(1), 4.
[4]   SI 1996/2803, reg 6(3).

[P23] There are special provisions where a payment has been made by the respondent before the day of calculation[1].

[1]   SI 1996/2803, reg 6(2).

[P24] The tribunal must stipulate, in the written statement of reasons, the total amount of interest awarded, together with a breakdown of its calculation[1].

[1]   SI 1996/2803, reg 7(1).

[P25] Once an award is made under the relevant discrimination regulation, the Employment Tribunals (Interest) Order 1990[1] will take effect, with interest accruing on the day immediately following the relevant decision day[2]. However, no interest will be payable under the Order if payment of the full amount of the award is made within 14 days after that date[3].

1   SI 1990/479.
2   SI 1996/2803, reg 8(1).
3   SI 1996/2803, reg 8(2).

6   Injury to Feelings

[P26]   The Court of Appeal has given guidance on the assessment of compensation for injury to feelings[1]. Earlier decisions indicating the proper limits for awards for injury to feelings should be treated with extreme caution, and it is not proposed to deal with them here.

1   *Vento v Chief Constable of West Yorkshire Police (No 2)* [2003] IRLR 102.

[P27]   In *Vento v Chief Constable of West Yorkshire Police (No 2)*[1], Ms Vento had joined the West Yorkshire Police as a probationary constable in December 1995. She had a long-held ambition to join the police force, but was unable to do so until the height requirements were relaxed in that year. After her marriage broke down in 1996, she claimed there was a change in attitude towards her from her superiors, alleging that they began to show an unwarranted interest in her private life, that they bullied her and subjected her to sexual harassment and that they placed her under undue scrutiny. She was not confirmed in post at the end of her probationary period in December 1997 and was therefore dismissed. One of the chief grounds given for this was that she had given a dishonest response to a superior officer. She successfully claimed that she had been discriminated against on the grounds of sex.

1   [2003] IRLR 102.

[P28]   The tribunal's award of compensation of £257,844 included £65,000 for injury to feelings, including £15,000 by way of aggravated damages and £9,000 for personal injury. The award of £50,000 for injury to feelings reflected the tribunal's finding that she had been subjected to bullying from her superiors following the breakdown of her marriage, that this contributed to clinical depression, and that she had then had the shock and disappointment of being dismissed and going through a tribunal hearing at which her private life had been subjected to minute scrutiny. She also lost a satisfying and congenial career. The additional award of £15,000 for aggravated damages reflected the tribunal's finding that the Chief Constable and his officers had acted throughout in a high-handed manner and that their attitude was one of institutional denial.

[P29]   The EAT reduced the award for injury to feelings, including aggravated damages, from £65,000 to £30,000, and the Court of Appeal awarded £18,000 for injury to feelings plus £5,000 aggravated damages, leaving the damages for psychiatric injury at £9,000. Mummery LJ gave general guidance at [65]–[68] of the decision:

> '65. Employment tribunals and those who practice in them might find it helpful if this court were to identify three broad bands of compensation for injury to feelings, as distinct from compensation for psychiatric or similar personal injury.

(i) The top band should normally be between £15,000 and £25,000. Sums in this range should be awarded in the most serious cases, such as where there has been a lengthy campaign of discriminatory harassment on the ground of sex or race. This case falls within that band. Only in the most exceptional case should an award of compensation for injury to feelings exceed £25,000.

(ii) The middle band of between £5,000 and £15,000 should be used for serious cases, which do not merit an award in the highest band.

(iii) Awards of between £500 and £5,000 are appropriate for less serious cases, such as where the act of discrimination is an isolated or one-off occurrence. In general, awards of less than £500 are to be avoided altogether, as they risk being regarded as so low as not to be a proper recognition of injury to feelings.

66. There is, of course, within each band considerable flexibility, allowing tribunals to fix what is considered to be fair, reasonable and just compensation in the particular circumstances of the case.

67. The decision whether or not to award aggravated damages and, if so, in what amount must depend on the particular circumstances of the discrimination and on the way in which the complaint of discrimination has been handled.

68. Common sense requires that regard should also be had to the overall magnitude of the sum total of the awards of compensation for non-pecuniary loss made under the various headings of injury to feelings, psychiatric damage and aggravated damage. In particular, double recovery should be avoided by taking appropriate account of the overlap between the individual heads of damage. The extent of overlap will depend on the facts of each particular case.'

The EAT has updated the *Vento* bands in *Da'Bell v National Society for the Prevention of Cruelty to Children*[1]. In that case, it confirmed the employment tribunal award which increased the *Vento* guidelines according to the retail prices index. The top of the bottom band increases from £5,000 to £6,000; the top of the middle band from £15,000 to £18,000; and the top of the top band from £25,000 to £30,000.

[1]   EAT/0227/09, 28 September 2009.

[P30]   In *London Borough of Hackney v Adams*[1], Elias J applied the *Vento* guidelines to trade union discrimination cases. He said at [9]:

'9. Personal injury comparisons

In our view, there is no need for a tribunal expressly to seek to locate where it would place the facts of the case before it in the framework of the awards given for injuries in personal injury cases. The court in *Vento* approved certain observations of Smith J in *HM Prison Service v Johnson* [1997] IRLR 162, when she said:

"Awards should bear some general broad similarity to the range of awards in personal injury cases. We do not think that this is done by reference to any particular type of personal injury award, rather to the whole range of such awards".'

[1]   [2003] IRLR 402.

[P31]   More recently, in *Virgo Fidelis Senior School v Boyle*[1], Judge Ansell (presiding) applied the *Vento* guidelines to 'whistleblower' cases[2].

[1]   [2004] IRLR 268, EAT.
[2]   ERA, s 47B.

[P32] In cases which involve multiple forms of prohibited discrimination, how is the tribunal to award injury to feelings? In *Al Jumard v Clwyd Leisure Ltd*[1], the employment tribunal had found that there had been discrimination on grounds of both race and disability, and made a single, composite award for injury to feelings. On appeal, the EAT ruled that this was not the correct approach as, in this case, the acts complained of fell separately into the different categories of discrimination and should, therefore, have been considered separately with respect to those acts. Where more than one form of discrimination arises out of the same facts, however, the EAT recognised that it could be artificial to ask to what extent each separate head of discrimination has contributed to the injury to feelings, and a single, composite award might well be appropriate. The correct approach will depend on the particular facts of the case, although at the end of any such exercise a tribunal must 'stand back and have regard to the overall magnitude of the global sum to ensure that it is proportionate and that there is no double counting in the calculation'.

[1]   [2008] IRLR 345, EAT.

7 Taxation of Awards for Injury to Feelings[1]

[P33] The EAT has recently decided that awards, insofar as they are for injury to feelings in a sex discrimination case, are not subject to taxation and therefore should not be grossed up accordingly[2].

[1]   It should be noted that the rest of the award is liable to be taxed, and therefore must be grossed up.
[2]   *Vince-Cain v Orthet Ltd* [2004] IRLR 857.

[P34] However, the position of the HM Revenue and Customs is more complicated. A termination payment is exempt from tax under the Income Tax (Earnings and Pensions) Act 2003 ('ITEPA'), s 401 if it is paid 'on account of an injury to the holder of an office or employment; or the disability of such a person'.

[P35] 'Injury' is construed as physical injury and does not include 'injury to feelings'[1].

[1]   ITEPA, s 406(b). See www.hmrc.gov.uk, Employment Income Manual EIM13610.

[P36] The High Court has decided in *Hasted v Homer*[1] that two tests have to be satisfied for the disability exception to apply:

(i)   there must be an identified medical condition that disables or prevents the employee from carrying out his or her other duties (this requires medical evidence[2]); and

(ii) the payment must be made on account of that disability and on account of nothing else.

[1]   (67TC439).
[2]   EIM13630.

[P37] Statutory compensation for discrimination is only taxable if it is 'connected'[1] with the termination. If the settlement or decision does not specify what payment is so connected, HM Revenue and Customs will apportion the payment on a just and reasonable basis[2]. Therefore, if the injury to feelings award is based in respect of a dismissal and acts of discrimination prior to dismissal, HM Revenue and Customs will tax that portion which it considers relates to the dismissal.

[1]   EIM13012.
[2]   EIM12965.

[P38]   In cases where the dismissal has contributed to the injury to feelings, it would be prudent to ask the tribunal to specify (or, if the case settles, to agree between the parties) that part of the injury to feelings award that relates to dismissal as opposed to the conduct of the employer prior to dismissal. The former is not taxable, but the latter is.

8   Personal Injury Awards

[P39]   In principle, injury to feelings and psychiatric injury are distinct[1]. In practice, however, the two types of injury are not always easily separable, giving rise to a risk of double recovery. In a given case, it may be impossible to say with any certainty or precision when the distress and humiliation that may be inflicted on the victim of discrimination becomes a recognised psychiatric illness, such as depression. Injury to feelings can cover a very wide range. At the lower end are comparatively minor instances of upset or distress, typically caused by one-off acts or episodes of discrimination. At the upper end, the victim is likely to be suffering from serious and prolonged feelings of humiliation, low self-esteem and depression; and, in these cases, it may be fairly arbitrary as to whether the symptoms are put before the tribunal as a psychiatric illness, supported by a formal diagnosis and/or expert evidence.

[1]   SDA, s 66(4) provides: 'For the avoidance of doubt it is hereby declared that damages in respect of an unlawful act of discrimination may include compensation for injury to feelings whether or not they include compensation under any other head'. The other anti-discrimination legislation has the same wording.

[P40]   There is nothing wrong, in principle, in a tribunal treating 'stress and depression' as part of the injury to be compensated for under the heading 'injury to feelings', provided it clearly identifies the main elements in the victim's condition which the award is intended to reflect (including any psychiatric injury) and the findings in relation to them. But, where separate awards are made, tribunals must be alert to the risk that what is essentially the same suffering may be being compensated twice under different heads[1].

[1]   As happened in *Birmingham City Council v Jaddoo* UKEAT/0448/04/LA.

[P41]   In appropriate cases, it will be possible to award, in addition to a sum for injury to feelings, a sum in respect of compensation for personal injuries caused by discrimination which results in psychiatric damage. In other cases the award may be a seamless whole. *HM Prison Service v Salmon*[1] illustrates this. Dawn Salmon was one of only three women out of 120 prison officers at Canterbury prison. She was employed there from September 1991. She was increasingly unhappy about the sexualised nature of her working environment. This culminated in an incident in October 1996, when a male colleague, Officer David, wrote offensive and sexually degrading comments about her in the dock book at Canterbury Crown Court. This led to her being off work with what was later diagnosed as a moderate to severe depressive illness. Eventually she took medical retirement in December 1997. Mrs Salmon successfully claimed that she had been discriminated against on grounds of sex by the Prison Service and by Officer David. The employment tribunal found that the Prison Service had created a humiliating working environment for women officers. Male colleagues openly read pornographic magazines and engaged in unacceptable sexual banter. The tribunal found that Officer David's comment in the dock book amounted to sexual harassment. The tribunal awarded compensation of £76,344.88 against the Prison Service. This included £45,094.88 in respect of loss of earnings, £20,000 for injury to feelings, and £11,250 compensation for personal injury in respect of the psychiatric damage caused to Mrs Salmon. This latter figure was arrived at by assessing 'full' compensation for her injury at £15,000, on the basis that her illness fell within the category of 'moderately severe' psychiatric damage as defined in the 1998 edition of the Judicial Studies Board Guidelines for personal injury damages, for which a bracket of £9,500 to £27,500 was given. The tribunal then reduced the £15,000 by 25% on the basis that her depressive illness was only caused to the extent of 75% by the acts of discrimination which had been proved. The award of £20,000 for injury to feelings included £5,000 aggravated damages. A further £1,000 under this head was awarded to be paid by Officer David.

1   [2001] IRLR 425.

[P42]   The EAT (Mr Recorder Underhill QC presiding) dismissed the appeal. It held that the employment tribunal did not err in assessing the applicant's damages for psychiatric injury resulting from sexual harassment at £15,000 and then discounting that by 25% on the basis that her depressive illness was only caused to the extent of 75% by the acts of discrimination which had been proved. The assessment of damages for psychiatric injury caused by an act of unlawful discrimination is a matter of fact to be determined by the employment tribunal, which can only be overturned on appeal if the tribunal has made an error of principle or arrived at a figure which is so high or so low as to be perverse. There was no error of law or principle in the figure of £15,000, which was entirely within the range of possible awards for a psychiatric illness of the severity and duration of that suffered by the applicant.

[P43]   The Court of Appeal held that the employment tribunal also did not err in making a 25% reduction to the compensation which it would otherwise have awarded in respect of the applicant's psychiatric injury, on the basis that this was an appropriate apportionment of the extent of the contribution which the unlawful conduct by the employers made to the causation of the applicant's illness. Such an exercise is inevitably a very broad assessment, which cannot be performed with any precision. Although the applicant was a vulnerable personality who might have suffered a serious psychiatric illness in any event, there was ample evidence on which the tribunal was entitled to reach the view that it was the matters which it held to constitute sex discrimination that were the main cause of the serious depression into which she fell. There was no cross-appeal on the question of the apportionment. The EAT commented that, conventionally, the claimant is entitled to recover on a 100% basis where the tortfeasor's act has materially contributed to the injury in question, even if there may have been other material causes. The other causes might well be relevant to the question as to whether the injury would have occurred in any event. However, in cases of indivisible injury (which most psychiatric injuries will be), subsequent Court of Appeal authority provides that the correct approach is not to apportion damages[1].

1   See *Dickins v O2* [2009] IRLR 58.

[P44]   The employment tribunal did not err in awarding aggravated damages against the appellant employers, as part of its award of compensation for injury to feelings, to reflect its view that the manner in which the employers dealt with an incident in which offensive and sexually degrading comments were written about the applicant by one of her colleagues in the court dock book suggested that the employers perceived the entire incident as trivial, and that the way the incident was dealt with communicated that perception to the applicant. The tribunal was entitled to find aggravating conduct, and it addressed the correct question, namely the extent to which that conduct aggravated the injury to the applicant's feelings.

[P45]   The employment tribunal's award of £20,000 for injury to feelings, including £5,000 aggravated damages, was not so excessive as to constitute an error of law. Although the award seemed to be high, it was not so high as to be perverse.

[P46]   The overlap between the injury to feelings for which the applicant would be compensated and the injury covered by the award of general damages for psychiatric injury was not such as to give rise to a substantial degree of double recovery. Although it was surprising on the face of it that the applicant should receive a higher award for injury to feelings than for psychiatric injury, considering the non-pecuniary award as a whole and the totality of the applicant's suffering, a total award of £31,250 could not be described as wholly excessive. In light of that, the award of £20,000 for injury to feelings was not vitiated by double counting.

9   Aggravated Damages

[P47]   Aggravated damages are available for an act of discrimination where, for example, the defendants have behaved in a high-handed, malicious, insulting or oppressive manner in committing the act of discrimination[1]. Malice or other bad intention on the part of the defendant will provide a reason for making an award of aggravated damages. Such award is likely to be reduced if an apology has been made. Aggravated damages may be awarded because of the lenient or favourable way in which an employer has treated the perpetrator of discrimination. It can also include damage caused by the unlawful act for actions taken by the employer (such as a disciplinary investigation or delay in resolving a grievance), even where the actions are not in themselves discriminatory[2].

1   *Armitage, Marsden and HM Prison Service v Johnson* [1997] IRLR 162, EAT, but not in Scotland.
2   *British Telecommunications plc v Reid* [2004] IRLR 327, CA.

[P48]   Aggravated damages may be appropriate in circumstances where the employer has treated a complaint about harassment in a trivial way[1]. They may also be awarded if the respondent is defending proceedings in a way that is currently inappropriate and intimidatory[2].

[1]   *HM Prison Service v Salmon* [2001] IRLR 45, EAT.
[2]   *Zaiwalla & Co v Walia* EAT, LTL 18/10/2002; (2002) Times, 1 August.

10   Exemplary Damages

[P49]   Exemplary damages may be awarded[1] if compensation is insufficient to punish the wrongdoer and: (a) if the conduct is oppressive, arbitrary or unconstitutional action by the agents of Government; or (b) where the defendant's conduct has been calculated by him or her to make a profit which may well exceed the compensation payable to the applicant.

[1]   *Kuddus v Chief Constable of Leicestershire Constabulary* [2001] UKHL 29.

11   The Ogden Tables

[P50]   The Ogden Tables are actuarial tables[1] produced by the Government Actuary's Department which are widely used in personal injury cases[2]. They provide a multiplier to be used for calculating future loss of earnings up to retirement in a case where a severely injured claimant will not be able to work again in their own field, and thus will be in less remunerative employment for the rest of their working life. In *Kingston upon Hull City Council v Dunnachie (No 3)*[3], the EAT discouraged the use of multipliers based on the Ogden Tables in order to calculate unfair dismissal compensation for future loss of earnings. According to the EAT, the Ogden Tables should only be used where the applicant has established a prima facie claim that their loss will last for the rest of their career.

[1]   They take into account accelerated payment and risks of mortality.
[2]   See Chapter H, Future Expenses and Losses.
[3]   [2004] ICR 227.

[P51]   The ordinary circumstances in which resort is had to the Tables, in cases of personal injury, are where a severely injured claimant will never be able to work again, or at any rate not in his or her own field, and thus for the rest of his or her working life will be in less remunerative employment, by virtue of the continuing handicap: and it is appropriate to calculate continuing loss of earnings up to retirement, with the appropriate discount for the risk of mortality prior to that age.

[P52]   In *Dunnachie (No 3)*, the EAT decided that the Ogden Tables should only be relied upon by employment tribunals in relation to the calculation of future loss in unfair dismissal claims, so far as concerns loss of remuneration and benefits, if it is sought to be, and once it is, established that there is a prima facie career-long loss. Before their applicability arises, such loss should first be addressed by reference to what we would call 'old job facts' and 'new job facts', and which we suggest by way of guidance, but in no way in derogation from the obligation of the 'industrial jury' to apply s 123 of the ERA:

(i)　Old job facts:

would include the following (dependent, of course, on the particular facts of each case):

- Would the applicant have remained in the job anyway: and, if so, for how long? Assuming he or she would otherwise have intended/wished to remain in such job, were there apparent factors, whether personal (health, family situations, location) or economic (new technology, fall-off in orders, lay-offs, redundancies) which on the available evidence, including the experience of the employment tribunal as industrial jury, should be taken into account? Would he or she have taken early retirement, or considered a second career?
- Would he or she have been promoted?
- Would his or her earnings have remained stable (other than by reference to the cost of living)?

(ii)　New job facts:

(a)　The first question is whether he or she would be likely (after using reasonable mitigation) to obtain a new job at all? If he or she has not yet obtained a new job, what steps (using reasonable mitigation) should he or she now take, and what new job is he or she likely to have obtained, by what date and at what remuneration?

(b)　The next question is whether (having taken reasonable steps and mitigation) he or she now has a job, but at a pay differential (or would have obtained a job at such differential if/when reasonable steps in mitigation were taken).

In the latter case:

- Will he or she stay in that job or (in accordance with the obligations of reasonable mitigation) change jobs to one which is better paid, thereby in whole or in part eliminating the differential?
- Will he or she be promoted: to the same effect?
- Will the earnings in the new job be stable (subject to the cost of living) or will they improve: to the same effect?

12　Procedural Guidance and the Ogden Tables

[P53]　The EAT in *Dunnachie (No 3)* endorsed the following points of general guidance in relation to the use of the Ogden Tables in claims for unfair dismissal compensation:

(i)　The employment tribunal should not consider the use of the Ogden Tables until a career-long loss (or differential loss) has been prima facie established. The Tables, which apply to loss to the relevant retirement age, can then appropriately be applied as a useful tool.

(ii)　A rate of return of 2.5% (or such rate as may from time to time be substituted by way of statutory instrument under the Damages Act 1996) should be adopted if the Tables are to be used.

(iii) If such Tables are to be useful, other tables could be produced under the supervision of the Employment Tribunal Service, for example giving answers for loss up to retirement for each year between 50 and 70.

(iv) Employment tribunals will need to develop a practice of giving directions in any case where future loss is sought, along the lines of the schedules and counter-schedules in the High Court. Each party can set out its respective case as to the 'old job facts' and 'new job facts' as a start. If there are to be any agreed schedules incorporating one set of figures, then it is essential that the basis of such agreement should be set out, ie whether the figures were agreed simply as figures or whether they were wholly agreed to be recoverable, subject only to liability.

More specifically:

(i) A party seeking to rely on the Ogden Tables should indicate in advance whether it wishes to rely on the tables and, if so, which table, preferably by way of a schedule submitted within 14 days of the presentation of a notice of appearance. Such schedule should set out the suggested multiplicand, by reference to relevant old job facts and new job facts, the relevant period relied upon, and what, if any, discount is to be made from the multiplier.

(ii) The other party, upon receipt of such a schedule, should submit a counter-schedule of loss within 14 days of receiving the first party's schedule, giving the same particulars.

(iii) In a case in which such steps have not been complied with, a chairman should be robust in issuing orders for further particulars and/or disclosure well in advance of the hearing, so that each party knows what case is to be met and what evidence needs to be called.

(iv) The Tables should not be used by an employment tribunal without giving the parties the opportunity to put forward their case.

(v) The use of actuarial evidence outside the Tables should be discouraged.

[P54] In *Birmingham City Council v Jaddoo*[1] the EAT (Burton J presiding) explained that the guidance in *Dunnachie (No 3)* was intended to apply not just to unfair dismissal claims but to employment tribunals generally and, indeed, in any case in courts or tribunals where there is a real issue as to whether career or lifelong losses arise.

[1]   [2004] UKEAT/0448/04.

[P55]   The EAT in *Abbey National and Hopkins v Chagger*[1] cautioned tribunals as to the use of the Ogden Tables in the assessment of future loss, warning that, if these are to be used, due regard should be given for all relevant contingencies.

[1]   [2009] IRLR 86.

13   Unfair Dismissal

[P56]   Compensation cannot be awarded for personal injury caused by the manner of dismissal[1]. Therefore, it is not proposed to deal with this.

[1]   *Johnson v Unisys* [2003] AC 809.

Q Precedents

Important notes regarding the Precedents

[Q1]

1. Please note that some of the example schedules **contain deliberate errors** so that these may be picked up in the corresponding counter-schedules.
2. Although all the example schedules are based upon fictitious claims, efforts have been made to ensure that figures contained within the examples are as realistic as possible. However, there is an obligation upon representatives to separately investigate and prepare each schedule on behalf of their clients. Appropriate evidence must be obtained in order to support any rates or amounts claimed within a schedule, and the authors take no responsibility for reliance placed upon the rates and amounts set out in the examples.
3. In some of the schedules, figures have been set out in respect of damages for pain, suffering and loss of amenity. There is no obligation under the CPR to detail such a claim, and it is a matter of personal taste and style as to whether items of general damage are to be included in the schedule. See further Chapters A and D.
4. You will see that there are schedules concerning two different Fatal Accidents Act claims. The first schedule has been pleaded on the traditional basis with the multiplier for future loss calculated from date of death; and the second schedule has been pleaded on the basis of the suggested approach of calculating the multiplier from date of trial. Please refer to Chapter L for more details.
5. In relation to the catastrophic schedule of loss, please note that:
   - There is only a very limited *Roberts v Johnstone*[1] calculation because this is dealt with by way of separate examples (one set out in this section and another set out in Chapter H). Likewise, there is no claim for pension loss, as this is covered in numerous separate examples in this section.
   - In a real claim of this size, there may be numerous other heads of loss that would be included in the schedule of loss. Please see further Chapters F and H regarding the potential heads of loss that might be recoverable in such a case. However, in order to keep the example relatively manageable, it has been necessary to be selective, and so only a number of the more common heads of loss have been detailed.
   - There are numerous different ways of presenting the claim for future aids and equipment. Many solicitors now use spreadsheets to calculate the discount factor for each replacement interval. This method tends to provide a more accurate calculation. However, for the purposes of this book, we have opted for the simpler method of using an average annual replacement cost. There are also different ways of calculating transport costs. In particular, it is possible to claim the annual difference in depreciation between the vehicle

that the claimant now has, or has to buy as a result of his or her injuries, and the vehicle that he or she already has and/or would have bought in any event. See further Chapters F and H.

6. All the schedules of loss should end the same way as shown in the schedule and counter-schedule to Claim 1. By virtue of para 1.4(3) of the Practice Direction to Pt 22, all schedules and counter-schedules, and any subsequent amendments, must be verified by a statement of truth.

7. Please note that, when preparing schedules of loss for use in the Employment Tribunal, certain claims may need to be grossed up in order to take account of taxation.

8. The majority of future loss multipliers have been calculated using the Ogden Tables (6th edn) and a discount rate of 2.5%.

9. Schedules of loss can be presented in a number of different styles and formats. A variety of styles have been adopted for the examples. Please note that some practitioners prefer to draft catastrophic injury schedules and Scott schedules in landscape rather than portrait format, because of the additional space allowed for tables with multiple columns. Please also note that, in the schedules regarding catastrophic injury, it is likely that an order for periodical payments would be more appropriate. However, the claim has been pleaded calculated using a conventional multiplier/multiplicand method for the purposes of exemplifying a lump sum calculation.

[1]   [1989] QB 878.

I Questionnaires

(i) General Accident Questionnaire

[Q2]

SECTION I – PERSONAL DETAILS	
TITLE: Mr/Ms/Miss/Mrs/other *please specify*	FAMILY NAME:
OTHER NAMES:	NATIONALITY:
DATE OF BIRTH:	MARITAL STATUS: single/married/ divorced/living with partner
ADDRESS::	
POSTCODE	
HOME TEL:	FAX:
WORK TEL:	MOBILE:
EMAIL:	NATIONAL INSURANCE No:
LEGAL EXPENSE INSURANCE (This should be checked on your household insurance and any other personal insurance policies)	
POLICY NUMBER: POLICY EXCESS: NAME OF PROVIDER: ADDRESS OF PROVIDER:	
(If under 18) LITIGATION FRIEND'S DETAILS IF DIFFERENT FROM ABOVE:	
GP's NAME AND ADDRESS:	
SECTION 2 – ACCIDENT DETAILS	
DATE OF ACCIDENT::	TIME OF ACCIDENT:
LOCATION OF ACCIDENT::	
BRIEF CIRCUMSTANCES OF ACCIDENT:	
NAMES AND ADDRESSES OF OTHER PARTIES INVOLVED IN ACCIDENT:	

NAMES AND ADDRESSES OF ANY WITNESSES TO ACCIDENT:

AMBULANCE CALLED?   Y / N
ATTEND HOSPITAL?   Y / N
IF YES, PLEASE STATE NAME AND ADDRESS OF HOSPITAL

SECTION 3 – DETAILS OF INJURIES

NATURE OF INJURIES:

TREATMENT RECEIVED

EFFECT OF INJURIES ON ABILITY TO WORK

EFFECT OF INJURIES ON DOMESTIC LIFE

EFFECT OF INJURIES ON HOBBIES / LEISURE ACTIVITIES:

EFFECT OF INJURIES ON SOCIAL LIFE

EFFECT OF INJURIES ON RELATIONSHIPS / SEX LIFE

SECTION 4 – LOSS AND DAMAGE

4.1 LOSS OF EARNINGS

Did you lose earnings as a result of the accident?   Y / N

If no, please go to 4.2. If yes, please answer (a) below if you were employed at the time of accident; (b) below if you were self-employed at the time of the accident; and (c) below if you were unemployed at the time of the accident.

(a) Employed Before Accident	
EMPLOYER'S NAME::	EMPLOYEE NUMBER:
EMPLOYER'S ADDRESS:	
JOB TITLE::	JOB DESCRIPTION:

AVERAGE GROSS SALARY:	
AVERAGE NET SALARY (after deductions for tax, NI etc):	
PAID: daily / weekly / monthly / other *please specify*	
BONUSES: Y / N	HOLIDAY PAY: Y / N
OVERTIME: Y / N	PERFORMANCE RELATED PAY: Y / N
OTHER REWARDS eg lunch vouchers, free petrol and private healthcare:	
DATE COMMENCED WORK:	
TIME OFF WORK TO DATE:	DATE RETURNED TO WORK:
MISSED PROMOTIONAL OPPORTUNITIES (IF ANY):	
BENEFITS RECEIVED TO DATE:	
(b) Self-Employed Before Accident	
NAME OF BUSINESS:	
TYPE OF BUSINESS:	
PAYMENT: cash in hand / cheques / BACS / Other *please specify*	
GROSS PROFIT IN LAST TAX YEAR:	
NET PROFIT IN LAST TAX YEAR (after deductions for expenses, tax, NI etc):	
TIME OFF WORK TO DATE:	DATE RETURNED TO WORK:
MISSED OPPORTUNITIES / LOSS OF GOODWILL:	
NAME AND ADDRESS OF ACCOUNTANT:	
(c) Unemployed Before Accident	
PRE-ACCIDENT VOCATION (IF ANY):	
QUALIFICATIONS, TRAINING AND EXPERIENCE:	
EMPLOYMENT HISTORY (INCLUDING DATES):	
NAMES AND ADDRESSES OF PREVIOUS EMPLOYERS:	

LENGTH OF TIME OUT OF WORK PRIOR TO ACCIDENT:

DETAILS OF ANY JOB OFFERS OR OPPORTUNTIES RECEIVED PRIOR TO ACCIDENT:

4.2 PENSION LOSS

If you have a company or private pension and by reason of the accident you have been unable to make pension contributions, please complete the section below. If not, please go to 4.3.

COMPANY PENSION: Y / N	PERSONAL PENSION: Y / N
POLICY No:	WAIVER OF PREMIUM BENEFIT: Y / N

DETAILS OF PENSION PROVIDER:

COPY OF PENSION SCHEME TRUST DEED ENCLOSED: Y / N

COPY OF PENSION POLICY BOOKLET/RULES ENCLOSED: Y / N

INTENDED RETIREMENT AGE: 50 / 55 / 60 / 65 / Other *please specify*

4.3 CLOTHING

(a) Clothing Destroyed / Damaged by the Accident (Including Shoes, Boots & Protective Clothing)

eg jacket ripped in accident bought 2 years ago for £100 value at time of accident £50

ITEM	NATURE OF DAMAGE	AGE	COST NEW	APPROX VALUE AT TIME OF ACCIDENT

(b) Clothing Bought as a Result of the Accident (Including Shoes, Boots & Protective Clothing)

eg larger shoes and socks to fit over plaster cast

DATE BOUGHT	ITEM	REASON BOUGHT	COST	RECEIPT ENCLOSED

4.4 POSSESSIONS

eg damaged jewellery

ITEM	NATURE OF DAMAGE	AGE	COST NEW	APPROX VALUE AT TIME OF ACCIDENT

4.5 MEDICAL EXPENSES

(a) Medical Treatment

eg private hospital and dental treatment as well as physiotherapy, osteopathy, chiropractic treatment, acupuncture etc

DATE	ITEM	COST	RECEIPT ENCLOSED: Y / N	COMMENT

ARE YOUR MEDICAL/DENTAL EXPENSES COVERED BY MEDICAL INSURANCE: Y / N

IF SO, PLEASE GIVE THE FOLLOWING DETAILS:		
MEDICAL INSURER:	ADDRESS:	POLICY NUMBER:
DENTAL INSURER:	ADDRESS:	POLICY NUMBER:

(b) Prescriptions and Medication

eg painkillers, sleeping tablets, anti-depressants, gels, creams and lotions

DATE	ITEM	COST	RECEIPT ENCLOSED: Y / N	COMMENT

(c) Other

eg supports, bandages and plasters etc

DATE	ITEM	COST	RECEIPT ENCLOSED: Y / N	COMMENT

4.6 TRAVEL

Please include all costs incurred travelling to and from hospital, physiotherapy appointments etc

(a) Public Transport

eg bus, tube and train etc

DATE	DESTINATION	MODE OF TRANSPORT	COST	RECEIPT ENCLOSED:Y / N

(b) Travel by Car / Motorcycle

DATE	DESTINATION	VEHICLE	ROUND TRIP MILEAGE	PARKING AND OTHER FEES

(c) Other

eg taxi fares, plane tickets etc

DATE	DESTINATION	MODE OF TRANSPORT	COST	RECEIPT ENCLOSED:Y / N

4.7   CARE AND ASSISTANCE

If you have required any assistance with washing, dressing, cooking, cleaning or driving please complete the following section. If not, go to 4.8.

(a) Professional Care

eg nurse, home help or cleaner

DATE	NAME OF CARER	TYPE OF CARE PROVIDED	TIME SPENT (IN HOURS)	COST (PER HOUR)

IS THE NEED FOR CARE CONTINUING?   Y / N

(b) Friends & Family

DATE	NAME OF CARER	TYPE OF CARE PROVIDED	TIME SPENT (IN HOURS)	ANY LOST EARNINGS

IS THE NEED FOR CARE CONTINUING?   Y / N

(c) Visits to hospital

Please complete this section if any friends or relatives incurred expenses visiting you in hospital

DATE	NAME OF VISITOR	EXPENSES	RECEIPT ENCLOSED: Y/N	COMMENT

4.8 AIDS & EQUIPMENT

Please complete this section if, as a result of the accident, you have had to buy any items to assist with daily life, eg a wheelchair, an orthopaedic pillow, a commode, a walking stick etc. If not, please go to 4.9 below.

ITEM	DATE BOUGHT	COST	RECEIPT ENCLOSED:Y / N	COMMENT

4.9 ACCOMMODATION

Please complete this section if you have had any difficulty with your present accommodation by reason of your injuries. If not, please go to 4.10.

IS YOUR PRESENT ACCOMMODATION SUITABLE FOR YOUR NEEDS?   Y / N

IF NO, PLEASE STATE THE REASONS WHY IT IS UNSUITABLE:

HAVE YOU CARRIED OUT ANY ADAPTATIONS TO YOUR HOME AS A RESULT OF THE ACCIDENT?   Y / N

IF YES, PLEASE DETAIL BELOW

DATE	ADAPTATION	COST	RECEIPT ENCLOSED:Y / N	COMMENT

4.10 DIY/DECORATING/CAR MAINTENANCE/GARDENING

(a) DIY and Decorating

PRIOR TO THE ACCIDENT DID YOU DO ANY MAINTENANCE, REPAIR OR DECORATION WORK AROUND YOUR HOUSE? Y / N

HAVE YOU HAD TO PAY ANYONE TO CARRY OUT ANY DIY OR DECORATING THAT, BUT FOR YOUR INJURIES, YOU WOULD HAVE DONE YOURSELF?   Y / N

IF YES, PLEASE DETAIL THE FOLLOWING MAKING SURE THAT ALL COSTS ARE FOR *LABOUR* COSTS ONLY

DATE	WORK DONE	COST	RECEIPT ENCLOSED:Y / N	COMMENT

DO YOU HAVE ANY OUTSTANDING JOBS THAT NEED TO BE DONE THAT, BUT FOR YOUR INJURIES, YOU WOULD HAVE DONE YOURSELF? Y / N				
IF YES, PLEASE PROVIDE THE FOLLOWING DETAILS				
WORK TO BE DONE	DATE TO BE COMPLETED	ESTIMATED COST	ESTIMATE ENCLOSED: Y / N	COMMENT

Do you have a continuing need for assistance with DIY and decorating?   Y / N

(b) Vehicle Maintenance

DID YOU UNDERTAKE YOUR OWN VEHICLE MAINTENANCE PRIOR TO THE ACCIDENT?   Y / N

IF YES, BY REASON OF YOUR INJURIES, HAVE YOU BEEN PROHIBITED FROM UNDERTAKING THIS WORK?   Y / N

IF YES, HAVE YOU PAID ANYONE TO DO REPAIR OR MAINTENANCE WORK THAT, BUT FOR YOUR INJURIES, YOU WOULD HAVE DONE YOURSELF?   Y / N

IF YES, PLEASE PROVIDE DETAILS BELOW

DATE	VEHICLE	WORK DONE	COST	COMMENT

Do you have any continuing need for assistance with vehicle maintenance?   Y / N

(c) Gardening

DO YOU HAVE A GARDEN?   Y / N

IF YES, PRIOR TO THE ACCIDENT, DID YOU TEND TO THE GARDEN YOURSELF?   Y / N

IF YES, BY REASON OF YOUR INJURIES, HAVE YOU HAD TO PAY ANYONE TO TEND TO YOUR GARDEN?   Y / N

IF YES, PLEASE COMPLETE THE FOLLOWING DETAILS

DATE	WORK DONE	COST	RECEIPT ENCLOSED: Y / N	COMMENT

Do you have a continuing need for assistance with your garden?   Y / N

4.11 SPECIAL ITEMS OF EXPENDITURE

Please set out any 'one-off' or special items of expenditure such as a new car, a special diet or a mobile phone. If you have no such expenses, please go to 4.12.

DATE	ITEM	COST	RECEIPT ENCLOSED:Y / N	COMMENT

4.12 DEBTS OR CHARGES

Have you incurred any debts or charges as a result of the accident such as overdraft interest or interest on loan: Y / N

If yes, please detail below. If not, please go to 4.13 below.

DATE	AMOUNT	CREDITOR	RECEIPT ENCLOSED:Y / N	COMMENT

4.13 MISCELLANEOUS

(a) Incidental Expenses

PLEASE ESTIMATE THE AMOUNT YOU HAVE SPENT TO DATE ON POSTAGE, TELEPHONE CALLS, STATIONERY, FAXES AND PHOTOCOPYING PURSUING YOUR CLAIM:

(b) Photographic charges

DATE	SUBJECT OF PICTURES	COST	RECEIPT ENCLOSED:Y / N	COMMENT

(c) Other

Please give details of any other items of loss or expenses not covered above

DATE	ITEM	COST	RECEIPT ENCLOSED:Y / N	COMMENT

SECTION 5 – CONSENT FORMS AND DECLARATION

5.1   GENERAL PRACTIONER RECORDS

I HEREBY AUTHORISE THE RELEASE OF ALL MY GENERAL PRACTIONER RECORDS TO CLAIMALOT SOLICITORS, 1 MILLION AVENUE, LONDON.

I CONFIRM THAT THE RECORDS ARE SOUGHT IN RELATION TO A CLAIM FOR PERSONAL INJURY ARISING OUT OF AN ACCIDENT AND THAT NO ACTION IS INTENDED AGAINST MY GENERAL PRACTITIONER.

SIGNED:	DATED

5.2 HOSPITAL RECORDS

I HEREBY AUTHORISE THE RELEASE OF ALL MY HOSPITAL RECORDS TO CLAIMALOT SOLICITORS, 1 MILLION AVENUE, LONDON.

I CONFIRM THAT THE RECORDS ARE SOUGHT IN RELATION TO A CLAIM FOR PERSONAL INJURY ARISING OUT OF AN ACCIDENT AND THAT NO ACTION IS INTENDED AGAINST THE NHS TRUST OR HEALTH AUTHORITY.

SIGNED:	DATED

5.3 DECLARATION	
I BELIEVE THE FACTS STATED IN THE ABOVE QUESTIONNAIRE ARE TRUE	
SIGNED:	DATED

NOTES

1. If any section or question is not relevant to you, please leave it blank, cross it through or write 'N/A'.
2. In order to be claimable any financial loss must be reasonably incurred as a result of the accident: losses which would have occurred in any event are not claimable.
3. Please keep a record of all expenditure that has been incurred as a result of the accident.
4. It is very important that you keep copies of all receipts and invoices in respect of any losses or expenses incurred as a result of the accident.
5. Where a claim is made for lost earnings please provide copies of payslips for a period of 13 weeks prior to the accident or provide copies of business records, accounts and tax returns for the last few years if self-employed.
6. Please obtain estimates for items or services that you wish to benefit from in the future.

(ii)   Road Traffic Questionnaire

[Q3]

SECTION 1 – PERSONAL DETAILS	
TITLE: Mr / Ms / Miss / Mrs / other *please specify*	FAMILY NAME:
OTHER NAMES:	NATIONALITY
DATE OF BIRTH	MARITAL STATUS: single / married / divorced / living with partner
ADDRESS:	
POSTCODE	
HOME TEL:	FAX:
WORK TEL:	MOBILE:
EMAIL:	NATIONAL INSURANCE No.
(If under 18) LITIGATION FRIEND'S DETAILS IF DIFFERENT FROM ABOVE:	
GP's NAME AND ADDRESS:	
SECTION 2 – ACCIDENT DETAILS	
DATE OF ACCIDENT:	APPROXIMATE TIME OF ACCIDENT:

LOCATION OF ACCIDENT:
BRIEF CIRCUMSTANCES OF ACCIDENT:
MAKE, MODEL AND REGISTRATION NUMBER OF THE VEHICLE YOU WERE IN:
MAKE, MODEL AND REGISTRATION NUMBER OF OTHER VEHICLE(S) INVOLVED IN ACCIDENT:
WERE YOU A PASSENGER OR DRIVER? IF PASSENGER PLEASE STATE WHERE YOU WERE SITTING:
WERE THERE OTHER PEOPLE IN YOUR VEHICLE? IF SO, PLEASE STATE WHO ELSE WAS IN YOUR VEHICLE, WHERE THEY WERE SITTING AND HOW YOU KNOW THEM
YOUR DIRECTION OF TRAVEL (NORTH/EAST/SOUTH/WEST):
OTHER VEHICLE(S) DIRECTION OF TRAVEL:
YOUR REASON FOR TRAVEL:
NAMES AND ADDRESSES OF OTHER PARTIES INVOLVED IN ACCIDENT:
NAMES AND ADDRESSES OF ANY WITNESSES TO ACCIDENT:
DETAILS OF ANY CONVERSATION(S) AT THE SCENE:

POLICE CALLED? Y / N	AMBULANCE CALLED? Y / N
ATTEND HOSPITAL? Y / N IF YES, PLEASE STATE NAME AND ADDRESS OF HOSPITAL:	

SECTION 3 – DETAILS OF INJURIES
NATURE OF INJURIES:
TREATMENT RECEIVED:
EFFECT OF INJURIES ON ABILITY TO WORK:
EFFECT OF INJURIES ON DOMESTIC LIFE:
EFFECT OF INJURIES ON HOBBIES / LEISURE ACTIVITIES:
EFFECT OF INJURIES ON SOCIAL LIFE:
EFFECT OF INJURIES ON RELATIONSHIPS / SEX LIFE:

SECTION 4 – LOSS AND DAMAGE

LOSS OF EARNINGS

Did you lose earnings as a result of the accident?   Y / N

If no, please go to 4.2. If yes, please answer (a) below if you were employed at the time of accident; (b) below if you were self-employed at the time of the accident; and (c) below if you were unemployed at the time of the accident.

Please answer (d) relating to benefits received in any event.

(a) Employed Before Accident	
EMPLOYER'S NAME:	EMPLOYEE NUMBER:
EMPLOYER'S ADDRESS:	
JOB TITLE:	JOB DESCRIPTION:
AVERAGE GROSS SALARY:	
AVERAGE NET SALARY (after deductions for tax, NI etc):	
PAID: daily / weekly / monthly / other *please specify*	
BONUSES: Y / N	HOLIDAY PAY: Y / N
OVERTIME: Y / N	PERFORMANCE RELATED PAY: Y / N
OTHER REWARDS eg lunch vouchers, free petrol and private healthcare:	
DATE COMMENCED WORK:	
DATE RETURNED TO WORK:	TIME OFF WORK TO DATE:

MISSED PROMOTIONAL OPPORTUNITIES (IF ANY):

(b) Self-Employed Before Accident

NAME OF BUSINESS:

TYPE OF BUSINESS:

PAYMENT: cash in hand / cheques / BACS / Other *please specify*

GROSS PROFIT IN LAST TAX YEAR:

NET PROFIT IN LAST TAX YEAR (after deductions for expenses, tax, NI etc):

TIME OFF WORK TO DATE:	DATE RETURNED TO WORK:

MISSED OPPORTUNITIES / LOSS OF GOODWILL

NAME AND ADDRESS OF ACCOUNTANT:

(c) Unemployed Before Accident

PRE-ACCIDENT VOCATION (IF ANY):

QUALIFICATIONS, TRAINING AND EXPERIENCE:

EMPLOYMENT HISTORY (INCLUDING DATES):

NAMES AND ADDRESSES OF PREVIOUS EMPLOYERS:

LENGTH OF TIME OUT OF WORK PRIOR TO ACCIDENT:

DETAILS OF ANY JOB OFFERS / OPPORTUNITIES RECEIVED PRIOR TO ACCIDENT:

(d) Benefits Received

BENEFITS RECEIVED PRIOR TO THE ACCIDENT? Y / N IF YES, PLEASE STATE WHEN FIRST STARTED RECEIVING BENEFITS: TYPE OF BENEFIT: AMOUNT OF BENEFIT:

FREQUENCY OF PAYMENTS:

ADDRESS OF BENEFIT OFFICE:

BENEFITS RECEIVED AFTER THE ACCIDENT? Y / N

IF YES, PLEASE STATE WHEN FIRST STARTED RECEIVING BENEFITS:

TYPE OF BENEFIT AND AMOUNT RECEIVED:

AMOUNT OF BENEFIT:

FREQUENCY OF PAYMENTS:

ADDRESS OF BENEFIT OFFICE (IF DIFFERENT FROM ABOVE):

4.2 PENSION LOSS

If you have a company or private pension and by reason of the accident you have been unable to make pension contributions, please complete the section below. If not, please go to 4.3.

COMPANY PENSION: Y / N	PERSONAL PENSION: Y / N
POLICY No.:	WAIVER OF PREMUIM BENEFIT: Y / N

DETAILS OF PENSION PROVIDER:

COPY OF PENSION SCHEME TRUST DEED ENCLOSED: Y / N

COPY OF PENSION POLICY BOOKLET/RULES ENCLOSED: Y / N

INTENDED RETIREMENT AGE: 50 / 55 / 60 / 65 / Other *please specify*

4.3 CLOTHING

(a) Clothing Destroyed / Damaged by the Accident (Including Shoes, Boots & Protective Clothing)

eg jacket ripped in accident bought 2 years ago for £100 value at time of accident £50

ITEM	NATURE OF DAMAGE	AGE	COST NEW	APPROX VALUE AT TIME OF ACCIDENT

(b) Clothing Bought as a Result of the Accident (Including Shoes, Boots & Protective Clothing)

eg larger shoes and socks to fit over plaster cast.

DATE BOUGHT	ITEM	REASON BOUGHT	COST	RECEIPT ENCLOSED: Y / N

4.4 POSSESSIONS

eg damaged jewellery

ITEM	NATURE OF DAMAGE	AGE	COST NEW	APPROX VALUE AT TIME OF ACCIDENT

4.5 MEDICAL EXPENSES

(a) Medical Treatment

eg private hospital and dental treatment as well as physiotherapy, osteopathy, chiropractic treatment, acupuncture etc

DATE	ITEM	COST	RECEIPT ENCLOSED: Y / N	COMMENT

ARE YOUR MEDICAL/DENTAL EXPENSES COVERED BY MEDICAL INSURANCE: Y / N		
IF SO, PLEASE GIVE THE FOLLOWING DETAILS:		
MEDICAL INSURER:	ADDRESS:	POLICY NUMBER:
DENTAL INSURER:	ADDRESS:	POLICY NUMBER:

(b) Prescriptions and Medication

eg painkillers, sleeping tablets, anti-depressants, gels, creams and lotions

DATE	ITEM	COST	RECEIPT ENCLOSED: Y / N	COMMENT

(c) Other

eg supports, plasters, bandages etc

DATE	ITEM	COST	RECEIPT ENCLOSED: Y / N	COMMENT

4.6 TRAVEL

Please include all costs incurred travelling to and from hospital, physiotherapy appointments, legal visits and experts.

(a) Public Transport

eg bus, tube and train etc

DATE	DESTINATION	MODE OF TRANSPORT	COST	RECEIPT ENCLOSED: Y / N

(b) Travel by Car / Motorcycle

DATE	DESTINATION	VEHICLE	ROUND TRIP MILEAGE	PARKING AND OTHER FEES

(c) Other

eg taxi fares, plane tickets etc

DATE	DESTINATION	MODE OF TRANSPORT	COST	RECEIPT ENCLOSED: Y / N

4.7   CARE AND ASSISTANCE

If you have required any assistance with washing, dressing, cooking, cleaning or driving please complete the following section. If not, go to 4.8.

(a) Professional Care

eg nurse, home help or cleaner

DATE	NAME OF CARER	TYPE OF CARE PROVIDED	TIME SPENT (IN HOURS)	COST (PER HOUR)

| IS THE NEED FOR CARE CONTINUING?   Y / N |

(b) Friends & Family

DATE	NAME OF CARER	TYPE OF CARE PROVIDED	TIME SPENT (IN HOURS)	ANY LOST EARNINGS

| IS THE NEED FOR CARE CONTINUING?   Y / N |

(c) Visits to hospital

Please complete this section if any friends or relatives incurred expenses visiting you in hospital.

DATE	NAME OF VISITOR	EXPENSES	RECEIPT ENCLOSED: Y / N	COMMENT

4.8   AIDS & EQUIPMENT

Please complete this section if, by reason of the accident, you have had to buy any items to assist with daily life, eg a wheelchair, an orthopaedic pillow, a commode, a walking stick etc. If not, please go to 4.9 below.

ITEM	DATE BOUGHT	COST	RECEIPT ENCLOSED: Y / N	COMMENT

4.9   ACCOMMODATION

Please complete this section if you have had any difficulty with your present accommodation by reason of your injuries. If not, please go to 4.10.

IS YOUR PRESENT ACCOMMODATION SUITABLE FOR YOUR NEEDS?   Y / N

IF NO, PLEASE STATE THE REASONS WHY IT IS UNSUITABLE:

HAVE YOU CARRIED OUT ANY ADAPTATIONS TO YOUR HOME AS A RESULT OF THE ACCIDENT?   Y / N

IF YES, PLEASE DETAIL BELOW

DATE	ADAPTATION	COST	RECEIPT ENCLOSED: Y / N	COMMENT

4.10   DIY/DECORATING/CAR MAINTENANCE/GARDENING

(a) DIY and Decorating

PRIOR TO THE ACCIDENT DID YOU DO ANY MAINTENANCE, REPAIR OR DECORATION WORK AROUND YOUR HOUSE ?   Y / N

HAVE YOU HAD TO PAY ANYONE TO CARRY OUT ANY DIY OR DECORATING THAT, BUT FOR YOUR INJURIES, YOU WOULD HAVE DONE YOURSELF?   Y / N

IF YES, PLEASE DETAIL THE FOLLOWING MAKING SURE THAT ALL COSTS ARE FOR *LABOUR* COSTS ONLY.

DATE	WORK DONE	COST	RECEIPT ENCLOSED: Y / N	COMMENT

DO YOU HAVE ANY OUTSTANDING JOBS THAT NEED TO BE DONE THAT, BUT FOR YOUR INJURIES, YOU WOULD HAVE DONE YOURSELF?   Y / N

IF YES, PLEASE PROVIDE THE FOLLOWING DETAILS

WORK TO BE DONE	DATE TO BE COMPLETED	ESTIMATED COST	ESTIMATE ENCLOSED: Y / N	COMMENT

DO YOU HAVE A CONTINUING NEED FOR ASSISTANCE WITH DIY AND DECORATING? Y / N				
(b) Vehicle Maintenance				
DID YOU UNDERTAKE YOUR OWN VEHICLE MAINTENANCE PRIOR TO THE ACCIDENT? Y / N IF YES, BY REASON OF YOUR INJURIES, HAVE YOU BEEN PROHIBITED FROM UNDERTAKING THIS WORK? Y / N IF YES, HAVE YOU PAID ANYONE TO DO REPAIR OR MAINTENANCE WORK THAT, BUT FOR YOUR INJURIES, YOU WOULD HAVE DONE YOURSELF? Y / N IF YES, PLEASE PROVIDE DETAILS BELOW.				
DATE	VEHICLE	WORK DONE	COST	COMMENT
DO YOU HAVE ANY CONTINUING NEED FOR ASSISTANCE WITH VEHICLE MAINTENANCE? Y / N				
(c) Gardening				
DO YOU HAVE A GARDEN? Y / N IF YES, PRIOR TO THE ACCIDENT, DID YOU TEND TO THE GARDEN YOURSELF? Y / N IF YES, BY REASON OF YOUR INJURIES, HAVE YOU HAD TO PAY ANYONE TO TEND TO YOUR GARDEN? Y / N IF YES, PLEASE COMPLETE THE FOLLOWING DETAILS:				
DATE	WORK DONE	COST	RECEIPT ENCLOSED: Y / N	COMMENT
DO YOU HAVE A CONTINUING NEED FOR ASSISTANCE WITH YOUR GARDEN? Y / N				

4.11 SPECIAL ITEMS OF EXPENDITURE

Please set out any 'one-off' or special items of expenditure such as a new car, a special diet or a mobile phone. If you have no such expenses, please go to 4.12.

DATE	ITEM	COST	RECEIPT ENCLOSED: Y / N	COMMENT

12   DEBTS OR CHARGES

Have you incurred any debts or charges as a result of the accident such as overdraft interest or interest on loan: **Y / N**

If yes, please detail below. If not, please go to 4.13 below.

DATE	AMOUNT	CREDITOR	RECEIPT ENCLOSED:Y / N	COMMENT

4.13   MISCELLANEOUS

(a) Incidental Expenses

PLEASE ESTIMATE THE AMOUNT YOU HAVE SPENT TO DATE ON POSTAGE, TELEPHONE CALLS, STATIONERY, FAXES AND PHOTOCOPYING PURSUING YOUR CLAIM

(b) Photographic charges

DATE	SUBJECT OF PICTURES	COST	RECEIPT ENCLOSED:Y / N	COMMENT

(c) Other

Please give details of any other items of loss or expenses not covered above

DATE	ITEM	COST	RECEIPT ENCLOSED:Y / N	COMMENT

SECTION 5 – ROAD TRAFFIC ACCIDENTS

Only complete this section if you sustained your injuries in a road traffic accident

5.1   INSURANCE

IS YOUR POLICY COMPREHENSIVE OR THIRD PARTY FIRE & THEFT?

HOW MUCH IS YOUR INSURANCE POLICY EXCESS?

DO YOU HAVE A RECEIPT FOR YOUR POLICY EXCESS?   Y / N

DID YOU LOSE YOUR NO CLAIMS BONUS AS A RESULT OF THE ACCIDENT? Y / N

HAVE YOUR INSURANCE PREMIUMS GONE UP AS A RESULT OF THE ACCIDENT? IF YES, PLEASE STATE BY HOW MUCH:

5.2   PRE-ACCIDENT VALUE/REPAIRS

(a) Write-offs

IF YOUR VEHICLE WAS AN ECONOMIC WRITE-OFF BY REASON OF THE ACCIDENT, PLEASE STATE THE APPROXIMATE PRE-ACCIDENT VALUE OF YOUR VEHICLE MINUS ANY SALVAGE OR SCRAP VALUE:

(b) Repaired

IF YOUR VEHICLE HAS BEEN REPAIRED ALREADY FOLLOWING THE ACCIDENT, PLEASE STATE HOW MUCH IT COST TO REPAIR (AND PROVIDE AN INVOICE FOR THE SAME):

(c) Awaiting Repairs

IF YOUR VEHICLE IS STILL AWAITING REPAIRS, PLEASE GIVE AN ESTIMATE REGARDING THE WORK THAT NEEDS TO BE DONE:

5.3   RECOVERY AND STORAGE CHARGES

DID YOU HAVE TO PAY SOMEONE TO RECOVER YOUR VEHICLE?   Y / N

IF YES, PLEASE STATE HOW MUCH IT COST:

INVOICE OR RECEIPT ENCLOSED?   Y / N

DID YOU HAVE TO PAY FOR YOUR VEHICLE TO BE STORED?   Y / N

IF YES, HOW LONG WAS IT STORED FOR?

HOW MUCH DID IT COST?

RECEIPT OR INVOICE ENCLOSED?   Y / N

5.4   CONTENTS OF VEHICLE

WERE ANY GOODS LOST, DAMAGED OR DESTROYED BY THE ACCIDENT, EG SHOPPING, CASSETTE TAPES OR CHRISTMAS PRESENTS?   Y / N

IF YES, PLEASE PROVIDE THE FOLLOWING DETAILS:

DATE	ITEM	COST	RECEIPT ENCLOSED: Y / N	COMMENT

5.5   HIRE CHARGES

DID YOU NEED TO HIRE A REPLACEMENT VEHICLE?   Y / N

IF YES, PLEASE STATE WHETHER YOU HAD TO PAY FOR THE HIRE CHARGES OR WHETHER THEY WERE GIVEN TO YOU ON CREDIT: PAID FOR / CREDIT

COPY OF HIRE RECEIPT/INVOICE ENCLOSED: Y / N

PLEASE COMPLETE THE FOLLOWING DETAILS:

DATE HIRED	DATE RETURNED	HIRE COMPANY	MAKE AND MODEL OF VEHICLE HIRED	COST

5.6 LOSS OF USE

WAS YOUR VEHICLE UNROADWORTHY FOR ANY PERIOD OF TIME BECAUSE OF THE ACCIDENT?   Y / N

IF YES, PLEASE STATE THE PERIOD OF TIME YOU WERE WITHOUT THE USE OF YOUR CAR:

HOW OFTEN DID YOU USE YOUR CAR PRIOR TO THE ACCIDENT?

WHAT DID YOU MAINLY USE YOUR CAR FOR PRIOR TO THE ACCIDENT?

WERE YOU ENTITLED TO A COURTESY CAR UNDER THE TERMS OF YOUR INSURANCE? Y / N

DID YOU HAVE ACCESS TO AN ALTERNATIVE VEHICLE FOLLOWING THE ACCIDENT? Y / N

WERE YOU ABLE TO RELY UPON FRIENDS AND FAMILY TO GIVE YOU A LIFT?   Y / N

PLEASE STATE ANY COSTS OR EXPENSES INCURRED BY BEING UNABLE TO USE YOUR VEHICLE:

PLEASE DETAIL ANY PARTICULAR INCONVENIENCE CAUSED BY BEING UNABLE TO USE YOUR VEHICLE:

5.7   LOSS OF PROFITS

WAS YOUR VEHICLE USED BY YOU FOR BUSINESS?   Y / N

DID YOU LOSE ANY MONEY AS A RESULT OF BEING UNABLE TO USE YOUR VEHICLE?   Y / N

IF SO, PLEASE STATE THE AMOUNT LOST AND HOW THAT MONEY WAS LOST:

5.8   LOST CAR TAX/INSURANCE/MOT

DID YOU LOSE THE USE OF ANY UNEXPIRED PORTION OF YOUR CAR TAX? Y / N

IF YES, PLEASE STATE THE APPROXIMATE AMOUNT LOST:

DID YOU ATTEMPT TO RECLAIM THE VALUE OF YOUR CAR TAX?   Y / N

IF YOU DID NOT ATTEMPT TO RECLAIM ITS VALUE, PLEASE STATE THE REASONS WHY NOT:

DID YOU LOSE THE USE OF ANY UNEXPIRED PORTION OF YOUR INSURANCE? Y / N

IF YES, PLEASE STATE THE APPROXIMATE AMOUNT LOST:

DID YOU ATTEMPT TO RECLAIM THE VALUE OF YOUR LOST INSURANCE?   Y / N

IF YOU DID NOT ATTEMPT TO RECLAIM ITS VALUE, PLEASE STATE THE REASONS WHY NOT
DID YOU LOSE THE USE OF ANY UNEXPIRED PORTION OF YOUR MOT?   Y / N
IF YES, PLEASE STATE THE APPROXIMATE AMOUNT LOST:

5.9   LOST PETROL

DID YOU HAVE ANY PETROL IN THE CAR THAT AS A RESULT OF THE ACCIDENT YOU WERE UNABLE TO USE?   Y / N
IF YES, PLEASE STATE THE TYPE OF PETROL: UN-LEADED / LEADED / DIESEL / SUPER / OTHER, *PLEASE SPECIFY*
HOW FULL WAS YOUR TANK PRIOR TO THE ACCIDENT?
WHAT WAS THE APPROXIMATE COST OF THE LOST PETROL?

SECTION 6 – CONSENT FORMS AND DECLARATION

6.1   GENERAL PRACTIONER RECORDS

I HEREBY AUTHORISE THE RELEASE OF ALL MY GENERAL PRACTIONER RECORDS TO CLAIMALOT SOLICITORS, 1 MILLON AVENUE, LONDON.

I CONFIRM THAT THE RECORDS ARE SOUGHT IN RELATION TO A CLAIM FOR PERSONAL INJURY ARISING OUT OF AN ACCIDENT AND THAT NO ACTION IS INTENDED AGAINST MY GENERAL PRACTITIONER.

SIGNED	DATED:

6.2   HOSPITAL RECORDS

I HEREBY AUTHORISE THE RELEASE OF ALL MY HOSPITAL RECORDS TO CLAIMALOT SOLICITORS, 1 MILLON AVENUE, LONDON.

I CONFIRM THAT THE RECORDS ARE SOUGHT IN RELATION TO A CLAIM FOR PERSONAL INJURY ARISING OUT OF AN ACCIDENT AND THAT NO ACTION IS INTENDED AGAINST THE NHS TRUST OR HEALTH AUTHORITY.

SIGNED	DATED:

6.3   DECLARATION

I BELIEVE THE FACTS STATED IN THE ABOVE QUESTIONNAIRE ARE TRUE

SIGNED:	DATED:

NOTES

1   If any section or question is not relevant to you, please leave it blank, cross it through or write 'N/A'.

2   In order to be claimable any financial loss must be reasonably incurred as a result of the accident: losses which would have occurred in any event are not claimable.

3   Please keep a record of all expenditure that has been incurred as a result of the accident.

4 It is very important that you keep copies of all receipts and invoices in respect of any losses or expenses incurred as a result of the accident.

5 Where a claim is made for lost earnings please provide copies of payslips for a period of 13 weeks prior to the accident or provide copies of business records, accounts and tax returns for the last few years if self-employed.

6 Please obtain estimates for items or services that you wish to benefit from in the future.

2   Claim 1 – Provisional Schedule of Loss and Response

(i)   Schedule of Loss

[Q4]

Schedule of Past and Future Losses and Expenses	In the SKYLIGHT County Court	
	Claim No	1
	Claimant	Mrs Unprepared
	(Including Ref)	Cl/Sol/1
	Defendant	Mr No Way
	(Including Ref)	Def/Sol/1

I. GENERAL DAMAGES

(1)   **Pain, Suffering and Loss of amenity**   To be assessed

(2)   **Handicap on the Labour Market**   To be assessed

(3)   **Interest at 2%**   To be assessed

II. PAST LOSSES AND EXPENSES

(1)   **Loss of Earnings**

More details will be provided in due course following the instruction of an   TBC
employment consultant.

(2)   **Travel and Transport**

More details will be provided in due course.   TBC

(3)   **Gratuitous Care**

The Claimant's husband and family have provided many hours of gratuitous   TBC
care to the Claimant. The Claimant is currently in the process of obtaining a
care report and will provide the necessary details of her claim in due course.

(4)   **Decorating, DIY and Gardening**

More details will be provided in due course.   TBC

(5)   **Medical Expenses**

Physiotherapy to date: £500

(6)   **Interest**

The Claimant claims interest at the full special account rate.   TBC

III. FUTURE LOSSES AND EXPENSES

(1)   **Loss of Earnings**

More details will be provided in due course following the instruction of an   TBC
employment consultant.

(2)   **Gratuitous Care**

The Claimant is currently in the process of obtaining a care report and will   TBC
provide the necessary details of her claim in due course.

(3)   **Aids and Equipment**

The Claimant is likely to benefit from a number of aids and equipment.   TBC
More details will be provided following receipt of the care report.

**The Claimant reserves the right to serve an updated schedule of past and future
expenses and losses.**

DATED this X day of Y

Statement of Truth

*   (I believe) (The Claimant believes)* that the facts stated in this Schedule of Loss are
    true.
*   I am duly authorised by the Claimant to sign this statement.

Full Name: ....

Name of Solicitor's Firm:...

Signed............................. position or office held...

*(Claimant)   (if signing on behalf of firm or company)

(Litigation Friend)

(Claimant's solicitor)

* delete as appropriate

Address for service of the Claimant's Solicitors: <u>PI-R-Us Solicitors</u>, 1 Crescent Rise,
Clapham, London SW8 9BZ. Tel: 0207 495 3333. Fax: 0207 495 4444. Ref: Cl/Sol/1.

TO: the Court; and the Defendant.

(ii) Counter-Schedule of Loss

[Q5]

Counter-Schedule of Past and Future Losses and Expenses	In the SKYLIGHT County Court	
	Claim No	I
	Claimant	Mrs Unprepared
	(Including Ref)	Cl/Sol/I
	Defendant	Mr No Way
	(Including Ref)	Def/Sol/I

PREAMBLE

In default of paragraph 4.2 of the Practice Direction to CPR, Part 16 the Claimant has failed to set out the details of her claimed losses and expenses. This claim involves a straightforward injury and given the length of time since the date of Claimant's accident, there is no reason why the claimed losses and expenses could not have been quantified to date. In the circumstances, this Counter-Schedule is served without prejudice to the contention that the Claimant has failed to serve a schedule of loss in compliance with the CPR.

GENERAL DAMAGES

Items (1)–(3) are to be assessed by the court. The Claimant is put to strict proof regarding her claimed handicap on the labour market.

PAST LOSSES AND EXPENSES

Items (1)–(6) are disputed. No details of the various losses and expenses have been provided. The Defendant is prejudiced from responding to the claim and is unable to take adequate steps to protect himself as to costs whilst the claim remains uncalculated. It is noted that the Claimant says that she is in the process of obtaining evidence from an employment consultant and a care expert. In light of the medical evidence that was served with the Particulars of Claim, a single report from Dr Quack dated 14.1.09, it is denied that evidence from either suggested expert is justified. In breach of the Personal Injury Pre-action Protocol the Defendant has not been put on prior notice of the intention to instruct either of these two experts nor does the Claimant have permission from the court to call evidence from experts in either discipline. As regards item (5), although the Claimant claims £500, no details are provided as to the nature of the medical expenses, the breakdown of the expenses claimed and the dates upon which the expenses are said to have been incurred. Further, no documentary evidence in support of the claim for medical expenses has been provided.

FUTURE LOSSES AND EXPENSES

Items (1)–(3) are disputed. The Defendant repeats the points made as regards past losses and expenses.

STRIKE OUT

The court is invited to summarily strike out the heads of loss claimed in the Claimant's defective schedule of loss or alternatively give the Claimant a limited time (say, 14 days) to properly detail the various heads of damage claimed failing which each head of damage be assessed at nil.

SERVICE OF AN UPDATED SCHEDULE

It is denied that the Claimant is able to reserve the right to serve an updated schedule of past and future expenses and losses as and when she chooses. This is a matter of discretion for the Court when exercising its case management powers. The Defendant repeats the contention that he remains prejudiced until such time as a fully pleaded schedule has been served.

DATED this Y day of Z

Statement of Truth
*   (I believe) (The Defendant believes)* that the facts states in this Counter-Schedule of Loss are true.
*   I am duly authorised by the Defendant to sign this statement.

Full Name: ....

Name of Solicitor's Firm:..

Signed............................. position or office held...

*(Defendant)   (if signing on behalf of firm or company)

(Litigation Friend)

(Defendant's solicitor)

* delete as appropriate

Address for service of the Defendant's Solicitors: Sledgehammers, 1 Field Court, London EC4Y 64E. Tel: 0207 333 4444. Fax: 0207 444 9999. Ref: Def/Sol/1.

TO: the Court; and the Claimant.

3   Claim 2 – Small Claims Track

(i)   Schedule of Loss

[Q6]

Schedule of Past and Future Losses and Expenses

In the FRONTDOOR County Court	
Claim No	2
Claimant (Including Ref)	Mr Whiplash CI/Sol/2
Defendant (Including Ref)	Mrs Airbag Def/Sol/2

		£
(1)	Repairs	1,000.00
(2)	Insurance Policy Excess	100.00
(3)	Loss of Earnings – 5 days to see physiotherapist @£50 each	250.00
(4)	Prescription Charges – June 2007	5.60
(5)	Physiotherapy – 5 sessions @£35 each	175.00
(6)	Travel Expenses	
	(a) to and from physiotherapist 5 visits @£1.00 bus fare each way	10.00
	(b) to and from GP 2 visits @£0.50 bus fare each way	2.00
	TOTAL:	**£1,542.60**

Interest is claimed at the full special account rate of 6% amounting to a total of £185.11 to date and continuing at the daily rate of £0.51 per day.

DATED etc as in CLAIM No 1

(ii)   Counter-Schedule of Loss

[Q7]

Counter-Schedule of Past and Future Losses and Expenses	In the FRONTDOOR County Court	
	Claim No	2
	Claimant (Including Ref)	Mr Whiplash CI/Sol/2
	Defendant (Including Ref)	Mrs Airbag Def/Sol/2

Item	Sum Claimed	Defendant's Figure	Defendant's comments
(1) Repairs	1,000	Nil	Denied. The Defendant disputes that the disclosed repair invoice relates to the accident in question. The Defendant contends that the damage alleged to have been caused by the Defendant pre-dated the accident.
(2) Policy Excess	100	Nil	Denied. The damage to the Claimant's vehicle was not caused by the Defendant and therefore the Defendant is not responsible for any subsequent insurance claim or policy excess.
(3) Loss of Earnings	250	Nil	Denied. The Claimant failed to mitigate his loss by taking days off work to see the physiotherapist. He could and should have visited the physiotherapist after work hours or at the weekend. In any event it is disputed that the accident was causative of the need for physiotherapy.
(4) Prescription	5.60	5.60	This claim may be agreed subject to disclosure of supporting documentary evidence.

Item	Sum Claimed	Defendant's Figure	Defendant's comments
(5) Physiotherapy	175	Nil	Denied. It is disputed that this treatment was required in order to treat the Claimant's injuries. The Claimant already needed such treatment by reason of her pre-existing degenerative changes.
(6) Travel Expenses	12	Nil	Travel costs to the physiotherapist are denied for the above reasons. Further, travel costs are denied regarding the Claimant's GP. His GP's surgery is in easy walking distance of his home and it was unreasonable for him to have incurred these costs.
TOTAL:	**£1,542,60**	**£5.60**	

The Claimant's claim for interest is denied. In any event, interest is awarded at the discretion of the court. It is argued that there has been unreasonable delay in bringing this action. The claim could and should have been brought sooner. In any event the full special account rate was reduced to 3% on 1.2.09 and further reduced to 1.5% on 1.5.09 and has been 0.5% since 1.7.09.

DATED etc as in Claim 1

4   Claim 3 – Fast Track

(i)   Schedule of Loss

[Q8]

Schedule of Past and Future Losses and Expenses	In the BACKDOOR County Court	
	Claim No	3
	Claimant (Including Ref)	Miss Trip CI/Sol/3
	Defendant (Including Ref)	Hazard Council Def/Sol/3

I. GENERAL DAMAGES

(1)   **Pain, suffering and loss of amenity**   To be assessed

(2)   **Handicap on the labour market**   To be assessed

II. PAST EXPENSES AND LOSSES

(1)   **Loss of Earnings**

(a) Period 1 – from 19.4.09 to 18.7.09

The Claimant's pre-accident average pay was £357 per week. She remained unable to work for a total period of 13 weeks: £4,641.00

(b) Period 2 – from 19.7.09 to 20.9.09

The Claimant returned to light duties for a total of 9 weeks @ £107 per week. She therefore claims the difference of £250 per week: £2,250.00

                                                                               £6,891.00

(2)   **Clothing**

Stained blouse   £100.00

Ripped trousers   £50.00

                                                                               £150.00

(3)   **Medical Expenses**

(a) Physiotherapy
10 sessions @ £35 per session: £350.00

(b) Acupuncture
5 sessions @ £25 per session   £125.00

	(c) Chinese herbal remedies		
	20 hand selected remedies @ £7.50 each	£150.00	
	(d) Prescription charges		
	15 prescriptions @ £5.50 each	£82.50	
			£707.50
(4)	**Travel Expenses**		
	(a) To and from GP		
	3 visits - 5 miles return trip @£0.50 per mile	£7.50	
	(b) To and from Physiotherapist		
	10 visits – 75 miles return trip @ £0.50 per mile	£375.00	
	(c) To and from Orthopaedic Expert		
	1 visit – train fare	£17.50	
			£400.00
(5)	**Aids and Equipment**		
	(a) Orthopaedic pillow	£25.00	
	(b) Orthopaedic mattress	£425.00	
(6)	**Miscellaneous**		
	(a) Policy excess	£100.00	
	(b) Postage, stationery, telephone calls and photocopying	£100.00	
			£200.00
			£8,798.50

III. FUTURE EXPENSES AND LOSSES

(1)	**Medical Expenses**	
	The claimant requires another 6 sessions of physiotherapy @ £35 each	£210.00
(2)	**Travel**	
	6 visits to the physiotherapist – 75 miles return trip @ £0.50 per mile	£225.00
		£435.00

IV. INTEREST

(1) **General Damages**

Interest is claimed at 2% from the date of service of the Claim Form.   To be assessed

(2) **Past Expenses and Losses**

Interest is claimed at the full special account rate.

DATED etc as in CLAIM No 1

(ii)   Counter-Schedule of Loss

[Q9]

Counter-Schedule of Past and Future Losses and Expenses	In the BACKDOOR County Court	
	Claim No	3
	Claimant (Including Ref)	Miss Trip CI/Sol/3
	Defendant (Including Ref)	Hazard Council Def/Sol/3

I. GENERAL DAMAGES

Item	Claim	Comment
(1) Pain, suffering and loss of amenity	To be assessed	The Defendant agrees that the Claimant should be entitled to an award under this head. However, the Defendant relies upon the evidence of Dr Botch who confirms that the Claimant should have been able to return to full-time work after 3 months post-accident with a full recovery taking place after 6 months.
(2) Handicap on the labour market	To be assessed	Denied. There is no 'real' or 'substantial' risk that the Claimant will lose her job by reason of her injuries.

II. PAST EXPENSES AND LOSSES

Item	Claim	Defendant's Figure	Defendant's Comments
(1) Loss of earnings	£6,891.00	£3,497.00	The Defendant agrees the initial 13-week period off work was reasonable. However, the figures claimed are gross. The Claimant's average weekly net earnings after deductions for tax and national insurance were £269. Therefore the Defendant allows the sum of £3,497.00.

Item	Claim	Defendant's Figure	Defendant's Comments
			The Defendant denies any loss after 13 weeks. The Claimant could and should have returned to full-time work.
(2) Clothing	£150.00	£50.00	No details have been provided regarding the age or make of the damaged clothing. Although receipts have been provided for the replacement items bought by the Claimant, she is only entitled to claim the second-hand value of the clothes at the time of the accident. In order to take account of the element of betterment the Defendant offers the sum of £50.00.
(3) Medical Expenses	£707.50	£280.00	The Defendant agrees that it was reasonable to have physiotherapy. However, 8 sessions would have been adequate. Subject to sight of supporting documentary evidence, the rate of £35 per session may be agreed.
			Acupuncture treatment is denied. It was not recommended by any doctor and was not necessary in addition to the physiotherapy treatment. From the physiotherapy records it can be seen that the Claimant made a full recovery without the need for further treatment.
			The claim for herbal remedies is denied. These were not taken in accordance with any medical advice. Furthermore, Chinese herbal remedies are not a clinically recognised treatment for the Claimant's injuries and have no scientifically proven medical benefit.
			The claim for prescriptions is denied. At the time of the accident the Claimant was already taking painkillers for her pre-existing arthritic condition. It is denied that the need for her prescriptions is related to the accident.

Item	Claim	Defendant's Figure	Defendant's Comments
(4) Travel	£400.00	£24.13	The Claimant is only entitled to recover the running costs which according to the AA motoring costs (2009) are 17.49 pence per mile for a car costing up to £12,000. Further, it is averred that it was unreasonable for the Claimant to see a physiotherapist so far away from her home. There are numerous people offering similar services in the Claimant's locality and the Defendant will allow for 8 sessions with a round trip of 10 miles each @ say £0.175 per mile.
			The Claimant could and should have bought her train ticket in advance to see the expert saving £7.50.
(5) Aids and Equipment	£425.00	Nil	Notice of this claim was first provided 23 months after the accident. It is denied that the Claimant required these items by reason of her injuries. This claim is not supported by the medical evidence. Any need for these items was caused by her pre-existing condition and she would have needed to buy them in any event. Furthermore, no documentary evidence has been provided in support of the claim.
(6) Miscellaneous	£200.00	£120.00	The Defendant agrees the Claimant's policy excess subject to supporting documentary evidence.
			The claim for postage, telephone calls and photocopying is excessive. The Defendant contends that £20 is reasonable.
Subtotal:	**£8,798.50**	**£3,971.13**	

III. FUTURE LOSS

(1) Medical Expenses	£210.00	Nil	The Defendant denies that the Claimant has any continuing need for physiotherapy. This is not supported by the medical evidence. Any need for continuing physiotherapy is not related to the accident.

(2) Travel	£225.00	Nil	This claim is denied. Any need for physiotherapy is not linked to the accident. In any event, a 75 mile round trip is excessive when there are physiotherapy services within the Claimant's locality.
Subtotal:	**£435.00**	**Nil**	

IV. INTEREST

The Claimant's claim for interest is not admitted. It is up to the court to award interest for whatever period and whatever rate is deemed appropriate.

DATED etc as in CLAIM No 1

5   Claim 4 – Multi-track Fatal Accidents Act (traditional approach using a multiplier calculated from the date of death)

(i)   Schedule of Loss

[Q10]

Schedule of Past and Future Losses and Expenses		

In the NIGHTMARE County Court		
Claim No	4	
Claimant	Mr Unlucky (Widower and Administrator of the Estate of Mrs Unlucky)	
(Including Ref)	Cl/Sol/4	
Defendant	Scaffolding UK Ltd	
(Including Ref)	Def/Sol/4	

Deceased's Date of Birth:	1 April 1954
Claimant's Date of Birth:	1 March 1956
Date of Accident:	1 April 2008
Date of Death:	1 April 2008
Age at Date of Death:	54
Pre-accident Employment:	Part-time retail manager
Intended Retirement Age:	65
Life Expectancy:	Normal
Multiplier for Future Financial Dependency:	6.41
Multiplier for Future Loss of Services:	18.7
Date of Issue:	1 April 2010
Date of Schedule:	1 April 2010
(Assumed) Date of Trial:	1 April 2011

Please note: expenses/losses have been rounded up to the nearest pound.

CLAIMS UNDER THE LAW REFORM (MISCELLANEOUS PROVISIONS) ACT 1934

1.   **General Damages**

   1.1   Pain, Suffering and Loss of Amenity   To be assessed

2.   **Special Damages**

   2.1   Jewellery

The Deceased's watch, bracelet and broach were all damaged beyond repair in the accident. The Claimant will rely upon the valuation report prepared by Mr E regarding the same.	£500

   2.2   Clothing

The Deceased's blouse and shawl were ruined by bloodstains. Her trousers were cut off her at hospital. Her shoes were damaged beyond repair.	£250

   2.3   Travel Expenses of Relatives

The Claimant spent £25 each way in a taxi to visit the morgue in order to identify the Deceased's body.	£50

Subtotal: £800

3.   **Other**

3.1	Funeral costs	£1,500	
3.2	Tombstone and coffin	£1,000	
Subtotal:			£2,500
TOTAL (1, 2 and 3):			£3,300

CLAIMS UNDER THE FATAL ACCIDENTS ACT 1976

4.   **Bereavement Award**

   4.1   Statutory Bereavement Award   £11,800

5.   **Financial Dependency**

At the time of the accident the Deceased was working part-time as a retail manager for Luxury Goods plc, Barking, Essex. Her earnings were £15,000 (gross) or £11,782 (net) per annum.

In line with the NAE index, the Deceased's earnings were likely to have risen by 4% to: £15,600 (gross) or £12,183 (net) on 01.04.95; to £16,224 (gross) or £12,601 (net) on 1.4.10; and £16,873 (gross) or £13,150 (net) on 1.4.10.

Since there are no dependent children, the financial dependency is claimed at two-thirds of the Deceased's earnings: *Harris v Empress Motors* [1983] 3 All ER 561.

5.1   Past Loss

    5.1.1   From 1.4.08 to 31.3.09
             £11,782 × 2/3 =   £7,855

    5.1.2   From 1.4.09 to 31.3.10
             £12,183 × 2/3 =   £8,122

    5.1.3   From 1.4.10 to 31.3.11
             £12,601 × 2/3 =   £8,400

    Subtotal: £24,377

5.2   Future Loss

The appropriate multiplier calculated from the Deceased's date of death is 9.41 (Table 10 of the Ogden Tables at a discount rate of 2.5%).

As 3 years of this multiplier would have been used up by the date of trial, the appropriate multiplier for future dependency is 6.41.

Therefore, the future dependency claim is £13,150   £56,194
× 2/3 x 6.41 =

6.   Services Dependency

6.1   Past Loss

    6.1.1   Cleaning

             Prior to her death the Deceased bore the   £1,440
             brunt of the household chores. Since
             the Deceased's death the Claimant has
             employed a cleaner to carry out the
             tasks that the Deceased used to do. The
             cleaner is paid at the rate of £40 per
             month. Therefore, the total claim for
             cleaning to date is 36 × £40 =

    6.1.2   Gardening

             The Deceased was a very keen gardener   £2,340
             and kept the family garden in immaculate
             condition. Since the Deceased's death, the
             Claimant has paid for a gardener during
             the growing season at the rate of £20
             per week. Therefore, the total claim for
             gardening to date is £20 × 39 × 3 =

    Subtotal: £3,780

6.2   Future Loss

The Claimant's need to replace the Deceased's domestic and gardening services will continue.

The Claimant contends for a lifetime multiplier of 21.7 (Table 2 of the Ogden Tables at a discount rate of 2.5%).

As 3 years of this multiplier would have been used up by the date of trial, the appropriate multiplier for future loss of services is 18.7.

6.2.1   Cleaning
These costs will continue at the rate of
£40 per month or £480 pa.

£480 × 18.7 =   £8,976

6.2.2   Gardening
These costs will continue at the rate of
£780 pa.

£780 × 18.7 =   £14,586

Subtotal: £23,562

TOTAL (4, 5 and 6):   **£119,713**

INTEREST

7.   **Interest**
7.1   Interest on Law Reform Act Claims
7.1.1   Interest on General Damages
The Claimant is entitled to and claims   To be assessed
interest at 2% on general damages from
the date of service of the Claim Form.
7.1.2   Interest on Special Damages
Interest on special damages is claimed   £56
at the full special account rate, from the
date of death to the date of trial (3 years),
making a total of 7.02%:
7.1.3   Interest on Other Items
Interest on funeral expenses is claimed   £176
at the full special account rate, from the
date of death to the date of trial (3 years),
making a total of 7.02%:
Subtotal: £232
7.2   Interest on Past FAA Claims
7.2.1   Interest on Bereavement Award
Interest on the bereavement award is   £828
claimed at the full special account rate,
from the date of death to the date of trial
(3 years), making a total of 7.02%:
7.2.2   Interest on Financial Dependency
Interest on past financial dependency is   £856
claimed at half the special account rate,
from the date of death to the date of trial
(3 years), making a total of 3.51%:
7.2.3   Interest on Services Dependency
Interest on past services is claimed at half   £133
the special account rate, from the date of
death to the date of trial (3 years), making
a total of 3.51%:
Subtotal: £1,817

TOTAL (7):   **£2,049**

TOTAL CLAIMS (1–7):   **£121,762**

DATED etc as in Claim 1

(ii)   Counter-Schedule of Loss

[Q11]

Counter-Schedule of Past and Future Losses and Expenses	In the NIGHTMARE County Court	
	Claim No	4
	Claimant	Mr Unlucky (Widower and Administrator of the Estate of Mrs Unlucky)
	(Including Ref)	CI/Sol/4
	Defendant	Scaffolding UK Ltd
	(Including Ref)	Def/Sol/4

Deceased's Date of Birth:	1 April 1954
Claimant's Date of Birth:	1 March 1956
Date of Accident:	1 April 2008
Date of Death:	1 April 2008
Age at Date of Death:	54
Pre-accident Employment:	Part-time retail manager
Likely Retirement Age:	60
Life Expectancy:	Normal
Multiplier for Future Dependency:	1.57
Multiplier for Future Loss of Services:	12.51
Date of Issue:	1 April 2010
Date of Schedule:	1 April 2010
Date of Counter-Schedule:	1 July 2010
(Assumed) Date of Trial:	1 April 2011

CLAIMS UNDER THE LAW REFORM (MISCELLANEOUS PROVISIONS) ACT 1934

	Claim	Claimant's Figure	Defendant's Figure	Defendant's Comments
1.	General Damages	To be assessed	Nil	The Deceased died instantly at the scene of the accident. There is no recoverable head of loss for fear of impending death: *Hicks v Chief Constable of South Yorkshire Police* [1992] 2 All ER 65, HL. Therefore no damages are recoverable under this head.
2.	Special Damages	£800	£800	Agreed.
3.	Funeral Expenses	£2,500	£2,500	Agreed.
TOTALS:		**£3,300**	**£3,300**	

CLAIMS UNDER THE FATAL ACCIDENTS ACT 1976

	Claim	Claimant's Figure	Defendant's Figure	Defendant's Comments
4.	Bereavement Award	£11,800	£11,800	Agreed.
5.	Financial Dependency	£80,571	£15,291	The Claimant's calculation of past earning dependency fails to take into account the Claimant's earnings of £15,000 net per annum. $^2/_3$'s of the joint earnings of £81,566 = £54,377 less the Claimant's earnings of £45,000 = £9,377.
				It is likely that the Deceased would have retired at age 60 rather than 65. Furthermore the actuarial multiplier of 5.51 should be discounted by a factor of 0.83 for contingencies (Table C). Therefore the adjusted multiplier is 4.57.

Claim		Claimant's Figure	Defendant's Figure	Defendant's Comments
				Since 3 years will have elapsed from the date of death to the date of trial, the Defendant will contend for a multiplier of 1.57 in respect of the unexpired portion of financial dependency.
				The multiplicand is joint earnings of £27,601 (£13,150 + £15,000) × $^2/_3$ = £18,767. Less the Claimant's earnings of £15,000 gives a multiplicand of £3,767. Future dependency is gives a total future dependency claim of £3,767 × 1.57 = £5,914.
6.	Services Dependency	£27,342	£9,929	It is noted that the Claimant and the Deceased already employed a cleaner prior to the accident. Therefore this loss cannot be related to the accident. Accordingly, the Defendant allows nothing for the claims in respect of past and future cleaning expenses.
				The claim for past gardening services is agreed in the sum of £2,340. However, the Defendant denies that the Deceased would have continued providing gardening services past the age of 70. From the Claimant's witness statement, it is clear that at this stage the Deceased and the Claimant would have moved to a private nursing home where these services would no longer be required.

Claim	Claimant's Figure	Defendant's Figure	Defendant's Comments
			The Defendant will contend for a full loss of services multiplier calculated from date of death of 12.73 (Table 12 of the Ogden Tables at a discount rate of 2.5%). Since 3 years will have elapsed from the date of death to the date of trial, the Defendant will contend for a multiplier of 9.73 in respect of the unexpired portion of lost services. Accepting the Claimant's multiplicand of £780, gives a total future lost services claim of £7,589.
TOTALS:	**£119,713**	**£37,020**	

INTEREST

	Claim	Claimant's Figure	Defendant's Figure	Defendant's Comments
7.	Interest	£2,049	£825	Interest should be awarded at half the special account rate, namely 3.51% on all past losses from the date of death to the date of trial. On the Defendant's figures, this amounts to £825.
GRAND TOTAL:		**£121,762**	**£41,145**	

DATED etc as in Claim 1

6 Claim 5 – Multi-track Fatal Accidents Act (modern approach using a multiplier calculated from the date of trial)

(i) Schedule of Loss

[Q12]

Schedule of Past and Future Losses and Expenses	In the SKYBLUE County Court

Claim No	5
Claimant	(1) Tracey Builder (Widow and Administratrix of the Estate of Bob-the-Builder)
	(2) Daisy Builder
	(3) Bill Builder
(Including Ref)	CI/Sol/5
Defendant	Scaffolding UK Ltd
(Including Ref)	Def/Sol/5

Contents   Page

I. RELEVANT INFORMATION

Deceased's Date of Birth:	26 August 1962
Date of Birth of Dependent Wife:	30 June 1963
Date of Marriage:	21 August 1964
Date of Birth of Dependent Daughter:	1 January 1994
Date of Birth of Dependent Son:	26 April 1999
Date of Accident:	21 August 2006
Date of Death:	26 August 2006
Cause of Death	Cerebral oedema
Age at Date of Death:	44
Age at Date of (Assumed) Trial:	47
Deceased's Pre-accident Employment:	Self-employed builder
First Claimant's Pre-accident Employment:	Housewife
Intended Retirement Age:	65
Life Expectancy:	Normal
Applicable Discount Rate:	2.5%
Multiplier for Future Financial Dependency:	13.97 (Table 9 of the Ogden Tables)
Multiplier for Future Loss of Services:	23.08 (Table 1 of the Ogden Tables)
Date of Issue:	1 January 2008
Date of Service:	1 June 2008
Date of Schedule:	26 August 2008
(Assumed) Date of Trial:	26 August 2009

2. SUMMARY OF CLAIMS

Item of Loss	Amount (£)
Law Reform (Miscellaneous Provisions) Act 1934 Claims	
(a) General Damages	5,000
(b) Special Damages	1,458
(c) Funeral Expenses	7,000
(d) Probate Fees	2,500
Subtotal:	**15,958**
Fatal Accidents Act 1976 Claims	
(a) Bereavement	11,800
(b) Past Losses and Expenses	
(i) Financial Dependency	47,664
(ii) Services Dependency	4,500
(c) Future Losses and Expenses	
(i) Financial Dependency	238,687
(ii) Services Dependency	34,620
(iii) Pension Loss	20,000
Subtotal:	**355,884**
Interest	
(a) Law Reform (Miscellaneous Provisions) Act 1934 Claims	1,858
(b) Past Fatal Accidents Act 1976 Claims	5,993
Subtotal:	**7,581**
TOTAL:	**381,080**

3. PRINCIPLES

The Claimant will rely upon the following principles:

(a)   **Multiplicand for Future Dependency**

From an analysis of the Deceased's accounts it is plain that he spent very little of his earnings upon himself and the vast majority of it was spent supporting his wife and two children, Daisy (DOB 1.1.94) and Bill (DOB 26.4.99). Both children are bright for their age and the Deceased spent a lot of money on additional tutoring in the hope that they would go on to higher education (an opportunity that the Deceased never had). Both children had expressed an interest in professional jobs and the Deceased was keen to support them through college and university.

The Claimant contends that, in the particular circumstances of this case, the correct percentage of the Deceased's income to be applied to the dependency is 80% up to when the youngest child, Bill, would have completed university in 2020. Thereafter a financial dependency of 75% of earnings is contended for.

(b)   **Multiplier for Future Dependency (Calculated from Date of Trial)**

The Deceased was 44 at the time of his death and would have been 47 at the date of trial. He planned to work until the age of 65. The correct multiplier for this period is 13.97 (Table 9 of the Ogden Tables at a discount rate of 2.5%).

This multiplier should be split as follows:

(i)   The first period (from trial to 2020). During this period both the deceased's wife and his children are dependants. The appropriate multiplier for this period of 11 years is 9.63 (Table 28 at a discount rate of 2.5%).

(ii)   The second period (from 2020 until the end of the dependency). During this time the deceased's wife will continue to be a dependant but the children will no longer be dependent. The appropriate multiplier is the whole dependency multiplier of 13.97 minus the multiplier for the first period of dependency of 9.63, making a total of 4.34.

As regards the service dependency, the appropriate multiplier is 23.08 (Table 1 of the Ogden Tables at 2.5% discount).

(c)   **Interest**

Interest should be awarded as follows:

(i)   At 2% from date of service of the Claim Form on general damages.

(ii)   At the full special account rate on the Bereavement Award.

(iii) At the full special account rate for one-off items of special damage (such as damaged clothing).

(iv)   At half the special account rate for continuing heads of damage.

4. CLAIMS UNDER THE LAW REFORM (MISCELLANEOUS PROVISIONS) ACT 1934

(a)   **General Damages**

The Deceased suffered a severe blow to the head when the scaffolding platform he was standing on collapsed. The Claimant relies upon the report of Dr Death which confirms that the deceased was in severe pain at the scene of the accident necessitating administration of morphine by the emergency services. He died five days later in hospital following several failed operations.   £5,000

(b)   **Special Damages**

(i) Damaged Items of Clothing Belonging to the Deceased

The Deceased's protective boots and gloves were all damaged beyond repair as a result of the accident.   £500

(ii) Travel Expenses

The Claimant made 3 return trips to hospital to see the Deceased. Each round trip was 50 miles. At @ £0.40 per mile, the total claim is: £60

(iii) Loss of Earnings

The Deceased was earning £90 per day working on site. Therefore the sum of 5 days @ £90 per day: £450

(iv) Child Minding

Whilst the Deceased was in hospital, it was necessary to pay a child-minder to baby-sit. In total 20 hours of child-minding was required @ £8 per hour, making a total of: £160

(v) Gratuitous Care

Whilst the Deceased was in hospital a member of his family was constantly in attendance during visiting hours. The sum of £6 per hour is claimed for 8 hours per day from 21.8.99 to 26.8.99, making a total of: £288

Subtotal: £1,458

(c) **Funeral Expenses**

(i) Burial Fees £1,000

(ii) Wake £500

(iii) Monument £5,500

Subtotal £7,000

(d) **Probate Fees**

Due to the distress caused by the Deceased's death the Claimant employed an outside agency to deal with all matters arising out of the administration of the Deceased's estate and to oversee the grant of probate. £2,500

TOTAL (Law Reform Act claims): **£15,958**

5. CLAIMS UNDER THE FATAL ACCIDENTS ACT 1976

(a) **Bereavement Award**

The First Claimant seeks and is entitled to the statutory award for bereavement under Section 1A of the Fatal Accidents Act 1976 (as amended). £11,800

(b) **Past Losses and Expenses**

(i) Financial Dependency

The Deceased's average monthly salary prior to the accident was £1,500 or £18,000 pa. This was likely to have risen by 10% to £19,800 in 2007–2008 and again by 10% to £21,780 in 2008–2009.

The Claimants are entitled to dependency at 80% of the Deceased's earnings.

Thus the total dependency claim to date is:

For 2006/2007 the dependency is 0.80 x £18,000 = £14,400

For 2007/2008 the dependency is 0.80 x £19,800 = £15,840

For 2008/2009 the dependency is 0.80 x £21,780 = £17,424

£47,664

(ii) Service Dependency

The Deceased provided a number of valuable services to the family (please see further the report of R Biggs dated 4 June 2004). In particular, the Deceased was an expert at DIY, plumbing and decorating. He had undertaken a number of large projects at the family home including retiling the roof, laying a patio and building an extension. The value of the Deceased's services was approximately £1,500 pa. Therefore the loss to date (× 3 years) is:

£4,500

Subtotal: £52,164

(c)   Future Expenses and Losses

(i) Financial Dependency

The Deceased's earnings would have continued at the rate of £21,780. Therefore the loss of financial dependency is as follows:

For the first period: 0.80 × £21,780 × 9.63   £167,793

For the second period: 0.75 × £21,780 × 4.34   £70,894

£238,687

(ii) Service Dependency

If the Deceased had lived he would have continued to provide services to the value of £1,500 pa. Applying a multiplier of 23.08 gives a total of:

£34,620

(iii) Pension Loss

It was the Deceased's intention to start a pension. He would have paid approximately 5% of his salary into the pension fund which would ultimately have benefited the Claimants. Had the Deceased survived, he would have been entitled to tax relief on his pension contributions to the extent of 5% of his salary. The Claimants rely upon the report prepared by Smith & Williamson dated 25 July 2000 and the calculations contained therein regarding the value of the Deceased's pension loss.

£20,000

Subtotal: £293,307

TOTAL (Fatal Accidents Act Claims):   **£357,271**

6. INTEREST

(a) **Interest on Law Reform Claims**

   (i)   General Damages (£5,000)

The Claimant is entitled to 2% from the date of service of the Claim Form to trial. 451 days at 2% interest, gives a total of: £124

   (ii)   Special Damages (£1,458)

Interest is claimed at the full special account rate from the date of death to the date of trial (3 years), making a total of 15.82%: £231

   (iii)   Funeral Expenses and Probate Fees (£9,500)

Interest is claimed at the full special account rate from the date of death to the date of trial (3 years), making a total of 15.82%:   £1,503

Subtotal: £1,858

(b) **Interest on (Past) Fatal Accidents Act Claims**

   (i)   Bereavement Award (£11,800)

Interest is claimed at the full special account rate from the date of death to the date of trial (3 years), making a total of 15.82%:   £1,867

   (ii)   Financial Dependency (£47,664)

Interest is claimed at half the special account rate from the date of death to the date of trial (3 years), making a total of 7.91%:   £3,770

   (iii)   Services Dependency (£4,500)

Interest is claimed at half the special account rate from the date of death to the date of trial (3 years), making a total of 7.91%:   £356

Subtotal: £5,993

TOTAL interest: **£7,851**

TOTAL Claims: **£381,080**

DATED etc as in Claim 1

(ii)   Counter-Schedule of Loss

[Q13]

Counter-Schedule of Past and Future Losses and Expenses	In the SKYBLUE County Court	
Claim No	5	
Claimant	(1) Tracey Builder (Widow and Administratrix of the Estate of Bob-the-Builder)	
	(2) Daisy Builder	
	(3) Bill Builder	
(Including Ref)	Cl/Sol/5	
Defendant	Scaffolding UK Ltd	
(Including Ref)	Def/Sol/5	

Please Note:

This counter-schedule is drafted in response to the schedule of past and future losses and expenses dated 26 August 2004.

The relevant dates as set out in the schedule of past and future losses and expenses are accepted save that it is denied that the Deceased intended to continue working until he was 65.

This counter-schedule is served without prejudice to the fact that it appears that the Claim Form was served beyond the expiry of the 4-month period of its validity.

I. SUMMARY OF CLAIMS

Item of Loss	Claimants' Figure (£)	Defendant's Figure (£)	Court's Award (£)
Law Reform Act Claims			
(a) General Damages	5,000	n/a	
(b) Special Damages	1,458	527	
(c) Funeral Expenses	7,000	1,500	
(d) Probate Fees	2,500	–	
Subtotal:	15,958	2,027	
Fatal Accidents Act Claims			
(a) Bereavement	11,800	10,000	
(b) Past Losses and Expenses			
(i) Financial Dependency	47,644	32,400	
(ii) Services Dependency	4,500	3,000	
(c) Future Losses and Expenses			
(i) Financial Dependency	238,687	60,454	
(ii) Services Dependency	34,620	15,200	
(iii) Pension Loss	20,000	–	
Subtotal:	357,271	121,054	
Interest			
(a) Law Reform Act Claims	1,858	320	
(b) Past FAA Claims	5,993	4,382	
Subtotal:	**7,851**	**4,702**	
TOTAL:	**381,080**	**127,783**	

2. NOTES ON THE MULTIPLICAND AND THE MULTIPLIERS

In response to the Claimants' contentions the Defendant will aver as follows:

(a) Multiplicand for Future Dependency

This case is not exceptional and there are no grounds for departing from the standard approach regarding the calculation of the Claimants' dependency.

It is denied that the Deceased spent very little on himself. The Deceased had a number of personal hobbies which took up a lot of his free time including stock car racing, parachuting and football. It is clear from the Deceased's credit card statements that he spent a reasonable amount of money on these hobbies as well as books, CDs, clothes etc.

In the circumstances, the Defendant aver that the usual starting point recognised in *Harris v Empress Motors Ltd* [1984] 1 WLR 212 should apply, ie that the dependency should be valued at 75% whilst there are dependent children and at 66.67% thereafter.

It is denied that the Second and Third Claimant's dependency will extend beyond the age of 18.

(b)   Multiplier for Future Dependency

(i) Multiplier for Financial Dependency

The Defendant agrees the discount rate of 2.5% used by the Claimants following the Lord Chancellor's Decision on 25 June 2001 to exercise his powers under the Damages Act 1996 to fix the rate at that level.

However, the Claimants' general approach to the calculation of future losses and expenses is disputed. The multiplier must be fixed at the date of death: *Cookson v Knowles* [1977] QB 913. See further ATH v MS [2002] 3 WLR 1179; White v ESAB Group UK [2002] PIQR Q76.

It is denied that the Claimant would have worked until 65. His job involved heavy manual work. His health was already fading and the Defendants will rely upon the evidence of Dr Lang that the Deceased would have been unlikely to work beyond the age of 60.

The multiplier advanced by the Claimant takes no account of contingencies other than mortality. The Deceased's locality was high in unemployment. Although it is accepted that the Deceased was a skilled builder, there is evidence of a general slow down in the building industry following the Deceased's death. As can be seen from the Deceased's accounts immediately prior to his death, his bookings had already started to tail off a little and there was no guarantee of regular work. The multiplier must also be adjusted downwards in order to reflect the risk that the Deceased would have died before the trial of this matter. The actuarial multiplier to a retirement age of 60 is 12.88. Table A suggests a discount of 0.79. However, on the facts of this case a discount of 0.70 is more realistic. Therefore the adjusted multiplier is 9.02. It is contended that the children's dependency would have ended on 26 August 2013 (when the Third Claimant turned 18). Deducting 3 for past loss, the remaining multiplier of 6.02 should be split as suggested by paragraph 22 of the Ogden guidance notes as follows.

Dates	Table 28 multiplier	% of whole Table 28 multiplier (11.12)	% applied to Cookson v Knowles multiplier of 6.02
From trial to 25.8.13	3.81	34.26%	2.06
From 27.8.26 to 26.8.22	7.31	65.74%	3.96
Total	11.12	100%	6.02

The multiplier should therefore be split as follows: (i) 3 in respect of the past loss; (ii) 2.06 for the second period; and (iii) 3.96 for the final period.

(ii) Multiplier for Service Dependency

As regards the pleaded service dependency, it is denied that a full life multiplier is appropriate. As he grew older, the Deceased was unlikely to have been able to continue providing the physically demanding DIY and decorating services that he had provided in the past. It is suggested that a fair cut-off point for this head of claim would be to age 70.

The appropriate lifetime multiplier for loss of services from date of death is therefore 18.20 (Table 11 of the Ogden Tables at a discount rate of 2.5%).

This multiplier should be split into: (i) 3 for the past loss; and (ii) 15.20 for future loss.

(c)   **Interest**

The Claimants' entitlement to interest is not admitted. It is for the Claimants to prove their entitlement to interest. In any event, interest is awarded at the discretion of the Court.

3. CLAIMS UNDER THE LAW REFORM (MISCELLANEOUS PROVISIONS) ACT 1934

Head of Damage	**Defendant's Response**
(a) **General Damages**	
Pain, suffering and loss of amenity – £5,000	It is agreed that the emergency services arrived on the scene promptly and provided the Deceased with pain relieving medication. The Deceased passed out shortly thereafter and did not regain consciousness before he died. The amount of pain and suffering he experienced is speculative and at most is limited to a matter of minutes.
(b) **Special Damages**	
(i) Clothing – £500	No documentary evidence has been supplied in support of this claim. It is understood that the items were all at least 2 years old. The sum of £250 is allowed in order to take account of the element of betterment.
(ii) Travel Expenses – £60	This head of loss is accepted in principle but the rate of mileage is disputed. The Claimant is only entitled to claim the running costs for the vehicle used. The Defendant offers 18 pence per mile (based upon the published AA figures), making a total of £27.
(iii) Loss of Earnings – £450	The Deceased was working 'cash-in-hand' without the benefit of a formal contract. Credit must be given for the tax and National Insurance that should have been paid. Further credit must be given for the expenses that the Deceased would have incurred hiring tools and travelling to work. In the circumstances the sum of £250 is offered for this head of loss.
(iv) Child Minding – £160	This head of loss is disputed – the costs would have been incurred in any event and are not related to the Deceased's death.

Head of Damage	Defendant's Response
(v) Gratuitous Care – £288	The Defendant does not accept that any gratuitous care or assistance was required whilst the Deceased was in hospital being treated for his injuries. The Deceased was unconscious during his stay in hospital and had no need for any care and assistance other than that provided by medical staff at the hospital. In any event, the Defendants will contend that the time spent with the Deceased was more akin to companionship falling short of that which is recoverable as costs of care.

(c)   Funeral Expenses

(i) Burial Fees – £1,000	Agreed.
(ii) Wake – £500	Denied this item is not recoverable in law: *Jones v Royal Devon & Exeter NHS Foundation Trust* [2008] EWHC 558 (QB); *Williams v Welsh Ambulance Services NHS Trust* [2008] EWCA Civ 81 LTL 15/2/2008.
(iii) Monument – £5,500	Denied. The Claimants are not entitled to recover this item of expense: *Gammell v Wilson* [1982] AC 27, CA. However, £500 is allowed for the headstone.

(d)   Probate Fees

Administrative fees etc – £2,500	Not admitted. The Claimants are put to strict proof regarding their entitlement to claim these expenses under the terms of the Law Reform (Miscellaneous Provisions) Act 1934.

4. CLAIMS UNDER THE FATAL ACCIDENTS ACT 1976

Head of Damage   **Defendant's Response**

(a)   **Bereavement Award**

£11,800

The statutory bereavement award for deaths occurring before 1.1.08 is £10,000.

(b)   **Past Losses and Expenses**

(i) Financial Dependency –
£47,664

The Defendant does not accept the Deceased's level of pre-accident earnings as advanced by the Claimants. The Defendant contends that the Deceased's net monthly earnings prior to the accident were more in the region of £1,200 per month or £14,400 pa. It is not admitted that the Deceased's earnings would probably have increased by 10% each year and the Claimants are put to strict proof regarding the same. It is noted from the Deceased's accounts that his gross takings were more or less consistent during the last two years before his death and do not support the increase contended for.

Given the current slow down in the building industry, it is not unrealistic to allow no increase in the Deceased's salary.

Therefore the calculation for past dependency is:

$0.75 \times £14,400 \times 3 = £32,400$

(ii) Service Dependency –
£4,500

The Defendant offers £3,000 in respect of this head of loss.

(c)   **Future Expenses and Losses**

(i) Financial Dependency –
£250,644

The Defendant allows:

$0.75 \times £14,400 \times 2.06 = £22,248$ plus

$0.67 \times £14,400 \times 3.96 = £38,206$

Making a total of £60,454.

(ii) Service Dependency –
£34,410

The Defendants offer £1,000 pa $\times$ 15.2 = £15,200.

(iii) Pension Loss – £20,000

Denied. The Deceased had not made any provision for a pension prior to his death. Any claim for dependency on the basis of a future pension is too remote or alternatively too speculative to calculate.

5. INTEREST

(a)   Interest on Law Reform Claims   Defendants' Response

    (i) General Damages – £124   Subject to the Court's discretion to award interest to the Claimants, the rate is agreed but the amount is disputed.

    (ii) Special Damages – £231   The rate and period of interest claimed is agreed, which on the Defendant's figures amounts to £83.

    (iii) Funeral Expenses and Probate Fees – £1,503   The rate and period of interest claimed is agreed, which on the Defendant's figures amounts to £237.

(b)   Interest on FAA claims

    (i) Bereavement Award – £1,800   Subject to the Court's discretion to award interest to the Claimants, the rate and amount of interest is agreed in the sum of £1,582.

    (ii) Financial Dependency – £4,290   The rate and period of interest is agreed, which on the Defendant's figures amounts to £2,563.

    (iii) Services Dependency – £405   The rate and period of interest is agreed, which on the Defendant's figures amounts to £237.

DATED etc as in Claim 1

7 Claim 6 – Multi-track Catastrophic Injury

(i) Schedule of Loss

[Q14]

IN THE HIGH COURT OF JUSTICE

QUEEN'S BENCH DIVISION

BETWEEN : -

Claim No. 6

MISS ANNIE YUCATAN

(By her Mother and Litigation Friend Mrs DEBORAH YUCATAN)

Claimant

– and –

LAMBETH HOSPITALS NHS TRUST

Defendant

SCHEDULE OF PAST AND FUTURE LOSSES AND EXPENSES

CONTENTS

A. RELEVANT DETAILS

Claimant's Date of Birth:	6 April 1993
Date of Defendant's Negligence:	6 April 2003
Date of Issue:	10 March 2008
Date of Service:	6 April 2008
(Assumed) Date of Trial:	6 April 2010
Claimant's Age at Date of Trial:	17
Claimant's life expectancy:	Normal
Applicable Discount Rate:	2.0%
Earnings Multiplier:	27.4 split into 5 equal multipliers of 5.48 each
Lifetime (Care) Multiplier:	37.8 split into 4 equal multipliers of 9.45 each
Equipment Multiplier:	36.8 (lifetime multiplier minus 1)
Date of Schedule:	6 April 2009

B. SUMMARY OF CLAIM

Head of Claim	Claimant's Figure	Defendant's Figure	Comment	Award
C.	**1. General Damages**			
1.1 Pain, Suffering and Loss of Amenity	£240,000			
Subtotal of General Damages:	**£240,000**			
D.	**2. Past Losses and Expenses**			
2.1 Care	£456,579			
2.2 Equipment Costs	£10,100			
2.3 Accommodation	£11,850			
2.4 Travel Expenses	£7,833			
2.5 Clothing	£3,360			
2.6 Medical Treatment	£26,975			
Subtotal of Past Losses and Expenses:	**£516,697**			
F.	**4. Future Losses and Expenses**			
4.1 Loss of Earnings	£1,260,400			
4.2 Care	£2,315,250			
4.3 Education	£166,600			

Head of Claim	Claimant's Figure	Defendant's Figure	Comment	Award
4.4 Aids and Equipment	£159,073			
4.5 Accommodation	£370,444			
4.6 Speech & Language Therapy and IT	£223,900			
4.7 Occupational Therapy	£37,800			
4.8 Transport	£516,180			
4.9 Treatment	£165,942			
4.10 Prescription Charges	£3,931			
4.11 Clothing	£18,900			
4.12 Holidays	£189,000			
4.13 Court of Protection Fees	£290,891			
Subtotal of Future Losses and Expenses:	**£5,718,311**			
G. 5. Interest				
5.1 Interest on General Damages	£9,600			
5.2 Interest on Past Losses and Expenses	£94,246			
Subtotal of Interest:	**£103,846**			
GRAND TOTAL:	**£6,578,854**			

C. 1. GENERAL DAMAGES

1.1   Pain, Suffering and Loss of Amenity

1.1.1   Introduction

By reason of the Defendant's negligence, the Claimant suffered severe brain damage resulting in significant physical and cognitive deficits as detailed in the medical reports of Dr X, Dr Y and Mr Z. Her continuing problems will be permanent. However, her life expectancy has been largely unchanged.

1.1.2   The Judicial Studies Board Guidelines

The Claimant contends that the appropriate category of the Judicial Studies Board Guidelines (9th Edition) is 2(A)(a) 'Very Severe Brain Damage': £180,000 to £257,750.

1.1.3   The Claim

The Claimant contends that her injuries are towards the top end of the appropriate bracket given the extent of the damage, the degree of insight, the young age of the Claimant (who will suffer the disability for that much longer) and the psychiatric effects upon her. In particular the Claimant's ability to communicate and form relationships has been severely affected. The Claimant will contend that the appropriate award in respect of general damages for pain, suffering and loss of amenity is in the region of £240,000.

D. 2. PAST LOSSES AND EXPENSES

2.1 Care

2.1.1 Background

Since the Claimant's injury, she has required constant care from her parents. Although she retains some mobility, she requires assistance with the vast majority of basic tasks such as washing, dressing and eating. Her need for fulltime care is permanent.

2.1.2 The Care Evidence

The Claimant will rely upon the written report of Mrs X regarding the rates and amount of past care costs.

2.1.3 The Calculation

The Claimant claims a total of £456,579 (rounded up) for past care costs as detailed in the breakdown at **Appendix 1**. Please note that no discount has been applied in order to take account of tax and National Insurance because no increase has been allowed in the rate for care provided at weekends or in holiday periods.

2.2 Equipment Costs

2.2.1	Quickie II Wheelchair	£2,000
2.2.2	Insurance for wheelchair	£50
2.2.3	Cordless telephone	£50
2.2.4	Plastic Sheets	£100
2.2.5	Portable hoist	£800
2.2.6	Slings	£100
2.2.7	Spa Bath	£6,000
2.2.8	TV and video	£500
2.2.9	Washing Machine/tumble dryer	£500
	Subtotal:	£10,100

2.3 **Accommodation**

2.3.1 Additional Household Expenses

2.3.1.1 Additional heating costs (gas)

84 months @£10 per month: £840

2.3.1.2 Additional electricity

84 months @£5 per month: £420

2.3.1.3 Wear and Tear

The Claimant relies upon the report of Mrs X regarding the additional wear and tear to the Claimant's home caused by her wheelchair. £10 per month is claimed for 84 months, giving a total of: £840

2.3.2 Adaptations

2.3.2.1 Widening doors for wheelchair access £2,000

2.3.2.2 Hand and grab rails £250

2.3.2.3 Walk-in shower £1,500

2.3.2.4 Installation of ramp outside back door £1,000

2.3.2.5 Installation of downstairs toilet £5,000

Subtotal: £11,850

2.4 **Travel Expenses**

2.4.1 Background

The Claimant has had to attend numerous hospital appointments. The Claimant has also had to attend rehabilitation, physiotherapy and hydrotherapy sessions. The Claimant's parents have driven the Claimant to the majority of the various appointments.

2.4.2 The Claim

The additional mileage is claimed @ £0.45 per mile.

2.4.3   The Calculation

The Claimant's past travel costs amount to £7,833 (rounded up). Please see attached detailed breakdown of past travel costs at **Appendix 2.**

2.5   Clothing

2.5.1   The Basis of the Claim

As a result of her injuries the Claimant has required additional clothing over and above that which she would have needed in any event.

2.5.2   The Claim

The additional cost of clothing is estimated @ £40 per month.

2.5.3   The Calculation

84 months @ £40 per month, making a total of: £3,360

2.6   Medical Treatment

2.6.1   The Background

The Claimant has the benefit of private health insurance and following her injury sought examination and treatment on a private basis. She is obliged to reclaim these expenses from the Defendant.

2.6.2   Medical Treatment

2.6.2.1	X-rays	£500
2.6.2.2	CT scans	£350
2.6.2.3	MRI scan (including operator)	£750
2.6.2.4	Consultations with Dr Q	£1,500
2.6.2.5	Rehabilitation course	£15,000

2.6.3 Physiotherapy

2.6.3.1 95 sessions of physiotherapy at the London Clinic

95 sessions @ £35 each: £3,325

2.6.3.2 45 sessions of physiotherapy at the Heatherwood Clinic

45 sessions @ £40 each: £1,800

2.6.4 Hydrotherapy

75 sessions @ £50 each £3,750

Subtotal: £26,975

TOTAL Past Losses and Expenses: **£516,697**

E. 3. NOTES ON MULTIPLIERS

3.1 Applicable Future Loss Discount Rate

3.1.1 Notwithstanding the Lord Chancellor's decision to fix the discount rate at 2.5%, the Claimant will contend that this is an appropriate case for the Court to exercise its discretion under Section 1(2) of the Damages Act 1996 to adopt a different rate. The Claimant will contend that the appropriate discount rate for this case is 2.0%. In support of this contention the Claimant relies upon the report of Mr R.

3.2 Applicable Ogden Tables (5th edition)

3.2.1 In this case the relevant tables are as follows:

- Table 2 (Pecuniary loss for life – females)
- Table 12 (Loss of earnings to pension age 70 – females)
- Table 28 (Pecuniary loss for term certain)

3.3 Future Earnings Multiplier

3.3.1 Background

The Claimant would probably have gone on to higher education. Her first job would have started at the age of 21. She was likely to continue working until age 70.

3.3.2 The Whole Life Earnings Multiplier

The Claimant will contend that the appropriate whole life earnings multiplier for a girl aged 21 to a retirement age of 70 is 30.80 (Table 12 of the Ogden Tables at a discount rate of 2.0%).

3.3.3 Discount for Contingencies

But for her injuries, the Claimant would probably have gone to university and obtained a degree. She would not have started work until age 21. The discount for contingencies for a female aged 21 with a degree is 0.89 (Table C), giving an adjusted multiplier for loss of 30.80 × 0.89 = 27.4.

3.3.4   Split Multiplier

For convenience, the multiplier is split into 5 equal multipliers of 5.48 each for the following earning periods: (i) age 21–29; (ii) 30–38; (iii) 39–47; (iv) 48–56; and (v) 57–65.

3.4   Lifetime Multiplier

3.4.1   The Claimant will contend that the appropriate lifetime multiplier is 37.80 (Table 2 of the Ogden Tables at a discount rate of 2.0%).

3.5   Care Multiplier

3.5.1   Background

The starting point for the Claimant's care multiplier is her whole life multiplier of 37.8.

3.5.2   Discount for Contingencies

Following *Wells v Wells* [1999] 1 AC 345 the Claimant contends that there should be no deduction from the whole life multiplier in respect of her future care claim.

3.5.3   Split Multiplier

It is apparent from the reports of Dr X that the Claimant's health is likely to deteriorate over time and she will require more intensive care from more highly qualified professionals. For convenience, the multiplier of 37.8 is split into 4 equal multipliers of 9.45.

3.6   Aids and Equipment Multiplier

3.6.1   The Claimant will contend that the appropriate multiplier for the replacement costs of aids and equipment that require immediate purchase is the lifetime multiplier minus 1, ie 36.8.

F. 4. FUTURE LOSSES AND EXPENSES

4.1   **Loss of Earnings**

4.1.1   The Medical Evidence

The Claimant is incapable of finding any sort of gainful employment.

4.1.2   The Basis of the Claim

The Claimant comes from a professional family. But for the Defendant's negligence, it is likely that she would have gone on to higher education and obtained a job as a lawyer or a doctor. The Claimant will rely upon the report of Mr C, employment consultant, regarding her likely level of earnings.

4.1.3   The Calculation

The Claimant claims £1,260,400 as detailed in the breakdown at **Appendix 3.**

4.2   **Care**

4.2.1   The Basis of the Claim

The Claimant's care needs are likely to continue at their current rate. However, it is unreasonable to expect the Claimant's parents to continuing providing gratuitous care. The claim is therefore based upon the rates of a professional carer (for which accommodation will have to be built) and a Case Manager.

4.2.2   The Care Evidence

The Claimant will rely upon the written report of Mrs X regarding the rates and amount of past care costs. Although the Claimant's parents have provided care to date, they should be allowed to pursue the option of obtaining professional care.

4.2.3   The Calculation

The Claimant claims £2,031,750 (as detailed in the breakdown at **Appendix 4**).

In addition the Claimant seeks the costs of employing a Case Manager @£7,500 per annum. Applying a life multiplier of 37.8, gives a total of: £283,500.

Thus the total future care claim amounts to: £2,315,250.

4.3   Education

4.3.1   The Basis of the Claim

As a result of her disabilities the Claimant has special educational needs which cannot be met with state provision.

4.3.2   The Education Evidence

The Claimant will rely upon the report of Mr P, Education Psychologist, regarding the Claimant's schooling needs.

4.3.3   The Calculation

The Claimant should attend St Peter's school between 2006 and 2011 which has special facilities for people with the Claimant's disabilities. The annual cost of school fees is £35,000. Applying a multiplier of 4.76 (Table 28 of the Ogden Tables at a discount rate of 2.0%), gives a total of: £166,600.

4.4   Aids and Equipment

4.4.1   The Basis of the Claim

As a result of her disabilities the Claimant requires special aids and equipment.

4.4.2   The Evidence

The Claimant relies upon the reports of Mrs J, Occupational Therapist.

4.4.3   The Calculation

The Claimant claims £159,073 as detailed in the breakdown at **Appendix 5**.

4.5   Accommodation

4.5.1   Additional Household Expenses

4.5.1.1   Additional heating costs (gas)

This will continue at the rate of £20 per month or £240 annually. Applying a lifetime multiplier of 37.8, gives a total of: £9,072

4.5.1.2   Additional electricity

This will continue at the rate of £10 per month or £120 annually. Applying a lifetime multiplier of 37.8, gives a total of: £4,536

4.5.1.3   Wear and Tear

This will continue at the rate of £10 per month or £120 annually. Applying a lifetime multiplier of 37.8, gives a total of: £4,536

4.5.2   Adaptations

4.5.2.1   Extension

The Claimant relies upon the housing report of Mr E in relation to the need to build an extension onto the Claimant's existing house in order to provide living accommodation for the Claimant's carers.   £45,000

4.5.2.2   Furnishing Extension

The Claimant will rely upon the report of Mrs J regarding the costs of adequately furnishing the extension for the Claimant's carers.   £5,000

4.5.2.3   Additional Garage

Additional garage to house the Claimant's Space Wagon.   £20,000

4.5.3　Hydrotherapy Pool

4.5.3.1　The Claimant reasonably requires a hydrotherapy pool at home.

4.5.3.2　Running costs of pool £3,500 × a lifetime multiplier of 37.8:　　£150,000

　　£132,300

Subtotal:　　£370,444

4.6　Speech & Language Therapy and IT

4.6.1　The Basis of the Claim

The Claimant's basic language skills should improve with treatment.

4.6.2　The Evidence

The Claimant relies upon the report of Miss V regarding the need for and likely costs of speech and language therapy.

4.6.3　The Claim

4.6.3.1　Information Technology

The Claimant requires a computer and software as detailed in the report of Miss V at an immediate cost of £20,000. These will need replacing every 5 years and therefore the annual cost is about £4,000. Applying a lifetime equipment multiplier of 36.8 gives a total of £147,200. Therefore the total cost for this head of claim amounts to:　　£167,200

4.6.3.2　Speech and Language Therapist

The annual cost of £1,500 is claimed. Applying a lifetime multiplier of 37.8, gives a total of:　　£56,700

Subtotal:　　£223,900

4.7 Occupational Therapy

4.7.1 The Basis of the Claim

The Claimant requires a bi-annual home review from an occupational therapist in order to ensure that her aids and equipment are adequately meeting her needs and that everything is working as it should.

4.7.2 The Evidence

The Claimant relies upon the reports of Mrs J, Occupational Therapist.

4.7.3 The Calculation

The annual cost of £1,000 is claimed × a lifetime multiplier of 37.8 gives a total of £37,800.

4.8 Transport

4.8.1 Purchase of Chrysler Voyager £52,500

4.8.2 Replacement costs of Chrysler Voyager

Replacement every 4 years. Resale value of 40%. Therefore the multiplicand is £31,500 / 4 = £7,875. £289,800
Applying a lifetime equipment multiplier of 36.8 = £289,800.

4.8.3 Additional Running Costs

The additional running costs of the Chrysler Voyager are estimated at £3,000 per annum based on £113,400
an annual mileage of 10,000 miles (see the report of Mrs X). Applying a lifetime multiplier of 37.8,
gives a total of:

4.8.4　Additional Insurance

Increased insurance to enable carers under 25 to driver vehicle. Multiplicand is £1,500 pa (see estimated from Quote you Happy insurance brokers). Applying a lifetime multiplier of 37.8 gives a total of:

£56,700

4.8.5　AA subscription

The Claimant claims the annual subscription to the AA rescue service in the sum of £100. Applying a lifetime multiplier of 37.8 to the annual figure of £100, gives a total of:

£3,780

Subtotal:

£516,180

4.9　Treatment

4.9.1　Annual review

The Claimant requires an annual review from a Consultant Neurologist together with an MRI scan at an annual cost of £750. Applying a lifetime multiplier of 37.8, gives a total of:

£28,350

4.9.2　Physiotherapy

The Claimant continues to require physiotherapy every two weeks at a cost of £40 per session, making an annual total of £1,040. Applying a multiplier of 37.8, gives a total of:

£39,312

4.9.3   Hydrotherapy

The Claimant continues to require hydrotherapy once a week at a cost of £50, making an annual total of £2,600. Applying a lifetime multiplier of 37.8, gives a total of: £98,280

Subtotal: £165,942

4.10   Prescription Charges

4.10.1   The Claimant claims the annual fee for prescriptions of £104. Applying a lifetime multiplier of 37.8 gives a total of: £3,931

4.11   Clothing

4.11.1   The Claimant's additional clothing costs will continue at the estimated amount of £500 per annum. Applying a lifetime multiplier of 37.8, gives a total of: £18,900

4.12   Holidays

4.12.1   As a result of the Claimant's injuries additional holiday costs will now be incurred because the Claimant is unable to travel without her carers. The estimated increased annual holiday costs are £5,000. Applying a lifetime multiplier of 37.8, gives a total of: £189,000

4.13   Court of Protection Fees

4.13.1   Background

The Claimant is incapable of managing her own affairs and is therefore a protected party under the Mental Capacity Act 2005. See further the report of Dr D, Consultant Neuropsychiatrist. An application will be made to the Court of Protection to appoint a professional deputy to look after the Claimant's damages.

4.13.2 One-off Expenses

4.13.2.1	Fixed costs	£600
4.13.2.2	Medical Opinion	£500
4.13.2.3	Commencement Fee	£250
4.13.2.4	Appointment Fee	£275
4.13.2.5	Statutory Will	£550

4.13.3 Annual Costs

The Claimant claims the annual cost of £6,500 plus VAT = £7,638. See further the statement of Mr Receiver. Applying a lifetime multiplier of 37.8 gives a total of: £288,716

Subtotal: £290,891

TOTAL Future Losses and Expenses: **£5,718,311**

G. 5. INTEREST

5.1   Interest on General Damages

5.1.1   The Basis of the Claim

Interest is claimed at 2% from the date of service of the Claim Form, amounting to 4%.

5.1.2   The Calculation

General damages of £240,000 × 4% =

£9,600

5.2   Interest on Past Losses and Expenses

5.2.1   The Basis of the Claim

Interest on past losses and expenses is claimed at half the special account rate, from the date of the negligence up to the (assumed) date of trial, amounting to 18.24%.

5.2.2   The Calculation

Past losses of £516,697 × 18.24% =

£94,246

Subtotal of Interest:

£103,846

GRAND TOTAL OF ALL CLAIMS (inclusive of interest):

£6,578,854

H. STATEMENT OF TRUTH

Statement of Truth

[I believe] [the Claimant believes] that the facts stated in this Schedule of Loss are true.

[I am duly authorised by the Claimant to sign this statement]

Signed: _____   Position or office held: _____

Dated: _____   The Claimant/Litigation Friend/Claimants' Solicitor

DATED etc. as in claim 1.

I. 6. APPENDICES

6.1

Appendix 1 – PAST CARE COSTS

6.1.1 Period One – 6.4.03 to 5.7.03 (90 days)

During this period the Claimant was an inpatient in hospital. The Claimant's parents visited her on a daily basis.

4 hours of care per day @ £7.73 per hour, making a total of: £2,782.80

6.1.2 Period Two – 6.7.03 to 31.3.04 (270 days)

After the Claimant's discharge from hospital she attended an intensive residential neuro-rehabilitation course and the care required was reduced.

2 hours of care per day @ £7.73 per hour, making a total of: £4,174.20

6.1.3 Period Three – 1.4.04 to 31.3.05 (365 days)

The Claimant returned home on 1.4.97 and has been cared for by her parents ever since. The Claimant will rely upon the report of Mrs X that she requires 24 hours of care per day. The Claimant will continue to require this level of care.

24 hours of care per day @ £7.94 per hour, making a total of: £69,554.40

6.1.4 Period Four – 1.4.05 to 31.3.06 (365 days)

24 hours of care per day @ £8.18 per hour, making a total of: £71,656.80

6.1.5 Period Five – 1.4.06 to 31.3.07 (366 days)

24 hours of care per day @ £8.43 per hour, making a total of: £74,049.12

6.1.6 Period Six – 1.4.07 to 31.3.08 (366 days)

24 hours of care per day @ £8.68 per hour, making a total of: £76,245.12

6.1.7 Period Seven – 1.4.08 to 31.3.09 (365 days)

24 hours of care per day @ £8.85 per hour, making a total of: £77,526

6.1.8 Period 8 – 1.4.09 to 31.3.10 (365 days) (estimated)

24 hours of care per day @ £9.07 per hour, making a total of: £79,453.20

6.1.9 Period 9 – 1.4.10 to 6.4.10 (6 days) (estimated)

24 hours of care per day @ £9.30 per hour, making a total of: £1,339.20

Subtotal: £456,578.52

6.2 **Appendix 2 – PAST TRAVEL COSTS**

6.2.1 Travel Costs Incurred Visiting the Claimant in Hospital

6.2.1.1 Parents

90 return trips of 15 miles @ £0.45 per mile, making a total of: £607.50

6.2.1.2 Other family members

10 return train tickets @ £27.50 each, making a total of: £275

6.2.2 Attending Hospital Appointments

6.2.2.1 Outpatient appointments

20 return trips of 50 miles to Northend Hospital @ 0.45 per mile, making a total of: £450

6.2.2.2 MRI scan

1 return trip of 70 miles to Laser Hospital @ £0.45 per mile, making a total of: £31.50

6.2.2.3 Annual check-up

6 return trips of 50 miles each to Northend Hospital @ 0.45 per mile, making a total of: £135

6.2.3 Attending Rehabilitation

6.2.3.1 Travel costs for Parents Visiting the Claimant at the Rehabilitation Centre

200 return trips of 45 miles each @ £0.45 per mile, making a total of: £4,050

6.2.3.2 Follow-up Sessions

    10 return trips of 45 miles each @ £0.45 per mile, making a total of: £202.50

6.2.4 Attending GP

6.2.4.1 25 return trips of 5 miles each @ £0.45 per mile, making a total of: £56.25

6.2.5 Attending Physiotherapy

6.2.5.1 At the London Clinic

    95 return trips of 30 miles each @ £0.45 per mile, making a total of: £1,282.50

6.2.5.2 At Heatherwood Hospital

    45 return trips of 20 miles each @ £0.45 per mile, making a total of: £405

6.2.6 Attending Hydrotherapy

6.2.6.1 75 return trips of 10 miles each @ £0.45 per mile, making a total of: £337.50

Subtotal: £7,832.75

6.3   **Appendix 3 – FUTURE LOSS OF EARNINGS**

6.3.1   Period One – Age 21 to 29

The Claimant is likely to have been earning in the region of £25,000 net per annum.

Applying a multiplier of 5.48 gives a total of: 137,000

6.3.2   Period Two – Age 30 to 38

The Claimant is likely to have been earning in the region of £35,000 net per annum.

Applying a multiplier of 5.48 gives a total of: 191,800

6.3.3   Period Three – Age 39 to 47

The Claimant is likely to have been earning in the region of £45,000 net per annum.

Applying a multiplier of 5.48 gives a total of: 246,600

6.3.4   Period Four – Age 48 to 56

The Claimant is likely to have been earning in the region of £55,000 net per annum.

Applying a multiplier of 5.48 gives a total of: 301,400

6.3.5   Period Five – Age 57 to 65

The Claimant is likely to have been earning in the region of £70,000 net per annum.

Applying a multiplier of 5.48 gives a total of: 383,600

Subtotal: £1,260,400

6.4   Appendix 4 – FUTURE CARE

6.4.1   Period One – age 17 to 35 years

The Claimant's care needs would be best met by the employment of two residential Home Care Assistants.

The annual cost for these carers is £40,000. Applying a multiplier of 9.45 gives a total of: £378,000

6.4.2   Period Two – age 35 to 53 years

The Claimant's health is likely to deteriorate and her care needs will increase. Although her care needs may still be met by employing two residential Home Care Assistants, the Claimant's level of dependency is likely to rise leading to an increase in the carers' salary.

The annual cost for these carers is £45,000. Applying a multiplier of 9.45 gives a total of: £425,250

6.4.3   Period Three – age 53 to 71 years

During this period, the Claimant's care needs would be best met by the employment of two residential Qualified Nurses.

The annual cost for these carers is likely to be £60,000. Applying a multiplier of 9.45 gives a total of: £567,000

6.4.4   Period Four – age 71 to 89 years

The Claimant's health is likely to further deteriorate. The Claimant's care is likely to become increasingly difficult to manage and the cost of employing two qualified nurses is likely to increase.

The annual cost for these carers is likely to be £70,000. Applying a multiplier of 9.45 gives a total of: £661,500

Subtotal: £2,031,750.00

6.5 Appendix 5 – FUTURE AIDS & EQUIPMENT

	Capital Cost (£)	Annual Cost (£)	Totals (£)
6.5.1 To Improve Mobility and Positioning			
6.5.1.1 Corbie Max III powered wheelchair			
Immediate cost of £6,500. Replacement every 5 years.	£6,500	£1,300	
6.5.1.2 Batteries, tyres etc for wheelchair			
Annual cost of £200 (although no items are needed during the first year).		£200	
6.5.1.3 Insurance and maintenance of wheelchair			
Annual cost of £200 (although first year is covered by warranty).		£200	
6.5.1.4 Motorised hoist for wheelchair			
Immediate cost of £1,000. Replacement every 10 years.	£1,000	£100	
6.5.1.5 Slings for motorised hoist			
Immediate cost £50. Replacement every 2 years.	£50	£25	
6.5.1.6 Parawalker			
Immediate cost of £1,500. Replacement every 6 years.	£1,500	£250	

	Capital Cost (£)	Annual Cost (£)	Totals (£)
6.5.1.7 Therapy stool			
Immediate cost of £100. Replacement every 10 years.	£100	£10	
6.5.1.8 Highpower armchair			
Immediate cost of £1,750. Replacement every 5 years.	£1,750	£350	
6.5.1.9 Highpower cushion			
Immediate cost of £30. Replacement every 2 years.	£30	£15	
6.5.2 Sleeping			
6.5.2.1 Spenco Anti-Pressure Mattress			
Immediate cost of £2,250. Replacement every 10 years.	£2,250	£225	
6.5.2.2 Waterproof cover for mattress			
Immediate cost of £5. Replacement annually.	£5	£5	
6.5.2.3 Superflux pillow			
Immediate cost of £15. Replacement annually.	£15	£15	
6.5.3 Versitrainer			
6.5.3.1 Immediate cost of £2,250. Replacement every 10 years.	£2,250	£225	

		Capital Cost (£)	Annual Cost (£)	Totals (£)
6.5.4	Hygiene			
	6.5.4.1 Shower chair			
	Immediate cost of £500. Replacement every 10 years.	£500	£50	
	6.5.4.2 Easy reach scrubber			
	Immediate cost of £5. Replacement annually.	£5	£5	
6.5.5	Stair lift			
	6.5.5.1 Stannah stair lift			
	Immediate cost of £2,500. Replacement every 10 years.	£2,500	£250	
	6.5.5.2 Installation of stair lift			
	One-off payment of £100.	£100		
	6.5.5.3 Insurance and maintenance of Stair lift			
	Annual cost of £200 (although first year is covered by warranty).		£200	
6.5.6	Miscellaneous			
	6.5.6.1 Padded toilet seat			
	Immediate cost and replacement annually of £75.	£75	£75	
	6.5.6.2 Transfer Board			
	Immediate cost of £65. Replacement every 5 years.	£65	£13	
	6.5.6.3 Advance 5000 door system			
	Immediate cost of £750. Replacement every 3 years.	£750	£250	
	6.5.6.4 Lap tray			
	Immediate cost of £9. Replacement every 3 years.	£9	£3	

	Capital Cost (£)	Annual Cost (£)	Totals (£)
6.5.6.5 Dispense trolley			
Immediate cost of £50. Replacement every 5 years.	£50	£10	
6.5.6.6 Diabalo bed table			
Immediate cost of £60. Replacement every 4 years.	£60	£15	
The total immediate capital outlay:			£19,564
The total annual cost amounts to £3,791. Applying an annual equipment multiplier of 36.8, gives a total of:			£139,509
Subtotal claim for aids and equipment:			£159,073

(ii) Counter-Schedule of Loss

[Q15]

IN THE HIGH COURT OF JUSTICE

QUEEN'S BENCH DIVISION

BETWEEN : -

Claim No. 6

MISS ANNIE YUCATAN

(By her Mother and Litigation Friend Mrs DEBORAH YUCATAN)

Claimant

– and –

LAMBETH HOSPITALS NHS TRUST

Defendant

COUNTER-SCHEDULE OF PAST AND FUTURE LOSSES AND EXPENSES

CONTENTS

PLEASE NOTE: This counter-schedule is served in response to the Claimant's schedule of loss dated 6 April 2009 which adopts an assumed trial date of 6 April 2010. It is served without prejudice to the Defendant's case on negligence and causation. The figures contained in this counter-schedule are on a full-liability basis.

NOTES ON MULTIPLIERS

The Defendant accepts the relevant details set out in the schedule of loss save as to the appropriate multipliers for future loss. The Defendant agrees that the Claimant's life expectancy has been largely unaffected by her injuries but does not accept that the Claimant would have continued working until age 70. The Defendant will contend that the Claimant would probably have retired earlier at age 60 and that the following multipliers are appropriate in this case.

Appropriate Discount Rate

The Defendant does not agree that this is an exceptional case in which the discount rate fixed by the Lord Chancellor at 2.5% should be departed from. The Defendant does not agree the report of Mr R and relies instead upon the report of Mr D. The Claimant is put to strict proof that it would be more appropriate to use a discount rate other than the rate set by the Lord Chancellor following extensive consultation and careful consideration.

Applicable Ogden Tables

The Defendant agrees that **Tables 2** and **28** of the Ogden Tables (6th edition) are the appropriate tables to be used in this case. However, in respect of loss of earnings, **Table 8** is the appropriate table to be used given the Claimant's likely retirement at age 60.

Future Loss of Earnings Multiplier

The Defendant accepts that the Claimant would probably have gone onto higher education and would not have begun working until at least age 21. The appropriate whole loss of earnings multiplier is therefore 24.8 (Table 8 of the Ogden Tables at a discount rate of 2.5%). This multiplier must be discounted for accelerated receipt by a factor of 0.9060 (Table 27 at a discount rate of 2.5%), giving a starting point multiplier of 22.47.

The starting point multiplier must be significantly discounted in order to take account of the following risks:

- Failing exams or training
- Periods of unemployment
- Redundancy
- Marriage (and children)
- Ill-health
- Career breaks

In the circumstances the Defendant will contend that the appropriate multiplier for future loss of earnings should be no higher than **15** (which equates to a discount of approximately 33%).

For convenience, the Defendant contends that this multiplier of 15 should be split into 4 earnings periods as follows (please see **Appendix 1**):

- 5.235 for the period 21-30
- 4.08 for the period 31-40
- 3.195 for the period 41-50
- 2.49 for the period 51-60

Lifetime Multiplier

The Defendant will contend that the appropriate lifetime multiplier is **33.15** (Table 2 of the Ogden Tables at a discount rate of 2.5%).

Care Multiplier

The Defendant accepts that the Claimant will require permanent continuous care. Therefore the appropriate starting multiplier is **33.15**. This should be split as follows (see **Appendix 2**):

- 14.53 for the period 17 to 35
- 9.28 for the period 35 to 53
- 6.01 for the period 53 to 71
- 3.83 for the period 71 to 89

Aids and Equipment Multiplier

On the basis of a discount rate of 2.5%, the appropriate multiplier for the replacement costs of aids and equipment is **32.15**.

	Claim (£)	Offer (£)

1. GENERAL DAMAGES

240,000 / 215,000

The Defendant agrees that the Claimant was catastrophically injured and is now wholly dependent upon others. The Defendant further agrees that the appropriate category of the Judicial Studies Board Guidelines (9th Edition) is 2(A)(a) 'Very Severe Brain Damage': £180,000 to £257,750. However, the Defendant will contend that the Claimant's injuries fall just below the middle of this bracket and the appropriate award in respect of pain, suffering and loss of amenity is £215,000.

2. PAST LOSSES AND EXPENSES

2.1 Care

456,579 / 134,279

The Defendant denies the claim for past care costs in the sum of £456,579. Whilst the Defendant agrees the various rates claimed, the number of hours claimed is excessive and the Defendant will rely upon the report Mrs G and the figures set out at **Appendix 3**. In any event, the claim falls to be reduced by one-third in order to take account of the 'gratuitous element'.

2.2 Equipment Costs

10,100 / 3,100

Items 2.2.1 to 2.2.6 in the schedule of loss are agreed. The cost of the spa bath is not agreed. The Defendant denies that this expenditure was reasonably required by reason of the Claimant's injuries. Further, the TV and video and washing machine/tumble dryer are normal household items which the Claimant probably would have bought in any event and therefore these items are not recoverable from the Defendant.

		Claim (£)	Offer (£)
2.3	**Accommodation**	11,850	10,590
	No details have been provided regarding the basis upon which the additional expenses have been calculated. The Claimant is put to strict proof regarding the cost of the same. In the absence of any documentary proof, the Defendant offers £10 per month to cover all the additional household expenses. The Defendant agrees the cost of adaptations claimed in the sum of £9,750. The total under this head is £840 + £9,750 = £10,590.		
2.4	**Travel Expenses**	7,833	2,794
	The Defendant agrees in principle that the various trips made were reasonably required. Train fares of £275 are agreed. However, the claimed rate of mileage at £0.45 is excessive. The Claimant is only entitled to recover the running costs of the vehicle used. Over the period in question the AA running costs were an average of approximately 15 pence per mile. 16,795 miles × £0.15 = £2,519.25 plus £275 = £2,794.25.		
2.5	**Clothing**	3,360	1,680
	In the absence of any documentary proof regarding the Claimant's additional expenditure on clothing, the Defendant offers the sum of £20 per month, making a total of £1,680.		
2.6	**Medical Treatment**	26,975	26,975
	Agreed in full.		
Subtotal:		**£516,697**	**£179,418**

3. NOTES TO MULTIPLIERS

Please see above.

	Claim (£)	Offer (£)
4. FUTURE LOSSES AND EXPENSES		
4.1 Loss of Earnings	1,260,400	479,400
4.2 Care	2,315,250	1,061,258
4.3 Education	166,600	47,000

4. FUTURE LOSSES AND EXPENSES

4.1 Loss of Earnings

The Claimant is put to strict proof regarding the claim for future loss of earnings. The Defendant does not agree the report of Mr C and instead relies upon the report of Mr F. The Defendant offers a total of £479,400 under this head of loss as detailed in **Appendix 4.**

4.2 Care

The Defendant puts the Claimant to strict proof regarding this head of loss. The report of Mrs X is not agreed and the Defendant relies upon the report of Mrs G. It is denied that professional care is required or would in fact be used until the Claimant reaches the age of 35. It is denied that a case manager is required. The tasks of a case manager have been adequately performed to date by the Claimant's family and there is no reason why they cannot continue to be satisfied in this way. The Defendant offers £1,061,258 under this head of loss as detailed in **Appendix 5.**

4.3 Education

It is agreed that the Claimant would benefit from attending a private school with special facilities. However, it is contended that St. Andrews school would more than satisfy the Claimant's needs between 2006 and 2011. Applying a multiplier of 4.7 (Table 28 at a discount rate of 2.5%) to the lower annual fees of St. Andrews of £10,000 p.a., gives a total of £47,000.

	Claim (£)	Offer (£)

4.4   Aids and Equipment

The Claimant is put to strict proof regarding the claim for future aids and equipment. The Defendant does not agree the report of Mrs J and instead relies upon the report of Ms R. The Defendant offers a total of £79,828 under this head of loss as detailed in **Appendix 6**.

	159,073	79,828

4.5   Accommodation

4.5.1   In the absence of any documentary proof, the Defendant will continue to offer £10 per month to cover all the Claimant's additional household expenses. This amounts to £120 annually. Applying a lifetime multiplier of 33.15, gives a total of £3,943.

	9,072	3,978

4.5.2.1   As regards the intended extension, the Defendant denies that this is necessary, particularly if the Claimant's parents continue to be responsible for the Claimant's care. In any event, credit should be given for the increase in the value of the Claimant's house by reason of the extension in the sum of £15,000. In the alternative therefore, the Defendant offers the sum of £30,000 under this head of loss.

	45,000	Nil (alternatively 30,000)

4.5.2.2   For the above reasons, the Defendant denies that the Claimant is entitled to recover the costs of furnishing the extension. If contrary to the Defendant's primary case, the Claimant does recover the cost of building an extension, the Defendant offers the sum of £3,000 to adequately furnish the extension.

	5,000	Nil (alternatively 3,000)

4.5.2.3   It is denied that it is reasonable or necessary for an additional garage to be built to house the new vehicle. Further, any need for an additional garage is not related to the Claimant's injuries. If contrary to the Defendant's primary case, the Claimant does recover the cost of building an extension, the Defendant offers the sum of £10,000 under this head of loss based upon the quote of Bob the Builder and the likely increase in value to the family home.

	20,000	Nil (alternatively 10,000)

	Claim (£)	Offer (£)
4.5.3 It is denied that the Claimant requires a hydrotherapy pool at home. This is not supported by the medical evidence. Further, there is a hydrotherapy pool 5 miles from the Claimant's home which she has been using without difficulty for the last few years. There is no reason why she cannot continue to use her local hydrotherapy pool. In any event, it is noted that the claim under this head of loss duplicates the claim made under 4.9.3. It is also clear that the claim under this head of loss far exceeds the claim detailed at 4.9.3 (taken together with the likely increased travel costs) and therefore fails to be reasonable or cost-effective.	282,300	Nil

4.6 Speech & Language Therapy and IT

	Claim (£)	Offer (£)
It is denied that the Claimant would derive any discernable benefit from the suggested treatment or equipment and therefore the Defendant does not allow anything under this head of loss. The report of Miss V is not agreed. The Defendant relies upon the report of Mr I.	223,900	Nil

4.7 Occupational Therapy

	Claim (£)	Offer (£)
The need for the Claimant's aids and equipment to be regularly reviewed is agreed in principle. However, the Defendant avers that an annual review would be sufficient for the Claimant's purposes. The Defendant does not agree the report of Mrs J. The Defendant relies upon the report of Ms R. Applying a lifetime multiplier of 33.15 to the annual cost of £250, gives a total of £8,288.	37,800	8,288

4.8 Transport

	Claim (£)	Offer (£)
4.8.1 The Defendant disputes the need for a Chrysler Voyager. A VW Sharan would be more than adequate to meet the Claimant's needs. The Defendant allows the list price of £25,000.	52,500	25,000

	Claim (£)	Offer (£)
4.8.2 The Defendant allows replacement of the VW Sharan every 5 years, less say £10,000 which the Claimant would have spent on a car in any event and residual value of 0.33 = £6,750 / 5 years = £1,350 per annum × a multiplier of 32.15 = £43,403.	289,800	43,403
4.8.3 The Defendant does not agree the report of Mrs X or the claimed additional running costs of £3,000 p.a. The Defendant relies upon the report of Mr U regarding the increased running costs of £1,000 p.a. Applying a lifetime multiplier of 33.15, gives a total of £33,150.	113,400	33,150
4.8.4 The Defendant disputes the amount claimed for additional insurance which has been overstated. £500 pa is allowed. Applying a lifetime multiplier of 33.15, gives a total of £16,575.	56,700	16,575
4.8.5 The Defendant denies that the claimed annual subscription to the AA is reasonable, necessary or related to the Claimant's injuries.	3,780	Nil
4.9 Treatment		
4.9.1 To date all the Claimant's treatment has been on the NHS and this is likely to continue in the future. There is no need for an annual MRI scan.	28,350	Nil
4.9.2 The need for physiotherapy every two weeks is agreed in the sum of £40 per week or £1,040 p.a. is agreed. Applying a lifetime multiplier of 33.15 gives a total of £34,476.	39,312	34,476
4.9.3 The need for hydrotherapy is agreed. It is noted that the claim under this head of loss is duplicated by the claim under 4.5.3. The Defendant will contend that the Claimant should continue to travel to her local hydrotherapy pool for treatment. However, the Defendant will rely upon the evidence of Dr E that sessions are now only required once every two weeks, making an annual total of £1,300. Applying a lifetime multiplier of 33.15, gives a total of £43,095.	98,280	43,095

	Claim (£)	Offer (£)
4.10 Prescription Charges	3,931	Nil
The Claimant is put to strict proof that she will incur any prescription charges in the future. It is understood that the Claimant currently receives free prescriptions and she is likely to continue to do so. In any event if they are not free at present, they will become free from age 60 so the Claimant's multiplier is excessive.		
4.11 Clothing	18,900	Nil
In the absence of the negligence, the Claimant probably would have spent more money on clothes for work and also clothes for sporting and leisure activities. Overall there is no additional cost under this head.		
4.12 Holidays	189,000	50,000
The Defendant accepts the claim for increased holiday costs in principle but relies upon the report of Mrs G that these costs amount to £2,000 p.a. Given that the Claimant may not have taken a holiday every year and it is unlikely that she would have continued to take annual holidays up until the end of her natural life, a lower multiplier of 25 is contended for. This gives a total under this head of claim of £50,000.		
4.13 Court of Protection Fees	290,891	157,980
The Defendant agrees the past expenses claimed of £2,175. As regards future expenses the Defendant allows the sum of £4,000 plus VAT = £4,700. Applying a lifetime multiplier of 33.15, gives a total of £155,805.		
Subtotal:	**5,306,133**	**2,083,431** (alternatively **2,126,431**)

	Claim (£)	Offer (£)

5. INTEREST

5.1   **The rate and period of interest is agreed.**

5.2   **Interest on General Damages**

| | 9,600 | 8,600 |

5.3   **Interest on Past Expenses and Losses**

| | 94,246 | 32,726 |

Subtotal interest:

| | 103,846 | 41,326 |

GRAND TOTAL:

	6,578,854	2,519,175
		(alternatively
		2,562,175)

6. STATEMENT OF TRUTH

Statement of Truth

[I believe] [the Defendant believes] that the facts stated in this counter-schedule are true.

[I am duly authorised by the Defendant to sign this statement]

Signed: _____   Position or office held: _____

Dated: _____   The Defendant / Litigation Friend / Defendant's Solicitor

---

DATED etc. as in claim 1.

7. SUMMARY OF CLAIM

Head Of Claim		Claimant's Figure (£)	Defendant's Figure (£)	Comment	Award (£)
C.	**1. General Damages**				
	1.1 Pain, Suffering and Loss of Amenity	240,000	**215,000**		
	Subtotal of General Damages:	**240,000**	**215,000**		
D.	**2. Past Losses and Expenses**				
	2.1 Care	456,579	134,279		
	2.2 Equipment Costs	10,100	3,100		
	2.3 Accommodation	11,850	10,590		
	2.4 Travel Expenses	7,833	2,794		
	2.5 Clothing	3,360	1,680		
	2.6 Medical Treatment	26,975	26,975		
	Subtotal of Past Losses and Expenses:	**516,697**	**179,418**		
F.	**4. Future Losses and Expenses**				
	4.1 Loss of Earnings	1,260,400	479,400		
	4.2 Care	2,315,250	1,061,258		
	4.3 Education	166,600	47,000		
	4.4 Aids and Equipment	159,073	79,828		

Head Of Claim		Claimant's Figure (£)	Defendant's Figure (£)	Comment	Award (£)
	4.5 Accommodation	370,444	3,978 (alt. 46,978)		
	4.6 Speech & Language Therapy and IT	223,900	Nil		
	4.7 Occupational Therapy	37,800	8,288		
	4.8 Transport	516,180	118,128		
	4.9 Treatment	165,942	77,571		
	4.10 Prescription Charges	3,931	Nil		
	4.11 Clothing	18,900	Nil		
	4.12 Holidays	189,000	50,000		
	4.13 Court of Protection Fees	290,891	157,980		
	Subtotal of Future Losses and Expenses:	**5,718,311**	**2,083,431** (alt 2,126,431)		
G.	**5. Interest**				
	5.1 Interest on General Damages	9,600	8,600		
	5.2 Interest on Past Losses and Expenses	94,246	32,726		
	Subtotal of Interest:	**103,846**	**41,326**		
	TOTAL CLAIM:	**£6,578,854**	**£2,519,175** (alt. £2,562,175)		

APPENDIX 1 – BREAKDOWN OF LOSS OF EARNINGS MULTIPLIER

The Defendant will contend for a whole loss of earnings multiplier until age 60 of 15. For convenience, the Defendant contends that this multiplier should be split into 4 separate earnings periods: (i) age 21 to 30; (ii) age 31 to 40; (iii) age 41 to 50; and (iv) 51 to 60. However, it would be wrong to split the multiplier equally because this would fail to take account of the effect of accelerated receipt and the fact that the Claimant has a greater chance of surviving the early years than the later years.

In order to calculate how the multiplier should be split as set out using the method set out at para 22 of the Ogden guidance notes. The 2.5% discount column of Table 28 is used to obtain the relevant multiplier for each time period. The appropriate whole multiplier for a fixed term of 40 years at 2.5% discount is 25.42. By deducting the relevant multipliers of the earlier periods from the later periods, it is possible to obtain the relevant factors by which to multiply the whole life earnings multiplier in order to achieve a pro rata split.

Time Period	Table 28 Multiplier	Factor
1–10	8.86	8.86/25.42 = 0.349
11–20	15.78 – 8.86 = 6.92	6.92/25.42 = 0.272
21–30	21.19 – 15.78 = 5.41	5.41/25.42 = 0.213
31–40	25.42 – 21.19 = 4.23	4.23/25.42 = 0.166

Thus applying the appropriate factors to the whole life earnings multiplier gives the following multipliers in respect of the different earning periods.

Earning Period	Calculation	Multiplier
21–30	0.349 × 15	5.235
31–40	0.272 × 15	4.08
41–50	0.213 × 15	3.195
51–60	0.166 × 15	2.49

APPENDIX 2 – BREAKDOWN OF CARE MULTIPLIER

The Defendant will contend for a care multiplier of 32.86 (Table 2 of the Ogden Tables at a discount rate of 2.5%). For convenience, the Defendant agrees that this multiplier should be split into 4 separate care periods: (i) age 17 to 35; (ii) age 35 to 53; (iii) age 53 to 71; and (iv) age 71 to 89. However, it would be wrong to split the multiplier equally because this would fail to take account of the effect of accelerated receipt and the fact that the Claimant has a greater chance of surviving the early years than the later years.

In order to calculate how the multiplier should be split the 2.5% discount column of Table 28 is used to obtain the relevant multiplier for each time period. The appropriate whole multiplier for a fixed term of 70 years at 2.5% discount is 33.31. By deducting the relevant multipliers of the earlier periods from the later periods, it is possible to obtain the relevant factors by which to multiply the whole life care multiplier in order to achieve a pro rata split.

Time Period	Table 28 Multiplier	Factor
1–18	14.53	14.53/33.65 = 0.4318
18–36	23.81 – 14.53 = 9.28	9.28/33.65 = 0.2758
36–54	29.82 – 23.81 = 6.01	6.01/33.65 = 0.1786
54–72	33.65 – 29.82 = 3.83	3.83/33.65 = 0.1138

Thus applying the appropriate factors to the whole life care multiplier gives the following multipliers in respect of the different care periods.

Care Period	Calculation	Multiplier
17 to 35	0.4318 × 33.65	14.53
35 to 53	0.2758 × 33.65	9.28
53 to 71	0.1786 × 33.65	6.01
71 to 89	0.1138 × 33.65	3.83

APPENDIX 3 – PAST CARE COSTS

General Comments

(1) The Claimant is entitled to recover damages for the 'services rendered voluntarily for a family member or other voluntary carer in nursing or providing other essential personal services for' a claimant (per Brooke LJ in *Hardwick v Hudson* [1999] 1 WLR 1770 at 1776).

(2) Damages are not recoverable in respect of the time spent visiting the claimant in hospital, chatting to her, generally improving her outlook on life and making the claimant feel cared for (see further the judgment of Beldam LJ in *Havenhand v Jeffrey*, unreported, 24 February 1997 reported *in Kemp & Kemp* at 5-031).

(3) The claim for gratuitous services is limited by the 'ceiling principle' to, at the most, claiming the cost of a professional carer: *Housecroft v. Burnett* [1986] 1 All ER 332, CA.

(4) Gratuitous carers may not be allowed to claim the higher weekend rates that professional carers charge for working weekends and bank holidays: *Fairhurst v St Helens and Knowsley Health Authority* [1995] PIQR Q1; *Noble v Owens* [2008] EWHC 359 (QB).

(5) Credit must be given for any care that was already being provided prior to the alleged negligence.

(6) A discount should be made to reflect the 'gratuitous element' of the care provided and the fact that a professional carer would have to pay tax and National Insurance and also to reflect the fact that the care provider has no relevant qualifications: *A and Others v The National Blood Authority and Others* [2001] Lloyd's Rep. Med. 187 at 273.

Discount

The Defendant will contend for a discount of one-third to reflect the 'gratuitous element' in this case.

The Calculation

The Defendant agrees the rates of care claimed by the Claimant but disputes the amount of care provided. The Report of Mrs X is not agreed and the Defendant will rely upon the report of Mrs G. The Defendant allows the amounts of past care as set out in the following table.

Period	Comment	No. of hours per day	No. of days	Rate per hour (£)	Amount (£)
6.4.03 to 5.7.03	During this period the Claimant was an inpatient in hospital. It is denied that 4 hours of gratuitous 'care' was provided to the Claimant per day. The responsibility for the care of the Claimant rested almost entirely upon the hospital staff and 1 hour per day is allowed for the gratuitous care provided by the family.	1	90	5.90	531
6.7.03 to 31.3.04	During this period, the Claimant's family provided little in the way of care that was not already provided by the staff at the rehabilitation centre. ½ an hour per day is allowed. For gratuitous care during this period.	0.5	270	5.90	796.50
1.4.04 to 31.3.05	The Defendant disputes that the Claimant has required 24-hour care, especially given the fact that she tends to sleep well through the night. 16 hours of care per day is allowed. However, this must be discounted for the care that was already being provided prior to the alleged negligence, estimated to be 2 hours per day. Therefore, in total 14 hours per day is allowed.	14	365	6.06	30,966.60
1.4.05 to 31.3.06	The level of care required continued at 14 hours per day.	14	365	6.24	31,886.40
1.4.06 to 31.3.07	The level of care required continued at 14 hours per day.	14	365	6.43	32,857.30
1.4.07 to 31.3.08	The level of care required continued at 14 hours per day.	14	366	6.62	33,920.88
1.4.08 to 31.3.09	The level of care required continued at 14 hours per day.	14	365	6.75	34,492.50
1.4.09 to 31.3.10	The level of care required continued at 14 hours per day.	14	365	6.92	35,361.20
1.4.10 to 6.4.10	The level of care required continued at 14 hours per day.	14	6	7.09	595.56
Subtotal:					**201,407.94**

Therefore the total claim for past care amounts to £201,407.94 66.67% = **£134,279**

APPENDIX 4 – FUTURE LOSS OF EARNINGS

Period	Likely Net Earnings p.a. (£)	Multiplier	Amount (£)
Age 21 to 30	20,000	5.235	104,700
Age 31 to 40	30,000	4.08	122,400
Age 41 to 50	40,000	3.195	127,800
Age 51 to 60	50,000	2.49	124,500
TOTAL:			**479,400**

APPENDIX 5 – FUTURE CARE COSTS

The Defendant does not agree the contents of Mrs X and relies upon the figures for care detailed by Mrs G in her report dated 1.2.05. It appears clear from the Claimant's witness statements that, if possible, the Claimant's family wish to continue to be the Claimant's primary carers. It is likely that the Claimant's parents will remain the Claimant's primary carers for the foreseeable future after which time the likelihood is that the Claimant's two brothers will share responsibility for the Claimant's care together with professional help.

Period	Comment	Annual Cost (£)	Multiplier	Amount (£)
Age 17 to 35	It is likely that the Claimant's family will continue to provide care at the level of 14 hours per day. Taking into account a discount of one-third to reflect the gratuitous element of the care provided, the annual cost is £19,691.	24,154	14.53	350,958
Age 35 to 53	It is accepted that the Claimant's care needs are likely to increase. During this period, the care provided by the Claimant's family may be supplemented by the employment of one non-residential Home Care Assistant. The annual cost would be £30,000.	30,000	9.28	278,400
Age 53 to 71	It is accepted that the Claimant's care needs will increase further. The Claimant's needs will be adequately met by the Claimant's family and one non-residential Home Care Assistant but it is accepted that the costs are likely to be slightly higher. The annual cost would be £40,000.	40,000	6.01	240,400
Age 71 to 89	It is accepted that the Claimant's health will further deteriorate. Her care needs at this stage would be best met by the Claimant's family together with the employment of one non-residential Qualified Nurse. The annual cost would be £50,000.	50,000	3.83	191,500
Subtotal:				**1,061,258**

APPENDIX 6 – FUTURE AIDS & EQUIPMENT

Item	Comment	Capital Cost (£)	Annual Cost (£)	Totals (£)
Corbie Max III powered wheelchair	Agreed.	6,500	1,300	
Batteries, tyres etc for wheelchair	Agreed.		200	
Insurance and maintenance of wheelchair	Agreed.		200	
Motorised hoist for wheelchair	Agreed.	1000	100	
Slings for motorised hoist	Agreed.	50	25	
Parawalker	Not reasonably required. The Defendant will rely upon the report of Mr K that the Claimant is unlikely to derive any discernible benefit from this item.	Nil	Nil	
Therapy stool	Agreed.	100	10	
Highpower armchair	The Defendant will aver that the Claimant's needs would be adequately met by the purchase of a Readymax armchair in the sum of £595. This requires replacement every 7 years.	595	85	

Item	Comment	Capital Cost (£)	Annual Cost (£)	Totals (£)
Highpower cushion	The Defendant will aver that the Claimant's needs would be adequately met by the purchase of a Readymax cushion in the sum of £15. This requires replacement every 3 years.	15	5	
Spenco Anti-Pressure Mattress	The Defendant will aver that the Claimant's needs are adequately met by her current Airlight mattress. This mattress requires replacement every 6 years at a cost of £750.		125	
Waterproof cover for mattress	Agreed.	5	5	
Superflux pillow	Agreed.	15	15	
Versitrainer	Not reasonably required. The Defendant will rely upon the report of Mr K that the Claimant is unlikely to derive any discernible benefit from this item.	Nil	Nil	
Shower chair	The Claimant's needs would be adequately met by the purchase of an Easysit shower chair at the cost of £200. This requires replacement every 10 years.	200	20	
Easy reach scrubber	Agreed.	5	5	
Stannah stair lift	This item is not agreed. The purpose of building the downstairs toilet and walk-in shower was to avoid the need to take the Claimant upstairs. Now there is no reasonable need for the Claimant to go upstairs and therefore no need for a stair lift.	Nil	Nil	
Installation of stair lift	Not agreed for the above reasons.	Nil	Nil	

Item	Comment	Capital Cost (£)	Annual Cost (£)	Totals (£)
Insurance and maintenance of Stair lift	Not agreed for the above reasons.	Nil	Nil	
Padded toilet seat	Agreed.	75	75	
Transfer Board	Agreed.	65	13	
Advance 5000 door system	Not agreed. There is no reasonable need for this item.	Nil	Nil	
Lap tray	Agreed.	9	3	
Dispenso trolley	Agreed.	50	10	
Diabalo bed table	Agreed.	60	15	
The total immediate capital outlay:				£8,744
The total annual cost amounts to £2,211. Applying an annual equipment multiplier of 32.15, gives a total of:				£71,084
Subtotal claim for aids and equipment:				**£79,828**

8 Example Scott Schedule

[Q16]

	HEAD OF CLAIM	CLAIMANT'S FIGURE (£)	DEFENDANT'S FIGURE (£)	AWARD (£)
(1)	**General Damages**			
	(a) Pain, Suffering and Loss of Amenity	To be assessed	To be assessed	
	(b) Loss of Congenial Employment	To be assessed	–	
	(c) Handicap on the Labour Market	To be assessed	–	
	Subtotal:	**To be assessed**	**To be assessed**	
(2)	**Interest on General Damages**	To be assessed	To be assessed	
(3)	**Past Losses and Expenses**			
	(a) Loss of Earnings	45,000	30,000	
	(b) Care	32,500	22,500	
	(c) Clothing*	500	500	
	(d) Medical Expenses**	2,500	2,500	
	(e) Travel Expenses**	750	750	
	(f) Gardening	1,500	1,000	
	(g) Miscellaneous*	300	300	
	Subtotal:	**83,050**	**57,550**	
(4)	**Future Losses and Expenses**			
	(a) Loss of Earnings	150,000	125,000	
	(b) Care	265,000	145,000	
	(c) Aids and Equipment	30,000	10,000	
	(d) Accommodation	137,500	–	
	(e) Treatment*	5,000	5,000	
	(f) Gardening	15,000	7,500	
	(g) Home Maintenance	8,900	5,000	
	(h) Medication*	2,750	2,750	
	(i) Holidays	20,000	–	
	Subtotal:	**634,150**	**300,250**	
(5)	**Interest on Past Losses and Expenses**	**17,500**	**8,000**	
(6)	**TOTAL**	**£734,700 (Plus assessments)**	**£365,800 (Plus assessments)**	

* Indicates that item is agreed
** Indicates that item is agreed and has already been paid

9   Examples of Interest Calculations

(i)   Example Interest Calculation on General Damages

[Q17]

The Claimant was injured in an accident at work on 6 May 2006. Proceedings were issued on 1 January 2009 and served on 1 March 2009. The trial is heard on 1 August 2012. General damages of £50,000 are awarded.

Period	No of Days	Rate of Interest (%)	Cumulative Total (%)
1.3.09 to 28.2.10	365	2	2
1.3.10 to 28.2.11	365	2	4
1.3.11 to 29.2.12	366	2	6
1.3.12 to 1.8.12	154	0.84	6.84

The interest on general damages is £50,000 × 6.84% = **£3,420**

(ii)   Example Interest Calculation on Past Losses and Expenses

[Q18]

The Claimant is injured in a road traffic accident on 4 December 2007. Proceedings are issued on 28 November 2009 and served on 20 February 2010. The trial is heard on 1 September 2010. The following awards for one-off past expenses and losses are made: (i) travel expenses in the sum of £5,000; (ii) physiotherapy and acupuncture in the sum of £2,000; and (iii) replacement car hire in the sum of £500. The following awards for continuing past losses and expenses are made: (i) £50,000 for loss of earnings; (ii) £20,000 for gratuitous care; and (iii) £5,000 for DIY and gardening.

I.   Summary of the Claim

1.1   The Claimant claims interest on past one-off expenses and losses totalling £7,500 at the full special account rate, namely 6% from the date of the accident up to 31 January 2009; 3% from 1 February 2009 to 31 May 2009; 1.5% from 1 June 2009 to 30 June 2009; and 0.5% from 1 July 2009.

1.2   The Claimant claims interest on continuing losses and expenses totalling £75,000 at half the full special account rate, namely 3% from the date of the accident up to 31 January 2009; 1.5% from 1 February 2009 to 31 May 2009; 0.75% from 1 June 2009 to 30 June 2009; and 0.25% from 1 July 2009.

1.3   The total amount of interest on past expenses and losses amounts to **£31,652.25**.

2. Interest on Past One-off Losses and Expenses

2.1 Interest is claimed from the day after the accident as set out in the following table.

Period	No of Days	Interest Rate (%)	Total Interest (%)
4.12.07 to 31.1.09	425	6	6.99
1.2.09 to 31.5.09	120	3	0.99
1.6.09 to 30.6.09	30	1.5	0.12
1.7.09 to 1.9.10	427	0.5	0.58
Total Interest			8.68

2.2 £7,500 × 8.68% = **£651**.

3. Interest on Continuing Losses and Expenses

3.1 Interest is claimed from the day after the accident as set out in the following table:

Period	No of Days	Interest Rate (%)	Total Interest (%)
4.12.07 to 31.1.09	425	3	3.4932
1.2.09 to 31.5.09	120	1.5	0.4932
1.6.09 to 30.6.09	30	0.75	0.0616
1.7.09 to 1.9.10	427	0.25	0.2925
Total interest			4.34

3.2 £75,000 × 4.34% = **£3,255**.

10   Information Required to Calculate a Claim for the Loss of a Final Salary/Defined Benefit Type of Pension

[Q19]

1.   Claimant's date of birth.

2.   Date of commencement of pensionable service.

3.   Claimant's intended retirement age.

4.   Date of termination of claimant's employment (ie the claimant's actual retirement age due to ill-health).

5.   Pension Policy No / Details of Pension Provider / copy trust deed and rules and/or scheme booklet.

6.   The commutable factor of the claimant's pension (which is often not in the pension scheme booklet), ie whether the claimant was entitled to a pension only or a lump sum and a reduced pension. In particular, did the claimant have any options on retirement regarding his or her pension or was the claimant forced to commute a certain proportion of his or her pension? If the claimant did have certain options available on retirement, documentary evidence should be sought regarding any stated intentions made by the claimant regarding which option he or she was planning to take and the claimant's instructions should be sought on the same and/or evidence obtained regarding which option the majority of the workforce in the claimant's position decide to take.

7.   Whether the claimant is married and if so: (i) whether the claimant's spouse is entitled to the pension after the claimant dies; (ii) the partner's date of birth; and (iii) any reason to suspect that the partner will outlive the claimant beyond the normal life expectancy tables.

8.   The likely level of the claimant's retirement pension and lump sum but for the accident, taking into account any promotional prospects and/or alternative job opportunities.

9.   The level of ill-health pension and/or lump sum actually received by the claimant.

10. Any pension entitlement received in alternative employment.

11 Examples of Pension Loss Calculations

(i) Single Man, Defined Benefit Pension and No Lump Sum (Traditional Auty v NCB Approach Using the Life Tables)

[Q20]

The claimant aged 45 at the date of trial is no longer able to work as a result of his injuries. But for the accident he would have retired at the age of 65 after 30 years of pensionable service. His pension entitlement accrues at the rate of 1/60 of his final salary for each year of service. His final salary would have been £30,000, which would have entitled him to an annual pension of £15,000 (gross), £10,000 (net). Following the accident the claimant was medically retired and now receives an ill-health benefit of £7,500 (gross), £5,000 (net) per annum.

Step 1	Calculate the annual net loss of pension The annual net loss of pension is £10,000 minus £5,000, ie £5,000.	
Step 2	Calculate the multiplier According to the current life tables, the claimant's life expectancy is 37.7 years beyond age 45, ie 17.7 years beyond age 65. The appropriate multiplier for this period is 14.34 (Table 28 of the Ogden Tables (6th edn) at 2.5% taking the 7/10 point between 17 and 18).	
Step 3	Apply multiplier Multiplying £5,000 by 14.34 gives a total of:	71,700
Step 4	Discount for advanced receipt This sum must be discounted by a factor of 0.6103 (Table 27 of the Ogden Tables (5th edn) at 2.5% discount) to take account of the fact that the claimant is receiving the money 20 years earlier.	(27,941.49)
Step 5	Discount for further eventualities This sum further needs to be discounted to take account of contingencies by say 10%.	(7,170)
TOTAL		**£36,588.51**

(ii) Single Man, Defined Benefit Pension and No Lump Sum (Modern Approach Using the Ogden Pension Loss Tables)

[Q21]

The claimant aged 45 at the date of trial is no longer able to work as a result of his injuries. But for the accident he would have retired at the age of 65 after 22 years of pensionable service. He was in a medium-risk job and his pension entitlement accrues at the rate of 1/60 of his final salary for each year of service. His final salary would have been £30,000, which would have entitled him to an annual pension of £11,000 (gross), £10,000 (net). Following the accident the claimant was medically retired and now receives an ill-health benefit of £5,000 net per annum.

Step 1   Calculate the annual net loss of pension
          The annual net loss of pension is £10,000 minus £5,000,
          ie £5,000.

Step 2   Apply multiplier
          The correct multiplier is taken from Table 21 of the
          Ogden Tables (6th edn) at 2.5% discount, ie 8.7 [NB
          this does not have to be further discounted for accelerated
          receipt because this has already been accounted for in the
          Ogden Tables]. Multiplying £5,000 by 8.7 gives a total of: 43,500

Step 3   Discount for further eventualities
          This sum further needs to be discounted to take account   (4,350)
          Contingencies other than mortality by say 10%.
          NB no further discount is applied for accelerated receipt
          because this has already been taken into account in the
          Ogden Tables.

                                                                                        _____

TOTAL   **£39,150**

(iii)   Married Man, Defined Benefit Pension and No Lump Sum (Traditional Approach Using the Life Tables)

[Q22]

The claimant is aged 50 at the date of trial and is no longer able to work as a result of his injuries. But for the accident he would have retired at the age of 60 after 17 years of pensionable service. His pension entitlement accrues at the rate of 1/50 of his final salary for each year of service. His final salary was likely to have been £50,000 but there were considerable risk factors in his industry. If he had continued to work at the same company until age 60 he would have been entitled to an annual pension of £17,000 (gross), £15,000 (net). Following the accident the claimant was medically retired and now receives an ill-health benefit of £7,500 net per annum. His wife who is also aged 50 at the date of trial is entitled to two-thirds of his pension in the event that she outlives him.

Step 1   Calculate the annual net loss of pension
          The annual net loss of pension is £15,000 minus £7,500,
          ie £7,500.

Step 2   Calculate the claimant's multiplier
          According to the current life tables, the claimant's life
          expectancy is 34.9 years at age 50. He therefore has 24.9
          years beyond age 60. The appropriate multiplier for this
          period would be 18.60 (Table 28 of the Ogden Tables
          (6th edn) at 2.5% discount taking the 9/10 point between
          24 and 25).

Step 3   Calculate the claimant's wife's multiplier
          According to the current life tables, the claimant's wife is
          likely to live another 38.1 years at age 50. She therefore
          has another 28.1 years beyond age 60. The multiplier for

this period would be 20.26 (Table 28 of the Ogden
Tables (6th edn) at 2.5% taking the 1/10 point
between 28 and 29).

Step 4   Calculate the adjusted multiplier
         Since the claimant's wife is entitled to two-thirds of
         his pension for the period that she outlives him, the
         claimant's multiplier should be increased by 1.11
         (representing two-thirds of the difference in
         multipliers of 1.66) making a total of 19.71.

Step 5   Apply the adjusted multiplier
         Multiplying £7,500 by 19.71 gives a total of: 147,825

Step 6   Discount for accelerated receipt
         This figure must be discounted by a factor of 0.7812
         (Table 27 of the Ogden Tables (6th edn) at 2.5%
         discount) to take account of the fact that the claimant
         is receiving his pension 10 years earlier   (32,344.11)

Step 7   Discount for further eventualities
         This figure also needs to be discounted to take
         account of the high contingencies other than
         mortality by a factor of say 20%.   (29,565)
                                                                       _____
TOTAL   **£85,915.89**

(iv)   Married Man, Defined Benefit Pension and Lump Sum Payment (Modern Approach Using the Ogden Pension Loss Tables)

[Q23]

The claimant is aged 55 at the date of trial and is no longer able to work as a result of his injuries. But for the accident he would have retired at the age of 65 after 34 years of pensionable service. His pension entitlement accrues at the rate of 1/80 of his final salary for each year of service. His final salary was likely to have been £40,000 in a low risk position. If he had continued to work at the same company until age 60 he would have been entitled to an annual pension of £17,000 (gross), £15,000 (net). Following the accident the claimant was medically retired and received a tax free lump sum of £50,000 and a reduced ill-health benefit of £5,000 net per annum. His wife who is aged 40 at the date of trial is entitled to one-half of his pension in the event that she outlives him.

Step 1   Calculate the annual net loss of pension
         The annual net loss of pension is £15,000 minus
         £5,000, ie £10,000.

Step 2   Calculate claimant's multiplier
         The claimant's multiplier is taken from Table 21 of
         the Ogden Tables (6th edn) at 2.5% discount, ie
         11.14 [NB this does not have to be further discounted
         for accelerated receipt because this has already been
         accounted for in the Ogden Tables].

Step 3   Calculate claimant's wife's multiplier
          According to the current life tables (Facts & Figures
          Table B3 Expectation of Life Table), the claimant's
          wife is likely to live another 48.5 years at age 40. She
          therefore has another 38.5 years beyond when the
          claimant reaches age 65. The multiplier for this period
          would be 24.85 (Table 28 at 2.5% taking the 1/2 point
          between 38 and 39). This figure must then be discounted
          for accelerated receipt by 10 years by applying a factor
          of 0.7812 (Table 27 of the Ogden Tables (6th edn) at
          2.5% discount) making a final multiplier for the claimant's
          wife of 19.41.

Step 4   Calculate the adjusted multiplier
          Since the claimant's wife is entitled to half of his pension
          for the period that she outlives him, the claimant's
          multiplier should be increased by 4.14 (representing
          half of the difference in multipliers of 8.27) making a
          total of 15.28.

Step 5   Apply adjusted multiplier
          Multiplying £10,000 by 15.28 gives a total of: 152,800

Step 6   Discount for further eventualities
          This sum needs to be discounted to take account of the
          low contingencies other than mortality by a factor of,
          say, 0.05.   (7,640)

Step 7   Discount lump sum received
          The claimant's whole life multiplier is 19.7 (Table 1
          of the Ogden Tables (6th edn) at 2.5%). The multiplier
          to pension age is 8.56 (Table 9 of the Ogden Tables
          (5th edn) at 2.5% discount). Therefore the post-retirement
          element of the claimant's pension is 11.14. The claimant
          must therefore give 11.14 divided by 19.7, ie 56.55%
          credit for the lump sum received of £50,000.   (28,275)

TOTAL   **£116,885**

(v)   Single Female, Defined Benefit Pension With Reduced Potential Lump Sum (Modern Approach Using the Ogden Pension Loss Tables)

[Q24]

The claimant is aged 30 at the date of trial and is no longer able to work as a result of her injuries. But for the accident she would have retired at the age of 55 after 22 years of pensionable service. Her pension entitlement accrues at the rate of 1/60 of her final salary for each year of service. Her final salary was likely to have been £30,000. If she had continued to work at the same company until age 50 she would have been entitled to an annual pension of £11,000 (gross), £10,000 (net). Following the accident the claimant was medically retired and received a reduced tax free lump sum of £10,000 instead of a potential lump sum of £20,000 and a reduced ill-health benefit of £7,500 (net) per annum.

Step 1	Calculate the annual net loss of pension The annual net loss of pension is £10,000 minus £7,500, ie £2,500.	
Step 2	Apply multiplier The claimant's multiplier is taken from Table 18 of the Ogden Tables (6th edn) at 2.5% discount, ie 11.65. Multiplying £2,500 by 11.65 gives a total of:	29,125
Step 3	Discount for further eventualities The sum of £29,125 needs to be discounted to take account of the contingencies other than mortality by say 10%.	(2,912.50)
Step 4	Add loss of potential lump sum But for the accident the claimant's potential tax free lump sum would have been £20,000.	20,000
Step 5	Discount for advanced receipt of potential lump sum The sum of £20,000 must be discounted by a factor of 0.5394 (Table 27 of the Ogden Tables (6th edn) at 2.5% discount) to take account of the fact that the claimant is receiving the money 25 years earlier.	(9,212)
Step 6	Discount for potential lump sum for mortality The subtotal of £10,788 (potential lump sum at today's value) has to be further discounted by a factor of 0.96 in order to take account of the fact that the claimant might die before she receives the potential lump sum (this factor is calculated from Facts & Figures Table A3, by which the probability of a 30-year-old woman not reaching the age of 55 is 95449.2 / 98963.4 = 3.55%).	(383)
Step 7	Discount lump sum received The claimant's whole life multiplier is 30.15 (Table 2 of the Ogden Tables (6th edn) at 2.5% discount). The multiplier to pension age 55 is 18.49 (Table 6 of the Ogden Tables at 2.5% discount). Therefore the post- retirement element of the claimant's pension is 11.66. The claimant must therefore give 11.66 divided by 30.15, ie 38.67% credit for the lump sum received of £10,000.	(3,867)
TOTAL		**£32,750.50**

(vi)   Female Employee in Occupational Money Purchase Scheme (Modern Approach Using the Ogden Pension Loss Tables)

[Q25]

The claimant is aged 43 at the date of the accident and 46 at the date of trial (exactly three years after the date of the accident). She is no longer able to work as a result of her injuries. For the first year after the accident she continued to be employed on full pay and her employer continued to make pension contributions on her behalf. Her employment was terminated exactly one year after the accident. But for the accident she would have retired at the age of 60. At the time of her retirement her pensionable pay was £25,000 but this would have increased by 5% per year. Each year her employer contributed 6% of her pensionable pay towards her pension. Assuming that the claimant's claim for loss of earnings is made net after deduction of the claimant's past and future pension contributions, the loss of her pension contributions is calculated as follows.

Step 1	Calculate past loss of pension contributions	
	The claimant has lost two years of pension contributions up to the date of trial.	
	In the first year her gross contributions would have amounted to 1,500 (6% of £25,000). After a deduction of tax at the marginal rate of 20% her net loss of pension contributions was £1,200.	
	In the second year her contributions would have amounted to £1,575 (6% of £26,250). After a deduction of tax at the marginal rate of 20% her net loss of pension contributions was £1,260.	
	Therefore her total net past loss of pension contributions is:	£2,460.00
Step 2	Calculate future loss of pension	
	The annual loss of net pension contributions will continue at the rate of £1,260 pa.	
	The correct multiplier is taken from Table 8 of the Ogden Tables (6th edn) at 2.5% discount, ie 11.64. Multiplying £1,260 by 11.64 gives a total of £14,666.40.	
	Applying a discount factor of, say, 0.95 for further contingencies gives a total future loss of pension of:	£13,933.08
TOTAL		**£16,393.08**

12   Example *Roberts v Johnstone*[1] Calculation

[Q26]

The claimant is currently aged 5 and will be 8 at the date of trial (with a normal life expectancy). As a result of her injuries she was forced to move to suitable three-bedroom ground floor accommodation near her school where she could live with her family. The house required various adaptations and an extension (funded by way of interim payment). At age 21 it is proposed that the claimant will leave her parents and live independently. At this stage her accommodation will need to be at least four-bedroom to provide adequate living accommodation for a live-in housekeeper/carer and overnight staying accommodation for her family. The property will also need to be adapted for her use and facilities built for the housekeeper/carer. But for her injuries, it is likely that the claimant would have had up to a 50% share in her own two-bedroom flat worth £150,000. In reliance upon the report of Mr Architect the claim for accommodation costs is advanced as follows.

1.   Accommodation to Age 21

		£	£	£
1.1	Additional capital costs Purchase price of three-bedroom property £350,000. 2.5% of cost = £8,750. Apply multiplier to age 21 of 11.12 (Table 28 of the Ogden Tables (5th edn) at 2.5% discount) making a total of:	97,300		
1.2	Extension costs	35,000		
1.3	Adaptation costs	30,000		
1.4	Discount for added value of extension	(15,000)		
Subtotal			147,300	

2.   Accommodation from Age 21

		£	£	£
2.1	Additional capital costs Purchase price of four-bedroom property £450,000. Less the half share in the starter flat which the claimant might have been expected to buy in any event (£75,000) = £375,000. 2.5% of increased capital cost = £9,375. Applying lifetime multiplier from age 21 of 23.61 (Life multiplier of 34.73 from Table 2 of the Ogden Tables (5th edn) at 2.5% discount minus 11.12) gives a total of:	221,343.75		
2.2	Adaptation costs	50,000		
2.3	Construction of carer's facilities	10,000		
2.4	Fitting out of carer's facilities	3,000		
Subtotal			284,343.75	

---

[1]   [1989] QB 878.

	£	£	£

3.   Additional Miscellaneous Costs

3.1 Removal, one-off expenses of, say: 1,500

3.2 Purchase and conveyancing, say: 2,000

3.3 Decoration, say: 5,000

3.4 Insurance
     Annual cost of £300 multiplied by lifetime
     multiplier of 34.73 (Table 2 of the Ogden
     Tables (5th edn) at 2.5% discount).   10,419

3.5 Council tax
     Annual cost of £300 multiplied by lifetime
     multiplier of 34.73 (Table 2 of the Ogden Tables
     (5th edn) at 2.5% discount).   10,419

3.6 Wear and tear
     Annual cost of £300 multiplied by lifetime
     multiplier of 34.73 (Table 2 at 2.5% discount).   10,419

3.7 Maintenance, heating and running costs
     Annual cost of £1,000 multiplied by lifetime
     multiplier of 34.73 (Table 2 at 2.5% discount).   34,730

Subtotal   74,487

TOTAL   **506,130.75**

13 Example of Schedule for Dying Claimant
[Q27]

IN THE HIGH COURT OF JUSTICE   HQ04X12345

QUEEN'S BENCH DIVISION

BETWEEN

DYING MANN

Claimant

-and-

MUCH ASBESTOS LIMITED

Defendants

SCHEDULE OF LOSS

INDEX

KEY FACTS

Claimant	Dying Mann
Date of birth	25 May 1955
Off work from	6 January 2009
Retirement date	25 May 2020
Wife	Lilian Mann
Address	20 Laurel Avenue Dagenham Essex
Date of service of claim form	3 June 2009
Date of schedule	21 July 2009
Date of hearing	25 November 2009
Date of death (estimated)	25 May 2010

GENERAL DAMAGES

Pain suffering and loss of amenities
(based on Dr ....'s reports)

Malignant mesothelioma of the pleura. Symptoms probably began around February 2009 with left chest pain. They have included increasingly severe left chest pain, shortness of breath on exertion, reduced appetite, weight loss, excessive sweating and progressive debility. He has undergone chemotherapy with some side effects including diarrhoea and anorexia but did not derive symptomatic benefit.

He ceased work due to mesothelioma. Had he not contracted it, he would have been able to work until the age of 65.

It is inevitable that there will be continued deterioration in his condition, probably with worsening pain, increasing breathlessness and debility. It is probable that he will need increasing levels of assistance during the last six months of his life. It is likely that he will become completely incapacitated and in need of constant nursing care towards the end of it.

He will probably die in 12 months time. The mesothelioma has accelerated his death by 20 years.

GENERAL DAMAGES   **£70,000.00**

INTEREST THEREON

General damages	£70,000.00
2% pa from 3/6/09 to 25/11/09 (175 days)	× 0.96%*
INTEREST THEREON	**£672.00**

* to 2 decimal places

SPECIAL DAMAGES

1. Claimant's earnings loss

Introduction

The Claimant was employed as a guard by Beta Security Ltd. His income, which consisted of salary and overtime, would have increased by 3% on 6 April 2009. There were no associated perks. Owing to his disease, he has been off work since 6 January 2009 and will never return to it.

a) Financial Year 2008/09

Claimant's gross pay totalled	£10,908.60
in the 6 months from 6/7/08 to 5/1/09	÷ 6
Claimant's gross pay	£1,818.10 pm
From 6/1/09 to 5/4/09	× 3
Claimant's gross pay should have been	£5,454.30
Instead he received sick pay of	£1,375.80
Loss of Claimant's gross pay	£4,078.50
Income tax @ 20%	-£815.70
National Insurance contributions @ 11%	-£448.64
Loss of net income	**£2,814.16 (a)**

b) Financial Year 2009/10

Claimant's gross pay of £1,810 pm × 12 =		£21,720.00 pa
Would have increased by 3%		+£651.60 pa
Claimant's increased gross pay		£22,371.60 pa
Tax free	£6,475.00	
20% tax on	£15,896.60 = £3,179.32	
Total tax		£3,179.32 pa
NIC free	£5,715 00	
11.0% NICs on	£16,656.60 = £1,832.23	
Total NICs		£ 1,832.23 pa
Claimant's net income		£17,360.05 pa
From 6/4/09 to 25/11/09		× 234/365
His net pay should have been		£12,556.31
Instead he received net sick pay of		£ 1,375.81
Loss of net income		**£11,180.50 (b)**

Earnings loss summary

a) FY 2008-09	£2,814.16
b) FY 2009-10	£11,180.50
Earnings Loss	**£13,994.66**

2. Care and assistance

(based on ....'s report)

Schedule 1
Care and assistance

1-31 May 2009
7 hours a week at £7.73 an hour

	4 weeks and 3 days	£239.63

1 June 2009 – 18 July 2009

8 hours a week at £7.73 an hour	7 weeks	£432.88

Schedule 2
Care and Assistance

19 July 2009 –

25 November 2009	18 weeks and 4 days	£1,292.01
9 hours a week at £7.73 an hour		

Value of wife's care	£1,964.52
25% non-commercial discount	-£491.13
Care and assistance	**£1,473.39**

3. Medical fees

Dr Physician's fees £80 + £70 =	£150.00
Private x-ray	£135.00
Medical fees	**£285.00**

4. Prescriptions

2008/09: 5 single prescriptions @ £7.10 =	£35.50
2009/10: Annual pre-payment certificate	£104.00
Prescriptions	**£139.50**

5. Equipment

Single bed, to sleep separately from wife	£349.99
Fan heater	£39.99
Equipment	**£389.98**

6. Bedding

2 single sheets @ £15 =	£30.00
2 pillows @ £9.99 =	£19.98
Bedding	**£49.98**

7. Claimant's hospital travel

(driven by daughter)

7 visits to A Hospital: 16 miles × 22.5p × 7 =	£25.20
Parking fees: £3 × 7 =	£21.00
4 visits to B. Hospital: 22 miles × 22.5p × 4	£19.80
Claimant's hospital travel	**£66.00**

8. Wife's hospital travel

(driven by daughter when Claimant in-patient)

6 visits to A Hospital: 16 miles × 22.5p × 6 =	£21.60
Parking fees: £3 × 6 =	£18.00
Wife's hospital travel	**£39.60**

9. Special foods

Extra cost of fresh fish, fruit, chicken and blackcurrant juice and nutritional calorific supplements	£15.00 pw
From 18/6/09 to 25/11/09	× 23
Special foods	**£345.00**

10. Tradesmen's fees

(Payments for tasks that Claimant would have performed if fit)

Painting main bedroom: £300 + 15% VAT =	£345.00
Gardener from 25/4/09 to 25/10/09: £27.50 pm × 6 =	£165.00
Tradesmen's fees	**£510.00**

Special Damages Summary

1. Earnings loss	£13,994.66
2. Care and assistance	£1,473.39
3. Medical fees	£285.00
4. Prescriptions	£139.50
5. Equipment	£389.98
6. Bedding	£49.98
7. Claimant's hospital travel	£66.00
8. Wife's hospital travel	£39.60
9. Special foods	£345.00
10. Tradesmen's fees	£510.00
SPECIAL DAMAGES	**£17,293.11**

INTEREST THEREON

Special damages £17,293.11

From	To	Days	Rate (p.a.)	Interest (£)
06/01/2009	31/01/2009	26	3.00%	£ 36.96
01/02/2009	31/05/2009	120	1.50%	£ 85.28
01/06/2009	30/06/2009	30	0.75%	£ 10.66
01/07/2009	25/11/2009	147	0.25%	£ 17.41
INTEREST THEREON				**£150.31**

FUTURE LOSS DURING LIFE DURING THE 'LOST YEARS'

1. Earnings loss

Annual loss of Claimant's net income (as above) £17,360.05 pa

from 25/11/09 to 25/5/10 × 6/12

Earnings loss **£8,650.30**

2. Care and assistance

(based on ....'s report)

Schedule 3

Care for the penultimate three months of life

Care and assistance

11 hours a week at £7.73 an hour 13 weeks £1,105.39 (a)

Personal carer

2 hours a day at £13.53 an hour weekdays 13 weeks £1,758.90(b)

Personal Carer

3 hours a day at £13.53 an hour weekdays 13 weeks £2,638.35(c)

Schedule 4

Care for the last three months of life

Month 1

Care and assistance

20 hours a week at £7.73 an hour 4 weeks £618.40(d)

Personal Carer

3 hours a day at £13.53 an hour weekdays 4 weeks £811.80 (e)

Month 2

Care and assistance

31 hours a week at £7.73 an hour	4 weeks	£958.52(f)

Personal Carer

5 hours a day at £13.53 an hour weekdays	4 weeks	£1,353.00 (g)

Month 3

Care and assistance

40 hours a week at £7.73 an hour	4 weeks	£1,236.80(h)

Personal Carer

6 hours a day at £13.35 an hour weekdays	4 weeks	£1,623.60(i)

Qualified nurse

4 hours a day at £17.39 an hour weekdays and £19.17 an hour weekends	4 weeks	£2,004.64(j)

Night nurse

10 hours a night at £14.89 an hour weekdays and £17.83 an hour weekends	4 weeks	£4,404.40 (k)

Care and assistance summary

Value of care from wife (a+d+f+h)	£3,919.11
25% non-commercial discount	- £979.78
Net value of wife's care	£2,939.33
Cost of professional care (b+c+e+g+i+j+k)	£14,594.69
Care and assistance	**£17,534.02**

3. Equipment

(based on ....'s report)

Stairlift	£1,800.00
Tintagel single motor rise and recline chair	£930.00
Delivery	£45.00
Propad original cushion (wipedown cover)	£50.60
Folding steel wheelchair	£361.70
Mangar Bath lift	£630.00
Delivery charge	£7.50
Adjustable toilet surround	£34.00
Blue comfort commode	£61.70

Therakair mattress rented for one month (inc delivery)	£1120.00
Equipment	**£5,040.50**

4. Sundry expenses

such as hospital travel, bedding, extra heating,
extra telephoning, special foods, extra clothes
and bed clothes, lotions and ointments,
cost of paying tradesmen to perform around
house and garden work which the Claimant
would have done himself if fit, collectively estimated at   **£1,000.00**

Lifetime loss summary

1. Earnings loss	£8,650.00
2. Care and assistance	£17,534.02
3. Equipment	£5,040.50
4. Sundry expenses	£1,000.00
FUTURE LOSS DURING LIFE	**£32,224.82**

FUTURE LOSS AFTER DEATH

1. Earnings loss

Owing to his premature death due to mesothelioma		
the Claimant will lose his net income (as above)		£17,360.05 pa
50% living expenses		÷ 2
Net income loss		£8,680.02 pa
from 25/5/10 to 25/5/20 (Ogden table 9, age 55):	8.56	
Allowance for contingencies	- 8%	
Earnings multiplier		× 7.88
Earnings loss		**£68,398.56**

2. Pensions loss

Owing to his premature death due to mesothclioma,		
the Claimant will lose his:		
a) state retirement pension: £111.87 p.w. × 52 1/7 =		£5,833.22 pa
b) occupational pension from Good Glaziers		£ 4,528.66 pa
Claimant's gross pensions		£10,361.88 pa
Total tax free	£9,490.00	
20% tax on	£871.88 = £174.38	
Total tax		£174.38 pa
Claimant's net pensions		£10,187.50 pa

50% living expenses		÷ 2
Net pensions loss		£5,093.75 pa
Life multiplier (Ogden table 28, 20* years) :	15.78	
Earnings multiplier (as above)		
Pensions multiplier		× 7.90
Pensions loss		**£40,240.62**

*based on Dr   's reports.

SUMMARY OF CLAIM

General Damages

General damages	£70,000.00	
Interest thereon	£ 672.00	
		£70,672.00

Special Damages

Special damages	£17,293.11	
Interest thereon	£ 150.31	
		£17,443.42

Future Loss During Life

Earnings loss	£8,650.30	
Care and assistance	£17,534.02	
Equipment	£5,040.50	
Sundry expenses	£1,000.00	
		£32,224.82

Future Loss After Death

Earnings loss	£68,398.56	
Pensions loss	£40,240.62	
		£108,639.18

TOTAL DAMAGES   **£228,979.42**

DATED etc

Example Periodical Payments Schedule of Loss
[Q28]

Schedule of Past and Future Losses and Expenses	In the FUTURE LOSS County Court

Claim No	1234
Claimant (Including Ref)	Mr Smith Smith1
Defendant (Including Ref)	Mrs Jones Jones20

1. PREAMBLE

The Claimant was 35 at the date of the accident and is currently aged 36. As a result of the Defendant's negligence, the Claimant suffered a fracture of his lower back at level L4/5. He has been unable to continue in his pre-accident work as a building site foreman. But for his injuries, it is contended that the Claimant would have been promoted to site manager by the age of 40 and company director by the age of 50. The Claimant has not returned to work since the accident and is unlikely to find remunerative employment in the future.

Liability for the accident is admitted and judgment was entered for the Claimant for an amount to be decided by the court on 2.10.09.

The Claimant seeks an order for periodical payments because: (i) it is the preferred method for meeting the Claimant's ongoing needs; (ii) the Claimant wishes to have periodical payments for reasons of security, ease of budgeting, avoidance of investment risk and avoidance of disputed evidence regarding life expectancy; and (iii) there is no good reason against periodical payments in the absence of any deduction for contributory negligence. The Claimant will maintain that periodical payments for care and case management should be linked to ASHE (6115).

2. RELEVANT INFORMATION

Date of Accident:	1.1.09
Date of Birth:	1.1.74
Intended Retirement Age:	70
Assumed Trial Date:	5.7.11
Date of Schedule:	5.7.10

3. EXPERT EVIDENCE

The Claimant relies upon the following expert evidence:

3.1   The report of Mr X, spinal consultant, dated 1.6.05.

3.2   The report of Mr Y, employment consultant, dated 1.8.05.

3.3   The report of Miss Z, occupational therapist, dated 1.8.05.

4. GENERAL DAMAGES

4.1	**Pain, suffering and loss of amenity**	TBA
4.2	**Loss of congenial employment**	TBA

5. INTEREST ON GENERAL DAMAGES

5.1   **Basis of the claim**

Interest is claimed at the rate of 2% pa from the date of service of the proceedings on 5.7.10.

5.2   **The Calculation**

The accrued interest to the assumed date of trial amounts to 2%.   TBA

6. PAST EXPENSES AND LOSSES

£   £

6.1   **Loss of earnings**

6.1.1 Basis of the Claim
At the time of the accident the Claimant was employed by RMT Contractors as a foreman. He was earning £42,500 (gross) or £30,000 (net) pa. He was paid in full up to 4.7.06 when he was medically retired as a result of his injuries. But for his injuries, he would have been entitled to a 3% annual increase in salary.

6.1.2 Calculation of Loss from 5.7.10 to 5.7.11
£30,000 × 1.03 =   30,900.00

6.2   **Care and Assistance**

6.2.1 Basis of the Claim
By reason of his injuries, the Claimant has required a significant amount of care and assistance from family and friends. Before the accident he used to share responsibility for domestic chores with his wife. The Claimant relies upon the expert evidence of Miss Z regarding the value of the care provided.

6.2.2 The Calculation
(i) From 1.1.09 to 30.6.09
50 hours of care per week × 26 weeks @ £6.50 per hour =   8,450.00
(ii) From 1.7.09 to 31.12.09
30 hours of care per week × 26 weeks @ £6.50 per hour =   5,070.00
(iii) From 1.1.10 to 5.7.11
20 hours of care per week × 78.57 weeks @ £7.00 per hour =   10,999.80
                                                            _____

Subtotal: 24,519.80

	£	£

6.3   Travel Expenses

The Claimant has incurred numerous travel expenses   350.00
travelling to and from various hospital and treatment
appointments. The total mileage is estimated at 1,000
miles × 35 ppm = £350.

6.4   Medical Expenses

6.4.1 Intensive Spinal Rehabilitation	10,000.00	
6.4.2 Physiotherapy	1,500.00	
6.4.2 Prescriptions and Medication	150.00	
Subtotal:		11,650.00

6.5   Miscellaneous

6.5.1 Labour charges for completing decoration of kitchen	200.00	
6.5.2 Replacement spinal brace	30.00	
6.5.3 Electric back massager 3100	50.00	
Subtotal:		280.00
Total Past Expenses and Losses:		**67,699.80**

7. INTEREST ON PAST EXPENSES AND LOSSES

	£	£

7.1   Basis of the Claim

Interest is claimed at half the special account rate from
the date of the accident until the assumed date of trial,
amounting to 1.31%.

7.2   The Calculation

£67,699.80 × 1.31% =   **886.87**

8. FUTURE LOSSES: EARNINGS AND OTHER INCOME

		Annual Loss Claimed (£)
8.1	**Loss of Earnings**	

8.1.1 The Basis of the Claim

The Claimant relies upon the expert evidence of Mr Y regarding his likely career earnings. But for the accident he would be earning £30,900 net at the date of trial. This would have risen to £35,000 net when he was promoted to site manager at the age of 40. His salary would have increased again to £40,000 net from the age of 50 when he was likely to have been promoted to company director. A retirement age of 70 is contended for bearing in mind the less physical nature of his managerial position, although the claimant accepts he may have reduced his hours in later life. In the circumstances a reduced claim is made for £30,000 net from age 65 to 69.

8.1.2 The Calculation

(i) Period 1 – from 5.7.11 to 31.12.13 (age 37 to 39)	30,900.00
(ii) Period 2 – from 1.1.14 to 31.12.23 (age 40 to 49)	35,000.00
(iii) Period 3 – from 1.1.24 to 31.12.38 (age 50 to 64)	40,000.00
(iv) Period 4 – from 1.1.39 to 31.12.43 (age 65 to 69)	30,000.00

8.2   Loss of Pension

8.2.1 Basis of the Claim

The Claimant had a final salary pension with his employer. But for his injuries he would have received annual pension payments of £20,000. His ill-health retirement pension is £10,000 pa.

8.2.2 The Claim

(i) Annual loss of pension from 1.1.44 for life	10,000.00

9. FUTURE LOSSES: CARE, MEDICAL COSTS AND OTHER RECURRING OR CAPITAL COSTS

9.1   Care and Assistance

9.1.1 Basis of the Claim

The Claimant requires ongoing assistance with physical care and domestic chores. It is likely that he will require additional help from the age of 50 onwards following the expected deterioration in his condition due to osteoarthritis. He relies upon the expert evidence of Miss Z regarding the value of the care/assistance required.

9.1.2 The Calculation

(i) Period 1 – from 5.7.11 to 31.12.23 (age 37 to 49)	
20 hours of care per week × 52 weeks per year @ £7.00 per hour = £7,280 pa.	7,280.00
(ii) Period 2 – from 1.1.24 for life	
25 hours of care per week × 52 weeks per year @ £7.00 per hour = £9,100 pa.	9,100.00

**Annual Loss
Claimed (£)**

9.2   Aids and Equipment

9.2.1 Basis of the Claim

The Claimant relies upon the evidence of Miss Z regarding the aids
and equipment he reasonably needs as a result of his injuries. An
allowance should be made to purchase the capital costs of these
items in year one to be paid as an addition to the lump sum award
under paras 4-7 above. Thereafter, the Claimant claims the average
annual replacement costs as set out in Miss Z's report.

9.2.2 The Claim

(i) Year 1 – (age 37) capital costs £10,000   10,000.00
(ii) Year 2 onwards – (from age 38 for life) replacement costs   1,250.00

9.3   Medical Expenses

9.3.1 Physiotherapy – from 5.7.11 to 31.12.13 (age 37 to age 39)
The Claimant relies upon the report of Mr X that he will need   1,000.00
physiotherapy at an annual cost of £1,000

9.3.2 Prescription charges – from 5.7.11 to 31.12.33 (age 37 to 59)
The Claimant claims the cost of an annual prepaid prescription card   104.00
until his prescriptions become free at age 60.

9.4   Gardening

9.4.1 Basis of Claim

Prior to the accident, the Claimant was responsible for carrying out
heavy gardening work such as lawn mowing and hedge trimming
etc. He greatly enjoyed this work and but for the accident, he would
have continued performing these services into his old age. A claim
is made for the full cost of these services up to age 75 and thereafter
at 50% to age 79.

9.4.2 The Calculation

(i) Period 1 – from 5.7.11 to 31.12.48 (age 37 to 74)
The Claimant relies upon the estimate obtained from JB & Sons   5,000.00
that the cost of providing the services that he would otherwise have
performed himself is £5,000 pa.

(ii) Period 2 – from 1.1.49 to 31.12.53 (age 75 to age 79)
The Claimant claims 50% of the annual total based upon the   2,500.00
estimate of JB & Sons in the sum of £2,500 pa.

9.5   Home Maintenance / DIY / Decorating

9.5.1 Basis of the Claim

The Claimant was a carpenter by trade and carried out much of his
own home maintenance. He was also responsible for carrying out
external and internal painting and decorating. An estimated claim
is made for £1,000 pa up to age 74 and thereafter @ £500 pa up to
age 79.

	Annual Loss Claimed (£)

9.5.2 The Calculation

(i) Period 1 – from 5.7.07 to 31.12.44 (age 37 to 74)
The Claimant claims £1,000 pa. — 1,000.00

(ii) Period 2 – from 1.1.45 to 31.12.49 (age 75 to age 79)
The Claimant claims £500 pa. — 500.00

9.6 Increased Holiday Expenditure

The Claimant relies upon the evidence of Miss Z that he is likely to incur additional holiday costs in terms of taxis and hiring suitable vehicles of £500 pa. This loss is claimed for life. — 500.00

9.7 Window Cleaning

But for the accident, the Claimant would have washed his own windows. He claims the cost of having this done professionally at a cost of £100 pa. This loss is claimed up to age 79. — 100.00

10. SUMMARY OF CLAIMS

	£
10.1 General Damages	TBA
10.2 Interest on General Damages at 2%	TBA
10.3 Past Expenses and Losses	67,699.80
10.4 Interest on Past Expenses and Losses	886.87

10.5 Future Periodical Payments	Annual loss of earnings and other income (£)	Annual care and medical costs etc (£)	Annual Total (£)
10.5.1 Age 37 (5.7.11)	30,900	24,984	55,884
10.5.2 Age 38 to 39 (1.1.12 to 31.12.13)	30,900	16,234	47,134
10.5.3 Age 40 to 49 (1.1.14 to 31.12.23)	35,000	15,234	50,234
10.5.4 Age 50 to 60 (1.1.24 to 31.12.33)	40,000	17,054	57,054
10.5.5 Age 60 to 64 (1.1.34 to 31.12.38)	40,000	16,950	56,950
10.5.6 Age 65 to 69 (1.1.39 to 31.12.43)	30,000	16,950	46,950
10.5.7 Age 70 to 74 (1.1.44 to 31.12.48)	10,000	16,950	26,950
10.5.8 Age 75 to 79 (1.1.49 to 31.12.53)	10,000	13,950	23,950
10.5.9 Age 80 for life (1.1.54 onwards)	10,000	10,850	20,850

DATED etc as in CLAIM No 1

Index

References are to paragraph numbers. Chapters are indicated in **bold**